T   H   E

Barnhart
Abbreviations
Dictionary

T H E

Barnhart
Abbreviations
Dictionary

Edited by
Robert K. Barnhart

John Wiley & Sons, Inc.
New York ▪ Chichester ▪ Brisbane ▪ Toronto ▪ Singapore

ISBN 0-471-57146-6

Printed in the United States of America

10 9 8 7 6 5 4 3 2 1

Contents

Preface

The evolution of this dictionary can be traced through a long series of collections of abbreviations. Our chief contribution to the study of abbreviations is in the organization and format of the material and the presentation of evidence from our files of developing English collected from newspapers, magazines, books, and other publications of current times. This dictionary is largely a result of consulting those files for abbreviations used today and for the form in which they are most likely to occur.

In editing material for a dictionary of abbreviations, it soon becomes evident that the breadth of human activity covered is so wide and varied that some identification is often necessary to distinguish one use from another. We have provided explanations or inserted subject labels for many terms to show the area of their application. When abbreviated forms are only a significant part of a longer form, the parts are shown in combination to help the user identify the usual context of usage. Because many abbreviations are ambiguous even in context, a primary aim of this book is to unravel the complexities and obscurities of usage. We have therefore confined our material to those common abbreviations in frequent use and sought to construct a style that makes each form readily identifiable.

The first part of this dictionary is an alphabetical list of abbreviations. The second part is an alphabetical reverse list of words, phrases, and written symbols with their abbreviated forms currently in use. We have also included in the reverse list notations showing what is recorded and in many cases is recommended, standard practice. Our selection of style sheets that we have quoted from is of a broad range and includes the largest printing house in the world for its breadth of coverage (the U.S. Government Printing Office), a newspaper of record (*The New York Times*), a standard American style sheet widely used in scholarly and academic work (by the Modern Language Association of America), a standard British scholarly and general publisher (Oxford University Press), and two Canadian style sheets (*Canadian Government Style Manual*

and *Civil Service of Canada Office Manual*). Although every entry and instance of usage in these style sheets is not included, we show, by a selection of their examples, what current practice is acceptable for various types of abbreviation in English.

Another feature of the organization in this dictionary is the distinction drawn between abbreviations and written symbols. Many entries are divided into two parts, the first showing use of a form as an abbreviation, the second as a symbol. The relevance of this separation lies in usage. Generally, a symbol does not take periods; sometimes a symbol is only remotely related to the phrase or concept or principle it stands for; often a symbol appears in a formula or some other scientific or technical notation. In essence, symbols are an extension of abbreviations and not strictly abbreviations. By separating symbols from abbreviations, we hope to make information easier for the user to find.

Many texts explaining the processes of language give only some attention to abbreviation. We have amplified these explanations in a longer discussion of abbreviation in English. The process is as much a function of speech as it is of writing, and we want to show the association of the two without overburdening the reader with details. It is often unclear from the record whether an abbreviation first developed in speech or in writing, so that the two forms of English are closely linked in Modern English. The discussion on the following pages explores this and other concepts and perhaps will stimulate more study of abbreviation in language.

This book has been many years in development. Much discussion and research has gone into compiling it and designing its form. The threads spun by many hands are evident in its fabric, not the least of which are those of my father, Clarence Barnhart, who first suggested the reverse list some thirty years ago. Others have added significant features, such as the notations of standard practice in the variously available style manuals, and given criticism of general execution, including my chief editor,

viii   **Preface**

Cynthia Barnhart. Two of my sons, Michael and David, have devoted much time and research to this project, and our style editor, Mrs. A. L. Bartling, has offered a legion of corrections and suggestions to enhance the quality of the dictionary. Albert Crocco has lent tireless assistance to all our labors, as has Katherine Barnhart. A former editor at Barnhart Books, Sol Steinmetz, brought the dictionary to the attention of the then publisher, Charles Levine. With the subsequent assistance of Judith McCarthy and Marcia Samuels, we developed our manuscript into a book.

For the editors and general users who consult the book, my hope is that they will find our efforts satisfactory and useful.

Robert K. Barnhart

Brewster, New York

The Structure of the Book

This dictionary is divided into two parts: first, a list of abbreviations and written symbols used in English, and second, a reverse list of words, phrases, concepts, and measurements accompanied by their abbreviations and symbols. Each part is arranged in alphabetical order.

Part I
Abbreviations List

The definitions in the abbreviations list are also given in alphabetical order, except for occasional instances where meanings are grouped by similar function or most common use. Where a form stands for both an abbreviation and a symbol, the definitions are given in separate sections of the entry, first for the abbreviations and then for the symbols.

> **i** *I an abbreviation for:* **1** jet *engineering.* **2** jewels *horology.*
> *II a symbol for:* **1** imaginary number $\sqrt{-1}$ (square root of minus one). **2** joule (unit of work) *physics.*

Definitions

Many definitions include illustrative phrases to show abbreviations used in the combination or type of combination in which they are most often found. This practice appears particularly in entries for single letters. Other entries have illustrative phrases for abbreviations that are found in a special context. All of these phrases are based on actual usage recorded in our quotation file.

> **L 8** last (as in price quoted of a stock) *finance.* **9** *also* **L.** late, in combination: *LGk.* = *Late Greek* (Greek from about 200 to 700 AD); *L.L.* = *Late Latin* (Latin from about 200 to 700 AD).
> **J 10** *also* **J.** Journal, esp. in combination: *WSJ* = *Wall Street Journal.*
> **P 6** per, esp. in combination: *MPH* = *miles per hour;* *RPM* = *revolutions per minute.*

Abbreviations with numbers or signs

Most abbreviations that start with or otherwise have a number in them (4WD) are placed nearest the abbreviation that contains the same letter or letters without a number. For example, I[131] is entered after **I**; **4WD** follows **WD**. Other abbreviations that use the ampersand (&) are placed in strict alphabetical order as if they were fully spelled with *and*, so that whether an abbreviation is found with ampersand or with *and* it can be found in the same alphabetical place.

> **I.A.N.C.**
> **I & C** *or* **I and C**
> **I and D** *or* **I & D**
> **I & O, etc.**

Variant forms

Variant forms are freely entered as they appear in our files. Usually the difference is a matter of periods and no periods for the same group of letters.

Although many style sheets try to regulate the use of periods, and dictionaries of abbreviations follow suit, usage in the same publication and even in the same article will escape the binding restrictions of an adopted style. As a matter of fact, close examination of several well-known style sheets attests to inconsistencies in the use of periods and also use of upper-case and lower-case letters. This dictionary departs from imposing a particular style and assigns alternate forms to specific abbreviations while still grouping various letter combinations under a common form so that the user will generally have but one place to look.

> **IDU 2** *also* **IdU** iododeoxyuridine.
> **inc. 2** *also* **inc** inclosure.
> **incalz.** *or* **Incalz** increasing tempo and tone *music.*

Labels

Subject labels and phrases are inserted to show the field, and thereby the application, of an abbreviation.

Defining phrases appear in parentheses to explain meaning or use.

> **KN 1** King's Knight *chess.*
> **KNP** King's Knight Pawn *chess.*
> **m 4** *also* **m.** maiden over *cricket...***7** *also* **m.** mare (in horse racing).

Area labels are used to show restrictions of dialect, especially British and American English. For example:

> **ICI** *or* **I.C.I. 1** *British* Imperial Chemical Industries.
> **KT 2** *Scottish also* **K.T.** Knight of the Order of the Thistle.
> **QB 2** *also* **Q.B.** *British* Queen's Bench *law.*

Foreign Abbreviations

From time to time foreign abbreviations are explained in brackets after a definition or entry. They appear in order to explain the order of letters and what the letters stand for.

> **Magn.** *or* **magn.** large. [Latin *magnus*]
> **quat. 1** four. [Latin *quattuor*]

Pronunciation

Pronunciations are given for abbreviations and acronyms where they apply or seem necessary. The word *pronounced* is used only where the abbreviation may be confused with the form of the pronunciation. Otherwise, the appearance of diacritics or stress marks in the pronounced form differentiates it from the abbreviation.

> **jep** (*pronounced* jep) jeopardy.
> **quango** (kwong′gō)
> **Rep 1** *also* **rep** (*pronounced* rep)

The key of symbols used to indicate pronunciation is the following familiar, simplified system found in many of the Barnhart dictionaries.

a	cap	i	pin	p	paper	v	very
ā	face	ī	five	r	run	w	will
ã	air			s	say	y	yet
ä	father			sh	she	z	zero
		j	jam	t	tell	zh	measure
		k	kin	th	thin		
b	bad	l	land	ᴛʜ	then		
ch	child	m	me			ə	represents:
d	did	n	no				
				u	cup	a	in about
				u̇	put	e	in taken
e	best	ng	long	ü	rule	i	in pencil
ē	be			yü	use	o	in lemon
ėr	term			yu̇	uric	u	in circus
		o	rock				
		ō	go				
f	fat	ô	order, all				
g	go	oi	oil				
h	he	ou	out				

Part II
Reverse List

The reverse list is arranged alphabetically by word, not letter by letter. (Hyphenated words are considered as single words, with hyphens preceding all letters alphabetically. Words followed by commas come after words followed by spaces.) For example:

acid number
acid value
acid, citrate, and dextrose
acid-resistant
acidity

In the reverse list, some entries or definitions are followed by one or more of the following abbreviations:

GPO   for Government Printing Office (of the United States)
NYT   for *The New York Times*
MLA   for Modern Language Association
CSM   for Canadian Style Manual (actually referring to either the *Canadian Government Style Manual* or the *Civil Service of Canada Office Manual* or both)
OUP   for Oxford University Press

Each of these abbreviations refers to a style manual whose significance, as noted in the preface to this dictionary, merely indicates a preference in form and is intended to serve as a guide.

Abbreviation in English

Linguistic science has demonstrated that a variety of mechanisms are at work within the structure of a language. And though speech is primary, and its mechanisms are reflected in the writing system of a language, the system of notation also generates differences peculiar to itself. These mechanisms, both of speech and of writing, are governed by underlying forces, such as the constant influence of economy in expression. This force is evident in English not only when simplifying the complexities of speech (as the loss of case and gender endings or the leveling of many strong verbs) but also when reducing notation, often by specialized mechanisms (as the substitution of the apostrophe for *e*, first for genitives ending in *e* and later applied in general to possessives). Reduction is particularly apparent in the processes of abbreviation, which create numerous types of shortened forms in the writing system of English. What is not so apparent is that some of these same processes are active in speech as well.

The Processes of Abbreviation

Many mechanisms of abbreviation in English are used to create a wide variety of forms. Some mechanisms produce forms generally common to speech and writing, such as clipping and the formation of acronyms; others yield forms primarily in written English, such as symbols and initialisms.

Clipping

The mechanism for clipping operates by omitting some part or parts at the end of a word. It is perhaps best known in popular slang or informal use, even though many such formations eventually gain acceptance in standard usage. Older forms include *auto* (for automobile), *dorm* for dormitory), *el* (for elevated railway), *memo* (for memorandum), and *polio* (for poliomyelitis); newer forms are *condo* (for condominium), *demo* (for demonstration), *deli* (for delicatessen), *limo* (for limousine), *mod* (for modern), and *specs* (for specifications).

Some clippings retain only the initial syllable of a word to satisfy comprehension, as *pop* (for popular), *prom* (for promenade: dance or concert), and *pro*

(for professional). However, where a prefix is present, a second syllable is included, as in *precip*, *prefab*, *prelim*; or, where an ambiguity obscures meaning, one or two following letters are included after the initial syllable, as in *prep* (for pre·par·a·to·ry), *prop* (for pro·pel·ler), and *mayo* (for may·on·naise). Clippings that are formed predominantly in written English also exhibit these two types of formation, as in *pop.* (for population) and *prep.* (for preposition), contrasted with *Prop* (for pro·pri·e·tor), *auto.* (for au·to·mat·ic), and *esp.* (for es·pe·cial·ly).

Some older written abbreviations formed by clipping have generated new uses almost exclusively confined to informal speech. This subgroup includes *Inc* (for incorporated, as in *Japan Inc*), *sync* or *synch* (for synchronized, synchronization as in *out of sync*), *sec* (for second or moment, as in *wait a sec*), *prob* (for problem, as in *what's the prob*), *hols* (for holidays, as in *going home for the hols*), and *Pres* (for president, earlier rendered *Prex* and *Prexy*, and now often *Prez*).

An offshoot of this group has developed into words based on phonetic spellings, some of which represent forms originally abbreviated. Examples include *perk* (for *perq.* perquisite), *pix* (for *pic.* pictures), *hi* (for *high* in hi-tech, a clipping of high technology). Other forms abbreviated by clipping that have generated words in English are *pro tem* (originally itself an abbreviation of *pro tempore*), *ad lib* (originally an abbreviation of *ad libitum*), and *op-ed* (for *opposite editorial* [page], later *opinion editorial*), and *ad* and British *advert* (for *advertisement*).

Many other examples exist (*lab, quad, stereo, intercom, strep, tarp, tech*), but it is unclear whether these forms, which are now well-established words, originated by clipping in speech or in writing. Available evidence tends to support clipping in speech, although there are ambiguous cases, such as *intercom*, which has spawned the shorter abbreviation *ICOM*.

Another type of clipping in English is produced in combination with suffixes. The form *Prexy*, given above, is an example of the suffix *-y* added to the older form *Prex*. Modern examples include diminutive *telly* from British English (*television* + doubling of *l* + *-y*), *veggie* (for *vegetable* or *vegetarian* + doubling of *g* + variant *-ie*), and *preemie*, or sometimes *premie* (*premature* + variant *-ie*). Another ending that assumes the function of a suffix is *-s*. And though it may appear to be an arbitrary ending, as found in *turps* (for turpentine), in this case it is a false plural that probably refers to "spirits of turpentine." However, in a form such as *cons* (*pros* and *cons*), the *-s* is a sign of the plural to the clipped form *con* (for contra).

Additionally, there are blends that derive exclusively by the process of clipping and are devised to be easily pronounceable. For this reason many are classified as acronyms and occur in such formations as *Comex* (for commodity exchange), *Conrail* (for Consolidated Rail Corporation), and *telex* (for teletype exchange). Others, such as *El-hi* (for elementary-high school), use specialized spelling devices to achieve their function as a blend.

Apheresis

The mechanism for apheresis, which is sometimes considered a special type of clipping, omits some part of the beginning of a word. As in clipping, many words formed by apheresis were originally considered to be nonstandard usage. Among the commonest examples of this mechanism are *bus* (for omnibus), *phone* (for telephone), *plane* (for airplane), *gator* (for alligator), and Australian *roo* (for kangaroo). A contemporary example is *corder* (for camcorder). Much-used older forms include the endings of cardinal numbers: 1st (for fir*st*), 2nd (for seco*nd*), 3rd (for thi*rd*), 4th (for four*th*), etc., which are amalgamated with number symbols.

A special type of apheresis is found in aphetic forms that omit an initial unstressed syllable, as in *state* (for estate), *possum* (for opossum), and *coon* (for raccoon).

A combination or type of clipping, sometimes broadly referred to as apocope, and apheresis occurs in *flu* (for influenza), *fridge* (for refrigerator, with addition of *d* from the spelling pattern *dge*). Additionally, numerous blends in English exhibit both clipping and apheresis. Examples include *motel* (for motor hotel), *camcorder* (for video camera recorder), *Oxbridge* (for Oxford-Cambridge), and *quasar* (for quasi-stellar), sometimes also classified further as acronyms. Some forms omit just a single letter in one of the elements of a blend, as *smog* (for smoke and fog) and *chunnel* (for Channel Tunnel).

Contraction

Other mechanisms have also developed to greatly extend the process of abbreviation in English. However, unlike clipping, they are largely rooted in written English and, except for acronyms, produce only occasional forms in spoken English. One of these mechanisms is contraction, which has produced *bldg.* (for building), *Dr.* (for doctor), *Agt* (for agent), *Capt* (for captain), *std* (for standard), *ft* (for foot), *Gk* (for Greek), *Spn* (for Spanish).

A few contractions have entered spoken English and become quite prominent, such as *TV* (for television), *TB* (for tuberculosis), *QT* (for quiet, especially in *on the QT*), *IV* (for intravenous), and *GI* (for gastrointestinal, as in *GI series* of x rays). These popular forms have assumed the capital letters associated with initialisms, as if their other syllables were separate words. Other examples combine syllables with distinct words as in *PVC* (for polyvinyl chloride) and *DMZ* (for demilitarized zone).

Another type of contraction incorporates the plural *s* of the full form, as *PJs* or *pj's* (for pajamas); and the abbreviation *Mrs.* has generated a specialized pronunciation (*mis'iz* for the full form mistress), while the form *pram* is a hybridization of contraction and clipping (for perambulator).

Initialism

The process of grouping initial letters to form initialisms is the most familiar and possibly the most productive form of written abbreviation. Most initialisms when used in spoken English are meant to be pronounced letter by letter. Some examples are *LA* (for Los Angeles), *FYI* (for your information), *SRO* (for standing room only or single room occupancy), *VCR* (for video cassette recorder), *RV* (for recreational vehicle or Revised Version, of the Bible), *CD* (for compact disk), *CO* (for commanding officer), *DH* (for designated hitter, in baseball), *EC* (for European Community), *LDL* (for low-density lipoprotein).

A special type of initialism has come to represent more than just the abbreviated word or words it stands for. In *GOP* (for Grand Old Party), the abbreviation is used to mean the Republican Party or its members, often as a special group in the Senate, the House of Representatives, or other legislative group; in *DWI* (for driving while intoxicated), the meaning refers not only to the offense of drunken driving but to the offender. *Non-U* (with *U* for upper class) is a humorous concoction for unsophisticated. In *OD* (for overdose), the initialism is used as a noun to mean the dose or the condition itself and has been extended to mean a person who has taken an overdose of some drug. *OD* is also inflected, as with '*d* (for *-ed*) in *OD'd* to describe a condition or fact of having taken an overdose as well as taking an overdose.

Of course, *OD* parallels the older *OK*, perhaps the most widely used abbreviation in the world. So far as available research can determine, *OK* is an initialism for "oll correct," said to be the product of a humorous dialectal rendering of "all correct." This abbreviation not only has inflected forms *Ok'd, OKd* and *Ok'ing, OKing*, but has been reinforced by the later form *A-OK* meaning all OK, which is an unconscious tautology of the original *OK*.

Other initialisms have come, often accidentally, to function as abbreviated forms pronounced according to the normal rules of spelling, as in *VAT* (for value-added tax) and *DOS* (for disk operating system). Special cases include *Seabee* (a pun on the pronunciation of *C.B.* for *Construction Battalion* of the U.S. Navy) and, more distantly, *Beeb* (an alteration of *B.B.C.* for British Broadcasting Corporation), and *Veep* (a similar alteration for Vice President). Another initialism affected by pronunciation is *QN* (replacing *QKt.* for Queen's Knight, in chess). This particular instance represents a phonetic spelling, similar to the substitution of *k* for *qu* in *perk* for perquisite. The military abbreviation *CINC* (pronounced *sē'n sē'*, for commander-in-chief) bridges the difference between initialisms and acronyms such as *CINCPAC* (pronounced *singk'pak'* for Commander-in-Chief Pacific Area).

In recent times the initialisms *DNA* and *RNA* have become especially well known, as biology advances in its understanding of life functions. We are now aware of the extended use of this knowledge in *DNA finger-printing* and in the research to trace the genetic formations in cell biology and disease control. An example of the extent to which this research has penetrated the descriptive language of biology and medicine is evident in *picornavirus* (pi kôr'nə vī'rəs), a combination of *pico* very small + *RNA* + *virus*. In this instance *RNA* is embedded, its identity obscured in adjacent syllables of this portmanteau word.

Acronyms

Although the process of acronymy in language derives from written forms, acronyms are specially contrived to be used as spoken forms or read as words and clearly demonstrate their dependence on the spelling patterns of writing. This type of formation has proliferated in English in comparatively recent times, though the acronym is of ancient origin said to be devised as a

mnemonic device used especially in religious study and medicine. Examples of this now widely distributed and popular mechanism of abbreviation are *radar* (for radio detection and ranging, with clipping of *radio*), *TEFL* (for teaching English as a foreign language, with omission of *as* and *a*), *AIDS* (for acquired immune deficiency syndrome), *GIGO* (gī'gō', for garbage in, garbage out, in computer jargon), *CAT* (for computerized axial tomography), *ECU* or *ecu* (ā'kü, for European Currency Unit), *OPEC* (for Organization of Petroleum Exporting Countries, with omission of *of*), *PAC* (for political action committee), and *ROM* (for read-only memory).

It is a curious fact that many acronyms stand for combinations of words that users cannot easily identify. A clear example is *amphetamine* (for alpha-methylbeta-phenyl-ethyl-amine). Others include *ECHO* or *Echo* virus (for enteric cytopathogenic human orphan virus), *GRAS* (for generally recognized as safe, of substances), *scuba* (for self-contained underwater breathing apparatus), and *Gulag* (in Russian, Glavnoye Upravleniye Lagerei, with clipping of *Lagerei*).

Many acronyms are artificially formed to convey a message or slogan. *MADD* (for Mothers Against Drunk Driving), *ASH* (for Action on Smoking and Health, with omission of *on, and*), *ACT UP* (for Aids Coalition to Unleash Power), and *NOW* (for National Organization for Women, with omission of *for*) are prominent examples.

Other acronyms have developed such strong advertising appeal or high recognition that, when what they originally stood for is changed for some reason, a different name or title is concocted using the same letters, thus preserving the original acronym. A good example of this is *CARE* (originally standing for Cooperative for American Relief to Europe, now, to Everywhere). Another, but more forced example, is *UNICEF* (originally, United Nations International Children's Emergency Fund, now United Nations Children's Fund).

A few acronyms in English combine with the suffix *-ie* or *-y* to produce a more euphonious form than the acronym alone. Perhaps the most successful of these is the currently popular *yuppie*, formed from the acronym *yup* (for young urban professional, with addition of *p* imitating the spelling pattern represented by pup/puppy, no doubt with a tinge of satire). The form *yuppie* also echoes *yippie*, from *YIP* (for Youth International Party) and earlier *hippie*, from *hip* (a word used especially as an adjective to mean up-to-date).

Substitution

Another process of abbreviation rooted in written forms is substitution, which often involves abbreviated forms of foreign words and expressions that are adopted in English contexts. Common examples of these abbreviations that derive in whole or in part from foreign languages are *AM* and *PM* (for morning and afternoon or evening, from Latin *ante meridiem* and *post meridiem*), *e.g.* (for example, from Latin *exempli gratia*), *lb* (for pound, from Latin *libra*), *x* (for *ex*, from Latin, as found in *x.d.* = ex dividend), and *X* (the Greek letter *chi* at the beginning of the name Christ written in Greek, and appearing in English *Xmas* which, incidentally, includes the form *mas* by apocope).

This device of using *x* to stand for its letter name has been extended in English to represent the initial syllable *ex-* (eks) of exchange as found in *Px* (for Post Exchange on a military base) and in *Tx* (for telephone exchange), and *ex-* of *extra* as found in *XL* (for extra large). Other equivalents include *ex-* as found in *xhst* (for exhaust) or *XPL* (for explosive), *xlnt* (for excellent), and *x'd* (for executed, of a legal or financial obligation).

The process of substitution is also evident in an abbreviation such as *xtal* (for crystal), in which *x* is a graphic representation of *kris-* in the initial syllable. In this example and the ones above, *x* assumes characteristics of a symbol.

A further extension of the use of *x* is found in its substitution for cross as a symbol of, and a visual pun on, the crossing strokes of the letter. Examples include *XING* (for crossing, as in *PED XING* for Pedestrian Crossing), *XC* or *X-C* (for cross-country), *XR* (for cross-reference), and *Xrds* (for crossroads).

The visual pun is also evident in *XFER*, in which the sense "cross" is identified with the meaning of the prefix "trans-" to produce an abbreviation for transfer, or *XMTR* (for transmitter) and *xstr* (for transistor).

Other visual puns in English include *EZ* (for easy, as in the tax form 1040EZ), *K-9* (for canine, and as in K-9 Corps), *MT* (for empty), and *IOU* (for the promissory note). The comic strip artist has also contributed *Z, z* (for sleep or snoring, in the form zzz, etc., now rendered *Z's* or *z's* in phrases such as *catch some z's*).

Development of Abbreviations

The origin of abbreviation probably lies in the speech mechanism of clipping longer words. But since the origin of speech is shrouded in antiquity, it is not possible to determine the origin of the process of abbreviation in speech.

The origin of abbreviation in writing is also unclear. However, the development of written abbreviation is traceable in some of its processes through available documents. In English, the development is rooted immediately in Latin, and more distantly in Greek—influenced to an indeterminate extent by Near Eastern practices of notation, such as those of the Phoenician traders.

In Latin inscriptions and documents it is possible to find examples of the basic processes used in our own times. Initialisms are frequent, such as the famous *SPQR* (*Senatus Populusque Romanus* for the Roman Senate and People), carried on standards before the Roman legions, and *A.U.C.* (*ab urbe condita* for after the foundation of Rome) to signify dates. Contraction is evident in *Cos.* (Consul), and examples of clipping are found in *Imp.* (imperium and imperator) and *Aet.* (*aetatis*, aged or at the age of).

Other devices used in Latin and then carried over into Medieval times include the horizontal line above a combination of letters to distinguish them as an abbreviation. Today the practice has been largely replaced by use of the period (in Medieval times, by a period at the midpoint above the line) and is found only as an archaism, especially in church carvings and stained glass windows, as in $\overline{IHS}$ (for Greek IHΣ, IHΣOYE Jesus) or $\overline{DNS}$ (for Latin *Dominus*). Another device used in Latin was a superscript to mark the terminal letter of an abbreviation. This practice still occurs in some European languages, typified in Spanish N^o for numero, but forms such as G^t, g^t (for great) and A^{gt} (for agent) are now found only occasionally in English, as printers have reduced all but D^r (for debtor), f^o (for folio), V^o (for verso), 1st, 2nd, etc. (for first, second, etc.), and occasionally q^n (for question) to a uniform letter size.

Medieval abbreviation used numerous other mechanical devices. Some are frequently employed today; others appear only as obscure vestiges of former practice. Although the virgule, or solidus, was replaced by the apostrophe fairly early on in such forms as *o'clock* and *y'day* (for yesterday), it is still found in a similar function separating parts of words in *u/s* (for unserviceable), *P/R* (for payroll), *w/h* (for withholding), and *w/o* (for without).

The virgule also separates letters in abbreviations that represent separate words, as in *F/L* (for focal length), and *c/o* (for carried over).

Another vestige of Medieval practice found in relatively few modern forms is the use of the circle. This device derives from the scribal practice of adding a curved stroke to the last letter of an abbreviation. Use of the curved terminal stroke appears in *oz* (for ounce) rendered ℥ and oʒ. Another Medieval form that displays the curved stroke as a terminal sign is the so-called "at" sign (@, sometimes considered an exaggerated form of Latin *ad*). The same device may be distantly operative in the modern notation © (for copyright) and ® (for registered trademark).

Medieval and perhaps earlier practice, certainly derivation from earlier practice, is evident in the ampersand (&) and in the abbreviation *viz* (for Latin *videlicet* namely). The *z* of *viz* is a blend of ancient Tironian notation 7 (for Latin *-et*, as in *videlicet*) and a Medieval midline dot (marking termination) that later developed into an approximation of the colon and semi-colon. Subsequently the mark was rendered in a single stroke similar to our cursive *ʒ*. In printed form, this character was set as *z* and did not originally require a period, which, of course, would have been a redundant use. Later, as the function of *ʒ* became obscure, a period was added. This situation is reminiscent of the development of *ye* (for *the*) in which Old English þ was replaced by *y*, in early printing being the best available approximation of the Old English character (þ thorn).

The development of ampersand (&) is not as clearly defined as that of *z* in *videlicet*. It is probably from a blending of 7 (for *-et*) and *c* or ɔ (for *cetera*), perhaps influenced by the ligature cͧ. Varying forms appear from earliest known cͧ, and in the 700's ⁊ᴄ, which is found as ⅋ in the 1100's and & in the 1200's.

The complex Medieval use of abbreviation, it is said, evolved to an extreme state in the hands of the Irish scribes. They became so facile at the art of abbreviation in later church manuscripts that there is scarcely a long word which is not shortened in some way. The early abundance of abbreviations in linear writing is not altogether a surprise if one recalls the conditions which preceded printing and the need to save space on precious vellum in the Medieval period.

The formation of acronyms transcends the history of all shortened forms. They are known from the time of early Hebrew literature and are found in many languages. As a product of speech and writing, the acronym's principal early function was that of a mnemonic device. The mnemonics are represented in modern times by *face* for the notes in the spaces of the staff of the treble clef in music, and much earlier in Hebrew by *Shas* (for shishak sedarim, an old name for the Talmud), or later *Besht* (for Baal Shim-Tov, founder of the Polish Hasidic movement).

By the time Ephraim Chambers was compiling his *Dictionary of the Arts and Sciences*, in 1728, the device of acronymy was known widely enough for him to state the following: "The Jewish authors and copyists . . . frequently take the initial letters of several succeeding words, join them together, and adding vowels to them, make a barbarous sort of word, representative of all the words thus abridged."

In our time W. Nelson Francis, in his text *The English Language*, refers to the same ancient practice: "The early Christians . . . took the initials of the Greek phrase . . . 'Jesus Christ, son of God, Savior' to make the Greek word ιχθυς ('fish') and adopted the fish as a symbol for Christ."

In spite of its long history, the acronym did not come to general public attention until World War II. This was after much popular use of three-letter abbreviations in the Depression, starting with the Hoover administration's *RFC* (for Reconstruction Finance Corporation), which was followed by Franklin Roosevelt's administration that generated what was popularly termed an alphabet soup of abbreviations for new agencies, such as *NRA* (for National Recovery Act) and *WPA* (for Works Project Administration), and even for the President himself (*FDR*). What is surprising about the use of acronyms during World War II was their easy acceptance at the time. Many have died away except for historical significance, such as *SHAEF*, *asdic*, and *WACs*, but some others from the war years have been absorbed in general use (*radar*, *Unesco*, *snafu*), possibly gaining currency even more easily than *AWOL* and *Anzac* (Australian and New Zealand Army Corps) from World War I. *AWOL* is generally held to have assumed the pronunciation *āʹwôl* during World War I, though as an abbreviation it was known in the Civil War.

What followed World War II (*Unicef*, *Nato*, *QUANGO*) has been greatly expanded by new technologies of space (*LEM*, *NASA*), the computer (*Fortran*, *ROM*, *DOS*), astronomy (*quasar*), physics (*laser*, *CERN*, *rad*), biology (*SIDS*, *REM*, *ECHO* virus or *echovirus*), and by society in turmoil (*SWAT*, *Nimby*, *posslq*). Even the international community now frequently uses acronyms (*SWAPO*, *SALT*, *OPEC*, *GATT*).

Symbols and Abbreviations

Letter symbols are traditionally distinguished from abbreviations by use, as in formulas; by function, as in mathematics for quantities, concepts, and processes; and by substitution for conditions and things, as in descriptive notation of chess or card games, or in schematic charts in genetics. Phonetic symbols abound in the pronunciation systems of dictionaries, and chemical symbols are used in every periodic table of the elements. The designation 2×4 of lumber for support timbers is purely by use of symbols; so, too, are the distress call *SOS*, devised because it is easy to transmit in Morse code, and the popular chemical name H_2O for water.

Many times the same letter or combination of letters serve as both symbol and abbreviation. In the formula $E = mc^2$ (where E stands for *energy*, m for *mass*, and c for *constant* speed of light), the letters, it is true, are abbreviations for particular words, but they stand as symbols in relation to one another for a concept and for quantities once the formula is applied in a specific instance. On the other hand, in the form *EMS* (energy management system), each letter standing for a specific word does not symbolize any operational concept of one member acting on another. Thus E for energy, depending on its context, can be either a symbol or an abbreviation.

The distinction between symbol and abbreviation is further blurred when symbols and abbreviations appear in combination, such as *4WD* (for four-wheel drive). This type of amalgamation is used in combinations of words and abbreviations to form new accretions, as in *triple A* (for *antiaircraft artillery*, from earlier *AA*, commonly known in World War II as *ack-ack*). Another example of amalgamation is found in the earlier-cited aphetic forms *-st*, *-nd* (for fir*st*, seco*nd*, etc.), which combine with number symbols to form *1st*, *2nd*, etc.

Some letter symbols have a distant and often obscure or even unknown relationship with the thing they stand for. The symbol *BB* (for small shot) is a size in the calibration of ammunition, but *Bx* in *Bx electrical cable* can only be conjectured as standing for box or boxed cable. *ABCs* (for fundamental concepts) is a figurative use that derives from the letters at the beginning of the alphabet, which in a transferred sense means basic facts or tenets. *Ms* (for "miz") is supposed to be a neutral concoction blended from *Miss* and *Mrs.* by omitting the medial letters that show a particular marital status. Use of Ms parallels that of the title *Mr.*

for a married or unmarried man. Other symbols seem impenetrably arbitrary in their selection, such as *H* for enthalpy and *S* for entropy in chemical engineering. Of course, the very arbitrariness of symbols contributes to their effectiveness.

Style and Abbreviations

The form and construction of abbreviations is principally a matter of prevailing convention. The use of periods, hyphens, the virgule, and spacing is complemented by the use of upper- and lower-case letters, italics, choice of letters, and grammatical function.

Use of Periods

In Medieval times a curved terminal stroke was often used so that there was little purpose for the period, and its use was very limited. When the period did appear, it was placed at a midpoint above the line. Today the period appears frequently but erratically. A modern tendency is to return to earlier practice by omitting it. This convention is considered to be more pronounced in Great Britain than in the United States, as typified by British *Dr*, U.S. *Dr.* (for doctor); however, an examination of current style in the United States in such widely consulted formats as that of telephone directory listings and mailing lists proves the practice of omitting periods here as well.

The period has been dropped generally in scientific and technical notation and specifically in forms such as *log* (for logarithm), *in* (for inch), *cot* (for cotangent), *C* (for Celsius), *cp* (for candlepower), *bhp* (for brake horsepower). Its absence is also fairly general in capitalized initialisms, such as *FBI*, *CAT* (for computerized axial tomography), *EMR* (for electromagnetic resonance), *GDP* (for gross domestic product), *LBJ*, *DNA*, *EC* (for European Community), *AC* and *DC*, *PC* (for politically correct and personal computer), *CD* (for certificate of deposit and compact disk), *OTB* (for off-track betting).

Regardless of practice, some style sheets persist in recommending use of the period in many forms, others in an erratic selection. Of course, there are special situations that demand periods, even in initialisms, to avoid the ludicrous, as in the headline PRESIDENT TAKES C.A.B. TO TASK. Where use of the period seems fixed is in abbreviations that can be confused with words. This condition occurs mostly in forms such as *Unit.* (for Unitarian), *art.* (for article), *Son.* (for sonata), *Sup.* (for Superior), and occasionally in nontechnical use of *in.* (for inch).

Other Marks of Punctuation

One of the marks from Medieval practice still appearing in abbreviations is the virgule. Not only does this slanted stroke serve to separate parts of words, such as *f/b* (for feedback, in electronics), *W/D* (for withdrawn) and *u/t* (for untrained), but it also separates letters that stand for separate words, as in *W/R* (for warehouse receipt). In *h/m/s* (for hours, minutes, seconds) and *W/L/T* (for win, lose, tie), the virgule assumes the function of a comma, a mark of punctuation that is not found in the body of abbreviations. In *P/L* (for profit *and* loss), *ac/* (for according *to*), *S/R* (for sale *or* return), *R/W* (for right *of* way), and *R/Q* (for request *for* quotation), the virgule stands for the implied use of *and, to, or, of,* and *for.* In a form such as *u/c* (for upper-case, of letters), the virgule emphasizes the contrast with *l/c* (for lower-case). Both of these forms alternate with *u.c.* and *l.c.,* and the virgule is an example of the older tendency to avoid use of periods, as is also found in *D/W* (for dead weight). In recent widespread use, the virgule is also a symbol of cancellation as in *P̸* (for No Parking) and *U̸* (for No U-Turn), similar to the use ≠ (not equal) in mathematics.

The hyphen is little noted in style sheets dealing with abbreviation. Sometimes it is interchangeable with the virgule, *T-R* and *T/R* (for transmit-receive); in other instances, it is not, as in *w-hr* (for watt-hour) and *w/hr* (for watts per hour). The hyphen has a tendency to disappear in abbreviated forms, as in *u/c* (for upper-case), *ZBB* (for zero-based budgeting), *IE* (for Indo-European), *kilovar* (for kilovolt-ampere reactive hour). It is sometimes retained in *x-r* (for cross-reference) and *x-c* (for cross-country), often in *kg-cal* (for kilogram-calorie), always in *l-glucose* (for levo- or levorotary glucose) and *K-9* (for canine).

The apostrophe is often lost in abbreviation, as in *KB* (for King's Bench), *KS* (for Kaposi's sarcoma), but is found, actually inserted, in *x's* (for atmospherics), *pj's* (for pajamas), and *cr's* (for cross-references), but not in *rms* (for reams and rooms). In addition to use in possessive and plural forms, the apostrophe also appears in inflected verbal forms, such as *Rev'g* (for reversing, of a lower court decision) and *resgn'd* (for resigned) but not in *unsgnd* (for unsigned) or *rfrd* (for referred), though *recd* and *rec'd* (for received) are both common.

Spacing

A particular characteristic of most abbreviations that represent more than one word is their tendency to be written as block compounds, without spaces. That is because the letters function as a word (*etc., ETA* for estimated time of arrival, *DOT* for Department of Transportation, *ASAP* for as soon as possible). It is also the style used in acronyms for the same reason (*Nafta* for North American Free Trade Association, *Zip* for Zone Improvement Plan, *FEMA* for Federal Emergency Management Agency).

Use of Upper- and Lower-case Letters

Another characteristic of many abbreviations is the use of capital letters. About two-thirds of all abbreviations are written either all capitals or beginning with a capital, regardless of whether the letters represent words that are usually capitalized or are derived from several words or the several syllables of one word. Examples of this practice abound in such multiple-word forms as free on board (*FOB*), true-false (*TF*), and very high frequency (*VHF*); in such multisyllabic words as chlorofluorocarbon (*CFC*) and trinitrotoluene (*TNT*); and can be found representing final letters as in the second syllable in quiet (*QT*).

Acronyms are also usually introduced with capital letters (*Nato*), or are written in all capitals, and often remain in that form to distinguish them from other words (*AIDS*). A few in common use eventually take on a form in lower-case letters (radar, scuba, quasar).

A noticeable exception to the preponderant use of capital letters occurs in rendering common units of measure (gal., in, hr, rpm), bibliographic references (op.cit., ibid.), and references written into prose (i.e., e.g., viz., etc.). Other common exceptions are found in *op-ed* (for opposite editorial page), *o.p.* (for out of print), *sit com* or *sitcom* (for situation comedy), and *sci-fi* or *si-fi* (for science fiction). It is interesting to note these last four abbreviations represent a group that in general mirrors their full written form by the use of lower-case letters, word division, and hyphenation.

Another kind of abbreviation combines upper- and lower-case letters to distinguish elements of a class within a particular group (*s* in *Ns* for nimbostratus, and *c* in *Nc* for nimbocumulus, referring to cloud types; *s* in *sRNA* for soluble RNA). A related use is found in such combinations as *kHz* (for kilohertz), *mL* (for milliliter), *Mw* (for megawatts), and *Tc* (for tera-cycles), in notation using the International Scientific units. A different use that combines upper- and lower-case letters is a part of the abbreviation for a single word (*Wb* for Weber, a unit of measure; *Au* for gold, Latin aurum; *Pl.* for Place, in an address; *Ms* for manuscript). Still another use of upper- and lower-case letters occurs in rendering such elements as the preposition or adverb within an abbreviation (*DOE* or *DoE*, Department of Energy; but always *b* in *SbW*, *sbw*, south by west).

Choice of Letters

While upper- and lower-case letters are a significant factor in the identification of abbreviations, primary to this is the selection and combination of letters. Sometimes a single letter is the only element (*b* for by; *v* for versus, now replacing older *vs*); in other abbreviations, letters stand for syllables within a single word (*PCB* for polychlorobiphenyl, *TV* for television) or for phrases (*etc.* for et cetera, *COD* for cash on delivery), and for phonetic equivalents (*x* in *Px* for Post Exchange).

Exceptions to the use of initial letters in clippings and initialisms are the easily recognized contractions that occur in *pd* (for paid), *St.* (for Saint), *pt* (for part), *Qn* (for question), *Jr.* or *Jnr.* (for junior), and *tbsp* (for tablespoon). Other variations occur in blends, such as *quasar* (for quasi-stellar object) and in substitutions, as in *xtal* (with the final syllable of crystal). In some forms, pronunciation is also a factor in identification (*Px*, *PR* for public relations, *TV*); in many others, understanding depends on a knowledge of context (*rd* for unit of radiation as contrasted with *rd* for measure of radioactive disintegration; *RV* or *R/V* for reentry vehicle as contrasted with *RV* or *R/V* for recreational vehicle; *Pet.* for Peter in the New Testament as contrasted with *Pet.* for Peters in Supreme Court Reports).

Grammar of Abbreviations

A special area that affects the form of abbreviations involves grammar, particularly in the change of form by inflection. The simple construction of plurals gen-erally uses *-s*, *-es* (GIs, WASPs, Amvets, telexes), or more popularly *-'s* (to separate *s* from the abbreviated form, as *cr's* (for cross references), *pj's* (for pajamas). A select group of perhaps fifty or so abbreviations regularly forms plurals by doubling a consonant (*Mss* manuscripts, *ff.* folios, *nn* notes, *pp.* pages, *VV* volumes, *qq* questions, and *qqv* see for references, *LLJ* Lord Justices, *LLD* Doctor of Laws).

Rhetoric also plays a part in the form of certain abbreviations. Emphasis is indicated by doubling, as in music (*f* loud, for Italian *forte*; *ff* very loud, for Italian *fortissimo*; *fff* very, very loud, for Italian *fortississimo*, and conversely *p* soft, for Italian *piano*; *pp* very soft, for Italian *pianissimo*; *ppp* very, very soft, for Italian *pianississimo*). Both the devices for creating plurals and for adding emphasis by doubling letters are borrowings of mechanisms from other languages, the former from Latin, the latter from Italian. And though the practices are firmly established for some common abbreviations, as in *ll* lines, *cc* copies, and in *HH* or *HHH* for hardness of pencil lead, they do not seem to be generating additional forms in English.

Verbal inflection also occurs in abbreviations as noted under use of the apostrophe. It is used in describing conditions or processes in which the form so used takes *-ed*, *'d*, *'ing* (*OD'd* for overdosed, *prepd* for prepared, lasered, *specing* or *specking* for specifying, *DJ'ing* for acting as a disk jockey). Again the apostrophe appears when the user feels a need to separate the abbreviation from its inflected sign for the sake of understandability.

Related to grammar, but more properly a part of word formation, is the process of combining abbreviations directly with suffixes, such as *-er* to form agent nouns (*CBer*, *CB'er*) or *-an*, *-ian* to form nouns of association (*Oxbridgian*). English also creates new forms by adding a diminutive suffix to clipped forms of longer words such as *preppie*, *preppy* (formed from *prep* as in prep school + doubling of *p* + *-ie* or *-y*) and by adding *-o*, in the sense of a person or thing associated with the meaning of a word in its full form, as in *combo* (formed from *combination* + *-o*). This final *-o* should not be confused with *-o* that is a part of a longer word (for example *porno* in pornography, now more often *porn*; *promo* in promotion; *pyro* in pyromaniac).

Borrowing

It is well known that many abbreviations have been borrowed into English from foreign languages, chiefly from Latin: *i.e.*, *op.cit.*, *cf.*, *Ib.*; but also from French:

RSVP, SI for International System (of units for scientific measurements), *Velcro* (Velours croché, hooked velvet); from Italian: *cresc* for crescendo, *GT* for Gran Turismo (type of sports car); German: *flak* for Fl.A.K. (Flieger Abwehr Kanone, usually written as one word), *Gestapo* for Geheime Staats-polizei; and Russian: *tokamak* for toroidal'naya kamera s aksial'nym magnitnym polem (device producing thermonuclear power). What is not so fully appreciated is how deeply such borrowing has penetrated English, producing bilingual blending, as in *PUO* for Latin *pyrexia* (fever) + English *(of) unknown origin; DWT* for Latin *denarius* (penny) + English *weight; cum d.* for Latin *cum* (with) + English *dividend.*

Conclusion

An examination of abbreviations shows that even though they use many of the mechanisms of language in their formation and are frequent at all levels of usage, most people, including editors, writers, and scholars, consider abbreviations to be a marginal element of language. Their variations in form, that is in the use of periods, upper- and lower-case letters, the inclusion or omission of prepositions and articles, etc., seem to be a matter of the moment. One does not have to look far in a magazine or newspaper to find more than one form for the same abbreviation, often in the same article. Because our citation files repeatedly demonstrate this striking fluidity, evidence suggests that, style rules to the contrary, it is usually the influence of the context that determines the form of an abbreviation in a given instance.

A

A *I an abbreviation for:* **1** ace (esp. a playing card). **2** acid. **3** acre. **4** *also* **A.** acting, esp. in combination: *APMG = Acting Postmaster General.* **5** adenine (one of four bases in RNA-DNA code). **6** adult (esp. adult entertainment in British motion-picture classification). **7 a** advance. **b** advanced: *the British A-level examinations.* **8** Afghani (Afghanistan unit of money). **9 a** air. **b** aircraft. **c** airman: *A-1 = Airman First Class.* **10** albedo (degree of whiteness or reflection of a surface). **11** Algeria, Algerian: *DA = Algeria dinar.* **12** Alpha (first letter of the Greek alphabet, used esp. as a symbol to denote first in order or degree). **13** alternate, esp. on aviation charts. **14** *also* **A.** alto *music.* **15** *also* **A.** amateur, esp. in combination: *AAU = Amateur Athletic Union.* **16** *also* **A.** America, American, esp. in combination: *AAU = American Astronomical Union.* **17** ammeter. **18** ampere. **19** amphibian. **20 a** amplification *physics.* **b** amplitude *physics.* **21** androecium (male parts of a flower). **22** angstrom unit (measure of wavelength of light). **23** annual *botany.* **24** anode. **25** answer. **26** antarctic or arctic (classification of an air mass) *meteorology.* **27** anterior, *esp. in anatomy.* **28** April. **29** *also* **A.** are (100 square meters). **30** area. **31** arrive, arrives at: *A 11:42, L 11:58.* **32** *also* **A.** assist *sports.* **33** *also* **A.** assistant, esp. in combination: *ADA = Assistant District Attorney.* **34** astragal *architecture, medicine.* **35** atomic: *A-Bomb.* **36** attendance *sports:* A 25,000. **37** August. **38** Australian, in combination: *A$ = Australian dollar.* **39** English (language, in tables). [French *anglais*]

II a symbol for: **1** absolute temperature. **2** argon (chemical element; replaced by Ar). **3** aspect ratio *aeronautics.* **4** atomic fission. **5** atomic weight or mass number. **6** attenuation constant *acoustics.* **7** average, esp. arithmetic average. **8 a** best of a kind. **b** highest grade given in school. **c** British road classification. **9** blood type A (one of the four major blood groups). **10** blue star of maximum hydrogen intensity *astronomy.* **11** dominant (Mendelian notation). **12** (medieval Roman numeral) **a** fifty; 50. **b** five hundred; 500. **13 a** first of a series (compare *Alpha* listed above). **b** first section (esp. in analysis of a music score). **c** first signature of a book *printing.* **14** hail *meteorology.* **15** Helmholtz function. **16** magnetic vector potential. **17** metric paper sizes of standard weights for stationery and printing, used by the International Organization for Standardization (ISO): *A3 = 297 mm × 420 mm, replacing 11 in × 17 in; A4 = 210 mm × 297 mm, replacing 8½ in × 11 in; A5 = 148 mm × 210 mm, replacing 6 in × 9 in and 5 in × 8 in; A6 = 105 mm × 148 mm, replacing 4 in × 6 in and 4 in × 5 in.* **18** quantity (esp. a known quantity in algebraic notation). **19** shoe width less than B. **20** sixth tone in the scale of C major. **21** strain of a virus: *A Victoria* (strain of influenza virus, first identified in 1975 in Victoria, Australia). **22** third highest ranking after AA *finance.* **23** work *physics.*

Ā in equal parts (of ingredients in a prescription). [Latin *ana*]

A **1** affinity *chemistry.* **2** dominant (Mendelian notation).

Å *or* **A°** angstrom unit (measure of wavelength of light).

A-1 *or* **A1** first class; excellent: *a book in A-1 condition.*
▶Though seldom used in running text, A-1 is often found in catalogs and newspaper advertisements. It was originally a shipping classification of *Lloyd's Register* indicating first-class condition of hull and rigging.

a *I an abbreviation for:* **1** abbreviation. **2** about (compare c). **3** absent. **4** absolute. **5** *also* **a.** accepted *commerce.* **6** accommodation (of the eyes) *medicine.* **7** account. **8** acid or acidity, esp. total acidity *medicine.* **9** acre. **10** active, in combination *esp. in grammar.* **11** addendum. **12** address. **13** *also* **a.** adjective. **14** adult. **15** advance, advanced. **16** advice or advise. **17** aerial. **18** after. **19** afternoon. **20** age. **21** air. **22** airplane. **23** alpha (first letter of the Greek alphabet). **24** alto *music, meteorology.* **25** amateur. **26** ampere. **27** angle. **28** angstrom unit (measure of wavelength of light). **29** annuity. **30** anode. **31** anonymous. **32** answer. **33** anterior *esp. in biology.* **34** *also* **a.** approved. **35** are (100 square meters). **36** area. **37** argent (silver tincture on a coat of arms). **38** arrive, arrive at: *a 11:42, l 11:58.* **39** article. **40** asbestos. **41** assist *sports.* **42** asymmetric *chemistry.* **43** at. **44** atmosphere *physics, meteorology.* **45 a** atomic. **b** atomic weight. **46** atto- (one quintillionth or 10^{-18}). **47** audit or auditor. **48** author *cataloging, printing.* **49** automatic. **50** aviation or aviator. **51** azimuth (angular distance east or west of north). **52** before: *a1450.* [Latin *ante*] **53** bright (of stars). **54** silver. [Latin *argentum*] **55** water. [Latin *aqua*]

II a symbol for: **1** acceleration, *esp. in physics.* **2** first in a series. **3** in equal parts (of ingredients in a prescription). [Latin *ana*] **4** linear acceleration, *esp. in physics.* **5** nucleus, heavily concentrated with closed spiral arms (of nebula) *astronomy.* **6** quantity, esp. a known quantity (in algebraic equations). **7** recessive (Mendelian notation). **8** recto leaf *botany.* **9** semimajor axis *astronomy.*

ā in equal parts (of ingredients in a prescription). [Latin *ana*]

a *I an abbreviation for:* **1** *also* **a.** abundant (occurrence of species) *biology.* **2** before: *a1600.* [Latin *ante*] **3** silver. [Latin *argentum*] **4** water. [Latin *aqua*]

II a symbol for: **1** absorption coefficient. **2** acceleration, *esp. in physics.* **3** accommodation coefficient. **4** first van der Waals constant. **5** recessive (Mendelian notation). **6** semimajor axis *astronomy.*

@ for, at (esp. in billing): *6 @ 25¢ = $1.50.*

AA *I an abbreviation for:* **1** absolute altitude. **2** accomplishment, achievement, or attainment age. **3** acting appointment. **4** Addicts Anonymous. **5** adenylic acid. **6** administrative assistant. **7** African Affairs (bureau of U.S. Department of State). **8** air-to-air missile. **9** *also* **A.A.** Alcoholics Anonymous. **10** antiaircraft. **11** antiproton accumulator *physics.* **12** approximate absolute temperature. **13** arithmetic average. **14** armature accelerator. **15** *also* **A.A.** Associate in Accounting. **16** *also* **A.A.**

1

Associate in Arts. **17** Augustinians of the Assumption. **18** *also* **A.A.** author's alteration. **19** Automobile Association (of Great Britain, Australia, New Zealand). **20** average audience, in rating radio and television programs *advertising*. **21** Foreign Office. [German *Auswärtiges Amt*]
II a symbol for: **1** highest grade (of aircraft fuel). **2** second highest rating after AAA *finance*. **3** shoe width less than A.

A-A air-to-air missile.

$\overline{AA}$ in equal parts (of ingredients in a prescription). [Latin *ana*]

Aa second highest rating after Aaa *finance*.

aa **1** *also* **a.a.** always afloat *shipping*. **2** antiaircraft. **3** approximate absolute temperature. **4** *also* **a.a.** author's alteration.

$\overline{aa}$ in equal parts (of ingredients in a prescription). [Latin *ana*]

a/a always afloat *shipping*.

AAA *I an abbreviation for:* **1** Actors and Artists of America. **2 a** Agricultural Adjustment Act (1933, defining the first farm parity prices). **b** Agricultural Adjustment Administration (1933–1936, created to control farm production). **3** Alaska. **4** Allied Artists of America. **5** Amateur Athletic Association (of Great Britain). **6** American Academy of Advertising. **7** *also* **A.A.A.** American Academy of Allergy. **8** *also* **A.A.A.** American Accounting Association. **9** American Anthropological Association. **10** *also* **A.A.A.** American Arbitration Association. **11** American Astronomers Association. **12** *also* **A.A.A.** American Automobile Association. **13** antiaircraft artillery (also called *triple A*). **14** Appraisers Association of America. **15** *also* **A.A.A.** Archives of American Art. **16** Australian Automobile Association.
II a symbol for: **1** highest rating *finance*. **2** shoe width less than AA.

Aaa highest rating *finance*.

AAAA *I an abbreviation for:* **1** Amateur Athletic Association of America. **2** American Association of Advertising Agencies. **3** Associated Actors and Artists of America. **4** *also* **A.A.A.A.** Association for the Advancement of American Art.
II a symbol for: shoe width less than AAA

AAAEE American Afro-Asian Educational Exchange.

A.A.A.G. Annals of the Association of American Geographers.

AAAI American Association for Artificial Intelligence.

A.A.A.L. American Academy of Arts and Letters.

AAAS **1** *also* **A.A.A.S.** American Academy of Arts and Sciences. **2** American Academy of Asian Studies. **3** American Association for the Advancement of Science (commonly referred to as *triple AS*). **4** Associate of the American Antiquarian Society.

AAASS American Association for the Advancement of Slavic Studies.

AAAUS Association of Average Adjusters of the United States.

AAB **1** American Association of Bioanalysts. **2** Association of Applied Biologists.

A.A.B.B. American Association of Blood Banks.

AABC American Amateur Baseball Congress.

AABD Aid to the Aged, Blind, or Disabled.

AABGA American Association of Botanical Gardens and Arboretums.

aaby as amended by.

AAC **1** aeronautical approach chart. **2** Alaskan Air Command. **3** American Alpine Club. **4** *also* **A.A.C.** Association of American Colleges. **5** automatic amplitude control. **6** automatic approach control (in landing aircraft). **7** *also* **A.A.C.** in the year before Christ. [Latin *anno ante Christum*]

AACCA *or* **A.A.C.C.A.** Associate of the Association of Certified and Corporate Accountants.

AACJC American Association of Community and Junior Colleges.

AACM Association for the Advancement of Creative Musicians.

AACP **1** American Academy for Cerebral Palsy. **2** *also* **A.A.C.P.** American Academy of Child Psychiatry.

AACR American Association for Cancer Research.

AACSE American Association of Classified School Employees.

AACTE American Association of Colleges for Teacher Education.

AAD **1** *also* **A.A.D.** American Academy of Dentists. **2** *also* **A.A.D.** American Academy of Dermatology.

AADA *or* **A.A.D.A.** American Academy of Dramatic Arts.

AADE *or* **A.A.D.E.** American Association of Dental Examiners.

AADLA Art and Antique Dealers League of America.

AADM *or* **A.A.D.M.** American Academy of Dental Medicine.

AADS American Association of Dental Schools.

A.A.E. *or* **AAE** American Association of Engineers.

AAEC Association of American Editorial Cartoonists.

A.A.E.C. Australian Atomic Energy Commission.

A.A.E.E. *or* **AAEE** American Association of Electrical Engineers.

A.Ae.E. Associate in Aeronautical Engineering.

AAES American Association of Engineering Societies.

AAF **1** American Advertising Federation. **2** American Astronautical Federation. **3** *also* **A.A.F.** Army Air Force. **4** ascorbic acid factor. **5** Auxiliary Air Force: *AAFB = Auxiliary Air Force Base.*

AAFP **1** American Academy of Family Physicians. **2** American Association of Film Producers.

AAFS **1** American Academy of Forensic Sciences. **2** American Association of Foot Specialists.

AAFSS advanced aerial fire-support system (helicopter gunship).

AAFSW Association of American Foreign Service Women.

AAG **1** Assistant Adjutant General. **2** *also* **A.A.G.** Assistant Attorney General. **3** *also* **A.A.G.** Association of American Geographers.

A.A.G.O. Associate of the American Guild of Organists.

AAGP American Academy of General Practice (of Medicine).

AAH advanced attack helicopter.

AAHA 1 *also* **A.A.H.A.** American Animal Hospital Association. **2** awaiting action of higher authority *military*.

A.A.H.E. Associate in Arts in Home Economics.

AAHM American Association for the History of Medicine.

AAHQ Allied Air Headquarters (in World War II).

AAI 1 African-American Institute. **2** American Association of Immunologists. **3** *also* **A.A.I.** Associate of the Auctioneers' and Estate Agents' Institute.

AAIA Association of American Indian Affairs.

A.A.I.E. *or* **AAIE** American Association of Industrial Engineers.

AAIS American Association for Italian Studies.

AAJC *or* **A.A.J.C.** American Association of Junior Colleges.

A.A.L. Academy of Art and Literature.

a.a.l. as the book opens. [Latin *ad aperturam libri*]

AALA American Automotive Leasing Association.

A.A.L.L. *or* **AALL** American Association of Law Libraries.

A.A.L.P.A. Associate of the Incorporated Society of Auctioneers and Landed Property Agents.

AALS 1 American Association of Language Specialists. **2** *also* **A.A.L.S.** Association of American Law Schools. **3** *also* **A.A.L.S.** Association of American Library Schools.

AAM 1 air-to-air missile. **2** American Academy of Microbiology. **3** American Association of Museums.

AAMA Architectural Aluminum Manufacturers Association.

AAMC *or* **A.A.M.C. 1** American Association of Marriage Counselors. **2** Association of American Medical Colleges. **3** Australian Army Medical Corps.

AAMD American Association on Mental Deficiency.

AAMES *or* **A.A.M.E.S.** American Association for Middle East Studies.

AAMW Association of Advertising Men and Women.

AAN 1 American Academy of Neurology. **2** American Academy of Nutrition. **3** *also* **A.A.N.** American Association of Nurserymen.

A & C Antony and Cleopatra (play by Shakespeare).

A & E *or* **A and E** aircraft and engine (of an aviation license).

A & F August and February.

a & h *or* **a. & h.** accident and health *insurance*.

a & i *or* **a. & i.** accident and insurance.

A & M *or* **A. and M. 1** Agricultural and Mechanical (in U.S. college names): *Arkansas A & M.* **2** *also* **A. & M.** Ancient and Modern (of hymns). **3** art and mechanical (graphics layout).

A. & N. Army and Navy Club.

A & O April and October.

A & P 1 anterior and posterior. **2** auscultation and percussion (a diagnostic technique in medicine). **3** Great Atlantic and Pacific Tea Company.

A&R 1 *also* **A. & R.** *or* **a. and r.** artists and repertory: *A&R man = person who supervises a recording company's list of recordings.* **2** assembly and repair.

A & T 1 acceptance and transfer. **2** *also* **A. and T.** Agricultural and Technical (in U.S. college names): *North Carolina A & T.*

AAO *or* **A.A.O. 1** American Academy of Ophthalmology. **2** American Academy of Optometry. **3** American Association of Orthodontists.

a.a.O. at the place quoted; ibid. or loc. cit. [German *am angeführten Orte*]

AAOG *or* **A.A.O.G.** American Association of Obstetricians and Gynecologists.

AAOMS American Association of Oral and Maxillofacial Surgeons (dentists who specialize in tooth implants).

AAONMS *or* **A.A.O.N.M.S.** Ancient Arabic Order of the Nobles of the Mystic Shrine.

AAOO *or* **AAO&O** American Academy of Ophthalmology and Otolaryngology.

AAP 1 affirmative action plan (of employment). **2** *also* **A.A.P.** American Association of Pathologists. **3** *also* **A.A.P.** American Academy of Pediatrics. **4** *also* **A.A.P.** Association of American Physicians. **5** Association of American Publishers. **6** *also* **A.A.P.** Australian Associated Press.

AAPB *or* **A.A.P.B.** American Association of Pathologists and Bacteriologists.

AAPCC American Association of Poison Control Centers.

AAPG American Association of Petroleum Geologists.

AAPL American Artists Professional League.

A.A.P.M.R. American Academy of Physical Medicine and Rehabilitation.

AAPOR American Association for Public Opinion Research.

AAPS *or* **A.A.P.S. 1** American Association for the Promotion of Science. **2** American Association of Plastic Surgeons.

A.A.P.S.S. American Academy of Political and Social Science.

AAPT American Association of Physics Teachers.

AAR 1 *also* **A.A.R.** *or* **a.a.r.** against all risks *insurance*. **2** American Academy in Rome. **3** *also* **A.A.R.** Association of American Railroads.

aarg. annual volume. [Swedish *aargang*]

AARP (*sometimes pronounced* ärp) American Association of Retired Persons.

A.A.R.S. All-American Rose Selections.

AAS *or* **A.A.S. 1** Acts of the Apostolic See. [Latin *Acta Apostolicae Sedis*] **2** All-American Selections: *AAS vegetable award.* **3** American Academy of Arts and Sciences; Fellow of the American Academy of Arts and Sciences. **4** American Antiquarian Society. **5** American Astronautical Society. **6** American Astronomical Society. **7** Army Air Service. **8** Associate in Applied Science. **9** Association for Asian Studies. **10** atomic absorption spectrometry. **11** Australian Academy of Science. **12** Fellow of the American Academy. [Latin *Academiae Americanae Socius*]

AASA American Association of School Administrators.

AASCU American Association of State Colleges and Universities.

AASDJ American Association of Schools and Departments of Journalism.

AASHO American Association of State Highway Officials (used to identify an association standard).

AASL or **A.A.S.L. 1** American Association of School Librarians. **2** American Association of State Libraries.

AASLH American Association for State and Local History.

AASM Association of American Steel Manufacturers.

AASO Association of American Ship Owners.

A.A.S.R. Ancient Accepted Scottish Rite (of Freemasonry).

A.A.S.S. Association of the American Antiquarian Society. [Latin *Americanae Antiquarianae Societatis Socius*]

A.A.T. Australian Antarctic Territory.

AATCC American Association of Textile Chemists and Colorists (used to identify an industry standard).

AATCLC American Association of Teachers of Chinese Language and Culture.

AATE amino adenosine triacid ester *biochemistry*.

AATEA American Association of Teacher Educators in Agriculture.

AATF American Association of Teachers of French.

AATG American Association of Teachers of German.

AATI American Association of Teachers of Italian.

AATNU United Nations Technical Assistance Administration. [French *Administration de l'assistance technique des Nations Unies*]

AATS American Association of Theological Schools.

AATSEEL American Association of Teachers of Slavic and East European Languages.

AATSP American Association of Teachers of Spanish and Portuguese.

AATU Association of Air Transport Unions.

A.A.T.U.F. All-African Trade Union Federation.

AAU or **A.A.U. 1** Amateur Athletic Union. **2** Association of American Universities.

AAUN 1 American Association for the United Nations. **2** Australian Association for the United Nations.

AAUP 1 American Association of University Presses. **2** also **A.A.U.P.** American Association of University Professors.

AAUSC American Association of University Supervisors and Coordinators.

AAUW or **A.A.U.W.** American Association of University Women.

AAV amphibious assault vehicle.

AAVMC Association of American Veterinary Medical Colleges.

AAVRPHS American Association for Vital Records and Public Health Statistics.

AAVS American Anti-Vivisection Society.

AAVSO or **A.A.V.S.O.** American Association of Variable Star Observers.

AAWS Advanced Anti-armor Weapon System.

AAWU Athletic Association of Western Universities.

AAZPA American Association of Zoological Parks and Aquariums.

AB *I an abbreviation for:* **1** also **A.B.** able-bodied seaman. **2** adapter booster. **3** advisory board. **4** afterburner. **5** Aid to the Blind. **6** Air Base. **7** airborne. **8** airman basic. **9** Alberta, Canada (U.S. postal abbreviation). **10** anchor bolt. **11** Assembly Bill (with a number, designating specific legislation in a state legislature). **12** also **A.B.** Bachelor of Arts. [Latin *Artium Baccalaureus*] **13** also **AB.** (times) at bat *baseball*.
II a symbol for: **1** blood type AB (one of four major blood groups). **2** having concealed nectar (of flowers).

A/B 1 also **a/b** or **a/b.** airborne. **2** airman basic. **3** joint stock company. [Swedish *Aktiebolaget*]

Ab *I an abbreviation for:* also **Ab.** Abbot.
II a symbol for: alabamine (chemical element; now astatine).

aB or **a.B.** on order. [German *auf Bestellung*]

a-b or **a.-b.** joint stock company. [Swedish *Aktiebolaget*]

ab 1 also **a.b.** able-bodied seaman. **2** also **ab. a** abort. **b** abortion. **3** also **ab.** about. **4** also **ab.** abstract. **5** also **a.b.** as before. **6** also **a.b.** (times) at bat *baseball*.

ABA 1 abscisic acid. **2** Amateur Boxing Association. **3** American Badminton Association. **4** also **A.B.A.** American Bankers Association. **5** also **A.B.A.** American Bar Association. **6** American Basketball Association (now NBA). **7** American Book Awards. **8** American Booksellers Association. **9** also **A.B.A.** Associate in Business Administration. **10** also **A.B.A. a** Association of British Archaeologists. **b** Associate of the British Archaeological Association.

A.B.A.A. 1 also **ABAA** Antiquarian Booksellers Association of America. **2** Associate of the British Association of Accountants and Auditors.

A.B.A.J. or **ABAJ** American Bar Association Journal.

abamp. abampere.

aband. abandoned.

Abb. 1 also **abb. a** abbess. **b** abbey. **c** abbot.
▶Generally the uppercase form is the title or the position and the lowercase form is only the position.
2 illustration. [German *Abbildung*]

abbr. or **abbrev. 1** abbreviate, abbreviated. **2** abbreviation. In computer work: *ABBR*

ABC *I an abbreviation for:* **1** advanced biomedical capsule (of a spacecraft). **2** airborne control: *ABC survey system developed by the US Geological Survey.* **3** airway, breathing, and circulation (essential bodily functions of cardiopulmonary resuscitation) *medicine*. **4** Alcoholic Beverage Control (former regulatory agency). **5 a** the alphabet: *the ABC's.* **b** alphabetical British railway guide of timetables (the *ABC* or *ABC Guide*). **6** American Book Collector (magazine title). **7** American Bowling Congress. **8** American, British, Canadian: *ABCSP = American, British, Canadian Standardization Program.* **9** American Broadcasting Company. **10** Argentina, Brazil, Chile: *ABC powers.* **11** Associated British Cinemas. **12** atomic, biological, and chemical: *ABC weapons.* **13** Audit Bureau of Circulation. **14** Australian Broadcasting Commission. **15** Australian Broadcasting Corporation. **16** automatic brightness control.
II a symbol for: a type of soil having a cross section of A, B, and C horizons: *ABC soil.*

ABCC 1 also **A.B.C.C.** Association of British Chambers of Commerce. **2** Atomic Bomb Casualty Commission.

ABCCC Airborne Battle Control and Command Center.

ABCD America, Britain, China, Dutch East Indies (opponents of Japan in the Pacific theater of World War II).

A.B.C.M. Association of British Chemical Manufacturers.

ABCST automatic broadcast.

ABCW American Bakery and Confectionery Workers Union.

ABD All but Dissertation (graduate student who has completed course requirements for a doctorate but has not written a dissertation).

abd. 1 abdicated. 2 abdomen. 3 aboard.

ABDA American-British-Dutch-Australian Command (in World War II).

abdom. 1 abdomen. 2 abdominal.

ABDPH American Board of Dental Public Health.

A.B.Ed. Bachelor of Arts in Education.

ABEND or **abend** abnormal end (interruption or termination of a computer program, usually because of an error).

A.B.E.P.P. American Board of Examiners in Professional Psychology.

Aber. Aberdeen.

ABET Accreditation Board for Engineering and Technology.

Ab Ex abstract expressionism.

ab ex. from without. [Latin *ab extra*]

A.B.F. Actors' Benevolent Fund.

A.B.F.M. American Board of Foreign Missions.

Abg. member of Parliament. [German *Abgeordneter*]

A.B.G.B.I. Associated Booksellers of Great Britain and Ireland.

abgk. abbreviated. [German *abgekürzt*]

abh. or **Abh.** records of a club or society. [German *Abhandlungen*]

ABI application binary interface (binary-based application to interface with a computer).

A.B.I.M. or **ABIM** American Board of Internal Medicine.

ab init. from the beginning. [Latin *ab initio*]

Abk. abbreviation. [German *Abkürzung*]

abk. abbreviated. [German *abgekürzt*]

Abl. April. [Spanish *Abril*]

abl. ablative.

ABLA Amateur Bicycle League of America.

A.B.L.S. Bachelor of Arts in Library Science. [Latin *Artium Baccalaureus Librarius Scientia*]

ABM 1 antiballistic missile. 2 automated or automatic batch mixing (of rocket fuel).

abm abeam.

ABMC or **A.B.M.C.** American Battle Monuments Commission.

ABMS American Bureau of Metal Statistics.

A.B.M.U. American Baptist Missionary Union.

ABN American Bank Note (a printer of U.S. postage stamps and commercial paper).

abn airborne.

abnd or **abnd.** abandon.

abni available but not installed.

ABNINF airborne infantry.

ABO a system of classifying blood factors.

abo. or **abor.** 1 aboriginal. 2 aborigines.

ABP 1 *also* **A.B.P.** American Board of Pediatrics. 2 American Business Press. 3 arterial blood pressure.

Abp. Archbishop.

ABPA Australian Book Publishers Association.

ABPC American Book Publishers Council (merged into *AAP*).

A.B.P.I. Association of the British Pharmaceutical Industry.

A.B.P.S. American Baptist Publishing Society.

Abr. or **abr.** 1 abridged. 2 abridgment. 3 abridger.

ABRA Advanced Biophysical Research Accelerator.

ABRC *British* Advisory Board for Research Councils.

ABRO (abʹrō) Animal Breeding Research Organisation.

abrsv. abrasive.

ABS 1 *also* **A.B.S.** able-bodied seaman. 2 absolute value *chemistry, physics, mathematics, computers.* 3 acrylonitrile butadiene styrene (plastic used in footwear, telephones, and small-boat hulls). 4 air break switch (of an electrical circuit). 5 alkyl benzene sulfonate (chemical bleach). 6 *also* **A.B.S.** American Bible Society. 7 *also* **A.B.S.** American Bureau of Shipping. 8 anti-lock brake system. 9 *British* Association of Broadcasting Staff. 10 *British also* **A.B.S.** Associate of the Building Societies Institute.

Abs. section, part, chapter, or division. [German *Abschnitt*]

abs. 1 absent. 2 *also* **abs a** absolute *or* absolute value *chemistry, physics, mathematics.* **b** absolutely. 3 abstract.

abse. re. the defendant being absent. [Latin *absente reo*]

abs. feb. in absence of fever *medicine.* [Latin *absente febre*]

absol. absolute, absolutely.

Absoluo. absolution.

abs. re. the defendant being absent. [Latin *absente reo*]

abst. abstract.

abstr. abstract, abstracted.

A.B.S.W. Association of British Science Writers.

ABT 1 American Ballet Theater. 2 Australian Broadcasting Tribunal (broadcast licensing authority).

Abt. division, part, department. [German *Abteilung*]

abt. about.

ABTA 1 American Board of Trial Advocates. 2 *also* **Abta** Association of British Travel Agents.

ABTF airborne task force.

A.B.U. United Bible Societies. [French *Alliance Biblique Universelle*]

abund. abundant.

abv. above.

AC 1 *also* **A.C.** account current *commerce.* 2 acre. 3 aerodynamic *or* aeronautical center. 4 *also* **A.C. a** after Christ. **b** year of the Lord; AD. [Spanish *año de Cristo*] 5 **a** air command. **b** air commodore. 6 air-conditioned, air conditioning. 7 *also* **A.C.** Air Corps. 8 **a** aircraft. **b** aircraft commander. **c** aircraftsman, aircraftswoman. 9 *also* **A.C.** *or* **A-C** alternating current. **10** altocumulus cloud *meteorology*. **11** ambulance corps. **12** amphibious corps. **13** analog computer. **14** *also* **A.C.** analytical chemist. **15** anodal closure. **16** *also* **A.C. a** appeal case. **b** Appeals Court. **17** *also* **A.C.** appellation contrôllée (of French wine). **18** area code (for telephones). **19** arithmetic computation test. **20** *also* **A.C. a** Army Corps. **b** Army Council. **21** *also* **A.C.** Arts Council of Great Britain. **22** asbestos cement (formerly in blueprints and other plans). **23** *also* **A.C.** Athletic Club, in combination: *N.Y.A.C.* = *New York Athletic Club*. **24** author's correction. **25** automobile club. **26** aviation cadet. **27 a** *also* **A.C.** before Christ; BC. [Latin *ante Christum*] **b** *also* **a.C.** *or* **A.C.** before Christ; BC. [Spanish *antes de Cristo*] **28** *also* **A.C.** Companion of the Order of Australia

A/C 1 absolute ceiling. **2** *commerce* **a** account. **b** account current. **3** air-conditioned, air conditioning. **4** aircraftsman, aircraftswoman. **5** airman (rank): *A/1C* = *airman first class*.

Ac *I an abbreviation for:* **1** accumulation. **2** acetyl. **3** altocumulus cloud *meteorology*.
II a symbol for: actinium (chemical element).

aC abcoulomb.

ac 1 air-conditioned, air conditioning. **2** alicyclic. **3** *also* **a.c.** *or* **a-c** alternating current. **4** *also* **a.c.** before meals *medicine*. [Latin *ante cibos*] **5** *also* **a.c.** current year. [French *année courante*] **6** *also* **a.c.** on account *commerce*. [French *à compte*]

a/c *commerce* **1** account. **2** account current. **3** on account. [French *à compte*]

ac. 1 account *commerce*. **2** acre.

ACA 1 adjacent channel attenuation *electronics*. **2** Adult Children of Alcoholics. **3** American Camping Association. **4** American Canoe Association. **5** American Chiropractic Association. **6** American College of Anesthesiologists. **7** American College of Apothecaries. **8** American Communications Association. **9** American Composers Alliance. **10** *also* **A.C.A.** American Congregational Association. **11** *also* **A.C.A.** Arts Councils of America. **12** Associate of the Institute of Chartered Accountants. **13** Association of Canadian Advertisers.

ACAA Agricultural Conservation and Adustment Administration.

ACAB Army Contract Adustment Board.

ACAC Association of College Admission Counselors.

Acad. Academy.

acad. academic.

Acad. Nat. Sci. Academy of Natural Science.

AC and U Association of Colleges and Universities.

ACARD Advisory Council for Applied Research and Development (British scientific advisory council).

ACAS 1 Advisory Conciliation and Arbitration Service (British organization for industrial relations). **2** airborne collision avoidance system. **3** Association of Casualty Accountants and Statisticians.

ACAT Accreditation Council for Accountancy and Taxation.

ACB 1 air circuit breaker. **2** asbestos cement board (formerly in blueprints and other plans). **3** Association of Customers'

Brokers. **4** Canadian Library Association. [French *Association Canadienne des Bibliothèques*]

ACBL American Contract Bridge League

ACB of A Associated Credit Bureaus of America.

ACBWS Automatic Chemical Biological Warning System.

ACC 1 *also* **A.C.C.** Accident Compensation Commission. **2** air control center. **3** Allied Control Commission. **4** *also* **Acc.** altocumulus castellatus cloud *meteorology*. **5** *also* **A.C.C.** American College of Cardiology. **6** American Conference of Cantors. **7** American Craftsmen's Council. **8** anodal closure contraction *medicine*. **9** Arab Corporation Council. **10** Army Chemical Center. **11** Association of Choral Conductors. **12** Association of County Councils. **13** astronomical great circle course. **14** Atlantic Coast Conference (collegiate athletic organization). **15** automatic contrast or color control *electronics*.

acc. 1 acceleration. **2** *commerce* **a** accept, accepted. **b** acceptance. **3** accompanied, accompaniment, *esp. in music*. **4** according. **5** *commerce* **a** account. **b** accountant. **6** accusative *grammar*.

ACCA 1 American Clinical and Climatological Association. **2** American Corporate Counsel Association. **3** Art Collectors Club of America. **4** *also* **A.C.C.A.** Association of Certified and Corporate Accountants.

ACCCE Association of Consulting Chemists and Chemical Engineers.

accdce. accordance.

acce. acceptance.

accel. 1 accelerate. **2** gradual increase in tempo *music*. [Latin *accelerando*]

ACCESS Automatic Computer-Controlled Electronic Scanning System.

access. accessory.

AccI accidental injury *insurance*.

ACCME American College of Continuing Medical Education.

A.C.C.O. Associate of the Canadian College of Organists.

accom. accommodation.

accomp. *or* **accpt.** accompaniment.

accrd. int. accrued interest.

accred. accredited.

A.C.C.S. Associate of the Corporation of Certified Secretaries.

acct. *commerce* **1** account. **2** accountant: *acct. & aud.* = *accountant and auditor*.

accum. accumulate, accumulation.

ACCUS Automobile Competition Committee for the United States.

accus. accusative *grammar*.

accy. accessory.

ACD 1 acid, citrate, and dextrose: *ACD solution* (substance to prevent coagulation of stored blood). **2** *also* **A.C.D.** American College of Dentists. **3** Australian College of Dentistry. **4** automatic call distribution (of telephone marketing).

ACDA 1 American Choral Directors Association. 2 Arms Control and Disarmament Agency (of U.S. Department of State).

AC/DC or **ac/dc** or **a-c/d-c** 1 alternating current, direct current. 2 *slang* bisexual.

acdnt. or **acdt.** accident.

ACE 1 adrenal cortical extract. 2 Advisory Center for Education. 3 aerospace control environment. 4 alcohol-chloroform-ether (a general anesthesia). 5 American Cinema Editors. 6 American Council on Education. 7 angiotensin-converting enzyme. 8 armored combat earthmover (armored bulldozer). 9 Army Corps of Engineers. 10 also **A.C.E.** Association of Consulting Engineers. 11 Australian College of Education. 12 automatic checkout equipment. 13 automatic circuit exchange *electronics*.

ACEC area of critical environmental concern (land protected by the U.S. Bureau of Land Management).

A.C.E.I. Association for Childhood Education International.

Ac Em actinium emanation.

ACER (ā'sər) Australian Council for Educational Research.

ACES automated camera effects system (used in filming animated cartoons).

acet or **acet.** 1 acetone. 2 acetylene.

ACF 1 Administration for Children and Families (of U.S. Department of Health and Human Services). 2 alternate communications facility. 3 American Checkers Federation. 4 also **A.C.F.** American Choral Foundation. 5 also **A.C.F.** Automobile Club de France. 6 also **A.C.F.** French-Canadian Academy. [French *Académie Canadienne Française*]

A.C.F.A.S. or **ACFAS** French-Canadian Association for the Advancement of Science. [French *Association Canadienne-Française pour l'avancement des sciences*]

a.c.f./min. actual cubic feet per minute.

acft aircraft.

ac.ft. or **ac.-ft.** acre-foot.

A.C.G. 1 American College of Gastroenterology. 2 Assistant Chaplain-General. 3 also **ACG** The Gaelic Society. [Gaelic *An Comuun Gaidhealach*]

AcG accelerator globulin, factor V (aid in blood clotting).

ACGB or **A.C.G.B.** Arts Council of Great Britain.

A.C.G.B.I. or **ACGBI** Automobile Club of Great Britain and Ireland.

A.C.G.I. Associate of the City and Guilds of London Institute.

ACH 1 also **Ach** acetylcholine. 2 also **A.C.H.** arm, chest, hip: the A.C.H. *index = arm girth, chest depth, and hip width.* 3 Association for Computers and the Humanities. 4 automated clearing house.

a.Ch. before Christ; BC [Latin *ante Christum*]

ACHA or **A.C.H.A.** American College of Hospital Administrators.

AChE or **ACHE** acetylcholinesterase.

ACHR American Council of Human Rights.

ACHS or **A.C.H.S.** Association of College Honor Societies.

ACI 1 acoustic comfort index. 2 airborne controlled intercept.

3 air combat information. 4 American Concrete Institute (used to identify an industry standard). 5 Automatic Car Identification (computer-operated system providing information on incoming freight cars to train yards). 6 also **A.C.I.** Automobile Club of Italy. 7 also **a.c.i.** insured against fire. [French *assuré contre l'incendie*]

ACIC Aeronautical Chart and Information Center.

A.C.I.L. American Council of Independent Laboratories.

ACIO Air Combat Intelligence Office or Officer.

ACIS 1 American Committee for Irish Studies. 2 also **A.C.I.S.** Associate of the Chartered Institute of Secretaries.

A.C.J. American Council for Judaism.

ACK acknowledge (in computer data and radio transmissions).

ack. or **ack** acknowledge, acknowledgment.

ackgt or **ackgt.** acknowledgment.

ACL 1 allowable cabin load (of an aircraft). 2 Association for Computational Linguistics. 3 automatic carrier landing system.

ACLA American Comparative Literature Association.

ACLD Association for Children with Learning Disabilities (compare *NCLD*).

ACLG air-cushion landing gear (for landing aircraft on rough or soft terrain and water).

ACLS 1 Advanced Cardiology Life Support. 2 also **A.C.L.S.** American Council of Learned Societies.

ACLT accelerate.

ACLU or **A.C.L.U.** American Civil Liberties Union.

ACM 1 advanced cruise missile. 2 also **A.C.M.** Air Chief Marshal (in the R.A.F.). 3 Air Commerce Manual. 4 American Campaign Medal. 5 Arab Common Market. 6 asbestos-covered metal (formerly in blueprints and other plans). 7 Association for Computing Machinery. 8 Association of Canadian Manufacturers.

ACMA 1 Air Carrier Mechanics Association. 2 Associate of the Institute of Cost and Management Accountants.

ACME 1 Advisory Council on Medical Education. 2 Association of Consulting Management Engineers.

A.C.M.F. Australian Commonwealth Military Forces.

A.C.M.P. Amateur Chamber Music Players.

acmp. or **acmp** accompany.

ACN 1 all concerned notified. 2 American Council on NATO. 3 assignment control number. 4 automatic celestial navigation. 5 also **A.C.N.** before the birth of Christ. [Latin *ante Christum notum*]

A.C.N.M. American College of Nurse Midwifery.

ACNO Assistant Chief of Naval Operations.

ACOE automatic checkout equipment.

ACOFS or **AC of S** Assistant Chief of Staff.

ACOG 1 aircraft on ground. 2 also **A.C.O.G.** American College of Obstetricians and Gynecologists.

A.C.O.P. Association of Chief Officers of Police.

ACORN automatic checkout and recording network.

ACOS Assistant Chief of Staff.

acous. acoustics.

ACP 1 acyl carrier protein (protein active in digestion of fatty acids). **2** African, Caribbean, and Pacific Association (trading group of developing nations). **3** air control point. **4** airline carriers of passengers. **5** *also* **A.C.P.** American College of Pharmacists. **6** *also* **A.C.P.** American College of Physicians. **7** Associate Computer Professional. **8** *also* **A.C.P.** Association of Clinical Pathologists. **9** *also* **A.C.P.** Association of Correctional Psychologists. **10** Association of Correctors of the Press. **11** Australian Country Party.

ACPA 1 Associate of the Institution of Certified Public Accountants. **2** Association of Computer Programmers and Analysts.

ACPM *or* **A.C.P.M.** American College of Preventive Medicine.

ACPRA American College Public Relations Association.

ACPT 1 accept. **2** *also* **acpt.** acceptance *commerce.*

acq *or* **acq.** acquire, acquired.

ACR 1 Admiral Commanding Reserves (in the Royal Navy). **2** aerial combat reconnaisance. **3** *also* **A.C.R** American College of Radiology. **4** approach control radar.

acrd. accrued.

ACRE automatic checkout and readiness equipment.

acre-ft. acre-foot.

ACRL Association of College and Research Libraries.

ACRR American Council on Race Relations.

ACRS 1 accelerated cost recovery system (U.S. Internal Revenue Service accelerated schedule of depreciation). **2** Advisory Committee on Reactor Safeguards (of the U.S. Nuclear Regulatory Commission).

acrs. across.

ACS 1 Airline Charter Service. **2** Alaskan Communications System. **3** American Cancer Society. **4** *also* **A.C.S.** American Chemical Society. **5** *also* **A.C.S.** American College of Surgeons. **6** anodal closing sound *medicine.* **7** Assistant Chief of Staff. **8** *also* **A.C.S.** Association of Clinical Scientists. **9** attitude control system (of a rocket or space capsule). **10** autograph card signed. **11** synchronous alternating current.

acs *or* **a.c.s. 1** anodal closing sound *medicine.* **2** autograph card signed.

ACSA Association of Collegiate Schools of Architecture.

A.C.S.C. Association of Casualty and Surety Companies.

ACSEA Allied Command in Southeast Asia (in World War II).

ACSF Attack Carrier Strike Force.

ACSL altocumulus clouds standing lenticular *meteorology.*

ACSM American Congress on Surveying and Mapping.

A.C.S.N. *or* **ACSN** Association of Collegiate Schools of Nursing.

ACSOC Acoustical Society of America.

ACSP Advisory Council on Scientific Policy, in Great Britain.

A/cs Pay. *or* **A/cs pay.** accounts payable.

ACSR aluminum cable, steel reinforced (used of transmission lines).

A/cs.Rec. *or* **A/cs.rec.** accounts receivable.

ACST 1 *also* **acst.** acoustic. **2** Army Clerical Speed Test.

ACSW Academy of Certified Social Workers.

ACT 1 active, activated. **2** actual. **3** advance corporation tax. **4** American College Testing Program: *ACT Battery = group of tests similar to the College Boards.* **5** Association of Classroom Teachers. **6** *also* **A.C.T.** Australian Capital Territory. **7** automatic credit transfer *finance.* **8** aviation classification test.

Act *I an abbreviation for: also* **Act.** actuary.
II a symbol for: actinium (chemical element).

act. 1 acting. **2** active, activated. **3** actor. **4** actual. **5** actuary. **6** actuate.

a cta. on account. [Spanish *á cuenta*]

A.C.T.C. Art Class Teacher's Certificate.

ACTFL American Council on the Teaching of Foreign Languages.

ACTG AIDS Clinical Trials Groups.

actg. 1 acting. **2** actuating.

Actg. Sec. Acting Secretary.

ACTH adrenocorticotropin *or* adrenocorticotropic hormone.

ACTL American College of Trial Lawyers.

actn. action, *esp. in law.*

actnt. accountant.

ACTR American Council of Teachers of Russian.

ACTRA (ak'trə) Association of Canadian Television and Radio Artists.

A.C.T.T. Association of Cinematograph and Television Technicians, in Great Britain.

ACTU *or* **A.C.T.U. 1** Association of Catholic Trade Unions. **2** Australian Council of Trade Unions.

ACT UP (akt'up') AIDS Coalition to Unleash Power (activist group for issues connected with AIDS).

actv. active.

ACTVT activate.

act. wt. actual weight.

ACTWU Amalgamated Clothing and Textile Workers Union.

ACU 1 *also* **A.C.U.** American Church Union. **2** *also* **A.C.U.** American Congregational Union. **3** *also* **A.C.U.** American Conservative Union. **4** American Cycling Union. **5** *also* **A.C.U.** Association of College Unions. **6** *also* **A.C.U.** Association of Commonwealth Universities. **7** automatic calling unit (electronic telephone calling device, used esp. to make telemarketing calls). **8** Automatic Calling Unit *electronics.*

a-cu altocumulus clouds *meteorology.*

A.C.U.H.O. Association of College and University Housing Officers.

ACUS Administrative Conference of the United States.

ACUTE Association of Canadian University Teachers of English.

ACV 1 *also* **acv** actual cash value. **2** air cushion vehicle.

ACW 1 aircraft control and warning. **2** aircraftswoman. **3** *also* **acw** alternating continuous waves *electronics.*

A.C.W.W. *or* **ACWW** Associated Country Women of the World.

ACYC anticyclonic *meteorology*.

ACYF Administration for Children, Youth, and Families.

AD 1 active duty. **2** adenoid-degenerating (of a type of respiratory disease). **3** *also* **A.D.** Administrative Department or Division. **4** advertising director. **5** aerodynamic decelerator. **6** air defense. **7** air depot. **8** air division. **9** air dried (of lumber). **10** alternate days *advertising*. **11** Alzheimer's disease. **12** *also* **A/D** analog to digital (system or device for converting information) *computers: ADC = analog to digital converter.* **13** Angel of the Lord. [Latin *Angelus Domini*] **14** Antitrust Division (of U.S. Department of Justice). **15** *also* **A.D.** Appellate Division. **16** Assembly District. **17** *also* **A.D.** Assistant or Associate Director. **18** Athletic Director. **19** attention display. **20** Australian Democrats (political party). **21** autograph document. **22** *also* **A.D.** average deviation *statistics*. **23** before the day. [Latin *ante diem*] **24** *also* **A.D.** daily proceedings *law*. [Latin *acta diurna*] **25** Dame of the Order of Australia. **26** *also* **A.D.** Democratic Action (Venezuelan political party). [Spanish *Acción Democrática*] **27** *also* **A.D.** *or* A.D. *or* AD in the year of the Lord. [Latin *anno Domini*]

a.D. 1 in the year of the Lord; AD. [Italian *anno Domini*] **2** retired. [German *ausser Dienst*]

ad 1 advantage *tennis*. **2** air dried (of lumber). **3** average deviation *statistics*.

ad. 1 a adapted. **b** adaptor. **2** adverb. **3** advertisement. **4** let them be added *or* to be added *medicine*.

a.d. 1 after date *commerce*. **2** autograph document. **3** before the day. [Latin *ante diem*] **4** right ear *medicine*. [Latin *auris dextra*]

ADA 1 acetone dicarboxylic acid (used in organic synthesis). **2** adenosine deaminase (enzyme active in breakdown of adenosine in metabolism of sugar and in muscle contraction). **3** American Dairy Association. **4** *also* **A.D.A. a** American Dental Association. **b** Australian Dental Association. **5** American Diabetes Association. **6** American Dietetic Association. **7** Americans for Democratic Action. **8** Americans with Disabilities Act. **9** angular differentiating accelerometer. **10** Assistant District Attorney. **11** *also* **A.D.A.** Australian Department of Agriculture. **12** average daily attendance.

Ada 1 action data automation (computerized defense system). **2** (ā′də) the name of a computer language. [for Augusta *Ada* Byron, 1815–1852, daughter of Lord Byron, who worked with Charles Babbage on an early computer]

A.D.A.A. *or* **ADAA** Art Dealers Association of America.

adag. slowly *music*. [Italian *adagio*]

ADAM angular distribution auger microscopy (used to map atomic structure of materials).

ADAMHA Alcohol, Drug Abuse, and Mental Health Administration (of U.S. Department of Health and Human Services).

ad an. at the year. [Latin *ad annum*]

ad. and ac. administrative and accounting purposes.

A.D. and C. advice, duration, and charge (British telephone service).

adap. adapted.

ADAPSO Association of Data Processing Service Organizations.

adapt. adaptation, adapted.

ADAS Agricultural Development and Advisory Service (of Great Britain).

ADB 1 *also* **adb** accidental death benefit *insurance*. **2** *also* **A.D.B.** Asian Development Bank. **3** *also* **A.D.B.** Bachelor of Domestic Arts.

ADC 1 active duty commitment. **2** advanced developing country. **3** advance delivery of correspondence. **4** *also* **A.D.C.** *or* **a.d.c.** aide-de-camp. **5** Aid to Dependent Children (U.S. Federal welfare program). **6** Air Defense Command. **7** Air Development Center. **8** Alaska Defense Command. **9** analog to digital converter (of computer data). **10** Army Dental Corps. **11** automatic digital computer.

ADCC 1 Air Defense Control Center. **2** antibody dependent cellular cytotoxicity *biochemistry, medicine*.

ADCCP advanced data communications control procedure *computer science*.

ADD 1 Administration on Developmental Disabilities. **2** attention deficit disorder.

add. 1 *also* **Add.** addendum, addenda. **2** addition, additional. **3** *also* **Add.** address. **4** let them be added *or* to be added *medicine*.

addend to be added.

addl. additional.

addn. addition.

addnl. additional.

addns, alts, & reprs additions, alterations, and repairs.

addsd. addressed.

ADE Association of Departments of English (of MLA).

A. de C. in the year of our Lord; AD. [Spanish *año de Cristo*]

ad effect. until effective *medicine*. [Latin *ad effectum*]

a. de J.C. before Christ; BC: *Aristóteles, 384–322 a. de J.C.* [Spanish *antes de Jesús Cristo*]

Adel. Adelaide (city in South Australia).

ADELA Atlantic Development Group for Latin America (investment organization of European, Japanese, and U.S. financial interests).

A Dep Air Depot.

ADEPT acoustic directed-energy pulse train.

ADERC Alzheimer's Disease Education Referral Center.

a des. to the right. [Italian *a destra*]

ad eund. admitted to the same degree. [Latin *ad eundem gradum*]

ADF 1 after deducting freight *commerce*. **2** aircraft direction finder. **3** automatic direction finder.

ADFA Australian Defence Force Academy.

ad fin. to the end. [Latin *ad finem*]

ADFL Association of Departments of Foreign Languages (of MLA).

ADG 1 *also* **A.D.G.** Assistant Director General. **2** average daily gain.

A.D.G.B. Air Defense of Great Britain.

adgo. leisurely *music*. [Italian *adagio*]

ADH 1 alcohol dehydrogenase (enzyme). **2** antidiuretic hormone (a pituitary hormone that contracts small blood vessels; vasopressin).

adh. adhesive.

ADHD attention deficit hyperactive disorder.

adhib. to be used *medicine*. [Latin *adhibeatur*]

ad h. l. on or at this passage. [Latin *ad hunc locum*]

ad hom. to the man. [Latin *ad hominem*]

ADI 1 acceptable daily intake (the maximum amount of a substance that can be safely ingested). **2** alien of declared intention. **3** American Documentation Institute (of the Library of Congress, for the collection of photographs, lists, charts, etc. appended to articles). **4** anti-detonation injection. **5** attitude direction indicator. **6** French Information Agency. [French *Agence de l'Informatique*]

Adidas (ə dē'dəz) Trademark of athletic equipment. [*Adi Dassler*, German manufacturer who founded company]

ad inf. *or* **ad infin.** to infinity. [Latin *ad infinitum*]

ad init. to or at the beginning. [Latin *ad initium*]

ad int. meanwhile. [Latin *ad interim*]

ADIS automatic data interchange system.

ADIZ Air Defense Identification Zone.

Adj. 1 adjacent. **2** Adjunct: *Adj.A.* = *Adjunct in Arts.* **3** adjutant: *Adj. Gen.* = *Adjutant General.*

adj. 1 adjacent. **2** adjective. **3** adjoining. **4** *also* **adjd.** adjourned: *adj. sum.* = *adjourned summons.* **5** adjudged. **6** adjunct. **7 a** adjust, adjusted. **b** adjustable: *adj. sp.* = *adjustable speed.* **c** adjustment, *esp. in banking.*

Adj. A. Adjunct in Arts.

adjac. adjacent, *esp. in medicine.*

adjd. sumns. adjourned summons.

Adj. Gen. *or* **Adj.-Gen.** Adjutant General.

Adjt. Adjutant: *Adjt. Gen.* = *Adjutant General.*

ADL 1 activities of daily living *medicine.* **2** Anti-Defamation League.

ad lib. at pleasure, as desired *music, pharmaceutics.* [Latin *ad libitum*]

ad libit. at pleasure, as desired *music.* [Latin *ad libitum*]

ad loc. 1 on or at this passage. [Latin *ad hunc locum*] **2** to or at the place. [Latin *ad locum*]

ADM 1 Admiral. **2** air defense missile. **3** Annual Delegate Meeting. **4** average daily membership.

Adm. 1 a administration. **b** administrative. **c** administrator. **2 a** admiral. **b** admiralty.

adm. 1 a administration. **b** administrative. **c** administrator. **2 a** admission. **b** admit, admitted.

ADMA American Drug Manufacturers Association.

Adm. Ct. Admiralty Court.

admin. 1 administration. **2** administrator.

admix. administratrix.

Adml. Admiral.

admor. administrator.

admov. apply *pharmaceutics.* [Latin *admoveatur*]

admr. administrator.

Adm. Rev. Very Reverend. [Latin *admodum reverendus*]

admrx. administratrix.

A.D.M.S. Assistant Director of Medical Services.

adms. *or* **admstr.** administrator.

admtrx. *or* **admx.** administratrix.

ADN 1 accession designation number. **2** *also* **A.D.N.** former East German news agency. [German *Allgemeines Deutsches Nachrichtenbureau*] **3** Assistant Director of Nursing.

A.D.O. *or* **ADO** Assistant District Officer.

Ado Much Ado About Nothing (play by William Shakespeare).

adop. adoption *law.*

ADP 1 *also* **A.D.P.** Academy of Dental Prosthetics. **2** adenosine diphosphate (compound formed in the body that aids in muscle contraction). **3** Australian Democratic Party. **4** automatic data processing.

ADPC automatic data processing center.

ADPE automatic data processing equipment.

ADPL average daily patient load (of a doctor or hospital).

ADPS automatic data processing system.

adpt. adapter.

ADR 1 alternative dispute resolution. **2** American Depositary Receipt (receipt for ownership of foreign stock) *commerce.* **3** automatic dialogue replacement.

Adr. in care of (in an address). [German, Norwegian, Danish *Adresse*]

ADRA Animal Diseases Research Association.

adrm. *or* **adrm** airdrome.

ADRMP automatic dialing recorded message program (for automatic dialing and presentation of a recorded sales message).

adrs. in care of (in an address). [Danish *Adresse*]

ADS 1 alternative delivery system. **2** American Daffodil Society. **3** American Dahlia Society. **4** American Dialect Society. **5** *also* **A.D.S.** *or* **a.d.s.** autograph document signed. **6** automatic door seal (used in blueprints and plans).

AdS Academy of Sciences. [French *Académie des Sciences*]

ads. at the suit of *law.* [Latin *ad sectam*]

ADSA American Dairy Science Association.

ADSM American Defense Service Medal.

ADSR attack, decay, sustain, release (music synthesizer functions).

adstadis advise status and disposition *commerce.*

ADT 1 alternate day therapy (of prescription). **2** American District Telegraph. **3** any desired thing *pharmaceutics.* **4** *also* **A.D.T.** *or* **a.d.t.** Atlantic Daylight Time. **5** automatic data transmission. **6** automatic debit transfer. **7** average daily traffic (referring to viewers of display advertising and to automotive traffic patterns). **8** *also* **a.d.t.** the same day. [German *an demselben Tage*]

ad us. according to custom *law, commerce.* [Latin *ad usum*]

Adv. 1 Advent. 2 advertisement. 3 advice *or* advise *commerce.* 4 advocate (lawyer).

adv. 1 according to the value *commerce.* [Latin *ad valorem*] 2 advance, advanced: *adv. chgs. = advance charges, adv. frt. = advance freight.* 3 a adverb. b adverbial, adverbially. 4 advertisement. 5 advice or advise. 6 advisory. 7 advocate (lawyer). 8 against *law.* [Latin *adversus*]

ad val. according to the value *commerce.* [Latin *ad valorem*]

advb. adverb.

advers. advertisement.

advert. *or* **Advert.** (*sometimes in Great Britain pronounced* ad'vert) advertisement.

Adv. Gen. *or* **Adv Gen** Advocate General.

advid (ad'vid) advertising video or videotape (used by applicants for college or job placement).

advl. adverbial.

adv. poss. adverse possession *law.*

advt. advertisement.

advtg. 1 advantage. 2 advertising.

ADX automatic data exchange.

AE 1 account executive. 2 adult education. 3 *also* **A.E.** Aeronautical Engineer. 4 *also* **A.E.** Agricultural Engineer. 5 air escape (in blueprints and other plans). 6 All England *sports.* 7 allergic encephalomyelitis. 8 *also* **A.E.** Architectural Engineer. 9 *also* **A.E.** a Associate in Education. b Associate in Engineering. 10 atomic energy.

Æ 1 *also* **A.E.** pen name of the Irish poet George William Russell. 2 third-class ship in Lloyd's Register.

ae. at the age of, aged. [Latin *aetatis*]

a.e. after end (in shipbuilding).

AEA 1 *also* **A.E.A.** Actors Equity Association. 2 Adult Education Association. 3 *also* **A.E.A.** Agricultural Engineers Association. 4 *also* **A.E.A.** Air Efficiency Award. 5 *also* **A.E.A.** American Economic Association. 6 *also* **A.E.A.** Atomic Energy Authority of Great Britain.

A.E. and P. *or* **A.E. & P.** Ambassador Extraordinary and Plenipotentiary.

AEB *or* **A.E.B.** 1 Area Electricity Board. 2 Associated Examining Board.

AEC 1 adenylate energy charge (measure of metabolic cell energy). 2 American Engineering Council. 3 Army Education Center. 4 Army Electronics Command. 5 *also* **A.E.C.** Association of Education Committees. 6 Atomic Energy Commission (of the United States, replaced in 1974 by the *NRC*).

AECL Atomic Energy of Canada, Limited (Crown Corporation for nuclear research).

AECT Association for Educational Communications and Technology.

AED *or* **A.E.D.** Doctor of Fine Arts. [Latin *Artium Elegantium Doctor*]

A Ed *or* **A. Ed.** Associate in Education.

A.E.D.E. *or* **AEDE** European Teachers Association. [French *Association Européenne des Enseignants*]

AEDS 1 Association for Educational Data Systems. 2 Atomic Energy Detection System.

AEE 1 absolute essential equipment. 2 *also* **A.E.E.** Atomic Energy Establishment (esp. in Great Britain).

Ae. E. *or* **Ae E** Aeronautical Engineer.

AEF 1 a *also* **A.E.F.** Allied Expeditionary Force. b *also* **A.E.F.** American Expeditionary Force. 2 American Economic Foundation. 3 Artists Equity Fund. 4 *also* **A.E.F.** Australian Expeditionary Force. 5 French Equatorial Africa. [French *Afrique Équatoriale Française*]

AEG *or* **aeg** air encephalogram.

A.E.G.M. Anglican Evangelical Group Movement.

AEI 1 American Enterprise Institute. 2 Associated Electrical Industries. 3 azimuth error indicator. 4 *also* **A.E.I.** International Schools Association. [French *Association des Écoles Internationales*]

AEJ Association for Education in Journalism.

A.E.L.T.C. All England Lawn Tennis Club.

AEM 1 Aircraft and Engine Mechanic. 2 architect, engineer, manager: *AEM plan.*

Aen. *or* **Æn.** the Aeneid (by Virgil).

aen. made of copper or bronze. [Latin *aeneus*]

A. Eng. Associate in Engineering.

AEP Adult Education Program.

AEPI American Educational Publishers Instiute.

aeq. *or* **æq.** equal, equals. [Latin *aequalis*]

AER 1 Aeronautical Engineering Report. 2 after engine room, in shipping. 3 *also* **A.E.R.** Army Emergency Reserve (of Great Britain).

Aer. 1 aerodrome. 2 *also* **aer.** aeronautics.

AERA 1 American Educational Research Association. 2 *also* **A.E.R.A.** Associate Engraver of the Royal Academy.

AERE Atomic Energy Research Establishment.

Aer. E. Aeronautical Engineer.

AERI *or* **A.E.R.I.** Agricultural Economics Research Institute.

aero. 1 aeronautical. 2 aeronautics.

aerodyn. aerodynamic, aerodynamics.

Aero. E. Aeronautical Engineer.

aerol. aerological.

aeromed. aeromedical.

aeron. aeronautics.

AES 1 *also* **A.E.S.** American Electrochemical Society. 2 American Entomological Society. 3 American Epidemiological Society. 4 American Ethnological Society. 5 atomic emission spectroscopy. 6 Audio Engineering Society. 7 Auger electron spectroscopy.

Aes. Aesop.

AESC *or* **A.E.S.C.** American Engineering Standards Committee.

Æsch. Aeschylus.

aesth. aesthetics.

AET 2-aminoethylisothiouronium (used in the prevention of radiation sickness).

A.E.T. Associate in Electrical Technology.

aet. at the age of, aged. [Latin *aetatis*]

AETA American Educational Theatre Association.

aetat. at the age of, aged. [Latin *aetatis*]

AETFAT Association for the Taxonomic Study of African Tropical Flora. [French *Association pour l'Étude Taxonomique de la Flore d'Afrique Tropicale*]

A. et M. Arts and Crafts. [French *Arts et Métiers*]

AETS Association for the Education of Teachers in Science.

AEU 1 *British* Amalgamated Engineering Union. **2** American Ethical Union.

AEW airborne early warning (defense system).

A.E.W.H.A. All England Women's Hockey Association.

AF 1 Admiral of the Fleet. **2** Air Force. **3** *also* **A.F.** *or* **AF.** *or* **A-F** Anglo-French. **4** *also* **A.F.** Associate Fellow. **5** *also* **A-F** audio frequency. **6** autofocus (of a camera). **7** family allowance. [French *allocations familiales*] **8** *also* **A.F.** French Academy. [French *Académie Française*] **9** *also* **A.F.** French Army. [French *Armée Française*]

Af 1 affix. **2** *also* **Af.** afghani (monetary unit of Afghanistan). **3** *also* **Af.** Africa, African. **4** *also* **Af.** Afrikaans.

aF abfarad.

af 1 affix. **2** *also* **a.f.** *or* **a-f** audio frequency. **3** *also* **a.f.** at or to the end. [Latin *ad finem*]

AFA 1 *also* **A.F.A.** Advertising Federation of America. **2** Air Force Association. **3** Amateur Fencing Association. **4** Amateur Football Association. **5** *also* **A.F.A.** American Federation of Arts. **6** American Foundrymen's Association. **7** *also* **A.F.A.** Associate in Fine Arts. **8** Associate of the Faculty of Actuaries.

AFAA 1 Airborne Flight Attendants Association. **2** Air Force Audit Agency.

A.F.A.M. *or* **A.F. & A.M.** Ancient Free and Accepted Masons.

A.F.A.S. 1 Associate of the Faculty of Architects and Surveyors. **2** French Association for the Advancement of the Sciences. [French *Association Française pour l'Avancement de Sciences*]

AFB 1 *also* **A.F.B.** Air Force Base. **2** American Foundation for the Blind. **3** antifriction bearing.

AFBCMR Air Force Review Board for Correction of Military Records.

A.F.B.F. American Farm Bureau Federation.

A.F.B.S. American and Foreign Bible Society.

AFC 1 *also* **A.F.C.** Air Force Cross (of Great Britain, Australia, or New Zealand). **2 a** Amateur or Association Football Club. **b** American Football Conference. **3** Area Forecast Center *meteorology*. **4** automatic flight control. **5** *also* **A.F.C.** *or* **afc** automatic frequency control.

AFCARA Air Force Civilian Appellate Review Agency.

AFCRL Air Force Cambridge Research Laboratories.

AFCS 1 Air Force Communications Service. **2** Automatic Flight Control System.

A.F.C.U. American and Foreign Christian Union.

AFD 1 accelerated freeze drying (process of preserving food by deep freezing and dehydrating). **2** Air Force Depot.

3 Associated Film Distribution. **4** *also* **A.F.D.** Doctor of Fine Arts; AED.

Afd. part, as of a publication. [Danish *Afdeling*]

AFDB African Development Bank.

AFDC Aid to Families with Dependent Children (U.S. Federal welfare program).

AFDF African Development Fund.

AFDOUS Association of Food and Drug Officials of the United States.

AFEA 1 American Farm Economic Association. **2** American Film Export Association.

AFF Army Field Forces.

aff. 1 affiliated. **2 a** affirmative. **b** affirming.

affret. *or* **affrett.** tenderly *music*. [Italian *affrettando*]

afft. affidavit.

AFFTC Air Force Flight Test Center.

Afg. Afghanistan.

AFGE *or* **A.F.G.E.** American Federation of Government Employees (compare *AFSCME*).

Afgh. Afghanistan.

AFH 1 Air Force Hospital. **2** *also* **A.F.H.** American Foundation for Homeopathy.

AFHQ Allied Forces Headquarters.

AFI 1 American Film Institute. **2** Armed Forces Institute.

AFIA American Foreign Insurance Association (for U.S. insurance companies doing business abroad).

AFII American Federation of International Institutes (organization for securing assurances required before visas can be issued to prospective immigrants).

AFIPS American Federation of Information Processing Societies.

AFIS American Forces Information Service.

AFL *or* **A.F.L. 1** American Federation of Labor. **2** American Football League.

afl. part (of a publication). [Dutch *aflevering*]

AFLA 1 Amateur Fencers League of America. **2** American Foreign Law Association. **3** *also* **A.F.L.A.** Asian Federation of Library Associations.

AFL-CIO *or* **A.F.L.-C.I.O.** labor organization merging the American Federation of Labor and the Congress of Industrial Organizations.

AFLD *or* **afld.** airfield.

AFM 1 *also* **A.F.M.** Air Force Medal (of Great Britain, Australia, or New Zealand). **2** Air Force Missile, esp. in combination: *AFMTC = Air Force Missile Test Center*. **3** *also* **A.F.M.** American Federation of Musicians. **4** antifriction metal. **5** atomic force microscopy. **6** audio frequency modulation (for recording on videotape and discs).

A.F.M.L.T.A. Australian Federation of Modern Language Teachers Association.

AFMS American Federation of Mineralogical Societies.

AFMUSC American Federation of Musicians of the United States and Canada.

AFN Armed Forces Network (broadcasting service).

AFNIL French Standard Book Number Agency. [French *Agence Francophone pour la Numération Internationale du Livre*]

AFNOR French Association for Standardization. [French *Association Française de Normalisation*]

AFO Accounting and Finance Office or Officer.

AFofL or **A.F.ofL.** American Federation of Labor: AF of L-CIO = *American Federation of Labor–Congress of Industrial Organizations.*

AFOSR Air Force Office of Scientific Research.

AFP 1 Air Force Pamphlet (used with a number). **2** alphafetoprotein (glycoprotein in amniotic fluid and blood serum of fetuses). **3** Alternate Flight Plan. **4** American Federation of Police. **5** Armed Forces Police. **6** *also* **afp** authority for purchase. **7** *also* **A.F.P.** French Press Agency. [French *Agence France Presse*]

AFPC Armed Forces Policy Council.

AFPEO Air Force Program Executive Offices.

AFPFL Anti-Fascist People's Freedom League (political party in Burma, now Myanmar, partly absorbed into the *BSPP*).

AFPI American Forest Products Industries.

AFPP Air Force Procurement Procedures.

AFPPS American Forces Press and Publications Service.

AFPR Air Force Plant Representative.

AFPS Armed Forces Press Service.

AFPTRC Air Force Personnel and Training Research Center.

AFQT Armed Forces Qualification Test.

AFR 1 Air Force Regulation (used with a number). **2** Air Force Reserve.

AFr or **AFr.** Anglo-French.

Afr. Africa, African.

afr. airframe.

AFRA 1 American Farm Research Association. **2** average freight rate assessment *commerce.*

A.F.R.Ae.S. Associate Fellow of the Royal Aeronautical Society.

AFRC Air Force Records Center.

AFRes or **AFRES** Air Force Reserve.

AFRI acute febrile respiratory infection or illness.

Afrik. Afrikaans.

AFROTC Air Force Reserve Officers Training Corps.

AFRRI Armed Forces Radiology Research Institute.

AFRS or **A.F.R.S.** Armed Forces Radio Service.

AFRTS or **A.F.R.T.S.** Armed Forces Radio and Television Service.

AFS 1 Air Force Station. **2** *also* **A.F.S.** American Field Service. **3** American Fisheries Society. **4** *also* **A.F.S.** American Folklore Society. **5** American Foundrymen's Society. **6** *also* **A.F.S.** Auxiliary Fire Service.

Afs. sender. [Danish *Afsender*]

AFSA American Foreign Service Association.

AFSC 1 *also* **A.F.S.C.** American Friends Service Committee. **2** Armed Forces Staff College.

AFSCME (afs′mē′) American Federation of State, County, and Municipal Employees.

afsd. aforesaid *law.*

AFSWC Air Force Special Weapons Center.

AFT 1 Air Freight Terminal. **2** *also* **A.F.T.** American Federation of Teachers. **3** *also* **aft** automatic fine tuning.

aft. 1 after. **2** afternoon.

A.F.T.A. or **AFTA** Australian Federation of Travel Agents.

AFTN Aeronautical Fixed Telecommunications Network.

aftn. afternoon.

AFTRA (af′trə) American Federation of Television and Radio Artists.

AG 1 *also* **A.G.** Accountant General. **2** *also* **A.G.** Adjutant General. **3** *also* **A.G.** Advocate General. **4** *also* **A.G.** Agent General. **5** *also* **A/G** air-to-ground (of rockets and missiles). **6** *also* **A/G** albumin-globulin: *A/G ratio.* **7** American Geologists (magazine title). **8** *also* **A.G.** or **A-G** Attorney General. **9** *also* **A.G.** Auditor General. **10** *also* **A.G.** joint stock company. [German *Aktiengesellschaft*]

Ag *I an abbreviation for:* **1** *also* **Ag.** agent. **2** *also* **Ag.** agriculture, agricultural. **3** atomic weight. [German *Atomgewicht*] **4** *also* **Ag.** August.
II a symbol for: silver (chemical element). [Latin *argentum*]

AGA 1 Amateur Gymnastics Association. **2** *also* **A.G.A.** American Gas Association.

AGAC American Guild of Authors and Composers.

AGACS Automatic Ground-to-Air Communications System.

a.g.b. any or a good brand.

AGC 1 Adjutant General's Corps. **2** advanced graduate certificate. **3** Association of General Contractors. **4** *also* **agc** automatic gain control *electronics.*

AGCA automatic ground-controlled approach (for landing aircraft).

AGCT Army General Classification Test.

agcy. agency.

AGD 1 Academy of General Dentistry. **2** Adjutant General's Department.

agd. agreed.

AGE 1 aerospace ground equipment. **2** *also* **A.G.E.** Associate in General Education.

Ag.E. Agricultural Engineer.

AGF 1 Army Ground Forces. **2** *also* **A.G.F.** French Geographers' Association. [French *Association des Géographes Français*]

agg. or **aggr.** aggregate.

agglut. agglutinated, agglutination.

AGI 1 adjusted gross income (after tax income). **2** American Geographical Institute. **3** American Geological Institute.

agit. shake or stir *pharmaceutics.* [Latin *agitatur*]

AGK Astronomical Association Catalogs: AGK_1, AGK_2 (listings of stars and their positions). [German AGK_1 *Zonenkatalog der Astronomischen Gesellschaft,* AGK_2 *Zweiter Katalog der Astronomischen Gesellschaft*]

AGL 1 above ground level (measurement of altitude) *navigation*. **2** acute granulocytic leukemia *medicine*.

AGM 1 air-to-ground missile. **2** American Guild of Music. **3** *also* **A.G.M.** *British* Annual General Meeting.

AGMA 1 American Gear Manufacturers Association. **2** *also* **A.G.M.A.** American Guild of Musical Artists.

AGN active galactic nuclei *astronomy*.

agn. again.

AGO 1 Adjutant General's Office. **2** *also* **A.G.O.** American Guild of Organists. **3** Attorney General's Opinion (advisory on interpretation of a point of law).

A.G.P.A. *or* **AGPA** American Group Psychotherapy Association.

AGR advanced gas-cooled reactor (atomic reactor).

agr. *or* **agri.** *or* **agric.** agriculture, agricultural.

AGRICOLA (ə grik′ə lə) Agricultural On Line Access.

agron. agronomy, agronomist.

AGRS American Graves Registration Service (of the U.S. military services).

AGS 1 abort guidance system (back-up guidance system of a spacecraft). **2** Aircraft General Standards. **3** *also* **A.G.S.** alternating gradient synchrotron. **4** American Gem Society. **5** *also* **A.G.S.** American Geographical Society. **6** *also* **A.G.S.** American Gynecological Society. **7** Army General Staff. **8** *also* **A.G.S.** Associate in General Studies. **9** automatic gain stabilization *electronics*.

A.G.S.M. Associate of the Guildhall School of Music.

A.G.S.S. American Geographical and Statistical Society.

agst. against.

Agt. 1 agent. **2** agreement.

agt. 1 against. **2** agent. **3** agreement.

AGTH adrenoglomeralotropin (a neurohormone).

AGU American Geophysical Union.

AGVA *or* **A.G.V.A.** American Guild of Variety Artists.

AGW *or* **agw** allowable gross weight (esp. of an aircraft at takeoff).

A.H. 1 *also* **AH** ampere-hour. **2** in the Hebrew year. [Latin *anno Hebraico*] **3** in the year of the Hegira, A.D. 622. [Latin *anno Hegirae*]

aH abhenry.

ah. hypermetropic astigmatism.

a.h. 1 after hatch *shipping*. **2** *also* **a-h.** ampere-hour.

A.H.A. 1 *also* **AHA** American Heart Association. **2** American Historical Association. **3** *also* **AHA** American Hospital Association. **4** American Hotel Association. **5** American Humane Association.

AHAUS Amateur Hockey Association of the United States.

AC Army Hospital Corps.

AHCPR Agency for Health Care Policy and Research (of U.S. Department of Health and Human Services).

AHD arteriosclerotic heart disease.

A.H.E. Associate in Home Economics.

AHEA American Home Economics Association.

AHF antihemophilic factor (a blood-clotting substance).

AHG antihemophilic globulin (a protein absent in the blood plasma of sufferers of hemophilia).

AHH aryl hydrocarbon hydroxylase (enzyme that converts chemicals in tobacco smoke to carcinogenic agents).

AHL American Hockey League.

a.h.l. on or at this passage. [Latin *ad hunc locum*]

AHMA American Hardware Manufacturers Association.

A.H.M.S. American Home Mission Society.

AHP 1 *also* **A.H.P.** actual horsepower. **2** *also* **ahp** air horsepower.

AHQ 1 Air Headquarters. **2** Allied Headquarters. **3** Army Headquarters.

AHR American Historical Review (magazine title).

AHS 1 American Helicopter Society. **2** *also* **A.H.S.** American Humane Society. **3** *also* **A.H.S.** in the year of human salvation. [Latin *anno humanae salutis*]

A.H.S.A. American Horse Shows Association.

a.h.v. at or on this word. [Latin *ad hanc vocem*]

AI 1 *also* **A.I.** Admiralty Islands. **2** airborne or aircraft interception. **3** Amnesty International (organization working for release of persons jailed for political and religious reasons). **4** *also* **A.I.** Anthropological Institute. **5** anti-icing. **6** *also* **A/I** aptitude index. **7** artificial insemination. **8** artificial intelligence. **9** associate or assistant instructor. **10** *also* **A.I.** Auctioneers' and Estate Agents' Institute. **11** auto-oxidation inhibitor (chemical that prevents the formation of free radicals). **12** *also* **A.I.** in the year of the discovery. [Latin *anno inventionis*]

a.i. 1 all iron (in foundry work, blueprints, and plans). **2** for the meantime. [Latin *ad interim*]

AIA 1 *also* **A.I.A.** Aerospace Industries Association. **2** Aircraft Industries Association. **3** American Insurance Association. **4** *also* **A.I.A.** American Institute of Accountants. **5** *also* **A.I.A.** American Insitute of Architects. **6** *also* **A.I.A.** Archaeological Institute of America. **7** *also* **A.I.A.** Associate of the Institute of Actuaries. **8** International Association of Allergology. [French *Association Internationale d'Allergologie*]

AIAA 1 American Institute of Aeronautics and Astronautics. **2** *also* **A.I.A.A.** Architect Member of the Incorporated Association of Architects and Surveyors. **3** Association of International Advertising Agencies.

A.I.A.C. 1 *also* **AIAC** Associate of the Institute of Company Accountants. **2** International Association for Classical Archaeology. [French *Association Internationale d'Archéologie Classique*]

A.I.A.E. Associate of the Institution of Automobile Engineers.

A.I. Arb. Associate of the Institute of Arbitrators.

A.I.A.S. *British* Associate Surveyor Member of the Incorporated Association of Architects and Surveyors.

AIAW Association of Intercollegiate Athletics for Women.

AIB 1 Accident Investigation Branch *British aviation*. **2** American Institute of Baking.

A.I.B. American Institute of Banking.

A.I.B.A. *or* **AIBA** International Amateur Boxing Association. [French *Association Internationale de Boxe Amateur*]

A.I.B.D. Associate of the Institute of British Decorators.

AIBS or **A.I.B.S.** American Institute of Biological Sciences.

A.I.C. or **AIC** American Institute of Chemists.

AICA International Association of Analog Computation. [French *Association Internationale pour le Calcul Analogique*]

A.I.C.E. or **AICE** 1 American Institute of Chemical Engineers. 2 American Institute of Consulting Engineers. 3 Associate of the Institution of Civil Engineers.

A.I.Ch.E. or **AIChE** American Institute of Chemical Engineers.

A.I.C.M.A. International Association of Aerospace Equipment Manufacturers. [French *Association Internationale des Constructeurs de Matériel Aerospatial*]

AICPA American Institute of Certified Public Accountants.

A.I.C.S. Associate of the Institute of Chartered Shipbrokers.

AID 1 Agency for International Development (of U.S. Department of State). 2 also **A.I.D.** American Institute of Decorators. 3 artificial insemination by donor.

AIDC Australian Industry Development Corporation.

AIDS (ādz) acquired immune deficiency syndrome (viral disease that attacks the body's immune system).

AIEA or **A.I.E.A.** International Atomic Energy Agency. [French *Agence Internationale de l'Énergie Atomique*]

AIEE or **A.I.E.E.** American Institute of Electrical Engineers.

AIG 1 Adjutant Inspector General. 2 all inertial guidance. 3 also **A.I.G.** International Association of Geodesy. [French *Association Internationale de Géodésie*]

aig. needle (in knitting): *aig. gche = left-hand needle.* [French *aiguille*]

AIGA 1 American Institute of Graphic Arts. 2 also **A.I.G.A.** International Association of Geomagnetism and Aeronomy. [French *Association Internationale de Géomagnétisme et d'Aéronomie*]

A.I.G.M. or **AIGM** International Association of Department Stores. [French *Association Internationale de Grands Magasins*]

AIH 1 artificial insemination by husband. 2 International Hotel Association. [French *Association Internationale de l'Hôtellerie*]

AIHA 1 American Industrial Hygiene Association. 2 autoimmune hemolytic anemia.

A.I.H.S. International Association of Scientific Hydrology. [French *Association Internationale d'Hydrologie Scientifique*]

AIIE or **A.I.I.E.** American Institute of Industrial Engineers.

AIJP International Association of Philatelic Journalists. [French *Association Internationale des Journalistes Philateliques*]

AIL 1 also **ail.** aileron. 2 American Institute of Laundering. 3 also **A.I.L.** International Association of Theoretical and Applied Limnology. [French *Association Internationale de Limnologie Théorique et Appliqué*]

A.I.L.A. or **AILA** American Institute of Landscape Architects.

AILAS automatic instrument landing approach system.

AIM 1 (ām) Accuracy in Media (private organization that monitors presentation of news, esp. on radio and television).

2 air intercept missile. 3 American Indian Movement (organization for protection of Native American civil rights and restoration of property taken by treaty). 4 also **A.I.M.** American Institute of Management. 5 Association for Information Management.

AIMA or **a.i.m.a.** as interest may appear (of insurance).

A.I.M.&M.E. American Institute of Mining and Metallurgical Engineers (compare *A.I.M.E.*).

A.I.Mar.E. Associate of the Institute of Marine Engineers.

A.I.M.E. 1 also **AIME** American Institute of Mining Engineers. 2 Associate of the Institution of Marine Engineers. 3 a American Institute of Mechanical Engineers. b also **A.I.Mech.E.** British Associate of the Institute of Mechanical Engineers. 4 British Associate of the Institution of Mining Engineers. 5 British Associate of the Institution of Mining and Metallurgy.

AIMME or **A.I.M.M.E.** American Institute of Mining and Metallurgical Engineers.

A.I.M.M.P.E. or **AIMMPE** American Institute of Mining, Metallurgical, and Petroleum Engineers.

A.I.M.P.A. or **AIMPA** International Association of Meteorology and Atmospheric Physics. [French *Association Internationale de Météorologie et de Physique de l'Atmosphère*]

A.I.M.T.A. or **AIMTA** Associate of the Institute of Municipal Treasurers and Accountants.

AIMU or **A.I.M.U.** American Institute of Marine Underwriters.

AINA 1 Arctic Institute of North America. 2 also **A.I.N.A.** Associate of the Institution of Naval Architects.

A-Ind or **A-Ind.** Anglo-Indian.

AIO Arecibo Ionospheric Observatory (a radio telescope at Arecibo, Puerto Rico).

A.I.O.P. International Association for Vocational Guidance. [French *Association Internationale d'Orientation Professionnelle*]

A.I.P. or **AIP** 1 American Institute of Physics. 2 also **A.Inst.P.** British Associate of the Institute of Physics.

A.I.P.A. International Association of Applied Psychology. [French *Association Internationale de Psychologie Appliquée*]

AIR 1 All India Radio. 2 American Institutes for Research. 3 also **A.I.R.** artist(s) in residence.

AIRA Air or Air Force attaché.

Aircav (ār'kav') or **Air Cav** Air cavalry (unit of the U.S. Army conveyed to battle area usually by helicopter).

AIREA or **A.I.R.E.A.** American Institute of Real Estate Appraisers.

AIREP aircraft report.

air hp. air horsepower.

AIRS U.S. Army Information Radio Service.

A.I.S.A. or **AISA** Associate of the Incorporated Secretaries Association.

AISC or **A.I.S.C.** American Institute of Steel Construction.

AISE or **A.I.S.E.** 1 Association of Iron and Steel Engineers. 2 International Economic Science Association. [French *Association Internationale des Sciences Économiques*]

AISI or **A.I.S.I.** American Iron and Steel Institute (also used to identify an industry standard).

AISP Association of Information Systems Professionals.

AIST U.S. Agency for Industrial Science and Technology.

AIT 1 Advanced Individual Training (level beyond basic training in the U.S. Army). **2** International Association of Workers. [French *Association Internationale des Travailleurs*] **3** International Tourism Alliance. [French *Alliance Internationale de Tourisme*]

A.I.V. International Association of Volcanology. [French *Association Internationale de Volcanologie*]

AIWM American Institute of Weights and Measures.

AJ 1 antijamming *electronics, communication*. **2** Associate in Journalism. **3** *also* **A.J.** Associate Justice.

AJA American of Japanese Ancestry.

AJC 1 a American Jewish Congress. **b** American Jewish Committee. **2** *also* **A.J.C.** in the year of Our Lord: *337 A.J.C.* [French *Année Jésus-Christ*]

AJIL American Journal of International Law (magazine title).

AJOJ April, July, October, January (month beginning each of the traditional financial quarters of the year).

AJS American Journal of Science (magazine title).

AK 1 Alaska (Zip Code). **2** assault or automatic rifle: *AK-47.* [Russian *Avtomat Kalashnikov*] **3** Knight of the Order of Australia.

a.k.a. or **a/k/a** or **AKA** also known as.

AKC American Kennel Club.

AKF Australian Koala Foundation.

AL 1 adaptation level *psychology*. **2** Alabama (Zip Code). **3** American League *baseball*. **4** *also* **A.L.** American Legion. **5** American Libraries (publication). **6** *also* **AL.** or **A-L** or **A.L.** Anglo-Latin.

Al aluminum (chemical element).

al 1 *also* **a.l.** after delivery of goods. [French *après livraison*] **2** alias **3** *also* **a.l.** all lengths (of lumber). **4** *also* **a.l.** autograph letter. **5** *also* **a.l.** light year *astronomy*. [French *année lumière*]

ALA 1 *also* **A.L.A.** Amalgamated Lithographers of America. **2** American Library Association. **3** American Literature Association. **4** amniolevulinic acid: *ALA-dehydratase = enyzme functioning in the synthesis of hemoglobin.* **5** *also* **A.L.A.** British Associate of the Library Association. **6** *also* **A.L.A.** Author's League of America. **7** Automobile Legal Association.

Ala. 1 Alabama. **2** *also* **ala. a** alanine (essential amino acid in protein). **b** alanyl.

ALADI Latin American Integration Association (trade association of Argentina, Bolivia, Brazil, Chile, Colombia, Ecuador, Mexico, Paraguay, Peru, Uruguay, and Venezuela). [Spanish *Asociación Latinoamericana de Integración*]

Al-Anon (al'ə non') Alcoholics Anonymous (a support group for family members of alcoholics).

ALARM Automatic Light Aircraft Readiness Monitor (checking system to determine an aircraft's airworthiness).

Alas. Alaska.

Alateen (al'ə tēn') Alcoholics Anonymous Teens (a support group for teen-age family members of alcoholics).

Alb. 1 Albania, Albanian. **2** Albany. **3** Alberta, Canada (not in official use). **4** *also* **Alb** white. [Latin *albus*]

alb. albumin.

ALBA American Lawn Bowling Association.

Alba. Alberta, Canada.

ALBM 1 Air Land Battle Management (command-and-control computer system for fighting battles). **2** air-launched ballistic missile.

ALC 1 *also* **A.L.C.** American Lutheran Church. **2** automatic level control (device to adjust recording level on audit equipment).

alc. or **alc** alcohol.

Alcan or **ALCAN** (al'kan) Alaska-Canada: *the Alcan Highway.*

ALCI appliance leakage current interrupter.

ALCM 1 air-launched cruise missile. **2** *also* **A.L.C.M.** Associate of the London College of Music.

alcoh. alcohol.

ALD adrenoleukodystrophy (metabolic disorder that affects development of myelin).

Ald. or **ald.** or **Aldm.** alderman.

ALE additional living expense *insurance*.

Alex. Alexander.

ALF 1 Animal Liberation Front (against exploitation of animals). **2** *British* automatic letter facer (device to stack and cancel letters). **3** Linguistic Atlas of France. [French *Atlas Linguistique de la France*]

Alf. 1 Alfonso. **2** Alfred.

ALG antilymphocyte globulin (used for immunosuppression in organ transplant operations).

Alg. 1 *also* **alg.** algebra. **2** Algerian, Algiers.

ALGOL or **Algol** (al'gol) Algorithmic language (algebraic language used in computer programming).

Alh. Alhambra.

A.L.I. 1 American Law Institute. **2** American Library Institute.

ali. elsewhere. [Latin *alibi*]

ALIDE Latin American Association of Development Financing Institutions. [Spanish *Asociación Latinoamericana de Instituciónes Financieros de Desarrollo*]

ALing Archivum Linguisticum (magazine title).

ALJ administrative law judge.

alk. alkali or alkaline.

All German (in language tables). [French *allemand*]

ALLC Association for Literary and Linguistic Computing.

allg. general or generally. [German *allgemein*]

allo. lively *music*. [Italian *allegro*]

A.L.M. or **ALM** Master of the Liberal Arts. [Latin *Artium Liberalium Magister*]

ALMACA Association of Labor-Management Administrators and Consultants on Alcoholism.

alnico (al'nə kō) aluminum, nickel, cobalt (an alloy).

ALO Air Liaison Officer.

ALOA Amalgamated Lithographers of America.

A.L.O.E. A Lady of England (pseudonym of Charlotte M. Tucker, 19th-century English author).

A.L. of H. American Legion of Honor.

ALP or **A.L.P. 1** American Labor Party. **2** Australian Labor Party. **3** Automated Library Program.

ALPA or **A.L.P.A.** Air Line Pilots Association.

Alph. Alphonse.

A.L.P.O. or **ALPO** Association of Lunar and Planetary Observers.

A.L.R. American Law Reports.

ALS 1 Advanced Launch System (NASA-Air Force project to construct rockets from common components). **2** advanced life support (system to provide emergency room services at the site of emergency medical calls). **3** also **a.l.s.** amyotrophic lateral sclerosis (commonly called *Lou Gehrig's disease*). **4** antilymphocyte serum (used against rejection in organ transplant). **5** also **A.L.S.** Associate of the Linnean Society. **6** also **A.L.S.** or **a.l.s.** autograph letter signed. **7** automatic-landing system.

ALSC Association for Library Service to Children.

Alsk. Alaska.

ALT alanine aminotransferase (an enzyme).

Alt. alternating (esp. of lights on navigation charts).

alt. 1 alternate, alternating, alternation. **2** alternative. **3** alternator. **4** altitude. **5** alto.

A.L.T.A. 1 American Land Title Association. **2** also **ALTA** American Literary Translators Association.

Alta. Alberta, Canada.

alt. dieb. every other day *pharmaceutics.* [Latin *alternis diebus*]

alter. alteration.

alt. hor. every other hour *pharmaceutics.* [Latin *alternis hora*]

altm. altimeter.

alt. noc. every other night *pharmaceutics.* [Latin *alternis noctibus*]

ALU arithmetic (and) logic unit (of a computer).

alum. 1 aluminum. **2** alumna, alumnae. **3** alumnus, alumni.

ALV avian leukemia virus.

alv. alveolar.

alw. or **Alw.** allowance, *esp. in horse racing.*

aly. alloy.

AM *I an abbreviation for:* **1** airlock module (of a spacecraft). **2** also **A/M** Air Marshal. **3** Air Medal. **4** also **A.M.** Air Ministry. **5** also **A.M.** or **A.-M.** Alpes-Maritimes (department of France). **6** amplitude modulation. **7** angular momentum. **8** arithmetic mean. **9** also **A.M.** Associate Member, esp. in combination: *A.M.E.I.C. = Associate Member of the Engineering Institute of Canada.* **10** also **A.M.** aviation medicine. **11** also **A.M.** Master of Arts. [Latin *Artium Magister*] **12** Member of the Order of Australia.
II a symbol for: **1** also **A.M.** before noon, time from midnight to noon. [Latin *ante meridiem*] **2** Hail, Mary! [Latin *Ave Maria*] **3** in the year of the world. [Latin *anno mundi*]

a.M. or **A/M** on the Main River, in Germany: *Frankfurt a.M.* [German *am Main*]

Am *I an abbreviation for:* **1** also **Am.** America or American: *Am. Emb. = American Embassy.* **2** also **Am.** ammeter. **3** also **Am.** Amos (book of the Old Testament). **4** also **Am.** ammunition.
II a symbol for: **1** alabamine (chemical element, now *astatine*). **2** americium (chemical element). **3** ammonium (hydrogen and nitrogen acting in a combined state). **4** amyl (carbon and hydrogen acting in a combined state).

am *I an abbreviation for:* **1** also **am.** amplitude. **2** amplitude modulation.
II a symbol for: **1** also **a.m.** before noon, time from midnight to noon. [Latin *ante meridiem*] **2** in the year of the world. [Latin *anno mundi*]

AMA 1 Aerospace Medical Association. **2** against medical advice. **3** also **A.M.A.** American Management Association. **4** also **A.M.A.** American Maritime Association. **5** also **A.M.A.** American Medical Association. **6** American Motorcycle Association. **7** Australian Medical Association. **8** Automobile Manufacturers Association.

amal. amalgamated.

Amb. 1 ambassador. **2** ambulance.

amb ambient.

AMC 1 Air Matériel Command (of the U.S. Air Force). **2** also **A.M.C.** American Maritime Cases. **3** Appalachian Mountain Club. **4** Army Medical Center. **5** arthrogryposis multiplex congenita (condition of joint impairment at birth). **6** also **A.M.C.** Art Master's Certificate. **7** automatic mixture control.

am. cur. friend of the court *law.* [Latin *amicus curiae*]

AMD 1 Aerospace Medical Division. **2** age-related macular degeneration (loss of the ability to see objects focused upon due to aging). **3 a** air movement data. **b** air movement designator. **4** Army Medical Department.

Am.Dec. American Decisions *law.*

A.M.D.G. to the greater glory of God. [Latin *ad majorem Dei gloriam*]

amdt. amendment.

AME 1 also **A.M.E.** African Methodist Episcopal. **2** American. **3** angle-measuring equipment.

AmE American English.

AMEDS or **AmedS** Army Medical Service.

amend. amendment.

Amep. American. [Russian *americahnskyi*]

Amer. America or American, esp. in combination: *Amer.G.S. = American Geographical Society.*

Amerind or **AmerInd** (am′ər ind) American Indian.

Ameslan (am′əs lan′) American Sign Language (manual language of the deaf).

Amex or **AMEX** (am′eks) American Stock Exchange.

A.M.E.Z. or **AMEZ** African Methodist Episcopal Zion: *A.M.E.Z.C. = African Methodist Episcopal Zion Church.*

A.M.F. 1 Australian Military Forces. **2** autocrine motility factor (protein in cancer research).

AM/FM or **am/fm** amplitude modulation/frequency modulation.

AMG automatic magnetic guidance.

amg. among.

amh hyperbolic amplitude *mathematics*.

AMI 1 acute myocardial infarction (damage caused to heart tissue by loss of blood). **2** air mileage indicator. **3** American Meat Institute.

A.M.I.A.E. *British* Associate Member of the Institution of Automobile Engineers.

A.M.I.C.E. 1 *also* **A.M.I.Chem.E.** *British* Associate Member of the Institution of Chemical Engineers. **2** *British* Associate Member of the Institution of Civil Engineers.

A.M.I.E.E. *British* Associate Member of the Institution of Electrical Engineers.

A.M.I.Mar.E. *British* Associate Member of the Institute of Marine Engineers.

A.M.I.Mech.E. *British* Associate Member of the Institution of Mechanical Engineers.

A.M.I.Min.E. *British* Associate Member of the Institution of Mining Engineers.

Am. Ind. *or* **Am Ind** American Indian.

Am. Inst. E.E. American Institute of Electrical Engineers.

AMIS audio media integration standard (for connection of computers with telephone communication).

A.M.J. World Assembly of Youth. [French *Assemblée Mondiale de la Jeunesse*]

AMLS *or* **A.M.L.S.** Master of Arts in Library Science.

AMM 1 anti-missile missile. **2** *also* **A.M.M.** Master of Mechanical Arts. **3** *also* **A.M.M.** World Medical Association. [French *Association Médicale Mondiale*]

A.M.M.I. American Merchant Marine Institute.

ammo (am′ō) *or* **ammo.** ammunition.

ammon. ammonia.

Amn. *or* **Amn** airman.

amn. ammunition.

AMNH American Museum of Natural History (in New York City).

AMO 1 *also* **A.M.O.** Air Ministry Order (with a number). **2** atomic, molecular, and optical *physics*.

AMORC *or* **A.M.O.R.C.** Ancient Mystical Order Rosae Crucis (Order of Rosicrucians).

amorph. amorphous.

AMOS Automatic Meteorological Observation System *or* Station.

AMP 1 acid mucopolysaccharides (a carbohydrate compound of the human body). **2** adenosine monophosphate: *AMPase* (enzyme present in cells and probably involved in ion transport across cell membranes).

amp (*sometimes pronounced* amp) *or* **amp. 1 a** amperage. **b** *also* **Amp.** ampere. **2** amplifier. **3** *also* **Amp.** amplitude. **4** ampule. **5** amputation.

AMPAC American Medical Political Action Committee.

AMPAS *or* **A.M.P.A.S.** Academy of Motion Picture Arts and Sciences.

AMPH *or* **amph. 1** amphibian. **2** amphibious.

amphetamine (am fet′ə mēn) drug used as a stimulant. [*alpha-methyl-beta phenyl-ethyl-amine*]

amp-hr. ampere-hour.

AMPTP Association of Motion Picture and Television Producers.

AMR Atlantic Missile Range.

AMRA American Mechanical Rights Association (recording rights, as on phonograph records, tapes, and discs).

Am.Repts. *or* **Am.R.** American Reports *law*.

AMS 1 accelerator mass spectroscopy (a form of chemical analysis). **2** aeronautical material specification. **3** Agricultural Marketing Service (of the U.S. Department of Agriculture, engaging in market research and regulation, inspection, and grading of farm products). **4** *also* **A.M.S.** American Mathematical Society. **5** *also* **A.M.S.** American Meteorological Society. **6** *also* **A.M.S.** American Microscopic Society. **7** American Montessori Society (organization of schools using the teaching methods advocated by Maria Montessori, Italian educator, 1870–1952). **8** American Musicology Society. **9** Army Map Service. **10 a** Army Medical Services. **b** Army Medical Staff. **11** *also* **A.M.S.** *or* **a.m.s.** autograph manuscript signed.

AMSA Advanced Manned Strategic Aircraft.

AMSGA Association of Manufacturers and Suppliers for the Graphic Arts.

AMSL *or* **amsl** above mean sea level.

AMSOC American Miscellaneous Society (part of the National Academy of Science).

Am. Soc. C.E. American Society of Civil Engineers.

Am. Soc. M.E. American Society of Mechanical Engineers.

Amst. Amsterdam.

AMSW *or* **A.M.S.W.** Master of Arts in Social Work.

AMT 1 advanced manufacturing technology (production using systems and machinery controlled by computers). **2** alternative minimum tax (U.S. tax to ensure that all taxable entities pay at least some tax). **3** amplitude modulation transmitter. **4** *also* **A.M.T.** Associate in Medical Technology. **5** astrograph mean time *astronomy*. **6** *also* **A.M.T.** Master's Degree in Teaching.

amt. amount.

A.M.T.C. Master of Arts Teaching Certificate.

Amtorg (am′tôrg) former Soviet trading company in the United States. [Russian *Amerikanskaja torgovlja* American trade]

Amtrak (am′trak′) American Track (trade name of National Railroad Passenger Corporation, providing interstate passenger rail service). [possibly *American Travel and Track*]

AMU 1 air mileage unit. **2** astronaut maneuvering unit (pack worn by astronauts outside a space vehicle, providing life-support systems). **3** *also* **A.M.U.** *or* **amu** atomic mass unit.

AMVER *or* **AMVERS** Atlantic Merchant Vessel Reporting System (program for aiding U.S. Coast Guard in search and rescue work).

AMVETS or **Amvets** (am'vets) American Veterans (of World War II, Korea, Vietnam, and the Gulf War).

AMWA or **A.M.W.A. 1** American Medical Women's Association. **2** American Medical Writer's Association.

AN 1 also **A.N.** acid number. **2** Air Force-Navy. **3** Airman. **4** also **AN.** or **A.N.** or **A-N** Anglo-Norman. **5** also **AN.** anode. **6** Army-Navy. **7** also **A.N.** arrival notice *shipping*. **8** also **A.N.** Associate in Nursing. **9** also **A.N.** autograph note.

An *I an abbreviation for:* **1** also **An.** annotated. **2** also **An.** annual.
II a symbol for: actinon (chemical element).

an. 1 also **an** above-named. **2** annotated. **3** annual. **4** anode. **5** anonymous. **6** before. [Latin *ante*] **7** in the year. [Latin *anno*]

a.n. 1 arrival notice *shipping*. **2** autograph note.

ANA 1 Administration for Native Americans (of the Department of Health and Human Services). **2** also **A.N.A.** American Neurological Association. **3** American Newspaper Association (compare *ANPA*). **4** American Numismatic Association. **5** also **A.N.A.** American Nurses' Association. **6** Arab Network of America. **7** *British* Article Numbering Association (manufacturers' group to supervise identification of products by a numbering system). **8** also **A.N.A.** Associate of the National Academy of Design. **9** Association of National Advertisers. **10** also **A.N.A.** Australian National Airways. **11** also **A.N.A.** Australian Natives' Association.

ANAF Army-Navy-Air Force.

anal. 1 a analogous. **b** analogy. **2 a** analysis. **b** analytic, analytical. **c** analyze, analyzed.

analyt. analytical.

ANARE Australian National Antarctic Research Expeditions.

anat. 1 anatomic, anatomical. **2** anatomist. **3** anatomy.

ANC 1 African National Congress. **2** Army Nurse Corps. **3** also **A.N.C.** before the birth of Christ; BC. [Latin *ante Nativitatem Christi*]

anc. ancient, anciently.

ANCAM Association of Newspaper Classified Advertising Managers.

ANCP African National Congress Party.

anct. ancient, anciently.

And Andromeda (constellation).

And. 1 Andorra. **2** Andrew.

and. moderately slow *music*. [Italian *andante*]

ANDB Air Navigation Development Board.

ANF 1 Atlantic Nuclear Force. **2** atrial natriuretic factor (hormone used as a diuretic and vasodilator).

A.N.F.M. August, November, February, May (quarter months of traditional financial year) *commerce*.

ANFO ammonium nitrate-fuel oil (dry blasting agent).

ANG 1 Air National Guard. **2** American Newspaper Guild.

Ang. 1 Angola. **2** in English: *s'il vous plaît*, Ang. [Medieval Latin *Anglice*]

ang. 1 angle. **2** angular.

Angl. 1 Anglican. **2** Anglicized.

angl. in English. [Latin *anglice*]

Ang.-Sax. Anglo-Saxon.

ANGUS Air National Guard of the United States.

Anh. 1 postscript; P.S. **2** supplement, appendix. [German *Anhang*]

anh. or **anhyd.** or **anhydr.** anhydrous.

a.n.i. international normal atmosphere. [French *atmosphère normale internationale*]

anim. lively *music*. [Italian *animato*]

ANL 1 Argonne National Laboratory (installation of the Nuclear Regulatory Commission). **2** Australian National Line (government-owned shipping organization). **3** also **anl** automatic noise limiter.

Anl. outline. [German *Anlage*]

anlys. analysis.

ANM Arab Nationalist Movement.

An M Annuale Medievale (magazine title).

Anm. note, footnote. [German *Anmerkung*]

ANMB Army-Navy Munitions Board.

ann. 1 also **Ann.** annals. **2** anniversary. **3** also **Ann.** annual, esp. in combination: *ann.rep.* = *annual report.* **4** annuity. **5** annunciator. **6** also **Ann a** in the year. [Latin *anno*] **b** years. [Latin *anni*]

anniv. anniversary.

annot. annotated, annotation, annotator.

Annunc. Annunciation (of the Virgin Mary).

anny. annuity *law*.

anod. anodize.

Anon. or **anon.** anonymous, anonymously.

A No. 1 first-class; A-1.

ANOVA analysis of variance.

ANP 1 atrial natriuretic peptide (hormone active in lowering blood pressure). **2** national news agency of the Netherlands. [Dutch *Algemeen Nederlands Persbureau*]

ANPA American Newspaper Publishers Association.

ANPT aeronautical national taper pipe threads.

ANQ American Notes and Queries (magazine title).

anr. another *law*.

ANRAC air navigation radio control.

ANRC or **A.N.R.C.** American National Red Cross (often *A.R.C.*).

ANS 1 American Name Society. **2** also **A.N.S.** American Nuclear Society. **3** also **A.N.S.** American Numismatic Society. **4** Army Nursing Service. **5** autograph note signed. **6** autonomic nervous system.

ans. answer, answered.

a.n.s. 1 autonomic nervous system. **2** autograph note signed.

ANSA Associated National Press Agency of Italy. [Italian *Agenzia Nazionale Stampa Associata*]

ANSI American National Standards Institute (U.S. government agency to establish standards in industry).

A.N.S.S. Associate of Normal School of Science.

Ant Antlia (constellation).

Ant. **1** Antarctica. **2** Anthony. **3** Antigua. **4** antiphon. **5** Antony and Cleopatra (play by Shakespeare). **6** Antrim, Ireland.

ant. **1** *also* **ANT** antenna. **2** anterior, esp. in combination: *ant. lobe.* **3 a** antiquarian, antiquary. **b** antique. **c** antiquities. **4** antonym.

ANTA (an'tə) (former) American National Theater (and) Academy.

Ant. & Cl. Antony and Cleopatra (play by Shakespeare).

Antarct. Antarctica.

ant. frt. anticipated freight *commerce.*

anth. *or* **anthol.** anthology.

anthr. *or* **anthro.** *or* **anthrop.** *or* **anthropol.** anthropological, anthropology.

anti *or* **anti.** antidote.

antilog antilogarithm.

antiq. **1** *also* **antiqn.** antiquarian. **2** antiquity, antiquities.

ANTS Anglo-Norman Text Society.

ANTU (an'tü) alpha-naphthylthiourea (powder used as rat poison).

A.N.U. *or* **ANU** Australian National University.

Anw. instruction, direction. [German *Anweisung*]

ANWR Arctic National Wildlife Refuge.

anx. annex.

ANZ Australian-New Zealand Bank Group.

ANZAAS (an'zəs, -zas') *or* **A.N.Z.A.A.S.** Australian and New Zealand Association for the Advancement of Science.

ANZAC (an'zak) Australia and New Zealand Army Corps, esp. in reference to a member of this corps.

ANZAM *or* **Anzam** (an'zam) Australia, New Zealand, and Malaysia (mutual defense pact).

ANZCERTA (anz'sèr'tə) Australia-New Zealand Closer Economic Relations Trade Agreement; CER.

A.N.Z.I.A. *or* **ANZIA** Associate of the New Zealand Institute of Architects.

A.N.Z.I.C. *or* **ANZIC** Associate of the New Zealand Institute of Chemistry.

A.N.Z.L.A. *or* **ANZLA** Associate of the New Zealand Library Association.

ANZUK (an'zuk) Australia, New Zealand, and United Kingdom (mutual defense pact).

ANZUS (an'zəs, -zus') Australia, New Zealand, and the United States (mutual defense pact, from which New Zealand withdrew in 1986).

A.O. **1** access opening *medicine, architecture.* **2** Accountant Officer. **3** account of. **4** *also* **AO** Administrative Officer. **5** Area Officer. **6** *also* **AO** Army Order (with a number). **7** *also* **AO** Officer of the Order of Australia.

a.O. *or* **a/O** on the Oder River, a boundary between Poland and Germany. [German *an der Oder*]

a/o *or* **A/o** *or* **a.o.** **1** account of. **2** and others.

AOA **1** *also* **AoA** Administration on Aging. **2** *also* **A.O.A.** American Optometric Association. **3** American Ordnance Association. **4** American Orthopedic Association. **5** American Osteopathic Association.

AOB **1** any other business. **2** at or below (as of a market price, or of a temperature indication).

AOC **1** Air Operations Center. **2** *also* **A.O.C.** anodal opening contraction. **3** in the year of the Creation. [Latin *anno Orbis Conditi*]

AOCP aircraft out of commission for parts.

AOD **1** *also* **A.O.D.** Ancient Order of Druids. **2** Army Ordnance Department.

A.O.F. Ancient Order of Foresters.

A.O.H. Ancient Order of Hibernians.

A-OK *or* **A-O.K.** All OK.

AOL **1** *also* **A.O.L.** absent over leave. **2 a** Atlantic Oceanographic Laboratory. **b** Atlantic Oceanographic Laboratories.

AONB *or* **A.O.N.B.** Area of Outstanding Natural Beauty (in Great Britain a scenic area under national protection).

A one first-class.

AOPA Aircraft Owners' and Pilots' Association.

AOPEC Arab Organization of Petroleum Exporting Countries.

AOQ average outgoing quality *commerce.*

AOR **1** adult-oriented rock: *AOR and classic-rock radio.* **2** advice of rights *law.* **3** at own risk (a hospital term).

a/or and/or, either or both.

aor. aorist (a past tense of Greek and Sanskrit verbs).

AORN Association of Operating Room Nurses.

AOS **1** acquisition of signal *aeronautics, astronautics.* **2** alternative operator service (telephone operators for users in hotels, airports, etc.). **3** *also* **A.O.S.** American Ophthalmological Society. **4** *also* **A.O.S.** American Oriental Society. **5** *also* **A.O.S.** American Otological Society.

A.O.S.E. *or* **AOSE** American Order of Stationary Engineers.

AOSO Advanced Orbiting Solar Observatory.

A.O.S.S. Fellow of the American Oriental Society. [Latin *Americanae Orientalis Societatus Socius*]

A.O.T.A. American Occupational Therapy Association.

A.O.U. American Ornithologists Union.

A.O.U.W. *or* **AOUW** Ancient Order of United Workmen.

AP **1** access panel *architecture.* **2** accounts payable. **3** acid-proof. **4** action potential *psychology.* **5** advanced placement: *AP calculus.* **6** advanced post *military.* **7** after perpendicular (esp. in blueprints of a ship). **8** airplane. **9** Air Police. **10** alkaline phosphatase (enzyme) *biochemistry.* **11** Alliance Party, of Ireland. **12** *also* **A.P.** American Pharmacopeia. **13** American Plan (hotel rate including cost of room plus three meals). **14** Annals of Philosophy (magazine title). **15** *also* **A.P.** anomalous propagation *meteorology.* **16** antipersonnel (of munitions). **17** aortic or arterial pressure *medicine.* **18** arithmetic progression. **19** *also* **AP** Associated Press. **20** Associate Presbyterian. **21** assumed position *astronomy, navigation.* **22** atomic power. **23** *also* **A.P.** Australia Party. **24** author's proof. **25** Popular Alliance, a Spanish political party. [Spanish *Alianza Popular*]

A/P **1** accounts payable. **2 a** authority to pay. **b** authority to purchase.

Ap. 1 Apostle. **2** *also* **Ap** April.

ap. 1 according to. [Latin *apud*] **2** apparent, esp. in combination: *ap. pos. = apparent position.*

a.p. 1 above proof (of alcoholic beverages). **2** additional premium *insurance.* **3** after perpendicular (esp. in blueprints of a ship). **4** armor piercing (of munitions). **5** assessment paid. **6** author's proof. **7** before dinner *pharmaceutics.* [Latin *ante prandium*] **8** before noon or time from midnight to noon; AM. [Finnish *aamupäivällä*]

APA 1 *also* **A.P.A.** Administrative Procedure Act *law.* **2** all points addressable *computers.* **3** American Pharmaceutical Association. **4** *also* **A.P.A.** American Philological Association. **5** American Philosophical Association. **6** American Physiotherapy Association. **7** American Protective Association. **8** American Protestant Association. **9** *also* **A.P.A.** American Psychiatric Association. **10** *also* **A.P.A.** American Psychological Association. **11** Architectural Photographers Association. **12** Ashton-Potter America (printer of U.S. postage stamps). **13** *also* **A.P.A.** Associate in Public Adminisration. **14** Austrian Cooperative Press Agency. [German *Österreichische Presse-Agentur*]

apa axial pressure angle (of gears).

Apart. apartment.

APB all points bulletin (general police announcement).

A.P.B.A. *or* **APBA** American Power Boat Association.

APC 1 adenoidal-pharyngeal-conjunctival: *APC virus.* **2** adenomatous polyposis coli (implicated in colon cancer). **3** *also* **A.P.C.** Aeronautical Planning Chart (of the U.S. Coast and Geodetic Survey). **4** *also* **A.P.C.** Alien Property Custodian. **5** area position control (of aircraft). **6** armored personnel carrier. **7** Army Pay Corps. **8** aspirin, phenacetin, caffeine (used as an analgesic) *medicine.*

apc automatic phase control.

A.P.C.N. in the year after the birth of Christ. [Latin *anno post Christum natum*]

APCS Air Photographic and Charting Service.

APD 1 air procurement district. **2** anti-phase domains (area of a substance consisting of highly ordered material). **3** Army Pay Department.

Apec (ā'pek) Asian-Pacific Economic Cooperation Council (trade group).

apers *or* **APERS** antipersonnel (of munitions).

APEX *or* **Apex** (ā'peks) Advanced Purchase Excursion (low-cost air fare for reservations paid in advance).

APF 1 acidproof floor. **2** animal protein factor (vitamin B_{12} added to animal feed).

APG 1 Aberdeen Proving Grounds, Maryland (of the U.S. Army). **2** air proving ground. **3** *also* **A.P.G.** American Professional Golfers.

APGA American Personnel and Guidance Association.

APH 1 anterior pituitary hormone. **2** Association of Private Hospitals.

aph. aphetic (of a word in which a phoneme, esp. an unaccented vowel, is omitted from the beginning).

APHA American Public Health Association.

A.Ph.A. *or* **APhA** American Pharmaceutical Association.

APHIS Animal and Plant Health Inspection Service (of the U.S. Departent of Agriculture).

API 1 air position indicator. **2** *also* **A.P.I.** American Petroleum Institute. **3** American Press Institute. **4** antecedent precipitation index *meteorology.* **5** application programming interface (functions or procedures used to operate a computer program). **6** Associated Photographers International.

APL 1 *also* **APLH** anterior pituitary-like hormone. **2** Applied Physics Laboratory (of Johns Hopkins University). **3** A Programming Language (a flexible computer program used esp. in mathematics).

Apl. April.

A.P.M. 1 Academy of Physical Medicine. **2** *also* **APM** Assistant Paymaster. **3** Assistant Provost Marshal.

apm. apomict (reproduction without union of sex cells) *biology.*

A.P.M.G. Assistant Postmaster General.

APN News Press Agency of Russia. [Russian *Agentstvo Pechati Novosti*]

APO 1 African Peoples Organization (of South Africa). **2** Air Force or Army Post Office.

apo. apogee.

Apoc. 1 Apocalypse. **2 a** *also* **Apocr.** Apocrypha. **b** Apocryphal.

APOD aerial port of debarkation.

APOE aerial port of embarkation.

apog. apogee.

apos. apostrophe.

Apost. 1 Apostle. **2** Apostolic: *Apost. Del. = Apostolic Delegate.*

APOTA automatic positioning of telemetering antenna.

Apoth. apothecary.

APP applications portability profile (standards for computer programs enabling wide use on different kinds of computer equipment).

App. 1 Apostles. **2** *law* **a** (esp. in combination) appeal: *U.S. App. D.C. = United States Court of Appeals, District of Columbia Circuit.* **b** appellate: *App. Ct. = Appellate Court.* **3** appendix.

app. 1 apparatus. **2** apparent, apparently. **3** appeal *law.* **4 a** appended. **b** appendix. **5** applied. **6** appointed. **7** appraise. **8** apprentice. **9 a** approval. **b** approved. **10** approximate, approximately.

appar. 1 apparatus. **2** apparent, apparently.

App. Ct. Appellate Court.

appd. 1 appraised. **2** approved.

App. D.C. District of Columbia Appeal Cases *law.*

App. Div. Appellate Division.

appl. 1 *law also* **Appl. a** appeal. **b** appellant. **2 a** applicable to. **b** application. **c** applied to.

appln. application.

appmt. appointment.

APPR Army Package Power Reactor.

appr. 1 apprentice. **2** approved. **3** *also* **Appr.** approximate, approximately.

appro. approval.

approx. 1 approximate, approximately. **2** approximation.

apps. appendices, appendixes.

appt. 1 appoint. **2** appointment.

apptd. appointed.

appurts. *or* **appurts** (ə pėrtz') appurtenances.

appx. appendix.

APR 1 American Public Radio (not to be confused with *NPR*). **2** annual percentage rate. **3** annual progress report. **4** approved.

Apr. *or* **Apr** April.

APRA *or* **Apra** (äp'rə) **1** American Popular Revolutionary Alliance (Peruvian political party). [Spanish *Alianza Popular Revolucionaria Americana*] **2** Australian Performing Rights Association.

A.P.R.C. in the year after the founding of Rome, 753 BC. [Latin *anno post Romam conditam*]

apr. J.-C. in the year of the Lord; AD. [French *après Jésus-Christ*]

APRO Aerial Phenomena Research Organization (principally engaged in UFO research).

APRT airport.

aprx. approximate.

A.P.S. 1 Aborigines Protection Society (of Australia). **2** American Peace Society. **3** American Pediatric Society. **4** *also* **APS** American Philatelic Society. **5** American Philosophical Society. **6** *also* **APS** American Physical Society. **7** American Physiological Society. **8** American Protestant Society. **9** American Psychological Society.

Aps the Bird of Paradise (constellation). [Latin *Apus*]

aps accessory or auxiliary power supply.

A.P.S.A. American Political Science Association.

Ap. Sed. Apostolic See. [Latin *Apostolica Sedes*]

APT 1 advanced passenger train (a train capable of speeds up to 150 miles per hour). **2** Association of Polytechnic Teachers. **3** automatically programmed tool (of machinery controlled by computer). **4** automatic picture transmission (by weather satellites with TV cameras).

apt. 1 *also* **Apt.** apartment. **2** aptitude.

APTA 1 *also* **A.P.T.A.** American Physical Therapy Association. **2** American Platform Tennis Association. **3** American Public Transit Association.

A.P.T.U. African Postal and Telecommunications Union.

APU 1 anti-poaching unit (of a game reserve). **2** Army Postal Unit. **3** authorized pickup *shipping*. **4** auxiliary power unit.

A.P.U. Arab Postal Union.

APV all-purpose vehicle.

APW architectural projected window (in blueprints and plans).

ap. wt. apothecaries' weight.

APWU American Postal Workers Union.

apx. appendix.

AQ 1 *also* **A.Q.** accomplishment, achievement, or attainment quotient *education*. **2** American Quarterly (magazine title). **3** any quantity.

aq any quantity.

aq. 1 aqueous. **2** water, esp. in combination: *aq. bull.* = *boiling water* for Latin *aqua bulliens; aq. dest.* = *distilled water* for Latin *aqua destillata*.

AQH average quarter hour (audience of a radio or television program).

AQI air quality index.

AQL acceptable quality level.

Aql the Eagle (constellation). [Latin *Aquila*]

Aqr Aquarius (constellation).

AR 1 *also* **A.R.** accomplishment, achievement, or attainment ratio *education*. **2** *also* **A/R** accounts receivable. **3** acid-resistant. **4** *also* **A.R.** acknowledgment of receipt *commerce*. **5** administrative ruling. **6** amateur radio station (in International Telecommunications Union symbols). **7** *also* **A.R.** analytical or analyzed reagent *chemistry*. **8** *also* **A.R.** Annual Register of World Events (annual contemporary review of history). **9** *also* **A.R.** British annual return. **10** Arkansas (Zip Code). **11 a** Army Regulation (with a number). **b** army regulations. **12** aspect ratio *electronics, aeronautics*. **13** *also* **A.R.** in the year of the reign. [Latin *anno regni*] **14** *also* **A.R.** Recollect Augustinian Fathers. **15** *also* **A.R.** right ascension *astronomy*.

Ar *I an abbreviation for:* **1** *also* **Ar. a** Arabian. **b** Arabic. **2** *also* **Ar.** Aramaic. **3** aromatic radical; aryl *chemistry*. **4** arrive, arrival.
II a symbol for: **1** argon (chemical element). **2** silver *heraldry, chemistry* (as a chemical element, now *Ag*). [Latin *argentum*]

a/r all risks (of insurance).

ar. 1 *also* **ar** area (of measure). **2** argent *heraldry*. **3** aromatic. **4** arrive, arrival.

a.r. 1 acknowledgment of receipt *commerce*. **2** all risks (of insurance). **3** analytical or analyzed reagent.

ARA 1 aerial rocket artillery: *ARA rocket firing helicopters.* **2** *also* **A.R.A.** Aircraft Research Association. **3** American Railway Association. **4** *also* **A.R.A.** Associate of the Royal Academy. **5** Australian Regular Army. **6** Australian Retailers Association. **7** Automatic Retailers of America.

Ar A arithmetic age *education*.

ara-A (ar'ə ā') drug used against viral infections. [*arabinose + Adenine*]

Arab. 1 Arabia. **2** Arabian, Arabic.

Arabsat (ar'əb sat') Arab Satellite (communications satellite system of the Arab League).

A.R.A.C. *or* **ARAC** Associate of the Royal Agricultural College.

ara-C (ar'ə sē') cytosine arabinoside (a drug used to treat cancer). [patterned on *ara-A*]

arach. arachnology (study of arachnids, such as spiders, mites, and ticks).

A.R.A.C.I. *or* **ARACI** Associate of the Royal Australian Chemical Institute.

A.R.A.D. *or* **ARAD** Associate of the Royal Academy of Dancing.

A.R.Ae.S. *or* **ARAeS** Associate of the Royal Aeronautical Society.

A.R.A.I.A. *or* **ARAIA** Associate of the Royal Australian Institute of Architects.

A.R.A.M. *or* **ARAM** Associate of the Royal Academy of Music.

Aram. Aramaic.

Aramco *or* **ARAMCO** (ə ram′kō) Arabian-American Oil Company (petroleum consortium).

ARAS 1 ascending reticular activating system (system of the brain stem involved in attention, awareness, and arousal processes). **2** *also* **A.R.A.S.** Associate of the Royal Astronomical Society.

ARB 1 a Accounting Research Bulletin (of the Institute of Certified Public Accountants). **b** Accountng Research Bureau. **2** Association of Radio Broadcasters.

arb 1 arbitrager, arbitrageur. **2** *also* **arb. a** arbitration. **b** arbitrator.

A.R.B.A. *or* **ARBA** Associate of the Royal Society of British Artists.

arbor. arboriculture.

A.R.B.S. *or* **ARBS** Associate of the Royal Society of British Sculptors.

ARC 1 AIDS-related complex (form of AIDS, characterized by swollen glands, loss of weight, and weakness). **2** *also* **A.R.C.** American Red Cross. **3** Ames Research Center (of NASA). **4** Appalachian Regional Commission.

Arc. Arctic.

ARCA 1 *also* **A.R.C.A. a** Associate of the Royal Canadian Academy of Arts. **b** Associate of the Royal College of Art. **2** Automobile Racing Club of America.

Arch. 1 Archbishop. **2** Archipelago. **3 a** Architect. **b** Architectural, esp. in combination: *Arch. E. = Architectural Engineer.*

arch. 1 archaeological, archaeology. **2 a** archaic. **b** archaism. **3** archery. **4** archipelago. **5 a** architect. **b** architectural, architecture. **6** archives.

archaeol. archaeological, archaeology.

Archbp. Archbishop.

Archd. Archdeacon.

Arch. E. Architectural Engineer.

archeol. archeological, archeology.

archit. architecture.

Archt. architect.

A.R.C.M. *or* **ARCM** Associate of the Royal College of Music.

A.R.C.O. *or* **ARCO** Associate of the Royal College of Organists.

A.R.C.S. *or* **ARCS 1** Associate of the Royal College of Science. **2** Associate of the Royal College of Surgeons. **3** Australian Red Cross Society.

Arct. Arctic.

ARD 1 acute respiratory disease. **2** Broadcasting Confederation of Germany. [German *Arbeitsgemeinschaft der öffentlich-rechtlichen Rundfunkanstalten der Bundesrepublik Deutschland*]

ARDC Air Research and Development Command.

ARDS adult respiratory distress syndrome.

A.R.E *or* **ARE** Associate of the Royal Society of Painter-Etchers and Engravers.

AREA American Railway Engineering Association.

ARENA National Renovating or Renewal Alliance (Brazilian political party). [Portuguese *Alliança Renovandro Nacional*]

ARF 1 acute renal failure *medicine*. **2** Advertising Research Foundation. **3** alkali-resistant factor (antianemic to replace both folic acid and vitamin B_{12}).

ARFOR 1 area forecast *meteorology*. **2** *also* **ARFORT** area forecast in English or traditional units *meteorology*.

Arg. 1 Argentina, Argentine. **2** arginine (an amino acid of plant and animal protein). **3** Argyll.

arg. 1 a argent (silver tincture in a coat of arms). **b** silver, *esp. medicine*. **2** arginine (an amino acid of plant and animal protein). **3** argument *mathematics*. **4** in arguing *law*. [Latin *arguendo*]

Arg. Rep. Argentine Republic.

a.Rh. *or* **a/Rh** on the Rhine River, in Germany: *Cologne or Köln a.Rh.* [German *am Rhein*]

A.R.H.A. *or* **ARHA** Associate of the Royal Hibernian Academy.

Ari Aries (constellation).

A.R.I.B.A. *or* **ARIBA** Associate of the Royal Institute of British Architects.

A.R.I.C. *or* **ARIC** Associate of the Royal Institute of Chemistry.

A.R.I.C.S. *or* **ARICS** Associate of the Royal Institute of Chartered Surveyors.

ARIS Advanced Range Instrumentation Ship.

Arist. Aristotle.

arith. arithmetic, arithmetical.

Ariz. Arizona.

Ark. Arkansas.

ARL 1 acceptable reliability level (of quality control). **2 a** *also* **A.R.L.** Aeronautical Research Laboratory. **b** *British* Aerospace Research Laboratory. **3** Arctic Research Laboratory. **4** *also* **A.R.L.** Association of Research Libraries. **5** Australian Radiation Laboratory.

ARM 1 adjustable rate mortgage (having an interest rate that fluctuates according to some market indicator). **2** antiradar or antiradiation missile. **3** artificial rupture of the membrane *medicine*. **4** atomic resolution microscope.

Ar.M. Master of Architecture. [Latin *Architecturae Magister*]

Arm. 1 Armagh. **2** Armenia, Armenian. **3** Armoric (of Brittany or the Breton language).

arm. armature.

A.R.M.C.M. *or* **ARMCM** Associate of the Royal Manchester College of Music.

ARMD age-related macular degeneration. (blood vessels growing underneath the retina that leak fluid, scarring the macula.

armd. armored *military*.

Armen. Armenian.

ARMET area forecast in metric units *meteorology*.

armor. arms and armor.

A.R.M.S. *or* **ARMS** Associate of the Royal Society of Miniature Painters.

armt. armament.

Army Ord Army Ordnance.

Arn. Arnold.

ARO 1 *also* **aro** after receipt of order *commerce*. 2 Army Research Office. 3 Army Routine Order (with a number).

ARP 1 aeronautical recommended practices. 2 Air Raid Precautions (British civil defense). 3 *also* **A.R.P.** Associated Reformed Presbyterian.

arp arpeggio *music*.

ARPA Advanced Research Projects Agency: *ARPAnet = Advanced Research Projects Agency Network* (now *DARPA,* a computer network to share resource data).

ARPS *or* **A.R.P.S.** Associate of the Royal Photographic Society.

ARQ automatic request for repetition *computers*.

Ar Q arithmetic quotient.

A.R.R. in the year of the King's or Queen's reign. [Latin *anno regni Regis or Reginae*]

Ar R arithmetic ratio.

arr. 1 *also* **Arr.** arranged or arranged by *music*. 2 arrangement, arrangements. 3 *also* **Arr.** arranger *music*. 4 arrestor. 5 *also* **ARR** arrive, arrived, arrival.

A.R.R.C. *or* **ARRC** Associate of the Royal Red Cross.

arrgt. arrangement.

ARRL American Radio Relay League (national association of radio amateurs).

Arron. *or* **Arrond.** administrative district. [French *arrondissement*]

ARRS *or* **A.R.R.S.** American Roentgen Ray Society.

ARRT *or* **A.R.R.T.** American Registry of Radiological Technologists.

ARS 1 Advanced Record System (computer-controlled routing of communications among the civilian agencies of the U.S. government). 2 Agricultural Research Service (of the U.S. Department of Agriculture). 3 Air Rescue Service. 4 American Rocket Society. 5 asbestos roof shingles (formerly in blueprints). 6 in the year of our redemption. [Latin *anno Reparatae Salutis*]

A.R.S.A. *or* **ARSA** 1 Associate of the Royal Scottish Academy. 2 Associate of the Royal Society of Arts.

A.R.S.S. Fellow of the Royal Society of Antiquaries. [Latin *Antiquariorum Regiae Societatus Socius*]

ARSTRIKE Army Strike Command.

A.R.S.W. *or* **ARSW** Associate of the Royal Scottish Society of Painting in Water Colours.

ART Accredited Record Technician.

Art. 1 Arthur. 2 article. 3 artillery.

art. 1 artery *medicine*. 2 article. 3 artificial. 4 artillery. 5 artist.

ARTC air route traffic control.

ARTCC air route traffic control center.

ARTFL American and French Research on the Treasury of the French Language.

Arth. 1 Arthur. 2 Arthurian.

arts. articles.

ARTU Automatic Range Tracking Unit.

Arty. *or* **arty.** artillery.

ARU 1 *also* **A.R.U.** American Railway Union. 2 audio response unit *computers*.

ARV 1 AIDS-related virus. 2 *also* **A.R.V.** American Revised Version (of the Bible).

ARVN *or* **Arvin** (är'vin) former Army of the Republic of Vietnam.

ARW 1 Air Raid Warden. 2 air raid warning.

A.R.W.S. *or* **ARWS** Associate of the Royal Society of Painters in Water Colours.

AS 1 *also* **A.S.** Academy of Science. 2 *also* **A.S.** or **A/S** account sales. 3 *British* Advanced Supplementary (examination for university admission and other higher education). 4 *commerce also* **A/S a** after sight. **b** at sight. 5 air speed. 6 *also* **A-S** air-to-surface: *ASM = air-to-surface missile.* 7 alongside (of commercial shipping). 8 American Samoa (Zip Code). 9 American Speech (magazine title). 10 *also* **A.S.** or **AS** or **A-S** Anglo-Saxon. 11 ankylosing spondylitis (spinal arthritis). 12 Annals of Science (magazine title). 13 antisubmarine. 14 apprentice seaman. 15 *also* **A-S** ascendance-submission *psychology*. 16 *also* **A.S.** Assistant Secretary: *ASD = Assistant Secretary of Defense*. 17 *also* **A.S.** Associate in Science. 18 *also* **A/S** association-sensation *psychology*: *A/S ratio*. 19 as stated *law*. 20 automatic sprinkler (in building specifications). 21 *also* **a/s** in care of; c/o. [French *aux soins de*] 22 *also* **A.S.** in the year of salvation. [Latin *Anno Salutis*] 23 joint stock company, as in *Greenex A/S.* [Danish *Aktieselskab,* Norwegian *Asjeselskap*] 24 *also* **A.S.** National Insurance. [French *assurance sociale*]

As *I an abbreviation for:* 1 altostratus cloud *meteorology*. 2 *also* **As. a** Asia. **b** Asian. **c** Asiatic. 3 astigmatism. *II a symbol for:* arsenic (chemical element).

as 1 asymmetric. 2 *also* **a.s.** at sight *commerce*. 3 *also* **a.s.** left ear *medicine*. [Latin *auris sinistra*]

ASA 1 acetylsalicylic acid (aspirin, esp. in Canada). 2 *also* **A.S.A.** Acoustical Society of America. 3 *British* Advertising Standards Authority. 4 Amateur Softball Association of America. 5 *British* Amateur Swimming Association. 6 American Society of Agronomy. 7 *also* **A.S.A.** American Society of Anesthesiologists. 8 American Society of Auctioneers. 9 *also* **A.S.A.** American Sociological Association. 10 American Standards Association (now *ANSI.* Use of *ASA* before film speeds has been replaced by *ISO*.). 11 American Statistical Association. 12 American Studies Association. 13 *also* **a.s.a.** angle side angle *geometry*. 14 Army Security Agency.

A.S.A.A. or **ASAA** *British* Associate of the Society of Incorporated Accountants and Auditors.

ASAE American Society of Agricultural Engineers.

ASALH Association for the Study of Afro-American Life and History.

A.S.A.M. Associate of the Society of Art Masters.

ASAP or **asap** as soon as possible.

ASAT 1 anti-satellite interceptor (satellite able to destroy another satellite). **2** Satellite Carrier Advisory Group. [German *Arbeitsgemeinschaft Satellitenträger*]

ASB 1 Alternative Book Service (in reference to the edition of the Anglican Book of Common Prayer used in a church service). **2** American Society of Bacteriologists.

asb. asbestos.

ASBC American Society of Biological Chemists.

ASBM air-to-surface ballistic missile.

ASC 1 Air Service Command. **2** altered state of consciousness. **3** also **A.S.C.** American Society of Cinematographers. **4** Army Signal Corps. **5** also **asc** auxiliary switch closed (designation for circuit breaker usually set in a closed position).

A.Sc. Associate in Science.

ASCAP or **A.S.C.A.P.** or **Ascap** (az′kap) American Society of Composers, Authors and Publishers.

ASCD Association for Supervision and Curriculum Development.

ASCE or **A.S.C.E.** American Society of Civil Engineers.

ASCEA or **A.S.C.E.A.** American Society of Civil Engineers and Architects.

A Sch American Scholar (magazine title).

ASChE or **A.S.Ch.E.** American Society of Chemical Engineers.

ASCI American Society for Clinical Investigation.

ASCII (as′kē) American Standard Code for Information Interchange (computer code representing letters, numbers, and symbols).

ASCLT American Society of Clinical Laboratory Technicians.

ASCP American Society of Clinical Pathologists.

ASCS Agricultural Stabilization and Conservation Service (of the U.S. Department of Agriculture).

ASCU or **A.S.C.U.** Association of State Colleges and Universities.

AScW or **A.Sc.W.** *British* Association of Scientific Workers.

A.S.D.A. American Stamp Dealers Association.

ASDE airport surface detection equipment.

a/s de in care of; c/o. [French *aux soins de*]

ASDF Air Self-Defense Force (air force of Japan).

Asdic or **asdic** (az′dik) or **A.S.D.I.C.** Sonar (British name for sonar because it was the subject of the *Allied Submarine Detection Investigation Committee* study).

ASDW Admiralty Sailing Directions for the World.

ASE 1 airborne search equipment. **2** also **A.S.E.** American Society of Engineers. **3** American Stock Exchange; Amex.

4 also **A.S.E.** *British* Associate of the Society of Engineers. **5** *British* Association for Science Education.

A.S.E. *British* Amalgamated Society of Engineers.

ASEA American Society of Engineers and Architects.

ASEAN (ä′sē ən) Association of South East Asian Nations (Brunei, Indonesia, Malaysia, the Philippines, Singapore, and Thailand, organized as a group in 1967 to promote economic progress and political stability in the area).

ASECS American Society for Eighteenth-Century Studies.

ASF 1 African swine fever. **2** Army Service Forces.

a.s.f. or **a./s.f.** amperes per square foot.

ASG 1 Aeronautical Standards Group. **2** also **A.S.G.** American Society for Genetics.

ASGB Aeronautical Society of Great Britain.

asgd. assigned.

asgmt. assignment.

ASH 1 (*pronounced* ash) Action on Smoking and Health. **2** American Society of Hematology.

ASHA or **A.S.H.A.** American School Health Association.

ASHRAE American Society of Heating, Refrigerating, and Air-Conditioning Engineers.

ASI air-speed indicator.

ASIC application specific integrated circuit (electronic circuit designed for a specific purpose).

ASID 1 American Society of Industrial Designers. **2** American Society of Interior Designers.

ASIH or **A.S.I.H.** American Society of Ichthyologists and Herpetologists.

ASIM or **A.S.I.M.** American Society of Internal Medicine.

ASIO Australian Security Intelligence Organization.

ASIS 1 abort sensing-implementation system (for rocket launching). **2** American Society for Information Science. **3** Australian Secret Intelligence Service.

ASL 1 also **asl** above sea level. **2** American Sign Language. **3** American Soccer League.

ASLA or **A.S.L.A.** American Society of Landscape Architects.

ASLB Atomic Safety and Licensing Board (of the U.S. Nuclear Regulatory Agency).

A.S.L.E.F. Associated Society of Locomotive Engineers and Firemen.

A.S.L.I.B. or **Aslib** Association of Special Libraries and Information Bureau (now *AIM*).

ASLO or **A.S.L.O.** American Society of Limnology and Oceanography.

ASM 1 also **A.S.M.** Aerospace Medical Association. **2** air-to-surface missile. **3** American Society for Metals. **4** American Society for Microbiology. **5** Association for Systems Management.

asm. assembly.

ASMC Army Supply and Maintenance Command (formerly Quartermaster Corps).

ASME or **A.S.M.E. 1** American Society of Magazine Editors. **2** American Society of Mechanical Engineers.

ASMI airfield surface movement indication (of a type of radar installation).

ASMP or **A.S.M.P.** American Society of Magazine Photographers.

ASMPTE or **A.S.M.P.T.E.** American Society of Motion Picture and Television Engineers.

asmt. assortment.

ASN or **asn 1** also **A.S.N.** Army Service Number. **2** asparagine (an amino acid found in many plants). **3** average sample number (in quality control).

Asn strength of association *psychology.*

ASNE 1 American Society of Naval Engineers. **2** also **A.S.N.E.** American Society of Newspaper Editors.

ASO 1 also **A.S.O.** American Symphony Orchestra. **2** Assistant Scientific Officer. **3** also **aso** auxiliary switch open (designation for circuit breaker usually set in an open position).

ASP 1 also **asp** accepted under protest (of bills). [French *accepté sous protêt*] **2** aerospace plane. **3** also **A.S.P.** American Selling Price (price charged by U.S. manufacturers, used to determine customs duty on imports). **4** (often pronounced asp) Anglo-Saxon Protestant. **5** British as soon as possible. **6** also **A.S.P.** Astronomical Society of the Pacific.

asp. or **Asp** aspartic acid (essential amino acid in protein).

ASPA Armed Services Procurement Act.

ASPAC or **Aspac** Asian and Pacific Council.

ASPC or **aspc** accepted under protest (of accounts). [French *accepté sous protêt, pour à compte*]

ASPCA American Society for the Prevention of Cruelty to Animals.

asph. asphalt.

Asp.N or **asp.N** asparagine (amino acid used as a diuretic and in bacteriology).

A spol. and company. [Czech *A spolecnost*]

ASPP 1 American Society of Picture Professionals. **2** steel alloy protective plating (in blueprints and plans).

ASPR Armed Services Procurement Regulations.

ASQC American Society for Quality Control.

ASR 1 Accounting Series Release (accounting procedures for reports filed with the Securities and Exchange Commission). **2** airport surveillance radar. **3** also **A/SR** Air-Sea Rescue. **4** authorized selling agent (of a literary property or of advertising for a publication). **5** automatic sending and receiving (of messages sent by radio and radio teletype). **6** available supply rate.

ASRE 1 British Admiralty Signal and Radar Establishment. **2** American Society of Refrigerating Engineers.

ASROC anti-submarine rocket.

ASRT or **A.S.R.T.** American Society of Radiologic Technologists.

Ass. 1 Assembly. **2** also **ass.** assistant, esp. in combination: *Ass.Com.Gen. = Assistant Commissary General.* **3** Association.

assd. 1 assessed. **2** assigned. **3** assured.

ASSE 1 American Society of Safety Engineers. **2** American Society of Sanitary Engineering.

ASSET 1 aerothermodynamic structural system environmental tests (of the U.S. Air Force). **2** also **A.S.S.E.T.** Association of Supervisory Staffs, Executives, and Technicians.

assim. assimilate, assimilated.

assmt. assessment.

Assn. or **assn.** association, esp. in combination: *Automobile Assn.*

assnd. assigned.

Assoc. or **assoc. 1 a** associate, esp. in combination: *Assoc. I. Min. E. = Associate of the Institute of Mining Engineers.* **b** associated: *assoc. w. = associated with.* **2** association.

Assoc. Sc. Associate in Science.

ASSR or **A.S.S.R.** (formerly) Autonomous Soviet Socialist Republic.

asst. 1 assessment. **2** also **Asst.** or **Ass't.** assistant, esp. in combination: *Asst. Surg. = assistant surgeon.* **3** assorted.

asstd. 1 assented. **2** assisted, assisted by. **3** associated. **4** assorted.

A.S.S.U. American Sunday School Union.

assy. or **ass'y** assembly.

Assyr. Assyria, Assyrian.

AST 1 aspartate aminotransferase (enzyme used in diagnosis of diseases of the liver and heart). **2** also **A.S.T.** or **a.s.t.** Atlantic Standard Time.

ASTA American Society of Travel Agents.

ASTD American Society for Training and Development.

ASTE American Society of Tool Engineers.

ASTEC advanced solar turbo-electric conversion.

ASTIA Armed Services Technical Information Agency.

ASTM or **A.S.T.M.** American Society for Testing and Materials.

ASTMH or **A.S.T.M.H.** American Society of Tropical Medicine and Hygiene.

ASTP Army Specialized Training Program.

astr. 1 astronomer. **2** astronomical, astronomy.

astro. astronautics.

astrol. 1 astrologer. **2** astrological, astrology.

astron. 1 astronomer. **2** astronomical, astronomy.

astrophys. 1 astrophysical. **2** astrophysics.

ASUC American Society of University Composers.

ASUUS Amateur Skating Union of the United States.

A.S.V. or **ASV** American Standard Version (of the Bible).

ASW 1 antisubmarine warfare. **2** also **A.S.W.** Association of Scientific Workers.

ASWG American Steel and Wire Gauge.

asym. asymmetric, asymmetrical.

AT 1 achievement test: *CAT = College Achievement Test.* **2** air temperature. **3** airtight or air-tight. **4** air transport: *MATS = Military Air Transport Service.* **5 a** alternative technology. **b** appropriate technology. **6** also **A/T** American terms *commerce.* **7** ampere turn. **8** antitank. **9** also **A.T.** Atlantic Time. **10** Atomic Time. **11** also **A/T** automatic transmission. **12** also **A.T.** the Old Testament. [German *Altes Testament*]

At *I an abbreviation for:* **1** *also* **A.t.** Atlantic Time. **2** attorney. *II a symbol for:* astatine (chemical element).

at. 1 atmosphere, atmospheric. **2** atomic, esp. in combination: *at. wt. = atomic weight.* **3** attorney.

a.t. 1 airtight. **2** ampere turn. **3** assay ton.

ATA 1 actual time of arrival. **2** Air Transport Association. **3** Air Transport Auxiliary. **4** American Translators Association. **5** American Trucking Association. **6** aurin tricarboxylic acid (antidote to beryllium poisoning).

ata atmosphere temperature absolute.

AT&T American Telephone and Telegraph.

ATB all-terrain bicycle.

ATC 1 a air traffic control, also in combination: *ATCRBS = air traffic control radar beacon system.* **b** air traffic controller. **2** *British* Air Training Centre. **3** Air Transport Command. **4** all-terrain cycle (balloon-tired motor tricycle). **5** Army Training Center. **6** automatic train control.

ATCC 1 Air Traffic Control Center. **2** American Type Culture Collection (depository for preserving and distributing samples of biological materials for research and patenting).

atch. attach, attachment.

A.T.C.L. Associate of Trinity College of Music, London.

ATD *or* **atd** actual time of departure.

ATE Automatic Test Equipment.

a tempo. in time, resume tempo *music.* [Italian *a tempo*]

ATF 1 actual time of fall. **2** Advanced Tactical Fighter. **3** Bureau of Alcohol, Tobacco, and Firearms (of the U.S. government).

ATG antithymocyte globulin (immunosuppressor) *medicine.*

ATGSB Admissions Test for Graduate Study in Business.

ath. *or* **athl.** athlete, athletics.

ATI Air Technical Intelligence, also in combination: *ATIC = Air Technical Intelligence Center.*

ATJ Association of Teachers of Japanese.

ATL adult T-cell leukemia.

Atl. 1 Atlantic, also in combination: *Atl. Oc. = Atlantic Ocean.* **2** Atlantic Reporter (journal title) *law.*

ATLA 1 American Theological Library Association. **2** *also* **A.T.L.A.** American Trial Lawyers Association.

ATLB Air Transport Licensing Board.

ATM 1 antitank missile. **2** *also* **A.T.M.** Association of Teachers of Mathematics. **3** automatic *or* automated teller machine (an electronic machine that dispenses cash, records deposits, and performs other banking services).

atm. 1 *also* **atm** atmosphere, atmospheres (esp. as a unit of pressure). **2** atmospheric, esp. in combination: *atm. press. = atmospheric pressure.*

atm. a. *or* **atma** absolute atmosphere (unit of pressure).

atmos. atmosphere.

ATMS assumption-based truth maintenance system (a program for building a system of facts in artificial intelligence).

ATN automatic transition network *communications.*

at. no. *or* **At. No.** atomic number.

ATO 1 assisted take-off, esp. in combination: *JATO = Jet Assisted Take-Off.* **2** automatic train operation.

A to A 1 *also* **A-to-A** air-to-air missile. **2** applicants-to-acceptance ratio.

A to J Appendices to the Journals (of New Zealand House of Representatives).

ATP 1 adenosine triphosphate (substance active in muscle contraction, sugar metabolism, and cell organization). **2** Admissions Testing Program (of the College Entrance Examination Board).

ATPAM Association of Theater Press Agents and Managers.

ATPase enzyme that assists in decomposition of adenosine triphosphatase. [*ATP* + *-ase* enzyme]

ATPI American Textbook Publishers Institute (now merged into *AAP*).

ATR 1 advanced test reactor (facility to test high performance reactor fuels). **2** airline transport rating. **3** Anglican Theological Review (magazine title). **4** Association of Teachers of Russian.

ATRAN automatic terrain recognition and navigation guidance system.

a.t.r.i.m.a. as their respective interests may appear *law.*

ATS 1 air-to-ship missile. **2** *also* **A.T.S.** American Temperance Society. **3** *also* **A.T.S.** American Tract Society. **4** American Transport Service. **5** antitetanus serum. **6** anxiety-tension-state *psychology.* **7** Army Transport Service. **8** Associate of Theological Study. **9** at the suit of *law.* **10** automated trading system (on a stock exchange). **11 a** automatic train stop. **b** automatic train supervision. **12** Auxiliary Territorial Service (now *WRAC*).

ats 1 antitetanus serum. **2** *also* **ats.** at the suit of *law.*

ATSDR Agency for Toxic Substances and Disease Registry (of U.S. Department of Health and Human Services).

att. 1 attach, attached. **2** *also* **Att.** attaché. **3** *also* **Att.** attention, used esp. in an address. **4** *also* **Att.** attorney. **5** leave on, of stitches in knitting. [French *attente*]

ATTD Alcohol and Tobacco Tax Division (of the Internal Revenue Service).

atten. attention.

Att. Gen. attorney general.

attn. *or* **Attn.** *or* **ATTN** attention, used esp. in an address: *Government Printing Office, Attn. Editorial Dept.*

attrib. 1 *also* **Attrib.** attribute, attributed to. **2** attributive or attributively *grammar.*

ATTU Atlantic to the Urals (area covered in arms-control negotiations).

atty. *or* **Atty.** attorney.

Atty. Gen. attorney general.

ATU Amalgamated Transit Union.

ATUC African Trade Union Confederation.

ATV 1 all-terrain vehicle. **2** *also* **A.T.V.** Associated Television (independent commercial television in Great Britain, now *I TV*).

at. vol. atomic volume.

ATW American Theatre Wing.

ATWS automated tracking while scanning (of radar).

at. wt. atomic weight.

AU 1 *also* **A-U** air-to-underwater missile. **2** Air University (of the U.S. Air Force). **3** *also* **A.U.** *or* **Å.U.** angstrom unit (a unit of the measurement of the wavelength of light; now *A* or *Å*). **4** *also* **A.U.** astronomical unit (mean distance from the center of the sun to the center of the earth, fundamental measurement of interplanetary distance). **5** author, esp. on proofs, followed by a query. **6** both ears *medicine*. [Latin *auries unitas*]

Au *I an abbreviation for*: **1** *also* **Au.** August. **2** *also* **Au.** *or* **au** author, esp. on proofs, followed by a query.
II a symbol for: gold (chemical element). [Latin *aurum*]

A.u. *or* **Å.u.** *or* **Åu.** angstrom unit (see *AU*, def. 3).

a.u. 1 according to custom. [Latin *ad usum*] **2** *also* **å.u.** angstrom unit (see *AU*, def. 3). **3** astronomical unit (see *AU*, def. 4).

A.U.A. American Unitarian Association.

A.U.B. (formerly) American University of Beirut.

A.U.B.C. Association of the Universities of the British Commonwealth.

A.U.C. *or* **AUC 1** Australian Universities Commission. **2** in the year since the founding of the city (Rome, in 753 BC.). [Latin *ab urbe condita* or *anno urbis conditæ*]

A-U-D agree-undecided-disagree (multiple choice test).

aud. 1 audible. **2** audit. **3** *also* **Aud.** auditor: *Aud.Gen.* or *Aud.-Gen.* = *Auditor General*.

AUDIT automatic unattended detection inspection transmitter (system for monitoring underground nuclear explosions).

AUEW *British* Amalgamated Union of Engineering Workers (now *AEU*).

Aufl edition (of a book). [German *Auflage*]

AUG adenine, uracil, guanine (sequence of bases forming DNA and RNA).

Aug. *or* **Aug 1** August. **2** Augustine. **3** Augustus.

aug. *or* **augm. 1** augmentative *grammar*. **2** augmented.

AUM air-to-underwater missile.

aum. enlarged. [Spanish *aumentado*]

AUMLA Australasian Universities Modern Language Association, also the title of its publication.

a.u.n. *or* **AUN** unmarked *commerce*; without annotation *bibliography* [Latin *absque ulla nota*]

AUPE Alberta Union of Provincial Employees.

Aur the Charioteer (constellation). [Latin *Auriga*]

aur. ear *medicine*. [Latin *auris*]

AURA Association of Universities for Research in Astronomy.

AUS *or* **A.U.S. 1** Army of the United States. **2** Australian Union of Students.

Aus. 1 Australia. **2** Austria, Austrian.

Ausg. edition or printing (of a book); issue. [German *Ausgabe*]

AUSSAT (ô'sat) Australian Telecommunications Satellite.

Aust. 1 Australia, Australian. **2** Austria, Austrian.

Austl. 1 Australasia, Australasian. **2** Australia, Australian.

Austr. Australia, Australian.

Austral. 1 Australasia, Australasian. **2** Australia, Australian.

AUT *or* **A.U.T.** Association of University Teachers.

Aut. 1 author. **2** Autonomous (of a region within a country or confederation).

aut. 1 author. **2** autograph, autographed. **3** automatic.

AUTEC Atlantic Undersea Test and Evaluation Center (of the U.S. Navy).

auth. 1 authentic (esp. of autographs, letters, documents, etc.). **2** *also* **Auth.** author. **3** *also* **Auth.** authority. **4** *also* **Auth.** authorized, also in combination: *Auth. Ver.* = *Authorized Version of the Bible*.

auto. 1 automatic. **2 a** automobile. **b** automotive.

autog. autograph, autographed.

aux. *or* **auxil.** auxiliary: *aux.v.* = *auxiliary verb*.

AV 1 *also* **A/V** *or* **a/v** according to the value *commerce*. [Latin *ad valorem*] **2** acid value. **3** *also* **A-V** Allport-Vernon (study of values) *psychology*. **4** anti-vivisectionist. **5** *also* **A-V a** arteriovenous: *AV shunt*. **b** atrioventricular: *AV node*. **6** *also* **A-V** *or* **A/V** audiovisual. **7** *also* **A.V. a** authorized version (of a play or other literary work). **b** Authorized Version of the Bible. **8 a** average value. **b** average variability.

Av. 1 Avenue. **2** Avestan.

aV abvolt, esp. in combination: *aV/cm* = *abvolt per centimeter*.

av 1 *also* **a.v.** according to the value. [Latin *ad valorem*] **2** *also* **a.v.** atomic volume. **3** *also* **av.** avenue. **4** *also* **av.** average, also in combination: *av. w.* = *average width*. **5** *also* **av.** avoirdupois, esp. in combination: *av. wt.* = *avoirdupois weight*. **6** *also* **a.v.** he or she lived so many years. [Latin *annos vixit*]

AVA 1 *also* **A.V.A.** American Vecturist Association (organization of collectors of transportation tokens). **2** American Vocational Association. **3** *also* **A.V.A.** Australian Veterinary Association.

avail. *or* **aval.** available.

AVC 1 *British* additional voluntary contribution (to a pension fund). **2** American Veterans Committee. **3** *also* **avc** *or* **a.v.c.** automatic volume control *electricity*.

AVCAT *or* **Avcat** aviation carrier turbine fuel.

AVCS advanced video camera system.

AVD Army Veteran Department.

avdp. avoirdupois.

AVE 1 *also* **ave** automatic volume expansion *electronics*. **2** *also* **Ave.** *or* **ave.** Avenue. **3** *also* **ave.** average.

aver. average.

AVF all-volunteer force (of the U.S. military, esp. the U.S. Army).

AVFR available for reassignment *military*.

AVG American Volunteer Group (the Flying Tigers of WWII).

avg. average.

AVGAS *or* **avgas** (av'gas') aviation gasoline *military*.

av. J.C. before Christ; BC. [French *avant Jésus-Christ*]

AVL *or* **A-V-L** Allport-Vernon-Livesey *psychology*.

av. l. average length (of lumber).

AVLIS atomic vapor laser isotope separation (a uranium enrichment process using a laser beam).

AVM 1 *also* **A/V/M** *or* **A.V.M.** Air Vice-Marshal of the Canadian Air Force. **2** arteriovenous malformation (malformation of a blood vessel). **3** automatic vehicle monitoring (used in controlling scheduled transportation, such as buses).

AVMA *or* **A.V.M.A.** American Veterinary Medical Association.

avn. *or* **Avn.** aviation.

AVO avoid verbal orders.

avoir. avoirdupois.

AVR 1 Army Volunteer Reserve (of Australia). **2** Avery (printer of U.S. postage stamps).

AVS 1 Anti-Vivisection Society. **2** Army Veterinary Service.

AVT *or* **A.V.T.** added value tax; VAT.

AW 1 above water. **2** Articles of War *military*. **3** *also* **A.W.** atomic weight. **4** automatic weapons *military*. **5** *also* **A.W.** azure wove (bookbinding cloth).

A/W 1 actual weight. **2** all water (of transportation) *commerce*. **3** alternate weeks *advertising*.

aw 1 air-to-water missile. **2** *also* **a.w.** all water (of transportation) *commerce*. **3** all widths (of lumber). **4** atomic weight.

a/w actual weight.

AWACS (ā′waks) Airborne Warning and Control System.

AWB 1 *also* **A.W.B.** Afrikaner Resistance Movement. [Afrikaans *Afrikaner Weerstandsbeweging*] **2** Australian Wheat Marketing Board. **3** Australian Wool Board.

A.W.B.A. American World's Boxing Association.

AWC 1 Air War College. **2** Army War College. **3** Association for Women in Computing. **4** Australian Wool Corporation (government-sponsored wool-marketing organization).

AWES Association of West European Shipbuilders.

AWG American Wire Gage (a gauge generally used for non-ferrous wire and tubing).

AWL *or* **A.W.L.** *or* **a.w.l. 1** absent with leave. **2** *Australian* absent without leave (compare *AWOL*).

AWLS All-Weather Landing System.

AWOC Agricultural Workers Organizing Committee.

AWOL (ā′wôl) *or* **A.W.O.L.** *or* **a.w.o.l.** absent without leave.

AWP Associated Writing Programs.

AWR Anglo-Welsh Review (magazine title).

AWRE Atomic Weapons Research Establishment (of Great Britain).

AWRI Australian Wine Research Institute.

AWRT American Women in Radio and Television.

AWS 1 American Watercolor Society. **2** American Welding Society. **3** Aviation Weather Service (of the U.S. National Weather Service).

AWSA American Water Ski Association.

AWT advanced waste treatment *ecology*.

AWU 1 *also* **awu** *or* **A.W.U.** atomic weight unit. **2** Australian Workers' Union.

A.W.V.S. American Women's Voluntary Services (group offering community support services).

AWW 1 All's Well That Ends Well (play by Shakespeare). **2** average weekly wage (used in cases of compensation) *law*.

ax. 1 axiom. **2** *also* **Ax.** axis, *esp. in medicine*.

AXAF Advanced X-ray Astronomy Facility (X-ray telescope).

AYH *or* **A.Y.H.** American Youth Hostels.

A.Y.L. *or* **A.Y.L.I.** As You Like It (play by Shakespeare)

A.Y.M. 1 Ancient York Mason. **2** Angry Young Man or Men.

Ayr. Ayrshire, Scotland.

AZ 1 Arizona (Zip Code). **2** azimuth (angular distance east or west of north).

Az. *or* **Az 1** azimuth (angular distance east or west of north). **2** Azores. **3** nitrogen. [French *azote*]

az 1 azimuth (angular distance east or west of north). **2** *also* **az.** azure.

Azerb. Azerbaijani.

AZT azidothymidine (drug used to treat HIV and AIDS virus).

A-Z test Ascheim-Zondek test (for human pregnancy).

B

B *I an abbreviation for:* **1** *also* **B.** *or* **B** bacillus: *B botulinus* (cause of food poisoning). **2** back of page (reverse side of page). **3** *also* **B.** bag. **4** Bahamas, in combination: *B$ = Bahamas dollar.* **5** Bahrain, in combination: *BD = Bahrain dinar.* **6** baht (Thai unit of money). **7** balboa (Panamanian unit of money). **8** *also* **B.** bale. **9** balk *baseball.* **10** *also* **B.** Balling (scale to measure a soluble in solution). **11** bandwidth *electronics.* **12** *also* **B.** Baron. **13** baryon number (number of subatomic particles in a system) *physics.* **14 a** base *baseball.*

b *also* **B.** base, in combination: *chemistry: B.HCl* **15** *also* **B.** bass *music.* **16** *also* **B.** basso (singer with a bass voice). **17** *also* **B.** bat or at bat *baseball.* **18** *also* **B.** battery (of artillery or percussion instruments in an orchestra). **19** baud (unit of measure expressing data transmission speed) *computers: KB = 1 kilobaud.* **20** *also* **B.** Baumé (scale to measure specific gravity). **21** *also* **B.** Bay. **22** beam (of a ship). **23** bearing (esp. of a compass reading). **24** bel *acoustics.* **25** Belize: *$B = Belize dollar.* **26** Bermuda, in combination: *$B = Bermuda*

dollar. **27** Beta (second letter of the Greek alphabet, used esp. as a symbol to denote second in order or degree). **28** also **B.** Bible. **29** bicuspid. **30** bid (as of a price offered for shares of stock). **31** billion, esp. in combination: *BeV = billion electron volts.* **32 a** bishop *chess.* **b** also **B.** Bishop (a religious). **33 a** black: *2B = double or soft black lead in a pencil.* **b** also **B.** blue. **34** also **B.** boatswain. **35** also **B.** boils or boils at, in combination. **36** bolivar (Venezuelan unit of money). **37** bomber, in combination: *B-1, B-29.* **38** bond *chemistry, finance.* **39** bonded *chemistry, electricity, finance.* **40** also **B.** book. **41** also **B.** born. **42** bottoms (in distilling). **43** bowels *medicine.* **44** breadth, width, or span. **45** brightness (compare *luminance* under symbols below). **46** also **B.** British, esp. in combination: *BBC = British Broadcasting Corporation.* **47** broadcast. **48** also **B.** Brother (in a religious order). **49** also **B.** Brotherhood, esp. in combination: *IBEW = International Brotherhood of Electrical Workers.* **50** Brunei, in combination: *B$ = Brunei dollar.* **51** buoyancy.
II a symbol for: **1** blood type B (one of the four major blood groups). **2** blue star of second class hydrogen intensity *astronomy.* **3** boron (chemical element). **4** brightness or luminance. **5** British thermal unit. **6** lymph cell that secretes antibodies against most infectious bacteria, in combination: *B cell.* [from *bone-derived,* earlier *Bursa of Fabricius*] **7** magnetic flux density or induction. **8** metric paper sizes of standard weights for card stock, used by the International Standards Organization (ISO): *B5 = 176 mm × 250 mm, replacing 7 in × 10 in; B6 = 125 mm × 176 mm, replacing 5 in × 7 in; B7 = 88 mm × 125 mm, replacing 3 in × 5 in.* **9** negative feedback. **10** New York (branch in the Federal regional banking system, found esp. on dollar bills). **11** quantity (esp. a known quantity in algebraic equations). **12 a** second best of a kind. **b** second highest grade in school. **c** British classification for secondary roads: *B312.* **13** second drive on a multidisk system *computers.* **14 a** second of a series or group (compare *Beta* listed above): *hepatitis B.; B chromosome; B unit of a diesel locomotive.* **b** second layer of soil next below the surface layer: *B horizon.* **15** seventh tone in the scale of C major. **16** shoe width greater than A and less than C. **17** sixth highest rating, after Ba *finance.* **18** susceptance *electricity.* **19** three hundred; 300 (medieval Roman numeral).

°**B.** Balling (scale to measure a soluble in solution).

b *I an abbreviation for:* **1** back of a book page (the reverse side of a piece of paper or left-hand side of a two-page spread). **2** also **b.** bag. **3** baht (Thai unit of money). **4** balboa (Panamanian unit of money). **5** also **b.** bale. **6** ball. **7** also **b.** bar (unit of pressure). **8** barn (smallest unit of square measure) *physics.* **9** base *architecture, baseball, electronics, geometry, mathematics, mechanics.* **10** baseman *baseball.* **11** bat or at bat *baseball.* **12** also **b.** bath. **13** battery *electronics.* **14** baud (unit of measure expressing data transmission speed) *computers.* **15** also **b.** beam (of a ship). **16** also **b.** bearing (esp. of a compass reading). **17** beauty *physics.* **18** bel *acoustics.* **19** also **b.** bicuspid. **20** also **b.** billion: *$100b.,* also in combination: *bcf = billion cubic feet.* **21 a** bit *computers: bps = bits per second.* **b** binary *electronics.* **22** also **b.** bitch (in pedigrees). **23** bituminous. **24** also **b.** blend or blend of. **25** also **b.** boils or boils at, in combination. **26** also **b.** boliviano (Bolivian unit of money). **27** also **b.** book. **28** also **b.** born. **29** bottom *physics: b quark = bottom quark.* **30** also **b.**

bound. **31** also **b.** bowled *sports.* **32** brass. **33** breadth, width, or span. **34** brick. **35** brother (sibling or companion). **36** bunt *baseball.* **37** also **b.** by: *NbW = North by West.* **38** bye *sports.* **39** byte (group of binary digits). **40** also **b.** in care of; at. [German *bei*] **41** volume (of a book). [Danish *bind;* German *Band;* Swedish *band*]
II a symbol for: **1** basic force (esp. as a subscript) *aeronautics.* **2** blue sky (in Beaufort weather notation). **3** galactic latitude *astronomy.* **4** magnetic flux density or induction. **5** nucleus (concentrated with slightly open spiral arms of nebula, in combination with S or SB) *astronomy.* **6** quantity (esp. a known quantity in algebraic equations). **7** regression coefficient *statistics.* **8** susceptance *electricity.*

BA 1 also **B.A.** Bachelor of Arts. [Latin *Baccalaureus Artium*] **2** batting average *baseball.* **3** blind approach *aviation.* **4** also **B.A.** Booksellers' Association (of Great Britain and Ireland). **5** also **B.A.** British Academy. **6** British America. **7** also **B.A.** British Association (for the Advancement of Science). **8** bronchial asthma. **9** Buenos Aires.

Ba *I an abbreviation for:* boliviano (Bolivian unit of money).
II a symbol for: **1** barium (chemical element). **2** fifth highest rating, after Baa *finance.*

BAA or **B.A.A.** *I an abbreviation for:* **1 a** Bachelor of Applied Arts. **b** Bachelor of Art and Architecture. **2** British Airports Authority. **3** British Archaeological Association. **4** also **B.A.A.A.** British Association of Accountants and Auditors. **5** British Astronomical Association.
II a symbol for: also **Baa** fourth highest rating, after A *finance.*

B.A.A.B. British Amateur Athletic Board.

BAAE or **B.A.A.E.** Bachelor of Aeronautical and Astronautical Engineering.

BAAS 1 British Association for American Studies. **2** also **B.A.A.S.** British Association for the Advancement of Science.

Bab. Babylonian.

BABS or **Babs** beam or blind approach beacon system *aeronautics.*

BABT British Approvals Board for Telecommunications.

BAC 1 blood alcohol concentration (measure of alcohol impairment of bodily reflexes and judgment). **2** also **B.A.C.** British Association of Chemists.

BACAT (ba'kat') barge aboard catamaran (a barge-carrying vessel developed for the European waterways systems).

B.Acc. Bachelor of Accounting.

Bach. or **bach.** bachelor.

back. or **Back.** backwardation (postponement on delivery of securities) *British finance.*

Bac. Mus. Bachelor of Music.

bact. or **Bact. 1** bacteria. **2** bacterial. **3** bacteriology.

bacteriol. bacteriology, bacteriological.

B.A.D.A. or **BADA** British Antique Dealers' Association.

BAE 1 Bureau of Agricultural Economics. **2** Bureau of American Ethnology.

B.A.E. 1 also **BAE** Bachelor of Aeronautical Engineering. **2** also **BAE** Bachelor of Architectural Engineering. **3** also **BAE** Bachelor of Arts in Education. **4** Badminton Association of England. **5** Belfast Association of Engineers.

BAEA or **B.A.E.A.** British Actor's Equity Association.

BAEC British Agricultural Export Council.

B.A.Econ. or **BAEcon** Bachelor of Arts in Economics.

B.A.Ed. or **BAEd** Bachelor of Arts in Education.

B.Ae.E. or **BAeE** Bachelor of Aeronautical Engineering.

baf baffle architecture, engineering.

BAFCOM or **BAFCom** (baf'com') Basic Armed Forces Communications Plan.

B.A.F.M.A. or **BAFMA** British and Foreign Maritime Agencies.

BAFTA (baf'tə) British Academy of Film and Television Arts.

B.Ag. or **BAg** Bachelor of Agriculture.

bag. or **bag** baggage.

B.Agr. Bachelor of Agriculture.

B.Agr.Sc. or **B.Ag.Sc.** or **B.Ag.Sci.** Bachelor of Agricultural Science.

Bah. Bahamas.

B.A.H.S. British Agricultural History Society.

B.A.I. **1** also **BAI** Bachelor of Engineering. [Latin Baccalaureus Artis Ingeniariae] **2** Book Association of Ireland.

Ba. Is. Bahama Islands.

B.A.J. or **B.A.Jour.** Bachelor of Arts in Journalism.

BAL **1** Bibliography of American Literature. **2** blood alcohol level (measure of alcohol impairment of bodily reflexes and judgment). **3** also **B.A.L.** British Anti-Lewisite (liquid used to combat prolonged metallic poisoning, originally developed to combat effects of lewisite gas in warfare; also known as dimercaprol).

Bal. **1** balance commerce. **2** Baluchistan.

bal. **1** balance commerce. **2** balancing. **3** balcony architecture.

Balc. balcony, esp. in theater.

Balk. Balkans.

Ball. Balliol College, Oxford.

ball. **1** ballast. **2** ballistics.

B.Alp. or **B.-Alpes** Basses-Alpes (department of France).

Balpa (bôl'pə) or **BALPA** British Air Line Pilots Association.

bals or **bals.** balsam.

Balt. **1** Baltic. **2** Baltimore.

Baluch. Baluchistan.

BALUN or **balun** balanced unbalanced (a balancing device in coaxial transmission cables).

BAM **1** AM broadcasting. **2** also **B.A.M.** Bachelor of Applied Mathematics. **3** Bachelor of Arts in Music. **4** Brooklyn Academy of Music.

B.A.Mus.Ed. Bachelor of Arts in Music Education.

BAN British Approved Name chemistry.

Banc. Sup. King's or Queen's Bench. [Latin Bancus Superior]

b & arp bare and acid resisting paint.

B & B **1** also **b & b** balled and burlapped agriculture. **2** also **B. and B.** benedictine and brandy. **3** also **b & b** bed and breakfast (of accommodations)

B & D or **B and D** bondage and discipline or bondage and domination (referring to sadomasochistic sexual practices).

B & E **1** breaking and entering (in police records). **2** also **b. & e.** beginning and ending.

B. & F.B.S. British and Foreign Bible Society.

B & L or **B and L** building and loan association (also known as savings and loan association, a bank that uses the deposits of members to make loans, usually for real estate and building).

b & p bare and painted.

B & S or **B & SG** Brown and Sharpe or Brown and Sharpe Gauge.

b & s beams and stringers building.

b & w or **B & W** or **B/W** black and white (of photographs or film).

BANK or **Bank** International Bank for Reconstruction and Development.

bank. **1** banking. **2** bankruptcy.

Bank. and Ins. R. Bankruptcy and Insolvency Reports.

bank clgs. bank clearings.

bank debs. bank debits.

Bankr. or **bankr.** bankruptcy: Bankr. Code = Bankruptcy Code.

BAOR or **B.A.O.R.** British Army of the Rhine.

BAP **1** 6-benzylaminopurine (plant growth hormone). **2** bromoform-allyl-phosphate (chemicals for flame-proofing cotton).

Bap. Baptist.

bap **1** also **bap.** baptized. **2** also **b. à p.** or **bàp** bills payable. [French billets à payer]

B.A.P.A. (bä'pə) British Airline Pilots Association (compare Balpa).

B.App. Arts Bachelor of Applied Arts.

B.App.Sc. Bachelor of Applied Science.

Bapt. Baptist.

bapt. baptized.

BAR or **B.A.R.** **1** Book Auction Records. **2** Browning Automatic Rifle.

B.Ar. Bachelor of Architecture.

Bar. **1** baritone. **2** barrister. **3** Baruch (book of the Apocrypha).

bar **1** also **bar.** baritone. **2** also **bar.** **a** barometer. **b** barometric. **3** also **bar.** barrel. **4** also **b. à r.** or **bàr** bills receivable. [French billets à recevoir]

Barb. Barbados.

B.A.R.C. British Automobile Racing Club.

B.Arch. Bachelor of Architecture.

Barit. or **barit.** baritone.

Barn. Barnard (star second closest to the sun).

BARP British Association of Retired Persons.

Barr. or **barr.** barrister.

bars. barrels.

BART (pronounced bärt) Bay Area Rapid Transit (transportation system in San Francisco).

Bart. (*pronounced* bärt) **1** Baronet. **2** Bartholomew.

Bart's or **Barts** (*pronounced* bärts) St. Bartholomew's Hospital (the first of the great London hospitals, founded in 1123).

BAS 1 *also* **B.A.S.** Bachelor of Agricultural Science. **2** *also* **B.A.S.** Bachelor of Applied Science. **3** *also* **B.A.S.** Bachelor of Arts and Sciences. **4** basic allowance for subsistence. **5** British Antarctic Survey.

Bas. 1 St. Basilius. **2** *also* **bas** basso. **3** Basutoland (now Lesotho).

B.A.Sc. 1 Bachelor of Agricultural Science. **2** Bachelor of Applied Science.

BASE Basic Adult Social Education (an Australian program to help underprivileged groups obtain basic skills and social awareness).

BASIC 1 *also* **Basic** (bā′sik) Beginners All-purpose Symbolic Instruction Code (a computer language). **2** Biological Abstract Subjects in Context.

BASW British Association of Social Workers.

BAT 1 best available technology (esp. for environmental standards). **2** brown adipose tissue. **3** *also* **B.A.T.** Technical Assistance Bureau. [French *Bureau de l'assistance technique*]

bat. 1 battalion. **2** *also* **bat** battery *military, electronics*.

BATF U.S. Bureau of Alcohol, Tobacco, and Firearms.

B.A. Theol. Bachelor of Arts in Theology.

B.A. Thread British Association Thread (of screws) *mechanics*.

batn. battalion.

batt. 1 battalion. **2** *also* **batt** battery *military, music*.

Bav. Bavaria, Bavarian.

b. à v. good at sight (of bills or drafts) *commerce*. [French *bon à vue*]

BB *I an abbreviation for:* **1** base on balls *baseball*. **2** *also* **B.B.** Blue Book (esp. a government publication, such as the list of official representatives or a report or manual). **3** *also* **B.B.** B'nai B'rith (Jewish fraternal society). **4** Bulletin of Bibliography (magazine title). **5** Bureau of the Budget; BOB.
II a symbol for: **1** *also* **BB.** drawing paper having a medium-rough surface. **2** fifth highest rating, after BBB *finance*. **3** shot somewhat less than $^1/_{16}$ of an inch in diameter, used in shot guns and air rifles, called "BB guns."

bb. 1 base box (unit of measure for tin). **2** *also* **bb** books.

b.b. 1 bail bond. **2** ball bearing. **3** bank book. **4** bearer bond (bond negotiable by the bearer) *finance*. **5** below bridges (in determining tolls for bridge openings for vessels) *shipping*. **6** bill book *commerce*. **7** break bulk (to remove cargo from a ship) *commerce*.

BBA 1 *also* **B.B.A.** Bachelor of Business Administration. **2** Big Brothers of America (child guidance agency). **3** *also* **B.B.A.** British Bankers Association.

BBB *I an abbreviation for:* **1** Bed, Breakfast, and Bath (of accommodations). **2** *also* **B.B.B.** Better Business Bureau. **3** blood-brain barrier *medicine*.
II a symbol for: fourth highest rating, after A *finance*.

BBBC British Boxing Board of Control.

BBC 1 body-centered cubic (of crystal structure). **2** Breeding Bird Census. **3** *also* **B.B.C.** (*also pronounced* bēb) British Broadcasting Corporation.

B.B.E. *or* **BBE** Bachelor of Business Education.

B.B.F.C. *or* **BBFC** British Board of Film Censors.

BBG Board of Broadcast Governors (Canadian regulatory agency).

bbl. barrel or barrels.

BBQ barbecue.

BBS 1 *also* **B.B.S.** Bachelor of Business Science. **2** *also* **B.B.S.** Bachelor of Business Studies. **3** *also* **BBS.** box bark strips (lumber used as rough siding in framing construction). **4** Breeding Bird Survey. **5** *also* **BBS.** or **B.B.S.** British Computer Society. **6** bulletin board system (electronic message center) *computers*. **7** *also* **B.B.S.** Bulletin of the Bureau of Standards.

BBT basal body temperature.

BC 1 *also* **B.C.** Bachelor of Chemistry. **2** *also* **B.C.** Bachelor of Commerce. **3** *also* **B.C.** Bachelor of Surgery. [Latin *Baccalaureus Chirurgiae*] **4** back cover (of a magazine, book, record album). **5** *also* **B.C. a** Bankruptcy Cases. **b** Bankruptcy Court. **6** base shield connection (of an electron tube). **7** bass clarinet. **8** *also* **B.C.** or **b.c.** or **bc** before Christ: *Caesar invaded Britain in 55 BC.* **9** between centers (in blueprints and diagrams). **10** Board Certified (of a physician). **11** bone conduction *medicine*. **12** Borough Council (in Great Britain). **13** British Columbia. **14** broadcast or broadcast band, also in combination: *BCI = broadcast interference.* **15** *also* **BC** figured bass (a continuous bass part in a piece of music indicated by figures to show its harmony). [Italian *basso continuo*] **16** The Book Collector (magazine title).

B/C 1 bill for collection *commerce*. **2** Board Certified (of a physician).

b.c. 1 bass clarinet. **2** bolt circle (in blueprints and diagrams). **3** *also* **bc** broadcast.

BCA 1 *also* **B.C.A.** Bachelor of Commerce and Administration. **2** Banknote Corporation of America (printer of U.S. postage stamps). **3** Boys' Clubs of America.

BCBG Parisian preppies. [French *bon chic, bon genre*]

BCC 1 *also* **bcc** or **b.c.c.** blind carbon copy (of a letter). **2** block check character (character added to a block of information that verifies the information has not been altered). **3** *also* **B.c.c.** body-centered cubic (of a crystal). **4** *also* **B.C.C.** British Council of Churches.

BCCB British Coordinating Committee for Biotechnology.

BCCI Bank of Credit and Commerce International (former world-wide banking company).

BCD 1 bad conduct discharge (formerly from military service). **2** binary coded decimal (computer system for coding decimal numbers in binary form).

b/c.d. barrels per charge day.

B.C.E. *or* **BCE 1** Bachelor of Chemical Engineering. **2** Bachelor of Civil Engineering. **3** *also* **B.C.E.** *or* **BCE** before the Christian or common era.

BCF 1 British Cycling Federation. **2** U.S. Bureau of Commercial Fisheries.

bcf billion cubic feet.

BCG 1 ballistocardiogram *medicine.* **2** Calmette-Guérin bacillus (vaccine tuberculosis).

BCH Beach (in postal address).

B.Ch. *or* **BCh** Bachelor of Surgery. [Latin *Baccalaureus Chirurgiae*]

bch. bunch.

B.Ch.D. *or* **BChD** Bachelor of Dental Surgery. [Latin *Baccalaureus Chirurgiae Dentalis*]

B.Ch.E. *or* **BChE** Bachelor of Chemical Engineering.

B.Chir. *or* **BChir** Bachelor of Surgery. [Latin *Baccalaureus Chirurgiae*]

BCI 1 broadcast interference. **2** Bureau of Criminal Investigation. **3** *also* **B.C.I.** International Cartographic Bibliography. [French *Bibliographie Cartographique Internationale*]

BCIE Central American Bank for Economic Integration; Cabei. [Spanish *Banco Centroamericano de Integración Economica*]

BCIS International Central Bureau of Seismology. [French *Bureau Central International de Séismologie*]

B.C.L. *or* **BCL 1** Bachelor of Canon Law. **2** Bachelor of Civil Law.

BCM Boston Conservatory of Music.

B.C.M.S. Bible Churchmen's Missionary Society.

BCN 1 Biomedical Communications Network (of the National Library of Medicine). **2** *also* **bcn** beacon, esp. on maps and charts.

BCNZ Broadcasting Corporation of New Zealand.

B.Comm. *or* **B.Com.** Bachelor of Commerce.

B.Com.Sc. Bachelor of Commercial Science.

B.C.P. *or* **BCP** Book of Common Prayer.

BCS 1 *also* **B.C.S.** Bachelor of Chemical Science. **2** *also* **B.C.S.** Bachelor of Commercial Science. **3** British Computer Society. **4** U.S. Bureau of Criminal Statistics. **5** theory of superconductivity: *BCS theory.* [after John *Bardeen*, Leon N. *Cooper*, J. Robert *Schrieffer*, its developers]

BCST broadcast.

BCTA British Canadian Trade Association.

BCURA British Coal Utilization Research Association.

BCW Bureau of Child Welfare (now Special Services for Children).

BD 1 *also* **B.D.** Bachelor of Divinity. **2** bank draft. **3** benday (screen used in photoengraving). **4** *also* **B.D.** bills discounted *commerce.* **5** blowing dust, esp. in aviation weather reports. **6** bomb disposal, esp. in combination: *BDS = bomb disposal squad.* **7** *also* **B.D.** Bonner Durchmusterung (German astronomical catalog of stars). **8** brought down *accounting.* **9** Federal Republic of Germany. [German *Bundesrepublik Deutschland*] **10** stories in comic-book form. [French *bande dessinée*]

B/D 1 bank draft. **2** bills discounted *commerce.* **3** brought down *accounting.*

Bd. 1 *also* **Bd** baud (unit of measure expressing data transmission speed). **2** board (esp. in a title): *Bd. of Ed. = Board of* Education. **3** bond. **4** Boulevard. **5** volume *or* book. [German *Band*]

bd. 1 *also* **bd** baud (unit of measure) *computers.* **2** bed, esp. in combination: *bd. & jt. = bed and joint; bd. & pt. = bed and point* (both used in masonry construction). **3** board, esp. in combination: *bd.ft. = board feet.* **4** bond, esp. in combination: *bd.rts. = bond rights.* **5** bound, esp. of books. **6** bundle.

b.d. 1 back dividend *finance.* **2** brought down *accounting.* **3** twice a day *medicine.* [Latin *bis in die*]

b/d 1 barrels per day. **2** brought down *accounting.*

b7d, b10d, b15d buyer has 7, 10, 15 days to take up stock.

BDA 1 bomb damage assessment. **2** *also* **B.D.A.** Bachelor of Dramatic Art. **3** *also* **B.D.A.** British Dental Association.

b.d.c. *or* **BDC** bottom dead center (of the position in a piston stroke nearest the crankshaft).

Bde. 1 brigade. **2** volumes or books. [German *Bände*]

bd.ft. board foot.

bdg. 1 binding (of a book). **2** bookbinding.

BDH British Drug Houses.

BDI 1 bearing deviation indicator. **2** *also* **b.d.i.** both dates inclusive.

B.D.L. British Drama League.

bdl. 1 *also* **bdle.** bundle. **2** bundled, as in *bdl.bk.s.* bundled bark strips (of rough siding shipped to a construction site).

BDM births, deaths, marriages.

BDOS basic operating system *computers.*

BDR bearer depositary receipt *finance.*

Bdr. 1 bombardier. **2** Brigadier.

bdr. border.

BDRM *or* **bdrm.** bedroom.

bdry boundary.

BDS 1 *also* **B.D.S.** Bachelor of Dental Surgery. **2** *also* **Bds** Barbados, in combination: *BDS$ = Barbados dollar.* **3** Bomb Disposal Squad.

bds. 1 bound in boards (of a book). **2** bundles.

b.d.s. to be taken twice a day *medicine.* [Latin *bis in die sumendus*]

BDSA U.S. Business and Defense Services Administration (developing economic growth and allocating strategic materials in emergency).

B.D.Sc. *or* **BDSc.** Bachelor of Dental Service.

BDST British Double Summer Time.

BDU 1 battle dress uniform. **2** Bomb Disposal Unit.

BDV breakdown voltage *physics, electronics.*

Bdx. Bordeaux.

bdy. boundary.

B.E. 1 *also* **BE** Bachelor of Education. **2** *also* **BE** Bachelor of Engineering. **3** Bank of England. **4** *also* **BE** bill of exchange *commerce.* **5** *also* **BE** Board Examined (of a physician). **6** Board of Education. **7** *also* **B.E.** *or* **BE** *or* **b.e.** Buddhist Era: *B.E. 2538 = A.D. 1995 in Thailand.*

BE *or* **B/E** Board of Eligibility (of a physician).

B/E 1 bill of entry *commerce*. **2** bill of exchange *commerce*.

Be beryllium (chemical element).

Bé Baumé (scale to measure specific gravity).

b.e. bill of exchange *commerce*.

BEA 1 *also* **B.E.A.** British Engineers Association. **2** Broadcast Education Association. **3** Bureau of Economic Analysis (of U.S. Department of Commerce).

BEAB British Electrical Approvals Board (corresponding to the American Underwriters' Laboratories).

Bearb. editor. [German *Bearbeiter*]

bearb. revised, compiled, edited. [German *bearbeitet*]

Beau. & Fl. Francis Beaumont and John Fletcher (17th-century English dramatists who collaborated on many plays).

BEC U.S. Bureau of Employees' Compensation.

B.Ec. Bachelor of Economics.

bec. because.

BECTU Broadcasting, Entertainment, and Cinematograph Technicians Union.

B. Ed. *or* **BEd 1** Bachelor of Education. **2** Board of Education.

Bedford. *or* **Beds.** Bedfordshire, England.

B.E.E. *or* **BEE** Bachelor of Electrical Engineering.

BEEM ballistic electron emission microscopy.

B.E.F. British Expeditionary Forces.

bef. before.

beg. begin, beginning (esp. as a direction in needlework).

begr. established *or* founded. [German *begründet*]

beh. 1 behavior *psychology*. **2** behaviorism.

Beibl. supplement [German *Beiblatt*]

beif. *or* **beiflgd.** enclosed. [German *beifolgend*]

beigeb. bound with (in a book). [German *beigebunden*]

BEL British Electrotechnical Committee.

Bel. 1 a Belgian. **b** Belgium. **2** Belgic (esp. Gaulish language of the Belgae). **3** Belize.

bel. below.

bel ex. fine copy, as of a book or print. [French *bel exemplaire*]

Belf. Belfast.

Belg. 1 a Belgian, also in combination: *Belg. pat.* = *Belgian patent*. **b** Belgium. **2** Belgic (esp. Gaulish language of the Belgae).

BEM 1 *also* **B.E.M.** Bachelor of Engineering of Mines. **2** *also* **B.E.M.** British Empire Medal. **3** bug-eyed monster (esp. in reference to science fiction writing).

Bem. note *or* comment. [German *Bemerkung*]

BEMA Business Equipment Manufacturers Association.

BEMF back electromotive force.

Ben. 1 blessing. [Latin *Benedictio*] **2** well, good. [Latin *Bene*]

B. en Dr. Bachelor of Law. [French *Bachelier en droit*]

Benelux (ben'ə luks) *or* **BENELUX** economic union of Belgium, the Netherlands, and Luxembourg.

Beng. Bengal, Bengali.

B.Eng. *or* **BEng** Bachelor of Engineering.

B.Eng.A. Bachelor of Agricultural Engineering.

Benj. Benjamin.

BEP Bureau of Engraving and Printing (U.S. government printer of postage stamps and currency).

Ber. 1 Berlin. **2** Bermuda.

Berb. Berber.

Ber. Is. Bermuda Islands.

Berk. Berkeley, California (usually in reference to the campus of the University of California at Berkeley, and esp. the scientific establishment there).

Berks. Berkshire, England.

Berw. Berwickshire, Scotland.

BES 1 *also* **B.E.S.** Bachelor of Engineering Science. **2** Bureau of Employment Security.

bes. especially. [German *besonders*]

B.E.S.A. *or* **BESA** British Engineering Standards Association.

B. ès A. Bachelor of Arts. [French *Bachelier ès Arts*]

BESC Binary Electronics Sequence Computer.

B.E.S.L. British Empire Service League.

B. ès L. Bachelor of Letters. [French *Bachelier ès Lettres*]

Bess. Bessemer.

B. ès S. Bachelor of Sciences. [French *Bachelier ès Sciences*]

BEST Basic Essential Skills Training.

BET 1 Brunauer, Emmett, Teller (absorption rate over a surface area): *BET equation*. **2** Business Experience Training.

bet. *or* **betw.** between.

betr. concerning. [German *betreffend*]

BEUC European Bureau of Consumers Unions. [French *Bureau Européen des Unions des Consommateurs*]

BEV (*also pronounced* bev) **1** billion electron volts. **2** black English vernacular.

Bev (*also pronounced* bev) *or* **BeV.** billion electron volts.

bev 1 *also* **Bev.** beveled. **2** *also* **bev.** beverage. **3** *also* **b.e.v.** billion electron volts.

BEW Board of Economic Warfare (in World War II).

Bez. brand. [German *Bezeichnung*]

bez. 1 paid. [German *bezahlt*] **2** referring. [German *bezüglich*]

bezw. respectively. [German *beziehungsweise*]

BF 1 *also* **B.F.** Bachelor of Finance. **2** *also* **B.F.** Bachelor of Forestry. **3** Banque de France. **4** beat frequency *electronics*. **5** *also* **B/F** brought forward *accounting*. **6** *also* **B.F. a** a good or proper deed *law*. [Latin *bonum factum*] **b** in good faith. [Latin *Bona Fide*]

bf 1 *also* **b.f.** *or* **bf.** boldface *printing*. **2** *also* **bf.** brief *law*. **3** *also* **b.f.** *or* **b/f** brought forward *accounting*. **4** firkin of beer.

B.F.A. *or* **BFA** Bachelor of Fine Arts.

B.F.B.S. British and Foreign Bible Society.

BFC Bureau of Foreign Commerce (U.S. Department of Commerce).

bfc or **b.f.c.** or **bf.c.** boldface caps (capitals) *printing.*

B.F.E. or **BFE** Bachelor of Forestry Engineering.

B.F.I. British Film Institute.

B.F.L. or **BFL** back focal length *photography.*

B.F.M.P. British Federation of Master Printers.

BFO or **bfo** beat frequency oscillator *electronics.*

BFOQ bona fide occupational qualification (special need because of sex, religion, race, or origin necessary to perform a job).

BFP biological false-positive (of a reaction to a test, esp. for syphilis).

BFPO British Forces Post Office.

BFS British Frontier Service.

BFT Biofeedback Training (conscious control of blood pressure or other bodily processes).

B.F.U.W. British Federation of University Women.

BFV Bradley Fighting Vehicle (military tank).

BG 1 best game *billiards.* **2 a** Birmingham Gage (gauge for steel tubing, plates, hoops, etc., copper sheets). **b** British Standard Gage (gauge for iron and steel sheets). **3** *also* **B.G.** Brigadier General. **4** *also* **B.G.** (formerly) British Guiana (now *Guyana*).

B/G bonded goods.

Bg. sheet or leaf of paper. [German *Bogen*]

bg. 1 background. **2** bag.

b.g. bay gelding (of a horse).

BGA 1 Better Government Association. **2** British Gaming Association. **3** *also* **B.G.A.** British Gliding Association.

B.G.B. Booksellers Association of Great Britain and Ireland.

bGH or **BGH** bovine growth hormone.

B.G.I. International Geographical Bibliography. [French *Bibliographie Géographique Internationale*]

BGN U.S. Board on Geographic Names (U.S. Department of the Interior).

BGS 1 *also* **B.G.S.** British Geriatrics Society. **2** Bulletin of the Geological Survey (magazine title).

bgs. bags.

BGSA Bulletin of the Geological Society of America (magazine title).

bgt. bought.

BH 1 *also* **B.H.** Bachelor of Humanities. **2** Base Hospital. **3** *also* **B.H.** both hands *music.* **4** Brinell hardness number (of a metal or alloy). **5** British Honduras (now *Belize*).

B/H bill of health.

Bh 1 Brinell hardness number (of a metal or alloy). **2** *also* **Bh.** supplement. [German *Beiheft*]

b.h. 1 *also* **bh.** base hit *baseball.* **2** bay horse. **3** *also* **bh** boiler horsepower. **4** candle hour. [French *bougie heure*]

BHA 1 British Hotels Association. **2** butylated hydroxyanisole (food preservative).

bha base helix angle *mechanics.*

B'ham Birmingham, England.

BHC 1 benzene hexachloride (insecticide). **2** *also* **B.H.C.** British High Commissioner.

bhd. bulkhead.

B.H.Ec. or **BHEc** Bachelor of Home Economics.

B.H.I. or **BHI** International Hydrographic Bureau. [French *Bureau Hydrographique International*]

BHK baby hamster kidney cells (used as a medium in virology).

B.H.L. or **BHL** Bachelor of Hebrew Letters or Literature.

BHN Brinell hardness number (of a metal or alloy).

B.H.N. Brotherhood of the Holy Name of Jesus.

Bhn Brinell hardness number (of a metal or alloy).

B.Hort. Bachelor of Horticulture.

B.Hort.Sc. Bachelor of Horticultural Science.

bhp or **BHP** or **b.hp.** brake horsepower, also in combination: *bhp-hr = brake horsepower hour.*

bhpric. Bishopric.

B.H.Sc. Bachelor of Household or Home Science.

BHT butylated hydroxytoluene (food preservative).

B. Hy. Bachelor of Hygiene.

B.I. 1 Balearic Islands. **2** Bermuda Islands. **3** *also* **BI** bodily injury *law, insurance.* **4** buffer index *biochemistry.*

Bi bismuth (chemical element).

BIA 1 *also* **B.I.A.** Bachelor of Industrial Arts. **2** Boating Industry Association. **3** Braille Institute of America. **4** British Insurance Association. **5** Bureau of Indian Affairs (of U.S. Department of Interior). **6** Bureau of Insular Affairs.

BIB Bureau of International Broadcasting.

Bib. Bible, biblical.

bib. drink *pharmaceutics.* [Latin *bibe*]

Bibl. Biblical.

bibl. 1 bibliographical, esp. in combination: *bibl.fn. = bibliographical footnote.* **2** bibliography. **3** library. [Latin *bibliotheca*]

bibliog. 1 bibliographer. **2** bibliographic, bibliographical, esp. in combination: *bibliog.fn. = bibliographical footnote.* **3** bibliography.

BIBRA or **Bibra** (bib'rə) British Industrial Biological Research Association.

BIC 1 International Containers Bureau. [French *Bureau International des Containers*] **2** U.S. Bureau of International Commerce.

bicarb (bī'kärb) or **bicarb.** sodium bicarbonate.

BICMOS bipolar complementary metal oxide semiconductor *electronics.*

B.I.D. or **BID 1** Bachelor of Industrial Design. **2** Bachelor of Interior Design.

b.i.d. twice a day *pharmaceutics.* [Latin *bis in die*]

BIE 1 *also* **B.I.E.** Bachelor of Industrial Engineering. **2** Bureau of International Expositions. **3** International Bureau of Education. [French *Bureau International d'Éducation*]

BIEE British Institute of Electrical Engineers.

BIEM International Bureau for Registration of Mechanical Rights (recording of music). [French *Bureau International des Sociétés Gérant les Droits d'Enregistrement et de Reproduction Mécanique*]

bien. biennial (of plants).

BIET British Institute of Engineering Technology.

BIFU Banking Insurance and Finance Union.

BIH International Bureau of Time. [French *Bureau International de l'Heure*]

BIL bilingual: *BIL temps = bilingual temporary employees.*

BILA Bureau of International Labor Affairs (of U.S. Department of Labor).

B.I.M. British Institute of Management.

bi-m bimonthly.

b.i.n. twice a night *pharmaceutics.* [Latin *bis in nocte*]

bind. binding (esp. of a book).

BINOVC breaks in overcast *meteorology.*

bio. 1 *also* **bio** (bī′ō′) biography. 2 biology, biological.

biochem. biochemistry.

biog. 1 biographer. 2 biography, biographical.

biogeog. biogeography.

biol. 1 biologist. 2 biology, biological.

BIOS basic input-output system *computers.*

BIOT British Indian Ocean Territory.

BIP Books in Print (index to the Publishers Trade List Annual).

BIPM International Bureau of Weights and Measures. [French *Bureau International des Poids et Mésures*]

BIR 1 *British* Board of Inland Revenue. 2 *also* **B.I.R.** British Institute of Radiology.

BIRD International Bank for Reconstruction and Development; IBRD (the World Bank). [French *Banque Internationale pour le Reconstruction et le Développement*]

B.I.R.E. British Institution of Radio Engineers.

BIRPI The Berne Convention on copyright (now *WIPO*). [French *Bureaux Internationaux Réunis pour la Protection de la Propriété Intellectuelle*]

BIRS British Institute of Recorded Sound.

BIS 1 *also* **B.I.S.** Bank for International Settlements. 2 best in show (of judging animals in competition). 3 *also* **B.I.S.** British Information Service. 4 British Interplanetary Society. 5 Business Information System *computers.*

bis. bissextile (having the extra day in leap year).

BISF British Iron and Steel Federation.

BISG Book Industry Study Group.

BISRA British Iron and Steel Research Association.

BIT International Labor Office. [French *Bureau International du Travail*]

bit (*pronounced* bit) binary digit *computers.*

BITNET a worldwide computer network. [*Because It's Time Network*]

BIV bovine immunodeficiency virus.

bitum. bituminous.

BIU International University Bureau. [French *Bureau International des Universités*]

biv. bivouac.

bi-w biweekly.

BIWF British Israel World Federation.

BIWS Bureau of International Whaling Statistics.

BIZ Bank for International Settlements. [German *Bank für Internationalen Zahlungsausgleich*]

biz (*pronounced* biz) *or* **biz.** *informal* business.

B.J. *or* **BJ** Bachelor of Journalism.

BJA Bureau of Justice Assistance.

BJCEB British Joint Communications Electronics Board.

BJP Bharatiya Janata Party (a Hindu fundamentalist party in India).

BJS Bureau of Justice Statistics.

B.Jur. *or* **B.Juris.** Bachelor of Jurisprudence.

BK balk *baseball.*

Bk *I also* **Bk.** an abbreviation for: 1 Bank. 2 Book.
II a symbol for: berkelium (chemical element).

bk. *or* **bk** 1 backwardation (postponement of delivery of securities) *finance.* 2 bank. 3 bark. 4 black. 5 block. 6 book. 7 brake.

bkbndr. bookbinder.

bkcy. bankruptcy.

bkfst. breakfast.

bkg. 1 banking. 2 bookkeeping.

bkgd. background.

bklr. black letter *printing.*

bklt. booklet.

Bklyn. Brooklyn.

bkm buckram (of a bookbinding).

bkpg. bookkeeping.

BKPR *or* **bkpr.** bookkeeper.

bkpt. bankrupt.

bkrtcy bankruptcy.

bks. 1 banks. 2 barracks. 3 blocks. 4 books.

bkt. 1 basket. 2 bracket.

bkts. baskets.

B.L. 1 *also* **BL** a *U.S.* Bachelor of Laws. b *British* Bachelor of Law. 2 *also* **BL** a Bachelor of Letters. b Bachelor of Literature. 3 barrister at law. 4 base line *sports, surveying.* 5 bill lodged *banking, commerce.* 6 *also* **B/L** bill of lading *commerce:* B/L att. = bill of lading attached. 7 black letter *printing.* 8 Bodleian Library. 9 breech-loading *ordnance.* 10 *also* **BL** British Library (formerly BM, British Museum). 11 Burkitt's lymphoma.

Bl. 1 Blessed (esp. in a title). 2 paper. [German *Blatt*]

bl. 1 bale. 2 barrel. 3 black. 4 block. 5 blue.

b.l. 1 base line *sports, surveying.* 2 *also* **b/l** bill of lading *commerce.* 3 breech-loading *ordnance.*

B.L.A. 1 *also* **BLA** Bachelor of Landscape Architecture. 2 *also* **BLA** Bachelor of Liberal Arts. 3 British Library Association.

BLAISE (blāz) British Library Automated Information Service.

BLC 1 *also* **blc.** balance *accounting.* **2** boundary layer control *aeronautics.*

bld. 1 blood. **2** bold or boldface *printing.*

bldg. *or* **Bldg.** building.

bldgs. buildings.

bldr. builder.

B.L.E. *or* **BLE** Brotherhood of Locomotive Engineers.

BLEU Belgium-Luxembourg Economic Union.

B.L.F.E. Brotherhood of Locomotive Firemen and Enginemen.

BLG betalactoglobulin (milk protein).

blg. building.

B.Lib. *or* **B.Lib.Sc.** Bachelor of Library Science.

B.Lit. Bachelor of Literature. [Latin *Baccalaureus Literarum,* sometimes *Litterarum*]

B.Litt. Bachelor of Letters. [Latin *Baccalaureus Litterarum*]

Blk. block.

blk. 1 black. **2** blank. **3** block. **4** bulk.

blkd. bulkhead.

B.LL. Bachelor of Laws. [Latin *Baccalaureus Legum*]

BLM Bureau of Land Management (of U.S. Department of the Interior).

B.L.M.R. Bureau of Labor-Management Reports.

BLMRCP Bureau of Labor-Management Relations and Cooperative Programs (of U.S. Department of Labor).

BLN. *or* **bln.** balloon.

BLS 1 *also* **B.L.S.** Bachelor of Library Science. **2** Bureau of Labor Statistics (of U.S. Department of Labor).

bls. 1 bales. **2** barrels.

BLST ballast.

BLT bacon, lettuce, and tomato (sandwich).

blt. built.

B.L.T.A. British Lawn Tennis Association.

BLVD Boulevard (in postal address).

Blvd. *or* **blvd.** boulevard.

BM 1 *also* **B.M.** Bachelor of Medicine. **2** *also* **B.M.** Bachelor of Music. **3** ballistic missile, esp. in combination: *ICBM = Intercontinental Ballistic Missile.* **4** basal metabolism. **5** *also* **B.M.** bench mark (survey marker). **6** *also* **B/M** bill of material. **7** *also* **B/M** binding margin, in book manufacturing. **8** Blessed Mary. **9** board measure (of lumber). **10** bowel movement. **11** *also* **B.M.** British Museum. **12** bronze medal or medalist, *esp. in sports.* **13 a** of blessed memory. [Latin *Beatae Memoriae*] **b** of happy memory. [Latin *Bonae Memoriae*] **14** to the well-deserving. [Latin *bene merenti*]

bm. 1 baromil (graduating unit of a mercury barometer in the centimeter-gram-second system). **2** beam.

b.m. 1 band measure. **2** board measure (of lumber).

B.M.A. *or* **BMA** British Medical Association.

BMD *or* **B.M.D.** Ballistic Missile Defense.

BME *or* **B.M.E. 1** Bachelor of Mechanical Engineering. **2** Bachelor of Mining Engineering. **3** *also* **B.M.Ed.** Bachelor of Music Education.

B.Mech.E. Bachelor of Mechancal Engineering.

B.Med.Sc. Bachelor of Medical Science.

BMEP *or* **b.m.e.p.** brake mean effective pressure (measure of the power stroke of an engine).

B.Met. *or* **BMet.** Bachelor of Metallurgy.

BMEWS (bē'myüz') Ballistic Missile Early Warning System.

BMFA Boston Museum of Fine Arts.

BMI 1 Ballistic Missile Interceptor. **2** body mass index (of human body weight). **3** Book Manufacturers Institute (also used as an industry standard, except for textbooks which are governed by *NASTA* specifications). **4** Broadcast Music Incorporated (association of broadcasting industry representing writers, composers, and publishers).

BMIC Bureau of Mines Information Circular.

BMJ British Medical Journal.

BML *or* **B.M.L.** British Museum Library.

BMO Ballistic Missile Offensive: *BMO deployment.*

B.M.O.C. *U.S. slang* big man on campus.

BMQ British Museum Quarterly (magazine title).

BMR *or* **B.M.R.** basal metabolic rate.

B.M.S. 1 *also* **BMS** Bachelor of Marine Science. **2** *also* **B.M.Sc.** Bachelor of Medical Science.

BMT 1 *also* **B.M.T.** Bachelor of Medical Technology. **2** bone marrow transplantation *medicine.* **3** Brooklyn-Manhattan Transit (division of the New York City subway system).

BMTP Bureau of Mines Technical Paper.

B.Mus. *or* **BMus.** Bachelor of Music.

B.Mus.Ed. Bachelor of Music Education.

B.M.V. Blessed Mary the Virgin. [Latin *Beata Maria Virgo*]

BMX bicycle motocross.

BN 1 *also* **B.N.** Bachelor of Nursing. **2** *also* **B.N.** bank note. **3** boron nitride (heat resistant and insulating material of great hardness). **4** Bureau of Narcotics. **5** National Library of France, Italy, or Spain. [French *Bibliothèque Nationale,* Italian *Bibliotèca Nazionale,* Spanish *Biblioteca Nacional*]

Bn 1 *also* **Bn.** Baron. **2** battalion. **3** beacon (on navigation charts).

bn. 1 *also* **bn** bassoon *music.* **2** battalion. **3** battens (boards used for flooring). **4** billion.

B.N.A. 1 Basel Anatomical Nomenclature (international terminology of anatomy, replaced by *NA*). [Latin *Basle Nomina Anatomica*] **2** British Naturalists' Association. **3** British North America, esp. in combination: *BNA Act* (Canadian Constitution of 1867, replaced by Constitution Act in 1982).

B.N.B. British National Bibliography (publication).

B.N.C.M National Library of Music, in Paris. [French *Bibliothèque Nationale du Conservatoire de Musique*]

bnd. bound.

BNDD Bureau of Narcotics and Dangerous Drugs (of U.S. Department of Justice).

B.N.E.C. British National Export Council.

BNF 1 Backus Naur Form (directions for computer programming language). **2** *also* **B.N.F.** British National Formulary (publication) *pharmaceutics*. **3** *also* **BNFL** British Nuclear Fuels Limited.

bnfts benefits (e.g., health insurance offered by employer).

bnk. bank.

BNL Brookhaven National Laboratory (research installation of the Atomic Energy Commission).

BNOA naphthoxyacetic acid (used to control plant growth).

BNOC 1 British National Oil Corporation. **2** *also* **B.N.O.C.** British National Opera Company.

BNP Bangladesh Nationalist Party.

BNRC Bulletin of the National Research Council (publication).

B.N.S. 1 *also* **BNS** Bachelor of Natural Science. **2** British Numismatic Society.

Bnss. baroness.

BNYPL Bulletin of the New York Public Library (publication).

BO 1 back order. **2** *also* **B.O.** best offer *commerce*. **3** Board of Ordnance. **4** body odor. **5** *also* **B.O.** box office. **6** branch office. **7** broker's order *commerce*. **8** *also* **B/O** brought over *accounting*. **9** buyer's option *commerce*. **10** government report. [French *Bulletin Officiel*]

b/o 1 back order. **2** box office. **3** brought over *accounting*.

b.o. 1 back order. **2** broker's order *commerce*. **3** brought over *accounting*. **4** buyer's option *commerce*.

B.O.A. 1 *also* **BOA** British Olympic Association. **2** British Optical Association. **3** *also* **BOA** British Orthopaedic Association.

BOB 1 best of breed (judging animals in competition). **2** Bureau of the Budget.

BOC Bureau of the Census (of U.S. Department of Commerce).

BOCES (bō'sēz') Board of Cooperative Educational Services.

BOD *or* **B.O.D.** biochemical or biological oxygen demand (amount of oxygen necessary for bacteria to metabolize organic matter in water, sewage, etc.).

Bod. *or* **Bodl.** Bodleian Library (Oxford University).

BOF 1 basic oxygen furnace, in steel making. **2** beginning of file *computers*.

B. of E. 1 Bank of England. **2** *also* **B of E** *or* **BOE** Board of Education.

B of H Board of Health.

B. of T. Board of Trade.

Boh. *or* **Bohem.** Bohemian.

boil. boiling.

Bol. Bolivia, Bolivian.

bol. pill *pharmaceutics*. [Latin *bolus*]

BOM 1 beginning of month *commerce*. **2** *also* **BoM** Bureau of Mines (of U.S. Department of the Interior). **3** *also* **bom** business office must (directive from management).

BOMC Book-of-the-Month Club.

Bon. Baron. [French *Baron*]

Bon. Mem. of happy memory. [Latin *Bonae Memoriae*]

Bonne. baroness. [French *baronne*]

Boo the Herdsman (constellation). [Latin *Boötes*]

BOP 1 basic oxygen process (for making steel, now usually *Q-BOP*). **2** Bureau of Prisons (of U.S. Department of Justice). **3** business owner's policy *insurance*.

BOQ bachelor officers' quarters *military*.

BOR Bureau of Reclamation (of U.S. Department of the Interior).

Bor. Borough.

B/Os binder's orders.

BOT 1 beginning of tape *electronics*. **2** Board of Trade.

bot. 1 botanist. **2** botany, botanical. **3** bottle. **4** bottom. **5** bought *commerce*.

B.O.U. *or* **BOU** British Ornithologists' Union.

Boul. *or* **boul.** Boulevard.

BP 1 *also* **B.P.** Bachelor of Pharmacy. **2** *also* **B.P.** Bachelor of Philosophy. **3** band pass *electronics*. **4** before the present: *The age is 18,460 years plus or minus 340 BP.* **5** Bermuda Plan (hotel rate including cost of room and breakfast). **6** *also* **B.P.** between perpendiculars (esp. of ship construction). **7** bills payable *commerce*. **8** *also* **B.P.** blood pressure. **9** boiling point, esp. in combination with a subscript indicating atmospheric pressure and a number indicating degrees of temperature. **10** *also* **B.P.** British Pharmacopoeia (publication). **11** *also* **B.P.** Most Holy Father. [Latin *Beatissime Pater*] **12** *also* **B.P.** Post Office Box; PO Box. [French *boîte postale*]

B/P 1 bill of parcels (invoice) *commerce*. **2** bills payable *commerce*. **3** blueprint.

Bp. Bishop.

b/p 1 bills payable *commerce*. **2** blueprint.

bp. 1 baptized. **2** birthplace.

b.p. 1 base pair *genetics*. **2** below proof, in distilling. **3** bill of parcels (invoice) *commerce*. **4** bills payable *commerce*. **5** boiler pressure. **6** *also* **bp** boiling point, esp. in combination with a subscript indicating atmospheric pressure and a number indicating degrees of temperature. **7** brick piers (in blueprints and diagrams). **8** the public good. [Latin *bonum publicum*]

BPA 1 *also* **B.P.A.** Bachelor of Public Administration. **2** Bonneville Power Administration. **3** *also* **B.P.A.** British Pediatric Association. **4** *also* **B.P.A.** British Philatelic Association.

B.Paed. *Canadian* Bachelor of Paedagogy.

B.Pay. *or* **b.pay.** bills payable.

B.P.B. *or* **b.p.b.** bank post bills *commerce*.

B.P.C. British Pharmaceutical Codex.

BPD borderline personality disorder.

B.Pd. Bachelor of Pedagogy.

b.p.d. barrels per day.

B.P.D.P.A. Brotherhood of Painters, Decorators, and Paperhangers of America.

B.P.E. *or* **BPE** Bachelor of Physical Education.

B.Pe. *or* **B.Ped.** Bachelor of Pedagogy.

b.p.f. good for (*stated number of*) francs. [French *bon pour ___ francs*]

BPH 1 *also* **B.P.H.** Bachelor of Public Health. **2** benign prostatic hyperplasia or hypertrophy (enlargement of the prostate gland).

B.Ph. *or* **BPh 1** Bachelor of Philosophy. **2** British Pharmacopoeia (publication).

B.Pharm. *or* **BPharm** Bachelor of Pharmacy.

B.P.H.E. *or* **BPHE** Bachelor of Physical and Health Education.

B.Phil. *or* **BPhil** Bachelor of Philosophy.

BPI Bureau of Plant Industry (of U.S. Department of Agriculture).

bpi bits or bytes per inch (unit of memory capacity in databanks).

bpl. birthplace.

BPM Bureau of Personnel Management (civil service).

bpm beats per minute *music.*

BPO benzylpennicilloyl (chief allergic factor in penicillin).

BPOE *or* **B.P.O.E.** Benevolent and Protective Order of Elks.

BPR Bureau of Public Roads (U.S. regulatory agency).

BPS Bureau of Product Safety (agency of the U.S. government).

bps bits or bytes per second (unit of transmission speed of data).

Bp. Suff. Suffragan Bishop.

BPSW Bulletin of the Philosophical Society of Washington (magazine title).

B.Q. may he or she rest well. [Latin *Bene Quiescat*]

BR 1 *also* **B.R.** bank rate. **2** bedroom. **3** *also* **B/R** bills receivable *commerce.* **4** *also* **B.R.** Book of Reference. **5** breeder reactor. **6** British Rail. **7** British Revision (of the BNA) *medicine.* **8** builder's risk *insurance.* **9** burning rate. **10 a** King's Bench (now *K.B.*). [Latin *Bancus Regis*] **b** Queen's Bench (now *Q.B.*). [Latin *Banco Reginae*]

Br *I an abbreviation for:* **1** *also* **Br.** Branch: *R.Br.* = *Rural Branch* (post office). **2** *also* **Br.** Breton (Brittany and language). **3** *also* **Br.** Britain, British. **4** *also* **Br.** Brother (member of a religious order). **5** viola. [German *Bratsche*]
II a symbol for: bromine (chemical element).

br. 1 bearing *navigation, machinery.* **2** bedroom. **3** branch *medicine, aeronautics.* **4** brand. **5** brass. **6** bridge *surveying.* **7** brief *law.* **8** brig. **9** bronze. **10** brother. **11** *also* **br** brown.

b.r. 1 *also* **b/r** bills receivable *commerce.* **2** boiling range *chemistry.* **3** builder's risk *insurance.*

B.R.A. British Records Association.

Br.Am. British America, British American.

Braz. Brazil, Brazilian.

BRB 1 Benefits Review Board (of U.S. Department of Labor). **2** *also* **B.R.B.** British Rail Board.

B.R.C.A. Brotherhood of Railway Carmen of America.

B.R.C.S. British Red Cross Society.

B.R.D. *or* **BRD** Federal Republic of Germany. [German *Bundesrepublik Deutschland*]

brd. board *architecture, bookbinding.*

B.R.D.C. British Racing Drivers' Club.

BRE 1 *also* **B.R.E.** Bachelor of Religious Education. **2** Building Research Establishment. **3** business reply envelope.

BrE British English.

Brec. *or* **Breck.** Brecknockshire, Wales.

B.Rec. *or* **b.rec.** *or* **b/rec.** bills receivable *commerce.*

b.rend. *or* **b/rend.** bill rendered *commerce.*

Bret. Breton (Brittany and language).

brev. 1 brevier (type size). **2** *also* **Brev.** (in titles) brevet or brevetted. **3** patent, patented. [French *breveté*]

brf. brief *law.*

brg. 1 *also* **BRG** bearing *navigation.* **2** bridge.

BRH Bureau of Radiological Health.

BRI 1 *also* **B.R.I.** Bank for International Settlements. [French *Banque des Règlements Internationaux*] **2** Biological Research Institute.

Brig. 1 Brigade. **2** Brigadier, also in combination: *Brig. Gen.* = *Brigadier General.*

brill. brilliant *music.* [Italian *brillante*]

Brit. 1 Britain, British. **2** Britannia. **3** Britannica. **4** Briticism.

BRITE Basic Research in Industrial Technology (an organization of the EEC).

Brit. Mus. British Museum.

Brit. Pat. British patent.

Britt. *or* **BRITT** of the Britons (used esp. on British coinage). [Latin *Brit(t)annicus*]

BRL Ballistic Research Laboratory.

brl. barrel.

brlp. burlap.

BRM 1 barometer. **2** binary rate multiplier *computers.* **3** *also* **B.R.M.** British Racing Motors.

brn brown.

Bro. *or* **bro. 1** brother. **2** brotherhood.

Bros. *or* **bros.** brothers.

B.R.S. 1 British Record Society. **2** *also* **BRS** British Road Services.

BRT 1 Belgian Radio and Television Company. [Dutch *Belgische Radio en Televisie*] **2** *also* **B.R.T.** Brotherhood of Railroad Trainmen.

Brt. gross tonnage. [German *Bruttoregister Tonne*]

brt. 1 bright. **2** brought.

Brux. Brussels. [French *Bruxelles*]

bryol. bryology (the study of mosses and liverworts).

brz. bronze.

BS 1 *also* **B.S.** Bachelor of Science. **2** *also* **B.S.** Bachelor of Surgery. **3** *also* **B.S.** balance sheet *commerce.* **4** Battle Squadron. **5** *also* **B.S.** Bibliographical Society. **6** *also* **B.S.** Blessed Sacrament. **7** blood sugar *medicine.* **8** blowing snow *meteorology.* **9** bottom settlings (of a vat or storage tank). **10** breath sound or sounds *medicine.* **11** *also* **B.S.** British Standard (usually with a catalog number for the publication of the BSI). **12** broadcasting station. **13** Suffragan Bishop.

B/S 1 *also* **b/s** bags. 2 *also* **b/s** bales. 3 bill of sale. 4 bill of sight (importation) *commerce.* 5 blood sugar *medicine.* 6 both sides *printing.*

B1S, B2S beaded one, two, sides (of lumber).

bs. 1 bags. 2 bales.

b.s. 1 back stage *theater.* 2 balance sheet *commerce.* 3 *also* **b/s** bill of sale *commerce.* 4 bill of sight (importation) *commerce.* 5 both sides, in construction. 6 bottom settlings (of a vat or storage tank).

BSA 1 *also* **B.S.A.** Bachelor of Science in Agriculture. 2 *also* **B.S.A.** Bibliographical Society of America. 3 body surface area *medicine.* 4 *also* **B.S.A.** Botanical Society of America. 5 Boy Scouts of America. 6 *also* **B.S.A.** Building Societies Association.

B.S.A.A. 1 *also* **BSAA** Bachelor of Science in Applied Arts. 2 British School of Archaeology at Athens.

BSAC British Sub-Aqua Club.

B.S.A.E. *or* **BSAE** 1 Bachelor of Science in Aeronautical Engineering. 2 *also* **B.S.Ag.** Bachelor of Science in Agricultural Engineering. 3 Bachelor of Science in Architectural Engineering.

B.S.&W. *or* **b.s.&w.** basic sediment and water.

B.S.Arch. Bachelor of Science in Architecture.

BSB 1 British Satellite Beam. 2 British Standard Beam (rolled steel beam made to standard measurement in Great Britain).

B.S.B.A. *or* **BSBA** Bachelor of Science in Business Administration.

B.S.B.I. Botanical Society of the British Isles.

BSC 1 *also* **B.S.C.** Bachelor of Science in Commerce. 2 *also* **bsc** basic. 3 *also* **B.S.C.** Bibliographical Society of Canada. 4 binary synchronous communication (for transmission of data in transactions by computer). 5 British Safety Council. 6 British Standard Channel (rolled steel channel made to standard in Great Britain). 7 Business Service Center.

B.Sc. Bachelor of Science.

B.Sc.Ag. *or* **B.Sc.Agr.** Bachelor of Science in Agriculture.

B.Sc.App. Bachelor of Applied Science.

B.S.C.E. *or* **BSCE** Bachelor of Science in Civil Engineering.

B.Sc.Econ. Bachelor of Science in Economics.

B.Sc.Eng. Bachelor of Science in Engineering.

B.Sc.F. *or* **B.Sc.For.** Bachelor of Science in Forestry.

B.S.Ch.E. Bachelor of Science in Chemical Engineering.

B.Sc.N Bachelor of Science in Nursing.

BSCP British Standard Code of Practice (publication of BSI).

BSCS Biological Sciences Curriculum Study.

B.Sc.Tech. Bachelor of Technical Science.

B.Sc.Vet. Bachelor of Veterinary Science.

B.S.D. *or* **BSD** Bachelor of Science in Design.

BSDA Business Services and Defense Administration (of U.S. Department of Commerce).

BSE 1 *also* **B.S.E.** *or* **B.S.Ed.** Bachelor of Science in Education. 2 *also* **B.S.E.** *or* **B.S.Eng.** Bachelor of Science in Engineering.

3 base support equipment. 4 bovine spongiform encephalopathy.

BSEE *or* **B.S.E.E.** 1 Bachelor of Science in Electrical Engineering. 2 Bachelor of Science in Elementary Education.

BSF 1 *also* **B.S.F.** Bachelor of Science in Forestry. 2 British Standard Fine (screw thread).

BSFC brake specific fuel consumption.

B.S.For. Bachelor of Science in Forestry.

B.S.F.S. Bachelor of Science in Foreign Service.

BSFW Bureau of Sport Fisheries and Wildlife.

BSG *or* **B.S.G.** British Standard Gauge.

b.s.g.d.g. patented without guarantee of the government. [French *breveté sans garantie du gouvernement*]

bsh. bushel.

B.S.H.E. *or* **B.S.H.Ec.** Bachelor of Science in Home Economics.

B.S.H.S. British Society for the History of Science.

BSI *or* **B.S.I.** 1 British Standards Institution (setting standards for industry, engineering, and science, used with a number): *BSI3700, for preparation of indexes.* 2 Building Societies' Institute.

BSIE *or* **B.S.I.E.** Bachelor of Science in Industrial Engineering.

BSJ *or* **B.S.J.** Bachelor of Science in Journalism.

BSJA British Show Jumping Association.

bskt. basket

BSL 1 *also* **B.S.L.** Bachelor of Sacred Literature. 2 *also* **B.S.L.** Bachelor of Science in Law. 3 *also* **B.S.L.** Bachelor of Science in Linguistics. 4 *also* **B.S.L.** Botanical Society of London. 5 Bulletin de la Société Linguistique (magazine title).

Bs/L bills of lading *commerce.*

BSLS *or* **B.S.L.S.** Bachelor of Science in Library Science.

BSM *or* **B.S.M.** Bachelor of Sacred Music.

BSME *or* **B.S.M.E.** 1 Bachelor of Science in Mechanical Engineering. 2 Bachelor of Science in Mining Engineering.

BSMT *or* **B.S.M.T.** Bachelor of Science in Medical Technology.

Bsmt *or* **bsmt** basement.

BSN *or* **B.S.N.** Bachelor of Science in Nursing.

BSO 1 blue stellar objects *astronomy.* 2 Boston Symphony Orchestra.

BSOAS Bulletin of the School of Oriental and African Studies (publication).

B.Soc.Sc. Bachelor of Social Science.

BSOT *or* **B.S.O.T.** Bachelor of Science in Occupational Therapy.

BSP 1 *also* **B.S.P.** Bachelor of Science in Pharmacy. 2 British Standard Pipe thread. 3 Bulgarian Socialist Party.

BSPA *or* **B.S.P.A.** Bachelor of Science in Public Administration.

BSPE *or* **B.S.P.E.** Bachelor of Science in Physical Education.

BSPH *or* **B.S.P.H.** Bachelor of Science in Public Health.

B.S.Phar. *or* **B.S.Pharm.** Bachelor of Science in Pharmacy.

BSPP Burma Socialist Programme Party.

BSPT *or* **B.S.P.T.** Bachelor of Science in Physical Therapy.

B.S.R.A. 1 British Ship Research Association. 2 British Society for Research on Ageing. 3 British Sound Recording Association.

B.S.S. 1 *also* BSS Bachelor of Social Science. 2 British Sailors' Society. 3 *also* BSS **a** British Standard Sizes. **b** British Standard Specification.

B.S.S.O. *or* **BSSO** British Society for the Study of Orthodontics.

B.S.S.S. *or* **BSSS** 1 Bachelor of Science in Secretarial Studies. 2 Bachelor of Science in Social Science.

BST 1 *also* **B.S.T.** Bachelor of Sacred Theology. 2 blood serological test. 3 bovine somatotrophin. 4 *also* **B.S.T. a** British Standard Time. **b** British Summer Time.

B/St *or* **b/st** bill of sight *commerce.*

BSTR booster *aeronautics, aerospace.*

BSW 1 *also* **B.S.W.** Bachelor of Social Work. 2 British Standard Whitworth (standard English screw thread).

BT 1 *also* **B.T.** Bachelor of Theology. 2 *also* **B.t.** Bacillus thuringiensis (microbial pesticide). 3 bathythermograph (device to measure oceanic water temperature). 4 body temperature *medicine.* 5 British Telecom (a telecommunications network of Great Britain).

Bt *or* **Bt.** Baronet.

bt. 1 beat. 2 bent. 3 boat. 4 bought.

BTA 1 best time available (for broadcasting a commercial) *advertising.* 2 *also* **B.T.A.** Board of Tax Appeals (of the Internal Revenue Service). 3 Boston Transportation Authority. 4 British Tourist Authority. 5 butylated hydroxyanisole (food preservative).

BTAM basic telecommunications access method.

°**BTDC** degrees before top dead center (spark advance) *engineering.*

B.T.E. *or* **BTE** Bachelor of Textile Engineering.

bté patent, patented. [French *breveté*]

B.Tech. Bachelor of Technology.

BTG British Technology Group (promoting application of research and development to industry).

BTH bathroom.

B.Th. Bachelor of Theology.

B.Th.U. *or* **B.th.u.** British thermal unit (used in Great Britain to distinguish abbreviation from *BTU* for Board of Trade Unit of electrical measure).

BTI *or* **B.T.I.** British Technology Index (publication).

BTL Bell Telephone Laboratories.

btl. bottle.

BTN *or* **B.T.N.** Brussels Tariff Nomenclature.

btn. 1 *also* **Btn.** battalion. 2 button.

BTO *or* **B.T.O.** British Trust for Ornithology.

B.T.R. British Tax Review (publication).

btr. *or* **BTR** better.

BTRY *or* **btry.** battery *military, music, technology.*

BTU *or* **B.T.U.** 1 Board of Trade Unit (commercial measure of electricity equivalent to one kilowatt hour). 2 *also* **Btu** *or* **B.t.u.** *or* **btu** *or* **b.t.u.** British thermal unit.

BTW by the way, in telecommunications.

btwn. between.

bty. 1 battery *electronics.* 2 *also* **Bty.** battery (artillery).

BU Boston University.

Bu 1 *also* **Bu.** Bureau, esp. in combination: *BuAer = Bureau of Aeronautics* (of the U.S. Navy). 2 butyl.

bu. 1 *also* **bu** blue. 2 bureau. 3 bushel.

buck. buckram.

Bucks. Buckinghamshire, England.

BUCOP *or* **B.U.C.O.P.** British Union Catalogue of Periodicals.

Budpst Budapest.

B.u.E. corrections and editions. [German *Berichtigungen und Ergänzungen*]

BUIC Back-Up Interceptor Control (computerized tracking system for directing missiles).

B.U.J. *or* **BUJ** Bachelor of Civil and Canon Law. [Latin *Baccalaureus Utriusque Juris* Bachelor of both Laws]

bul. bulletin.

Bulg. Bulgaria, Bulgarian.

bull. bulletin.

BUN blood, urea, nitrogen (indicator of protein catabolism).

BUNAC British Universities North America Club (student travel organization).

BUP *or* **B.U.P.** British United Press.

Bur. 1 Bureau, esp. in combination: *Bur. Stds. = National Bureau of Standards.* 2 Burma, Burmese (now Myanmar).

bur. buried.

Burg. 1 burgess. 2 burgomaster.

burl. burlesque.

Burs. bursar.

Bus. business, esp. in combination: *Bus. Agt. = business agent.*

bus. bushel.

Bus. Admin. Business Administration.

BUSE Boston University Studies in English (magazine title).

bush. 1 bushel. 2 bushing *mechanics, electricity.*

Bus. Mgr. Business Manager.

Busn Business.

but. 1 butter. 2 button.

Bute. Buteshire (county in Scotland).

BV 1 *also* **B.V.** Bible Version (in reference to Psalms, esp. in the Book of Common Prayer, that differ in wording from Psalms in the Bible). 2 *also* **B.V.** Blessed Virgin. 3 blood volume. 4 *also* **B/v** book value *commerce.* 5 *also* **B.V.** farewell. [Latin *bene vale*] 6 private company, of the Netherlands. [Dutch *Besloten Vennootschap*] 7 *also* **B.V.** Your Holiness. [Latin *Beatitude Vestra*]

b.v. 1 *also* **bv** balanced voltage. 2 book value *commerce.* 3 for example. [Dutch *bij voorbeeld*]

B.V.A. 1 *also* BVA British Veterinary Association. **2** Bureau of Veterans Affairs.

BVD 1 bovine diarrhea virus (used to protect pigs from hog cholera). **2** *also* **B.V.D.** Bradley, Vorhees, and Day (clothing manufacturer, esp. formerly of underwear for men and boys).

B.V.I. British Virgin Islands.

B.V.M. 1 *also* BVM Bachelor of Veterinary Medicine. **2** Blessed Virgin Mary.

B.V.S. *or* BVS *or* **B.V.Sc.** Bachelor of Veterinary Science.

bvt. brevet, brevetted.

BW 1 biological or bacteriological warfare. **2** *also* **B/W** black and white. **3** *also* **B.W.** Black Watch. **4** body weight *medicine*. **5** bonded warehouse.

b.w. turn page; PTO. [German *bitte wenden*]

BWA *or* **bwa** backward wave amplifier.

B'way Broadway (theater district in New York City).

BWB British Waterways Board.

BWC Biological and Toxic Weapons Convention.

B.W.D. bacillary white diarrhea or Salmonellosis (infectious disease of fowl, caused by salmonella).

bwd. backward.

BWG Birmingham Wire Gage (for steel tubing, plates, hoops).

BWI 1 boating while intoxicated. **2** *also* **B.W.I.** British West Indies.

bwk. 1 brickwork. **2** bulwark, esp. on navigation charts.

BWO *or* **bwo** backward wave oscillator.

BWR boiling water reactor (nuclear reactor, formerly used esp. to generate electricity).

B.W.S. *or* BWS British Watercolour Society.

B.W.T.A. British Women's Temperance Association.

BWV index of J. S. Bach's works (used with a number). [German *Bach Werke-Verzeichnis*]

BX 1 base exchange (general store on a U.S. Air Force base). **2** flexible armored electrical cable.

Bx. 1 Beatrix (used esp. in cataloging and indexing). **2** biopsy. **3** *also* **Bx** Bronx.

bx. box.

bxd. boxed.

bxs. boxes.

b.y. billion years: *The Cobalt Beds of Canada are thought to be 2.2 b.y. old.*

Bye. Byelorussia (now *Belarus*).

BYOB bring your own booze or bottle.

byp. *or* **BYP** bypass *computers*.

Byz. 1 Byzantine. **2** Byzantium.

BZ 1 Belousov-Zhabotinsky (of a chemical reaction possibly affecting the biological clock in humans and other animals). **2** code name for a nerve gas that incapacitates without killing.

Bz 1 benzene. **2** benzoyl.

bzgl. referring to. [German *bezüglich*]

bzw. respectively. [German *beziehungsweise*]

C

C *I an abbreviation for:* **1** calculated *or* calculation, *esp. in astronomy.* **2** *also* **C.** can (navigational buoy). **3** candle *physics.* **4** *also* **C-** canoe, in combination: *C-2.* **5** *also* **C.** capacitance. **6** capacitor. **7** *also* **C.** Cape, esp. in combination: *C. Verde Is. = Cape Verde Islands.* **8 a** cargo. **b** *also* **C-** cargo aircraft, in combination: *C-59, C-164.* **9** cathode. **10** *also* **C.** *or* °**C** Celsius scale; centigrade: *100°C* **11** *also* **C.** center, esp. in combination: *TDC = top dead center.* **12** centimeter. **13** Central, esp. in combination: *CAR = Central African Republic.* **14** *also* **C.** century. **15** *also* **C.** cervical spinal nerve. **16 a** *also* **C.** chair, chairman, chairperson. **b** *also* **C.** Chief, in combination: *C.J. = Chief Justice.* **17** chapter, *esp. in law.* [Latin *caput*] **18** Church, esp. in combination: *RCC = Roman Catholic Church.* **19** City, in combination: *NYC = New York City.* **20** class. **21** cold (esp. cold water). **22** color (of a telecast, esp. in a newspaper listing). **23** Commander, in combination: *C-in-C = Commander-in-Chief.* **24** common, as in common time or common meter *music.* **25** Congress, in combination: *CORE = Congress on Racial Equality.* **26** Conservative. **27** contralto. **28** corolla (the petals of a flower). **29 a** correct (esp. in marking school papers). **b** correction (esp. signifying a correction factor). **30** coulomb (measure of electricity). **31** *also* **C.** Court, in combination: *C.Cls. = Court of Claims.* **32** Cyprus, in combination: *£C = Cyprus pound.* **33** cytosine (one of four bases in RNA-DNA code). **34** gallon *pharmaceutics.*[Latin *congius*]

II a symbol for: **1 a** capacity (esp. heat capacity). **b** capacity (electrical capacity). **2** carbon (chemical element). **3 a** charge (electrical charge) *physics.* **b** charge conjugation (interchange of signs of all electrical charges, one of the three operations of symmetry) *physics.* **4** circumference: $C = \pi d$ means circumference equals pi times diameter. **5** coefficient. **6** *also* <u>C</u> concentration, such as concentration by volume of a solution. **7** conductance of heat or electricity. **8** constant (esp. in mathematical formulas of physics and chemistry). **9** first tone in the scale of C major. **10** hundred; 100 (Roman numeral). [Latin *centum*] **11** molecular heat. **12** ninth rating after CC or Ca *finance.* **13** Philadelphia (branch in the Federal Reserve regional banking system, found esp. on dollar bills). **14** quantity, esp. a known quantity (in algebraic equations). **15** shoe width greater than B and less than D. **16 a** third best of a kind, average. **b** third highest grade in school, usually considered the average grade and of no distinction. **17** third of a series. **18** a programming language for small computers and its later version *C++*. **19** viruses of a group that produce tumors and cause leukemia and other cancers in animals: *C-type virus.*

© Copyright: *Copyright © 1939, Copyright © 1955.*

¹²C carbon¹²

¹⁴C or **C₁₄** carbon¹⁴ (radioactive isotope of carbon absorbed by most living things. The time absorption ceases is determined by amount of decayed isotope present which is used to calculate age of fossil remains).

c *I an abbreviation for:* **1** *also* **c.** about, approximately: *c1500.* [Latin *circa*] **2** call (stock or commodity to buy). **3** *also* **c.** calm *meteorology.* **4** calorie. **5** *also* **c.** candle *physics.* **6** *also* **c.** canine tooth, cuspid. **7** *also* **c.** carat (unit of weight). **8** *also* **c. a** carton. **b** case. **9** *also* **c. a** catcher *baseball.* **b** caught *cricket.* **10** *also* **c.a** cent (coin of the United States and Canada). **b** centavo (coin of Brazil, Mexico, Philippines, Portugal, etc.). **c** centime (coin of France, Switzerland, Haiti, etc.). **11** *also* **c.** center, esp. in combination: *t.d.c. = top dead center, esp. in engineering.* **12** centi- (hundredth or 10^{-2}). **13** centimeter. **14** *also* **c.** chapter, *esp. in law.* [Latin *caput*] **15 a** cirrus (cloud) *meteorology.* **b** cloudy *meteorology.* **16** *also* **c.** cognate with *linguistics.* **17** cold (esp. cold water). **18** *also* **c.** column *bibliography.* **19** conductor *physics.* **20** continental air mass *meteorology.* **21** contralto. **22** *also* **c.** copy. **23** copyright (often as superscript): *ᶜ1962.* **24** *also* **c.** cup, in cooking. **25** *also* **c.** curie (unit of radioactivity). **26** cycle, esp. in combination: *cps = cycles per second.* **27 a** *also* **c.** gallon *pharmaceutics.* [Latin *congius*] **b** with *pharmaceutics.* [Latin *cum*]
II a symbol for: **1** coefficient. **2** concentration (esp. as subscript such as for concentration by volume of a solution) *chemistry.* **3** diminished nucleus with open spiral arms (of nebula in combination with S or SB) *astronomy.* **4** specific heat capacity *physics.* **5** *also* **c** speed of light: $E = mc^2$ *means energy equals mass times the speed of light squared.*

¢ **1** cedi (monetary unit of Ghana). **2** cents. **3** *also* **₡** colón (monetary unit of El Salvador and Costa Rica). **4** *also* **₡** cordoba (monetary unit of Nicaragua).

CA 1 California (Zip Code). **2** *also* **C.A.** Catholic Action. **3** *also* **C.A.** Central America. **4** *also* **C.A.** Chartered Accountant (in Scotland). **5** Chemical Abstracts (professional journal). **6** *also* **C.A.** chief accountant. **7** chronological age *psychology.* **8** *also* **C.A.** claim agent. **9** Coast Artillery. **10** *also* **C.A.** commercial agent. **11** *also* **C.A. a** Consular Affairs (section of U.S. Department of State). **b** Consular Agent. **12** *also* **C.A.** controller of accounts. **13** *also* **C.A.** County Alderman. **14** *also* **C.A.** Court of Appeals. **15** croup associated viruses. **16** *also* **C.A.** Crown Agent (criminal prosecutor, in Scotland, or a colonial agent, in England).

C/A 1 capital account. **2** course of action. **3** credit account. **4** current account.

Ca *I an abbreviation for:* **1** *also* **Ca. a** California. **b** Canada, Canadian. **2** cancer. **3** *also* **Cᵃ** company. [Portuguese *Companhia,* Spanish *Compañia*]
II a symbol for: **1** calcium (chemical element). **2** eighth rating, after Caa *finance.*

cA continental air mass having antarctic air within it.

ca 1 *also* **ca.** about, approximately: *ca1770.* [Latin *circa*] **2** *also* **c.a.** alternating current. [French *courant alternatif,*

Spanish *corriente alterna*] **3** cable *electronics.* **4** case *commerce, law.* **5** *also* **ca.** cathode. **6** *also* **ca.** centiare (one square meter). **7** *also* **c.a.** with the bow *music.* [Italian *coll'arco*]

CAA 1 Canadian Authors' Association. **2 a** Civil Aeronautics Administration (of the United States). **b** Civil Aviation Authority (of Great Britain). **3** Community Action Agency.

Caa *a symbol for:* seventh rating, after B *finance.*

CAAA Canadian Association of Advertising Agencies.

CAAE Canadian Association for Adult Education.

CAB 1 *also* **C.A.B.** Canadian Association of Broadcasters. **2** captured air bubble (of an air-cushion vehicle). **3** cellulose acetate butyrate (substance to give a smooth, hard finish to metals). **4** chemical-atomic-biological (referring to agents used in warfare). **5** *also* **C.A.B.** Citizens' Advice Bureau (a British social services agency). **6** Civil Aeronautics Board. **7** *also* **C.A.B.** Contract Appeals Board (of U.S. Department of Transportation).

cab. 1 cabin. **2** cabinet. **3** cable.

CABEI or **Cabei** Central American Bank for Economic Integration; BCIE.

C.A.B.M. or **CABM** Commonwealth of Australia Bureau of Meteorology.

cabt. or **cabnt.** cabinet.

CAC 1 Central Arbitration Committee (an arbitration body for labor disputes in Great Britain). **2** *also* **C.A.C.** Chemical Addiction Certification (for the treatment of drug addiction). **3 a** Consumer Advisory Council. **b** Consumers Association of Canada. **4** Continental Air Command (of the U.S. Air Force Reserve). **5** Corrective Action Commission or Committee. **6** County Agricultural Committee.

CACM 1 Central American Common Market (trade association of Costa Rica, El Salvador, Guatemala, Honduras, and Nicaragua). **2** Communications of the Association for Computing Machinery.

CACUL Canadian Association of College and University Libraries.

CAD 1 cash against documents *commerce.* **2** computer-aided or -assisted design. **3** coronary artery disease.

Cad. 1 Cadet. **2** cadmium (chemical element; symbol *Cd*).

C.-à-d. or **c-à-d** that is to say. [French *c'est-à-dire*]

cad. 1 cadenza *music.* **2** cadet.

CADAM computer-aided design and manufacturing.

CADC central air data computer.

CAD-CAM computer-aided design and computer-aided manufacturing.

CADD computer-aided design and drafting.

CAE 1 common applications environment (programs to develop computer application). **2** computer-aided engineering

Cae the Chisel (constellation). [Latin *Caelum*]

Caern. Caernarvonshire, Wales.

CAES compressed air energy storage (for generating electricity).

Caes. Caesar.

CAF 1 *also* **C.A.F.** Canadian Armed Forces (unified Army, Navy, and Air Force since 1968). **2** clerical, administrative, and fiscal *accounting*. **3** consider all factors. **4** *also* **c.a.f.** **a** cost and freight. **b** cost, assurance, and freight.

caf cafeteria.

CAFE cooperative average fuel economy (automotive fuel consumption standard).

CAG 1 Composers and Authors Guild. **2** Concert Artists Guild.

C.A.G.S. *or* **CAGS** Certificate of Advanced Graduate Study.

CAH 1 chronic active hepatitis. **2** congenital adrenal hyperplasia (often leading to malformation of genitalia).

CAHA Canadian Amateur Hockey Association.

CAI 1 *also* **C.A.I.** Canadian Aeronautical Institute. **2** computer-assisted instruction. **3** Italian Alpine Club. [Italian *Club Alpino Italiano*]

Caith. Caithness County, Scotland.

cAK Arctic or Antarctic continental cold air mass.

CAL 1 Center for Applied Linguistics. **2** computer-assisted learning. **3** Cornell Aeronautical Laboratory.

Cal. 1 Calcutta, India. **2** calendered paper (glossy paper). **3** California. **4** large calorie *physics, medicine*.

cal. 1 calendar. **2** caliber. **3** diminish in tone and tempo *music*. [Italian *calando*] **4** small calorie *physics, medicine*.

calc. calculate.

calcd. calculated.

calef. warmed *pharmaceutics*. [Latin *calefactus*]

Calg. Calgary, Canada.

calibr. 1 calibrate. **2** calibration.

Calif. California.

caln. calculation.

CALPA (kal′pə) Canadian Air Line Pilots Association.

CALS computer-assisted acquisition and logistic support.

Caltech (kal′tek′) *or* **Cal. Tech.** California Institute of Technology.

CAM 1 cellular-automata (or automation) machine (computer circuitry designed to simulate physical processes). **2** chorioallantoic membrane (of chicken eggs, used for testing chemical substances in place of live-animal tests). **3** *also* **C.A.M.** commercial air movement. **4** computer-aided manufacture. **5** content-addressable memory *computers*. **6** crassulacean acid metabolism (modification of photosynthesis).

Cam 1 *also* **Cam.** Cambridge. **2** the Giraffe (constellation). [Latin *Camelopardalis*]

cam. camouflage.

Camb. Cambridge.

Cambs Cambridgeshire, England.

CAMC Canadian Army Medical Corps.

Camd. Soc. Camden Society (English historical society).

CAMO computer-aided manual operation.

CAMP computer-assisted menu planning.

Camp. Campeche (state in Mexico).

cAMP cyclic adenosine monophosphate (regulator in cellular and enzymatic processes).

CaMV cauliflower mosaic virus.

Can. 1 *also* **CAN** Canada, Canadian: *CAN$* = *Canadian dollar*. **2** canal. **3** Canberra, Australia. **4** Canon (a religious). **5** Canto.

can. 1 canal. **2** *also* **CAN** cancel, canceled, cancellation. **3** cannon. **4** canon *music*. **5** canto.

Canad. Canadian.

Canc. Chancellor. [Latin *cancellarius*]

canc. canceled, cancellation.

c & b caught and bowled *cricket*.

C & D *or* **c & d** collection and delivery *commerce*.

C & F *or* **c & f** cost and freight *commerce*.

C & GS 1 Coast and Geodetic Survey. **2** Command and General Staff, esp. in combination: *C&GSC* = *Command and General Staff College*.

C & I *or* **c & i** cost and insurance *commerce*.

C & J clean and jerk, in weight lifting.

c & lc capitals and lower case (typesetting instruction).

c & p 1 carriage and packing *commerce*. **2** collated and perfect *bookbinding*.

c & sc capitals and small capitals (typesetting instruction).

CANDU *or* **Candu** (kan dü′) Canadian deuterium uranium (atomic reactor and electrical generating station).

C&W country and western *music*.

Can.F. *or* **Can.Fr.** Canadian French.

Can.I. Canary Islands.

Can. pat. Canadian patent.

Cant. 1 Canterbury. **2** Canticles. **3** *also* **cant.** Canto. **4** Canton, Cantonese.

Cantab. of Cambridge (University). [Latin *Cantabrigiensis*]

cantab. in a smooth or flowing manner *music*. [Italian *cantabile*]

CANTAT transatlantic cable to Britain from Canada.

Cantaur. of Canterbury (in reference to the Archbishop and therefore used as a signature). [Latin *Cantuariensis*]

CANUKUS Canada, United Kingdom, and United States.

canv *or* **canv.** canvas.

CAO 1 Chief Accounting Officer. **2** *also* **C.A.O.** Chief Administrative Officer. **3** *British* County Agricultural Officer. **4** *also* **C.A.O.** Crimean Astrophysical Observatory.

CaOC. cathodal opening contracture *medicine*.

CAORG Canadian Army Operational Research Group.

CAP 1 Canada Assistance Plan (benefit system for Canadian citizens). **2** catabolite activator protein (regulates chromosome transmission) *genetics*. **3** *also* **C.A.P.** Certificate of Professional Ability (French vocational or technical degree). [French *Certificat d'Aptitude Professionnelle*] **4 a** *also* **C.A.P.** Civil Air Patrol (civilian auxiliary of the U.S. Air Force). **b** Combat Air Patrol. **5** *also* **C.A.P.** College of American Pathologists. **6** Common Agricultural Policy (to stabilize markets within the European Economic Community). **7** computer-aided production.

Cap 1 *also* **Cap.** capital. **2 a** capitalize (proofreader's correction). **b** capital letter. **3** Capricorn, the Goat (constellation). **4** *also* **Cap.** Captain. **5** *also* **Cap.** chapter. [Latin *capitulum, caput*, Spanish *capitulo*]

cap 1 capacitance. 2 capacitor. 3 *also* **cap.** capacity. 4 *also* **cap.** **a** capitalize (proofreader's correction). **b** capital letter. 5 *also* **cap.** capsule *pharmaceutics.* 6 caption (for an illustration). 7 *also* **cap.** chapter. [Latin *capitulum, caput,* Spanish *capitulo*] 8 foolscap (paper 15 to 17 inches long and 12 to 13 1/2 inches wide) *printing.* 9 *also* **c.a.p.** Italian postal code. [Italian *codice di avviamento postale*] 10 *also* **cap.** let the patient take *pharmaceutics.* [Latin *capiat*]

CAPAC *or* **C.A.P.A.C.** Composers, Authors, and Publishers Association of Canada.

CAPCOM (kap'kom') capsule communicator (NASA communications center for manned space exploration).

CAPD continuous ambulatory peritoneal dialysis *medicine.*

capel. chapel. [Latin *capella*]

CAPO Canadian Army Post Office.

Caprice Capricorn (constellation).

caps *or* **Caps** 1 capitalize (proofreader's correction). 2 capital letters.

caps. capsule.

caps and lc capitals and lower case (typesetting instruction).

caps and sc capitals and small capitals (typesetting instruction).

Capt. *or* **Captn.** Captain.

CAR 1 Canadian Association of Radiologists. 2 *also* **C.A.R.** Central African Republic. 3 Civil Air Regulations. 4 *also* **C.A.R.** Commonwealth Arbitration Reports (of Australia). 5 computer-assisted retrieval. 6 conditioned avoidance response *psychology.*

Car 1 *also* **Car.** Carlow (county in Republic of Ireland). 2 *also* **Car.** Charles. [Latin *Carolus*] 3 the Keel (of the ship Argo, an old and very large constellation). [Latin *Carina*]

car. 1 carat (unit of weight of precious stones or measure of purity of gold). 2 cargo.

carb. 1 carbon. 2 carburetor.

carbo. carbohydrates, *esp. in medicine.*

Card. 1 Cardiganshire, Wales. 2 Cardinal.

CARDE Canadian Armament Research and Development Establishment.

CARE 1 continuous aircraft reliability evaluation. 2 Cooperative for American Relief Everywhere, Inc.

Carib. Caribbean.

CARICOM *or* **Caricom** (kär'ə kom', kär'-) Caribbean Common Market or Caribbean Community (an association of Caribbean countries replacing the Caribbean Free Trade Association).

CARIFTA Caribbean Free Trade Association (an association of Caribbean countries replaced by *CARICOM*).

Carliol. of Carlisle (in reference to the Bishop and therefore used as a signature). [Latin *Carliolensis*]

Carm. Carmarthenshire, Wales.

Carp. Carpathian Mountains.

carp. 1 carpentry, carpenter. 2 carpeting.

CARR carrier *computers.*

carr. 1 carriage. 2 carrier *commerce.*

CART Championship Auto Racing Team.

cart. cartage *commerce.*

Cartog. cartographer, cartography.

CAS 1 calibrated air speed. 2 *also* **C.A.S.** Certificate of Advanced Study. 3 Chemical Abstract Service. 4 Chief of the Air Staff (of the Royal Australian Air Force). 5 Children's Aid Society. 6 collision-avoidance system (for commercial aircraft). 7 Fellow of the Connecticut Academy of Arts and Sciences. [Latin *Connecticutensis Academiae Socius*]

Cas 1 Cassiopeia (constellation). 2 *also* **Cas.** castle.

cas. 1 casing. 2 casualty.

CASA *or* **C.A.S.A.** Contemporary Art Society of Australia.

Ca. Sa. *or* **ca. sa.** writ of execution, directing a sheriff to hold a person for appearance in court to satisfy debt or damages.

CASC 1 California Association of Student Councils. 2 Canadian Automoile Sports Club. 3 Council for the Advancement of Small Colleges (association of four-year, private colleges).

CASE 1 Committee on Academic Science and Engineering. 2 computer-aided software engineering.

cash. cashier.

cass *or* **Cass** cassette.

Cast. Castile.

CASW Council for the Advancement of Science Writing.

CAT 1 *also* **C.A.T.** California Achievement Test. 2 Children's Apperception Test. 3 Civil Air Transport (a paramilitary air force). 4 clear air turbulence. 5 **a** College Ability Test. **b** College Achievement Test. 6 *British* College of Advanced Technology. 7 community antenna television; CATV. 8 computer-assisted teaching; CAT. 9 computer-assisted testing *engineering.* 10 computer-assisted training. 11 computer-assisted typesetting. 12 (*pronounced* kat) computerized axial tomography: CAT scan, CAT scanner. 13 Conventional Arms Transfer. 14 *also* **C.A.T.** Technical Assistance Committee of the United Nations. [French *Comité de l'Assistance Technique*]

Cat. Catalan (esp. referring to a dialect spoken in Catalonia).

cat. 1 catalog. 2 *also* **cat** catalysis. 3 cataplasm (a hot poultice). 4 catapult. 5 cataract *medicine.* 6 catechism. 7 category.

Catal. Catalan (esp. referring to a dialect spoken in Catalonia).

Cath. 1 Cathedral. 2 **a** Catherine. **b** St. Catherine's College (of Oxford University). 3 Catholic.

cath. 1 cathartic. 2 **a** catheter. **b** catheterize. 3 cathode.

CATOR Comprehensive Assessment of Treatment Outcome Research (a research organization assessing drug treatment programs).

CATV 1 cable television. 2 community antenna television (system of television reception using a common antenna).

Cauc. Caucasian (esp. referring to any of the languages of the Caucasus region).

caus. causative *grammar.*

CAV 1 constant angular velocity (method of tagging information in computer storage). 2 *also* **C.A.V.** the court desires to consider *law.* [Latin *curia advisari vult*]

Cav. 1 Cavalier (esp. as a title of honor). 2 *also* **Cav** (kav) Cavalry: *the 1st U.S. Air Cav.*

cav. 1 caveat (notice restraining a legal authority until the person asking restraint can be heard). **2** cavity.

CAVD a scale used to measure intelligence. It is based on four tests: completion, arithmetic, vocabulary, and direction following. [the initial letter of each kind of test used to make the abbreviation]

CAVU ceiling and visibility unlimited *aviation.*

CAW computer-assisted writing.

cAw Arctic or Antarctic, continental warm air mass.

CB 1 *also* **C.B.** Bachelor of Surgery. [Latin *Chirurgiae Baccalaureus*] **2** *also* **C.B.** Cape Breton Island, Nova Scotia. **3** cashbook *accounting.* **4** cast in brass *foundry.* **5** catch basin, in blueprints and other drawings. **6** Cavalry Brigade. **7** cement base, in blueprints and other drawings. **8** Census Bureau. **9** center back *sports.* **10** center of buoyancy (of a boat or ship), in blueprints or other drawings. **11** chemical and biological: *CB weapons.* **12** Chief Baron (of the Court of Exchequer in Great Britain). **13** Citizens Band (radio frequency). **14** *also* **C.B.** *British* Common Bench *law.* **15** *also* **C.B.** Companion of the Order of the Bath. **16** compass bearing. **17** Confidential Book (in the British Navy). **18** confined to barracks *military.* **19** Construction Battalion *military, esp. U.S. Navy* (when pronounced it is written *Seabee*). **20** *also* **C.B. a** contrabass *music.* **b** with the bass *music.* [Italian *col basso*] **21** *also* **C.B.** county borough, esp. in combination: *CBC = County Borough Council.* **22** *also* **C.B.** Cumulative Bulletin (of the Internal Revenue Service, followed by a number): *CB518.* **23** currency bond.

C/B 1 cashbook *accounting.* **2** circuit breaker. **3** cost benefit *finance.*

Cb 1 columbium (chemical element, now *niobium*). **2** cumulonimbus (cloud).

cb 1 center back *sports.* **2** center of buoyancy (of a boat or ship). **3** centibar *meteorology.* **4** *also* **c.b.** *or* **c/b** circuit breaker. **5** *also* **c.b.** common brick *construction.*

CBA 1 *also* **C.B.A.** Canadian Bankers Association. **2** *also* **C.B.A.** Canadian Bar Association. **3** *also* **C.B.A.** Canadian Booksellers Association. **4** Chinese Bridge Association (of card players). **5** Christian Broadcasting Association.

CBAT Central Bureau for Astronomical Telegrams (clearinghouse for citings of celestial phenomena).

CBC 1 Canadian Broadcasting Corporation. **2** *also* **C.B.C.** Children's Book Council. **3** complete blood count.

CBCC Chemical-Biological Coordination Center.

C.B.C.S. *or* **CBCS** Commonwealth Bureau of Census and Statistics (of Australia).

CBD 1 *also* **C.B.D.** *or* **cbd** cash before delivery. **2** *also* **C.B.D.** central business district. **3** common bile duct *medicine.*

CBE 1 *also* **C.B.E.** Commander of the Order of the British Empire. **2** competency-based education (educational program based on certain skills or objectives). **3** Council for Basic Education.

C.B.E.L. *or* **CBEL** Cambridge Bibliography of English Literature.

CBF cerebral blood flow.

CBI 1 Cape Breton Island, Nova Scotia. **2** Caribbean Basis Initiative (trade agreement). **3** Central Bureau of Identifica-

tion. **4** *also* **C.B.I.** China, Burma, India (combat theater in World War II). **5** *also* **c.b.i.** complete background investigation. **6** computer-based instruction. **7** Confederation of British Industry. **8** Cumulative Book Index (publication).

CBJO Coordinating Board of Jewish Organizations.

CBL 1 *also* **cbl.** cable. **2** *also* **c.bl.** carte blanche. **3** *also* **CB/L** *or* **cb/l** commercial bill of lading. **4** computer-based learning.

CBM 1 cognitive behavioral modification *psychology.* **2** *also* **cbm** constant boiling mixture. **3** *also* **cbm** cubic meter.

CBMS Conference Board of Mathematical Sciences.

CBN 1 *also* **cbn** carbine (in the U.S. Army). **2** Christian Broadcasting Network.

CBO 1 confirmation of broadcast order *advertising.* **2** Congressional Budget Office (agency of the U.S. Congress that advises on the nation's economy, federal budget, and federal programs).

CBOE Chicago Board Options Exchange.

CBOT Chicago Board of Trade.

CBPC *or* **C.B.P.C.** Canadian Book Publishers Council.

CBR 1 Center for Brain Research. **2** chemical, biological, radiological: *CBR warfare.* **3** cost-benefit ratio.

CBRT Canadian Brotherhood of Railway, Transport, and General Workers Union.

CBS 1 *also* **C.B.S.** Canadian Biochemical Society. **2** Center for Bibliographical Services (of the MLA, compiling an annual bibliography of articles or studies in language and literature). **3** chronic brain syndrome *medicine.* **4** Columbia Broadcasting System. **5** *also* **C.B.S.** Confraternity of the Blessed Sacrament (in the Roman Catholic Church).

CBSO City of Birmingham Symphony Orchestra.

CBT 1 Chicago Board of Trade, also *CBOT.* **2** computer-based training.

CBU cluster bomb unit.

CBW chemical and biological warfare.

CC *I an abbreviation for:* **1** Caribbean Community, also known as *CARICOM.* **2** *also* **C.C.** cash credit (credit given a depositor for overdraft of a bank account). **3** cashier's check. **4** cast copper. **5** Challenge Certificate (best of sex of a breed), in dog shows. **6** *also* **C.C.** Chamber of Commerce, also in combination: *ACC = American Chamber of Commerce.* **7** *also* **C.C.** Chief Clerk. **8** *also* **C.C.** Chief Commissioner. **9** Chief Counsel. **10** *also* **C.C.** U.S. Circuit Court. **11** *also* **C.C. a** City Council. **b** City Councilor. **12** *also* **C.C.** civil cases *law.* **13** *also* **C.C.** civil code *law.* **14** civil commotion (used to specify exclusions in an insurance policy). **15** *also* **C.C.** Civil Court. **16** closed caption (caption on a television screen visible through a decoding device for use by people who are deaf or hard of hearing). **17** coefficient of correlation (measure of the relationship between two variables) *statistics.* **18 a** color code, *esp. in electronics.* **b** color correction: *CC filter.* **19** Command Center *military.* **20** common carrier. **21** *also* **C.C. a** Common Council. **b** Common Councilman. **22** *also* **C.C.** Community College, in combination: *WCC = Westchester Community College.* **23** *also* **C.C.** Companion of the Order of Canada. **24** Company Commander *military.* **25** confined to camp *military.* **26** *also* **C.C.** Consular Clerk. **27** continuation clause, in an insurance policy. **28** counterclockwise. **29** *also* **C.C.** County

Clerk. **30** County Commissioner. **31** *also* **C.C. a** County Council, esp. in combination: *L.C.C.= London County Council.* **b** County Councilor. **32** *also* **C.C.** County Court. **33** credit card or cards. **34** *also* **C.C.** criminal cases. **35** *also* **C.C.** Crown Clerk. **36** cubic centimeter or centimeters. **37** *also* **C.C.** direct current. [French *courant continu*, Italian *corrènte continua*, Spanish *corriente continua*]
II a symbol for: **1** eighth rating, after CCC *finance.* **2** two hundred; 200 (Roman numeral).

C/C 1 account current. [French *compte courant*, Italian *conto corrènte*] **2** change of course (notation in ship or aircraft log).

Cc cirrocumulus (cloud).

cc 1 *also* **cc.** centuries. **2** *also* **cc.** chapters, *esp. in law.* [Latin *capita*] **3** compass course. **4** *also* **cc.** copies. **5** *also* **cc.** or **c.c.** cubic centimeter or centimeters. **6** *also* **c.c.** cubic contents. **7** *also* **c.c.** current account. [French *compte courant*] **8** direct current. [French *courant continu*, Italian *corrènte continua*, Spanish *corriente continua*]

CCA 1 chicken cell agglutination (factor used in vaccine). **2** *also* **C.C.A.** Chief Clerk of the Admiralty. **3** *also* **C.C.A.** U.S. Circuit Court of Appeals. **4** Consumers Cooperative Association. **5** controlled circulation audit (of a publication). **6** *also* **C.C.A.** County Court of Appeals. **7** current cost accounting.

CCAA Citizens' Civic Action Association (of Canada).

C.C.B. Civil Cooperation Bureau (South African Defense Forces, undercover organization).

CCC *I an abbreviation for:* **1** Canadian Chamber of Commerce. **2** Central Computer Complex. **3** *also* **C.C.C** Central Criminal Court (Old Bailey in London). **4** *also* **C.C.C.** Certificate of Clinical Competence (in speech). **5** Civilian Conservation Corps (construction and reforestation corps to employ young men from 1933–1942). **6** Commodity Credit Corporation. **7** Corpus Christi College, Oxford and Cambridge universities. **8** Council for Cultural Cooperation (of the European Economic Community). **9** Customs Cooperation Council. **10** cycocel (gene altering chemical). **11** one hundred call seconds (telecommunications unit of measuring use).
II a symbol for: **1** seventh rating, after B *finance.* **2** three hundred; 300 (Roman numeral).

CCCC *I an abbreviation for:* Conference on College Composition and Communication (of the National Council of Teachers of English).
II a symbol for: four hundred; 400 (Roman numeral).

CCCO Coordinating Council of Community Organizations.

CCCP (formerly) Union of Soviet Socialist Republics. [Russian *Soyuz Sovetskikh Sotsialisticheskikh Respublik*]

CCD 1 carbonate or calcite compensation depth (ocean level where calcium carbonate dissolves rapidly). **2** charge-coupled device (light-sensitive mechanism to convert light into electronic signals for storage on an electronic disk, as in a computer or camera): *CCD camera.* **3** countercurrent distribution (separation of different substances by solubility, as in the manufacture of drugs and synthetic hormones) *chemistry.*

CCDM Consultation Committee for the Definition of the Metre (of the International Standards Organization).

CCDS Consultative Committee for the Definition of the Second (of the International Standards Organization).

CCE 1 Consultative Committee for Electricity (of the International Standards Organization). **2** *also* **C.C.E.** Council of European Municipalities. [French *Conseil des Communes d'Europe*] **3** Council on Chiropractic Education.

CCEA Cabinet Council on Economic Affairs.

CCEI *or* **ccei** composite cost-effectiveness index.

CCEMRI Consultative Committee for the Standards of Measurement of Ionizing Radiations (of the International Standards Organization). [French *Comité Consultatif pour les Standards des Mesurement Radiations Ionizant*]

CCF 1 *also* **ccf** congestive cardiac failure. **2** Cooperative Commonwealth Federation of Canada (now incorporated in the *NDP*).

C.C.G. (formerly) Allied Control Commission Germany.

CCH 1 Commerce Clearing House (publisher of business and tax information). **2** cubic capacity of holds, in shipping.

CCI 1 chronic coronary insufficiency *medicine.* **2** *also* **C.C.I.** International Chamber of Commerce. [French *Chambre de Commerce International*]

CCIA Commission of the Churches on International Affairs (of the World Council of Churches).

CCIF International Telephone Consultative Committee. [French *Comité Consultatif International Fernsprecht*]

CCIR International Radio Communication Consultative Committee. [French *Comité Consultatif International des Radiocommunications*]

CCITT International Telegraph and Telephone Consultative Committee. [French *Comité Consultatif International Telegraphique et Telephonique*]

CCJ *or* **C.C.J.** Circuit or County Court Judge.

CCK cholecystokinin (hormone of the small intestine that helps regulate food consumption).

cckw. counterclockwise.

C.Cls. Court of Claims, also in combination: *C.Cls.R. = Court of Claims Reports.*

CCM Chawa Cha Mapinduzi (ruling political party of Tanzania).

ccm 1 centimeters. **2** *also* **c.cm.** cubic centimeters.

CCN contract change notice or notification.

CCNY *or* **C.C.N.Y.** City College of New York (division of CUNY).

C.C.O. *or* **CCO** Comprehensive Certificate of Origin (of goods imported into the United States).

CCP 1 Certificate in Computer Programming. **2** Chinese Communist Party. **3** *also* **C.C.P. a** Code of Civil Procedure. **b** Code of Criminal Procedure. **4** *also* **C.C.P.** Court of Common Pleas. **5** *also* **ccp** credit card purchase or purchases. **6** cubic close packed or packing (of molecular structure) *chemistry.* **7** Postal Checking Account. [French *Compte Chèques Postaux*]

C.C.P.A. Court of Customs and Patent Appeals.

CCPD continuous cycling peritoneal dialysis *medicine.*

C.C.P.E. *or* **CCPE** Canadian Council of Professional Engineers.

CCPR Consultative Commitee for Photometry and Radiometry (of the International Standards Organization).

CCR 1 cassette camera recorder (a camcorder). **2** Commission on Civil Rights.

CCRS Capital Cost Recovery System.

CCS 1 Canadian Cancer Society. **2** Casualty Clearing Station. **3** collective call sign. **4** Combined Chiefs of Staff. **5** common channel signaling *communications.*

CCST Center for Computer Sciences and Technology.

CCT Consultative Committee for Thermometry (of the International Standards Organization).

CCTA Central Computing and Telecommunications Agency (of Great Britain).

CCTV closed-circuit television.

CCU 1 camera control unit (for selecting TV camera signal to be broadcast). **2** Cardiac or Coronary Care Unit (of a hospital). **3** Consultative Committee for Units (of the International Standards Organization).

CC.VV. illustrious men. [Latin *clarissimi viri*]

CCW or **ccw.** counterclockwise.

CD 1 *also* **C.D.** Canadian Forces Decoration. **2** *also* **C.D.** certificate of deposit. **3** Civil Defense. **4** Civil Division (of U.S. Department of Justice). **5** cluster of differentiation (of leucocytes) or cluster designation *immunology.* **6** coastal defense, esp. coastal defense radar. **7** compact disk, also in combination: *CD-I = compact disk interactive.* **8** *also* **C.D.** companion dog (certification of standards in obedience). **9** *also* **C.D.** confidential document. **10** Congressional District: *the 10th CD.* **11** *also* **C.D.** contagious *or* communicable disease *medicine.* **12** *also* **C.D.** convulsive disorder *medicine.* **13** Criminal Division (of U.S. Department of Justice). **14** curative dose *medicine:* CD_{50} = *half or median curative dose.* **15** current density of electricity. **16** Customs Declaration. **17** Diplomatic Corps.

C/D 1 carried down *finance.* **2** cerificate of deposit.

Cd *I an abbreviation for:* also **Cd.** commissioned, esp. in combination: *CdEng = Commissioned Engineer.*
II a symbol for: cadmium (chemical element).

c/d 1 carried down *finance.* **2** with the right hand *music.* [Italian *colla dèstra*]

cd 1 candela (unit of luminous intensity) *physics.* **2** *also* **c.d.** carried down *finance.* **3** *also* **c.d.** cash discount *commerce.* **4** *also* **cd.** cord: *cd.ft. = cord foot.* **5** cum dividend (with dividend) *commerce.*

CDA 1 *also* **C.D.A.** Canadian Dental Association. **2** Civil Defense Act. **3** *also* **C.D.A.** Colonial Dames of America. **4** command and data acquisition.

CDAPC Comprehensive Drug Abuse Prevention and Control Act (1970).

CDBG Community Development Block Grant (of U.S. Department of Housing and Urban Development).

CDC 1 Call Directing Code (to route a command to a computer automatically). **2** *also* **C.D.C.** Canadian Development Corporation (for capital to Canadian companies). **3** Center(s) For Disease Control (agency of the U.S. Public Health Service). **4** U.S. Combat and Development Command. **5** command and data-handling console *computers.* **6** *also* **C.D.C** Commissioners of the District of Columbia. **7** *also* **C.D.C.** Curriculum Development Centre (Australian schools).

CDD certificate of disability for discharge *military.*

C.de G. Croix de Guerre (French decoration for bravery under fire).

CDF Collider Detector at Fermilab (particle accelerator used in high-energy physics).

CDFR commercial demonstration fast reactor.

cd.ft. cord foot.

CDI 1 cartilage derived inhibitor (protein inhibitor). **2** category development index (ratio of a product's local sale to national sale) *marketing, advertising.* **3** *also* **CD-I** compact disc-interactive (a video system for graphic images on compact disc).

CDL Citizens for Decent Literature.

CDM code division multiplex (system for separating different messages transmitted over the same line or channel).

CDMA code division multiple access (transmission of different messages over a single line or channel).

CDN 1 a Canada. **b** *also* **Cdn.** Canadian. **2** Chicago Daily News (a newspaper and news service).

CDOS concurrent DOS (multiple user system for personal computers).

CDP 1 *also* **C.D.P.** Certificate in Data Processing. **2** *also* **C.D.P.** Christian Democratic Party (in Germany). **3** cytidine diphosphate (substance used in body growth), also in combination: *CDPC = cytidine diphosphate choline.*

CDR 1 Center for Democratic Renewal. **2** child development research. **3** *also* **C.D.R.** Committee for the Defense of the Revolution (in Cuba).

CDr. *or* **CDR** Commander.

CD-Rom compact disk–read only memory (compact disk for computer storage).

CDS 1 *also* **C.D.S.** *British* Chief of the Defense Staff. **2** *British* Civil Defense Services.

CDT 1 *also* **Cdt. a** Cadet. **b** Commandant. **2** *also* **C.D.T.** *or* **c.d.t.** Central Daylight Time.

CDTV compact disk television (a compact disk system that displays on a television screen).

CDU *or* **C.D.U.** Christian Democratic Union (in Germany).

CDV compact disk video (picture recording with sound stored on a compact disk).

c.d.v. visiting card. [French *carte de visite*]

CDW Collision Waiver (insurance for a rental car).

CE 1 *also* **C.E.** Canada East (Quebec, 1841–1867). **2** *also* **C.E. a** Chemical Engineer. **b** Chief Engineer. **3** *also* **C.E.** Christian Education. **4** *also* **C.E.** Christian Endeavor. **5** *also* **C.E.** *or* **ce** *or* **c.e. a** Christian Era. **b** Common Era: *50CE is equivalent to 50 AD.* **6** *also* **C.E.** *or* **C. of E.** Church of England. **7** *also* **C.E.** Civil Engineer. **8** College English (magazine title). **9** *also* **C.E.** Common Entrance. **10** constant error *psychology.* **11** Continuing Education. **12** *also* **C.E.** (U.S. Army) Corps of Engineers. **13** *also* **C.E. a** Council of Europe. **b** European Community. [French *Communauté Européenne*] **14** counterespionage. **15** Customer Engineer *computers.*

Ce cerium (chemical element).

c.e. 1 buyer's risk, let the buyer beware. [Latin *caveat emptor*] **2** compass error.

CEA 1 carcinoembryonic antigen (protein found in cells of some cancer patients and in fetal tissue, considered a clinical sign of the presence of cancer). **2** *also* **C.E.A.** Central Electricity Authority (of Great Britain). **3** College English Association. **4** Commodity Exchange Authority. **5** Council of Economic Advisers (to the President of the United States). **6** European Confederation of Agriculture. [French *Confédération Européenne de l'Agriculture*] **7** *also* **C.E.A.** French Atomic Energy Commission. [French *Commissariat à la énergie atomique*]

CEAO West African Economic Community. [French *Communauté Économique de l'Afrique Ouest*]

CEB *British* Central Electricity Board.

CEBAF Continuous Electron Beam Accelerator Facility.

CEC 1 Canadian Electrical Code. **2** *also* **C.E.C.** Commonwealth Economic Committee. **3** Council for Exceptional Children.

C.E.C.A. (formerly) European Coal and Steel Community. [French *Communauté Européenne du Charbon et de l'Acier*]

CECLES European Launching Development Organization (for launching commercial space satellites). [French *Conseil Européen pour la Construction de Lancers d'Engins Spatiaux*]

CED 1 *also* **C.E.D.** Committee for Economic Development (research and education organization). **2** computer entry device.

CEDA 1 *also* **C.E.D.A.** Committee for Economic Development of Australia. **2** Confederation of Autonomous Rightist Parties (in Spain). [Spanish *Confederación Española de Derechas Autónomas*]

CEE 1 *also* **C.E.E.** Certificate of Extended Education. **2** Common Entrance Examination. **3** *also* **C.E.E.** European Economic Community. [French *Communauté Économique Européenne*, Spanish *Comunidad Económica Europea*] **4** International Commission on Rules for the Approval of Electrical Equipment.

CEEA *or* **C.E.E.A.** European Atomic Energy Community. [French *Communauté Européenne de l'Énergie Atomique*]

CEEB College Entrance Examination Board.

CEEC *or* **C.E.E.C.** Council for European Economic Cooperation.

CEED *or* **C.E.E.D.** Council for Economic and Environmental Development.

CEEP *or* **C.E.E.P.** European Center for Population Studies. [French *Centre Européen d'Études de Population*]

CEG School of General Instruction (one of three types of French state high schools). [French *Collège d'Enseignement Général*]

CEGB Central Electricity Generating Board (of Great Britain).

CEI 1 communications electronics instructions. **2** cost effectiveness index. **3** *also* **C.E.I.** Council of Engineering Institutions. **4** International Electrotechnical Commission. [French *Commission Électro-technique Internationale*]

CEIF *or* **C.E.I.F.** Council of European Industrial Federations.

ceil. ceiling: *cath.ceil.* = *cathedral ceiling*.

CEIR *or* **C.E.I.R.** Corporation for Economic and Industrial Research.

CEL Central European Line (part of the oil pipeline network of Europe).

Cel. Celsius (centigrade scale).

cel. 1 celebrated. **2** celesta *music*. **3 a** celluloid. **b** cellulose.

Cels. Celsius (centigrade scale).

Celt. Celtic.

CEM combination export manager (exporter of products made by small companies).

cem. 1 *also* **cem** cement: *cem.p.* = *cement paint*. **2** cemetery.

CEMA 1 Conveyor Equipment Manufacturers Association. **2** Council for Mutual Economic Assistance (former Soviet trading bloc). **3** *also* **C.E.M.A.** Council for the Encouragement of Music and the Arts.

cemf *or* **CEMF** counter-electromotive force.

CEMO Canada Emergency Measures Organization.

C.E.M.S. Church of England Men's Society.

CEN European Committee for Standardization, also in combination: *CENEL* = *European Committee for Standardization of Electrical (terms, units, and practices)*. [French *Comité Européen de Normalisation*]

Cen Centaur (constellation).

cen. 1 center. **2** central. **3** century.

CEng chartered engineer.

cens. 1 censor. **2** censorship.

Cent. Central, in combination: *Cent. Afr.* = *Central Africa*, *Cent. Amer.* = *Central America*.

cent. 1 center, centered. **2** *also* **cent** centiare ($1/100$ of an are or one square meter). **3** centigrade. **4** *also* **cent** centime ($1/100$ of a franc). **5** centimeter. **6** central. **7** centrifugal. **8** century, in combination: *15th cent.* **9 a** hundred, esp. in combination: *per cent.* = *hundredths*. [Latin *centum*] ▶The period gradually disappeared as *per cent* has become Anglicized and is often written as one word today. **b** hundredweight.

CENTO Central Treaty Organization (dissolved in 1979).

Centr. central, in combination: *Centr. Afr.* = *Central Africa*.

CENTS Consortium for the Education of Non-Traditional Students (organization that recruits older students to college).

centy. *or* **Centy.** century: *Centy. Assoc.* = *Century Association*.

CEO 1 Chief Education Officer. **2** Chief Executive Officer.

CEP 1 Center of Experimentation in the Pacific Ocean. [French *Centre d'Expérimentation du Pacifique*] **2** circle of equal probability. **3** circular probable error *mathematics*. [originally, *circular error probability*]

Cep Cepheus (constellation).

CEQ Council on Environmental Quality.

CER 1 (*also pronounced* sir) Closer Economic Relations (Australia–New Zealand Closer Economic Relations Trade Agreement). **2** conditioned emotional response.

Cer. Ceramic, Ceramics, esp. in combination: *Cer.E* = *Ceramics Engineer*.

CERA Civil Engineering Research Association (of Great Britain).

ceram. ceramics.

CERC centralized engine room control (of a ship).

CERCHAR French Carbon Research Center. [French *Centre d'Études et Recherches des Charbonnages de France*]

CERCLA Comprehensive Environmental Response, Compensation and Liability Act, the Superfund (legislation holding liable parties responsible for cleaning up hazardous waste sites).

CERI Center for Educational Research and Innovation (of the Organization for Economic Cooperation and Development).

CERL Central Electricity Research Laboratory.

CERN (*pronounced* sèrn) European Organization for Nuclear Research, often referred to as European Laboratory for Particle Physics, and originally known as European Council for Nuclear Research. [French *Conseil Européen pour la Recherche Nucléaire*]

CERT Council of Energy Resources Tribes (American Indian organization to control exploitation of tribal lands).

cert. 1 *also* **Cert. a** certificate: *Cert.H.E. = Certificate in Higher Education.* **b** certification. **c** certified: *cert. inv. = certified invoice.* **d** certify. **2** certiorari (order of a higher court calling for lower court's record of a case for review), esp. in combination: *cert. den. = certiorari denied.*

certif. 1 certificate, certificated. **2** certify.

cerv. cervical: *cerv. vert. = cervical vertebra.*

CES 1 Committee of European Shipowners. **2** School of Secondary Instruction (one of three types of French state high schools). [French *Collège d'Enseignement Secondaire*]

CESA Canadian Engineering Standards Association.

Cestr. of Chester (in reference to the Bishop and therefore used as a signature). [Latin *Cestrensis*]

CET 1 *also* **C.E.T.** Central European Time. **2** School of Technical Instruction (one of three types of French state high schools). [French *Collège d'Enseignement Technique*] **3** *also* **Cet** the Whale (constellation). [Latin *Cetus*]

CETA 1 *also* **C.E.T.A.** Center for the Study of Agricultural Techniques (in France). [French *Centre d'Étude Techniques Agricoles*] **2** (*pronounced* sē'tə) Comprehensive Employment and Training Act (of the United States).

CETEX 1 Committee on Extraterrestrial Exploration. **2** Contamination by Extraterrestrial Exploration.

CETI communication with extraterrestrial intelligence.

cet. par. other things being equal. [Latin *ceteris paribus*]

CETS 1 *also* **C.E.T.S.** Church of England Temperance Society. **2** European Conference on Satellite Communications. [French *Conférence Européenne du Télécommunication Satellite*]

C.E.U. Christian Endeavour Union.

C.E.W.M.S. *or* **CEWMS** Church of England Working Men's Society.

Cey. Ceylon (now *Sri Lanka*).

CF 1 Canadian Forces (armed forces, unified since 1968). **2** *also* **C/F** carried forward *accounting* **3** carrier frequency *electronics.* **4 a** center field *or* center fielder *baseball.* **b** center forward *sports.* **5** center of flotation, in ship diagrams. **6 a** centrifugal force. **b** centripetal force. **7** certainty factor *mathematics.* **8** *also* **C.F.** British Chaplain to the Forces. **9** coefficient of friction *physics.* **10** Comédie Française. **11** complement fixation (used in diagnosis of viral disease): *CF test.* **12** constant frequency. **13** conversion factor. **14** *also* **C.F.** Corresponding Fellow. **15** cystic fibrosis.

Cf californium (chemical element).

c/f 1 cannot find (esp. of a book in library or in answer on publisher's book order). **2** carried forward *accounting.*

cf. 1 calf (of a book binding). **2** compare. [Latin *confer*]

c.f. 1 carried forward *accounting.* **2** cost and freight (compare *c.f.i.*) *commerce.* **3** plain chant or fixed song *music.* [Latin *cantus firmus*]

CFA 1 African Financial Community (countries formerly French territories in northern and central Africa), esp. in combination: *CFA franc = monetary unit of the African Financial Community.* [French *Communauté Financière Africaine*] **2** Canadian Federation of Agriculture. **3** *also* **C.F.A.** Chartered Financial Analyst. **4** College Football Association. **5** Commission of Fine Arts. **6** complement fixing antigen (substance produced by a virus early in infection). **7** Consumer Federation of America (organization to promote consumer interests). **8** Council on Foreign Affairs.

CFAF African Financial Community franc (monetary unit of former French Territories in northern and central Africa). [French *Communauté Financière Africaine*]

CFC 1 chlorofluorocarbon (carbon compounds containing fluorine, formerly used as refrigerants, aerosols, and solvents). **2** colony-forming cells *biology.* **3** Combined Forces Command. **4** Consolidated Freight Classification.

CFCC Canadian Forces Communication Command.

cfd *or* **c.f.d.** cubic feet per day.

CFDT French Democratic Confederation of Labor. [French *Confédération Française Démocratique du Travail*]

CFE 1 Canadian Forces Europe (of the Canadian Armed Forces). **2** contractor-furnished equipment, in construction. **3** Conventional Forces in Europe: *CFE Treaty.*

CFF 1 critical flicker frequency *psychology.* **2** *also* **C.F.F.** Swiss National Railroad. [French *Chemins de Fer Fédéraux*]

cfh *or* **c.f.h.** cubic feet per hour.

CFI 1 *also* **c.f.i.** cost, freight, and insurance *commerce.* **2** *also* **C.F.I.** Court of First Instance.

CFL Canadian Football League.

CFM 1 chlorofluoromethane (type of chlorofluorocarbons). **2** *also* **cfm.** confirm *esp. in the military.* **3** Council of Foreign Ministers.

cfm *or* **c.f.m.** cubic feet per minute.

CFO 1 *also* **C.F.O.** channel for orders *commerce.* **2** Chief Financial Officer.

CFP 1 Common Fisheries Policy (of the European Economic Community). **2** Financial Community of the Pacific, esp. in combination: *CFP francs = monetary unit of the former French Colonies in the Pacific.* [French *Communauté Financière du Pacifique*]

CFR 1 Code of Federal Regulations, also in combination: *CFR Supp. = Code of Federal Regulations Supplement.* **2** *also* **C.F.R.** Cooperative Fuel Research. **3** Council on Foreign Relations.

CFS 1 *also* **C.F.S.** Central Flying School (of the RAF). **2** chronic fatigue syndrome *medicine.*

cfs *or* **c.f.s.** cubic feet per second.

CFSA Canadian Figure Skating Association.

CFT 1 complement fixation test *medicine.* **2** French Television Company. [French *Compagnie Francaise de Télévision*]

cft. craft.

c.ft. cubic foot.

CFTC Commodity Futures Trading Commission.

CFU colony-forming unit *biology.*

C.F.X. Brothers of St. Francis Xavier. [Latin *Congregatio Fratrum Xaverianorum*]

C.F.Y. Clinical Fellow Year (study and field experience after award of a Master's degree).

CG 1 *also* **C.G.** Captain General. **2** Captain of the Guard. **3** *also* **c.g.** center of gravity. **4** *also* **C.G.** Coast Guard. **5** Coldstream Guards. **6** color graphics *computers:* CGA = color graphics adaptor. **7** *also* **C.G.** Commanding General: *General H. H. Arnold, CG, USAAF.* **8** Commissary General. **9** completed games pitched *baseball.* **10** computer graphics. **11** Consul General. **12** Croix de Guerre (French decoration for bravery). **13** wholesale. [French *commerce de gros*]

cg. *or* **cg** centigram.

CGA 1 *also* **C.G.A.** Certified General Accountant. **2** *also* **C.G.A. a** Coast Guard Academy. **b** Coast Guard Auxiliary. **3** color graphics adaptor *computers.* **4** *also* **C.G.A.** General Agricultural Union. [French *Confédération Générale de l'Agriculture*]

c.g.a. *or* **cga** cargo's proportion of general average *commerce.*

C.G.C. *or* **CGC** Coast Guard Cutter: *C.G.C. "Storis".*

CGD 1 Christian Trade Union Federation of Germany. [German *Christlicher Gewerkschaftsbund Deutschlands*] **2** chronic granulomatosis disease (genetic disorder).

cge. carriage, esp. in combination: *cge. free = carriage or delivery free.*

C.G.H. Cape of Good Hope.

c.g.i. corrugated galvanized iron, in blueprints and other drawings.

CGIAR Consultative Group on International Agricultural Research.

CGIL 1 *also* **C.G.I.L.** *or* **C.G.I.** City and Guilds of London Institute. **2** Italian General Confederation of Labor. [Italian *Confederazione Generale Italiana del Lavoro*]

CGM 1 computer graphics metafile. **2** *also* **C.G.M.** British Conspicuous Gallantry Medal.

cgm. *or* **cgm** centigram, centigrams.

cGMP cyclic GMP (cyclic guanosine monophosphate, a constituent of nucleic acid active in cellular metabolism).

cgo. 1 cargo. **2** contango (British term for charge to postpone payment for stock purchase) *finance.*

CGOT Canadian Government Office of Tourism.

CGPM General Conference on Weights and Measures. [French *Conférence Générale des Poids et Mesures*]

CGS 1 Canadian Geographical Society. **2** *also* **cgs** *or* **c.g.s.** centimeter-gram-second (system of measurement). **3** *also* **C.G.S.** Chief of the General Staff. **4** Coast and Geodetic Survey

CGT 1 capital gains tax *finance.* **2** *also* **C.G.T.** General Confederation of Labor (of France and Argentina). [French *Confédération Générale du Travail,* Spanish *Confederación General de Trabajo*]

CH 1 *also* **C.H.** Captain of the Horse. **2** casehardened (process of hardening the surface of iron or steel). **3** center halfback *sports.* **4** choke or choke coil *electronics.* **5** *also* **C.H.** clearing house. **6** *also* **C.H.** Companion of Honour (British Order): *The Rt.Hon. Richard Austen Butler, C.H., M.P.* **7** compass heading. **8** *also* **C.H.** Courthouse. **9** *also* **C.H.** Customs House.

Ch. 1 Chairman. **2** chamber, in blueprints. **3** *also* **Ch** champion: *Ch. Philabeg Heilas, a 2-year-old border terrier.* **4** Chancellor. **5** Chancery, esp. in combination: *Ch.D. = Chancery Division.* **6** *also* **Ch** channel *television, navigation.* **7** Chaplain, esp. in combination: *Ch.F. = Chaplain of the Fleet.* **8** *also* **Ch** chapter (of a book or organization). **9** Charles. **10** *also* **Ch** check *chess.* **11** chemistry, esp. in combination: *Ch.D. = Doctor of Chemistry.* **12** *also* **Ch** Chief, esp. in combination: *Ch. Acct. = Chief Accountant.* **13** child, children. **14** China, Chinese. **15** choir. **16** church, esp. in combination: *R.C.Ch. = Roman Catholic Church.* **17** *also* **Ch** horsepower. [French *cheval-vapeur*]

ch. 1 *also* **ch** chain (surveyor's measure and referring to a stitch in needlework). **2** *also* **ch** channel *television.* **3** chapter (of a book). **4** *also* **ch** check *chess.* **5** chest, esp. as a measurement of the girth of the chest, *esp. in dressmaking, tailoring, medicine.* **6** chestnut, esp. as the color of a horse. **7** child, children. **8** chimney. **9** chronic. **10** church, esp. on a survey. **11** *also* **ch** each, every. [French *chaque*]

c.h. 1 *also* **c-h.** candle hour (unit of light energy). **2** *also* **ch** central heating. **3** *also* **ch** horsepower. [French *cheval-vapeur*]

Cha 1 *also* **Cha.** Channel. **2** the Chameleon (constellation).

Chal. *or* **Chald.** Chaldean.

Chamb. Chamberlain.

champ. *or* **champ** *or* **Champ.** champion.

CHAMPVA Civilian Health and Medical Program of the Veterans Administration.

chan. *or* **Chan.** channel.

Chanc. 1 *also* **Chanc** Chancellor: *Chanc.Ex. = Chancellor of the Exchequer.* **2** Chancery.

Chap. 1 a Chapel. **b** Chaplain. **2** *also* **chap.** chapter: *Chap.II.*

char. 1 *also* **CHAR** character *printing, computers.* **2** characteristic. **3** charity. **4** *also* **Char.** charter.

chart. paper, *esp. in pharmaceutics.* [Latin *charta*]

Chas. Charles.

Chauc. Chaucer.

chauf. chauffeur.

Ch.B. *or* **ChB** Bachelor of Surgery. [Latin *Chirurgiae Baccalaureus*]

CHC choke coil *electronics.*

Ch. Clk. Chief Clerk.

CHD 1 congenital heart disease. **2** congestive heart disease. **3** coronary heart disease.

Ch.D. *or* **ChD** Doctor of Chemistry.

chd. chord *mathematics.*

ChE 1 *also* **Ch.E.** *or* **Che.E.** Chemical Engineer. **2** Chief Engineer. **3** *also* **chE** cholinesterase (enzyme that prevents accumulation of acetylcholine at nerve endings).

CHEKA (*pronounced* chek′ə) Russian Political Police (active from the Revolution to 1921). [Russian *Chrezvychainaya Kommissia*]

C.H.E.L. *or* **CHEL** Cambridge History of English Literature.

chem. 1 chemical. **2** chemist. **3** chemistry.

Chem.E. *or* **ChemE** Chemical Engineer.

chemfet chemical field effect transistor (electronic sensor placed inside the body to gather data).

CHEOPS (kē′ops) chemical engineering optimization system (system of mathematical models used in chemical manufacture).

Ches. *or* **Chesh.** Cheshire, England.

Chev. Chevalier.

chev. chevron.

CHF congestive heart failure.

Chf. chief, esp. in combination: *Chf. Eng.* = *Chief Engineer.*

chg. 1 change. **2** charge, in combination: *chg. acct.* = *charge account.*

chgd. 1 changed. **2** charged.

Chgo Chicago, esp. in commodity quotations *finance.*

Chi. *or* **Chic.** Chicago.

Chih. Chihuahua (state in Mexico).

Chin. China, Chinese.

Chino-Jap. Chino-Japanese.

Chi. R. Chicago Review (magazine title).

Chir. B. Bachelor of Surgery. [Latin *Chirurgiae Baccalaureus*]

Chi. Trib. Chicago Tribune (newspaper).

Ch.J. Chief Justice.

CHK *or* **chk.** check, also in combination: *CHK PT* = *checkpoint.*

CHKR *or* **chkr** checker.

chl *or* **chlo. 1** chloride. **2** *also* **chloro.** chloroform.

Ch.M. Master of Surgery. [Latin *Chirurgiae Magister*]

Chm. 1 Chairman. **2** *also* **CHM** (in a degree) choirmaster.

chm. 1 chamber. **2** checkmate *chess.*

CHMC Children's Hospital Medical Center (in Boston, MA).

Chn. 1 Chairman, Chairperson. **2** *also* **Chmn.** Chairman.

chn. chain (surveyor's measure).

CHO carbohydrate.

choc. chocolate.

chol. cholesterol.

Chor. 1 Choral, *esp. in titles of choral societies.* **2** chorus.

CHP 1 *also* **chp.** championship. **2** combined heat and power (in calculating use of energy).

Chpn chairperson.

ch.ppd. charges prepaid.

CHQ Corps Headquarters.

chq. cheque.

Chr. 1 Christ. **2** Christian. **3** Christmas. **4** Christopher.

chr. 1 *also* **c-hr.** candle hour (unit of light energy). **2** chrestomathy (collection of passages, esp. from one author). **3** chronic.

Christ. 1 Christian: *Christ. Mart.* = *Christian Martyr.* **2** Christmas.

Chrm. *or* **Chrmn.** Chairman: *Chrmn. of Council of Ministers.*

Chron. 1 Chronicle: *A.-S.Chron.* = *The Anglo-Saxon Chronicle.* **2** Chronicles (two books of the Old Testament): *I Chron.* = *One or First Chronicles; II Chron.* = *Two or Second Chronicles.* **3** chronometry (science of measuring time).

chron. *or* **chronol. 1** chronological, chronologically. **2** chronology.

Chrp. Chairperson.

CHS *or* **C.H.S.** Canadian Hydrographic Service.

chs. chapters.

CHT cylinder head temperature.

cht. chest.

CHU centigrade heat unit.

CHUNNEL *or* **Chunnel** (chun′əl) Channel Tunnel (tunnel across the English Channel).

chw *or* **c.h.w.** constant hot water.

Chwdn. churchwarden.

chy. *or* **chy** chimney.

CI 1 cardiac index. **2 a** cast iron. **b** *also* **c.i.** corrugated iron. **3** Cayman Islands: *CI$* = *Cayman Islands dollar.* **4** *also* **C.I.** cephalic index *anthropology, medicine.* **5** cerebral infarction. **6** *also* **C/I** certificate of insurance. **7** *also* **C.I.** Channel Islands: *La Corbiere, Jersey, C.I.* **8** chemotherapeutic index *pharmaceutics, medicine.* **9** Chief Inspector. **10** Chief Instructor. **11** *also* **c.i.** class interval *statistics, psychology.* **12** Color Index, *esp. in astronomy.* **13** *also* **C.I.** *or* **c.i.** compression ignition. **14** consular invoice. **15** *also* **c.i.** cost and insurance *commerce.* **16** *also* **C.I. a** counterinsurgency: *Special Group C.I.* **b** counterintelligence. **17** cropping index *agriculture.*

Ci 1 cirrus (cloud) *meteorology.* **2** curie (unit of measure to express radioactivity, replaced by *Bq* becquerel).

CIA 1 Central Intelligence Agency. **2** Certified Internal Auditor. **3** *also* **Cia.** *or* **C^{ia}** company. [Spanish *compañia*, Italian *compagnia*] **4** Culinary Institute of America. **5** International Council on Archives. [French *Conseil International des Archives*]

C.I.A.M. International Congress of Modern Architecture. [French *Congrès Internationaux d'Architecture Moderne*]

CIAT International Center for Tropical Agriculture. [French *Centre International de l'Agriculture Tropique*]

CIB 1 Central Intelligence Board. **2** *also* **C.I.B.** Criminal Investigation Branch (of New Zealand). **3** International Council for Building Research, Studies, and Documentation. [French *Conseil International du Bâtiment pour la Recherche, l'Étude et la Documentation*]

CIC 1 Capital Issues Committee (financial regulatory body of Great Britain). 2 Chemical Institute of Canada. 3 Combat Information Center (of a warship). 4 *also* **C-I-C** Commander in Chief. 5 Consumer Information Center. 6 Counterintelligence Corps (of the U.S. Army).

Cic. Cicero.

Cicestr. of Chichester (in reference to the Bishop and therefore used as a signature).

CICS customer information control system (used in automatic teller machine systems).

CICT International Council of Film and Television. [French *Conseil International du Cinéma et de la Télévision*]

CID 1 charge-injection device (an image sensor) *electronics*. 2 combined immunodeficiency *medicine*. 3 Council of Industrial Design. 4 *also* **C.I.D.** Criminal Investigation Department (of Scotland Yard). 5 cytomegalic inclusion disease.

CIDA *or* **C.I.D.A.** Intergovernmental Copyright Committee. [French *Comité Intergouvernemental du Droit d'Auteur*]

CIDOC Center for Intercultural Documentation (in Mexico). [Spanish *Centro Intercultural de Documentación*]

CIDS Computer Information Delivery Service.

CIE 1 *also* **Cie.** *or* **Cⁱᵉ** Company. [French *compagnie*] 2 counterimmunoelectrophoresis *medicine*. 3 *also* **C.I.E.** International Commission on Illumination; ICI: *C.I.E. system of color measurement and specification.* [French *Commission Internationale de l'Éclairage*] 4 Tranport Organization of Ireland. [Gaelic *Coras Iompair Eireann*]

CIES Council for International Exchange of Scholars.

CIF 1 *also* **C.I.F.** Canadian Institute of Forestry. 2 central information file *computers*. 3 computer-integrated factory. 4 contact-inhibiting factor. 5 *also* **c.i.f.** cost, insurance, and freight, also in combination: *c.i.f. & c. = cost, insurance, freight, and commission.*

CIFT Contextual Indexing and Faceted Taxonomic Access System (computer-based system of bibliographic referencing).

CIG 1 Compliance and Investigations Group (of the U.S. Office of Personnel Management, making background checks on prospective employees). 2 International Committee on Geophysics. [French *Comité International de Géophysique*]

CIGRE International Conference on Large Electric Systems. [French *Conférence Internationale des Grands Réseaux Electriques a Haute Tension*]

C.I.I. *or* **CII** Chartered Insurance Institute.

CIIT Chemical Industry Institute of Toxicology.

CIM 1 *also* **C.I.M.** Canadian Institute of Mining. 2 *also* **C.I.M.** Commission for Industry and Manpower. 3 computer input microfilm. 4 computer-integrated manufacturing. 5 International Music Council. [French *Conseil International de la Musique*]

Cin. Cincinnati, also in combination: *Cin.L.Rev. = Cincinnati Law Review.*

CINC (sē'ən sē' *or* sink) Commander-in-Chief *military*, the usual military abbreviation, esp. in combination: *CINCPAC = Commander-in-Chief, Pacific Fleet* (of the U.S. Navy). *CINC-SOUTH = Commander-in-Chief, Allied Forces Southern Europe.*

C-in-C *or* **CinC** (sē'ən sē') Commander-in-Chief: *A C-in-C must draw up a master plan for the campaign he envisages.*

Cinn. Cincinnati.

CINS (*pronounced* sinz) Child or Children In Need of Supervision.

CIO *or* **C.I.O.** Congress of Industrial Organizations (national labor union, now merged into the AFL-CIO).

CIOB Chartered Institute of Building.

CIOCS communications input and output control system *computers.*

CIOMS Council for International Organizations of Medical Sciences.

CIO-PAC Congress of Industrial Organizations Political Action Committee.

C.I.O.S. International Committee of Scientific Management. [French *Comité International de l'Organisation Scientifique*]

CIP 1 cataloging in publication (of the Library of Congress). 2 computer-integrated production.

CIPA *or* **C.I.P.A.** 1 Canadian Institute on Public Affairs. 2 Chartered Institute of Patent Agents.

C.I.P.L. Permanent International Committee of Linguists. [French *Comité International Permanent des Linguistes*]

CIPM 1 Council for International Progress in Management. 2 International Committee of Weights and Measures. [French *Comité International des Poids et Mesures*]

CIPS Canadian Information Processing Society.

CIPSH *or* **C.I.P.S.H.** International Council for Philosophy and the Humanities. [French *Conseil International de la Philosophie et des Sciences Humaines*]

C.I.P.W. *or* **CIPW** Cross, Iddings, Pirsson, and Washington (system of rock classification).

CIR 1 Circle (in postal address). 2 Council on Industrial Relations.

Cir the pair of Compasses (constellation). [Latin *Circinus*]

cir. *or* **circ.** 1 about, approximately. [Latin *circa*] 2 *also* **Cir.** circle: *159 North Terrace Cir.* 3 *also* **Circ.** circuit: *cir. bkr. = circuit breaker, Circ.Ct. = Circuit Court.* 4 circular: *cir. mil = circular mil* (a unit measure for wire gauge). 5 circulation. 6 circumference.

circe. circumstance.

circs (*pronounced* sirks) *or* **circs.** *British* circumstances: *under the circs! What chance has she in the circs?*

circum. circumference.

CIRM International Radio Medical Center (free, long-range doctor to sick or injured seamen on board ship). [Spanish *Centro Internazionale Radio Medico*]

cir mil *or* **cir. mil** circular mil (a unit measure for wire gauge).

CIS 1 *also* **cis.** cataloging in source, *in bibliography*. 2 *also* **C.I.S.** Catholic Information Society. 3 Center for International Studies. 4 Commonwealth of Independent States (current name for Russia and some other states of the former USSR).

CISAC *or* **C.I.S.A.C.** International Confederation of Societies of Authors and Composers. [French *Confédération Internationale des Sociétés d'Auteurs et Compositeurs*]

CISC 1 complex instruction set computer (computer with instructions corresponding to an assembly language). 2 International Federation of Christian Trade Unions. [French *Confédération Internationale des Syndicats Chrétiens*]

CISL 1 International Confederation of Free Trade Unions. [French *Confédération Internationale des Syndicats Libres*] 2 Italian Confederation of Trades Union Workers. [Italian *Confederazione Italiana Sindicati Lavoratori*] 3 Italian Free Trades Union Confederation. [Italian *Confederazione Italiana Sindicati Liberi*]

CISPR International Special Committee on Radio Interference. [French *Comité International Spécial des Perturbations Radioélectriques*]

CIT *or* **C.I.T.** 1 California Institute of Technology. 2 Carnegie Institute of Technology. 3 Compact Ignition Tokamak (for research in fusion-generated electricity). 4 computer-integrated telephony (for connecting computers to telephone networks).

cit. 1 citation, esp. of a source. 2 cited, esp. in combination: *op. cit.* = *work cited.* 3 citizen. 4 citrate (salt or ester of citric acid). 5 *also* **c.i.t.** compression in transit, *in shipping.*

CITES Convention on International Trade in Endangered Species.

CITI International Confederation of Professional and Intellectual Workers. [French *Confédération Internationale des Travailleurs Intellectuels*]

cito disp. let it be dispensed quickly *pharmaceutics.* [Latin *cito dispensetur*]

CIU computer interface unit (to connect peripheral equipment).

CIUS International Council of Scientific Unions. [French *Conseil International des Unions Scientifiques*]

civ. 1 *also* **Civ.** civil: *Civ. Eng.* = *Civil Engineer; Civ. Ct.* = *Civil Court.* 2 civilian. 3 civilization.

CIW *or* **C.I.W.** Carnegie Institute of Washington.

CIWS close-in weapons system.

C.J. 1 body of law, esp. in combination: *C.J.S.* = *Corpus Juris Secundum* (encyclopedic treatise of American law). [Latin *corpus juris*] 2 Chief Judge. 3 Chief Justice. 4 Circuit Judge.

cj. conjectural.

C.J.Can. body of the canon law. [Latin *Corpus Juris Canonici*]

C.J.Civ. body of the civil law. [Latin *Corpus Juris Civilis*]

CJD *or* **C-J disease** Creutzfeldt-Jakob Disease (a disease of the brain).

CJI Criminal Justice Institute.

CJM *or* **C.J.M.** Code of Military Justice. [French *Code de Justice Militaire*]

CJR Columbia Journalism Review (publication).

CK creatine kinase (enzyme active in vertebrate muscle contraction).

ck. 1 cask. 2 *also* **ck** centistoke (unit of viscosity). 3 check. 4 cook.

CKD 1 *also* **C.K.D.** Certified Kitchen Designer. 2 completely knocked down (of machinery, furniture, building parts, etc., too large to send assembled) *commerce.*

CKG cardiokymograph.

cks. 1 casks. 2 checks *commerce.*

ckt. circuit: *ckt. bkr.* = *circuit breaker.*

ckw. clockwise.

CL 1 *also* **C/L** cash letter *commerce.* 2 center line *sports, printing, theater,* and in mechanical drawings. 3 *also* **C.L.** Civil Law. 4 *also* **C.L.** Common Law. 5 control leader (signal indicating that code of operation is to follow) *computers.* 6 *also* **c/l** craft loss (a commercial insurance term used of shipping). 7 critical list.

Cl *I an abbreviation for:* 1 *also* **Cl.** claim, claims: *Cl. Ct.* = *Claims Court.* 2 class (kind or type), esp. in combination: *Cl. A-1.* 3 *also* **Cl.** Classical, esp. in combination: *Cl. L.* = *Classical Latin.* 4 *also* **Cl.** clause, esp. in combination: *Cl. 4.* 5 clay (as on surveys and navigational charts). 6 cleric, clergyman. 7 *also* **Cl.** clerk, esp. in combination: *Ct. Cl.* = *court clerk.* 8 *also* **Cl.** club.
II a symbol for: **a** chloride. **b** chlorine (chemical element).

cl 1 *also* **cl.** carload *commerce.* 2 centiliter. 3 *also* **cl.** claim. 4 clarinet *music.* 5 *also* **cl.** **a** class (kind or type). **b** classification. 6 *also* **cl.** clause, esp. in combination: *n. cl.* = *noun clause.* 7 clearance. 8 closet, in blueprints and other drawings. 9 *also* **cl.** cloth, esp. in combination: *cl. bds.* = *cloth boards.*

c.l. 1 carload lots *commerce.* 2 corpus luteum (endocrine substance in the sac of ova that produces progesterone in pregnancy).

CLA 1 *also* **C.L.A.** Canadian Library Association. 2 *also* **C.L.A.** Catholic Library Association. 3 College Language Association (or their publication). 4 Commission for Local Administration (oversees local authorities in Great Britain).

Clar. *or* **clar.** 1 clarendon (a style of printing type). 2 clarinet.

class. 1 classic, classical. 2 classification. 3 classified.

CLAT communication line adapter for teletype *computers.*

CLC 1 *also* **C.L.C.** Canadian Labor Congress. 2 course line computer *navigation.*

C.L.D. *or* **CLD** Doctor of Civil Law. [Latin *Civilus Lex Doctor*]

cld. 1 called (of bonds) *commerce.* 2 *also* **CLD** cancelled *commerce, computers, meteorology.* 3 **a** cleared (of checks) *commerce.* **b** cleared (of the sky) *meteorology.* **c** *also* **CLD** cleared (of a computer register or memory). 4 colored. 5 cooled. 6 could.

CLEP College Level Examination Program.

Clerg. clergyman.

Clev. *or* **Cleve.** Cleveland.

clg. 1 ceiling. 2 clearing, *esp. in finance.*

CLI 1 command language interpreter (part of computer system that converts user commands into computer functions). 2 cost-of-living index.

clim. climate.

climat climatology, climatological.

Clin. 1 Clinic. 2 *also* **clin.** clinical: *Clin.Psych.* = *Clinical Psychology.*

C.Lit. *or* **C.Litt.** Companion of Literature.

clk. 1 clerk. 2 *also* **CLK** clock.

clkg. caulking.

CLL chronic lymphocytic leukemia.

Cl Lat. Classical Latin.

Cllr. British Councillor: *Cllr. A. S. Gringe, chairman of the Highways Committee.*

clm. column.

CLML Current List of Medical Literature.

clo. 1 closet. 2 clothing.

CLNS connectionless network service (data communications service through which messages can be sent without first establishing a hookup).

CLP Constituency Labour Party.

C.L.P.A. *or* **CLPA** Common Law Procedure Acts.

CLR 1 Central London Railway (the underground or subway). 2 clear *computers.* 3 computer language recorder. 4 *also* **C.L.R.** Council on Library Resources.

clr. 1 clear. 2 clearance. 3 color.

CLRB Canadian Labor Relations Board.

Clrm. classroom.

CLRU Cambridge Language Research Unit.

CLS 1 *also* **C.L.S.** Certificate in Library Science. 2 close *computers.* 3 Comparative Literature Studies (publication). 4 *also* **C.L.S.** Courts of London Sessions.

C.L.S.C. Chautauqua Literary and Scientific Circle.

CLSH corpus luteum stimulating hormone.

Clst. *or* **clst.** clarinetist.

CLT 1 Canadian Law Times (publication). 2 communication line terminal *computers.* 3 computer language translator.

C.L.U. *or* **CLU** Chartered Life Underwriter.

CLV 1 *also* **Clv.** Cleveland. 2 constant linear velocity *computers.*

clvd clavichord *music.*

CM 1 *also* **C.M.** Canada Medal. 2 Career Minister (of government). 3 center of mass *physics.* 4 *also* **C.M.** Certificate of Merit. 5 circulation manager. 6 command module (part of spacecraft). 7 Common Market. 8 *also* **C.M.** common meter *music.* 9 common mode *electronics.* 10 *also* **C.M.** Corresponding Member, esp. in combination: *C.M.Z.S. = Corresponding Member of the Zoological Society.* 11 countermeasure, esp. in combination: *COMCM = communications countermeasures.* 12 *also* **C.M.** courtmartial. 13 *also* **C.M.** Master in Surgery. [Latin *Chirurgiae Magister*] 14 *also* **C.M.** Member of the Order of Canada.

cm see or compare; cf. [Russian *smotri*]

Cm curium (chemical element).

C/m call of more (in a stock transaction) *finance.*

cM centimorgan (unit of distance on a map of chromosomes).

cm 1 *also* **c.m.** in expectation of death, *esp. in law.* [Latin *causa mortis*] 2 *also* **c.m.** center matched (of lumber). 3 *also* **c.m.** center of mass *physics.* 4 *also* **cm.** centimeter. 5 *also* **cm.** circular mil (a unit measure for wire gauge). 6 *also* **c.m.** metric caret. [French *caret metrique*] 7 *also* **c.m.** tomorrow morning *pharmaceutics.* [Latin *cras mane*]

CMA 1 Canadian Manufacturers' Association. 2 *also* **C.M.A.** Canadian Medical Association. 3 Census or Consolidated Metropolitan Area.   4 certificate of management account-

ing. 5 *also* **C.M.A.** Certified Medical Assistant. 6 *also* **C.M.A.** Cooperative Merchandising Agreement. 7 Country Music Association. 8 Court of Military Appeals.

CMa Canis Major (constellation).

CMB 1 *also* **C.M.B.** Central Medical Board. 2 Coastal Motor Boat.

CMBI Caribbean Marine Biological Institute.

CMC 1 Canadian Meteorological Center. 2 Canadian Music Council. 3 carboxymethylcellulose (used in manufacture of cotton goods to stiffen and make easily cleaned). 4 *also* **C.M.C.** Certified Management Consultant. 5 Collective Measures Committee (of the United Nations). 6 *also* **C.M.C.** Commandant of the Marine Corps. 7 critical micelle concentration *chemistry.* 8 compact molecular cloud (of a substance dissolving) *chemistry.*

CMC-CT sodium carboxymethylcellulose (used in detergents).

CMD Common Meter Double *music.*

Cmd. 1 Command. 2 Command Paper, in combination with a number (White Paper): *Cmd.8980 dealt with Communist organizations.*

Cmdg. Commanding: *Cmdg. Gen. = Commanding General.*

Cmdr. Commander.

Cmdre. Commodore.

Cmdt. Commandant.

CME 1 Chicago Mercantile Exchange. 2 *also* **C.M.E.** Christian Methodist Episcopal: *CME ministers.* 3 continuing medical education. 4 coronal mass ejection (of the sun).

CMEA (formerly) Council for Mutual Economic Assistance; Comecon.

CMF Citizen Military Force (of Australia).

C.M.G. *or* **CMG** Companion of the Order of St. Michael and St. George.

c./m./g. *or* **c/m/g** counts per minute per gram.

C.M.H. *or* **CMH** Congressional Medal of Honor.

C.M.H.A. *or* **CMHA** Canadian Mental Health Association.

CMHC 1 Central Mortgage and Housing Corporation (of Canada). 2 community mental health center.

CMI 1 cell-mediated immunity (specific immunity caused by the presence of T-cells). 2 complete marked inversion (method of obtaining a genetically pure strain of laboratory animals). 3 computer-managed instruction.

CMi Canis Minor (constellation).

C.M.I.A. Coal Mining Institute of America.

CML 1 chronic myelocytic leukemia. 2 current mode logic *computers.*

cml. 1 *also* **Cml** chemical: *Cml C. = Chemical Corps.* 2 commercial.

c.mm. cubic millimeter.

cmml. commercial.

cmmz commercial zone.

CMN *or* **Cmn.** commission.

Cmnd. Command Paper, in combination with a number: *White Paper (Cmnd.1290).*

CMO 1 Chief Medical Officer. **2** Collateralized Mortgage Obligation.

CMOS complementary metal oxide semiconductor (integrated circuit used in small computers) *electronics*.

CMP 1 Commissioner of Metropolitan Police. **2** *also* **cmp** compare *computers*. **3** Controlled Materials Plan (for allocating basic metals in time of shortage). **4** Corps of Military Police. **5** cytidine monophosphate (building unit of nucleic acid).

cmp. compromise.

cmpd *or* **CMPD** compound, compounded.

cm.pf. cumulative preferred stock *finance*.

CMPL *or* **Cmpl** complement *computers*.

cmps *or* **cm.p.s.** centimeters per second.

CMPT *or* **Cmpt** compute *computers*.

CMR common mode rejection (of an amplifier signal), also in combination: *CMRR = common mode rejection ratio*.

CMRRA Canadian Musical Reproduction Rights Agency.

CMS 1 *also* **C.M.S.** Center for Measurement Science. **2** *also* **C.M.S.** Church Missionary Society. **3** Consumer and Marketing Service (of the U.S. government). **4** Conversational Monitor System *computers*.

cm/s *or* **cm./s** centimeters per second.

c.m.s. to be taken tomorrow morning *pharmaceutics*. [Latin *cras mane sumendus*]

CMSA Consolidated Metropolitan Statistical Area (of the U.S. Census Bureau).

cm/sec *or* **cm./sec.** centimeters per second.

C.M.T.C. Citizens Military Training Camp.

Cmte Committee.

CMU 1 Canadian Maritime Union. **2** chlorophenyldimethylurea (used to keep ground free of vegetation as along railroad beds and in lumber yards).

CMV cytomegalovirus (cause of enlarged cells in newborns that affect many organs).

CMYK cyan (blue-green), magenta, yellow, key or black (colors of a system used in high-quality color printing).

CN 1 Canada (used especially with numbers), in bibliography. **2** Canadian National Railways. **3** carbon-nitrogen: *CN cycle*. **4** chloroacetophenone (fragrant-smelling tear gas that also irritates the skin). **5** *also* **C.N.** Code Napoleon. **6** compass north. **7 a** consignment note (bill of lading). **b** cover note (binder on insurance coverage of a shipment).

C/N 1 *also* **C:N** carbohydrate-nitrogen ratio. **2** carbon-nitrogen ratio *chemistry*. **3** circular note (letter of credit). **4** consignment note (bill of lading). **5** credit note.

Cn 1 *also* **Cn.** Canon. **2** cumulonimbus (cloud).

c.n. 1 consignment note (bill of lading). **2** tomorrow night *pharmaceutics*. [Latin *cras nocte*]

CNA *or* **C.N.A. 1** Canadian Nurses Association. **2** Chemical Notation Association.

CNBC Consumer News and Business Channel (a television cable network).

CNC computer numerical control (of a computer in a system used to control machinery, as in an assembly line).

Cnc the Crab (constellation). [Latin *Cancer*]

CNCE *or* **C.N.C.E.** National Center of Foreign Commerce (of France). [French *Centre National du Commerce Extérieur*]

CNCL 1 *also* **Cncl** cancel *computers*. **2** National Commission of Communication (government agency of French broadcasting). [French *Commission Nationale de la Communication et des Libertés*]

Cncl. Council.

Cnclr. Councilor.

CNCMH Canadian National Committee for Mental Hygiene.

cncr. *or* **Cncr.** concurrent.

CND Campaign for Nuclear Disarmament.

CNEN Spanish Atomic Energy Commission. [Spanish *Comisión Nacional de Energía Nuclear*]

CNES National Center for Space Research (French space agency). [French *Centre National d'Études Spatiales*]

CNET National Center for the Study of Telecommunications. [French *Centre National d'Études des Télécommunications*]

CNG compressed natural gas.

CNIPA Committee of National Institutes of Patent Agents.

CNL 1 Canadian National Library. **2** Commonwealth National Library (of Australia).

CNLA Council of the National Library Association.

CNM Certified Nurse Midwife.

CNN Cable News Network.

CNO 1 carbon, nitrogen, oxygen, esp. in combination: *CNO cycle*. **2** *also* **C.N.O.** Chief of Naval Operations.

C.N.P.F. *or* **CNPF** French National Council of Employers. [French *Conseil National du Patronat Français*]

CNR Canadian National Railways.

cnr. *or* **cnr** corner.

CNRS National Center for Scientific Research. [French *Centre National de la Recherche Scientifique*]

CNS *or* **C.N.S.** *or* **c.n.s.** central nervous system.

CNSL *or* **Cnsl** console *computers*.

CNT 1 *also* **Cnt** count *commerce, computers*. **2** National Confederation of Labor. [Spanish *Confederación Nacional de Trabajo*]

cntn contain.

cntr 1 *also* **Cntr. a** center. **b** container. **2** *also* **cntr.** contribution.

CNTU Confederation of National Trade Unions (of Canada).

CNV *or* **cnv** contingent negative variation *biology*.

CNVA Committee for Nonviolent Action (former group that pioneered nonviolent action for peace in the South).

Cnvt *or* **cnvt** convert or converts to *chemistry, commerce, computers, mathematics, physics*.

CO 1 carbon monoxide: *CO laser*. **2** cardiac output. **3** *also* **C.O.** cash order. **4** central office. **5** Colorado (Zip Code). **6** *also* **C.O.** Commanding Officer. **7** conscientious objector: *draft-age CO's*. **8** *also* **C.O.** criminal offense. **9** *also* **C.O.** Crown Office. **10** crystal oscillator *electronics*. **11 a** cutoff. **b** cut out.

CO₂ carbon dioxide.

C/O 1 *also* **c/o** *or* **c.o.** carried over *accounting.* **2** cash order. **3** *also* **C.O.** Certificate of Origin (of imported goods). **4** *also* **c.o.** *or* **c/o** change over. **5** *also* **c/o** *or* **c.o.** in care of (in an address).

Co *I also* **Co.** an abbreviation for: **1** Colorado. **2** Company: *New York Times Co.* **3** coral (as on navigational charts). **4** County: *Westchester Co.* *II a symbol for:* **1** cobalt (chemical element): CO^{60} = radioactive cobalt. **2** coenzyme, esp. in combination: CoA = coenzyme A.

co. 1 coaxial. **2** colatitude.

COAC clutter-operated anti-clutter (radar).

Coad. Coadjutor.

COAM customer owned and maintained (computer equipment).

coax 1 coaxial. **2** coaxial cable.

C.O.B. coordination of benefits (of health insurance between two or more insurers of one family or person).

COBE Cosmic Background Explorer (spacecraft measuring background radiation).

COBOL Common Business Oriented Language (language for writing instructions to computers).

C.O.B.Q. May He Rest With All Good Souls. [Latin *Cum Omnibus Bonis Quiescat*]

COC 1 Chamber of Commerce. **2** Cleveland Open Cup (measure of flashpoint) *chemistry.* **3** Combat Operations Center (Air Defense Command).

coch. *or* **cochl.** spoonful *pharmaceutics,* esp. in combination: *coch.amp.* = *tablespoonful* [Latin *cochleare amplum*]; *coch.parv.* = *teaspoonful.* [Latin *cochleare parvum*]

COCOM Coordinating Committee (for East-West Trade, to control export of technology).

COCU Consultation on Church Union (of the Episcopal Church).

COD 1 *also* **C.O.D.** *or* **c.o.d. a** cash on delivery. **b** collect on delivery. **2** cause of death. **3** chemical oxygen demand. **4** Concise Oxford Dictionary.

cod. *or* **Cod. 1** code, esp. in combination: *Cod. Civ.* = *Civil Code.* **2** codicil (of a will). **3** manuscript. [Latin *codex*]

CODAG combined diesel and gas (of turbine-propulsion).

codan carrier-operated device, anti-noise (device to activate a radio receiver on signal or shut a receiver down when a signal ceases).

CODAR correlation, detection, and ranging (electronic method of submarine detection by use of buoys equipped with SONAR).

CODASYL Conference on Data Systems Languages (group to coordinate development of programming languages for computers).

codd. codices (plural of *codex*).

Codec (kō'dek) Coder and Decoder (a network interface unit that connects a computer terminal to a transmission line).

CODIC computer-directed communications.

COE Corps of Engineers.

coed *or* **co-ed** (kō'ed) coeducational (of students, dormitory facilities, educational programs, etc.).

Co-edn. co-edition, *in cataloging.*

coef. *or* **coeff.** coefficient.

COENCO Committee for Environmental Conservation.

C. of A. certificate of airworthiness.

C. of B. *or* **C of B** confirmation of balance *banking.*

C of C Chamber of Commerce.

C. of E. Church of England.

C of F Chief of Finance; CFO.

COFI Committee on Fisheries (of the Food and Agriculture Organization of the United Nations).

C. of I. Church of Ireland.

C of L *or* **COFL** cost of living.

C of M certificate of maintenance *aeronautics.*

COFO Council of Federated Organizations (consisting of four civil rights organizations and the National Council of Churches).

COFS *or* **C of S 1** Chief of Section. **2** Chief of Staff.

C. of S. Church of Scotland.

cog 1 *also* **c.o.g.** *or* **COG** center of gravity. **2** *also* **cog.** cognate *linguistics.* **3** *also* **cog.** cognizant (having legal cognizance or jurisdiction).

Cogas coal-oil-gas (in reference to gasification of coal or oil).

COGB *British* certified official government business.

COGO coordinate geometry (computer language used in engineering).

COGSA *or* **C.O.G.S.A.** Carriage of Goods by Sea Act (of a bill of lading and the responsibilities of a shipper).

COH 1 carbohydrate. **2** *also* **c.o.h.** cash on hand *accounting.*

COHA Council on Hemispheric Affairs.

co-hab cohabit, cohabitation.

COHMAP Cooperative Holocene Mapping Project.

COHO coherent oscillator *electronics.*

COHSE *or* **C.O.H.S.E.** Confederation of Health Service Employees.

COI *or* **C.O.I.** Central Office of Information (of Great Britain).

COIN counterinsurgency.

coin-op coin-operated: *coin-op self-service laundries.*

Cointelpro (kō'in tel'prō') counterintelligence program (FBI program to disrupt activities of groups regarded as a threat to national security).

COIR Commission on Intergroup Relations.

COJO Conference of Jewish Organizations.

COL 1 computer-oriented language. **2** *also* **col** *or* **c.o.l.** cost of living, in combination: *COLA* = *cost of living allowance.*

Col 1 *also* **Col. a** College. **b** Collegiate. **2** *also* **Col.** Colombia. **3** colon (large intestine). **4** *also* **Col.** Colonel. **5** *also* **Col. a** Colonial. **b** Colony. **6** *also* **Col.** Colorado. **7** *also* **Col.** Colossians (book of the New Testament). **8** *also* **Col.** Columbia. **9** the Dove (constellation). [Latin *Columba*]

col. 1 *also* **col** colatitude *astronomy, navigation.* 2 collated. 3 a collect. b collected. c collector. 4 colloquial. 5 colony (esp. of bacteria, etc.). 6 colophon (trade mark, esp. publisher's imprint on the spine of a book). 7 color, colored. 8 *also* **col** column. 9 *also* **col** strain (to remove impurities) *pharmaceutics.* [Latin *cola*]

COLA (kō′lə) cost-of-living allowance or adjustment.

Coll. College, Collegiate.

coll. 1 collated. 2 collateral: *coll.tr. = collateral trust.* 3 colleague. 4 a collect. b collected. c collection. d collective: *coll.vol. = collective volume.* e collector. 5 college. 6 colloidal. 7 colloquial.

collab. 1 collaborate. 2 collaboration, in collaboration with. 3 collaborator, esp. in literary and musical composition.

collat. collateral.

collect. collective.

colloq. 1 colloquial. 2 colloquialism. 3 colloquially.

Coll'ott. (play) in octaves *music.* [Italian *coll'ottava*]

collut. mouthwash *pharmaceutics.* [Latin *collutorium*]

coll.vol. collective volume *chemistry.*

collyr. eye lotion *pharmaceutics.* [Latin *collyrium*]

colm. column.

Colo. Colorado.

colog cologarithm.

Coloss. Colossians (book of the New Testament).

col.p. adapted to the principal part *music.* [Italian *colla parte*]

COLS communications for on-line systems *computers.*

cols. 1 colonies (of bacteria). 2 columns.

Col.-Sgt. Color-Sergeant.

col.vo. adapted to the principal voice *music.* [Italian *colla voce*]

COM 1 a command *computers,* esp. in combination: *COM file.* b Commander *military,* esp. in combination: *COMAIR-LANT = Commander Air Force, Atlantic.* 2 communications, in combination: *COMSAT = Communications Satellite.* 3 computer, esp. in combination: *COMPAC = Computer Program for Automatic Control.* 4 *also* **com** computer output microfilm (computer printout made directly on microfilm). 5 customer's own merchandise.

Com Berenice's Hair (constellation). [Latin *Coma Berenices*]

Com. 1 Commander *military: Com.-in-Chf. = Commander-in-Chief.* 2 Commercial: *Com. Lic. = Commercial License.* 3 Commissary, esp. in combination: *Com. Sub. = Commissary of Subsistence.* 4 a Commission: *West. Lnd. Com. = Westchester Land Commission.* b Commissioner. 5 Committee: *Cent. Com. = Central Committee.* 6 Commodore. 7 Common, esp. in combination: *Com.Ver. = Common Version of the Bible.* 8 Commonwealth, esp. in combination: *Com. Sec. = Commonwealth Secretariat.* 9 Communist. 10 Community, esp. in combination: *Comes = Community of European Writers.* 11 Company *commerce.*

com. 1 comedy. 2 comma. 3 a comment. b commentary. 4 a commerce. b commercial. 5 common, commonly. 6 a communicate. b communicated. c communication.

COMAL Common Algorithmic Language.

comb. 1 a combination: *LR–DR comb. = living room–dining room combination.* b combine, combined, combining. 2 a combustible. b combustion.

combi (kom′bē) *British* combination.

combo (kom′bō) combination.

combs. combinations (two-piece underwear or tights).

COMD Commanding *military.*

Comd. 1 Command. 2 Commander.

Comdg. Commanding.

Comdr. Commander.

Comdt. Commandant.

COMECON *or* **Comecon** (kom′ə kon) (former) Council for Mutual Economic Assistance (of the USSR and its satellites).

Com.Err. The Comedy of Errors (play by Shakespeare).

Comes Community of European Writers.

COMEX *or* **Comex** (kō′meks) Commodity Exchange (of New York City).

COMEXO Committee for Exploitation of the Oceans.

COMIBOL Bolivian Mining Corporation. [Spanish *Corporación Minería de Bolivia*]

Com.-in-Chf. Commander-in-Chief.

Cominform (kom′in fôrm) Communist Information Bureau (former organization to coordinate Communist Party propaganda throughout the world).

COMINT communications intelligence.

Comintern (kom′in tèrn) Communist International (former organization to coordinate Communist activities throughout the world).

COMISCO Committee of the International Socialist Conference.

COMIT Computing System M.I.T. (computer language that is verbal instead of numerical).

coml. commercial.

Comm. 1 Commander. 2 a Commerce, esp. in combination: *Comm.Ct. = Commerce Court.* b Commercial: *Comm. Art. = Commercial Artist.* 3 Commissary: *Comm.Gen. = Commissary General.* 4 a Commission. b Commissioner: *Comm. of Hwys. = Commissioner of Highways.* 5 Committee: *Sen.Comm. = Senate Committee.* 6 Commonweal (magazine title). 7 Commonwealth. 8 Communist. 9 Community.

comm. 1 commence, begin, as of stitches in knitting. [French *commencer*] 2 a commentary. b commentator. 3 commercial. 4 communication.

commem. commemorative.

Commn. Commission.

Commr. Commissioner.

commun. communication.

Commw. Commonwealth: *Commw.Ct. = Commonwealth Court.*

Com.Off. commissioned officer.

Comp. 1 a compiled: *Comp.St.* = *Compiled Statutes.* **b** compiler, compiled by (of a literary work or a file). **2** Comptroller, esp. in combination: *Comp.Gen.* = *Comptroller General.*

comp. 1 companion. **2 a** comparative. **b** compare. **c** comparison. **3** compass, in combination: *comp.pt.* = *compass point.* **4 a** compensating. **b** compensation (of insurance). **5 a** compilation. **b** compiler, compiled by (of a literary work or a file). **6** component. **7 a** compose. **b** composer, composed by. **8 a** composite. **b** composition: *comp.bd.* = *composition board.* **c** compositor. **9 a** compound. **b** compounded *pharmaceutics.* **10** comprehensive. **11** compress, compressed, in combination: *comp.g.* = *compressed gas.* **12** comprising.

Compa. company. [Spanish *Compañia*]

COMPAC (kom′pak′) Commonwealth-Pacific (referring to a telephone cable system across the Pacific).

compander device to enhance electromagnetic signals. [*compressor-expander*]

compar. 1 comparative. **2** comparison.

compd. compound, compounded *chemistry, pharmaceutics.*

Comp.Dec Comptroller's Decisions (decisions of the Comptroller General of the United States).

Comp.Gen. Comptroller General, esp. in reference to decisions of the Comptroller General of the United States.

Compl. A Lover's Complaint (poem usually attributed to Shakespeare).

compl. 1 complement. **2** complete, completed.

complt. complainant.

compn. or **compo.** composition.

comps. 1 compilers. **2** also **comps** (*pronounced* komps) comprehensives (comprehensive examinations).

Compt. or **Comptr.** comptroller.

compt. 1 compartment. **2** comptometer.

compt. rend. reports. [French *comptes rendus*]

Comr. Commissioner.

COMSAT or **Comsat** communications satellite.

Com. Ver. Common Version (of the Bible).

CON 1 console *computers.* **2** continental, esp. in combination: *CONAD* = *Continental Air Defense Command.*

Con. 1 Conservative *politics.* **2** also **Con** Consolidated: *Con Ed* = *Consolidated Edison Co. of New York.* **3** Consul. **4** Contralto *music.*

con (*pronounced* kon) **1** against: *pro and con.* [Latin *contra*] **2** confidence: *con game.* **3** convict: *ex-con.*

con. 1 concerning. **2** concerto. **3** conclusion. **4** concrete *construction: con.p.* = *concrete piers.* **5** conic, conics: *con.sec.* = *conic section.* **6** connection. **7** console. **8** consolidated. **9** *British* consols (consolidated bonds or stocks). **10** constant *computers.* **11** continued. **12** control, controlled. **13** *British* conveniences: *a mansion and all mod. con.* **14** conversation. **15** wife or consort *law.* [Latin *conjunx*]

CONAC Continental Air Command (of the U.S. Air Force).

CONAD Continental Air Defense Command (of the U.S. Air Force).

CONARC Continental Army Command (of the U.S. Army).

Conc. Council.

conc. 1 a concentrate, concentrated. **b** concentration. **2** concentric. **3** concerning. **4** concerto. **5** concrete.

CONCACAF Confederation of North, Central American, and Caribbean Association Football.

concast continuous casting (of steel).

concd. or **concentr.** concentrated.

conch. conchology (study of shells and shellfish).

concl. conclusion.

concn. concentration, *esp. in chemistry, geology.*

cond. 1 a condense. **b** condensed. **c** condenser. **2 a** condition. **b** conditional. **c** conditioner. **3 a** conduct. **b** conducted by *music.* **c** *also* **Cond.** conductor *music.* **4** conductivity.

condr. conductor.

Conelrad or **CONELRAD** (kon′əl rad) control of electromagnetic radiation (former system to confuse enemy radio direction-finding equipment; replaced by *EBS* in 1963).

con esp. with expression *music.* [Italian *con espressione*]

Conf. 1 Confederation. **2** Conference. **3** Confessor: *Conf. Pont.* = *Confessor and Bishop.* [Latin *Confessor Pontifex*] **4** Confucius.

conf. 1 compare. [Latin *confer*] **2** conference. **3** confidential.

Confed. 1 Confederacy. **2** Confederate. **3** Confederation.

config. configuration.

Cong. 1 a Congregation. **b** Congregational. **c** Congregationalist. **2 a** Congress. **b** Congressional: *Cong. Comm.* = *Congressional Committee.*

cong. gallon *pharmaceutics.* [Latin *congius*]

Cong. Rec. Congressional Record.

conj. 1 a conjugate *mathematics, grammar.* **b** conjugation *grammar.* **2 a** conjunction. **b** conjunctive.

CONLIS Committee on National Library and Information Systems.

Conn. Connecticut.

conn. 1 a connected. **b** connection. **c** connector. **2** connotation.

Conrail (kon′rāl′) Consolidated Rail (corporation that administers the freight operations of many eastern and midwestern railroads; formed by the U.S. government, now privately held).

CONS connection-oriented network service (data service that must make a connection before sending a mesage).

Cons. 1 a consecrated. **b** consecration. **2** Conservative. **3** Conservatory. **4** Constable. **5 a** Constitution. **b** Constitutional: *Cons. Amend.* = *Constitutional Amendment.* **6** Consul.

cons. 1 consecrated. **2** consecutive. **3** consequence. **4** conservation. **5** conserve *medicine.* **6 a** consigned. **b** consignment *commerce.* **7** consolidated. **8** *British* consols (consolidated bonds or stocks). **9** consonant. **10** constant, esp. in combination: *cons.sp.* = *constant speed.* **11 a** constitution. **b** constitutional. **12** construction. **13** consulting. **14** *British* conveniences: *a small flat with all mod.cons.*

consec. consecutive: *consec.ds.* = *consecutive days.*

con.sec. *or* **con.sect.** conic section.

Conserv. 1 *also* **conserv.** Conservation. **2** Conservatory.

Cons.Gen. Consul General.

consgt. consignment *commerce.*

consol. consolidated.

Consols *or* **consols** (kən solz') Consolidated Annuities (of the Consolidated Funds, which are an issue of British Government bonds at fixed interest).

consperg. dust or sprinkle *pharmaceutics.* [Latin *consperge*]

Const. 1 Constable: *Head Const. J.N.W. Swart.* **2** Constantinople. **3 a** Constitution. **b** Constitutional.

const. 1 constant. **2** constituency. **3 a** constitution. **b** constitutional. **4** construction.

constit. constituent.

constr. 1 construction. **2** construed.

Cont. 1 contemporary. **2 a** Continent. **b** Continental. **3 a** continue. **b** continued. **c** continuous. **4** controller.

cont. 1 against. [Latin *contra*] **2 a** containing. **b** contents. **3 a** continent. **b** continental. **4 a** continuation. **b** continue. **c** continued. **d** continuous. **5** contract. **6** contrary. **7 a** control. **b** *also* **Cont.** controller.

contam. contaminate.

contbd. contraband.

Contbg. contributing: *Contbg. Ed.* = *Contributing Editor.*

contd. *or* **Contd.** continued.

contemp. contemporary.

conter. rub together *pharmaceutics.* [Latin *contere*]

contg. 1 containing. **2** continuing.

contl. *or* **Contl.** continental.

contn. continuation.

contr. 1 a contract. **b** contracted. **c** contraction. **d** *also* **Contr.** contractor. **2** *also* **Contr.** contralto. **3** contrary. **4 a** *also* **Contr.** contributor. **b** contribution. **5 a** control. **b** *also* **Contr.** controller.

contra. contraindication *medicine.*

contrail condensation or vapor trail *meteorology.*

contr. bon. mor. contrary to good manners. [Latin *contra bonos mores*]

cont. rem. let the remedy be continued *pharmaceutics.* [Latin *continuetur remedium*]

contrib. 1 *also* **Contrib.** contributing. **2** contribution. **3** *also* **Contrib.** contributor.

CONUS Continental United States.

Conv. 1 convent. **2** convocation.

conv. 1 convalescent. **2** convenient. **3 a** convention. **b** conventional. **4** conversation. **5 a** converted. **b** converter. **c** convertible.

coop. *or* **co-op. 1** cooperation. **2** cooperative (party, stores, society, union, etc.).

coord. 1 coordinate. **2** coordination.

COP 1 coefficient of performance (of heat) *physics.* **2** customer-owned property *commerce.*

Cop. Coptic.

CoP copilot.

cop. 1 copper. **2** copulative *grammar.* **3** copy. **4** copyright, copyrighted.

C.O.P.A. *or* **COPA** Committee of Agricultural Organizations (of the EEC). [French *Comité des Organisations Professionnelles Agricoles de la CEE*]

COPANT Pan American Technical Standards Commission. [Spanish *Comisión Panamericana de Normas Técnicas*]

COPD chronic obstructive pulmonary disease.

COPE *or* **C.O.P.E.** Committee on Political Education (of the AFL-CIO).

copr. *or* **copy.** copyright: *Copy.Bull.* = *Copyright Bulletin.*

Copt. Coptic.

coq. boil *pharmaceutics.* [Latin *coquatur*]

Cor. 1 Corinthians (two books of the New Testament): *I Cor.* = *One or First Corinthians; II Cor.* = *Two or Second Corinthians.* **2** Coriolanus (play by Shakespeare). **3** Coroner. **4** Corsica.

cor. 1 corner. **2** cornet *music.* **3** coroner. **4** corpus. **5 a** correct. **b** corrected. **c** correction. **d** corrective. **6** correlative. **7 a** correspondence. **b** correspondent. **c** corresponding. **8** corrugated. **9 a** corrupted *linguistics.* **b** corruption *linguistics.*

CORAL graphical communications and control language (a high-level machine language for programming computers).

Cord. cordillera (long chain of mountains).

CORE (*pronounced* kôr) Congress of Racial Equality.

Coriol. Coriolanus (play by Shakespeare).

Cor. Mem. corresponding member.

Corn. 1 Cornish *linguistics.* **2** *also* **Cornw.** Cornwall.

corol. *or* **coroll.** corollary.

Corp. 1 Corporal. **2** Corporation. **3** Corpus: *Corp.Jur.* = *the body of law.* [Latin *Corpus Juris*]

Corpl. Corporal.

corr. 1 a correct. **b** corrected. **c** correction. **2** correlative. **3 a** correspond. **b** corresponding. **4 a** correspondence. **b** correspondent. **5** corrigenda. **6** corrosion. **7** corrugated. **8 a** corrupt *linguistics.* **b** corrupted, corruption *linguistics.*

correl. correlative.

corresp. 1 correspondence. **2 a** corresponding. **b** corresponds.

Corr. Fell. Corresponding Fellow.

Corr. Mem. Corresponding Member.

corrs. corrections.

Corr. Sec. Corresponding Secretary.

Cors. Corsica.

Cor. Sec. Corresponding Secretary.

cort. cortex.

COS *or* **C.O.S. 1** Canadian Ophthalmological Society. **2** cash on shipment *commerce.* **3** Charity Organization Society (of Great Britain). **4** Chief of Section. **5** Chief of Staff. **6** Clinical Orthopedic Society.

Cos. 1 *also* **cos.** companies. **2** *also* **cos.** counties. **3** Consul.

cos 1 *also* **c.o.s.** cash on shipment *commerce.* **2** cosine.

co.sa. as above *music.* [Italian *come sopra*]

COSAG *or* **Cosag** combined steam and gas (turbine engines).

COSAR compression scanning array radar.

COSATI Committee on Scientific and Technical Information.

COSATU Congress Of South African Trade Unions.

COSBA Computer Services and Bureaus Association.

cosec cosecant *mathematics.*

COSFPS Commons, Open Spaces and Footpaths Preservation Society (of Great Britain).

cosh hyperbolic cosine *mathematics.*

CoSIRA Council for Small Industries in Rural Areas (of Great Britain).

cosmog. cosmography (science of the structure of the universe).

Cosmop. cosmopolitan.

COSPAR *or* **Cospar** (kō'spär) Committee on Space Research (of the International Council of Scientific Unions).

COSPUP Committee on Science and Public Policy (of the National Academy of Sciences).

Coss. Consuls. [Latin *consules*]

cot 1 cotangent *mathematics.* **2** *also* **cot.** cotter pin. **3** *also* **cot.** cotton (thread or material).

COTA Certified Occupational Therapy Assistant.

COTAL Confederation of Latin American Travel Organizations. [Spanish *Confederación de Organizaciónes Turísticas de l'América Latina*]

COTC Canadian Officers' Training Corps.

coth hyperbolic cotangent *mathematics.*

COTR Contracting Officers Technical Representation.

couch. couchant (lying down with the head raised) *heraldry.*

Coun. 1 a Council (group). **b** Councilor. **2** Counsel, Counselor (lawyer).

counter emf counter electromotive force.

coup. coupling *electronics.*

cour. *or* **Cour.** of the current month (in letters). [French *courant*]

Cov. Covenant.

c.o.v. cross-over value *genetics.*

covers coversed sine *mathematics.*

COWAR Committee on Water Research.

Cox. *or* **cox.** coxswain.

Coy. company, *esp. military.*

COZI communications zone indicator (of radio transmission).

CP 1 Camp (in postal address). **2** Canadian Press (news distribution service). **3** candlepower. **4** cardinal point (of the compass). **5** carriage paid *commerce.* **6** center of pressure. **7** central processor *computers.* **8** cerebral palsy. **9** *also* **C.P.** change point *surveying.* **10** charge conjugation, parity *physics,* esp. in combination: *CP invariance.* **11** charter party (group chartering transportation). **12** *also* **C.P.** chemically pure. **13** *also* **C.P.** Chief Patriarch. **14** *also* **C.P.** Civil Procedure. **15** *also* **C.P.** Clarendon Press. **16** Classical Philology (publication). **17** *also* **C.P.** British Clerk of the Peace. **18** *also* **C.P.** Code of Procedure *law.* **19** Command Post. **20** *also* **C.P.** Common Plea. **21** *also* **C.P.** (Book of) Common Prayer (Anglican services). **22** Communist Party. **23** Congress Party (of India). **24** constant pressure. **25** construction permit. **26** control panel. **27** *also* **C.P.** Country Party (of Australia). **28** *also* **C.P.** Court of Probate.

C/P custom of the port.

Cp. Cassiopeia (constellation).

cP continental polar air.

cp 1 accompanying the solo part *music.* [Italian *colla parte*] **2** *also* **cp.** *or* **c.p.** candlepower. **3** *also* **c.p.** carriage paid *commerce.* **4** *also* **c.p.** center of pressure. **5** *also* **cp.** centipoise (unit of viscosity). **6** *also* **c.p.** chemically pure. **7** *also* **c.p.** circular pitch. **8** cold-punched (of metal). **9** *also* **cp.** compare. **10** *also* **c.p.** constant pressure. **11** *also* **cp.** coupon, in combination: *cp. on = coupon on (of investment bonds).*

CPA 1 *also* **C.P.A.** Canadian Pharmaceutical Association. **2** *also* **C.P.A.** Canadian Psychological Association. **3** *also* **C.P.A.** Certified Public Accountant. **4** *also* **C.P.A.** Chartered Patent Agent. **5** *also* **C.P.A.** Chartered Public Accountant. **6** color phase alternation (system of color television transmission). **7** *also* **C.P.A.** Commonwealth Parliamentary Association. **8** constant phase angle (element in electrical circuitry). **9** Consumer Protection Agency. **10** *also* **c.p.a.** cost, planning, and appraisal. **11** critical path analysis; CPM (system of charting and diagraming steps of a complex operation, esp. by computer).

CPAP continuous positive airway pressure *medicine.*

CPB 1 Charged Particle Beam (weapon). **2** competitive protein binding (bonding of protein molecules) *biology.* **3** Corporation for Public Broadcasting.

CPC 1 City Planning Commission. **2** *also* **C.P.C.** Clerk of the Privy Council. **3** Clinical Pathological Conference *medicine.*

CPCIZ Permanent Committee of International Zoological Congresses. [French *Comité Permanent des Congrès Internationaux de Zoologie*]

C.P.C.U *or* **CPCU** Chartered Property and Casualty Underwriter.

CPD 1 *also* **C.P.D.** charterers pay dues (for shipping). **2** chronic pulmonary disease. **3** contact potential difference *electronics.*

cpd. compound.

CPE 1 Cape (in postal address). **2** Certificate of Physical Education. **3** chronic pulmonary emphysema. **4** *also* **c.p.e.** circular probable error *navigation.* **5** computer performance evaluation. **6** contractor performance evaluation. **7** cytopathic effect (effect on cells, as of a virus) *medicine.*

cpe. centipoise (unit of viscosity).

C.Pen. penal code. [French *code pénal*]

CPFF *or* **c.p.f.f.** cost plus fixed fee (government reimbursement of a contractor for all the costs of a project).

CPFS Council for the Promotion of Field Studies.

C.P.H. Certificate in Public Health.

c.p.h. cycles per hour.

CPHA or **C.P.H.A.** Canadian Public Health Association.

CPhA or **C.Ph.A.** Canadian Pharmaceutical Association.

CPI 1 also **cpi** characters per inch printing. **2** also **C.P.I.** Consumer Price Index (of the cost of standard specific goods and services purchased at a given time).

CPIF or **cpif** cost plus incentive fee.

C.P.J.I. Permanent Court of International Justice. [French Cour Permanente de Justice Internationale]

CPK creatine phosphokinase (substance present in muscle contraction).

cPk continental polar cold air mass.

CPL 1 also **cpl** characters per line computers, printing. **2** Combined Programming Language computers.

Cpl. Corporal.

cpl. 1 carpel (part of the flower that produces seeds). **2** complete.

CPM 1 a characters per minute (of a computer printer or typist). **b** cycles per minute. **2** also **C.P.M.** common particular meter music. **3** cost per thousand. **4** critical path method; CPA (system of charting and diagraming steps of a complex operation, esp. by computer).

CP/M Control Program for Microcomputers.

cpm or **c.p.m. 1** characters per minute (of a computer printer or typist). **2 a** counts per million. **b** counts per minute (of radioactive substance monitored in medical diagnosis). **3** cycles per minute.

Cpn Copenhagen.

CPO 1 Chief Petty Officer. **2** concurrent peripheral or processing or program operation computers.

CPP 1 Canada Pension Plan. **2** also **c.p.p.** characters per pica printing. **3** critical path planning computers, also in combination: CPPS = critical path planning and scheduling. **4** also **cpp** current purchasing power.

CPPCC Chinese People's Political Consultative Conference (originally to enact the constitution of Communist China and later an advisory body).

CPR 1 Canadian Pacific Railroad. **2** cardiopulmonary resuscitation (emergency procedure to revive victim of cardiac arrest).

cpr. copper.

CPRA Council for the Preservation of Rural America.

CPRE or **C.P.R.E.** Council for the Preservation of Rural England.

CPS 1 also **C.P.S.** Certified Professional Secretary. **2** characters per second (of a computer printer). **3** also **C.P.S.** Clerk of Petty Sessions. **4** Congregational Publishing Society. **5** cycles per second physics, electronics. **6** also **C.P.S.** Keeper of the Privy Seal. [Latin Custos Privati Sigilli]

cps or **c.p.s. 1** characters per second (of a computer printer). **2** cycles per second.

cps. 1 centipoise (unit of viscosity). **2** coupons.

cp.s. candlepower second.

CPSA or **C.P.S.A.** Civil and Public Services Association (British union of civil servants).

CPSC Consumer Product Safety Commission.

cpse. centipoise (unit of viscosity).

CPSU or **C.P.S.U.** (formerly) Communist Party of the Soviet Union.

CPT 1 also **C.P.T.** certified public accountant. [Spanish Contador Público Titulado] **2** charge conjugation, parity, time physics: a CPT-reversed galaxy. **3** Paraguay Confederation of Workers. [Spanish Confederación Paraguaya de Trabajadores]

Cpt. Captain.

cpt. counterpoint music.

CPTP Civil Pilot Training Program.

cptr. carpenter.

CPU 1 central processing unit (of a computer). **2** also **C.P.U.** Commonwealth Press Union.

CPUOS Committee on the Peaceful Uses of Outer Space (of the United Nations).

CPV canine parvo virus.

CPW Certified Pediatric Worker.

cPw continental polar warm air mass.

CQ 1 also **C.Q.** Charge of Quarters (non-commissioned officer in charge of quarters). **2** commercial quality. **3** also **C.Q.** conceptual or creativity quotient. **4** conditionally qualified. **5** general call to receive (code in amateur radio broadcasting).

CQD or **C.Q.D.** radio distress signal (this original signal has been changed to SOS).

CQM Chief or Company Quartermaster, also in combination: CQMS = Company Quartermaster Sergeant.

CQSW or **C.Q.S.W.** Certificate of Qualification in Social Work.

CR 1 carriage return (of a printing head or cursor moving to the following line) computers. **2** also **C.R.** or **C/R** carrier's risk commerce. **3** cathode ray. **4** center of resistance engineering. **5** also **C.R.** Chancery Reports law. **6** chloroprene (neoprene, a synthetic rubber). **7** cold rolled (of steel). **8** color response psychology. **9** also **C.R.** or **C/R** company's risk commerce. **10** compression ratio engineering. **11** conditioned response or reflex psychology. **12** consciousness raising: CR group. **13** Consumer Reports (publication). **14** Consumers' Research. **15** control routine computers. **16** also **C.R.** Costa Rica, Costa Rican. **17** also **C.R.** cost reimbursable (of contracts). **18** also **C.R.** credit rating. **19** critical ratio. **20** crossroads (esp. on government maps and navigation charts). **21** also **C.R.** current rate commerce. **22** also **C.R.** Keeper of the Rolls. [Latin Custos Rotulorum] **23** riel (monetary unit of Cambodia or Kampuchea).

Cr I an abbreviation for: **1** also **Cr.** Center: Cty.Cr. = City Center. **2** also **Cr.** Cranch's Reports (U.S. Supreme Court Reports). **3** creatinine (substance produced by the breakdown of creatine in muscle contraction). **4** also **Cr. a** credit. **b** creditor. **5** Creek (watercourse, American Indian tribe). **6** also **Cr.** Criminal, esp. in combination: Cr. Code. **7** Crown (authority of the head of state). **8** cruzeiro (monetary unit of Brazil): Cr$. II a symbol for: chromium (chemical element).

cr 1 a also **cr.** center. **b** also **c.r.** center of resistance engineering. **2** also **cr.** crate. **3** cream. **4** created. **5** also **cr. a** credit.

b creditor. **6** crew, also in combination: *cr/m = member of the crew.* **7** crimson. **8** crochet. **9** *also* **cr.** crown (paper size).

CRA 1 California Redwood Association. **2** *also* **C.R.A.** Colorado River Authority.

CrA the Southern Crown (constellation). [Latin *Corona Australis*]

CRAC Careers Research and Advisory Centre (of Great Britain).

CRAF Civil Reserve Air Fleet (commercial airliners designated for military use in time of emergency).

CRAM Card Random Access Memory *computers.*

craniol. craniology (study of the physical characteristics of the skull).

CRB Civilian Review Board (as of conduct in a police department).

CrB the Northern Crown (constellation). [Latin *Corona Borealis*]

CRC 1 camera-ready copy *printing.* **2** Certified Rehabilitation Counselor. **3** *also* **C.R.C.** Civil Rights Commission. **4** Control and Reporting Center. **5** *also* **C.R.C.** Coordinating Research Council. **6** cyclic redundancy check (used to check accuracy of transmitted data) *computers.*

CRD 1 chronic respiratory disease. **2** Civil Rights Division (of U.S. Department of Justice). **3** Crop Research Division (of the U.S. Department of Agriculture). **4** *also* **crd** crude, esp. referring to a grade of oil.

CRE corrosion resistant, esp. in combination: *CRES = corrosion-resistant steel.*

CREEP (formerly) Committee to Re-elect the President (campaign committee for reelection of President Nixon, whose activities led to the Watergate Scandal).

cres. *or* **cresc.** crescendo *music.*

CRF 1 chronic renal failure *medicine.* **2** corticotropin releasing factor *medicine.* **3** *also* **C.R.F.** French Red Cross. [French *Croix-Rouge Française*]

CRH corticotropin releasing hormone.

CRI 1 *also* **C.R.I.** Caribbean Research Institute. **2** color reversal intermediate (duplicate negative) *photography, printing.* **3** *also* **C.R.I.** Italian Red Cross. [Italian *Croce Rossa Italiana*]

crim. *or* **Crim.** criminal, also in combination: *crim.con. = criminal conversation* (adultery) *law.*

criminol. 1 criminologist. **2** criminology.

crit. 1 critic. **2** critical. **3 a** criticism. **b** criticized.

CRK Creek (in postal address).

C.R.L. *or* **CRL 1** Certified Record Librarian. **2** Certified Reference Librarian.

C.R.L.A. California Rural Legal Assistance (a legal advocate group).

CRM 1 cross-reacting material. **2** cruise missile. **3** cultural resource management (for the protection of archaeological sites).

C.R.N.A. Certified Registered Nurse Anesthetist.

CRO 1 cathode-ray oscilloscope. **2** County Registrars or Recorders Office. **3** *also* **C.R.O.** Criminal Records Office.

Croat. Croatia, Croatian.

CROM Control Read Only Memory *computers.*

cross. crossing.

CRP 1 Conservation Reserve Program (program which pays farmers to keep easily eroded farmland out of production). **2** C-reactive protein *biochemistry.*

CRPL Central Radio Propagation Laboratory (of the National Bureau of Standards)

C.R.R. Curia Regis Roll (the King's court or King's Bench of the Norman kings of England).

CRREL Cold Region Research and Engineering Laboratory.

CRS 1 cold-rolled steel. **2** Community Relations Service (agency of U.S. Department of Justice). **3** congenital rubella syndrome (birth defects caused by rubella). **4** Congressional Research Service. **5** *also* **crs** constant rate of solution. **6** *also* **crs.** **a** credits. **b** creditors. **7** French Security or Riot Police. [French *Compagnie Republicaine de Sécurité*]

cr.st. crushed stone.

CRT 1 cathode-ray tube: *CRT display.* **2** computer terminal having a cathode-ray tube.

Crt 1 *also* **Crt.** Court. **2** crater *astronomy, geology.* **3** the Cup (constellation). [Latin *Crater*]

crt 1 crate. **2** crater *astronomy, geology.*

CRTC Canadian Radio-television and Telecommunications Commission.

CRTT Certified Respiratory Therapy Technician.

CRU *or* **cru** collective reserve unit (central banking reserves of international currencies).

Cru the Southern Cross (constellation). [Latin *Crux*]

Cruz. cruzeiro (monetary unit of Brazil).

Crv the Crow (constellation). [Latin *Corvus*]

crypto. *or* **CRYPTO 1** cryptographic. **2** *also* **Crypto.** cryptography.

cryst. 1 a crystal. **b** crystalline. **2** crystallized. **3** *also* **crystall.** crystallography.

crystn. crystallization.

CS 1 *also* **C.S.** *finance* **a** capital stock. **b** common stock. **2 a** carbon steel. **b** cast steel. **3** Cesarean section *medicine.* **4** Chief of Staff. **5** *also* **C.S.** Christian Science. **6** *also* **C.S.** **a** Civil Servant. **b** Civil Service. **7** *also* **C.S.** **a** Clerk of Session or Sessions. **b** Court of Session or Sessions. **8** close-up shot *photography.* **9** *also* **C.S.** cloth sides *bookbinding.* **10** color separation *printing*, also in combination: *CSO = color separation overlay.* **11** commercial standard. **12** conditioned stimulus *psychology.* **13** corticosteroid *medicine.* **14** current strength or intensity *electronics.* **15** cyclosporin (immunosuppressive drug) also in combination: *CSA = cyclosporin-A.* **16** *also* **C.S.** Keeper of the Seal. [Latin *Custos Sigilli*] **17** tear gas. [Carson and Staughton, its inventors]

C/S 1 call signal (of a radio station). **2** cases *commerce.*

C1S coated one side (of a sheet of paper) *printing.*

C2S coated both sides (of a sheet of paper) *printing.*

Cs *I an abbreviation for:* **1** *also* **Cs.** case *law.* **2** cirrostratus (cloud). **3** conscious *medicine, psychology.* **4** market

quotation. [French *cours*]
II *a symbol for:* cesium (chemical element).

c/s cycles per second.

cs. 1 case *commerce.* **2** census. **3** centistoke (unit of viscosity). **4** common. [Latin *communis*]

c.s. 1 *also* **cs** *finance* **a** capital stock. **b** common stock. **2** with the left hand *music.* [Italian *colla sinistra*]

CSA 1 Canadian Standards Association. **2** *also* **C.S.A.** Child Study Association (formally *C.S.A.A.* Child Study Association of America). **3** Community Services Administration. **4 a** Computer Science Association (of Canada). **b** Computing Services Association (of Great Britain). **5 a** Confederate States Army. **b** Confederate States of America.

CSB 1 *also* **C.S.B.** Bachelor of Christian Science. **2** Central Statistical Board. **3** chemical stimulation of the brain *medicine.*

CSBM confidence and security-building measures (of battlefield forces).

CSC 1 *also* **C.S.C.** Civil Service Commission. **2** Commonwealth Science Council. **3** Congregation of the Holy Cross. [Latin *Congregatio Sanctae Crucis*]

csc cosecant *mathematics.*

CSCC *or* **C.S.C.C.** Civil Service Commission of Canada.

CSCE Conference on Security and Cooperation in Europe.

csch hyperbolic cosecant *mathematics.*

CSCPRC Committee on Scholarly Communication with the People's Republic of China.

CSD 1 Children's Services Division (of the American Library Association). **2** constant speed drive *engineering.* **3** *also* **C.S.D.** Doctor of Christian Science.

CSE 1 *also* **C.S.E.** Certificate of Secondary Education (now *GCSE*). **2** *also* **cse** course.

C.S.E.A. *or* **CSEA** Civil Service Employees Association.

CSF 1 *also* **C.S.F.** Canadian Standard Freeness (laboratory test of paper composition). **2** *also* **c.s.f.** cerebrospinal fluid *medicine.* **3** colony stimulating factor (substance that stimulates formation of antibodies). **4** critical success factor (assessment of a user's essential needs of a computer).

csg. casing.

CSI 1 cholesterol, saturated-fat index. **2** compact source iodide (referring to a lamp used to illuminate TV and motion picture sets). **3** Construction Specifications Institute. **4** International Sports Commission. [French *Commission Sportif International*]

CSICC Canadian Steel Industries Construction Council (for standards).

CSIR Council for Scientific and Industrial Research (in any of various countries associated with Great Britain; under the general auspices of the CSIRO).

CSIRO Commonwealth Scientific and Industrial Research Organization (of Australia).

csk. *or* **csk 1** cask *commerce.* **2** countersink, in carpentry and design plans.

CSL 1 Commonwealth Serum Laboratories (of Australia). **2** computer simulation language.

CSLATP *or* **C.S.L.A.T.P.** Canadian Society of Landscape Architects and Town Planners.

CSLP Center for Short Lived Phenomena (of the Smithsonian Institution).

CSLT *or* **C.S.L.T.** Canadian Society of Laboratory Technologists.

CSM 1 *also* **CSMA** carrier sense multiple access (system of controlling use of a single line of communication) *computers.* **2** cerebrospinal meningitis. **3** Christian Science Monitor (newspaper). **4** command service module (of a spacecraft). **5** Commission for Synoptic Meteorology (of the United Nations). **6** corn, soya, milk (a powdered food supplement).

C.S.M.M.G. Chartered Society of Massage and Medical Gymnastics.

C.S.N. Confederate States Navy.

CSO 1 Central Statistical Office. **2** *also* **C.S.O. a** Chicago Symphony Orchestra. **b** Cincinnati Symphony Orchestra. **3** *also* **C.S.O. a** Chief Scientific Officer. **b** Chief Signal Officer. **c** Chief Staff Officer.

CSP 1 Certified System Professional *computers.* **2** *also* **C.S.P.** Congregation of St. Paul (Paulist Fathers). **3** Council for Scientific Policy (of Great Britain).

C-Span (sē'span') Cable Satellite Public Affairs Network.

CSPCA *or* **C.S.P.C.A.** Canadian Society for the Prevention of Cruelty to Animals.

CSPI Center for Science in the Public Interest.

C.S.R. *or* **CSR 1** Certified Shorthand Reporter. **2** Chartered Stenographic Reporter.

CSRS Cooperative State Research Service.

CSS 1 Canada Standard Size (a system of standardized clothing measurements). **2** Canadian scientific ship: *CSS "Hudson."* **3** Central Security Service. **4** Commodity Stabilization Service (of U.S. Department of Agriculture, now *ASCS*). **5** computer systems simulator.

CSSB compatible single side-band transmission *electronics.*

CSSDA Council for Social Service Data Archives.

CST 1 *also* **C.S.T.** *or* **c.s.t.** Central Standard Time. **2** channel status table *computers.*

Cst. coast.

cst. centistoke (measure of viscosity).

cstg. casting.

CSU 1 Christian Social Union (German political party affiliated with the Christian Democratic Union). **2** Combined State Unions (of New Zealand). **3** *also* **c.s.u.** constant speed unit *engineering.*

CSV *or* **C.S.V.** community service volunteer.

CSW 1 *also* **C.S.W.** Certificate in Social Work. **2** channel status word *computers.* **3** continuous seismic wave *geology.*

CSWY Causeway (in postal address).

CT 1 *also* **C/T** cable transfer (dispatch of money or credit by cable or telegraph). **2** cell therapy (unconfirmed medical technique of cell injection). **3** center tap *electronics.* **4** *also* **C.T.** Central Time. **5** *also* **C.T. a** certified teacher. **b** certified technician. **6** coated tablet *pharmaceutics.* **7** computer or computerized tomography: *CT scan = computer tomography scan.* **8** Connecticut (Zip Code). **9** contraterrene (anti-matter in science fiction). **10** Court (in postal address). **11** current transformer.

Ct *I an abbreviation for:* **1** *also* **Ct.** Canton. **2** *also* **Ct.** Certificate. **3** *also* **Ct.** Connecticut. **4** *also* **Ct.** Count. **5** countertenor *music.* **6** *also* **Ct.** County, esp. in combination: *Ct. Clk. = County Clerk.* **7** *also* **Ct.** Court, esp. in combination: *Ct. Cl. = Court of Claims.*
II a symbol for: celtium (chemical substance, once considered an element).

cT tropical continental air mass.

ct. **1** *also* **ct** carat (unit of weight or content of alloy). **2 a** carton. **b** crate. **3** caught *cricket.* **4** cent. **5** centime (French monetary unit). **6** circuit. **7** count. **8** court *sports.* **9** current, esp. of electricity.

c.t. **1** Central Time. **2** *also* **C.T.** career trainee.

CTA **1** Canadian Tuberculosis Association. **2** *also* **C.T.A.** Caribbean Tourist Association. **3** Chicago Transit Authority. **4** Commodities Trading Advisor. **5** *also* **C.T.A.** *or* **c.t.a.** with the will annexed *law.* [Latin *cum testamento annexo*]

CTAS center tracon automation system (for spacing planes in air traffic control).

CTB *or* **CTBT** Comprehensive Test Ban Treaty.

CTC **1** Canadian Transport Commission. **2** carbon tetrachloride. **3** Centralized Traffic Control (of trains). **4** chlortetracycline (a wide spectrum antibiotic). **5** Citizens' Training Corps. **6** *also* **C.T.C.** Civil Technical Corps. **7** critical trauma care *medicine.* **8** *also* **C.T.C.** Cyclists' Touring Club.

CTCL Cutaneous T-Cell Lymphoma.

Ct. Cls. Court of Claims.

CTE *or* **cte** coefficient of thermal expansion *engineering, physics.*

CTEB Council of Technical Examining Bodies.

CTETOC Council for Technical Education and Training for Overseas Countries.

CTF Canadian Teachers' Federation.

ctf. **1 a** certify. **b** certified. **2** certificate.

ctg. *or* **ctge.** **1** cartage. **2** cartridge. **3** cottage.

ctgh hyperbolic cotangent *mathematics.*

Ct.Ho. *or* **Cths.** Courthouse.

cTk tropical continental cold air mass.

CTL **1** *also* **Ctl.** Central. **2** *also* **c.t.l.** constructive total loss *insurance.* **3** cytotoxic T-lymphocyte (immune cell in the body that destroys virus-infected cells).

ctl. cental (unit of weight equal to 100 pounds).

CTM Mexican Federation of Labor. [Spanish *Confederación de Trabajo de Mexico*]

Ctmo. **1** centesimo (a coin of Chile, Panama, Italy, Uruguay, Somalia worth $^1/_{100}$ of the basic monetary unit). **2** centimo (a coin of Costa Rica, Spain, Venezuela, Paraguay worth $^1/_{100}$ of the basic monetary unit).

CTN New York Cotton Exchange.

ctn **1** *also* **ctn.** carton. **2** cotangent *mathematics.*

CTNE National Telephone Company of Spain. [Spanish *Compañía Telefónica Nacional de España*]

ctnh hyperbolic cotangent *mathematics.*

CTO **1** *also* **c.t.o.** canceled to order (of postage stamps for collecting). **2** Chief Technical Officer.

cto. concerto.

c. to c. *or* **c-to-c** center to center, in blueprints and drawings.

CTOL (se'tol') conventional takeoff and landing *aeronautics.*

c. to s. carting to shipside *commerce.*

CTP **1** cytidine triphosphate (a nucleotide) *biochemistry.* **2** Peruvian Confederation of Labor. [Spanish *Confederación de Trabajadores del Perú*]

ctp *or* **ctpt** counterpoint *music.*

CTR **1** Center (in postal address). **2 a** Central Tumor Registry *medicine.* **b** Certified Tumor Registrar *medicine.* **3** *also* **CTRL** control *computers.* **4 a** controlled thermonuclear reaction. **b** controlled thermonuclear reactor. **5** Currency Transaction Report.

ctr. **1** *also* **Ctr.** center. **2** counter.

CTS **1** carpal tunnel syndrome (nerve damage to the hands and fingers caused by excessive use, as in typing). **2** clear to send *computers.* **3** Courts (in postal address).

cts. **1** carats (unit of weight or content of alloy). **2** cartons. **3** centimes (French monetary unit). **4** cents. **5** certificates. **6** crates.

Ctss. Countess.

CTT *British* capital transfer tax.

Cttee. Committee.

CTU *or* **C.T.U.** Celsius or centigrade thermal unit.

CTV **1** cable television. **2** Canadian Television (a national TV network of Canada). **3** Venezuelan Confederation of Workers. [Spanish *Confederación de Trabajadores de Venezuela*]

Ctvo. centavo (coin of Argentina, Bolivia, Colombia, Mexico, and many other South and Central American countries, worth $^1/_{100}$ of the basic monetary unit).

CTW Children's Television Workshop (program development group associated with Public Broadcasting System).

cTw tropical continental warm air mass.

Cty. **1** City. **2** County.

CU **1** *also* **C.U.** Cambridge University. **2** close-up (shot) *photography.* **3** Columbia University. **4** Consumers Union. **5** container unit *commerce.* **6** control unit *computers.* **7** Cooper Union. **8** Cornell University. **9** crosstalk unit (measure of coupling between two circuits) *electronics.* **10** crystal unit *electronics.*

Cu *I an abbreviation for:* cumulus (cloud).
II a symbol for: copper (chemical element). [Latin *cuprum*]

cu. **1** cubic, esp. in combination: *cu.m. = cubic meter.* **2** cumulative.

CUA *or* **C.U.A.** Canadian Underwriter Association.

CUC chronic ulcerative colitis.

cu.cm. cubic centimeter.

CUE control unit end *computers.*

C.U.E.W. Congregational Union of England and Wales.

CUFOS Center for UFO Studies.

CUFT Center for Utilization of Federal Technology (of U.S. Department of Commerce).

cu.ft. cubic foot.

CUG closed user group (computer terminals that are confined to communicating within a group).

cu.in. cubic inch.

cuis. cuisine.

cuj. of which *pharmaceutics*. [Latin *cujus*], and in combination: *cuj.lib.* = of any. [Latin *cujus libet*]

CUKT *or* **C.U.K.T.** Carnegie United Kingdom Trust.

cul. culinary.

cult. 1 a cultivated. **b** cultivation. 2 a cultural. **b** culture *anthropology, law*.

cu.m. cubic meter.

cum *or* **cum.** cumulative: *cum files*.

Cumb. *or* **Cumbld.** Cumberland, England.

cum cp. with coupon *commerce*.

cum d. *or* **cum div.** with dividend *commerce*.

cum int. with interest *commerce*.

cu.mm. cubic millimeter.

cum. pref. cumulative preference (of shares of stock) *commerce*.

cun. cuneiform.

CUNA Credit Union National Association.

CUNY (kyü′nē) City University of New York.

CUP 1 *also* **C.U.P.** Cambridge University Press. 2 Christian Democratic People's Party of Switzerland. [German *Christlichdemokratische Volkspartei der Schweiz*] 3 Columbia University Press.

CUPE Canadian Union of Public Employees.

cur. 1 *also* **Cur.** court, esp. in combination: *cur. adv. vult.* = *the court wishes to consider*. [Latin *curia advisari vult*] 2 currency. 3 current (this month or instant).

curr. 1 currency. 2 *also* **curt.** current (esp. this month).

CURV Controlled Underwater Recovery Vehicle (of the U.S. Navy to retrieve from water of great depth).

CUS Canadian Union of Students.

cusec (kyü′sek′) cubic second (measure of rate of flow of a cubic foot per second).

CUSIP Committee on Uniform Securities Identification Procedures (of the American Bankers Association).

CUSO Canadian University Students Overseas.

CUSP Central Unit for Scientific Photography (research group in Great Britain).

CUSRPG Canada-U.S. Regional Planning Group (of NATO).

cust. 1 customer. 2 *also* **Cust.** customs. 3 *also* **Cust.** *or* **Custod.** custodian. 4 custody.

C.U.T. United Confederation of Workers (formerly in Chile). [Spanish *Confederación de Uniti Trabajadores*]

cu.yd. cubic yard.

CV 1 calorific value. 2 cardiovascular, esp. in combination: *CVA = cardiovascular accident; CVRD = cardiovascular renal disease.* 3 check valve. 4 coefficient of variation *psychology, statistics.* 5 *also* **C.V.** Common Version (of the Bible). 6 controlled variable *psychology.* 7 Cove (in postal address). 8 *also* **C.V.** horsepower. [French *cheval-vapeur*, Spanish *caballo de vapor*] 9 *also* **C.V.** résumé or biographical summary. [Latin *curriculum vitae*]

cv 1 convertible (as of bonds, etc.): *cv db = convertible debentures.* 2 *also* **cv.** cultivar (plant variety produced by selective breeding). 3 horsepower. [French *cheval-vapeur*, Spanish *caballo de vapor*]

c.v. 1 chief value or current value, esp. in customs evaluation. 2 with the voice *music*. [Italian *colla voce*]

CVA 1 cerebrovascular accident (a stroke). 2 Columbia Valley Authority.

c-v-c *or* **cvc** *or* **CVC** consonant, vowel, consonant (of three-letter words, such as *cat, bin, get,* used in early reading) *education.*

CVD 1 *also* **c.v.d.** cash versus documents *commerce.* 2 chemical vapor deposition (technique for producing thin sheets of crystalline substance, such as synthetic diamond).

CVI 1 *also* **C.V.I.** Cape Verde Islands. 2 common variable immunodeficiency (condition of decreased numbers of antibodies).

CVIS Computerized Vocational Information System.

C.V.M.A. Canadian Veterinary Medical Association.

CVn the Hounds *or* the Hunting Dogs (constellation). [Latin *Canes venatici*]

C.V.O. *or* **CVO** Commander of the Royal Victorian Order.

C.Voc. *or* **c.voc.** with the voice *music.* [Italian *colla voce*]

CVP 1 central venous pressure *medicine.* 2 Christian People's Party (of Flemish Belgium). [Flemish *Christelijke Volkspartij*]

CVR Contingent Value Rights.

CVS 1 cardiovascular system. 2 chorionic villus sampling (of placental tissue to test for birth defects).

CVT 1 constant or continuous variable transmission (of an automobile). 2 *also* **cvt.** *or* **cv't.** convertible (of bonds, etc.) *commerce.*

CW 1 call waiting (an electronic system of holding one or more calls on the same telephone). 2 *also* **C.W.** Canada West: *From 1841 to Confederation in 1867, Ontario was listed CW and Quebec CE.* 3 carrier wave *electronics,* esp. in broadcasting. 4 chemical warfare: *CW agents.* 5 Child Welfare. 6 clockwise. 7 code wave. 8 cold weld *mechanics, engineering.* 9 commercial weight. 10 continuous wave *electronics: CW laser.* 11 Country and Western *music.*

cw 1 clockwise. 2 *also* **c.w.** continuous wave *electronics.*

CWA 1 Civil Works Administration. 2 *also* **C.W.A.** Clean Water Act. 3 Communications Workers of America (labor union).

CWAS Contractor Weighted Average Share (in cost risks of a project).

CWD civilian war dead.

C.W.L. *or* **CWL 1** Catholic Women's League. **2** Child Welfare League.

Cwlth. *or* **C'wealth** Commonwealth.

CWO 1 *also* **c.w.o.** *or* **C.W.O.** cash with order *commerce.* **2** Chief Warrant Officer.

CWP Communist Workers Party.

CWR *or* **c.w.r.** continuous welded rail (of a railroad).

CWS 1 Canadian Wildlife Service. **2** Child Welfare Service. **3** coal water slurry.

cwt. *or* **cwt** hundredweight (100 lbs. U.S.; 112 lbs. U.K.). [Latin *centum* and English *weight*]

CWU Chemical Workers Union.

cx. 1 convex. **2** *also* **CX** correct (proofreader's mark).

CXT common external tariff (of the Common Market, applied to imports from nonmember countries).

CY 1 calendar year. **2** current year.

Cy 1 *also* **Cy.** County. **2 a** cyanide (chemical). **b** cyanogen (gas).

cy 1 *also* **cy.** capacity. **2** *also* **cy.** currency *commerce.* **3 a** cyanide (chemical). **b** cyanogen (gas). **4** cycle *physics, chemistry, electronics, medicine.*

cyath. glassful *pharmaceutics,* sometimes in combination: *cyath. vinos.* = *wineglassful.* [Latin *cyathus*]

cyber. *or* **Cyber.** cybernetics (comparative study of animal nervous systems with the functions of electromechanical systems).

cyborg (sī'bôrg) cybernetic organism (living organism whose functions are partly controlled by electronic devices).

cyc 1 cycle *physics, chemistry, etc.* **2** *also* **cyc.** *or* **Cyc. a** cyclopedia (specialized encyclopedia). **b** cyclopedic. **3** (sīk) cyclorama (curved curtains forming the back and sides of the stage).

cycl. *or* **cyclo. 1** *also* **Cycl.** *or* **Cyclo.** cyclopedia (specialized encyclopedia). **2** cyclotron.

Cyg Cygnus, the Swan (constellation).

cyl. 1 cylinder. **2** cylindrical (as of a lens).

Cym. 1 *also* **Cymb.** Cymbeline (play by Shakespeare). **2** Cymric (of the Welsh or their language).

CYMS *or* **C.Y.M.S.** Catholic Young Men's Society.

CYN Canyon (in postal address).

CYO *or* **C.Y.O.** Catholic Youth Organization.

Cyp. 1 Cyprian. **2** Cypriot. **3** Cyprus.

CYS compression yield strength *engineering.*

cys. *or* **Cys. 1** cysteine (an essential amino acid in protein). **2** cystine (an amino acid essential in protein building).

cysto cystology.

cyt 1 cytochrome (cell pigments essential to organic oxidation). **2** *also* **cytol. a** cytology (study of cells) *biology.* **b** cytological.

CZ 1 *also* **C.Z.** Canal Zone. **2** Cenozoic *geology, biology.* **3** combat zone *military.* **4** commercial zone.

Cz 1 Cenozoic *geology, biology.* **2** cruzeiro (monetary unit of Brazil): *Cz$.* **3** *also* **Cz. a** Czech. **b** (former) Czechoslovakia. **c** (former) Czechoslovakian.

Czech. 1 (former) Czechoslovakia. **2** (former) Czechoslovakian.

D

D *I* an abbreviation for: **1** dalasi (monetary unit of Gambia). **2** Dallas: *The Big D.* **3** *also* **D.** dam (in pedigrees). **4** *also* **D.** Dame, in combination: *D.B.E.* = *Dame Commander of the Order of the British Empire.* **5** *also* **D.** date. **6** *also* **D.** daughter. **7 a** *also* **D.** day, esp. in combination: *D.B.* = *Day Book.* **b** D day: *The H hour is always on D day. D plus 2 or D+2 means two days later.* **8** *also* **D.** Deacon. **9** debit, esp. in combination: *D/N* = *debit note.* **10** December. **11** *also* **D.** decree. **12 a** defense *sports.* **b** Defense, esp. in combination: *DoD* = *Department of Defense; D notice* = *Defense notice* (a formal request of the British government to withhold publication of a news item for reasons of national security). **13** *also* **D.** Democrat, Democratic (political party): *D for Democrat, R for Republican, I for independent.* **14** Denmark, Danish, in combination: *DKr.* = *Danish Krone.* **15** *also* **D.** Department, in combination: *DAPC* = *Department of Air Pollution Control.* **16** *also* **D.** Deputy, in combination: *DAAG* = *Deputy Assistant Advocate General.* **17** *also* **D.** *or* **ᴅ** Deutsch (used with a number in cataloging music of Schubert). **18** Deutsche, esp. in combination: *D–mark.* **19** diameter. **20** *also* **D.** died, deceased; laid to rest [Latin *depositus*]: *D.1527.* **21** dinar (monetary unit of Algeria, Bahrain, Iraq, Jordan, Kuwait, Libya, Tunisia, Yemen). **22** *also* **D.** Director, in combination: *D.G.* = *Director General.* **23** distance: *R × T* = *D means Rate multiplied by Time equals Distance.* **24** *also* **D.** district, in combination: *D.C.* = *District of Columbia.* **25** Division, esp. in combination. **26** *also* **D.** Doctor, in combination: *M.D.* = *Doctor of Medicine; D.D.* = *Doctor of Divinity.* **27** dong (monetary unit of Vietnam). **28** *also* **D.** door. **29** *also* **D.** dose *medicine.* **30** *also* **D.** double. **31** Dounias (used with a number in cataloging music of Tartini). **32** *also* **D.** Dowager. **33** drachma (monetary unit of Greece). **34** draperies (of long bands of aurora) *astronomy.* **35** drive (of a stimulus) *psychology.* **36** *also* **D. a** Duchess. **b** Duke, esp. in combination: *D.C.L.I.* = *Duke of Cornwall's Light Infantry.* **37** *also* **D.** duodecimo. **38** dust *meteorology* **39** *also* **D.** Dutch, esp. in combination: *ModD*

= *Modern Dutch.* **40** *also* **D. a** God. [Latin *Deus*] **b** Lord. [Latin *Dominus*] **c** Sir *or* Madam (form of address). [Spanish *Don/Doña,* Portuguese *Dom/Dona*]
II a symbol for: **1** density, *esp. in physics.* **2 a** Denver (designating coins minted in Denver). **b** Cleveland (branch in the Federal Reserve regional banking system, found esp. on dollar bills). **3** *also D* derivative, esp. derivative operator *mathematics.* **4** desynchronized: *D sleep.* **5** deuterium (heavy hydrogen). **6** *also* **D.** *or* ᴅ Deutsch (in classifying Schubert's music). **7** deviation *statistics.* **8** *also D* dextro, dextrorotatory *chemistry.* **9** dimensional, in combination: *3-D = three-dimensional.* **10** didymium (rare-earth metal; formerly believed to be an element, it is a mixture of neodymium and parseodymium). **11** *also D* dielectric flux density. **12** *also D* difference *statistics.* **13** *also D* diffusion coefficient *physics.* **14** displacement *physics.* **15** distortion. **16** drag *aeronautics.* **17** *also D* electric displacement *chemistry.* **18** five hundred; 500 (Roman numeral). **19 a** fourth best of its kind. **b** fourth highest grade in school, considered below average and indicating passing work. **c** fourth of a series. **20** lowest rating, after C *finance.* **21** second tone in the scale of C major. **22** shoe width greater than C and less than E. **23 a** sodium line in solar spectrum *astronomy.* **b** layer of the atmosphere (between the mesosphere and the E layer): *D layer.* **24** vitamin D.

2,4-D *or* **2:4-D** dichlorophenoxyacetic acid (a synthetic plant auxin, used for weed control; auxins control plant growth and development).

4-D dead, dying, diseased, or disabled (of animals slaughtered to make pet food, a category of the U.S. Department of Agriculture).

d *I an abbreviation for:* **1** *also* **d.** customs. [French *douane*] **2** *also* **d.** dam (in pedigrees). **3** *also* **d.** date. **4** *also* **d.** daughter. **5** day: **a** *d/a = days after acceptance.* **b** *also* **d.** in combination: *d.d. = days after date.* **6** *also* **d.** dead, esp. in combination: *dw = dead weight.* **7** deci- (tenth or 10⁻¹): *dm = decimeter.* **8** *also* **d.** deciduous *botany, dentistry.* **9** *also* **d.** decree. **10** *also* **d.** defeated *sports.* **11** *also* **d.** degree. **12** *also* **d.** delete. **13** departs, esp. in schedules. **14** *also* **d.** depth, height, altitude. **15** diameter: *c = πd means circumference equals pi times diameter.* **16** *also* **d.** died, deceased: *A. Lincoln b.1809 d.1865.* **17** *also* **d.** dime. **18** diode. **19** *also* **d.** discharged. **20** distal (terminal) *anatomy.* **21** distance: *r × t = d means rate times time equals distance.* **22** *also* **d.** dividend: *cum d. = with dividend.* **23** *also* **d.** dollar. **24** *also* **d.** door. **25** *also* **d.** dorsal. **26** *also* **d.** dose *medicine.* **27** *also* **d.** driving (esp. in horse racing). **28** *also* **d.** drizzle *meteorology.* **29** *also* **d.** duration *medicine.* **30** *also* **d.** dyne (unit of force). **31** *also* **d.** give *pharmaceutics.* [Latin *da*]
II a symbol for: **1** dalton unit (one sixteenth of the mass of an oxygen atom) *biochemistry.* **2** density, *esp. in physics.* **3** deuteron. **4** *also d* dextro, dextrorotatory *chemistry.* **5** *also d* differential (esp. differential operator) *mathematics.* **6** diopter (unit of optical refractive power). **7** dominant (of a species in a biosphere). **8 a** *also* **d.** penny (of nail sizes): *10d nails = 2 ½″ nails.* **b** penny, in former unit of money (replaced by p forpence): *3d per gallon.* [Latin *denarius*] **9** right. [French *droit*]

d- *or* **d-** **1** dextro- (dextrorotatory) *chemistry.* **2** down *or* downward (in the spin of an atomic particle): *d-quark.*

DA 1 data acquisition *computers,* also in combination: *DA&A = data acquisition and analysis.* **2** delayed action (of an explosive device). **3** *also* **D.A.** Dental Assistant. **4** Department of Agriculture, esp. in combination: *USDA = United States Department of Agriculture.* **5** Department of the Army. **6** *also* **D.A.** deposit account *commerce.* **7** desk accessory *computers.* **8** Developmental Age *medicine, psychology.* **9** *also* **D.A.** Dictionary of Americanisms. **10** dinar (monetary unit of Algeria). **11** *also* **D.A.** Diploma of Art. **12** direct access *computers.* **13** Dissertation Abstracts International (publication). **14** *also* **D.A.** District Attorney. **15** *also* **D.A.** Doctor Of Arts. **16** documents attached *or* for acceptance *commerce.* **17** don't answer, *esp. in telegraphy.*

D/A 1 *also* **d/a** days after acceptance *commerce.* **2** deposit account *commerce.* **3** *also* **D-A** digital-to-analog: *D/A conversion computers.* **4** documents attached *or* for acceptance *commerce.*

Da. 1 *also* **Da** dalton unit (one sixteenth of the mass of an oxygen atom) *biochemistry.* **2** Danish.

da 1 *also* **da.** daughter. **2** *also* **da.** day. **3** deca- (ten or 10¹): *dal = decaliter,* usually written *dkl.* **4** direct action.

DAA Drug Amendments Act (1962 law requiring pharmaceutical manufacturers to show drug is effective and safe).

DAAD German Academic Exchange Service. [German *Deutscher Akademischer Austauschdienst*]

DAAG *or* **D.A.A.G. 1** Deputy Assistant Adjutant General. **2** Deputy Assistant Advocate General.

DAB 1 *also* **D.A.B.** Dictionary of American Biography. **2** German pharmacopoeia. [German *Deutsches Apothekerbuch*]

DABS discrete address beacon system *aeronautics.*

DAC 1 data acquisition and control *computers.* **2** Development Assistance Committee (a part of the Organization for Economic Cooperation and Development). **3** *also* **D/AC** *or* **D-AC** digital-to-analog converter *computers.*

DAD Deputy Assistant Director, esp. in combination: *DADOS = Deputy Assistant Director of Ordnance Services.*

DAE *or* **D.A.E.** Dictionary of American English.

daf *or* **d.a.f.** described as follows.

DAG 1 Deputy Adjutant General. **2** *also* **D.A.G.** Development Assistance Group (international aid group including United States, Japan, Canada, and eight European countries). **3** Union of Salaried Staff Workers. [German *Deutsche Angestellten-Gewerkschaft*]

dag. decagram, decagrams.

D. Agr. Doctor of Agriculture.

DAH 1 *also* **D.A.H** Dictionary of American History. **2** disordered action of the heart *medicine.*

Dah. Dahomey.

DAI 1 *also* **d.a.i.** death by accidental injury. **2** Dissertation Abstracts International (publication).

Dak. Dakota (territory or aircraft).

dal. decaliter, decaliters.

Dall. Dallas's United States Supreme Court Reports.

Dal S. from the sign (play or sing the passage marked again) *music.* [Italian *Dal Segno*]

dam. 1 damage or damaged commerce, insurance. 2 decameter, decameters.

Dan. 1 Daniel (book of the Old Testament). 2 Danish.

DANCOM Danube Commission (regulating use of the Danube River).

D&B or **D and B** discipline and bondage; B&D (referring to sadomasochistic sexual practice).

D&C also **D. and C.** Dean and Chapter. 2 dilation and curettage (gynecological procedure).

D and D 1 also **D&D** death and dying (psychological, social, and physical aspects now studied by doctors, nurses, and clergy). 2 also **D&D** decontamination and deconstruction, in nuclear technology. 3 drunk and disorderly (a criminal charge).

D and E or **D&E** dilation and evacuation (method of abortion).

D&H dressed and headed (of lumber).

D.&J. December and June (of accounting statements).

D&M dressed and matched (of lumber).

D&O directory and officers (of business liability insurance).

D. and P. or **D&P** develop and print photography.

d. and s. demand and supply economics.

Danl. Daniel (book of the Old Testament).

DANTES (dan'tēz) Defense Activity for Non-Traditional Education Support.

DAP 1 diallyl phthalate (a moisture-resistant plastic). 2 also **d.a.p.** documents against payment commerce. 3 also **DAPT** Draw a Person test psychology.

DAR 1 also **D.A.R.** Daughters of the American Revolution. 2 delayed allergic response (as the reaction to a tuberculin test). 3 Directorate of Atomic Research (of Canada).

D.Arch. Doctor of Architecture.

DARE 1 Dictionary of American Regional English (American dialect dictionary). 2 Drug Abuse Resistance Education.

Darpa (där'pə) Defense Advanced Research Projects Agency (of U.S. Department of Defense).

DAS 1 Data Acquisition System computers. 2 also **das** delivered alongside ship commerce. 3 direct access storage computers.

DASD direct access storage device (usually a computer disk and its drive).

DAT 1 Differential Aptitude Test psychology. 2 digital audiotape. 3 dynamic address translator computers.

dat. dative grammar.

DATA 1 Defense Air Transportation Administration. 2 Draughtsmen's and Allied Technicians' Association.

DATEL (dā'tel) data telecommunications (trade name for commercial telephone transmission of computer data).

DATO Discover America Travel Organizations.

dau. daughter.

D.A.V. or **DAV** Disabled American Veterans.

Dav. David.

DAX (daks) German index of stock prices. [German Deutscher Aktien Index]

DB 1 also **D.B.** Bachelor of Divinity. 2 database computers. 3 also **D.B. a** date book. **b** day book (diary or bookkeeping journal). 4 deals and battens (wood for flooring). 5 delayed broadcast (of a radio or television program broadcast). 6 Domesday Book. 7 double-break (of relay contacts). 8 double-breasted. 9 dry bulb (esp. of a temperature reading taken with a dry-bulb thermometer). 10 German Federal or Central Bank. [German Deutsche Bundesbank] 11 German Federal Railways. [German Deutsche Bundesbahn]

dB decibel, decibels.

db 1 database computers. 2 also **db.** decibel, decibels. 3 double-breasted.

d.b. 1 **a** date book. **b** day book (bookkeeping journal). 2 double bass music.

DBA 1 Database Administrator computers. 2 also **D.B.A.** Doctor of Business Administration.

dBA decibels at A-level (within normal human range).

dba 1 decibels adjusted. 2 also **d.b.a.** or **d/b/a** doing business as: Beaver Meadow Creamery, Inc., d.b.a. Beaver Creamery.

DBB 1 deals, battens, and boards (wood, esp. for flooring). 2 German Civil Servants' Union. [German Deutscher Beamtenbund]

D.B.E. or **DBE** Dame Commander of the Order of the British Empire.

d.b.h. diameter breast high forestry.

DBI Dittler Brothers Inc. (printer of U.S. postage stamps).

D.Bib. Douay Bible.

dBk or **dbk** decibels (calculated from a base of one kilowatt).

dbk. drawback commerce.

dbl. or **dble.** double.

DBM or **D.B.M.** Diploma in Business Management.

dBm or **dbm** decibels (calculated from a base of one milliwatt).

DBMS database management system computers.

D.B.N. or **d.b.n.** of the goods not yet administered (of letters of administration of an executor) law. [Latin de bonis non]

dbn double bassoon music.

DBP 1 diastolic blood pressure medicine. 2 German Federal Patent. [German Bundespatent]

dBrn or **DBRN** decibels above reference noise.

DBS 1 direct broadcasting by satellite. 2 direct broadcast satellite.

DBST or **D.B.S.T.** Double British Summer Time.

DBT dry bulb temperature (thermometer reading).

dbt. debit.

dBv or **dbv** decibels (calculated from a base of one volt).

dBw or **dbw** decibels (calculated from a base of one watt).

DBX or **dbx** Dolby noise reduction electronics.

DC 1 also **D.C.** or **d.C.** after Christ; AD. [Italian dopo Cristo, Spanish después de Cristo] 2 Christian Democratic Party (of Italy). [Italian Democrazia Cristiana] 3 **a** data communication computers, esp. in combination: DCCU = data communication control unit. **b** data conversion computers. 4 also **D.C.**

death certificate. **5** *also* **D.C.** decimal classification (Dewey system of library cataloging). **6** Dental Corps. **7** depth charge (antisubmarine explosive). **8** Deputy Consul (in a diplomatic corps). **9** design change *engineering*. **10** *also* **D/C** deviation clause *insurance*. **11** digital computer. **12** direct coupled *computers*, esp. in combination: *DCTL = direct-coupled transistor logic*. **13** *also* **D.C.** *or* **d-c** direct current (of electricity). **14** *also* **D.C.** Disciples of Christ (Protestant sect). **15** *also* **D.C.** District Commissioner. **16** *also* **D.C.** District Court. **17 a** District of Columbia (Zip Code). **b** *also* **D.C.** District of Columbia. **18** *also* **D.C.** Doctor of Chiropractic. **19** double crochet (direction in needlework). **20** repeat from the beginning *music*. [Italian *da capo*]

d.c. 1 *also* **dc** dead center *engineering*, in combination: *t.d.c. = top dead center*. **2** deviation clause *insurance*. **3** *also* **dc** direct current *electricity*. **4** *also* **d/c** double column, *esp. in accounting and printing*. **5** double crochet (direction in needlework). **6** repeat from the beginning *music*. [Italian *da capo*]

DCA 1 Defense Communications Agency (of U.S. Department of Defense). **2** deoxycorticosterone acetate (used for adrenal insufficiency). **3** Department of Civil Aviation (of Australia). **4** document content architecture *computers*.

DCAA Defense Contract Audit Agency (of U.S. Department of Defense).

D.Cap. *or* **d cap.** double foolscap (paper size).

DCASR Defense Contract Administration Services Region.

DCB dichlorobenzidine (chemical used in processing of dyes).

DCC digital compact cassette (digital tape recording).

DCE 1 data circuit terminal equipment (modem, terminal, etc.) *computers*. **2** data communications equipment. **3** *also* **D.C.E.** Doctor of Civil Engineering. **4** domestic credit expansion (British measure of money supply excluding foreign reserves and overseas borrowing).

DCEP *or* **D.C.E.P** Diploma of Child and Educational Psychology.

DCF 1 data collection form. **2** *also* **d.c.f.** *British* discounted cash flow.

dcg. decagram.

DCH *or* **D.C.H.** Diploma in Child Health.

D.Ch. Doctor of Surgery. [Latin *Doctor Chirurgiae*]

D.Ch.E. *or* **DChE** Doctor of Chemical Engineering.

DCI 1 data communication interrogate *computers*. **2** Director of Central Intelligence. **3** *also* **dci** double column inch *advertising*.

DCJ District Court Judge.

D.C.L. *or* **DCL 1** Doctor of Canon Law. **2** Doctor of Civil Law.

dcl. 1 decaliter. **2** *also* **Dcl.** declaration *commerce, insurance, law*.

D.C.M. *or* **DCM 1** *British* Distinguished Conduct Medal. **2** Doctor of Comparative Medicine.

dcm. decameter.

D.Cn.L. Doctor of Canon Law.

DCO diffusing capacity *medicine*.

DCofS Deputy Chief of Staff.

D.Com.L. Doctor of Commercial Law.

D.Comp.L. Doctor of Comparative Law.

DCP *or* **D.C.P. 1** Diploma in Clinical Pathology. **2** Diploma in Clinical Psychology.

DCR Democratic Constitutional Rally (a Tunisian political party).

DCS 1 Defense Communications System. **2** Deputy Chief of Staff. **3** *also* **D.C.S.** Deputy Clerk of Sessions. **4** Direct Coupled System. **5** *also* **D.C.S.** Doctor of Christian Science. **6** *also* **D.C.S.** Doctor of Commercial Science. **7** dorsal column stimulator (electrical device that supplies impulses to stimulate the spinal nerves and relieve pain).

DCT 1 *also* **D.C.T.** Doctor of Christian Theology. **2** *also* **dct** document.

DCTL direct-coupled transistor logic *computers*.

D.C.V.O. Dame Commander of the Royal Victorian Order.

DCWV *or* **dcwv** direct current working voltage.

DD 1 *also* **D/D** *commerce*. **a** days after date. **b** days after delivery. **2** *also* **D.D.** dedicated. [Latin *dedicavit*] **3** *also* **D.D.** *or* **D/D** demand draft *commerce*. **4** Deputy Director, esp. in combination: *DDST = Deputy Director of Supplies and Transportation*. **5** dichloropropane-dichloroprene (chemical soil sterilant). **6** dishonorable discharge *military*. **7** District Director (esp. of the U.S. Internal Revenue Service or the U.S. Customs Service). **8** *also* **D.D.** Doctor of Divinity. **9** due date *commerce, obstetrics*.

D.d. he or she gave to God. [Latin *Deo dedit*]

dd 1 *also* **d.d.** dated. **2** *also* **d.d.** *or* **d/d** *commerce*. **a** days after date. **b** days after delivery. **3** *also* **d.d.** day's date. **4** *also* **dd.** dedicated. [Latin *dedicavit*] **5** *also* **d.d.** delayed delivery *commerce*. **6** *also* **dd** delivered. **7** *also* **d.d.** *or* **d/d** delivered at dock *commerce*. **8** *also* **d.d.** demand draft *commerce*. **9** drydock. **10** *also* **d.d.** he or she gave as a gift. [Latin *dono dedit*]

DDA 1 Demand Deposit Account, in banking. **2** digital differential analyzer *computers*.

D-Day 1 June 6, 1944 (day of the Allied assault on the Germans at Normandy in World War II). **2** any appointed time to begin something.

DDB double declining balance *commerce*.

DDC 1 Dewey Decimal Classification (library cataloging system). **2** direct digital control *computers*.

DDD 1 Direct Distance Dialing (signified by a three-digit telephone number). **2** *also* **D.D.D. a** he or she gave and consecrated as a gift. [Latin *dono dedit dedicavit*] **b** he or she gives, devotes, and dedicates. [Latin *dat, dicat, dedicat*]

d. de J.C. year of the Lord; after Christ; AD: *Vespasiano, 9–72 d. de J.C.* [Spanish *después de Jesús Cristo*]

DDH *or* **D.D.H.** Diploma in Dental Health.

DDI 1 dideoxyinosine (drug used to treat AIDS). **2** *also* **D.D.I.** Directorate of Intelligence.

d.d. in d. from day to day, esp. in medicine. [Latin *de die in diem*]

DDL Data Description Language *computers*.

DDM *or* **D.D.M. 1** Diploma in Dermatological Medicine. **2** Doctor of Dental Medicine.

DDO Directorate of Operations.

DDP distributed data processing *computers.*

D.D.R. (formerly) German Democratic Republic (East Germany). [German *Deutsche Demokratische Republik*]

DDS 1 Deep Diving System. **2** Department of Defense Support (purchasing agent of Australia Department of Defence). **3** diaminodiphenyl sulfone (drug used to treat Hansen's disease, leprosy). **4** digital data service (for transmitting data) *computers.* **5** *also* **D.D.S. a** *also* **D.D.Sc.** Doctor of Dental Science. **b** Doctor of Dental Surgery.

dd/s delivered sound (of grain).

DDST Denver Developmental Screening Test (measure of childhood development).

DDT dichlorodiphenyl-trichloroethane (powerful and very harmful insecticide).

ddt. deduct *commerce.*

DDTA derivative differential thermal analysis (investigation of chemical structure of materials).

DDVP dimethyl dichlorovinyl phosphate (insecticide).

DE 1 *also* **D.E.** deckle edge (rough untrimmed edge on paper). **2** defensive end, in football. **3** Delaware (Zip Code). **4** Department of Employment (of Great Britain). **5** Department of Energy; DOE (of the United States). **6** diesel engine. **7** *also* **D.E.** Doctor of Engineering. **8** double entry *accounting.* **9** lower house of parliament of the Irish Republic. [Irish Gaelic *Dail Eireann*]

DEA 1 diethanolomine (wetting agent used in soaps and detergents). **2** Drug Enforcement Administration (agency of U.S. Department of Justice).

Dea. Deacon.

Deb (*pronounced* deb) debutante.

deb. 1 *also* **deben.** debenture. **2** debit.

D.Ec. *or* **D. Econ.** Doctor of Economics.

Dec. 1 Dean. [Latin *Decanus*] **2** *also* **Dec** December. **3** decile (division on a scale of data equaling one tenth of the whole) *statistics.*

dec. 1 deceased. **2** decimal. **3** decimeter. **4 a** declaration. **b** declared. **5** declension *grammar.* **6** declination. **7** decompose *chemistry, physics.* **8 a** decorated. **b** decoration. **c** decorative. **9** decrease. **10** decrescendo *music.*

decaf (dē′kaf) decaffeinated (coffee).

decd. 1 deceased. **2** declared. **3** decreased.

decid. deciduous.

decim. decimeter.

decl. 1 declaration. **2** declension *grammar.* **3** declination.

decn. 1 *also* **Decn.** decision *law.* **2** *also* **decon** decontamination.

decomp. 1 decompose. **2** *also* **decompn.** decomposition.

decres. decrescendo *music.*

decub. lying down *medicine.* [Latin *decubitus*]

D.Ed. Doctor of Education.

ded. 1 dedicated to, dedication. **2 a** deduct. **b** *also* **deduct.** deduction.

de d. in d. from day to day, *esp. in medicine.* [Latin *de die in diem*]

Deet (dēt) diethyltoluamide (chemical insect repellent).

def. 1 deceased. [Latin *defunctus*] **2** defecation *medicine.* **3** defective. **4** defendant. **5** defense. **6** deferred. **7** deficit. **8 a** defined. **b** definition. **9** definite, also in combination: *def.art.* = *definite article.*

DEFCON *or* **Defcon** (def′kon) defense condition (of a country), used with a number: *DEFCON 1 to 4 are stages of alert.*

defect. defective.

deft. defendant.

deg. 1 degeneration *medicine.* **2** degree (of temperature or angularity).

D.E.I. Dutch East Indies (*now* Indonesia).

DEL delete (character) *computers.*

Del 1 *also* **Del.** Delaware. **2** *also* **Del. a** Delegation. **b** Delegate. **3** the Dolphin (constellation). [Latin *Delphinus*]

del. 1 delegate. **2** delete. **3 a** deliver. **b** *also* **DEL** delivered. **c** delivery. **4** he or she drew it. [Latin *delineavit*]

deld. delivered.

Deleg. Delegate.

deli (del′ē) delicatessen.

delin. 1 *also* **delinq.** delinquent *commerce, law.* **2** he or she drew it. [Latin *delineavit*]

deliq. *or* **deliquesc.** deliquescent *chemistry.*

delt. he or she drew it. [Latin *delineavit*]

delvy. *or* **dely.** delivery.

Dem. Democrat, Democratic.

dem 1 *also* **dem.** demand *commerce, law.* **2** *also* **dem.** demise *law: Frank dem. Clark = Frank on the demise of Clark.* **3** *also* **dem.** democracy. **4** demodulator *electronics.* **5** demonstrative *grammar,* esp. in combination: *dem pron = demonstrative pronoun.* **6** *also* **dem.** demurrage (failure to meet a loading or unloading schedule in shipping). **7** *also* **dem.** demy (paper size) *printing.* **8** Deutsche mark (unit of money in Germany).

Demo (dem′ō) Democrat.

demo (dem′ō) demonstration.

demob. demobilization: *military demob. numbers.*

demon. demonstrative.

Den. Denmark.

den. 1 *also* **den** denier (unit of weight in silk and synthetic yarn). **2** denotation.

dend. *or* **Dend.** dendrology (study of trees).

D.Eng. Doctor of Engineering.

DENK (*pronounced* denk) dual employed, no kids; DINK (designation of a couple, esp. in personal advertisements).

denom. denomination.

dens. *or* **dens** density.

Dent. dentist.

dent. 1 a dental. **b** dentist. **c** dentistry. **2** let them be given *medicine, pharmaceutics.* [Latin *dentur*]

DEP 1 Department of Environmental Protection. **2** diethyl phthalate (used in insecticides and perfumes). **3** *also* **DEP.** laid to rest. [Latin *depositus*]

Dep. 1 Department. 2 deposit *banking.* 3 Depot. 4 Deputy: *Dep. Premier.*

dep. 1 depart, departs, departure: *dep. and arr.* 2 department. 3 dependent. 4 deponent *grammar, law.* 5 deposed. 6 a deposit: *dep.ctf. = deposit certificate.* b depositor.

DEPA Defense Electric Power Administration.

depr. 1 depreciation *commerce.* 2 depression *geology, medicine.*

dept. 1 *also* **Dept.** Department: *Dept. of Agr. = Department of Agriculture.* 2 departure: *airport dept. tax.* 3 deponent *grammar, law.* 4 *also* **Dept.** Deputy: *Dept. Sheriff.*

DER 1 Department of Environmental Resources. 2 reaction of degeneration (of nerves to muscle fibers).

der. 1 a derivation. b derivative. 2 derived.

Derby. *or* **Derbys.** Derbyshire County, England.

deriv. 1 derivation. 2 derivative.

derm. 1 dermatitis. 2 a dermatologist. b *also* **dermatol.** dermatology.

dern *or* **dern.** last. [French *dernier*]

derr *or* **derr.** back. [French *derrière*]

DES 1 data encryption standard (system to encode data sent over a communication link). 2 *also* **D.E.S.** Department of Education and Science (in Great Britain). 3 diethylstilbestrol (a substitute for estrogen).

Des. 1 Desert, esp. in geographical place names. 2 Designer: *Des. RCA = Designer of the Royal College of Arts.*

des. 1 desertion. 2 design. 3 designation. 4 dessert.

desc. 1 descendant. 2 describe.

D. ès L. Doctor of Letters. [French *Docteur ès Lettres*]

desp. despatch.

D. ès S. Doctor of Sciences. [French *Docteur ès Sciences*]

destn. destination.

DET 1 diethyltoluamide; DEET (insecticide). 2 diethyltryptamine (a hallucinogenic drug).

Det. detective, also in combination: *Det.Sgt. = Detective Sergeant; Det.Insp. = Detective Inspector.*

det. 1 detach, detached. 2 detachment *military.* 3 detail. 4 detector. 5 determiner *grammar.* 6 let it be given *medicine, pharmaceutics.* [Latin *detur*]

detn. determination.

DEU data entry unit *computers.*

Deut. Deuteronomy (book of the Old Testament).

DEV Duck Embryo Virus (used in antirabies vaccine).

Dev. 1 a Developer. b Development. 2 Devonian *geology.* 3 Devonshire County, England.

dev. 1 a develop. b developer. c *also* **devel.** development. 2 deviation, esp. in navigation. 3 *also* **dev** front. [French *devant*]

Devon. Devonshire County, England.

devp. develop.

devpt. development.

Devt. Development.

DEWAT deactivated war trophy.

DEWK (dēk) dual employed with kids (in personal advertisements).

DEW Line (dü) Distant Early Warning line (network of radar stations).

dex 1 (deks) Dexedrine (drug used to control appetite). 2 right. [Latin *dexter*]

DEZ diethylzinc (chemical used in preservation of books).

DF 1 *also* **D.F.** Dean of the Faculty. 2 decontamination factor (of radioactive exposure). 3 *also* **D.F.** Defender of the Faith (title given to Henry VIII for denunciation of Luther). 4 *also* **D/F** direction finder (electronic navigational device). 5 disk file *computers* (file of information stored on a computer disk). 6 dissipation factor *electronics.* 7 *also* **D.F.** Doctor of Forestry. 8 drop forge, in metal work. 9 Federal District (in Mexico). [Spanish *Distrito Federal*]

df 1 degrees of freedom *statistics.* 2 draft.

d.f. 1 damage free *commerce.* 2 dead freight *commerce.*

DFA *or* **D.F.A.** Doctor of Fine Arts.

DFAS Defense Finance and Accounting Service (agency of U.S. Department of Defense).

DFC 1 Development Finance Corporation (of New Zealand). 2 disk file check *computers.* 3 *also* **D.F.C.** Distinguished Flying Cross.

DFDT difluorodiphenyl-trichloroethane (powerful insecticide).

DFI developmental flight instrumentation.

D.fl. Dutch florin.

DFM 1 decayed, missing, and filled teeth *dentistry.* 2 *also* **D.F.M.** Distinguished Flying Medal.

D.F.M.S. Domestic and Foreign Missionary Society.

DFO desferrioxamine, also in combination: *DFOM = desferrioxamine-B* (for treatment of iron poisoning).

DFP diisopropyl fluorophosphate (for treatment of glaucoma).

DFS 1 disk filing system *computers.* 2 *also* **D.F.S.** German Research Institute for Soaring. [German *Deutsches Forschungsinstitut für Segelflug*]

DFT 1 Diagnostic Function Test (for program reliability). 2 discrete Fourier transform; FFT (for analysis of an acoustic signal, and for algorithmic functions in mathematics, spectrometry, physics, and chemistry).

dft. 1 defendant. 2 *also* **Dft.** draft.

DFVLR German Aerospace Research Center. [German *Deutsche Forschung und Versuchsanstalt für Luft und Raumfahrt*]

DG 1 *also* **D.G.** a by the grace of God. [Latin *Dei Gratia*] b thanks to God. [Latin *Deo Gratias*] 2 degauss (demagnetize) 3 differential generator (in a servo-system) *electricity.* 4 directional gyro *navigation.* 5 *also* **D.G.** *or* **D-G** Director General: *D.G.M.S. = (British) Director General of Medical Services.*

dg 1 *also* **dg.** decigram. 2 diglyceride *medicine.*

d.g. double gummed (paper).

DGA Directors Guild of America.

DGB German Trade Unions Federation. [German *Deutscher Gewerkschaftsbund*]

D.G.O. *British* Diploma in Gynaecology and Obstetrics.

DGRST General Delegation for Scientific and Technical Research. [French *Délégation Général pour Recherche Scientifique et Technique*]

DGRST General Delegation for Scientific and Technical Research. [French *Délégation Général pour Recherche Scientifique et Technique*]

dgt digit *mathematics, computers.*

DGZ desired or designated ground zero (designated target area, as for a nuclear weapon).

DH 1 dead heat (of a race) *sports.* **2** designated hitter *baseball.* **3** dirham (monetary unit of Morocco and United Arab Emirates). **4** *also* **D.H.** Doctor of Humanities.

dh 1 deadhead (airplane, train, etc. without passengers or freight). **2** designated hitter *baseball.* **3** double hung (of windows) *building.* **4** *also* **d.h.** that is to say, namely. [German *das heisst*]

DHA 1 dehydroepiandrosterone (an androgen or sex hormone). **2** dihydroxyacetone (artificial tanning agent).

DHEW (former) Department of Health, Education, and Welfare; HEW (of the United States).

DHHS Department of Health and Human Services (of the United States).

DHI dairy herd improvement.

D.H.L. *or* **DHL 1** Doctor of Hebrew Literature or Letters. **2** Doctor of Humane Letters.

DHQ Division Headquarters *military.*

D.Hum. Doctor of Humanities.

D.Hy. Doctor of Hygiene.

DI 1 *also* **D.I.** Department of the Interior. **2** *also* **D.I.** Detective Inspector. **3** diabetes insipidus *medicine.* **4** diplomatic immunity. **5** disability insurance. **6** *also* **D.I.** discomfort index; THI. **7** District Inspector. **8** *also* **D.I.** drill instructor *military.*

Di didymium (rare-earth metal; formerly believed to be an element).

di 1 *also* **di.** diameter. **2** *also* **d.i.** that is; i.e. [German *das ist*]

DIA 1 Defense Intelligence Agency (of U.S. Department of Defense). **2** *also* **D.I.A.** Design and Industries Association. **3** Document Interchange Architecture (system for computer database exchange).

dia. 1 diagram. **2** diameter. **3** diathermy *medicine.*

diag. 1 a diagnosis. **b** diagnostic. **2** diagonal. **3** *also* **diagr.** diagram.

DIAL differential absorption lidar (for detection of atmospheric gases).

dial. 1 dialect, dialectal. **2** dialectic, dialectical. **3** dialogue.

diam. diameter.

DIANE (dī'an) **1** Digital Integrated Attack Navigation Equipment (device that gives visual image of terrain contours, buildings, etc. for pilot and navigator). **2** Direct Information Access Network for Europe.

diap. diapason *music.*

DIC 1 *also* **D.I.C.** Diploma of the Imperial College. **2** disseminated intravascular coagulation *medicine.*

dict. 1 a dictated. **b** dictation, esp. of letters and memorandums. **2** diction. **3** *also* **Dict.** dictionary.

DID direct inward dialing (of a telephone system that connects calls to the appropriate extension).

DIDA diisodecyl adipate (in manufacture of a material to make it soft or flexible).

DIDP diisodecyl phthalate (in manufacturing of a material to make it soft or flexible).

DIDS Digital Information Display System *computers.*

dieb. alt. on alternate days *pharmaceutics.* [Latin *diebus alternis*]

diet. 1 dietary. **2** *also* **Diet.** dietician.

DIF data interchange format *computers.*

dif. *or* **diff. 1 a** difference. **b** different. **2** differential.

D.I.G. *British* Disabled Income Group.

dig. 1 *also* **Dig.** digest, esp. in combination: *Am.Dig.* = *American Digest* (of decisions in law cases); *Rdr.Dig.* = *Reader's Digest* (a commercial publication). **2 a** digit. **b** digital.

DIH Diploma in Industrial Health.

dil. 1 a dilute. **b** dilution. **2** dissolve.

dilat. dilatation.

dild. 1 diluted. **2** dissolved.

diln. dilution *chemistry.*

DIM Diploma in Industrial Management.

dim. 1 dimension. **2** *also* **dimin.** *music* **a** diminished. **b** diminuendo. **3** diminutive. **4** half *pharmaceutics.* [Latin *dimidius*]

DIN German Industrial Standards. [German *Deutsche Industrienormen*]

Din dinar (monetary unit of former Yugoslavia).

din. 1 *also* **din** dining, in combination: *din rm* = *dining room; paneled din rm.* **2** dinner.

DINFOS Defense Information School.

D.Ing. Doctor of Engineering. [Latin *Doctor Ingeniariae*]

DINK (*pronounced* dink) *or* **dink** double income, no kids; DENK (designation of a couple in demographics and in personal advertisements).

Dioc. Diocese, Diocesan.

DIP 1 dual in-line package (integrated circuit board in a printed circuit) *electronics: DIP switch.* **2** *also* **D.I.P.** sleeps in peace. [Latin *Dormit In Pace*]

Dip. 1 diploma, esp. in combination: *Dip.Econ.* = *Diploma of Economics; Dip.A.D.* = *Diploma in Art and Design; Dip.Ed.* = *Diploma in Education; Dip.T.* = *Diploma in Teaching.* **2** Diplomat.

DIPA diisopropanolamine (substance used in manufacture of water-base paints, insecticides, etc.).

DI particle defective interfering particle, defective agent (a class of viruses).

DIPEC Defense Industrial Plant Equipment Center.

diph. diphtheria.

Dipl. 1 Diploma, esp. in combination: *Dipl.Econ.* = *Diploma in Economics.* **2 a** Diplomat. **b** Diplomatic.

dipl. 1 diplomacy. **2 a** diplomat. **b** diplomatic.

DIR developer inhibitor release (of an emulsion on photographic film).

Dir. 1 directed by, *esp. in music.* **2** Director, also in combination: *Dir. Gen. = Director General.*

dir. 1 *also* **dir** direct, also in combination: *dir.coup. = direct coupling.* **2** direction.

DIS 1 Defense Intelligence School. **2** Defense Investigative Service (agency of U.S. Department of Defense). **3** disseminated intravascular coagulation *medicine.*

dis. 1 disabled. **2** discharge, discharged. **3** discipline. **4** disconnect, disconnected. **5 a** discontinued, esp. of a publisher's listing of titles. **b** *also* **dis** discontinuity *geology, mathematics, physics.* **6** discount. **7** distance, distant. **8** distribute, distributed, as of type. **9** distribution.

DISA 1 Defense Information Services Activity. **2** Defense Information Systems Agency.

disab. 1 disability. **2** disabled.

DISAM Defense Institute of Security Assistance Management.

disbs. disbursements *accounting.*

DISC 1 differential scatter (for detecting particles in the atmosphere). **2** *also* **D.I.S.C.** Domestic International Sales Corporation (subsidiary corporation whose income is derived from foreign sales).

disc. 1 *also* **Disc.** discography. **2** disconnect. **3** discontinue. **4** *also* **disc** discotheque. **5** discount. **6 a** discovered. **b** discoverer.

disch. or *military* **DISCH** discharge, discharged.

disco (dis′kō) discotheque.

discon 1 disconnect. **2** disorderly conduct: *discon arrests.*

disct. discount.

dishon. dishonorable.

disj. disjunctive *grammar,* esp. in combination: *disj. pron. = disjunctive pronoun.*

dismd. dismissed.

disp. 1 a *also* **Disp.** dispensary. **b** dispenser. **2 a** disperse. **b** dispersion.

displ. displacement.

diss. 1 *also* **Diss.** dissertation. **2** dissolve.

Dist. 1 Distributor. **2** District, also in combination: *Dist. Admin. = District Administrator.*

dist. 1 a distance. **b** distant. **2** distilled. **3 a** distinguish. **b** distinguished. **4 a** distributed. **b** distributor. **5** *also* **Dist.** district.

Dist. Atty. District Attorney.

Dist. Ct. District Court.

distn. distillation.

distr. or **distrib. 1** *also military* **DISTR a** distribute. **b** distribution. **c** distributor. **2** distributive *mathematics.*

Div. 1 *also* **Div** dividend *commerce, law.* **2 a** Divine. **b** Divinity. **3** Division, esp. in combination: *App. Div. = Appellate Division.*

div. 1 a divergence *mathematics, meteorology.* **b** diverse. **c** diversion. **2 a** divide. **b** divided, *esp. in music.* **3** *also* **divd.** dividend *commerce, law, mathematics.* **4** division. **5 a** divorce. **b** divorced.

divid. let it be divided *pharmaceutics.* [Latin *dividatur*]

div. in p. aeq. divide into equal parts *pharmaceutics.* [Latin *dividatur in partes aequales*]

divn or **Divn.** division, also in combination: *Divn.Hq. = Division Headquarters.*

Divnl. Divisional.

divs dividends.

DIY or **d.i.y.** do-it-yourself (esp. in reference to home improvement and other projects).

DJ 1 Department of Justice; DOJ. **2** dinner jacket. **3** *also* **dj** disk jockey: *DJ programs.* **4** *also* **D.J.** District Judge. **5** *also* **D.J.** Doctor of Jurisprudence, Doctor of Law. [Latin *Doctor Juris*] **6** *also* **D.-J.** Dow Jones *commerce,* also in combination referring to stock trading indexes: *DJIA = Dow Jones Industrial Average; DJTA = Dow Jones Transportation Average.* **7** *also* **dj** or **d.-j.** dust jacket (of a book or computer disk).

Dj. mountain *or* hill. [Arabic *djebel*]

d.J. 1 *also* **dJ** Junior; Jr. [German *der Jüngere*] **2** this year: *i.d.J. = in this year.* [German *dieses Jahres*]

DJD degenerative joint disease.

DJI Dow Jones Index.

DJS *or* **D.J.S.** Doctor of Juridical Science.

DJur or **D.Jur.** Doctor of Jurisprudence.

dk 1 *also* **dk.** dark. **2** deca (ten), esp. as a prefix: *dkg = decagram.* [*deka-* variant spelling, used esp. in many European languages] **3** *also* **dk.** deck. **4** *also* **dk.** dock. **5** *also* **DK** don't know *commerce.*

DKA diabetic ketoacidosis *medicine.*

DKDP deuterated potassium dihydrogen phosphate (an electrooptical crystal) *electronics.*

dkg or **dkg.** decagram, decagrams.

dkl or **dkl.** decaliter, decaliters (10 liters).

dkm or **dkm.** decameter, decameters.

DKP 1 Danish Communist Party. [Danish *Danmarks Kommunistike Parti*] **2** dipotassium phosphate (used in antifreeze, household fertilizers, culturing antibiotics, pharmaceuticals). **3** German Communist Party. [German *Deutsche Kommunistische Partei*]

Dkr Danish krone (monetary unit of Denmark).

dks or **dks.** decastere, decasteres (10 cubic meters).

dkt. or **Dkt.** docket, also in combination: *Civ. Dkt. = Civil Docket.*

Dkyd. Dockyard.

DL 1 *also* **D/L** data link *computers.* **2** *also* **D/L** demand loan *commerce.* **3** Department of Labor. **4** difference limen (difference in threshold of perception) *psychology.* **5** *also* **D.L.** Doctor of Law.

dl 1 *also* **dl.** deciliter, deciliters ($1/10$ of a liter). **2** dextro- and levorotatory molecules, racemic (of an optically inactive compound formed by combination).

DLA 1 Defense Logistics Agency (of U.S. Department of Defense). **2** Department of Labor Academy (of U.S. Department of Labor).

DLAT or **D.Lat.** difference of or in latitude.

DLB dead letter box (of the Postal Service).

DLC or **D.L.C.** Democratic Leadership Council (of the Democratic Party in the U. S.).

dld 1 deadline data. **2** also **dld.** delivered.

DLE 1 data link escape *computers*. **2** discoid lupus erythematosus (skin disorder).

DLES 1 Division of Law Enforcement Sciences (of the Bureau of Indian Affairs). **2** also **D.L.E.S.** Doctor of Letters in Economic Studies.

D.Lett. Doctor of Letters. [French *Docteur en Lettres*]

DLF 1 Designers Lighting Forum. **2** also **D.L.F.** Development Loan Fund (for credits to underdeveloped countries).

DLI Defense Language Institute (of U.S. Army).

D.-Lib. Democrat Liberal (usually a fusion ticket in an election).

DLIS or **D.L.I.S.** Desert Locust Information Service.

D.Lit. or **DLit.** or **D.Litt.** or **DLitt.** Doctor of Letters or Literature. [Latin *Doctor Lit(t)erarum*]

d.l.M. or **dlM** of the current month. [German *des laufenden Monats*]

DLO 1 Dead Letter Office (of the Postal Service, now RLO in Great Britain). **2** also **d.l.o.** dispatch loading only *commerce*.

DLONG or **D.Long.** difference of or in longitude.

DLP Democratic Labour Party (of Barbados and South Korea).

dlr. 1 dealer. **2** also **dlr** dollar.

DLS or **D.L.S. 1** debt liquidation schedule *law, commerce*. **2** also **DLSc.** or **D.L.Sc.** Doctor of Library Science.

dls. dollars.

DLSA Defense Legal Services Agency (of U.S. Department of Defense).

DLT data loop transceiver *computers*.

dlvd. delivered.

dlvr. 1 deliver. **2** also **dlvy.** delivery.

dly. 1 also **Dly.** daily. **2** delivery.

DM 1 also **dM** dark matter *astronomy*. **2** also **D.M.** Deputy Master. **3** also **DM.** Deutsche mark (monetary unit of Germany). **4** diabetes mellitus *medicine*. **5** diastolic murmur (of the heart) *medicine*. **6** digital modulation (for coding radio waves). **7** diphenylaminochloroarsine, adamsite (disabling gas, used in riot control). **8** direct marketing. **9** also **D.M.** Doctor of Mathematics. **10** also **D.M.** Doctor of Medicine. **11** also **D.M.** Doctor of Music. **12** also **D.M.** with the right hand *music*. [Italian *destra mano*]

dm or **dm.** decimeter, decimeters.

DMA 1 also **D.M.A.** Dance Masters of America. **2** Defense Mapping Agency (of U.S. Department of Defense). **3** designated market area (of a radio or television station) *advertising*. **4** dimethylamine (used in missile fuel and soap). **5** Direct Marketing Association (formerly DMAA and DMMA). **6** direct memory access *computers*.

DMAA or **D.M.A.A.** Direct Mail Advertising Association (now *DMA*).

DMAC dimethylacetamide (chemical reactant and catalyst, solvent for plastics, resins, gums, and paint remover).

DMAT Decision-Making Ability Test *psychology*.

DMath. or **D.Math.** Doctor of Mathematics.

DMB dimethoxybenzene (used in plastics, perfumes, dyes, and suntan oils).

DMBA dimethylbenzanthracene (carcinogenic substance used to determine resistance to skin cancer).

DMC 1 digital microcircuit *electronics*. **2** dimethylaminoethyl chloride hydrochloride (used in antihistamines). **3** direct manufacturing cost *commerce*.

DMCT demethylchlortetracycline (antibiotic).

DMD 1 decision-making device. **2** also **D.M.D.** Doctor of Dental Medicine. [Latin *Dentariae Medicinae Doctor*] **3** also **D.M.D.** Doctor of Mathematics and Didactics. **4** Duchennes Muscular Dystrophy *medicine*.

DMDT dimethoxy-diphenyl-trichloro-ethane (insecticide).

DME 1 distance-measuring equipment (used in air navigation): *DME radar*. **2** drilling mud emulsifier (used in drilling very deep wells). **3** dropping mercury electrode *electronics*.

DMet. or **D.Met. 1** Doctor of Metallurgy. **2** Doctor of Meteorology.

DMEU dimethylol ethylene urea (basis of crease-resistant finishes for fabrics).

DMF 1 decayed, missing, and filled teeth: *DMF rates*. **2** dimethylformamide (universal organic solvent) *chemistry*.

DMFO Defense Medical Facilities Office.

dmg. damage, *esp. in insurance, commerce*.

DMHF dimethylhydantoin formaldehyde (used in paper and textile manufacturing).

DMI 1 desmethylimipramine (antidepressant). **2** Director of Military Intelligence.

DMJ or **D.M.J.** Diploma in Medical Jurisprudence.

DMJS December, March, June, September (months ending each of the traditional financial quarters of the year).

DMK or **D.M.K.** Dravida Munnetra Kazhagam (political party in India).

DML 1 data manipulation language *computers*. **2** also **dml** demolition. **3** also **D.M.L.** Doctor of Modern Languages.

DMLS Doppler Microwave Landing System *aviation*.

DMLT or **D.M.L.T.** Diploma in Medical Laboratory Technology.

DMM digital multimeter.

dmm or **dmm.** decimillimeter, decimillimeters.

DMMA Direct Mail and Marketing Association (now *DMA*).

DMN or **DMNA** dimethylnitrosamine (chemical in certain foods and tobacco smoke that is a carcinogenic compound).

dmn dimension.

DMO 1 Director of Military Operations. **2** District Medical Officer.

DMOS diffused metal oxide semiconductor *electronics*.

DMP dimethylphthalate (used as a softening agent in plastics and rubber, coating for safety glass, insect repellent).

DMPA 1 Defense Materials Procurement Agency. **2** Depo-Provera (Depo-Medroxyprogesterone acetate, a contraceptive drug). **3** dimethylolpropionic acid (used in the manufacture of textiles, cosmetics, plastics). **4** zytron (dichlorophenyl-methyl-isopropylphosphoramidothioate, insecticide and herbicide).

DMPE dimethoxyphenylethylamine (chemical associated with schizophrenia).

DMPI desired mean point of impact *military*.

DMPP dimethylphenylpiperazinium iodide (adrenalin stimulant).

dmpr. damper.

DMPS deepwater motion-picture system.

DMR 1 defective material report. **2** digital mobilized radio. **3** *also* **D.M.R.** Diploma in Medical Radiology.

DMRE or **D.M.R.E.** Diploma in Medical Radiology and Electrology.

DMS 1 data management system *computers*. **2** Defense Mapping System. **3** Defense Materials System (sets military requirements for strategic materials). **4** dimethylsulfide (protects against high salt concentration). **5** Directorate of Military Survey (of Great Britain). **6** *also* **D.M.S.** Director of Medical Services. **7** *also* **D.M.S.** or **D.M.Sc.** Doctor of Medical Science. **8** Documentation of Molecular Spectroscopy (service issuing spectral diagrams). **9** drilling mud surfactant (used in drilling very deep wells).

DMSA Defense Medical Support Activity.

DMSO dimethyl sulfoxide (industrial solvent and topical analgesic).

DMSSC Defense Medical Systems Support Center.

dmst. or **dmstn.** demonstration.

dmstr. demonstrator.

DMT 1 *also* **D.M.T.** dimethylterephthalate (main ingredient in polyester fiber). **2** dimethyltryptamine (hallucinogenic drug). **3** Director of Military Training.

DMTS delayed matching to sample *psychology* (and in studying animal behavior).

DMU 1 decision-making unit (group in an organization). **2** dimethylolurea (used in manufacture of plywood).

D.Mus or **DMus** Doctor of Music.

DMV 1 Department of Motor Vehicles. **2** *also* **D.M.V.** Doctor of Veterinary Medicine.

DMZ demilitarized zone (buffer area to reduce chances of conflict).

D.N. 1 *also* **DN** Department of the Navy. **2** *also* **DN** Diploma in Nursing. **3** *also* **DN** Diploma in Nutrition. **4** Our Lord. [Latin *Dominus Noster*] **5** To Our Lord. [Latin *Domino Nostro*]

D/N 1 debit note *commerce*. **2** *also* **D:N** dextrose to nitrogen ratio *medicine*.

Dn sir, Mr. [Spanish *Don*]

dn. 1 down. **2** dun (esp. as the color of a horse).

DNA 1 Defense Nuclear Agency (of U.S. Department of Defense). **2** deoxyribonucleic acid (substance of most genes). **3** German Committee on Standards. [German *Deutscher Normenausschuss*] **4** Norwegian Labor Party. [Norwegian *Del Norske Arbeiderparti*]

Dna Mrs. [Spanish *Doña*]

DNase or **DNAase** deoxyribonuclease (enzyme of DNA).

DNB 1 *also* **D.N.B.** Dictionary of National Biography. **2** dinitrobenzene (used in making dyes). **3** German News Agency. [German *Deutsches Nachrichtenbüro*]

DNC 1 Democratic National Committee. **2** dinitrocresol (insecticide). **3** direct or distributed numerical control (as in computer-directed machine tool work) *computers*.

DNCB dinitrochlorobenzene (used in AIDS treatment and in measuring antibody production).

DND 1 Department of National Defense (of Canada). **2** German News Service. [German *Deutscher Nachrichten Dienst*]

Dne customs (taxes paid to import goods). [French *douane*]

DNF did not finish (of a race) *sports*.

DNI *British* Director of Naval Intelligence.

D.N.J.C. Our Lord Jesus Christ. [Latin *Dominus Noster Jesus Christus*]

DNOC dinitro-ortho-cresol (insecticide).

D Notice or **D notice** *British* Defense Notice (government request not to publish specific information for national security).

DNP 1 dinitrophenol (used in dyes, in preservative for timber, in explosives). **2** dinitrophenyl (substance that unites to form an antigen).

D.N.P.P. Our Lord the Pope. [Latin *Dominus Noster Papa Pontifex*]

D.N.R. or **DNR 1** Director of Naval Recruiting (British Admiralty). **2** do not resuscitate (on hospital patient record).

Dns or **Dns.** or **dns** Downs, on maps and in gazetteers: *S.Dns of Kent.*

D.N.Sc. Doctor of Nursing Science.

DNT dinitrotoluene (explosive).

DNUS or **Dnus** Lord. [Latin *Dominus*]

DO *I an abbreviation for:* **1** Defense Order (military order of priority to industry). **2** *also* **D/O** delivery order *commerce.* **3** *also* **D.O.** Diploma in Ophthalmology. **4** *also* **D.O.** direct order *commerce, military.* **5** dissolved oxygen (as in a body of water). **6** *also* **D.O. a** District Office. **b** District Officer. **7** *also* **D.O.** Doctor of Optometry. **8** Doctor of Oratory. **9** *also* **D.O.** Doctor of Osteopathy and Surgery. **10** Duty Officer. *II a symbol for:* action (an instruction range in a computer program loop).

do. or **d°** ditto.

DOA 1 *also* **d.o.a.** dead on arrival *medicine*. **2** Department of Agriculture; USDA. **3** *also* **DoA** Department of the Army.

DOB or **d.o.b.** date of birth.

DOC 1 *also* **D.O.C.** Commanding District Officer. **2** deoxycorticosterone (adrenal hormone, often synthetically produced). **3** *also* **DoC** Department of Commerce (of the U.S.). **4** direct operating cost *commerce*.

Doc. 1 Doctor, also in combination: *Doc.Eng. = Doctor of Engineering.* **2** *also* **doc.** document.

DOCA deoxycorticosterone acetate (synthetic adrenal hormone).

docu or **docu. 1** *also* **docum.** document. **2** documentary.

DOD 1 *also* **d.o.d.** date of death. **2** *also* **DoD** Department of Defense. **3** *also* **d.o.d.** died of disease. **4** direct outward dialing (of a telephone system that connects extensions to outside lines).

DODDS Department of Defense Dependents Schools.

DOE 1 *also* **DoE a** Department of Education (of the U.S.). **b** *also* **DoE** Department of Energy (of the U.S.). **2** *also* **DoE** Department of the Environment (of Great Britain). **3** Director of Education.

DOF *or* **dof** degree of freedom (variables) *physics, chemistry, statistics.*

DOH *or* **DoH** Department of Health.

DOHSA Death on High Seas Act (covering death from negligence at sea).

DOI 1 *also* **d.o.i.** dead of injuries *medicine.* **2** *also* **DoI** Department of Industry. **3** *also* **DoI** Department of the Interior (of the U.S.). **4** Director of Information.

DOJ *or* **DoJ** Department of Justice (of the U.S.).

DOL 1 *also* **DoL** Department of Labor (of the U.S.). **2** *also* **D.O.L.** Doctor of Oriental Learning.

dol (dōl) unit of pain *medicine.* [Latin *dolor*]

dol. 1 dollar. **2** sweetly or softly *music.* [Italian *dolce*]

dolciss. very sweetly or very softly *music.* Italian *dolcissimo*]

D.O.M. 1 God the Lord of all. [Latin *Dominus Omnium Magister*] **2** to God, the Best and Greatest. [Latin *Deo Optimo Maximo*]

Dom. 1 Domestic, esp. in combination:d *Dom. Rel. Ct.* = *Domestic Relations Court.* **2** Dominion: *Dom. Can.* = (former) *Dominion of Canada.* **3** Lord, Master. [Latin *Dominus*]

dom. 1 domestic, also in combination: *dom. sci.* = *domestic science.* **2** domicile. **3** dominant.

Dom. Proc. the House of Lords *law.* [Latin *Domus Procerum*]

Dom. Rep. Dominican Republic.

DOMS *or* **D.O.M.S.** Diploma in Ophthalmic Medicine and Surgery.

domsat *or* **Domsat** (dom'sat') domestic satellite (communications satellite restricted in operation to a particular country).

Don. Donegal, Northern Ireland.

don. until *medicine, pharmaceutics.* [Latin *donec*]

DOPA *or* **dopa** (dō'pə) dihydroxyphenylalanine (see also **L-DOPA**).

D.Ops. (dē'ops') Director of Operations.

DOR dance-oriented rock *music.*

Dor 1 Dorado (constellation). **2** *also* **Dor.** Doric.

D.O.R.A. Defense of the Realm Act (passed in Great Britain during World War I).

DORAN Doppler ranging (system to determine missile range).

dorm (dôrm) *or* **dorm.** dormitory.

Dors. Dorset, England.

DOS 1 *also* **d.o.s.** day of sale *commerce.* **2** *also* **DoS** Department of State. **3** (*pronounced* dos) disk operating system (program on disk that controls a computer and its peripheral equipment). **4** Doctor of Optical Science.

dos. dosage, dose.

D.O.S.T. *Dictionary of the Scottish Tongue.*

DOSV deep ocean survey vessel.

DOT 1 *also* **D.O.T.** Department of Overseas Trade (of Great Britain). **2** *also* **D.O.T.** Department of Transport (of Canada). **3** *also* **DoT** Department of Transportation (of the U.S.). **4** designated order turnaround (of a stock transaction of less than 1200 shares, completed directly by a floor specialist in the exchange). **5** *Dictionary of Occupational Titles.* **6** *also* **D.O.T.** Diploma in Occupational Therapy.

DOVAP (dō'vap) Doppler velocity and position (system for tracking objects in flight).

DOW *or* **d.o.w.** died of wounds *military.*

DOW. Dowager.

doz. dozen.

DP 1 at the direction of the President. **2** data processing *computers.* **3** degree of polymerization *chemistry.* **4** delivery point *commerce.* **5** Democratic Party. **6** departure point *commerce.* **7** dew point. **8** diametral pitch (a measure of teeth per inch on a pitched gearwheel). **9** diastolic pressure *medicine.* **10** direct port (of ship transport) *commerce.* **11 a** disabled person. **b** displaced person. **12** *also* **D.P.** Doctor of Pharmacy. **13** *also* **D/P** documents against payment *commerce.* **14** double play, *esp. in baseball.* **15** double pole *electricity, electronics.* **16** durable press (of clothing). **17** duty paid *commerce.* **18** dynamic programming *computers.* **19** *also* **D.P.** the House of Lords. [Latin *Domus Procerum*]

dp 1 damp proof. **2** degree of polymerization *chemistry.* **3** *also* **d.p.** double point (a type of knitting needle). **4** double pole, esp. of an electrical switch: *dpst* = *double pole, single throw.*

DPA 1 *also* **d.p.a.** deferred payment account. **2** diphenylamine (used in making dyes, explosives, pharmaceuticals, pesticides, etc.). **3** *also* **D.P.A.** Doctor of Public Administration. **4** *also* **D.P.A.** German Press Agency. [German *Deutsche Presse Agentur*]

D.P.A.S. Discharged Prisoners' Aid Society (of Great Britain).

DPB deposit passbook *commerce.*

DPC data-processing control *computers.*

d.p.c. *British* damp proof course (seal around the foundation of a building).

DPDT *or* **dpdt** double pole, double throw (of an electrical switch).

DPE Diploma in Physical Education.

DPG *or* **DPGA** diphosphoglyceric acid (controlling the ability of red blood cells to absorb oxygen).

DPH *or* **D.P.H. 1 a** Department of Public Health. **b** Diploma in Public Health. **c** Doctor of Public Health. **2** diamond pyramid hardness.

D.Ph. *or British* **D.Phil.** Doctor of Philosophy.

D.Pharm. Doctor of Pharmacy.

D.P.I. *British* Director of Public Instruction.

dpi dots per inch (measure of density of image on a CRT screen or an optical scanner).

Dpl. 1 Diploma, esp. in combination: *Dpl.P.H.* = *Diploma in Public Health.* **2** *also* **DPL** diplomat, diplomatic (corps): *the DPL license plate.*

dpl. *or* **dplx** duplex.

DPM *or* **D.P.M.** 1 Diploma in Psychological Medicine. 2 Doctor of Pediatric Medicine. 3 Doctor of Podiatric Medicine.

dpm *or* **d.p.m.** disintegrations per minute *physics.*

DPMA Data Processing Management Association.

DPN (oxidized) *or* **DPNH** (reduced) diphosphopyridine nucleotide (enzyme in metabolic processes, now *NAD*).

DPO *or* **D.P.O.** Distributing Post Office.

dpob date and place of birth.

D.Pol.Sc. Doctor of Political Science.

DPP 1 Democratic Progressive Party (of Taiwan). 2 *also* **D.P.P.** Diploma in Plant Pathology. 3 *also* **D.P.P.** *British* Director of Public Prosecutions.

dpp. double. [German *doppelt*]

DPPH diphenylpicrylhydrazyl (chemical reagent).

DPR Director of Public Relations.

DPRK Democratic People's Republic of Korea.

DPS 1 data-processing system. 2 Department of Public Services (of Great Britain). 3 *also* **D.P.S.** Doctor of Political Science.

DPSA Data Processing Supplies Association.

DPSK differential phase shift keying (for modulation of transmission in conveying electronic data).

DPST *or* **dpst** double pole, single throw (of an electrical switch).

DPT 1 diphosphothiamine (coenzyme active in movement of muscles). 2 diphtheria, pertussis (whooping cough), tetanus: *DPT shots.*

dpt. 1 department. 2 deponent *grammar, law.* 3 *also* **Dpt.** deposition. 4 depth.

dpty. *or* **Dpty.** deputy.

DPW 1 Department of Public Welfare. 2 *also* **D.P.W.** Department of Public Works.

DQ 1 deterioration quotient. 2 *also* **D.Q.** developmental quotient (average level of development) *psychology.* 3 *also* **D.Q.** direct question, *esp. in law.* 4 disqualify, disqualified *sports, law.*

DR 1 *also* **D/R** dead reckoning *navigation,* also in combination: *DRAI = dead reckoning analog indicator.* 2 deficiency report. 3 *also* **D.R.** degeneration reaction *physiology.* 4 *also* **D/R** deposit receipt *commerce.* 5 dining room. 6 direct reduction (process for converting ore into metallic iron). 7 District Registry. 8 *also* **D/R** dock receipt *commerce.* 9 double reduced (in metal rolling to reduce thickness). 10 a Drive (in postal address). b drive *computers.*

Dr *or* **Dr.** 1 debit. [possibly abbreviation of Latin *debere* to owe] 2 debtor. 3 a Director: *Dr Gen = Director General, Mus.Dr. = Music Director.* b directed by. 4 Doctor. 5 drachma (monetary unit of Greece). 6 drawer (used with a number). 7 Drive: *Riverside Dr., New York City.*

dr *or* **dr.** 1 debit [possibly abbreviation of Latin *debere* to owe] 2 debtor. 3 door, esp. in combination: *2dr. = two-door automobile.* 4 drachma (monetary unit of Greece). 5 dram, drams (a unit of weight). 6 drawer, esp. in plans. 7 a drawing. b drawn, drawn by. 8 drill. 9 drive. 10 drum *mechanics, music.* 11 right (side, hand, etc.). [French *droite*]

Dra Draco, the Dragon (constellation).

DRAM (dē'ram') dynamic random-access memory *computers,* also in combination: *DRAMS = dynamic random-access memory systems.*

dram. 1 dramatic. 2 dramatist.

dram. pers. dramatis personae (characters in a play, motion picture, or sometimes a novel or other work).

dr.ap. apothecaries' dram.

Drav. Dravidian (family of languages of southern India and Sri Lanka, including Tamil and Telugu).

DRB Defense Research Board (of Canada).

D.R.C. Dutch Reformed Church.

drch. drachma (monetary unit of Greece).

Dr.Chem. Doctor of Chemistry.

DRDO Defence Research and Development Organization (of India).

DRE 1 Defense Research Establishment (of Canada). 2 *also* **D.R.E.** Doctor of Religious Education.

DREE Department of Regional Economic Expansion (of Canada).

Dr.Eng. Doctor of Engineering.

DRF dose-reduction factor (of radiation).

DRG Diagnosis Related Group (for reducing hospital costs).

drg. drawing.

DRGM *or* **D.R.G.M.** German registered design. [German *Deutsches Reichsgebrauchsmuster*]

Dr.h.c. Honorary Doctor. [Latin *Doctor honoris causa*]

Dr.Hy. Doctor of Hygiene.

DRI 1 Defense Research Institute. 2 directly reduced iron (produced by direct reduction).

DRIE Department of Regional Industrial Expansion (of Canada).

Dr.Ing. Doctor of Engineering. [German *Doktor Ingenieur,* Italian *Dottore in Ingegneria,* etc.]

DRIP dividend reinvestment program *finance.*

Dr.Jur. 1 Doctor of Jurisprudence. 2 Doctor of Law. [Latin *Doctor Juris*]

DRK German Red Cross. [German *Deutsches Rotes Kreuz*]

DRM direction of relative movement *navigation.*

DRL daytime running lights.

Dr.Med. Doctor of Medicine.

drn. drawn.

Dr.Nat.Sci. Doctor of Natural Science.

DRO destructive read-out (destruction of data read from storage) *computers.*

DRP 1 direct reduction process (for converting ore into iron). 2 *also* **D.R.P.** German patent. [German *Deutsches Reichspatent*]

Dr.P.H. 1 Doctor of Public Health. 2 Doctor of Public Hygiene.

Dr.Phil. Doctor of Philosophy.

Dr.Pol.Sc. Doctor of Political Science.

DRQ discomfort-relief quotient *psychology.*

DRSAMD or **D.R.S.A.M.D.** Diploma of the Royal Scottish Academy of Music and Dance.

Dr.Sc. or **Dr.Sci.** Doctor of Science.

DRT 1 dead reckoning tracer (of ships). **2** diagnostic rhyme test *psychology*.

Drt. Dartmouth.

DRTE Defense Research Telecommunications Establishment (of Canada).

Dr.Theol. Doctor of Theology.

Dr. und Vrl. printed and published by. [German *Druck und Verlag*]

Dr.Univ.Par. Doctor of University of Paris.

DRV or **DRVN** Democratic Republic of (North) Vietnam.

DS 1 data set (device, such as a modem, also a file) *computers*. **2** *commerce* **a** days after sight. **b** also **D/S** days' sight: *30 D/S = payable within 30 days after presentation*. **3** also **D.S.** degree of substitution *chemistry*. **4** also **D.S.** Dental Surgeon. **5** Department of State. **6** also **D.S.** detached service, *esp. military*. **7** diethyl sulfate (used in organic synthesis) *chemistry*. **8** dilute strength *medicine, chemistry*. **9** Diplomatic Security (of U.S. Department of State). **10** also **D.S.** Doctor of Science. **11** also **D.S.** document signed, in autograph collecting. **12** Doppler sonar (for underwater tracking). **13** also **D.S.** Down's Syndrome. **14** dressed sides (of lumber): *D2S = dressed two sides*. **15** also **D.S.** from the sign *music*. [Italian *dal segno*] **16** God. [Latin *Deus*]

Ds 1 dysprosium (discarded symbol for chemical element, now *Dy*). **2** God. [Latin *Deus*]

ds 1 also **d.s.** *commerce* **a** days after sight. **b** days' sight: *15 d.s. = payable within 15 days after presentation*. **2** also **ds.** decistere, decisteres ($1/10$ of a cubic meter). **3** also **d.s.** document signed, in autograph collecting. **4** double-stranded *biology*: ds RNA. **5** also **d.s.** double strength *building*. **6** also **d.s.** from the sign *music*. [Italian *dal segno*]

DSA 1 daily subsistance allowance (for business travel on an expense account). **2** Defense Supply Agency. **3** digital subtraction angiography *medicine*. **4** Direct Selling Association. **5** also **D.S.A.** Distinguished Service Award. **6** division service area *military*.

DSAA Defense Security Assistance Agency (of U.S. Department of Defense).

D.S.A.O. Diplomatic Service Administration Office (of Great Britain).

DSAR daily subsistance allowance rates (schedules for business travel on expense account).

DSARC Defense Systems Acquisition Review Council.

DSAS Division of Substance Abuse Services.

DSB 1 double sideband *radio*. **2** Drug Supervisory Board (of the United Nations).

DSC 1 also **D/Sc** data-to-synchro converter *computers*. **2** also **D.S.C.** Distinguished Service Cross. **3** also **D.S.C.** Doctor of Surgical Chiropody. **4** also **dsc** double silk covered (of wire insulation).

D.Sc. Doctor of Science.

DSCB data set control block *computers*.

D.Sc.Eng. Doctor of Science in Engineering.

DSCM or **D.S.C.M.** Diploma of the Sydney Conservatory of Music.

DSDP Deep Sea Drilling Project.

DSE or **D.S.E.** Doctor of Science in Economics.

DSECT or **DSect.** dummy section (of a memory) *computers*.

Dsf Düsseldorf, Germany.

dsgn or **dsgn. 1 a** design. **b** designer. **2** designation *computers*.

DSI Dairy Society International.

DSIF Deep Space Information Facility (of NASA).

DSIR Department of Scientific and Industrial Research (now *SERC* in Great Britain).

DSKY (dis'kē) display and keyboard (used esp. by astronauts to communicate with an on-board computer).

DSL deep scattering layer.

DSM or **D.S.M. 1** Diagnostic and Statistical Manual (of the American Psychiatric Association). **2** Distinguished Service Medal. **3** Doctor of Sacred Music.

DSMA disodium methylarsonate (chemical used esp. to control crabgrass).

Dsmd. or **dsmd.** dismissed.

DSN Deep Space Network *astronautics*.

DSNA Dictionary Society of North America.

DSO 1 a Dallas Symphony Orchestra. **b** Detroit Symphony Orchestra. **2** also **D.S.O.** Distinguished Service Order.

D.Soc.Sci. Doctor of Social Science.

DSP 1 Democratic Socialist Party. **2** diarrheic shellfish poison *medicine*. **3** also **d.s.p.** died without issue. [Latin *decessit sine prole*] **4** digital signal processor (high-speed data processing) *computers*. **5** Digital Sound Processing. **6** also **d/sp.** double spacing.

dspl. disposal, esp. in combination: *med.wt. dspl. = medical waste disposal*.

DSPS delayed sleep phase syndrome (sleeping disorder).

DSR 1 also **D.S.R.** Director of Scientific Research. **2** dynamic spatial reconstructor *medicine*.

DSRV Deep Submergence Rescue Vehicle.

DSS 1 decision support system (data to help make decisions) *computers*. **2** also **D.S.S.** Doctor of Holy Scripture. [Latin *Doctor Sacrae Scripturae*] **3** also **D.S.S.** or **D.S.Sc.** Doctor of Social Science.

d.s.s. dioctyl sodium sulfosuccinate (wetting agent and laxative).

DSSP Deep Submergence Systems Project (for research and submarine escape and rescue).

DSSV Deep Submergence Search Vehicle (for rescue and research).

DST 1 also **D.S.T.** or **d.s.t.** Daylight Saving Time. **2** Defense and Security of the Country (French intelligence service). [French *Défense et Sécurité du Territoire*] **3** also **D.S.T.** Doctor of Sacred Theology. **4** *British* Double Summer Time.

dstl. distill.

dstn. destination.

dstrib. distribution.

D.Surg. Dental Surgeon.

DSW 1 Department of Social Welfare. **2** device status word *computers*. **3** *also* **D.S.W. a** Doctor of Social Welfare. **b** Doctor of Social Work.

DT 1 data transmission. **2** *also* **D.T.** Daylight Time. **3** defensive tackle, in football. **4** delirium tremens. **5** *also* **D.T.** Dental Technician. **6** Department of Transportation. **7** displacement ton (unit of ship displacement in water). **8** *also* **D.T.** Doctor of Theology. **9** double throw (of an electrical switch).

dt 1 *also* **d.t.** delirium tremens. **2** *also* **d.t.** displacement ton (unit of ship displacement in water). **3** double throw (of an electrical switch). **4** double time.

DTA differential thermal analysis (investigation of mineral structure, chemical analysis of polymers, carbohydrates, study of radiation damage).

DTC direct to consumer.

D.T.C.D. Diploma in Tuberculosis and Chest Disease.

DTCU data transmission control unit *computers*.

DTD Directorate of Technical Development (of the British Ministry of Supply).

dtd *or* **dtd.** dated, *esp. in commerce*.

d.t.d. give of such doses *medicine*. [Latin *dentur tales doses*]

DTE data terminal equipment *computers*.

D.Tech. *or* **DTech.** Doctor of Technology.

DTH 1 delayed type hypersensitivity (of an allergic reaction) *medicine*. **2** *also* **D.T.H.** Diploma in Tropical Hygiene.

D.Th. *or* **D.Theol.** Doctor of Theology.

DTI Department of Trade and Industry (of Great Britain).

DTL diode transistor logic *electronics*.

DTM *or* **D.T.M. 1** Diploma in Tropical Medicine. **2** Doctor of Tropical Medicine.

D.T.M.H. Diploma in Tropical Medicine and Hygiene.

DTP 1 desktop publishing *computers*. **2** diphtheria, tetanus, pertussis (whooping cough): *DTP shots*. **3** distal tingling on percussion *medicine*.

DTPA diethylenetriaminepentaacetic acid (a chelating agent) *chemistry*.

DTR 1 *also* **D.T.R.** deep tendon reflex *medicine*. **2** *also* **D.T.R.** Diploma in Therapeutic Radiology. **3** *computers* **a** disposable tape reel. **b** distribution tape reel.

DTS digital termination system *computers*.

d.t.'s delirium tremens.

DTSA Defense Technology Security Administration.

DTTU data transmission terminal unit *computers*.

DTU data transmission or transfer unit *computers*.

3-DTV three-dimensional television.

D.T.V.M. *or* **DTVM** Diploma in Tropical Veterinary Medicine.

DU 1 diagnosis undetermined *electronics, medicine*. **2** digital unit. **3** display unit *computers, aeronautics*. **4** duodenal ulcer *medicine*.

Du. 1 Duke. **2** Dutch.

du 1 *also* **du.** dilution units. **2** *also* **d.U.** the undersigned. [German *der Unterzeichnete*]

Dub. *or* **Dubl.** Dublin, Ireland.

dub. dubious.

DUI *or* **D.U.I.** driving under the influence (of alcohol or, sometimes, drugs).

DUKW *or* **Dukw** (duk) amphibious truck of the U.S. Army. [group of letters from manufacturer's code: *d* boat, *u* truck body, *kw* chassis, given name *duck* for their fanciful similarity to the animal]

Dul. Duluth, Minnesota.

Dumf. Dumfries, Scotland.

du./mg. dilution units per milligram.

Dun. Dundee, Scotland.

dun. dunnage (loose packing around cargo).

Dunelm. of Durham (in reference to the Bishop and therefore used as a signature). [Latin *Dunelmensis*]

D.Univ. Doctor of the University.

duo. duodecimo (paper size) *printing*.

DUP 1 Democratic Unionist Party (of Northern Ireland). **2** *also* **D.U.P.** Doctor of the University of Paris. [French *Docteur de l'Université de Paris*] **3** (*pronounced* dŭp) duplicate.

dup *or* **dup.** *or* **dupl. 1** duplex *commerce, biology*. **2** (*pronounced* dŭp) duplicate.

Dur. 1 Durban, South Africa. **2** Durham, England.

dur. dolor. for the duration of the pain *medicine*. [Latin *durante dolore*]

DUSA *Dispensatory of the United States of America* (description of drugs, chemicals, and tests used in medicine).

DUSC Deep Underground Support Center *military*.

Dut. Dutch.

DUV data-undervoice (digital microwave transmission).

DV 1 *also* **d.V.** author. [German *der Verfasser*] **2** dependent variable *statistics*. **3** dilute volume. **4** distinguished visitor. **5** dorsiventral *botany*. **6** *also* **D.V.** Douay Version. **7** *also* **d.v.** double vibration (one complete cycle of a sound wave, used to determine pitch). **8** God willing. [Latin *Deo volente*]

DVA Disabled Veterans Administration (of Canada).

D.V. & D. Diploma in Venereology and Dermatology.

D.V.H. Diploma in Veterinary Hygiene.

DVI digital video interactive (system for recording video and audio signals on CD-ROM) *computers*.

DVM 1 digital voltmeter. **2** *also* **D.V.M.** Doctor of Veterinary Medicine.

D.V.M.S. Doctor of Veterinary Medicine and Surgery.

DVP 1 Digital Voice Privacy network (radio system of the FBI for secure communications). **2** *also* **d.v.p.** died in his or her father's life. [Latin *decessit vita patris*]

Dvr. driver.

DVS 1 Descriptive Video Service (TV programming for the blind). **2** *also* **D.V.S. a** *also* **D.V.Sc.** Doctor of Veterinary Science. **b** Doctor of Veterinary Surgery.

DVST direct view storage tube *computers.*

DW 1 *also* **D/W** dead weight, also in combination: *DWC = dead weight capacity.* **2** dishwasher. **3** distilled water. **4** *also* **D/W** dock warrant *commerce.* **5** dust wrapper (of a book or compact disk).

d.w. 1 *also* **dw** dead weight: *210,000-ton dw tanker.* **2** *also* **d/w** *or* **DIW** dextrose and water *medicine.* **3** *also* **d-w** dust wrapper.

DWC *or* **d.w.c.** deadweight capacity.

dwg. 1 drawing. **2** *also* **dwel.** dwelling.

DWI *or* **D.W.I. 1** died without issue. **2** driving while intoxicated.

DWL 1 design waterline (of a ship at rest without cargo). **2** dominant wavelength.

dwl dowel, doweling.

dwn *or* **Dwn 1** down. **2** *also* **Dwn.** Down (esp. on maps, in gazetteers).

DWPF Defense Waste Processing Facility.

DWR Daily Weather Report.

dwr 1 drawer, as in plans and designs. **2** *also* **Dwr** Drawer, as in a postal address.

DWT 1 *also* **d.w.t.** deadweight ton *commerce.* **2** *also* **dwt.** pennyweight. [denarius weight]

DWU *or* **D.W.U.** Distillery, Wine and Allied Workers Union.

DWV drain, waste, and vent *plumbing.*

DX *I an abbreviation for:* **1** daylight exposure (of photographic film). **2** *also* **dx** differential. **3** *also* **D.X.** distance or distant, esp. of radio reception. **4** duplex *electronics.*
II a symbol for: **1** *also* **Dx** diagnosis *medicine.* **2** highest priority.

DXF data exchange format (file format for computers).

DXR *or* **D.X.R.** *or* **DX-R** deep X-ray, also in combination: *DXRT = deep X-ray therapy.*

Dy dysprosium (chemical element).

dy. 1 delivery. **2** *also* **dyd.** dockyard. **3** duty. **4** *also* **d.y.** the younger, junior: *Sigval Bergesen d.y.* [Norwegian *den yngre*]

dyn. 1 *also* **dynam.** dynamics. **2** dynamite. **3** dynamo. **4** *also* **dyn** dyne, dynes (unit of force).

DZ 1 dizygotic (of twins). **2** *also* **D.Z.** *or* **D. Zool.** Doctor of Zoology. **3** drop zone (in parachuting) *military,* also in combination: *DZA = drop zone area.*

dz. dozen.

E

E *I an abbreviation for:* **1** *also* **E.** East, Eastern (the compass point or in combination): *EbS = East by South, EIC = East India Company.* **2** edge (of lumber or paper in bookbinding): *DE = deckle edge.* **3** efficiency, esp. in combination: *EER = energy efficiency ratio.* **4** effort, in combination: *ME = maximum effort.* **5** Egyptian, in combination: *£E = Egyptian pound.* **6 a** electron, in combination: *ECO = electron coupled oscillator.* **b** electronic, in combination: *EDP = electronic data processing.* **7** emalangeni (plural of *lilangani,* monetary unit of Swaziland). **8** *also* **E.** emmetropia (normal condition of the lenses of the eyes). **9** end *football.* **10** energy, esp. in combination: *ME = metabolized energy.* **11** Engineer, Engineering, esp. in combination: *EM = Engineering Manual.* **12** *also* **E.** English, esp. in combination: *ME = Middle English.* **13** enhanced, enhancement *electronics, medicine,* esp. in combination: *E-HEMT = enhancement mode high electron mobility transistor, E-IPV = enhanced inactivated poliovirus vaccine.* **14** equatorial (esp. equatorial air) *meteorology.* **15** error *statistics, sports.* **16** estimated, esp. in combination: *ETA = estimated time of arrival.* **17** European, esp. in combination: *EEC = European Economic Community, E$ = European dollar or Eurodollar.* **18** evaporation. **19** excellence, excellent. **20** export. **21** extra, in combination: *EHV = extra high voltage.* **22** *also* **E.** eye, esp. in combination: *RE = right eye.* **23** Spanish (language, in tables). [French *espagnol,* Spanish *español*]

II a symbol for: **1** eddy diffusivity (mixing of fluids in motion) *chemistry, physics.* **2** einsteinium (chemical element; approved symbol *Es*). **3** electric field strength. **4** *also* **E** electromotive force (esp. of a voltaic cell). **5** elliptical nebula (in combination with a number from 0, circular, to 7). **6** energy (in ergs): $E = MC^2$. **7** erbium (chemical element; approved symbol *Er*). **8** exa- (10^{18}, one quintillion): *E-volt = exavolt or one quintillion volts.* **9 a** fifth of a series. **b** conditional grade given in school until unfinished work is completed. **c** shoe width greater than D; the greatest standard shoe width. **d** third tone in the scale of C major. **10** *physics* **a** illumination. **b** irradiance. **11** iron line in solar spectrum *astronomy.* **12** layer of the atmosphere (between the *D layer* and the *F layer*): *E layer.* **13** linear strain. **14** modulus of elasticity. **15** oxidation-reduction potential, esp. when written with subscript: E_h. **16** Richmond (branch in the Federal Reserve regional banking system, found esp. on dollar bills). **17** second class (a merchant shipping classification of Lloyd's Register). **18** two hundred fifty; 250 (medieval Roman numerals).

e *I an abbreviation for:* **1** *also* **e.** east, eastern, esp. in combination: *e.d.t. = eastern daylight time.* **2** *also* **e.** eldest. **3 a** electron, esp. in combination: *eV = electron volt.* **b** electronic, esp. in combination: *e-mail.* **4** emitter (of a transistor, esp. in a circuit diagram). **5** *also* **e.** entrance (a direction in plays). **6** epoch *astronomy, geology.* **7** erg *physics.*
II a symbol for: **1** coefficient of impact. **2 a** eccentricity *math-*

ematics, physics. **b** eccentricity of the orbit *astronomy*. **3** *also* **e a** electric charge. **b** electron (e⁺ = positron, e⁻ = electron). **4** elementary charge *chemistry*. **5** emissivity (reflective ability) *physics*. **6** molar extinction coefficient *chemistry*. **7** *also* **e.** partial water vapor pressure *meteorology*. **8** permittivity (amount of resistance to electric current) *physics*. **9** specific energy *physics*. **10** 2.71828... (base of the system of natural or Naperian logarithms). **11** voltage. **12** *also* **e.** wet air without rain *meteorology*.

EA 1 Corporation (autonomous entity). [Italian *Ente Autonomo*] **2** *also* **E.A.** economic advisor. **3** *also* **E.A.** educational age. **4** effective address *computers*. **5** enemy aircraft. **6** environmental assessment or analysis (preliminary to an environmental impact statement).   **7** erythrocyte with antigen, in immunology.

ea. each.

EAA *or* **E.A.A.** Engineer and Architects Association.

EAAP European Association for Animal Production.

EAC 1 East African Community (former economic union of Kenya, Tanzania, and Uganda, dissolved in 1977). **2** erythrocyte with antigen and complement, in immunology.

EACA epsilon amino caproic acid (used to control blood flow).

ead. the same *pharmaceutics*. [Latin *eadem*]

EADI electronic altitude direction indicator *aeronautics*.

EAEC European Atomic Energy Community, also known as Euratom.

EAEG European Association of Exploration Geophysicists.

EAES European Atomic Energy Society.

EAF emergency action file.

EAFFRO East African Freshwater Fisheries Organization.

EAGGF European Agricultural Guidance and Guarantee Fund (to help finance improvements in European agriculture and stabilize world prices for agricultural products).

EAM 1 electronic accounting machine. **2** National Liberation Front (Greek underground movement in World War II). [Greek *Ethniko Apeleftherotiko Metopo*]

EAMF European Association of Music Festivals.

EAMFRO East African Marine Fisheries Research Organization.

EAN 1 Emergency Action Notification (defense warning system of the United States). **2** European Academic Network (computer network for researchers and scholars). **3** experimental allergic neuritis.

E&C edge and center (of lumber), esp. in combination: *E&CB2S = edge and center, bead 2 sides*.

E.&O.E. *or* **E.&o.e.** errors and omissions excepted *commerce, civil engineering*.

E&P 1 Editor and Publisher (magazine title). **2** *also* **E. and P.** Extraordinary and Plenipotentiary.

E and R Evangelical and Reformed Church (part of the United Church of Christ).

EAON *or* **e.a.o.n.** except as otherwise noted.

EAP 1 Employee Assistance Program. **2** Experimental Aircraft Program.

EAPA East Asian and Pacific Affairs (section of U.S. Department of State).

EARN European Academic Research Network (computer network for researchers and scholars).

EAROM electrically alterable read-only memory *computers*.

EAS 1 electronic article surveillance (tagging articles of clothing, etc. in stores with a plastic piece embedded with a metal strip that is removed on purchase). **2** equivalent air speed *aeronautics*. **3** extended area service (of telephone billing). **4** external archival storage (data files, on tape or disk) *computers*.

EASE Experimental Assembly of Structures in Extravehicular Activity (for use in space station assembly).

East. *or* **east.** eastern.

Eastw. eastward.

EAT 1 earliest arrival time. **2** earnings after taxes *finance*.

EAVRO East African Veterinary Research Organization.

EAW The *Effects of Atomic Weapons* (report by U.S. Department of Defense and the Atomic Energy Commission June 1950).

EAX electronic automatic exchange *computers, communications*.

EB 1 eastbound. **2** electron beam, also in combination: *EBW = electron beam weapon*. **3** *also* **E.B.** elementary body (of a virus). **4** *Encyclopaedia Britannica*. **5** Epstein-Barr (virus, associated with various types of human cancers). **6** Ethiopian birr (monetary unit of Ethiopia).

EBA English Bowling Association.

EBAM electron-beam addressed memory *computers*.

EBC European Brewery Convention.

EBCDIC extended binary coded decimal interchange code *computers*.

EBDC ethylene bisdithiocarbamate (a strong fungicide used in agriculture).

EBICON electron bombardment induced conductivity (of TV camera tube).

EBIS electron beam ion source (to ionize gas) *electronics, physics*.

EBIT earnings before interest and taxes *finance*.

EBM electron beam machining, in metalwork.

EbN east by north.

Ebor. of York (in reference to the Bishop of York and therefore used as his official signature). [Latin *Eboracensis*]

EBR 1 electron beam recording (recording of data or graphic images on microfilm). **2** (formerly) Experimental Breeder Reactor.

EBRA Engineer Buyers and Representatives Association.

EBRD European Bank for Reconstruction and Development (to finance rebuilding of Eastern Europe).

EBS 1 Emergency Broadcast System (to inform the public of special and often dangerous conditions). **2** *also* **E.B.S.** English Bookplate Society.

EbS east by south.

EBU 1 *also* **E.B.U.** European Boxing Union. **2** European Broadcasting Union (operating the Eurovision network).

EBV Epstein-Barr virus (associated with various types of human cancers).

EBW electron beam welding.

EBWR experimental boiling-water reactor (nuclear generator).

E by N east by north.

E by S east by south.

EC 1 East Caribbean: *EC$ = East Caribbean dollar* (monetary unit of Anguilla, Antigua and Barbados, Dominica, Grenada, Montserrat, St. Kitts–Nevis, St. Lucia, and St. Vincent). **2** electron capture *physics, chemistry.* **3** environmental control. **4 a** *also* **E.C.** Episcopal Church. **b** Established Church. **5** error correction or corrected. **6** European Community. **7** *also* **E.C.** Executive Committee. **8** extended coverage *broadcasting.* **9** extension course *education.*

Ec. Ecuador.

e.c. 1 enamel covered (as of wire insulation). **2** *also* **ec** for example. [Latin *exempli causa*]

ECA 1 Economic Commission for Africa (of the UN Economic and Social Council). **2** Economic Cooperation Administration. **3** European and Canadian Affairs (section of U.S. Department of State). **4** European Confederation of Agriculture.

ECAB Employees' Compensation Appeals Board (of U.S. Department of Labor).

ECAC 1 *also* **E.C.A.C.** Eastern College Athletic Conference. **2** European Civil Aviation Conference.

ECAFE Economic Commission for Asia and the Far East (of the UN, now *ESCAP*).

ECAP Electronic Circuit Analysis Program *computers.*

ECB 1 electronic components board. **2** *also* **E.C.B.** Evangelical Christians and Baptists (in the former Soviet Union).

ECC 1 earth continuity conductor *electricity.* **2** Employees' Compensation Commission. **3** European Cultural Center.

ecc. and so forth; etc. [Italian *eccetera*]

Eccl. 1 Ecclesiastes (book of the Old Testament). **2** Ecclesiastic, Ecclesiastical.

Eccles. Ecclesiastes (book of the Old Testament).

eccles. ecclesiology (study of church organization or of church architecture).

Ecclus. Ecclesiasticus (book of the Apocrypha).

ECCM electronic counter-countermeasures.

ECCS emergency core cooling system (of a reactor).

ECD estimated completion date.

ECDC electrochemical diffused collector transistor.

ECE 1 Early Childhood Education. **2** Economic Commission for Europe (of the UN Economic and Social Council). **3** extended coverage endorsement (in insurance).

ECF 1 eosinophilic chemotactic factor (active substance in an allergic reaction) *medicine.* **2** extended care facility *medicine.* **3** extracellular fluid *medicine.*

ECFA European Committee for Future Accelerators (of the European Laboratory for Particle Physics).

ECFMG Educational Council for Foreign Medical Graduates (also in reference to the examination given by the Council).

ECG 1 electrocardiogram. **2** electrocardiograph.

E.C.G.D. Export Credits Guarantee Department.

Ech. echelon *military.*

ECHO *or* **Echo** (ek'ō) enteric cytopathogenic human orphan (class of viruses): *ECHO virus.*

EC/IC extracranial-intracranial (in reference to arterial bypass) *medicine.*

ECITO European Central Inland Transport Organization.

ECJ European Court of Justice (of the EC).

ECL emitter coupled logic *electronics.*

ECLAC Economic Commission for Latin America and the Caribbean (of the UN Economic and Social Council).

eclec. 1 eclectic. **2** eclecticism.

ecli. eclipse.

ECLO emitter-coupled logic operator *electronics.*

ECM 1 chronic migrating red rash (of Lyme Disease). [Latin *erythema chronicum migrans*] **2** electrochemical machining. **3** electronic coding machine. **4** electronic countermeasures (against radio signals). **5** end center matched (of lumber).

ECMA European Computer Manufacturers Association.

ECMO extracorporeal membrane oxygenation (procedure used to cleanse blood of diseased newborn babies).

ECMT European Conference of Ministers of Transport (regulating international road transport).

EC(No.) Enzyme Commission (Number, for the classification of enzymes under the International Union of Biochemistry).

ECO 1 electron-coupled oscillator. **2** engineering change order. **3** English Chamber Orchestra.

eco. (ē'kō) **1** *also* **eco** ecological. **2** economics.

ecol. 1 ecological. **2** ecology.

E. coli Escherichia coli (a common intestinal bacteria).

Ecol. Soc. Am. Ecological Society of America.

econ. 1 a *also* **Econ.** economic. **b** economical. **2** *also* **Econ.** economics. **3** *also* **Econ.** economist. **4** economy.

ECOR Engineering Committee on Ocean Resources.

ECOSOC Economic and Social Council (of the UN).

ECOWAS Economic Commission of West African States.

ECP 1 engineering change proposal. **2** estradiol cyclopentylpropionate (drug used to increase fertility in domestic animals).

ECPD Engineers Council for Professional Development.

ECPS European Center for Population Studies.

ECQAC Electronic Components Quality Assurance Committee.

ECR 1 electron cyclotron resonance (source) *physics.* **2** electronic cash register (electronic system with a cash register connected to a scanner to read bar codes).

ECS 1 electroconvulsive shock (a treatment for mental patients). **2** environmental control system (controlling the living conditions in an enclosed area, such as a space capsule, the cab of some machinery, or interior areas of a ship). **3** European Communications Satellite.

ECSC European Coal and Steel Community (free trade area for coal and steel industries, no part of the European Community).

ECT electroconvulsive therapy (a treatment for mental patients).

ECU 1 *also* **E.C.U.** English Church Union. **2** environmental control unit. **3** *also* **ecu** (*sometimes* ā′kü) European Currency Unit (a money of account in the European Market). **4** extreme closeup (camera shot).

Ecua. Ecuador.

ECV energy conservation vehicle (experimental automobile).

ECWA Economic Commission for Western Africa (of the UN).

ED 1 *also* **E.D.** Doctor of Engineering. **2** Education Department (of the U.S.). **3** effective dose (of a drug or medicine): *ED$_{50}$ = median effective dose.* **4** *also* **E.D.** Efficiency Decoration (of Canada and Great Britain). **5** election district. **6** error detection or detecting, also in combination: *EDAC = Error detection and correction.* **7** erythema dose *medicine.* **8** everyday (of insertion of an advertisement in a publication). **9** existence doubtful (used chiefly to mark possible underwater obstruction on navigational charts). **10** extra duty.

ed. 1 *also* **Ed. a** edited. **b** editor. **c** editorial. **d** edition: *text ed. = text edition.* **2 a** *also* **éd.** edition. [French *édition*] **b** edition. [Spanish *edición*, Italian *edizione*] **3 a** educated. **b** *also* **Ed.** education, educational.

e.d. ex dividend *finance.*

EDA *or* **E.D.A. 1** Economic Development Administration (of U.S. Department of Commerce). **2** United Democratic Left Party (of Greece). [Greek *Eniae Demokratiki Aristera*]

EDB ethylene dibromide (solvent, fumigant, gasoline purifier).

Ed.B. Bachelor of Education.

EDC 1 *British* Economic Development Committee. **2** *also* **edc** error detection and correction. **3** European Defense Community (plan for a common W. European army, defeated by the French Assembly Aug. 30, 1954). **4** expected date of confinement (for delivery of a baby) *medicine.*

ed.cit. edition cited.

EDD 1 *also* **E.D.D.** English Dialect Dictionary. **2** expected date of delivery, *esp. in obstetrics, commerce.*

Ed.D. Doctor of Education.

EDES Hellenic National Democratic Party. [Greek *Ellinikos Democratikos Ethnikos Stratos*]

EDF 1 Environmental Defense Fund. **2** European Development Fund (of the EC). **3** *also* **E.D.F.** French National Electrical Corporation. [French *Électricité de France*]

EDH efficient deck hand (grade of seaman below Able Seaman).

EDHE experimental data handling equipment.

EDI electronic data interchange (information transfer from one computer to another).

Edin. Edinburgh, Scotland.

EDIS Engineering Data Information System.

edit. *or* **Edit. 1** edited. **2** edition. **3** editor. **4** editorial.

EDK Conference of Directors of Education (of Switzerland). [German *Erziehungsdirektorenkonferenz*]

e.d.l. deluxe edition.

EDM 1 electrical or electronic discharge machining. **2 a** electric dipole moment *physics.* **b** electron dipole moment *nuclear physics.*

Ed.M. Master of Education.

e.d.m. early day motion (usually followed by a number; British parliamentary motion to call attention to an issue or other matter, formerly raised on days when sessions ended early).

Edn. edition.

EDOC effective date of change, *esp. in commerce.*

EDP electronic data processing: *EDP auditor.*

EDPE electronic data processing equipment.

EDPS electronic data processing system.

EDR 1 electrodermal response (esp. in a lie detector or other test). **2** *also* **E.D.R.** European Depositary Receipts.

edr equivalent direct radiation (of heat in engineering).

EDRF endothelium-derived relaxing factor (substance produced by the body to prevent blood vessel constriction).

EDS 1 *also* **E.D.S.** English Dialect Society. **2** Environmental Data Service. **3** exchangeable disk store *computers.*

Ed.S. Specialist in Education.

eds. 1 editions. **2** editors.

EDSAC electronic delayed storage automatic calculator (first stored-program computer, went into operation in May 1949).

EDST *or* **E.D.S.T.** *or* **e.d.s.t.** Eastern Daylight Saving Time.

EDT *or* **E.D.T.** *or* **e.d.t.** Eastern Daylight Time.

EDTA edetic acid (chelating agent used in preserving food, in detecting lead poisoning, and in geological analysis of rock samples).

EDTV extended or enhanced definition television (giving a wider picture with greater density).

EDU European Democratic Union.

educ. 1 educated. **2** education. **3** educational.

EDV end diastolic volume *medicine.*

EDVAC Electronic Discrete Variable Automatic Computer (early computer).

Edw. Edward.

E.E. 1 *also* **EE** Early English. **2 a** *also* **EE** electrical engineer. **b** electrical engineering. **3** Envoy Extraordinary. **4** *also* **EE** errors excepted.

e.e. errors excepted.

EEA European Economic Area.

E.E.&M.P. Envoy Extraordinary and Minister Plenipotentiary.

EEB European Environmental Bureau.

EEC *or* **E.E.C.** European Economic Community (Common Market).

EEE eastern equine encephalomyelitis (inflammation of the brain and spinal cord).

EEG 1 electroencephalogram. **2** electroencephalograph. **3** electroencephalography.

EEI 1 Edison Electric Institute. **2** Environmental Equipment Institute. **3** essential elements of information.

EELS electron energy loss spectroscopy (spectrographical analysis by bombardment with a beam of electrons) *chemistry, physics.*

EEMS enhanced expanded memory specification (expanded data storage) *computers.*

EENT eye, ear, nose, and throat (now generally limited to ear, nose, and throat: *ENT) medicine.*

EEO equal employment opportunity (of a company's hiring policy), also in combination: *EEOC = Equal Employment Opportunity Commission.*

EEPROM (ē'prom or ē'ē'prom) electrically erasable programmable read-only memory *computers.*

EER energy efficiency ratio (an electric appliance in relation to electric power used).

EEROM (ē'rom or ē'ē'rom) electrically erasable read-only memory *computers.*

EET *or* **E.E.T.** Eastern European Time.

E.E.T.S. Early English Text Society.

EE.UU. United States; U.S.A. [Spanish *Estados Unidos*]

EEZ Exclusive Economic Zone.

EF 1 elevation finder. **2** English finish (of paper). **3** erythroblastosis fetalis (Rh-factor blood disease that causes death in newborn children and fetuses). **4** Expeditionary Force, esp. in combination: *AEF = American Expeditionary Force.* **5** extra fine.

EFA 1 essential fatty acid or acids *biochemistry.* **2** European Fighter Aircraft.

EFAS electronic flash approach system (of an airport runway).

EFC 1 European Federation of Corrosion. **2** European Forestry Commission.

EFD electrofluid-dynamic (method of converting fluid energy into electricity).

EFDSS *or* **E.F.D.S.S.** English Folk Dance and Song Society.

EFE 1 Eastern Fishermen's Association. **2** endocardial fibroelastosis (thickening of the inner lining of the heart).

eff. 1 a *also* **Eff.** effect. **b** effective. **2** efferens, efferent *biology.* **3** efficiency.

EFI electronic fuel injection (in an internal-combustion motor).

EFL 1 emitter-follower logic *computers.* **2** English as a foreign language. **3** *also* **E.F.L.** equivalent focal length. **4** error frequency limitcomputers. **5** External Financing Limits *commerce.*

EFLA Educational Film Library Association.

EFM 1 electronic fetal monitor *medicine.* **2** European Federalist Movement.

EFNS Educational Foundation for Nuclear Science.

EFP electronic field production (of material photographed or televised outside a studio).

EFPD equivalent full-power day.

EFPH equivalent full-power hour.

e.f.p.h. effluent flow per hour.

EFPW European Federation for the Protection of Waters.

EFRC Edwards Flight Research Center.

EFSA European Federation of Sea Anglers.

EFT electronic funds transfer (system of transferring money by computer).

EFTA European Free Trade Association (rival of the European Common Market, consisting of Austria, Finland, Iceland, Norway, Sweden, Switzerland).

EFTPOS *or* **Eftpos** *or* **Eft/pos** electronic funds transfer at point of sale.

EFTS electronic funds transfer system (for transferring money by computer).

EFU European Football Union.

EFVA Educational Foundation for Visual Aids.

EG ethylene glycol (used in antifreeze, hydraulic fluid), also in combination: *EGT = ethylene glycol bis-trichloroacetate* (used as a herbicide).

Eg. Egypt, Egyptian.

e.G. registered company. [German *eingetragene Gesellschaft*]

e.g. 1 edges gilt (of a book). **2** for example. [Latin *exempli gratia*]

EGA 1 effluent gas analysis; GEA *chemistry.* **2** enhanced graphics adaptor *computers.* **3** *also* **E.G.A.** European Golf Association.

EGADS (ē gadz') electronic ground automatic destruct sequencer (used to blow up missiles that have gone astray).

EGCR experimental gas-cooled reactor (nuclear reactor).

EGD 1 effluent gas detection. **2** electrogasdynamic.

EGF epidermal growth factor (a natural protein that promotes growth of body hair and cells in the skin, cornea, liver, blood, thyroid, etc.)

EGG 1 electrogastrogram. **2** electrogastrograph.

EGIFO Edward Grey Institute of Field Ornithology.

EGM extraordinary general meeting (of shareholders in a corporation).

e.G.m.b.H. limited liability company. [German *einetragene Gesellschaft mit beschränkter Haftung*]

EGO eccentric (orbiting) geophysical observatory.

EGPC Egyptian General Petroleum Corporation (state-owned corporation).

EGR exhaust gas recirculation.

EGT exhaust gas temperature.

EGU *or* **E.G.U.** English Golf Union.

Egypt. Egyptian.

Egyptol. 1 Egyptology. **2** Egyptologist.

EH English horn *music.*

EHD electrohydrodynamic *physics.*

EHEC ethyl hydroxyethyl cellulose.

EHF 1 European Hockey Federation. **2** *also* **ehf** extremely high frequency *electronics.*

EHL 1 Eastern Hockey League. **2** *also* **ehl** effective half-life *nuclear physics.*

ehp *or* **EHP 1** effective horsepower. **2** electric horsepower.

EHR English Historical Review (magazine title).

EHS Emergency Health Service.

EHT *or* **eht** extra-high tension.

EHV *or* **ehv** extra-high voltage *electronics.*

EI or **E.I. 1 a** East Indies. **b** East Indian. **2** also **E/I** endorsement irregular, in banking. **3** exposure index (of film) *photography.*

EIA 1 Electronic Industries Association. **2** Energy Information Administration (of U.S. Department of Energy). **3 a** environmental impact assessment. **b** Environmental Investigation Agency.

EIB 1 European Investment Bank (for long-term financing of EEC projects). **2** Export-Import Bank (of U.S.)

EIC 1 earned income credit (of U.S. tax code). **2** Engineering Institute of Canada.

eidem the same (authors, etc.) as given before. [Latin plural of *idem*]

Eigw. adjective. [German *Eigenschaftswort*]

EIK eat-in kitchen (of a kitchen large enough to have a counter or table to eat at).

EIN Employers Identification Number (for reporting taxes and working conditions).

E-in-C 1 Editor-in-Chief. **2** Engineer-in-Chief.

einschl. inclusive. [German *einschliesslich*]

Einw. inhabitant. [German *Einwohner*]

EIR environmental impact report.

EIRMA European Industrial Research Management Association.

EIRT equivalent isotropic radiated power (of a satellite signal) *communications.*

EIS 1 Economic Information Service. **2** Egyptian Intelligence Service. **3** electronic ignition system (of an automobile). **4** Environmental Impact Statement. **5** Epidemic Intelligence Service (of the U.S.).

EISA extended industry standard architecture (of computer design).

EISEP Expanded In-home Services for the Elderly Program.

EIT electrical impedance tomography *medicine.*

EIU or **E.I.U.** Economist Intelligence Unit.

EJ English Journal (publication).

ej. example. [Spanish *ejemplo*]

EJC or **E.J.C.** Engineers Joint Council.

ejusd. of the same *pharmaceutics.* [Latin *ejusdem*]

EK 1 Center Union Party of Greece. [Greek *Enosis Kentron*] **2** electrocardiogram.

e.K. or **eK** in the year of the Lord; AD. [Danish *efter Kristus*, Norwegian *etter Kristi*]

EKD or **EKID** Evangelical (Protestant) Church of Germany. [German *Evangelische Kirche in Deutschland*]

EKG 1 electrocardiogram. **2** electrocardiograph.

ekw electrical kilowatt.

EKY electrokymogram (record of uterine contraction) *medicine.*

EL 1 elevation. **2** enter left (stage direction).

el. 1 elected. **2 a** electric, electrical: *el.cond.* = *electrical conductivity.* **b** electricity. **3** element. **4 a** also **El.** elevation. **b** also **el** or **El** (*pronounced* el) elevated railway.

ELAS Hellenic People's Army of Liberation (in World War II). [Greek *Ellinikos Laikos Apeleftherotikos Stratos*]

elas. elasticity.

ELBS or **E.L.B.S.** English Language Book Society.

ELCH Evangelical Lutheran Church in America.

elct. electronics.

ELD electroluminescent display (of a flat panel, such as that of a calculator).

eld. elder, eldest.

elec. 1 a also **Elec.** electric, electrical: *Elec.Eng.* = *Electrical Engineer.* **b** also **Elec.** electrician. **c** electricity. **2** electuary (sweet paste containing medicine to be administered to animals).

elect. 1 a elected. **b** election. **2 a** also **Elect.** electric, electrical. **b** also **Elect.** electrician. **c** electricity. **3** electuary (sweet paste containing medicine to be administered to animals).

electrochem. 1 electrochemical. **2** electrochemistry.

electron. electronics.

electrophys. electrophysical.

elem. 1 element. **2** elementary.

elev. 1 elevation. **2** elevator.

ELF or **elf 1** also **e.l.f.** early lunar flare. **2** extra-low or extremely-low frequency *astronomy, physics, electronics*: *ELF signals.*

ELH Journal of English Literary History (publication).

El-hi (el'hī') elementary-high school (of a curriculum or textbook).

Eli. or **Elij.** Elijah (Hebrew prophet).

elim. eliminated, *esp. in sports.*

ELINT electronic intelligence.

ELISA or **Elisa** (i lī'sə, i lē'sə) enzyme-linked immunosorbent assay (test of blood supplies for contamination by the AIDS virus).

elix. elixir *pharmaceutics.*

Eliz. Elizabeth, Elizabethan (esp. of Queen Elizabeth I of England or during the period of her reign).

ELLA European Long Lines Agency.

ellipt. elliptical.

ELMA electromechanical aid.

ELMINT electromagnetic intelligence.

ELN 1 English Language Notes (magazine title). **2** National Liberation Army (of Colombia). [Spanish *Ejército de Liberación Nacional*]

elo. 1 also **eloc.** elocution. **2** also **eloq.** eloquence.

ELOISE (el'ō ēz') European Large Orbiting Instrumentation for Solar Experiment.

E.long. east longitude.

elong. elongation.

ELR export licensing regulations.

ELS electrophoretic light scattering (for measuring particle velocity in a magnetic field) *physics.*

El Salv. El Salvador.

ELT 1 emergency locator transmitter, also in combination: *ELTR = emergency locator transmitter receiver.* **2 a** English language teaching. **b** English Language Teaching (magazine title).

ELV 1 Expendable Launch Vehicle. **2** *also* **elv** extra-low voltage.

ELW extreme low water, also in combination: *ELWS = extreme low water, spring* (tides).

Ely easterly.

Elz. Elzevir (family of 16th, 17th century Dutch printers noted for their fine editions; also printing type).

EM 1 *also* **E.M.** Earl Marshal. **2** East Mark (the mark of former East Germany). **3** electromagnetic, esp. in combination: *EMU = electromagnetic unit.* **4** electromotive, esp. in combination: *EMF = electromotive force.* **5 a** electron microscope. **b** electron microscopy. **6** emergency maintenance. **7** emergency medicine. **8** end of medium *computers.* **9** ends matched (of lumber). **10** *also* **E.M.** Engineer of Mines. **11** enlisted man or men. **12** expanded metal.

Em 1 emanation (of radioactivity), esp. in combination: *AcEm = actinium emanation.* **2** *also* **Em.** Emanuel. **3** *also* **Em.** Eminence.

em 1 *also* **em.** afternoon, time from noon to midnight; PM. [Danish *eftermiddag*] **2** *also* **e.m.** electromagnetic, esp. in combination: *emu = electromagnetic unit.* **3** *also* **e.m.** electromotive, esp. in combination: *e.m.f. = electromotive force.* **4** emanation (of radioactivity). **5** (*pronounced* em) unit of type area in printing.

EMA 1 electron microprobe analysis (of small particles). **2** European Monetary Agreement (brought into force in 1958 when member countries restored external convertibility for their currencies).

e-mail (ē'māl') electronic mail (communications sent by computer).

EMB 1 eosin methylene blue (agar, culture medium for bacteria). **2** ethambutol (drug administered in treatment of tuberculosis).

Emb. embassy.

emb. 1 embargo. **2 a** embark. **b** embarkation. **3** embossed. **4** embroidered. **5 a** embryo. **b** embryology.

EMBO European Molecular Biology Organization.

emboff (em bôf', -bof') embassy officer (of the U.S.).

embr. 1 a embroider. **b** embroidery. **2 a** embryo. **b** *also* **embryol.** embryological. **c** *also* **embryol.** embryology.

EMC 1 emergency medical care. **2** encephalomyocarditis.

EMDP *or* **e.m.d.p.** electromotive difference of potential.

emend. *or* **Emend.** emendation, emendations.

Emer. 1 *also* **emer.** *or* **emerg.** emergency, esp. in combination: *Emer. Ct. App. = Emergency Court of Appeals.* **2** Emeritus.

E.Met. Engineer of Metallurgy.

EMF 1 electromagnetic field. **2** *also* **e.m.f.** electromotive force. **3** erythrocyte maturing factor *medicine.*

EMG 1 electromyogram. **2** electromyography (recording of electrical potential of muscle tissue).

EMI 1 Electric and Musical Industries (worldwide recording company). **2** electromagnetic interference.

EMIC emergency maternity and infant care.

EMK electromotive force. [German *elektromotorische Kraft*]

E.MnE. Early Modern English (1500–1700).

EMO Emergency Measures Organization (in Canada).

E.Mod.E. Early Modern English (1500–1700).

EMOS *or* **emos** earth's mean orbital speed.

EMP 1 electromagnetic pulse (extremely high and powerful electromagnetic radiation). **2** electromolecular propulsion (using an electric field to separate constituent molecules). **3** ethyl mercury phosphate (fungicide for seeds).

Emp. 1 Emperor, Empress. **2** Empire.

emp. 1 a plaster. [Latin *emplastrum*] **2** employment: *emp. agcy = employment agency.*

e.m.p. after the manner prescribed *pharmaceutics.* [Latin *ex modo prescripto*]

EMR 1 Department of Energy, Mines and Resources (of Canada). **2** educable mentally retarded. **3** electromagnetic resonance (used for medical diagnosis of internal conditions of the body).

EMRIC Educational Media Research Information Center.

EMS 1 Emergency Medical Service. **2** eosinophilia-myalgia syndrome (blood disorder with an increase of a type of white blood cells). **3** European Monetary System (to create economic stability in Europe). **4** expanded memory specification *computers.*

EMSA Electron Microscope Society of America.

EMSC Electrical Manufacturers Standards Council.

EMSS experimental manned space station.

EMT 1 electrical metallic tubing. **2** emergency medical technician, also in combination: *EMT-P = emergency medical technician paramedic.* **3** equivalent megatons (measure of the destructive capacity of an arsenal of stored weapons).

EMU 1 Economic and Monetary Union (European Community agreement to adopt a single currency). **2** *also* **emu** electromagnetic unit. **3** (*sometimes* ē myü') European Monetary Unit.

emul. emulsion.

eMW megawatts of electricity.

EN 1 exceptions noted. **2** National Highway. [Spanish *Estrada Nacional*]

En. *or* **En 1** Engineer. **2** English.

en (*pronounced* en) unit of type area in printing matter, being the same depth and one-half the breadth of an *em.*

en. 1 enema. **2** enemy.

ENA 1 English Newspaper Association. **2** National School of Administration. [French *École Nationale d'Administration*]

enam. enameled.

enc. 1 *also* **encl. a** enclosed. **b** enclosure. **2** *also* **Enc.** encyclopedia, esp. in combination: *Enc.Brit. = Encyclopaedia Britannica.*

ency. *or* **Ency.** encyclopedia, esp. in combination: *Ency. Brit. = Encyclopaedia Britannica.*

encyc. *or* **Encyc.** *or* **encycl.** *or* **Encycl.** encyclopedia.

end 1 *also* **end. a** endorsed. **b** endorsement. **2** endosperm. **3** front, front of. [French *endroit*]

ENDOR electron nuclear double resonance (technique used in spectroscopy)

end p. *or* **endp.** end paper, in bookbinding.

ENE *or* **E.N.E.** *or* **e.n.e.** east-northeast.

ENEA European Nuclear Energy Agency.

ENEL National Electric Power Agency (of Italy). [Italian *Ente Nazionale per l'Energia Elettrica*]

ENF *or* **E.N.F.** European Nuclear Force.

ENG 1 electronic news gathering (by videotape, usually for broadcast by television). **2** electronystagmograph (measures electrical activity in the brain).

Eng. 1 Engineering. **2 a** England. **b** English. **3 a** engraved. **b** engraver.

eng. 1 a *also* **eng** engine: *Turbo II eng.* **b** engineer. **c** engineering. **2 a** engraved. **b** engraving. **c** engraver.

Eng.D. Doctor of Engineering.

engg. *or* **Engg.** engineering.

eng hn *or* **Eng hn** English horn *music.*

engin. engineering.

Engl. 1 England. **2** English.

Eng. Lit. English Literature.

Engr. 1 engraved. **2** engraver.

engr. 1 engineer. **2 a** engraved. **b** engraver. **c** engraving.

Eng.Sc.D. Doctor of Engineering Science.

ENI National Hydrocarbons Corporation (state-owned oil and gas combine of Italy). [Italian *Ente Nazionale Idrocarburi*]

ENIAC (ē'nē ak) Electronic Numerical Integrator And Calculator (first large-scale digital electronic computer).

ENIT Italian State Tourist Agency. [Italian *Ente Nazionale Industrie Turistiche*]

ENL erythema nodosum leprosum (a condition of skin eruptions, esp. in leprosy).

enl. 1 enlarged. **2** enlisted.

ENO English National Opera.

ENP estimated time at or over next position (used in aircraft surveillance and navigational reporting).

ENQ *or* **enq** enquiry, esp. in computer work.

ENR Environment and Natural Resources Division (of U.S. Department of Justice).

ENS School of the Fine Arts (in Paris). [French *École Normale Supérieure des Beaux-Arts*]

ens 1 ensemble *music.* **2** together. [French *ensemble*]

ENSA *or* **E.N.S.A.** Entertainments National Service Association (Britain's equivalent of the USO in World War II).

ENSO El Niño-Southern Oscillation *meteorology.*

ENT ear, nose, and throat *medicine.*

ent. 1 *also* **Ent.** entertainment. **2** entomology (study of insects). **3 a** *also* **Ent.** entrance. **b** *also* **entd.** entered.

entom. *or* **entomol. 1** entomological. **2** entomology (study of insects).

entspr. corresponding. [German *entsprechend*]

Ent. Sta. Hall Entered at Stationers' Hall (former copyright notice in Great Britain. Stationers' Hall was the old copyright office).

Env. 1 environmental, esp. in combination: *Env.L.* = *environmental law.* **2** Envoy, also in combination: *Env.Ext.* or *Env.Extr.* = *Envoy Extraordinary.*

env. 1 envelope. **2** *also* **envtl.** environmental.

ENW The *Effects of Nuclear Weapons* (report prepared by the U.S. Department of Defense and published by the former Atomic Energy Commission, June 1957).

EO 1 *also* **E.O.** Eastern Orthodox. **2** *also* **E.O.** Education Officer. **3** Engineer Officer. **4** Executive Officer. **5** *also* **E.O.** Executive Order (followed by a number).

e.o. by authority of the office, officially. [Latin *ex officio*]

EOA 1 end of address *computers.* **2** examination, opinion, and advice *medicine.*

EOB 1 end of block *computers.* **2** Executive Office Building.

EOC 1 emergency operating center. **2** end of cycle. **3** Equal Opportunities Commission (also compare *EEOC*).

Eoc. Eocene (second epoch of the Cenozoic Era).

EOCR Equal Opportunity and Civil Rights (bureau of U.S. Department of State).

EOD 1 *also* **e.o.d.** every other day (publication schedule of an advertisement; delivery schedule for mail, etc.). **2** Explosive Ordnance Disposal (clearing of mines, shells, etc. from an area of hostilities).

EOE 1 equal opportunity employer. **2** *also* **E.O.E.** *or* **e.o.e.** errors and omissions excepted *commerce.*

EOF 1 Educational Opportunity Fund. **2** Emergency Operating Facility. **3** end of file *computers.*

EOG 1 *also* **E.O.G.** Educational Opportunity Grant. **2 a** electrooculogram. **b** electrooculograph (device to measure speed and direction of eye movements and changes in electric potential between the cornea of the eye and the retina).

e.o.h.p. *or* **EOHP** except as otherwise herein provided *commerce, law.*

EOIR Executive Office for Immigration Review (of U.S. Department of Justice).

EOJ end of job *computers.*

EOKA *or* **Eoka** National Organization of Cypriot Struggle (to consolidate in union with Greece). [Greek *Ethniki Organosis Kypriakou Agonos*]

EOL end of line *computers.*

EOM 1 end of message *computers.* **2** *also* **e.o.m.** end of the month, *esp. in accounting.* **3** *also* **e.o.m.** every other month *advertising.*

EOMB Explanation of Medical Benefits (of Medicare and private health insurance).

e.o.o.e. *or* **EOOE** errors or omissions excepted.

EOP 1 emergency operations plan. **2** employee ownership plan (compare *ESOP*). **3** Executive Office of the President.

EOQ economical order quantity (of inventory ordering).

EOQC European Organization for Quality Control.

EOR 1 end of record *computers.* **2** enhanced oil recovery.

EORTC European Organization for Research on Treatment of Cancer.

EOS 1 *also* **EoS** *or* **Eos** Earth Observing System (polar orbiting satellites to study the earth's environment). **2** Earth Orbiting Satellite.

eos. eosinophil (white blood cell having an affinity to eosin, a red stain).

EOT 1 end of tape *computers.* **2** end of transmission *computers.*

EOUSA Executive Office for United States Attorneys (of Department of Justice).

EOUST Executive Office for United States Trustees (of Department of Justice).

EOW *or* **e.o.w.** every other week (publication of an advertisement).

EP 1 earned points (in recording a sports event). **2** electrically polarized. **3** electroplate. **4** *also* **E.P.** end point, *esp. in distillation.* **5** erythrose phosphate *biochemistry.* **6** estimated position (in a navigational logbook). **7** European Parliament. **8** European Plan (charges for room without including meals). **9** extreme pressure: *EP lubricants.*

Ep. 1 *also* **EP.** Bishop. [Latin *Episcopus*] **2** *also* **ep.** Epistle.

ep 1 electrically polarized. **2** electric primer. **3** end paper, in bookbinding. **4** *also* **e.p.** in passing *chess.* [French *en passant*] **5** probable error.

EPA 1 *also* **E.P.A.** educational priority area (of Great Britain, area requiring extra educational facilities). **2** Emergency Powers Act. **3** Environmental Protection Agency (of U.S. government). **4** Equity Principle Auditions (open casting auditions for a stage production). **5** European Productivity Agency.

EPAA Emergency Petroleum Allocation Act.

EPAQ electronic parts of assessed quality.

EPB Environmental Protection Board (of Great Britain).

EPC 1 Economic and Planning Council. **2** Economic Policy Committee. **3** Educational Publishers Council.

EPCA 1 Energy Policy and Conservation Act. **2** European Petro-Chemical Association.

EPCOT Experimental Prototype Community of Tomorrow, in combination: *EPCOT Center.*

EPD 1 earliest practicable date *commerce.* **2** equilibrium peritoneal dialysis *medicine.* **3** excess profits duty *commerce.*

EPDA Emergency Powers Defense Act.

EPDM ethylene propylene diene monomer (used for shoes, coating cables and electrical wires, hosiery, etc.).

EPG electronic program guide (a scroll of programming on a TV screen).

Eph. 1 *also* **Ephes.** Ephesians (book of the New Testament). **2** Ephraim.

EPI 1 electronic position indicator *surveying, navigation.* **2** elevation position indicator (an aircraft instrument). **3** Emergency Public Information.

epid. epidemic.

EPIE Educational Products Information Exchange.

epig. 1 epigram. **2** epigraphy (study of inscriptions, esp. ancient writings).

epil. epilogue.

Epiph. Epiphany (12th day after Christmas).

Epis. 1 Episcopal, Episcopalian. **2** Epistle.

Episc. 1 Bishop. [Latin *Episcopus*] **2** Episcopal, Episcopalian.

epit. 1 *also* **Epit.** epitaph. **2** epitome.

EPLF Eritrean People's Liberation Front.

EPM electron probe microanalysis.

EPN ethylparanitrophenyl (insecticide).

EPNdB effective perceived noise decibel.

EPNS 1 electroplated nickel silver. **2** *also* **E.P.N.S.** English Place-Name Society.

EPO 1 earth parking orbit (orbit of a spacecraft around the earth). **2** erythropoietin (kidney hormone that stimulates production of red blood cells and is used against anemia). **3** European Patent Office (of the European Community).

EPOS electronic point of sale (bar code scanner, electronic cash register, and other devices to record sales) *computers.*

EPP European People's Party.

EPPO European and Mediterranean Plant Protection Organization.

EPR 1 electron paramagnetic resonance (to study free radicals, transition metals, and unpaired electrons in bacterial extracts). **2** engine-pressure ratio. **3** ethylene-propylene rubber.

EPRI Electric Power Research Institute.

EPRLF Eelam People's Revolutionary Liberation Front (Tamil guerrilla group operating in Sri Lanka).

EPROM erasable programmable read-only memory *computers.*

EPS 1 *also* **Eps.** Bishop. [Latin *Episcopus*] **2** *also* **eps** earnings per share *commerce.* **3** electrophysical study (of the heart). **4** encapsulated PostScript (system for files of graphics) *computers.* **5** Engineered Performance Standard (of the air traffic capacity of an airport). **6** English Philological Studies (publication). **7** exophthalmos-producing substance *medicine.*

EPSF encapsulated PostScript format (system for files of graphics) *computers.*

EPSP excitatory postsynaptic potentials (depolarizing potentials produced in the cell membrane by excitatory synapses).

EPT 1 early pregnancy test. **2** ethylene propylene terpolymer (used for shoes, coating cables and electrical wires, hosiery, etc.). **3** excess-profits tax.

EPTA Expanded Program of Technical Assistance (of the United Nations).

EPU European Payments Union.

Epus. Bishop. [Latin *Episcopus*]

EPW enemy prisoner of war.

EQ 1 *also* **E.Q.** educational quotient. **2** *also* **E.Q.** encephalization quotient (ratio of body weight to brain weight, used to describe animal development of a species). **3** equalization or equalizer *electronics, engineering.* **4** equivalence, esp. in combination: *EQ Gate* (in computer logic).

Eq. 1 a Equator. **b** Equatorial. **2** Equerry.

eq. 1 equal. **2** equation. **3** equipment. **4 a** equitable. **b** *also* **eq** equity, also in combination: *eqi = equity income*. **5** equivalent.

EQI environmental quality index.

eqn. equation.

Equ the Little Horse (constellation). [Latin *Equuleus*]

Equat. Equatorial.

equip. equipment.

equiv. 1 equivalence. **2** equivalent.

ER 1 earned runs *baseball*. **2** *also* **E.R.** East Riding, Yorkshire. **3** East River (flowing on the eastern side of Manhattan Island). **4** echo ranging. **5** Edinburgh Review (magazine title). **6** *also* **E.R.** educational ratio. **7** effectiveness report. **8 a** electronic recorder (for keeping a court record). **b** electronic reporting (of a courtroom proceeding). **9** electroreflectance (in spectroscopic study of substances in an electric field) *physics*. **10** electrorheological, in combination: *ER fluids* (fluids that increase in viscosity in an electric field) *physics*. **11** emergency room (of a hospital). **12** endoplasmic reticulum (network in cell cytoplasm active in cell construction) *biology*. **13** engine room. **14** enhanced radiation (weapon). **15** *also* **E/R** en route. **16** error recovery *computers*. **17** external resistance *medicine*. **18** *also* **E.R.** Queen Elizabeth. [Latin *Elizabeth Regina*]

Er erbium (chemical element).

ERA 1 earned-run average *baseball*. **2** Electrical Research Association (of Great Britain). **3** electron ring accelerator *physics*. **4** Energy Regulatory Administration (of U.S. Department of Energy). **5** *also* **E.R.A.** Equal Rights Amendment.

ERAB Energy Resources Advisory Board (of U.S. Department of Energy).

Eras. Erasmus.

ERC 1 Economic Research Council. **2** Electronics Research Center. **3** Energy Research Center.

ERD equivalent residual dose (of gamma radiation).

ERDA Energy Research and Development Administration.

ERDE Explosives Research and Development Establishment (of Great Britain).

ERDL Engineering Research and Development Laboratory.

ERE 1 Edison Responsive Environment (voice-activated typewriter). **2** National Radical Union (in Greece). [Greek *Etniki Rizospastiki Enosis*]

ERF 1 electrorheological fluid (fluid that increases in viscosity in an electric field) *physics*. **2** *also* **erf** error function.

ERFA European Radio Frequency Agency.

ERG 1 electrical resistance gauge. **2** electroretinogram (recording of electrical reaction of the retina to light).

ergon. ergonomics.

Eri the River Eridanus (constellation). [Latin *Eridanus*]

ERIC 1 Educational Research Information Center (of U.S. Department of Education). **2** Energy Rate Input Controller.

ERIM Environmental Research Institute of Michigan.

Erint Extended Range Intercept Technology (advanced antimissile missile guided by on-board radar and computers).

ERIS *or* **Eris** Exoatmospheric Reentry Vehicle Interceptor System (antimissile missile guided by on-board radar and computers).

ERISA Employee Retirement Income Security Act.

ERL Environmental Research Laboratory (of the National Oceanic and Atmospheric Administration).

ERM exchange rate mechanism (monetary system within the EC to control exchange rates of members' currencies).

erm. ermine.

ERNIE Electronic Random Number Indicating Equipment.

E.R.O. European Regional Organization (of Free Trade Unions).

EROS Earth Resources Observation Satellite (compare *Landsat*).

ERP 1 early receptor potential (rapid change recorded in the eye after exposure to light). **2** effective radiated power (of an antenna) *communications*. **3** *also* **E.R.P.** European Recovery Program (Marshall Plan). **4** event-related potential (electrical activity in the brain associated with response to various outside stimuli).

ERPF effective renal plasma flow *medicine*.

Err. 1 The Comedy of Errors (play by Shakespeare). **2** *also* **err.** error.

erron. erroneous, erroneously.

ERS 1 Economic Research Service (of U.S. Department of Agriculture). **2** Experimental Research Society.

ERT 1 estrogen-replacement therapy *medicine*. **2** Greek national radio and television agency. [Greek *Elliniki Radiophonia Tileorasis*]

ERTS Earth Resources Technology Satellite (now *Landsat*).

ERU *or* **E.R.U.** English Rugby Union.

ERV 1 *also* **E.R.V.** English Revised Version (of the Bible). **2** expiratory reserve volume (maximum volume of air exhaled after regular breathing).

ERW enhanced radiation weapon.

erw. *or* **erweit.** enlarged (esp. of a book). [German *erweitert*]

ES 1 *also* **E.S.** Educational Specialist. **2** electrostatic. **3** English Studies (publication). **4** enzyme substrate (complex, rate of formation and decay of enzymes in combination of concentration) *biochemistry*. **5** *also* **es** equal section (in blueprints and other plans). **6** Executive Schedule (of U.S. Civil Service).

Es 1 einsteinium (chemical element). **2** *also* **Es.** Esther (book of the Old Testament).

ESA 1 Ecological Society of America. **2** Employment and Standards Administration (of U.S. Department of Labor). **3** Entomological Society of America. **4** European Space Agency. **5** Euthanasia Society of America.

ESANZ *or* **E.S.A.N.Z.** Economic Society of Australia and New Zealand.

ESB electrical stimulation of the brain.

ESC 1 Economic and Social Council (of the UN, acting on economic, social, health, educational, and technical affairs). **2** Entomological Society of Canada. **3** *also* **Esc.** escadrille (now *squadron;* former French unit of warships or airplanes, more esp. six airplanes in WWI). **4** escape *computers.* **5** *also* **esc.** escudo (monetary unit of Portugal and Cape Verde).

esc. 1 discount. [French *escompte*] **2** *also* **esc** escape, escaping, escaped.

ESCA electron spectroscopy for chemical analysis.

ESCAP Economic and Social Commission for Asia and the Pacific (of the UN Economic and Social Council).

ESCES Experimental Satellite Communication Earth Station (any one of 22 stations throughout the world).

eschat. eschatology (branch of theology that deals with death, final judgment, etc.).

ESCO Educational, Scientific, and Cultural Organization (of the UN).

ESCWA Economic and Social Commission for Western Asia (of the UN Economic and Social Council).

ESD 1 echo sounding device. **2** external symbols dictionary (list of symbols for linking computer programs).

Esd. Esdras (two books of the Apocrypha, or two books of the Douay Bible called Ezra and Nehemiah in the Protestant and Jewish Bibles).

ESDAC European Space Data Center.

ESDI enhanced small device interface (a device that connects a hard disk, tape drive, etc. to a small computer).

ESDIAD electron stimulated desorption ion angular distribution (used to study bonding in crystals).

ESE *or* **E.S.E.** *or* **e.s.e.** east-southeast.

ESEA Elementary and Secondary Education Act.

ESECA Energy Supply and Environmental Coordination Act.

ESF 1 erythropoietic stimulating factor *biochemistry.* **2** *also* **E.S.F.** European Science Foundation.

ESG 1 electrically suspended gyroscope. **2** electronic sports gathering. **3** English Standard Gauge.

E.S.H. European Society of Haematology.

ESHP *or* **eshp** equivalent shaft horsepower.

ESI externally specified index (system providing for operation of several networks over an input-output channel).

Esk. Eskimo.

ESL English as a Second Language.

ESLAB European Space Research Laboratory.

ESM 1 edible structural material (compound of milk, hominy grits, and banana flakes, a food for astronauts). **2** ends standard matched (of lumber).

ESN 1 *British* educationally subnormal. **2** *also* **esn** essential.

ESO European Southern Observatory.

ESOC European Space Operation Center.

ESOL (ē'səl) English for Speakers of Other Languages.

ESOP (ē'sop) Employee Stock Ownership Plan (plan for ownership among employees).

ESP 1 electron spin polarization *physics.* **2** electrosensitive pattern. **3** English for Special Purposes. **4** extrasensory perception. **5** *also* **Esp. a** Spain. [French *Espagne,* Spanish *España*] **b** Spanish. [French *Espagnol,* Spanish *Español*]

esp. 1 *also* **espec.** especially. **2** *also* **esp** with expression *music.* [Italian *espressivo*]

ESPN Entertainment and Sports Network (a cable TV station).

ESPRIT European Strategic Research Program in Information Technology.

Esq. *or* **Esqr.** *or* **Esqre.** Esquire.

▶**Esq., Esquire** written following a person's name no longer carries any meaning, though it is frequently used by lawyers when writing to one another. Modern usage has abandoned the dictum of omitting *Mr., Dr., Hon.,* etc. when using *Esq.*

ESR 1 *also* **e.s.r.** electron spin resonance (a form of spectroscopy used to study paramagnetic materials and in dating artifacts by measuring absorption of radiation). **2** erythrocyte sedimentation rate *medicine.*

ESRC Economic and Social Research Council.

ESRIN European Space Research Institute.

ESRO European Space Research Organization (U.K., France, Germany, Italy, Switzerland, Sweden, Netherlands, Belgium, Spain, Denmark).

ESS 1 electronic still store (file of still pictures for use in TV broadcasting). **2** Electronic Switching System *communications.* **3** executive support system *computers.*

Ess. Essex County, England.

ess. essence.

ESSA 1 Environmental Science Services Administration (of U.S. Department of Commerce). **2** Environmental Survey Satellite.

EST 1 earliest start time. **2** *also* **E.S.T.** *or* **e.s.t.** Eastern Standard Time. **3** electroshock therapy. **4** Estates (in postal address).

Est. 1 established: *John Markham Co., Est. 1822.* **2 a** Estonia. **b** Estonian. **3** Estuary.

est. 1 established. **2** estate. **3 a** estimate. **b** estimated, esp. in combination: *est. wt. = estimated weight.* **c** estimation. **4** estuary.

Estab. *or* **estab. 1** established. **2** Establishment.

estd. 1 *also* **Estd.** established. **2** estimated.

ESTEC European Space Technology Center (a part of European Space Research Organization).

estg. estimating.

Esth. Esther (book of the Old Testament).

ESTRACK European Satellite Tracking and Telemetry Network.

ESU 1 electronic setup (assembly of equipment for a television broadcast). **2** *also* **esu** electrostatic unit *physics.* **3** engineering setup (still shot displayed in background of a scene on television, esp. on a news program). **4** *also* **E.S.U.** English Speaking Union.

ESV earth satellite vehicle.

ESWL extracorporeal shock wave lithotripsy (use of sound waves to break up kidney stones) *medicine.*

ET 1 *also* **E.T.** *or* **e.t.** Eastern Time. **2** *also* **E.T.** *British* Easter Term. **3** educational therapy. **4** egg transfer (ovum implantation) *medicine.* **5** *also* **e.t.** elapsed time (of a race, endurance test, celestial event, etc.). **6** Emergency (Medical) Technician.

7 emerging technology. **8 a** engineering test, also in combination: *ETR = Engineering Test Reactor.* **b** engineering time. **9** *also* **E.T.** English translation. **10** ephemeris time (time figured by orbital planetary motion as a correction of solar time). **11** extraterrestrial (being).

Et ethyl: Et_2O = *ether.*

ETA 1 *also* **E.T.A.** Basque Country and Liberty (a political movement). [Basque *Euzkadi ta Azkatasuna*] **2** Employment and Training Administration (of U.S. Department of Labor). **3** *also* **e.t.a.** estimated time of arrival. **4** European Teachers Association.

et al. 1 and elsewhere. [Latin *et alibi*] **2** and others. [Latin *et alii*]

ETAP Expanded Technical Assistance Program.

ETB end of transmission block *computers.*

ETBE ethyl tertiary butyl ether (gasoline additive).

ETC 1 *also* **E.T.C.** Electrical or Electronic Technicians Certificate. **2** electrothermal chemical, esp. in ETC propulsion (chemical charge to propel a missile without damaging its electronic guidance system). **3** estimated time of completion. **4** *also* **E.T.C.** European Translation Center.

etc. *or* **&c.** and so forth. [Latin *et cetera*]

ETD *or* **e.t.d.** estimated time of departure.

ETE estimated time en route *navigation.*

ETEC enterotoxigenic E. coli (a cause of traveler's diarrhea).

ETH Confederation Technical Institute (of Switzerland). [German *Eidgenössische Technische Hochschule*]

Eth. 1 Ethiopia. **2** Ethiopian, also in combiation: *$Eth.* = *Ethiopian dollar.* **3** Ethiopic.

eth. 1 ether. **2 a** ethical. **b** ethics.

ethn. 1 ethnological. **2** ethnology (science of characteristics of different peoples, customs, etc.).

ethnog. ethnography or ethnographic (classification and description of races).

ethnol. 1 ethnological. **2** ethnology (science of characteristics of different peoples, customs, etc.).

ETI 1 *also* **eti** elapsed time indicator. **2** extraterrestrial intelligence.

etiol. etiology (cause of disease).

ETO European Theater of Operations: *ETOUSA = European Theater of Operations, United States Army.*

E to E end to end (of piping in blueprints and other plans).

EtOH ethyl alcohol.

ETP 1 electron transport particles *physics.* **2** estimated turnaround point.

ETR 1 Eastern Test Range (for U.S. missiles). **2** Engineering Test Reactor. **3** estimated time of return.

Etr. Etruscan.

ETS 1 Educational Testing Service. **2** environmental tobacco smoke. **3** estimated time of separation (from military service).

et seq. and (the) following: *192 et seq.* [Latin *et sequens*]

et seqq. *or* **et sqq.** and (those) following. [Latin *et sequentes, et sequentia*]

ETSU Energy Technology Support Unit (of British Department of Energy).

ETU 1 *also* **E.T.U.** Electrical Trades Union. **2** ethylene thiourea (a carcinogenic substance produced by the decomposition of the fungicide EBDC).

ETUC European Trade Union Confederation.

et ux. and wife. [Latin *et uxor*]

ETV 1 Educational Television. **2** *also* **etv** engine test vehicle.

ETX end of text *computers.*

ety. *or* **etym.** *or* **etymol. 1** etymological. **2** etymology.

EU *or* **E.U. 1** *also* **e.u.** entropy unit. **2** European Union (economic bloc of European countries). **3** Evangelical Union. **4** *also* **E-U** United States. [French *États Unis*, Spanish *Estados Unidos*, etc.]

Eu *I an abbreviation for: also* **Eu.** Europe, European. *II a symbol for:* europium (chemical element).

EUA 1 European Unit of Account (of the EC). **2** examination under anesthesia *medicine.* **3** *also* **E.U.A.** United States of America. [French *États-Unis d'Amérique*, Spanish *Estados Unidos de America*, etc.]

E.U.B. Evangelical United Brethren.

EUCARPIA European Association for Research on Plant Breeding.

EUCOM U.S. European Command (administrative center for all U.S. forces in Europe).

EUDISED European Documentation and Information System in Education (of the EC).

EUFTT European Union of Film and Television Technicians.

EUI energy utilization index.

EUM United States of Mexico. [Spanish *Estados Unidos Mexicanos*]

EUMETSAT European Meteorological Satellite (Agency, system of weather reporting).

EUP 1 *also* **E.U.P.** English Universities Press. **2** Experimental Use Permit (granted by the Environmental Protection Agency for field testing of prohibited substances, esp. in genetic engineering).

euphem. euphemism.

E.U.R. Universal Exhibition of Rome. [Italian *Esposizione Universale di Roma*]

Eur. Europe, European.

EURAILPASS (yü′rāl pas′) European Railway Pass (ticket permitting transportation for a specified period of time on European railroads).

Euratom (yü rat′əm) European Atomic Energy Community.

Euronet (yür′ō net′) European Network (information database for member groups within the EC on scientific, medical, technological, economic topics).

Eur. pat. European patent.

Eus. Eusebius (bishop and historian of the early Christian Church).

EUTELSAT European Telecommunications Satellite (agency).

EUV extreme ultraviolet (radiation) *physics: EUV astronomy.*

EUVE Extreme Ultraviolet Explorer (satellite for monitoring environment of the sun).

EUW European Union of Women.

EV 1 electric vehicle. **2** *also* **eV** *or* **e.v.** electron volt. **3** *also* **E.V.** English Version (of the Bible). **4** exhaust valve. **5** expected value *mathematics*. **6** *also* **E-V** exposure-value system *photography*. **7** *also* **E.V.** in town (in an address). [French *en ville*]

Ev. *or* **Evid.** evidence *law*.

e.V. incorporated. [German *eingetragener Verein*]

EVA 1 ethylene vinyl acetate (resin used for adhesives and coatings of metals). **2** extravehicular activity (space walk).

evac. 1 evacuated. **2** evacuation.

eval. 1 a evaluate. **b** evaluated. **2** evaluation.

Evang. *or* **evang. 1** evangelical. **2** evangelist.

EVAO estimated value of agricultural operations.

evap. 1 a evaporate. **b** evaporated. **2** *also* **evapn.** evaporation.

Eve *or* **eve** evening (as of a performance).

Eves. evenings: *Eves. call John 899-5314.*

EVF electronic view finder.

EVG European Defense Community. [German *Europäische Verteidigungsgemeinschaft*]

evg. evening.

E VIV DISC departed from life. [Latin *E Vivis Discessit*]

evol. evolution.

EVOP evolutionary operation (incremental adjustments in the development of a plan or device) *engineering*.

EVP electromagnetic vector potential *physics*.

EVR electronic video recording (and reproduction).

EVT educational and vocational training.

evy every, also in combination: *evythg = everything.*

EW 1 electronic warfare, also in combination: *EWTR = electronic warfare test range.* **2** emergency ward (in a hospital). **3** sleet shower *meteorology*.

EWA *or* **E.W.A.** Education Writers Association.

EWL evaporation water loss.

EWR early warning radar.

EWRC European Weed Research Council.

EWS emergency water supply.

E.W.T. *or* **EWT** taken elsewhere *construction*.

EX 1 Exchange, esp. in combination: *COMEX = Commodity Exchange.* **2** experimental, esp. as part of a number or other designation for some device.

Ex 1 *also* **Ex.** example. **2** excellent. **3** excerpt. **4** *also* **Ex.** Exchange. **5** *also* **Ex.** Executive: *Ex. Doc. = Executive Document.* **6** Exodus (book of the Old Testament). **7** Express, esp. in combination: *FedEx = Federal Express, AMEX = American Express* (both trademarks). **8** *also* **Ex.** extra, esp. in combination: *Ex.Sess. = Extra Session.* **9** out of (a ship or dock, referring to merchandise, etc.).

ex. 1 a examination. **b** examined. **2** example. **3 a** except. **b** exception. **4** exchange, also in combination: *Telex = telegraphic exchange.* **5** excluding. **6** excursion. **7** executed. **8** executor. **9** exempt. **10** exercise. **11** export. **12** express. **13** extra: *ex.fcy. = extra fancy.* **14** extract.

EXAFS extended X-ray absorption fine structure (in X-ray spectrometry) *physics*.

Exam. examiner.

exam. 1 (eg zam') examination. **2** examined.

Examg. examining.

EXC exciter *electronics*.

Exc. 1 Excellency. **2 a** excommunicated. **b** excommunication.

exc. 1 excellent. **2 a** except, excepted. **b** exception. **3** exciter *electronics*. **4** he or she engraved it. [Latin *excudit*]

Exch. 1 Exchange. **2** *also* **Exchq.** Exchequer.

excl. 1 *also* **Excl** excellent: *Excl w/details = excellent with details.* **2** *also* **exclam.** exclamation, exclamatory. **3 a** exclude, excluding. **b** exclusive, exclusively.

Ex.Com. Executive Committee.

ex cp. ex coupon (stocks sold without the most recent dividend coupons).

exd. examined.

ex d. *or* **ex div.** ex dividend (stock sold without right to next dividend).

Ex.Doc. executive document.

EXEC 1 execute *computers*. **2** executive *computers*: *EXECP = executive program.*

Exec. (*sometimes pronounced* eg zek') Executive, esp. in combination: *Exec.Dir. = Executive Director.*

exec. 1 executed, execution, esp. *in law*. **2** executor *law*.

exer. exercise.

ex.gr. for example; e.g. [Latin *exempli gratia*]

exh. 1 exhaust, also in combination: *exh.v. = exhaust vent.* **2 a** exhibit. **b** *also* **Exh.** exhibition.

Exhib. *or* **Exhbn.** Exhibition.

exhib. 1 exhibit. **2** let it be given *pharmaceutics*. [Latin *exhibeatur*]

Ex-Im (eks'im') *or* **Eximbank** Export-Import Bank (of Washington).

ex int. ex interest (of a note, bond, or other security without the next interest payment).

ex lib. from the library or books of. [Latin *ex libris*]

Exmr. examiner.

Exod. Exodus (book of the Old Testament).

ex off. by authority of the office; officially. [Latin *ex officio*]

Exon. 1 Exeter, England. [Latin *Exonia*] **2** of Exeter (in reference to the Bishop and therefore used as his official signature). [Latin *Exoniensis*]

exor. executor.

exp. 1 *also* **EXP** expansion. **2** expense, expenses. **3** *also* **Exp a** experience: *2 yrs exp.* **b** *also* **expd.** *or* **Expd** experienced. **4 a** experiment. **b** *also* **EXP** experimental. **5** expired. **6** exponent, exponential *mathematics*. **7 a** export, exported. **b** exportation. **8** exposure *photography, physics, medicine*. **9** express. **10** expurgated.

ex p. on behalf. [Latin *ex parte*]

expat (eks'pat) expatriate.

expd or **edp'd** experienced.

Expdn. expedition.

exper. 1 a experience: *post-grad exper.* = *post-graduate experience.* b *also* **experd.** experienced. 2 experimental.

expl. 1 a explanation. b explanatory. 2 a explosion. b explosive.

Expn. or **Expo** (eks'pō) exposition: *Canadian Expo.*

expr. 1 expires. 2 *also* **Expr.** express.

expt. 1 experiment. 2 export.

exptl. experimental.

Exptr. exporter.

Expwy Expressway, esp. on maps and road signs.

EXPY Expressway (in postal address).

exr. executor.

ex rel or **ex rel.** by or on the information of *law: The opinion quoted a statement in "United States ex rel Milwaukee Social Democratic Pub.Co. v. Burleson," (41 Sup.Ct. 352).* [Latin *ex relatione*]

exrx. executrix *law.*

exs expenses *accounting.*

exsec exsecant *mathematics.*

EXT 1 Extension (in postal address). **2** exterior. **3** extinguisher.

ext. 1 extant (still in existence). **2 a** extend. **b** *also* **Ext.** extension (as of a telephone). **3** exterior. **4** external, externally. **5** extinct. **6** extra. **7 a** extract *pharmaceutics.* **b** extraction *dentistry.* **8** extreme.

extd. 1 *also* **Extd.** or **EXTD** extended (as of a weather forecast). **2** extracted *medicine, dentistry.*

exte outside; exterior.

extern. externally *medicine.*

ext.liq. liquid extract *pharmaceutics.* [Latin *extractum liquidum*]

extn. extension.

extr. 1 extraordinary. **2** extruded.

extrad. extradition.

exx. 1 examples. **2** executrix.

EYC European Youth Center.

EZ or **E-Z** easy, as of tax forms: *940-EZ.*

Ez. or **Ezr.** Ezra (book of the Old Testament).

Ezek. Ezekiel (book of the Old Testament).

F

F *I an abbreviation for:* **1** *also* **F.** brother. [Latin *frater*, French *frère*, etc.] **2** face, as of a gear: *F to F* = *face to face.* **3** *also* **F.** Fahrenheit. **4** *also* **F.** fair. **5** false. **6 a** fast, esp. on a regulating device. **b** fast, esp. in combination: *FTC* = *fast time constant.* **7** *also* **F.** Father (of the Roman Catholic Church). **8** *also* **F.** February. **9** *also* **F.** Federal, in combination: *FHA* = *Federal Housing authority; F. (2nd)* = *Federal Reporter, second series.* **10** *also* **F.** Fellow (of the), in combination: *FAGS* = *Fellow of the American Geographical Society; F.A.A.A.S.* = *Fellow of the American Academy of Arts and Sciences.* **11** *also* **F.** female or feminine. **12** fertility, esp. in combination: *F factor* = *Fertility factor* (enabling bacteria to donate genetic material or to receive such material). **13** fiction (esp. in library cataloging). **14** field, esp. in combination *medicine, mathematics, military,* etc.: *FA* = *Field Artillery.* **15** field of vision *medicine.* **16** Fiji or Fijian, in combination: *$F* = *Fiji dollar.* **17** filament (esp. of a radio tube). **18** film. **19** fine (of lead pencils and pen points). **20** fire: *FD* = *fire department.* **21** firm (of pencil lead). **22** fixed. **23** flat *construction.* **24** florin (monetary unit of Aruba and the Netherlands). **25** *also* **F.** fluid ounce. **26** force. **27** *also* **F.** formula. **28** foul *sports.* **29** fragment (of immunoglobulin) *biochemistry.* **30** franc (monetary unit of Belgium, Burundi, Djibouti, France, French Guinea, Guadeloupe, Guinea Republic, Liechtenstein, Luxembourg, Madagascar, Martinique, Miquelon, Monaco, Reunion, Rwanda, St. Pierre, Switzerland) and in combination: *CFAF* = *CFA franc of former French colonies in Africa.*

31 *also* **F.** France or French, esp. in combination: *OF* = *Old French.* **32** frequency, esp. in combination: *FM* = *frequency modulation.* **33** *also* **F.** Friday. **34** fuse. **35** *also* **F.** son (esp. after the name of an author). [Latin *filius*]

II a symbol for: **1** Atlanta (branch in the Federal Reserve regional banking system, found esp. on dollar bills). **2** blue second hydrogen line in the solar spectrum. **3** distribution function *physics.* **4** farad (unit of electrical capacitance). **5** Faraday constant or faraday. **6** filial generation, esp. in combination: F_1 = *the first filial generation;* F_2 = *the second filial generation.* **7** fluorine (chemical element). **8** force. **9** forty; 40 (medieval Roman numerals). **10** fourth tone in the scale of C major. **11** free energy *physics.* **12** Fresh Water Load Line (Plimsoll mark). **13** function (of), esp. in combination: *Fx* = *function of x,* in mathematics. **14** hyperfine structure quantum number *physics.* **15** loud *music.* [Italian *forte*] **16** lowest grade in school, indicating failure. **17** luminous flux. **18** magnetomotive force. **19** noise factor *electronics.* **20** *British* quantum number of total angular momentum *physics.* **21** sixth of a series. **22** thrust. **23** upper ionized layer of the ionosphere. **24** weight *physics.*

F- fighter, in combination: *F-100.*

F₀ pure parental type *biology* (see *F* the symbol).

°F degrees Fahrenheit.

1F, 2F editions of Shakespeare's plays, usually designated 1st folio edition (1623) and 2nd folio edition (1632).

4F classification in the U.S. Selective Service System (physically or mentally unfit for military service).

f I *an abbreviation for:* **1** *also* **f.** born. [Danish, Norwegian *født*] **2** *also* **f.** family. **3** *also* **f.** farad. **4** *also* **f.** farthing. **5** *also* **f.** father. **6** *also* **f.** fathom. **7** *also* **f. a** female. **b** feminine *grammar.* **8** femto- (one quadrillionth or 10^{-15}): *fa, fA = femtoampere.* **9** fermi (unit of length) *physics.* **10** filament (esp. as a subscript). **11** *also* **f.** filly, in horse racing. **12** *also* **f.** florin (an old coin of Europe; the English silver florin was worth 2 shillings; there was a gold florin issued in Florence and numerous gold and silver pieces issued by different countries of Medieval Europe). **13** *also* **f.** fluid or fluid ounce. **14** *also* **f.** fog. **15** *also* **f.** folio. **16** *also* **f.** following. **17** *also* **f.** foot or feet, esp. in combination: *fps = foot-pound-second system; f.p.s. = feet per second.* **18** *also* **f.** formula. **19** *also* **f.** franc. **20** free, in combination: *fob = free on board.* **21** frequency, in combination: *fm = frequency modulation.* **22** frequent (occurrence of species) *biology.* **23** *also* **f.** from. **24** fugacity *botany* (tendency to fall or fade early), *thermodynamics* (measure of the volatility of gas). **25** *also* **f.** furlong: *7f.* **26** *also* **f.** furnished: *Large barely f. room. Tel. –.* **27** loud *music.* [Italian *forte*] II *a symbol for:* **1** activity of molar concentration *chemistry.* **2** cut-off frequency (of transistors) *electronics.* **3** *also* **f.** focal length *optics, photography.* **4** frequency. **5** friction *or* friction factor. **6** function (of), in combination: *f(x) = function of x, in mathematics.* **7** fusion (esp. as a subscript). **8** *also* **f.** let it be made *pharmaceutics.* [Latin *fiat*] **9** partition function *chemistry.* **10** relative humidity.

f: focal length *photography.*

FA 1 family allowance. **2** fatty acid. **3** field ambulance. **4** field artillery. **5** fielding average *baseball.* **6** *also* **F.A.** Financial Adviser. **7** fine arts. **8** first aid. **9** fluorescent antibody *medicine.* **10** folic acid. **11** *also* **F.A.** British, Australian, Irish Football Association: *the F.A. Cup.* **12** free association *psychology.* **13** freight agent. **14** *also* **F/A** friendly aircraft *military.*

Fa. 1 business firm. [German *Firma*, Danish, Norwegian *firma*] **2** Faeroese (Islands between Britain and Iceland; the language spoken there). **3** Florida.

f.a. free alongside ship *commerce.*

FAA 1 Federal Aviation Administration (of U.S. Department of Transportation). **2** *also* **F.A.A. a** Fellow of the American Association (for the Advancement of Science). **b** Fellow of Australian Academy (of Science). **3** *also* **F.A.A.** *British* Fleet Air Arm. **4** *also* **f.a.a.** free of all average *commerce.*

FAAA *or* **F.A.A.A.** Fellow of the American Academy of Allergy.

FAAAS *or* **F.A.A.A.S. 1** Fellow of the American Academy of Arts and Sciences. **2** Fellow of the American Association for the Advancement of Science.

FAAO *or* **F.A.A.O.** Fellow of the American Academy of Optometry.

FAAOS *or* **F.A.A.O.S.** Fellow of the American Academy of Orthopedic Surgeons.

FAAP *or* **F.A.A.P.** Fellow of the American Academy of Pediatrics.

FAB *or* **F.A.B. 1** fast atom bombardment (for spectrographic analysis of solids). **2** free on board; FOB. [French *franco à bord*]

fab. 1 fabric. **2** *also* **fabr.** fabricate, fabricated.

Fab.Soc. Fabian Society.

FAC Forward Air Controller (military observer who directs artillery fire or aerial attack).

fac. 1 facsimile (now more often *fax*). **2** factor. **3** factory. **4** *also* **Fac.** faculty.

FACA *or* **F.A.C.A.** Fellow of the American College of Anesthesiologists.

FACB Federation of Australian Commercial Broadcasters.

FACC *or* **F.A.C.C.** Fellow of the American College of Cardiology.

FACCA *or* **F.A.C.C.A.** Fellow of the Association of Certified and Corporate Accountants.

FACD *or* **F.A.C.D.** Fellow of the American College of Dentists.

FACE 1 *also* **F.A.C.E.** Fellow of the Australian College of Education. **2** *also* **Face** Field Artillery Computer Equipment.

facet. 1 facetiae (collection of humorous remarks or sometimes books of rough humor). **2** facetious.

FACG *or* **F.A.C.G.** Fellow of the American College of Gastroenterology.

FACHA *or* **F.A.C.H.A.** Fellow of the American College of Hospital Administration.

facil. *or* **Facil.** facility.

FACO *or* **F.A.C.O.** Fellow of the American College of Otolaryngology.

FACOG *or* **F.A.C.O.G.** Fellow of the American College of Obstetricians and Gynecologists.

FACP *or* **F.A.C.P. 1** Fellow of the American College of Pathologists. **2** Fellow of the American College of Physicians.

FACR *or* **F.A.C.R.** Fellow of the American College of Radiology.

FACS 1 *also* **facs** (pronounced faks) facsimile copy *or* machine. **2** *also* **F.A.C.S.** Fellow of the American College of Surgeons. **3** fluorescence activated cell sorter (device to measure DNA content of cells) *biochemistry.*

FACSM *or* **F.A.C.S.M.** Fellow of the American College of Sports Medicine.

facsim. *or* **facsm.** facsimile copy *or* machine.

FACT fully automatic compiler translator.

fact. 1 factory. **2** *also* **Fact.** invoice. [Spanish *factura*]

FACTS Federation of Australian Commercial Television Stations.

FAD 1 flavin adenine dinucleotide (coenzyme essential to utilization of oxygen). **2** *also* **f.a.d.** free air delivered *commerce.*

FAE fuel-air explosive (a fire bomb weapon).

Faer. Faeroe Islands.

FAF 1 fatty acid fraction *biochemistry.* **2** final approach fix *aeronautics.*

FAGMS field artillery guided missile.

F.A.G.O. *or* **FAGO** Fellow of the American Guild of Organists.

FAGS 1 Federation of Astronomical and Geophysical Services. **2** *also* **F.A.G.S.** Fellow of the American Geographical Society.

Fah. or **Fahr.** Fahrenheit: *300 degrees Fah.*

FAI 1 fresh air intake *construction, refining.* **2** International Aeronautical Federation. [French *Fédération Aéronautique Internationale*]

F.A.I.A. or **FAIA** Fellow of the American Institute of Architects.

FAIC or **F.A.I.C.** Fellow of the American Institute of Chemists.

FAIDS Feline Acquired Immune Deficiency Syndrome.

Fak. or **Fakt.** invoice *commerce.* [German *Faktura*]

Falk.Is. Falkland Islands.

FALN or **F.A.L.N.** Armed Forces for National Liberation (of Puerto Rico, Venezuela, etc.). [Spanish *Fuerzas Armadas de Liberación Nacional*]

F.A.M. or **F.& A.M.** Free and Accepted Masons (a fraternal order).

fam. 1 familiar. **2** *also* **Fam.** family, also in combination: *Fam.L.Q.* = *Family Law Quarterly*

FAMA or **F.A.M.A.** Fellow of the American Medical Association.

FAME fatty acid methyl ester (used to identify microorganisms) *biochemistry.*

FAMEME or **F.A.M.E.M.E.** Fellow of the Association of Mining, Electrical, and Mechanical Engineers.

FAN Armies of the North (military government of Chad). [French *Forces Armées du Nord*]

f&a or **f. and a.** fore and aft.

F. and A.M. Free and Accepted Masons.

F&B food and beverage: *F&B Supervisor, F&B hotel experience.*

f&d or **f. and d.** freight and demurrage *commerce.*

f&f or **f. and f.** furniture or fittings and fixtures *insurance.*

f&g or **f&gs** or **F&G** or **F&Gs** folded and gathered (printed pages folded and stacked, ready for binding).

F&M foot and mouth disease (of livestock).

F. and R. force and rhythm (of the pulse) *medicine.*

F&T fire and theft *insurance.*

Fannie Mae (fan′ē mā′) Federal National Mortgage Association; FNMA.

F.A.N.Y. First Aid Nursing Yeomanry.

FAO 1 Finance and Accounts Office, esp. in combination: *FAOUSA = Finance and Accounts Office of the U.S. Army.* **2** *also* **f.a.o.** finish all over. **3** Food and Agriculture Organization (of the UN).

FAP 1 familial adenomatous polyposis (genetically inherited condition of numerous small polyps in the colon that frequently become cancerous). **2** Family Assistance Program. **3** First Aid Post. **4** fixed action pattern (of behavior) *psychology.*

F.A.P.H.A. or **FAPHA** Fellow of American Public Health Association.

F.A.P.S. or **FAPS** Fellow of the American Physical Society.

FAQ or **f.a.q. 1** fair average quality. **2** free alongside quay. **3** frequently asked questions, in electronic communications.

FAR 1 Federal Acquisition Regulations (for contracting services, purchases, etc.). **2** Federal Aviation Regulation.

Far. or **far.** farad, faradic (of induced current of electricity).

Farmer Mac (far′mər mak) Federal Agricultural Mortgage Corporation.

FAS 1 *also* **F.A.S.** Federation of American Scientists. **2** *also* **F.A.S. a** Fellow of the Anthropological Society. **b** Fellow of the Antiquarian Society. **c** Fellow of the Society of Arts. **3** fetal alcohol syndrome *medicine.* **4** *also* **f.a.s.** firsts and seconds (grading of lumber). **5** Foreign Agricultural Service (of U.S. Department of Agriculture, to promote foodstuff exports). **6** *also* **F.A.S.** or **f.a.s.** free alongside ship (delivery to the ship without charge to the buyer). **7** Strategic Air Force (of France). [French *Forces Aériennes Stratégique*]

FASB Financial Accounting Standards Board (of the American Institute of Certified Public Accountants).

fasc. fascicle (one of the parts of a long book, etc., printed and issued a part at a time).

FASCE or **F.A.S.C.E.** Fellow of the American Society of Civil Engineers.

FASE Fundamentally Analyzable Simplified English (system for transcribing English language texts into less complex prose).

FASEB or **F.A.S.E.B.** Fellow of the American Societies for Experimental Biology.

FAST factor analysis system.

FAT 1 file allocation table (for management of disk space). **2** fluorescent antibody test *biochemistry.*

fath. fathom.

FATIS Food and Agriculture Technical Information Service (of the Organization for Economic Cooperation and Development).

fav. 1 favorable. **2** favorite.

FAWA or **F.A.W.A.** Federation of Asian Women's Associations.

FAWS Flight Advisory Weather Service.

fax (*pronounced* faks) **1** facsimile. **2** facsimile machine.

FB 1 *also* **F.B.** Fenian Brotherhood. **2** fighter bomber (with number designation as to type). **3** fire brigade: *FBH = fire brigade hydrant.* **4** Fishery Board. **5** *also* **F.B.** Free Baptist. **6** fullback *sports.*

f.b. 1 *also* **f/b** feedback *electronics.* **2** flat bar. **3** fog bell (on navigation charts). **4** foreign body *medicine.* **5** freight bill. **6** fullback *sports.*

FBA or **F.B.A. 1** Federal Bar Association. **2** Fellow of the British Academy.

FBAA or **F.B.A.A.** Fellow of the British Association of Accountants and Auditors.

FBC fluidized bed combustion *engineering.*

FBCS Fellow of the British Computer Society.

FBFM or **F.B.F.M.** Federation of British Film Makers.

FBHI or **F.B.H.I.** Fellow of the British Horological Institute.

FBI or **F.B.I.** Federal Bureau of Investigation.

FBIM or **F.B.I.M.** Fellow of the British Institute of Management.

FBIS Foreign Broadcast Information Service.

f.bk. flat back (of lumber).

FBM fleet ballistic missile.

fbm foot board measure.

FBO fixed base operator (in airports).

F.B.O.U. or **FBOU** Fellow of the British Ornithologists' Union.

FBP 1 also **F.B.P.** Federal Bureau of Prisons. **2** also **fbp** final boiling point.

FBR fast breeder reactor.

fbr. fiber.

FBS 1 also **F.B.S.** Fellow of the Botanical Society (of Great Britain). **2** forward-based system *military*. **3** frontal bovine serum *medicine*.

FC 1 fielder's choice *baseball*. **2** fire control. **3** also **F/C** first class. **4** follow copy *printing*. **5** also **F.C.** Football Club. **6** foot candle. **7** foreign consul. **8** free cholesterol *biochemistry*. **9** Free Church (of Scotland). **10** also **F/C** full charge: *Bookkeeper F/C.*

fc 1 also **f.c.** bequeathed in trust. [Latin *fidei commissum*] **2** also **f.c.** follow copy. **3** foot candle. **4** also **fc.** franc.

FCA 1 Farm Credit Administration. **2** also **F.C.A.** Federation of Canadian Artists. **3** Fellowship of Christian Athletes. **4** also **F.C.A.** Fellow of the Institute of Chartered Accountants (of Great Britain). **5** frequency control and analysis *aeronautics*.

f.c.& s. free of capture and seizure *commerce*.

FCAP or **F.C.A.P.** Fellow of the College of American Pathologists.

fcap. or **f/cap** foolscap (paper 15 to 17 inches long and 12 to 13 1/2 inches wide) *printing*.

FCASI or **F.C.A.S.I.** Fellow of the Canadian Aeronautics and Space Institute.

FCB file control block (part of a file to hold information about its contents, etc.) *computers*.

FCC 1 face-centered cubic (of a crystal) *chemistry*. **2** also **F.C.C.** Federal Communications Commission **3** also **F.C.C.** Federal Council of Churches. **4** first class certificate. **5** flight control center *aeronautics*. **6** fluid catalytic cracking.

FCCA or **F.C.C.A.** Fellow of the Chartered Association of Certified Accountants.

F.C.C.O. or **FCCO** Fellow of the Canadian College of Organists.

FCCS or **F.C.C.S.** Fellow of the Corporation of Certified Secretaries (of Great Britain).

FCDA Federal Civil Defense Administration.

fcg or **fcg.** facing.

F.C.G.I. Fellow of the City and Guilds of London Institute.

FCGP or **F.C.G.P.** Fellow of the College of General Practitioners.

FCIA or **F.C.I.A.** **1** Fellow of the Canadian Institute of Actuaries. **2** Fellow of the Corporation of Insurance Agents. **3** Foreign Credit Insurance Association.

FCIC or **F.C.I.C.** **1** Federal Crop Insurance Corporation (of U.S. Department of Agriculture). **2** Fellow of the Chemical Institute of Canada.

FCII or **F.C.I.I.** Fellow of the Chartered Insurance Institute.

F.C.I.S. or **FCIS** Fellow of the Chartered Institute of Secretaries.

FCM futures commission merchant.

FCO Foreign and Commonwealth Office (of Great Britain).

f.co. fair copy.

FCP 1 fatigue crack propagation, in refining. **2** final common pathway *anatomy*.

fcp. foolscap (see *fcap.*).

FCPA or **F.C.P.A.** Fellow of the Canadian Psychological Association.

FCPS or **F.C.P.S.** Fellow of the College of Physicians and Surgeons.

FCS 1 Farm Credit System (of U.S. Department of Agriculture). **2** frame check sequence (redundancy check) *computers*.

fcs or **fcs.** francs.

f.c.s. free of capture and seizure *commerce*.

FCSC or **F.C.S.C.** Foreign Claims Settlement Commission (of U.S. Department of Justice).

FCST or **F.C.S.T.** Federal Council for Science and Technology.

FCT 1 also **F.C.T.** Federal Capital Territory (of Australia). **2** also **fct** filament center tap *electronics*.

fcty. factory.

FCU Federal Credit Union.

fcy or **fcy.** fancy.

FD 1 also **F.D.** Defender of the Faith (reference to King Henry VIII of England). [Latin *Fidei Defensor*] **2** also **F.D.** fire department, esp. in combination: *NYFD = New York Fire Department.* **3** floppy disk *computers*, esp. in combination: *FDOS = floppy disk operating system.* **4** also **f/d** focal distance. **5** also **f.d.** free delivery or dispatch. **6** full duplex (data processing) *computers*.

Fd. 1 Fiord. **2** founded.

fd 1 ferredoxin (protein, possible agent of energy transfer in photosynthesis). **2** also **fd.** field. **3** also **fd.** fund, funds.

FDA or **F.D.A.** Food and Drug Administration (of U.S. Department of Health and Human Services).

FDAA or **F.D.A.A.** Federal Disaster Assistance Administration.

FD&C Food, Drug, and Cosmetic Act (of the U.S.).

FDAU flight data acquisition unit.

FDC 1 Federal Detention Center. **2** Fire Direction Center. **3** first-day cover (envelope with stamp mailed on first day of issue) *philately*. **4** flight director computer.

FDD Food and Drug Directorate (of Canada).

FDDI fiber distributed data interface (fiber-optic network) *computers*.

Fdg. or **fdg.** funding.

FDHD floppy disk, high density *computers*.

FDI International Dental Federation. [French *Fédération Dentaire Internationale*]

FDIC or **F.D.I.C.** Federal Deposit Insurance Corporation.

FDIM fluorescence digital imaging microscopy.

FDJ Free German Youth. [German *Freie Deutsche Jugend*]

FDM frequency division multiplex (technique of separating a bandwidth to share transmission space), also in combination: *FDMA = frequency division multiplex access.*

fdn. foundation.

FDNB fluorodinitrobenzene (insecticide).

FDOT Regional Defense Forces (of Spain). [Spanish *Fuerzas de Defensa Operativa del Territorio*]

FDP 1 fibrin degradation products (fragments of degraded fibrin in the circulatory system) *medicine.* **2** Field Developed Program *computers.* **3** foreign duty pay. **4** *also* **F.D.P.** **a** Free Democratic Party. [German *Freie Demokratische Partei*] **b** Radical Democratic Party of Switzerland. [German *Freisinnige Demokratische Partei der Schweiz*] **5** fructose diphosphate (used in the study of cell carbohydrate metabolism).

FDR 1 Democratic Revolutionary Front (of El Salvador). [Spanish *Frente Democrática Revolucionaria*] **2** flight data recorder *aeronautics.* **3** formal dining room. **4** Franklin Delano Roosevelt (U.S. President during the Great Depression and WWII).

Fdr. founder.

fdry. foundry.

FDS Fermi, Dirac, Sommerfeld (originators of a principle to describe velocity of atomic particles) *physics.*

FDX full duplex (simultaneous transmission in both directions on a single channel) *electronics.*

FE field engineer.

Fe iron (chemical element). [Latin *ferrum*]

fe 1 *also* **f.e.** first edition. **2** *also* **fe.** wet fog *meteorology.*

FEA 1 Federal Energy Administration (later *Department of Energy*). **2** Federal Executive Association.

FEANI European Federation of National Associations of Engineers. [French *Fédération Européenne d'Associations Nationales d'Ingénieurs*]

FEB 1 Federal Executive Board. **2** functional electronic block (of an integrated circuit) *computers.*

Feb. February.

FEBS Federation of European Biochemical Societies.

FEC 1 European Cultural Foundation. [French *Fondation Européenne de la Culture*] **2** Federal Election Commission. **3** Freestanding Emergency Clinic. **4** in vitro fertilization. [French *fécondation extra-corporelle*]

fec. he or she made it. [Latin *fecit*]

FECA *or* **F.E.C.A.** Federal Employees' Compensation Act.

FED 1 European Development Fund; EDF. [French *Fond Européen de la Développement*] **2** Fusion Engineering Device.

Fed (*pronounced* fed) **1** any federal law-enforcement agency or officer, as of the FBI or DEA. **2** Federal Reserve Bank or District: *NY Fed = New York Federal Reserve Bank or District.* **3** Federal Reserve Board.

Fed. *or* **fed. 1 a** Federal, also in combination: *Fed.Comm. = Federal Commission.* **b** Federal District. **2** Federalist. **3** Federal Reporter. **4** Federated. **5** Federation.

FEDC Federation of Engineering Design Consultants.

Fedex *or* **FEDEX** *or* **FedEx** (fed'eks') Federal Express (trade name of a private mail and shipping service).

FEDLINK (fed'lingk') Federal Library and Information Network.

Fed. Reg. Federal Register.

FEDRIP Federal Research in Progress (database summarizing U.S. government research projects).

FEI 1 Federal Executive Institute (executive training for managers of U.S. government organizations). **2** *also* **F.E.I.** International Equestrian Federation. [French *Fédération Équestre Internationale*]

FEIA Flight Engineers' International Association.

FEIN Federal Employer Identification Number.

FEL free electron laser.

FELA *or* **F.E.L.A.** Federal Employer's Liability Act.

FELABAN Latin American Banking Federation. [Spanish *Federación Latinoamericana de Bancos*]

FeLV feline leukemia virus.

fem. 1 female. **2** *also* **Fem** feminine, often in combination: *Fem Lib. = Feminine Liberation.*

FEMA (fē'mə) Federal Emergency Management Agency.

fenc. fencing.

FENSA Film Entertainments National Service Association.

FEO *or* **F.E.O.** Federal Energy Office.

FEOGA European Agricultural Guidance and Guarantee Fund (of EC). [French *Fonds Européen d'Orientation et de Garantie Agriculturel*]

FEP 1 fair employment practices: *FEP law;* also in combination: *FEPA = Fair Employment Practices Act; FEPC = Fair Employment Practices Commission.* **2** fluorinated ethylene propylene (resin with nonstick properties). **3** front-end processor *computers.*

Fer. Fermanagh County, Ireland.

FERA Federal Emergency Relief Administration.

FERC Federal Energy Regulatory Commission.

Ferd. Ferdinand.

FERES International Federation of Catholic Institutes of Social and Socio-Religious Research. [French *Fédération Internationale des Instituts Catholiques de Recherches Socio-Religieuses*]

Ferm. Fermanagh County, Ireland.

Fermilab (fér'mē lab') Fermi National Accelerator Laboratory.

ferv. boiling. [Latin *fervens*]

FES 1 *also* **F.E.S.** Fellow of the Ethnological Society. **2** *also* **F.E.S.** Fellow of the Entomological Society. **3** fine error sensor (camera guiding telescope on a target star).

Fest. festival.

FET 1 a Federal Estate Tax. **b** Federal Excise Tax. **2** field effect transistor (modulating transistor used esp. in oscillators, amplifiers, etc.) *electronics.*

feud. 1 feudal. **2** feudalism.

FEV 1 *also* **fev.** fever. **2** forced expiratory volume (from the lungs) *medicine.*

FF *I an abbreviation for:* **1** *also* **FF.** Brothers (esp. of religious). [Latin *fratres,* French *frères*] **2** fast forward (esp. of a tape machine). **3** Fianna Fáil (Militia of Ireland, a political party). **4** *also* **F-F** flip-flop (of alternating circuits, esp. in transistors) *electronics.* **5** folded flat. **6** form feed, form feeding *computers.*

7 French fried. **8** full-fashioned (of hose, sweaters, or other garments knitted to fit the shape of the foot, leg, or body). **9** furniture and fixtures, *esp. in insurance.* **10** also **F.F.** Most Fortunate Brothers. [Latin *Felicissimi Fratres*]
II *a symbol for:* thick fog *nautical, meteorology.*

ff. I *an abbreviation for:* **1** also **f.f.** or **f/f** fixed focus (esp. of a camera). **2** folios. **3** following, esp. the following pages. **4** they made it. [Latin *fecerunt*]
II *a symbol for:* also **ff** very loud *music.* [Italian *fortissimo*]

FFA 1 also **F.F.A.** Fellow of the Faculty of Actuaries. **2** also **F.F.A.** foreign freight agent *commerce.* **3** for further assignment. **4** free fatty acids. **5** free foreign agency *commerce.* **6** also **f.f.a.** free from alongside ship *commerce.* **7** Future Farmers of America.

F.F.A.S. or **FFAS** Fellow of the Faculty of Architects and Surveyors (of Great Britain).

FFB 1 also **F.F.B.** Federal Financing Bank (of U.S. Treasury). **2** Frequent Flier Bonus (of a category of airline passengers and tickets for flying the same airline or group of airlines a certain number of times in a given period).

FFC 1 Foreign Funds Control. **2** free from chlorine *chemistry.*

FFDCA Federal Food, Drug, and Cosmetic Act (1938, controlling purity, labeling, ingredients, safety).

fff as loud as possible *music.* [Italian *fortississimo*]

F.F.I. 1 free from infection *medicine.* **2** French Forces of the Interior (section of the Maquis in WWII). [French *Forces Françaises de l'Intérieur*]

F.F.L. 1 finished floor level. **2** Free French Forces (section of the Maquis in WWII). [French *Forces Françaises Libres*]

FFP 1 firm fixed price (of a contract). **2** Frequent Flier Program. **3** fresh frozen plasma *medicine.*

FFPS or **F.F.P.S.** Fellow of the Faculty of Physicians and Surgeons.

FFR or **F.F.R.** Fellow of the Faculty of Radiologists.

FFT 1 Fast Fourier Transform (system using algorithms to decrease calculation for analysis of curves, wave forms in acoustics and crystals, spectroscopy, etc.). **2** final form text (ready to print from a computer file), esp. in combination: *FFTDCA = final form text in Document Center Architecture.* **3** also **F.F.T.** flicker fusion threshold (test to determine when the flicker of a light is so fast that the patient sees a continuous light).

F.F.V. or **FFV** First Families of Virginia: *The University of Virginia has educated many sons of the F.F.V.s.*

FG 1 also **F.G.** Federal Government, esp. in combination: *FGAA = Federal Government Accountants Association.* **2** field goal, *esp. in football.* **3** Fine Gael (Irish Tribe, political party). **4** fine grain. **5** flat grain. **6** also **F.G.** friction glazed (of paper).

fg. fog over low ground.

f.g. 1 fine grain. **2** friction glazed (of paper). **3** fully good *commerce.*

FGA or **f.g.a. 1** foreign general average *insurance.* **2** free of general average (not involved in the costs for loss of cargo at sea) *insurance.*

FGD flue gas desulfurization *engineering.*

f.g.f. fully good, fair *commerce.*

fgg. the following. [German *folgende*]

FGIS Federal Grain Inspection Service (of U.S. Department of Agriculture).

fgn. or **Fgn.** foreign.

F.G.O. Fellow of the Guild of Organists.

FGP Foster Grandparent Program.

FGS or **F.G.S. 1** Fellow of the Geographical Society (of Great Britain). **2** Fellow of the Geological Society (of Great Britain).

FGSA or **F.G.S.A.** Fellow of the Geological Society of America.

FGT 1 Federal Gift Tax. **2** also **fgt.** freight.

FH 1 familial hypercholesterolemia (disease of liver cells that are unable to remove cholesterol from the bloodstream). **2** also **F.H.** family history, *esp. in medicine.* **3** field hospital *military.* **4** fire hydrant (esp. on maps). **5** flat head (esp. of screws). **6** fog horn (esp. on navigational charts). **7** also **F/H** freeholder (of real estate).

f.h. 1 fog horn (esp. on navigational charts). **2** make a draft *pharmaceutics.* [Latin *fiat haustus*]

FHA 1 Farmers Home Administration (of U.S. Department of Agriculture, supplement credit from private sources). **2** Federal Highway Administration (of U.S. Department of Transportation). **3** Federal Housing Administration. **4** Future Homemakers of America.

fha. date. [Spanish *fecha*]

FHAA Field Hockey Association of America.

F.H.B. family hold back (expression reputedly warning members of a family to take small enough portions of food served at a meal so that guests will have enough to eat).

FHD ferrohydrodynamic, esp. in reference to suspension of a ferromagnetic solid in a liquid.

FHFB Federal Housing Finance Board.

FHH fetal heart heard *medicine.*

FHLB Federal Home Loan Bank.

FHLBB Federal Home Loan Bank Board.

Fhld freehold.

FHLMC (*often pronounced* fred' ē mak' *and written Freddie Mac*) Federal Home Loan Mortgage Corporation.

fhp or **FHP 1** fractional horsepower. **2** also **F.H.P.** friction horsepower.

FHR 1 Federal House of Representatives (of Australia). **2** fetal heart rate *medicine.*

FHWA Federal Highway Administration.

FI 1 fade in (gradual increase in sound, as of broadcast music, or gradual brightening of an image, as in television or motion pictures). **2** also **F.I.** Falkland Islands. **3** fire insurance. **4** free in *commerce.* **5** fuel injection (of an internal combustion motor).

Fi. 1 Finland. **2** Finnish.

f.i. for instance.

FIA 1 Federal Insurance Administration. **2** also **F.I.A.** Fellow of the Institute of Actuaries (of Great Britain). **3** fluorescent indicator analysis. **4** fluoro-immuno-assay *biochemistry.*

5 Freedom of Information Act. **6** *also* **f.i.a.** full interest admitted *commerce.* **7** International Automobile Federation. [French *Fédération Internationale de l'Automobile*]

FIAA *or* **F.I.A.A.** Fellow of the Incorporated Association of Architects.

FIAC *or* **F.I.A.C.** **1** Federation of International Amateur Cycling. **2** Fellow of the Institute of Company Accountants.

FIAF International Federation of Film Archives. [French *Fédération Internationale des Archives du Film*]

FIAJ International Federation of Youth Hostels. [French *Fédération Internationale des Auberges de la Jeunesse*]

FIAT Field Information Agency, Technical (report).

FIAV *or* **F.I.A.V.** International Federation of Travel Agencies. [French *Fédération Internationale des Agences de Voyages*]

FIB **1** foreground-initiated background (program involving lengthy computations that do not require human intervention). **2** *also* **f.i.b.** *commerce* **a** free into barge. **b** free in bunker.

fib. fibrillation *medicine.*

F.I.B.A. International Amateur Basketball Federation. [French *Fédération Internationale de Basketball Amateur*]

FIBT *or* **F.I.B.T.** International Bobsleighing and Tobogganing Federation. [French *Fédération Internationale de Bobsleigh et de Tobogganing*]

FIC **1** Federal Information Center. **2** *also* **F.I.C.** Fellow of the Institute of Chemistry (of Great Britain). **3** Flight Information Center. **4** frequency interface control *communications.*

fic. **1** fiction. **2** fictitious.

FICA (fīʹkə) Federal Insurance Contributions Act.

FICC *or* **F.I.C.C.** International Federation of Camping and Caravanning. [French *Fédération Internationale de Camping et de Caravanning*]

FICD *or* **F.I.C.D.** Fellow of the International College of Dentists.

FICO Financing Corporation.

FICS *or* **F.I.C.S.** **1** Fellow of the Institute of Chartered Shipbrokers. **2** Fellow of the International College of Surgeons.

fict. **1 a** fiction. **b** fictitious. **2** (made) of pottery, earthenware. [Latin *fictilis*]

FID **1** Field Intelligence Department (of the U.S. Army). **2** International Federation for Documentation. [French *Fédération Internationale de Documentation*]

fid. **1** fidelity. **2** fiduciary.

FIDAC film input to digital automatic computer.

FIDE International Chess Federation. [French *Fédération Internationale Des Échecs*]

Fid.Def. Defender of the Faith (reference to King Henry VIII of England). [Latin *Fidei Defensor*]

F.I.D.I.C. *or* **FIDIC** International Federation of Consulting Engineers. [French *Fédération Internationale des Ingénieurs Conseils*]

FIDO **1** *also* **Fido** Flight Dynamics Officer (engineer responsible for management of the dynamics of a space flight). **2** Fog Investigation Dispersal Operations.

F.I.D.S. Falkland Islands Dependencies Survey (now *British Antarctic Survey*).

FIE **1** feline infectious enteritis. **2** International Fencing Federation. [French *Fédération Internationale d'Escrime*]

F.I.E.J. *or* **FIEJ** International Federation of Newspaper Publishers and Editors. [French *Fédération Internationale des Éditeurs de Journaux et Publications*]

FIERE *or* **F.I.E.R.E.** Fellow of the Institute of Electronic and Radio Engineers.

FIFA International Federation of Association Football. [French *Fédération Internationale de Football Association*]

fi.fa. cause to be done: *issue a writ of fi.fa. to enforce payment.* [Latin *fieri facias*]

FIFCLC International Federation of Business and Professional Women. [French *Fédération Internationale de Femmes de Carrières Libérales et Commerciales*]

FIFDU International Federation of University Women. [French *Fédération Internationale des Femmes Diplômées des Universités*]

Fife. Fifeshire County, Scotland.

FIFO *or* **fifo** (fīʹfō) first in, first out (a method of inventory) *commerce.*

FIFOR flight forecast *meteorology.*

FIFRA Federal Insecticide, Fungicide, and Rodenticide Act.

FIG International Federation of Gymnastics. [French *Fédération Internationale de Gymnastique*]

fig **1** *also* **fig.** figurative, figuratively. **2** *also* **Fig.** *or* **fig.** figure, figures (illustrations or graphs and tables in a book).

FIGCM Fellow of the Incorporated Guild of Church Musicians.

FIGO *or* **F.I.G.O.** International Federation of Gynecology and Obstetrics. [French *Fédération Internationale de Gynécologie et de l'Obstétrique*]

FIGS figures shift *computers.*

figs. figures (illustrations or graphs and tables in a book).

FIH **1** *also* **F.I.H.** International Federation of Hospitals. [French *Fédération Internationale des Hôpitaux*] **2** International Hockey Federation. [French *Fédération Internationale de Hockey*]

FIIA *or* **F.I.I.A.** Fellow of the Institute of Industrial Administration.

FIInfSc *or* **F.I.Inf.Sc.** Fellow of the Institute of Information Scientists.

FIJ **1** International Federation of Journalists. [French *Fédération Internationale des Journalistes*] **2** International Judo Federation. [French *Fédération Internationale de Judo*]

FIL Fellow of the Institute of Linguistics.

fil. **1** filament. **2** fillet. **3 a** filter. **b** filtration.

FILO *or* **filo** (fīʹlō) first in, last out: **a** a method of inventory *commerce.* **b** a system of adding items to a list *computers.*

filt. filter.

FIM **1** field ion microscope. **2** *also* **F.I.M.** International Federation of Musicians. [French *Fédération Internationale des Musiciens*] **3** International Motorcycle Federation. [French *Fédération Internationale Motocycliste*]

FIMS field ion mass spectroscopy.

Fin. 1 finish, in horse racing. 2 a Finland. b Finnish.

fin. 1 final. 2 a finance. b financial. 3 a finish. b finished. 4 a the end. [Latin *finis*] b to the end. [Latin *ad finem*]

FINA 1 also **f.i.n.a.** following items not available *commerce*. 2 also **F.I.N.A.** International Amateur Swimming Federation. [French *Fédération Internationale de Natation Amateur*]

FINCEN Financial Crimes Enforcement Network.

Fincl or **fincl** financial: *Fincl Statmnt = financial statement.*

Finn. Finnish.

Fin.Sec. Financial Secretary.

F.Inst.P. Fellow of the Institute of Physics.

fin-syn or **fin/syn** financial interest and syndication (referring to rules of the Federal Communications Commission that govern syndication rights of TV network programming).

FIO or **f.i.o.** 1 for information only. 2 free in and out (shipper pays for loading and unloading) *commerce*.

FIOS or **f.i.o.s.** free in and out stowage (shipper pays for loading, unloading, and stowage) *commerce*.

FIP 1 also **f.i.p.** finite intersect property *mathematics*. 2 also **F.I.P.** International Philatelic Federation. [French *Fédération Internationale de Philatélie*]

FIPS Federal Information Processing Standards.

FIQ International Bowling Federation. [French *Fédération Internationale des Quilleurs*]

FIR flight information region.

fir. firkin (measure equal to a quarter of a barrel).

FIRA 1 Foreign Investment Review Agency (of Canada). 2 Furniture Industry Research Association (of Great Britain). 3 International Amateur Rugby Federation. [French *Fédération Internationale de Rugby Amateur*]

F.I.R.E. or **FIRE** Fellow of the Institute of Radio Engineers.

FIRS Federal Information Relay Service.

FIRST 1 far infrared space telescope. 2 fast interactive retrieval system technology (computer language).

FIS 1 *British* Family Income Supplement. 2 Flight Information Service. 3 International Ski Federation. [French *Fédération Internationale de Ski*] 4 also **F.I.S.** Islamic Salvation Front (Islamic party in Algeria). [French *Front Islamique de Salut*]

FISA 1 also **F.I.S.A.** Fellow of the Incorporated Secretaries Association. 2 International Federation of Automotive Sports. [French *Fédération Internationale du Sport Automobile*] 3 International Rowing Federation. [French *Fédération Internationale des Sociétés d'Aviron*]

fisc. fiscal.

FISE or **F.I.S.E.** International Federation of Teachers Union. [French *Fédération Internationale Syndicale de l'Enseignement*]

fish. 1 fishery. 2 fishing.

FIST Federal Investigative Strike Team (law-enforcement groups to capture important fugitives).

F.I.S.U. or **FISU** International Federation of University Sports. [French *Fédération Internationale du Sport Universitaire*]

FIT 1 also **F.I.T.** Fashion Institute of Technology. 2 Federal Income Tax. 3 free and independent travelers (tourists not in a tour group). 4 also **f.i.t.** a free in and trim *shipping*. b free in truck *commerce*. 5 free of income tax. 6 also **F.I.T.** International Federation of Translators. [French *Fédération Internationale des Traducteurs*]

FITA International Federation of Archery. [French *Fédération Internationale de Tir à l'Arc*]

FITC fluorescein isothiocyanate (used to label proteins) *biochemistry*.

FITW or **fitw** Federal Income Tax Withheld.

fix. fixture.

Fj. or **Fjd.** Fjord.

F.J.I. or **FJI** Fellow of the Institute of Journalists.

Fk. 1 Fork (in place names). 2 Frank.

f.k. before Christ; BC [Norwegian *før Kristus*]

FKA or **fka** formerly known as.

FL 1 flashing (esp. of lights on navigation charts): *FLR = flashing red light.* 2 also **F/L** Flight Lieutenant. 3 Florida (Zip Code). 4 flush (even). 5 also **F/L** focal length. 6 foot-lambert (unit of luminance). 7 Foreign Language.

Fl *I an abbreviation for:* 1 also **Fl.** a Flanders. b Flemish. 2 flashing (esp. of lights on navigation charts). 3 florin (monetary unit of Aruba and the Netherlands). 4 also **Fl.** river (esp. in place names). [German *Fluss*, French *fleuve*] *II a symbol for:* fluorine (chemical element).

fl 1 also **f.l.** false reading (of a document). [Latin *falsa lectio*] 2 also **fl.** floor. 3 also **fl.** a floret (small flower in the head of a composite flower). b flower. 4 also **fl.** florin (monetary unit of Aruba and the Netherlands). 5 flour. 6 also **fl.** flourished: *Eusebius of Caesarea, fl. 4th century.* 7 also **fl.** fluid. 8 also **fl.** flush (even). 9 flute *music*. 10 also **f-l** or **fL** foot-lambert (unit of luminance).

FLA 1 Federal Loan Agency. 2 also **F.L.A.** Fellow of the Library Association. 3 Foreign Language Annuals (magazine title).

Fla. Florida.

f.l.a. make by the rules of the art *pharmaceutics*. [Latin *fiat lege artis*]

F.L.A.A. or **FLAA** Fellow of the Library Association of Australia.

flak (*pronounced* flak) antiaircraft gunfire. [German *Fl.A.K.* for *Flieger Abwehr Kanone*, usually written as one word]

flav. yellow *pharmaceutics*. [Latin *flavus*]

FLB Federal Land Bank.

FLCM or **F.L.C.M.** Fellow of the London College of Music.

fld. 1 also **FLD** field. 2 flowered (of plants). 3 fluid.

fldg. folding.

fl.dr. fluid dram.

Flem. Flemish.

FLES Foreign Language in the Elementary Schools.

FLETC Federal Law Enforcement Training Center.

FLEX Foreign Licensing Examination (of doctors who have received their training outside the U.S.) *medicine*.

flex. *or* **FLEXBL** flexible.

flg. 1 flange. **2** flooring.

FLIH first level interrupt handler (to route signals from peripherals) *computers.*

FLIP 1 Flexible Loan Insurance Program. **2** Floating Instrument Platform.

FLIR forward-looking infrared (night vision equipment for combat).

F.L.N. National Liberation Front (of various French and Spanish-speaking countries). [French *Front de Libération Nationale;* Spanish *Frente de Liberación Nacional*]

FLOP floating point operation (operational capacity of a computer).

FLOPS floating point operations per second (measure of the operating speed of a computer).

flor. flourished. [Latin *floruit*]

flot. flotation.

FLOX fluorine and liquid oxygen.

fl.oz. fluid ounce.

FLP Foreign Language Program.

fl.pl. with double flowers *botany.* [Latin *flore pleno*]

fl.pt. flash point.

FLQ Liberation Front of Quebec (Quebec Separatist party, also *PQ*). [French *Front de Libération Québécois*]

flr. 1 *also* **Flr** floor. **2** florin. **3** flower.

FLRA Federal Labor Relations Authority.

F.L.S. *or* **FLS** Fellow of the Linnean Society.

Fls falls (esp. in an address): *Croton Fls.*

fls. flowers.

FLSA Fair Labor Standards Act.

FLT 1 fleet, esp. in combination: *FLTSATCOM = fleet satellite communications system.* **2** force, length, time (system of units, used esp. in rocket dynamics and propulsion).

Flt. 1 fleet: *Flt.Adm. = Fleet Admiral.* **2** flight: *Flt.Lt. = Flight Lieutenant.*

flt. 1 filter. **2** flight. **3 a** float. **b** flotation.

fltg. floating.

fluc. 1 fluctuate. **2** fluctuation.

fluor. fluorescent.

FLV Friend Leukemia Virus.

flx. *or* **flx** flexible.

FM 1 Federated States of Micronesia (in postal address) **2** *also* **F.M.** field magnet. **3** (U.S. Army) field manual (followed by a number). **4** *also* **F.M.** Field Marshall. **5** *also* **F.M.** Foreign Minister. **6** *also* **F.M.** Foreign Missions. **7** frequency modulation *electronics.*

Fm *I* an abbreviation for: *also* **Fm.** farm.
II a symbol for: fermium (chemical element).

fm 1 *also* **f.m.** before noon *or* time from midnight to noon; AM [Danish, Norwegian *formiddag*] **2** farm. **3** *also* **fm.** fathom. **4** femtometer, femtometers (unit of length) *physics.* **5** fine measurement. **6** *also* **fm.** form. **7** frequency modulation *electronics.* **8** *also* **fm.** from. **9 a** front matter (of a book). **b** facing matter (advertisement or illustration on a facing page). **10** *also* **f.m.** make a mixture *pharmaceutics.* [Latin *fiat mistura*]

FMB Federal Maritime Board.

FMC 1 Federal Maritime Commission. **2** Forces Mobile Command (of the Royal Canadian Army).

FMCS Federal Mediation and Conciliation Service.

FM-CW frequency modulation-continuous wave (radar).

FMD *or* **f.m.d.** foot-and-mouth disease.

FMDS Flight Model Discharge System (producing a conducting plasma cloud to protect spacecraft from ionized electrical charges in space).

FMF 1 Familial Mediterranean Fever *medicine.* **2** Fleet Marine Forces (of Great Britain).

FMG foreign medical graduate (of a doctor applying to practice in the U.S.).

FmHA Farmers Home Administration (of U.S. Department of Agriculture).

FMI Food Marketing Institute.

Fmk markka (monetary unit of Finland).

FMLN National Liberation Front (former guerrilla group in El Salvador). [Spanish *Farabundo Marti Liberación Nacional*]

FMLT force, mass, length, time (system of units, used esp. in rocket dynamics and propulsion).

FMN flavin mononucleotide (a coenzyme essential to human nutrition).

fmn. formation.

FMP 1 Finance and Management Policy (bureau of U.S. Department of State). **2** fructose-monophosphate (constituent of cell metabolism) *biochemistry.*

fmr. former, formerly.

FMRS *or* **F.M.R.S.** Foreign Member of the Royal Society.

FMS 1 Financial Management Service (of U.S. Department of the Treasury). **2** flexible manufacturing system.

FMV 1 fair market value *commerce.* **2** full motion video (of compact disk technology to reproduce a picture).

FMVSS Federal Motor Vehicle Safety Standards.

FN 1 government armament factory of France: *FN automatic rifles.* [French *Fabrique Nationale*] **2** *also* **F.N.** National Front (conservative French political party). [French *Front National*]

fn 1 *also* **fn.** *or* **f.n.** footnote **2** *also* **fn.** fusion, esp. in combination: *fn.p. = fusion point.*

FNAA *or* **F.N.A.A.** Fellow of the National Association of Auctioneers.

fnd. 1 *also* **Fnd.** foundation (institution or structural support). **2 a** found. **b** *also* **fdd.** founded.

fndr. *or* **Fndr** founder.

fndry. *or* **Fndry** foundry.

F.N.I. Fellow of the National Institute of Sciences of India.

FNIF *or* **F.N.I.F.** Florence Nightingale International Foundation.

fnl. 1 final. **2** finally.

FNLA National Liberation Front of Angola. [Portuguese *Frente Nacional de Libertação de Angola*]

FNMA (fan'ē mā', often written *Fannie Mae*). Federal National Mortgage Association.

FNN Financial News Network (cable TV broadcast network).

FNP *or* **fn.p.** fusion point.

FNS 1 Food and Nutrition Service (of U.S. Department of Agriculture). 2 Nuclear Strategic Force (nuclear weapons defense system of France). [French *Forces Nucléaire Stratégiques*]

F.N.S.E.A. National Federation of Farmers Union (of France). [French *Fédération Nationale des Syndicats d'Exploitants Agricoles*]

FNU 1 full name unknown. 2 United Nations Forces. [French *Forces des Nations Unies*]

FNZIA *or* **F.N.Z.I.A.** Fellow of the New Zealand Institute of Architects.

FNZIC *or* **F.N.Z.I.C.** Fellow of the New Zealand Institute of Chemistry.

FNZIE *or* **F.N.Z.I.E.** Fellow of the New Zealand Institution of Engineers.

FNZLA *or* **F.N.Z.L.A.** Fellow of the New Zealand Library Association.

FNZSA *or* **F.N.Z.S.A.** Fellow of the New Zealand Society of Accountants.

FO 1 fade out (of an image on television or in a motion picture). 2 *also* **F.O.** field office. 3 Field Officer. 4 field order (with a number). 5 *also* **F.O.** Finance or Financial Officer, esp. in combination: *CFO = Chief Financial Officer*. 6 a *also* **f.o.** firm offer *commerce*. **b** formal offer (of securities). 7 Flag Officer. 8 *also* **F/O** Flying Officer. 9 Foreign Office. 10 forward observer *military*. 11 *also* **f.o.** free overside *shipping*. 12 *also* **f.o.** fuel oil. 13 *also* **F.O.** full organ *music*.

fo. *or* **f°** folio.

f/o 1 fade out (of an image on television or in a motion picture). 2 for orders *commerce*. 3 full out (terms in trading grain) *commerce*.

FOB 1 Field Operations Bureau (of the Federal Communications Commission). 2 *also* **F.O.B.** *or* **f.o.b.** free on board *commerce*: *manufacturers' prices are quoted F.O.B. Detroit*.

FOBS Fractional Orbital Bombardment System.

FOC 1 *also* **F.O.C.** Father of the chapel (archaic term for master of a shop in the printers' union). 2 *also* **f.o.c.** free of charge *commerce*.

FOCA Freedom of Choice Act (legislation to protect pro-choice or abortion rights).

FOD 1 foreign object damage (inside a turbine or jet engine). 2 *also* **f.o.d.** free of damage *commerce*.

FOE 1 *also* **F.O.E.** Fraternal Order of Eagles. 2 *also* **FoE** Friends of the Earth (British activist environmental group). 3 fuel oil equivalent.

FOFA follow on forces attack (use of artillery and missiles to reinforce and follow up an attack) *military*.

FOI freedom of information: *file FOI requests*.

FOIA Freedom of Information Act.

f.o.k. *or* **FOK** free of knots (of lumber).

FOL Federation of Labour (of New Zealand).

fol. 1 folio. 2 followed, following.

foll. 1 folios. 2 following.

fols. folios.

FOM figure of merit (in evaluating statistics).

FOMC Federal Open Market Committee.

FONAR field focusing nuclear magnetic resonator.

foot. footings *building*.

FOP forward observation post *military*.

FOQ *or* **f.o.q.** free on quay *shipping*.

FOR 1 Fellowship of Reconciliation (human rights group). 2 *also* **f.o.r.** free on rails *commerce*.

For Fornax, the Furnace (constellation).

for. 1 *also* **For.** foreign. 2 forensic. 3 a *also* **For.** forest. **b** forestry.

for'd. forward.

Forgn. foreign: *Forgn. Affairs Com. chairman*.

form 1 formation. 2 former, formerly.

For. Rts foreign rights, esp. of a book or patent.

fort. 1 fortification. 2 fortified.

FORTH *or* **Forth** (*pronounced* fôrth) a computer programming language (distinguished by its adaptability to many functions).

FORTRAN *or* **Fortran** (fôr'tran') Formula Translation (computer programming language).

Forts. continuation. [German *Fortsetzung*]

forz. with force or emphasis *music*. [Italian *forzando*]

FOS *or* **f.o.s.** free on station or ship *commerce*.

FOSDIC (foz'dik) film optical sensing device for input to computers (optical scanning device).

FOT 1 *also* **f.o.t.** free of tax *commerce*. 2 *also* **f.o.t.** free on truck *commerce*. 3 optimum working frequency *electronics*.

Found. Foundation.

FOUR Federation of Union Representatives.

4×4 (fôr'bī fôr') four-wheel drive, esp. a pick-up truck or car with four-wheel drive.

401k (fôr'ō'wun'kā') a retirement savings plan allowing deferment of income that is taxed after retirement.

4WD four-wheel drive.

FOUSA Finance Office of the U.S. Army.

FOV field of view.

f.o.w. 1 first open water (after ice clears in a port) *shipping*. 2 free on wagon *commerce*.

FP 1 *also* **F.P.** family practitioner *medicine*. 2 *also* **F.P.** fine paper (edition of a book). 3 fireplace. 4 *also* **F.P.** fixed price: *FP Contract*. 5 flash point. 6 flavoprotein (energy-producing enzyme in body cells). 7 *also* **F.P.** floating policy *insurance*. 8 *also* **fp.** foot-pound. 9 forward pass *football*. 10 forward perpendicular (esp. of ship construction). 11 freezing point. 12 *also* **F.P.** fully paid *commerce*.

Fp. or **fp.** frontispiece.

fp 1 also **f.p.** flameproof. **2** freezing point. **3** also **f.p.** fully paid commerce. **4** loud and then soft music. [Italian fortepiano] **5** also **f.p.** make a pill pharmaceutics. [Latin fiat pilula]

FPA 1 Family Planning Association. **2** also **F.P.A.** Foreign Policy Association. **3** also **F.P.A.** Foreign Press Association. **4** also **f.p.a.** free of particular average insurance, esp. in combination: FPAAC = free of particular average American conditions.

FPC 1 Federal Power Commission. **2** fish protein concentrate. **3** also **F.P.C.** fixed price contract commerce. **4** flat plate collector (solar collector) engineering.

f.p.c. for private circulation.

FPF or **fpf** frames per foot photography.

fph full-power hours.

FPHA Federal Public Housing Authority.

FPHC Foreign Personal Holding Company.

F.Ph.S. Fellow of the Philosophical Society (of Great Britain).

F.Phys.S. Fellow of the Physical Society (of Great Britain).

FPI 1 Federal Prison Industries. **2** also **F.P.I.** fixed price incentive (of a contract) commerce.

f.pil. make a pill pharmaceutics. [Latin fiat pilula]

FPIS forward propagation ionospheric scatter electronics, physics.

FPL Popular Liberation Forces (in Spanish-speaking countries). [Spanish Fuerzas Populares de Liberación]

fpl or **fplc** fireplace.

FPLA field programmable logic array computers.

fpm or **f.p.m.** feet per minute.

FPMR Federal Property Management Regulation.

FPO 1 Field Post Office. **2** Field Project Office. **3** Fire Prevention Officer. **4** Fleet Post Office.

FPP floating point processor computers.

FPRF fireproof.

FPRS Federal Property Resources Service.

FPS or **F.P.S. 1** Fellow of the Philological Society. **2** Fellow of the Philosophical Society. **3** Fluid Power Society.

fps or **f.p.s. 1** feet per second. **2** also **FPS** foot-pound-second (system of measure). **3** frames per second photography.

fpsps or **f.p.s.p.s.** feet per second per second.

FPT fixed price tenders commerce.

FPV or **F.P.V.** free piston vessel.

FQ 1 Faerie Queene (poem by Edmund Spenser). **2** also **f.q.** fiscal quarter accounting.

fqcy frequency.

FQS Federal Quarantine Service.

FR 1 family room. **2** also **F.R.** Federal Register. **3** fire resistant. **4** freight release commerce.

Fr I an abbreviation for: **1** Brother (a religious). [Latin frater, French frère] **2** also **Fr.** Father. **3** fragment law. **4 a** France. **b** also **Fr.** French. **5** Friar. **6** Friday. **7** also **Fr.** Mrs. [German Frau]

II a symbol for: **1** francium (chemical element). **2** Froude number (of fluids) physics.

fr. 1 fragment. **2** frame computers, construction, photography. **3** also **fr** franc: fr. 10,000. **4** frequent. **5** from. **6** front. **7** fruit botany. **8** furring (in building).

f.r. right-hand side of a two-page spread. [Latin folio recto]

FRA Federal Railroad Administration (of U.S. Department of Transportation).

FRACGP or **F.R.A.C.G.P.** Fellow of the Royal Australian College of General Practitioners.

FRACI or **F.R.A.C.I.** Fellow of the Royal Australian Chemical Institute.

FRACP or **F.R.A.C.P.** Fellow of the Royal Australian College of Physicians.

FRACS or **F.R.A.C.S.** Fellow of the Royal Australian College of Surgeons.

FRAeS or **F.R.Ae.S.** Fellow of the Royal Aeronautical Society.

frag. 1 fragile. **2** also **frag** (pronounced frag) **a** fragment. **b** fragmentation.

FRAgS or **F.R.Ag.S.** Fellow of the Royal Agricultural Societies.

F.R.A.H.S. Fellow of the Royal Australian Historical Society.

F.R.A.I. Fellow of the Royal Anthropological Institute.

FRAIA or **F.R.A.I.A.** Fellow of the Royal Australian Institute of Architects.

FRAIC or **F.R.A.I.C.** Fellow of the Royal Architectural Institute of Canada.

F.R.A.M. or **FRAM** Fellow of the Royal Academy of Music.

Franc. Franciscan.

f.r.&c.c. free of riot and civil commotion (clause of an insurance policy).

Frank. Frankish.

FRAP 1 also **F.R.A.P.** Federal Rules of Appellate Procedure. **2** also **F.R.A.P.** Fellow of the Royal Academy of Physicians. **3** Popular Action Front (a political party of Chile). [Spanish Frente de Acción Popular]

F.R.A.S. or **FRAS 1** Fellow of the Royal Asiatic Society. **2** Fellow of the Royal Astronomical Society.

Frat. fraternity.

fraud. fraudulent.

FRB or **F.R.B. 1** Bolivian Revolutionary Front. [Spanish Frente de la Revolución Boliviana] **2 a** Federal Reserve Bank. **b** Federal Reserve Board. **c** Federal Reserve Branch. **3** Fisheries Research Board (of Canada).

F.R.B.S. 1 also **FRBS** Fellow of the Royal Botanic Society. **2** Fellow of the Royal Society of British Sculptors.

FRC 1 Federal Radiation Council. **2** Federal Radio Commission (now FCC). **3** Flight Research Center (division of National Aeronautics and Space Administration). **4** Foreign Relations Council. **5** functional residual capacity (the resting lung volume).

FRCA or **F.R.C.A.** Fellow of the Royal College of Art.

F.R.C.M. or **FRCM** Fellow of the Royal College of Music.

F.R.C.O. or **FRCO** Fellow of the Royal College of Organists.

FRCOG or **F.R.C.O.G.** Fellow of the Royal College of Obstetricians and Gynaecologists.

F.R.C.P. or **FRCP 1** Federal Rules of Civil Procedure. **2** Fellow of the Royal College of Physicians, also in combination: *F.R.C.P.E.* = *Fellow of the Royal College of Physicians of Edinburgh.*

F.R.C.S. or **FRCS** Fellow of the Royal College of Surgeons, also in combination: *F.R.C.S.I.* = *Fellow of the Royal College of Surgeons of Ireland.*

FRCSc or **F.R.C.Sc.** Fellow of the Royal College of Science.

F.R.C.V.S. or **FRCVS** Fellow of the Royal College of Veterinary Surgeons.

F.R.D. Federal Rules Decisions.

frd. framed (of a building under construction).

fre invoice. [French *facture*]

F.R.Econ.S Fellow of the Royal Economic Society.

FRED figure reading electronic device.

Fred. Frederic, Frederick.

Freddie Mac (fred'ē mak') FHMC (Federal Home Loan Mortgage Corporation).

Fredk. Frederick.

Frelimo or **FRELIMO** (frā'lē mō) Liberation Front of Mozambique (political party of Mozambique). [Portuguese *Frente de Liberação de Moçambique*]

freq. 1 frequency. **2** frequent, frequently. **3** frequentative (that expresses frequent or repetitive action, as -*gle* added to *wag* in *waggle*).

FRES or **F.R.E.S.** Fellow of the Royal Entomological Society.

FRFPS or **F.R.F.P.S.** Fellow of the Royal Faculty of Physicians and Surgeons.

FRG Federal Republic of Germany.

FRGS or **F.R.G.S.** Fellow of the Royal Geographical Society.

frgt. freight.

F.R.Hist.S. Fellow of the Royal Historical Society.

F.R.Hort.S. Fellow of the Royal Horticultural Society.

F.R.H.S. 1 Fellow of the Royal Historical Society. **2** also **FRHS** Fellow of the Royal Horticultural Society.

Fri. Friday.

FRIA or **F.R.I.A.** Fellow of the Royal Irish Academy.

FRIBA or **F.R.I.B.A.** Fellow of the Royal Institute of British Architects.

FRIC or **F.R.I.C.** Fellow of the Royal Institute of Chemistry.

fric. 1 fricative (of a speech sound, such as those represented by *f, s,* or *z*). **2** friction.

FRICS or **F.R.I.C.S.** Fellow of the Royal Institution of Chartered Surveyors.

Fries. Friesland.

Fris. 1 a Frisia. **b** Friesland. **2** Frisian (language of Friesland).

FRISCO fast reaction integrated submarine control.

Frl. Miss. [German *Fräulein*]

frl. fractional.

frm. 1 former. **2** framing (of lumber, in building construction). **3** from.

FRMCM or **F.R.M.C.M.** Fellow of the Royal Manchester College of Music.

F.R.Met.S. Fellow of the Royal Meteorological Society.

F.R.M.S. or **FRMS** Fellow of the Royal Microscopical Society.

F.R.N.S. or **FRNS** Fellow of the Royal Numismatic Society.

f.r.o.f. fire risk on freight (of insurance).

Frolinat National Liberation Front (political party of Chad). [French *Front de Libération Nationale*]

front. frontispiece.

FRP 1 fiber reinforced plastic. **2** fuel reprocessing plant.

FRPA Feather River Project Association (a nongovernmental group active in California water planning).

FRPF fireproof.

F.R.P.S. or **FRPS** Fellow of the Royal Photographic Society.

F.R.P.S.L. or **FRPSL** Fellow of the Royal Philatelic Society (of London).

frq. or **FRQ** frequent, frequently.

FRS 1 Federal Reserve System. **2** also **F.R.S.** Fellow of the Royal Society. **3** fuel research station.

Frs. Frisian.

frs. or **frs 1** francs. **2** fruits *botany*.

F.R.S.A. or **FRSA** Fellow of the Royal Society of Arts.

F.R.S.A.I. or **FRSAI** Fellow of the Royal Society of Antiquaries of Ireland.

F.R.S.C. or **FRSC 1** Fellow of the Royal Society of Canada. **2** Fellow of the Royal Society of Chemistry.

F.R.S.E. or **FRSE** Fellow of the Royal Society of Edinburgh.

F.R.S.G.S. or **FRSGS** Fellow of the Royal Scottish Geographical Society.

F.R.S.L. or **FRSL 1** Fellow of the Royal Society of Literature. **2** Fellow of the Royal Society of London (the *L* is generally omitted).

F.R.S.M. or **FRSM** Fellow of the Royal Society of Medicine.

F.R.S.N.Z. or **FRSNZ** Fellow of the Royal Society of New Zealand.

F.R.S.S. or **FRSS** Fellow of the Royal Statistical Society, also in combination: *F.R.S.S.S.* = *Fellow of the Royal Statistical Society of Scotland.*

F.R.S.S.A. or **FRSSA** Fellow of the Royal Scottish Society of Arts.

frt. 1 freight, also in combination: *frt.fwd.* = *freight forwarded.* **2** fruit.

fru. fructose (sugar present in many fruits and in honey).

frust. in small pieces. [Latin *frustillatim*]

Frwd. foreword.

frwk framework.

frwy. freeway.

fry or **Fry. 1** ferry. **2** freeway.

F.R.Z.S. or **FRZS** Fellow of the Royal Zoological Society.

FS 1 *also* **F.S.** Fabian Society. **2** *also* **f/s** factor of safety. **3** feasibility study. **4** *also* **F.S.** Federal Specification. **5** Field Service: *FSR = Field Service Representative.* **6** financial statement. **7 a** Foreign Secretary. **b** Foreign Service. **8** Forest Service (of U.S. Department of Agriculture). **9** forward (of mail, etc.). [French *faire suivre*]

fs 1 *also* **fs.** facsimile. **2** film strip. **3** *also* **f.s.** *or* **f-s a** foot-second. **b** *also* **f/s** feet per second. **4** *also* **f.s.** forward (of mail, etc.). [French *faire suivre*] **5** *also* **f.s.** full scale or size, also in combination: *f.s.d. = full scale detail.* **6** times (a number of occurrences). [French *fois*]

FSA 1 Farm Security Administration. **2** Federal Security Agency. **3** *also* **F.S.A.** Fellow of the Society of Antiquaries, also in combination: *F.S.A.L. = Fellow of the Society of Antiquaries of London.* **4** *also* **F.S.A.** Fellow of the Society of Arts. **5** Field Survey Association.

FSAA *or* **F.S.A.A.** Fellow of the Society of Incorporated Accountants and Auditors.

fsbo *or* **FSBO** (fiz′bō) for sale by owner (of real estate, for sale without the services of an agent).

FSC 1 *also* **F.S.C.** Brothers of the Christian Schools, Christian Brothers. [Latin *Fratres Scholarum Christianorum*] **2** Federal Safety Council. **3 a** Federal Supply Catalog. **b** Federal Stock or Supply Code, also in combination: *FSCM = Federal Supply Code for Manufacturers.* **4** Federal Supreme Court.

FSCA Fellow of the Society of Company and Commercial Accountants.

FSD full-scale deflection *electronics, physics, engineering.*

FSE 1 *also* **F.S.E.** Fellow of the Society of Engineers. **2** field support equipment.

FSF Flight Safety Foundation.

FSH follicle-stimulating hormone (stimulates enlargement of the Graafian follicle).

FSI 1 Foreign Service Institute (of U.S. Department of State). **2** *also* **F.S.I.** Free Sons of Israel. **3** free standing insert (an advertisement folded into a newspaper or magazine).

FSIA *or* **F.S.I.A.** Fellow of the Society of Industrial Artists.

FSIS Food Safety and Inspection Service (of U.S. Department of Agriculture).

FSK frequency-shift keying *computers.*

FSLIC Federal Savings and Loan Insurance Corporation.

FSLN Sandinista National Liberation Front (in Guatemala and Nicaragua). [Spanish *Frente Sandinista Liberación Nacional*]

FSM 1 Federated States of Micronesia. **2** flying spot microscope (instrument that illuminates its field with a scanning spot of intense light). **3** World Federation of Trade Unions. [French *Fédération Syndicale Mondiale*]

FSN Federal Stock Number.

FSO 1 Field Security Officer. **2** Foreign Service Officer.

FSP 1 *also* **F.S.P.** fiber saturation point (of drying lumber). **2** food stamp program. **3** foreign service pay.

Fspr. telephone. [German *Fernsprecher*]

FSPT Federation of Societies for Paint Technology.

FSR 1 Field Service Regulations. **2** Field Service Representative.

FSS 1 Federal Supply Service (of the General Services Administration). **2** *also* **F.S.S.** Fellow of the (Royal) Statistical Society: *F.S.S.I. = Fellow of the Statistical Society of Ireland.*

fst. fast (esp. of the condition of a race track).

FSTS Federal Secure Telephone Service.

FSTV fast scan television.

FSU *British* Family Service Unit.

F.Supp. Federal Supplement (to the Federal Reporter of U.S. Federal Court decisions).

FSV full-screen video (on compact disk) *electronics.*

FSX fighter support experimental (an advanced fighter airplane).

FT 1 *also* **F.T.** field test or trial: *F.T.Ch. = field test champion* (of a dog). **2** The Financial Times (publication). **3** Fort (in postal address). **4** Fourier transform *mathematics.* **5** freight ton (one of several units of cubic measure each applied to a specific commodity, as of stone which has a ton weight equal to about 16 cubic feet or lumber which has a ton weight equal to about 40 cubic feet). **6** *also* **F/T** full-time (of employment). **7** fume tight.

Ft. 1 forint (monetary unit of Hungary). **2** Fort.

ft. 1 faint. **2** flat (esp. of paper). **3** *also* **ft** foot, feet. **4** fortification. **5** fortified. **6** make *pharmaceutics.* [Latin *fiat*]

f.t. 1 freight ton (unit of cubic measure; see *FT*). **2** full terms *commerce.*

FTA 1 fluorescent treponemal antibody (antigen found in a test for syphilis). **2 a** Free Trade Agreement (superseded by *NAFTA*). **b** Free Trade Area. **3** Future Teachers of America.

FTAM file transfer, access, and management *computers.*

ft.b.m. foot board measure.

FTC 1 *also* **ftc** fast time constant (of a radar circuit with short signals). **2** *also* **F.T.C.** Federal Trade Commission. **3** Flight Test Center.

ft-c *or* **ftc** foot-candle.

FTD 1 Federal Tax Deposit. **2** Florists' Transworld Delivery (formerly, Florists' Telegraph Delivery).

FTE 1 full-time employee. **2 a** full-time equivalent (measure based on one person working full time). **b** full-time equated (student, funding formula).

ftg. fitting.

fth. *or* **fthm.** fathom.

FTI federal tax included.

FTIA Financial Times Institute of Actuaries (index of 500 stocks).

FTIR *or* **FT-IR** Fourier transform infrared (spectroscopy).

ftL *or* **ft-l** foot-lambert (unit of luminance).

ft-lb *or* **ft lb** foot-pound (unit of energy).

FTLV feline T-lymphotropic lentivirus.

FTM fractional test meal.

FTP 1 *also* **F.T.P.** fear, tension, pain (syndrome) *psychology.* **2** file transfer protocol *computers.* **3** folded, trimmed, and packed (in bookbinding).

FTPAA *or* **F.T.P.A.A.** Film and Television Production Association of Australia.

FT/PT full-time or part-time (referring to employment).

FTS 1 Federal Telecommunications System. **2** Federal Transfer Surcharge (on telephone service).

ft/s *or* **ft/sec** feet per second.

FTSE Financial Times Stock Exchange (Index, of 100 companies traded).

Ft.s.m. foot surface measure (of lumber).

FTV flight test vehicle.

FTZ 1 Foreign Trade Zone. **2** Free Trade Zone.

FU 1 finsen unit (measure of ultraviolet radiation). **2** fluorouracil (used in chemotherapy for cancer). **3** *also* **fu** flux unit (measure of a signal in radio astronomy).

5-FU fluorouracil (used in treating lymphatic cancer).

FUN fluorine, uranium, and nitrogen (technique for dating artifacts) *archaeology.*

FUNAI National Indian Foundation (of Brazil). [Portuguese *Fundação Nacional do Indio*]

func. *or* **funct.** function.

fund. fundamental.

FUO *or* **F.U.O.** fever of unknown origin *medicine.*

fu.p. fusion point.

fur. 1 furlong. **2** furnished. **3** further.

furl. furlough.

furn. 1 furnace. **2** furnished. **3** furniture.

fus. fuselage.

Fussn. footnote. [German *Fussnote*]

fut. future.

FUTA (füʹtə) Federal Unemployment Tax Act (esp. in reference to the tax itself).

fV *or* **fv** femtovolt.

f.v. 1 fire vent. **2** flush valve. **3** *also* **FV** on the back of the page. [Latin *folio verso*]

FVC forced vital capacity (test of respiratory function) *medicine.*

FW *or* **f.w. 1** fire wall, esp. in blueprints. **2** formula weight *chemistry.* **3** fresh water.

FWA 1 Factories and Workshops Act (of Great Britain). **2** *also* **F.W.A.** Family Welfare Association (of Great Britain). **3** Federal Works Agency.

FWB 1 *also* **f.w.b.** four-wheel brakes. **2** *also* **F.W.B.** Free Will Baptists.

FWD 1 four-wheel drive. **2** *also* **fwd** fresh water damage (of cargo in shipping). **3** *also* **f.w.d.** front-wheel drive.

fwd. forward.

fwdg. forwarding.

fwh *or* **FWH** flexible working hours.

fwhm *or* **FWHM** full width at half maximum (of the intensity of a line or resonance curve in spectroscopy).

F.W.I. *or* **FWI** Federation of West Indies.

FWP Federal Writers Project (employment of American authors under the Works Project Administration in the 1930's and early 1940's).

FWPCA Federal Water Pollution Control Administration.

FWS Fish and Wildlife Service or Federal Wildlife Service.

fwt. featherweight (a class in boxing).

FWY Freeway (in postal address).

FX 1 *also* **Fx** fixed (weather station, area, etc.). **2** *also* **F/X** foreign exchange. **3** *also* **fx.** foxed (of discolored book pages). **4** *also* **F/X** special effects (in motion pictures and television).

fxd. 1 fixed. **2** foxed (of discolored book pages).

FY fiscal year: *FY 2000.*

Fy. *or* **fy.** ferry.

FYE for your eyes.

FYI for your information.

fz. 1 *also* **FZ** freeze, freezing. **2** with force *music.* [Italian *forzando*]

F.Z.S. Fellow of the Zoological Society.

G *I an abbreviation for:* **1** gain *electronics, statistics.* **2** games (esp. in giving a sports record of a person or team). **3** Garrison, in combination *military: GA = Garrison Adjutant.* **4** gas, esp. as subscript. **5** gate. **6** *also* **G.** gauge. **7** gauss (unit of magnetic induction of flux density). **8** general **a** esp. of motion pictures for general audience. **b** *also* **G.** esp. in combination: *A.G. = Attorney General; G.H.Q. = General Headquarters.* **9** general factor (of intelligence) in testing. **10** Geography (magazine title). **11** *also* **G.** German or Germany, esp. in combination: *MHG = Middle High German.* **12** giga- (one billion or 10⁹): *GW = gigawatt.* **13** goalkeeper *sports.* **14** goals (scored) *sports.* **15** good. **16** gourde (monetary unit of Haiti). **17** *also* **G.** grain. **18** *also* **G.** gram. **19** *also* **G.** Grand, esp. in combination: *G.A.R. = Grand Army of the Republic; G.O.P. = Grand Old Party.* **20** *also* **G.** gravel, as on surveys and navigational charts. **21** gravity. **22** *also* **G.** Greek, esp. in combination: *LG = Late Greek.* **23** *also* **G.** green. **24** grid, *esp. in physics and cartography.* **25** ground. **26** *also* **G.** group: *G.Capt. = Group Captain.* **27** guanine (base compound of DNA). **28** guard *sports.* **29** *also* **G.** British guinea. **30** *also* **G.** Gulf. **31** Guyana, in combination: *G$ = Guyana dollar.* **32** gynoecium (pistil of a flower).

II *a symbol for:* **1** cell activity (indicated by degree with a subscript number): G_0 = *resting stage of a cell cycle.* **2** Chicago (branch in the Federal Reserve regional banking system, found esp. on dollar bills). **3** *also* **G** conductance *physics.* **4** fifth tone in the scale of C major *music.* **5** four hundred; 400 (medieval Roman numeral). **6** General Staff, in combination: *G1, G2, G3, and G4* = *staff functions of divisions, corps, and armies.* **7** *also* **G** Gibbs function *physics.* **8** *also* **G** gravitational constant. **9** gravitational force (one G equals the force of gravitation at the surface of the earth). **10** increased presence of metals in yellow stars *astronomy.* **11** iron line in solar spectrum *astronomy.* **12** mass velocity, *esp. in aeronautics.* **13** *also* **G** modulus of rigidity or shear modulus *mechanics.* **14** one thousand dollars: *twenty Gs* = $20,000. **15** seventh of a series. **16** vitamin B_2 (or riboflavin).

G-3 Group of Three (an organization for trade–Mexico, Colombia, Venezuela).

G-7 Group of Seven (an organization of seven industrialized nations–Canada, Great Britain, France, Germany, Italy, Japan, and the United States).

G_{11} or **G-11** hexachlorophene (germicide).

g *I an abbreviation for:* **1** *also* **g.** gauge. **2** *also* **g.** gelding (of a race horse). **3** *also* **g.** gender. **4** *also* **g.** general. **5** general intelligence *psychology.* **6** *also* **g.** genitive. **7** gilbert (unit of magnetomotive force). **8** *also* **g.** gilt. **9** *also* **g.** gloom *meteorology.* **10** *also* **g.** gold: *14kt. g = 14 carat gold.* **11** good. **12** *also* **g.** grain (unit of measure). **13** *also* **g.** gram. **14** gravity. **15** *also* **g.** green. **16** grid *physics.* **17** gross (unit of measure = 144). **18** *also* **g.** guide. **19** *also* **g.** guinea (monetary unit). **20** *also* **g.** left. [French *gauche*]
II *a symbol for:* **1** acceleration of gravity *physics.* **2** classical gyromagnetic ratio *physics.* **3** g-factor or nuclear gyromagnetic ratio or Landé factor. **4** statistical weight or degeneracy *physics.*

GA *I an abbreviation for:* **1** *also* **G.A.** Gamblers Anonymous. **2** gas amplification. **3** *also* **G.A.** General Agent. **4** General American (speech area of American English). **5** *also* **G.A. a** General Assembly (of the UN). **b** also in combination: *G.A.P.C.E.* = *General Assembly of the Presbyterian Church of England.* **6** general assistance. **7** *also* **G/A** general average, in insurance: *GA con.* = *general average contribution.* **8** general aviation (civilian commercial and private aviation). **9** General of the Army. **10** Georgia (Zip Code). **11** gibberellin (any of a group of hormones that regulate plant growth). **12** glutamic acid (most abundant amino acid). **13** glyceric acid. **14** go ahead (esp. in radio and telex communications). **15** Golfers' Association: *Senior GA.* **16** graduate assistant. **17** *also* **G/A** or **G-A** ground-to-air (of missiles or aircraft communication).
II *a symbol for:* nerve gas (later developed into **GB**).

Ga *I an abbreviation for:* **1** *also* **Ga.** Gallic. **2** *also* **Ga.** Georgia.
II *a symbol for:* gallium (chemical element).

g.a. **1** gauge atmosphere. **2** general average, in insurance.

GAA Gay Activists' Alliance.

GAAP generally accepted accounting principles.

GAAS generally accepted auditing standards.

GaAs gallium arsenide (used in lasers, semiconductors, etc.).

GAB General Agreement or Arrangements to Borrow (of the International Monetary Fund to obtain resources among member nations).

Gab Gabon (country in West Africa).

GABA (gab′ə) gamma-aminobutyric acid (amino acid in central nervous system of mammals).

GAC **1** General Advisory Committee (of the Nuclear Regulatory Commission). **2** granular activated carbon (used in filters).

GAD glutamic acid decarboxylase (enzyme found in diabetes patients).

Gael. gaelic.

GAFTA Grain and Feed Trade Association.

GAG glycosaminoglycan (polysaccharide found in connective tissue, used in creating artificial skin and gene therapy research).

GAI guaranteed annual income.

Gal **1** galactose (monosaccharide found in milk, sugar beets, etc.) *biochemistry.* **2** *also* **Gal.** Galatians (book of the New Testament). **3** *French* General. **4** unit of acceleration (of gravity). [from *Galileo*]

gal. **1** gallon. **2** *also* **gal** galvanized. **3** unit of acceleration (of gravity). [from *Galileo*]

GALCIT Guggenheim Aeronautical Laboratory of the California Institute of Technology.

gall. **1** *also* **Gall.** gallery. **2** gallon, gallons.

gal/min. gallons per minute.

gals. gallons.

galv. **1 a** galvanic (producing or caused by electric current, esp. from chemical action). **b** galvanism (electric current produced by chemical reaction). **2** galvanized (covered with a thin coat of zinc to inhibit rust). **3** galvanometer.

GAM guided aircraft missile.

Gam. Gambia.

G & I growth and income *finance.*

G & N guidance and navigation (system).

G & S Gilbert and Sullivan (composers of operettas in the 19th century).

gänz. or **gänzl.** complete, entire. [German *gänzlich*]

GAO General Accounting Office (agency responsible to the U.S. Congress for U.S. Federal spending).

g.a.o.f. *British* gummed all over flap (of envelopes).

GAP **1** General Assembly Program *computers.* **2** gross agricultural product *economics.* **3** Group for the Advancement of Psychiatry.

GaP gallium phosphide (used in semiconductors) *electronics.*

GAPA or **Gapa** ground-to-air pilotless aircraft.

GAPAN Guild of Air Pilots and Air Navigators.

G.A.R. Grand Army of the Republic (Union Army in the U.S. Civil War).

GAR guided aircraft rocket.

Ga R Georgia Review (magazine title).

gar. garage.

garb. garbage.

GARD general address reading device.

Gard. Gardens.

gard. garden.

garg. gargle.

GARIOA Government and Relief in Occupied Areas.

GARP Global Atmospheric Research Program.

GAS 1 *also* **G.A.S.** general adaptation syndrome (animal physiological reaction to stress or injury). **2** Government of American Samoa.

GASC German-American Securities Corporation.

GASP Group Against Smokers Pollution.

Gastroent. gastroenterology.

GAT *or* **G.A.T.** Greenwich Apparent Time.

GATA *or* **G.A.T.A.** Graphic Arts Trade Association.

GATB General Aptitude Test Battery *psychology*.

GATC *or* **gatc** guanine, adenine, thymine, cytosine *genetics*.

GATCO Guild of Air Traffic Control Officers.

GATF Graphic Arts Technical Foundation.

GATT *or* **Gatt** (*pronounced* gat) General Agreement on Tariffs and Trade (agreement among major world trading countries to fix tariffs on a reciprocal basis).

GAU Gay Academic Union.

Gaul. Gaulish (Celtic language of the ancient Gauls).

GAV gross annual value.

GAW *or* **G.A.W.** *or* **Gaw** guaranteed annual wage.

GAX gaseous oxygen.

G.A.Z. Comprehensive Index of Foreign Periodicals (German list of foreign periodicals). [German *Gesamtverzeichnis der Ausländischen Zeitschriften*]

gaz. 1 *also* **Gaz.** gazette. **2** gazetted. **3** *also* **Gaz.** gazetteer.

GB *I an abbreviation for:* **1** gallbladder *medicine*. **2** gigabyte *computers*. **3** *also* **G.B.** Great Britain. **4** grid bias *electronics*. **5** *also* **G.B.** guide book.
II a symbol for: nerve gas (sarin).

Gb *or* **gb** gilbert (unit of magnetomotive force).

G.B. & I. *or* **GB & I** Great Britain and Ireland.

GBAT Graduate Business Admissions Test.

GBE 1 *also* **g.b.e.** gilt beveled edge, in bookbinding. **2** *also* **G.B.E.** Grand Cross of the Order of the British Empire.

G.B.H. *or* **GBH** grievous bodily harm.

GB/L *or* **GBL** government bill of lading.

GBO *or* **g.b.o.** goods in bad order *commerce*.

GBS *or* **G.B.S.** George Bernard Shaw (playwright, critic, and political activist 1856–1950).

GC 1 gas chromatography (process of vaporizing a material into its constituent compounds). **2** *also* **G.C.** general counsel *law*. **3** *also* **G.C.** *British* **a** George Cross. **b** Grand Cross. **4** gonococcus *medicine*. **5** *also* **G.C.** Grand Chancellor. **6** *also* **G.C.** Grand Chaplain. **7** *also* **G.C.** Grand Chapter. **8** *also* **G.C.** Grand Commander. **9** *also* **G.C.** Grand Conductor, in freemasonry. **10** *also* **G.C.** Grand Council. **11** great circle *navigation, geography*. **12** *also* **G/C** Group Captain (in the British or Canadian Air Force). **13** guanine and cytosine (base compounds of DNA).

gc. gigacycle (now *gigahertz*) *electronics*.

GCA 1 Girls Clubs of America. **2** ground control approach (radar) *aviation*.

g.cal. *or* **g-cal** gram calorie.

GCAU grain-consuming animal unit, in agricultural statistics.

G.C.B. *or* **GCB** Grand Cross of the Order of the Bath.

GCBS *or* **G.C.B.S.** General Council of British Shipping.

GCC Gulf Cooperation Council (of the Persian Gulf).

GCD 1 General and Complete Disarmament. **2** *also* **g.c.d.** greatest common divisor *mathematics*.

GCE 1 *also* **G.C.E.** General Certificate of Education. **2** General College Entrance (examination).

GCF *or* **g.c.f.** greatest common factor *mathematics*.

GCFR gas controlled fast reactor.

GCHQ Government Communications Headquarters (of Great Britain).

GCI ground control interception (of radar): *GCI radar installations*.

G.C.I.E. *or* **GCIE** Grand Commander of the Order of the Indian Empire.

GCIU Graphics Communication International Union.

GCL ground control landing *aviation*.

G.C.L.H. *or* **GCLH** Grand Cross of the Legion of Honor.

GCM 1 general circulation model (of the atmosphere). **2** general court-martial. **3** Good Conduct Medal. **4** *also* **g.c.m.** *mathematics*. **a** greatest common measure. **b** greatest common multiple.

G.C.M.G. Grand Cross of the Order of St. Michael and St. George.

GCMS *or* **GC/MS** gas chromatography mass spectrometry or spectrometer (used in spectrographic analysis) *chemistry*.

GCR ground-controlled radar.

gc./s. gigacycles (now *gigahertz*) per second.

GCSE *or* **G.C.S.E.** General Certificate of Secondary Education.

G-CSF granulocyte colony stimulating factor (a substance that increases production of white blood cells, used to treat some cancers).

G.C.S.I. *or* **GCSI** Grand Commander of the Star of India.

GCT *or* **G.C.T.** *or* **G.c.t.** Greenwich civil time (formerly *GMT*) *astronomy, navigation*.

GCU generator control unit.

G.C.V.O. *or* **GCVO** Grand Cross of the (Royal) Victorian Order.

GCVS General Catalog of Variable Stars.

GD 1 general delivery (of mail). **2 a** General Duty. **b** general duties. **3** *also* **G.D.** **a** Grand Duchy. **b** Grand Duke, Grand Duchess. **4** ground detector. **5** soman (type of nerve gas).

Gd *I an abbreviation for:* **1** *also* **Gd.** Grand. **2** *also* **Gd.** Guard, esp. in combination: *Gdhse = Guardhouse*.
II a symbol for: gadolinium (chemical element).

gd 1 *also* **gd.** good, esp. good condition. **2** *also* **g.d.** granddaughter. **3** *also* **g.d.** gravimetric density. **4** *also* **gd.** ground, esp. in electronics.

GDBA Guide Dogs for the Blind Association.

gde. gourde (monetary unit of the Republic of Haiti).

G.D.F. French National Gas Company. [French *Gaz de France*]

GDG general data group *computers*.

GDH 1 glutamate dehydrogenase (enzyme active in converting ammonia to protein in bacteria) *biochemistry*. **2** growth and development hormone *biochemistry*.

Gdk Gdansk, Poland (formerly *Danzig*).

GDL gas dynamic laser.

gdn. 1 garden. **2** *also* **Gdn.** guardian.

GDNS Gardens (in postal address).

Gdns. Gardens: *Bnx. Bot. Gdns.* = *Bronx Botanical Gardens*.

GDOP geometrical dilution of precision (of attitude control) *navigation*.

GDP 1 gross domestic product *economics*. **2** guanosine diphosphate *biochemistry*.

GDR *or* **G.D.R.** German Democratic Republic (former East Germany).

gds. goods.

Gdsm. Guardsman.

GE 1 gastroenterology. **2** general election (esp. in Great Britain). **3** General Electric (Company). **4** gross energy.

Ge germanium (chemical element).

g.e. gilt edged, in bookbinding.

GEA gas evolution analysis; GEA *chemistry*.

geb. 1 born. [German *geboren*] **2** bound (of volumes). [German *gebunden*]

Gebr. brothers. [German *Gebrüder*, Dutch *gebroed*]

G.E.C. General Equivalency Certificate.

GECOM general compiler (computer language).

GED 1 *also* **GED test** *or* **GEDT** General Educational Development Test (tests given on high school and college levels to determine general educational achievement). **2** General Equivalency Diploma. **3** gross earnings deflator (measure of the effect of rising prices and taxes on earnings) *economics*.

GEEIA Ground Electronics Engineering Installation Agency (of U.S. Air Force).

gegr. founded. [German *gegründet*]

GEK geomagnetic electrokinetograph (device to measure ocean currents).

gel. 1 gelatin. **2** gelatinous.

GEM 1 ground effect machine (air cushion vehicle). **2** growing equity mortgage.

Gem. Gemini, the Twins (constellation).

gem. geminate.

GEMS Global Environmental Monitoring System.

Gen. 1 General: *Gen. Eisenhower; Gen. Assem.* = *General Assembly; Gen.St.* = *General Statutes*. **2** Genesis (book of the Old Testament). **3** Geneva, Genevan.

gen. 1 gender. **2 a** genealogy. **b** genealogical. **3** genera. **4 a** general, also in combination: *gen.av.* = *general average*.

b generally. **5** generation. **6** generator. **7** generic. **8** genetics. **9** genitive *grammar*. **10** genuine. **11** genus.

geneal. 1 genealogy. **2** genealogical.

genit. genitive *grammar*.

Genl. General, esp. of rank or title.

genl. general.

GENOT general notice (esp. in aviation communications).

genr. 1 generate. **2** generation. **3** generator.

Gent. *or* **gent.** gentleman, gentlemen.

GEO geosynchronous orbit (of an artificial satellite).

Geo. 1 George. **2** Georgia.

geod. 1 geodesy. **2** geodetic.

GEODSS ground electro-optical deep space surveillance (for tracking in space).

Geoff. Geoffrey.

geog. *or* **geogr. 1** geographer. **2** geographic, geographical. **3** geography.

geol. 1 geologic, geological. **2** geologist. **3** geology.

geom. 1 geometer. **2** geometric, geometrical. **3** geometry.

geophys. 1 geophysical. **2** geophysics.

geopol. geopolitics.

GEOREF World Geographic Reference System.

Georg. Georgian.

Ger. 1 a German: *Ger. pat.* = *German patent*. **b** Germanic. **2** Germany.

ger. 1 gerund. **2** gerundive.

Germ. 1 German. **2** Germany.

GERT Graphical Evaluation and Review Technique *computers*.

Ges. 1 canto. [German *Gesang*] **2** company, association, or society. [German *Gesellschaft*] **3** *also* **ges.** registered, as of a trademark or patent. [German *gesetzlich geschützt*]

GESP General Extrasensory Perception (technique to test the occurrence of ESP).

gest. deceased, late. [German *gestorben*]

Gestapo (gə stä′pō) Nazi secret state police. [German *Geheime Staatspolizei*]

GET ground elapsed time *navigation*.

GETOL ground effects takeoff and landing *aeronautics*.

GEV 1 *also* **GeV** *or* **Gev** *or* **g.e.v.** giga-electron-volt (one billion electron volts). **2** ground effect vehicle.

gez. signed. [German *gezeichnet*]

GF 1 goal for *sports*. **2** government form (followed by a number). **3** government furnished, esp. in combination: *GFAE* = *government furnished aircraft equipment*. **4** ground fog *meteorology*. **5** Guggenheim Foundation. **6** Portuguese customs and tax service. [Portuguese *Guarda Fiscal*]

gf gram-force *physics*.

GFA 1 General Freight Agent. **2** *also* **g.f.a.** good fair average *commerce*.

GFCI ground fault circuit interrupter *electricity*.

GFE government-furnished equipment.

GFM government-furnished materials.

GFP government-furnished part or parts.

GFR 1 *also* **G.F.R.** German Federal Republic (formerly West Germany, now *FRG*). **2** glomerular filtration rate (rate waste products are filtered from the blood in the kidneys).

GFRP glass fiber reinforced plastic.

GFS *or* **G.F.S.** Girls' Friendly Society.

GFTU General Federation of Trade Unions.

GFWC General Federation of Women's Clubs.

GG 1 *also* **G.G.** gamma globulin. **2** gas generator. **3** *also* **G.G.** Girl Guides. **4** *also* **G.G.** Governor General. **5** great gross (144 dozen). **6** Grenadier Guards. **7** *also* **G/G** *or* **G-G** ground-to-ground (of a missile).

G.G.A. Girl Guides Association.

g.gd. great granddaughter.

GGP gross global product.

g.gr. great gross (144 dozen).

g.gs. great grandson.

GGSM *or* **G.G.S.M.** Graduate of the Guildhall School of Music (and Drama).

GH 1 general headquarters. **2** general hospital. **3** grid heading *navigation*. **4** growth hormone.

Gh *or* **Gh.** Ghana.

GHA Greenwich hour angle *navigation, astronomy*.

GHI Group Health Insurance.

GHOST global horizontal sounding technique (atmospheric data monitoring from radio-equipped balloons transmitting at specified altitudes).

GHP *or* **ghp** gas horsepower.

GHQ General Headquarters *military*.

GHRF growth-hormone releasing factor.

GHz gigahertz (one billion hertz, unit of frequency).

GI 1 *also* **g.i.** galvanized iron. **2** *also* **G.I.** gastrointestinal. **3** general issue *law*. **4** *also* **G.I.** globin insulin *medicine*. **5** *also* **G.I.** Government issue, esp. referring to enlisted personnel in the U.S. Army: *The GI Bill covers the education costs of former GIs.*

gi. gill (unit of measure).

GIA *or* **G.I.A.** Gemological Institute of America.

Gib. Gibraltar.

GIC guaranteed investment contract.

GIF Graphics Interchange Format *computers*.

GIFT gamete intra-fallopian transfer (injection of mature unfertilized eggs and sperm into Fallopian tube).

GIGO (gī′gō′) garbage in, garbage out (of computer data).

Ginnie Mae (jin′ē mā′) GNMA (Government National Mortgage Association).

GIP *British* glazed imitation parchment (packaging paper).

GIR 1 graduated interest rate *finance*. **2** greens in regulation, in golf.

gir. girder.

GIS 1 Generalized Information System *computers*. **2** Geographical Information System *computers*. **3** Government Information Service. **4** Guaranteed Income Supplement (in Canada).

GIT Group Inclusive Tour.

GK goalkeeper *sports*.

Gk *or* **Gk.** Greek.

GKS graphics or graphical kernel system (standardized system to interface graphics for input, output, and transfer on computers).

GL 1 *also* **G/L** general ledger *accounting*. **2** Gothic letter or letters *printing*. **3** Government Laboratory. **4** *also* **G.L.** Grand Lodge (of Freemasons). **5** ground level.

4-GL fourth-generation language (of computers).

Gl glucinum (chemical element, former name of beryllium).

gl. 1 gill (unit of measure). **2** glass. **3** *also* **Gl.** glory: *gl. in excelsis.* [Latin *gloria*] **4 a** gloss (of a surface, *or* of a text giving equivalent words). **b** glossy. **5** glossary.

g./l. *or* **g/l** grams per liter.

GLA gross leasable area.

glab. glabrous (smooth without down) *botany*.

Glam. Glamorganshire, Wales.

Glas. *or* **Glasg.** Glasgow.

glau. glaucous (covered with a powdery waxy substance) *botany*.

glav. red. editor-in-chief. [Russian *glavnyi redaktor*]

GLC 1 gas-liquid chromatograph or chromatography (chemical analysis). **2** *also* **G.L.C.** Greater London Council (replaced *L.C.C.* and in 1986 itself taken over by City and borough governments).

GLCM 1 *also* **G.L.C.M.** Graduate of the London College of Music. **2** ground-launched cruise missile.

Gld. *or* **gld.** *or* **gldr.** guilder, guilders (unit of currency of the Netherlands).

GLE gravitational lens effect.

GLF Gay Liberation Front.

gliss. glissando (with a gliding effect) *music*.

GLM graduated length method (of ski instruction).

gln. *or* **Gln.** glutamine (amino acid found in many plants and animals).

Glo. 1 *also* **Glo** global. **2** *also* **glo.** glossary.

Glos. Gloucester, Gloucestershire.

Gloss. 1 *also* **gloss.** glossary. **2** Gloucester, Gloucestershire.

Gloucester. Gloucestershire.

glt. gilt.

glu. 1 glucose. **2** *also* **Glu.** glutamic acid (most abundant amino acid in living protein).

GluN glutamine (amino acid found in many plants and animals).

gly. *or* **Gly.** glycine (sweet crystalline amino acid formed by boiling gelatin).

GM 1 *also* **G.M.** general manager. **2** general merchandise. **3** general mortgage. **4** General Motors. **5** geometric mean. **6** *also* **G.M. a** *British* George Medal. **b** gold medal. **7** Grand Marshal. **8** *also* **G.M. a** Grand Master, in freemasonry. **b** Grand Master, in combination: *G.M.M.G.* = *Grand Master of the Order of St. Michael and St. George.* **9** group mark *computers.* **10** guessed mean *psychology.* **11** guided missile. **12** gunner's mate.

gm *I an abbreviation for:* **1** *also* **gm.** gram, grams. **2** grammass.
II a symbol for: also **Gm** mutual conductance or transconductance.

GMA Grocery Manufacturers of America, or Australia.

GMAG Genetic Manipulation Advisory Group (for genetic engineering in Great Britain).

G-Man (jē'man) government man, *esp. an FBI agent.*

GMAT 1 General Mathematical Aptitude Test. **2** Graduate Management Admission Test (as for qualifying in graduate studies of business management). **3** *also* **G.M.A.T.** *or* **G.m.a.t.** Greenwich mean astronomical time.

GMB 1 General, Municipal, Boilermakers (trade union, of Great Britain). **2** *also* **g.m.b.** good merchandisable brand *commerce.* **3** *also* **G.M.B.** Grand Master of the Order of the Bath.

G.m.b.H. *or* **GmbH** company with limited liability. [German *Gesellschaft mit beschränkter Haftung*]

G.M.C. General Medical Council.

Gmc. Germanic.

G-M Counter *or* **GM Counter** Geiger-Müller counter (commonly referred to as a Geiger counter, a device to measure radioactivity).

GM-CSF granulocyte macrophage colony stimulating factor (experimental drug used in cancer treatment).

GMHC Gay Men's Health Crisis (support group for people with AIDS).

G.M.I.E. *or* **GMIE** Grand Master of the Order of the Indian Empire.

G.M.M.G. *or* **GMMG** Grand Master of the Order of St. Michael and St. George.

g mol *or* **g.-mol.** gram molecule.

GMP 1 good manufacturing practices. **2** guanosine monophosphate (substance used to keep blood fresh for transfusion).

GMQ *or* **g.m.q.** good merchandisable quality.

GMR ground mapping radar.

GMS 1 general maintenance system *computers.* **2** geostationary meteorological satellite.

gms *or* **gms.** grams.

G.M.S.I. *or* **GMSI** Grand Master of the Order of the Star of India.

GMT *or* **G.M.T.** *or* **G.m.t.** Greenwich mean time.

G-M tube *or* **GM tube** Geiger-Müller tube: **1** the sensing tube of a Geiger counter. **2** a Geiger counter.

GMV 1 *also* **g.m.v.** gram-molecular volume. **2** *also* **gmv** guaranteed minimum value.

GMW *or* **g.m.w.** gram-molecular weight.

GMWU General and Municipal Workers Union (of Great Britain, now *GMB*).

G:N glucose nitrogen ratio.

G.N. Graduate Nurse.

gn. 1 *also* **Gn.** general. **2** *also* **gn** green. **3** *also* **Gn.** guinea (in former English money, one pound, one shilling or 21 shillings, now equal to one pound, five pence).

gnd. *or* **GND** ground.

GNI *or* **G.N.I.** gross national income.

Gnl. *or* **gnl.** general.

GNMA (jin'ē mā', for *Ginnie Mae*) Government National Mortgage Association.

GNP *or* **G.N.P.** gross national product *economics.*

Gnr. gunner.

GnRH gonadotropin-releasing hormone (stimulates hormones that make testes and ovaries function).

gns. *or* **Gns.** guineas (see *gn.*, def.3).

GO 1 gas operated. **2** *also* **G.O.** General Office. **3** *military* **a** General Officer. **b** general order or orders. **4** government-owned: *GOM* = *government-owned materials.* **5** *also* **G.O.** great organ *music.*

g.o. gummed only (of an envelope flap).

GOB *or* **g.o.b.** good ordinary brand.

GOC *or* **G.O.C. 1** *British* general officer commanding. **2** Greek Orthodox Church.

GOCO government-owned contractor-operated.

G.O.E. General Ordination Examination.

GOES geostationary operational environmental satellite.

GOGAT glutamate synthase (enzyme that assimilates ammonia into glutamic acid).

GOM 1 government-owned materials. **2** *also* **G.O.M. a** Grand Old Man (William Ewart Gladstone). **b** grand old man (any venerated leader): *The GOMs of jazz get grander.*

GONG Global Oscillation Network Group.

GOP *or* **G.O.P.** Grand Old Party (Republican Party of the U.S.).

GOPAC Grand Old Party Political Action Committee (of the Republican Party).

GOR general operational requirement.

GORK *Slang* God only really knows *medicine.*

Gos. *or* **Gosud.** state. [Russian *Gosudarstvo*]

GOT glutamic-oxaloacetic transaminase (enzyme in the blood having to do with nitrogen transfer).

Got. *or* **Goth.** Gothic.

Gov. *or* **gov. 1** Government. **2** Governor.

Gov. Gen. Governor General.

Govt. *or* **govt.** Government.

GOX *or* **gox** gaseous oxygen.

GP *I an abbreviation for:* **1** *also* **G.P.** Gallup Poll. **2** general paralysis *medicine.* **3** general pause *music.* **4** *also* **G.P.** general practitioner (of medicine). **5** *also* **G.P.** general public: *the G.P. scene.* **6** general purpose. **7** geographic position (of a celestial body in reference to earth). **8** geometric progression. **9** *also* **G.P.** glory be to the Father. [Latin *Gloria Patri*] **10** *also* **G.P.** Graduate in Pharmacy. **11** Grand Prix (international sports-car race; also an automobile model style). **12** *also* **G.P.** great primer (18-point printing type).

II *a symbol for:* general with parents' consent (of a motion picture considered appropriate for any audience with parents' approval suggested).

Gp. *or* **gp.** group: *Gp.Capt.* = *Group Captain.*

g.p. 1 *also* **gp** gene protein *biochemistry: gp 120, gp 160.* **2** great primer (18-point printing type).

GPA 1 grade-point average *education.* **2** *also* **G.P.A.** general passenger agent. **3** *also* **G.P.A.** British General Practitioners' Association.

GPC general purpose computer.

GPD 1 *also* **g.p.d.** gallons per day. **2** glass plasma display *electronics.* **3** glucose phosphate dehydrogenase (catalyst in carbohydrate metabolism).

GPDC general purpose digital computer.

GPDH glucose phosphate dehydrogenase (catalyst in carbohydrate metabolism).

g.p.g. *or* **GPG** grams per gallon.

GPH *or* **g.p.h.** gallons per hour.

G.Ph. Graduate in Pharmacy.

GPI *or* **G.P.I. 1** general paralysis of the insane *medicine.* **2** ground position indicator *aeronautics.*

GPM 1 *also* **g.p.m.** gallons per minute. **2** geopotential meter. **3** graduated payment mortgage. **4** *also* **G.P.M.** Grand Past Master, in freemasonry.

GPN graduate practical nurse.

GPO 1 *also* **G.P.O.** General Post Office. **2** general purpose oscillograph. **3** *also* **G.P.O.** Government Printing Office.

GPS 1 *also* **g.p.s.** gallons per second. **2** Global Positioning System (computerized navigation system). **3** *also* **G.P.S.** British Graduated Pension Scheme.

GPSS General Purpose Simulation System *engineering.*

GPT group projective test *psychology.*

GPU 1 *also* **G.P.U.** State Political Administration (Soviet secret police organization of the 1920's). [Russian *Gosudarstvennoi Politicheskoi Upravlenie*] **2** ground power unit (diesel-electric unit to power military field operations).

GQ *or* **G.Q.** general quarters (general alarm in the Navy, esp. on shipboard).

GR 1 gamma ray or rays. **2** general reconnaissance *military.* **3** General Reserve. **4** *also* **G.R.** Grand Recorder. **5** guard ring (of an electric field). **6** King George. [Latin *Georgius Rex*]

Gr. 1 grade. **2** Grand. **3** Grashof number (of heat transfer). **4** (Asa) Gray *botany.* **5** Great, in combination: *Gr. Brit.* = *Great Britain.* **6 a** Greece. **b** Greek. **c** Grecian. **7** gross (144 articles). **8** British gunner.

gr. 1 grade. **2** *also* **gr** grain, grains (unit of measure). **3** *also* **gr** gram, grams. **4** grammar. **5** *also* **gr** gravity. **6** gray. **7** great, *esp. in combination: gr.gdf.* = *great grandfather.* **8 a** gross (144 items). **b** gross (whole, entire): *gr.wt.* = *gross weight.* **9** group.

GRACE (grās) graphic arts composing equipment *printing.*

grad. 1 gradient. **2** gradual. **3** *also* **grad** (*pronounced* grad) graduate. **4** graduated.

Grad.I.A.E. Graduate of the Institute of Automobile Engineers.

Grad.I.M. Graduate of the Institute of Metallurgists.

Grad.Inst.B.E. Graduate of the Institution of British Engineers.

Grad.Inst.P. Graduate of the Institute of Physics.

Grad.S.E. Graduate of the Society of Engineers.

GRAE generally recognized as effective *medicine.*

Gral. general. [Spanish *general*]

gram. 1 grammar. **2** grammatical.

GRAS generally regarded as safe (list of manufactured substances surveyed by the U.S. Food and Drug Administration).

grat. free. [Latin *gratis*]

GRB gamma-ray burst *astronomy.*

GRBM Global-Range Ballistic Missile.

Gr. Br. *or* **Gr. Brit.** Great Britain.

G.R.C.M. *or* **GRCM** Graduate of the Royal College of Music.

grd. 1 grind. **2** *also* **GRD** ground. **3** guard.

GRE Graduate Record Examination.

Green. *or* **Greenl.** Greenland.

Greg. 1 Gregorian. **2** Gregory.

Grepo border patrol (of former East Germany). [German *Grenzpolizei*]

GRF 1 *also* **grf.** group repetition frequency *electronics.* **2** growth hormone-releasing factor *biochemistry.*

gr. gro. great gross (144 dozen).

GRI 1 Government of the Ryukyu Islands. **2** guaranteed retirement income.

grm. 1 germination. **2** gram.

grn. 1 *also* **gr.n.** *or* **GRN** gram-negative. **2** green.

gRNA guide RNA (ribonucleic acid which aids in transcription of DNA).

GRO 1 (Compton) Gamma Ray Observatory (NASA satellite to complete mapping of gamma ray distribution). **2** *British also* **G.R.O.** General Register Office (of births, deaths, etc.). **3** *also* **G.R.O.** Greenwich Royal Observatory.

gro. gross (144 items).

GRP *or* **grp 1** glass reinforced plastic or polyester. **2** *also* **gr.p.** gram-positive (of bacteria or viruses). **3** gross rating point *commerce.*

Grp. group.

GRS 1 *also* **GR-S** government rubber-styrene (synthetic rubber produced in WWII). **2** *also* **G.R.S.** Graves Registration Service (responsible for burial and transmittal of war dead). **3** great red spot (atmospheric disturbance on surface of planet Jupiter).

grs. 1 grains (unit of weight). **2** *also* **Grs.** grass (as on navigational charts).

GRSE *or* **G.R.S.E.** Guild of Radio Service Engineers.

GRSM *or* **G.R.S.M.** Graduate of the Royal Schools of Music.

GRT 1 *also* **g.r.t.** gross registered tons or tonnage. **2** *also* **grt** gross tons.

Grt *or* **grt** great *advertising.*

GRU Russian military intelligence. [Russian *Glavnoye Razvedyvatelnoye Upravleniye*]

Gru the Crane (constellation). [Latin *Grus*]

GRV Grove (in postal address).

gr.wt. gross weight.

gry or **g.r.y.** gross redemption yield.

GS 1 General Schedule (followed by a number for civil service grade): GS-13. **2** General Secretary. **3 a** General Service. **b** General Services (Bureau of the UN Secretariat). **4** also **G.S.** General Sessions law. **5** General Staff military. **6** General Studies education. **7 a** Geological Society. **b** Geological Survey. **8** giant slalom, in skiing. **9** also **G.S.** Girl Scouts. **10** glutamine synthetase biochemistry. **11** Government Service. **12** grand speed. **13** ground station. **14** group separator computers.

Gs 1 gauss (unit of magnetic induction of flux density). **2** also **Gs.** guarani (monetary unit of Paraguay).

g/s gallons per second.

gs. guineas.

g.s. 1 grandson. **2** ground speed.

GSA 1 General Services Administration (of the U.S.). **2** also **G.S.A.** Geological Society of America. **3** also **G.S.A.** Girl Scouts of America.

GSC 1 gas-solid chromatography (chemical analysis). **2** General Staff Corps.

GSCE General Certificate of Secondary Education.

GSDF Ground Self-Defense Force (the army of Japan).

GSE ground support equipment (for aircraft and missiles).

GSEE General Confederation of Greek Workers (trade union). [Greek Geniki Synomospondia Ergaton Hellados]

GSFC Goddard Space Flight Center.

GSFLT Graduate School Foreign Language Test.

GSG Galvanized Sheet Steel Gauge.

GSGB or **G.S.G.B.** Geological Survey of Great Britain.

GSGS or **G.S.G.S.** Geographical Section of the British General Staff.

GSH glutathione (a polypeptide important in organic oxidation).

GSI 1 also **G.S.I.** Geological Survey of India. **2** ground speed indicator.

GSL 1 also **G.S.L.** Geological Society of London. **2** also **G/SL** ground or sea-launched (of a missile): GSLCM = ground or sea-launched cruise missile. **3** guaranteed student loan.

GSLP Guaranteed Student Loan Program.

GSM 1 General Sales Manager. **2** also **gsm** grams per square meter.

GSMD or **G.S.M.D.** Guildhall School of Music and Dance.

GSP 1 Generalized System of Preferences. **2** also **G.S.P.** good service pension military. **3** gross social product (gross national product minus the value of services) economics.

GSR galvanic skin response (degree of skin resistance detected by electrodes and regulated by the autonomic nervous system).

GSS 1 geostationary satellite. **2** global surveillance system.

GST 1 goods and services tax (Canadian and New Zealand sales tax). **2** also **G.S.T.** or **G.s.t.** Greenwich sidereal time astronomy, navigation.

gst garter stitch knitting.

GSV guided space vehicle.

GSW gunshot wound, also in combination: GSWA = gunshot wound to the abdomen.

GT 1 grand total. **2 a** Gran Turismo (class of two-seater sports cars). **b** Grand Touring (automobile). **3** greater than mathematics, computers. **4** gross ton.

Gt. Great, esp. in combination: Gt. Marlborough Street, London.

gt 1 also **gt.** drop. [Latin gutta] **2** also **g.t.** gas tight. **3** also **g.t.** gilt top, of pages in bookbinding. **4** glass tube. **5** also **g.t.** gross ton.

GTA 1 gas tungsten arc. **2** also **G.T.A.** graduate teaching assistant.

Gt. Br. or **Gt. Brit.** Great Britain.

GTC 1 Girls Training Corps. **2** also **g.t.c.** good till canceled or countermanded (of an order to buy stock) finance. **3** Government Training Center.

gtd. guaranteed.

GTE or **g.t.e.** gilt top edges, of pages in bookbinding.

GTF glucosyltransferase (an enzyme) genetics.

GTH gonadotropic hormone.

GTM 1 General Traffic Manager. **2** also **g.t.m.** good this month commerce.

GTO 1 gate turnoff. **2** geosynchronous or geostationary transfer orbit (of an artificial satellite).

GTP guanosine triphosphate (active in DNA transfer).

Gtr. Greater, in combination: Gtr. Man. = Greater Manchester.

GTS 1 gas turbine ship. **2** General Theological Seminary. **3** global telecommunications system (of the World Meteorological Organization). **4** Greenwich time signal (used in broadcasting).

GTT glucose tolerance test.

gtt. drops. [Latin guttae]

GTV gas turbine vessel.

GTW or **g.t.w.** good this week commerce.

GU 1 gastric ulcer. **2** also **G.U.** genitourinary. **3** Guam (Zip Code).

guar. guarantee, guaranteed.

Guat. Guatemala.

GUI (gü'ē) graphical user interface (a computer program using pictures or symbols to display commands) computers.

Gui. Guiana.

gui. guitar.

guid. guidance.

GUIDO or **Guido** Guidance Officer astronautics.

Guin. Guinea.

gulag or **Gulag** (gü'läg) state detention and forced labor camp (in former Soviet Union). [Russian Glavnoye Upravleniye Lagerei]

G.U.M. or **GUM** state operated Department Store (in former Soviet Union). [Russian Glavnoye Universalny Magazin]

gun. gunnery.

GUS or **G.U.S.** Great Universal Stores.

GUT Grand Unified Theory *physics*.

GUTS grand unification theories.

gutt. drops. [Latin *guttae*]

g.u.v. correct and complete. [German *gerecht und vollkommen*]

GV granulosis virus.

gv 1 gate valve. **2** *also* **g.v.** gravimetric volume.

GVH graft-versus-host: *GVH disease*.

gvl. gravel.

GVT 1 *also* **Gvt.** *or* **gvt** government. **2** gravity-vacuum transportation.

GVW gross vehicle weight.

GW 1 George Washington. **2** *also* **gw** gigawatt or gigawatts. **3** gross weight. **4** guided weapon.

GWEN Ground Wave Emergency Network.

GWP gross world product *economics*.

GY or **gy.** gray.

gym (*pronounced* jim) **1** gymnasium. **2** gymnastics.

GYN or **gyn.** or **gynecol. 1** gynecological. **2** gynecology: *GYN/OB = gynecology and obstetrics*.

Gyp (*pronounced* jip) gypsum.

GZ ground zero.

Gz gigahertz.

G.Z.V. list of German periodicals. [German *Gesamt Zeitschriften Verzeichnis*]

H *I an abbreviation for:* **1** *also* **H.** harbor. **2** hard or hardness (of a lead pencil, rock sample or stratum etc.). **3** haze *meteorology*. **4** heater *electronics*. **5 a** heavy, esp. in medicine: *H chain disease = disease similar to lymphoma*. **b** *also* **H.** heavy sea. **6** hecto- (one hundred or 10^2). **7** heel (on organ music). **8 a** height or altitude. **b** thickness or depth. **9** helicopter. **10** *also* **H.** *or* н Helm (used with a number in cataloging music of C.P.E. Bach). **11** *also* **H.** hence. **12** King Henry (in listing plays by Shakespeare): *H5 = King Henry the Fifth; 1H4 = King Henry the Fourth, Part 1; 2H6 = King Henry the Sixth, Part 2*. **13** heroin. **14** high **a** high-pressure area *meteorology*. **b** the highest price quoted of a stock *finance*. **15 a** histamine *biochemistry*. **b** histamine receptor, in combination: H_1, H_2. **16** hit *baseball*. **17** *also* **H.** *or* н Hoboken (used with a number in cataloging music of Haydn). **18** *also* **H.** Holy, esp. in combination: *H.R.E. = Holy Roman Empire*. **19** *also* **H.** horizontal. **20** horn *music*. **21** hospital. **22** hot. **23** *also* **H.** hour: *H minus 3 = 3 hours before the appointed hour*. **24** *also* **H.** House of Representatives: *H.Conf.Report = House of Representatives Conference Report*. **25** humanities (in library cataloging). **26** humidity. **27** *also* **H.** hundred. **28** *also* **H.** husband. **29** *also* **H.** part (number of a periodical publication). [German *Heft*]
II a symbol for: **1** Boltzmann function *physics*. **2** calcium line in solar spectrum. **3** eighth of a series. **4** enthalpy (heat content of a unit mass). **5** Hamiltonian function *physics*. **6** henry (unit of induction) *electricity*. **7** hydrogen (chemical element). **8 a** intensity of magnetic field strength. **b** horizontal force of the magnetic field of the earth *physics, electronics, astronomy*. **9** irradiance *physics*. **10** St. Louis (branch in the Federal Reserve regional banking system, found esp. on dollar bills). **11** tone B in the German system *music*.

H- helicopter (followed by model number): *H-19*.

H° hydrogen ion concentration.

H₀ Hubble constant.

H⁺ *or* **H⁻** hydrogen ion (positive or negative).

H¹ protium (isotope of hydrogen).

H¹⁺ proton.

H² deuterium (heavy hydrogen).

H³ tritium (isotope of hydrogen, used in hydrogen bomb).

4-H a group of clubs for young people in agricultural areas of the United States, sponsored by the Department of Agriculture (their symbol stands for *head, heart, hands, health*).

h *I an abbreviation for:* **1** *also* **h.** hail *meteorology*. **2** half. **3** *also* **h.** hand *music*, esp. in combination: *r.h. = right hand*. **4** *also* **h.** handily, in horse racing. **5** hard or hardness, (esp. of rock sample or stratum). **6** hazy, *esp. in spectroscopy*. **7** heat. **8** heater, *esp. as a subscript electronics*. **9** hecto- (100 or 10^2): *hg. = hectogram*. **10 a** height or altitude. **b** depth or thickness. **11** *also* **h.** heir. **12** *also* **h.** heller (coin of former Czechoslovakia). **13** *also* **h.** hence. **14** *also* **h.** horizontal. **15** horn *music*. **16** *also* **h.** horse, in horse racing. **17** hot. **18** *also* **h.** hour. **19** house. **20** *also* **h.** hundred. **21** *also* **h.** husband. **22** hydrolysis *physics*.
II a symbol for: **1** head (unit of pressure) *physics, chemistry*. **2** height of an arc, as in the height of an arch, the sag of a cable, or the radius of a lens zone. **3** henry (unit of induction) *electricity*. **4** index of precision *statistics*. **5** Planck constant *physics*. **6** specific enthalpy (heat content of a unit).

ℏ Dirac's constant (unit of electronic spin).

HA 1 *also* **H.A.** hardy annual (plant whose seeds are able to withstand heavy frost). **2** *also* **H.A.** Hautes-Alpes (department of France). **3 a** heavy artillery. **b** *also* **H.A.** Horse Artillery. **4** hemaglutinin (surface protein of flu virus). **5** high altitude, in combination: *HARP = High Altitude Research Project*. **6** hour angle *astronomy*. **7** hyaluronic acid (constituent of connective tissue).

Ha *I an abbreviation for: also* **Ha.** 1 Haiti. 2 Hawaii.
II a symbol for: hahnium (chemical element 105).

ha 1 *also* **ha.** hardy annual (plant whose seeds can withstand heavy frost). 2 hectare.

h.a. 1 in this year. [Latin *hoc anno*] 2 of this year. [Latin *huius anni*]

HAA 1 heavy antiaircraft. 2 height above airport. 3 hepatitis-associated antigen.

H.A.& M. hymns ancient and modern.

HAB high-altitude bombing.

Hab. Habakkuk (book of the Old Testament).

hab. 1 habitat. 2 habitation.

hab. corp. habeas corpus (a writ to order judgment of detention).

habit. habitat.

HABS Historic American Buildings Survey.

habt. let him have *pharmaceutics.* [Latin *habeat*]

HAC 1 high-alumina cement *construction.* 2 *also* **H.A.C.** Honorable Artillery Company.

HACCP hazard analysis critical control point (control in processing foods).

had. hereinafter described.

HAF 1 high-abrasion furnace. 2 high-altitude fluorescence.

Haf. port or harbor. [German *Hafen*]

Hag. Haggai (book of the Old Testament).

hagiol. hagiology (lives and literature of the saints).

HAHO high altitude, high opening (of parachute jumping).

HAI hospital-acquired infection.

Hal. Halifax, Nova Scotia.

hal *or* **hal.** halogen (any element combining directly with a metal to form a salt).

HALO high altitude, low opening (of parachute jumping).

HAM 1 human (serum) albumin microspheres *medicine.* 2 *also* **H.A.M.** hymns ancient and modern.

Ham. *or* **Haml.** Hamlet, Prince of Denmark (play by Shakespeare).

Hamb. Hamburg, Germany.

H.& B. Humboldt and Bonpland (catalog) *botany.*

h.and c. hot and cold (running water).

H & D system to indicate film emulsion speed, from the names of Hunter and Driffield.

H.& I. harassment and interdiction (of an enemy) *military.*

H & J hyphenation and justification (in preparing copy or checking printing proofs).

Hants *or* **Hants.** Hampshire County, England.

Har. 1 *also* **har.** harbor. 2 Harold.

hard. hardware.

HARM high-speed anti-radiation missile (designed to avoid heat-detecting counter devices).

Harm. harmonics *music.*

harp. harpsichord.

Hart. Hartford.

Harv. Harvard, esp. in combination: *Harv. Intl. L. J.* = *Harvard International Law Journal.*

HAS Health Advisory Service.

HASP Houston Automatic Spooling Program (system, mass storage of data).

HAT 1 height above touchdown *aeronautics.* 2 hypoxanthine, aminopterin, thymidine (a medium for tissue culture).

haut. length or height. [French *hauteur*]

HAV hepatitis A virus.

hav haversine (half of the reversed sine) *mathematics.*

Haw. Hawaii, also in combination: *Haw. App.* = *Hawaii Appellate Reports.*

HAWK tactical missile of the U.S. [*homing all the way killer*]

HAWT horizontal axis wind turbine.

haz. 1 hazard. 2 hazardous.

HB 1 halfback *sports.* 2 handbook. 3 hard and black (of pencil lead). 4 hardy biennial (of seeds or a plant that can withstand winter cold) *botany.* 5 *also* **H/B** hatchback (of automobile design). 6 hepatitis B. 7 high band. 8 hit by ball *baseball.* 9 homing beacon. 10 horizontal band. 11 House (of Representatives) Bill (followed by a number).

Hb 1 *also* **Hb.** half. [German *Halb*] 2 *also* **hb.** hemoglobin, also in combination: *Hbf = fetal hemoglobin.*

hb. hardy biennial (of seeds or a plant that can withstand winter cold) *botany.*

h.b. 1 halfback *sports.* 2 hardback (book). 3 human being.

H.B. & K. Humboldt, Bonpland, and Kunth (catalog) *botany.*

HBC 1 high breaking capacity *engineering.* 2 *also* **H.B.C.** Hudson's Bay Company (1610–1869).

HBD 1 *also* **H.B.D.** had been drinking (in accident reports). 2 hydroxybutyric dehydrogenase (present in heart muscle of some heart attack victims).

HBGF heparin-binding growth factor (protein stimulating the growth of blood vessels).

HBK 1 *also* **h.bk.** *or* **hbk** handbook. 2 *also* **hbk** hardback (book). 3 hollow back (of lumber).

HBLV human B lymphotropic virus (now *CFS*).

HBM *or* **H.B.M.** Her or His Britannic Majesty.

HBO Home Box Office (cable TV broadcasting service).

H-bomb hydrogen bomb.

HBP 1 *also* **hbp** high blood pressure. 2 hit by pitched ball.

HBR Harbor (in postal address).

hbr. *or* **Hbr.** harbor.

HBV hepatitis B virus.

HC 1 *also* **H.C.** habitual criminal. 2 hand control. 3 hard copy (printed copy on pages as contrasted with microfilm or computer tape or disk copy). 4 hardcover (book). 5 *also* **H/C** held covered (of a shipment) *insurance.* 6 *also* **H.C.** Heralds' College. 7 high capacity. 8 High Church. 9 *also* **H.C.** High Commissioner. 10 high compression. 11 Holy Communion. 12 *also* **H.C.** Hospital Corps. 13 *also* **H/C** hot and cold water (esp. of running water in living accommodations). 14 *also* **H.C.** House (of Representatives) Committee, in combination: *HCIS = House Committee on Internal Security.* 15 *also* **H.C.** House of Commons. 16 hydrocarbon.

h.c. 1 for the sake of honor. [Latin *honoris causa*] **2** *also* **h/c** hot and cold water (esp. of running water in living accommodations).

hcap handicap.

HCB 1 hexachlorobenzene (fungicide, wood preservative). **2** House of Commons Bill (followed by a number).

HCC *or* **hcc** hydraulic cement concrete.

HCD *or* **hcd** high current density.

h.c.e. 1 hard–coal equivalents (of various energy sources). **2** human-caused error.

HCF 1 high carbohydrate and fiber (of a diet). **2** *also* **h.c.f.** highest common factor *mathematics*. **3** hundred cubic feet.

HCFA Health Care Financing Administration (of U.S. Department of Health and Human Services, administering Medicare).

HCFC hydrochlorofluorocarbon, also in combination: *HCFC-22* (a chlorofluorocarbon less damaging to the atmosphere).

HCG human chorionic gonadotrophin (triggers the release of ova).

HCH hexachlorocyclohexane (insecticide).

H.C.J. High Court of Justice.

HCL *or* **h.c.l. 1** high cost of living. **2** horizontal center line.

HCl hydrochloric acid.

HCN hydrogen cyanide.

HCO Harvard College Observatory.

H.Conf.Rept. House (of Representatives) Conference Report (used with a number).

H.Con.Res. House (of Representatives) Concurrent Resolution (used with a number).

hcp 1 handicap. **2** *also* **HCP** hexagonal close-packed (of a crystal structure). **3** *also* **HCP** House of Commons Paper.

HCR Highway Contract Route (private mail carrier for U.S. Postal Service).

hcptr helicopter.

HCS 1 *also* **hcs** high-carbon steel. **2** *also* **H.C.S.** British Home Civil Service. **3** human chorionic somatomammotrophin (hormone that promotes growth, mammary development, and milk secretion).

HCT *or* **Hct.** hematocrit (centrifuge for determining blood volume of plasma and cells).

HCTBA Hotel and Catering Trades Benevolent Association.

HCU hydraulic cycling unit.

HD 1 half duplex *computers*. **2 a** Hansen's disease (leprosy). **b** Hodgkin's disease. **c** Huntington's disease. **3** hard-drawn *metallurgy*. **4 a** hard disk (computer storage on a rigid disk). **b** hard drive (computer mechanism for reading a hard disk). **5** harmonic distortion, also in combination: *HDM = harmonic distortion meter*. **6** *also* **H.D.** hearing distance (measure of a person's ability to hear). **7** heavy duty, also in combination: *HDT = heavy duty truck*. **8** Henry Draper (astronomical catalog). **9** high definition, esp. in combination: *HDV = high-definition video*. **10** high density, also in combination: *HDP = high-density polyethylene*. **11** honorable discharge *military*. **12** hourly difference *navigation, astronomy*. **13** *also* **H-D** Hunter and Driffield (system to indicate film emulsion speed): *H-D curve*.

H.D. 1 Henry Draper (astronomical catalog). **2** Hilda Doolittle (American poet 1886–1961).

Hd. Head, in place names: *Duncansby Hd.*

hd 1 *also* **h.d.** at bedtime, esp. *pharmaceutics*. [Latin *hora decubitus*] **2** *also* **hd.** hand. **3** *also* **hd.** head. **4** *also* **hd.** hogshead. **5 a** hundred. **b** *also* **hds** in hundreds (of a given company's shares in stock transaction for a particular day).

HDA high duty alloy.

HDATZ high-density air traffic zone.

Hdb. manual, handbook. [German *Handbuch*]

hdbk. handbook.

HDBMS hierarchical database management system *computers*.

HDC *or* **hdc** holder in due course *commerce, law*.

HDD head-down display (instrument information display in an aircraft cockpit).

HDDS high-density data system *computers*.

Hdg. *or* **hdg** heading.

HDF Hungarian Democratic Forum (political party).

hdkf. handkerchief.

HDL high-density lipoprotein (containing more protein than lipids and carrying off cholesterol to the liver).

hdl. handle.

HDLC high-level data link control *computers*.

hdlg. handling.

HDM high-duty metal.

HDN hemolytic disease of newborns.

hdn. harden.

H.Doc. House (of Representatives) Document (used with a number).

HDP *or* **HDPE** high-density polyethylene.

Hdqrs. headquarters.

HDR hot dry rock: *HDR geothermal source*.

HDS Office of Human Development Services.

HDTV high-definition television.

HDV 1 heavy-duty vehicle. **2** high-definition video.

hdw. *or* **hdwe.** hardware.

hdwd. hardwood (lumber).

HDX half duplex *computers*.

HE 1 heat engine. **2** high energy, esp. in combination: *HEAO = High-Energy Astronomy Observatory*. **3** high explosive. **4** *also* **H.E. a** His Eminence (cardinal of the Roman Catholic Church). **b** His or Her Excellency. **5** horizontal equivalent. **6** hub end. **7** hydrogen embrittlement (of crytals).

He helium (chemical element).

h.e. 1 that is. [Latin *hoc est*] **2** this is. [Latin *hic est*]

HEA Higher Education Act.

HEAO High-Energy Astronomy Observatory (artificial satellite that gathers data on astronomical phenomena).

HEAP Home Energy Assistance Program.

Heb. *or* **Hebr. 1 a** Hebrew (esp. language). **b** Hebraic (of the language). **2** Hebrews (book of the New Testament). **3** Hebrides.

hect. hectare (unit of 100 ares).

hectog. hectogram (unit of 100 grams).

hectol. hectoliter (unit of 100 liters).

hectom. hectometer (unit of 100 meters).

hed (*pronounced* hed) headline, *esp. in printing.*

HEED high-energy electron diffraction.

HEF high-energy fuel.

HEI high-explosive incendiary (of a bomb).

HEL 1 high-energy laser. **2** house or home equity loan.

Hel. 1 Helsinki, Finland. **2** Switzerland. [Latin *Helvetia*]

hel or **heli** (hel'ē) helicopter.

Hellen. 1 Hellenic. **2** Hellenism. **3** Hellenistic.

helo. heliport.

HELP helicopter electronic landing path.

Helv. Switzerland. [Latin *Helvetia*]

HEM hybrid electromagnetic (wave).

hem. or **hemo. 1** hemoglobin. **2** hemorrhage.

HEMT high-electron mobility transistor.

Hen. Henry, *esp. King Henry* (in listing plays by Shakespeare); *Hen.V = King Henry the Fifth; 1 Hen. IV = King Henry the Fourth, Part 1.*

He-Ne helium-neon (laser).

HEOS Highly Eccentric Orbital Satellite.

HEP 1 high energy phosphate. **2** high-explosive plastic.

HEPA high-efficiency particulate air (filter).

HEPC Hydroelectric Power Commission.

HEPL High Energy Physics Laboratory.

HER Harvard Educational Review (publication).

Her Hercules (constellation).

her. 1 heir. [Latin *heres*] **2 a** heraldic. **b** heraldry.

Herb. herbarium.

hered. heredity.

Heref or **Heref.** or **Hereford.** Herefordshire County, England.

HERF high-energy rate forming (metal press).

HEREIU Hotel Employees and Restaurant Employees International Union.

Herod. Herodotus (ancient Greek historian).

herp. or **herpet.** herpetology.

Herts or **Herts.** Hertfordshire County, England.

HET heavy equipment transporter.

HETP 1 height equivalent of theoretical plate (in distillation calculations) *chemical engineering.* **2** hexaethyl tetraphosphate (organic insecticide).

HEU hydroelectric unit.

HEW Health, Education, and Welfare (former Department of U.S. government).

HEX or **hex** hexadecimal *computers.*

hex. 1 hexachord. **2 a** hexagon. **b** hexagonal.

HF 1 Hageman factor (a coagulating factor of the blood). **2** hard firm (a grade of pencil). **3** high fidelity. **4** also **H-F** high frequency. **5** *British* **a** Home fleet. **b** Home forces. **6** hydrogen fluoride (catalyst in rocket fuel). **7** hyperfine *biology.*

Hf hafnium (chemical element).

hf 1 *also* **hf.** half. **2** high fidelity. **3** *also* **h-f** high frequency.

Hfa Haifa, Israel.

H.F.A.R.A. or **HFARA** Honorary Foreign Associate of the Royal Academy.

hf.bd. half-bound (in leather, of a book), also in combination: *hf.bd.cf. = half-bound in calf.*

HFBR High Flux Beam Reactor.

HFC 1 *also* **hfc** high-frequency current. **2** hydrofluorocarbon (refrigerant proposed as an environmentally safer replacement for CFC).

hf.cf. half calf (binding of a book).

HFCS high-fructose corn syrup.

HF-DF or **HF/DF** high-frequency direction finder or finding.

HFG heavy free gas.

HFIR High Flux Isotope Reactor.

HFM hold for money *commerce.*

hf.mor. half morocco (binding of a book).

HFO 1 heavy fuel oil. **2** high-frequency oscillation *electronics.*

HFR 1 *also* **Hfr** high frequency (of) recombination (of chromosomal material). **2** hold for release (of a press release or advertising copy).

H.F.R.A. or **HFRA** Honorary Fellow of the Royal Academy.

hfs or **HFS** hyperfine structure (of spectral lines in chemical analysis).

Hft. part or number, *esp. of a magazine or fascicle of a book.* [German *Heft*]

Hfx Halifax, Nova Scotia.

HG 1 *also* **H-G** Haute-Garonne (department of France). **2** High German (of language). **3** high grade. **4** *also* **H.G.** His or Her Grace (title). **5** *also* **H.G.** *British* **a** Home Guard. **b** Horse Guards.

Hg *I an abbreviation for:* **1** hectogram (unit of 100 grams). **2** hemoglobin. **3** *also* **Hg.** Hungarian.
II a symbol for: mercury (chemical element). [Latin *hydrargyrum*]

hg 1 *also* **hg.** hectogram (unit of 100 grams). **2** hemoglobin.

HGB commercial code. [German *Handelsgesetzbuch*]

Hgb hemoglobin.

HGCA Home Grown Cereals Authority (of America).

HGE Human granulocytic ehrlichiosis.

HGF hyperglycemic (glycogenolytic) factor (hormone secreted by the pancreas).

HGH human growth hormone.

HGPRT or **HGPTase** hypoxanthine-guanine phosphoribosyl transferase (a catalyzing enzyme).

hgr 1 *also* **Hgr** hangar (for airplanes). **2** hanger.

HGT high-grade tax-exempt (bonds) *finance.*

hgt. height.

Hgts Heights (in a place name).

HGV *British* heavy goods vehicle.

HGW heat-generating waste.

Hgwy. highway.

HH 1 heavy hydrogen (deuterium). **2** Herbig-Haro *astronomy*: *HH object* (small bright star). **3** *also* **H.H.** His or Her Highness. **4** *also* **H.H.** His Holiness. **5** very hard (of pencil lead).

hh 1 *also* **h.h.** half hard *metallurgy*. **2** hands, hands high (measure of height of horses).

hha. *or* **HHA** half-hardy annual (plant that must be started indoors or the seeds of which must be protected from heavy frost).

hhb. *or* **HHB** half-hardy biennial (plant that must be protected from heavy frost).

HH.D. Doctor of Humanities. [Latin *humanitatum doctor*: the *HH* is a conventional sign of the plural]

hhd. hogshead.

HHF household furniture *insurance*.

HHFA Housing and Home Finance Agency (of U.S. Department of Housing and Urban Development).

HHG household goods *insurance*.

HHH very hard (of pencil lead).

HHMU hand-held maneuvering unit (astronaut's personal space maneuvering device).

hhp. *or* **HHP** half-hardy perennial (plant that must be protected from heavy frost).

HHS *or* **H.H.S.** Health and Human Services (department of the U.S. Government).

HHV human herpes virus, esp. in combination: *HHV-6*.

HI 1 a Hawaii (Zip Code). **b** *also* **H.I.** Hawaiian Islands. **2** height of instrument *surveying*. **3** hemagglutination inhibition or inhibiting *medicine*. **4** *also* **H.I.** here lies. [Latin *hic iacet*] **5** *also* **H.I.** high intensity: *HI arc*. **6** hospital or hospitalization insurance. **7** *also* **H.I.** human interest (of feature stories in a newspaper, magazine, or TV production). **8** humidity index.

Hi. Hindi (language).

H.I.A. Horological Institute of America.

HIAC *or* **hi. ac.** high accuracy.

HIAS Hebrew Immigration Aid Society.

HIB Hemophilus or Haemophilus influenza type B (bacteria).

Hib. Hibernian.

HIC hybrid integrated circuit *electronics*.

HICAT high-altitude clear air turbulence, also in combination: *HI-HICAT = high, high-altitude clear air turbulence*.

Hi. Com. 1 High Command. **2** *also* **Hi-Com** High Commissioner.

HID high-intensity discharge.

hi-def (hī′def′) high-definition TV: HDTV.

Hier. Jerusalem. [Latin *Hierosolyma*]

hier. 1 hieroglyphics. **2** hieroglyphic.

HIF Housing Implementation Fund (of U.S. Department of Housing and Urban Development).

hi-fi *or* **Hi-Fi** (hī′fī′) high fidelity.

HIFOR high-level forecast.

HIG hermetic-integrating gyroscope *navigation*.

HIH *or* **H.I.H.** His or Her Imperial Highness.

Hil. Hilary (term, Spring Session of British courts or universities, esp. Oxford).

HILAC *or* **Hilac** (hī′lak′) heavy-ion linear accelerator.

HILAT *or* **Hilat** high latitude (satellite).

HIM hepatitis infectious mononucleosis *medicine*.

HIMAT high-maneuverable aircraft technology.

Hind. 1 Hindu. **2 a** Hindustan. **b** *also* **Hindu.** Hindustani.

HIOMT hydroxyindole-O-methyltransferase (enzyme present in the pineal gland).

HIP 1 (*pronounced* hip) Health Insurance Plan. **2** high-impact plastic.

HIPAC heavy ion plasma accelerator *physics*.

HIPAR high-power acquisition radar.

HIPC Health Insurance Purchasing Cooperative.

HIPERNAS high-performance navigation system.

HIPO hierarchy plus input-process-output *computers*.

HIPOE (hip′ō) high-pressure oceanographic equipment.

hipot. high potential.

Hipp. Hippocrates (ancient Greek physician, 460–380 BC).

HIPS high-impact polystyrene.

HIRAN (hī′ran) high-precision short-range navigation.

hi-res high resolution, *esp. in physics*.

HIS hospital information system.

H.I.S. here lies buried. [Latin *hic iacet sepultus*]

his. *or* **His.** histidine (amino acid in simple proteins).

hist. 1 histology. **2 a** *also* **histn** historian. **b** *also* **Hist.** historic, historical, esp. in combination: *Hist.Dist. = Historic District*. **c** history.

histol. histology.

H.I.T. Holtzman Inkblot Technique (psychological test).

hi-tech (hī′tek′) high technology.

Hitt. Hittite.

H.I.U.S. Hispanic Institute of the United States.

HIV *or* **HIV-1** human immunodeficiency virus (cause of AIDS).

HIV-2 human immunodeficiency virus (producing symptoms similar to those of AIDS).

HJ *or* **H.J.** here lies. [Latin *hic iacet*]

HJD heliocentric Julian date *astronomy*.

H.J.Res. *or* **HJR** House (of Representatives) Joint Resolution (used with a number).

HJS *or* **H.J.S.** here lies buried. [Latin *hic iacet sepultus*]

HK 1 Hong Kong, also in combination: *HK$ = Hong Kong dollar*; *HKSE = Hong Kong Stock Exchange*. **2** *also* **H.K.** House of Keys (lower house of the legislature of the Isle of Man).

hkf. handkerchief.

HKJ Hashemite Kingdom of Jordan.

HL 1 *also* **H-L** Haute Loire (department of France). **2** Honours List (of titles bestowed by the British monarch). **3** *also* **H.L.** House of Lords.

HI latent hyperopia *medicine.*

hl 1 *also* **hl.** hectoliter (unit of 100 liters). **2** *also* **h.l. a** in this place. [Latin *hoc loco*] **b** of this place. [Latin *hujus loci*]

HLA human leucocyte antigen or histocompatibility locus antigen (determining the compatibility of tissue types in white blood cells of humans).

HLB 1 Harvard Library Bulletin (publication). **2** hydrophilic-lipophilic balance (in emulsifying agents) *chemistry.*

HLBB *or* **H.L.B.B.** Home Loan Bank Board.

HLL high-level language.

HLLV heavy-lift launch vehicle *aeronautics.*

HLNW high-level nuclear waste.

Hlpr. helper.

H.L.S. *or* **HLS** laid in this place. [Latin *hoc loco situs*]

Hl.S. Holy Scripture. [German *Heilige Schrift*]

HLT highly leveraged transactions *finance.*

HLW high-level waste.

HM 1 hallmark. **2** *also* **H.M.** handmade, esp. of paper. **3** *also* **H.M.** Harbor Master. **4** harmonic mean *mathematics.* **5** *also* **H-M** Haute-Marne (department of France). **6** hazardous materials. **7** headmaster, headmistress. **8** *also* **H.M.** Her or His Majesty. **9** Home Mission.

Hm manifest hypermetropia (farsightedness) *medicine.*

hm 1 *also* **hm.** hectometer (unit of 100 meters). **2** *also* **h.m. a** in this month. [Latin *hoc mense*] **b** of this month. [Latin *hujus mensis*]

H.M.A. Headmasters' Association.

HMAS *or* **H.M.A.S.** Her or His Majesty's Australian Ship.

H.M.C. 1 *also* **HMC** Her or His Majesty's Customs. **2** Historical Manuscripts Commission (of Great Britain). **3** Horticultural Marketing Council (of Great Britain).

HMCS *or* **H.M.C.S.** Her or His Majesty's Canadian Ship.

HMCSS *or* **H.M.C.S.S.** Her or His Majesty's Civil Service Commissioners.

HMD 1 hollow metal door *construction,* also in combination: *HMDF = hollow metal door frame.* **2** hyaline membrane disease. **3** hydraulic mean depth.

HMF *or* **H.M.F.** Her or His Majesty's Forces.

HMG 1 *also* **H.M.G.** Her or His Majesty's Government. **2** human menopausal gonadotrophin *biochemistry.*

HMI *or* **H.M.I.** Her or His Majesty's Inspector (of schools), also in combination: *H.M.I.T. = Her or His Majesty's Inspector of Taxes.*

HMLR *or* **H.M.L.R.** Her or His Majesty's Land Registry.

hmlt. hamlet.

HMMWV (hum'vē') High-Mobility, Multiple-purpose Wheeled Vehicle (later modification of the jeep).

HMNZ *or* **H.M.N.Z.** Her or His Majesty's New Zealand Ship.

HMO Health Maintenance Organization.

HMOW *or* **H.M.O.W.** Her or His Majesty's Office of Works.

HMP 1 *also* **hmp** handmade paper. **2** *also* **H.M.P.** he erected this monument. [Latin *hoc monumentum posuit*] **3** *also* **H.M.P.** Her or His Majesty's Prison.

HMS 1 *also* **H.M.S.** Her or His Majesty's Service. **2** *also* **H.M.S.** Her or His Majesty's Ship. **3** *also* **h/m/s** *or* **hms** hours, minutes, seconds.

HMSA hydroxymethanesulfonate (a strong-acid component of acid rain).

HMSO *or* **H.M.S.O.** Her or His Majesty's Stationery Office.

Hmstd homestead.

HMV His Master's Voice (a recording label).

HMW high molecular weight *chemistry.*

HN *or* **H.N.** head nurse.

hn *or* **Hn** horn *music.*

H.N.C. Higher National Certificate (of education).

H.N.D. Higher National Diploma (of education).

hnd 1 hand, esp. in combination: *hndpt = handprinted.* **2** *also* **HND** hundred.

hndbk. handbook.

HNIS Human Nutrition and Information Service (of U.S. Department of Agriculture).

Hnos. brothers. [Spanish *Hermanos*]

HnRNA heterogeneous nuclear RNA (also called heteronuclear RNA, form of ribonucleic acid found in mammalian cells).

Hnrs honors, honours.

H.O. *or* **HO 1** Head Office. **2** Health Officer. **3** Home Office (of British government). **4** hostilities only (designation of enlisted personnel who sign up for the duration of hostilities). **5** Hydrographic Office (of U.S. Navy).

3HO Happy, Healthy, Holy Organization (form of Sikhism practiced in North America).

Ho *I an abbreviation for:* also **Ho.** *or* **ho.** house. *II a symbol for:* holmium (chemical element).

h.o. hold or held over *theater, commerce.*

HOA Home Owners' Association.

Hob. Hoboken (catalog of Haydn's music).

HOC *or* **h.o.c.** held on charge.

H.O.D. Hoffer-Osmond Diagnosis (test for schizophrenia).

HOE Homing Overlay Experiment (a defensive weapon against incoming ballistic missiles).

H of C *or* **HoC** House of Commons.

H of L *or* **HoL** House of Lords.

H of R House of Representatives.

Hol. Holland.

hol *or* **hol. 1** (*pronounced* hol) holiday: *on hol abroad.* **2** hollow.

HOLC Home Owners' Loan Corporation.

Holl. Holland.

hols *or* **hols.** (*pronounced* holz) holidays: *the Christmas hols.*

Hom. Homer (ancient Greek poet, possibly 800–700 BC).

hom homonym (word having same pronunciation and spelling as another: *mail* armor—*mail* letter).

homeo. 1 homeopathy. **2** homeopathic.

HOMO highest occupied molecular orbital *chemistry.*

homo. 1 a homeopathy. **b** homeopathic. **2 a** homosexual. **b** homosexuality.

hom. sap. homo sapiens: *discontent is inherent in hom. sap.*

Hon. or **Hon 1** Honorable, Honourable, also in combination: *Rt.Hon. = Right Honorable.* **2** Honorary: *Hon.Sec. = Honorary Secretary; Hon. F.R.A.M. = Honorary Fellow of the Royal Academy of Music.*

hon. 1 honor, honour. **2 a** honorable. **b** honorably. **3** honorary.

Honble. Honorable, Honourable.

Hond. Honduras.

Hons. British Honours: *Hons. degree in physics.*

HOP high oxygen pressure.

HOPE Health Opportunity for People Everywhere (charitable organization donating medical service).

Hor the Clock (constellation). [Latin *Horologium*]

Hor. Horace (Roman poet, 65–8 BC).

hor. 1 horizon. **2** horizontal. **3 a** horology. **b** horological.

horol. horology.

hort. horticulture, horticultural.

Hos. Hosea (book of the Old Testament).

Hosp. hospital.

HOTOL horizontal takeoff and landing (aircraft).

HOV high-occupancy vehicle.

How. Howard (U.S. Supreme Court Reports).

how. howitzer.

HP 1 *also* **hp.** hardy perennial (plant or seeds that can stand severe frost). **2** *also* **H-P** Hautes Pyrénées (department of France). **3** high performance, esp. in combination: *HPRR = High Performance Research Reactor.* **4** high potency. **5** *also* **H.P.** high power. **6** *also* **H.P.** high pressure. **7** British hire purchase: *goods acquired on HP.* **8** hit by pitcher *baseball*. **9** *also* **H.P.** horsepower. **10** *also* **H.P.** hot-pressed (of paper smoothed by pressing between heated rollers). **11** house physician. **12** *also* **H.P.** Houses of Parliament. **13** hydroxymethyl phenylalanine (amino acid essential for mental development and for building new proteins and tissues).

hp 1 *also* **h.p.** half pay. **2** *also* **hp.** hardy perennial (plant or seeds that can withstand severe frost). **3** high-pass (electronic filter). **4** *also* **h.p.** high pressure. **5** British hire purchase. **6** *also* **h.p.** horizontal parallax *astronomy*. **7** *also* **h.p.** horsepower.

HPA 1 high-power amplifier. **2** hypothalamic-pituitary-adrenal (a rhythmic system of the body controlling the secretion of ACTH and other corticotropins).

HPBW half-power beamwidth *electronics*.

HPC history of present complaint *medicine*.

hpcd or **hpch** harpsichord.

HPF highest possible frequency.

HPH or **hph** or **hp-hr** horsepower-hour (work done in one hour at constant rate of one horsepower).

HPI 1 Heifer Project International (distribution of livestock to subsistence farmers who give firstborn female to another). **2** history of present illness *medicine*.

HPLC high-performance liquid chromatography *chemistry*.

HPMV high-pressure mercury vapor.

HPN or **hp.n.** horsepower nominal *mechanics*.

HPNS high-pressure nervous syndrome.

HPS 1 high-pressure steam. **2** high-protein supplement.

HPT high-pressure test.

HPV 1 human papillomavirus. **2** human-powered vehicle.

HQ 1 *also* **hq.** headquarters. **2** high quality.

h.q. look for this. [Latin *hoc quaere*]

HR 1 hail and rain *meteorology*. **2** heart rate *medicine*. **3** heat resistant, also in combination: *HRP = heat-resistant plastic.* **4** high resolution, esp. in combination: *HRSEM = High-Resolution Scanning Electron Microscope.* **5** high run, in billiards. **6** Home Relief (aid program for assistance with costs of housing). **7** Home Rule. **8** home run *baseball*. **9** hot rolled **a** of steel. **b** *also* **H.R.** of paper. **10 a** House of Representatives. **b** House of Representatives Bill (with a number).

Hr. Mister. [German *Herr*]

hr. 1 hairspace, in typography. **2** hour.

HRA 1 Health Resources Administration. **2** *also* **H.R.A.** Honorary Member of the Royal Academy. **3** Human Resources Administration.

HRAF Human Relations Areas Files (cultural background information on societies in all parts of the world).

H-ras (āch'ras') human-ras (human gene of the ras group).

HRC Human Rights Commission.

HRCA or **H.R.C.A.** Honorary Member Royal Cambrian Academy.

hrd. hard.

H-R diagram Hertzsprung-Russell diagram (plot of a star's total energy output against surface temperature).

H.R.E. 1 Holy Roman Emperor. **2** Holy Roman Empire.

HREM High-Resolution Electron Microscope.

H.Rept. House (of Representatives) Report (with a number).

H.Res. House (of Representatives) Resolution (with a number).

HRGC high-resolution gas chromatography (in spectrographic analysis).

HRH or **H.R.H.** Her or His Royal Highness.

HRHA 1 *also* **H.R.H.A.** Honorary Member of Royal Hibernian Academy. **2** Human Rights and Humanitarian Affairs (bureau of U.S. Department of State).

HRI height-range indicator.

H.R.I.P. or **HRIP** here rests in peace. [Latin *hic requiescit in pace*]

HRIR High-Resolution Infrared Radiometer (for measuring heat radiation).

HRMS high-resolution mass spectrometry.

Hrn. plural of mister. [German *Herren*]

HRP 1 heat resistant plastic. **2** horizontal radiation pattern (of a transmission antenna).

H-R-R Hardy-Rand-Ritter (color blindness test).

hrs. hours.

HRSA 1 Health Resources and Services Administration (of U.S. Department of Health and Human Services). **2** *also* **H.R.S.A.** Honorary Member of the Royal Scottish Academy.

HRSEM High-Resolution Scanning Electron Microscope.

hrsg. edited or published. [German *herausgegeben*]

HRT 1 hormone replacement therapy. **2** Hostage Rescue Team.

hrt. heart.

hrtwd. heartwood.

HRWMC House of Representatives Ways and Means Committee.

HS 1 *also* **H-S** Hute-Saône (department of France). **2** *also* **H.S. a** here is buried. [Latin *hic sepultus*] **b** here lies. [Latin *hic situs*] **3** *also* **H.S.** High School, esp. in combination: *GWHS = George Washington High School.* **4** high speed, esp. in combination: *HSGT = high-speed ground transportation.* **5** *also* **H.S.** British Home Secretary. **6** house.

Hs. manuscript. [German *Handschrift*]

h.s. 1 at bedtime, esp. in pharmaceutics. [Latin *hora somni*] **2** in this sense. [Latin *hoc sensu*]

HSA human serum albumin *medicine.*

HSAA Health Sciences Advancement Award.

HSCT High-Speed Civil Transport (supersonic airbus).

HSD high-speed diesel (lubricating oil).

HSDA high-speed data acquisition *computers.*

H.S.E. *or* **HSE** here is buried. [Latin *hic sepultus est*]

Hse. House.

HSF Home Service Force (of Great Britain, formerly the Home Guard).

hsg. housing.

Hsgbr. editor. [German *Herausgeber*]

HSGT high-speed ground transport.

HSH *or* **H.S.H.** Her or His Serene Highness.

HSI heat stress index (of people).

hskpr housekeeper.

HSLA high-strength low-alloy (steel).

HSM 1 *also* **H.S.M.** Her or His Serene Majesty. **2** high-speed memory *computers.*

HSMCDR (hus muk'dər) High-Speed Multichannel Data Recorder.

HSP high-speed printer *computers.*

HSPG heparan sulfate protoglycan (protein found near nerve synapses).

HSR 1 high-speed rail (transportation). **2** high-speed reader *computers.* **3** homogeneous staining region *biochemistry.*

HSRI Highway Safety Research Institute.

H.S.S. *or* **HSS** Fellow of the Historical Society. [Latin *Historiae Societatis Socius*]

HST 1 *also* **H.S.T.** *or* **H.S T.** Harry S Truman. **2** *also* **H.S.T.** *or* **h.s.t.** Hawaiian Standard Time. **3** *also* **hst** highest spring tide. **4** high-speed train. **5** Hubble Space Telescope. **6** hypersonic transport.

HSUS Humane Society of the United States.

HSV herpes simplex virus (now designated as HSV-1, HSV-2).

HT 1 half-time, *esp. in sports, education.* **2** half title *printing.* **3** halftone *photography, printing.* **4** *also* **H.T.** Hawaii Time. **5** heat treatment. **6** hibernation trigger (substance in the blood of hibernating animals). **7** high temperature. **8** high tension *electricity.* **9** high tide. **10** serotonin; HTP (5-hydroxytryptamine, vasoconstrictor and neurotransmitter).

ht 1 *also* **h.t. a** at this time. [Latin *hoc tempore*] **b** by or under this title. [Latin *hoc titulo*] **2** halftone *photography, printing.* **3** *also* **ht.** heat. **4 a** *also* **ht.** height. **b** high or long. [French *haut*] **5** *also* **h.t.** high tension *electricity.*

HTA heavier than air.

HTB high-tension battery.

Htbk *or* **htbk** hatchback (automobile design).

HTC heat transfer coefficient.

Htd *or* **htd.** heated: *Htd Rm = heated room.*

htg. heating.

HTGC *or* **HTGCR** *or* **HTGR** high-temperature gas-cooled reactor.

HTH high-test hypochlorite (purifying agent for swimming pools, laundry bleach).

HTK hed (headline) to come.

HTLV human T-cell lymphotropic virus (any of several retroviruses linked to various forms of leukemia, now designated HTLVI, II, III, or IV).

HTM heat transfer medium *engineering.*

HTP hydroxytryptophan; HT (serotonin).

HTR 1 hard tissue replacement (substance injected into areas of bone loss to prevent teeth from loosening). **2** Harvard Theological Review (magazine title). **3** high-temperature reactor.

htr. heater.

HTS 1 Heights (in postal address). **2** high-tensile steel.

Hts. Heights.

HTST high-temperature short-time (form of pasteurization).

HTU 1 heat transfer unit. **2** height of transfer unit *engineering.*

HTV Hypersonic Test Vehicle (research tool to gather data at hypersonic speeds).

ht. wkt. hit wicket *cricket.*

HUAC (hyü'ak') House (of Representatives) Un-American Activities Committee (replaced by Committee on Internal Security 1969, abolished 1975).

HUCR highest useful compression ratio *engineering.*

HUD (*pronounced* hud) **1** Department of Housing and Urban Development. **2** head-up display (display of aircraft instrument readings on windshield or piece of sloping glass in the cockpit).

HUGO Human Genome Organization.

HUK hunter-killer (naval designation for search groups hunting enemy submarines, also in combination: *HUKS = hunter-killer submarine.*

Hum. 1 *also* **HUM** human, also in combination: *HUMRRO = Human Resources Research Office.* **2** humane. **3** the Humanities.

hum. 1 human. **2** humorous.

humint or **HUMINT** (hyü'mənt) human intelligence (the gathering of secret intelligence by spies).

Hun. or **Hung.** 1 Hungary. 2 Hungarian.

hun. or **hund.** hundred.

hunth. hundred thousand.

Hunts or **Hunts.** Huntingdonshire County, England.

HUP Harvard University Press.

Hur 1 homes using radio *advertising.* 2 *also* **hur.** or **HURCN** hurricane.

HUSAT Human Sciences and Advanced Technology (Institute).

Husb. or **husb.** husbandry.

HUSTLE helium underwater speech translating equipment (for divers).

HUT homes using television *advertising.*

HV 1 *also* **H&V** heating and ventilating. 2 high vacuum: *HVGO = high-vacuum gas oil.* 3 high velocity: *HVAR = high-velocity aircraft rocket.* 4 *also* **h.v.** high voltage: *HVDC = high-voltage direct current.* 5 home video: *HVE = home video entertainment.*

HVA homovanillic acid.

HVAC heating, ventilation, and air conditioning.

HVCA Heating and Ventilating Contractors Association.

HVEM high-voltage electron microscope.

HVPS high-voltage power supply.

HVRA Heating and Ventilating Research Association.

hvy. or **hvy** heavy.

HW 1 *also* **H.W.** hazardous waste, also in combination: *H.W.M.D. = Hazardous Waste Management Division.* 2 headwaiter. 3 heavy water, esp. in combination: *HWOCR = heavy water organic cooled reactor.* 4 *also* **H.W.** high water, also in combination: *HWOST = high water ordinary spring tides.* 5 hot water.

hw 1 herewith. 2 *also* **h.w.** hit wicket *cricket.* 3 *also* **h.w.** hot water: *h.w. cylinder.*

h/w husband and wife.

HWC circulating hot water.

HWF hardwood floor.

HWI high-water interval.

HWL or **hwl** high-water line.

HWM or **hwm** high-water mark, also in combination: *HWMNT = high-water mark neaptide.*

HWR heavy water reactor.

HWS 1 hot water soluble. 2 Hurricane Warning System.

hwt. hundredweight.

Hwy. or **hwy.** 1 highway. 2 *also* **HWY** Highway (in postal address).

H-Y histocompatibility Y-chromosome (antigen, protein that determines the action of the male or Y chromosome in mammals).

hy. 1 heavy. 2 *also* **Hy.** henry (unit of induction) *electricity.* 3 *also* **Hy** highway.

Hya Hydra, the Water Snake (constellation of the Northern sky).

hyb. hybrid.

HYCOTRAN hybrid computer translator.

hyd. 1 **a** hydraulic. **b** hydraulics. 2 **a** hydrography. **b** hydrographic. 3 **a** hydrostatic. **b** hydrostatics.

Hydr. hydrographer.

hydr. or **hydraul.** hydraulics.

hydro. 1 hydrodynamic. 2 hydroelectric. 3 **a** *also* **hydrog.** hydrographic. **b** *also* **HYDRO** Hydrographic Office.

HYDROLANT (hī'drō lant') hydrography, Atlantic Ocean (service of U.S. Naval Oceanographic Office, to safeguard all shipping).

HYDROPAC (hī'drō pak') hydrography, Pacific Ocean (service of U.S. Naval Oceanographic Office, to safeguard all shipping).

hydros. hydrostatics.

hydt. hydrant.

Hyg. or **hyg.** hygiene.

Hyi Hydrus (constellation of the Southern sky, erroneously confused in many tables of constellations with *Hydra,* because of the misapplication of the name "water snake").

HYMA Hebrew Young Men's Association.

Hyp hydroxyproline (amino acid used in biochemical research).

hyp. 1 hypodermic (needle or injection). 2 hypotenuse. 3 **a** hypothesis. **b** hypothetical.

hypo. 1 hypodermic (needle or injection). 2 *also* **hypo** (hī'pō') sodium thiosulphate (fixing solution used in photographic developing, formerly hyposulfite).

hypoth. 1 hypothesis. 2 hypothetical.

hys. or **hyst.** hysteria.

HYT high-yield tax-exempt (bonds) *finance.*

Hz or **Hz.** hertz (unit of frequency equivalent to one cycle per second).

hz. haze.

Hzk. Hezekiah (a king of Judah).

hzy. hazy.

I

I *I an abbreviation for:* **1** *also* **I.** Emperor. [Latin *Imperator*] **2** Empress. [Latin *Imperatrix*] **3** Iceland, Icelandic, in combination: *Ikr = Icelandic króna; OI = Old Icelandic.* **4** *also* **I.** Idaho. **5** impulse *aeronautics.* **6** incomplete (esp. to indicate a grade held until school work is completed). **7** independent: *D for Democrat, R for Republican, I for Independent.* **8** index or index number, *esp. in statistics.* **9** indicated, in combination: *IHP = indicated horsepower.* **10** industrial. **11** inertia (esp. moment of inertia) *physics, chemistry.* **12** inosine (a compound obtained from adenosine). **13** inside. **14** inspector, in combination: *IG = Inspector General.* **15** intensity (esp. radiant or acoustic intensity). **16** International: *IBT = International Brotherhood of Teamsters.* **17** interstate highway (used with a number): *I-84.* **18** Iraq, Iraqi, in combination: *ID = Iraqi dinar.* **19** *also* **I.** Ireland, Irish, in combination: *IRA = Irish Republican Army.* **20** iron, in blueprints and other drawings. **21** irregular (esp. irregular nebula in astronomy). **22** *also* **I.** Island, Isle. **23** Israel, Israeli: *I£ = Israeli shekel.*
II a symbol for: **1** acoustic intensity. **2** candlepower *or* luminous intensity. **3** current, such as convection current, conduction current, and electric current *physics.* **4** iodine (chemical element). **5** ionic strength. **6** Minneapolis (branch in the Federal Reserve regional banking system, found esp. on dollar bills). **7** ninth of a series. **8** nuclear or isotopic spin. **9** one; 1 (Roman numeral).
▶Though the ancients knew and used *J*, originally Latin did not often account for *J*. This affected English, in which many proper names, esp. abbreviations in inscriptions, such as *IHS* for "Jesus," are still common.

I^{131} radioactive iodine.

i *I an abbreviation for:* **1** *also* **i.** incisor. **2** *also* **i.** interest, in combination: *x.i. = ex interest.* **3** *also* **i.** intransitive, in combination: *vi = verb intransitive.*
II a symbol for: **1** angle of incidence *physics.* **2** class interval or width *statistics.* **3** imaginary number $\sqrt{-1}$ (square root of minus one) *mathematics.* **4** inclination (of the orbit of a planet). **5** instantaneous current. **6** one; 1 (Roman numeral). **7** Van't Hoff factor (ratio of dissolved particles in a solution to number of particles if ionization has not taken place). **8** vapor pressure constant *physics.*

IA **1** immediately available *commerce.* **2** impedance angle. **3** incorporated accountant. **4** *also* **I.A.** Indian Army. **5** indicated altitude *aeronautics, surveying, geography.* **6** infected area. **7** Institute of Actuaries. **8** *also* **I.A.** international angstrom. **9** Iowa (Zip Code).

Ia. Iowa.

i.A. by order of. [German *im Auftrage*]

i.a. **1** among other things. [Latin *inter alia*] **2** in one's absence. [Latin *in absentia*]

IAA **1** indoleacetic acid (commonest auxin, regulating plant growth and development). **2** Inter-American Affairs (bureau of U.S. Department of State). **3** International Academy of Astronautics. **4** International Advertising Association. **5** International Association of Allergology.

IAAA Irish Amateur Athletic Association.

IAAAA Intercollegiate Association of Amateur Athletes of America.

IAAC International Antarctic Analysis Center (esp. for meteorological studies).

IAAE Institution of Automotive and Aeronautical Engineers.

IAAF International Amateur Athletic Federation.

IAAOPA International Association of Aircraft Owners and Pilots Association.

I.A.A.S. Incorporated Association of Architects and Surveyors.

IAB Industrial Advisory Board.

IABA International Association of Aircraft Brokers and Agents.

IABSE International Association for Bridge and Structural Engineering.

IABSIW International Association of Bridge, Structural, and Ornamental Iron Workers.

IAC **1** Industry Advisory Committee. **2** international analysis code *meteorology.* **3** interposed abdominal compressions (modified form of cardiopulmonary resuscitation).

IACA International Air Carriers Association.

IACB International Advisory Committee on Bibliography (of the UN).

IACCP Inter-American Council of Commerce and Production.

IACHR Inter-American Commission on Human Rights.

IACOMS International Advisory Committee on Marine Sciences (of the UN).

I.A.C.P. International Association of Chiefs of Police.

IACP **1** *also* **IACP & AP** International Association for Child Psychiatry and Allied Professions. **2** International Association of Culinary Professionals.

IACR International Association of Cancer Registries.

IADB **1** Inter-American Defense Board. **2** Inter-American Development Bank.

IADR International Association for Dental Research.

IAE Institution of Automobile Engineers.

IAEA International Atomic Energy Agency (of the UN).

IA-ECSOC Inter-American Economic and Social Council.

IAEE International Association of Earthquake Engineers.

IAF **1** Indian Air Force. **2** Inter-American Foundation. **3** International Astronautical Federation.

IAFC International Association of Financial Consultants.

IAFF International Association of Fire Fighters.

IAG 1 International Association of Geodesy. **2** International Association of Gerontology.

IAGA International Association of Geomagnetism and Aeronomy.

IAGS or **I.A.G.S.** Inter-American Geodetic Survey.

I.A.G.U.S. International Association of Genito-Urinary Surgeons.

IAH International Association of Hydrology.

IAHP International Association of Horticultural Producers.

IAHR International Association for Hydraulic Research.

IAI International African Institute.

IAIA Institute for American Indian Arts.

IAL 1 International Algebraic Language. **2** International Association of Theoretical And Applied Limnology. **3** also **I.A.L.** Irish Academy of Letters.

IALA International African Law Association.

IALS International Association of Legal Science.

IAM or **I.A.M.** **1** Institute of Aviation Medicine. **2** International Association of Machinists and Aerospace Workers. **3** International Association of Meteorologists. **4** International Association of Microbiologists.

IAMAP International Association of Meteorology and Atmospheric Physics.

IAMAT International Association for Medical Assistance to Travelers.

IAMS International Association of Microbiological Societies.

IANAP Interagency Noise Abatement Program (of aircraft noise).

I.A.N.C. International Airline Navigators Council.

I & C or **I and C** installation and checkout, (esp. of electronics equipment).

I and D or **I & D** incision and drainage *medicine*.

I & O input and output (of data) *computers*.

I & P or **i. and p.** indexed and paged (of printing proofs or manuscript).

I and R or **I & R** **1** information and retrieval. **2** initiative and referendum, (esp. of a voting petition).

I & S or **I and S** installation and service.

IANEC or **I.A.N.E.C.** Inter-American Nuclear Energy Commission.

I.A.O.S. Irish Agricultural Organization Society.

IAP International Academy of Pathology.

IAPA Inter-American Press Association.

I.A.P.B. International Association for Prevention of Blindness.

IAPG International Association of Physical Geography.

I.A.P.H. International Association of Professional Numismatists.

IAPO International Association of Physical Oceanography.

IAPSO International Association for Physical Sciences of the Oceans.

IAPT International Association for Plant Taxonomy.

I.A.P.T.A. International Allied Printing Trades Association.

IAR instruction address register *computers*.

IARC International Agency for Research on Cancer.

IARF International Association for Religious Freedom.

IARI Indian Agricultural Research Institute.

IARU International Amateur Radio Union.

IAS 1 immediate access storage *computers*. **2** also **I.A.S.** Indian Administrative Service. **3** indicated air speed. **4** Institute for Advanced Study. **5** also **I.A.S.** Institute of the Aerospace Sciences. **6** instrument approach system *aeronautics*.

IASA International Air Safety Association.

IASH International Association of Scientific Hydrology.

IASI Inter-American Statistical Institute.

IASMW International Association of Sheet Metal Workers.

IASPEI International Association of Seismology and Physics of the Earth's Interior.

IASS International Association of Soil Science.

IAT 1 inside air temperature. **2** international atomic time.

IATA International Air Transport Association.

IATEFL International Association of Teachers of English as a Foreign Language.

IATSE International Alliance of Theatrical Stage Employees and Moving Picture Machine Operators (of U.S. and Canada).

IATUL International Association of Technical University Libraries.

IAU 1 International Association of Universities. **2** International Astronomical Union.

IAUPL International Association of University Professors and Lecturers.

IAV International Association of Volcanology.

IAW or **i.a.w.** in accordance with.

IAWPR International Association of Water Pollution Research.

IB 1 also **I.B.** in bond *commerce*. **2** in bound. **3** inclusion body (cluster of viral particles or proteins). **4** industrialized building. **5** inner bottom (in blueprints and other technical drawings, esp. in shipbuilding). **6** instruction book. **7** internal browning (of fruits and vegetables). **8** invoice book.

ib. in the same place. [Latin *ibidem*]

IBA 1 Independent Bankers Association. **2** Independent Broadcasting Authority (of Great Britain). **3** indolebutyric acid (used to regulate plant growth and development). **4** also **I.B.A.** Institute of British Architects. **5** International Bar Association. **6** International Bauxite Association. **7** Investment Bankers Association, in combination: *IBAA = Investment Bankers Association of America.*

IBB 1 *rarely* **IBBISBBFH** International Brotherhood of Boilermakers (Iron Shipbuilders, Blacksmiths, Forgers and Helpers). **2** International Brotherhood of Bookbinders.

IBC inside back cover (of a magazine) *advertising*.

IBD Institute of Business Designers.

IBE 1 also **I.B.E.** Institute of British Engineers. **2** International Bureau of Education (in the UN). **3** International Bureau of Exhibition.

IBEC International Bank for Economic Cooperation.

IBEW International Brotherhood of Electrical Workers.

IBF 1 immunoglobulin-binding factor *biochemistry*. **2** International Badminton Federation. **3** international banking facilities (accounting device to maintain separation between domestic and foreign funds and transactions). **4** International Boxing Federation.

IBG 1 *also* **I.B.G.** Institute of British Geographers. **2** interblock gap (space between blocks of information) *computers*.

IBI *or* **i.b.i.** invoice book inwards *accounting*.

IBIB isobutyl isobutyrate (used in insect repellent and as flavoring).

IBID International Bibliographical Description.

ibid. *or* **ibid** (i'bid) in the same place. [Latin *ibidem*]

IBM 1 intercontinental ballistic missile. **2** *also* **I.B.M.** International Business Machines (corporation).

IBO *or* **i.b.o.** invoice book outwards *accounting*.

IBP 1 *also* **i.b.p.** *or* **ibp** initial boiling point. **2** International Biological Program.

I.B.P. 1 Institute of British Photographers. **2** International Biological Program (for conservation of species).

IBPAT International Brotherhood of Painters and Allied Trades.

IBPGR International Board for Plant Genetic Resources.

IBR 1 infectious bovine rhinotracheitis. **2** Institute of Boiler and Radiator Manufacturers (also identifying a standard of rating in engineering). **3** integral boiling reactor.

IBRD International Bank for Reconstruction and Development (the World Bank).

IBT *or* (rarely) **IBTCHW** International Brotherhood of Teamsters (Chauffeurs, Warehousemen, and Helpers of America).

ibuprofen (ī'byü prō'fən) isobutylphenylpropionic acid (a drug that reduces inflammation).

IBWM International Bureau of Weights and Measures.

IC 1 identity card. **2** immediate constituent (any one of the largest structural components of a sentence). **3** immune complex, esp. in combination: *IC disease, IC reaction*. **4** Index Catalogue *astronomy*. **5** index correction. **6** information center. **7** *also* **I & C** inspected and condemned, (esp. of a building). **8** inspiratory capacity (of the lungs). **9** integrated circuit *electronics*. **10** interior communications. **11** internal combustion (of an engine). **12** *also* **I.C.** Jesus Christ. [Latin *Iesus Christus*]

i/c 1 in charge: *Surg. i/c = Surgeon in charge*. **2** intercom.

i.c. between meals *pharmaceutics*. [Latin *inter cibos*]

ICA *or* **I.C.A. 1** Institute of Chartered Accountants. **2** Institute of Contemporary Arts. **3** International Cartographic Association. **4** International Commercial Arbitration. **5** International Communication Agency. **6** International Communication Association. **7** International Cooperation Administration. **8** International Cooperative Alliance. **9** International Council on Archives.

ICAA Investment Counsel Association of America.

ICAAAA *or* **IC4A** Intercollegiate Association of Amateur Athletes of America.

ICAE 1 International Commission on Agricultural Engineering. **2** International Conference of Agricultural Economists.

ICAF Industrial College of the Armed Forces.

ICAI International Commission for Agricultural Industries.

ICAN International Commission for Air Navigation (of the International Civil Aviation Organization).

ICAO International Civil Aviation Organization (also used to identify standards).

ICAR Indian Council of Agricultural Research.

ICAS 1 Interdepartmental Committee for Atmospheric Sciences. **2** intermittent commercial and amateur service. **3 a** International Council of Aeronautical Sciences. **b** International Council of Aerospace Science.

ICB 1 Institute of Comparative Biology. **2** International Container Bureau.

ICBA International Community of Booksellers Associations.

ICBD International Council of Ballroom Dancing.

ICBM intercontinental ballistic missile.

ICBN International Code of Botanical Nomenclature.

ICBO International Congress of Building Officials.

ICBP International Council for Bird Preservation.

ICC 1 Indian Claims Commission (former agency of the U.S. government). **2** *also* **I.C.C.** International Chamber of Commerce. **3** International Congregational Council (of the United Church of Christ). **4** *also* **I.C.C.** International Copyright Convention. **5** International Cricket Conference. **6** *also* **I.C.C.** Interstate Commerce Commission.

ICCA International Consumer Credit Association.

ICCR International Consultative Council for Radio Communications.

ICCS International Center for Criminological Studies.

ICD International Classification of Diseases (usually followed by a number signifying the edition): *ICD9*.

IC/DV import certification, delivery verification *commerce*.

ICE 1 Institution of Chemical Engineers (of Great Britain). **2** Institution of Civil Engineers (of Great Britain). **3** internal combustion engine. **4** International Cultural Exchange.

Ice. 1 Iceland. **2** Icelandic.

ICED International Council for Educational Development.

ICEF International Children's Emergency Fund.

Icel. Icelandic.

ICES 1 Integrated Civil Engineering System. **2** International Council for the Exploration of the Sea.

ICETT Industrial Council for Educational and Training Technology.

ICF 1 inertial confinement fusion (program for research into development of inertial fusion). **2** intracellular fluid.

I.C.F.C. *or* **ICFC** Industrial and Commercial Finance Corporation.

ICFTU *or* **I.C.F.T.U.** International Confederation of Free Trade Unions.

ICG 1 icing, *esp. in meteorology*. **2** interactive computer graphics, esp. in combination: *ICGS = interactive computer graphics system*. **3** International Commission on Glass.

ich. *or* **ichth.** *or* **ichthyol.** ichthyology.

ICHA International Cargo Handling Association.

I.Chem.E. Institution of Chemical Engineers.

ICI *or* **I.C.I.** 1 *British* Imperial Chemical Industries. 2 International Commission on Illumination (known outside the U.S. as *CIE* Commission Internationale de L'Éclairage).

ICID International Commission on Irrigation and Drainage.

ICIE International Council of Industrial Editors.

ICIP 1 International Communications and Information Policy (bureau of U.S. Department of State). 2 International Conference on Information Processing.

ICITA International Cooperative Investigations of the Tropical Atlantic.

ICJ *or* **I.C.J.** 1 International Commission of Jurists. 2 International Court of Justice.

ICJW International Council of Jewish Women.

ICL International Confederation of Labor.

ICLA 1 International Committee on Laboratory Animals. 2 International Comparative Literature Association.

ICM 1 Intergovernmental Committee for Migration. 2 International Confederation of Midwives.

ICMA International Circulation Managers Association.

ICN 1 *also* **I.C.N.** in Christ's name. [Latin *in Christi nomine*] 2 International Council of Nurses.

ICNAF International Commission for Northwest Atlantic Fisheries.

ICO 1 Interagency Committee on Oceanography. 2 International Coffee Organization. 3 International Commission for Optics. 4 Islamic Conference Organization.

ICOM 1 intercom. 2 International Council of Museums.

ICOMOS International Council of Monuments and Sites.

icon. iconography.

ICOR Intergovernmental Conference on Oceanic Research.

I.C.O.S. International Committee of Onomastic Sciences.

ICOT Institute for New Generation Computer Technology.

ICP 1 inductively coupled plasma *physics*. 2 International Council of Psychologists.

ICPA International Commission for the Prevention of Alcoholism.

ICPHS International Council for Philosophy and Humanistic Studies.

ICPO International Criminal Police Organization; Interpol.

ICR 1 Institute of Cancer Research. 2 intelligent character recognition *computers*. 3 *also* **icr** ion cyclotron resonance *physics*.

ICRC *or* **I.C.R.C.** International Committee of the Red Cross.

I.C.R.F. *or* **ICRF** Imperial Cancer Research Fund.

ICRP International Commission on Radiological Protection.

ICRU International Commission on Radiological Units and Measurements.

ICS 1 Indian Civil Service (now *IAS*). 2 installment credit selling. 3 Interagency Communications System. 4 *also* **I.C.S.** International College of Surgeons. 5 International Correspondence Schools.

ICSH interstitial cell-stimulating hormone.

ICSI International Conference on Scientific Information.

ICSID International Council of Societies of Industrial Design.

ICSLS International Convention for Safety of Life at Sea.

ICSPE International Council of Sport and Physical Recreation.

ICSS intracranial self-stimulation.

I.C.S.T. *or* **ICST** Imperial College of Science and Technoloy.

ICSU *or* **I.C.S.U.** International Council of Scientific Unions.

ICSW International Council of Social Welfare.

ICT 1 insulin coma therapy. 2 International Critical Tables.

I.C.T. with Jesus Christ as our protector. [Latin *Iesu Christo Tutore*]

ICTA 1 Industry Council for Tangible Assets (organization to certify companies and individuals dealing in valuable coins, art objects, etc.). 2 International Council of Travel Agents.

ICTMM International Congresses on Tropical Medicine and Malaria.

ICTP International Center for Theoretical Physics.

ICTU Irish Congress of Trade Unions.

ICU 1 Intensive Care Unit (of a hospital). 2 International Code Use.

ICVA International Council of Voluntary Agencies.

ICW 1 *also* **icw** in connection with. 2 Institute of Child Welfare. 3 International Council of Women. 4 *also* **i.c.w.** interrupted continuous wave *electronics*.

ICWM International Commission for Weights and Measures.

ICWU International Chemical Workers Union.

ICZN International Commission or Code on Zoological Nomenclature.

ID 1 Idaho (Zip Code). 2 *also* **I.D.** identification: *an ID card.* 3 identifier sequence (of nucleotides) *biochemistry.* 4 independent distributor (of magazines and newspapers). 5 *also* **I.D.** induced-draft: *ID fan.* 6 industrial design. 7 infectious disease. 8 infective dose: ID_{50} (dose required to produce infection in 50 percent of subjects). 9 inside or inner diameter. 10 *also* **I.D.** Intelligence Department. 11 intradermal *medicine.* 12 Iraqi dinar (monetary unit).

Id. 1 Idaho. 2 Island.

id 1 *also* **i.d.** inside or inner diameter. 2 *also* **id.** the same. [Latin *idem*]

IDA 1 iminodiacetic acid (used in manufacturing). 2 Institute for Defense Analyses. 3 International Development Association (of the World Bank). 4 Islamic Democratic Alliance (Pakistani political party).

Ida. Idaho.

I.D.B. *or* **IDB** 1 illicit diamond buyer or buying. 2 Inter-American Development Bank.

IDC Industrial Development Certificate.

IDCA International Development Cooperation Agency.

IDD 1 *also* **IDDM** insulin-dependent diabetes mellitus. 2 international direct dialing (of a telephone circuit).

IDEC Interior Design Educators Council.

iden. *or* **ident.** 1 identification. 2 identity.

IDF 1 intermediate distribution frame (for circuits). 2 International Dairy Federation. 3 Internatinal Diabetes Federation. 4 Israel Defense Forces. [Hebrew *Zahal, Zua Haganah Israel*]

IDG integrated drive generator *electronics.*

IDIOT instrumentation digital on-line transcriber *computers.*

IDL 1 intermediate-density lipoprotein *biochemistry.* 2 International Date Line.

IDMA International Dancing Masters Association.

I.D.N. in the name of God. [Latin *In Dei nomine*]

IDO International Disarmament Organization.

IDP 1 inosine diphosphate. 2 integrated data processing. 3 International Driving Permit.

IDR international drawing rights *commerce.*

IDRC International Development Research Center.

IDS 1 Integrated Data Store *computers.* 2 *also* **I.D.S.** Interior Design Society. 3 *also* **I.D.S.** Investigative Dermatological Society.

IDSO *or* **I.D.S.O.** International Diamond Security Organization.

IDT 1 industrial design technology. 2 insured deposits transferred (in a bank liquidation).

IDU 1 International Dendrology Union. 2 *also* **IdU** iododeoxyuridine (prevents viral replication, as of herpes simplex).

IDV *or* **I.D.V.** International Distillers and Vintners.

IE 1 index error. 2 *also* **I.E.** Indo-European (referring to a group of languages or the hypothetical language from which they were derived). 3 *also* **I.E.** Industrial Engineer. 4 *also* **I.E.** inside edge. 5 Institute of Electronics. 6 ion exchange.

i.e. that is: *31 per cent of all married women were in the labor force, i.e. actually working or looking for a job.* [Latin *id est*]

IEA 1 *also* **I.E.A.** Institute of Economic Affairs. 2 *also* **I.E.A.** International Economic Association. 3 International Energy Agency (of the EC). 4 International Project for the Evaluation of Educational Achievement.

IEC International Electrotechnical Commission.

IED 1 *also* **I.E.D.** improvised explosive device. 2 Institution of Engineering Designers.

IEE 1 Institute of Electrical Engineers. 2 Institute of Environmental Engineers. 3 Institution of Electrical Engineers (of Great Britain).

IEEE Institute of Electrical and Electronics Engineers.

IEEIE Institution of Electrical and Electronics Incorporated Engineers.

IEETE Institution of Electrical and Electronics Technician Engineers.

I.E.F. International Equestrian Federation.

IEI 1 Industrial Engineering Institute. 2 Institute for Educational Innovation.

IEME Inspectorate of Electrical and Mechanical Engineering.

IEP 1 individual education plan (for a student with learning difficulties). 2 instruments for the evaluation of photographs.

IER 1 Institute for Environmental Research. 2 Institute of Educational Research.

IERE Institution of Electronic and Radio Engineers.

IES 1 Illuminating Engineering Society. 2 Indian Educational Service.

I.E.T. interest equalization tax.

IEVS Income Eligibility Verification Systems.

IF 1 information feedback. 2 interferon *biochemistry.* 3 *also* **I-F** *or* **i-f** intermediate frequency.

i.f. 1 he did it himself. [Latin *ipse fecit*] 2 intermediate frequency.

IFA 1 International Federation of Actors. 2 International Fertility Association. 3 International Fiscal Association.

IFAC International Federation of Automatic Control.

IFAD International Fund for Agricultural Development (of the UN).

IFALPA International Federation of Airline Pilots' Association.

IFAP International Federation of Agricultural Producers.

IFATCA International Federation of Air Traffic Controllers' Association.

IFAW International Fund for Animal Welfare.

IFB invitation for bid *commerce.*

IFBB International Federation of Bodybuilders.

IFBPW International Federation of Business and Professional Women.

IFC 1 *also* **I.F.C.** International Finance Corporation (of the UN). 2 International Fisheries Commission. 3 International Freighting Corporation.

IFCATI International Federation of Cotton and Allied Textile Industries.

IFCC International Federation of Camping and Caravanning.

IFCCTE International Federation of Commercial, Clerical, and Technical Employees.

IFCO International Fisheries Cooperative Organization.

IFCS International Federation of Computer Sciences.

IFCTU International Federation of Christian Trade Unions (now *WCL*).

IFDA International Fund for Agricultural Development (of the UN).

IFEMS International Federation of Electron Microscope Societies.

IFF 1 identification, friend or foe (esp. an electronic device to identify combat aircraft). 2 *also* **iff** if and only if *mathematics.*

IFFA International Federation of Film Archives.

IFGO International Federation of Gynecology and Obstetrics.

IFHP International Federation for Housing and Planning.

IFIP International Federation of Information Processing.

I.F.J. *or* **IFJ** International Federation of Journalists.

IFLA 1 International Federation of Landscape Architects. 2 *also* **I.F.L.A.** International Federation of Library Association.

IFO identified flying object.

I.F.O.P. French Institute of Public Opinion. [French *Institut Français d'Opinion Publique*]

IFOR International Federation of Operational Research Societies.

IFPM International Federation of Physical Medicine.

IFPW International Federation of Petroleum Workers.

IFR 1 instrument flight rules (popularly used to describe the weather and/or flight conditions to which these rules apply). **2** integral fast reactor *physics*. **3** internal function register *computers*.

IFRB International Frequency Registration Board.

IFRF International Flame Research Foundation.

IFRU interference frequency rejection unit *electronics*.

IFS 1 Indian Forest Service. **2** International Federation of Surveyors. **3** *also* **I.F.S.** Irish Free State.

IFST Institute of Food Service and Technology.

IFSTAD Islamic Foundation for Science, Technology and Development.

IFSW International Federation of Social Workers.

IFT International Federation of Translators.

IFTC International Film and Television Council.

I.F.T.U. International Federation of Trade Unions (now *WFTU*).

IFUW or **I.F.U.W.** International Federation of University Women.

IFYE International Farm Youth Exchange.

IG 1 *also* **I-G** Indo-Germanic. **2** inertial guidance. **3** inground, esp. in combination: *IGP = inground pool.* **4** *also* **I.G.** Inspector General, also in combination: *IGDOD = Inspector General, Department of Defense.* **5** *also* **I.G.** combination or trust. [German *Interessengemeinschaft*]

Ig immunoglobulin (any one of several classes of antibodies categorized as **IgA**, found in saliva and other secretions; **IgD**, found in cell receptors; **IgF1**, promoting cell growth and reproduction; etc.).

ig. ignition.

IGA 1 Independent Grocers Alliance. **2** International Geographical Association.

IGAS International Graphic Arts Society.

IGC 1 *also* **I.G.C.** intellectually gifted child or children. **2** *also* **I.G.C.** Intergovernmental Conference. **3** International Geophysical Cooperation. **4** International Grassland Congress.

IGCC Intergovernmental Copyright Committee.

IGD 1 *also* **i.g.d.** illicit gold dealer. **2** Inspector General's Department.

IGE Individualized Guided Education.

IGES initial graphics exchange specification *computers*.

IGF insulin-like growth factor.

IGFA International Game Fish Association.

IGFET insulated gate field effect transistor.

IGIA Interagency Group for International Aviation.

ign. 1 ignition. **2** *also* **Ign.** unknown. [Latin *ignotus*]

IGO or **I.G.O.** Intergovernmental Organization.

IGOR intercept ground optical recorder *astronautics*.

IGPP Institute of Geophysics and Planetary Physics.

Igr. therefore. [Latin *igitur*]

IGS inertial guidance system *aeronautics*.

IGST Intergovernmental Committee on Science and Technology.

IGU 1 International Gas Union. **2** International Geographical Union.

IGY International Geophysical Year (July 1, 1957 to Dec. 31, 1958).

IH 1 *also* **I-H** Indo-Hittite. **2** infectious hepatitis.

i.h. 1 here lies. [Latin *iacet hic*] **2** *also* **ih** inside height.

IHA 1 Indian Housing Authority (for Native Americans). **2** *also* **I.H.A.** Individual Housing Account.

IHAB International Horticultural Advisory Bureau.

IHB International Hydrographic Bureau.

IHD 1 International Hydrological Decade (1965 to 1974). **2** ischemic heart disease.

IHE Institute of Highway Engineers.

IHF 1 Industrial Hygiene Foundation. **2** International Hockey Federation. **3** International Hospital Federation.

IHP or **ihp** or **i.hp.** indicated horsepower, also in combination: *IHP-hr* or *ihp-hr.* = *indicated horsepower hour.*

IHR Institute of Historical Research.

IHS 1 *also* **I.H.S.** an abbreviation of the name of Jesus. ▶IHS is a Latinate form of the Greek IHΣ (iota, eta, sigma) for IHΣOYΣ, in which the second letter (the Greek *eta*) was transcribed as the capital *H* of Latin, though normally the abbreviation would have read *IES*. Various popular interpretations have therefore been contrived, *Iesus Hominum Salvator*, Jesus Saviour of men; *In Hoc Signo (vinces),* By this sign (conquer); or *In Hoc (cruce) Salus,* In this (cross) is salvation; or even the English phrase *In His Sign.* **2** Indian Health Service (bureau of U.S. Department of Health and Human Services).

IHSA iodinated human serum albumin.

IHSS idiopathic hypertrophic subaortic stenosis (lack of blood flow from the left ventricle).

II 1 indorsement irregular, in banking. **2** inventory and inspection.

IIA 1 Information Industry Association. **2** International Information Administration (of U.S. Department of State).

IIAC Industrial Injuries Advisory Council.

IIAL International Institute of Arts and Letters.

IIALC International Institute of African Languages and Culture.

IIB International Patent Institute. [French *Institut International des Brevets*]

IIC International Institute for Conservation of Historic and Artistic Works.

IIE 1 Institute of Industrial Engineers. **2** *also* **I.I.E.** Institute of International Education (for cultural exchange programs). **3** International Institute of Embryology.

IIEA International Institute for Environmental Affairs.

IIEP International Institute for Educational Planning.

IIHF International Ice Hockey Federation.

III International Institute of Interpreters (of the UN).

IIL or **I²L** integrated injection logic (electronic circuits made with transistors).

I.Inf.Sc. Institute of Information Scientists.

IIOE International Indian Ocean Expedition.

IIP 1 International Ice Patrol. **2** International Institute of Philosophy.

IIR isobutylene-isoprene rubber.

IIS 1 Institute of Information Scientists. **2** integrated information system (computer-based coordination of information within a company).

IIT 1 Illinois Institute of Technology. **2** Indian Institute of Technology.

IIW International Institute of Welding.

i.J. in the year. [German *im Jahre*]

IJC International Joint Commission (created by the 1909 treaty to investigate all border-water disputes between Canada and the U.S.).

IJLP Islamic Jihad for Liberation of Palestine.

IL 1 Illinois (Zip Code). **2** *also* **I/L** import license. **3** inside left, in soccer and association football. **4** inside length. **5** instrument landing *aviation*. **6** interleukin, also in combination: *IL2*.

Il *I an abbreviation for: also* **Il.** *Iliad*.
II a symbol for: illinium (chemical element, now called *promethium*).

il 1 *also* **il. a** illustrated. **b** illustration. **2** *also* **i.l.** inside length.

ILA 1 Institute of Landscape Architects. **2** instrument landing approach *aviation*, also in combination: *ILAS = instrument landing approach system.* **3** International Language for Aviation. **4** *also* **I.L.A.** International Law Association. **5** *also* **I.L.A.** International Longshoremen's Association. **6** serum insulin-like activity (factors that together result in effective action of insulin).

ILAA 1 Independent Literary Agents Association. **2** International Legal Aid Association.

ILAB International League of Antiquarian Booksellers.

ILAR Institute of Laboratory Animal Resources.

ILAS Institute for Latin American Studies.

ILC International Law Commission (of the UN).

Ile *or* **ileu.** isoleucine (amino acid common in protein).

ILF 1 infralow frequency. **2** International Landworkers Federation.

ILGA Institute of Local Government Administration.

ILGWU *or* **I.L.G.W.U.** International Ladies' Garment Workers' Union.

Ill. Illinois.

ill. 1 illuminated: *ill. ms = illuminated manuscript.* **2 a** illustrated. **b** illustration. **c** *also* **Ill.** illustrator. **3** most distinguished. [Latin *illustrissimus*]

illegit. illegitimate.

illit. illiterate.

illog. antilog *mathematics*.

illum. illuminated, as of a manuscript.

illus. *or* **illust. 1** illustrated. **2** illustration.

ILN Illustrated London News (publication).

ILO 1 *also* **ilo** in lieu of. **2** *also* **I.L.O. a** International Labor Office (permanent staff of the International Labor Organization). **b** International Labor Organization (of the UN).

I.L.P. Independent Labour Party (of Great Britain).

ILR independent local radio (of Great Britain).

ILS 1 instrument landing system *aviation*. **2** International Latitude Service. **3** International Lunar Society.

ILSR Institute for Local Self-Reliance (group concerned with private and government action to solve urban problems).

ILT infectious laryngotracheitis.

ILTF *or* **I.L.T.F.** International Lawn Tennis Federation.

ILU inventory of land use, also in combination: *ILURP = Inventory of Land Use Restraints Program.*

ILW intermediate level waste (classification of risk in handling garbage).

ILWU *or* **I.L.W.U.** International Longshoremen's and Warehousemen's Union.

IM 1 infectious mononucleosis. **2** *also* **i.m.** intramuscular, intramuscularly (esp. of an injection) *medicine*. **3** *also* **I.M.** Isle of Man.

im. 1 immature. **2** impulse.

imag. imaginary.

I.Mar.E. Institute of Marine Engineers.

IMAS International Marine and Shipping (Conference).

IMAWU International Molders' and Allied Workers' Union.

Imax (ī′maks′) image maximum (giant TV screen).

IMB Institute of Marine Biology.

IMC 1 image motion compensation *photography*. **2** Institute of Management Consultants. **3** instrument meteorological conditions *aviation*. **4** International Maritime Committee. **5** International Music Council.

IMCC Integrated Mission Control Center (of NASA in Houston).

IMCO 1 Intergovernmental Maritime Consultative Organization (now *IMO*). **2** International Metered Communication Service.

imdt. immediately.

IME 1 Institute of Marine Engineers. **2** *also* **I.Mech.E.** Institution of Mechanical Engineers.

IMEMO Institute of World Economics and International Affairs (in Moscow). [from Russian acronym]

IMEP *or* **i.m.e.p.** indicated mean effective pressure.

IMF *or* **I.M.F.** International Monetary Fund.

I.Min.E. Institution of Mining Engineers.

IMINT (im′int) image intelligence (intelligence obtained through aerial photography).

imit. 1 imitation. **2** imitative.

IMM 1 Institution of Mining and Metallurgy. **2** International Monetary Market.

immed. immediate.

IMMS International Material Management Society.

immun. *or* **immunol.** immunology.

IMO 1 interband magneto-optic: *IMO effect.* 2 International Maritime Organization (of the UN). 3 International Meteorological Organization.

IMP 1 indeterminate mass particle (hypothetical nuclear particle). 2 inosine monophosphate (nucleotide of purine). 3 Interface Message Processors *computers.* 4 *also* **I.M.P.** International Match Point (unit of scoring used in European contract bridge). 5 **a** interplanetary monitoring platform (satellite). **b** interplanetary monitoring probe (to measure magnetic fields, cosmic rays, and solar winds beyond the earth's magnetic field).

Imp 1 *also* **Imp. a** Emperor. [Latin *Imperator*] **b** Empress. [Latin *Imperatrix*] 2 imperial (size of paper, about $2 \times 2\frac{1}{2}$ feet). 3 indeterminate mass particle (hypothetical nuclear particle).

imp. 1 imperative. 2 imperfect. 3 imperial: *imp. gal. = imperial gallon.* 4 impersonal. 5 **a** import. **b** imported. **c** importer. 6 important. 7 impression. 8 imprint. 9 **a** improved. **b** improvement. 10 **a** let it be printed. [Latin *imprimatur*] **b** printed. [French *imprimé*]

IMPACT implementation, planning, and control techniques, *esp. in computers.*

IMPATT IMP(act) Avalanche Transit Time *computers*, esp. in combination: *IMPATT amplifier, IMPATT diode.*

imp. bu. imperial bushel.

imper. imperative.

imperf. 1 imperfect. 2 imperforate, (esp. of postage stamps).

impf. interperfect *grammar*, esp. in combination: *3sg. impf. = third person singular imperfect.*

imp. gal. imperial gallon.

impl. implement.

impr. 1 **a** improved. **b** improvement. 2 printer, printing house, press. [French *imprimeur* and *imprimerie*; Spanish *imprenta*] 3 edition. [Spanish *impresión*]

Impr. Nat. French Government Printing Office. [French *Imprimerie Nationale*]

improp. 1 improper. 2 improperly.

impt. important.

imptr. importer.

IMR 1 infant mortality rate. 2 Institute for Motivational Research. 3 Institute of Medical Research.

IMS 1 Indian Medical Service. 2 industrial methylated spirits. 3 Information Management System *computers.* 4 Institute of Museum Services (of the National Foundation on the Arts and the Humanities). 5 International Magnetospheric Study. 6 International Musicological Society.

IMU 1 inertial measurement unit. 2 International Mathematical Union.

IMV intermittent mandatory ventilation.

IMVIC indole, methyl red, Voges-Proskauer, and citrate tests (to distinguish bacteria).

IMVS Institute of Medical and Veterinary Science.

IMW 1 Institute of Masters of Wine. 2 International Map of the World.

IN 1 Indiana (Zip Code). 2 Indian Navy. 3 *also* **I.N.** inertial navigation. 4 *also* **in** input *electronics.*

In *I an abbreviation for:* 1 **a** India. **b** Indian. 2 *also* **In.** Inner: *In. Mong. = Inner Mongolia.* 3 Instructor.
II a symbol for: indium (chemical element).

in. *or* **in** 1 inch, inches. 2 interest.

INA 1 Indian National Army. 2 *also* **I.N.A.** Institution of Naval Architects. 3 *also* **I.N.A.** International Neurological Association. 4 international normal atmosphere.

INAA instrumental neutron activation analysis (technique used to identify presence of trace elements).

INAH 1 interstitial nuclei of the anterior hypothalamus (segment of the brain possibly active in regulating sexual activity). 2 isonicotinic acid hydrazide (anti-tubercular drug).

INaLF National Institute for French Language. [French *Institut National de la Langue Française*]

INAO National Institute of Names of Origin (of wine). [French *Institut National des Appellations d'Origine*]

inaug. inaugurated.

inbd. 1 inboard. 2 inbound.

INC *or* **I.N.C.** 1 Indian National Congress. 2 in the name of Christ. [Latin *in nomine Christi*]

Inc. Incorporated.

inc. 1 engraved. [Latin *incisus*] 2 *also* **inc** inclosure (esp. with a letter of correspondence). 3 **a** included. **b** including. **c** inclusive. 4 income. 5 incomplete. 6 incorporated. 7 *also* **inc** increase. 8 *also* **inc** incumbent.

INCA Information Council of America.

incalz. *or* **Incalz** increasing tempo and tone *music.* [Italian *incalzando*]

INCAP Institute of Nutrition of Central America and Panama.

INCB International Narcotics Control Board (of the UN).

inch. *or* **incho.** inchoate, inchoative (incomplete, unfinished, imperfect) *law, grammar.*

incl. 1 **a** incline. **b** inclined. 2 inclosure. 3 **a** included. **b** including. **c** inclusive.

INCO instrumentation and communications officer (on a spaceflight).

incog. incognito.

incompat. incompatibility.

incompl. incomplete.

Incorp. Incorporated.

incorr. incorrect.

INCOSPAR Indian National Committee for Space Research.

incr. 1 **a** increase. **b** increased. **c** increasing. 2 **a** increment. **b** incremental.

incun. *or* **Incun.** incunabula (book printed before 1501), *esp. in cataloging.*

IND 1 Independent (division of the New York City subway system). 2 investigational new drug (the status of a drug approved by a regulatory agency for experimentation and research).

Ind. 1 a Independent, in combination: *Ind. Lib.* = *Independent Liberal*. **b** Independence, in combination: *Ind. Day* = *Independence Day*. **2** India. **3 a** Indian. **b** *also* **Ind** the Indian, American Indian (constellation) *astronomy*. [Latin *Indus*] **4** Indiana. **5** Indies, in combination: *W Ind.* = *West Indies*. **6** Indonesia. **7 a** Industry. **b** Industrial, in combination: *Ind. Eng.* = *Industrial Engineer*.

ind. 1 a independence. **b** independent. **2 a** index. **b** indexed. **3 a** indicated. **b** indication. **c** indicative *grammar*, esp. in combination: *pres. ind.* = *present indicative*. **4** indigo. **5** indirect. **6** individual. **7 a** industry. **b** industrial, in combination: *ind. pol.* = *industrial pollution*.

in d. daily *pharmaceutics*. [Latin *in dies*]

INDC Indian National Democratic Congress (of India).

Ind.E. Industrial Engineer.

INDECS Immigration and Nationality Department Electronic Computer System.

indef. indefinite, in combination: *indef.art.* = *indefinite article*.

indem. indemnity.

indic. 1 indicated. **2** indicating. **3** indicative *grammar*. **4** indicator.

Indig. indigenous, *esp. in botany*.

indiv. *or* **individ.** *or* **indiv'l** individual.

Indo-Eur. Indo-European.

Indo-Ger. Indo-Germanic.

Indon. 1 Indonesia. **2** Indonesian.

induc. induction.

indust. 1 industrial. **2** industry.

ined. unpublished. [Latin *ineditus*]

INF 1 Intermediate-Range Nuclear Forces, esp. in combination: *INF Treaty*. **2** International Naturalist Federation.

Inf. Infantry.

inf. 1 below. [Latin *infra*] **2** infectious. **3** inferior. **4 a** infinite. **b** infinity. **5** infinitive. **6** information. **7** infuse, infusion *medicine, pharmaceutics*.

infin. infinitive.

Infirm. Infirmary.

infl. 1 inflammable. **2** inflorescence *botany*. **3 a** influence. **b** influenced.

Infm. Information.

info (in'fō) information.

infobit (in'fō bit') information bit (item of information in a databank).

infra dig *or* **infra dig.** (in'frə dig') undignified, beneath one's dignity. [Latin *infra dignitatem*]

infreq. infrequent.

ING Intense Neutron Generator.

INGO International Non-Governmental Organization (esp. of the UN).

INH isonicotinic acid hydrazide, isoniazid (used to treat tuberculosis).

Inh inhibitor *medicine*: *C1 Inh* = *C1 esterase inhibitor*.

inhab. 1 inhabited. **2** inhabitants.

INI National Industries Institute (state holding company of Spain). [Spanish *Instituto Nacional de Industria*]

in init. in or at the beginning. [Latin *in initio*]

INIS International Nuclear Information System.

init. initial (beginning).

I.N.J. in the name of Jesus (often found in secular music scores of J. S. Bach). [Latin *in nomine Jesu*]

inj. 1 inject. **2** *also* **inject.** injection.

inkl. inclusive. [German *inklusive*]

INLA 1 International Nuclear Law Association. **2** Irish National Liberation Army.

in.-lb. *or* **in-lb** inch-pound ($^1/_{12}$ of a foot-pound).

in lim. at the outset. [Latin *in limine*]

in loc. in its place. [Latin *in loco*]

in loc. cit. in the place cited. [Latin *in loco citato*]

INMARSAT International Maritime Satellite Organization (mobile land, sea, and air communications satellite system).

in mem. in memory of. [Latin *in memoriam*]

INMHO in my humble opinion (used in electronic communication).

INN 1 Independent News Network. **2** International Nonproprietary Name (esp. of a drug).

inns. innings *cricket*.

inorg. inorganic.

INOSHAC Indian Ocean and Southern Hemisphere Analysis Center.

INP 1 *also* **I.N.P.** inert nitrogen protection (process). **2** in peace. [Latin *in pace*] **3** International News Photo.

INPO Institute of Nuclear Power Operations.

in pr. in or at the beginning. [Latin *in principio*]

in pro in proportion.

inq. inquiry.

INQUA International Association on Quaternary Research.

in. req. information requested.

INRI *or* **I.N.R.I.** Jesus of Nazareth, King of the Jews. [Latin *Iesus Nazarenus, Rex Iudaeorum*]

INS 1 Immigration and Naturalization Service (of U.S. Department of Justice). **2** Inertial Navigation System. **3** (former) International News Service (now merged with United Press to form *UPI*). **4** ion neutralization spectroscopy.

Ins. 1 Inspector. **2** insurance.

ins. 1 inches. **2** *also* **insc.** inscribed. **3** insular. **4 a** insulated. **b** insulation. **c** insulator. **5** insurance.

Inscr. *or* **inscr. 1** inscribed. **2** inscription.

INSEA International Society for Education through Art.

insep. inseparable.

insol. insoluble.

insolv. insolvent.

Insp. Inspector, also in combination: *Insp. Gen.* = *Inspector General*.

I.N.S.T. in the name of the Holy Trinity. [Latin *in nomine Sanctae Trinitatis*]

Inst. 1 a Institute. b Institution. 2 Instructor.

inst. 1 installment. 2 instant: a (present month). b (immediate). 3 instantaneous. 4 a institute. b institution. 5 a instructor. b instruction. 6 a instrument. b instrumental.

in stat. pup. subject to the rule of the institution (implied by the literal translation, being in the condition of a pupil or in the position of a ward). [Latin *in statu pupillari*]

Inst.C.E. Institution of Civil Engineers.

Inst.E.E. Institution of Electrical Engineers.

instl. 1 installation. 2 *also* **Instl.** Intitutional.

Inst.M.E. 1 Institute of Marine Engineers. 2 *also* **Inst. Mech.E.** Institution of Mechanical Engineers.

Inst.M.M. Institution of Mining and Metallurgy.

Instn Institution.

Inst.N.A. Institution of Naval Architects.

instns. instructions.

Inst.P. Institute of Physics.

Instr. Instructor.

instr. 1 instructions. 2 a instrument. b instrumental.

INSTRAW International Research and Training Institute for the Advancement of Women (of the UN).

instrns instructions.

Int. 1 intelligence (information gathering). 2 *also* **INT** Internal: *Int. Rev. = Internal Review.* 3 International.

int. 1 integral. 2 intelligence. 3 interest: *ex int. = without interest.* 4 interim. 5 interior. 6 interjection *grammar.* 7 intermediate. 8 internal: *int. med. = internal medicine.* 9 international. 10 interpreter. 11 interval.

int. al. among other things. [Latin *inter alia*]

INTELPOST International Electronic Post (high-speed electronic mail service).

INTELSAT (in'tel sat') International Telecommunications Satellite.

intens. intensive.

Inter. 1 Intermediate. 2 International.

inter. 1 interleave. 2 intermediate. 3 a interrogation. b interrogative.

intercom (in'tər kom') 1 *also* **intercom.** intercommunication. 2 intercommunication system.

interj. interjection.

intern. 1 internal. 2 *also* **Intern.** international.

internat. *or* **Internat.** international.

Internet (in'tər net') internetwork or International network (of computer systems for worldwide communications).

Interpol (in'tər pōl') International Criminal Police Organization.

interrog. 1 interrogation. 2 interrogative.

intgr. 1 interrogate 2 interrogator.

INTIPS Integrated Information-Processing System.

intl. *or* **Intl.** international.

intmt. intermittent.

intpr. interpreter.

intr. 1 intransitive. 2 a introduce. b introduced. c introducing. 3 a introduction. b introductory.

intrans. intransitive.

in trans. in passing *or* in transit. [Latin *in transitu*]

Int. Rev. Internal Revenue (Service).

intro. *or* **introd.** 1 a introduce. b introduced. c introducing. 2 *also* **Intro.** *or* **Introd.** a introduction. b introductory.

INTUC Indian National Trades Union Congress.

I.Nuc.E. Institute of Nuclear Engineering.

Inv. 1 Inverness. 2 invoice.

inv. 1 he or she invented or designed it. [Latin *invenit*] 2 a invented, invented by. b invention. c inventor. 3 inventory. 4 inversion. 5 investment. 6 invoice.

invert. invertebrate.

invest. 1 investigation. 2 investment.

invol. involuntary.

invt. 1 he or she invented or designed it. [Latin *invenit*] 2 *also* **invty.** inventory.

INWATS inward wide-area telephone service.

IO 1 image orthicon (tube in a television camera). 2 information officer. 3 input/output *computers,* also in combination: *IOPS = input/output processing system.* 4 intelligence officer. 5 interpersonal orientation (exploring potential reaction among groups of different types of people). 6 investigating or investigation officer. 7 issuing office.

I/O 1 *also* **I-O** inboard-outboard, (esp. of motorboat with an inboard engine attached to an outboard drive shaft or the engine itself). 2 industrial and organizational (psychology). 3 *also* **i/o** input/output *electronics, computers.* 4 investigating or investigation officer.

Io I *an abbreviation for:* also **Io.** Iowa.
II *a symbol for:* ionium (chemical element).

IOA International Organization Affairs (bureau of U.S. Department of State).

IOB *or* **i/ob** input/output buffer *computers.*

IOBC Indian Ocean Biological Center.

IOC 1 Initial Operational Capability (period from initial integration to combat-ready missile). 2 input/output controller *computers.* 3 integrated optical circuit *electronics.* 4 Intergovernmental Oceanographic Commission (of the UN). 5 *also* **I.O.C.** International Olympic Committee.

IOCS input/output control system *computers.*

IOCU International Oranization of Consumers Unions.

IOCV International Organization of Citrus Virologists.

I.O.D.E. *Canadian* Imperial Order of the Daughters of the Empire.

IOE International Organization of Employers.

IOF 1 *also* **I.O.F.** Independent Order of Foresters. 2 International Oceanographic Foundation.

I.O.G.T. Independent Order of Good Templars (fraternal organization).

IOJ 1 *also* **IoJ** Institute of Journalists. 2 International Organization of Journalists.

IOM 1 *also* **I.O.M.** Indian Order of Merit. 2 Institute of

Metals. **3** Institute of Office Management. **4** *also* **I.O.M.** Isle of Man. **5** International Organization for Migration.

IOME Institute of Marine Engineers.

Ion. Ionic.

I.O.O.F. Independent Order of Odd Fellows (fraternal organization).

IOP 1 input/output processor *computers*. **2** *also* **I.O.P.** Institute of Painters in Oil Colors. **3** Institute of Physics.

IOPAB International Organization for Pure and Applied Biophysics.

I.O.R.M. Improved Order of Red Men (fraternal organization).

IOS International Organization for Standardization; ISO.

I.O.S.M. Independent Order of the Sons of Malta (fraternal organization).

IOT 1 initial orbit time. **2** *also* **IoT** Institute of Transport.

IOU 1 industrial operations unit. **2** investor-owned utilities. **3** *also* **I.O.U. a** I owe you. **b** note showing a debt, such as a commercial paper or an unsecured note.

IOVST International Organization for Vacuum Science and Technology.

IOW 1 Institute of Welding. **2** *also* **I.O.W.** Isle of Wight.

IP 1 identification point. **2** impact point. **3** incentive pay. **4** *also* **I&P** indexed and paged (of a manuscript or printer's proofs). **5** *also* **I.P.** India paper. **6** initial phase *or* point. **7** innings pitched *baseball*. **8** inpatient (in a hospital). **9** installment plan. **10** *also* **I.P.** Institute of Petroleum. **11** *also* **i.p.** intermediate pressure, also in combination: *IPC = intermediate pressure cylinder.*

IPA 1 Individual Practice Association *medicine*. **2** *also* **I.P.A.** Institute of Practitioners in Advertising (part of the British Advertising Association). **3** intermediate power amplifier. **4 a** International Phonetic Alphabet. **b** *also* **I.P.A.** International Phonetic Association. **5** International Police Association. **6** *also* **I.P.A.** International Press Association. **7** International Psychoanalytical Association. **8** *also* **I.P.A.** International Publishers' Association. **9** isopropyl alcohol.

i.p.a. including particular average *insurance*.

IPAA 1 Independent Petroleum Association of America. **2** International Prisoners Aid Association.

IPBMM International Permanent Bureau of Motor Manufacturers.

IPC 1 industrial process control. **2** International Polar Commission. **3** Iraq Petroleum Company. **4** isopropylphenylcarbamate (insecticide).

IPCC Intergovernmental Panel on Climate Change (of the UN).

IPCS Institution of Professional Civil Servants (of Great Britain).

IPD 1 individual package delivery. **2** insertion phase delay *electronics*. **3** intermediate peritoneal dialysis *medicine*. **4** *also* **I.P.D.** in the presence of the Lords of Session (of Scotland) *law*. [Latin *in praesentia Dominorum*]

I.P.E. 1 Institute of Plant Engineers. **2** Institute of Production Engineers. **3** *also* **IPE** individual protection equipment.

IPFC Indo-Pacific Fisheries Council.

IPH *or* **iph** inches per hour.

IPI 1 Industrial Production Index *finance*. **2** *also* **I.P.I.** International Press Institute. **3** *also* **i.p.i.** in the regions of unbelievers. [Latin *in partibus infidelium*]

IPL 1 information-processing language *computers*. **2** initial program load or loading *computers*.

IPM 1 *also* **ipm** inches per minute. **2** Institute of Personal Management. **3** integrated pest management. **4** interruptions per minute.

IPN infectious pancreatic necrosis.

IPO 1 initial public offering (of a stock). **2** input, process, output *computers*.

IPP independent power producer (of electrical energy).

I.P.P.A.U. International Printing Pressmen and Assistants' Union (of North America).

IPPB intermittent positive pressure breathing *medicine*.

IPPF International Planned Parenthood Federation (of voluntary and government agencies in 35 countries).

IPR 1 *also* **ipr** inches per revolution. **2** Institute of Public Relations.

IPRA International Public Relations Association.

IPRE Incorporated Practitioners in Radio and Electronics.

IPS 1 *also* **ips** inches per second, as of recording tape. **2** Indian Police Service. **3** Institute of Population Studies. **4** interpretive programming system *computers*. **5** *also* **ips** iron pipe size.

IPSA International Political Science Association.

IPSE integrated program support environment (to develop computer applications without programming language).

IPSJ Information Processing Society of Japan.

IPSP inhibitory postsynaptic potential *medicine*.

IPT 1 *also* **i.p.t.** indexed, paged, and titled (of a manuscript or printer's proofs). **2** *also* **ipt** internal pipe thread.

IPTPA International Professional Tennis Players Association.

IPTS International Practical Temperature Scale.

IPU 1 input preparation unit *computers*. **2** *also* **I.P.U.** Inter-Parliamentary Union.

IPV inactivated poliovirus vaccine.

i.p.v. instead of. [Dutch *in plaats van*]

IPW interrogation prisoner of war.

ipy inches per year (of precipitation).

IQ 1 import quota. **2** *also* **I.Q.** intelligence quotient (indicates general level of mental ability).

Iq. Iraq.

i.q. the same as. [Latin *idem quod*]

IQA Institute of Quality Assurance.

i.q.e.d. that which is to be proved. [Latin *id quod erat demonstrandum*]

IQS Institute of Quantity Surveyors.

IQSY International Quiet Sun Year (Jan. 1, 1964 to Dec. 31, 1964 to study the sun and its effects on the earth).

IR *I an abbreviation for:* **1** industrial relations. **2 a** information request. **b** information retrieval, *esp. of computers.* **3 a** infrared. **b** infrared radiation. **4** *also* **I.R.** British Inland Revenue. **5** inside radius. **6** inside right, in soccer and association football. **7** instantaneous replay. **8** Intelligence and Research (bureau of U.S. Department of State). **9** *also* **I.R.** intelligence ratio. **10** interim report. **11** international registration. **12** Ireland, Irish: *IR£= Irish pound.*
II a symbol for: current resistance.

Ir *I an abbreviation for:* **1** immune response: *Ir gene.* **2** internal resistance *medicine.* **3** *also* **Ir.** Iran. **4** *also* **Ir.** Ireland, Irish: *£Ir = Irish pound.*
II a symbol for: iridium (chemical element).

i.r. **1** *British* infrared. **2** inside radius.

IRA **1** (ī′rə) Individual Retirement Account. **2** *also* **I.R.A.** International Reading Association. **3** Irish Republican Army.

IRAC **1** Industrial Relations Advisory Committee. **2** Interdepartmental Radio Advisory Committee.

IRAD Institute for Research on Animal Diseases.

IRAL International Review of Applied Linguistics (publication).

Iran. Iranian.

IRAS Infrared Astronomical Satellite.

IRASER infrared laser.

IRB **1** Institutional Review Board *medicine.* **2** Insurance Rating Board. **3** *also* **I.R.B.** Internal Revenue Bulletin (followed by a number). **4** *also* **I.R.B.** Irish Republican Brotherhood (secret organization in the early 1900s that sought independent Irish republic).

IRBM Intermediate Range Ballistic Missile.

IRC **1** inductance, resistance, capacitance *electronics.* **2** *also* **I.R.C.** Industrial Relations Counselors. **3** Industrial Reorganization Corporation (of Great Britain). **4** Internal Revenue Code (of U.S. Internal Revenue Service). **5** *also* **I.R.C.** International Red Cross. **6** International Rescue Committee (private group to assist political refugees). **7** International Research Council.

IRD immune renal disease *medicine.*

IRDA Industrial Research and Development Authority (of Great Britain).

IRE **1** Institute of Radio Engineers. **2** Investigative Reporters and Editors.

Ire. Ireland.

IREX International Research and Exchange Board.

IRF **1** International Road Federation. **2** International Rowing Federation.

IRG interrecord gap (space between blocks of information stored on disk or tape).

IRI **1** *also* **I.R.I.** Industrial Research Institute. **2** Institute for Industrial Reconstruction. [Italian *Istituto per La Ricostruzione Industriale*]

irid. iridescent *biology.*

IRIS Industrial Research Information Service.

IRL information retrieval language.

IRLS interrogation recording location system *navigation.*

IRM **1** Information Resource Manager *computers.* **2** innate releasing mechanism (for regulating behavior). **3** intermediate

range missile. **4** *also* **irm** isothermal remanent magnetization *physics.*

IRMA individual retirement mortgage account.

IRMS Information Resources Management Service.

IRN Independent Radio News.

IRO **1** *also* **I.R.O.** British Inland Revenue Office or Officer. **2** Internal Revenue Office or Officer. **3** International Refugee Organization (former organization to resettle displaced persons after World War II). **4** International Relief Organization.

IRP Islamic Republican Party.

IRPA International Radiation Protection Association.

IRR **1** infrared rays. **2** Institute of Race Relations. **3** internal rate of return *finance.*

irr. **1** irredeemable, *esp. in finance.* **2** *also* **irreg. a** irregular. **b** irregularly.

IRRI International Rice Research Institute (of the Philippines).

irrig. irrigation.

IRS **1** *also* **i.r.s.** independent rear suspension (of a car). **2** information retrieval system *computers.* **3** infrared star (with a number): *IRS-16.* **4** Internal Revenue Service (of U.S. Department of the Treasury). **5** *also* **I.R.S.** International Rorschach Society.

IRT Interborough Rapid Transit (part of New York City subway system).

IRTS International Radio and Television Society.

IRU **1** international radium unit. **2** International Road Transport Union.

IRV inspiratory reserve volume (of the lungs).

IS **1** independent school, esp. in combination: *IS3; ISA = Independent School Association.* **2** information science, also in combination: *ISAD = Information Science and Automation Division.* **3** information service. **4** information system. **5** insertion sequence (followed by a number) *genetics: IS 1.* **6 a** Inspection Service (of U.S. Internal Revenue Service). **b** Investigation Service (of the Canadian Post Office). **7** *also* **I.S.** intercostal space *medicine.* **8** *also* **I.S.** intermediate school (followed by a number): *IS 102.* **9** internal shield *electronics.* **10** *also* **I.S.** Irish Society. **11** Island (in postal address). **12** secondary input *electronics.*

Is. **1** *also* **Isa.** Isaiah (book of the Old Testament). **2 a** Islam. **b** Islamic. **3** *also* **is.** island, isle. **4 a** Israel. **b** Israeli.

ISA **1** Independent Schools Association. **2** Instrument Society of America. **3** International Society of Appraisers. **4** International Sociological Association. **5** International Standards Association (Basel). **6** International Standard Atmosphere: *ISA Conditions.*

ISAB Institute for the Study of Animal Behavior.

ISAM indexed sequential access method *computers.*

I.S.A.P.C. or **ISAPC** Incorporated Society of Authors, Playwrights, and Composers.

ISAS Institute of Space and Aeronautical Science (responsible for Japanese scientific satellites).

i.s.b. or **ISB** independent sideband *electronics.*

ISBA Incorporated Society of British Advertisers.

ISBB International Society for Bioclimatology and Biometeorology.

ISBD international standard bibliographic description, in cataloging.

ISBN International Standard Book Number (for distinguishing titles, esp. in ordering books and in cataloging).

ISC 1 a Inter-American Society of Cardiology. **b** International Society of Cardiology. **2** International Seismology Center. **3** International Society of Chemotherapy.

ISCB International Society for Cell Biology.

ISCE *or* **I.S.C.E.** International Society for Christian Endeavor.

ISCEH International Society for Clinical and Experimental Hypnosis.

I.S.C.M. *or* **ISCM** International Society for Contemporary Music.

ISCO International Standard Classification of Occupations.

ISCP International Society of Clinical Pathology.

ISD 1 international standard depth. **2** international subscriber dialing (of telephones).

ISDN integrated-services digital network (communications network providing immediate connection for voice, music, video, and computer data transmission on public access lines).

ISE 1 Institution of Structural Engineers. **2** International Stock Exchange (of Great Britain).

ISEF International Science and Engineering Fair.

ISETU International Secretariat of Entertainment Trade Unions (agency for copyright protection).

ISF 1 industrial space facility. **2** International Science Foundation. **3** International Shipping Federation.

ISFA International Scientific Film Association.

ISG *or* **isg** imperial standard gallon.

ISGE International Society of Gastroenterology.

ISH International Society of Hematology.

ISHAM International Society for Human and Animal Mycology.

ISHS International Society for Horticultural Science.

ISI 1 Indian Standards Institute. **2** International Statistical Institute. **3** Iron and Steel Institute.

ISIC International Student Identity Card.

I.S.I.D. International Society of Interior Designers.

ISIM International Society of Internal Medicine.

ISIS (*sometimes pronounced* ī′sis) **1** Independent Schools Information Service. **2** International Satellites for Ionospheric Studies. **3** International Shipping Information Services.

Isl. *or* **isl.** island or isle.

ISLIC Israel Society of Special Libraries and Information Centers.

Isls. *or* **isls.** islands or isles.

ISLWF International Shoe and Leather Workers Federation.

ISM 1 a Incorporated Society of Musicians. **b** International Society for Musicology. **2** Institute of Sports Medicine. **3** interstellar matter. **4** *also* **I.S.M.** Jesus, Savior of the World. [Latin *Iesus Salvator Mundi*]

ISME International Society for Music Education.

ISO 1 independent sales organization. **2** Information Systems Office (of the Library of Congress). **3** International Science Organization. **4** International Standards Organization; IOS: *ISO metric threads; ISO film speed.*

iso *or* **iso. 1** isolated. **2** isotope.

isoln isolation.

isos. isosceles.

ISP 1 Intensively Supervised Probation *law.* **2** Inter-American Society of Psychology.

ISPA International Society for the Protection of Animals.

ISPHS International Society of Phonetic Science.

ISPO 1 International Society for Prosthetics and Orthotics. **2** International Statistical Programs Office.

ISQ *or* **isq** in status quo.

ISR 1 information storage and retrieval *computers.* **2** Institute for Social Research. **3** International Society of Radiology. **4** intersecting storage rings *physics.*

Isr. Israel, Israeli.

I.S.R.D. International Society for Rehabilitation of the Disabled.

ISRO Indian Space Research Organization.

ISS 1 inertia survey system. **2** Institute of Space Sciences. **3** International Seismological Summary. **4** International Space Station. **5** International Student Service. **6** ionosphere sounding satellite. **7** ion-scattering spectroscopy. **8** Islands (in postal address).

iss. issue (of a publication).

ISSA International Social Security Association (to promote improvement of social security programs).

ISSC International Social Science Council.

ISSN International Standard Serial Number (for periodical publications).

ISSS International Society of Soil Science.

IST 1 Indian Standard Time. **2** Information Sciences Technology. **3** insulin shock therapy *medicine.*

ISTA International Seed Testing Association.

ISTAT Italian Central Statistical Institute. [Italian *Instituto Centrale de Statistica*]

ISTD International Society of Tropical Dermatology.

Isth. *or* **isth.** isthmus.

ISTM *or* **I.S.T.M.** International Society for Testing Materials.

ISTP international solar terrestrial physics (program to study effects of solar radiation on the earth).

ISU 1 International Seamen's Union. **2** *also* **I.S.U** International Skating Union. **3** International Society of Urology.

ISV 1 independent software vendor *computers.* **2** International Scientific Vocabulary (technical and scientific vocabulary of the international community of scientists).

ISWG *or* **i.s.w.g.** Imperial Standard Wire Gauge (for wire in Great Britain).

IT 1 immunity test *medicine.* **2** *also* **I.T.** inclusive tour: *The IT business includes airlines, travel agents, and hotels.* **3** income tax: *IT form 1040.* **4** (formerly) Indian Territory (of the U.S.). **5 a** information technology. **b** information theory. **6** internal thread, in machining. **7** international tolerance *engineering.*

It. Italian, Italy.

it. item.

i.t. in transit.

ITA 1 *British* Independent Television Authority (now *IBA*). **2** International Trade Administration (of U.S. Department of Commerce).

ITAI Institute of Technical Authors and Illustrators.

Ital. Italian, Italy.

ital *or* **ital.** italic, italics.

I.T. & T. International Telephone and Telegraph Corporation.

ITAR International Traffic in Arms Regulations.

ITB 1 International Time Bureau. **2** Irish Tourist Board.

ITC 1 *also* **I.T.C.** Industrial Training Council. **2** *also* **I.T.C.** International Tin Council. **3** International Trade Commission. **4** *also* **ITCZ** Intertropical Convergence Zone (sometimes known as the equatorial front). **5** investment tax credit.

ITcal International Table calorie.

ITDA indirect target damage assessment.

ITE 1 Institute of Telecommunications Engineers. **2** Institute of Terrestrial Ecology. **3** Institute of Traffic Engineers.

ITER International Thermonuclear Experimental Reactor.

I.T.F. 1 International Tennis Federation. **2** International Trade Federations. **3** International Transport Workers' Federation. [German *Internationale Transportarbeiter Föderation*] **4** intertropical front *meteorology.*

ITFS Instructional Television Fixed Service.

ITI 1 International Technical Institute. **2** *also* **I.T.I.** International Theater Institute.

itin. itinerary.

Itl. Italian.

ITMA Institute of Trade Mark Agents.

ITN Independent Television News (international news service of Great Britain).

ITO 1 India Tourist Office. **2** *also* **I.T.O.** International Trade Organization.

ITS 1 integrated trajectory system. **2** Intermarket Trading System (of securities) *finance.* **3** International Trade Secretariats (an organization of international trade unionism). **4** invitation to send (of a message) *computers.*

ITT 1 insulin tolerance test. **2** International Telephone and Telegraph Corporation.

I.T.T.F. *or* **ITTF** International Table Tennis Federation.

ITTO International Tropical Timber Organization (of the UN).

ITU 1 International Telecommunications Union (of the UN). **2** *also* **I.T.U.** International Typographical Union.

ITV 1 *also* **I.T.V.** Independent Television (in Great Britain). **2** Industrial Television (system used typically for deep sea exploration and salvage, medical instruction, combating shoplifters). **3** instructional television. **4** instrumented test vehicle.

IU *or* **I.U. 1** immunizing unit. **2** instrument unit (as of a space

vehicle). **3** international unit *medicine.* **4** interval of uncertainty *psychology.*

I.U.A. *or* **IUA** International Union of Architects.

IUAES International Union of Anthropological and Ethnological Sciences.

IUAPPA International Union of Air Pollution Prevention Associations.

IUB International Union of Biochemistry.

IUBCTW International Union of Bakery, Confectionery, and Tobacco Workers.

IUBS International Union of Biological Sciences.

IUC International Union of Chemistry.

IUCN International Union for Conservation of Nature and Natural Resources.

IUCr International Union of Crystallography.

IUCSTP Inter-Union Commission on Solar Terrestrial Physics.

IUD 1 Industrial Union Department (research department of the AFL-CIO). **2** intrauterine device (prevents conception).

IUE 1 International Ultraviolet Explorer (satellite). **2** *also* **I.U.E.** International Union of Electrical Workers (now formally known as International Union of Electronic, Electrical, Technical, Salaried, and Machine Workers).

IUF International Union of Food and Allied Workers Associations.

IUFRO International Union of Forest Research Organizations.

IUGG International Union of Geodesy and Geophysics.

IUGS International Union of Geological Sciences.

IUHPS International Union of the History and Philosophy of Science.

I.U.L.A. International Union of Local Authorities.

IUMMSW International Union of Mine, Mill, and Smelter Workers.

IUNS International Union of Nutritional Sciences.

IUOE International Union of Operating Engineers.

IUOPAB International Union of Pure and Applied Biophysics.

IUOTO International Union of Official Travel Organizations.

IUPA International Union of Police Associations.

IUPAC International Union of Pure and Applied Chemistry.

IUPAP International Union of Pure and Applied Physics.

IUPS International Union of Physiological Sciences.

I.U.S. International Union of Students.

IUSP International Union of Scientific Psychology.

IUSSI International Union for the Study of Social Insects.

IUTAM International Union of Theoretical and Applied Mechanics.

IV 1 independent variable *statistics.* **2** initial velocity. **3** *also* **I.V.** intravenous, intravenously, also in combination: *IVIG = intravenous immunoglobulin.*

i.V. acting for. [German *in Vollmacht*]

i.v. 1 increased value. **2** initial velocity. **3** intravenous, intravenously. **4** invoice value. **5** under the word. [Latin *in verbo* or *in voce*]

IVA Value Added Tax; VAT. [Spanish *impuesto de valor agregado*]

IVCD intraventricular conduction delay (heart blockage).

IVF in vitro fertilization.

IVI incremental velocity indicator (of a rocket).

IVOX intravenous oxygenator (an implant that acts as an artificial lung when connected to an oxygen supply).

IVP intravenous pyelogram (X-ray picture of the kidneys and bladder done with dye).

IVR international vehicle registration.

I.V.S. *or* **IVS** International Voluntary Service (volunteer work on social welfare programs).

IVT intravehicular transfer (in space vehicles).

IVU intravenous urography *medicine*.

IW 1 index word. **2** indirect waste. **3** *also* **i.w.** inside width or diameter. **4** *also* **I.W.** Isle of Wight. **5** *also* **i.w.** isotopic weight.

IWA 1 Inland Waterways Association. **2** Institute of World Affairs. **3** International Wheat Agreement. **4** International Woodworkers of America.

IWC 1 *also* **I.W.C.** International Whaling Commission. **2** International Wheat Council.

IWP Indicative World Plan (for the development of agriculture).

IWS International Wool Secretariat.

IWSA International Water Supply Association.

IWW *or* **I.W.W.** Industrial Workers of the World (early radical labor organization known as the "wobblies").

IWY International Women's Year.

IX 1 ion exchange *chemistry*. **2** *also* **I.X.** Jesus Christ. [Greek Ιησους Χριστος; in the Greek alphabet χ represents a sound equated with English *ch*, as in *Christ* and is so transliterated]

IYHF International Youth Hostels Federation.

I.Y.R.U. International Yacht Racing Union.

izd. *or* **Izd.** edition. [Russian *izdanie*]

Izdat. publisher. [Russian *izdatel*]

J

J *I an abbreviation for:* **1** jack (connecting plug or playing card). **2** Jacobean (referring to arts and culture in the time of James I of Great Britain, 1603–1625). **3** Jacobian *mathematics* (in allusion to German mathematician Karl G. J. Jacobi, 1804–1851). **4** Jamaica, Jamaican, esp. in combination: *J$ = Jamaica dollar*. **5** January. **6** *also* **J.** Japan, esp. in combination: *JA = Japan Association*. **7** jet, esp. in combination: *JP = jet propulsion*. **8** *also* **J.** John or James. **9** Jordan, Jordanian, esp. in combination: *JD = Jordanian dinar*. **10** *also* **J.** Journal, esp. in combination: *WSJ = Wall Street Journal*. **11** *also* **J.** Judge, esp. in combination: *J.Prob. = Judge of Probate; Hon. David Franklin, J.* **12** July. **13** junction *electronics, communication*. **14** June. **15** *also* **J.** Justice, esp. in combination: *J.P. = Justice of the Peace*. **16** juvenile (in library cataloging). **17** *also* **J.** law, laws, in combination: *J.C.D. = Doctor of Canon Law*. [Latin *juris*]
II a symbol for: **1** action variable *physics*. **2** angular momentum *physics*. **3** curve on a graph showing the relationship between dropping currency value and trade deficits: *J-curve*. **4** electric current density. **5** gram-equivalent weight. **6** intensity, esp. radiant or emissive intensity (of light, sound, energy or power) *astronomy, physics*. **7** joule (unit of work) *physics*. **8** J particle *physics*. **9** Kansas City (branch in the Federal Reserve regional banking system, found esp. on dollar bills). **10** magnetic polarization *physics, electronics*. **11** (formerly) mechanical equivalent of heat (now specific heat capacity of water) *physics*. **12** moment of inertia *physics*. **13** tenth of a series (though often omitted in a series). ▶See usage note at I.

J- jet engine: *J-50*.

j *I an abbreviation for:* **1** jet *engineering*. **2** jewels *horology*. *II a symbol for:* **1** imaginary number $\sqrt{-1}$ (square root of minus one). **2** joule (unit of work) *physics*. **3** one; 1 (medieval Roman numeral, used esp. in prescriptions to mark the end of a series of i's standing for one: *iij*). ▶See usage note at I. **4** tenth of a series (though often omitted in a series).

JA 1 Japan Association. **2** *also* **J.A.** *or* **J/A** joint account *commerce*. **3** joint agent. **4** *also* **J.A. a** Judge Advocate. **b** Justice of Appeal. **5** Junior Achievement. **6** Yearbook for American Studies (publication). [German *Jahrbuch für Amerikastudien*]

Ja January.

J.A.A. Japan Aeronautic Association.

jaarg. annual (volume, supplement, edition). [Dutch *jaargang*]

JAC Junior Association of Commerce.

Jac. Jacobean *or* Jacobus (in reference to laws, furniture style, etc., dating from the reigns of the English kings James I and II).

JACM *Journal of the Association for Computing Machinery*.

JACS *Journal of the American Chemical Society*.

JADB Joint Air Defense Board *military*.

JAEC Japan Atomic Energy Commission.

JAERI Japan Atomic Energy Research Institute.

JAFC Japan Atomic Fuel Corporation.

JAG or **J.A.G.** Judge Advocate General.

Jahrg. annual publication. [German *Jahrgang*]

JAIEG Joint Atomic Information Exchange Group.

Jam. 1 Jamaica. **2** James (figure in the New Testament; also a disparaged abbreviation for *Jas.*, the book of the New Testament).

JAMA (*sometimes pronounced* jam'ə) Journal of the American Medical Association.

JAN joint Army-Navy (usually in supply specifications).

Jan. or **Jan** January.

jan. janitor (now usually referred to as custodian).

j. & w.o. jettison and washing overboard *commerce, insurance.*

JANET (jan'ət) Joint Academic Network (used by academic institutions in Great Britain) *computers.*

JAP (*pronounced* jap) or **J.A.P.** Jewish American Princess (used disparagingly to refer to a rich or spoiled Jewish girl or woman).

Jap. 1 Japan. **2** *also* **Japan.** Japanese.

jap. japanned (finished with a hard, glossy varnish).

JAPC or **JAPAC** Japan Atomic Power Company.

jar. jargon.

JAS Jamaica Agricultural Society.

Jas. James (esp. a book of the New Testament).

JATCRU Joint Air Traffic Control Radar Unit.

JATO jet-assisted takeoff (rockets used to provide extra power to piston-engine planes at takeoff).

jaund. jaundice.

Jav. 1 Javanese. **2** javelin.

JB 1 *also* **J.B.** Bachelor of Law. [Latin *Jurum Baccalaureus*] **2** junction box (used in blueprints and diagrams of electrical construction).

JBC Jamaica Broadcasting Corporation.

JC 1 *also* **J.C.** Jesus Christ. **2 a** *also* **J.C.** Julius Caesar (Roman emperor). **b** Julius Caesar (play by Shakespeare). **3** member of a local Junior Chamber of Commerce. **4** *also* **J.C.** British Justice Clerk. **5** juvenile court.

Jc. Junction, *esp. in place names: White River Jc.*

JCAE Joint Committee on Atomic Energy.

JCAH Joint Commission on Accreditation of Hospitals, usually referred to as **JCAHO** Joint Commission on Accreditation of Healthcare Organizations.

J.C.B. or **JCB 1** Bachelor of Canon Law. [Latin *Juris Canonici Baccalaureus*] **2** Bachelor of Civil Law. [Latin *Juris Civilis Baccalaureus*]

JCC 1 Jewish Community Center. **2** Joint Communications Center. **3** Junior Chamber of Commerce.

J.C.D. or **JCD 1** Doctor of Canon Law. [Latin *Juris Canonici Doctor*] **2** Doctor of Civil Law. [Latin *Juris Civilis Doctor*]

JCEE Joint Council on Economic Education.

JCEWS Joint Command, Control, and Electronic Warfare School.

JCI Junior Chamber (of Commerce) International.

JCL 1 Job Control Language *computers.* **2** *also* **J.C.L.** Licentiate in Canon Law. [Latin *Juris Canonici Licentiatus*]

JC of C Junior Chamber of Commerce.

JCP Japan Communist Party.

JCRC Jewish Community Relations Council.

JCRR Joint Commission on Rural Reconstruction.

JCS Joint Chiefs of Staff.

JCSOS Joint and Combined Staff Officer School.

JCT Junction (in postal address).

jct. or **jctn.** junction.

JC virus a slow virus that causes progressive multifocal leukoencephalopathy (named for the first patient diagnosed as having this virus).

JCWI Joint Council for the Welfare of Immigrants, *esp. in Great Britain.*

JD 1 *also* **J.D. a** Doctor of Jurisprudence. [Latin *Juris Doctor*] **b** Doctor of Laws. [Latin *Jurum Doctor*] **2** Jordan dinar (monetary unit of Jordan). **3** *also* **J.D.** Julian Day (used esp. to determine the interval in days between two observations) *astronomy.* **4** Junior Deacon. **5** jury duty. **6** Justice Department (U.S. Department of Justice). **7 a** *also* **j.d.** juvenile delinquency. **b** *also* **J.D.** juvenile delinquent.

jd joined.

JDA Japan Defense Agency.

JDB Japan Development Bank.

JDC Joint Distribution Committee.

JDL or **J.D.L. 1** Jewish Defense League. **2** job descriptor language.

JDS job data sheet.

Je June.

JEA joint export agent.

JEC Joint Economic Committee (of U.S. House and Senate).

JEDEC Joint Electron Device Engineering Council.

JEMC Joint Engineering Management Conference.

JEN Committee on Nuclear Energy. [Spanish *Junta de Energía Nuclear*]

Jep (*pronounced* jep) jeopardy.

Jer. 1 Jeremiah (book of the Old Testament). **2** Jersey. **3** Jerusalem.

JERC Joint Electronic Research Committee.

JES job entry subsystem.

Jes. Jesus.

JESA Japan Engineering Standards Association.

JET Joint European Torus (tokamak experiment to produce energy by fusion of deuterium and tritium).

JETEC Joint Electron Tube Engineering Council.

JETRO Japan External Trade Organization.

Jew. Jewish.

jew. jewelry.

JFET junction field-effect transistor.

JFK John Fitzgerald Kennedy: **a** U.S. President (1961–1963). **b** major airport in New York City.

JFM Young World Federalists. [French *Jeunesses Fédéralistes Mondiales*]

JFRCA Japanese Fisheries Resources Conservation Association.

JFS Japan Fishery Society.

Jg. 1 annual (volume, supplement, edition). **2** vintage, esp. of wine. [German *Jahrgang*]

jg. *or* **j.g.** junior grade, in combination: *Lieut.(j.g.).*

JGA juxtaglomerular apparatus (near the kidney, secreting renin).

JGE *Journal of General Education.*

J.G.T.C. Junior Girls' Training Corps.

J.G.W. Junior Grand Warden, in Masonry.

JH juvenile hormone *biochemistry.*

Jh. century. [German *Jahrhundert*]

JHA job hazard analysis.

JHI *Journal of the History of Ideas.*

JHS *or* **J.H.S. 1** Jesus, Savior of Men (see *IHS*). **2** Junior High School, usually followed by a number: *JHS 285 at Beverly Road and Ralph Avenue.*

JHVH *or* **JHWH** the Tetragrammaton (a complex of four consonant letters applied to the sacred Hebrew name for Jehovah).

J.I.B. 1 *also* **JIB** Joint Information Bureau (news pool for reporters covering a military operation). **2** *British* Joint Intelligence Bureau.

J.I.C. 1 Joint Industrial Council. **2** *also* **JIC** Joint Intelligence Center. **3** *also* **JIC** Joint Intelligence Committee (of U.S. House and Senate).

JICST Japan Information Center of Science and Technology.

JIM Japan Institute of Metals.

JINS (*pronounced* jinz) Juvenile In Need of Supervision *law, social work.*

JIRA *or* **J.I.R.A.** Japan Industrial Robot Association.

JIS Japan Industrial Standard.

JIT 1 job instruction training. **2** just in time (a computer inventory system to minimize accumulation of parts needed in manufacturing).

JJ. 1 Judges (in referring to arbiters of the law or a book of the Old Testament). **2** Justices.

JKT job knowledge test.

jkt. jacket.

Jl 1 *also* **Jl.** Journal. **2** July.

JLA Jewish Librarians Association.

JLP Jamaica Labour Party.

JMA 1 Japan Medical Association. **2** Japan Meteorological Agency.

JMD Justice Management Division (of U.S. Department of Justice).

J.M.J. Jesus, Mary, and Joseph (Holy Family).

J.M.P. jen min piao or yuan (the People's Money of China).

JMSDF Japan Maritime Self-Defense Force.

JMT job methods training.

Jn. 1 John: **a** esp. King John (play by Shakespeare). **b** book of the New Testament. **2** Junction, in place names.

jn 1 join. **2** junction, on maps and in electrical wiring diagrams.

Jnc. Junction, in place names.

JND *or* **j.n.d.** just noticeable difference (in comparative tests) *psychology.*

JNF 1 Jewish National Fund. **2** Japan Nuclear Fuel.

Jnl. journal.

Jno. John (personal name or a book of the New Testament).

J.N.O.V. judgment notwithstanding verdict *law.* [English *judgment* + Latin *non obstante veredicto*]

JNR Japanese National Railways.

Jnr. *or* **jnr.** junior: *Henry Morgenthau, Jnr.*

jnt. *or* **jnt** joint: *jnt. stk. = joint stock.*

JNTO Japan National Tourist Organization.

JO 1 job order. **2** *also* **J.O.** junior officer. **3** Official Journal (recording business of government). [French *Journal Officiel*] **4** *also* **J.O.** ombudsman. [Swedish *justitieombudsmannen*]

Jo. 1 Joel (book of the Old Testament). **2** John (personal name or a book of the New Testament).

JOA joint operating agreement (permitting competing newspapers to combine production and business operations while maintaining separate newsrooms).

Jo. Bapt. John the Baptist.

JOC 1 joint operations center. **2** Young Christian Workers. [French *Jeunesse Ouvrière Chrétienne Internationale*]

joc. 1 jocose. **2** jocular.

JOD joint occupancy date.

JODC Japan Oceanographic Data Center.

Johan. Johannesburg, South Africa.

JOIDES Joint Oceanographic Institutions Deep Earth Sampling.

join. joinery.

Jon. 1 Jonah (book of the Old Testament). **2** *also* **Jona.** Jonathan.

Jos. 1 Joseph. **2** *also* **Josh.** Joshua (book of the Old Testament). **3** Josiah, esp. in the Bible.

Jour. Journal.

jour. 1 a journalism. **b** journalist. **2** journey. **3** journeyman.

JOVIAL Jules Own Version of the International Algorithmic Language (early computer language).

JP 1 a jet propulsion. **b** jet propellant (followed by a number designating the type of fuel): *JP-10.* **2** *also* **J.P.** Justice of the Peace.

J.P.C. 1 Joint Planning Council. **2** Joint Production Council.

J.P.G. Joint Planning Group.

JPL Jet Propulsion Laboratories (at California Institute of Technology).

Jpn. Japanese.

JPS Jewish Publication Society.

J.R. 1 Joint Resolution, esp. in combination: *H.J.R. = House (of Representatives) Joint Resolution.* **2** King James. [Latin *Jacobus Rex*]

Jr. 1 Journal. **2** *also* **Jr** *or* **jr.** Junior: *John Parker, Jr.* ▶**Jr.** is written after the name and only if the father is living. It should not be used without the Christian name or initials, but may be used with a title and initials (*Mr. J. A. Parker, Jr.,* not *Mr. Parker, Jr.*). **3** Juror.

jr. day. [French *jour*]

JRA Japanese Red Army (radical group originally based in Lebanon).

JRC 1 Joint Research Council (of the EC). **2** Junior Red Cross.

J.Res. Joint Resolution.

JS 1 Japan Society. **2** judgment summons *law.*

JSA job safety analysis.

JSC 1 Japan Science Council. **2** Johnson Space Center (of NASA at Houston, Texas). **3** joint stock company.

J.S.D. *or* **JSD** Doctor of Juristic Science, Doctor of the Science of Law. [Latin *Jurum Scientiae Doctor*]

JSP *or* **J.S.P.** Japan Socialist Party.

JSPS Japan Society for the Promotion of Science.

JSS joint services standard (for military procurement).

JST Japanese Standard Time.

JT Japan Times (newspaper).

Jt. *or* **jt.** joint: *jt. auth. = joint author.*

JTC joint technical committee.

JTCCCA *or* **JTC³A** Joint Tactical Command, Control, and Communications Agency.

JTF Joint Task Force.

Jth. Judith, esp. in the Bible.

JTIDS Joint Tactical Information Distribution System (providing integrated communication, navigation, and identification).

jtly. jointly.

JTPA Job Training Partnership Act (formerly CETA, 1982).

JTS job training standards.

JU *or* **j.u.** joint use.

Ju 1 June. **2** July.

J.U.D. *or* **JUD** Doctor of Both Canon and Civil Laws. [Latin *Juris Utriusque Doctor*]

Jud. 1 Judges (book of the Old Testament). **2** Judith (book of the Apocrypha and the Douay Bible).

jud. 1 a a judge. **b** judgment. **2 a** judicial. **b** judiciary.

Judg. Judges (book of the Old Testament).

judgt. judgment.

JUG Joint Users Group (computer users who have a common interest).

Jul. 1 Julian. **2** July.

Jul. Caes. *or* **Jul. C.** Julius Caesar (play by Shakespeare).

Jun. 1 June. **2** Junior.

Junc. *or* **junc.** Junction.

Jup Jupiter (planet).

jur. juridical.

Jur. D. Doctor of Law. [Latin *Juris Doctor*]

Juris. 1 *also* **jurisd.** jurisdiction. **2** *also* **jurisp.** jurisprudence.

Jus. Justice.

J.U.S.E. Japan Union of Scientists and Engineers.

Just. 1 Justice. **2** Justinian.

Juv. 1 Juvenal (Roman poet, 60–130 AD). **2** *also* **juv.** juvenile, esp. in cataloging books and in legal work: *Juv. Ct. = Juvenile Court.*

jux *or* **jux.** juxtaposition.

J.V. *or* **JV 1** joint venture *commerce.* **2** *also* **j.v.** junior varsity *sports.*

J.W. *or* **JW** Jehovah's Witnesses.

J.W.B. *or* **JWB** Jewish Welfare Board.

jwlr. jeweler.

J.W.V. *or* **JWV** Jewish War Veterans.

JX Jesus Christ. [the *X* is a confused transliteration of Greek χ (chi) in Χριστος from the Middle Ages]

K

K *I an abbreviation for:* **1** calends. [Latin *kalendae*] **2** carat, karat: *14K g = 14 carat gold.* **3** cathode, kathode. **4** keel. **5** *also* **K.** Kelvin scale; kelvin. **6** Kenya, esp. in combination: *KSh. = Kenya shilling.* **7** kicker *football.* **8 a** kilo- (one thousand or 10³): *KEV = kilo electron volts.* **b** kilobyte (1024 in the binary system) *computers.* **9** kilogram. **10** kina (monetary unit of Papua, New Guinea). **11** Kindergarten: *K-12 = Kindergarten through 12th grade.* **12** kinetic, as in kinetic energy. **13** *also* **K.** King, esp. in cards, checkers, chess. **14** Kings

(books of the Old Testament, in the Douay version including Samuel): *IK and IIK = One and Two,* or *First and Second, Kings.* **15** *also* **K.** kip (monetary unit of Laos). **16** *also* **K.** or **K** *or* к Kirkpatrick (used with a number in cataloging music of Domenico Scarlatti). **17** kitchen, also in combination: *EIK = eat-in-kitchen; K&B = kitchen and bath.* **18** *also* **K.** Knight, esp. in combination: *K.C.B. = Knight Commander of the Order of the Bath.* **19** knit (direction in knitting). **20** *also* **K.** or к Köchel (used with a number in cataloging music of Mozart):

K.551, *"The Jupiter Symphony."* **21** kopeck (monetary unit of Russia). **22** kosher (used as a food label). **23** Kuwait, esp. in combination: *KD = Kuwait Dinar.* **24** kwacha (monetary unit of Malawi and Zambia). **25** kyat (monetary unit of Burma). *II a symbol for:* **1** atomic shell of two maximum electrons per shell. **2** bulk modulus *physics.* **3** calcium in the solar spectrum *astronomy.* **4** calyx *botany.* **5** constant, factor, or quantity, as in: **a** Boltzmann's constant. **b** constant or continuous *astronomy.* **c** dielectric constant. **d** equilibrium constant *chemistry.* **e** Kerr constant. **f** solar absorption index. **6** curvature *physics.* **7** Dallas (branch in the Federal Reserve regional banking system, found esp. on dollar bills). **8** eleventh of a series (tenth when *J* is omitted). **9** luminous efficiency *physics.* **10** potassium (chemical element). [Latin *kalium*] **11** red star of maximum intensity of metal *astronomy.* **12** rotational quantum number *physics.* **13** smoke *meteorology.* **14** strikeout *baseball.* **15** two hundred fifty; 250 (medieval Roman numeral).

K- kayak: *K-4.*

°K formerly, degrees Kelvin (now *kelvins*).

K-9 canine: *K-9 Corps* (a police unit using dogs).

k *I an abbreviation for:* **1** *also* **k.** capacity *electricity.* **2** *also* **k.** carat, karat. **3** cathode, kathode. **4** *also* **k.** keg. **5** key. **6 a** kilo- (one thousand or 10^3): *kw. = kilowatt.* **b** kilogram. **c** kilobyte (1024 in the binary system) *computers.* **7** knit (direction in knitting). **8** *also* **k.** knot (nautical unit of speed). *II a symbol for:* **1** circular wave number *physics.* **2** coefficient, constant, factor, or quantity, as in: **a** Boltzmann's constant. **b** coefficient of alienation *statistics.* **c** compressibility factor *physics.* **d** force constant *physics.* **e** multiplication or reproduction factor (of a chain reaction). **f** per unit of time, area, etc. **g** torsion constant *physics.* **h** velocity, esp. reaction velocity. **3** cold air mass *meteorology.* **4** eleventh of a series (tenth when *j* is omitted). **5** magnetic susceptibility *physics.* **6** radius gyration *physics.* **7** thermal conductivity.

K.A. King of Arms.

Ka **1** cathode, kathode. **2** *also* **Ka.** Company. [Finnish *Komppania*]

kA kiloampere.

ka. cathode, kathode.

KADU Kenya African Democratic Union (former political party).

kal. calends. [Latin *kalendae*]

KAMI Kesatuan Aksi Mahasiswa Indonesia (political party).

Kan. *or* **Kans.** Kansas.

KANU Kenya African National Union (the legal political party of Kenya).

kao. kaolin (clay used in porcelain).

Kap. **1** chapter. [German *Kapitel*] **2** *also* **kap.** chapter. [Danish, Norwegian, Swedish *kapitel*]

KAPI Kesatuan Aksi Peladjar Indonesia (political party).

Kar. Karachi, Pakistan.

Kas. Kansas.

Kash. Kashmir.

Kath. Katharine.

KAU Kenya African Union.

KB **1** *also* **KB.** double bass *music.* [German *Kontrabass*] **2** keyboard, esp. in combination: *KBM = keyboard monitor.* **3** kilobyte *computers.* **4** *also* **K.B.** King's Bench: *K.B.C. = King's Bench Court.* **5** King's Bishop *chess.* **6** Knight Bachelor. **7** Knight of the Order of the Bath.

Kb **1** kilobit *computers.* **2** knit into back of stitch, in knitting.

kb **1** *also* **kbar** kilobar *meteorology.* **2** kilobase *genetics.* **3** kilobit *computers.*

K.B.E *or* **KBE** Knight Commander of the Order of the British Empire.

K.B.I. *or* **KBI** Kansas Bureau of Investigation.

Kbit kilobit *computers.*

KBP King's Bishop's Pawn *chess.*

kbps *or* **kb/s** kilobits per second.

K byte kilobyte *computers,* also in combination: *K byte/S = kilobytes per second.*

KC **1** *also* **K.C.** Kansas City, also in reference to the Kansas City Board of Trade. **2** Kennel Club: *AKC = American Kennel Club.* **3** kilocycle. **4** *also* **K.C.** King's Counsel. **5** *also* **K.C.** Knight Commander: *KCB.* **6** *also* **K.C.** Knights of Columbus (Roman Catholic fraternal society).

Kč *or* **Kc** koruna (Czech coin). [Czech *koruna česk*]

kc. **1** kilocurie. **2** *also* **Kc.** kilocycle (now *kHz* kilohertz), also in combination: *kc/s = kilocycles per second.*

Kcal. *or* **kcal** Kelvin calorie (temperature).

kcal. kilocalorie.

K.C.B. *or* **KCB** Knight Commander of the Order of the Bath.

kCi kilocurie.

KCIA Korean Central Intelligence Agency.

K.C.I.E. Knight Commander of the Order of the Indian Empire.

K.C.M.G. Knight Commander of the Order of Saint Michael and Saint George.

kcps *or* **kc/s** *or* **kcs** kilocycles per second.

KCS KCS Industries (a printer of U.S. postage stamps).

Kčs koruna (coin of former Czechoslovakia). [Czech *koruna československà*]

K.C.S.I. Knight Commander of the Star of India.

K.C.V.O. Knight Commander of the Royal Victorian Order.

KD **1** kiln-dried (of lumber). **2** Kingdom of Denmark. [Danish *Kongeriget Danmark*] **3 a** knock down, in boxing. **b** *also* **kd.** knocked down *commerce.* **4** Kuwaiti dinar (monetary unit of Kuwait).

kd killed.

K-Day Kuwait Day (commencement of hostilities in the Gulf War in 1991).

KDCL knocked down, in carloads *commerce.*

KDF knocked down flat *commerce.*

KDLCL knocked down, in less than carloads *commerce.*

KDM Royal Danish Navy. [Danish *Kongelige Danske Marine*]

Kdm kingdom.

KdN Kingdom of the Netherlands. [Dutch *Koninkrijk der Nederlanden*]

KE kinetic energy, also in combination: *KEW = kinetic energy weapon.*

KEAS *or* **keas.** knots equivalent airspeed.

Ken. 1 *also* **Kens** Kensington (esp. area of London). **2** Kentucky.

KEPZ Kaohsiung Export Processing Zone, Taiwan (for firms manufacturing products for re-export).

Ker. Kerry County, Ireland.

KEV *or* **keV** *or* **kev** kiloelectron volt.

KG 1 *also* **K.G.** Knight of the Order of the Garter. **2** limited partnership *commerce.* [German *Kommanditgesellschaft*]

kg 1 keg. **2** *also* **kg.** *or* **kG** kilogauss. **3** *also* **kg.** kilogram.

K.G.B. *or* **KGB** Committee of State Security (Russian civilian intelligence service). [Russian *Komitet Gosudarstvennoj Bezopasnosti*]

K.G.C. *or* **KGC 1** Knight Grand Commander. **2** Knight of the Golden Circle. **3** Knight of the Grand Cross.

kg. cal. *or* **kg-cal** kilogram-calorie.

kgf kilogram-force (unit of force used for calibration of most specific instruments).

kgm *or* **kgm. 1** kilogram. **2** *also* **kg. m.** *or* **kg-m** kilogram-meter.

kgps kilograms per second.

kgr. kilograin.

KGS ketogenic steroid *medicine.*

K.G.V. Knight of Gustavus Vasa (of Sweden).

KHN Knoop hardness number (of ceramics).

kHz *or* **kHz.** kilohertz (formerly *kc*).

Ki. Kings (two books of the Protestant Old Testament or four books of the Douay Version).

ki. kitchen.

KIA killed in action, also in combination: *KIA/BNR = killed in action, body not recovered.*

KIAS *or* **kias.** knots indicated airspeed.

kid. kidney.

K.i.H. Kaiser-i-Hind (a medal formerly given by the British for service in India; the British monarch as ruler of India was styled as such).

kil. 1 kilderkin (unit of measure). **2** kilogram. **3** kilometer.

Kild. Kildare County, Ireland.

kild. kilderkin (unit of measure).

Kilk. Kilkenny County, Ireland.

kilo. 1 *also* **kilo** (kē′lō′) kilogram. **2** kilometer.

kilog. kilogram.

kilol. kiloliter.

kilom. kilometer.

kilovar kilovolt-ampere reactive (hour).

kind. kindergarten.

King. *or* **Kingd.** Kingdom.

kip kilopound (1000 pounds).

KISS Keep It Simple, Stupid (a rule of procedure, said to have developed in the U.S. Army).

kit. *or* **kitch** kitchen, in advertisement.

KJ knee jerk *medicine.*

kj. *or* **kJ** kilojoule.

K.J.V. King James Version (of the Bible).

KKE *or* **K.K.E.** Communist Party of Greece. [Greek *Kommunistiko Komma Ellados*]

KKK *or* **K.K.K.** Ku Klux Klan.

K.Kt. *or* **KKt** King's Knight *chess.*

K.Kt.P. *or* **KKtP** King's Knight's Pawn *chess.*

kl. *or* **kl** kiloliter.

KLH 1 *also* **klh** keyhole limpet hemocyanin *biology.* **2** *also* **K.L.H.** Knight of the Legion of Honor (of France).

KLM Royal Dutch Airlines. [Dutch *Koninklijke Luchtvaart Maatschappij*]

K.M. Knight of Malta.

Km. *or* **Km** Kingdom.

kM kilomega (10^9 or 1 billion).

km *or* **km.** kilometer.

kMc *or* **kmc** *or* **kmc.** kilomegacycle, gigacycle (one billion cycles).

km/h kilometers per hour.

KMO Kobe Marine Observatory.

km/s kilometers per second.

KMT Kuomintang (Chinese Nationalist party, now restricted to Taiwan).

kmw *or* **kMw** kilomegawatt (one billion watts), also in combination: *kmwh = kilomegawatt-hour.*

KN 1 King's Knight *chess.* **2** Norway. [Norwegian *Kongeriket Norge*]

kn 1 knot (nautical unit of speed). **2** *also* **kn. a** krona (Swedish coin). **b** króna (Icelandic coin). **c** krone (Danish and Norwegian coin).

KNM Royal Norwegian Navy. [Norwegian *Kongelige Norske Marine*]

KNP King's Knight's Pawn *chess.*

Knt. 1 Knight. **2** Knight Bachelor.

KNUFNS Kampuchean National United Front for National Salvation (Vietnam-supported political party in Kampuchea or Cambodia).

knwldg. knowledge.

KO 1 kickoff *football.* **2** *also* **K.O.** *or* **k.o.** (kā′ō′) knockout *boxing.*

K. of C. Knights of Columbus (Roman Catholic fraternal society).

K. of L. Knights of Labor (early labor organization in U.S.).

K. of P. Knights of Pythias (fraternal charitable organization in U.S. and Canada).

Komintern (kom′in tèrn′). *See* **Comintern.**

Komp. Company. [German *Kompanie*]

Kor. 1 *also* **Kor** the Koran. **2 a** Korea. **b** Korean.

KP 1 King's Pawn *chess.* **2** *also* **K.P.** kitchen police: *K.P. duty.* **3** Knights of Pythias (fraternal charitable organization in U.S.

and Canada). **4** knotty pine (of boards or furniture made of such boards).

kPa kilopascal (unit of pressure in metric system).

kpc kiloparsec (unit in computing star distance).

KPD German Communist Party. [German *Kommunistische Partei Deutschlands*]

KPH *or* **kph** kilometers per hour.

Kpr. keeper.

KPU Kenya People's Union (former political party).

Kq line squall *meteorology*.

KR 1 Kenyon Review (publication). **2** Khmer Rouge. **3** King's Rook *chess*.

Kr *I an abbreviation for:* **1** krona (monetary unit of Sweden). **2** krone (monetary unit of Norway).
II a symbol for: krypton (chemical element).

kr 1 kilorad (unit of radiation). **2** *also* **kr. a** króna (monetary unit of Iceland). **b** krone (monetary unit of Denmark). **c** krone (former coin of Germany and Austria).

K-ration emergency high-concentration field ration. [named after Ancel *Keys*, American nutritionist, consultant in World War II]

K.R.C. Knight of the Red Cross.

KREEP potassium, rare-earth elements, and phosphorus (components of lunar rock).

KRL knowledge representation language (programming language for an expert computer system).

KRP King's Rook's Pawn *chess*.

Krs kurus (Turkish coin).

KS 1 Kansas (Zip Code). **2** Kaposi's sarcoma (often a complication of AIDS) *medicine*. **3** *also* **K.S.** keep standing (of printing forms). **4** ketosteroid *medicine*. **5** Kingdom of Sweden. [Swedish *Konungariket Sverige*] **6** *also* **KS.** storm of drifting snow *meteorology*.

KSAM keyed sequential access method (direct access to computer files).

KSC Kennedy Space Center.

KSh. Kenya shilling (monetary unit of Kenya).

K.s.i. *or* **ksi** one thousand pounds (kip) per square inch.

KSM 1 Korean Service Medal. **2** Royal Swedish Navy. [Swedish *Kungliga Svenska Marinen*]

KSR keyboard send and receive (keyboard transmitter and receiver).

K.St.J. Knight of the Order of St. John of Jerusalem (Hospitalers, knights originally of a monastery in Jerusalem).

KT 1 *also* **K-T** *or* **K/T** Cretaceous-Tertiary (separate geologic periods, with particular reference to artifacts not absolutely attributable to one period). **2** *Scottish also* **K.T.** Knight of the Order of the Thistle. **3** *also* **K.T.** Knight Templar, Knight Templars (religious and military order that in late Middle Ages turned to banking).

Kt. 1 *also* **Kt** Knight *chess*. **2** Knight Bachelor.

kt 1 *also* **kt.** carat, karat. **2** *also* **kT.** kiloton. **3** knot (nautical unit of speed, also used to indicate wind speed).

KTA Kindergarten Teachers Association.

KTAS *or* **ktas.** knots true airspeed.

Kt. Bach. Knight Bachelor.

KTO Kuwait Theater of Operations (of the Gulf War, 1991).

Ku 1 kurchatovium (Russian name for chemical element 104). **2** Kurtosis (describing frequency distribution) *statistics*.

KUB kidney, ureter, bladder *medicine*.

Kuw. Kuwait.

KV *or* **K.V. 1** kilovolt (1000 volts). **2** Köchel catalog (used with a number in cataloging music of Mozart): *K.V. 551, "The Jupiter Symphony."* [German *Köchel Verzeichnis*]

kV *or* **kv.** kilovolt (1000 volts).

KVA *or* **kVA** *or* **kva** kilovolt-ampere.

kVAH *or* **kvah** kilovolt-ampere-hour.

kVAr *or* **kvar** kilovar (kilovolt-ampere reactive).

KVP *or* **kVp** *or* **kvp** kilovolt peak.

Kw. motor vehicle. [German *Kraftwagen*]

kW *or* **kw.** kilowatt.

KWAC Keyword and Context (form of computer-generated index with surrounding context).

kWe *or* **KWE** *or* **kwe** kilowatt electrical.

kWh *or* **KWH** *or* **kwh** kilowatt-hour.

kWhr *or* **kw-hr** *or* **kwhr.** kilowatt-hour.

KWIC Key Word in Context (form of index to documents within surrounding context).

KWIT Keyword in Title (form of computer-generated index by a keyword appearing in context of documents).

Kwl *or* **kwl** knowledge, esp. in advertising: *Kwl of French.*

KWOC Keyword out of Context (form of index to documents by keyword only).

kWt *or* **kwt** kilowatt thermal.

KY Kentucky (Zip Code).

Ky. Kentucky.

kybd keyboard.

Kyo Kyoto, Japan.

KZ *or* **kz** sandstorm or dust storm *meteorology*.

K-Z concentration camp, esp. referring to symptoms found in liberated prisoners: *K-Z syndrome.* [German *Konzentrationslager*]

Kz kwanza (monetary unit of Angola).

L

L *I an abbreviation for:* **1** *also* **L.** book. [Latin *liber*] **2** lactobacillus (bacteria that produces acid in milk). **3** *also* **L.** Lady. **4** *also* **L.** Lake. **5** *also* **L.** land. **6** Language: **a** esp. in combination: *ESL = English as a second language.* **b** magazine title, but Lg. preferred. **7** large, as in clothing sizes: *S, M, L, XL (extra large).* **8** last (as in price quoted of a stock) *finance.* **9** *also* **L.** late, in combination: *LGk. = Late Greek* (Greek from about 200 to 700 AD); *L.L. = Late Latin* (Latin from about 200 to 700 AD). **10** *also* **L.** Latin. **11** latitude. **12** *also* **L.** law, esp. in combination: *Yale L.J. = Yale Law Journal.* **13** *also* **L.** leaf (esp. of a book). **14** learner: *the L plate on a student driver's car.* **15** leave, leave at: *A11:42 L11:58.* **16** Lebanese: *L£ or LL = Lebanese pound.* **17** *also* **L.** left, such as left hand *music,* or left side of a stage *theater,* or left foot *dancing.* **18** lek (monetary unit of Albania). **19** lempira (monetary unit of Honduras). **20** length (span or distance). **21 a** leu (monetary unit of Romania). **b** lev (monetary unit of Bulgaria). **22** Liberal (a political party). **23** Libra *astrology.* **24** Libyan, in combination: *LD = Libyan dinar.* **25** *also* **L.** ligament *biology.* **26** light (illumination, shade, consistency, weight). **27** lilangeni (monetary unit of Swaziland). **28** *also* **L.** Linnean (of the binomial system of animal and esp. plant classification). **29** lira (monetary unit of Italy and Turkey): *LT = Turkish lira.* **30** local (esp. of a train schedule). **31** *also* **L.** London. **32** long *physics:* L-wave. **33** longitude (esp. in specialized application, such as mean longitude in orbit, in astronomy). **34** Longo (used in cataloging keyboard compositions of Domenico Scarlatti). **35** lost (of a game or record of play). **36** loti (monetary unit of Lesotho). **37 a** low *meteorology.* **b** *also* **L.** Low, esp. in combination *linguistics: LG = Low German.* **c** low, lowest (price quoted of a stock) *finance.* **38** *also* **L.** place. [Latin *locus*]
II a symbol for: **1** atomic shell of eight maximum electrons per shell. **2** drizzle *meteorology.* **3** electromagnetic radiance (esp. luminance, luminosity) *astronomy, physics.* **4** fifty; 50 (Roman numeral). **5** inductance (esp. self-inductance) *electricity.* **6** Lagrangian function (kinetic potential) *physics.* **7** latent heat *physics.* **8** *also* **L-** levo (levorotatory) *chemistry:* L-asparaginase = an enzyme of the levorotatory form of the amino acid asparagine. **9** lift *aeronautics.* **10** lithium (chemical element). **11** orbital angular momentum quantum number *physics.* **12** pound. [Latin *libra*] **13** relative heat *physics.* **14** San Francisco (branch in the Federal Reserve regional banking system, found esp. on dollar bills). **15** twelfth of a series (eleventh when *J* is omitted).

£ 1 pound (monetary unit of Cyprus, Egypt, Falkland Islands, Ireland, Lebanon, Sudan Republic, Syria, United Kingdom). **2** new shekel (monetary unit of Israel).

l *I an abbreviation for:* **1** *also* **l.** book. [Latin *liber,* Spanish *libro,* French *livre*] **2** *also* **l.** lake. **3** latitude. **4** *also* **l.** law. **5** *also* **l.** leaf (esp. of a book). **6** *also* **l.** leave (esp. in a timetable). **7** *also* **l.** left, in combination: *l.h. = left hand, music.* **8** length (span or distance). **9** *also* **l.** lightning *meteorology.* **10** *also* **l.** line. **11** *also* **l.** lira (monetary unit of Italy). **12** *also* **l.** liter (metric wet or dry measure of capacity). **13** local. **14** long. **15** longitude. **16** place. [Latin *locus*]
II a symbol for: **1** lambert (unit of brightness) *physics.* **2** levo (levorotatory) *chemistry.* **3** lumen (unit of light or luminous flux). **4** mean free path (distance a molecule of gas travels before colliding with another molecule). **5** twelfth of a series (eleventh when *j* is omitted).

l- 1 *also* **l-** levo (levorotatory) *chemistry:* l-glucose. **2** *also* **L-** left or levorotatory (of organic compounds having such an asymmetric configuration around carbon atoms).

LA 1 *also* **L.A. a** Latin America. **b** Latin American. **2** left atrium (of the heart). **3** *also* **L.A.** Legal Advisor. **4** *also* **L.A.** Legislative Assembly. **5** *also* **L/A** *or* **l/a** letter of advice *commerce.* **6** *also* **L/A** letter of authority *commerce, law.* **7** light alcohol or low alcohol (content in beer and, sometimes, wine). **8** lightning arrester. **9** Local Authority. **10** Los Angeles. **11** Louisiana (Zip Code). **12** low altitude, also in combination: *LAB = low-altitude bombing.*

La *I an abbreviation for:* **1** *also* **La.** lane (in a place name). **2** *also* **La.** Louisiana.
II a symbol for: lanthanum (chemical element).

la 1 *also* **l.a.** as directed *pharmaceutics.* [Latin *lege artis*] **2** *also* **la.** last (weight, esp. wool measure of 3900 pounds).

LAA 1 League of Advertising Agencies. **2** *also* **L.A.A.** Library Association of Australia. **3** Life Assurance Advertisers.

Lab. 1 Labor or Labour Party. **2** Laboratory. **3** Laborite, Labourite. **4** Labrador, also in combination: *Lab. Cur. = Labrador Current.*

lab. 1 label. **2** labor, laborer. **3** laboratory.

LABS low-altitude bombing system.

LAC 1 *also* **L.A.C.** law-abiding citizen. **2** leading aircraftsman (in RAF). **3** *also* **L.A.C.** Licentiate of the Apothecaries' Company. **4** linear aeronautical chart. **5** load accumulator *electronics.*

Lac the Lizard (constellation). [Latin *Lacerta*]

lac. 1 lacquer. **2** lactation.

LACE liquid air cycle engine (proposed for a spaceplane).

LACONIQ (lə kon'ik) laboratory computer on-line inquiry.

LACR low-altitude coverage radar.

LACW leading aircraftswoman (in RAF).

lad. ladder.

ladar *or* **LADAR** (lā'där) laser detection and ranging (laser radar).

Ladp. Ladyship.

LADR linear accelerator–driven reactor.

LAF French Academy. [French *L'Académie Française*]

LAFC Latin-American Forestry Commission.

LAFTA Latin Am Free Trade Association (now *LAIA* or *ALADI*).

Lag. Lagoon.

Lah. Lahore, Pakistan.

LAI 1 leaf area index (ratio of leaves of a plant or crop to soil available). **2** *also* **L.A.I.** Library Association of Ireland.

LAIA Latin American Integration Association; ALADI (economic union of Argentina, Bolivia, Brazil, Chile, Colombia, Ecuador, Paraguay, Peru, Uruguay, Venezuela, and Mexico).

LAK lymphokine activated killer (cell that attacks cancer cells, used in cancer treatment).

LAL Linear Accelerator Laboratory (in France).

L.A.M. 1 London Academy of Music. **2** *also* **LAM** Master of Liberal Arts. [Latin *Liberalium Artium Magister*]

Lam. 1 Lamarck (name of species) *biology*. **2** Lamentations (book of the Old Testament).

lam. 1 laminated. **2** lamination.

LAMCO Liberian, American, Swedish Mineral Corporation.

L.A.M.D.A. London Academy of Music and Dramatic Art.

LAMP Lunar Analysis and Mapping Program.

LAMPS light airborne multipurpose system.

LAMS launch acoustic measuring system.

LAMSAC Local Authorities Management Services and Computer Committee.

LAN 1 *also* **l.a.n.** local apparent noon, in navigation. **2** local area network (a system in which a series of computers, printers, and other devices are linked by telephone lines, as in an office or building).

LANAC laminar navigation, anticollision.

LANBY large automatic navigational buoy.

Lancs *or* **Lancs.** Lancashire or Lancaster County, England.

L & A light and accommodation (of the eye) *medicine*.

L & D 1 loans and discounts (of bank transactions). **2** loss and damage *insurance*.

Landsat (land′sat′) Land satellite (U.S. artificial satellite designed to gather data about the earth's natural resources).

lang. language.

LANL Los Alamos National Laboratory.

LANS local area networks (of computers).

LANTIRN (lan′tərn) low-altitude navigation and targeting infrared system (for night targeting location).

Lap. Lapland.

lap. laparotomy (surgical incision through the abdominal wall, esp. for examination).

LAR limit address register *computers*.

LARO Latin American Regional Office (of the UN Food and Agricultural Organization).

LARP local and remote printing *computers*.

LARR linear accelerator regenerator reactor (device to irradiate nuclear fuel).

laryngol. laryngology.

LAS 1 large astronomical satellite. **2** League of Arab States (a group of 22 Arab states including the PLO that promotes and protects the political interests of its members including the Arab Common Market). **3** *also* **L.A.S.** Legal Aid Society.

4 linear alkylate sulfonate (a biodegradable detergent). **5** *also* **L.A.S.** Lord Advocate of Scotland.

LASA 1 large aperture seismic array. **2** *also* **L.A.S.A.** Latin American Studies Association.

LASCR light-activated silicon-controlled rectifier.

LASCS light-activated silicon-controlled switch.

laser (lā′zər) light amplification by stimulated emission of radiation (device that produces a narrow beam of light of a single wavelength).

LASH lighter aboard ship (freighter with barge to transport cargo to shore).

LASO Latin American Solidarity Organization; OLAS.

LASP low-altitude space platform.

LAT *or* **l.a.t.** local apparent time.

Lat. 1 Latin. **2 a** Latvia. **b** Latvian.

lat. 1 latent, esp. in combination: *lat. ht.* = *latent heat.* **2** lateral. **3** latitude.

LATA Local Access and Transport Area (esp. of telephone communications).

LATCOM Latin American Common Market.

LATS long-acting thyroid stimulator (agent found in the blood of a hyperthyroid person).

Latv. 1 Latvia. **2** Latvian.

L.A.U.K. *or* **LAUK** Library Association of the United Kingdom.

laun. launched.

LAV 1 light armored vehicle. **2** lymphadenopathy-associated virus (the original French label for HIV).

lav. lavatory.

LAW 1 League of American Writers. **2** Light Antitank Weapon.

law. lawyer.

lax (*pronounced* laks) lacrosse. [*la* + *x* visual pun for cross, French *crosse*]

lax. laxative.

LB 1 *also* **L.B.** Bachelor of Letters or Literature. [Latin *Lit(t)erarum Baccalaureus*] **2** Labrador (postal code). **3** left back or fullback *sports*. **4** line buffer *computers*. **5** *also* **L.B.** local board (of an authority, such as education or selective service).

lb 1 *also* **l.b.** leg bye, in cricket. **2** *also* **lb.** pound. [Latin *libra*]

lb. ap. apothecaries' pound.

lb. av. pound avoirdupois.

LBBB left bundle branch block (of nerves).

Lbc Lübeck, Germany.

LBCH London Bankers Clearing House.

LBD 1 *also* **L.B.D.** League of British Dramatists. **2** lower back disorder *medicine*.

LBDI Liberian Bank of Development and Investment.

lbf pound-force (to express weight and force).

lb-ft pound-foot.

LBH *or* **lbh** length, breadth, height.

lb-in pound-inch.

LBJ Lyndon Baines Johnson (U.S. president 1963–1970).

lbm *or* **lb-m** pound-mass.

LBNP lower-body negative pressure.

LBO leveraged buyout *finance.*

LBP 1 length between perpendiculars, *esp. in shipbuilding.* **2** lower back pain. **3** low blood pressure.

lbr. 1 labor. **2** lumber.

LBS 1 Libyan Broadcasting Service. **2** *also* **L.B.S.** to the kind reader, greeting. [Latin *Lectori Benevolo salutem*]

lbs. pounds. [Latin *librae*]

lb. t. pound troy weight.

LBTS land-based test site.

LBV late-bottled vintage (of wine).

LBW 1 *also* **l.b.w.** leg before wicket, in cricket. **2** low birth weight *medicine.*

LC *I an abbreviation for:* **1** landing craft, esp. in combination: *LCT = landing craft tank.* **2** Law Courts. **3** lead covered (of cable). **4** *also* **L.C.** leading cases (important cases setting precedent, standards, form, etc.) *law.* **5** *also* **L.C.** left center, esp. as a stage direction. **6** legal currency. **7** lethal concentration (of a drug). **8** *also* **L/C** letter of credit *commerce.* **9** level crossing (of a road over railroad tracks, used on maps). **10** *also* **L.C.** Library of Congress. **11** liquid chromatography. **12** *also* **L.C.** liquid crystal, also in combination: *LCD = liquid crystal display.* **13** *also* **L.C.** *British* **a** Lord Chamberlain. **b** Lord Chancellor. **14** A Lover's Complaint (poem usually attributed to Shakespeare). **15** low calorie (usually in tabular description of some commercially prepared food or drink). **16** low carbon. **17** Lower Canada (designation for Quebec from 1791 to 1841).
II a symbol for: inductance capacitance ratio *electricity.*

lc 1 *also* **l.c.** in the place cited. [Latin *loco citato*] **2** *also* **lc.** or **l/c** lower case (in small letters).

LCA 1 low-cost automation. **2** Lutheran Church in America.

LCAC landing craft air cushion (military hovercraft troop carrier).

LCAO linear combination of atomic orbitals *physics, chemistry.*

LCAT lecithin cholesterol acyltransferase (enzyme that decomposes cholesterol).

LCB 1 Liquor Control Board, esp. in combination: *LCBO = Liquor Control Board of Ontario.* **2** *also* **l.c.b.** longitudinal center of buoyancy.

LCC 1 life cycle cost *accounting.* **2** London County Council (replaced in 1986 by the Court of Common Council and 32 borough governments).

LCCC *or* **L.C.C.C.** Library of Congress Catalog Card.

LCD 1 a liquid crystal diode. **b** liquid crystal display (as in watches). **2** *also* **L.C.D.** lower court decision. **3** *also* **l.c.d.** lowest or least common denominator, *esp. among fractions mathematics.*

LCDR Lieutenant Commander.

LCF *or* **l.c.f. 1** longitudinal center of flotation. **2** lowest or least common factor *mathematics.*

LCFA long-chain fatty acid *chemistry.*

LCG *or* **l.c.g.** longitudinal center of gravity.

L.Ch. Licentiate in Surgery. [Latin *Licentiatus Chirurgiae*]

LCI landing craft infantry.

L.C.J. Lord Chief Justice.

LCL 1 *also* **l.c.l.** *commerce* **a** less than carload lot: *LCL shipments.* **b** less than container load. **2** Liberal Country League (Australian political party). **3** lifting condensation level *meteorology.* **4** lower control limit.

lcl. local.

LCM 1 life cycle management *computers.* **2** *also* **L.C.M.** London College of Music. **3** *also* **l.c.m.** lowest or least common multiple *mathematics.* **4** lymphocytic choriomeningitis *medicine.*

LCN 1 load classification number. **2** local civil noon.

LCO Launch Control Officer (of a rocket takeoff).

LCP 1 last complete program *computers.* **2** *also* **L.C.P.** Liberal-Country Party (of Australia). **3** liquid crystal polymer. **4** low-cost production.

L Cpl Lance Corporal.

l/cr. letter of credit.

L.C.S.W. Licensed Counseling Social Worker.

LCT 1 landing craft tank. **2** *also* **l.c.t.** local civil time.

lcty. locality.

LCU large closeup *photography.*

LCUSA Lutheran Council in the United States of America.

LCV 1 League of Conservative Voters. **2** longer combination vehicles (tandem trailer trucks).

LD 1 *also* **L.D.** Doctor of Letters. [Latin *Lit(t)erarum Doctor*] **2** *also* **L.D.** Lady Day (Annunciation Day). **3 a** learning disability. **b** learning disabled. **4** lethal dose (of radiation or a chemical): *LD₁₀₀ = fatal to all exposed.* **5** Libyan dinar (monetary unit of Libya). **6** light difference (of the differential sensitivity of each eye) *medicine.* **7** line of duty. **8** Linz-Donawitz: *LD process* (in which oxygen replaces air as the agency to refine steel). **9** low density. **10** Low Dutch (Dutch as spoken in the Netherlands). **11** Lyme Disease.

L/D 1 length-to-diameter ratio *engineering.* **2** letter of deposit *finance.* **3** lift-drag or lift-drag ratio *aeronautics.*

Ld. 1 Limited. **2** Lord (part of title).

ld. 1 land. **2** lead. **3** load: *ld. lmt. = load limit.*

LDA localizer directional aid *aeronautics.*

LDC 1 less-developed country. **2** long-distance call. **3** *also* **l.d.c.** lower dead center *engineering.*

LDDS low-density data system.

LDEF (el'def') Long Duration Exposure Facility (satellite acting as an unmanned laboratory for studying the effects of space and radiation on materials and living tissue).

LDF Legal Defense Fund (of the National Association for the Advancement of Colored People).

LDG Lodge (in postal address).

ldg. 1 landing: *ldg. & dely. = landing and delivery.* **2** leading. **3** loading. **4** lodging.

LDH lactic dehydrogenase (enzyme active in metabolism of lactic acid).

L.d'H. Legion of Honor. [French *Légion d'Honneur*]

LDL low-density lipoprotein (a lipoprotein containing more lipids than protein and believed to contribute to coronary artery disease).

Ldmk landmark.

Ldn. London.

LDO limited duty officer.

Ldo. licensed. [Spanish *licenciado*]

L-DOPA or **L-dopa** (el'dō'pə) levodopa or L-dihydroxyphenylalaline (drug used in treating Parkinson's disease).

LDP 1 Liberal-Democratic Party (of Japan). **2** *also* **LDPE** low-density polyethylene.

Ldp. 1 Ladyship. **2** Lordship.

LDR light-dependent resistor *electronics*.

ldr. 1 leader. **2** ledger.

LDRI low data rate input *computers*.

ldry. laundry.

L.D.S. 1 Latter-day Saints (of the Church of Jesus Christ of the Latter-day Saints, or Mormons): *L.D.S. Chapel*. **2** *also* **LDS** light distillate spirit (form of refined petroleum).

LDT logic design translator (to facilitate coordination of components in a computer system).

LDV or **L.D.V.** Local Defence Volunteers or Volunteer (successor to the former British Home Guard).

LDW Licensed Driver's Waiver (of insurance for a rental car).

LDX Long-Distance Xerography.

LE 1 *British* Labour Exchange. **2** *also* **L.E.** law enforcement, also in combination: *LEAJ = Law Enforcement and Administration of Justice*. **3** leading edge *aeronautics, computers, meteorology*. **4** left end *football*. **5** *also* **L.E.** left eye *medicine*. **6** lupus erythematosus (disease that affects the connective tissues): *LE factor*.

£E Egyptian pound (monetary unit of Egypt).

Le 1 *also* **Le. a** Lebanon. **b** Lebanese. **2** leone (monetary unit of Sierra Leone).

L.E.A. *British* Local Education Authority.

lea. 1 league. **2** leather.

LEAA 1 Law Enforcement Assistance Act. **2** (*sometimes pronounced* lē'ə) Law Enforcement Assistance Administration.

LEAR (lēr) Low-Energy Anti-Proton Ring (for the study of particle physics).

Leb. 1 Lebanese. **2** Lebanon.

lect. 1 a lecture. **b** *also* **Lect.** lecturer. **2** lesson, esp. a lesson from the Bible. [Latin *lectio*]

LED light-emitting diode (crystalline semiconducting device used especially in electronic displays).

L.Ed. Lawyer's Edition (U.S. Supreme Court Reports).

led. ledger.

LEED 1 laser-energized explosive device. **2** low-energy electron diffraction.

LEFM linear elastic fracture mechanics.

Leg. 1 a Legate. **b** Legation. **2 a** Legislative. **b** Legislature.

leg. 1 legal, also in combination: *leg.wt. = legal weight*. **2** legend (esp. under an illustration in a book). **3** legislation. **4** smooth *music*. [Italian *legato*]

legg. light and rapid, light and lively *music*. [Italian *leggiero*]

legis. 1 *also* **Legis.** legislature. **2** legislative. **3** legislation.

Legit. legitimate, legally.

legit. (*often pronounced* lə jit') legitimate: *legit. theater*.

LEGT High School for General and Technical Studies. [French *Lycée d'Enseignement Général et Technologique*]

LEI leading economic indicators (government measure of economic activity).

Leic. or **Leics.** Leicestershire County, England.

Le. Is. Leeward Islands.

LEM 1 lateral eye movement. **2** (*pronounced* lem) Lunar Excursion Module: *LEM vehicle*.

LEO low earth orbit.

LEP 1 large electron-positron (synchroton). **2** lowest effective power. **3** Professional Secondary School for Advanced Studies. [French *Lycée d'Enseignement Professionel*]

Lep Lepus, the Hare (constellation).

LEPD low-energy positron diffraction.

LEPORE Long-Term and Expanded Program of Oceanic Research and Exploration.

LES 1 launch escape system (to free astronauts and their spacecraft if a launch vehicle fails). **2** *also* **les** local excitatory state *physics*. **3** lower esophageal sphincter (area in lower esophagus).

L. ès L. or **LèsL** Licentiate in Letters (equivalent to B.A.). [French *Licencié ès Lettres*]

L. ès Sc. or **LèsS** Licentiate in Science (equivalent to B.S.). [French *Licencié ès Sciences*]

LET linear energy-transfer (energy loss per unit distance of penetration, stopping power).

let. letter.

Lett. Lettish (language of the Letts or the group of languages Lettish belongs to).

lett. letters.

lett'd lettered (of the spine of a book in binding).

leu. or **Leu.** leucine (amino acid produced in the digestion of protein).

LEV lunar excursion vehicle.

Lev. 1 Levant. **2** *also* **Levit.** Leviticus (book of the Old Testament).

Lex. Lexicon.

lex. lexical.

lexicog. 1 lexicography. **2** lexicographer. **3** lexicographical.

Lexis Lexicography Information Service.

Ley or **Leyd.** Leyden, Netherlands.

LF 1 *also* **l.f.** ledger folio *accounting*. **2 a** left field *baseball*. **b** left forward *sports*. **c** left fullback *sports*. **3** left foot, esp. in dance notation. **4** *also* **Lf** limit of flocculation (extent of forming clumps) *medicine*. **5** line feed (line-by-line advance of a cursor or paper feed) *computers*. **6** *also* **L-F** low frequency.

lf 1 *also* **lf.** leaf *botany*. **2** *also* **lf.** or **l.f.** lightface *printing*. **3** *also* **l-f** low frequency, also in combination: *lfo = low-frequency oscillator*.

LFB or **l.f.b.** left fullback *sports*.

LFC 1 laminar flow control. **2** *also* **lfc** low-frequency current. **3** Lutheran Free Church.

LFD 1 least fatal dose *medicine.* **2** *also* **L.F.D.** low-fat diet.

LFO 1 light fuel oil. **2** low-frequency oscillator.

lft 1 *also* **lft.** leaflet *botany.* **2** *also* **l.ft.** linear foot or feet.

LG 1 *also* **L.G.** Lady of the Order of the Garter. **2** *also* **L.G.** or **l.g.** large grain (esp. of a surface or a size or grade of granule). **3** *also* **l.g.** left guard *sports.* **4** Life Guards (British cavalry regiment). **5** *also* **LG.** Low German (a language of North Germany).

Lg. 1 Lagoon. **2** Language (publication).

lg. *or* **lg 1** language. **2** large: *lg. light liv. rm. w/fireplace.* **3** long.

L.G.B. local government board.

lge. 1 large. **2** *also* **Lge.** league.

L.Ger. Low German (a language of North Germany).

LGk *or* **LGk.** Late Greek or, sometimes, Low Greek.

LGM little green man or men (whimsical reference to intelligent extraterrestrial life).

LGO Lamont Geological Observatory.

LGP liquefied petroleum gas.

LGr. Low Greek or, sometimes, Late Greek.

lgr. 1 lager (beer). **2** larger. **3** longer.

LGS landing guidance system.

L.G.S.M. *or* **LGSM** Licentiate of the Guildhall School of Music.

lgt. *or* **Lgt.** light (of ingredients or illumination).

lgth. length.

lg. tn. long ton.

LGU Ladies' Golf Union.

LGV lymphogranuloma venereum (a venereal disease of the lymph nodes).

LH 1 left halfback *sports.* **2** *also* **L.H.** left hand, *esp. in music.* **3** *also* **L.H.** Legion of Honor. [French *Légion d'Honneur*] **4** lighthouse (esp. on maps and navigation charts). **5** lower half. **6** luteinizing hormone (triggers ovulation and makes the ovary produce progesterone).

lh 1 *also* **l.h.** left hand, also in combination: *lhd = left-hand drive.* **2** lighthouse (esp. on maps and navigation charts). **3** lower half, esp. in combination: *lha = lower half assembly.*

LHA 1 landing helicopter assault. **2 a** local hour angle *astronomy, navigation.* **b** lower hour angle *astronomy.*

LHB *or* **l.h.b.** left halfback *sports.*

L.H.D. Doctor of the Humanities or Doctor of Humane Letters. [Latin *Lit(t)erarum Humaniorum Doctor*]

lhr *or* **l-hr.** lumen-hour.

LHRF luteinizing hormone releasing factor.

LHRH *or* **LH-RH** luteinizing hormone releasing hormone (hormone that causes the pituitary gland to release luteinizing hormone).

lhs *or* **LHS** left-hand side.

LHSV liquid hourly space velocity *engineering.*

LI 1 *also* **L.I.** Leeward Islands. **2** *also* **L.I.** Licentiate of Instruction. **3** Long Island. **4** *also* **l.i.** longitudinal interval.

Li lithium (chemical element).

li. 1 link (unit of surveyor's measure). **2** lira (Italian monetary unit).

Lib 1 Libra; the Balance or Scales (constellation). [Latin *Libra*] **2** *also* **Lib.** Book. [Latin *Liber*] **3** *also* **Lib. a** Liberal. **b** Liberal Party. **3** liberation: *Women's Lib.* **4** *also* **Lib.** Liberia. **5** *also* **Lib. a** Library. **b** Librarian.

lib. 1 book. [Latin *liber*] **2** *also* **lib** liberation (chiefly in reference to women's liberation). **3 a** library. **b** librarian. **4** *also* **lib** libretto.

lib. cat. library catalog.

Lib. Cong. Library of Congress.

Libn. *or* **Libr.** librarian.

LIC linear integrated circuit.

Lic. 1 a License. **b** Licensed. **2** Licentiate: *Lic. Med. = Licentiate in Medicine.*

lidar (lī'där) light detection and ranging (device using infrared laser light pulses to define cloud patterns and atmospheric disturbances).

LIE Long Island Expressway.

Lieut. Lieutenant, also in combination: *Lieut. Col. = lieutenant colonel, Lieut. Gov. = Lieutenant Governor.*

LIF laser-induced fluorescence.

LIFE long instruction format engine (multitask chip) *computers.*

LIFFE London International Financial Futures Exchange.

LIFO *or* **Lifo** (lī'fō') last in, first out: **a** method of inventory *commerce.* **b** description of a data file *computers.*

lig. ligament.

LILO (lī'lō') last in, last out: **a** method of inventory *commerce.* **b** description of a data file *computers.*

LIM *or* **L.I.M.** linear induction motor.

lim. limit.

limo (lim'ō) *or* **limo.** limousine.

lin. 1 lineal. **2** linear. **3** liniment.

LINAC *or* **linac** linear accelerator.

LINC laboratory instrument computer (for research).

Linc. Lincoln: **a** U.S. president 1861–1865. **b** capital of Nebraska. **c** College of Oxford University.

Lincs *or* **Lincs.** Lincolnshire County, England.

lin. ft. linear foot.

ling. linguistics.

Linn. 1 Linnean. **2** Linnaeus (Swedish botanist, 1707–1778).

lino. *or* **Lino.** linotype (method of typesetting).

LINS Laser Inertial Navigation System.

L.I.O.B. Licentiate of the Institute of Building.

LIOCS (lī'oks) logical input-output control system *computers.*

LIP *or* **l.i.p.** life insurance policy.

LIPL Linear Information Programming Language.

LIPS *or* **lips** (*pronounced* lips) logical inferences per second (measure of the speed with which a computer solves a problem).

liq. 1 liquid. **2** liquor.

LIS Library Information Service, also in combination: *LISA = Library Information Service Abstracts*.

Lis. Lisbon, Portugal.

L.I.S.M. Licentiate of the Incorporated Society of Musicians.

Lisp *or* **LISP** list processing (a computer language, used esp. in artificial intelligence research).

Lit lira Italy or lira italiana (monetary unit of Italy).

lit. 1 *also* **lit** liter. **2 a** literal **b** literally. **3** *also* **Lit. a** literary: *lit.crit. = literary criticism*. **b** literature: *Eng. Lit. = English literature*.

Lit.B. Bachelor of Letters or Literature. [Latin *Lit(t)erarum Baccalaureus*]

lit.crit. (*sometimes* lit'krit') literary criticism.

Lit.D. Doctor of Letters or Literature. [Latin *Lit(t)erarum Doctor*]

Lith. 1 Lithuania. **2** Lithuanian.

lith. 1 *also* **litho.** lithograph. **2** *also* **lithog.** lithography.

lithol. lithology (study of rocks or the branch of medicine dealing with calculi).

Lit. Hum. the Humanities, Classics. [Latin *Literae Humaniores*]

Litt.B. Bachelor of Literature or Letters. [Latin *Lit(t)erarum Baccalaureus*]

Litt.D. Doctor of Literature or Letters. [Latin *Lit(t)erarum Doctor*]

Litt.M. Master of Literature or Letters [Latin *Lit(t)erarum Magister*]

Liturg. 1 Liturgies. **2** Liturgy.

liturg. 1 liturgics. **2** liturgical.

LIUNA Laborers International Union of North America.

Liv. 1 Book. [French *Livre*] **2** Liverpool.

liv. 1 book. [French *livre*] **2** *also* **livr.** number or part (of a publication). [French *livraison*]

liv. rm. living room.

LJ 1 *also* **L.J.** Law Journal: *Yale L.J.* **2** Library Journal. **3** *also* **l.j.** life jacket. **4** long jump *sports* **5** *also* **L. J.** Lord Justice.

L.JJ. Lord Justices.

LK Lake (in postal address).

Lk l Lake, also in combination: *Lk view.* **2** *also* **Lk.** Luke (book of the New Testament) .

lkd locked.

lkg 1 *also* **lkge** leakage. **2** locking.

Lkr. locker.

LKS Lakes (in postal address).

Lkt. map. [German *Landkarte*]

Lkw truck. [German *Lastkraftwagen*]

LL 1 *also* **L.L.** Late Latin. **2** *also* **L.L.** Law Latin. **3** *also* **£L** Lebanese pound. **4** limited liability *commerce, insurance.* **5** *also* **L/L** line by line. **6** Little League, also in combination: *BLL = Brewster Little League.* **7** live load (vehicles, people, etc., supported by a bridge, floor, etc.). **8** lower left, esp. in combination: *LLQ = lower left quadrant.* **9** lower limit *electronics.* **10** low level, also in combination: *LLW = low-level waste* (low radioactivity).

ll. 1 laws. **2** leaves. **3** lines.

l.l. 1 in the place cited. [Latin *loco laudato*] **2** *also* **l/l.** loose leaf.

LLat. Late Latin.

LL.B. Bachelor of Laws. [Latin *Legum Baccalaureus*]

LLC *or* **llc** lower left center.

L.L.C.M. Licentiate of the London College of Music.

LL.D. Doctor of Laws. [Latin *Legum Doctor*]

LLD factor lactobacillus lactis Dorner factor (vitamin B-12).

LLE low-level exposure (of radioactivity).

LLI latitude and longitude indicator.

LLL 1 *also* **LL.L.** Licentiate of Laws. [Latin *Legum Licentiatus*] **2** *also* **L.L.L.** Love's Labor's Lost (play by Shakespeare). **3** low-level logic *computers: LLL circuit.*

LL.M. Master of Laws. [Latin *Legum Magister*]

L.L.P. *or* **LLP** Limited Liability Partnership.

LLR 1 line of least resistance. **2** load-limiting resistor *electronics.*

LLS lunar logistic system.

LLTV low-light television *electronics.*

LLW low-level waste (of radioactive waste).

LM 1 Legion of Merit. **2** *also* **L.M. a** Licentiate in Medicine. **b** Licentiate in Midwifery. **3** light metal. **4** light microscope. **5** *also* **L.M.** long meter *music.* **6** *also* **L.M.** Lord Mayor. **7** lunar module.

Lm Maltese lira (monetary unit of Malta).

l.M. of the current month. [German *laufenden Monats*]

lm lumen (unit of measurement of light).

LMBC Liverpool Marine Biological Committee.

LMC 1 Large Magellanic Cloud *astronomy.* **2** *also* **L.M.C.** Lloyd's machinery certificate. **3** *also* **l.m.c.** low middling clause (of cotton trade).

LMD 1 *also* **lmd** leaf mold. **2** *also* **L.M.D.** long meter double *music.*

L.M.E. London Metal Exchange.

LMEC Liquid Metal Engineering Center.

LMFBR liquid metal fast breeder reactor.

LMFR liquid metal fuel reactor.

LMH Lady Margaret Hall (college of Oxford University).

lmhr *or* **lm-hr.** lumen-hour.

LMi the Little Lion (constellation). [Latin *Leo Minor*]

lmn. lineman.

LMO 1 lens-modulated oscillator. **2** *also* **lmo** light machine oil.

LMP 1 last menstrual period *medicine.* **2** Literary Market Place (directory of the publishing industry).

LMR liquid metal reactor.

LMRDA Labor Management Reporting and Disclosure Act.

LMS 1 laser mass spectrometry *chemistry.* **2** *also* **L.M.S.** London Mathematical Society. **3** *also* **L.M.S.** London Missionary Society.

LMT 1 *also* **l.m.t.** length, mass, time *physics.* **2** *also* **lmt** limit. **3** *also* **l.m.t.** *or* **lmt** local mean time.

LMTD 1 *also* **lmtd** limited. **2** logarithmic mean temperature difference.

L.M.V.D. Licensed Motor Vehicle Dealer (of Australia and New Zealand).

lm/w lumen per watt.

LN 1 Lane (in postal address). **2** *also* **LN$_2$** liquid nitrogen. **3** lymph node *medicine*, also in combination: *LNPF = lymph node permeability factor*.

Ln lanthanide *or* lanthanide series (rare-earth elements) *chemistry*.

ln 1 *also* **ln.** liaison. **2** loan. **3** natural logarithm *mathematics*.

LNCP Liberal National Country Party (of Australia).

Lndg. Landing (in place names).

LNDR lender.

lndsc landscape.

LNG liquefied natural gas.

lng. 1 length. **2** lining.

LO 1 *also* **L.O.** Liaison Officer. **2** *also* **LO$_2$** liquid oxygen. **3** local origination (TV station that originates programming). **4** lubricating oil. **5** Trade Unions Federation: **a** of Denmark. [Danish *Landsorganisation i Danmark*] **b** of Norway [Norwegian *Landsorganisasjon i Norge*] **c** of Sweden. [Swedish *Landsorganisationen i Sverige*]

LOA 1 leave of absence. **2** *also* **l.o.a.** length over all. **3** letter of agreement.

LOB 1 left on base *baseball*. **2** line of balance.

LOBAR long-baseline radar.

LOC 1 Launch Operation Center (of NASA). **2** letter of credit. **3** Library of Congress. **4** lines of communication.

loc. 1 local. **2** location.

LOCA loss of coolant accident (of a nuclear reactor).

LOCAL load on call (putting data into storage as needed) *computers*.

loc. cit. in the place cited. [Latin *loco citato*]

locn location.

loco. 1 locomotion. **2** locomotive.

loc. primo cit. in the place first cited. [Latin *loco primo citato*]

LOD line of duty.

lodg 1 lodging. **2** lodgings.

LOF loss of fluid *mechanics, medicine*.

L of C 1 Library of Congress. **2** line of communications.

LOFT 1 loss of fluid test. **2** (*pronounced* lôft) low-frequency radio telescope.

log. 1 *also* **log** (*pronounced* lôg) logarithm. **2** logic. **3 a** logistic. **b** logistical. **c** *also* **Log.** logistics.

LOGANDS logic or logical commands *computers*.

log-dec logarithmic decrement (of a ratio in oscillation between amplitudes) *physics*.

log$_e$ natural logarithm.

LOGO programming language, esp. for use with graphics.

LOGRAM logical program *computers*.

LOH light observation helicopter.

LOI 1 *also* **l.o.i.** limit of impurities *chemistry*. **2** *also* **loi** loss on ignition. **3** lunar orbit insertion (putting a spacecraft into orbit around the moon).

LOLA (lō'lə) library on-line acquisition.

L.O.M. *or* **LOM** Loyal Order of Moose (patriotic fraternal organization).

Lomb. Lombardy, Italy.

Lon. London.

lon. longitude.

Lond. 1 London. **2** Londonderry, Northern Ireland.

long. longitude.

longl. longitudinal.

L.O.O.M. Loyal Order of Moose (fraternal organization).

LOP line of position *navigation*.

LOPAR low-power acquisition radar.

loq. he or she speaks. [Latin *loquitur*]

LORAC (lôr'ak) long-range accuracy (radio navigational system).

LORAD (lôr'ad) long-range active detection.

LORAN *or* **loran** (lôr'an) long-range navigation (radio navigational system).

LOS 1 Law of the Sea. **2** line of scrimmage *football*. **3** line of sight. **4** loss of signal, esp. in electronic communications.

LOSS large-object salvage system.

LOT large orbiting telescope.

lot. a lotion *pharmaceutics*.

Loth. Lothian, esp. in combination: *W.Loth. = West Lothian*.

Lou. Louisiana.

LOX *or* **lox** (*pronounced* loks) liquid oxygen.

loy. loyalty.

LOZ liquid ozone.

LP 1 a Labor Party. **b** Labour Party. **c** Liberal Party (of Australia). **2** *also* **L.P. a** large paper (edition of a book, printed on larger than standard paper). **b** large post (paper size) *printing*. **c** large print (edition of a book, magazine, or newspaper printed in larger than normal type). **3** laser printer *computers*. **4** launch platform (of a rocket). **5** limited partnership *commerce, law*. **6** linear programming *computers*. **7 a** liquefied petroleum, esp. in combination: *LPG or LP gas*. **b** liquid or liquefied propane. **c** liquid propellant, esp. for a missile. **8** list price. **9** long-playing (phonograph record, originally a trademark of Columbia Records, Inc.). **10** *also* **L.P.** long primer (printing type). **11** low pass (filter) *electronics*. **12** low power. **13** *also* **L.P.** *or* **l.p.** low pressure, also in combination: *LPC = low-pressure chamber*. **14** lumbar puncture.

Lp. 1 Ladyship. **2** Lordship.

LPBT Ladies Professional Bowlers Tour.

LPC 1 leaf protein concentrate. **2** linear predictive coding (method of coding speech for data transmission) *computers*. **3** low-pressure chamber. **4** low-pressure coolant.

LPD liquid protein diet.

LPE liquid phase epitaxy (for layering crystals used in electronic circuits).

LPF **1** leach-precipitate float: *LPF process* (for recovering metal from ore and tailings). **2** leukocytosis-promoting factor *medicine*.

LPG liquefied petroleum gas (bottled gas).

L.P.G.A. Ladies Professional Golfers' Association.

LPH lipotropic hormone (lipotropin promoting the breakdown of fats and the precursor of endorphins).

lpi lines per inch.

LPL List Processing Language *computers*.

LPM **1** lines per minute (of a computer printer). **2** *also* **L.P.M.** long particular meter *music*.

LPMC Liberia Produce Marketing Corporation.

LPN *or* **L.P.N.** Licensed Practical Nurse.

LPNA Lithographers and Printers National Association.

LPO **1** *also* **L.P.O.** London Philharmonic Orchestra. **2** Lunar Polar Orbiter (satellite).

Lpool *or* **L'pool** Liverpool.

LPR liquid propellant rocket.

LPS **1** *also* **lps** lipopolysaccharide (esp. in the membrane of some bacteria). **2** *also* **L.P.S.** Lord Privy Seal.

LPTB London Passenger Transport Board.

LPTV low-power television (station of limited range).

LPW *or* **l.p.w.** lumens per watt.

Lpz Leipzig, Germany.

LQ lowest quartile *statistics*.

LR **1** *also* **L.R.** Law Reports. **2** *also* **L.R.** living room: *Foldaway doors provide L.R. and two bedrooms.* **3** *also* **L.R.** Lloyd's Register. **4** log run (of timber). **5** long range, esp. in combination: *LRCM = long-range cruise missile.* **6** long run, also in combination: *LRAC = long-run average cost.* **7** lower right, also in combination: *LRC = lower right center.*

Lr *I an abbreviation for:* **1** *also* **Lr.** King Lear (play by Shakespeare). **2** *also* **Lr.** Lower, in combination: *Lr. Calif. = Lower California.*
II a symbol for: lawrencium (chemical element).

lr. lira (monetary unit of Italy, Malta, and Turkey).

LRAACA long-range air antisubmarine capability aircraft.

L.R.A.M. *or* **LRAM** Licentiate of the Royal Academy of Music.

LRBM long-range ballistic missile.

LRC longitudinal redundancy check (of data) *computers*.

L.R.C.M. *or* **LRCM** Licentiate of the Royal College of Music.

L.R.C.P. *or* **LRCP** Licentiate of the Royal College of Physicians.

L.R.C.S. *or* **LRCS** **1** League of Red Cross Societies. **2** Licentiate of the Royal College of Surgeons.

L.R.C.V.S. *or* **LRCVS** Licentiate of the Royal College of Veterinary Surgeons.

LRD long-range data *computers*.

LRF luteinizing (hormone) releasing factor (secreted by the hypothalamus stimulating release of luteinizing hormone).

lrg. large.

LRINF Long-Range Intermediate Nuclear Forces.

LRL Lunar Receiving Laboratory.

LRP long-range planning.

LRRP lowest required radiating power.

LRS Legislative Reference Service.

LRT light rapid transit (transit system using electrically powered cars, such as streetcars and monorails).

LRTNF Long-Range Theater Nuclear Forces.

LRU **1** least recently used (of computer data). **2** line replacement unit.

LRV **1** light-rail vehicle. **2** lunar-roving vehicle.

LS **1** *also* **L.S.** British Leading Seaman. **2** *also* **L.S.** Letter Service. **3** *also* **L.S.** letter signed. **4** *also* **L.S.** Library Science: *M.S. in L.S. = Master of Science in Library Science.* **5** *also* **L.S.** Licensed Surveyor. **6** liminal sensitivity *physiology*. **7** *also* **L.S.** Linnean Society (of London). **8** (time of) local sunset. **9** longitudinal section *biology*. **10** long shot *photography*. **11** loudspeaker. **12** low speed, also in combination: *LSL = low-speed logic.* **13** *also* **£S a** Sudanese pound (monetary unit). **b** Syrian pound (monetary unit). **14** *also* **L.S.** the place of the seal (on a document). [Latin *locus sigilli*]

l.s. **1** left side. **2** letter signed. **3** the place of the seal (on a document). [Latin *locus sigilli*]

LSA **1** Leukemia Society of America. **2** limited space charge accumulation (of oscillations) *electronics*. **3** Linguistic Society of America.

LSAT Law School Admission Test.

LSB least significant bit *computers*.

LSC **1** least significant character *computers*. **2** liquid scintillation counter.

LSD **1** landing ship dock. **2** large-screen display (of TV). **3** Law Student Division (of the American Bar Association). **4** least significant digit *mathematics, computers*. **5** liquid scintillation detector. **6** lysergic acid diethylamide (hallucinogenic drug). [German *Lysergsäure-diäthylamid*]

lsd. leased, also in combination: *lsd.l. = leased line.*

L.S.E. *or* **LSE** **1** *also* **l.s.e.** limited signed edition (of a book or lithograph). **2** London School of Economics (and Politics). **3** London Stock Exchange.

LSI *or* **L.S.I.** large-scale integration *electronics*, also in combination: *LSIC = large-scale integration, or integrated, circuit.*

LSL low-speed logic *computers*.

LSM linear synchronous motor.

LSO **1** landing signal officer (on an aircraft carrier). **2** *also* **L.S.O.** London Symphony Orchestra.

LSS life-support system.

LST **1** landing ship tank. **2** large space telescope. **3** *also* **l.s.t. a** local sidereal time *astronomy*. **b** local standard time.

L. Sup. Lake Superior.

LT **1** landed terms *commerce*. **2** laptop (small computer). **3** left tackle *football*. **4** *also* **L.T.** Licentiate in Theology. **5** Lieutenant *military*. **6** local time. **7** London Transport (authority). **8** long ton (British ton, 2240 pounds). **9** low temperature *meteorology, physics*. **10** low tension (of electricity or physical strain) *engineering, physics*.

Lt. 1 Lieutenant, *1st Lt. = First Lieutenant; Lt.(jg.) = Lieutenant (junior grade); Lt.Gov. = Lieutenant Governor.* **2** Light: *Lt.Cav. = Light Cavalry; Montauk Lt. = Montauk Light (meaning lighthouse).*

lt 1 *also* **l.t.** landed terms *commerce.* **2** *also* **lt.** light. **3** *also* **lt.** literature, literary. **4** *also* **l.t.** local time. **5** long ton (British ton, 2240 pounds). **6** *also* **l.t.** loop test *electricity.* **7** *also* **l.t.** low tension (of electricity or physical strain) *engineering, physics;* also in combination: *l.t.b. = low-tension battery.*

LTA 1 Lawn Tennis Association. **2** lighter-than-air: *LTA transport.*

LTAA Lawn Tennis Association of Australia.

LTBT Limited Test Ban Treaty (prohibiting atmospheric nuclear testing).

LTC Land Trust Commission.

Lt.Col. Lieutenant Colonel.

Lt.Com. *or* **Lt.Comdr.** Lieutenant Commander.

Ltd. *or* **ltd.** limited: **a** of corporate liability *commerce: J.& J. Paton, Ltd.* **b** of or for restricted use, publication, etc.: *ltd. ed. = limited edition.*

ltg lighting.

Lt.Gen. Lieutenant General.

Lt.Gov. Lieutenant Governor.

LTH *or* **LtH** luteotrophic hormone (stimulates production of milk and progesterone).

L.Th. Licentiate in Theology.

lthr leather.

LTI light transmission index.

Lt.Inf. Light Infantry.

LTL *or* **l.t.l.** less than truckload *shipping.*

LTM long-term memory (of a person).

ltng. lightning, also in combination: *ltng. arr. = lightning arrester.*

l. to r. *or* **l-to-r** left-to-right (of a picture caption).

LTPD lot tolerance percent defective (percent of units in a lot that are defective) *engineering.*

LTR long terminal repeat (of nucleic chains) *biology.*

ltr. 1 *also* **Ltr.** letter. **2** lighter (barge).

LTRS letter shift *computers.*

LTS 1 launch telemetry station (of a rocket takeoff). **2** launch tracking system (of a rocket flight).

LTTE Liberation Tigers of Tamil Eelam (revolutionary group in Sri Lanka).

LTU 1 line termination unit *computers.* **2** long ton unit.

LTV long-tube vertical (multiple effect distillation process, for distillation of seawater).

lt-yr light-year *astronomy.*

Lu lutetium (chemical element).

lu 1 *also* **LU** logic unit *computers.* **2** lumen (unit of light).

LUA 1 Life Underwriters Association (in combination with: *C = of Canada; NZ = of New Zealand,* etc.). **2** London Underwriters Association.

lub. (*often pronounced* lŭb) **1** lubricant. **2** lubricate. **3** lubricating, esp. in combination: *self-lub. brakes.*

l.u.b. least upper bound (smallest of the upper bounds of a set) *mathematics.*

LUC Land Use Commission.

Luc. *or* **Lucr.** The Rape of Lucrece (poem by Shakespeare).

L.U.E. left upper entrance (a stage direction).

LUF *or* **LUHF** *or* **luhf** lowest useful or usable high frequency.

lug. luggage.

LULAC League of United Latin-American Citizens.

lum. 1 *also* **lumb.** lumber. **2** luminosity. **3** luminous.

LUMAS lunar mapping system.

Lup the Wolf (constellation). [Latin *Lupus*]

L.U.S. *or* **LUS** Land Utilization Survey (of Great Britain).

LUSI lunar surface inspection.

Lusing. caressing or coaxing (a direction to play a passage) *music.* [Italian *lusinghiero*]

LUT launch umbilical tower (of a rocket).

Luth. Lutheran.

Lux. Luxembourg.

LV 1 land value. **2** launch vehicle (of a rocket). **3** left ventricle or ventricular, also in combination: *LVAD = left ventricular assist device.* **4** light and variable (of wind) *meteorology.* **5** *also* **L/V** light vessel (ship). **6** limited voting (of stock rights). **7** *also* **l.v.** low voltage. **8** *also* **L.V.** luncheon voucher.

Lv 1 a Latvia. **b** Latvian. **2** *also* **lv** *or* **lv.** leave, leave at (on schedule). **3** lev (monetary unit of Bulgaria). **4** *also* **lv.** book. [French *livre*]

LVA Literacy Volunteers of America.

LVCD least voltage coincidence detection (of an electronic circuit gate).

lvd. leaved *botany.*

LVDT linear variable-differential transformer.

LVH left ventricular hypertrophy *medicine.*

LVI low viscosity index.

LVL laminated-veneer lumber (an engineered wood, used in building).

LVN *or* **L.V.N.** Licensed Vocational Nurse.

LVR 1 line voltage regulator. **2** longitudinal video recording (with audio and video tracks recorded on one tape).

LVS light value system (exposure-value system for photographic film).

lvs. leaves *botany.*

LVT landing vehicle tracked *military.*

LW 1 lightweight, esp. in combination: *LWCP = lightweight coated paper.* **2** long wave (of radio signals or of a seismic shock wave, also *L-wave*). **3** low water, also in combination: *LWOST = low-water ordinary spring tide.*

Lw lawrencium (former symbol for chemical element 103, now *Lr*).

l/w lumens per watt.

LWB *or* **lwb** long wheelbase (of a truck).

LWF Lutheran World Federation.

LWL 1 *also* **l.w.l. a** (of a ship or boat) length at water line. **b** (of a ship) load water line. **2** low-water line (of tide).

LWM low-water mark (of tide).

lwop or **l.w.o.p.** leave without pay.

LWR light-water reactor.

LWT London Weekend Television (British television production company).

LWV League of Women Voters.

lx 1 light. [Latin *lux*] **2** lux (unit of illumination).

LXX or **LXX.** the Septuagint.

▶The Septuagint is the Greek translation from the Hebrew Old Testament, represented by the Roman numeral for seventy because Ptolemy II was thought to have commissioned seventy Greek scholars for seventy days to complete the work.

ly 1 langley (unit of solar radiation) *astronomy, physics.* **2** *also* **l.y.** light-year *astronomy.*

Lyn the Lynx (constellation).

Lyr Lyra, the Lyre (constellation).

lyr. 1 lyric, lyrical. **2** lyricist.

lys. or **Lys.** lysine (amino acid essential for growth).

LZ landing zone (for a helicopter) *military.*

LZT lead zirconate titanate *metallurgy.*

M *I an abbreviation for:* **1** hand. [French *main*] **2** Mach (the speed of sound): *M2 = twice the speed of sound.* **3** *also* **M.** Magistrate. **4** *also* **M.** Majesty, in combination: *HMS Ark Royal = His Majesty's Ship Ark Royal.* **5** Malaysia, Malaysian: *M$ = Malaysian dollar.* **6** *also* **M.** male. **7** Mali: *MF = Mali franc.* **8** maloti (plural of loti, monetary unit of Lesotho). **9** *also* **M.** manual *music.* **10** March (the month). **11** *also* **M.** mark (monetary unit of Germany). **12** *also* **M.** Marquis. **13** *also* **M.** married. **14** *also* **M.** Master, esp. in combination: *MA = Master of Arts.* **15** mature. **16** May (the month). **17** mean, esp. in combination: *MHW = mean high water.* **18** *also* **M.** medical, medicine, esp. in combination: *MD = Doctor of Medicine, MT = Medical Technician.* **19** medium: *S (34), M (36–38), L (40–42), XL (44–46).* **20** mega- (one million or 10^6): *MW = megawatt (1,000,000 watts).* **21** *also* **M.** member, in combination: *MASME = Member of the American Society of Mechanical Engineers.* **22** memorandum. **23** *also* **M.** meridian. **24** mesh. **25** Messier (catalog of bright clusters and nebulae): *M31 (a nebula of the Milky Way).* **26** Metropolitan, in combination: *MTA = Metropolitan Transportation Authority.* **27** *also* **M.** Middle, in combination: *ME = Middle English (English from about 1100 to about 1500).* **28** mile. **29** milligram, esp. of explosive material, as in fireworks: *M-80.* **30 a** Minister, in combination: *MOH = Minister of Health.* **b** Ministry, in combination: *MOT = Ministry of Transport.* **31** missile, in combination: *TM-76 tactical guided missile.* **32** *also* **M.** mix *pharmaceutics.* **33** model (usually followed by a number): *M-16 (type of U.S. Army rifle).* **34** moderate. **35** modulation, in combination: *FM = frequency modulation.* **36** module, esp. in combination: *LEM = lunar excursion module.* **37** molar *physics, chemistry, dentistry.* **38** Monday. **39** monophonic (of a recording). **40** *also* **M.** Monsieur. **41** *also* **M.** monsoon air *meteorology.* **42** month, monthly: *A, annual; M, monthly; Q, quarterly. IRS Form 941-M = Employer's Monthly Federal Tax Return.* **43** *also* **M.** morning. **44** *also* **M.** Mother (esp. in a religious order). **45** motor, in combination: *M/V Bluenose = Motor Vessel Bluenose.* **46** British motorway (with a route number): *M6.* **47** *also* **M.** mountain: *MRS = mountain rescue service.* **48** *also* **M.** mud, esp. on nautical charts and in hydrology.
II a symbol for: **1** absolute magnitude *astronomy.* **2** arithmetic mean. **3** atomic shell of 18 maximum electrons per shell. **4 a** atomic weight *physics, chemistry.* **b** molecular weight *physics, chemistry.* **5** luminous emittance. **6** magnetization *physics.* **7** Maxwell (magnetic flux, usually represented by *B*). **8** measured ceiling *meteorology* **9** moment, esp. bending moment or moment of force *physics.* **10** money *economics* (measure of a country's money supply): *M1* or M_1 = *amount of currency and demand deposits; M2* or M_2 = *M1 plus amount in savings accounts, time deposits, money market accounts, and overnight bank borrowings; M3* or M_3 = *M1 and M2 plus large time deposits and borrowings, institutional money market funds, and other large financial instruments.* **11** mutual inductance *physics.* **12** noon. [Latin *meridies*] **13** red star of prominent titanium oxide intensity *astronomy.* **14** thirteenth of a series (twelfth when *J* is omitted). **15** thousand; 1000 (Roman numeral). [Latin *mille*]

$\overline{\text{M}}$ million; 1,000,000 (Roman numeral).

M′ arbitrary or working origin.

M′ Mac: *John M'Clintock.*

M molar mass *physics.*

m *I an abbreviation for:* **1** *also* **m.** handful. [Latin *manipulus*] **2** magnetic. **3** magnification. **4** *also* **m.** maiden over *cricket.* **5** *also* **m.** male. **6** *also* **m.** manual. **7** *also* **m.** mare, in horse racing. **8** maritime air mass *meteorology.* **9** *also* **m.** married. **10** *also* **m.** masculine. **11** mean: *mcp = mean candle power.* **12** *also* **m.** measure (of size, quantity, etc., or a bar of music): *In Bach's Italian Concerto the melodic line in the left hand starts from m.29.* **13** *also* **m.** melting at. **14** *also* **m.** meridian. **15** mesh. **16** *also* **m.** meter (unit of measure), metric: *m.t. = metric ton.* **17** micro- (one millionth or 10^{-6}) ▶Often in

printed work *y* is substituted for *m*, while *u* is often used in typewritten or handwritten material. **18** mile. **19** *also* **m.** mill (monetary unit of the United States, used esp. in computing tax rates). **20** milli- (one thousandth or 10^{-3}): *ma. = milliampere.* **21** million: *£1,000m = one thousand million pounds or one billion pounds in the United States.* **22** *also* **m.** minim (about a drop or $1/60$ of a dram; the smallest unit of liquid measure). **23** minor. **24** *also* **m.** minute. **25** *also* **m.** mist *meteorology.* **26** *also* **m.** mix *pharmaceutics.* **27** modulation, in combination: *am = amplitude modulation.* **28** *also* **m.** modulus *mathematics, physics.* **29** molar *physics, chemistry.* **30** *also* **m.** moon. **31** *also* **m.** muscle, in anatomy. **32** stitch, in knitting. [French *maille*]
II a symbol for: **1** apparent magnitude *astronomy.* **2** before noon, time from midnight to noon; AM [Spanish *mañana*] **3** magnetic moment, esp. magnetic dipole moment. **4** magnetic pole strength. **5** magnetic quantum number of *spin* m_S or *orbit* m_1 (see abbreviations above). **6** mass *physics:* m_e = electron mass; m_n = neutron mass; m_p = proton mass. **7** modulation factor *electronics.* **8** molality (measure of concentration of a solution). **9** noon. [Latin *meridies*] **10** thirteenth of a series (twelfth when *j* is omitted).

m- meta- (having both the 1 and 3 positions in the benzene ring) *chemistry: m-dichlorobenzene.*

MA 1 Maritime Administration (of the U.S. Department of Transportation). **2** Massachusetts (Zip Code). **3** *also* **M.A.** Master of Arts. [Latin *Magister Artium*] **4** mental age *psychology.* **5** metropolitan area: *San Diego proper has only 322,000 population, but the MA is 536,000.* **6** *also* **M/A.** Middle Ages. **7** Military Attaché.

Ma *I an abbreviation for:* **1** Mach number. **2** *also* **Ma.** major *music, military.*
II a symbol for: masurium (chemical element, now *Tc* technetium).

ma. 1 maritime antarctic air mass *meteorology.* **2** milliampere.

mA. 1 milliampere. **2** *also* **mÅ** milliangstrom.

MAA 1 master-at-arms. **2** Mathematical Association of America. **3** *also* **M.A.A.** Medieval Academy of America. **4** *also* **M.A.A.** British Motor Agents' Association.

MAAG Military Assistance Advisory Group.

MAAS *or* **M.A.A.S.** Member of the American Academy of Arts and Sciences.

MAB Medical Advisory Board.

MAC 1 machine-aided cognition *computers.* **2** maximum allowable concentration. **3** mean aerodynamic chord. **4** message authentication code *computers.* **5** Military Airlift Command. **6** motion analysis camera *biophysics.* **7** multiple-access computer (a computer system for simultaneous use from several inputs). **8** multiplexed analog components (color TV signal coding). **9** *also* **M.A.C.** Municipal Assistance Corporation. **10** mycobacterium aviumintracellulare complex (secondary bacterial infection associated with AIDS).

Mac. 1 *also* **Macb.** Macbeth (play by Shakespeare). **2** *also* **Macc.** Maccabees (two books of the Old Testament Apocrypha).

mac. 1 macadam. **2** macerate.

MACC military aid to the civilian community.

Maced. 1 Macedonia. **2** Macedonian.

mach. 1 machine. **2** machinery. **3** machinist.

Mackenz. Mackenzie, esp. Mackenzie District, Canada.

macroeco. macroeconomics.

MAD 1 a Magnetic Anomaly Detection (to trace differences in a magnetic field, originally for detecting submarines—and called Magnetic Airborne Detection—and now used in geology). **b** Magnetic Anomaly Detector. **2** maintenance, assembly, and disassembly. **3** Mutual Assured Destruction (in nuclear warfare).

Mad. 1 *also* **Madag.** Madagascar. **2** Madam. **3** Madrid.

MADD Mothers Against Drunk Driving (national organization to combat use of alcohol before driving).

MADGE Microwave Aircraft Digital Guidance Equipment.

MADI maximum acceptable daily intake.

Madm. Madam.

MADR minimum adult daily requirement *nutrition.*

MADRE magnetic drum receiving equipment (over-the-horizon search radar).

MADT microalloy diffused-base transistor.

M.A.E. *or* **MAE 1** Master of Aeronautical Engineering. **2** Master of Art Education. **3** *also* **M.A.Ed** Master of Arts in Education.

Ma.E. *or* **MaE** Master of Engineering.

M.A.Econ. Master of Arts in Economics.

Maesto. majestically *music.* [Italian *maestoso*]

MAF 1 macrophage activating factor *biology, medicine.* **2** million acre-feet: *a reservoir capacity of 4.1 MAF.* **3** minimum admissible flow. **4** minimum audible field. **5** *also* **m.a.f.** moisture and ash free (of coal).

M.A.F.F. Ministry of Agriculture, Fisheries, and Food (of Great Britain).

MAG 1 magnesium. **2** Maritime Air Group (of the Canadian Maritime Command), esp. for surveillance, customs, fisheries, and pollution monitoring. **3** maximum available gain *electronics.* **4** Military Advisory Group.

M.Ag. Master of Agriculture.

Mag. 1 large. [Latin *magnus*] **2** Magyar.

mag. 1 magazine. **2** *also* **mag** magnesium: *shiny mag wheels of a sports car.* **3 a** magnet. **b** *also* **mag** magnetic, esp. in combination: *maglev = magnetic levitation.* **c** magnetism. **4** magneto. **5** *also* **mag** magneton (unit of magnetic moment). **6** magnetron (tube used to produce microwaves). **7** magnitude. **8** magnum (of wine, esp. champagne). **9** British university master. [Latin *magister*]

MAGAMP magnetic amplifier.

magg. major *music.* [Italian *maggiore*]

maglev (mag'lev') magnetic levitation (a high-speed train supported above the ground and guided on a track of superconducting electromagnets).

Magn. *or* **magn.** large. [Latin *magnus*]

M.Agr. Master of Agriculture.

mah. *or* **mahog.** mahogany.

MAI 1 *also* **M.A.I.** Master of Engineering. [Latin *Magister in Arte Ingeniaria*] **2** *also* **mai** mean annual increment (of tree growth).

maint. maintenance.

Maj. 1 Major. **2** majority.

Maj.Gen. Major General.

mAk maritime Arctic cold air *meteorology*.

M.A.L. Member of the Legislative Assembly. [French *Membre de l'Assemblée législative*]

Mal. 1 Malachi (book of the Old Testament). **2 a** Malay. **b** Malaya. **c** Malayan. **3 a** Malaysia. **b** Malaysian. **4** Malta.

malac. malacology (study of mollusks).

M.A.L.D. *or* **MALD** Master of Arts in Law and Diplomacy.

mall malleable.

MALS 1 *also* **M.A.L.S. a** Master of Arts in Liberal Studies. **b** Master of Arts in Library Science. **2** Medium or Minimum Intensity Approach Lights System (airplane guidance to a runway).

m. à m. word for word. [French *mot à mot*]

MAMBO Mediterranean Association of Marine Biology and Oceanography.

MAMOS Marine Automatic Meteorological Observing Station (one of a series of floating buoys to transmit weather information).

Man. 1 *also* **Man** managing: *Man. Dir.* = *Managing Director; Man Ed* = *Managing Editor.* **2** Manila (of paper). **3** *also* **Man** Manitoba, Canada. **4** manual: **a** *also* **MAN.** (of an organ). **b** (of a mechanical device): *Man. trans.* = *manual transmission.* **c** (of a book of directions): *Man.Op.* = *Manual of Operation.* **5 a** manufactured: *Man. in U.S.A.* **b** manufacturer.

man. 1 manual. **2** manually: *man. op.* = *manually operated.*

manc. gradually decreasing *music.* [Italian *mancando*]

M&A mergers and acquisitions *finance.*

M&B *British* a sulphonamide. [from May and Baker, pharmaceutical house]

M&E music and effects.

M&R maintenance and repairs.

M&S maintenance and supply.

MANF May, August, November, February (months ending quarters in the financial year).

manf. manufacturer.

Mang. management.

MANIAC (mā'nē ak) Mathematical Analyzer Numerical Integrator And Computer (computer used in development of the hydrogen bomb).

Manit. Manitoba, Canada.

manuf. 1 manufacture. **2** manufactured. **3** manufacturer. **4** manufacturing.

MAO 1 *also* **M.A.O.** *British* Master of Arts in Obstetrics. **2** monoamine oxidase (enzyme).

MAOI monoamine oxidase inhibitor (antidepressant drug).

MAP 1 macro assembly program *computers.* **2** manufacturing automated protocol (data exchange between supplier and factory). **3** maximum average price. **4** mean arterial pressure *medicine.* **5** medical aid post. **6** Medical Assistance Program. **7** Military Assistance Program: *MAPAG = Military Assistance Program Advisory Group.* **8** minimum audible pressure (of noise). **9** *also* **M.A.P.** Ministry of Aircraft Production (of Great Britain). **10** Modified American Plan (room, breakfast, and dinner). **11** modified atmospheric packaging (food packaging with a gas mixture to retard spoiling; also the wrapper used in such packaging). **12** Mutual Assistance Program.

MAPI Machinery and Allied Products Institute.

M.App.Sc. Master of Applied Science.

MAQ monetary allowance for quarters.

MAR 1 memory address register *computers.* **2** microanalytical reagent *chemistry.* **3** Multifunction Array Radar.

Mar. March.

mar. 1 marine. **2** maritime. **3** married.

MARAD Maritime Administration (of U.S. Department of Commerce).

MARC 1 Machine Readable Catalog or Cataloging (computer tapes of a collection, esp. of the Library of Congress or the British Library). **2** Metropolitan Applied Research Center.

marc. in a marked or emphatic way *music.* [Italian *marcato*]

March. Marchioness.

M.Arch. Master of Architecture.

MARCOM Maritime Command (of the Canadian Armed Forces).

marg 1 margarine. **2 a** margin. **b** *also* **marg.** marginal, also in combination: *marg. trans.* = *marginal translation.*

Marisat (mar'ə sat') maritime satellite (any one of a group of satellites positioned over the world's oceans for transmission of marine weather conditions).

Marit. Maritime.

MARMAP (mar'map') Marine Resources Monitoring Assessment and Prediction (survey of living marine resources available to the U.S.).

Marq. Marquess or Marquis.

MARS 1 Meteorological Automatic Reporting Station. **2** Military Affiliated Radio System. **3** Mobile Atlantic Range Stations.

Mart. 1 Martinique. **2 a** martyr. **b** martyrology.

MARV (*pronounced* marv) Maneuverable Reentry Vehicle (missile with multiple warheads that can be maneuvered to avoid interception).

MAS 1 Military Agency for Standardization (agency of NATO). **2** *also* **mAs** milliampere second.

M.A.S. *or* **M.A.Sc.** Master of Applied Science.

masc. masculine.

maskon (mas'kon') mass concentration (of dense material lying below the surface of a planet or moon).

maser (mā'zər) microwave amplification by stimulated emission of radiation.

MASH (*pronounced* mash) Mobile Army Surgical Hospital.

Mass. Massachusetts.

MAT 1 machine-aided translation. **2** *also* **M.A.T.** Master of Arts in Teaching. **3** material *military.* **4** Mechanical Aptitude Test. **5** microalloy transistor *electronics.* **6** Miller Analogy Test (for qualifying in graduate studies in education).

Mat 1 maternity: *Mat Ward.* **2** *also* **Mat.** matinee: *Evgs. 7:30, Mats. Sats. 2:30.* **3** Matthew. **4** maturity (of a financial obligation).

mat. 1 matinee. **2** matins. **3** maturity.

MATCOM Materials Command *military.*

math. 1 *also British* **maths** (*pronounced* maths) mathematics. **2** mathematical. **3** mathematician.

MATIF Financial Futures Exchange. [French *Marché à Terme des Instruments Financiers*]

matl. material.

matr. matrimony, marriage.

Matric. 1 matriculated. **2** matriculation.

MATS (*pronounced* mats) Military Air Transport Service.

Matt. 1 Matthew (book of the New Testament). **2** Matthias (the disciple who took Judas's place).

Matts multiple airborne target trajectory system.

MATV master antenna television (now generally replaced by cable).

Mau *or* **Mau.** Mauritius (island country in the Indian Ocean): *Mau Rs = Mauritius rupee* (monetary unit).

MAUDE Morse Automatic Decoder.

MAW medium assault weapon.

mAw maritime Arctic warm air mass *meteorology.*

m.a.W. in other words. [German *mit anderen Worten*]

Max. Maximilian.

max. 1 maxim. **2** *also* **MAX** (*often pronounced* maks) maximum.

MB 1 *also* **M.B. a** *British* Bachelor of Medicine. [Latin *Medicinae Baccalaureus*] **b** Bachelor of Music [Latin *Musicae Baccalaureus*] **2** *also* **m.b.** magnetic bearing *navigation, surveying.* **3** Manitoba (postal code). **4** Marketing Board. **5** *also* **M.B.** Medical Board. **6** *also* **Mb** megabit (one million bits). **7** megabyte (one million bytes): *1,600 MB disk memory.* **8** memory buffer *computers.* **9** *also* **M.B.** Municipal Borough: *M.B.C. = Municipal Borough Council.*

mb 1 *also* **mb. a** millibar, millibars *meteorology.* **b** millibarn *nuclear physics.* **2** *also* **m.b.** mix well *pharmaceutics.* [Latin *misce bene*]

MBA Master of Business Administration.

mbar millibar, millibars *meteorology.*

MBC maximum breathing capacity *medicine.*

MBD minimal brain dysfunction.

mbd million barrels per day.

MBDA Minority Business Development Administration (of U.S. Department of Commerce).

MBE 1 *also* **M.B.E.** Member of the Order of the British Empire. **2** Minority Business Enterprise. **3** molecular beam epitaxy *physics.* **4** Multistate Bar Examination.

MBF *or* **mbf** thousand board feet.

MBFR mutual and balanced force reduction (plan for simultaneous and proportionate reduction of armed forces of Western Europe and the former Soviet Union).

m.b.H. limited liability (corresponding to British *Ltd.* and American *Inc.* or *Corp.*). [German *mit beschränkter Haftung*]

mbit megabit *computers.*

MBK missing, believed killed (of military casualties).

M.B.L. *or* **MBL** Marine Biological Laboratory.

mbl. mobile.

MBM 1 Master of Business Management. **2** *also* **m.b.m.** thousand feet or foot board measure: *income from forest products was derived from spruce planks and boards, $4,438,908 (57,552 MBM).*

MBO management by objective (esp. in public sector).

MBP 1 major basic protein. **2** mean blood pressure.

Mbps megabits per second *computers.*

MBR 1 master bedroom. **2** memory buffer register *computers.*

Mbr. *or* **mbr.** member.

MBRF Ministry for Security of the Russian Federation. [Russian *Ministerstvo Bezopasnosti Rossiyskaya Federatsiya*]

MBS 1 mortgage-backed security. **2** Mutual Broadcasting System (radio and television network).

M.B.Sc. *or* **MBSc** Master of Business Science.

MBT 1 main battle tank. **2** many-body theory (method used to determine physical properties of particles in a system) *physics.* **3** mean body temperature. **4** mercaptobenzothiazole (used in making rubber). **5** metal base transistor.

MBTA Metropolitan Boston Transit Authority.

Mbyte (em'bīt') megabyte *computers.*

MC 1 *also* **M.C.** machinery certificate (of a ship). **2** magnetic course *navigation.* **3** Marine Corps: *USMC = United States Marine Corps.* **4** master control, also in combination: *MCL = master control log.* **5** *also* **M.C.** master of ceremonies. **6** *also* **M.C.** British Master of Surgery. [Latin *Magister Chirurgiae*] **7** Medical Center, in combination: *NYUMC = New York University Medical Center.* **8** medical certificate. **9** Medical Corps. **10** *also* **M.C.** Member of Congress. **11** *also* **M.C.** British Member of Council. **12** *also* **M.C.** British Military Cross. **13** Mission Control (of a space flight). **14** molecular cloud *astronomy.* **15** Morse Code. **16** motorcycle. **17** multiple contact *electronics.*

M/C marginal credit *finance, commerce.*

Mc- Mac: *Ruth G. McClair.*

mc. 1 *also* **Mc.** *or* **mc** megacycle, megacycles (for radio, now represented as megahertz, MHz). **2** *also* **mc** millicurie, millicuries.

m.c. 1 master of ceremonies. **2** metric carat. **3** *also* **mc** moving coil (current carrying coil in a magnetic field), also in combination: *mcm = moving coil motor.*

MCA 1 *also* **M.C.A.** Management Consultants Association. **2** *also* **M.C.A.** Manufacturing Chemists Association. **3** methylcyanoacrylate (an adhesive). **4** microchannel architecture *computers.* **5** monetary compensatory amounts. **6** multichannel analyzer *electronics.*

MCAE mechanical computer-aided engineering.

mcal. microcalorie (small calorie).

MCAT (em'kat') Medical College Admission Test.

MCC 1 also **M.C.C.** Marylebone Cricket Club (accepted worldwide as the source of cricket regulations). **2** midcourse correction *navigation*. **3** Mission Control Center (for NASA).

MCD 1 magnetic circular dichromism *physics*. **2** mean corpuscular diameter.

MCE or **M.C.E.** Master of Civil Engineering.

Mcf or **M c.f.** or **MCF** thousand cubic feet: *Mcfd = thousand cubic feet per day.*

MCG magnetocardiograph *medicine*.

mcg microgram.

MCGA multicolor graphics array *computers*.

MCH 1 Maternal and Child Health, also in combination: *MCHS = Maternity and Child Health Services*. **2** mean corpuscular hemoglobin, also in combination: *MCHC = mean corpuscular hemoglobin concentration*.

Mch 1 Manchester. **2** March.

M.Ch. *British* Master of Surgery. [Latin *Magister Chirurgiae*]

M.Ch.D. *British* Master of Dental Surgery. [Latin *Magister Chirurgiae Dentalis*]

M.Ch.E. Master of Chemical Engineering.

M.C.H.R. Medical Committee for Human Rights.

mcht merchant.

mchy machinery.

MCI 1 malleable cast iron. **2** Microwave Communications Incorporated (independent telephone service).

MCi megacurie.

mCi millicurie.

MCL 1 Marine Corps League. **2** also **M.C.L. a** Master of Civil Law. **b** Master of Comparative Law. **3** maximum contaminant level.

MCM 1 Monte Carlo method (computational technique using random samples for solutions to mathematical and physical problems) *mathematics, physics*. **2** one thousand circular mils (1 MCM = 0.000785 sq.in.).

MCO mill cull outs (of lumber).

Mco. Morocco (leather).

M.Com. Master of Commerce (business degree).

MCP 1 male chauvinist pig (epithet to describe excessive male pride). **2** master control program. **3** Master of City Planning. **4** microchannel plate *biology*.

MCPA methylchlorophenoxyacetic acid (herbicide).

M/CPO Master Chief Petty Officer.

mcps megacycles per second (now *MHz/s*).

MCR 1 master control routine *computers*. **2** metabolic clearance rate *medicine*. **3** military compact reactor: *MCR power plant*. **4** mobile control room *military*.

MCS 1 also **M.C.S. a** Master of Commercial Science. **b** Master of Computer Science. **2** medium close shot *photography*. **3** also **M.C.S.** multiple chemical sensitivities (an allergic condition) *medicine*.

mc/s megacycles per second (now *MHz/s*).

M-CSF monocyte colony stimulating factor (of the blood) *medicine, biology*.

MCT maximum continuous thrust (of a rocket motor).

MCU 1 medium close-up *photography*. **2** microprogrammed control unit (computer memory storing microoperations).

MCV mean corpuscular volume *medicine*.

MCW modulated continuous wave *electronics*.

Mcy/sec megacycles per second (now *MHz/s*).

MD 1 also **M.D.** Doctor of Medicine. [Latin *Medicinae Doctor*] **2** machine direction. **3** also **M.D.** Managing Director. **4** map distance. **5** Maryland (Zip Code). **6** mean deviation *navigation, statistics*. **7** also **M.D.** Medical Department. **8** also **M.D.** memorandum of deposit *commerce*. **9** mentally deficient. **10** also **M.D.** Middle District (a U.S. judicial district, esp. in a large political division, such as a State). **11** Middle Dutch (from about 1100 to about 1500). **12** mini disk (small compact disk). **13** muscular dystrophy. **14** also **M.D.** music director. **15** right hand *music*. [Italian *mano destra*, French *main droite*]

M/D 1 memorandum of deposit *commerce*. **2** *commerce* **a** months after date. **b** month's date. **3** mother/daughter (referring to a small apartment in a private house).

Md *I an abbreviation for:* **1** also **Md.** Maryland. **2** median. *II a symbol for:* mendelevium (chemical element).

m/d or **m.d.** *commerce* **1** months after date. **2** month's date.

md or **mD** millidarcy (measure of permeability).

MDA 1 methylenedioxy-amphetamine (a hallucinogenic drug). **2** minimum detectable activity. **3** monochrome display adaptor *computers*. **4** multidimensional access *computers*. **5** Muscular Dystrophy Association.

MDAP Mutual Defense Assistance Program (1949, later *Mutual Security Program*).

M-day mobilization day *military*.

MDB Brazilian Democratic Movement (political party). [Brazilian Portuguese *Movimento Democrático Brasileiro*]

M.d.B. Member of the German Parliament. [German *Mitglied des Bundestages*]

MDC More Developed Country (designation in political economic geography).

Md D median deviation *statistics*.

mdd milligrams per square decimeter per day.

Mddx. Middlesex County, England.

M.Des. Master of Design.

MDF 1 macrodefect-free cement. **2** main distribution frame (of circuits in a computer). **3** manual direction finder.

MDG muscular dysgenesis.

MDH magnetohydrodynamic *physics*: *MDH generator*.

MDI magnetic direction indicator.

m. dict. as directed, *esp. in pharmaceutics*. [Latin *modo dictu*]

M.Div. Master of Divinity.

M.d.L. Member of the State Parliament (any of the states of Germany). [German *Mitglied des Landtages*]

mdl. *or* **Mdl.** 1 middle. 2 model.

Mdlle. Mademoiselle.

Mdm. madam.

MDMA methylenedioxy-methamphetamine (stimulating hallucinogenic drug).

Mdme. *British* Madame.

mdn. *or* **Mdn** median.

mdnt. midnight.

MDR 1 memory data register *computers*. 2 *also* **mdr** minimum daily requirement: *900 times the mdr of various nutrients.* 3 multichannel data recorder *computers*.

MDS 1 *also* **M.D.S.** Master of Dental Surgery. 2 medical-dental service. 3 minimum data set (forms to record a patient's condition). 4 minimum discernible signal *electronics*. 5 multipoint distribution service (microwave broadcasting to subscribers).

M.D.Sc. Master of Dental Science.

mdse merchandise.

mdsg. *or* **Mdsg** merchandising.

MDST *or* **M.D.S.T.** *or* **m.d.s.t.** mountain daylight saving time.

MDT 1 mean downtime (time of malfunction of a computer or other machinery). 2 *also* **M.D.T.** *or* **m.d.t.** mountain daylight time.

mdt. moderate.

MDTA Manpower Development and Training Act.

MDu *or* **MDu.** Middle Dutch (from about 1100 to about 1500).

M.D.V. *or* **MDV** Doctor of Veterinary Medicine.

M.D.Z. Maritime Defense Zone (area surrounding the U.S. protected by the U.S. Coast Guard).

ME 1 Maine (Zip Code). 2 *also* **M.E.** Managing Editor. 3 marbled edges (in book manufacturing). 4 *also* **M.E.** Marine Engineer. 5 marriage encounter (discussion group for support of married couples). 6 maximum effort. 7 *also* **M.E.** Mechanical Engineer. 8 *also* **M.E.** Medical Examiner. 9 metabolizable energy. 10 Middle East, esp. in combination: *MECAS = Middle East Centre for Arab Studies.* 11 *also* **ME.** *or* **M.E.** Middle English (from 1100 to 1475 or 1500). 12 *also* **M.E.** Mining Engineer. 13 Mössbauer Effect *nuclear physics*.

Me methyl *chemistry*.

Me. 1 Madame. 2 Maine. 3 Master (title of French advocate). [French *maître*] 4 Messerschmitt (German fighter plane of WWII): *Me. 109.*

me. milliequivalent.

MEA monoethanolamine (cleaning agent and carbon dioxide absorbent).

meas. 1 measurable. 2 measure.

Meas. for M. Measure for Measure (play by Shakespeare).

MEBA Marine Engineers Beneficial Association.

M.E.C. 1 Member of the Executive Council. 2 *also* **M.E.Ch.** Methodist Episcopal Church.

M.Ec. Master of Economics.

MECA molecular emission cavity analysis *biology*.

mech. *or military* **MECH** 1 mechanic. 2 mechanical. 3 mechanics. 4 mechanism. 5 mechanized.

Mech.E. Mechanical Engineer.

MECO main engine cutoff (the point in a space flight when the main engine of a spacecraft is shut down).

M.Econ. Master of Economics.

MED 1 *also* **M.E.D.** Middle English Dictionary. 2 *medicine* a minimum effective dose b minimum erythema dose (to produce an allergic reaction). 3 Offices of Medical Services.

Med. 1 Medical: *Med.R.C. = Medical Reserve Corps.* 2 Medieval: *Med. Lat. = Medieval Latin.* 3 Mediterranean: *Med. Sea.*

med. 1 medalist. 2 median. 3 *also military* **MED** medical, medicine: *med. tech. = medical technology; MEDEVAC = Medical Evacuation.* 4 medium.

M.Ed. Master of Education.

MEDEVAC *or* **medevac** (med′ə vak′) medical evacuation (military helicopter to carry combat wounded).

Medibank (med′ə bangk′) Medical Bank (national health insurance program of Australia).

Medicaid *or* **medicaid** (med′ə kād′) medical aid (government program helping to pay medical costs).

Medicare *or* **medicare** (med′ə kãr′) medical care (government program of medical care: in the U.S., benefits for those over 65; in Canada and Australia, the government health insurance program).

MEDICO (med′ə kō′) Medical International Cooperation Organization (to build hospitals in remote areas).

Medit. Mediterranean.

MEDLARS *or* **Medlars** (med′lärz′) Medical Literature Analysis and Retrieval System (computerized bibliography of medical literature from magazines).

MEDLINE (med′līn′) MEDLARS on-line (direct-line computer system for bibliographical data in MEDLARS).

MEDO Middle East Defense Organization.

Med.Sc.D. Doctor of Medical Science.

M.E.E. Master of Electrical Engineering.

meg 1 magneto-encephalograph (used in diagnosis of epilepsy). 2 *also* **MEG** mega (10^6 or 1,000,000). 3 megabyte, megabytes *computers*. 4 megacycle (now *MHz*). 5 megohm.

megarep. mega roentgen equivalent physical.

MEK methyl ethyl ketone (solvent).

MEL Master or Mistress of English Literature.

Mel 1 *also* **Melan.** a Melanesia. b Melanesian. 2 *also* **Melb** Melbourne.

MELUS Society for the Study of Multi-Ethnic Literature of the United States.

mem. 1 member. 2 memento. 3 memoir. 4 memorandum. 5 *also* **Mem.** memorial.

MEMC methoxyethylmercury chloride (fungicide).

memcon (mem′kon′) memorandum of a conversation.

memo (mem′ō) memorandum.

MEN multiple endocrine neoplasia *medicine.*

Men Table Mountain (constellation). [Latin *Mensa*]

MENC Music Educators National Conference.

M.Eng. 1 Master of Engineering. 2 Mechanical Engineer. 3 Mining Engineer.

mensur. mensuration (measuring or study of measurement).

mentd mentioned.

MEP 1 *also* **M.E.P.** Master of Engineering Physics. 2 *also* **mep** mean effective pressure. 3 Member of the European Parliament.

meq *or* **m.eq.** *or* **mEq.** milliequivalent.

MER 1 maximum efficient rate. 2 methanol extraction residue.

mer. 1 mercury. 2 meridian.

merc. 1 mercantile. 2 *also* **merc** (*pronounced* mèrk) mercenary. 3 mercury.

Merch. V. The Merchant of Venice (play by Shakespeare).

Merry W. The Merry Wives of Windsor (play by Shakespeare).

MES 1 *also* **M.E.S.** Methodist Episcopal Church, South (southern branch that broke away from the Methodists over slavery). 2 Mössbauer Emission Spectroscopy *chemistry.*

MESA Marine Ecosystems Analysis.

M. ès A. Master of Arts. [French *Maître ès Arts*]

MESBIC minority-enterprise small-business investment company.

M. Esc Mozambique escudo (monetary unit).

MESFET metal semiconductor field-effect transistor *electronics.*

MeSH Medical Subject Headings (reference guide used with MEDLARS).

Messrs. Messieurs, Gentlemen.

Met 1 *also* **Met.** methionine (an essential amino acid). 2 *also* **Met.** Metropolitan. 3 (*pronounced* met) Metropolitan Opera House or Company, New York.

met. 1 *also* **metab.** metabolism. 2 metallic. 3 a metallurgy. b metallurgical. 4 a metaphor. b metaphorical. 5 a metaphysics. b metaphysical. 6 *also* **met** a meteorology. b meteorological: *met satellites.* 7 methionine (an essential amino acid). 8 metronome.

metal. *or* **metall.** 1 metallurgy. 2 metallurgical.

metaph. 1 a metaphor. b metaphorical. 2 a metaphysics. b metaphysical.

Met.E. Metallurgical Engineer.

meteor. *or* **meteorol.** 1 meteorology. 2 meteorological.

Meteosat meteorological satellite (of the European system of weather observation): *Meteosat-3.*

Meth. Methodist.

meth 1 (*pronounced* meth) methamphetamine (hallucinogenic drug). 2 *also* **meth.** methane (principal constituent of natural gas). 3 *also* **Meth.** methylated, esp. methylated spirits (in British English reduced to *meths*, alcohol mixed with methyl alcohol to make it unfit to drink).

methadone (meth'ə dōn) synthetic narcotic used to treat heroin addiction. [(di)*meth*(yl) *a*(mino) *d*(iphenyl) (heptan)*one*]

M-et-L Maine-et-Loire (department of France).

M-et-M Meurthe-et-Moselle (department of France).

meton. metonymy (figure of speech; use of words in a transferred sense).

metro (met'rō) 1 *also* **Metro** metropolitan area. 2 subway system, esp. the Paris subway system and later that of London, Washington, D.C., and Los Angeles. [Although Parliament created London's Metropolitan railway in 1853, the name *metro* seems to derive from the French *métro*, for *métropolitain*, a shortened form of *chemin de fer métropolitain*, whose construction was started some 45 years after London's Metropolitan railway.]

metrol. metrology (science of weights and measures).

metrop. 1 metropolis. 2 *also* **metropol** metropolitan.

metsat (met'sat') meteorological satellite.

m. et sig. mix and write a label *pharmaceutics.* [Latin *misce et signa*]

MEV *or* **MeV** *or* **Mev** *or* **mev** (*pronounced* mev) million electron volts.

meV millielectron volt.

MEW Microwave Early Warning (high-power warning radar, built in 1942 to protect the West Coast from Japanese attack).

Mex. 1 Mexican, also in combination: *Mex.Sp.* = *Mexican Spanish.* 2 Mexico.

MEZ *or* **M.E.Z.** Middle European Time. [German *Mitteleuropäische Zeit*]

mez mezzo *music.*

Mezz. mezzanine (in a theater).

MF 1 machine finish (of paper). 2 *also* **M.F.** Master of Forestry. 3 Medal of Freedom (Presidential Medal of Freedom, highest U.S. civilian award). 4 *also* **mf** medium frequency *electronics.* 5 melamine-formaldehyde (resin). 6 microfiche. 7 *also* **MF.** Middle French (about 1400 to about 1600). 8 mill finish (of lumber). 9 multifrequency (of a telephone operated by tones, Touch-Tone): *MF switching.*

M-F Monday through Friday.

mf. 1 manufacture. 2 *also* **mf** *or* **mF** a microfarad, microfarads (one millionth of a farad). b millifarad, millifarads (one thousandth of a farad).

m.f. moderately loud (direction in playing or singing) *music.* [Italian *mezzo forte*]

m/f male, female, esp. in advertisements for employment.

MFA 1 *also* **M.F.A.** Master of Fine Arts: *M.F.A. Mus.* = *Master of Fine Arts in Music.* 2 Multifiber Arrangement (textile and apparel importing quotas in the EC)

M.F.B. *or* **MFB** British Metropolitan Fire Brigade.

MFBM *or* **m.f.b.m.** thousand feet or foot board measure; MBM.

M.F.D. *or* **MFD** minimum fatal dose *medicine.*

mfd. 1 manufactured. 2 *also* **mfd** a microfarad, microfarads (one millionth of a farad). b *also* **mfd** millifarad, millifarads (one thousandth of a farad).

mfg. manufacturing.

MFH mobile field hospital *military.*

m/f/h/v male, female, handicapped, veteran (in advertisements for employment).

MFlem Middle Flemish (from about 1300 to about 1550).

mflops million floating-point operations per second *computers*.

MFM modified frequency modulation (encoding for computer storage of data).

MFN most favored nation.

MFO Multinational Peacekeeping Force (Canadian military forces attached to the UN for truce observance and other peacekeeping functions).

MFP mean free path (of subatomic particles or sound waves) *physics*.

M.Fr. Middle French (from about 1400 to about 1600).

mfr. 1 manufacture. 2 manufacturer.

MFS *or* **M.F.S.** 1 Master of Food Science. 2 Master of Foreign Study.

MFSK multiple-frequency-shift keying *computers*.

MFT 1 motor freight tariff *commerce*. 2 multiprogramming with fixed task *computers*.

m.ft. let a mixture be made *pharmaceutics*. [Latin *mixtura fiat*]

mftL millifoot lamberts *physics*.

MG 1 *also* **M.G.** *or* **m.g.** left hand. [French *main gauche*] 2 *also* **m.g.** machine glazed (of paper). 3 machine gun, also in combination: *MGC = machine gun company or corps*. 4 Military Government: *MGO = Military Government Officer*. 5 Morris Garage (originally British manufacturer of sports cars, and the name of the automobiles). 6 motor generator. 7 myasthenia gravis (muscular disease).

Mg *I an abbreviation for: also* **Mg.** megagram (one million grams).
II a symbol for: magnesium (chemical element).

mg. 1 a margin. b marginal. 2 *also* **mG** milligauss (thousandth of a gauss, unit of magnetic induction). 3 *also* **mg a** milligram, milligrams (thousandth of a gram). b microgram (millionth of a gram).

MGA *or* **M.G.A.** Member of the General Assembly.

Mgal million gallons, also in combination: *Mgal/d = million gallons per day*.

mgal. milligal (thousandth of a gal, measure of gravity).

mgawd *or* **MGAWD** make good all works distributed (esp. in contracts) *law*.

M.G.B. *or* **MGB** Ministry of State Security (former internal security force). [Russian *Ministerstvo Gosudarstvennoi Bezopasnosti*]

m.g.d. *or* **MGD** million gallons per day (as of sewage).

MGE Minneapolis Grain Exchange (a commodities market) *commerce*.

mge message.

M.G.H. Massachusetts General Hospital.

mgh milligram hour.

MGk. Medieval or Middle Greek (from about 700 to 1500).

MGM Metro-Goldwyn-Mayer (motion picture studio).

mgm. *or* **mgm** milligram, milligrams (thousandth of a gram).

Mgmt. management.

MGN membranous glomerulonephritis (type of kidney disease).

MGOe megagauss-oersted (measure of magnetic energy).

MGr. Medieval or Middle Greek (from about 700 to 1500).

Mgr. 1 *also* **mgr.** Manager. 2 Monseigneur (French title of honor). 3 Monsignor (title in Roman Catholic Church).

mgs *or* **m.g.s.** *or* **MGS** meter-gram-second (system of measurement).

Mgt management.

MGW 1 Manchester Guardian Weekly (newspaper). 2 *also* **mgw** maximum gross weight (as of a vehicle carrying cargo or passengers).

MH 1 magnetic heading (of a compass). 2 main hatch (of a ship). 3 maleic hydrazide (chemical that prevents sprouting in plants). 4 Marshall Islands (in postal address). 5 *also* **M.H.** Medal of Honor. 6 Mental Health, also in combination: *MHT = mental health technician*. 7 Military Hospital.

mh. *or* **mh** *or* **mH** millihenry, millihenries (thousandth of a henry).

MHA 1 Master in Hospital Administration. 2 *also* **M.H.A.** Member of the House of Assembly.

MHC major histocompatibility complex (genes controlling human antigens).

MHCP *or* **mhcp** mean horizontal candlepower.

MHD 1 a magnetohydrodynamic (generator). b magnetohydrodynamics. 2 minimum hemolytic dose.

MHG *or* **M.H.G.** Middle High German (language of south and central Germany from about 1050 to about 1500).

M.H.K. *or* **MHK** Member of the House of Keys (lower house of the legislature of the Isle of Man).

M.H.L. Master of Hebrew Literature.

M.H.L.G. *or* **MHLG** British Ministry of Housing and Local Government.

MHMA Mobile Homes Manufacturers Association.

mho (mō) unit of electrical conductance (reciprocal of the ohm, now called *siemens: S*).

M.Hort. Master of Horticulture.

M.H.R. *or* **MHR** Member of the House of Representatives.

MHSS Military Health Services System.

MHT mean high tide.

MHW mean high water: *MHWNT = mean high-water neap tide*.

M.Hy. Master of Hygiene.

MHz megahertz (term now used to replace *megacycles*).

MHz/s megahertz per second.

mHz millihertz.

MI 1 malleable iron (malleable cast iron or wrought iron). 2 metabolic index. 3 Michigan (Zip Code). 4 Military Intelligence: *MID = Military Intelligence Division; MI5 = counterespionage and security branch of British military intelligence*. 5 mitotic index (percentage of cells in mitosis) *biology*.

6 moment of inertia *physics.* **7** *also* **M.I.** myocardial infarction (obstruction of blood supply to the heart muscle).

Mi. minor *astronomy, music, military.*

mi. 1 a *also* **mi** mile, miles, also in combination: *mi/gal = miles per gallon; mi/h = miles per hour.* **b** mileage. **2** mill, mills (monetary unit). **3** minute, minutes.

MIA 1 missing in action. **2** *also* **M.I.A.** Murrumbidgee Irrigation Area (in Australia). **3** *also* **M.I.A.** Mutual Improvement Association (Mormon youth movement).

MIC 1 microwave integrated circuit *electronics.* **2** military-industrial complex.

Mic Microscope (constellation).

Mic. Micah (book of the Old Testament).

MICA Mentally Ill Chemical or Chronic Abuser.

Mich. 1 Michael. **2** Michaelmas (esp. of the festival honoring St. Michael). **3** Michigan.

MICR magnetic ink character recognition (on bank checks, etc.).

micr. microscopic.

Micro. 1 Micronesia. **2** Micronesian.

microcryst. microcrystalline.

micros. microscopy.

MICU Mobile Intensive Care Unit.

MID 1 military intelligence division. **2** *also* **M.I.D.** minimum infective dose *medicine.*

Mid. 1 Midlands (the Midland counties of England). **2** *also* **Mid** Midshipman.

mid. 1 middle. **2** midnight.

MIDAS (mī′dəs) measurement information data analysis system (analog computing program).

Middx. Middlesex County, England.

MIDI musical instrument digital interface (system connecting various electronic instruments).

Mids.N.D. A Midsummer Night's Dream (play by Shakespeare).

MIF migration inhibitory factor *medicine.*

MIFS multiplex interferometric Fourier spectroscopy (technique used in infrared astronomy).

MIG 1 metal-inert gas (method for welding aluminum). **2** *also* **Mig** Russian jet fighter (followed by number indicating model): *MIG 21.* [Russian *Mikoyan* and *Gurevich*, aircraft designers]

Mij. joint stock company. [Dutch *Maatschapij*]

MIL military: *MILSPEC = military specifications.*

mil. 1 mileage. **2** *also* **Mil.** Military: *Mil. Att. = Military Attaché.* **3** *also* **Mil.** Militia. **4** millieme (unit of money worth one thousandth of country's monetary unit). **5** million.

Milit. military.

mill. million.

millisec millisecond.

Milt. Milton (English poet, 1608–74).

Milw. Milwaukee.

MIMD Multiple Instruction, Multiple Data (computer system for different instructions to operate on different data simultaneously).

Min. 1 a mineralogy. **b** mineralogical. **2 a** Minister: *Defense Min.* **b** Ministry. **3** minor, *esp. in music.*

min 1 microinch, microinches. **2** *also* **min.** mineral. **3** *also* **min. a** mineralogy. **b** mineralogical. **4** minim (about a drop or 1/60 of a dram, smallest unit of liquid measure). **5** *also* **min.** minimum, also in combination: *min. wt. = minimum weight.* **6** *also* **min.** mining. **7** *also* **min.** minor. **8** *also* **min.** minute, minutes.

mineral. 1 mineralogy. **2** mineralogical.

Minn. Minnesota.

Min.Plen. Minister Plenipotentiary (minister of government having full authority).

MINS (*pronounced* minz) Minor In Need of Supervision *law, social work.*

MIO minimal identifiable odor.

MIP 1 Marine Insurance Policy. **2** *also* **M.I.P.** *or* **m.i.p.** mean indicated pressure. **3** Monthly Investment Plan (stock purchase through New York Stock Exchange member firms monthly or quarterly on a pay-as-you-go basis).

MIPR Military Interdepartmental Purchase Request.

MIPS (*pronounced* mips) million instructions per second (measure of computer capacity).

MIR 1 *also* **M.I.R.** Leftist Revolutionary Movement (of South America). [Spanish *Movimiento de Izquierda Revolucionaria*] **2** memory information register *computers.* **3** Music Information Retrieval.

M.Ir. *or* **MIr** Middle Irish (Irish from about 900 to about 1400).

mir. mercifully. [Latin *misericorditer*]

MIRA Motor Industry Research Association (of Great Britain).

MIRAS mortgage interest relief at source.

MIRB Mutual Insurance Rating Bureau.

MIRD medical internal radiation dose.

MIRV (*pronounced* mèrv) Multiple Independently-targeted Reentry Vehicle (space weaponry which splits off warheads as it approaches target).

MIS 1 Management Information System. **2** metal insulator semiconductor (transistor).

misc *or* **misc. 1** *also* **miscl. a** miscellaneous. **b** miscellany. **2** miscible (that can be mixed).

Misc. Doc. Miscellaneous Document (followed by number, of the U.S. House of Representatives or the Senate).

MISD Multiple Instruction, Single Data (computer system for different instructions to operate on one set of data; compare *MIMD*).

MISFET metal insulator semiconductor field effect transistor.

misn. misnumbered.

Miss. 1 a Mission. **b** *also* **miss.** Missionary. **2** Mississippi.

mist. mixture. [Latin *mistura*]

mistrans. mistranslation.

MIT 1 *also* **M.I.T.** Massachusetts Institute of Technology. **2** master instruction tape *computers*. **3** *also* **m.i.t.** milled in transit. **4** monoiodotyrosine (precursor of thyroid hormone).

M.I.T.I. *or* **MITI** Ministry of International Trade and Industry (of Japan).

mIU milli-International Unit.

mixt. mixture.

mj. 1 *also* **MJ** megajoule. **2** *also* **mj** *or* **mJ** millijoule.

MJD management job description.

M.J.S. Member of the Japan Society.

MJSD March, June, Setember, December (quarterly months in accounting).

Mk 1 a *also* **MK** Mark (car model): *the Austin Cambridge MK II*. **b** *also* **Mk.** Mark (book of the New Testament). **2** *also* **mk. a** mark (monetary unit of Germany). **b** *also* **mk** markka (monetary unit of Finland). **3** *also* **MK** system of classifying stars in order of luminosity (formerly *MKK*): *MK system*.

mk 1 *also* **MK** meter-kilogram. **2** *also* **mK** millikelvin.

mkd. marked.

mkg *or* **m-kg.** meter-kilogram.

MKK Morgan, Keenan, Kellman (tabulation of stellar luminosity, now *MK* or *Mk*): *MKK system*.

mkm. *or* **Mkm.** marksman.

MKO Mauna Kea Observatory (astronomical observatory in Hawaii).

mkr. marker.

mks *or* **MKS** meter-kilogram-second (system of measurement).

mksa *or* **MKSA** meter-kilogram-second-ampere, or Giorgi, system (system of measurement).

mkt. market.

mktg *or* **mktg.** marketing, *esp. in advertising*.

Mkw.h. *or* **MkWh** million kilowatt hours.

ML 1 *also* **M.L.** Licentiate in Medicine. [Latin *Medicinae Licentiatus*] **2** machine language. **3** *also* **m.l.** mean level. **4** *also* **ML.** Medieval Latin. **5** medium large. **6** *also* **M.L.** mineral lease. **7** *also* **m.l.** *or* **M/L** mixed lengths (of lumber). **8** mold line, in technical drawings. **9** motor launch. **10** *also* **M.L.** muzzle-loading: *M.L. shooting*. **11** regular oil (a grade of motor oil).

Ml. *British* mail.

mL 1 millilambert (unit of brightness). **2** milliliter.

ml. 1 *British* mail. **2** mile. **3** *also* **ml** milliliter.

MLA 1 *also* **M.L.A.** Master in Landscape Architecture. **2** Medical Library Association. **3** *also* **M.L.A.** Member of the Legislative Assembly. **4** Modern Language Association (professional organization for teachers and scholars in all the modern languages and literatures). **5** Music Library Association.

MLB Multiple Listing Board or Bureau (of real estate and employment).

MLBM modern large ballistic missile.

MLC 1 *also* **M.L.C.** Member of the Legislative Council. **2** mixed lymphocyte culture (test for compatibility of tissues for transplant).

MLD 1 *also* **m.l.d. a** median lethal dose. **b** minimum lethal dose. **2** metachromatic leukodystrophy (disease inhibiting metabolism of fat).

Mld. report. [German *Meldung*]

mld. 1 molded. **2** *also* **mldg.** molding (of lumber).

MLDNA mitochondrial DNA.

mldr. molder.

MLE 1 maximum likelihood estimate *statistics*. **2** maximum loss expectancy.

mle model *or* pattern. [French *modèle*]

MLF 1 Feminist Liberation Movement. [French *Mouvement de Libération de la Femme*] **2** multilateral force (Pres. Kennedy's proposed Nato fleet of ships armed with nuclear weapons and manned by multinational crews. It was one of the issues that led to French withdrawal from NATO).

MLG *or* **MLG.** Middle Low German (language of northern Germany from about 1050 to 1500).

M.Lib.Sc. Master of Library Science.

M.Lit. *or* **M.Litt.** Master of Letters or Literature. [Latin *Magister Lit(t)erarum*]

MLJ Modern Language Journal (publication).

Mlle. Mademoiselle.

Mlles. Mesdemoiselles.

MLM multilevel marketing (door-to-door sales).

MLN 1 Modern Language Notes (publication). **2** National Liberation Movement (of Latin America). [Spanish *Movimiento (de) Liberación Nacional*]

MLNS mucocutaneous lymph node syndrome *medicine*.

MLO Military Liaison Officer.

MLQ Modern Language Quarterly (publication).

MLR 1 main line of resistance *military*. **2** *also* **M.L.R.** maximum legal rent: *the M.L.R. for every dwelling unit* (under rent control). **3** minimum lending rate (the official interest rate of the Bank of England). **4** mixed lymphocyte reaction (test to determine compatibility of donor and recipient in organ transplant). **5** Modern Language Review (publication). **6** multiple (linear) regression *statistics*. **7** muzzle-loading rifle: *MLRG = muzzle-loading rifled gun*.

MLRS Multi-Launch Rocket System.

MLS 1 *also* **M.L.S.** Master of Library Science. **2** Microwave Landing System (for aircraft). **3** mixed or multi-language system. **4** Multiple Listing Service (of real estate).

MLT 1 mass, length, time (system of units, used esp. in rocket dynamics and propulsion). **2** mean length per turn *electronics*. **3** mean low tide. **4** median lethal time (for 50% mortality of microorganisms or experimental animals).

MLV 1 magnetic levitation vehicle (high-speed train, car, etc., guided on a track of superconducting electromagnets). **2** murine leukemia virus, used esp. in viral studies.

MLW mean low water, also in combination: *MLWST = mean low-water spring tide*.

MM 1 *also* **M.M.** machine made (of paper). **2** Machinist's Mate (specialist in U.S. Navy). **3** *also* **M.M.** Maelzel's metronome (used as a standard of measure) *music*. **4** maintenance manual. **5** (Their) Majesties. **6** *also* **MM.** *or* **Mm.** martyrs

7 *also* **M.M.** Maryknoll Missioner. **8** *also* **M.M.** Master Mason, in Freemasonry. **9** *also* **M.M.** master mechanic. **10** *also* **M.M.** Master of Music. **11** *also* **MM.** masters. **12** Measure for Measure (play by Shakespeare). **13** *also* **M.M.** Medal for Merit (for civilian activity in wartime). **14** Merchant Marine. **15 a** *also* **MM.** Messieurs. **b** *also* **M/M** Mr. and Mrs., Mr. and Ms. **16** *also* **M.M.** mucous membrane *medicine*. **17** two thousand; 2000.

mM millimole, millimoles (unit of molecular weight).

mm 1 *also* **mm.** millimeter, millimeters. **2** millimicron (now *nm*). **3** micrometer. **4** thousands. [Latin *millia*]

m.m. with the necessary changes. [Latin *mutatis mutandis*]

MMA 1 Metropolitan Museum of Art (in New York City). **2** monomethyl aniline (fuel additive for internal-combustion engines). **3** multiple module access *computers*.

MMAP Medicare, Medicaid Assistance Program (of American Association of Retired Persons).

M.Math. Master of Mathematics.

MMC 1 metal-matrix composite. **2** Monopolies and Mergers Commission (of Great Britain).

mmc *or* **mmc.** micromicrocuries (now *pC*).

MMDA money market deposit account.

M.M.E. *or* **MME 1** *also* **M.Mech.Eng.** Master of Mechanical Engineering. **2** *also* **M.M.Ed.** Master of Music Education.

Mme. Madame.

Mmes. Mesdames.

mmf. *or* **mmf** micromicrofarad, micromicrofarads (now *pF*).

MMF *or* **m.m.f.** magnetomotive force.

mmfd. *or* **mmfd** micromicrofarad, micromicrofarads (now *pF*).

MMH monomethyl hydrazine (rocket fuel).

mmHg millimeter of mercury (unit of pressure, esp. atmospheric, or barometric, pressure).

MMI macrophage migration inhibition *biology, medicine*.

MMIC monolithic microwave integrated circuit *electronics*.

MMLA Midwest Modern Language Association.

MMM 1 Mauritian Militant Movement. **2** Member of the Order of Military Merit.

MMO 1 main meteorological office. **2** medium machine oil.

MMP 1 *also* **M.M.P.** International Organization of Masters, Mates and Pilots. **2** Maritime Mobile Phone.

MMPI Minnesota Multiphasic Personality Inventory (to identify persons who may have or develop serious personality disorders).

MMR measles, mumps, and rubella (inoculation).

MMRBM mobile medium-range ballistic missile.

MMS 1 methyl methanesulphonate *biochemistry*. **2** Minerals Management Service (of U.S. Department of the Interior). **3** *also* **M.M.S.** multimission modular spacecraft.

M.M.Sc. Master of Medical Science.

MMT 1 methylcyclopentadienyl manganese tricarbonyl (fuel additive for internal-combustion engines). **2** Multiple Mirror Telescope.

MMU 1 manned maneuvering unit (compact rocket unit fitted on an astronaut's back for walking in space). **2** memory management unit *computers*.

mmu millimass unit (one-thousandth of an atomic mass unit).

M.Mus. Master of Music, also in combination: *M.Mus.Ed.* = *Master of Music Education*.

MN *I an abbreviation for:* **1** magnetic north. **2** *also* **M.N.** Master of Nursing. **3** *also* **M.N.** Merchant Navy. **4** Minnesota (Zip Code). **5** national currency, esp. M$N for Argentine peso. [Spanish *moneda nacional*]
II a symbol for: also **M-N** presence of M and N antigens in blood.

Mn *I an abbreviation for:* **1** house. [French *maison*] **2** *also* **Mn.** midnight.
II a symbol for: manganese (chemical element).

mn 1 million: £mn = *million pounds*. **2** *also* **m.n.** *or* **m/n** national currency [Spanish *moneda nacional*]

MNA 1 *also* **M.N.A.** Master of Nursing Administration. **2** *also* **M.N.A.** Member of the National Assembly (of Quebec). **3** multinetwork area (of radio or television) *advertising*.

MNAM National Museum of Anthropology of Mexico. [Spanish *Museo Nacional de Antropología Mexicano*]

M.N.A.S. *or* **MNAS** Member of the National Academy of Sciences.

MNC multinational corporation.

MND 1 Midsummer Night's Dream, A (play by Shakespeare). **2** motor neurone disease or diseases (such as myasthenia gravis and muscular dystrophy).

M.N.E. Merchant Navy Establishment: *training Officers of the M.N.E.*

MnE *or* **MnE.** Modern English (from about 1500 to the present; Early Modern English from 1500 to 1700; Late Modern English from 1700 to present).

Mng. Managing: *Mng.Ed.* = *Managing Editor*.

Mngr. 1 Manager. **2 a** Monseigneur (French title of honor). **b** Monsignor (title in Roman Catholic Church).

Mnl. Manila, Philippines.

mnm *or* **mnm.** minimum.

MNOS metal-nitride-oxide semiconductor *electronics*.

MNP microcom (microcommunications) networking protocol (for transmission of data over telephone lines).

MNR National Resistance Movement (formerly of Zimbabwe, and of Mozambique).

Mnr. Manor (esp. in place names).

MNS 1 *also* **M.N.S.** Member of the Numismatic Society. **2** system of classifying blood groups, based on genetically controlled antigens (anti-M, anti-N, anti-S) found in the membranes of red blood cells.

mntn. maintenance.

M.Nurs. Master of Nursing.

MO 1 *also* **M.O.** mail order. **2 a** manually operated, esp. in combination: *MOPB* = *Manually Operated Plotting Board*. **b** mechanically operated, esp. in combination: *MOIV* = *Mechanically Operated Inlet Valve*. **3** *British* mass observation (wide-ranging survey of opinions, habits, or attitudes). **4** master oscillator *electronics*. **5** Medical Officer. **6** *also* **M.O.** Meteorological Office. **7** *also* **M.O.** method of operation. [Latin *modus operandi*] **8** *also* **M.O.** Military Observer (of the UN). **9** Missouri (Zip Code). **10** molecular orbital (indication of electron energy level). **11** money (esp. referring to money in circulation). **12** *also* **M.O.** money order. **13** *also* **M.O.** mustered out (of military service).

Mo *I an abbreviation for:* **1** *also* **Mo.** Missouri. **2** mode *statistics*. **3** Monday.
II a symbol for: molybdenum (chemical element).

mo 1 *also* **m.o. a** mail order. **b** money order. **2** *also* **m.o.** method of operation [Latin *modus operandi*] **3** *also* **mo. a** month **b** monthly

MOA 1 memorandum of agreement *commerce*. **2** Music Operators of America.

mob. 1 *also* **Mob.** mobile, esp. in combination: *Mob. Lib. = Mobile Library*. **2** mobilization. **3** mobilized.

Mobidic (mō′bē dik′) mobile digital computer *military*.

MOBS (*pronounced* mobz) Multiple Orbit Bombardment System (nuclear-weapon system carried in earth satellites).

MOC magnetic oxide conversion (method of refining jasper ore).

Moçam. Mozambique. [Portuguese *Moçambique*]

MOCVD metal-organic chemical vapor deposition (technique for creating layers on electronic chips).

MOD 1 mail order department. **2** *also* **MoD** *British* Ministry of Defence **3** *British* Ministry of Overseas Development. **4** modulator *electronics*.

mod. 1 model. **2 a** moderate. **b** *also* **Mod.** moderator. **3** moderately quick *music*. [Italian *moderato*] **4** *also* **mod** (*pronounced* mod) *or* **Mod.** modern, also in combination: *mod styles; mod-con = modern conveniences*. **5** *also* **mod a** modification. **b** modified. **6** modulus *physics, mathematics*.

modem (mō′dem) *or* **MODEM** Modulator-Demodulator (unit that converts computer signals for telephone communications).

MODFET modulation-doped field effect transistor.

mod. praes. as prescribed *pharmaceutics*. [Latin *modo praescripto*]

Mods (*pronounced* modz) Moderations (one of a series of examinations for degree at Oxford).

MOE measure of effectiveness *computers*.

Moho (mō′hō′) Mohorovicic discontinuity (boundary between the earth's crust and mantle).

MOI 1 Military Operations and Intelligence. **2** multiplicity of infection (number of infectious particles in relation to number of surrounding cells) *biology, medicine*

MOL 1 Machine-Oriented Language *computers*. **2** Manned Orbital Laboratory. **3** *also* **M.O.L.** Master of Oriental Languages.

mol 1 mole (amount of substance). **2** *also* **mol. a** molecule. **b** molecular.

mold. molding.

mol wt molecular weight.

MOM *or* **m.o.m. 1** middle of the month *accounting, finance*. **2** milk of magnesia.

MOMA Museum of Modern Art, New York.

MON motor octane number.

Mon 1 *also* **Mon.** Monaco. **2** Monastery. **3** *also* **Mon.** Monday. **4** Monsignor. **5** *also* **Mon.** Montana. **6** Monument: *Wash Mon = Washington Monument*. **7** the Unicorn (constellation). [Latin *Monoceros*]

mon. 1 monetary. **2** monitor. **3** *also* **mon** monsoon.

Mong. 1 Mongolia. **2** Mongolian.

mono (mon′ō′) **1** monaural *or* monophonic (of sound reproduction). **2** mononucleosis.

mono. monotype.

monocot. monocotyledon *biology*.

monog. *or* **monogr.** monograph.

Mons. 1 Monsieur. **2** Monsignor.

Monsig. Monsignor.

Mont. Montana.

MOP 1 *also* **MoP** Member of Parliament. **2** methoxypsoralen (for treatment of skin blemishes and increasing skin's tanning ability). **3** multiple on-line programming (enabling many programmers to talk simultaneously with a large computer). **4** *also* **M.o.P.** mustering-out pay *military*.

m.o.p. mother of pearl.

MOPA master oscillator power amplifier *electronics*.

Mopac (mō′pak′) Missouri Pacific Railroad.

moped (mō′ped′) motorbicycle. [*motor* and *pedal*]

MOPH Military Order of the Purple Heart (U.S. decoration for personnel wounded or killed in combat).

MOR middle-of-the-road (used esp. in reference to broadcast programming).

Mor. 1 Morocco. **2** Moroccan.

mor. 1 gradually diminishing *music*. [Italian *morendo*] **2** morocco (leather). **3** mortar.

MORC Medical Officers Reserve Corps.

mor. dict. as directed *pharmaceutics*. [Latin *more dictu*]

MORI (môr′i) Market and Opinion Research Institute.

MORL Manned Orbital Research Laboratory (proposed NASA project).

morn. morning.

morph. 1 morphine. **2 a** *also* **morphol.** morphological. **b** morphology.

mor. sol. in the usual manner *pharmaceutics*. [Latin *more solito*]

mort. 1 mortar. **2** mortgage. **3** mortuary.

MOS 1 man on the street (in advertising and broadcasting), also in combination: *MOSbite = man on the street bite* (interview). **2** metal or metallic oxide semiconductor. **3** metal oxide sensor. **4** metal oxide silicon (components of a semiconductor). **5** military occupational specialty.

Mos. Moscow.

mos. months.

MOSE Electromechanical Experimental Module (proposed system of gates to protect Venice from flooding). [Italian *Modulo Sperimentale Elettromeccanico*]

MOSFET (mos'fet') metal oxide semiconductor field effect transistor (used in microprocessors, computer memories, and other electronic circuits).

mOsm milliosmol (unit of osmotic pressure).

MOST 1 metal oxide semiconductor transistor. **2** Motorcycle Operator Skills Test.

MOT *or* **MoT** *British* Ministry of Transport: *MOT vehicle test.*

mot. 1 motor: *mot. op. = motor operated.* **2** motorized.

MOTNE Meteorological Operational Telecommunications Network Europe.

MOU *or* **m.o.u.** memorandum of understanding *commerce, law.*

mov 1 *also* **movt** movement, esp. section of large musical composition. **2** movement (as a direction for playing music rapidly). [Italian *movimento*]

Moz. 1 *also* **Mozamb.** Mozambique. **2** Mozart (composer, 1756–1791).

MP 1 medium pressure. **2** melting point. **3** *also* **M.P.** Member of Parliament. **4** *also* **M/P** memorandum of partnership *commerce, law.* **5** Mercator's Projection. **6 a** Metropolitan Police (of London). **b** Military Police or Policeman. **7** *also* **M.P.** Minister Plenipotentiary (minister with full authority). **8** multipolar. **9** multiprocessor. **10** Northern Mariana Islands (in postal address). **11** Roman mile of 1000 of a legionary's double pace. [Latin *milia passum*]

mP maritime polar air *meteorology.*

mp 1 as directed, as prescribed *pharmaceutics.* [Latin *modo praescripto*] **2** melting point. **3** *also* **mp.** millipoise (measurement of viscosity). **4** *also* **m.p.** moderately soft *music.* [Italian *mezzo piano*]

MPA 1 Magazine Publishers Association. **2** *also* **M.P.A.** Master of Public Administration. **3** maximum permissible amount (of exposure to radioactivity). **4** *also* **MPAA** Motion Picture Association of America. **5** Music Publishers Association.

MPa *or* **mpa** megapascal (unit of pressure).

MPB Missing Persons Bureau.

MPC 1 *also* **mpc** maximum permissible concentration (of radioactivity). **2** *also* **M.P.C.** Member of Parliament, Canada. **3** military payment certificate (military scrip). **4** Military Police Corps (of the U.S. Army). **5** multimedia personal computer.

Mpc *or* **mpc** megaparsec (equivalent to three million light-years).

MPD 1 magnetoplasmadynamic: *MPD generators.* **2** maximum permissible dose (of medicine or radioactivity). **3** Movement for Democracy (political party, Cape Verde Islands). **4** multiple personality disorder *psychiatry.* **5** myofascial pain dysfunction (muscle spasms of the jaw area) *medicine.*

M.Pd. Master of Pedagogy.

MPE 1 *also* **M.P.E.** Master of Physical Education. **2** maximum permissible exposure (to radioactivity or sunlight).

MPEG (em'peg) Motion Picture Experts Group (computer standard for compressing video, animation, and audio files).

M.P.F. *or* **MPF** multipurpose food (a precooked fifty-percent-protein powder).

mpg *or* **m.p.g.** miles per gallon.

MPGN membranoproliferative glomerulonephritis (type of kidney disease).

M.P.H. *or* **MPH** Master of Public Health.

M.Ph. Master of Philosophy.

mph *or* **m.p.h.** miles per hour.

M.Pharm. Master of Pharmacy.

M.Phil. Master of Philosophy.

mphps *or* **mphp/s** miles per hour per second.

MPI 1 magnetic-particle inspection. **2** Maudsley Personality Inventory *psychology.* **3** Max Planck Institute. **4** mean point of impact.

mPk cold maritime Polar air mass *meteorology.*

MPL 1 *also* **M.P.L.** Master of Patent Law. **2** maximum permissible level (of radiation).

MPLA Popular Movement for Liberation of Angola (since independence, the only legal political party). [Portuguese *Movimento Popular de Libertação de Angola*]

MPM *or* **mpm** meters per minute.

MPN most probable number *mathematics.*

MPO 1 Management and Personnel Office (of the British civil service). **2** *also* **M.P.O.** Metropolitan Police Office (New Scotland Yard, London). **3** myeloperoxidase (generates bacteriocidal activity) *biochemistry.*

MPP 1 massively parallel processor (computer able to perform many computations simultaneously). **2** *also* **M.P.P.** Member of the Provincial Parliament (member of the legisature of a province of Canada). **3** mission-planning program, *esp. in aerospace.* **4** most probable position *navigation.*

MPPDA *or* **M.P.P.D.A.** Motion Picture Producers and Distributors of America.

MPR 1 Mongolian People's Republic. **2** People's Consultative Assembly. [Bahasa Indonesia *Madjelis Permusjawaratan Rakjat*] **3** Popular Movement of the Revolution (in Zaire). [French *Mouvement Populaire de la Révolution*]

MPRP Mongol People's Revolutionary Party.

MPS 1 mail preference service (for customer-requested removal of a name from direct-mail lists). **2** marbled paper sides, in bookbinding. **3** *also* **M.P.S.** Master of Public Services. **4** *also* **mps** meters per second. **5** microprocessor system. **6** mucopolysaccharidoses (genetic biochemical disorders, designated MPS I through VII). **7** multiprogramming system *computers.* **8** Patriotic Salvation Movement. [French *Population Patriotique Salvation*]

M.Ps. *or* **M.Psych.** Master of Psychology.

MPTA Mechanical Power Transmission Association.

MPU microprocessor unit *computers.*

mPw warm maritime Polar air mass *meteorology.*

MPX 1 multiplex: *MPX broadcasting.* **2** multiplexer (electronic device for multiple transmissions on a single line).

MQ 1 metol quinal (developer) *photography.* **2** multiplier quotient *computers*: *MQ register.*

Mq *or* **mq.** mosque.

Mqe Martinique.

MR 1 magnetic resonance *physics.* **2** map reference. **3** *also* **M.R.** Master of the Rolls (in Great Britain, judge of the court of appeal or senior judge who is in charge of the Public Record Office). **4** medical record. **5** medium range (of aircraft or missiles). **6** *also* **M.R.** medullary ray (tissue separating vascular bundles and connecting bark and pith in certain plants and trees). **7** *also* **M/R** memorandum (of) receipt *commerce.* **8** mental retardation. **9** metabolic rate *medicine.* **10 a** millirem (thousandth of a rem, unit of absorbed radiation). **b** milliroentgen (thousandth of a roentgen, unit of intensity of X or gamma rays). **11** mill run (of lumber). **12** *also* **M.R.** Minister Resident (diplomatic representative to a small country). **13** Morning Report (daily muster) *military.* **14** motivational research.

Mr 1 March (as in a financial or other crowded listing). **2** *also* **Mr.** (mis′tər) mister: *Mr. Richard Baxter; Mr. President; Mr. Chairman.*

mr. 1 megarad (one million rads, unit of absorbed radiation). **2 a** *also* **mr** *or* **m/R** milliroentgen (thousandth of a roentgen, unit of intensity of X or gamma rays). **b** *also* **mr** *or* **m/R** microroentgen (one millionth of a roentgen).

MRA 1 minimum reception altitude *aeronautics.* **2** Moral Re-Armament (religious movement).

M.Rad. Master of Radiology.

mrad millirad (one thousandth of a rad, a unit of radiation).

MRB Medical Review Board (of a hospital).

MRBM Medium-Range Ballistic Missile.

MRC 1 *also* **M.R.C.** *British* **a** Medical Research Council. **b** Council standard of units of measurement. **2** Medical Reserve Corps. **3** Military Representatives Committee.

MRCA multirole combat aircraft.

MRCC *or* **M.R.C.C.** Medical Research Council of Canada.

MRD minimum reacting dose *medicine.*

MR/DD mentally retarded and developmentally disabled.

MRE 1 *also* **M.R.E.** Master of Religious Education. **2** meals, ready to eat (packaged army field rations). **3** Microbiological Research Establishment (of Great Britain).

M.R.E.I.N.Z. Member of the Real Estate Institute of New Zealand.

mrem millirem (thousandth of a rem, unit of absorbed radiation).

MRF 1 material recovery facility (recycling facility). **2** maternal resistance factor. **3** Mutual Reduction in Forces (disarmament).

MRG Minority Rights Group (of Great Britain).

MRI 1 magnetic resonance imaging (a process using the effects of a magnetic field to produce computer images of structures of the body, somewhat like an X ray). **2** medical records indexing.

MRIR medium-resolution infrared radiometer.

mrkr. marker.

Mrkt. Market.

MRL 1 *also* **M.R.L.** Medical Records Librarian. **2** medium-power loop range *electronics.*

MRM mechanically recovered meat (during processing).

mRNA *or* **m-RNA** messenger ribonucleic acid.

mrng morning.

MRO maintenance, repair, and operating (esp. of buses and trucks).

MRP 1 *also* **M.R.P.** Master in Regional Planning. **2** material requirements planning (method of inventory control by monitoring production needs). **3** Popular Republican Movement. [French *Mouvement Républicain Populaire*]

MRS 1 magnetic resonance spectroscopy. **2** monitored retrievable storage *computers.*

Mrs. *or* **Mrs** (mis′iz, miz′iz) mistress (title put in front of a married woman's name: *Mrs. Jackson,* but now often replaced by *Ms*).

MRT magnetic resonance tomography.

mrtm. maritime.

MRU mobile repair unit.

MRV (*often pronounced* mėrv) multiple reentry vehicle.

MS 1 *also* **M.S.** left hand *music.* [Italian *mano sinistra*] **2** *also* **M.S.** machinery survey (of a ship). **3** machine screw *mechanics.* **4** main switch, esp. in blueprints and schematic drawings. **5** manuscript. **6** margin of safety. **7** mass spectrometry *astronomy, chemistry.* **8** *also* **M.S.** Master of Science. **9** maximum stress (of materials). **10** mean square *mathematics.* **11** Medical Services (bureau of U.S. Department of State). **12** medium shot *photography, television.* **13** medium steel. **14** metric system. **15** military science. **16 a** Military Specification. **b** Military Standard, esp. with a number identifying the designated product. **17** mint state (of coins). **18** Mississippi (Zip Code). **19** mitral stenosis (hardening or narrowing of the mitral valve). **20** motorship. **21** multiple sclerosis. **22** *also* **M.S.** sacred to the memory of. [Latin *memoriae sacrum*]

M/S 1 margin of safety. **2** month's sight or months after sight (usually of bills payable 30 days or a month after presentation or of notes due a given number of months after presentation) *commerce.* **3** motorship.

mS millisiemens (thousandth of a siemens, unit of electrical conductance).

Ms 1 manuscript. **2** *also* **Ms.** megasecond (one million seconds). **3** *also* **Ms.** (*pronounced* miz) mistress, miss, Mrs (used before the name of a woman either married or unmarried).

ms 1 manuscript. **2** *also* **ms.** **a** megasecond (one million seconds). **b** millisecond (thousandth of a second).

m/s *or* **m.s.** month's sight or months after sight (usually of bills payable 30 days or a month after presentation or notes due a given number of months after presentation) *commerce.*

MSA 1 *also* **M.S.A.** Master of Science and Arts. **2** *also* **M.S.A.** *or* **M.S.Agr.** Master of Science in Agriculture. **3** Metropolitan Statistical Area (Bureau of the Census unit). **4** Mineralogical Society of America.

MSAT Minnesota Scholastic Aptitude Test.

MSB 1 Minority Small Business. **2** most significant bit (highest-order bit of a binary number) *computers.*

MSBA *or* **M.S.B.A.** *or* **MSBus** *or* **M.S.Bus.** Master of Science in Business Administration.

MSC 1 *also* **M.S.C.** Manchester Ship Canal. **2** Manned Spacecraft Center (of NASA). **3** Manpower Services Commission (of Great Britain). **4** Military Sealift Command. **5** moved, seconded, and carried (of a motion or rule).

M.Sc. *or* **MSc** Master of Science.

msc 1 millisecond (thousandth of a second). **2** miscellaneous. **3** *also* **m.s.c.** moved, seconded, and carried (of a motion or rule).

M.Sc.D. Doctor of Medical Science.

MSCE *or* **M.S.C.E.** Master of Science in Civil Engineering.

MS.Ch.E. Master of Science in Chemical Engineering.

M.Sc.Econ. Master of Science in Economics.

M.Sc.Eng. Master of Science in Engineering.

m.s.c.p. *or* **MSCP** mean spherical candlepower.

MSD 1 *also* **M.S.D.** Doctor of Medical Science. **2** *also* **M.S.D.** Master of Science in Dentistry. **3** modem sharing device (modem that permits connection of several computer terminals at one time). **4** most significant digit (highest-order digit of a number or word) *computers*.

MSDF Maritime Self-Defense Force (Japanese Navy after World War II).

MS/DOS *or* **MS-DOS** Microsoft Disk Operating System *trademark*.

MSE 1 *also* **M.S.E.** Master of Science in Education. **2** *also* **M.S.E.** Master of Science in Engineering. **3** mean square error *mathematics*. **4** Montreal Stock Exchange.

msec. *or* **msec** millisecond (thousandth of a second).

M.S.Ed. *or* **MSEd.** Master of Science in Education.

MSEE *or* **M.S.E.E.** Master of Science in Electrical Engineering.

MSEM *or* **M.S.E.M.** Master of Science in Engineering Mechanics.

MSF 1 Doctors Without Frontiers (volunteer medical service). [French *Médecins Sans Frontières*] **2** *also* **M.S.F.** Master of Science in Forestry. **3** medium standard frequency. **4** Mobile Strike Force.

MSFC Marshall Space Flight Center.

MSG monosodium glutamate, used esp. as a flavor enhancer for food.

Msg. Monsignor.

msg. message.

Msgr. 1 Monseigneur (French title of honor). **2** Monsignor (official of the Roman Catholic Church).

msgr. messenger.

M.Sgt. *or* **M/Sgt.** Master Sergeant.

MSH melanocyte-stimulating hormone, intermedin.

MSHA 1 *also* **M.S.H.A.** Master of Science in Hospital Administration. **2** Mine Safety and Health Administration (of U.S. Department of Labor).

MSHE *or* **M.S.H.E.** Master of Science in Home Economics.

Mshl marshal.

M.S.Hyg. Master of Science in Hygiene.

MSI 1 Italian Social Movement. [Italian *Movimento Sociale Italiano*] **2** medium-scale integration (a number of integrated circuits on a single computer chip).

M.S.J. *or* **MSJ** Master of Science in Journalism.

MSL 1 Major Soccer League. **2** *also* **M.S.L.** Master of Science in Linguistics. **3** *also* **m.s.l.** mean sea level.

MSLS *or* **M.S.L.S.** Master of Science in Library Science.

MSM 1 Manhattan School of Music. **2** *also* **M.S.M.** Master of Sacred Music. **3** Meritorious Service Medal (of Great Britain). **4** Militant Socialist Movement (in Mauritius). **5** *also* **M s.m.** thousand feet surface measure.

MSMA monosodium acid methanearsenate (herbicide).

M.S.M.E. *or* **MSME** Master of Science in Mechanical Engineering.

M.S.Mus. Master of Science in Music.

M.S.N. *or* **MSN** Master of Science in Nursing.

Msn. mission.

msngr. messenger.

MSO multiple systems operator (company owning more than one cable TV system).

M.Soc.Sc. Master of Social Science.

MSP 1 *also* **M.S.P.** *or* **M.S.Pharm.** Master of Science in Pharmacy. **2** monobasic sodium phosphate (used in baking powders, cleansers, water treatment, foods, etc.).

MSPB Merit Systems Protection Board.

MSPH *or* **M.S.P.H.** Master of Science in Public Health.

MSPHE *or* **M.S.P.H.E.** Master of Science in Public Health Engineering.

MSR 1 machine stress-graded lumber *building*. **2** missile-site radar.

MSS 1 *also* **Mss** *or* **mss** manuscripts. **2** mass storage system *computers*. **3** *also* **M.S.S.** Master of Social Science. **4** multi-spectral scanner *medicine, photography*.

MSSD Model Secondary School for the Deaf.

M.S.S.E. *or* **MSSE** Master of Science in Sanitary Engineering.

MSSW *or* **M.S.S.W.** Master of Science in Social Work.

MST 1 *also* **M.S.T.** Master of Sacred Theology. **2** Master of Science in Taxation. **3** *also* **M.S.T.** Master of Science in Teaching. **4** *also* **mst a** mean solar time. **b** mean survival time (to weather or water conditions). **5** minimum spanning tree (mathematical model for designing networks, such as computer circuits, supply and manufacturing locations, etc.). **6** *also* **M.S.T.** *or* **m.s.t.** Mountain Standard Time.

mst. measurement.

M.Stat. Master of Statistics.

Ms-Th *or* **MsTh** mesothorium (an isotope either of radium or actinium).

Mstr. *or* **Mstr** master: *Mstr. Mech.* = *Master Mechanic*.

MSTS Military Sea Transportation Service.

MSTV medium-scan television.

MSU main storage unit *computers*.

M.Surv. Master of Surveying.

MSV murine sarcoma virus.

MSW 1 magnetic surface wave. **2** *also* **M.S.W.** Master of Social Work. **3** Medical Social Worker.

MSY maximum sustainable yield (greatest amount of a renewable natural resource that can be consumed yearly without impairing replacement).

MT 1 empty (of a container or railroad car). **2** machine translation. **3** magnetic tape. **4** *also* **M/T** mail transfer. **5** malignant tertian (malaria, formerly a common cause of death among Europeans). **6** malignant tumor. **7** *also* **M.T.** Masoretic Text (corrected text with marginal notes of the Old Testament or Hebrew Bible). **8** mass transportation. **9** mean tide, also in combination: *MST = mean spring tide.* **10** mean time (average time), esp. in combination: *MTBF = mean time between failures.* **11** mechanical transport. **12** *also* **M.T.** medical technologist. **13** megaton (measure of force of nuclear explosion). **14** metric ton. **15** Montana (Zip Code). **16** motor transport *British military.* **17** Mount (in postal address). **18** mountain time.

mT Maritime tropical air mass *meteorology.*

Mt. 1 Mount: *Mt. Everest.* **2** mountain.

mt 1 a *also* **mt.** megaton (measure of force of nuclear explosion). **b** *also* **m.t.** metric ton. **2** mountain time.

M.T.A. *or* **MTA** Metropolitan Transportation Authority.

MTB 1 Materials Transportation Bureau. **2** motor torpedo boat.

MTBE methyl tert-butyl ether (gasoline additive).

MTBF mean time between failures.

MTCA Ministry of Transport and Civil Aviation (of Great Britain).

MTCR Missile Technology Control Regime (for export control of U.S. technology).

MTD 1 maximum tolerated dose. **2** mean temperature difference.

Mtd. *or* **Mtd** mounted.

mtDNA mitochondrial DNA (genetic material in the cytoplasm of cells).

M.Tech. Master of Technology.

MTF 1 mechanical time fuse. **2** Mississippi Test Facility (of NASA). **3** modulation transfer function *photography.*

mtg. *or* **mtg 1** meeting. **2** mortgage. **3** mounting.

mtgd. *or* **mtgd** mortgaged.

mtge. *or* **mtge** mortgage.

mtgee. *or* **mtgee** mortgagee.

Mtgne mountain. [French *montagne*]

mtgor. *or* **mtgor** mortgagor.

M.Th. Master of Theology.

Mth. *or* **Mth** Mouth (of a river) *geography.*

mth. *or* **mth** month.

MTI 1 Hungarian News Agency. [Hungarian *Magyar Tavviati Iroda*] **2** moving-target indicator.

MTIRA Machine Tool Industry Research Association (of Great Britain).

mTk Tropical maritime cold air mass *meteorology.*

MTL 1 *also* **mtl.** material. **2** mean tidal level. **3** merged transistor logic *computers.*

MTM methods time measurement (of work measurement).

MTN 1 Medical Television Network. **2** Mountain (in postal address). **3** multilateral trade negotiations.

mtn. mountain.

MTOC microtubule-organizing center.

M.T.P. Master of Town Planning.

MTR 1 Materials Testing Reactor. **2** mean time to restore. **3** *also* **mtr** motor. **4** multiple-track radar.

Mt. Rev. Most Reverend.

MTS motor turbine ship: *MTS Argonaut.*

Mts. *or* **mts.** mountains.

MTTF mean time to failure, also in combination: *MTTFF = mean time to first failure.*

MTTR mean time to repair.

MTU magnetic tape unit *computers.*

MTV 1 mammary tumor virus. **2** Music Television.

mTw Tropical maritime warm air mass *meteorology.*

MU 1 Maintenance Unit. **2** mobile unit. **3** *also* **M.U.** *or* **m.u.** mouse unit *biology.* **4** multiple unit (as of railroad cars).

mu 1 mapping unit, of genes. **2** micron (millionth of a meter). **3** millimicron (thousandth of a micron).

MUA main urban area (of a population and administration unit in New Zealand).

muc. mucilage.

MUF *or* **muf** maximum usable frequency.

MUFON Mutual UFO Network.

mult. 1 multiple. **2** multiply.

MUN munitions *military.*

mun. *or* **Mun.** municipal.

munic. *or* **Munic. 1** municipal. **2** municipality.

MUPO maximum undistorted power output *electronics.*

MURA Midwest Universities Research Association.

MURI mild upper-respiratory infection.

Mus the Fly (constellation). [Latin *Musca*]

mus. *or* **Mus. 1** museum. **2 a** music. **b** musical. **c** musician. **3** Muslim.

MUSA multiple-unit steerable antenna.

Mus.B. *or* **Mus.Bac.** Bachelor of Music. [Latin *Musicae Baccalaureus*]

Mus.D. *or* **Mus.Doc.** Doctor of Music. [Latin *Musicae Doctor*]

Mus.M. Master of Music. [Latin *Musicae Magister*]

MUST Manned Underwater Station.

mut. 1 mutation. **2** mutilated. **3** *also* **Mut.** mutual.

muv microvolt (millionth of a volt).

muw microwatt (millionth of a watt).

MUX multiplexer *computers.*

MV 1 market value. **2** mean variation. **3** medium voltage. **4** megavolt (million volts). **5** *also* **M/V** motor vessel: *MV*

Bluenose. **6** muzzle velocity. **7** The Merchant of Venice (play by Shakespeare). **8** *also* **M.V.** Veterinary Physician. [Latin *Medicus Veterinarius*]

Mv Mendelevium (chemical element).

mv 1 *also* **m.v.** market value. **2** *also* **m.v.** mean variation. **3** medium voltage. **4** *also* **Mv** megavolt (million volts). **5** *also* **mV** millivolt (thousandth of a volt). **6** muzzle velocity. **7** *also* **m.v.** somewhat softly *music.* [Italian *mezza voce*]

MVA 1 *also* **mv.a.** megavolt-ampere. **2** Mississippi Valley Authority. **3** Missouri Valley Authority.

MVAR *or* **mvar** megavar (million volt ampere): *mvarh = megavar-hour.*

MVBR multivibrator *electronics.*

MVD 1 *also* **M.V.D.** Doctor of Veterinary Medicine. **2** Ministry of Internal Affairs (of the former Soviet Union, dissolved 1958). [Russian *Ministerstvo Vnutrennikh Del*] **3** Motor Vehicles Department.

MVP most valuable player (of the year) *sports.*

M.V.Sc. Master of Veterinary Science.

MVT Multiprogramming for Variable Tasks *computers.*

mvt. movement.

MW 1 medium wave *electronics.* **2** megawatt (million watts). **3** mixed widths (of lumber). **4** *also* **M.W.** molecular weight. **5** *also* **M.W. a** Most Worshipful, in combination: *MWGM = Most Worshipful Grand Master.* **b** Most Worthy, in combination: *MWGCP = Most Worthy Grand Chief Patriarch.*

mw 1 *also* **Mw** megawatt (million watts). **2** *also* **mW** milliwatt (thousandth of a watt). **3** *also* **m.w.** *or* **m.wt.** molecular weight.

M.W.A. 1 Modern Woodmen of America (fraternal organization). **2** Mystery Writers of America.

M-way British motorway.

MWD *or* **Mwd** *or* **mwd** megawatt day: *MWD/T = megawatt-days per ton.*

MWE *or* **MWe** *or* **Mw(e)** megawatts of electrical power.

MWF 1 Medical Women's Federation. **2** Monday, Wednesday, Friday (order of occurrence).

MWG *or* **m.w.g.** Music Wire Gauge.

MWGM *or* **M.W.G.M.** Most Worshipful Grand Master (of a Masonic order).

MWH *or* **Mwh** *or* **mwh** megawatt-hour.

MWIA Medical Women's International Association.

MWO Mount Wilson Observatory.

MWP 1 maximum working pressure. **2** mechanical wood pulp (of paper). **3** *also* **M.W.P.** Most Worthy Patriarch (of a Masonic order).

MWR morale, welfare, and recreation (program of U.S. Army).

MWT *or* **Mwt** *or* **mwt** megawatt, thermal.

MWV maximum working voltage.

MWW The Merry Wives of Windsor (play by Shakespeare).

MWYE *or* **Mwye** *or* **mwye** megawatt year of electricity.

MX 1 missile, experimental. **2** motocross (cross-country motorcycle racing). **3** multiplex (multiple transmission in a single circuit or wavelength).

Mx 1 *also* **mx** maxwell (unit of magnetic flux). **2** Middlesex County, England. **3** *also* **mx** multiplex (multiple transmission on a single circuit or wavelength).

mxd. *or* **mxd** mixed.

mxm maximum.

MY motor yacht.

My May (esp. in cataloging).

my 1 *also* **m.y.** million years *astronomy, anthropology, geology.* **2** muddy track, in horse racing. **3** *also* **my.** myopia (nearsightedness).

mya 1 million years ago *geology.* **2** *also* **mya.** myriare (one square kilometer, about 250 acres).

Myc. Mycenaean.

myc. *or* **mycol. 1** mycology (study of fungi). **2** mycological.

myg *or* **myg.** myriagram (ten kilograms, about 22 pounds).

myl *or* **myl.** myrialiter (ten kiloliters; about 2600 gallons).

mym *or* **mym.** myriameter (100 square kilometers; about 39 square miles).

MYOB mind your own business.

myst. mystery, mysteries.

myth. 1 mythology. **2** *also* **mythol.** mythological.

MZ monozygotic, *esp. of identical twins.*

N

N I an abbreviation for: **1** nadir. **2** naira (monetary unit of Nigeria). **3** *also* **N.** name. **4** narrow (as of shoe size). **5** *also* **N.** National, in combination: *NAACP = National Association for the Advancement of Colored People; N.A.M. = lored People; N.A.M. = National Association of Manufacturers.* **6** Navy, Naval, in combination: *USN = United States Navy; USNA = United States Naval Academy.* **7** Nepal, in combination: *NRs = Nepal rupees.* **8** neutral. **9** neutron: *N-ray.* **10** *also* **N.** New, in combination: *N.B. = New Brunswick; NED = New English Dictionary; NL = New Latin; N$ = new peso (of Mexico).* **11** ngultrum (monetary unit of Bhutan). **12** Nigerian, in combination: *N£ = Nigerian pound.* **13** nimbus cloud. **14** no or not, in combination: *N/F = no funds; N/S = not to scale.* **15** nones: **a** a religious office or hour once celebrated nine hours after sunrise. **b** ninth day before the ides in calendar of ancient Rome. **16** *also* **N.** noon. **17** normal (of the strength of

a solution in chemistry or the strength of a force in physics), esp. in combination: $Nm.^3$ = *normal cubic meter.* **18** Norse (language of Scandinavia to about 1300 or the language of Iceland in the Middle Ages; usually now classified as Old Icelandic), esp. in combination: *ON = Old Norse.* **19** *also* **N.** North, Northern (compass point, pole of a magnet, or in combination): *NbW = North by West; Nato = North Atlantic Treaty Organization; N.W.T. = Northwest Territory.* **20** Norwegian, in combination: *NKr. = Norwegian krone.* **21** November. **22 a** nuclear: *N reactor.* **b** nucleus. **23** number, *esp. as a symbol in science and math.* **24** *also* **N.** nun (navigational marker). **25** report. [German *Nachricht*]
II a symbol for: **1** atomic shell of 32 maximum electrons per shell. **2** *also* **N** or N_A Avogadro's number (number of molecules in a mole). **3** carbon star *astronomy.* **4** factor of safety *physics.* **5** fourteenth of a series (thirteenth when *J* is omitted). **6** Knight *chess.* **7** negative (electric pole). **8** neutron number. **9** newton (measure of force) *physics.* **10** ninety; 90 (medieval Roman numeral). **11 a** nitrogen (chemical element). **b** (of a group of organic compounds) attached to nitrogen: *N-methyl acetamide = methyl group attached to the nitrogen atom in the acetamide molecule.* **12** number of conductors *electronics* **13** number of factors or variables. **14** number of grating lines of an atom. **15** number of observation, *esp. in psychology.* **16** number of windings of a coil.

n *I an abbreviation for:* **1** *also* **n.** born. [Latin *natus*] **2** *also* **n.** nail (unit of cloth measure, $2\frac{1}{4}$ inches). **3** *also* **n.** name. **4** nano- (billionth or 10^{-9}): *ng. = nanogram.* **5** *also* **n.** nasal *medicine.* **6** neper (measure of power ratio equal to about 8.7 decibels). **7** *also* **n.** nephew. **8** *also* **n.** nerve *medicine.* **9** net: *n wt = net weight.* **10** *also* **n.** neuter. **11** neutron *physics.* **12** *also* **n.** night. **13** *also* **n.** no or not: *n.d. = no date.* **14** *also* **n.** nominative. **15** *also* **n.** noon. **16** *also* **n** normal (esp. of the strength of a solution) *chemistry.* **17** *also* **n.** note: *p.364n. = page 364 foot note.* **18** *also* **n.** noun, also in combination: *n.pl. = plural noun.* **19** nozzle. **20** *also* **n.** number, esp. as a symbol in science and math.
II a symbol for: **1** efficiency *physics.* **2** fourteenth of a series (thirteenth when *j* is omitted). **3** indefinite number *mathematics.* **4** index of refraction. **5** load factor *aeronautics.* **6** modulus of rigidity *physics.* **7** number of components. **8** number of variables. **9** principal quantum number. **10** revolutions or rotations (esp. per unit of time). **11** transport number of an ion.

n- normal (of the straight-chain structure of a radical): *n-methyl.*

n haploid number of chromosomes or haploid generation.

2 *n* diploid number of chromosomes or diploid generation.

NA 1 *also* **N.A.** Narcotics Anonymous. **2** *also* **N.A.** National Academician. **3** *also* **N.A.** Nautical Almanac. **4** *also* **N.A.** Naval Academy. **5** *also* **N.A.** Naval Architect. **6** Naval Attaché. **7** neuraminidase (surface protein on a flu virus). **8** *also* **N/A** no advice *banking.* **9** no answer. **10** *also* **N/A** nonacceptance *commerce.* **11** *also* **N.A. a** North America. **b** North American, also in combination: *NAFTA = North American Free Trade Agreement.* **12 a** not allowed. **b** *also* **N/A** not applicable. **c** not assigned. **d** *also* **N.A.** not available. **13** numerical aperture (the index of resolving power on a microscope objective). **14** nurse's aide.

Na sodium (chemical element). [Latin *natrium*]

nA 1 nanoampere. **2** transitional antarctic coastal air mass *meteorology.*

n/a 1 no account *banking.* **2** nonacceptance *commerce.* **3** *also* **n.a.** not applicable. **4** *also* **n.a.** not available.

NAA 1 naphthylacetic acid (synthetic auxin). **2** National Aeronautics Association. **3** National Archery Association. **4** neutron activation analysis. **5** Newspaper Association of America.

naa not always afloat *shipping.*

NAACP National Association for the Advancement of Colored People.

NAAFI *British* Navy, Army, and Air Force Institutes.

NAAG National Association of Attorneys General.

NAAQS National Ambient Air Quality Standards.

NAAS National Agricultural Advisory Service (of Great Britain).

NAB 1 National Alliance of Businessmen. **2** National Association of Broadcasters. **3** naval air base. **4** New American Bible. **5** Newspaper Advertising Bureau.

NABE National Association of Business Economists.

NABET National Association of Broadcast Employees and Technicians.

NABISCO National Biscuit Company.

NABLOC Brussels Tariff Nomenclature for the Latin American Free Trade Association: *NABLOC nomenclature.*

N.A.B.M. National Association of British Manufacturers.

NABT National Association of Biology Teachers.

NAC 1 National Advisory Council. **2** National Association of Counties. **3** North Atlantic Council.

NACA 1 National Advisory Committee for Aeronautics. **2** National Air Carrier Association. **3** National Association for Children of Alcoholics. **4** *also* **N.A.C.A.** National Association of Cost Accountants. **5** National Association of County Administrators.

NACAC National Association of College Admissions Counselors.

NACAM National Association of Corn and Agricultural Merchants.

NACC National Association of Childbearing Centers (organization promoting standards of quality).

Nachtr. supplement. [German *Nachtrag*]

NACOR National Advisory Committee on Radiation.

NACSE *or* **N.A.C.S.E.** National Association of Civil Service Employees.

NAD 1 *also* **N.A.D.** National Academy of Design. **2** nicotinamide adenine dinucleotide (coenzyme in cell metabolism). **3** *also* **n.a.d.** no appreciable disease. **4** *also* **n.a.d.** nothing abnormal discovered. **5** not on active duty.

NADA 1 National Association of Dealers in Antiques. **2** National Automobile Dealers Association.

Nadar (nā'där) North American Data Airborne Recorder (recorder to log information about flights).

NADH hydrogen nicotinamide adenine dinucleotide (coenzyme in metabolism).

NADL National Association of Dental Laboratories.

NADP nicotinamide adenine dinucleotide phosphate (coenzyme in metabolism); TPN.

NADPH hydrogen nicotinamide adenine dinucleotide phosphate (coenzyme in metabolism).

NAE National Academy of Engineering.

NAEB National Association of Educational Broadcasters.

N.A.E.B.M. National Association of Engine and Boat Manufacturers.

NAEC National Aerospace Education Council.

NAEMT National Association of Emergency Medical Technicians.

NAEP National Assessment of Educational Progress (U.S. government body to monitor student achievement).

NAFC National Association of Food Chains.

N.A.F.D. National Association of Funeral Directors.

NAFEC National Aviation Facilities Experimental Center (of U.S. Federal Aviation Administration).

NAFO Northwest Atlantic Fisheries Organization.

N. Afr. 1 North Africa. 2 North African.

NAFTA (naf′tə) 1 New Zealand, Australia Free Trade Agreement. 2 North American Free Trade Agreement. 3 North Atlantic Free Trade Area.

NAG 1 N-acetylglucosamine (an amino sugar). 2 also **n.a.g.** net annual gain commerce.

N.A.G.C. National Association for Gifted Children.

NAGE National Association of Government Employees.

NAGCP National Association of Greeting Card Publishers.

Nah. Nahum (book of the Old Testament).

NAHB National Association of Home Builders.

NAHCAC National Ad Hoc Committee Against Censorship.

NAIA 1 also **N.A.I.A.** National Association of Insurance Agents. 2 National Association of Intercollegiate Athletics.

N.A.I.B. National Association of Insurance Brokers.

NAIR national arrangements for incidents involving radioactivity.

NAIRU Nonaccelerating Inflation Rate of Unemployment (measure of rise and decline of wage levels).

N.A.I.S. National Association of Independent Schools.

NAK negative acknowledgment communications.

NAL 1 National Accelerator Laboratory. 2 National Aerospace Laboratory.

NALC National Association of Letter Carriers (formally **NALCUSA** National Association of Letter Carriers of the United States of America).

NALF New Linguistic Atlas of France. [French Le Nouveau Atlas Linguistique de la France]

NALGO National and Local Government Officers' Association (of Great Britain).

N.A.L.U. National Association of Life Underwriters.

NAM 1 N-acetylmuramic acid (sugar component of bacterial cell walls). 2 also **N.A.M.** National Association of Manufacturers. 3 also **nam** nautical air miles, also in combination: NAM/LB = nautical air miles per pound (of fuel). 4 also **nam** Non-Aligned Movement.

N. Am. 1 North America. 2 North American.

NAME 1 National Association of Marine Engineers. 2 also **N.A.M.E.** National Association of Medical Examiners.

NAMH National Association for Mental Health.

naml. namely. [German nämlich; Swedish namligen]

NAMP National Association of Magazine Publishers.

NAMS National Association of Marine Surveyors.

NAN neutron activation analysis physics.

n.a.n. unless otherwise noted. [Latin nisi aliter notetur]

NANA 1 N-acetylneuraminic acid (a sialic acid). 2 also **N.A.N.A.** North American Newspaper Alliance.

NANAC National Aircraft Noise Abatement Council.

NAND Not AND (logic operator) computers.

N.&Q. Notes and Queries (publication, Notes and Queries for Readers and Writers, Collectors and Librarians).

nanosec. nanosecond (billionth of a second).

N.A.P. Paris Anatomical Nomenclature (international terminology of anatomy). [Latin Nomina Anatomica Parisiensa]

Nap 1 Naples. 2 also **Nap.** Napoleon.

nap. naphtha.

NAPA 1 also **N.A.P.A.** National Association of Performing Artists. 2 National Association of Purchasing Agents.

napalm (nā′päm, -pälm) naphthenic and palmitic acids (a thickened jellied gasoline).

NAPAN National Association for the Prevention of Addiction to Narcotics.

NAPAP National Acid Precipitation Assessment Program.

NAPCA National Air Pollution Control Administration.

NAPF National Association of Pension Funds.

naph. naphtha.

N.A.P.L. 1 National Association of Photo Lithographers. 2 also **NAPL** National Association of Printers and Lithographers.

NAPLPS North American Presentation Level Protocol Syntax (computer language).

NAPM 1 National Association of Paper Merchants. 2 also **N.A.P.M.** National Association of Photographic Manufacturers. 3 National Association of Purchasing Management (issuing a business index).

NAPNAP National Association of Pediatric Nurse Associates and Practitioners.

NAPNES National Association for Practical Nurse Education and Service.

NAPO 1 (nā′pō′) National Association of Police Organizations (police-sponsored community service groups). 2 National Association of Probation Officers. 3 National Association of Property Owners.

NAPT National Association of Physical Therapists.

NAR 1 National Association of Realtors. 2 National Association of Rocketry.

nar 1 also **nar.** narrow. 2 also **n.a.r.** net assimilation rate biology.

NARA National Archives and Records Administration.

NARAL National Abortion Rights Action League.

NARAS National Academy of Recording Arts and Sciences.

NARC National Agricultural Research Center.

narc 1 *also* **narc. a** narcotic. **b** narcotics. **2** (*pronounced* närk) narcotics agent.

NARCO (när′kō′) United Nations Narcotics Commission.

N.A.R.D. National Association of Retail Druggists.

N.A.R.E.B. *or* **NAREB** National Association of Real Estate Boards.

NARM National Association of Record Merchandisers.

narr. narrator, narrated by.

NARS National Archives and Records Service.

NARTB National Association of Radio and Television Broadcasters.

NAS 1 National Academy of Sciences. **2** National Aerospace or Aircraft Standards. **3** National Airspace System (air-traffic control). **4** *also* **N.A.S.** National Audubon Society. **5** Naval Air Station. **6** Noise Abatement Society. **7** Nursing Auxiliary Service.

NASA (na′sə) National Aeronautics and Space Administration.

NASC 1 National Aeronautics and Space Center. **2** National Aeronautics and Space Council. **3** National Association of Student Councils.

NASCAR (nas′cär′) National Association of Stock Car Auto Racing.

NASCO National Academy of Science Committee on Oceanography.

NASD 1 *also* **N.A.S.D.** National Amalgamated Stevedores and Dockers (of Great Britain). **2** National Association of Securities Dealers.

NASDA *or* **Nasda** National Space Development Agency (of Japan).

NASDAQ (naz′dak′) National Association of Securities Dealers Automated Quotations (listing of over-the-counter stock transactions).

NASE National Association of Stationary Engineers.

Nash. Nashville.

NASL North American Soccer League.

NASM National Association of Schools of Music.

NAS-NRC National Academy of Science–National Research Council.

NASP 1 National Achievement Scholarship Program. **2** (*pronounced* nasp) National Aero-Space Plane (hydrogen-powered, supersonic plane under consideration). **3** National Airport System Plan. **4** National Association of School Psychologists.

NASPAA National Association of Schools of Public Affairs and Administration.

NASPO National Association of State Purchasing Officials.

NASS National Agricultural Statistics Service (of U.S. Department of Agriculture).

Nass. Nassau.

NASW 1 National Association of Science Writers. **2** National Association of Social Workers.

Nat. 1 Natal. **2** National: *Nat. Bk.* = *National Bank; Nat. Gal.* = *National Gallery.* **3** Natural: *Am. Mus. Nat. Hist.* = *American Museum of Natural History.*

nat. 1 native. **2** *also* **nat.** natural: *nat. phil.* = *natural philosophy.* **3** *also* **nat.** naturalist. **4** naturalized. **5** *also* **n.a.t.** normal allowed time.

NATA 1 National Association of Tax Accountants. **2** National Association of Testing Authorities. **3** National Association of Transportation Advertisers.

NATAS National Academy of Television Arts and Sciences.

N.A.T.B. National Automobile Theft Bureau.

NATCA National Air Traffic Controllers Association.

Nat. Con. Nature Conservancy.

Nath. Nathaniel.

Nat. Hist. natural history.

Nativ. Nativity.

Natl. *or* **natl.** national: *natl. economy.*

NATO 1 National Association of Theater Owners. **2** National Association of Travel Organizations. **3** *also* **Nato** (nā′to′) North Atlantic Treaty Organization.

Nat. Ord. natural order (of the "natural classification" in botany, roughly equivalent to a plant family).

Nat. Phil. natural philosophy.

Nat. Pk. National Park.

NATS Naval Air Transport Service.

Nat. Sci. *or* **Nat. Sc.** natural science.

NATTS National Association of Trade and Technical Schools.

natur. naturalist.

Natzd. naturalized (established but not native), *esp. in biology.*

NAUCA Central American Standard Tariff Terminology (commodity classification for the Free Trade Area of Latin America). [Spanish *Nomenclatura Arancelaria Uniforme Centroamericano*]

naut. nautical: *naut. mi.* = *nautical mile.*

NAUW National Association of University Women.

Nav. Navaho.

nav. 1 *also* **NAV** naval *military: NAVCOMMSTA* = *Naval Communication Station.* **2 a** navigable. **b** navigation. **c** navigator.

n.a.v. *or* **NAV** net asset value *finance.*

NAVA National Audio-Visual Association.

navaid (nav′ād′) navigational aid.

NAVAIR Naval Air (Systems Command Headquarters).

NAVAR navigation and radar.

NAVDAC navigation data assimilation computer.

navig. 1 navigation. **2** navigator.

NAVOBSY Naval Observatory.

NAVPERS U.S. Navy Papers (esp. manuals followed by a number): *NAVPERS 12-1526.*

NAVSAT navigation satellite.

NAVSTAR (nav′stär′) navigation system based on time and ranging.

NAWAPA North American Water and Power Alliance (plan to redistribute the waters of North America through Canada, U.S., and Mexico).

NAWAS National Warning System.

NAWB National Associations of Workshops for the Blind.

Nazi (nät′sē) National Socialist German Workers Party (party structure of Hitler's dictatorship of Germany from 1933 to 1945). [German *Nationalsozialist*]

NB 1 narrow band *electronics*. **2** National Battlefield: *Antietam NB*. **3** Naval Base. **4** newborn. **5** New Brunswick (postal code). **6** no bias *electronics*. **7** no bid. **8** northbound. **9** note well or observe carefully. [Latin *nota bene*]

Nb *I an abbreviation for:* nimbus (cloud) *meteorology*. *II a symbol for:* niobium (chemical element).

n.b. 1 no ball *cricket*. **2** *also* **n/b** northbound. **3** note well or observe carefully. [Latin *nota bene*]

NBA 1 *also* **N.B.A.** National Bankers Association. **2** *also* **N.B.A.** National Bar Association. **3** National Basketball Association. **4** *also* **N.B.A.** National Book Awards. **5** National Boxing Association. **6** Net Book Agreement.

NBBB National Better Business Bureau.

NBC 1 *also* **N.B.C.** National Book Council (former name of the National Book League). **2** *also* **N.B.C.** National Broadcasting Company. **3** nuclear, biological, chemical (weapons in warfare).

NBD negative binomial distribution *statistics*.

NbE north by east.

NBER National Bureau of Economic Research.

NBFI nonbank financial institutions (of Australia).

NBFM narrow band frequency modulation.

NBFU National Board of Fire Underwriters.

NBI *or* **n.b.i.** no bone injury *medicine*.

NBL 1 *also* **N.B.L.** National Book League (book industry organization to promote the product). **2** National Bowling League.

NBP 1 National Battlefield Park: *Richmond NBP*. **2** *also* **nbp** normal boiling point.

N.B.P.I. National Board for Prices and Incomes (of Great Britain).

NBR N-acrylonitrile-butadiene rubber.

NBRT National Board for Respiratory Therapy.

NBS 1 National Battlefield Site: *Brice Cross Roads NBS*. **2** National Broadcasting Service (of New Zealand). **3** National Bureau of Standards (now *NIST*). **4** *also* **N.B.S.** New British Standard (wire gauge).

NBT narrow-beam transducer.

NBTS National Blood Transfusion Service.

NBV *or* **n.b.v.** net book value *commerce*.

NBW National Book Week.

NbW *or* **N by W** north by west.

N by E north by east.

NC 1 national coarse (American screw thread). **2** Nature Conservancy. **3** Navy Cross. **4** *also* **N.C.** *or* **n.c.** nitrocellulose. **5** no change (of conditions). **6** *also* **n/c** no charge. **7** no comment. **8** no connection, esp. in electronics. **9** *also* **N/C** no credit *commerce*. **10** normally closed (of a door, switch, etc.). **11** North Carolina: **a** (in Zip Code). **b** *also* **N.C.** (in general use). **12** nose cone. **13** not cataloged, esp. in bibliography. **14** *also* **n/c** numerical control: *NC machines or other fully automatic machines*. **15** *also* **N.C.** Nurse Corps, esp. in combination: *ANC = Army Nurse Corps*.

NC-17 *or* **NC 17** no children under 17 years of age admitted (motion picture rating indicating a film with material not suitable for young audiences).

NCA 1 National Cattlemen's Association. **2** National Chiropractic Association. **3** National Coal Association. **4** National Coffee Association. **5** *also* **N.C.A.** National Commission on Accrediting (accredits accrediting agencies). **6** National Council for the Arts. **7** National Council on Aging. **8** National Credit Association. **9** National Cricket Association (of Great Britain). **10** neurocirculatory asthenia (syndrome of fatigue more commonly known as cardiac neurosis). **11** *also* **n.c.a.** no copies available.

NCAA National Collegiate Athletic Association.

NCAC National Copyright Advisory Committee.

NCAE National Council on Adult Education.

NCAI National Congress of American Indians.

NCAM nerve cell adhesion molecule.

NCAR National Center for Atmospheric Research.

N. Car. North Carolina.

NCATE *or* **N.C.A.T.E.** National Council for the Accreditation of Teacher Education.

NCB no-claim bonus *insurance*.

NCBA National Cattle Breeders Association.

NCBE National Conference of Bar Examiners.

NCBI National Center for Biotechnology Information (of the National Library of Medicine).

NCC 1 National Computing Centre (of Great Britain). **2** National Coordinating Committee. **3** *also* **N.C.C.** National Council of Churches. **4** Nature Conservancy Council (of Great Britain).

NCCD National Council on Crime and Delinquency.

NCCI National Committee for Commonwealth Immigrants (of Great Britain).

N.C.C.J. National Conference of Christians and Jews.

NCCS National Climbing Classification System (for rating the difficulty of climbing rock faces).

N.C.D. no one dissenting *law*. [Latin *nemine contra dicente*]

NCDC 1 National Center for Disease Control. **2** National Climatic Data Center (of the National Environmental Satellite, Data, and Information Service). **3** National Communicable Disease Center.

NCEA *or* **N.C.E.A.** National Catholic Education Association.

NCEP National Cholesterol Education Program.

NCER National Center for Earthquake Research.

NCERT National Council for Educational Research and Training.

NCES National Center for Educational Statistics.

NCET 1 National Conference of English Teachers. **2** National Council for Educational Technology.

NCEW National Conference of Editorial Writers.

NCG new college graduate.

NCGE National Council for Geographic Education.

NCH number or name changed (of a telephone listing).

NCHGR National Center for Human Genome Research (of the National Institutes of Health).

n.Chr. in the year of the Lord; AD. [German *nach Christus* after Christ]

NCHS National Center for Health Statistics.

NCI 1 National Cancer Institute. **2** New Community Instrument (for borrowing and lending among members of the EC). **3** *also* **n.c.i.** no common interest.

nCi nanocurie (billionth of a curie).

NCIC 1 National Cartographic Information Center. **2** National Crime Information Center.

NCJRS National Criminal Justice Reference Service.

NCL National Chemical Laboratory (of Great Britain).

NCLEX National Council Licensing Examination (for nursing).

NCM National Congress of Mothers.

NCNA New China News Agency.

N.C.N.C. National Council of Nigerian Citizens (Nigerian political party).

NCNR National Center for Nursing Research (of the National Institutes of Health).

NCO *or* **n.c.o.** Noncommissioned Officer.

N.C.O.M.P. National Catholic Office for Motion Pictures.

NCP 1 national cycling proficiency. **2** *also* **n.c.p.** normal circular pitch *engineering*.

NCPAC National Conservative Political Action Committee.

NCPC National Capital Planning Commission.

NCPT National Congress of Parents and Teachers.

NCR 1 National Crime Survey. **2** no carbon required (of multiple-copy forms).

NCRP National Committee on Radiation Protection.

NCRR National Center for Research Resources (of the National Institutes of Health).

NCS 1 National Cemetery System. **2** National Communications System.

NCSC 1 National Companies and Securities Commission (of Australia). **2** National Council of Senior Citizens.

NCSS National Council for the Social Studies.

NCTA National Cable Television Association.

NCTC National Collection of Type Cultures *medicine*.

NCTE National Council of Teachers of English.

NCTEPS National Commission on Teacher Education and Professional Standards.

NCTI National Consumer Testing Institute.

NCTM National Council of Teachers of Mathematics.

NCTS National Council of Technical Schools.

NCU 1 National Communications Union. **2** *also* **N.C.U.** National Cyclists' Union. **3** Navigation Computer Unit.

NCUA National Credit Union Administration.

n.c.u.p. *or* **NCUP** no commission until paid *commerce*.

n.c.v. *or* **NCV** no commercial value.

N.C.W. National Council of Women.

N.C.W.C. *or* **NCWC** National Catholic Welfare Conference.

NCz new cruzado (monetary unit of Brazil): *NCz$*.

ND 1 National Debt. **2** Navy Department. **3** Neuropathic Doctor. **4** neutral density (esp. of a filter). **5** *also* **N/D** next day *commerce*. **6** *also* **N.D.** no date *or* not dated. **7** *also* **N.D.** *or* **N/D** no decision. **8** *also* **N.D.** no deed. **9** *also* **N.D.** *or* **N/D** *or* **n/d** no discount *commerce*. **10** *also* **N/D** nondelivery. **11** nondirectional (microphone). **12** North Dakota: **a** (in Zip Code). **b** *also* **N.D.** (in general use). **13** *also* **N.D.** Northern District (of a judicial administrative division). **14** *also* **N.D.** Our Lady. [French *Notre Dame*]

Nd neodium (chemical element).

2nd *or* **2ⁿᵈ** second (rank, order): *2nd ed.* = *second edition.*

n.d. 1 no date or not dated. **2** nondelivery.

NDA 1 National Dairy Association. **2** *also* **N.D.A.** National Dental Association. **3** new drug application. **4** *also* **n.d.a.** nondestructive analysis *chemistry, engineering*.

NDAC 1 National Defense Advisory Commission. **2** Nuclear Defense Affairs Committee (of NATO).

N. Dak. North Dakota.

NDB nondirectional (radio) beacon *aeronautics*.

NDC 1 National Dairy Council. **2** National Democratic Committee. **3** NATO Defense College.

NDE 1 near-death experience. **2** nondestructive evaluation (for materials testing).

NDEA National Defense Education Act.

NDGA nordihydroguaiaretic acid (food preservative).

NDHQ National Defence Headquarters (of the Canadian armed forces).

NDI nondestructive inspection (of materials testing).

Ndl. the Netherlands. [Dutch *Nederland*]

NDMB National Defense Mediation Board.

NDP 1 National Democratic Party (of Germany). **2** Net Domestic Product *economics*. **3** New Democratic Party (of Canada). **4** nucleoside diphosphate (active in metabolism of sugar).

NDPS National Data Processing Service (of Great Britain).

NDR North German Radio: *the NDR Symphony Orchestra of Hamburg*. [German *Norddeutscher Rundfunk*]

NDRC National Defense Research Committee.

NDRO nondestructive readout (of materials testing results) *computers*.

NDSB Narcotic Drugs Supervisory Body (of the UN).

NDT 1 neurodevelopmental treatment (motor therapy as for cerebral palsy). **2** nondestructive testing (of materials).

NDTA National Defense Transportation Agency.

NDU National Defense University.

NE 1 National Emergency, esp. in combination: *NEMTC = National Emergency Management Training Center.* **2** *also* **N.E.** Naval Engineer. **3** Nebraska (Zip Code). **4** *also* **N.E.** new edition. **5** *also* **N.E.** New England, also in combination: *NEJM = New England Journal of Medicine.* **6** *also* **NE.** New English. **7** *also* **N.E. a** northeast. **b** northeastern. **8** not essential.

N/E no effects (without funds) *banking.*

Ne neon (chemical element).

n.e. 1 a northeast. **b** northeastern. **2** *also* **n/e** not exceeding.

NEA 1 National Editorial Association. **2** *also* **N.E.A.** National Education Association (formally **NEAUS** National Education Association of the United States). **3** *also* **N.E.A.** National Endowment for the Arts. **4** negative electron affinity. **5** *also* **N.E.A.** Newspaper Enterprise Association. **6** Nuclear Energy Agency (of the Organization for Economic Cooperation and Development).

NEACP National Emergency Airborne Command Post (for use in a nuclear war).

NEAFC North East Atlantic Fisheries Commission.

NEB 1 National Electricity Board. **2** National Energy Board (of Canada). **3** New English Bible.

Neb. *or* **Nebr.** Nebraska.

NEbE *or* **NE by E** northeast by east.

NEbN *or* **NE by N** northeast by north.

NEC 1 National Electrical Code. **2** National Electronics Conference. **3** National Executive Committee. **4** *also* **NECM** New England Conservatory of Music.

nec 1 *also* **nec.** necessary. **2** *also* **n.e.c.** not elsewhere classified (in a cataloging or classification system).

NECC National Emergency Coordination Center.

necrol. necrology.

NECS National Electrical Code Standards.

necy necessary.

NED 1 New English Dictionary (original name of Oxford English Dictionary). **2** no evidence of disease *medicine.*

NEDC (*often pronounced* ned′ē) National Economic Development Council (of Great Britain).

NEDO National Economic Development Office (of Great Britain).

NEF noise exposure forecast (to evaluate noise level).

NEFA 1 nonesterified fatty acid. **2** *also* **N.E.F.A.** North East Frontier Agency (of India).

neg. 1 a negation. **b** negative, negatively. **2 a** negligent. **b** negligence. **3** negotiable: *neg. ins. = negotiable instrument.*

NEH National Endowment for the Humanities.

Neh. Nehemiah (book of the Old Testament).

NEI National Eye Institute (of the National Institutes of Health).

n.e.i. 1 he or she has not been found (indicated by a court officer when a subpoena cannot be served). [Latin *non est inventus*] **2** not elsewhere indicated.

NEIC National Earthquake Information Center.

NEL 1 National Engineering Laboratory. **2 a** Naval Electronics Laboratory. **b** National Electronics Laboratory.

NELA National Electric Light Association.

NEM 1 New Economic Mechanism (reform in Hungary, enacted in 1968). **2** *also* **n.e.m.** not elsewhere mentioned.

NEMA National Electrical Manufacturers Association.

nem. con. nobody opposing: *all resolutions passed nem. con.* [Latin *nemine contradicente*]

nem. dis. nobody dissenting. [Latin *nemine dissentiente*]

NEMLA Northeast Modern Language Association.

NEMTC National Emergency Management Training Center.

N. Eng. New England.

neol. neologism.

NEP 1 *also* **N.E.P.** New Economic Policy (of the former Soviet Union from 1921 to 1927, restoring private marketing and taxes). **2** *also* **n.e.p.** new edition pending. **3** *also* **nep** noise equivalent power.

Nep. 1 Nepal. **2** Neptune.

NEPA National Environmental Policy Act.

NEQ nonequivalence *computers: NEQ gate.*

NERC 1 National Electronics Research Council (of Great Britain). **2** Natural Environment Research Council (of Great Britain).

NEROC Northeast Radio Observatory Corporation.

NERVA Nuclear Engine for Rocket Vehicle Applications.

NES 1 National Employment Service (of Canada). **2** *also* **n.e.s.** not elsewhere specified.

NESA National Environmental Study Area.

NESAA Near Eastern and South Asian Affairs (bureau of U.S. Department of State).

NESC 1 National Electrical Safety Code. **2** National Environmental Satellite Center.

NESDIS National Environmental Satellite, Data, and Information Service (of the National Oceanic and Atmospheric Administration).

NEST Nuclear Emergency Search Team.

NET 1 National Educational Television. **2** *also* **net** *or* **Net** network, esp. a computer network: *the net;* also in combination: *NETNORTH = Network North* (of Canada). **3** *also* **n.e.t.** not earlier than.

Neth. the Netherlands.

n. et m. night and morning. [Latin *nocte et mane*]

netwrkg networking.

neubearb. revised. [German *neubearbeitet*]

neur. 1 neurology. **2** *also* **neurol.** neurological.

neut. 1 neuter. **2 a** neutral. **b** neutralize.

Nev. Nevada.

NEW net economic welfare.

New Eng. New England.

Newf. Newfoundland.

New M. New Mexico.

New Test. New Testament.

NF 1 national fine (American screw thread). **2** *also* **N.F.** National Formulary (U.S. Pharmacopeia—The National Formulary, a book of registered drugs and drug products, their characteristics and doses). **3** near face *engineering*. **4** neurofibromatosis (disorder affecting the nervous system and skin). **5** Newfoundland: **a** (postal code). **b** *also* **N.F.** *or* **NF.** (in general use). **6 a** noise factor. **b** noise figure *electronics*. **7** nonferrous (of metals containing no iron). **8 a** nonfundable. **b** *also* **N/F** *or* **N.F.** no funds *banking*. **9** *also* **N.F.** *or* **N-F** Norman-French (French of the Normans who conquered England).

nF 1 nanofarad (billionth of a farad) *electronics*. **2** *also* **n.F.** new series. [German *neue Folge*]

nf 1 nanofarad (billionth of a farad) *electronics*. **2** *also* **n.f.** *or* **n/f** no funds *banking*. **3** *also* **n.f.** noun feminine *grammar*.

NFA 1 National Futures Association. **2** *also* **nfa** net financial assets *commerce*. **3** *also* **n.f.a.** no further action.

NFAH National Foundation for the Arts and Humanities.

NFB 1 National Federation of the Blind. **2** National Film Board (of Canada). **3** negative feedback or no feedback *electronics*.

N.F.B.P.W.C. *or* **NFBPWC** National Federation of Business and Professional Women's Clubs.

NFC 1 National Football Conference. **2** *also* **nfc** not favorably considered.

Nfd. Newfoundland.

n.f.d. no fixed date.

NFDM nonfat dry milk.

N.F.E.R. National Foundation for Educational Research (of Great Britain).

N.F.F.E. *or* **NFFE** National Federation of Federal Employees.

NFI National Flood Insurance (for designated areas).

N.F.I.B. National Federation of Independent Business.

NFIP 1 National Flood Insurance Program. **2** National Foreign Intelligence Program.

N.F.I.P. National Foundation for Infantile Paralysis.

NFL 1 National Film Library. **2** *also* **N.F.L.** National Football League. **3** National Liberation Front (in various countries). [French *Front National de Libération*]

Nfld. Newfoundland.

NFLPA National Football League Players Association.

NFM *or* **nFM** narrow band frequency modulation.

NFMC National Federation of Music Clubs.

N.F.O. *or* **NFO** National Farmers Organization.

NFP natural family planning.

NFPA 1 National Fire Protection Association. **2** National Fluid Power Association. **3** National Forest Products Association.

N.F.P.W. *or* **NFPW** National Federation of Professional Workers.

NFR *or* **n.f.r.** no further requirements.

NFS 1 *also* **N.F.S.** National Fire Service (of Great Britain). **2** National Forest System. **3** not for sale.

NFSAIS National Federation of Science Abstracting and Indexing Services.

N.F.T.C. National Foreign Trade Council.

NFU 1 *also* **N.F.U.** National Farmers' Union (of Great Britain). **2** National Film Unit.

NFWA National Farm Workers Association.

NFZ no-fly zone *military*.

NG 1 *British* National Gallery. **2** National Guard. **3** natural gas. **4** *also* **N.G.** New Guinea. **5** nitroglycerine. **6** *also* **N.G.** *or* **N/G** no good: *manuscript is NG.* **7** nuclear galaxy (distinguished by a starlike central nucleus).

Ng. Norwegian.

ng 1 *also* **ng.** *or* **nG** nanogram (billionth of a gram). **2** *also* **n.g.** new genus *biology*. **3** *also* **n.g.** *or* **n/g** no good.

NGA 1 *also* **N.G.A.** National Gallery of Art. **2** National Governors Association.

NGC New General Catalogue (of stars): *NGC 2444-45.*

NGDC National Geophysical Data Center (of the National Oceanic and Atmospheric Administration).

n.gen. new genus *biology*.

NGF nerve growth factor *biochemistry*.

NGI not guilty (by reason of) insanity.

NGk. *or* **NGk** *or* **NGr.** New Greek.

NGL natural gas liquids.

NGO nongovernmental organization (of the UN).

NGS 1 National Geographic Society. **2** nuclear generating station.

NGSDS National Geophysical and Solar Terrestrial Data Center.

NGSIC National Geodetic Survey Information Center.

NGTE National Gas Turbine Establishment (of Great Britain).

NGU nongonococcal urethritis *medicine*.

NGUS National Guard of the United States.

NGV natural gas vehicle.

NH 1 Naval Hospital. **2** New Hampshire: **a** (in Zip Code). **b** *also* **N.H.** (in general use). **3** *also* **N.H.** Northern Hemisphere.

nh. *or* **nH** nanohenry (billionth of a henry).

NHA 1 National Health Association. **2** National Hockey Association. **3** National Housing Agency or Act.

NHANES National Health and Nutrition Examination Survey.

NHB National Harbours Board (of Canada).

NHBRC National House Builders' Registration Council.

NHC 1 National Health Council. **2** National Hurricane Center.

NHCIC National Hazardous Chemicals Information Center.

NHEA National Higher Education Association.

N.Heb. 1 New Hebrew. **2** New Hebrides.

NHG. *or* **NHG** New High German (of language).

NHI *or* **N.H.I.** National Health Insurance (of Great Britain or Canada).

NHK Japanese National Broadcasting Station. [Japanese *Nippon Hoso Kyokai*]

NHL *or* **N.H.L.** National Hockey League.

NHLBI National Heart, Lung, and Blood Institute (of the National Institutes of Health).

NHMRCA National Health and Medical Research Council of Australia.

NHO 1 National Hospice Organization. **2** Navy Hydrographic Office.

NHP 1 National Historic Park. **2** *also* **nhp** *or* **n.hp.** nominal horsepower.

NHPRC National Historical Publication and Records Commission.

NHRP National Hurricane Research Project.

NHS 1 *also* **N.H.S.** National Health Service. **2** National Historic Site. **3** *also* **N.H.S.** National Honor Society.

NHSC National Health Service Corps.

NHTSA National Highway Traffic Safety Administration (of U.S. Department of Transportation).

NI 1 *also* **N.I.** National Insurance (of Great Britain). **2** naval intelligence. **3** Northern Ireland. **4** *also* **N.I.** North Island (one of the two main islands of New Zealand).

Ni nickel (chemical element).

ni 1 *also* **n/i** new impression, in casting, die casting, or printing. **2** *also* **ni.** night.

NIA 1 National Institute on Aging (of the National Institutes of Health). **2** National Intelligence Authority. **3** Neighborhood Improvement Association.

NIAB National Institute of Agricultural Botany.

NIAID National Institute of Allergy and Infectious Diseases.

NIAMSD National Institute of Arthritis and Musculoskeletal Diseases.

NIB noninterference basis (curtailment of scientific studies for purposes of military security).

Nibmar *or* **NIBMAR** (nib'mär') no independence before majority African rule (a British Commonwealth policy demanding proportional representation of black populations in dependencies before granting independence).

NIBSC National Institute for Biological Standards Control.

NIC 1 National Incomes Commission (of Great Britain). **2** National Institute of Corrections. **3** network interface card *computers*. **4** newly industrialized country. **5** nineteen-hundred indexing and cataloging *computers*. **6** *also* **nic** not in contact *electronics*.

Nic. *or* **Nicar. 1** Nicaragua. **2** Nicaraguan.

nicad *or* **NiCad** nickel-cadmium (of an electrical battery).

NICB 1 National Industrial Conference Board. **2** National Insurance Crime Bureau (investigative arm of the American insurance industry).

NICHHD *or* **NICH** National Institute of Child Health and Human Development (of the National Institutes of Health).

NICU neonatal intensive care unit.

NID 1 a National Institute on Deafness (fully *NIDCD*). **b** National Institute of Diabetes (fully *NIDDKD*). **2** Naval Intelligence Department.

NIDA 1 National Institute of Dramatic Art. **2** *also* **Nida** (nī'də) National Institute on Drug Abuse.

NIDCD National Institute on Deafness and Other Communication Disorders (of the National Institutes of Health).

NIDD noninsulin-dependent diabetes.

NIDDKD National Institute of Diabetes and Digestive and Kidney Diseases (of the National Institutes of Health).

NIDDM noninsulin-dependent diabetes mellitus.

NIDR National Institute of Dental Research.

NIE National Institute of Education (U.S. government agency).

NIEHS National Institute of Environmental Health Sciences (of the National Institutes of Health).

N.I.E.S.R. National Institute of Economic and Social Research.

nif nitrogen-fixing (of a gene) *biology*.

NIFO (nī'fō') next in, first out (method of inventory control).

Nig. 1 Nigeria. **2** Nigerian.

NIGMS National Institute of General Medical Sciences (of the National Institutes of Health).

NIH National Institutes of Health (principal biomedical research agency of U.S. Government).

NIHGR National Institute for Human Genome Research (of the National Institutes of Health).

NIJ National Institute of Justice (research and development agency of U.S. Department of Justice).

NIMBY *or* **Nimby** (nim'bē) not in my back yard (opposition to establishment of a public facility in one's area).

NIMH National Institute of Mental Health (of the National Institutes of Health).

NIMR *British* National Institute for Medical Research.

NINDS National Institute of Neurological Disorders and Stroke (of the National Institutes of Health).

NIO National Institute of Oceanography.

NIOSH National Institute for Occupational Safety and Health.

Nip. 1 Nippon (Japan). **2** Nipponese (Japanese).

NIPH National Institute of Public Health.

NIPO negative input, positive output *electronics*.

ni. pri. unless before (stipulated, mentioned, provided for, etc.). [Latin *nisi prius*]

N.Ir. *or* **N.Ire.** Northern Ireland.

NIRA 1 National Industrial Recovery Act (of the New Deal under Franklin Roosevelt). **2** National Industrial Recreation Association.

NIRC National Industrial Relations Court (of Great Britain).

NIRD National Institute of Research in Dairying.

NIREX (nī'reks) Nuclear Industry Radioactive Waste Executive (of Great Britain).

NIRI National Investor Relations Institute.

NIRNS National Institute for Research in Nuclear Science.

NIRS National Institute of Radiological Science.

NIS 1 Naval Investigation Service. **2** *also* **n.i.s.** not in stock *commerce*.

NIST National Institute of Standards and Technology (replacing the National Bureau of Standards in 1988).

NIT 1 National Intelligence Test. **2** National Invitational Tournament. **3** negative income tax.

NJ New Jersey: **a** (Zip Code). **b** also **N.J.** (in general use).

N.J.A.C. or **NJAC** British National Joint Advisory Council (of the Ministry of Labour).

NJCAA National Junior College Athletic Association.

NK 1 natural killer, of a cell: *NK cells*. **2** also **N.K.** Nomenclature Commission, esp. in combination: *NK-INA = Nomenclature Commission of the Jena Nomina Anatomica*. [German *Nomenklatur Kommission*] **3** also **N.K.** or **nk** not known, also in combination: *NKA = not known as* (in law).

nk. neck, in horse racing.

N.K.B.A. or **NKBA** National Kitchen and Bath Association.

NKGB People's Commissariat of State Security (of the former Soviet Union). [Russian *Narodnyi Komissariat Gosudarstvennoi Bezopasnosti*]

Nkr Norwegian krone (monetary unit).

NKVD People's Commissariat of Internal Affairs (of the former Soviet Union). [Russian *Narodnyi Komissariat Vnutrennikh Del*]

NL or **N.L. 1** National Lakeshore: *Indiana Dunes NL*. **2** National League *baseball*. **3** native language (first language a person learns to speak; also, the predominant language of most inhabitants of a country). **4** British Navy League. **5** also **NL.** New Latin. **6** new line (next line on a computer). **7** also **N.L.** no load (as of a mutual fund that does not charge a commission to buyers). **8** north latitude.

Nl National.

n.l. 1 a it is not clear. [Latin *non liquet*] **b** it is not permitted. [Latin *non licet*] **2** natural log or logarithm. **3** new line *printing*.

NLA 1 National Library of Australia. **2** National Lumbermen's Association.

N.Lat. or **N.lat.** north latitude.

NLB 1 National Labor Board. **2** National Library for the Blind.

N.L.C. National Library of Canada.

N.L.C.A. Norwegian Lutheran Church of America.

NLD National League for Democracy (political party in Burma or Myanmar).

NLF National Liberation Front; FLN.

NLGI National Lubricating Grease Institute (used with a number, classifying lubricating grease).

N.L.I. National Library of Ireland.

N.L.L. or **NLL** or **NLLST** National Lending Library for Science and Technology (of Great Britain).

NLM National Library of Medicine (of U.S. Department of Health and Human Services).

NLN National League for Nursing.

NLP 1 natural language processing *computers*. **2** neighborhood loan program (government-sponsored low-rate mortgages).

NLQ near letter quality (of a computer printer).

NLR noise load ratio.

NLRB or **N.L.R.B.** National Labor Relations Board (preventing unfair labor practices and conducting labor organizing and bargaining).

N.L.S. National Library of Scotland.

NLT 1 normal lymphocyte transfer (test for tissue compatibility). **2** also **n.l.t. a** not later than. **b** not less than.

NM 1 also **nm** nautical mile. **2** New Mexico: **a** (Zip Code). **b** also **N.M.** (in general use).

Nm newton meter *physics*.

N/m or **n/m** no mark or not marked *commerce*.

nm 1 also **n.m.** or **nm.** afternoon, time from noon to midnight; PM. [Dutch *namidday*, German *Nachmittag*] **2** nanometer (billionth of a meter). **3** also **n.m.** new moon. **4** also **n.m.** night and morning *pharmaceutics*. [Latin *nocte et mane*]

NMA or **N.M.A. 1** National Management Association. **2** National Medical Association (professional organization). **3** National Mortgage Association.

NMB 1 National Maritime Board (of Great Britain). **2** National Mediation Board.

NMC 1 National Marketing Council. **2** National Meteorological Center. **3** Naval Medical Center.

n.m.c. no more credit *commerce*.

NMCC National Military Command Center.

NMCS National Military Command System.

NMDA N-methyl-D-aspartate (receptor in the brain, involved in memory).

NME National Military Establishment.

N. Mex. New Mexico.

NMFS National Marine Fisheries Service.

NMI or **nmi** no middle initial.

n.mi. or **n.mi** nautical mile.

NML National Measurement Laboratory.

NMN nicotinamide mononucleotide *biochemistry*.

NMNH National Museum of Natural History (of the Smithsonian Institution).

NMOS (en'môs) N(negative)-channel metal oxide semiconductor *electronics*.

NMP net material product (total value of goods produced and services used in their production).

NMPA National Music Publishers Association.

NMR nuclear magnetic resonance (scanner) *medicine*.

NMRR normal-mode rejection ratio (measure of ability to screen outside electronic interference).

NMS 1 National Market System (of American stock exchanges). **2** National Merit Scholarship, also in combination: *NMSC = National Merit Scholarship Corporation; NMSQT = National Merit Scholarship Qualifying Test*. **3** neuroleptic malignant syndrome (complication after treatment with antipsychotic drugs).

NMT or **nmt** not more than.

NMTBA National Machine Tool Builders' Association.

NMTF National Market Traders' Federation.

NMU National Maritime Union.

NN or **N.N.** neutralization number *chemistry*.

N/N or **n/n** not to be noted *commerce*.

nn. 1 also **NN.** names. [Latin *nomina*] **2** nerves *medicine*. **3** notes.

n.n. no name.

NNA National Newspaper Association.

N.N.D. New and Nonofficial Drugs (publication).

NNE or **N.N.E.** or **n.n.e.** north-northeast.

NNI or **n.n.i.** noise and number index (in acoustic evaluation of ambient noise).

n. nov. new name *taxonomy*. [Latin *nomen novum*]

NNP Net National Product (Gross National Product after deduction for depreciation and value of capital and business services used in production).

NNPA National Newspaper Publishers Association.

N.N.R. New and Nonofficial Remedies (publication).

NNSS Navy Navigation Satellite System.

NNW or **N.N.W.** or **n.n.w.** north-northwest.

NO 1 also **N.O.** natural order (family in plant classification) *botany*. **2** naval officer. **3** Navigation Officer. **4** also **N.O.** New Orleans. **5** also **N/O** no orders *commerce*. **6** also **n.o.** normally open: *NO circuit or switch*. **7** also **N/O** not operating.

No *I an abbreviation for:* **1** also **No.** north, northern. **2** number. [Latin *numero*]
II a symbol for: nobelium (chemical element).

no 1 net. [German *netto*] **2** also **no.** north, northern. **3** nose (esp. in horse racing). **4** also **n.o.** not out *cricket*. **5** also **no.** number. [Latin *numero*]

NOA 1 betanaphthoxyacetic acid (plant growth hormone). **2** also **N.O.A.** National Opera Association. **3** new obligation authority (U.S. Government commitment to future expenditures). **4** also **n.o.a.** not otherwise authorized.

NOAA (nō'e) National Oceanic and Atmospheric Administration (of U.S. Department of Commerce).

NOAO National Optical Astronomy Observatories.

Nob. noble.

nob. for or on our part. [Latin *nobis*]

NOC 1 National Olympic Committee. **2** also **n.o.c.** not otherwise classified.

Noct. nocturne *music*.

noct. during the night *pharmaceutics*. [Latin *nocte*]

NOD night observation device.

NODC National Oceanographic Data Center.

NODL National Office for Decent Literature (of the Catholic Church in the U.S.).

NOE or **n.o.e.** not otherwise enumerated.

NOFI National Oil Fuel Institute.

NoHo (nō'hō') North of Houston Street (area in New York City that is a center of avant-garde art, music, film, and fashion).

NOHP or **n.o.h.p.** not otherwise herein provided.

NOIBN or **n.o.i.b.n.** not otherwise indexed by name (esp. of goods subject to tariff) *commerce*.

nok or **NOK** next of kin.

NOL Naval Ordnance Laboratory.

nol. con. I do not wish to contend *law*. [Latin *nolo contendere*]

nol. pros. will not continue or not willing to prosecute *law*. [Latin *nolle prosequi*]

nom. 1 nomenclature. **2** nominal. **3** nominated. **4** nominative *grammar*.

NOMA National Office Management Association.

NOMAD Navy Oceanographic Meteorological Automatic Device (fixed broadcasting station for monitoring oceanic conditions of temperature, barometric pressure, and wind speed and direction).

nom. cap. nominal capital *commerce*.

nomen. nomenclature.

nomin. nominative *grammar*.

nom. nov. new name *taxonomy*. [Latin *nomen novum*]

nom. nud. name alone (unsupported by technical description) *taxonomy*. [Latin *nomen nudum*]

NOMSS National Operational Meteorological Satellite System.

Non. nones (the religious office or hour once celebrated about nine hours after sunrise or the ninth day before the ides in the calendar of ancient Rome).

noncom (non'kom') or *military* **NONCOM** noncommissioned officer.

non cul. not guilty *law*. [Latin *non culpabilis*]

non obs. or **non obst.** notwithstanding. [Latin *non obstante*]

non pros. he or she does not prosecute *law*. [Latin *non prosequitur*]

non rep. do not repeat *pharmaceutics*. [Latin *non repetatur*]

non res (non'rez') or **Non Res.** nonresident: *non res. num. = nonresident number*.

non seq (non'sek') it does not follow (of the logic or subject of a statement or argument). [Latin *non sequitur*]

nonstand or **nonstd** nonstandard.

non-U (non'yü) not upper class (original British informal usage for something tending to be common or informal).

NOO Naval Oceanographic Office.

no op or **No op 1** nonoperational. **2** no operation *computers*.

NOP 1 *British* National Opinion Polls. **2 a** no operation *computers*. **b** nonoperation, nonoperational. **3** also **n.o.p.** not otherwise provided for. **4** not our publication.

NOPA National Office Products Association.

no par. no paragraph (in preparing copy).

NOPEC (nō'pek) non-OPEC (of oil-producing countries, not members of OPEC).

NOPHN National Organization for Public Health Nursing.

NOR 1 not operationally ready, also in combination: *NORS = not operationally ready (until) supplied*. **2** NOT-OR (logic operator) *mathematics, computers*.

Nor. 1 Norman (French). 2 North, Northern. 3 a Norway. b Norwegian. 4 *also* **Nor** the Level (constellation). [Latin *Norma*]

nor. 1 normal. 2 north, northern.

NORAD (nôr'ad') North American Air Defense Command.

NORC 1 *also* **Norc** National Opinion Research Center. 2 Naval Ordnance Research Computer.

Norf. Norfolk County, England.

Norm. Norman: *Norm.Fr.* = *Norman-French.*

norm. 1 normal. 2 a normalize. b normalized.

NORPAC North Pacific *military.*

North. *or* **north.** northern.

Northants Northamptonshire County, England.

Northum. *or* **Northumb.** Northumberland County, England.

Northw. *or* **northw.** northward.

Norw. 1 Norway. 2 Norwegian.

NOS 1 National Ocean Service (of National Oceanic and Atmospheric Administration). 2 National Ocean Survey.

Nos. *or* **nos.** numbers.

n.o.s. not otherwise specified.

Not. 1 Notary. 2 *also* **not.** notice.

NOTAM notice to airmen.

NOTB National Ophthalmic Treatment Board.

Notts. Nottinghamshire County, England.

notwg notwithstanding.

nouv. new (of an edition of a book). [French *nouveau, nouvelle*]

Nov. 1 *also* **nov.** a novel. b novelist. 2 *also* **Nov** November. 3 *also* **nov.** novice.

n.o.v. *or* **N.O.V.** notwithstanding the verdict *law.* [Latin *non obstante veredicto*]

NOVS National Office of Vital Statistics.

NOW 1 (*pronounced* now) National Organization for Women. 2 negotiated order of withdrawal (of an interest-bearing bank account from which withdrawals can be made by check).

NO$_x$ (noks) nitrogen oxide, nitrogen oxides.

N.O.Y. *or* **n.o.y.** not out yet (of the publication of a book).

noz nozzle.

NP 1 National Park, also in combination: *NPS = National Park Service; ZCNP = Zion Canyon National Park.* 2 National Party (political party of Australia, New Zealand, or South Africa). 3 a neuropsychiatric. b neuropsychiatry. 4 *also* **N.P.** New Providence, Bahamas. 5 *also* **N.P.** Nobel Prize. 6 nondeterministic polynomial (of or belonging to a class of problems that are impractical to solve because no polynomial algorithm can be given): *NP-complete.* 7 nonpolice. 8 nonprofit. 9 *also* **N/P** no protest, in banking. 10 normal pressure. 11 *also* **N.P.** Notary Public. 12 nucleoprotein. 13 a Nurse Practitioner. b nursing procedure. 14 *also* **N.P.** unless before (used of certain actions, trials, etc.) *law.* [Latin *nisi prius*]

Np *I an abbreviation for:* neper (measure of power equal to about 8.7 decibels).
II a symbol for: neptunium (chemical element).

n.p. 1 *also* **n/p** net proceeds. 2 *also* **np** new paragraph. 3 *also* **np** nonparticipating (of stock rights). 4 *also* **np** no paging *printing.* 5 a no place of publication. b no publisher. 6 normal pressure. 7 *also* **np** noun phrase *grammar.*

NPA 1 National Personnel Authority (Japanese civil service board). 2 National Petroleum Association. 3 National Planning Association. 4 National Production Authority (to provide vital materials and production facilities in time of national crisis). 5 New People's Army (communist guerrilla group in the Philippines). 6 *also* **N.P.A.** Newspaper Publishers Association.

NPAC National Program for Acquisition and Cataloging (of the Library of Congress).

NPC 1 National People's Congress (of China). 2 National Petroleum Council. 3 National Press Club.

NPCA National Pest Control Association.

NPD 1 *also* **N.P.D.** National Democratic Party (neo-Nazi political party of Germany). 2 no pathologic diagnosis *medicine.* 3 *also* **n.p.d.** north polar distance.

np/d no place or date (listing in a bibliographic reference).

n.p.f. not provided for.

NPFL National Patriotic Front of Liberia.

NPG 1 *also* **N.P.G.** National Portrait Gallery. 2 a Naval Proving Grounds. b Nevada Proving Ground. 3 Nuclear Planning Group.

NPH neutral protein Hagedorn (a type of insulin).

NPK *or* **N-P-K** nitrogen-phosphorous-potassium (ingredients of fertilizers).

NPL 1 *also* **N.P.L.** *British* National Physical Laboratory. 2 New Programming Language *computers.* 3 noise pollution level. 4 no personal liability *insurance.*

n.pl. noun plural.

NPN 1 *also* **npn** negative-positive-negative (of a transistor configuration) *electronics.* 2 nonprotein nitrogen (an indicator of protein catabolism).

n.p.n.a. *or* **NPNA** no protest nonacceptance *banking.*

NPNP *or* **npnp** negative-positive-negative-positive (of a transistor configuration) *electronics.*

NPO 1 Navy Post Office. 2 *also* **n.p.o.** nothing by mouth *medicine.* [Latin *nil per os*]

n.p. or d. (listing in bibliographic reference): 1 no place or date. 2 *also* **n.p./n.d.** not published and no date.

NPP nuclear power plant.

n.p.p. no passed proof *printing.*

NPPA National Press Photographers Association.

NPPD nitrophenyl pentadienal (so-called spy dust).

NPPF National Planned Parenthood Federation.

NPR 1 National Public Radio. 2 noise-power ratio *electronics.* 3 nuclear paramagnetic resonance *physics.*

NPS 1 National Park Service (of U.S. Department of Interior). 2 *also* **N.P.S.** National Portrait Society. 3 Nonprofessional

Staff (clerical staff of a hospital, university, or technical institution). **4** no prior service.

NPSH net positive suction head (total pressure at the impeller eye of a pump).

NPT 1 *also* **N.P.T. a** nonproliferation treaty. **b** Nuclear Proliferation Treaty. **2** *also* **n.p.t.** normal pressure and temperature.

NPTA National Paper Trade Association.

NPTRL Naval Personnel Training Research Laboratory.

NPU 1 National Pharmaceutical Union. **2** National Postal Union. **3** *also* **npu** not passed urine *medicine*.

n.p.u. the ultimate or perfect state, nothing beyond. [Latin *ne plus ultra*]

NPV 1 *also* **n.p.v.** *finance* **a** net present value (expected costs and revenues from a project back to the present). **b** no par value. **2** nuclear polyhedrosis virus (a baculovirus).

N.P.W.S. National Parks and Wildlife Service (of Australia).

NQ Notes and Queries (for Readers and Writers, Collectors and Librarians; publication).

n.q.a. net quick assets *finance*.

NQR nuclear quadrupole resonance *physics*.

NR 1 natural rubber. **2** Navy Regulations (usually in combination with a number). **3** Nepalese rupee. **4** net register *shipping*. **5 a** noise ratio. **b** noise reduction (of recorded sound on phonograph records, tapes, and discs). **6** nonreactive *electronics*. **7** *also* **N.R.** or **N-R** nonresident. **8** *also* **N.R.** no response or return (to a poll or questionnaire). **9** *also* **N/R** no risk *insurance*. **10** *also* **N.R.** or **n/r** not reported, esp. in law. **11** *also* **n.r.** not to be repeated *pharmaceutics*. [Latin *non repetatur*]

Nr. number. [German *Nummer*]

nr. 1 near. **2** number. [Norwegian, Swedish, Danish *nummer*]

NRA 1 National Reclamation Association. **2** *also* **N.R.A.** (of the New Deal under Franklin Roosevelt): **a** National Recovery Act. **b** National Recovery Administration. **3 a** National Recreation Association. **b** National Recreational Area. **4** National Restaurant Association. **5** *also* **N.R.A.** National Rifle Association.

NRAD or **n.r.a.d.** no risk after discharge *insurance*.

NRAO National Radio Astronomy Observatory.

NRC 1 National Republican Convention (Nigerian political party). **2** National Research Council. **3** Nuclear Regulatory Commission.

NRCA National Retail Credit Association.

NRCC 1 National Republican Campaign Committee. **2** National Research Council of Canada.

NRDC 1 *also* **N.R.D.C.** National Research Development Corporation. **2** Natural Resources Defense Council (group concerned with quality of the environment).

NRDL Naval Radiological Defense Laboratory.

NRDS Nuclear Rocket Development Station.

NRe Reynolds number (factor of fluid in a flow system, used esp. in aerodynamics).

NREC National Resources Evaluation Center.

NRECA National Rural Electric Cooperative Association.

NREM non-REM (rapid eye movement), also in combination: *NREMS* = *non-REM Sleep* (form of sleep in which little dreaming occurs and breathing and pulse are slow to normal and regular).

N.R.F. 1 National Relief Fund. **2** Nouvelle Revue Française (publication of Gide and Rivière).

NRHQ Northern Region Headquarters (of the Canadian Armed Forces).

N.R.H.S. National Railway Historical Society.

NRI or **N.R.I.** National Radio Institute.

NRL 1 National Radiation Laboratory. **2** *also* **N.R.L.** National Reference Library (of Science and Invention). **3** Naval Research Laboratory.

NRM 1 National Resistance Movement (in Uganda). **2** natural remanent magnetization. **3** next to reading matter (direction for placement of an ad on a page). **4** Northern Rocky Mountains (esp. referring to NRM wind scale).

N.R.M.A. National Retail Merchants Association.

NRMC National Records Management Council.

nrml normal.

N.R.O.T.C. or **NROTC** Naval Reserve Officer Training Corps.

NRP 1 *also* **N.R.P.** National Religious Party (of Israel). **2** net rating point or points (for calculating radio or television audience).

NRPB National Resources Planning Board.

NRPC National Railroad Passenger Corporation.

NRR net reproductive rate.

NRS nuclear reaction spectrometry.

NRT 1 *also* **N.R.T.** National Repertory Theater. **2** *also* **nrt** net registered tonnage *shipping*.

N.R.T.A. National Retired Teacher Association.

NRTS National Reactor Testing Station.

NRV 1 net realizable value *commerce*. **2** *also* **nrv** nonreturn valve.

Nrw. Norwegian.

NRZ nonreturn to zero (maintains computer write mechanism at the end of an operation).

NS 1 National Assembly (of Bulgaria). [Bulgarian *Narodno Sŭbranie*] **2** National Seashore: *Cape Cod NS*. **3** National Service. **4** Natural Science. **5** Naval Standard (esp. with a number identifying the designated product). **6** near side (left-hand side, esp. of an automobile). **7** *also* **N.S.** New Series. **8** *also* **N.S.** New Style (Gregorian calendar, adopted in 1752 in English-speaking countries, but in general use in Europe by 1582). **9** *also* **N.S.** not significant, esp. in biology. **10** *also* **N/S** not sufficient (of funds) *banking*. **11 a** Nova Scotia (esp. in postal code). **b** *also* **N.S.** Nova Scotia (in general use). **12** nuclear science. **13** nuclear ship: *NS Savannah*. **14** *also* **N.-S.** Our Lord. [French *Notre-Seigneur*] **15** postscript; P.S. [German *Nachschrift*]

Ns nimbostratus (clouds) *meteorology*.

ns 1 nanosecond (billionth of a second). **2** *also* **n.s.** new series. **3** nonstandard, esp. in combination: *nsi* = *nonstandard item*.

4 a nonstop. **b** not scheduled. **5** *also* **n/s** no service. **6** not specified. **7** *also* **n/s** not sufficient (of funds) *banking*.

NSA 1 National Security Agency (of U.S. Department of Defense). **2** National Shipping Authority. **3** National Skating Association. **4** National Ski Association. **5** National Standards Association. **6** National Student Association. **7** *also* **N.S.A.** Neurological Society of America. **8** *British* Nursery School Association.

NSAC National Society for Autistic Children.

NSAE National Society of Art Education.

NSAFA *British* National Service Armed Forces Act.

NSAID nonsteroidal anti-inflammatory drug.

NSB National Science Board.

NSC 1 National Safety Council. **2** National Security Council. **3** National Service Center.

N.S.C.C. *or* **NSCC** National Society for Crippled Children.

n.s.d. no significant difference.

NSDD National Security Decision Directive (authorizing covert action).

NSE neuron-specific enolase (enzyme associated with nerve cell cancer).

nsec. nanosecond (billionth of a second).

NSERC Natural Science and Engineering Research Council.

NSF 1 National Sanitary Foundation. **2** *also* **N.S.F.** National Science Foundation. **3** National Ski Federation. **4** *also* **nsf** not sufficient funds *banking*: *NSF drafts*.

NSGT Non-Self-Governing territory.

NSIA National Security Industrial Association.

NSIC *or* **N.S.I.C.** Our Saviour Jesus Christ. [Latin *Noster Salvator Iesus Christus*]

N.S.I.D. National Society of Interior Designers.

NSL *or* **N.S.L. 1** National Science Library. **2** National Standards Laboratory.

NSLI National Service Life Insurance (insurance for military personnel).

NSLS National Synchrotron Light Source (X-ray laser holograph).

NSMR National Society for Medical Research.

N.S.N.A. *or* **NSNA** National Student Nurses Association.

NSO naval staff officer.

n.sp. new species *biology*.

NSPA National Scholastic Press Association.

N.S.P.B. *or* **NSPB** National Society for the Prevention of Blindness.

NSPCA *or* **N.S.P.C.A.** National Society for the Prevention of Cruelty to Animals.

NSPCC *or* **N.S.P.C.C.** National Society for the Prevention of Cruelty to Children.

NSPE *or* **N.S.P.E.** National Society of Professional Engineers.

n.s.p.f. *or* **nspf** not specifically provided for.

NSRB National Security Resources Board.

NSRDS National Standard Reference Data System (critically evaluated data in the physical sciences).

NSS 1 National Sample Survey. **2** National Sculpture Society. **3** *also* **n.s.s.** normal saline solution *medicine*.

NSSA National Sportscasters and Sportswriters Association.

NSSFC National Severe Storm Forecast Center.

NSSL National Severe Storms Laboratory.

NST *or* **N.S.T.** Newfoundland Standard Time.

NSTA 1 National Science Teachers Association. **2** National Security Traders Association.

NSTL National Space Technology Laboratories.

NSU nonspecific urethritis *medicine*.

NSV net sales value.

N.S.W. *or* **NSW** New South Wales (state in Australia).

N.S.W.G. *or* **NSWG** New South Wales Government.

NSWMA National Solid Waste Management Association.

N.S.Y. *or* **NSY** New Scotland Yard (headquarters of the London Metropolitan Police, esp. the detective division).

NT 1 *British* National Trust. **2** *also* **n.t.** net ton. **3** *also* **N.T.** *or* **NT.** New Testament. **4** *also* **N.T.** new translation. **5** *also* **N.T.** Northern Territory (state in Australia). **6** Northwest Territories (Canada, postal code). **7** *also* **N.T.** no-trump, in playing cards.

Nt niton (former name of radon).

N/t new terms *commerce*.

nt 1 *also* **nt.** net: *nt wt = net weight*. **2** newton (unit of force). **3** night: *4-7 nt. stay*. **4** nit (unit of luminance). **5** not traded (of a stock) *commerce*.

NTA 1 National Technical Association. **2** *also* **N.T.A.** National Tuberculosis Association. **3** net tangible assets *finance*. **4** nitrilotriacetic acid (used in detergents).

NTB 1 Nontariff Barrier. **2** Norwegian News Agency. [Norwegian *Norsk Telegrambrya*]

NTC *or* **n.t.c.** negative temperature coefficient *electronics*.

ntfy notify.

NTGk *or* **N.T.Gk** New Testament Greek.

Nth 1 Netherlands. **2** North.

Nthn *or* **nthn.** northern.

NTHP *or* **N.T.H.P.** National Trust for Historic Preservation.

NTI 1 Nielsen Television Index (audience rating system). **2** noise transmission impairment.

NTIA 1 National Technical Information Service (of U.S. Department of Commerce). **2** National Telecommunications and Information Administration (of U.S. Department of Commerce).

NTID National Technical Institute for the Deaf.

n.t.l. no time lost.

NTM *or* **n.t.m.** net ton mile.

n.t.o. *or* **NTO** not taken out.

nto. net (amount remaining after deductions). [Spanish *neto*]

NTP 1 *also* **ntp** normal temperature and pressure. **2** *also* **n.t.p.** no title page.

NTR nothing to report.

NTS 1 National Traffic System. **2** Naval Transport Service. **3** Nevada Test Site (atomic and chemical weapons test site). **4** *also* **ntc** not to scale.

NTSB National Transportation Safety Board.

NTSC National Television System Committee: *NTSC standards.*

NTT 1 New Technology Telescope (producing computer-enhanced images). **2** Nippon Telegraph and Telephone Corporation.

NTU 1 National Taxpayers Union. **2** nephelometric turbidity unit (measure of water turbidity by determination of light-scattering effect of suspended particles).

NTV Nippon Television.

ntwrk network.

nt wt *or* **nt. wt.** net weight.

NU 1 *also* **N.U.** National Union, in combination: *NUAW = National Union of Agricultural Workers.* **2** number unobtainable. **3** United Nations. [French *Nations Unies*]

Nu Ngultrum (currency of Bhutan).

n.u. 1 name unknown. **2** number unobtainable.

NUAAW National Union of Agricultural and Allied Workers.

N.U.B.E. *or* **NUBE** National Union of Bank Employees (of Great Britain).

NUC not under control: *NUC lights.*

nuc nuclear.

NUCEA National University Continuing Education Association (association of correspondence schools).

nud. 1 nudism. **2** nudist.

NUDETS nuclear detonation or detection system.

NUG 1 necrotizing ulcerative gingivitis *medicine.* **2** nonutility generator.

NUGMW National Union of General and Municipal Workers (of Great Britain).

NUI 1 *also* **N.U.Irel.** National University of Ireland. **2** network user identifier *computers.*

N.U.J. *or* **NUJ** National Union of Journalists (of Great Britain).

NUL 1 *also* **N.U.L.** National Urban League. **2** null character *computers.*

NUM 1 National Union of Mineworkers (of Great Britain). **2** numeric *computers.*

Num. Numbers (book of the Old Testament).

num. 1 number. **2 a** numeral. **b** numerical.

numb. numbered (as of copies of a limited edition).

NUMEC Nuclear Materials Equipment Corporation.

numis. *or* **numism. 1** numismatics. **2** numismatic.

NUPE National Union of Public Employees (of Great Britain).

NUS National Union of Students (of Great Britain).

NUSAS National Union of South African Students.

NUSC Naval Underwater Systems Center.

NUT National Union of Teachers (of Great Britain).

nut. nutrients.

NUTN National Union of Trained Nurses (of Great Britain).

nutr. nutrition.

NUWW National Union of Women Workers (of Great Britain).

NV 1 *also* **N.V.** limited company or Dutch corporation. [Dutch *naamloze vennootschap*] **2** Nevada (Zip Code). **3** *also* **N.V.** New Version (edition of the Psalms in 1696). **4** night vision, esp. in combination: *NVD = night vision device.* **5** *also* **N.V.** *or* **N/V** nonvintage (of wine). **6** nonvoting (of stock rights). **7** noun-verb (description of syntactical order).

nv 1 needle valve. **2** neutron flux.

NVGA *or* **N.V.G.A.** National Vocational Guidance Association.

NVM 1 *also* **N.V.M.** Nativity of the Virgin Mary. **2** nonvolatile matter.

NVMA *or* **N.V.M.A.** National Veterinary Medical Association.

NVR no voltage release.

NVRS National Vegetable Research Station (of Great Britain).

nvt neutron flux time integral.

NW 1 *also* **N.W.** North Wales. **2** *also* **N.W.** *or* **n.w. a** northwest. **b** northwestern. **3** nuclear warfare.

nW nanowatt (billionth of a watt).

nw 1 *also* **n.w.** *or* **n/w** net weight. **2** *also* **n/w** net worth.

NWbN *or* **NW by N** northwest by north.

NWbW *or* **NW by W** northwest by west.

NWC National War College.

NWF National Wildlife Federation.

Nwfld Newfoundland.

N.W.F.P. North-West Frontier Province (Pakistan).

NWG 1 national wire gauge. **2** Neighborhood Watch Group.

N.W.I. *or* **NWI** Netherlands West Indies.

NWLB National War Labor Board (of WWII).

NWM nuclear waste material.

N.W.M.P. North West Mounted Police (1873–1920, now *RCMP*).

N.W.O. New World Order (of the post Cold War).

NWP numerical weather prediction.

N.W.P. North-West Provinces (India).

NWPC National Women's Political Caucus.

NWQSS National Water Quality Surveillance System.

NWR 1 National Wildlife Refuge. **2** National Wildlife Reserve. **3** NOAA (National Oceanic and Atmospheric Administration) Weather Radio.

NWS 1 National Weather Service. **2** *also* **nws** normal water surface.

NWSA National Women's Studies Association.

NWSC National Weather Satellite Center.

NWSCA National Water and Soil Conservation Agency.

NWSF Nuclear Weapons Storage Facility.

N.W.T. *or* **NWT** Northwest Territories (Canada).

n.wt. *or* **nwt** net weight.

NWTD *or* **nwtd** nonwatertight door (of a ship).

nx *or* **nxt** next, esp. in combination: *nx wk = next week.*

NY 1 New Year. 2 New York: **a** (Zip Code). **b** *also* **N.Y.** (in general use).

NYA National Youth Administration.

N.Y.B.F.U. New York Board of Fire Underwriters.

N.Y.B.S.B.C. New York Bureau of State Building Codes.

NYC *or* **N.Y.C.** New York City.

NYCB New York City Ballet.

NYCE 1 New York Cash Exchange. 2 New York Cocoa Exchange. 3 New York Commodity Exchange.

NYD not yet diagnosed *medicine.*

NYFE New York Futures Exchange.

N.Y.H.S. New York Historical Society.

nyl nylon.

NYME New York Mercantile Exchange.

NYNEX (nī′neks) New York Telephone Company (New York and New England Exchange).

NYO National Youth Orchestra.

NYP *or* **n.y.p.** not yet published.

NYPD New York (City) Police Department.

NYPL New York Public Library.

NYR *or* **n.y.r.** not yet returned.

N.Y.R.A. New York Racing Association.

NYS *or* **N.Y.S.** New York State.

NYSAC New York State Athletic Commission.

NYSE *or* **N.Y.S.E.** New York Stock Exchange.

NYT New York Times.

NYTA New York (City) Transit Authority.

NYZS New York Zoological Society.

NZ *or* **N.Z.** *or* **N.Zeal.** New Zealand: *NZ$ = New Zealand dollar.*

NZAEC New Zealand Atomic Energy Committee.

NZAP New Zealand Associated Press.

NZBC *or* **N.Z.B.C.** New Zealand Broadcasting Corporation.

NZCTU New Zealand Council of Trade Unions.

NZEI *or* **N.Z.E.I.** New Zealand Educational Institute.

NZFS New Zealand Forest Service.

NZL New Zealand.

NZLP New Zealand Labour Party.

N.Z.M.A. New Zealand Medical Association.

N.Z.P.A. *or* **NZPA** New Zealand Press Association.

NZPO *or* **N.Z.P.O.** New Zealand Post Office.

NZR *or* **N.Z.R.** New Zealand Railways.

NZRFU New Zealand Rugby Football Union.

NZRN New Zealand Registered Nurse.

NZUSA *or* **N.Z.U.S.A.** New Zealand University Students Association.

NZWB New Zealand Wool Board.

O *I an abbreviation for:* 1 died. [Latin *obiit*] 2 *also* **O.** East. [German *Osten*] 3 *also* **O.** eye, *esp. in medicine.* [Latin *oculus*] 4 observation, observer. 5 *also* **O.** Ocean. 6 *also* **O.** octavo (page size of a book in which the printing sheet is folded and cut into eight pages, now usually about 6 × 9 inches). 7 *also* **O.** October. 8 Office, in combination: *USOE = United States Office of Education; OC = office copy.* 9 Officer, in combination: *OD = Officer of the Day.* 10 *also* **O.** Ohio. 11 ohm (unit of electrical resistance). 12 *also* **O.** Old, in combination: *OE = Old English.* 13 *also* **O.** Ontario. 14 opening price (of shares in stock trading). 15 orange, Orange, also in combination: *OFS = Orange Free State; OJ = orange juice.* 16 *also* **O.** **a** Order, in combination: *O.R.C. = Order of the Red Cross.* **b** order: *M.O. = money order.* 17 ordinary: *the British O-level examinations.* 18 *also* **O.** Oregon. 19 Organization, in combination: *OAS = Organization of American States.* 20 oscillation: *O-factor.* 21 over, in combination: *PTO = please turn over; O/D = overdraft.* 22 owner, in combination: *O/R = owner's risk.* 23 *also* **O.** pint *pharmaceutics.* [Latin *octarius*] 24 *also* **O.** West. [French *ouest*]

II a symbol for: 1 atomic shell of 50 maximum electrons per shell. 2 blood type O (one of the four major blood groups). 3 eleven; 11 (medieval Roman numeral). 4 fifteenth of a series (fourteenth when *J* is omitted). 5 New Orleans (mint mark on U.S. coins). 6 oxygen (chemical element). 7 star of great heat showing ionized helium, oxygen, and hydrogen in spectral analysis *astronomy.*

O₂ oxygen.

O₃ ozone.

o *I an abbreviation for:* 1 *also* **o.** best. [Latin *optimus*] 2 *also* **o.** bone *medicine.* [Latin *os*] 3 *also* **o.** occasional, as occasional occurrence of a species. 4 *also* **o.** octavo (page size of a book in which the printing sheet is folded and cut into eight pages, now usually about 6 × 9 inches). 5 *also* **o.** off. 6 ohm. 7 *also* **o.** outs *baseball.* 8 *also* **o.** over *cricket.* 9 *also* **o.** overcast *meteorology.* 10 *also* **o.** pint *pharmaceutics.* [Latin *octarius*] *II a symbol for:* fifteenth of a series (fourteenth when *j* is omitted).

o- ortho (of, bonded to, substituting for two adjacent carbon atoms in a benzene ring): *o-dichlorobenzene.*

OA 1 office automation. **2** Office of Administration (esp. of various U.S. government departments and agencies). **3** old account. **4** operations analysis. **5** osteoarthritis. **6** also **o.a.** over all: *LOA = length over all.* **7** also **O.A.** Overeaters Anonymous.

O/A or **o/a** or **o.a. 1** on account *commerce.* **2** on or about.

OAA 1 Food and Agriculture Organization; FAO (of the UN). [French *Organisation pour l'Alimentation et l'Agriculture,* Spanish *Organización para la Alimentación y la Agricultura*] **2** Office of Administrative Appeals (of U.S. Department of Labor). **3** Old Age Assistance. **4** Older Americans Act (funding programs for the aged). **5** Outdoor Advertising Association.

OAAA Outdoor Advertising Association of America.

OAAU Organization of Afro-American Unity.

OABETA Office Appliance and Business Equipment Trade Association.

OACI International Civil Aviation Organization. [French *Organisation d'Aviation Civile Internationale,* Spanish *Organización de Aviación Civil Internacional*]

OAD or **o.a.d.** depth over all.

OAG 1 Office of the Attorney General. **2** Official Airline Guide.

OAH or **o.a.h.** height over all.

OAL 1 also **o.a.l.** length over all; LOA. **2** Office of Administrative Law.

OAM Order of Australia (medal).

OAMS Orbital Attitude Maneuvering System (of a spacecraft).

O&A October and April (of author royalty statements, semiannual billings, etc.).

O&M 1 Operations and Maintenance. **2** also **O. & M.** Organization and Method: *persons with experience of O. & M.*

O&O owned and operated.

OAO 1 also **o.a.o.** off and on (of a switch). **2** orbiting astronomical observatory.

OAP 1 Office of Alien Property, also in combination: *OAPC = Office of Alien Property Custodian.* **2** Old Age Pension or Pensioner.

OAPEC (ō'ä'pek) Organization of Arab Petroleum Exporting Countries (a group within OPEC).

OAR Office of Aerospace Research (of the U.S. Air Force).

OART Office of Advanced Research and Technology (of NASA).

OAS 1 Office of Airline Statistics (of the U.S. Department of Transportation). **2** Old Age Security (social security system of Canada). **3** on active service *military.* **4** also **O.A.S.** Organization of American States (association of over 30 Latin American states and the U.S. to maintain peace and security among members and to promote economic and social development in Latin America). **5** Secret Army Organization (former French clandestine Army group formed to maintain French control of Algeria). [French *Organisation de l'Armée Secrète*]

OASAS Office of Alcoholism and Substance Abuse Services (of U.S. Department of Health and Human Services).

OASDHI Old Age, Survivors, Disability, and Health Insurance (formerly *OASDI,* a revision of the *OASI* Old Age and Survivors Insurance).

OASP organic acid-soluble phosphorus.

OAST Office of Aeronautics and Space Technology (of NASA).

OASTP Office of the Assistant Secretary for Technology Policy (of U.S. Department of Commerce).

OAT 1 Office of Automated Tariffs (of the U.S. Department of Transportation). **2** outside air temperature.

OATC Oceanic Air Traffic Control.

OAU Organization of African Unity.

OB 1 also **OB. a** obstetrical. **b** obstetrician. **c** obstetrics, also in combination: *OB/GYN = obstetrics and gynecology.* **2** also **oB** off-Broadway (of a theatrical production). **3** also **O/B** opening of books. **4** ordered back. **5** outside broadcast (from outside the studio). **6** outward bound, esp. in a list of shipping.

Ob Obadiah (book of the Old Testament).

ob 1 also **ob.** or **Ob.** he, she, or it died. [Latin *obiit*] **2** also **ob.** in passing, incidentally. [Latin *obiter*] **3** oblong. **4** also **ob.** oboe. **5** observation. **6** also **o.b.** on board. **7** also **o/b** or **o.b.** outboard. **8** also **o/b** out of bounds.

Obad. Obadiah (book of the Old Testament).

obb. or **obbl.** not to be omitted *music.* [Italian *obbligato*]

OBC 1 Outboard Boating Club (of America). **2** outer or outside back cover (of a magazine) *advertising.*

OBD omnibearing direction *navigation.*

obdt. obedient.

OBE 1 Office of Business Economics. **2** also **O.B.E.** (Officer of the) Order of the British Empire. **3** out-of-body experience.

OB/GYN 1 obstetrician and gynecologist. **2** obstetrics and gynecology (esp. as a department of a hospital).

OBI omnibearing indicator *navigation.*

obit (ō'bit) or **obit.** obituary.

obj. 1 object. **2** objection. **3** also **object.** objective.

obl. 1 obligation. **2** oblique. **3** oblong.

OBO or best offer (preceded by a dollar figure) *advertising:* *$1200 OBO.*

O/B/O ore-bulk-oil (carrier, in reference to a type of ship).

ob.ph. oblique photograph *surveying.*

Obre. October. [French *Octobre,* Spanish *Octubre,* etc.]

Obs. or **OBS 1** observed. **2 a** obstetrician. **b** obstetrics.

obs. 1 obscure. **2** observation. **3** also **Obs.** observatory. **4** observe, observed. **5** also **Obs.** obsolete. **6** obstacle.

obsc. or **Obsc.** obscured, esp. on navigation charts.

obsol. or **obsoles.** obsolescent.

ob.s.p. he or she died without issue. [Latin *obiit sine prole*]

obstet. 1 obstetrics. **2** obstetrical.

obt. obedient.

obtd. obtained.

OBulg. Old Bulgarian (Old Slavic, in Eastern Orthodox religious texts of the 800s and 900s AD).

obv. obverse.

OC 1 *also* **O.C.** by aid and counsel *law*. [Latin *ope (et) consilio*] **2** office copy. **3** Officer Candidate. **4** *also* **O.C.** British Officer Commanding. **5** official classification. **6** Old Catholic (Catholics who broke away from Rome about 1870 in opposition to doctrine of Papal infallibility). **7** oleoresin capsicum (made from cayenne peppers, a substitute for MACE). **8** *also* **O/C** on camera, in television. **9** on course. **10** *also* **O/C** open charter *commerce*. **11** open circuit. **12** operating characteristic. **13** oral contraceptive. **14** *also* **O/C** order canceled. **15** *also* **O.C.** (Officer of the) Order of Canada. **16** *also* **O.C.** original cover (of a postage stamp issue). **17** *also* **O/C** *or* **o/c** overcharge. **18** *also* **O-C** over-the-counter; OTC, in securities trading.

Oc. *or* **oc.** ocean, esp. in combination: *Oc.B/L = ocean bill of lading.*

o.c. 1 in the work cited; op. cit. [Latin *opere citato*] **2** on center. **3** only child.

OCA 1 Office of Consumer Affairs. **2** Organization of Cooperatives of America (in Latin America).

OCAL On-line Cryptanalytic Aid Language *computers*.

OCAM African and Malagasy Common Organization. [French *Organisation Commune Africaine et Malgache*]

O.Cart. Carthusian Order. [Latin *Ordo Cartusiensis*]

OCAS Organization of Central American States.

OCAT Optometry College Admissions Test.

OCAW *or* **OCAWIU** Oil, Chemical and Atomic Workers International Union.

OCB 1 oil circuit breaker *engineering*. **2** Organized Crime Bureau (of the FBI).

OCC 1 *also* **O.C.C.** Carmelite Friars. [Latin *Ordo Carmelitarum Calceatorum*] **2** Office of the Controller of the Currency. **3** Operations Control Center.

occ. 1 *also* **occas. a** occasionally. **b** occasional. **2** occupation.

occn. occasion.

occup. 1 occupation. **2** occupational.

OCD 1 obsessive compulsive disorder *medicine*. **2** on-line communications driver *computers*.

O.C.D.E. Organization for Economic Cooperation and Development; OECD. [French *Organisation de Coopération et de Développement Économiques*]

oceanog. oceanography.

OCG Office of Challenge Grants (of the National Endowment for the Humanities).

och. ochre.

OCHAMPUS Office of Civilian Health and Medical Program of the Uniformed Services.

OCIAA Office of Coordinator of Inter-American Affairs.

OCLA Office of Congressional and Legislative Affairs (of U.S. Department of Interior).

OCLC 1 Ohio College Library Center (a major research library catalog). **2** Online Computer Library Center.

OCO open-close-open (of a circuit) *electronics*.

OCP output control pulses *electronics*.

OCR 1 Office of Civil Rights (of U.S. Department of Transportation). **2** *computers*: **a** optical character reader. **b** optical character recognition.

OCRWM Office of Civilian Radioactive Waste Management (of U.S. Department of Energy).

OCS 1 Office of Community Services (of U.S. Public Health Services). **2** Office of Computer Services (of U.S. Department of Commerce). **3** Office of Contract Settlement. **4** Officer Candidate School. **5** optical character scanner *computers*. **6** Outer Continental Shelf.

OCSE Office of Child Support Enforcement (of U.S. Public Health Services).

OCST 1 Office of Commercial Space Transportation (of U.S. Department of Transportation). **2** overcast *meteorology*.

Oct 1 octant (instrument for measuring arcs in navigation, whose name was borrowed for this constellation, Octans, of the southern sky). **2** *also* **Oct.** October.

oct. 1 octagon. **2** octave. **3** octavo (page size of a book in which the printing sheet is folded and cut into eight pages, now usually about 6×9 inches).

OCTV open-circuit television.

OCU operational conversion unit.

OCV open circuit voltage.

OD 1 *also* **O.D.** Doctor of Optometry. **2** Officer of the Day. **3** *also* **OD.** Old Dutch (before 1100). **4** olive drab (former uniform color). **5** *also* **O/D** on demand *finance*. **6** on duty. **7** optical density *biology, chemistry, medicine*. **8 a** ordnance data. **b** Ordnance Department. **9** organizational development. **10** origin and destination. **11** *also* **O.D. a** outside diameter. **b** outside dimensions. **12** overdose (of narcotics; also a person suffering from such a dose). **13** *also* **O/D** *banking*: **a** overdraft. **b** overdrawn. **14** *also* **O.D.** right eye *medicine*. [Latin *oculus dexter*]

od *or* **o/d 1** on demand *finance*. **2** *also* **o.d. a** outside diameter. **b** outside dimensions. **3** overdose (of narcotics; also a person suffering from such a dose).

ODA 1 office document architecture (system of storage for documents in a computer). **2** Official Development Assistance (to underdeveloped nations). **3** Orphan Drug Act (1983, to encourage development of new drugs for rare diseases).

ODan. Old Danish (before 1100).

ODB Office of Dependency Benefits.

ODECA *or* **O.D.E.C.A.** Organization of Central American States; CACM. [Spanish *Organización de Estados Centroamericanos*]

ODP Ocean Drilling Program (study of tectonic plates under the oceans).

ODR 1 Office of Defense Resources. **2** omnidirectional ranging *navigation*.

ODS 1 Ocean Data Station. **2** oxide dispersion strengthened (of steel).

ODT Office of Defense Transportation.

OE 1 Office of Education. **2** Office of Exploration (of space, division of NASA). **3** *also* **O.E.** Old English (from 600 to about 1100). **4** *also* **O.E.** omissions excepted. **5** original equipment. **6** original error.

Oe *or* **Oe.** oersted (unit of magnetic intensity).

o.e. 1 omissions excepted. **2** open end. **3** original equipment. **4** original error.

OEA 1 Office of Economic Adjustment. **2** Office of Environmental Affairs. **3** *also* **O.E.A.** Organization of American States. [Spanish *Organización de Estados Americanos*] **4** Overseas Education Association.

OEC 1 Office of Energy Conservation. **2** Office of the Chief of Engineers of the U.S. Army.

OECD Organization for Economic Cooperation and Development.

OECS Organization of Eastern Caribbean States.

OED Oxford English Dictionary.

OEEC Organization for European Economic Cooperation (replaced by *OECD* in 1961).

OEIU Office Employees International Union.

OEM original equipment manufacturer (company that manufactures component parts of machinery or equipment).

OEO 1 Office for Equal Opportunity (of U.S. Department of the Interior). **2** Office of Economic Opportunity.

OEP Office of Emergency Planning (later Office of Emergency Preparedness, now a part of Federal Emergency Management Agency).

OER 1 Office of Energy Research (of U.S. Department of Energy). **2** officer efficiency report. **3** Officers' Emergency Reserve.

OERWM Office of Environmental Restoration and Waste Management (of U.S. Department of Energy).

OES 1 Office of Economic Stabilization (during WWII). **2** Office of Employment Stability. **3** optical emission spectroscopy. **4** orbital escape system (of a spacecraft). **5** *also* **O.E.S.** Order of the Eastern Star. **6** Organization of European States.

OEZ *or* **O.E.Z.** East European Time. [German *Osteuropäische Zeit*]

OF 1 *also* **O.F.** Odd Fellows (fraternal organization). **2** *also* **O.F.** old face (printing type). **3** *also* **O.F.** Old French (before 1350 or 1400). **4** Operating Forces *military*. **5** outfield *baseball*. **6** oxidizing flame.

OFA 1 Office For the Aging. **2** Office of Family Assistance.

ofc. *or* **Ofc.** office.

OFCC Office of Federal Contract Compliance.

ofcl. *or* **Ofcl.** official.

OFEMA French Office for the Export of Aeronautical Material. [French *Office Français d'Exportation de Matériel Aéronautique*]

off. 1 offered. **2** *also* **Off.** office. **3** *also* **Off.** officer. **4** *also* **Off.** official: *off. nom. = official nomenclature*. **5** officinal (of a drug kept in stock or the drug itself).

offg. officiating.

Off. Gaz. Official Gazette (of U.S. Patent Office).

offic. *or* **Offic.** official.

offr. *or* **Offr.** officer.

OFHC oxygen-free high-conductivity (of copper).

OFlem. Old Flemish (before 1100).

OFM 1 Office of Financial Management. **2** Office of Foreign Missions (of U.S. Department of State). **3** *also* **O.F.M.** Order of Friars Minor (Observant Franciscans). [Latin *Ordo Fratrum Minorum*]

OFPP Office of Federal Procurement Policy.

OFR Office of the Federal Register (of the National Archives).

OFr *or* **O.Fr.** Old French (before 1350 or 1400).

OFRC Office of Federal Records Centers (of the National Archives).

OFris. Old Frisian (before 1500).

OFS *or* **O.F.S.** Orange Free State (province in Republic of South Africa).

OFT Office of Fair Trading (of Great Britain).

Oftel *or* **OFTEL** Office of Telecommunications (British regulatory commission for telecommunications).

OG 1 Officer of the Guard. **2** *also* **O.G.** ogee (esp. a pointed arch with S-shaped sides) *architecture*. **3** *also* **O-G** O-Gravity (weightlessness). **4** *also* **O.G.** Olympic Games. **5** original gravity, in brewing. **6** *also* **o.g.** original gum (of a postage stamp). **7** outgassing (steel-making process). **8** outside guard, *esp. in sports*.

OGE Office of Government Ethics.

OGM ordinary general meeting (of a corporation).

OGO Orbiting Geophysical Observatory.

OGPS Office of Grants and Program Systems.

OGPU *or* **O.G.P.U.** Unified State Political Administration (earlier form of former Soviet secret police, MVD). [Russian *Obedinennoe Gosudarstvennoi Politicheskoi Upravlenie*]

OGTT oral glucose tolerance test *medicine*.

OH *I an abbreviation for:* **1** Official Hostess (woman who officiates at social functions for a bachelor or widower, usually in government). **2** office hours. **3** Ohio (Zip Code). **4** Olduvai Hominid (of prehuman remains found at Olduvai gorge) *anthropology*. **5** on hand. **6** open hearth (steel-making process). **7** *also* **O/H** overhead, *esp. in accounting*. *II a symbol for:* hydroxyl.

o.h. 1 every hour *pharmaceutics*. [Latin *omni hora*] **2** on hand.

OHA Office of Hearings and Appeals (of U.S. Department of the Interior).

O.H.B.M.S. *or* **OHBMS** On His or Her Britannic Majesty's Service.

OHC *or* **o.h.c.** overhead camshaft.

OHCS hydroxycorticosteroid: *17-OHCS*.

OHD organic heart disease.

OHDETS over-horizon detection system.

OHE *or* **O.H.E.** Office of Health Economics (of Great Britain).

OHG *or* **O.H.G. 1** Old High German (used in southern Germany before 1100). **2** regular partnership *commerce*. [German *Offene Handelsgesellschaft*]

OHI ocular hypertension indicator.

OHIA Oil Heat Institute of America.

O.H.M.S. *or* **OHMS** On His or Her Majesty's Service.

OHN occupational health nurse.

OHP overhead projector.

OHS 1 Office of Highway Safety. 2 open hearth steel.

OHV 1 *also* **o.h.v.** overhead valve: *o.h.v. engine.* 2 overhead vent.

OI 1 oil immersed. 2 Old Icelandic (before 1500). 3 *also* **O.I.** operating instructions. 4 *also* **O.I.** osteogenesis imperfecta (disease of the bone structure).

OIA 1 Office of Impact Analysis (of the Environmental Protection Agency). 2 Office of International Affairs (of U.S. Department of Justice).

OIC 1 International Trade Organization. [French *Organisation Internationale du Commerce*] 2 Officer-in-Charge. 3 Office of Independent Counsel (of U.S. Department of Justice). 4 Ohio Improved Chester White (kind of pig). 5 *also* **O.I.C.** Opportunities Industrialization Center. 6 Organization of the Islamic Conference (promoting unity among Islamic countries).

OICD Office of International Cooperation and Development.

OIcel. Old Icelandic (before 1500).

OID original-issue discount (bond purchased at less than face amount when first marketed).

OIESA Oceans and International Environmental and Scientific Affairs (of U.S. Department of State).

OIG Office of the Inspector General (of various U.S. government departments and agencies).

O.I.J. International Organization of Journalists. [French *Organisation Internationale des Journalistes*]

oint. ointment.

OIPC Interpol (International Police Organization). [French *Organization Internationale de Police Criminelle*]

OIPR Office of Intelligence Policy and Review (of U.S. Department of Justice).

OIr. Old Irish (before 1200).

OIRT International Radio and Television Organization. [French *Organisation Internationale de Radio-diffusion et Télévision*]

OISA Office of International Scientific Affairs.

OIT 1 International Labor Organization. [French *Organisation Internationale du Travail*] 2 Office of International Trade.

OIt. Old Italian (before 1550).

OITF Office of International Trade Fairs.

OJ 1 open joint *building.* 2 *also* **o.j.** orange juice: *instant o.j.*

o.J. no date (of publication). [German *ohne Jahr*]

OJAJ October, January, April, July (months ending quarters) *accounting.*

OJC Order of Jacques-Cartier (secret society in Canada).

OJJDP Office of Juvenile Justice and Delinquency Prevention.

OJP Office of Justice Programs (supervising national criminal justice system, of U.S. Department of Justice).

OJT on-the-job training: *trainees in OJT courses.*

OJTP Office of Job Training Programs (of U.S. Department of Labor).

OK 1 *also* **O.K.** *or* **o.k.** (ō′kā′) all correct or approved. 2 Oklahoma (Zip Code).

o.k.a. *or* **o/k/a** otherwise known as: *Samuel Langhorne Clemens o.k.a. Mark Twain.*

Okla. Oklahoma.

O.K.W. High Command of the Armed Forces (in WWII). [German *Oberkommando der Wehrmacht*]

OL 1 *also* **O.L.** left eye *medicine.* [Latin *oculus laevus*] 2 *also* **O.L.** Old Latin (before 100 BC). 3 on-line *computers,* esp. in combination: *OLRT = on-line real time.* 4 *also* **O.L.** (Officer of the) Order of Leopold. 5 outside left, in soccer and association football. 6 overflow level. 7 overhead line. 8 overload *electricity.*

Ol. Olympiad (period of four years, by which the ancient Greeks computed time).

ol. oil. [Latin *oleum*]

OLA Office of Legislative Affairs (of U.S. Department of Justice).

OLAFS Orbiting and Landing Approach Flight Simulator.

OL and T *or* **OL&T** owners, landlords, and tenants.

OLC 1 oak leaf cluster (decoration) *military.* 2 Office of Legal Counsel (of U.S. Department of Justice). 3 on-line computer.

Old Test. Old Testament.

OLF Oromo Liberation Front (insurgent group in the Sudan-Ethiopian civil war).

OLG *or* **O.L.G.** Old Low German (in northern Germany and the Netherlands before 1100).

OLMR organic liquid-moderated reactor.

OLMS Office of Labor-Management Standards (of U.S. Department of Labor).

OLRT on-line real time operation *computers.*

OLS 1 Office of Liaison Service (of U.S. Department of Justice). 2 ordinary least squares *statistics.*

Olym. 1 Olympiad (period of four years, by which the ancient Greeks computed time). 2 Olympics *or* Olympic Games.

OM 1 *also* **O.M.** *or* **o/m** operation and maintenance. 2 *also* **O.M.** Order of Merit (of Great Britain). 3 *also* **O.M.** ordnance map (issued in Great Britain). 4 organic matter *biology.*

o.m. 1 every morning *pharmaceutics.* [Latin *omni mane*] 2 old measurement.

OMA (ō′mə) 1 Office of Management and Administration (of the National Archives). 2 orderly marketing agreement (agreement between governments to regulate trade).

omarb. revised. [Swedish *omarbetad*]

OMB *or* **O.M.B.** Office of Management and Budget.

OMBE Office of Minority Business Enterprise.

OMEI Office of Minority Economic Impact (of U.S. Department of Energy).

OMH Office of Mental Health.

O.M.I. Oblates of Mary Immaculate.

OMIP Office of Minority Institutions Program (of U.S. Department of the Interior).

OMIS Office of Management and Information Systems.

OMM World Meteorological Organization; WMO. [French *Organisation Météorologique Mondiale*]

omn. bih. every two hours *pharmaceutics*. [Latin *omni bihorio*]

omn. hor. every hour *pharmaceutics* [Latin *omni hora*]

omn. man. every morning *pharmaceutics*. [Latin *omni mane*]

omn. noct. every night *pharmaceutics*. [Latin *omni nocte*]

OMPA octomethyl pyrophosphoramide (used to restore muscular strength as in myasthenia gravis).

OMR Optical Mark Reading *or* Recognition (of bar codes, meter readings, test markings, etc.).

OMS 1 Orbital-Maneuvering System (of an artificial satellite). **2** output per man shift (measure of productivity). **3** ovonic memory switch *electronics*. **4** World Health Organization; WHO. [French *Organization Mondiale de la Santé*]

ON 1 octane number. **2** *also* **O.N.** Old Norse (Old Icelandic and Old Norwegian collectively, the North Germanic language of Scandinavia to about 1300). **3** Ontario (postal code). **4** order number. **5** *also* **O.N.** orthopedic nurse.

o.n. every night *pharmaceutics* [Latin *omni nocte*]

ONA Office of the National Archives.

O.N.C. Ordinary National Certificate (in Great Britain, high-school diploma).

Onco *or* **Oncol. 1** oncology (medical study and treatment of tumors). **2** oncological.

O.N.D. Ordinary National Diploma (in Great Britain, high-school diploma).

ONERA National Office for Aerospace Study and Research. [French *Office National d'Études et de Recherches Aérospatiales*]

ONF *or* **O.N-F.** Old Norman French (dialects, esp. of Picardy and Normandy before 1500).

ONI Office of Naval Intelligence.

ONO *or* **o.n.o.** *or* the nearest offer *advertising*: *$1500 ONO.*

onomat. onomatopoeia.

ONP operating nursing procedure *medicine*.

ONPR Office of New Production Reactors (of U.S. Department of Energy).

ONR Office of Naval Research.

ONS Office of Nuclear Safety (of U.S. Department of Energy).

Ont. Ontario.

ONU United Nations Organization. [French *Organisation des Nations Unies*, Spanish *Organización de las Naciones Unidas*]

onz. ounce. [Spanish *onza*]

OO 1 a Observation Officer. **b** Ordnance Officer. **2** Office of Operations (of U.S. Public Health Service). **3** orbiting observatory (artificial satellite).

O/O 1 *also* **o/o** on order. **2** operations order. **3** *also* **O/o** order of. **4** ore or oil (carrier, type of ship).

OOB 1 *also* **ooB** off-off-Broadway (of a theatrical production). **2** out of bed *medicine*.

OOD *or* **O.O.D. 1** Officer of the Day. **2** Officer of the Deck.

OOG *or* **O.O.G.** Officer of the Guard.

OOP 1 object-oriented programming *computers*. **2** out-of-pocket (expenses). **3** *also* **o.o.p.** out of print.

OOR Office of Ordnance Research (of U.S. Army).

OOS *or* **o.o.s.** out of stock.

OOT out of town.

o.O.u.J. with no date or place of publication. [German *ohne Ort und Jahr*]

OOW *or* **O.O.W.** Officer of the Watch.

OP 1 observation post *military*. **2** open policy (of insurance). **3 a** operating procedure, esp. in combination: *SOP = standard operating procedure.* **b** operation: *OP code.* **c** operational, esp. in combination: *OPCON = operational control.* **4** *also* **O.P.** opposite prompter (right side or wing of a stage). **5** *also* **O.P.** Order of Preachers (Dominicans). [Latin *Ordo Praedicatorum*] **6** organophosphorus: *OP compounds* (often used as insecticides). **7** osmotic pressure *chemistry*. **8** other people's, esp. in facetious combination: *OPM = other people's money; OPC = other people's cigarettes.* **9** *also* **o.p.** out of print. **10** outpatient (of a hospital), also in combination: *OPD = Outpatient Department.* **11** *also* **o.p.** *or* **O.P.** overprint (esp. of a postage stamp marked with another denomination). **12** *also* **O.P.** overproof (of liquor).

Op 1 *also* **Op. a** Operation, Operations. **b** operator. **2** optical: *Op art.* **3** *also* **Op.** opus (esp. a musical composition): *Brahms's Piano Quartet in G minor (Op. 25).*

op 1 operation. **2** *also* **op.** opposite. **3** optical: *op artist; optk = optical tracking.* **4** *also* **op.** opus (composition, writing, etc.).

OPA 1 *also* **O.P.A.** Office of the Pardon Attorney (of U.S. Department of Justice). **2** Office of Price Administration (in WWII). **3** Office of Public Affairs (of a U.S. government department, such as Energy, Interior, or Justice). **4** opto-electronic pulse amplifier.

op-amp operational amplifier.

Op. Atty. Gen. Opinions of the U.S. Attorney General.

OPB Office of Planning and Budget (of various U.S. government departments and agencies).

OPC 1 Office of Policy Coordination (a branch of the CIA). **2** *also* **opc** ordinary portland cement. **3** Outpatient Clinic. **4** *also* **O.P.C.** Overseas Press Club.

op. cit. (*pronounced* op'sit') in the work cited or article or book referred to. [Latin *opere citato*]

OPCON *or* **op con** (*pronounced* op'kon') *or* **ops-con** (*pronounced* ops'kon') operation or operations control.

OPD 1 Office of Policy Development (of a U.S. government agency or department, such as Justice or the White House). **2** Outpatient Department (of a hospital).

OPDAR Optical Direction and Ranging (of missiles in flight).

OPEC *or* **Opec** (ō'pek) Organization of Petroleum Exporting Countries.

Op-Ed *or* **op-ed** (op'ed') Opposite Editorial (page), of a newspaper page featuring articles of opinion by columnists and other writers.

OPEIU Office and Professional Employees International Union.

OPEP Organization of Petroleum Exporting Countries. [French *Organisation des Pays Exportateurs de Pétrole*]

OPer. *or* **OPers.** Old Persian (ancient language of Persia in cuneiform).

OPEX Operational Executive and Administrative Personnel (of the UN Secretariat).

OPFI Office of Program and Fiscal Integrity.

OPFOR Opposing Forces (in war games).

opg. opening.

Oph Serpent Holder (constellation). [Latin *Ophiuchus*]

oph. 1 ophthalmic. 2 a *also* **Oph.** ophthalmologist. b *also* **Oph.** ophthalmology. c ophthalmoscope.

ophth. *or* **ophthal.** 1 *also* **Ophth.** *or* **Ophthal.** a ophthalmologist. b ophthalmology. 2 a opthalmoscope. b opthalmoscopy.

OPI Office of Public Information (of NASA).

OPIC Overseas Private Investment Corporation.

Opinc options income.

OPL Office of Presidential Libraries (of the National Archives).

opl. operational.

OPM 1 Office of Personnel Management (replaced Civil Service Commission). 2 operations per minute *computers*. 3 other people's money.

opn. 1 *also military* **OPN** operation. 2 opinion.

OPO 1 Office of Program Organization (of Equal Employment Opportunity Commission). 2 Organ Procurement Organization (for medical transplants).

OPP 1 Office of Public Programs (of the National Archives). 2 Ontario Provincial Police (Canada). 3 oriented polypropene (used in packaging). 4 *also* **O.P.P.** *or* **o.p.p.** out of print at present.

Opp. opera or opuses (works).

opp. 1 opportunity. 2 opposed. 3 opposite. 4 opposition.

OPPA 1 Office of Policy Planning and Analysis (of U.S. Department of Energy). 2 Office of Publications and Public Affairs (of National Endowment for the Humanities).

OPPRB Office of Policy, Planning, Research, and Budget (of the National Endowment for the Arts).

oppy. opportunity.

OPR 1 Office of Planning and Research. 2 Office of Primary Responsibility.

OPr. *or* **OPruss.** Old Prussian (a Baltic language found in records of the 15th and 16th centuries).

opr. 1 operate. 2 *also* **Opr.** operator.

OProv. Old Provençal (before 1500, principal language of the troubadours).

OPS Office of Price Stabilization (in WWII).

Ops. *or* **Ops** (*sometimes pronounced* ops) Operations, esp. in combination: *D.Ops = Director of Operations.*

opt. 1 best, optimal. [Latin *optimus*] 2 operation. 3 optative (expressing a desire or wish, esp. of verbs in Greek). 4 a optical: *opt. mineral. = optical mineralogy.* b optics. c optician. 5 a optimal. b optimum. 6 a option. b optional.

Optacon (op'tə kon) optical-to-tactile converter (trademark for an electronic device that enables a blind person to read ordinary printed matter by touch).

Opt.D. Doctor of Optometry.

OPTUL optical pulse transmitter using laser *electronics*.

OPV oral polio vaccine.

O.Q.M.G. Office of Quartermaster General.

OR 1 *also* O/R *or* o/r on request. 2 operating room *medicine*. 3 operational requirement, *esp. in military*. 4 *also* **O.R.** Operational Research (using scientific methods to make decisions of chance or mischance). 5 operations research. 6 operations room *military*. 7 Oregon (Zip Code). 8 other ranks *military*. 9 outside radius. 10 outside right, in soccer and association football. 11 *also* **O.R.** owner's risk (of cargo) *insurance*. 12 *also* **O-R** oxidation reduction.

Or. 1 orange. 2 Oregon. 3 Oriental. 4 original.

or 1 *also* **or.** orange. 2 *also* **or.** other. 3 out of range. 4 *also* **o.r.** outside radius. 5 *also* o/r *or* o&r overhaul and repair. 6 *also* **o.r.** owner's risk (of cargo) *insurance*.

ORA Office of Records Administration (of the National Archives).

orat. 1 oration. 2 orator. 3 *also* **Orat.** oratorio. 4 oratory. 5 petitioner. [Latin *orator*]

ORB 1 oceanographic research buoy. 2 omnidirectional radio beacon. 3 *also* **O.R.B.** *or* **o.r.b.** owner's risk of breakage (of cargo) *insurance*.

ORBIS Orbiting Radio Beacon Ionospheric Satellite.

ORC *or* **O.R.C.** 1 Officers Reserve Corps. 2 Organized Reserve Corps (of the U.S. Army).

ORCA Ocean Resources Conservation Association.

ORCH Orchard (in postal address).

orch. 1 orchard. 2 a *also* **Orch.** orchestra. b orchestral. c *also* **Orch.** orchestrated by.

ORD 1 optical rotary dispersion (of wavelengths). 2 *also* **o.r.d.** owner's risk of damage *insurance*.

Ord. 1 a Ordained. b Ordination. 2 Order. 3 Ordnance. 4 Ordinary. 5 *also military* **ORD** ordnance: *Ord.Sgt. = Ordnance Sergeant.*

ord. 1 *also military* **ORD** order. 2 ordinal. 3 ordinary.

Ordn. *or* **ordn.** ordnance.

Ore. *or* **Oreg.** Oregon.

ORF 1 Austrian Broadcasting Corporation. [German *Österreichischer Rundfunk*] 2 *also* **o.r.f.** owner's risk of fire (of cargo) *insurance*.

Org. 1 Organist. 2 *also* **Orgn.** Organization.

org. 1 *also* **org** organ. 2 organic. 3 organism. 4 organist. 5 a organized. b *also* **org** (*pronounced* ôrg) *or* **orgn.** organization. c organizational.

ORI Ocean Research Institute.

Ori Orion (constellation).

Orient. *or* **orient.** oriental.

orig. 1 origin. 2 a *also* **Orig.** original: *Orig. Bds. = original boards* (of a book, in original binding). b originally. 3 originated. 4 *also* **Orig.** originator.

ORINS Oak Ridge Institute for Nuclear Studies.

ORIT Inter-American Labor Organization. [Spanish *Organización Regional Interamericana de Trabajadores*]

Ork. Orkney Islands.

ORL *or* **o.r.l.** owner's risk of leakage (of cargo) *insurance.*

ORM Office of Regional Management.

orn. 1 ornament. 2 a *also* **ornith.** ornithology. b *also* **ornithol.** ornithological.

ORNL Oak Ridge National Laboratory.

ORP ordinary, reasonable, and prudent (of a person) *law.*

Orph. orphanage.

ORR 1 Office of Refugee Resettlement (of U.S. Department of Health and Human Services). 2 *also* **o.r.r.** owner's risk rates *insurance.*

ORS 1 Operational Research Society. 2 *also* **o.r.s.** owner's risk of shifting (of cargo) *insurance.*

ors. others.

O.R.S.A. Operations Research Society of America.

ORT 1 oral rehydration therapy (for diarrhea). 2 (ôrt) Organization for Rehabilitation through Training.

Orth. 1 Orthodox. 2 a Orthopedics. b Orthopedic.

orth. *or* **ortho.** orthography (esp. a type of projection of maps and technical drawings).

ORuss. Old Russian (before 1500).

ORV off-road vehicle (esp. a type of motorcycle).

ORW *or* **o.r.w.** owner's risk of wetting (of cargo) *insurance.*

OS 1 *also* **O.S.** left eye *medicine.* [Latin *oculus sinister*] 2 ocean station. 3 *British* offside (right-hand side, esp. of an automobile). 4 oil switch. 5 *also* **OS.** Old Saxon (German language of northwest Germany from about 800 to about 1100). 6 *also* **O.S.** Old Series *law.* 7 a Old Style (Julian calendar, used in English-speaking countries until 1752, but generally replaced by the Gregorian calendar in 1582). b *also* **O.S.** old style (printing type). 8 one side. 9 *also* **O/S** on sale. 10 *also* **O/S** on schedule. 11 on station. 12 *also* **O.S.** opening snap (of a heart valve) *medicine.* 13 operating system *computers:* OS/2. 14 *also* **O.S.** Ordinary Seaman. 15 *also* **O.S.** Ordnance Survey (used with a number in labeling maps made from geographical survey of Great Britain and Ireland). 16 *also* **O/S** out of stock. 17 output secondary *electronics.* 18 a outside. b *also* **O.S.** outsides (sheet of paper at either end of a ream). 19 outsize (of clothing). 20 *also* **o/s** outstanding *banking.*

Os osmium (chemical element).

o.s. 1 left eye *medicine.* [Latin *oculus sinister*] 2 Old Series *law.* 3 only son. 4 *also* **o/s** out of stock.

OSA 1 Office of the Secretary of the Army. 2 *also* **O.S.A.** *British* Official Secrets Act. 3 *also* **O.S.A.** Ontario Society of Artists. 4 Optical Society of America. 5 Order of St. Augustine (Augustinians).

OSAF Office of the Secretary of the Air Force.

o. s. & d. over, short, and damaged *commerce.*

OSAP Office of Substance Abuse Prevention (of U.S. Public Health Service).

O.S.B. Order of Saint Benedict (Benedictines).

OSC 1 Office of Space Communications (of NASA). 2 Office of Special Counsel (of various U.S. government departments and agencies). 3 *also* **osc.** a oscillate. b oscillation. c oscillator.

OSCAR Orbital Satellite Carrying Amateur Radio.

OSD 1 Office of the Secretary of Defense. 2 *also* **O.S.D.** Order of Saint Dominic (Dominicans). 3 *also* **O.S.D.** *British* Ordnance Survey Department. 4 *also* **OS/D** over, short, and damaged *commerce.*

OSDBU Office of Small and Disadvantaged Business Utilization (of several U.S. government departments, such as Interior, Transportation, and Labor).

OSE operational support equipment.

OSF 1 Office of Space Flight (of NASA). 2 *also* **O.S.F.** Order of Saint Francis (Franciscans).

OSHA (ō′shə) Occupational Safety and Health Administration.

OSHRC Occupational Safety and Health Review Commission.

OSI 1 Office of Scientific Integrity (of National Institutes of Health, overseeing experimentation and publication of reports). 2 Office of Special Investigations (of various U.S. departments and agencies, such as Justice). 3 open systems interconnection (standard plan for computer network). 4 *also* **o.s.i.** out of stock indefinitely.

OSIA On-Site Inspection Agency (of U.S. Department of Defense).

OSL Office of the Secretary of Labor.

OSl. *or* **OSlav.** Old Slavic or Old Church Slavic (language no longer spoken but occurring and therefore preserved in some Orthodox liturgy).

OSM 1 *also* **OSMRE** Office of Surface Mining Reclamation and Enforcement (of U.S. Department of Interior). 2 *also* **O.S.M.** Order of the Servants of Mary (Servites).

OSN Office of the Secretary of the Navy.

OSO orbiting solar observatory.

OSP 1 *also* **O.S.P.** *or* **o.s.p.** he or she died without issue. [Latin *obiit sine prole*] 2 offshore procurement.

OSp. Old Spanish (from about 1100 to about 1500).

OSRD Office of Scientific Research and Development (in WWII).

OSS Office of Strategic Services (U.S. secret intelligence oranization of WWII, developed into CIA).

OSSA Office of Space Science and Applications (of NASA).

OSSD Office of Space Systems Development (of NASA).

OST 1 Office of Science and Technology (abolished 1973, now part of National Science Foundation). 2 *also* **o.s.t.** ordinary spring tides.

Osteo. 1 osteopath. 2 *also* **osteo.** *or* **osteop.** osteopathy.

OSTI Office of Scientific and Technical Information or Infrastructure (of National Science Foundation).

OSTP Office of Science and Technology Policy (of the Executive Office of the President).

OSTS Office of Surface Transportation Safety (of National Transportation Safety Board).

O.S.U. Order of St. Ursula.

OSV ocean station vessel.

OSW or **O.S.W.** 1 Office of Saline Water (of U.S. Department of Interior, for investigation of distillation of seawater). 2 Office of the Status of Women (coordinating Australian government policy on issues affecting women).

OT 1 also **O.T.** occupational therapy. 2 occupied territories (by Israel). 3 Office of Transportation. 4 oiltight. 5 a also **O.T.** old term or terminology, *esp. in medicine.* b also **O/t** or **O/T** old terms *commerce.* 6 also **O.T.** or **OT.** Old Testament. 7 a old tuberculin. b a patch test for tuberculosis, using old tuberculin. 8 also **O/T** overtime.

o.t. 1 also **ot** on time. 2 also **o/t** overtime.

OTA Office of Technology Assessment.

OTAA Office of Trade Adjustment Assistance.

OTAN or **Otan** North Atlantic Treaty Organization; NATO. [French *Organisation du Traité de l'Atlantique Nord*]

OTB 1 off-track betting (esp. in reference to New York City's agency for betting on horse races and other sporting events). 2 open to buy *commerce.*

otbd. outboard.

OTC 1 officer in tactical command. 2 also **O.T.C.** *British* Officer Training Corps. 3 also **O.T.C.** one-stop-inclusive tour charter (combining low-cost air fares and discount for accommodations at a single destination). 4 Organization for Trade Cooperation. 5 ornithine transcarbanylase *biochemistry.* 6 Overseas Telecommunications Commission of Australia (operating Radio Australia). 7 over-the-counter (esp. of a stock transaction or of nonprescription pharmaceuticals). 8 oxytetracycline (antibiotic).

OTD organ tolerance dose *medicine.*

OTEC ocean thermal-energy conversion.

OTeut. Old Teutonic (now referred to as Old Germanic).

OTF off-the-film (of light) *photography.*

OTH over-the-horizon (a radar system), also in combination: *OTH-B = over-the-horizon backscatter.*

Oth. Othello, the Moor of Venice (play by Shakespeare).

OTI 1 Office of Treatment Improvement (of U.S. Public Health Service). 2 official test insecticide.

OTO 1 one time only (to show an ad) *advertising.* 2 a otolaryngology (branch of medicine dealing with diseases of the ear, nose, and throat). b otolaryngologist.

otol. otology (branch of medicine dealing with diseases of the ear).

OTR 1 Office of U.S. Trade Representative. 2 a Registered Occupational Therapist. b also **O.T., Reg.** Certified Occupational Therapist (in Canada).

OTS 1 Office of Technical Services (of U.S. Department of Commerce). 2 Office of Thrift Supervision (of U.S. Department of the Treasury). 3 Officer Training School (of the U.S. Air Force). 4 Organization for Tropical Studies.

Ott. Ottawa, Canada.

ott. octave *music.* [Italian *ottava*]

OTU 1 operational taxonomic unit (in numerical biological taxonomy). 2 Operational Training Unit.

OU or **o.u.** each eye *medicine.* [Latin *oculus uterque*]

O.U.A.M. Order of United American Mechanics.

OUI operating under the influence (of alcohol, referring to operation of any conveyance) *law.*

OUP or **O.U.P.** Oxford University Press.

out. 1 outlet. 2 output.

outbd. outboard.

OV or **o.v.** over voltage.

Ov or **Ov.** 1 Overture *music.* 2 Ovid (Roman poet, 43 BC to 17 AD).

ov 1 also **ov.** ovary. 2 over, esp. in combination: *ovc = overcast.* 3 overture *music.*

ova. octaves *music.* [Italian *ottava*]

ovbd overboard.

OVC Office for Victims of Crime.

ovc 1 also **o.v.c.** other valuable considerations *commerce.* 2 also **ovc.** or **ovcst** overcast *meteorology.*

ovfl. overflow.

ovhd. overhead.

OVI Office of Volunteerism Initiatives.

OVIR Office of Visas and Registration (in former Soviet Union and in Russia). [from Russian acronym]

ovld. overload.

ovo. octavo (printing sheet folded and cut into eight pages, now usually about 6 × 9 inches).

OVP 1 Austrian Peoples Party. [German *Österreichische Volkspartei*] 2 also **OVPUS** Office of the Vice President of the United States.

ovpd. overpaid *commerce.*

ovrd. override.

OW 1 Old Welsh (before 1200). 2 also **O.W.** one way (of a fare).

O/W 1 oil in water. 2 one way (of a fare).

OWBL Office of Work-Based Learning (of U.S. Department of Labor).

OWBO Office of Women's Business Ownership.

OWCP Office of Workers' Compensation Programs (of U.S. Department of Labor).

OWF optimum working frequency *electronics.*

OWI Office of War Information (in WWII).

OWL Older Women's League.

OWM Office of War Mobilization (in WWII).

OWRAP Office of Worker Retraining and Adjustment Programs (of U.S. Department of Labor).

OWS Ocean Weather Service.

Ox. Oxford.

ox 1 oxidizer, esp. of rocket fuel. 2 oxygen.

Oxbridge (oks'brij') Oxford and Cambridge Universities.

Oxf. 1 Oxford. **2** Oxfordshire, England.

Oxfam *or* **OXFAM** (oks' fam') Oxford Committee for Famine Relief.

Oxon. *or* **oxon. 1** of Oxford (of an academic degree or in reference to the Bishop of Oxford and therefore used as his official signature). [Latin *Oxoniensis*] **2** Oxford, Oxfordshire. [Latin *Oxonia*]

oxy oxygeny.

OY *or* **O/Y** corporation (in Finland). [Finnish *Osakeytio*]

oys. oysters.

Oz ozone.

oz. *or* **oz** ounce. ▶The *z* is a blend of ancient Tironian notation 7 (for Latin *-et*, as in *videlicet*) and a medieval midline dot that later approximated a semicolon and was subsequently rendered in a single stroke ʒ similar to our cursive ɀ. In printed form, this character was set as *z*, reminiscent of the Old English Þ, which in printing was early set as *y*, producing the anomaly *ye* for modern *the*.

oz. ap. *or* **oz. apoth.** ounce apothecaries' weight.

oz. av. ounce avoirdupois.

OZNA (former) Yugoslavian secret police. [Serbo-Croatian *Odeljenje Zastite Naroda*]

ozs. ounces.

oz. t. ounce troy (weight).

P *I an abbreviation for:* **1** *also* **P.** holy. [Latin *pius*] **2** parity *physics.* **3** parking. **4** Parkway, in combination: *GSP = Garden State Parkway.* **5** *also* **P.** Pastor. **6** per, esp. in combination: *MPH = miles per hour; RPM = revolutions per minute.* **7** percentile. **8** perianth (surrounding or enclosing part of a flower). **9** perimeter. **10** period (of time, motion, cycle, etc.). **11** personal foul *basketball.* **12** peseta (monetary unit of Spain and Andorra). **13** peso (monetary unit of Argentina, Bolivia, Chile, Columbia, Cuba, Guinea-Bissau, Mexico, Uruguay, and the Philippines). **14** peta- (one quadrillion or 10^{15}): *PHz = petahertz.* **15** petite (size, esp. for women's clothing). **16** Philadelphia (mint mark on U.S. coins). **17** phrase, in combination: *NP = noun phrase* (description of syntactical form). **18** piaster (monetary unit of Vietnam, Egypt, Lebanon, Libya, Sudan, Syria, Turkey). **19** Pincherle (catalog of music of Vivaldi, followed by a number). **20** planed (of lumber). **21** points, in a game. **22** poise (unit of viscosity). **23** polar *meteorology, astronomy.* **24** polarization *physics.* **25** *also* **P.** Pope. **26** port (harbor; left side of a ship or boat and in combination): *POE = port of entry.* **27** *also* **P.** position. **28** positive (electric pole). **29** posterior. **30** power *physics.* **31** premolar. **32** *also* **P.** President, in combination: *VP = Vice President.* **33** pressure *physics, chemistry, geology: P-wave = pressure wave.* **34** *also* **P.** Priest *or* Father. **35** *also* **P.** Prince, esp. in combination: *PEI = Prince Edward Island.* **36** probability. **37** *also* **P.** prompter, in theater. **38** pula (monetary unit of Botswana). **39** pulse: *the initial P wave of an earthquake at long range.* **40** *also* **P.** pupil, esp. in medicine. **41** purl (a stitch), in knitting. **42** weight *or* by weight. [Latin *pondere*]
II a symbol for: **1** atomic shell of 72 maximum electrons per shell. **2** parental (specifically the original parental generation or in combination: $P_1 = $ *first parental generation;* $P_2 = $ *second parental generation.* **3** parity (reversal of space coordinates, one of the three operations of symmetry) *physics.*

4 pass, passed (esp. as a grade in school). **5** pawn *chess.* **6** permeance *physics.* **7** phosphorus (chemical element). **8** sixteenth of a series (fifteenth when *J* is omitted).

P- pursuit (now replaced by F- for fighter plane): *P-38, P-51.*

p *I an abbreviation for:* **1** *also* **p.** by. [Latin *per*] **2** *also* **p.** first. [Latin *primus*] **3** *also* **p.** for. [Latin *pro*] **4** *also* **p.** in part. [Latin *partim*] **5** *also* **p.** little *music.* [Italian *poco*] **6** *also* **p.** near *medicine.* [Latin *proximum*] **7** *also* **p.** page. **8** pamphlet, in cataloging. **9** parallax (the apparent change in position of an object viewed from a distant point). **10** *also* **p.** part. **11** *also* **p. a** particle. **b** past, in combination in grammar: *p.p. = past participle.* **12** *also* **p.** passing showers *meteorology.* **13 a** new pence (British unit of currency). **b** *also* **p.** penny, esp. of nails: *10p = ten penny nail* (more often written *10d*). **14** per, in combination: *mph = miles per hour; cps = cycles per second.* **15** percentage, esp. in statistics. **16** *also* **p.** perch (unit of measure). **17** perforated (of blocks of stamps, in collecting). **18** *also* **p.** perishable. **19** pico- (one trillionth or 10^{-12}): *pf. = picofarad.* **20** *also* **p.** pint. **21** *also* **p.** pipe. **22** pitch (amount of slope or inclination). **23** *also* **p.** pitcher *baseball.* **24** *also* **p.** plate (electrode). **25** *also* **p.** pole (unit of measure and magnetic or electric pole of force) *physics.* **26** poor. **27** *also* **p.** population. **28** positive, as of layers in a transistor. **29** posterior. **30** *also* **p** pressure *physics.* **31** *also* **p.** priest *or* father. **32** proportion. **33** proton. **34** purl (a stitch), in knitting. **35** put (of a stock or commodity option to sell). **36** soft *music.* [Italian *piano*] **37** weight *or* by weight. [Latin *pondere,* French *poids*]
II a symbol for: **1** electric dipole moment. **2** four hundred; 400 (medieval Roman numeral). **3** *also* **p** momentum *physics.* **4** pawn *chess.* **5** sixteenth of a series (fifteenth when *j* is omitted).

p- para (having the 1 and 4 positions in the benzene ring) *chemistry.*

PA 1 particular average (loss on special cargo or interests and not on the whole) *insurance.* **2** Pennsylvania (Zip Code). **3** *also* **P.A.** pernicious anemia *medicine.* **4 a** *British* personal assistant. **b** physician's assistant. **c** production assistant. **5** points against, esp. in tabulating play in sports. **6** *also* **P.A.** Port Authority: *bridges, tunnels, bus terminals, piers, and airports fathered by the P.A.* **7** Post Adjutant *military.* **8** power amplifier. **9** *also* **P.A.** *or* **P/A** power of attorney. **10** *also* **P.A.** Press Agent: *a high-powered secretary who's more of a PA.* **11** *also* **P.A.** Press Association. **12** *also* **P.A.** *or* **P/A** private account *banking, commerce.* **13** *also* **Pa.** professional association. **14** *also* **P.A.** Prothonotary Apostolic (chief registrar in the Roman Catholic Church or chief clerk in a court of law). **15** public address *or* public-address system (loudspeakers connected to a power amplifier to boost sound). **16** Public Affairs (office, esp. of various U.S. government departments and agencies, such as State). **17** public assistance (relief program). **18** *also* **P.A.** Purchasing Agent.

Pa *I an abbreviation for:* **1** *also* **Pa.** pascal (unit of pressure). **2** *also* **Pa.** Pennsylvania.
II a symbol for: protactinium (chemical element).

pA picoampere (unit of one billionth of an ampere).

pa. paper.

p.a. 1 annually: *scholarships in value of $10,000 p.a.* [Latin *per annum*] **2** participial adjective *grammar.* **3** particular average (loss on special cargo or interests and not on the whole) *insurance.* **4** public address or public-address system (loudspeakers connected to a power amplifier to boost sound).

p.a.a. to be applied to the affected part *pharmaceutics.* [Latin *parti affectae applicandus*]

PAAA Premium Advertising Association of America.

PAB *or* **PABA** *or* **paba** para-aminobenzoic acid (constituent of vitamin B complex).

PABX private automatic branch exchange (permitting a telephone caller to dial directly through to the wanted extension).

PAC 1 packaged assembly circuit *electronics.* **2** *also* **P.A.C.** Pan Africanist Congress. **3** *also* **P.A.C.** Pan-American Congress (esp. of 1889–90 establishing the Pan-American Union). **4** *also* **P-A-C** Parent, Adult, Child (designating the three ego-states within every individual according to transactional analysis). **5** phenacetin, aspirin, caffeine (nonprescription compound for pain relief). **6** (*pronounced* pak) Political Action Committee. **7** polycyclic aromatic compound (or hydrocarbon) *chemistry.* **8** *British* Public Assistance Committee. **9** put and call (of a commercial agreement to sell, *put,* or buy, *call,* securities at a specific price within a specified time).

Pac. 1 a Pacific. **b** *also military* **PAC,** esp. in combination: *PACAF = Pacific Air Forces; PACOM = Pacific Command.* **2** Pacific Reporter (publication) *law.*

PACE 1 performance and cost evaluation *commerce.* **2** precision analog computing equipment.

Pacif. Pacific.

PACNIC Pacific newly industrializing countries.

Pac. O. *or* **Pac. Oc.** Pacific Ocean.

PACS Pacific Area Communications System.

PACTO Professional, Administrative, Clerical, Technical, and Other (categories of white-collar U.S. government civilian employees).

PACU Post-Anesthesia Care Unit (after surgery).

PAD 1 packet assembler and disassembler (allowing dissimilar units to use a computer network). **2** payable after death *insurance.* **3 a** peripheral arterial disease. **b** peripheral artherosclerotic disease. **4** permissible accumulated dose.

pad. 1 padding. **2** padlock.

PADC Pennsylvania Avenue Development Corporation (Washington, D.C.).

p. ae. equal parts (of ingredients in a prescription). [Latin *partes aequales*]

PAF 1 peripheral address field *computers.* **2** platelet-activating factor *medicine.*

PAG periaqueductal gray matter (of the mesencephalon) *medicine.*

pAg pressure silver ion.

PAGEOS Passive Geodetic Earth-Orbiting Satellite (plastic balloon satellite).

PAH 1 para aminohippuric acid (used for measuring renal blood flow). **2 a** polycyclic aromatic hydrocarbon. **b** polyhalogenated aromatic hydrocarbon (found in gasoline engine exhaust). **c** polynuclear aromatic hydrocarbon.

PAHO Pan-American Health Organization.

PAICV African Party for the Independence of Cape Verde.

paint. 1 painter. **2** painting.

PAIS Public Affairs Information Service.

PAIT Program for the Advancement of Industrial Technology.

Pak. 1 Pakistan. **2** Pakistani.

PAL 1 parcel airlift mail (military reduced-rate airmail). **2** peripheral availability list *computers.* **3** permissive action link (unlocks arming circuits on nuclear weapons). **4** phase-alternating line (color television transmission system in Britain and Europe). **5** *also* **P.A.L.** Police Athletic League. **6** programming assembly language (used esp. in robotics).

Pal. Palestine.

pal. 1 paleography (study of ancient forms of writing). **2** paleontology (science of prehistoric life).

paleob. paleobotany.

paleog. paleography (study of ancient forms of writing).

paleon. *or* **paleont.** *or* **paleontol.** paleontology (science of prehistoric life).

PALM precision altitude and landing monitor.

PALS permissive action link system *computers.*

PAM 1 payload assist module (of a spacecraft). **2** polyacrylamide (used to cleanse waste water). **3** procaine penicillin in oil and aluminum monostearate (treatment for syphilis). **4** process automatic monitor *computers.* **5** protopam chloride (antidote for insecticide poisoning). **6** *also* **pam** pulse amplitude modulation *electronics.*

pam. *or* **pamph.** pamphlet.

P.A.M.A. *or* **PAMA** Pan-American Medical Association.

PAN 1 National Action Party (conservative Catholic political party of Mexico). [Spanish *Partido Acción Nacional*] **2** peroxyacetyl nitrate (chemical air pollutant). **3** polyacrylonitrile (used in synthetic fibers).

Pan. 1 Panama. **2** Panamanian.

pan. 1 panchromatic (of black-and-white film, sensitive to light reflected from all colors). **2** panoramic. **3** pantomime. **4** pantry.

PANAFTEL (pan'af'tel) Pan-African Telecommunications (network).

PANAMSAT (pan'am'sat) Pan-American satellite system.

Pan. Can. *or* **PanCan** Panama Canal.

P&A 1 Personnel and Administrative. **2** Professional and Administrative.

P&C put and call (of a commercial agreement to sell, *put*, or buy, *call*, securities at a specific price within a specified time).

P&D pick up and delivery *or* deliveries (of freight).

P&H postage and handling *commerce*.

P&I protection and indemnity (against accidents to passengers and crew) *insurance*.

P&L *or* **p&l** profit and loss *commerce*: *P & L statements*.

P&O planning and operations.

P&S *or* **p&s** port and starboard.

P&W pension and welfare.

PANS Procedures for Air Navigation Services.

PAO Public Affairs Officer.

PAP 1 *also* **P.A.P.** People's Action Party (now *Barisan Sosialis*, of Malaysia). **2** *also* **P.A.P.** Polish news agency. [Polish *Polska Agencja Prasowa*] **3** primary atypical pneumonia. **4** Progressive Australia Party. **5** prostatic acid phosphatase.

Pap 1 (*pronounced* pap) Papanicolaou (test or smear, esp. for cancer): *Pap test*. **2** *also* **Pap. a** Papua, New Guinea. **b** Papuan.

pap. paper.

PAR 1 perimeter acquisition radar. **2** precision approach radar; GCA (air navigation). **3** program appraising and review. **4** pulse acquisition radar.

Par. 1 Paraguay. **2** Parish.

par. 1 parabolic. **2** paragraph. **3** parallax (the apparent change in position of an object viewed from increasingly distant points). **4** parallel. **5** parenthesis, parentheses. **6** parochial. **7** part, esp. in combination: *par. aff. = part affected, pharmaceutics.* [Latin *pars affecta*]

Para. *or* **Parag. 1** Paraguay. **2** Paraguayan.

para. 1 *also* **parab. a** parabola. **b** parabolic. **2** paragraph. **3** paraphrase.

param parameter, parameters.

paramp parametric amplifier (microwave amplifier).

parch. parchment.

PARCS Perimeter Acquisition Radar Attack Character System (in missile detection).

paren (pə ren') parenthesis, *pl.* **parens** (pə renz') parentheses.

Parl. *or* **parl. 1** Parliament. **2** Parliamentary: *Parl. Agt. = Parliamentary Agent; Parl.S. = Parliamentary Secretary.*

parq 1 parquet, also in combination: *parq flr = parquet flooring.* **2** *also* **Parq.** main floor of a theater.

PARS perimeter acquisition radar sites.

pars. paragraphs.

parsec (pär'sek) parallax second (unit in computing the distance of stars).

part. 1 participating. **2 a** participle. **b** participial, esp. in combination: *part. adj. or part.a. = participial adjective.* **3** particle. **4** particular. **5 a** partner. **b** *also* **Part.** partnership.

part. aeq. equal parts (of ingredients in a prescription). [Latin *partes aequales*]

part. vic. in divided doses or parts *pharmaceutics*. [Latin *in partibus vicibus*]

PAS 1 *also* **PASA** para-aminosalicylic acid (used to treat tuberculosis). **2** periodic acid Schiff (stain used in histology). **3** photoacoustic spectroscopy. **4** proven as safe, esp. of a food substance or drug.

pas. 1 passage (right of entry). **2** passive *grammar*.

PAS-INAH para-aminosalicylic acid and isonicotinic acid hydrazide (used to treat tuberculosis and other chest diseases).

PASOK Panhellenic Socialist Movement (political party of Greece). [Greek *Panallenio Socialistiko Kinema*]

Pass. 1 Passage: *N.W. Pass. = Northwest Passage.* **2** Passover.

pass. 1 here and there (in a book, article, or other work, referring to a symbol, word or phrase, concept, etc.). [Latin *passim*] **2** passage. **3** passenger. **4** passive *grammar*.

PAT 1 paroxysmal atrial tachycardia (sudden increase in heart rate) *medicine*. **2** point after touchdown *football*. **3** pollution-added tax. **4** Professional Association of Teachers (of Great Britain).

pat. 1 *also* **Pat.** patent, patented. **2** patient. **3** pattern.

pa.t. past tense *grammar*.

PATA Pacific Area Travel Association.

Pata. Patagonia.

PATCO (pat'kō) Professional Air Traffic Controllers Organization (disbanded 1981).

patd. patented.

PATH 1 pituitary adrenotrophic hormone *biochemistry*. **2** Port Authority Trans-Hudson Corporation.

path. *or* **pathol. 1** pathology. **2** pathological. **3** pathologist.

Pat.Off. Patent Office.

pat. pend. patent pending.

patt. pattern.

P.A.U. *or* **PAU** Pan American Union.

Pav the Peacock (constellation). [Latin *Pave*]

PAX private automatic exchange (telephone network within a business or organization connected by automatic switching to outside lines).

PAYE 1 *also* **P.A.Y.E.** *British* pay-as-you-earn (tax system). **2** pay as you enter.

Paymr. or **Payr.** Paymaster.

payt. payment.

PB 1 also **P.B.** Bachelor of Philosophy. [Latin *Philosophia Baccalaureus*] **2** also **P.B.** British Pharmacopoeia. [Latin *Pharmacopoeia Britannica*] **3** paperback (binding of a book). **4** passbook *banking.* **5** also **pb** passed ball or balls *baseball.* **6** also **P.B.** Plymouth Brethren (Protestant sect having no formal creed or order of ministers). **7** power brakes. **8** also **P.B.** Prayer Book. **9** also **P.B.** Presiding Bishop. **10** Publication Board (of U.S. Department of Commerce): *PB Report* (on commerce, science, and industry) **11** also **p/b** pushbutton, esp. in combination: *PBC = pushbutton control.*

Pb *I an abbreviation for:* purl into back of stitch, in knitting. *II a symbol for:* lead (chemical element). [Latin *plumbum*]

PBA 1 also **P.B.A.** Patrolmen's Benevolent Association. **2** Proceedings of the British Academy (publication). **3** also **P.B.A.** Professional Bowlers Association. **4** Public Buildings Administration.

PBB polybrominated biphenyl (formerly widely used as a flame retardant).

PBD or **PBd** or **pbd** particle board.

PBFA particle beam fusion accelerator.

PBGC Pension Benefit Guaranty Corporation.

PBI 1 also **P.B.I.** *British* poor bloody infantry: *He spent four years in the P.B.I.* **2** protein-bound iodine: *PBI test for thyroid activity.*

PBK 1 also **pbk** paperback (binding of a book). **2** Phi Beta Kappa (undergraduate academic honor society).

PBM permanent bench mark *surveying.*

PBR payment by results *commerce.*

PBS 1 phosphate-buffered saline. **2 a** Public Broadcasting Service (network of public noncommercial television stations in U.S.). **b** Public Broadcasting System. **3** Public Buildings Service (of U.S. General Services Administration).

PBSA Papers of the Biographical Society of America (publication).

PBT 1 permeable base transistor *electronics.* **2** profits before taxes *finance.*

PBX private branch exchange (telephone network within a business or organization connected by manual or automatic switching to outside lines).

PBZ pyribenzamine (antihistamine, in topical form as a salve).

PC 1 Pacific Command (of U.S. Department of Defense). **2** also **P.C.** Panama Canal. **3** also **P.C.** Parliamentary Cases *law.* **4** participation certificate (in Government loans). **5** also **P.C.** Patent Cases *law.* **6** Peace Corps. **7** Penal Code. **8** personal computer. **9** also **P.C. a** personal corporation. **b** professional corporation (business providing professional services). **10** personnel carrier (military vehicle). **11** phosphocreatine (energy-giving substance in muscle tissue). **12** pitch circle (of a gearwheel). **13** also **P.C.** Pleas of the Crown *law.* **14 a** Police Commissioner. **b** *British* Police Constable. **15** also **P.C.** politically correct (socially acceptable). **16** portland cement. **17** Post Commander. **18** prestressed concrete. **19** printed circuit *electronics.* **20** *British* **a** Privy Council. **b** Privy Councilor. **21** *computers* **a** processor controller. **b** program controller. **c** program

counter. **22** Progressive Conservative (political party, esp. in Canada).

pc 1 also **p.c.** pharmaceutics **a** after eating. [Latin *post cibo*] **b** after a meal. [Latin *post cibum*] **2** also **pc.** parsec (unit of computing the distance of stars). **3** also **p.c. a** percent: *Within a month he expects to be 90 p.c. fit again.* **b** also **Pc** percentage (in tabulating performance) *sports.* **4** also **p.c.** personal computer. **5** also **p/c** petty cash. **6** pica (measure of type). **7** also **pc.** piece. **8** politically correct (socially acceptable). **9** also **p.c.** postcard. **10** power cord (of an appliance, camera, computer, etc.). **11** also **pc. a** price. **b** also **p/c** price current.

PCA 1 also **P.C.A.** Parliamentary Commissioner for Administration (ombudsman in Great Britain). **2** patient-controlled analgesia *medicine.* **3** Permanent Court of Arbitration. **4** polar cap absorption (of shortwave radio signals). **5** principal component analysis *mathematics.* **6** Production Code Administration (of the film industry).

PCB 1 also **p/cb.** petty cash book. **2** plenum chamber burning (short-term thrust increase for lift-off of a rocket). **3** also **pcb** polychlorinated biphenyl (poisonous chemical used in plastic manufacture). **4** also **pcb** printed circuit board *electronics.*

PCC 1 Communist Party of Cuba (ruling group in Cuba). [Spanish *Partido Communista de Cuba*] **2** Pacific Coast Conference (collegiate athletic association). **3** Panama Canal Commission. **4** Poison Control Center. **5** program-controlled computer.

PCD polychlorinated dibenzo- (toxic chemical found in fish and some other wildlife), esp. in combination: *PCDF = polychlorinated dibenzofuran; PCDP = polychlorinated dibenzo-p-dioxin.*

PCE 1 also **P.C.E.** Spanish Communist Party. [Spanish *Partido Comunista Española*] **2** polychloroethylene. **3** also **pce** pyrometric cone equivalent (unit of measurement for heat in a pottery kiln).

PCF 1 also **P.C.F.** French Communist Party. [French *Parti Communiste Français*] **2** also **pcf** pounds per cubic foot.

PCG phonocardiogram *medicine.*

PCGN Permanent Committee on Geographical Names.

PCGS Professional Coin Grading Service.

PCI 1 Italian Communist Party. [Italian *Partito Comunista Italiano*] **2** programmed control interrupt *computers.*

PCL printer control language *computers.*

pcl. parcel.

PCM 1 also **P.C.M.** Mexican Communist Party. [Spanish *Partido Comunista Mexicano*] **2** phase-change material. **3** plug-compatible manufacturer. **4** protein-calorie malnutrition. **5** also **pcm** Pulse Code Modulation (system of transmission in telephone communication).

PCMB parachloromercuribenzoate (reagent in biochemistry).

PCMI photochromic microimage (trademarked process for miniature reproduction).

PCN 1 part control number, in inventory or ordering. **2** personal communications network *computers.*

PCNB pentachloronitrobenzene (fungicide).

PCP 1 also **P.C.P.** British Parliamentary Conservative Party. **2** also **P.C.P.** Past Chief Patriarch. **3** pentachlorophenol (fungicide and wood preservative). **4** phenylcycloexylpiperidine (phencyclidine, trademark for depressant used as an animal tranquillizer and illegally in powder form as a narcotic, Angel Dust). **5** pneumocystis carinii pneumonia (infection associated with AIDS). **6** primary control program *computers*.

PCPA 1 para-chlorophenoxyacetic acid (plant growth regulator). **2** para-chlorophenylalanine (reduces level of serotonin in the blood; used in medical research to treat such conditions as intestinal tumors and schizophrenia).

pcpt. perception.

PCR 1 polymerase chain reaction (technique for making multiple copies of a particular gene and for studying and detecting the presence of the AIDS virus). **2** program control register *computers*.

PCS 1 permanent change of station. **2** personal communication service (miniaturized cellular phone system). **3** also **P.C.S.** Principal Clerk of Session (in Scotland). **4** print contrast signal.

pcs 1 pieces. **2** also **Pcs.** preconscious *psychology*.

PCSIR Pakistan Council of Scientific and Industrial Research.

PCT 1 Patent Cooperation Treaty. **2** plasmacrit test (test for syphilis). **3** Workers' Party of the Congo. [French *Parti Congolais du Travail*]

pct. or **Pct. 1 a** percent. **b** percentage. **2** precinct.

PCTE portable common tools environment (European standard for computer software).

PCTFE polychlorotrifluoroethylene (protective coating).

pcu 1 passenger-car unit: *In Britain, the total flow of vehicles was 76 billion pcu-miles.* **2** also **PCU** power control unit. **3** also **PCU** pressurization control unit.

PCV 1 packed cell volume (of blood, esp. for transfusion). **2** Peace Corps Volunteer. **3** positive crankcase ventilation (system to reduce automobile exhaust pollution): *PCV valve.* **4** also **P.C.V.** Venezuelan Communist Party. [Spanish *Partido Comunista Venezolana*]

PCZ Panama Canal Zone, also in combination: *PCZST = Panama Canal Zone Standard Time.*

PD 1 also **P.D.** by the day, as of expenses or fees. [Latin *per diem*] **2** also **P.D. a** Doctor of Pharmacy. **b** Doctor of Philosophy. **3** interpupillary distance, in measuring for eyeglasses. **4** Parkinson's disease. **5** also **P.D.** Police Department. **6 a** port dues *shipping*. **b** port of debarkation. **7** position doubtful (of a vessel or aircraft). **8** postage due. **9** also **P.D.** or **P/D** postdated, *esp. in banking*. **10** potential difference. **11** also **P.D.** preventive detention. **12** also **P.D.** program director. **13** property damage *insurance*. **14** also **P.D.** public defender. **15** public domain (of publications, computer programs, etc.).

Pd palladium (chemical element).

pd 1 also **p.d.** or **p/d** by the day, as of expenses or fees. [Latin *per diem*] **2** also **pd.** paid. **3** also **pd.** passed. **4** pond. **5** also **p/d** postdated, *esp. in banking*. **6** also **p.d.** potential difference. **7** also **pd.** pound (weight). **8** prism diopter (refractive power of a prism).

PDA 1 also **P.D.A.** Democratic Party of Angola. [Portuguese *Partido Demócrata Angolano*] **2** personal digital assistant (personal computer that performs whole tasks at a single command). **3** postdeflection acceleration *physics*. **4** predicted drift angle *navigation*. **5** probability distribution analyzer.

p.d.a. to say good-by. [French *pour dire adieu*]

PDB paradichlorobenzene (insecticide).

Pd.B. Bachelor of Pedagogy. [Latin *Pedagogiae Baccalaureus*]

Pd.D. Doctor of Pedagogy. [Latin *Pedagogiae Doctor*]

PDF probability density function *engineering*.

PDFLP Popular Democratic Front for the Liberation of Palestine.

PDG Democratic Party of Guinea. [French *Parti Démocratique Guinéé*]

PDGF platelet-derived growth factor (necessary for blood clotting).

PDH packaged disaster hospital (medical supplies and equipment for a 200-bed hospital).

PDI 1 picture description instruction, in computer graphics. **2** predelivery inspection *commerce*.

PDL 1 page description language *computers*. **2** Patent Depository Library. **3** British poverty datum line (minimum level of income for subsistence).

pdl poundal (unit of force) *physics*, esp. in combination: *ft-pdl = foot poundal.*

PDM pulse duration modulation *electronics*.

Pd.M. Master of Pedagogy. [Latin *Pedagogiae Magister*]

PDMS plasma desorption mass spectrometry.

PDN public data network (data communications system).

PDP 1 parallel distributed processing *computers*. **2** Program Development Plan.

PDPA People's Democratic Party of Afghanistan.

PDPS parts data-processing system.

PDQ or **p.d.q.** *slang* pretty damn quick.

PDR 1 Physician's Desk Reference (publication). **2** precision depth recorder.

pdr. 1 pounder, *esp. in combination: 25-pdr. gun.* **2** also **pdr** powder.

PDS programming documentation standards *computers*.

PDST or **P.D.S.T.** or **p.d.s.t.** Pacific Daylight Saving Time.

PDT or **P.D.T.** or **p.d.t.** Pacific Daylight Time.

PDU power distribution unit.

PE 1 pentaerythritol (resin in paint and varnish). **2** permanent echo (of radar). **3** personal effects. **4** also **P.E.** Petroleum Engineer. **5** physical education. **6** physical examination. **7** Plant Engineer. **8** polyethylene (widely used durable thermoplastic). **9** port of embarkation. **10** also **P.E.** Presiding Elder. **11** Prince Edward Island (postal code). **12** printer's error. **13** also **P.E.** probable error *statistics*. **14** processing elements *computers*. **15** also **P.E.** Professional Engineer.

P/E 1 port of embarkation. **2** also **P-E** precipitation, evaporation (quotient index of aridity): *P/E ratio.* **3** also **P-E** price-to-earnings ratio (the price of a share of stock in relation to the annual earnings of a company).

p.e. 1 equal parts (of ingredients in a prescription). [Latin *partes equales*] **2** *also* **pe** printer's error. **3** probable error statistics.

P.E.A. Public Education Association.

PEB party election broadcast (political party advertisement on British radio and television during elections).

PEC 1 *also* **pec** photoelectric cell. **2** photoelectrochemical cell (producing electricity by exposure to sunlight).

ped. 1 *also* **PED.** *or* **Ped.** pedal, esp. as an instruction on piano music. **2** pedestal. **3** pedestrian. **4** *also* **Ped. a** pediatrics. **b** pediatrician.

Ped.D. Doctor of Pedagogy. [Latin *Pedagogiae Doctor*]

PEE Proof and Experimental Establishment (of Great Britain).

PEEP Pilot's Electronic Eye-level Presentation (of instrumentation and aiming devices).

PEF personal effects floater (policy) *insurance*.

PEG 1 pneumoencephalogram (X-ray examination of the brain by creating air pockets in circulating cerebrospinal fluid). **2** polyethylene glycol (polymer used in food, drugs, lubricants, and cosmetics). **3** public, educational, and governmental (referring to required access to cable TV channels).

Peg Pegasus (constellation).

P.E.I. Prince Edward Island.

pel *or* **PEL** (*pronounced* pel) picture element, pixel *computers*.

PELL Papers in English Language and Literature (publication).

PEM 1 photoelectromagnetic. **2** proton exchange membrane (used in fuel cells).

PEN (*pronounced* pen) *or* **P.E.N.** International Association of Poets, Playwrights, Editors, Essayists, and Novelists.

Pen. *or* **pen. 1** penicillin. **2** peninsula. **3** penitentiary.

P.Eng. Professional Engineer.

Penn. *or* **Penna.** Pennsylvania.

penol. penology.

Pent. 1 Pentateuch (first five books of the Old Testament) **2** Pentecost (celebrating descent of the Holy Ghost; marking gift of Torah to Moses).

pent. pentagon.

PEO polyethylene oxide.

PEP 1 peak envelope power *communications*. **2** phosphoenolpyruvic acid (in glucose metabolism). **3** *British* Political and Economic Planning. **4** pre-eradication program (in controlling disease-producing carriers). **5** Program Evaluation Procedure *computers*.

pep. 1 pepper. **2** peppermint.

PEPI (pep′ē) post-menopausal estrogen and progestin intervention.

PEPP Professional Engineers in Private Practice.

PER protein efficiency ratio *agriculture*.

Per 1 *also* **Per.** Pericles, Prince of Tyre (play by Shakespeare). **2** Perseus (constellation). **3** *also* **Per. a** Persia. **b** Persian.

per. 1 perennial. **2** period. **3** periodical (of a publication). **4** person.

PERA Production Engineering Research Association (of Great Britain).

per an. *or* **per ann.** annually. [Latin *per annum*]

perc. percussion *medicine, music*.

per cap. per capita.

per cent. by the hundred (now usually written as a phrase *per cent* or a word *percent*). [Latin *per centum*]

perd. dying away, subsiding *music*. [Italian *perdendosi*]

perf. 1 perfect. **2** perforated, esp. of postage stamps. **3 a** performance. **b** performed by.

perh. perhaps.

peri. 1 *also* **perig.** perigee (point closest to earth in the orbit of a celestial body). **2** *also* **perih.** perihelion (point closest to the sun in the orbit of a celestial body). **3** *also* **perim.** perimeter.

period. periodical (a publication).

perk (pėrk) perquisite (often found in pl. **perks**).

perm 1 *also* **perm.** permanent. **2** (pėrm) permanent wave (of the hair). **3** *British* permutate (a football pool).

per M per thousand.

perp. 1 perpendicular. **2** *also* **perp** (pėrp) perpetrator (person who has committed a crime). **3** perpetual (bond).

per pro. *or* **per proc.** by procuration, by agent, by proxy. [Latin *per procurationem*]

perq (pėrk) perquisite (often found in pl. **perqs**).

Pers. Persia, Persian.

pers. 1 person. **2** personal. **3** personnel.

persh. perishable.

persp. perspective.

PERT Program Evaluation Review Technique (computer program for project management, originally developed by U.S. Navy).

pert. pertaining.

Peruv. Peruvian.

PES photoelectric scanner.

pes. peseta (monetary unit of Spain and Andorra).

PET 1 paper equilibrium tester. **2** *also* **P.E.T.** Parent Effectiveness Training. **3** polyethylene terephthalate (used esp. in manufacturing plastic bottles). **4** (*pronounced* pet) positron-emission tomograph or tomography: *PET scan*. **5** production environmental test.

Pet. 1 Peter (two books of the New Testament): *I Pet.* = *One or First Peter; II Pet.* = *Two or Second Peter.* **2** Peters (U.S. Supreme Court Reports).

pet. 1 petroleum. **2 a** petrology (study of the origin and structure of rock). **b** petrologist.

Peta (pē′tə) *British* portable electronic traffic analyzer (radar speed monitor).

PETN pentaerythritol tetranitrate (an explosive).

petn. petition.

petr. 1 petrified. **2** petroleum.

petro (pet′rō) petrochemical: *the petro industry*.

petrog. petrography (classification of rocks).

petrol. petrology (study of the origin and structure of rocks).

PETT positron emission transverse tomography (used in examining internal structures of the body).

p. ex. for example. [French *par exemple*]

PF 1 page footing (division of computer memory at the end of each segment). **2** page format *printing*. **3** personal foul *sports*. **4** points for (in tabulating performance) *sports*. **5** preflight. **6** *also* **P.F.** Procurator-Fiscal (county public prosecutor in Scotland whose duties correspond to those of coroner). **7** pulse frequency *electronics*. **8** punch off *computers*.

Pf. proof (of coins).

pF picofarad (trillionth of a farad).

pf 1 *also* **p.f.** a little louder *music*. [Italian *più forte*] **2** *also* **pf.** perfect. **3** personal foul *sports*. **4** *also* **Pf.** pfennig (German coin). **5** pianoforte (piano). **6** picofarad (trillionth of a farad). **7** plain face (having a flat face, as of a hammer, molding, etc.). **8** power factor (ratio of actual power to apparent power). **9** preferred (of stock in a company). **10** pro forma (esp. referring to a business invoice sent as notice of shipment). **11** proof (of coins or printer's proofs). **12** to congratulate. [French *pour féliciter*]

PFA pulverized fuel ash.

PFBC pressurized fluidized bed combustion (reduces emissions from burning coal to produce power).

PFC 1 plaque-forming cells. **2** polychlorinated fluorocarbon.

Pfc *or* **pfc** private first class *military*.

pfce. *or* **Pfce** performance.

PFD 1 personal flotation device (such as a life jacket). **2** position-fixing device.

pfd. *or* **pfd** preferred, as of stock in a company or in combination: *pfd. sp. = preferred spelling.*

pfg. pfennig (German coin).

PFI physical fitness index.

PFK phosphofractokinase (an enzyme).

PFLP Popular Front for the Liberation of Palestine.

PFM *or* **pfm** pulse frequency modulation *electronics*.

PFP Progressive Federal Party (of South Africa).

PFR 1 peak flow rate. **2** prototype fast reactor (nuclear reactor).

PFRA *Canadian* Prairie Farm Rehabilitation Act.

PFRT preliminary flight rating test (of aircraft engines).

p.f.s.a. to say good-by. [French *pour fair ses adieux*]

Pft. *or* **Pfte** pianoforte (piano), also in combination: *Pft. acct. = pianoforte accompaniment.*

pfu plaque-forming unit, in study of viruses.

pfx. prefix (of a number or word element).

PG 1 parental guidance (motion picture rating for a film not suited for young children). **2** *also* **P.G.** paste grain (of leather, esp. that used in bookbinding). **3** *also* **p.g.** *or* **P.G.** paying guest. **4** *also* **P.G.** plate glazed (of paper). **5** polygalacturonase (enzyme active in metabolism of many plant sugars and gums). **6** postgraduate. **7** prostaglandin (hormonelike substance active in muscle contraction, nerve-impulse transmission, metabolism, and regulation of blood pressure). **8** proving ground (for testing materials and equipment). **9** pulse generator *electronics*.

Pg. *or* **Pg 1** Portugal. **2** Portuguese.

pg 1 *also* **p.g.** page. **2** picogram (trillionth of a gram).

PG-13 parental guidance 13 (motion picture rating for a film not suitable for children under 13 years of age).

PGA 1 phosphoglyceric acid (active in carbohydrate metabolism). **2** pin grid array (for mounting chips on boards) *computers*. **3** *also* **P.G.A.** Professional Golfers' Association. **4** pteroylglutamic acid (folic acid).

PGC *or* **pgc** per gyrocompass, esp. as a notation in a ship's log or flight report.

PGCE Postgraduate Certificate of Education.

PgDn page down *computers*.

PGE one of two groups of prostaglandins (the other being *PGF*).

PGF one of two groups of prostaglandins (the other being *PGE*).

PGI₂ prostacycline (substance in lining of the arteries which prevents blood clotting). [from *prostaglandin* + I_2 designation for this type of prostaglandin]

PGK phosphoglycerate kinase (enzyme of carbohydrate metabolism).

PGM 1 *also* **P.G.M.** Past Grand Master. **2** platinum group metals. **3** precision-guided munition.

pgm. program.

PGR 1 population growth rate. **2** psychogalvanic response (skin resistance to electrode monitoring).

PGT *or* **pgt** per gross ton.

PgUp page up *computers*.

PH 1 page heading (division of computer memory at the beginning of each segment). **2** past history (of a patient) *medicine*. **3** phase. **4** pinch hitter *baseball*. **5** *also* **P.H.** Public Health. **6** *also* **P.H.** Purple Heart (decoration) *military*.

Ph 1 pharmacopoeia (official list of drugs and medicines). **2** phenyl (radical of benzene) *chemistry*.

pH *or* **pH** symbol for the degree of acid or alkaline condition by measurement of hydrogen ion concentration in solution: *Acid solutions have pH values lower than 7.* [*p*(otential for) H(ydrogen)]

ph 1 phase. **2** *also* **ph.** phone. **3** *also* **ph.** phosphor. **4** phot (unit of illumination).

PHA 1 phytohemagglutinin (plant substances that cause clumping and change of shape in blood cells). **2** primary human amnion, in cell biology. **3** *also* **P.H.A.** Public Housing Administration. **4** pulse height analyzer *electronics*.

Phar. *or* **phar. 1** pharmaceutical. **2 a** pharmacist. **b** pharmacy: *Phar.B. = Bachelor of Pharmacy.* [Latin *Pharmaciae Baccalaureus*] **3** pharmacopoeia (official list of drugs and medicines).

Pharm. *or* **pharm. 1** pharmaceutical. **2** pharmacology. **3 a** pharmacist. **b** pharmacy: *Pharm.D. = Doctor of Pharmacy.* [Latin *Pharmaciae Doctor*] **4** pharmacopoeia (official list of drugs and medicines).

pharmacol. pharmacology.

Ph.B. *or* **PhB** Bachelor of Philosophy. [Latin *Philosophiae Baccalaureus*]

ph.bz. phosphor bronze (hard alloy used in marine fittings).

PHC 1 primary health care. **2** primary health center (community medical center).

Ph.C. Pharmaceutical Chemist.

P.H.D. *or* **PHD** Doctor of Public Health.

Ph.D. *or* **PhD** Doctor of Philosophy. [Latin *Philosophiae Doctor*]

PHE Public Health Engineer.

Phe 1 *also* **phe** *or* **Phe.** phenylalanine (amino acid, deficient in phenylketonuria). **2** Phoenix (constellation).

phenom (*sometimes pronounced* fē′nom′) phenomenon.

Ph.G. 1 German Pharmacopoeia. **2** Graduate in Pharmacy.

Phil. 1 Philadelphia. **2** Philemon (book of the New Testament). **3** Philharmonic, esp. in combination: *NYPhil.* = *New York Philharmonic.* **4** Philip. **5** Philippians (book of the New Testament). **6** Philippines, Philippine. **7** *also* **phil. a** philology (study of literature and language). **b** philological. **8** *also* **phil. a** philosophy. **b** philosophical.

Phila. Philadelphia.

Philem. Philemon (book of the New Testament).

Phil.I. *or* **Is.** Philippine Islands.

Philipp. Philippines.

philol. *or* **Philol 1** philology (study of literature and language). **2** philological. **3** philologist.

philos. *or* **Philos 1** philosophy. **2** philosopher. **3** philosophical.

Phil. Soc. 1 Philharmonic Society (as of New York). **2** Philological Society (of London). **3** Philosophical Society (of America).

Phil. Trans. Philosophical Transactions (of the Royal Society of London).

PHM Patrol Hydrofoil Missileship.

Ph.M. Master of Philosophy. [Latin *Philosophiae Magister*]

Phm.B. Bachelor of Pharmacy.

PHN *or* **P.H.N.** public health nurse.

phon. 1 *also* **phonol.** phonology (study of sounds of a language). **2** *also* **phonet.** phonetics (study of speech sounds and pronunciation).

phono. phonograph.

phos. 1 phosphate. **2** phosphorescence.

phot. 1 photography. **2** photographer. **3** photograph. **4** photographic.

PHOTINT photographic intelligence.

photo (fō′tō) *or* **photo.** photograph, also in combination: *photo op* = *photographic opportunity.*

photog. 1 photography. **2** photographer. **3** photographic.

photom. 1 photometry (study of measurement and intensity of light). **2** photometrical.

PHP 1 *also* **p/hp** pounds per horsepower. **2** *also* **php** pump horsepower.

phr. 1 phrase. **2** phraseology.

PHS Public Health Service (of U.S. Department of Health and Human Services).

PhT The Phoenix and the Turtle (poem by Shakespeare).

phys. 1 physical, also in combination: *phys. chem.* = *physical chemistry; phys. exam.* = *physical examination.* **2** physician. **3** physics. **4 a** physiology (study of normal function of organisms). **b** physiological.

phys. ed. physical education.

physiol. 1 physiology (study of normal function of organisms). **2** physiologist. **3** physiological.

phytogeog. phytogeography (study of the geographical distribution of plants).

PI 1 *also* **P.I.** International Pharmacopoeia. [Latin *Pharmacopoeia Internationalis*] **2 a** personal income. **b** personal injury *law, insurance.* **3** *also* **P.I.** Philippine Islands. **4 a** photo interpretation. **b** photo interpreter. **5** position indicator. **6** present illness *medicine.* **7** principal investigator (in a scientific experiment or study). **8** *also* **P.I.** private investigator. **9** program indicator (of codes) *computers.* **10** programmed instruction (learning in small sequential units). **11** protamine insulin. **12** Public Information.

Pi inorganic phosphate or orthophosphate.

pi 1 *also* **Pi.** piaster (monetary unit and coin of Egypt, Lebanon, Libya, Sudan, Syria, Turkey). **2** pica (measure of type). **3** poison ivy.

PIA 1 peripheral interface adapter *computers.* **2** Plastics Institute of America. **3** *also* **P.I.A.** Printing Industries of America.

PIANC Permanent International Association of Navigation Congresses.

PIARC Permanent International Association of Road Congresses.

PIB 1 polyisobutylene (used esp. in insulators). **2** Publishers Information Bureau.

PIC 1 personal identification code. **2** program interrupt control *computers.*

Pic Painter or, sometimes Easel, for its older name *Equuleus Pictoris*, Painter's Easel (constellation). [Latin *Pictor*]

pic. 1 piccolo. **2** picture.

PICGC Permanent International Committee for Genetic Congresses.

pict. 1 pictorial. **2** picture.

PID 1 pelvic inflammatory disease. **2** personal identification device (usually a card read by electronic device). **3** prolapsed intervertebral disk *medicine.*

PIE Proto-Indo-European (hypothetical prehistoric language, ancestor of the Indo-European languages). **2** *also* **P.I.E.** pulmonary infiltrates with eosinophilia *medicine.*

PIF prolactin inhibitory factor.

pig. *or* **pigm. 1** pigment. **2** pigmentation.

PIK payment in kind.

PIL payment in lieu.

pil. pill *pharmaceutics.* [Latin *pilula*]

Pilgr. 1 The Passionate Pilgrim (group of poems, some of which are attributable to Shakespeare). **2** The Pilgrim's Progress (story by Bunyan).

PILOT Programmed Inquiry, Learning or Teaching (interactive program) *computers.*

PIM pulse interval modulation *electronics.*

PIN 1 (*pronounced* pin) personal identification number (esp. for use at automatic teller machines): *PIN code.* **2** positive-intrinsic-negative (semiconductor construction) *electronics.*

Pind. Pindar (Greek poet, 518–438 BC).

PINO positive input, negative output *electronics.*

PINS (*pronounced* pinz) Person *or* Persons In Need of Supervision (child or adolescent with socially disruptive behavioral problems) *law.*

pinx. he or she painted it. [Latin *pinxit*]

PIO public information office *or* officer.

PIOB President's Intelligence Oversight Board.

PIOCS (pī′oks) physical input/output control system *computers.*

pion pi-meson (an unstable nuclear particle).

PIOSA Pan-Indian Ocean Science Association.

PIP 1 Peripheral Interchange Program *computers.* **2** persistent internal polarization (used in computer memory, photography, and energy storage devices). **3** picture in picture (of TV screens, showing simultaneous pictures, usually of what is being recorded on a VCR).

PIRA 1 Paper Industries Research Association (of Great Britain). **2** Printing Industry Research Association.

PIREP pilot report (of weather conditions).

PIRG Public Interest Research Group.

PIS Postal Inspection Service.

Pisc the Fishes (constellation). [Latin *Pisces*]

pist. pistil, pistillate (of flowers).

PITI *or* **p.i.t.i.** principal, interest, taxes, insurance *commerce.*

Pitts. Pittsburgh.

PIUS Process Inherent Ultimate Safety (nuclear reactor with a core in borated water).

PIV 1 *also* **piv** peak inverse voltage. **2** *also* **P.I.V.** positive infinity variable.

pix (*pronounced* piks) picture.

PIXE (pik′sē) proton-induced X-ray emission.

pixel (pik′səl) picture element (esp. of an electronic screen); pel.

pizz. pizzicato (played by plucking) *music.*

P.J. 1 Police Justice. **2** Presiding Judge. **3** Probate Judge.

P.J.M. Pennsylvania, New Jersey, Maryland Interconnection (first power pool in the world, started in 1928).

pjs *or* **p.j.'s** (pē′jāz′) pajamas.

PK 1 *also* **P-K** Prausnitz-Küstner reaction (for typing allergic antibodies). **2** psychokinesis (supposed mental influence on events).

pk. 1 *also* **pk** pack. **2** *also* **Pk.** park. **3** *also* **Pk.** peak. **4** *also* **pk** peck (unit of measure).

pK symbol for a measure of the strength of acids, based on the negative logarithm of the ionization constant.

pkg. package.

pkr. *or* **Pkr.** packer.

PKPA Parental Kidnapping Prevention Act.

pkt. 1 packet. **2** pocket.

PKU phenylketonuria (inability to metabolize phenylalanine, chemical in all proteins, resulting in brain and physical damage).

Pkw. passenger car. [German *Personenkraftwagen*]

Pkwy *or* **Pkwy.** Parkway: *Eastern Pkwy. at Utica.*

PKY Parkway (in postal address).

pky. pecky (of lumber).

PL 1 *also* **P.L.** London Pharmacopoeia. [Latin *Pharmacopoeia Londinensis*] **2** partial loss *insurance.* **3 a** passenger liability *insurance.* **b** product liability. **c** public liability *insurance:* *PL&PD = public liability and property damage.* **4** perception of light. **5 a** phone line. **b** private line. **6** Place (in postal address). **7** *also* **P.L.** Plimsoll Line (load line on merchant vessel). **8** power locks (on automobiles). **9** *also* **P/L** *or* **P-L** profit and loss *commerce.* **10** Programming Language *computers.* **11** proportionality limit. **12** *also* **P.L.** Public Law (followed by a number). **13** *also* **P.L.** Public Library, esp. in combination: *NYPL = New York Public Library.*

pl. 1 *also* **Pl.** place. **2** plain. **3** *also* **Pl.** plasma. **4** *also* **Pl.** plate. **5** *also* **Pl.** platoon, also in combination: *Pl.Sgt. = Platoon Sergeant.* **6** plural, also in combination: *n.pl. = noun plural.*

p.l. partial loss *insurance.*

PLA 1 Palestine Liberation Army. **2** People's Liberation Army (China's single-service armed forces). **3** *also* **P.L.A.** Port of London Authority. **4** Programmable Logic Array *computers.*

Pla. Plaza.

PLACE programming language for automatic checkout equipment.

PLAM price-level adjusted mortgage.

plan. 1 planet. **2** planetarium. **3** *also* **planet.** planetary.

plas. 1 plaster. **2** plastic.

plat. 1 *also* **Plat.** plateau. **2** *also* **platf.** platform. **3** platoon.

PLATO *or* **Plato** (plā′tō) Programmed Logic for Automatic Teaching Operations (computer-based individualized system of instruction).

Plaut. Plautus (Roman writer of comedies, 254–184 BC).

PLBB Patent Licensing Bulletin Board (of U.S. Department of Commerce, listing government inventions available for licensing).

PLC 1 power line carrier. **2** programmable logic controller *computers.* **3** Public Limited Company.

Plcy policy.

Pld *or* **pld** payload.

Plen. *or* **plen.** plenipotentiary (with full authority): *Amb. Plen. = Ambassador Plenipotentiary.*

plf *or* **p.l.f.** pounds per linear foot.

plf. *or* **plff.** plaintiff.

pli *or* **p.l.i.** pounds per linear inch.

PLL phase-locked loop *electronics.*

PLM 1 *also* **PL/M** programming language for microprocessors. **2** Progressive Labor Movement. **3** pulse length modulation *electronics*.

plmb. plumbing.

PLN National Liberal Party. [Spanish *Partido Liberal Nacionalista*]

pln. plain.

plng planning.

PLO *or* **P.L.O.** Palestine Liberation Organization.

PLOP pressure line of position.

PLP 1 *also* **P.L.P.** Parliamentary Labour Party (of Great Britain). **2** Progressive Liberal Party (of the Bahamas).

PLR public-lending right (proposed royalty paid to authors based on the circulation rate of their books in libraries).

pls. *or* **Pls.** please.

PLSS (*pronounced* plis) Portable Life-Support System.

plt. 1 pilot. **2** plate.

pltf. plaintiff.

plu. plural.

plup. *or* **plupf.** pluperfect *grammar*.

plur. 1 plural. **2** plurality.

plwd plywood.

Ply. Plymouth.

PLYRM playroom.

PLZ Plaza (in postal address).

PLZT lead lanthanum zirconate titanate (used in electronic display units).

PM *I an abbreviation for:* **1** *also* **P.M.** Paymaster. **2** permanent magnet: *PM audio speaker.* **3** *electronics* **a** phase modulation. **b** pulse modulation. **4** *also* **P.M.** Police Magistrate. **5** *also* **P.M.** Postmaster. **6** *also* **P.M.** postmortem. **7** preventive maintenance. **8** *also* **P.M.** Prime Minister. **9 a** product manager. **b** program manager. **c** project manager. **10** *also* **P.M.** proper motion *astronomy*. **11** Provost Marshal (officer in charge of keeping order on military establishment). *II a symbol for:* *also* **P.M.** after noon, time from noon to midnight. [Latin *post meridiem*]

Pm promethium (chemical element, formerly *illinium*).

pm. 1 premium. **2** premolar.

p.m. *I an abbreviation for:* postmortem. *II a symbol for:* *also* **pm** after noon, time from noon to midnight. [Latin *post meridiem*]

PMA 1 *also* **P.M.A.** papillary, marginal, attached (of gingivitis) *medicine*. **2** Pharmaceutical Manufacturers' Association. **3** phenylmercuric acetate (herbicide). **4** phosphomolybdic acid (used in paints and plastics). **5** Politico-Military Affairs (bureau of U.S. Department of State). **6** primary mental abilities *psychology*. **7** Production and Marketing Administration.

PMAC Pharmaceutical Manufacturers' Association of Canada.

PMD postmortem dump *computers*.

PMDA pyromellitic dianhydride (used in curing epoxies).

PME photomagnetoelectric effect.

PMF probable maximum flood.

PMG *or* **P.M.G. 1** Paymaster General. **2** Postmaster General. **3** Provost Marshal General.

PMH 1 previous medical history. **2** *also* **pmh** production man-hour.

PMI point of maximal impulse (of the heart) *medicine*.

pmk postmark.

pmkd postmarked.

PML 1 probable maximum loss *insurance*. **2** progressive multifocal leukoencephalopathy (a fatal slow virus).

PMLA Publications of the Modern Language Association (of America).

PMMA polymethylmethacrylate (an acrylic resin).

PMMU paged memory management unit *computers*.

PMN polymorphonuclear leukocyte.

PMO Principal Medical Officer.

PMOS (pē'môs) P(positive) channel metal oxide semiconductor *electronics*.

PMP Participative Management Program (worker participation).

PMQ *British* Prime Minister's Question (Time).

PMR 1 Pacific Missile Range. **2** proton magnetic resonance.

PMS 1 Pantone matching system (of colored inks) *printing*. **2** pregnant mare's serum (to control ovulation in ewes and cows) *veterinary medicine*, also in combination: *PMSG = pregnant mare's serum gonadotrophin.* **3** premenstrual syndrome. **4** processor-memory-switch *computers*. **5** Project Management System *commerce*. **6** Public Message Service *computers*.

PMT 1 photomechanical transfer. **2** photomultiplier tube. **3** premenstrual tension.

pmt payment.

PMU pregnant mare's urine (source of estrogen in animal husbandry) *veterinary medicine*.

PMX private manual (telephone) exchange *communications*.

PN 1 *also* **P/N** part number. **2** *also* **p.n.** *or* **P/N** please note. **3** *also* **P-N** *or* **p-n** positive-negative *electronics*: *P-N junction.* **4** *also* **P.N.** Practical Nurse. **5** *also* **P/N** *or* **p.n.** promissory note *commerce*. **6** pseudorandom noise (code) *computers*. **7** psychoneurotic.

pn. partition.

PNA pentose nucleic acid (nucleic acid containing pentose, a sugar in animal tissue).

PNC *or* **P.N.C. 1** Palestine National Council (PLO parliament). **2** People's National Congress (political party in Guyana).

PND principal neutralizing determinant (AIDS virus outer coat, used in a test for the disease).

PNdb *or* **PNdB** perceived noise decibel (measure of noise, as of aircraft).

pndg pending.

PNET Peaceful Nuclear Explosions Treaty (nonaggressive use of such explosions).

P.N.E.U. Parents' National Educational Union (of Great Britain).

pneu. or **pneum.** pneumatic.

PNG 1 also **P.N.G.** Papua New Guinea. **2** also **p.n.g.** person, esp. a diplomat, whose presence in a foreign country is not acceptable to its government. [Latin *persona non grata*]

PNI Indonesia Nationalist party. [Indonesian *Partai National Indonesia*]

PNIN or **p-n-i-n** positive-negative-intrinsic-negative (of a transistor's intrinsic element between two negative elements) *electronics*.

PNIP or **p-n-i-p** positive-negative-intrinsic-positive (of a transistor's intrinsic element between a negative and a positive element) *electronics*.

pnl. panel.

PNLD or **pnld.** paneled.

PNM 1 Nationalist Party of Mexico. [Spanish *Partido Nacionalista de México*] **2** People's National Movement (in Trinidad and Tobago).

PNP 1 also **P.N.P. a** New Progressive Party (of Puerto Rico). [Spanish *Partido Nuevo Progresista*] **b** People's National Party (of Jamaica). **2** also **P.N.P.** Pediatric Nurse Practitioner. **3** also **p-n-p** positive-negative-positive (of a transistor composed of a negative element between two positive elements).

PNPN or **p-n-p-n** positive-negative-positive-negative (of poles of an electrical switch).

p.n.r. prior notice required *commerce*.

PNS peripheral nervous system.

pnso or **PNSO** pull next stitch over, in knitting.

Pnt Pentagon (U.S. Department of Defense or building housing it).

pntd 1 painted (with date). **2** painted by (with name).

pntr. painter (with name).

PNU protein-nitrogen unit.

pnxt. he or she painted it. [Latin *pinxit*]

PO 1 also **P.O.** by order. [Spanish *por orden*, French *per ordre*] **2** also **P.O. a** parole officer. **b** probation officer. **3** Passport Office. **4** also **P.O.** Patent Office. **5** Personnel Officer. **6** Petty Officer: *PO 1/C = Petty Officer First Class.* **7** also **P/O** phosphate to oxygen (ratio of phosphate atoms to oxygen atoms). **8** also **P/O** pilot officer (in the Royal Air Force). **9** *British* postal order (money order). **10** also **P.O.** Post Office, also in combination: *APO = Army Post Office; POB = Post Office box.* **11** power oscillator. **12** also **P.O.** Province of Ontario. **13** purchase order. **14** putout *baseball*.

Po polonium (chemical element).

po 1 also **p.o.** orally *medicine*. [Latin *per os*] **2** polarity *physics*. **3** also **po.** pole (unit of measure). **4** also **p.o.** *British* postal order (money order). **5** also **p.o.** putout *baseball*.

POB or **P.O.B.** Post Office Box.

POC 1 also **P.O.C.** port of call. **2** process operator's console *computers*.

POD 1 payable on death *commerce, insurance*. **2** also **p.o.d.** pay on delivery. **3** also **P.O.D.** port of debarkation. **4** also **P.O.D.** Project Operations Director.

Pod.D. Doctor of Podiatry.

POE or **P.O.E. 1** port of embarkation. **2** port of entry: *models from $11,990 POE N.Y.*

poet. poetry, poetic.

POGO (pō'gō') Polar Orbiting Geophysical Observatory.

pois. poisonous.

POL 1 Pacific Oceanograph Laboratory. **2** petroleum, oil, and lubricant, *esp. in military*. **3** problem-oriented language *computers*.

Pol. 1 Poland. **2** Polish.

pol. 1 a polar. **b** polarization. **2** polished. **3 a** politics. **b** political: *pol. econ. = political economy; pol. sci. = political science.* **c** also **pol** (*pronounced* pol) politician: *not a radiant knight, but a real pol.* **4** polymerase (a gene that encodes a polymerase): *pol I.*

pol. ad. or **Pol. Ad.** political advisor.

polar. polarization.

pol ind pollen index.

polit. 1 political: *polit. econ. = political economy.* **2** politics.

poll. 1 pollutants. **2** pollution.

Poly. 1 Polynesia. **2** Polynesian. **3** polytechnical school or institute.

poly. 1 polyester fiber. **2** polyethylene. **3** polymer. **4 a** polytechnic. **b** polytechnical. **c** *British* (pol'ē) a polytechnical school or institute.

poly I:C (pol'ē ī'sē) polyinosinic:polycytidylic acid (synthetic chemical compound that stimulates the body to produce interferon).

polytech (pol'ē tek') polytechnical, esp. a polytechnical school.

POM 1 polyoxymethylene (a thermoplastic resin). **2** Project Operations Manager.

pom. 1 pomology (science of fruit growing). **2** pomological.

POMAR Position Operational Meteorological Aircraft Report (system for gathering weather data over a wide area).

POMR problem-oriented medical record.

pon or **pont.** pontoon: *pont.br. = pontoon bridge.*

PONA paraffins, olefins, naphthenes, aromatics (constituents that determine octane rating of gasoline): *PONA analysis.*

pond. by weight. [Latin *pondere*]

Pont. Pontiff or Pontificate: *Pont. Max. = Supreme Pontiff.* [Latin *Pontifex Maximus*]

POP 1 plaster of paris. **2** also **P.O.P.** point of purchase: *an erosion of advertising funds from the P.O.P. medium.* **3** printout or printing-out paper.

pop. 1 a also **pop** (*pronounced* pop) popular: *pop. ed. = popular edition.* **b** popularly. **2** population.

POR or **p.o.r. 1** payable on receipt. **2** pay on return.

por. 1 a porous. **b** porosity. **2** portage: *por. 242c. = portage of 242 chains, or approximately three miles.* **3** portion. **4** portrait.

porc. porcelain.

porn or **porn. 1** (pôrn) pornography. **2** also **porno** (pôr'nō) pornographic.

Port. 1 Portugal. 2 Portuguese: *Port. Guin.* = *Portuguese Guinea.*

port. 1 portable. 2 portfolio. 3 *also* **portr.** portrait.

POS 1 point of sale: *POS card, POS terminal.* 2 product of sums *mathematics.*

pos 1 position. 2 positive. 3 **a** possession. **b** possessive. 4 **a** possible. **b** possibly. **c** possibility.

posh a word with the meaning of elegant, stylish. The often quoted derivation for the initial letters of *port outside, starboard home* is without substance.

POSIX Portable Operating System Interface (in reference to a standard of the Institute of Electrical and Electronic Engineers).

POSM patient-operated selector mechanism.

posn. position.

POSS passive optical surveillance system.

poss. 1 **a** possession, possessions. **b** possessive *grammar,* also in combination: *poss. pron.* = *possessive pronoun.* 2 **a** possible. **b** possibly. **c** possibility.

posslq or **POSSLQ** (pos'əl kyü') person of the opposite sex sharing living quarters (used in census reports and advertisements).

post. 1 postal. 2 posterior.

post cib. after eating *pharmaceutics.* [Latin *post cibo*]

posth. posthumous (of a composition in music or literature published after the composer's or author's death): *Schubert's Sonata in A (posth.).*

pot. 1 potash. 2 potential. 3 *also* **pot** potentiometer (instrument to measure electromotive force). 4 pottery.

potass. potassium (chemical element).

POTUS President of the United States.

POV 1 point of view. 2 *also* **pov** privately owned vehicle.

POW or **P.O.W.** or **PoW** prisoner of war.

POY partially oriented yarn (synthetic materials requiring processing before use).

PP 1 *also* **PP.** Fathers (priests). [Latin *Patres*] 2 *also* **P.P.** in one's own person *law.* [Latin *propria persona*] 3 inorganic pyrophosphate *biochemistry.* 4 near point (of focus of the eyes). [Latin *punctum proximum*] 5 *also* **P.P.** Parcel Post. 6 *also* **P.P.** Past President: *P.P.R.A.* = *Past President of the Royal Academy.* 7 *also* **p-p** peak to peak, *esp. in electronics.* 8 **a** personal property *insurance.* **b** private property. 9 Planned Parenthood. 10 *also* **PP.** Pope. 11 postpaid. 12 post position, in horse racing. 13 postprandial, after meal(s), *esp. in pharmaceutics.* 14 power plant. 15 prepaid. 16 proper forms being observed. [Latin *praemissis praemittendis*] 17 The Passionate Pilgrim (group of poems, some of which are attributable to Shakespeare).

pp 1 *also* **p.p.** by agent or proxy (power of attorney) *commerce, law.* 2 *also* **pp.** pages. 3 *also* **p.p.** partly paid *commerce.* 4 *also* **pp.** or **p.p.** past participle *grammar.* 5 *also* **p.p.** postprandial, after meal(s), *esp. in pharmaceutics.* 6 *also* **p.p.** **a** privately printed. **b** published, put before the public. [Latin *publice proponit*] 7 *also* **p-p** push-pull (of a circuit). 8 very softly *music.* [Italian *pianissimo*]

PPA 1 *also* **P.P.A.** Periodical Publishers Association (of America). 2 phenylpropanolamine (mild stimulant used in nonprescription diet pills). 3 Professional Photographers of America.

p.p.a. 1 after first shaking the bottle *pharmaceutics.* [Latin *phiala prins agitata*] 2 per power of attorney.

PP. AA. Cardinals (of the Roman Catholic Church). [Latin *Patres Amplissimi*]

PPB 1 paper, printing, and binding (costs of book manufacturing). 2 *also* **ppb** or **p.p.b.** parts per billion. 3 political party broadcast (political party advertisement on British radio and television between elections). 4 programming, planning, and budgeting, also in combination: *PPBS* = *programming-planning-budgeting system* (method of trying to measure the benefits of a program in relation to its costs).

PPBF Pan-American Pharmaceutical and Biochemical Federation.

PPC 1 plain paper copier *commerce.* 2 Policy Planning Council (of U.S. Department of State). 3 progressive patient care *medicine.*

p.p.c. 1 picture postcard. 2 to take leave. [French *pour prendre congé*]

PPD 1 Party for Peace and Democracy (of South Korea). 2 Popular Democratic Party (of Puerto Rico). [Spanish *Partido Popular Democrático*] 3 *British* Preferred Policyholders' Discount (of automobile insurance). 4 **a** purified protein derivative (of tuberculin). **b** patch test for tuberculosis that uses this substance.

ppd. 1 postpaid. 2 prepaid.

PPE philosophy, politics, and economics: *Oxford is strong in the classics and PPE.*

PPF 1 personal property floater *insurance.* 2 Plumbers and Pipefitters Union.

PPFA Planned Parenthood Federation of America.

pph 1 pages per hour (of a press run). 2 *also* **pph.** pamphlet. 3 parts per hundred, esp. in combination: *pphm* = *parts per hundred parts of mix.*

PPI 1 plan position indicator (radar data). 2 *also* **p.p.i.** policy proof of interest *insurance.* 3 Producer Price Index (of the cost of raw materials used in production of new goods).

PPL private pilot license.

ppl. participle.

PPLO pleuropneumonia-like organism (cause of primary atypical pneumonia).

PPM 1 *also* **ppm** or **p.p.m.** parts per million (concentration of some substance in a mixture). 2 *also* **p.p.m.** or **p/m** pounds per minute. 3 pulse position modulation *communications.*

PPN Niger Progressive Party. [French *Parti Progressiste Nigérien*]

PPO 1 polyphenylene or polyphene oxide (polymer used in making synthetic materials, such as piping). 2 preferred provider organization (for health care).

PPP 1 Pakistan People's Party. 2 People's Progressive Party (of Gambia and Guyana). 3 purchasing power parity (of exchange rates).

ppp. very, very softly *music.* [Italian *pianississimo*]

PPPI precision plan-position indicator (of radar).

P.P.R. permanent personal registration (for voting).

ppr. 1 *also* **Ppr.** paper. 2 *also* **p.pr.** present participle.

PPS 1 *also* **P.P.S.** British Parliamentary Private Secretary: *serving as a PPS to Churchill.* 2 Popular Socialist Party (of Mexico). [Spanish *Partido Popular Socialista*] 3 post-polio sequelae (symptoms afflicting polio survivors). 4 pounds per second. 5 *also* **P.P.S.** second postscript. [Latin *post postscriptum*]

p.p.s. 1 *also* **p/s** pounds per second. 2 *also* **pps** pulses per second. 3 second postscript. [Latin *post postscriptum*]

ppt 1 *also* **p.p.t. a** parts per thousand. **b** parts per trillion. 2 *also* **ppt.** precipitate *chemistry.*

pptd *or* **pptd.** precipitated *chemistry.*

pptg *or* **pptg.** precipitating *chemistry.*

pptn *or* **pptn.** precipitation *chemistry.*

ppty *or* **Ppty** property.

PPV 1 pay-per-view (television). 2 poly p-phenylene vinylene (electrically conducting plastic).

PPWP Planned Parenthood–World Population.

PQ 1 *also* **P.Q.** Parliamentary Question. 2 perceptual quotient. 3 permeability quotient. 4 *also* **P.Q.** personality quotient. 5 *also* **P.Q.** *or* **p.q.** previous question. 6 *also* **P.Q.** Province of Quebec. 7 Quebec Party. [French *Parti Québécois*]

PQLI physical quality of life index.

PR 1 far point (of focus of the eyes). [Latin *punctum remotum*] 2 *also* **P.R.** Parliamentary Report. 3 Partisan Review (magazine title). 4 *also* **P/R** payroll. 5 percentile rank *statistics.* 6 **a** performance report. **b** preliminary report. **c** progress report. 7 periodic reverse (of electric current). 8 pitch ratio. 9 *also* **P.R.** press release. 10 *also* **P.R.** proportional representation. 11 *also* **P.R.** *or* **p.r.** public relations. 12 Puerto Rico: **a** (Zip Code). **b** *also* **P.R.** (in general use). 13 *also* **P.R.** Republican Party. [French *Parti Républicain,* Spanish *Partido Republicano*]

Pr *I an abbreviation for:* 1 preferred (stock, in an exchange listing). 2 *also* **Pr.** presbyopia (inelasticity of the lens of the eye, causing farsightedness). 3 *also* **Pr.** Press. 4 Priest. 5 Prince. 6 *also* **Pr.** Printer. 7 *also* **Pr.** Private. 8 Provençal.

II a symbol for: 1 Prandtl number (unit of fluid heat transfer). 2 praseodymium (chemical element). 3 propyl (radical of propane) *chemistry.*

pr 1 *also* **pr.** pair. 2 paper. 3 *also* **p/r** payroll. 4 power. 5 *also* **pr.** preferred (stock listing of transactions). 6 *also* **pr.** present. 7 price. 8 **a** *also* **pr.** printed, printed by. **b** *also* **pr.** printer. **c** printing. 9 *also* **pr.** prior. 10 *also* **pr.** pronunciation. 11 *also* **p.r.** *or* **p/r** pro rata. 12 proved.

PRA 1 phosphoribosylamine (derivatives in purine biosynthesis). 2 planetary radio astronomy. 3 *also* **P.R.A.** President of the Royal Academy. 4 Private Retirement Account. 5 probabilistic risk assessment (of nuclear reactors). 6 Purchase and Resale Agreement (short-term loans by the Bank of Canada to money-market investment dealers).

prac. 1 practice. 2 *also* **Prac.** practitioner.

prag. 1 pragmatic. 2 pragmatism.

P.R.B. Pre-Raphaelite Brotherhood (group of artists in England in the mid-1800s who vowed to portray the simplicity of nature).

PRBS pseudorandom binary sequence *computers.*

PRC 1 *also* **P.R.C.** after the building of Rome. [Latin *Post Roman Conditam*] 2 People's Republic of China. 3 Postal Rate Commission.

PRD 1 Dominican Revolutionary Party. [Spanish *Partido Revolucionario Dominicano*] 2 Revolutionary Democratic Party (of Mexico) [Spanish *Partido Revolucionario Democratico*]

pre. prefix.

preamp (prē'amp') preamplifier.

Preb. *or* **preb.** 1 prebend (salary paid to clergy of a cathedral or property, or tax from which this salary is paid). 2 prebendary (clergy with a prebend).

Prec. Precentor (director of church choir).

prec. 1 **a** preceding. **b** preceded. 2 precision.

precip. 1 precipitate, *esp. in chemistry.* 2 (prē'sip') precipitation *meteorology.*

PRECIS preserved context index system.

pred. 1 predicate. 2 predicative.

Pref. 1 Preface. 2 Prefect. 3 preferred stock *commerce.*

pref. 1 preference. 2 *also* **prefd** preferred. 3 **a** prefix. **b** prefixed.

prefab (prē'fab') prefabricated.

preg. pregnant.

prehist. *or* **prehis.** prehistoric.

prej. prejudice.

prel. *or* **prelim.** (pri'lim') 1 preliminary, esp. a preliminary examination. 2 *also* **prelims** (pri'limz') preliminary proofs or pages of a book.

Prem. Premier.

prem. 1 *also* **prem** premature (when referring to infants, usually written **preem** or **preemie,** *pronounced* prē'mē). 2 premium.

premed 1 (prē'med') premedical student. 2 *also* **premed.** premedical.

preop (prē'op') *or* **preop.** preoperation or preoperative (before surgery).

prep. *or* **prep** 1 **a** (*also pronounced* prep) preparation. **b** preparatory (*also pronounced* prep, esp. in *prep school*). **c** prepare. **d** *also* **prepd** (*also pronounced* prept) prepared. 2 preposition *grammar.*

prepn. preparation.

prepreg (prē'preg') pre-impregnation (of fibers with resins prior to forming).

prepub (prē'pub') prepublication.

prereq. prerequisite, as of a course that must be taken before enrolling in a more advanced course.

Pres. 1 *also* **Presb.** *or* **Presbyt.** Presbyterian. 2 Presentation. 3 (*also pronounced* prez) President.

pres. 1 present, esp. in combination in grammar: *pres.ind.* = *present indicative; pres.part.* = *present participle.* 2 **a** presidency. **b** (*also pronounced* prez) president. **3** pressure. **4** presumptive.

press. *or* **press** pressure.

PRESTO program reporting and evaluation system for total operation.

presv. preservation.

pret. preterit (past tense) *grammar*.

prev. 1 previous. **2** previously.

PRF 1 prolactin releasing factor. **2** pulse recurrence or repetition frequency (of radar).

prf. proof, also in combination: *prfr = proofreader*.

PRI 1 *also* **P.R.I.** (prē) Institutional Revolutionary Party (of Mexico). [Spanish *Partido Revolucionario Institucional*] **2** Italian Republican Party. [Italian *Partito Republicano Italiano*] **3** periodic review instrument (assesses patient care needs).

pri. 1 primary. **2** primer. **3** private.

prim. 1 primary. **2** primate. **3** primitive.

primip. primipara (woman who has borne one child or is giving birth to first child).

prin. 1 a *also* **Prin.** principal. **b** principally. **2** *also* **Prin.** Principality. **3** principle.

print. 1 printer. **2 a** printed, printed by. **b** printing.

prion proteinaceous infectious particle (protein particle about 100 times smaller than a normal virus).

pris. prisoner.

PRISE program for integrated shipboard electronics.

PRISM (priz′əm) program reliability information system for management.

prism. prismatic.

PRIST paper radioimmunosorbent test (for allergic and immunological reaction).

priv. 1 a private. **b** privately: *priv.pr. = privately printed*. **2** privative (expressing denial or negation) *grammar*. **3** privilege.

Private Res. private resolution (with number).

PRK photo-reactive keratectomy (surgical procedure to correct corneal defects with laser).

P.R.L. Republican Liberal Party. [French *Parti Républicain de la Liberté*]

prm. premium.

Pr.Min. Prime Minister.

PRN 1 *also* **p.r.n.** *or* **P.R.N.** for the occasion *or* as needed *medicine, pharmaceutics* [Latin *pro re nata*] **2** phenyltoloxamine (a tranquilizer). **3** *also* **prn** print numerically.

prntr printer.

PRO 1 peer review organization, esp. in treatment covered by Medicare. **2** Problem Resolution Officer (in the Internal Revenue Service). **3** *also* **P.R.O.** Public Record Office. **4** public relations officer. **5** *also* **Pro.** proline (an essential amino acid).

Pro *or* **Pro.** Provost.

pro 1 *also* **pro.** procedure. **2** *also* **pro.** (prō) professional, also in combination: *Pro-am = professional-amateur* (category in

sports). **3** *also* **Pro.** progressive (political party or other group). **4** *also* **pro.** propyl (radical of propane). **5** protein.

prob. 1 a probability. **b** probable. **c** probably. **2** *also* **Prob. a** probate. **b** probation: *Prob.Off. = Probation Officer*. **3** (*also pronounced* prob) problem.

Proc. 1 proceedings. **2** Proclamation. **3** Proctor. **4** *also military* **PROC a** procure. **b** procurement.

proc. 1 procedure. **2** process.

proc′g processing.

PROCLIB (prok′lib) procedure library (file of procedures for a computer).

prod. 1 a produce. **b** produced. **2** producer. **3 a** product. **b** production.

Prof. 1 professional, also in combination: *Prof.Eng. = Professional Engineer*. **2** *also* **Prof** (*also pronounced* prof) professor, also in combination: *Prof.Eng. = Professor of English*.

prof. 1 profession. **2** professional.

Prog. Progressive (political party or other group).

prog. 1 prognosis *medicine*. **2 a** program: *prog.bk. = program book*. **b** programmed. **3 a** progress. **b** progressive.

proj. *or* **proj 1** *also* **Proj.** project, also in combination: *Proj.Eng. = Project Engineer*. **2** projection. **3** projector.

prol. prologue.

PROLOG (prō′lôg) Programming in Logic (computer language).

PROLT procurement lead time *military*.

PROM 1 premature rupture of the membranes (of newborns) *medicine*. **2** (*pronounced* prom) programmable read-only memory *computers*.

prom. 1 *also* **prom** (*pronounced* prom) **a** promenade (dance). **b** *also* **Prom** *British* promenade (concert). **2** *also* **Prom.** promontory. **3** promoted. **4** promotion: **a** advancement. **b** *also* **promo** (prō′mō) announcement of a program or product.

pron. 1 a pronoun. **b** pronominal. **2 a** pronunciation. **b** pronounced.

PRONTO program for numerical tool operation.

prop 1 (*pronounced* prop) propeller. **2** *also* **prop. a** proper. **b** properly. **3** *also military* **PROP**, *or in the theater* **prop.** (*pronounced* prop) property. **4** *also* **prop. a** proposition (often with a number). **b** proposed. **5 a** *also* **Prop.** proprietor. **b** proprietary.

propl. proportional.

propn. proportion.

Propr. proprietor.

props. *or* **props** (*pronounced* props) properties, in the theater.

pros. prosody.

Pros. Atty Prosecuting Attorney.

prost. 1 prostate. **2** prostitution.

Prot. 1 Protectorate. **2** *also* **Protest.** Protestant.

prot. 1 protected. **2** protection.

pro tem or **Pro tem.** (prō tem′) for the time being. [Latin *pro tempore*]

Prov. 1 provenance (source or origin of a work of art or antique). **2** Provençal. **3** Provence (area in SE France). **4** Proverbs (book of the Old Testament). **5 a** Province. **b** Provincial. **6** Provost.

prov. 1 a proverb. **b** proverbial. **2** provincialism. **3 a** provision. **b** provisional.

Provo (prō′vō) **1** Provisional (member of the provisional wing of the Irish Republican Army). **2** also **provo** provocateur (member of a group of Dutch or German political agitators).

prox. next month. [Latin *proximo (mense)*]

PRP 1 platelet-rich plasma *medicine.* **2** potentially responsible parties (of toxic waste dumps) *insurance, law.* **3** also **Prp** prion protein (protein in neurons responsible for transmitting scrapie). **4** progressive rubella panencephalitis (disease resulting from previous infection of rubella). **5** pseudo-random pulse *electronics.* **6** pulse repetition period *electronics.*

pr.p. present participle.

PRPB Popular Revolutionary Party of Benin. [French *Parti de la Révolution Populaire du Bénin*]

PRQ Republican Party of Quebec. [French-Canadian *Parti Républicain du Québec*]

PRR pulse repetition rate *electronics.*

PRS 1 pattern recognition system *computers.* **2** also **P.R.S.** Performing Right Society (of Great Britain). **3** also **P.R.S. a** President of the Royal Society. **b** Proceedings of the Royal Society (publication).

Prs. Printers.

prs. pairs.

PRSA or **P.R.S.A.** Public Relations Society of America.

prsd pressed.

P.R.S.E. 1 President of the Royal Society of Edinburgh. **2** Proceedings of the Royal Society of Edinburgh (publication).

PRT 1 personal rapid transit (a proposed elevated, rapid transit sysem of small passenger cars that would stop at individual destinations by pushing a button). **2** Port (in postal address). **3** program reference table *computers.* **4** pulse repetition time *electronics.*

prt print, also in combination: *prtg = printing, prtr = printer.*

PRTase hypoxanthine-guanine phosphoribosyltransferase (enzyme in brain cell metabolism).

Prus. or **Pruss. 1** Prussia. **2** Prussian.

PRV 1 peak reverse voltage. **2** pressure-reducing valve.

p.r.v. to return a call. [French *pour rendre visite*]

PS 1 also **P.S. a** British Parliamentary Secretary. **b** British Permanent Secretary (highest civil service rank). **c** Press Secretary. **d** private secretary. **2** phrase structure *grammar.* **3** pipe size. **4** Police Sergeant. **5** polystyrene. **6** also **P.S.** postscript. [Latin *post scriptum*] **7** also **P/S** power steering. **8** power supply. **9** also **P.S.** Privy Seal. **10** also **P.S.** prompt side (right-hand side of the stage facing the audience), in the theater. **11** proton synchrotron *physics.* **12** public school (usually with a number): *P.S. 12.* **13** also **P.S.** Public Statutes. **14** pull switch,

in blueprints and diagrams. **15** Socialist Party (of France). [French *Parti Socialiste*]

Ps. 1 also **ps.** peseta (monetary unit of Andorra and Spain). **2 a** Psalm. **b** Psalms (book of the Old Testament).

ps 1 picosecond (trillionth of a second). **2** also **ps.** pieces. **3** also **p.s.** postscript. [Latin *post scriptum*] **4** pressure sensitive: *ps tape, ps switch.* **5** also **ps.** pseudonym.

PSA 1 also **P.S.A.** Photographic Society of America. **2** prostate-specific antigen (an indication present in the blood of possible prostate cancer). **3** public service announcement.

PsA the Southern Fish (constellation). [Latin *Piscis Austrinus*]

Psa. a Psalm. **b** Psalms (book of the Old Testament).

PSAC President's Science Advisory Committee.

PSAT Preliminary Scholastic Aptitude Test.

PSBR public sector borrowing requirement (of some governments' budgets, used to balance taxation and borrowing).

PSC 1 also **psc** per standard compass (in a ship's log or flight report). **2** polar stratospheric cloud (in which ice crystals react with ozone to deplete it and create an ozone hole). **3** also **P.S.C.** Public Service Commission. **4** Social Christian Party (of French Belgium). [French *Parti Social Chrétien*]

P.S.D. Social Democratic Party. [French *Parti Social Démocratique,* Italian *Partito Socialista Democratico,* Portuguese *Partido Social Democratica,* etc.]

PSE 1 Pacific Stock Exchange. **2** point of subjective equality *psychology.*

psec. or **psec** picosecond (trillionth of a second).

pseud. pseudonym.

psf or **p.s.f.** pounds per square foot.

PSGN poststreptococal glomerulonephritis (a disease of the kidneys).

psgr. passenger.

PSI 1 Italian Socialist Party. [Italian *Partito Socialista Italiano*] **2** personalized system of instruction. **3** Pollution Standard Index (used by U.S. Environmental Protection Agency). **4** Public Services International (international alliance of trade unions operating among public employees).

psi or **p.s.i.** pounds per square inch.

psia or **p.s.i.a.** pounds per square inch, absolute.

ᵖsid sidereal period of revolution *astronomy.*

psid or **p.s.i.d.** pounds per square inch, differential.

psig or **p.s.i.g.** pounds per square inch gauge.

PSK Phase Shift Keying (of phase modulation) *electronics.*

PSM product sales manager.

PSMSL Permanent Service for Mean Sea Level (data collection for navigational charts).

PSN 1 also **psn** position. **2** Public Switched Network *computers.*

PSO Procurement Services Office.

PSOE Spanish Socialist Workers Party. [Spanish *Partido Socialista Obrero Español*]

p sol partly soluble.

PSP 1 phenolsulfonphthalein (used in a kidney excretion test). **2** pseudostatic spontaneous potential *engineering*.

p.s.p. postsynaptic potential.

PSR 1 plow steel rope. **2** *also* **P.S.R.** Presidential Special Representative. **3** pulsar (with a number).

PSRO *or* **P.S.R.O.** professional standards review organization (regional medical review board and hospital inspection group).

PSS 1 *also* **P.SS.** *or* **p.ss.** postscripts. **2** Professional Services Section. **3** psychological saline solution.

Pss. Psalms (indicating selected Psalms from the Book of Psalms of the Old Testament).

p.s.s.o. *or* **PSSO** pass slipped stitch over, in knitting.

PST *or* **p.s.t. 1** *also* **P.S.T.** Pacific Standard Time. **2** *also* **pst.** pounds static thrust.

Pstl. postal.

PSU power supply unit.

p.surg plastic surgery.

PSV 1 probability state variable. **2** Public Service Vehicle.

PSW 1 program status word *computers*. **2** psychiatric social worker.

psy. 1 psychiatry. **2** psychoanalysis. **3** psychology.

psych. 1 a psychiatric. **b** psychiatry. **2** psychic. **3** *also* **psychol. a** psychology. **b** psychological. **c** psychologist.

Psyn synodic time of revolution *astronomy*.

psyop (*also pronounced* sī'op) psychological warfare operations.

psywar psychological warfare.

PSZ partially stabilized zirconia (ceramic material used to make dies and bearings).

PT 1 *also* **P.T.** Pacific time. **2** *also* **P/T** part time. **3** patrol torpedo (boat, often followed by a number): *PT 103.* **4** *also* **P.T. a** physical therapy or therapist. **b** physiotherapy, physiotherapist. **c** psychotherapy, psychotherapist. **5** potential transformer. **6** prime time, esp. in television programming. **7** prothrombin time (in generation of thrombin during clotting) *medicine.* **8** pupil-teacher, esp. in combination: *PTR = pupil-teacher ratio.* **9** British purchase tax.

Pt *I an abbreviation for:* **1** *also* **Pt.** part: *Henry IV Pt.1.* **2** *also* **Pt.** Point: *King's Pt.* **3** *also* **Pt.** Port: *Pt. Washington. II a symbol for:* platinum (chemical element).

pt 1 part. **2** *also* **p.t.** *or* **p/t** part time. **3** past. **4** *grammar* **a** *also* **p.t.** past tense. **b** *also* **pt.** preterit (past tense). **5** patient. **6** *also* **pt.** payment. **7** *also* **pt.** pint. **8** point, as in printing (meaning *period*). **9** port. **10** *also* **p.t.** pro tem, for the time being. [Latin *pro tempore*] **11** *also* **p.t.** British purchase tax.

PTA 1 Parent-Teacher Association. **2** phosphotungstic acid (reagent in chemical testing). **3** plasma thromboplastin antecedent (a precoagulant usually deficient in hemophiliacs). **4** post-traumatic amnesia. **5** prior to admission *medicine.*

Pta. 1 *also* **pta.** peseta (monetary unit of Spain and Andorra). **2** Point. [Spanish *Punta*]

ptbl. portable.

PTC 1 phenylthiocarbamide (substance used to test inherited traits by ability to taste). **2** photo-type composition. **3** plasma thromboplastin component (a clotting factor). **4** positive temperature coefficient.

PTD post-tuning drift (of a radio).

Ptd. printed.

Pte. *British* Private (in the Army).

PTF plasma thromboplastin factor: *PTF-A* (antihemophilic factor in blood).

PTFCE polytrifluorochloroethene (easily molded plastic).

PTFE polytetrafluoroethylene (used for bearings, sliding parts, and other nonstick surfaces).

Ptg. 1 a Portugal. **b** Portuguese. **2** *also* **ptg.** printing.

PTH parathyroid hormone.

PTI 1 Physical Training Instructor. **2** Press Trust of India (news agency). **3** previously taxed income. **4** pretrial intervention.

Ptl. patrolman.

PTM 1 phase time modulation. **2** pulse time modulation.

Ptn. *or* **ptn.** partition.

Ptnr. partner.

PTO 1 Patent and Trademark Office (of U.S. Department of Commerce). **2** *also* **P.T.O.** Perlsucht tuberculin original *medicine.* **3** *also* **p.t.o.** please turn over (the page). **4** power take-off (flywheel or pulley and a belt, or driveshaft that provides power to machines from a tractor motor). **5** *also* **P.T.O.** Public Trustee Office.

Pto. Port. [Spanish *Porto*]

PTP *or* **p-t-p** point to point *electronics.*

PTR pool test reactor.

ptr. 1 painter. **2** *also* **Ptr.** printer.

PTRM partial thermoremanent magnetization *geophysics.*

pts 1 parts. **2** *also* **pts.** payments. **3** *also* **pts.** pints. **4** points.

PTSA Parent-Teacher-Student Association.

PTSD post-traumatic stress disorder.

PTT 1 *also* **P.T.T.** Mail, Telegraph, and Telephone (national service of France and of Switzerland). [French *Postes Télégraphes et Téléphones*] **2** partial thrombin time (in generation of thrombin during clotting) *medicine.*

pt/tm *or* **pt tm** part time.

PTU propylthiouracil (used to control thyroid activity).

PTV public television.

ptw per thousand words.

Pty. *or* **pty. 1** party. **2** *also* **Pty** proprietary: *Pty. Ltd. = proprietary limited.*

PU 1 *also* **P/U** pickup *electronics.* **2** polyurethane (plastic). **3** *also* **P.U.** pregnancy urine (of humans and animals). **4** processor unit *computers.* **5** propellant utilization.

Pu plutonium (chemical element).

p.u. plant unit *botany.*

Pub. 1 Public: *Pub. Aff. = Public Affairs.* **2** publication (often with a number). **3** publicity: *Pub. Agent.*

pub. *or* **publ. 1** public. **2** publicity: *pub. notice.* **3 a** *also* **pubd.** published. **b** publication. **c** publisher. **d** publishing.

Pub. Doc. public document.

Public Res. Public Resolution (used with a number).

Pubn or **pubn.** publication.

PUC 1 also **p.u.c.** papers under consideration. **2** also **P.U.C.** Public Utilities Commission.

PUD 1 pickup and delivery. **2** planned unit development. **3** public utility district.

pud. (pud) pudding.

PUFA polyunsaturated fatty acids.

pug. pugilist.

pul. or **pulm.** pulmonary.

pulv. 1 powder *pharmaceutics: pulv.gros. = coarse powder.* [Latin *pulvis* and *pulvis grossus*] **2** pulverized.

pun. 1 punish. **2** punishment.

punc. punctuation.

PUO pyrexia (fever) of unknown origin *medicine.*

Pup the Poop (of the ship Argo, an old and very large constellation). [Latin *Puppis*]

PUPP pruritic urticarial papules and plaques (skin eruption, esp. during pregnancy).

pur. 1 a purchase. **b** purchaser. **c** also **purch** purchasing. **2 a** pure or clean. [Latin *purus*] **b** purification. **3** pursuit.

purp purple.

PURV (perv) powered underwater research vehicle.

PUS or **P.U.S. 1** *British* **a** Parliamentary Undersecretary. **b** Permanent Undersecretary (second-highest rank in civil service). **2** Pharmacopoeia of the United States.

PUSH People United to Serve Humanity.

PUVA (pü've) Psoralen Ultraviolet A (treatment for psoriasis using psoralen with exposure to ultraviolet A light).

PV or **P.V.** *British* positively vet (examine, investigate thoroughly).

PVA 1 polyvinyl acetate (a latex paint). **2** polyvinyl alcohol.

PVC 1 polyvinyl chloride (tough, fire-resistant plastic, now prohibited as a dangerous polluting agent). **2** premature ventricular contraction (of the heart) *medicine.*

PVD peripheral vascular disease.

PvdA Labor Party, of the Netherlands. [Dutch *Partij van de Arbeid*]

PVDC polyvinyl dichloride (a plastic; modified form of PVC).

PVDF polyvinylidene difluoride (protective plastic).

PVE 1 polyvinyl ethyl ether (used esp. in manufacturing pressure-sensitive adhesives). **2** prosthetic valve endocarditis (inflammation of the lining around the heart caused by an artificial valve implanted in the heart).

PVF polyvinyl fluoride (plastic film used to protect building material, electric cable, etc.).

PVI polyvinyl isobutyl ether (synthetic resin used as a lubricant and adhesive).

PVM polyvinyl methyl ether (synthetic compound used as an adhesive in printing and dyeing).

PVP polyvinyl pyrrolidone (synthetic substance used to make antiseptics and cosmetics and as a substitute for blood plasma).

PVS or **P.V.S. 1** persistent vegetative state (of a comatose patient) *medicine.* **2** Post-Vietnam Syndrome (complex of emotional problems experienced by veterans of the Vietnam War).

PVT 1 page view terminal (display of whole page) *computers.* **2** polyvinyl toluene (a thermoplastic). **3** pressure, volume, temperature *chemical engineering.*

Pvt. Private (soldier of the lowest rank).

pvt. or **pvt** private.

p.v.t. by telegraph. [French *par voie télégraphique*]

PW 1 also **p.w.** packed weight. **2** Palau (in postal address). **3** power windows (of an automobile). **4** also **P.W.** prisoner of war. **5** private wire (telephone). **6** psychological warfare. **7** also **P.W.** public works, esp. in combination: *DPW = Department of Public Works.* **8** Publishers' Weekly (trade magazine). **9** pulse width *electronics.*

pw or **pw.** picowatt (trillionth of a watt).

PWA 1 person with AIDS. **2** Public Works Administration (in government of Franklin Roosevelt).

PWBA Pension and Welfare Benefits Administration (of U.S. Department of Labor).

pwd. 1 also **pwd** plywood. **2** powder. **3** also **pwd** powered.

P.W.L.B. Public Works Loans Board (of Great Britain).

PWM pulse width modulation *electronics.*

PWP personal word processor (electronic typewriter).

PWR 1 also **pwr.** or **pwr** power, also in combination: *PWR windows; pwr. sup. = power supply.* **2** pressurized water reactor.

PWS plasma-wave sensor (measures low-frequency electromagnetic waves, aboard a spacecraft).

pwt. pennyweight.

PX 1 physical examination. **2** also **P.X.** please exchange. **3** also **Px** pneumothorax *medicine.* **4** Post Exchange (store on a military establishment). **5** private telephone exchange.

pxt. he or she painted it. [Latin *pinxit*]

Py pyridine (organic base used as a solvent and in various drugs and vitamins).

pymt. payment.

PYO pick your own (usually in an orchard or field indicating the customer must harvest what is purchased).

pyro. 1 also **pyro** (pī'rō) pyrogallol (used in photographic developer, in medicine, and as a reagent). **2** also **pyro** (pī'rō) pyromaniac. **3** also **pyrotech.** pyrotechnic (display or use or manufacture of fireworks). **4** also **pyrox.** pyroxylin (used in guncotton, cellulose, and collodion).

Pyx the Compass (of the ship Argo, an old and very large constellation). [Latin *Pyxis*]

PZA pyrazinamide (drug given in treatment of tuberculosis).

PZD partial zonal drilling (technique of in vitro fertilization).

PZI protamine zinc insulin.

PZM pressure-zone microphone.

PZPR Polish United Workers' Party. [Polish *Polska Zjednoczona Partia Robotnicza*]

PZT lead zirconate titanate (used in electrical devices that convert pressure into electrical energy, as in microphones or computer controls).

Q

Q *I an abbreviation for:* **1** Qatar, in comination: *QRI = Qatar Riyal* (monetary unit). **2** quality: *Q-factor* (see symbols def. 5). **3** quantity (see symbols def. 6). **4 a** Quarterly (of a report or publication), in combination: *QJS = Quarterly Journal of Speech.* **b** quarterly (as in a report of stock dividends). **5 a** quartile: *Q₁ = first quartile.* **b** quartile deviation *statistics.* **6** *also* **Q.** quarto: **a** page size of a book in which the printing sheet is folded and cut into four pages, now usually about 9 × 12 inches. **b** applied to early editions of works by Shakespeare: *Q1, Q2, Q3,* etc. **7** *also* **Q.** Quebec: *P.Q. = Province of Quebec.* **8** *also* **Q. a** Queen, in combination: *QAB = Queen Anne's Bounty.* **b** Queen (esp. in cards and chess). **9** *also* **Q.** Queensland (state in Australia), esp. in combination: *QLTA = Queensland Lawn Tennis Association.* **10** question. **11** quetzal (monetary unit of Guatemala). **12** quinone (coal-tar derivative). **13** *also* **Q.** quire (24 sheets of paper of the same quality and trim size). **14** quotient.
II a symbol for: **1** atomic shell of 98 electrons per shell. **2** Gospel passages common to Matthew and Luke that were not derived from the Gospel of Mark. **3** moment of area. **4** quadrupole moment *physics.* **5** quality factor (of an atomic reactor or an electrical circuit). **6** quantity, *esp. in science and math:* **a** quantity of heat. **b** quantity of light, electricity, or electric charge; coulomb. **d** quantity of reactive power. **7** Querwellen (of transverse seismic waves measured by their time of absorption and disappearance): *Q scale.* **8** seventeenth of a series (sixteenth if *J* is omitted). **9** thermoelectric power *physics.*

q *I an abbreviation for:* **1** farthing. [Latin *quadrans*] **2** quantity. **3** *also* **q. a** quart. **b** quarter. **c** quarterly. **4** *also* **q.** quarto (page size of a book in which the printing page is folded and cut into four pages, now usually about 9 × 12 inches). **5 a** query (question): *A/q = author's query by proofreader on galley proofs.* **b** question. **6** *also* **q.** quintal (a hundredweight). **7** *also* **q.** quire (24 sheets of paper of the same quality and trim size).
II a symbol for: **1** dynamic pressure. **2** every, *esp. pharmaceutics:* *q⁴ʰ = every 4 hours.* [Latin *quaque*] **3** generalized coordinate *physics.* **4** perihelion distance *astronomy.* **5** quantity, *esp. in science and math:* **a** quantity or rate of flow, as of heat flow or volumetric flow. **b** quantity of electricity or electric charge. **6** quark *physics.* **7** seventeenth of a series (sixteenth if *j* is omitted). **8** squalls *meteorology.*

QA 1 qualification approval. **2** quality assurance (as of health care or in manufacturing): *QA Coordinator; QADS = quality assurance data system.* **3** *British* quarters allowance. **4** *British* **a** *also* **QAIMNS** Queen Alexandra's Imperial Military Nursing Service (of WWI). **b** (later allocated to each service): *QARANS* of the Royal Army, *QARAFNS* of the Royal Air Force, and *QARNNS* of the Royal Navy. **5** *also* **Q/A** or **Q&A** or **Q. and A.** question and answer: *a long session of QA.*

Q.A.B. *British* Queen Anne's Bounty (trust fund whose income is used to pension poor clergy and finance church mortgages, etc.).

QALY quality-adjusted life years (in evaluating medical procedures).

QAM 1 quadrature amplitude modulation (for high-speed data transmission). **2** queued access method (synchronizing high-speed input and output of data).

Qantas (kwon'tis) Queensland and Northern Territory Aerial Service, or Qantas Empire Airways.

QB 1 *also* **q.b.** quarterback, in football and soccer. **2** *also* **Q.B.** *British* Queen's Bench *law.* **3** Queen's Bishop *chess.*

Q.B.An. who lived (number of) years. [Latin *Qui Bixit* (number of) *Annos*]

Qbc Quebec.

Q.B.D. *British* Queen's Bench Division *law.*

QBE query by example (a computer program in the form of a checkoff procedure that asks questions of the user).

QBO quasi-biennial oscillation (of stratospheric winds over the tropics that usually reverse direction once a year).

Q-BOP Quell basic oxygen process (for producing steel). [Q for German *Quell* fountain]

QBP Queen's Bishop's Pawn *chess.*

q.b.s.p. or **Q.B.S.P.** (I) who kisses your feet: *a letter bearing the old-fashioned Spanish salutation q.b.s.p.* [Spanish *que besa sus pies*]

QC 1 quality control. **2** Quartermaster Corps. **3** *also* **Q.C.** *British* Queen's Counsel *law.* **4** quickchange (as of an aircraft, easily converted from a freighter to a passenger carrier). **5** quick connect, esp. in combination: *QCV = quick-connect valve.* **6** quitclaim (document or action giving up a claim) *law.*

QCB queue control block (regulation of job order) *computers.*

QCD quantum chromodynamics (theory of quantum properties of quarks based on forces called color).

QCE quality control engineering.

QCF unlawful entry *law.* [Latin *quare clausum fregit*]

QCT 1 quality control technology. **2** quantitative computed tomography *medicine.*

q.d. 1 as if said. [Latin *quasi dictum*] **2** *pharmaceutics:* **a** every day [Latin *quaque die*] **b** *also* **Q.D.** four times a day; q.i.d. [Latin *quater in die*]

q.d.a. or **QDA** quantity discount agreement *commerce.*

QE 1 quantum electronics. **2** *British* Queen's evidence *law.*

q.e. which is. [Latin *quod est*]

QE 2 Queen Elizabeth the Second (a British ocean liner).

QED 1 quantum electrodynamics. **2** also **Q.E.D.** or **q.e.d.** which was to be proved, *esp. in mathematics.* [Latin *quod erat demonstrandum*]

Q.E.F. or **q.e.f.** which was to be done, *esp. in mathematics.* [Latin *quod erat faciendum*]

Q.E.I. or **q.e.i.** which was to be found out, *esp. in mathematics.* [Latin *quod erat inveniendum*]

Q.E.N. wherefore execution should not be issued *law.* [Latin *quare executionem non*]

QF 1 quality factor. **2** quench frequency *electronics.* **3** quick-firing. **4** quick freeze.

QFIA quantitative fluorescence image analysis (test for bladder cancer using a fluorescent dye).

QFT quantum field theory (of particles and forces) *physics.*

QG Quartermaster General.

q.h. every hour *pharmaceutics:* q.2 h. = every two hours. [Latin *quaque hora*]

Q.H.C. Queen's Honorary Chaplain.

Q.H.P. Queen's Honorary Physician.

Q.H.S. Queen's Honorary Surgeon.

QI quality improvement: *QI Manager.*

q.i.d. four times a day *pharmaceutics.* [Latin *quater in die*]

Q.I.P. may he or she rest in peace. [Latin *quiescat in pace*]

QISAM queued indexed sequential access method *computers.*

QJS Quarterly Journal of Speech (publication).

Qk quick (as of flashing lights marked on navigation charts): *IQk = interrupted quick.*

QKt or **Qkt** Queen's Knight *chess.*

QKtP or **Qktp** Queen's Knight's Pawn *chess.*

QL query language *computers.*

ql 1 also **q.l.** or **q.lib.** as much as you please *pharmaceutics.* [Latin *quantum libet*] **2** quintal (hundredweight).

Qld. Queensland (state in Australia).

qlty. quality.

QM 1 quantum mechanics. **2** Quartermaster, also in combination: *QMS = Quartermaster Sergeant.* **3** also **Q.M.** Queen's Messenger.

q.m. every morning *pharmaceutics.* [Latin *quaque mane*]

QMB quick make-and-break (contact) *electronics.*

QMC Quartermaster Corps.

QMG or **QMGen.** Quartermaster General.

QMR 1 qualitative material requirement. **2** also **Qmr.** Quartermaster.

QMRP qualified (to work with) mentally retarded people.

QN 1 also **Q.N.** qualified nurse. **2** Queen's Knight *chess.*

Qn. Queen.

qn 1 also **q.n.** every night *pharmaceutics.* [Latin *quaque nocte*] **2** also **qn.** or **q^n** question. **3** also **qn.** quotation.

QNP or **QNp** Queen's Knight's Pawn *chess.*

QNS or **q.n.s.** quantity not sufficient.

Qnsld. Queensland (state in Australia).

qnt quintet *music.*

qnty quantity.

QOL quality of life.

QOR qualitative operational requirement.

QP Queen's Pawn *chess.*

qp or **q.p.** or **q.pl.** as much as you please *pharmaceutics.* [Latin *quantum placet*]

QPI qualitative personnel information.

QPL qualified products list.

QPM quality-protein maize (nutritionally improved corn).

QPO quasiperiodic object (celestial object that emits a varying pulse).

QPRI qualitative personnel requirements information.

QPSK quarternary phase-shift keying *computers.*

Qq or **Qq.** quartos: **a** of a book, usually of large page size, *esp. in antiquarian bookselling.* **b** early editions of works by Shakespeare: *Qq 1, 2, 3.*

qq 1 each, every. [French *quelque*] **2** also **qq.** questions.

q.q.h. every four hours *pharmaceutics.* [Latin *quaque quater hora*]

qq.hor. every hour *pharmaceutics.* [Latin *quaque hora*]

qq.v. which see (used in referring to more than one item). [Latin *quae vide*]

QR 1 Quarterly Review (publication). **2** also **Q.R.** Queen's Regulations: *QRs, section 1298, subsection 3.* **3** Queen's Rook *chess.* **4** quick response *commerce.* **5** quiet room.

qr. 1 a quarter. **b** quarterly. **c** quarter ton: *a crop from 5 to 9 qrs. per acre.* **2** also **qr** quire (24 sheets of paper of the same quality and trim size).

QRA quality reliability assurance.

QRM electronic interference *communications.*

QRP or **QRp** Queen's Rook's Pawn *chess.*

qrs. 1 also **Qrs** quarters. **2** also **qrs** quires (of 24 sheets of paper).

QRZ who is calling, in amateur radio.

QS 1 quadratic sieve (a factoring method) *computers.* **2** quarter section (about 160 acres). **3** also **Q.S.** quarter session (court of law held quarterly).

q.s. 1 as much as necessary, sufficient quantity *pharmaceutics:* q.s./ad = quantity sufficient to make. [Latin *quantum sufficit addum*] **2** quarter section (about 160 acres).

QSAM queued sequential access method *computers.*

QSE *British* qualified scientist and engineer.

QSG quasi-stellar galaxy *astronomy.*

QSO 1 contact, in amateur radio. **2** quasi-stellar object (quasar) *astronomy.*

QSR or **QSS** quasi-stellar radio source (quasar) *astronomy.*

QSTOL (kyü'stôl) quiet short takeoff and landing (aircraft).

QST 1 general call preceding a message, in amateur radio. **2** publication of the American Radio Relay League.

QT 1 quality test. **2** also **Q.T.** questioned trade (of stock) *commerce.* **3** queueing theory (for organizing data) *computers.*

4 *also* **Q.T.** who sues (on behalf of a government authority) *law.* [Latin *qui tam*]

qt 1 *also* **qt.** quantity. **2** *also* **qt.** quart. **3** quartet *music.* **4** *also* **q.t.** (kyü′tē) *slang* quiet: *on the q.t. = very quietly or secretly.*

QTAM queued telecommunications access method *computers.*

qtd. quartered.

qtly. *or* **Qtly** quarterly.

qto. *or* **Qto.** quarto: **a** of a book, usually of large page size, *esp. in antiquarian bookselling.* **b** page size about 9 × 12 inches. **c** early edition of works by Shakespeare.

QTOL (kyü′tôl) quiet takeoff and landing (aircraft).

qtr. 1 quarter. **2** *also* **Qtr.** quarterly.

qtrs. *or* **Qtrs** quarters.

qts. quarts.

qty. quantity.

qtz. quartz.

Qu. 1 Queen. **2** *also* **Qu a** query. **b** question.

qu. 1 quart. **2 a** quarter. **b** quarterly. **3** *also* **qu a** query. **b** question.

quad. 1 *also* **quad** *or* **Quad** (*pronounced* kwod) quadrangle. **2** quadrant. **3** quadraphonic (of sound reproduction). **4** quadrilateral. **5 a** quadruple. **b** quadruplicate.

qual. 1 a qualify. **b** qualified. **c** qualification. **2 a** quality. **b** qualitative.

quango (kwong′gō) *British* **1** quasi-autonomous national government organization. **2** quasi-autonomous nongovernmental organization.

quant. 1 quantitative. **2** quantity.

quant. suff. as much as necessary, sufficient quantity *pharmaceutics.*

quar. *or* **quart. 1** quarter. **2** quarterly.

quasar (kwā′sär) quasi-stellar object *astronomy.*

quat. 1 four. [Latin *quattuor*] **2** *also* **Quat.** quaternary.

Que. 1 Quebec. **2** Quechua (language of the Incas).

Queens. *or* **Queensl.** Queensland (state in Australia).

ques. question.

questn questionnaire.

QUIL quad in-line (of an integrated circuit package) *electronics.*

quint. 1 fifth. [Latin *quintus*] **2 a** quintuple. **b** quintuplicate.

quor. *or* **Quor** quorum.

quot. 1 quotation. **2** quoted.

quotid. daily *pharmaceutics.* [Latin *quotidie*]

q.v. 1 as much as you wish *pharmaceutics.* [Latin *quantum vis*] **2** which see (used in cross-referring to a single item). [Latin *quod vide*]

QVEC Qualified Voluntary Employee Contribution Plan (tax shelter for employees).

qwerty *or* **QWERTY** (kwér′tē) *Informal* the standard English language typewriter keyboard. [*q, w, e, r, t, y,* the first six keys in the upper row of letters]

QWL quality of working life (esp. in design of computer systems).

Qy. 1 Quay. **2** *also* **qy.** query.

qz. quartz.

R *I an abbreviation for:* **1** *also* **R. a** king. [Latin *rex*] **b** queen. [Latin *regina*] **2** *also* **R.** rabbi. **3** radar. **4** radiancy, radiance *physics.* **5** radical *chemistry.* **6** radius. **7** *also* **R.** railroad or railway, in combination: *CPR = Canadian Pacific Railway.* **8** Raleigh wave (seismic wave on or slightly below surface of the earth). **9** rand (monetary unit of the Republic of South Africa). **10** range, in combination: *Rmax = maximum range.* **11** Rankine (temperature scale). **12** rate: $R = D \div T$, *Rate = Distance divided by Time.* **13** ratio. **14** reaction. **15** reaffirmed. **16** real *mathematics.* **17** *also* **R.** Réaumur (temperature scale). **18** received (of a radio message). **19** recto (right-hand page of a two-page spread). **20** *also* **R.** red. **21** *also* **R.** redactor (editor). **22** reference. **23** refraction. **24** *also* **R.** registered. **25** reluctance *physics.* **26 a** repeat. **b** reprint (of a book) **c** rerun, in television schedules. **27** Republican: *D for Democrat, R for Republican, I for Independent.* **28** Reserve, esp. in combination: *USNR = United States Navy Reserve.* **29** resistance: **a** *physics* (esp. electrical or acoustic or radiation resistance); **b** *biology* (esp. genetic factor in bacteria that codes for resistance to antibiotics): *R-factors;* **c** *construction* (resistance to heat flow provided by insulating material): *R-value.* **30** resistor. **31** *also* **R.** respiration. **32** *also* **R.** respond, response (in liturgies). **33** restricted, restriction (of a government publication, a military area, a motion picture rating indicating a film not suitable for audiences under 17 years old). **34** retard (slow the action of clock movements), retarder. **35** return, as on a round-trip ticket, typewriter keyboard, blueprint of a circulation system. **36** reverse, esp. of machinery such as the transmission of an automobile. **37 a** rial (monetary unit of Iran, Oman, and Yemen Arab Republic). **b** riyal (monetary unit of Qatar and Saudi Arabia). **38** King Richard (in listing plays by Shakespeare): *R2 = King Richard the Second; R3 = King*

Richard the Third. **39 a** *also* **R.** right (as a direction such as right hand) *music*; right side of a stage *theater*; right foot *dancing*. **b** right (correct). **40** *also* **R.** ring (closed chain of atoms) *chemistry*. **41** *also* **R.** river, esp. on maps or in combination: *Ohio R.* **42** *also* **R.** road. **43** rocket. **44** roentgen (unit of intensity of X- or gamma radiation). **45** Rook *chess*. **46** roots: R_a = secondary roots. **47** rough (of a bacterial colony, condition of the sea, etc.). **48** *also* **R.** royal, in combination: *HRH = His Royal Highness; R.A. = Royal Academy*. **49** ruble (monetary unit of Russia and other areas of the former Soviet Union). **50** *also* **R.** rule. **51** run *baseball, cricket*. **52** rupee (monetary unit of India, Pakistan, Sri Lanka, Bhutan, Nepal, Muscat and Oman, and Maldive Islands). **53** *also* **R.** rural, in combination: *R.Br. = Rural Branch* (post office). **54** Ryom (catalog of music of Vivaldi, followed by a number). **55** street, in combination: *R. Madelaine*. [French *rue*]
II a symbol for: **1** alkyl. **2** carbon stars *astronomy*. **3** correlation coefficient *statistics*. **4** eighteenth of a series (seventeenth if *J* is omitted). **5** gas constant *physics, chemistry*. **6** halogen (any element combining directly with a metal to form a salt). **7** Reynolds number (factor of fluid in a flow system) *aerodynamics*. **8** Rydberg constant (number used in a formula to express wave function in a spectral series) *astronomy*.

R_x take *pharmaceutics*. [Latin *recipe*]

°R Rankine (temperature scale).

r *I an abbreviation for:* **1** radius. **2** *also* **r.** rain. **3** range. **4** *also* **r.** rare (of species) *biology*. **5** rate: $r \times t = d$ means *rate multiplied by time equals distance*. **6** *also* **r.** received *commerce*. **7** recto (right-hand page of a two-page spread). **8** red. **9** *also* **r.** residence, resides at. **10** resistance *physics*. **11** *also* **r.** retired. **12** *also* **r.** right, esp. as a direction. **13** *also* **r.** rises. **14** *also* **r.** rod (measure of length). **15** roentgen (unit of intensity of X- or gamma radiation): *10-r/wk = 10 roentgens per week*. **16** *also* **r.** rood (square rod, unit of measure). **17** *also* **r.** Rook *chess*. **18** *also* **r.** royal (paper size). **19** *also* **r.** rubber. **20** *also* **r.** run *baseball, cricket*. **21** take. [Latin *recipe*]
II a symbol for: **1** angle of reflection *physics*. **2** correlation coefficient *statistics*. **3** eighteenth of a series (seventeenth if *j* is omitted). **4** not traded, as of a commodity on a given stock exchange. **5** position or radius vector *physics*. **6** relative humidity *meteorology*. **7** specific refraction.

RA 1 a radioactive. **b** radioactivity. **2** *also* **R.A.** Rear Admiral. **3** reduction of area. **4** *also* **R/A** refer to acceptor *commerce*. **5** Regular Army. **6** *also* **R.A.** Republic of Argentina. **7 a** Resident Advisor (in undergraduate housing). **b** *also* **R.A.** resident alien. **8** *also* **R/A** returned to author (of proofs or manuscript). **9** rheumatoid arthritis. **10** *also* **R.A.** right ascension *astronomy*. **11** right atrium *medicine*. **12** *also* **R.A.** British **a** Royal Academy. **b** Royal Academician. **13** *British* Royal Artillery.

Ra *I an abbreviation for:* also **Ra.** Range: *Sierra Nevada Ra.*
II a symbol for: radium (chemical element).

R.A.A. 1 Rabbinical Alliance of America. **2** Royal Academy of Arts.

RAAF Royal Australian Air Force.

RAB Radio Advertising Bureau.

Rab. Rabbi.

RABAL radiosonde balloon.

Rabb. 1 Rabbinate. **2** Rabbinic (Hebrew language). **3** Rabbinical.

RAC 1 Railway Association of Canada. **2** Research Analysis Corporation. **3** *also* **R.A.C.** Royal Agricultural College. **4** Royal Armored Corps. **5** *also* **R.A.C.** Royal Automobile Club.

RACA *or* **R.A.C.A.** Royal Automobile Club of Australia.

RACE 1 rapid automatic checkout equipment *electronics*. **2** Research and Development in Advanced Communications Technology in Europe (of the E.E.C.).

RACEP random access and correlation for extended performance.

RACES Radio Amateur Civil Emergency Service.

racon *or* **RACON** (rā′kon) radar beacon.

RAD 1 (*pronounced* rad) unit of radiation (amount of absorbed dose). **2** *military*, esp. in combination: **a** radio or radiological: *RADWAR = radiological warfare; RADNOS = no radio signal*. **b** radar: *RADCM = radar countermeasures*.

Rad. Radical, in politics.

rad 1 *also* **rad.** radial. **2** radian (unit of circular measure). **3** *also* **rad.** radical or radix (root) *mathematics*. **4** *also* **rad.** radio. **5** *also* **rad.** radius. **6** (*pronounced* rad) unit of radiation (amount of absorbed dose).

RADA 1 random access and discrete address (of telephone communications and in computer use). **2** *also* **R.A.D.A.** Royal Academy of Dramatic Art.

RADAN (rā′dan) radar navigation.

radar *or* **RADAR** (rā′där) radio detecting and ranging (device for measuring the distance and often displaying an outline of an object that is usually out of view by reflecting transmitted microwaves off the object).

RADAS random access discrete address system *computers*.

RADAT (rā′dat) radar data (transmission to network of remote radar scopes).

radiac radioactivity detection, identification, and computation (measurement of amount of radiation in an area).

R.Adm. *or military* **RADM** Rear Admiral.

radn radiation.

radome (rā′dōm) radar dome (covering for radar antenna).

RADVS Radar Altimeter and Doppler Velocity Sensor (controls altitude of rocket).

RAE 1 radio astronomy explorer. **2** Royal Aircraft Establishment (now Royal Aerospace Establishment).

RAEC Royal Army Educational Corps.

R.Ae.C. Royal Aero Club.

R.Ae.S. Royal Aeronautical Society.

RAF 1 Red Army Faction (of former East Germany). **2** Royal Air Force.

RAFVR Royal Air Force Volunteer Reserve.

RAG recombination activation gene (designated as *RAG-1, RAG-2*).

RAH Royal Albert Hall (concert hall, London).

R.A.H.S. Royal Australian Historical Society.

RAI Radio and Television Agency of Italy. [Italian *Radio Audizioni Italiane*, now *Radiotelevisione Italiana*]

RAIA Royal Australian Institute of Architects.

RAIC Royal Architectural Institute of Canada.

Raj. Rajasthani (language of Rajasthan, India).

RAL resorcylic acid lactone (used in manufacture of dyes and pharmaceutics).

rall. or **rallen.** becoming slower *music*. [Italian *rallentando*]

RALS remote augmented lift system (similar to an afterburner).

RALU register and arithmetic logic unit *computers*.

RAM 1 radar-absorbing material (as used in STEALTH aircraft). **2** (*pronounced* ram) random access memory *computers*. **3** *also* **r.a.m.** relative atomic mass. **4** reverse annuity mortgage. **5** *also* **R.A.M.** Royal Academy of Music. **6** *British* Royal Arch Mason.

RAMAC random access memory accounting.

RAMARK radar marker (radar beacon).

RAMC Royal Army Medical Corps.

RAMPS resource allocation in multiprocess scheduling.

R.A.M.S. right ascension of the mean sun *navigation*.

RAN 1 request for authority to negotiate. **2** Royal Australian Navy.

RANC Royal Australian Naval College.

Rand or **RAND** research and development: *Rand Corporation*.

R&A Royal and Ancient Golf Club (Saint Andrews, Scotland).

R&B or **R and B** or **r&b** rhythm and blues (rock'n'roll with blues as its melodic element).

R&D or **R and D** research and development.

R&R or **R and R 1** rescue and recovery. **2** rest and recreation or rehabilitation. **3** *also* **r&r** or **r'n'r** rock'n'roll.

R&W or **r. and w.** rail and water *commerce*.

RANN Research Applied to National Needs (program of the National Science Foundation, to explore solutions to social, environmental, and health problems).

RANR or **R.A.N.R.** Royal Australian Naval Reserve.

RAO radio astronomy observatory.

RAOB radiosonde or radio observation, *esp. in meteorology*.

RAOC Royal Army Ordnance Corps.

RAP 1 random access programming *computers*. **2** recurrent abdominal pain. **3** redundancy adjustment of probability.

rap. rapid.

RAPCON Radar Approach Control (Center).

RAPPI random access plan position indicator.

RAR 1 radioacoustic ranging. **2** revenue agent's report (after an IRS audit).

RAREP radar report *meteorology*.

RAS 1 reticular activating system (of the cortex). **2** *also* **R.A.S.** Royal Aeronautical Society. **3** *also* **R.A.S.** Royal Agricultural Society. **4** *also* **R.A.S.** Royal Astronomical Society.

RASD or **R.A.S.D.** Reference and Adult Services Division (of the American Library Association).

RAST radioallergosorbent test (for allergic substance) *medicine*.

RASTI rapid speech transmission index (technique for electronic measurement of the intelligibility of speech).

RAT 1 ram-air turbine. **2** remote-association test. **3** rocket-assisted homing torpedo.

rat. 1 rating. **2** ration.

RATAN radio, television aid to navigation.

RATE remote automatic telemetry equipment.

RATO or **rato** rocket-assisted takeoff *aeronautics*.

RATT radio teletype.

RAV Rous-associated virus (a cause of leukemia in chickens).

RAVO Royal Army Veterinary Corps.

RAWARC radar warning circuits (National Weather Service teletype circuits to collect radar reports and other data to forecast severe weather).

RAWIN radar wind measurements.

RB 1 a radio bearing or beacon. **b** relative bearing. **2** Republic of Bolivia. **3** return to bias *computers*. **4** Rifle Brigade. **5 a** right back or fullback *sports*. **b** running back, in football.

Rb rubidium (chemical element).

rb rubber band.

RBA 1 rare bird alert (of the Linnaean Society). **2** *also* **R.B.A.** Royal Society of British Artists.

RBAF Royal Belgian Air Force.

RBC 1 a red blood cell. **b** red blood count. **2** red blood corpuscle: *RBC anemia*.

RBE relative biological effectiveness (of the doses of two different radiations necessary to produce the same biological effect).

RBI 1 require better information. **2** *also* **rbi** runs batted in *baseball*.

rbl. ruble (monetary unit of former Soviet Union).

R.Bn. radio beacon (on navigation charts).

RBS 1 *also* **R.B.S.** Royal Society of British Sculptors. **2** rutherford backscattering spectrometry *physics*.

RC 1 a radio code. **b** radio coding. **2** *also* **R.C.** Red Cross. **3** Regional Commissioner (U.S. Customs Service). **4** reinforced concrete. **5** *also* **R/C a** remote control or controlled. **b** radar control or controlled. **c** radio controlled. **6** Reserve Corps. **7** resin coated (photographic paper). **8** *also* **R-C** resistance-capacitance *electronics*. **9** reverse course. **10** *also* **R.C.** right center (esp. as a stage direction). **11** *also* **R.C.** Roman Catholic. **12** rotary combustion. **13** rough cut (of lumber in building).

r.c. release clause.

RCA 1 *also* **R.C.A.** Rabbinical Council of America. **2** Radio Corporation of America. **3** *also* **R.C.A.** Royal Canadian Academy of Arts. **4** *also* **R.C.A.** Royal College of Art.

RCB reactor containment building (of a nuclear power plant).

RCC 1 Radio Chemical Center (source of processed radioisotopes in Great Britain). **2** radio common carrier. **3** Rescue Coordination Center. **4** resistance-capacitance coupling *electronics*. **5** Revolutionary Command Council (Iraqi governmental body). **6** *also* **R.C.C.** or **R.C.Ch.** Roman Catholic Church.

rcd. or **Rcd** received.

RCDS or **R.C.D.S.** Royal College of Defence Studies.

RCE right center entrance (stage direction).

RCF 1 relative centrifugal force. **2** remote call forwarding (for telephone customers).

RCG 1 radioactivity concentration guide (description of the amount of radioactive contamination in air and water). **2** *also* **rcg** reverberation-controlled gain *electronics*.

RCI 1 radar coverage indicator. **2** Republic of the Ivory Coast. [French *République de la Cote d'Ivoire*] **3** Royal Canadian Institute.

RCJ reaction control jet.

RCL ruling case law.

RCM 1 a radar countermeasures. **b** radio countermeasures. **2** *also* **R.C.M.** Royal College of Music.

RCMP *or* **R.C.M.P.** Royal Canadian Mounted Police.

RCN *or* **R.C.N. 1** Reactor Centrum Netherlands (for planning and construction of nuclear reactors and peaceful application of atomic energy). **2** Royal College of Nursing.

RCNC Royal Corps of Naval Constructors (for design, construction, and repair of British naval ships).

RCNT Registered Clinical Nurse Teacher.

RCO 1 remote control oscillator. **2** *also* **R.C.O.** Royal College of Organists.

RCOG *or* **R.C.O.G.** Royal College of Obstetricians and Gynecologists.

RCP 1 reinforced concrete pipe. **2** *also* **R.C.P.** Royal College of Physicians.

rcpt. receipt.

RCR Regional Customs Representative (U.S. Customs Service).

RCRA Resource Conservation and Recovery Act.

RCS 1 radar cross section. **2** reaction control system (of a rocket engine). **3** reactor cooling system. **4** reentry control system (of a spacecraft). **5** remote computing service. **6** remote control system. **7** *also* **R.C.S.** Royal College of Science. **8** *also* **R.C.S.** Royal College of Surgeons.

RCSS random communication satellite system.

RCT 1 *also* **Rct.** recruit. **2** regimental combat team.

rct. receipt.

RCTL resistor-capacitor-transistor logic *electronics*.

RCU remote control unit.

RCVR *or* **rcvr** receiver, esp. a radio receiver.

RCVS *or* **R.C.V.S.** Royal College of Veterinary Surgeons.

RD 1 Dominican Republic: *RD$ = Dominican Republic peso.* [Spanish *República Dominica*] **2** reaction of degeneration *medicine.* **3** recorded demand. **4** *also* **R/D** *British* refer to drawer (of a check in banking). **5** Registered Dietitian. **6** research and development (usually *R&D*), also in combination: *RD&D = research, development, and demonstration.* **7** Road (in postal address). **8** *also* **R.D.** Rural Delivery (of post).

Rd *I an abbreviation for: also* **Rd.** road: *54 South State Rd.* *II a symbol for:* radium (chemical element; symbol replaced by *Ra*).

rd *I an abbreviation for:* **1** rad (unit of radiation, amount of absorbed dose). **2** red (esp. on surveys and navigational charts). **3** reduction. **4** *also* **rd.** rod (unit of measure). **5** *also*

rd. round (esp. of a game or sport). **6** *also* **r.d.** running days (of a ship in transit). *II a symbol for:* rutherford (measure of radioactive disintegration).

3rd *or* **3rd** third (order, rank, group): *23rd Reg. = Twenty-third Regiment.*

RDA 1 *also* **R.D.A.** African Democratic Party (replaced by *PDCI*). [French *Rassemblement Démocratique Africain*] **2** *nutrition:* **a** recommended daily allowance. **b** recommended dietary allowance. **3** retail display agreement (for book promotion). **4** Rural Development Administration.

RD&D research, development, and demonstration.

RD&E research, development, and engineering.

RDB Research and Development Board.

RDBMS relational database management system *computers.*

RDC 1 Central African Democratic Assembly (legal political party of the Central African Republic). [French *Rassemblement Démocratique Centrafricain*] **2** rail-diesel-car (self-propelled railroad passenger car). **3** running-down clause *insurance.* **4** *also* **R.D.C.** *British* Rural District Council.

RDD random digit dialing (telephone market surveys, dialing last four numbers randomly).

RDE 1 *British* Research and Development Establishment. **2** receptor-destroying enzyme.

RDF 1 radio direction finder or finding. **2** *also* **R.D.F.** Rapid Deployment Force (military unit or units immediately available for an operation).

rdg. 1 reading. **2** *also* **Rdg.** ridge.

RDGE resorcinol diglycidyl ether (used in epoxy resins).

rd hd roundhead (of a wood or machine screw).

rdm. random.

rDNA ribosomal DNA *biology.*

RDOS real time disk operating system *computers.*

RDP 1 Portuguese National Radio. [Portuguese *Radiodifusão Portuguese*] **2** rectifying-demodulating phonopneumograph (sound device used in diagnosing arthritis).

rdr radar.

RDS 1 respiratory distress syndrome. **2** *also* **R.D.S.** Royal Drawing Society.

RDT&E research, development, testing, and evaluation.

RdTh radiothorium.

rdv *or* **rdvu.** rendezvous.

RDX cyclonite (a powerful explosive used in bombs, shells, etc.). [Research and Development Explosive]

rdy ready.

RDZ radiation danger zone.

RE 1 radium emanation. **2** rare earth (element, one of the group of chemical elements 58 through 71). **3** *also* **R/E** rate of exchange. **4** real estate, esp. in combination: *REMB = Real Estate Marketing Board.* **5** religious education. **6** *also* **R.E.** revised edition. **7** right end *football.* **8** *also* **R.E.** right eye *medicine.* **9** rotary engine. **10** *British* Royal Engineers.

Re *I an abbreviation for:* **1** real: *Re z = real part of z.* **2** rupee (monetary unit of India, Mauritius, Nepal, Pakistan, Seychelles, and Sri Lanka).

II a symbol for: **1** Reynolds number (factor of fluid in a flow system, used esp. in aerodynamics). **2** rhenium (chemical element).

r.e. 1 *also* **r/e** rate of exchange. **2** reticuloendothelial (referring to cellular system that functions in freeing the body of diseased and foreign matter).

REA Rural Electrification Administration (of U.S. Department of Agriculture).

react. 1 reactance *electricity*. **2** *also* **reac.** reactor.

READI rocket engine analyzer and decision instrumentation (to warn a spacecraft pilot of trouble or to take corrective measures automatically).

Rear Adm. Rear Admiral.

Réaum. *or* **Réau.** Réaumur (temperature scale).

REB relativistic electron beam *physics*.

Rec. 1 fresh or new, *esp. in pharmaceutics*. [Latin *recens*] **2 a** Recorder (office or musical instrument). **b** Recording, esp. in combination: *Rec. Sec.* = *Recording Secretary*.

rec. 1 receipt. **2** *also* **REC a** receive. **b** receiver. **3** recent. **4** reception. **5** recipe. **6 a** record. **b** recorded. **c** recorder (device). **d** recording. **7** (*pronounced* rek) recreation: *rec. room*.

recap (rē'kap') **1** recapitulate. **2** recapitulation.

recd. *or* **rec'd.** received.

recep. reception.

recid. 1 recidivism (habitual relapse into crime). **2** recidivous.

recip. 1 reciprocal. **2** reciprocating: *recip. engn = reciprocating engine*. **3** reciprocity.

recirc. 1 recirculating. **2** recirculation.

recit. 1 recitation. **2** *also* **Recit.** recitative *music*.

reclam. reclamation.

recm. *or* **recom.** recommend.

RECMF Radio and Electronic Component Manufacturers Federation (of Great Britain).

recog. 1 recognition. **2** recognize.

recon. 1 reconcentration. **2** reconciliation. **3** recondition. **4** *also* **RECON** (rē'kon) reconnaissance. **5** reconsignment. **6** *also* **reconst.** reconstruction. **7** reconveyance.

recp. 1 reception. **2 a** reciprocal. **b** reciprocating.

recr. receiver.

Rec. Rm. recovery room.

recryst. recrystallize.

recrystn recrystallization.

Rec. Sec. Recording Secretary.

Rect. 1 Rector. **2** Rectory.

rect. 1 receipt. **2 a** rectangle. **b** rectangular. **3 a** rectified. **b** rectifier.

recur. 1 recurrent. **2** recurring.

rec.v. *or* **recvee** (rek'vē') recreational vehicle.

red. 1 *also* **Red.** redactor (editor). **2** redeemable. **3 a** reduced, reduction. **b** reducer, *esp. in photography*.

réd. edited or compiled. [French *rédigé*]

redisc. rediscount.

redox. reduction oxidation.

redup. *or* **redupl.** reduplication.

REE rare earth element (one of a group of chemical elements 58 through 71).

ref. *or* **Ref. 1** refer, refer to. **2** *also* **ref** (*pronounced* ref) referee. **3** *also* **ref a** reference: *ref. lib. = reference library*. **b** referred, referred by. **4** refined, refining. **5 a** Reformation (social, cultural, and political movement in Europe during the 16th century). **b** reformation. **c** reformed. **6** refraction. **7 a** refrigerated. **b** refrigeration. **8** refund.

Re.fa.lo. have the record before the court. [Latin *recordari facias loquelam*]

refash. refashioned.

Ref. Ch. Reformed Church.

REFCORP Resolution Funding Corporation (funding the Resolution Trust Corporation).

refd. 1 referred. **2** refund, refunded.

refg. 1 refrigerated. **2** refrigeration.

refl. 1 a reflection. **b** reflective. **2 a** reflex. **b** reflexive *grammar*, esp. in combination: *refl. pron. = reflexive pronoun*.

Reform. Reformatory.

Ref. Pres. Reformed Presbyterian.

refr. 1 refraction. **2** *also* **refrig. a** refrigerate. **b** refrigeration.

Ref.Sp. reformed spelling (any of various methods to simplify spelling of English words, usually by closer correlation with pronunciation and reduction of variety in spelling patterns).

Reg. 1 Queen. [Latin *regina*] **2** Regent. **3** Regiment. **4** Region: *Pac. Reg.* = *Pacific Region*. **5 a** Register. **b** Registered, esp. in combination: *Reg. Pharm. = Registered Pharmacist*. **c** Registrar, also in combination: *Reg. Gen. = Registrar General*. **d** Registry. **6** Regular: *Reg. Army*. **7 a** Regulation. **b** (*plural pronounced* regz) Regulations.

reg. 1 region: *metro. reg. = metropolitan region*. **2 a** register. **b** registered. **c** registration. **3 a** registrar. **b** registry. **4 a** regular. **b** regularly. **c** regulation. **d** regulator.

REGAL (rē'gəl) range and elevation guidance for approach and landing *aeronautics*.

regd. *or* **Regd** registered.

regen. 1 regenerate. **2** regeneration.

reg. gen. general rule (of the court). [Latin *regula generalis*]

Reg. Jud. register of judicial writs *law*. [Latin *registrum judiciale*]

Reg. Lib. register book (of decrees, laws). [Latin *registrarii liber*]

Reg. Pl. rule of pleading *law*. [Latin *regula placitandi*]

Reg. Prof. Regius Professor (Crown appointment to a university chair).

Regr. Registrar.

Regs (*pronounced* regz) Regulations (as of the Internal Revenue Service).

Regt. 1 Regent. **2** Regiment.

Regtl. Regimental.

Reg. TM registered trademark.

Reg. US Pat. Off. registered at the United States Patent Office (of a trademark, product, or process).

rehab. *or* **Rehab** (rē'hab') rehabilitation.

reinf. 1 reinforced. 2 reinforcing.

REINS (rānz) radar-equipped inertial navigation system.

REIT (rēt) real estate investment trust.

rej. 1 reject. 2 rejection.

rejasing (rē jā'sing) reusing junk as something else.

REL rate of energy loss.

rel. *I an abbreviation for:* 1 **a** relating. **b** related. **c** relation. 2 **a** relative: *rel. pron. = relative pronouns.* **b** relatively. 3 relay. 4 **a** release. **b** released. 5 relic, relics. 6 **a** relief, esp. of a valve. **b** relieve. **c** relieved. 7 *also* **Rel. a** religion. **b** religious.
II a symbol for: reluctance (resistance to magnetic lines of force).

Relig. 1 religion. 2 *also* **relig.** religious.

REM (*pronounced* rem) 1 rapid eye movement (movement of the eyes during period of dreaming). 2 *also* **rem** roentgen equivalent man (old unit of absorbed dose of radiation).

rem. 1 **a** remainder. **b** remaining. 2 remarks. 3 remittance. 4 removed.

REMC Radio and Electronics Measurements Committee.

R.E.M.E. *or* **REME** Royal Electrical and Mechanical Engineers.

REMS (*pronounced* remz) rapid eye movement sleep (period of sleep accompanied by movement of the eyes during dreaming).

REMT radiological emergency medical team.

Ren. Renaissance (cultural revival in Europe during the 14th to 17th centuries).

Renamo *or* **RENAMO** Mozambique National Resistance. [Portuguese *Resistência Nacional Moçambicana*]

RENFE national rail system of Spain. [Spanish *Red Nacional de los Ferrocarriles Españoles*]

R.Eng. Royal Engineers.

renv. 1 renovate. 2 renovation.

reo (rē'ō) respiratory enteric orphan: *reovirus.*

reorg. reorganization.

REP *or* **r.e.p.** roentgen equivalent physical (superceded by *rad*).

Rep 1 *also* **rep** (*pronounced* rep) **a** repertory. **b** Repertory Company *or* Theater. 2 **a** *also* **rep** (*pronounced* rep) representative, esp. a sales representative. **b** *also* **Rep.** Representative (usually an elected official). 3 *also* **Rep.** Republic: *French Rep.* 4 *also* **Rep.** Republican.

rep. 1 repair. 2 repeat. 3 **a** report. **b** reported. **c** reporter. 4 reputation.

REPC Regional Economic Planning Council.

repet. let it be repeated *pharmaceutics.* [Latin *repetatur*]

repl. 1 replace. 2 replacement.

REPM rare earth permanent magnet (made from cobalt).

repo (rē'pō') 1 **a** repossess. **b** repossessed property. 2 repossession.

repr. 1 **a** represented. **b** representing. 2 **a** reprint. **b** reprinted.

repro (rē'prō') *or* **repro.** reproduction.

rept. 1 receipt. 2 *also* **Rept.** report. 3 reptile.

Repub. 1 Republic. 2 Republican.

repub republication.

repunit (rep'yü'nit) repeating unit (number having one or more identical integers, such as 11, 111, 1111, etc.).

req. 1 request. 2 **a** require. **b** *also* **req'd** required. **c** *also* **reqn** requisition.

RER rough-surfaced endoplasmic reticulum *medicine.*

RERP Radiological Emergency Response Plan.

RES 1 restore *computers.* 2 reticuloendothelial system (cellular system that functions in freeing the body of diseased and foreign matter).

Res. 1 Research: *Res. Asst. = Research Assistant.* 2 Reservation. 3 Reserve. 4 Reservoir. 5 Resident: *Res. Phys. = Resident Physician.* 6 Resolution: *Jt.Res. = Joint Resolution.*

res. 1 resawed (of lumber). 2 *also* **resc.** rescue. 3 research. 4 **a** reserve. **b** reserved. 5 reservoir. 6 **a** resident. **b** residence. **c** resides, resides at. 7 *also* **res a** *also* **resid** residual, as of oil. **b** residue. 8 **a** *also* **resign.** resignation. **b** *also* **resgn'd** resigned. 9 *also* **resist.** *physics, electronics:* **a** resistance. **b** resistor. 10 resolution *optics.* 11 resonator *electronics.*

RESA Research Society of America.

resp. 1 respective, respectively. 2 *also* **respir. a** respiration. **b** respiratory. 3 respondent. 4 responsible.

RESPA Real Estate Settlement Procedures Act (disclosure of closing costs in real estate transactions).

rest. 1 *also* **restr.** restaurant. 2 **a** restoration. **b** restored. 3 **a** restrict. **b** *also* **restr.** restriction.

resub. resubmit.

Resurr. Resurrection.

Ret the Net (constellation). [Latin *Reticulum*]

ret. 1 **a** retain. **b** retainer (fee for services). 2 retard. 3 retired. 4 return, returned.

retd. 1 retained. 2 retired. 3 *also* **ret'd.** returned.

R. et I. 1 King and Emperor. [Latin *Rex et Imperator*] 2 Queen and Empress. [Latin *Regina et Imperatrix*]

RETMA Radio, Electronics, Television Manufacturers Association (now *EIA*).

retnr. retainer (fee for services).

RETRF Rural Electrification and Telephone Revolving Fund.

RETRO *or* **Retro** (ret'rō) retrofire officer (engineer in charge of firing retrorockets of a spacecraft).

retro (ret'rō) *or* **retro.** 1 retroactive. 2 retrofire. 3 retrofit. 4 retrorocket.

retrog. retrogressive.

Rev. 1 Revelation (book of the New Testament). 2 Revenue (of the U.S. Internal Revenue Service): *Rev. Rul. = Revenue Ruling.* 3 Reverend: *Very Rev.* 4 Review: *Sewanee Rev.; Rev. Proc. = Review Procedures.* 5 Revised: *Rev. Ver. = Revised Version.* 6 Revolution: *Am. Rev. = American Revolution.*

rev. 1 revenue. 2 **a** reverse. **b** reversed. 3 **a** review. **b** reviewed. 4 **a** revise. **b** revised: *rev. ed. = revised edition.*

c revision. **5 a** also **rev** (pronounced rev) revolution: rev/min = revolutions per minute. **b** revolving. **6** revolver.

Revd. Reverend.

Rev'g. reversing (lower-court decision).

revol. 1 revolution. **2** also **Revol. a** Revolution: French Revol. **b** Revolutionary (of a political group).

revs (pronounced revz) revolutions: revs/sec = revolutions per second.

Rev. Stat. Revised Statutes.

Rev. Ver. Revised Version (of the Bible).

Rew. 1 reward. **2** also **REW** rewind (of a film or tape).

REX robotic excavator (sonar-guided to find buried utility pipelines).

RF 1 also **R.F.** forested routes (on walking maps). [French routes forestières] **2** also **R.F.** French Republic. [French République Française] **3** also **R-F** radio frequency. **4** range finder. **5 a** rapid-fire. **b** rim-fire (of ammunition). **6** releasing factor (of a hormone). **7** replicating form (of DNA in a virus) genetics. **8** representative fraction (in constructing map quadrants). **9** also **R.F.** Reserve Force. **10 a** rheumatic fever. **b** rheumatoid factor. **11** right field, right fielder baseball. **12** right foot, esp. in dance notation. **13** right forward sports. **14** right fullback sports. **15** rough finish (of paper).

Rf rutherfordium (chemical element; accepted form Ru).

rf 1 also **r.f.** or **r-f** radio frequency . **2** also **r.f.** rapid-fire. **3** reducing flame (flame used as a reducing agent) chemistry. **4** reinforcing (sudden crescendo) music. [Italian rinforzando] **5** roof.

RFA Royal Field Artillery.

R.F.A.C. Royal Fine Art Commission.

RFB 1 Recording for the Blind. **2** also **r.f.b.** right fullback sports.

RFC 1 also **rfc** radio frequency choke electronics. **2** Reconstruction Finance Corporation (part of economic program in Herbert Hoover's and Franklin Roosevelt's administrations). **3** also **R.F.C.** Royal Flying Corps (now RAF). **4** also **R.F.C.** Rugby Football Club.

RFD 1 Reentry Flight Demonstration (simulator for flight training). **2** Rural Free Delivery: an RFD mail carrier.

RFE Radio Free Europe.

RFFSA Federal Railways of Brazil. [Portuguese Rede Ferrocarril Federal Sedada Anonima]

RFG reformulated gas (oxygenated gasoline to reduce emissions).

rfg. roofing.

RFH Royal Festival Hall (concert hall, London).

RFI 1 radio frequency interference. **2** request for information.

rfl. refuel.

RFLP (rif'lip) **1** restriction fragment-length polymorphism (fragments of DNA cut by restriction enzyme, used as genetic markers).

RFN or **R.F.N.** Registered Fever Nurse.

RFP 1 request for proposals. **2** reverse field pinch physics.

RFQ request for quotation commerce.

RFR radio-frequency radiation.

rfrd referred.

RFU Rugby Football Union.

rfz reinforcing (sudden crescendo) music. [Italian rinforzando]

RG 1 also **R.G.** general rule or order of court law. [Latin Regula Generalis] **2** Reader's Guide to Periodical Literature. **3** red-green (of colorblindness). **4** also **r.g.** right guard sports.

rg row, esp. in needlework. [French rang]

RGA residual gas analyzer.

RGB red-green-blue (color separations of light for photographic film or electronic transmission).

Rgd. registered.

Rge Range: Mt. Rge = mountain range.

RGG Royal Grenadier Guards.

RGN or **R.G.N.** Registered General Nurse.

Rgn or **rgn** region.

RGO or **R.G.O.** Royal Greenwich Observatory.

R.G.S. or **RGS** Royal Geographical Society.

RGT resonant gate transistor.

Rgt. Regiment.

RGU red, green, and ultraviolet (of a method of assessing the magnitude of a star by viewing through filters): RGU system.

RH 1 relative humidity. **2** right halfback sports. **3** also **R.H.** right hand. **4** Rockwell hardness (measure of hardness of a metal or alloy). **5** roundhead (of a screw or bolt). **6** also **R.H.** Royal Highness, esp. in combination: HRH = His Royal Highness. **7** running head (title or other matter at the top of a printed page).

Rh 1 Rhesus factor (antigen found in red blood cells of most humans and higher mammals): Rh+ = Rhesus factor positive (indicating presence of the Rh antigen; its absence is noted by Rh−). **2** rhodium (chemical element).

rh 1 also **r.h.** relative humidity. **2** also **rh.** rheumatic. **3** also **r.h.** right hand.

rhap. rhapsody.

RHB or **r.h.b.** right halfback sports.

RHC regional holding company (any of various satellite telephone companies formed from breakup of AT&T).

RHEED reflection high-energy electron diffraction.

RHEL Rutherford High Energy Laboratory.

rheo. rheostat.

rhet. 1 rhetoric. **2** rhetorical.

RHI range-height indicator.

R. Hist. S. Royal Historical Society.

RHM roentgens per hour at one meter distance.

rhom 1 a rhombic. **b** rhomboid. **2** rhombus.

rhp or **r.h.p.** rated horsepower.

RHQ Regimental Headquarters.

RHR 1 resting heart rate. **2** Royal Highland Regiment (popularly known as the Black Watch).

r/hr roentgens per hour.

R.H.S. or **RHS** 1 Royal Historical Society. 2 Royal Horticultural Society. 3 Royal Humane Society.

rhs 1 right-hand side. 2 roundheaded screw.

RI 1 also **R.I. a** King and Emperor. [Latin *Rex et Imperator*] **b** Queen and Empress. [Latin *Regina et Imperatrix*] 2 radio inertial (guidance). 3 read in *computers*. 4 refractive index (index of refraction). 5 reinsurance. 6 also **R.I.** religious instruction. 7 respiratory infection *or* illness. 8 retroactive inhibition (failure to remember or learn something because a similar fact or action has interrupted the learning process) *psychology*. 9 Rhode Island: **a** (Zip Code). **b** also **R.I.** (in general use). 10 also **R.I.** Rotary International. 11 also **R.I. a** Royal Institute (of Painters in Water Colours). **b** Royal Institution (for dissemination of scientific knowledge, London).

r.i. 1 refractive index (index of refraction). 2 **a** rubber insulated. **b** rubber insulation.

RIA 1 radioimmunoassay (chemical analysis by labeling a substance with a radioactive substance). 2 also **R.I.A.** Research Institute of America. 3 also **R.I.A.** Royal Irish Academy.

RIAA Recording Industry Association of America (esp. referring to a standardized curve of the acoustic characteristics in phonograph recording frequencies).

RIAI or **R.I.A.I.** Royal Institute of Architects of Ireland.

RIAM or **R.I.A.M.** Royal Irish Academy of Music.

RIAS or **R.I.A.S.** Royal Incorporation of Architects of Scotland.

rib. 1 ribbon. 2 ribose (sugar present in all plant and animal cells).

RIBA or **R.I.B.A.** Royal Institute of British Architects.

RIC 1 Remote Interactive Communications (expert computer systems). 2 Royal Institute of Chemistry (now *RSC*). 3 also **R.I.C.** Royal Irish Constabulary.

Rich. Richard, also in combination: *Rich.II* = *King Richard the Second*; *Rich.III* = *King Richard the Third* (plays by Shakespeare).

RICO (rē'kō') Racketeer Influenced and Corrupt Organizations (referring to laws to investigate and prosecute organized crime).

RID Radio Intelligence Division (of the Federal Communications Commission).

RIF 1 Reading Is Fundamental (literacy group). 2 **a** also **R.I.F.** reduction in force (notice of dismissal of government employees). **b** reduction in forces; MRF (usually, mutual reduction in forces, a term used in disarmament talks). 3 Resistance-Inducing Factor.

RIFF raster (rectangular pattern of lines) image file format (conversion of a picture in pixels for graphics storage) *computers*.

riflip or **RIFLIP** (rif'lip) restriction fragment-length polymorphism (fragments of DNA cut by restriction enzymes, used as genetic markers); RFLP.

R.I.I.A. or **RIIA** Royal Institute of International Affairs.

RIM 1 reaction injection molding. 2 receipt, inspection, and maintenance (as of a missile received at its operational base).

rinf. reinforcing (sudden crescendo) *music*. [Italian *rinforzando*]

RIOP or **R.I.O.P.** Royal Institute of Oil Painters.

RIP 1 also **R.I.P.** may he or she rest in peace. [Latin *requiescat in pace*] 2 raster (rectangular pattern of lines) image processor (conversion of pixel data into a picture) *computers*. 3 remote instrument package. 4 rest in proportion (instruction for enlarging or reducing printing type or parts of a layout).

rip 1 full orchestra *music*. [Italian *ripieno*] 2 also **rip.** ripped (of lumber).

RISA radioactive iodine serum albumen (for testing blood volume).

RISC reduced instruction set computer.

rit. or **ritard.** becoming slower *music*. [Italian *ritardando*]

riten. slower *music*. [Italian *ritenuto*]

riv. 1 revised. [Italian *riveduto*] 2 also **Riv.** river.

RJE remote job entry *computers*, also in combination: *RJET* = *remote job entry terminal*.

RK 1 also **rk** radial keratotomy (incision of the cornea) *medicine*. 2 run of kiln (of pottery).

Rk or **rk** rock (on surveys and navigational charts).

RKO Radio-Keith-Orpheum (motion-picture company).

rkt. rocket.

rky rocky **a** (on surveys and navigational charts). **b** also **Rky.** (in place names): *Rky. Mts.* = *Rocky Mountains*.

RL 1 Radio Liberty (of U.S. Information Service, transmitting to the former Soviet Union and Afghanistan). 2 radio location. 3 random length (of lumber). 4 reference library. 5 research laboratory. 6 also **R.L.** Revised Laws. 7 rocket launcher.

RLF 1 reduced layer formation. 2 retrolental fibroplasia (fibrous thickening of tissue behind the lens in the eye).

RLIN Research Libraries Information Network.

RLL run-length limited (of data stored by code rather than character-by-character).

R.L.O. Returned Letter Office.

RLS Robert Louis Stevenson.

RLT Registered Laboratory Technician.

Rltr. Realtor.

Rly. or **rly.** railway: *Rly. Sta.* = *Railway Station*.

RM 1 registered midwife. 2 also **r.m.** reichsmark. 3 also **R.M.** resident magistrate (former British justice in a colony or in Ireland). 4 Rocky Mountains: *NRM* = *northern Rocky Mountains*. 5 also **R.M.** Royal Mail. 6 also **R.M.** Royal Marines.

r/m revolutions per minute.

rm. 1 ream (of paper). 2 room.

r.m. ring micrometer.

R.M.A. Royal Military Academy.

RMB People's Currency (of the People's Republic of China). [Chinese pinyin *Renminbi*]

R.M.C.M. Royal Manchester College of Music.

r.m.d. ready money down.

R.Met.S. Royal Meteorological Society.

RMI radio magnetic indicator.

r/min revolutions per minute.

R.M.I.T. Royal Melbourne Institute of Technology.

r.m.m. or **rmm** relative molecular mass.

RMN or **R.M.N.** Registered Maternity Nurse.

R.M.O. Resident Medical Officer, in Australia, New Zealand, and India.

RMP Royal Military Police.

RMR 1 resting metabolic rate *medicine*. **2** Royal Marine Reserve.

RMS 1 remote manipulator system (arm on a spacecraft, used to launch or retrieve payloads in space). **2** root mean square *mathematics*. **3 a** Royal Mail Service. **b** *also* **R.M.S.** Royal Mail Steamship. **4** Royal Meteorological Society. **5** *also* **R.M.S.** Royal Microscopical Society.

rms 1 *also* **rms.** reams (of paper). **2** *also* **rms.** rooms. **3** *also* **r.m.s.** root mean square *mathematics*.

RMSE or **rmse** or **r.m.s.e.** root mean square error *mathematics*.

RMT Registered Medical Technician.

RN *I an abbreviation for*: **1** radionavigation. **2** *also* **R.N.** Registered Nurse. **3** *also* **R.N.** Royal Navy.
II a symbol for: Reynolds number (factor of fluid in a flow system).

Rn radon (chemical element).

RNA 1 National Radio of Angola. [Portuguese *Rádio Nacional de Angola*] **2** *also* **rna** ribonucleic acid (molecule carrying instructions from a gene to the assembly of proteins).

RNAase or **RNase** ribonuclease (enzyme active in breakdown of ribonucleic acid).

RNAP ribonucleic acid phosphorus.

r'n'b rhythm and blues (rock'n'roll with blues as its melodic element) *music*.

RNC 1 Republican National Committee. **2** *also* **R.N.C.** Royal Naval College.

RNCM Royal Northern College of Music (of Manchester).

rnd. 1 round. **2** *also* **rnd** round, as a direction in knitting.

Rng. Range.

R.N.L.I. Royal National Lifeboat Institution (British sea rescue service).

RNP ribonucleoprotein (involved in the synthesis of proteins in cells).

RNR or **R.N.R.** Royal Naval Reserve.

r.'n'r. rock'n'roll (popular music with strong beat).

R.N.S.C. or **RNSC** Royal Naval Staff College.

RNSS or **R.N.S.S.** Royal Naval Scientific Service.

RNTE Royal Naval Training Establishment.

RNWMP or **R.N.W.M.P.** Royal Northwest Mounted Police (now *RCMP*).

rnwy runway.

RNXS Royal Naval Auxiliary Service.

RNZ or **R.N.Z.** Radio New Zealand.

RNZAC Royal New Zealand Armoured Corps.

RNZAF or **R.N.Z.A.F.** Royal New Zealand Air Force.

RNZAS Royal New Zealand Astronomical Society.

RNZIR Royal New Zealand Infantry Regiment.

RNZN or **R.N.Z.N.** Royal New Zealand Navy.

RO 1 a radar operator. **b** radio operator. **2** *also* **R.O. a** Receiving Office. **b** Receiving Officer. **3** recombinant organism (virus produced by genetic engineering and contained in a vaccine). **4** Record Office, also in combination: *PRO = Public Record Office*. **5** Recruiting Officer. **6** *also* **R.O.** Regimental Order (with a number). **7** reverse osmosis (process for purification of liquid by forcing it through a semipermeable membrane). **8** *printing*: **a** a run-on (matter continued or added without a break). **b** runover (matter that is longer than the space assigned to it).

ro. 1 *also* **r°** recto (right-hand page of a two-page spread). **2** roan (color). **3** rood (unit of measure).

ROA 1 received on account *commerce*. **2** return on assets *commerce*, also in combination: *ROAM = return on assets managed*.

ROAD Reorganization of Army Divisions.

ROAR right of admission reserved.

rob remaining on board (of cargo) *shipping*.

Robt. or **Rob.** Robert.

ROC 1 receiver operator characteristic *communications*. **2** *also* **R.O.C.** Republic of China (Taiwan). **3** return on capital *commerce*.

ROD rewritable optical disk *computers*.

ROE return on equity *commerce*.

Roffen of Rochester (in reference to the Bishop and therefore used as his official signature). [Latin *Roffensis*]

ROFOR (rō'fôr) route forecast (of aircraft) *meteorology*.

r.o.g. or **ROG** receipt of goods *commerce*.

ROI 1 return on investment *commerce*. **2** *also* **R.O.I.** Royal Institute of Oil Painters.

ROJ range of jamming, in radio communications.

ROK a Republic of Korea (South Korea). **b** *also* **rok** (pronounced rok) soldier in the South Korean Army.

ROM (*pronounced* rom) read-only memory (computer storage system for holding permanent data).

Rom. 1 Roman: *Rom. Ant. = Roman antiquities; Rom. Hist. = Roman History*. **2** Romance, Romanic (referring to those languages derived from Latin): *Rom. Lang. = Romance Languages*. **3 a** Romania. **b** Romanian. **4** Romans (book of the New Testament). **5** *also* **Rom. & Jul.** Romeo and Juliet (play by Shakespeare).

rom. roman (type).

Rom. Cath. Roman Catholic: *Rom. Cath. Ch. = Roman Catholic Church*.

ROP 1 run of paper: *ROP advertisements* (placed anywhere in publication). **2** run of press.

ROR 1 *also* **R.O.R.** released on own recognizance *law*. **2** rocket-on-rotor (of helicopter rotor blades).

ro-ro or **RO/RO** (rō'rō') roll-on roll-off (of a ship carrying vehicles, especially loaded trucks, driven directly on board at one port and driven off at another).

ROS 1 read-only storage *computers*. **2** review of symptom *medicine, psychology*. **3 a** run-of-station (of an advertising announcement placed any time in broadcasting schedule). **b** run-of-schedule (of an advertising announcement to be kept in the same presentation).

Rosat *or* **ROSAT** Roentgen Satellite (X-ray monitoring satellite).

ROSE Research Open Systems in Europe (basis for network research) *computers*.

Rospa Royal Society for the Prevention of Accidents.

ROT remedial occupational therapy.

Rot. Rotterdam, Netherlands.

rot. 1 rotary. **2 a** *also* **Rot.** rotating (as of navigational lights). **b** rotation. **3** rotor.

R.O.T.C. *or* **ROTC** (rot′sē) Reserve Officers' Training Corps.

ROTI Recording Optical Tracking Instrument (for tracking the flight of guided missiles).

rotn. rotation.

ROTP *Canadian* Regular Officer Training Plan.

roul. roulette (separation in a sheet of postage stamps).

Roum. Roumania, Roumanian.

ROV remotely operated vehicle.

R.O.W. right of way.

Roy. Royal.

RP 1 readiness potential. **2** rear projection (of a motion picture to produce a background). **3** Received Pronunciation (type of southern British educated speech). **4** *also* **R.P.** Reformed Presbyterian. **5** Reform Party (Canadian political party). **6** *also* **R.P.** Regius Professor (Crown-appointed university chair). **7** relief pitcher *baseball*. **8** *also* **R.P.** reprint, reprinted. **9** *also* **R.P.** **a** Republic of Panama. **b** Republic of Portugal. **10** research paper. **11** retinitis pigmentosa (progressive retinal degeneration). **12** return premium *insurance*. **13** *also* **R.P.** Reverend Father. [Latin *Reverendus Pater*, French *Révérend Père*] **14** ribose phosphate (active in purine biosynthesis and pentose metabolism). **15 a** rocket powered. **b** rocket projectile. **c** rocket propellant. **16** Royal Society of Portrait Painters. **17** Rules of Procedure.

Rp *or* **Rp.** rupiah (monetary unit of Indonesia).

RPA Regional Planning Association.

RPAR Rebuttable Presumption Against Registration (procedure for regulation of the use of a hazardous substance).

RPB recognized professional body.

RPC 1 remote position control. **2** reply postcard.

RPCF Reiter Protein Complement Fixation (test for Reiter's Syndrome).

R.P.D. *or* **RPD 1** Doctor of Political Science. [Latin *Rerum Politicarum Doctor*] **2** Rocket Propulsion Department.

RPE 1 *also* **R.P.E.** Reformed Protestant Episcopal. **2** retinal pigmented epithelium (part of the retina that converts vitamin A to its original structure after absorption of light). **3** rotating platinum electrode (used in amperometric titrations).

RPF renal plasma flow *medicine*.

RPG 1 Radiation Protection Guides (amount of permissible radiation to certain body organs, measured in rems). **2** Report Program Generator (computer programming language).

R.Ph. Registered Pharmacist.

rph *or* **r.p.h.** revolutions per hour.

RPI retail price index.

RPM 1 reliability performance measure. **2** *also* **R.P.M.** British resale price maintenance (industry price fixing). **3** *also* **rpm** *or* **r.p.m.** revolutions per minute.

RPMI revolutions per minute indicator.

RPN Registered Psychiatric Nurse. **2** reverse Polish notation (algebraic notation usually without parentheses and with operating signs before or after factors).

RPO 1 Returned by Post Office. **2** *also* **R.P.O.** Royal Philharmonic Orchestra.

RPQ request for price quotation *commerce*.

RPR 1 rapid plasma reagin (test for venereal disease). **2** Union for the Republic (Gaullist republican party). [French *Rassemblement pour La République*]

RPROM reprogrammable programmable ROM (read-only memory) *computers*.

RPRT 1 rapid plasma reagin test (for venereal disease). **2** *also* **rprt.** report.

RPS 1 renal pressor substance (active in elevation of blood pressure). **2** *also* **rps** *or* **r.p.s.** revolutions per second . **3** *also* **R.P.S.** Royal Philharmonic Society. **4** Royal Photographic Society.

RPT Registered Physical Therapist.

rpt. 1 repeat. **2** *also* **Rpt.** report. **3** reprint.

RPU remote pickup unit (emergency civil defense transmitter, receiver).

RPV remotely piloted vehicle (an aircraft).

RQ 1 *also* **R/Q** request for quotation *commerce*. **2** *also* **r.q.** respiratory quotient (index of the body's use of carbohydrates and other foods).

rqmt *or* **Rqmt** requirement.

RR 1 radio range. **2** railroad. **3** *also* **R/R** raised ranch (type of domestic architecture). **4** *also* **R.R.** recovery room (in a hospital). **5** Republic of Romania. **6** Research Report. **7** respiration rate. **8** *also* **R.R.** Right Reverend. **9** rural route.

rr 1 ragged right (margin in printing). **2** *also* **rr.** of this subject. [Latin *rerum*] **3** *also* **rr.** very rare (esp. of a rule). [Latin *rarissime*]

RRB Railroad Retirement Board.

R.R.C. Royal Red Cross.

RRDC Road Racing Drivers Championship.

RRE Royal Radar Establishment (now *RSRE*).

RRL Registered Record Librarian.

RRM renegotiable rate mortgage.

rRNA ribosomal ribonucleic acid.

RRP 1 recommended retail price. **2** *also* **R.R.P.** Rotterdam Rhine Pipeline (part of the European pipeline system for carrying crude oil).

RRS 1 reciprocal recurrent selection, in stock breeding. **2** retrograde rocket system. **3** Royal Research Ship.

RRSP *Canadian* Registered Retirement Savings Plan.

RRT 1 rail rapid transit. **2** Registered Respiratory Therapist.

RRTA railroad retirement tax.

RS 1 radio station, esp. on maps. **2** receiving station. **3** recommended *or* requirement standard (of Electrical Industries Association). **4** *also* **R.S.** Recording Secretary. **5** Reformed Spelling. **6** reinforcing stimulus *psychology*. **7** *also* **R/S** rejection slip (of a manuscript). **8** related subjects. **9** *also* **rs** remote sensing, esp. in combination: *RSS = remote sensing system.* **10** respiratory syncytial (a virus). **11** *also* **R.S.** Revised Statutes. **12** *also* **r.s.** right side. **13** *also* **R.S.** Rolls Series. **14** *also* **R.S.** Royal Society.

Rs 1 reis (former monetary unit of Portugal and Brazil). **2** rupees (monetary unit of Bhutan, India, Nepal, Pakistan).

r/s revolution per second.

rs. sleet *meteorology*.

RSA 1 radar signature analysis (to identify the shape of an object). **2** Rehabilitation Services Administration. **3** Republic of South Africa. **4** Returned Services Association. **5** Rivest-Shamir-Adleman (system of algorithmic notation used for complex computation). **6** *also* **R.S.A. a** Royal Scottish Academician. **b** Royal Scottish Academy. **7** Royal Society of Antiquarians. **8** Royal Society of Arts. **9** *also* **R.S.A.** Royal Society of Australia.

RSAC Reactor Safety Advisory Committee (of Canada).

RSB 1 range safety beacon. **2** rolled steel beam.

RSC 1 Royal Shakespeare Company. **2** *also* **R.S.C.** Royal Society of Canada. **3** Royal Society of Chemistry (formerly *RIC*).

Rsch *or* **rsch** research.

RSD *or* **R.S.D.** Royal Society of Dublin.

RSE *or* **R.S.E.** Royal Society of Edinburgh.

RSG regional seat of government.

RSGB Radio Society of Great Britain (amateur radio).

R.S.G.C. *or* **RSGS** Royal Scottish Geographical Society.

RSI 1 repetitive stress *or* strain injury (as of the hand from computer typing). **2** *also* **R.S.I.** Royal Sanitary Institute.

RSJ rolled steel joint.

RSL 1 *also* **RSLA** Returned Services League of Australia. **2** *also* **R.S.L.** Royal Society of Literature.

RSM 1 Regimental Sergeant Major. **2** *also* **R.S.M.** Royal Society of Medicine.

rsn reason.

RSNA *or* **R.S.N.A.** Radiological Society of North America.

R.S.N.Z. *or* **RSNZ** Royal Society of New Zealand.

RSO 1 Radiation Safety Officer. **2** Range Safety Officer (person in charge of destroying a missile or rocket that goes off course).

RSP recirculating single pass (hemodialyzer, kidney machine).

RSPA Research and Special Programs Administration (of U.S. Department of Transportation).

RSPCA *or* **R.S.P.C.A.** Royal Society for the Prevention of Cruelty to Animals.

RSPE *or* **R.S.P.E.** Royal Society of Painter-Etchers and Engravers.

RSPP *or* **R.S.P.P.** Royal Society of Portrait Painters.

RSRE Royal Signals and Radar Establishment.

RSS 1 *also* **R.S.S.** Fellow of the Royal Society. [Latin *Regiae Societatis Socius*] **2** *also* **rss** root-sum-squares *mathematics*. **3** *also* **R.S.S.** Royal Statistical Society.

RSTR *or* **Rstr** restricted.

RSV 1 research safety vehicle. **2** respiratory syncytial virus. **3** *also* **R.S.V.** Revised Standard Version (of the Bible). **4** Rous sarcoma virus.

RSVP 1 *also* **R.S.V.P.** *or* **r.s.v.p.** please answer. [French *répondez, s'il vous plaît*] **2** restartable solid variable pulse (rocket engine). **3** Retired Senior Volunteer Program.

Rsvr. *or* **rsvr** reservoir.

RSWC *or* **R.S.W.C.** right side up with care *shipping*.

RT 1 Radio Technician. **2** *also* **R/T a** radiotelephone. **b** radiotelephony. **3** reaction time. **4** real time: *RTO = real time operation.* **5** recreational therapy. **6** *also* **R.T.** Registered Technician, esp. X-ray technician. **7** Respiratory Therapist. **8** *also* **R/T a** return trip (of a fare). **b** round trip. **9** right tackle *football*. **10** room temperature. **11** running time (of a trip or of a tape or movie).

rt 1 *also* **r.t.** reverberation time *acoustics*. **2** *also* **rt.** right.

RTA 1 Algerian Radio and Television (network). [French *Radiodiffusion Télévision Algérien*] **2** *also* **R.T.A.** Reciprocal Trade Agreement (originally passed in the R.T.A.A., Reciprocal Trade Agreements Act 1934; many are now part of GATT, General Agreement on Tariffs and Trade). **3** Regional Transportation Authority. **4** renal tubular acidosis. **5** Retired Teachers Association.

RTB 1 return to base *military*. **2** Rural Telephone Bank.

RTBF Belgian Radio and Television in French. [French *Radio-Télévision Belge de la Communauté Française*]

RTC Resolution Trust Corporation (U.S. government agency replacing FSLIC, Federal Savings and Loan Insurance Corporation).

RTCA Radio Technical Committee for Aeronautics.

RTD resistance temperature detector *physics*.

rtd. returned.

RTDS real time data system *computers*.

RTE Radio and Television of Ireland. [Gaelic *Radio Telefis Eireann*]

Rte. Route: *N.Y. Rte. 22.*

RTECS Registry of Toxic Effects of Chemical Substances.

RTF 1 French National Radio and Television. [French *Radiodiffusion Télévision Française*] **2** resistance-transfer factor (controlling genetic replication and transferability).

RTG radioisotope thermoelectric generator.

Rt. Hon. Right Honourable (title of respect): *Rt. Hon. John Green, Prime Minister of Canada.*

RTL 1 resistor transistor logic *computers*. **2** Right-to-Life (opposed to legally induced abortion).

RTM registered trademark.

RTMA Radio and Television Manufacturers Association (now *EIA*).

rtn return.

RTNDA Radio-Television News Directors Association.

RTO radiotelephone operator.

RTOL (är'tōl) reduced takeoff and landing (of an aircraft that uses less than half the standard runway).

RTP Portuguese National Radio and Television. [Portuguese *Radiotelevisão Portuguesa*]

r-tPA recombinant tissue plasminogen activator.

RTRA Radio and Television Retailers Association.

Rt. Rev. Right Reverend: *The Rt. Rev. J. P. Dee, Bishop of the Diocese of Long Island.*

Rts. rights, *esp. in finance.*

RTTY radio teletype.

RTU 1 remote terminal unit *computers.* 2 returned to unit *military.*

RTVE Spanish National Radio and Television. [Spanish *Radio Televisión Española*]

r-t-w *or* **rtw** ready-to-wear (clothes).

rty *or* **Rty** realty.

RU *or* **R.U.** 1 rat unit (unit of measure of some substance or effect sufficient to produce a detectable change in experimental animals, esp. rats) *biology, biochemistry.* 2 Rugby Union.

Ru *I an abbreviation for:* also **Ru.** 1 Rumania, Rumanian. 2 Russia, Russian.
II a symbol for: ruthenium (chemical element).

R.U. 486 *or* **RU 486** Reussel Uclaf 486 (drug that causes abortion, registered to the French pharmaceutical manufacturer Reussel Uclaf).

rub. 1 red. [Latin *ruber*] 2 rubber.

RUBISCO *or* **RuBisCO** (rü bis'kō) ribulose biphosphate carboxylase oxygenase (enzyme in photosynthesis).

RUBP *or* **RuBP** ribulose biphosphase (material acted upon by RUBISCO).

RUC *or* **R.U.C.** Royal Ulster Constabulary.

rud. rudder.

R.U.E. right upper entrance (a stage direction).

RUG resident utilization group (places nursing home patients in a care category).

RUKBA Royal United Kingdom Beneficent Association.

RULEG rule then example (in computer programming).

RUM Remote Underwater Manipulator (submersible tank with a long, jointed arm and TV system, operated from onshore).

Rum. Rumania, Rumanian.

RUN rewind and unload *computers.*

rupt. rupture.

R.U.R. Rossum's Universal Robots (play by Karel Čapek in which he introduced the word *robot*).

rurp realised ultimate reality piton (a type of small, thin piton, used in rock climbing).

Rus. *or* **Russ.** Russia, Russian.

RV 1 *also* **R/V** recreational vehicle. 2 *also* **R/V** reentry vehicle. 3 regular variable star *astronomy.* 4 relief valve. 5 *also* **Rv** rendezvous. 6 *also* **R/V** research vessel: *RV Chain.* 7 residual volume (of the lungs) *medicine.* 8 *also* **R.V.** Revised Version (of the Bible). 9 right ventricle *or* ventricular *medicine.* 10 Ryom-Vivaldi (catalog of music of Vivaldi).

rva *or* **RVA** reactive volt ampere.

R.V.C. Royal Veterinary College.

RVH right ventricular hypertrophy *medicine.*

R.V.O. Royal Victorian Order.

RVP Reid vapor pressure *aeronautics.*

RVR runway visual range *aviation.*

RVRA renal vein renin activity *medicine.*

RVSVP *or* **R.V.S.V.P.** *or* **rvsvp** please answer at once. [French *répondez vite, s'il vous plaît*]

RW 1 radiological warfare. 2 railway. 3 rain shower *meteorology.* 4 random widths (of lumber). 5 *also* **R/W** read, write *computers: R/W storage.* 6 *also* **R/W** right of way. 7 *also* **R.W. a** Right Worshipful: *R.W.G.M. = Right Worshipful Grand Master.* **b** Right Worthy: *R.W.G.T. = Right Worthy Grand Templar.* 8 runway.

r.w.b. *or* **RWB** rear-wheel brakes.

r.w.d. *or* **RWD** rear-wheel drive.

R.W.F. Royal Welsh Fusiliers.

R.W.S. *or* **RWS** Royal Society of Painters in Water Colours.

R.W.T. right when tested (of machinery).

Rwy. railway.

RX receive, receiver, also in combination: *RXD = receive data* (of computers).

Rx 1 **a** take *pharmaceutics.* **b** prescription: *Rx for a healthy summer.* [Latin *recipe*] 2 *also* **rx** tens of rupees.

Ry 1 *also* **Ry.** railway. 2 *also* **ry** Rydberg (constant in nuclear physics, usually *R*).

RZ *or* **rz** return to zero (in recording analog functions).

S

S *I an abbreviation for:* **1** *also* **S.** label *or* mark *pharmaceutics.* [Latin *signa*] **2** *also* **S.** left hand *music.* [Latin *sinister*] **3** *also* **S.** Mr. [Italian *Signor*] **4** *also* **S.** page. [German *Seite*] **5** *also* **S.** Sabbath. **6** safety (position) *football.* **7** *also* **S.** saint, esp. in combination: *S.P.S.P. = Saint Peter and Saint Paul.* **8** salinity. **9** *also* **S.** sand (on surveys and nautical charts). **10** satisfactory. **11** *also* **S.** Saturday. **12** scalar *mathematics, physics.* **13** *also* **S.** schilling (monetary unit of Austria). **14** *also* **S.** Schmieder (catalog of J. S. Bach's works). **15** *also* **S.** school, esp. in combination: *P.S.12 = Public School 12.* **16** *also* **S.** Sea. **17** *also* **S.** seaman, esp. in combination: *A.B.S. = able-bodied seaman.* **18 a** second (order in a series or unit of measurement). **b** secondary (esp. of electrical winding). **19** secret. **20 a** *also* **S.** section, as of a report, legislation, etc. (followed by a number): *S3606.* **b** cross section. **21** *also* **S.** sen (coin of Japan, Cambodia, and Indonesia). **22** *also* **S. a** Senate. **b** Senate bill (followed by a number): *S2021.* **23 a** sensation *psychology.* **b** sensitivity (of a phototube) *physics.* **24** sentence *linguistics.* **25** September. **26** sets *sports, mathematics, etc.* **27** short, esp. in clothing sizes. **28** sickle (of a gene): *SS = blood containing double genes for sickle hemoglobin.* **29** side: *C1S = coated one side of a sheet of paper; B2S = beaded two sides of a board.* **30** signature (printed on the spine or a page of each section of a book for binding). **31** *also* **/s/** signed, (referring to the name as fixed to the original copy of a letter, contract, etc.). **32** Singapore: *S$ = Singapore dollar.* **33** single, esp. in combination: *DPST = double-pole single-throw switch; SE = single-entry bookkeeping.* **34** *also* **S.** sire (in pedigrees). **35** *also* **S.** Sister (in a religious order). **36** slow, *esp. on a regulating device.* **37** small: *S (34), M (36–38), L (40–42).* **38** smooth (of a bacterial colony, condition of the sea, etc.). **39** Socialist (political party). **40** *also* **S.** society, in combination: *ASPCA = American Society for the Prevention of Cruelty to Animals; R.S. = Royal Society.* **41** soft. **42** sol (monetary unit of Peru). **43** *also* **S.** solo. **44** *also* **S.** son. **45** *also* **S.** soprano (voice). **46** *also* **S.** South, Southern (the compass point or the pole of a magnet): *SbW = South by West; SCLC = Southern Christian Leadership Conference; SC = South Carolina.* **47** *also* **S.** Spain, Spanish, esp. in combination: *AATSP = American Association of Teachers of Spanish and Portuguese.* **48** *also* **S.** spar (navigational marker). **49** *also* **S.** spherical. **50** spiral (of nebula) *astronomy.* **51** stage (of a rocket), in combination: *the first flight of the S-1C first-stage booster.* **52** *also* **S.** standard, esp. in combination: *STP = standard temperature and pressure; RSV = Revised Standard Version (of the Bible); USASI = United States of America Standards Institute; E.S.T. = eastern standard time.* **53** *also* **S.** steel, esp. in combination: *SS = stainless steel.* **54** stereo: *Stereo (S) and monophonic versions.* **55** stimulus, also in combination: *SR = stimulus response.* **56** subject: *S-V-O = subject, verb, object.* **57** sucre (monetary unit of Ecuador). **58** Sudan, Sudanese: *£S = Sudanese pound.* **59** *also* **S.** sun. **60** *also* **S.** Sunday. **61** superior. **62** surface. **63** *also* **S.** surplus. **64** Sweden, Swedish: *Skr. = Swedish krona.* **65** *also* **S.** symbol. **66** synchronized: *S sleep = synchronized sleep* (a stage of deep sleep marked by presence of synchronized delta waves). **67** Syria, Syrian: *S£ = Syrian pound.* **68** write *pharmaceutics.* [Latin *signa*]

II a symbol for: **1** action *physics.* **2** apparent power (of electrical magnetic power). **3** current density (of electrical energy). **4** elastance (of resistor capacity in electricity). **5** entropy (measure of random motion of a system) *physics.* **6** nineteenth of a series (eighteenth when *J* is omitted). **7** Poynting vector (product of electric and magnetic fields). **8** sabin (unit of measure of sound absorption). **9** San Francisco (on coins minted in San Francisco). **10** siemens (unit of electrical conductance). **11** spin quantum number *physics.* **12** Staff *military,* in combination: *S1, S2, S3, and S4 = staff functions of units smaller than a division.* **13** star of approximately equal presence of carbon and oxygen in spectrum. **14** steradian (unit of measure of solid angles). **15** stoke (unit of viscosity). **16** sulfur (chemical element). **17** Summer Load Line (Plimsoll mark to show maximum depth a ship may ride when loaded for summer sea conditions). **18** surface area. **19** Svedberg unit (measure of sedimentation).

$ 1 dollar (monetary unit of various Caribbean countries, Australia, Canada, Fiji, Hong Kong, Liberia, New Zealand, Taiwan, United States, and Zimbabwe). [origin unknown] **2** peso (monetary unit of Argentina, Bolivia, Chile, Colombia, Cuba, Dominican Republic, Guinea-Bissau, Mexico, Uruguay, and the Philippines). **3** ringgit (monetary unit of Malaysia).

s *I an abbreviation for:* **1** *also* **s.** century. [French *siècle*] **2** *also* **s.** half. [Latin *semi*] **3** *also* **s.** left. [Latin *sinister*] **4** *also* **s.** on: *Bar-s.-Seine.* [French *sur*] **5** second (order in a series or unit of measurement, esp. of time). **6** *also* **s.** section. **7** *also* **s.** series. **8** *also* **s.** set *sports, mathematics, etc.* **9** shield *electronics.* **10** shilling (former coin of Great Britain). **11** *also* **/s/** signed (referring to the name fixed to the original copy of a letter, contract, etc.). **12** silver. **13** *also* **s.** singular. **14** *also* **s.** sire (in pedigrees). **15** *also* **s.** sister. **16** slip (esp. of machinery) *physics.* **17** snow. **18** soft. **19** solid. **20** soluble, solubility, esp. in combination: *sRNA.* **21** *also* **s.** son. **22** *also* **s.** soprano (instrument). **23** *also* **s.** south, southern (the pole of a magnet or the compass point). **24** split (of a stock) *finance.* **25** *also* **s.** standard, as standard deviation or in combination: *scf = standard cubic foot; e.s.t. = eastern standard time.* **26** steel. **27** *also* **s.** stem *botany.* **28** stere (unit of cubic measure, esp. as used for firewood). **29** strange *physics: s quark = strange quark.* **30** stratus (cloud): *Ns = nimbostratus cloud.* **31** strike price (of a commodity) *finance.* **32** *also* **s.** substantive, in combination: *n.s. = noun substantive.* **33** *also* **s.** succeeded. **34** *also* **s.** sun. **35** surface, in combination: *sfpm = surface feet per minute.* **36** *also* **s.** symbol. **37** *also* **s.** without, *esp. in pharmaceutics.* [Latin *sine*]

II a symbol for: **1** condensation *physics.* **2** displacement *physics.* **3** distance or length (of a line, path, arc) *physics.*

4 entropy, esp. specific entropy (measure of random motion of a system) *physics.* **5** nineteenth of a series (eighteenth when *j* is omitted). **6** symmetrical *botany, chemistry, mathematics.*

SA 1 *also* **S.A.** according to art *pharmaceutics.* [Latin *secundum artem*] **2** *also* **S.A.** or **S/A** corporation. [French *Société Anonyme,* Spanish *Sociedad Anónima,* Italian *Società Anonima,* etc.] **3** Salvation Army. **4** *also* **S.A. a** Saudi Arabia. **b** Saudi Arabian. **5** seaman apprentice. **6** semiannual. **7** semiautomatic (of a weapon). **8** *also* **S.A.** Seventh Avenue (of fashion or the garment industry that is located on this street in New York City). **9** *also* **S.A.** sinoatrial: *S.A. node of the heart.* **10** small arms. **11** *also* **S.A.** Society of Authors. **12** *also* **S.A. a** South Africa. **b** South African. **13** *also* **S.A. a** South America: *Industries Dante Ramenzoni S.A.* **b** South American. **14** *also* **S.A. a** South Australia (state in Australia). **b** South Australian. **15** special agent. **16** storm troopers (Hitler's private army of terrorists formed in 1923). [German *Sturmabteilung*] **17** subsistence allowance. **18** surface area. **19** surface-to-air (of a missile or other weapon).

Sa *I an abbreviation for:* **1** sable (in heraldry). **2** *also* **Sa.** Saturday. **3** *also* **Sa.** or **S^a** Spanish Señora. **4** Sierra. *II a symbol for:* **1** normal spiral with pronounced nuclear regions and closely coiled arms *astronomy.* **2** samarium (chemical element).

s.a. 1 according to art *pharmaceutics.* [Latin *secundum artem*] **2** semiannual. **3** subject to approval. **4** undated or without year. [Latin *sine anno*] **5** under the year. [Latin *sub anno*]

SAA 1 small arms ammunition. **2** *also* **S.A.A.** South Atlantic Anomaly. **3** Speech Association of America. **4** Standards Association of Australia. **5** *also* **S.A.A.** systems application architecture *computers.*

SAAB (säb) Swedish aircraft and automobile manufacturer. [Swedish *Svenska Aeroplan Aktiebolaget*]

SAAEB South African Atomic Energy Board.

SAAF South African Air Force.

SAARC South Asian Association for Regional Cooperation.

S.A.B. 1 *also* **SAB** School of American Ballet. **2** Science Advisory Board. **3** Society of American Bacteriologists. **4** soprano, alto, bass *music.*

Sab. Sabbath.

SABA South African Black Alliance.

SABC South African Broadcasting Corporation.

SABR Society for American Baseball Research.

SABRA South African Bureau of Racial Affairs.

SABS South African Bureau of Standards.

SAC 1 Science Advisory Committee. **2** (*pronounced* sak) Strategic Air Command (of U.S. Department of Defense).

SACEM Society of Authors, Composers, and Editors of Music (French performing-rights organization). [French *Société des Auteurs, Compositeurs et Éditeurs de la Musique*]

SACEUR Supreme Allied Command or Commander, Europe (in Nato).

SACLANT Supreme Allied Command or Commander, Atlantic (in Nato).

SACO Swedish Confederation of Professional Organizations. [Swedish *Sveriges Aakademikers Centralorganisation*]

SACOL South African Confederation of Labor.

SACP South African Communist Party.

SACS Southern Association of Colleges and Schools.

SACSIR South African Council for Scientific and Industrial Research.

SACTU South African Congress of Trade Unions.

SAD seasonal affective disorder (mild form of depression occurring at certain seasons of the year, especially in winter).

SADCC South African Development Co-ordination Council.

SADD Students Against Drunk Driving.

SADF South African Defense Force.

SAE 1 *also* **S.A.E.** Society of American Etchers. **2** Society of Automotive Engineers: *SAE specifications.* **3** *also* **s.a.e.** stamped addressed envelope (enclosed with correspondence to hold a reply).

saec. century. [Latin *saeculum*]

SAF 1 Society of American Foresters. **2** Strategic Air Force.

S.Af. or **S.Afr. 1** South Africa: *Cape Town, S.Af.* **2** *also* **SAfr** South African, also in combination: *S.Afr.D. = South African Dutch.*

saf. safety.

SAG Screen Actors' Guild.

SAGA Society of American Graphic Artists.

SAH 1 *also* **S.A.H.** Society of American Historians. **2** subarachnoid hemorrhage *medicine.* **3** Supreme Allied Headquarters (for Nato).

SAHR Society for Army Historical Research.

SAI 1 *also* **S.A.I.** Italian corporation. [Italian *Società Anonima Italiana*] **2** Statement of Additional Information (information about an investment in addition to what is given in a prospectus, such as the financial statement of a fund).

SAIDS simian AIDS.

SAIF 1 Savings Association Insurance Fund (replacing *FSLIC*). **2** *also* **S.A.I.F.** South African Industrial Federation.

S.A.I.M.R. South African Institute of Medical Research.

SAL survey analysis language.

sal. salary.

s.a.l. according to the rules of art, esp. in pharmaceutics. [Latin *secundum artis leges*]

Sallie Mae (sal'ē mā') Student Loan Marketing Administration; SLMA.

SALP 1 South African Labour Party. **2** Systematic Assessment of Licensee Performance (evaluation of nuclear power station).

SALR saturated adiabatic lapse rate (of air) *meteorology.*

SALT (sôlt) Strategic Arms Limitation Talks.

Salv. El Salvador.

salv. salvage.

SAM 1 sampling and automatic measurement. **2** scanning acoustic microscope. **3** shared appreciation mortgage. **4** social-accounting matrix. **5** space available mail (for military, sent by U.S. Postal Service at reduced rate as space is available). **6** *also* **S-A-M** surface-to-air missile, also in combination: *SAM-D = surface-to-air missile defense.* **7** synchronous amplitude modulation.

Sam. 1 Samaritan (esp. the good Samaritan of the New Testament). 2 *also* **Sam a** Samoa. **b** Samoan. 3 Samuel (two books of the Old Testament, usually distinguished as **I Sam.**, **II Sam.**).

S.Am. *or* **S.Amer.** South America, South American.

SAMA 1 Saudi Arabian Monetary Agency (financial fund of the government of Saudi Arabia). 2 Scientific Apparatus Makers Association.

S.A.M.E. *or* **SAME** Society of American Military Engineers.

Saml. Samuel (two books of the Old Testament, usually distinguished as **I Saml.**, **II Saml.**).

SAMOS satellite and missile observation system (reconnaissance satellite of USAF).

SAMTEC Space and Missile Test Center.

SAN 1 standard address number *computers*. 2 styrene acrylonitrile (thermoplastic).

san. 1 sanitary. 2 sanitarium.

S&C 1 *also* **S.&C.** shipper and carrier. 2 *also* **s. and c.** sized and calendered (of paper).

S&D song and dance: *S&D man.*

S&F *or* **s. and f.** stock and fixtures (of a store) *insurance*.

S.&F.A. shipping and forwarding agents.

S&H 1 shipping and handling (charges) *commerce*. 2 Sundays and holidays.

S&I Directorate of Security and Intelligence (branch of the Royal Canadian Mounted Police).

S&L Savings and Loan Association.

S and M *or* **S&M** 1 sadism and masochism. 2 sadist and masochist.

S&P Standard & Poor (referring to a financial rating system and a stock-indexing system): *S&P 500.*

S&SC *or* **s. and s.c.** sized and supercalendered (of paper).

S&T 1 science and technology. 2 scientific and technical: *all S&T information.*

SANE National Committee for a Sane Nuclear Policy.

San Fran. San Francisco.

sanit. 1 sanitary. 2 sanitation.

SANR *or* **s.a.n.r.** subject to approval, no risk.

Sans. 1 *also* **sans** sans serif. 2 *also* **Sansk.** Sanskrit (ancient sacred and literary language of India).

SANZ Standards Association of New Zealand.

SAO Smithsonian Astrophysical Observatory.

SAP 1 secondary audio program (of TV, providing bilingual soundtrack, descriptive programming for the blind, etc.). 2 Social Democratic Party (of Sweden). [Swedish *Socialdemokratiska Arbetarepartiet*] 3 *also* **s.a.p.** soon as possible. 4 South African Police. 5 System Assurance Program *computers*.

sap. 1 *also* **sapon.** saponification (process of making a soap by heating an ester with an alkali), also in combination: *sap.no. = saponification number.* 2 sapwood (of lumber).

SAPA *or* **S.A.P.A.** 1 South African Press Association. 2 South African Publishers' Association.

SAPS Secondary Audio Program Services (TV channel providing bilingual soundtrack, descriptive programming for the blind, etc.).

SAR 1 safety analysis report. 2 search and rescue: *SARO = Search and Rescue Operation.* 3 semiautomatic rifle. 4 *also* **S.A.R.** Society of Authors' Representatives. 5 *also* **S.A.R.** Sons of the American Revolution. 6 *also* **S.A.R.** South African Republic. 7 synthetic-aperture radar.

Sar. 1 Sarawak. 2 **a** Sardinia. **b** Sardinian.

SARAH (sãr′ə) Search and Rescue Automatic Homing (device sending radio signal from people lost at sea).

SARBE Search and Rescue Beacon Equipment.

SARDA State and Regional Disaster Airlift.

S.A.R.L. corporation of limited liability; Ltd. [French *Société à Responsabilité Limitée*]

SARPS standards and recommended practices.

SARSAT search and rescue satellite-aided tracking.

Sarum (sãr′əm) of Salisbury (in reference to the Bishop of Salisbury and therefore used as his official signature). [Latin *Sarumensis*]

SARUS (sãr′əs) search and rescue using satellites (system to search out missile nose cones, space capsules or conventional aircraft, and ships).

SAS 1 limited liability partnership or corporation. [Italian *Società in Accomandita Semplice*] 2 *also* **s.a.s.** side, angle, side *geometry*. 3 small-angle scattering *physics, electronics*. 4 small astronomical satellite. 5 **a** sodium alkane sulfonate (detergent). **b** sodium aluminum sulfate (used in tanning, matches, as water purifier, food additive, etc.). 6 Special Air Service. 7 stability augmentation system (of an aircraft autopilot system).

SASC 1 Senate Armed Services Committee. 2 senior appointments selection committee.

SASE *or* **s.a.s.e.** self-addressed stamped envelope.

Sask. Saskatchewan.

SASOL South African coal, oil, and gas corporation.

SASP small acid-soluble spore protein.

SASS swath-sounding sonar.

SAT 1 satellite, esp. in combination: *SATCOM = satellite communications.* 2 Scholastic Aptitude Test (measure of academic skills for entrance to college). 3 *also* **S.A.T.** ships apparent time *navigation*. 4 *also* **S.A.T.** systematic assertiveness training.

SAt *or* **S.At.** South Atlantic (ocean): *SAt current.*

Sat. 1 satellite. 2 satisfactory. 3 Saturday. 4 Saturn.

sat. 1 *also* **satd.** saturated. 2 *also* **satn.** saturation.

S.A.T.B. *or* **SATB** soprano, alto, tenor, bass *music*: *Standard carolbooks gear their arrangements to the S.A.T.B. church choir.*

SATCO (sat′kō) signal automatic air traffic control.

SATCOM (sat′kom) satellite communications.

SATF Site Activation Task Force.

SATIF Scientific and Technical Information Facility (of NASA).

SATS Short Airfield for Tactical Support.

sat. sol. saturated solution.

SATW Society of American Travel Writers.

SAU standard advertising unit (unit of measure for advertising space in a publication).

S. Aus. South Australia.

SAV *British* stock at value (price quoted separately from the advertised price).

sav. savings.

SAVE Systematic Alien Verification for Entitlement.

SAW 1 space at will *advertising*. 2 surface acoustic wave *electronics*.

SAWRS supplementary airways weather-reporting station.

Sax. 1 Saxon. 2 Saxony.

sax (*pronounced* saks) saxophone.

SAYE *British* save as you earn (savings plan).

SB *I an abbreviation for:* 1 *also* **S.B.** Bachelor of Science. [Latin *Scientiae Baccalaureus*] 2 *also* **S.B.** sales book *commerce*. 3 Savings Bank, esp. in combination: *SBLI = Savings Bank Life Insurance*. 4 Senate bill (with a number). 5 short bill *commerce*. 6 simultaneous broadcast (transmission from more than one transmitter). 7 *British* single-breasted: *three-button SB suits*. 8 a small bore (of a rifle). b smooth bore (of a rifle or cannon). 9 southbound. 10 *also* **S.B.** South Britain (England and Wales). 11 *British* Special Branch (of police). 12 *also* **S-B** Stanford-Binet (an intelligence test). 13 *also* **S/B** statement of billing. 14 stolen base or bases *baseball*.
II a symbol for: barred spiral (of extragalactic nebulae) *astronomy*.

Sb 1 antimony (chemical element). [Latin *stibium*] 2 spiral having nuclear regions less conspicuous than Sa class and greater than Sc with arms wider open than Sa class *astronomy*.

sb *I an abbreviation for:* 1 *also* **s/b** should be. 2 *also* **s.b.** stolen base or bases *baseball*. 3 *also* **sb.** substantive *grammar*.
II a symbol for: stilb (unit of brightness).

SBA 1 Small Business Administration. 2 Standard Beam Approach (guided aircraft landing system).

SBAC Society of British Aeronautics Companies.

SBB Federal Railroads of Switzerland. [German *Schweizerische Bundesbahnen*]

SBC 1 small business computer. 2 *also* **S.B.C.** Southern Baptist Convention.

SBDT surface barrier diffused transistor *electronics*.

SBE subacute bacterial endocarditis *medicine*.

SbE south by east.

SBI Steel Boiler Institute (standard of rating in engineering).

SBIC *or* **S.B.I.C.** Small Business Investment Company (authorized to help finance small business).

SBLI Savings Bank Life Insurance.

SBMI School Bus Manufacturers Institute.

SBN Standard Book Number (now *ISBN*).

SBO classification of galactic nebulae between elliptical and spiral types having a bright nucleus and dark bands of matter but no distinguishable arms *astronomy*.

SBP systolic blood pressure.

SBR 1 Society for Biological Rhythm. 2 styrene-butadiene rubber (used for most domestic tires).

SBS 1 shaken baby syndrome. 2 Special Broadcasting Service (noncommercial Australian television service).

SBT surface barrier transistor *electronics*.

SBU strategic business unit.

SbW south by west.

S by E south by east.

S by W south by west.

SC 1 *also* **S.C.** same case *law*. 2 *also* **S.C.** a Sanitary Corps. b Signal Corps. c Staff Corps. 3 school certificate (examination taken by secondary school students in New Zealand, usually at the U.S. tenth-grade level). 4 *also* **S.C.** Security Council (of the UN). 5 service charge *commerce*. 6 *also* **S/C** short circuit. 7 South Carolina: a (Zip Code). b *also* **S.C.** (in general use). 8 Southern Command (of U.S. Department of Defense). 9 Space Command (of U.S. Department of Defense). 10 Staff College. 11 *also* **S.C.** steel casting. 12 *also* **S-C** sudden commencement type (magnetic storm associated with sunspots). 13 supercalendered (of paper). 14 *also* **S.C.** Supreme Court.

Sc *I an abbreviation for:* stratocumulus (cloud) *meteorology*.
II a symbol for: 1 scandium (chemical element). 2 spiral having the least conspicuous nuclear regions and with arms very loosely coiled *astronomy*.

Sc. 1 Scandinavia. 2 scene (of a play). 3 science. 4 a Scotch, Scottish. b Scotland, Scots.

sc 1 *also* **sc.** he or she engraved or carved it. [Latin *sculpsit*] 2 *also* **sc.** namely. [Latin *scilicet*] 3 scale. 4 *also* **sc.** scene (of a play). 5 screw. 6 *also* **sc.** scruple (apothecaries' weight). 7 *also* **s.c.** *or* **s/c** single column, esp. in accounting and printing. 8 *also* **s.c.** single crochet (a direction in needlework). 9 *also* **s.c.** (of paper): a sized and calendered. b supercalendered. 10 *also* **s.c.** small capitals (typesetting instruction). 11 *also* **s.c.** subcutaneous *medicine*.

SCA 1 Science Clubs of America. 2 sex chromosome abnormalities. 3 sickle cell anemia. 4 Standard Consolidated Area. 5 Supervising Customs Agent (of U.S. Customs Service).

SCAF Supreme Commander Allied Forces.

SCAMA switching, conference, and monitoring arrangements (system by which one operator can hold telephone conferences worldwide).

Scan. *or* **Scand.** Scandinavia, Scandinavian.

SC&S *or* **s.c. and s.** strapped, corded, and sealed *shipping*.

scan. mag. defamation of dignity *law*. [Latin *scandalum magnatum*]

SCAP 1 silent, compact auxiliary power. 2 Supreme Commander for the Allied Powers (former position of Douglas MacArthur in Japan after WWII).

SCAPA *or* **S.C.A.P.A.** Society for Checking the Abuses of Public Advertising.

s.caps. small capitals (typesetting instruction).

SCAR 1 Scandinavian Council for Applied Research. 2 Special Committee on Antarctic Research. 3 Submarine Celestial Altitude Recorder (system of determining latitude and longitude under water).

SCAT 1 School and College Ability Test. 2 security control of air traffic. 3 sheep cell agglutination test. 4 silicon controlled avalanche transistor *electronics*. **5** supersonic commercial air transport.

SCATS sequential controlled automatic transmitter start *computers*.

Sc.B. Bachelor of Science: *Sc.B.E.* = *Bachelor of Science in Engineering*. [Latin *Scientiae Baccalaureus*]

SCBU special care baby unit.

SCC 1 Science Council of Canada. **2** stress corrosion cracking *engineering*.

S.C.C.A. *or* **SCCA** Sports Car Club of America.

SCD 1 *also* **scd.** screwed (of construction). **2** sudden cardiac death *medicine*.

Sc.D. Doctor of Science: *Sc.D.Med.* = *Doctor of Medical Science*. [Latin *Scientiae Doctor*]

Scd. *or* **scd** scheduled.

SCDE schools, colleges, and departments of education.

SCE 1 schedule compliance evaluation. **2** *also* **S.C.E.** Scottish Certificate of Education. **3** standard calomel electrode (for measuring potential of electrodes) *physics*.

SCEAR Scientific Committee on the Effects of Atomic Radiation (UN agency to study radiation effects on environment).

S.C.EE.RR. Sacred Congregation of Bishops and Regulars. [Latin *Sacra Congregatio Episcoporum et Regularium*]

SCEL Signal Corps Engineering Laboratories.

SCERT Systems Computer Evaluation and Review Technique (descriptions of computers and ancillary equipment).

SCF Save the Children Fund.

scf *or* **s.c.f.** standard cubic foot, esp. in combination: *scfm* or *s.c.f.m.* = *standard cubic feet per minute*.

SCG *or* **S.C.G.** seismocardiography.

scg scoring.

Sc. Gael. Scotch Gaelic (Gaelic as spoken in Scotland).

SCGB *or* **S.C.G.B.** Ski Club of Great Britain.

Sch. 1 *also* **SCH** schedule (esp. on tax forms): *Sch.D.* **2** schilling (monetary unit of Austria). **3 a** School. **b** Scholar. **4** schooner.

sch. 1 school (esp. on maps). **2** *also* **sch** note or explanation. [Latin *scholium*]

sched. schedule.

schem. schematic.

Scherz. lively, sportive *music*. [Italian *scherzando*]

schol. 1 a scholarship. **b** scholastic. **2** note *or* explanation. [Latin *scholium*]

Schr. *or* **schr.** schooner: *The Schr. Rival, wrecked on McNab's Island.*

SCI 1 Science Citation Index (publication). **2** *also* **sci** single column inch (in measuring advertising space in a publication). **3** *also* **S.C.I.** Society of the Chemical Industry.

Sci. *or* **sci. 1** science. **2** scientific.

SCID severe combined immunodeficiency disease.

sci. fa. that you cause to know *law*. [Latin *scire facias*]

sci-fi (sī′fī′) science fiction: *the sci-fi world of monsters.*

scil. namely. [Latin *scilicet*]

S.C.J. Society of Priests of the Sacred Heart of Jesus. [Latin *Societas Cordis Jesu*]

S.C.L. Scottish Central Library. **2** Student of Civil Law.

Scl the Sculptor (constellation).

scl. scale.

SCLC Southern Christian Leadership Conference (founded by Martin Luther King Jr.).

SCM 1 *also* **S.C.M.** Student Christian Movement. **2** Summary Court-Martial.

Sc.M. Master of Science: *Sc.M.Hyg.* = *Master of Science in Hygiene*. [Latin *Scientiae Magister*]

SCMS Serial Copy Management System (mechanism to prevent copying of audio and video tapes).

SCN suprachiasmatic nucleus (cluster of brain cells identified with the body's biological clock).

SCNA sudden cosmic noise absorption (absorption by the earth's atmosphere of radio-frequency radiation from cosmic sources).

SCO selective conscientious objector.

Sco Scorpius *or* Scorpio (constellation).

S.Con.Res. Senate concurrent resolution (followed by a number).

SCOR Scientific Committee on Oceanic Research (of the International Council of Scientific Unions).

SCORE Service Corps of Retired Executives (of Small Business Administration).

Scot. 1 a Scotch (esp. of whiskey). **b** Scottish. **2** Scotland.

Scotl. Scotland.

SCOTUS Supreme Court of the U.S.

SCP 1 *also* **S.C.P.** single-cell protein. **2** Social Credit Party (of Canada). **3** *also* **scp** *or* **s.cp.** *or* **s.c.p.** spherical candlepower.

SCPC single channel per carrier *electronics*.

S/CPO Senior Chief Petty Officer.

SCPS Society of Civil and Public Servants (of Great Britain).

SCR 1 selective catalytic reduction (exhaust-gas treatment technology). **2** silicon-controlled rectifier (type of transistor).

scr. 1 *also* **scr** screw. **2** scrip *commerce*. **3** scruple (apothecaries' weight).

Script. 1 *also* **script.** manuscript. **2** *also* **Scrip. a** Scripture, Scriptures. **b** Scriptural.

scrn screen.

scRNA small cytoplasmic RNA.

SCRTD Southern California Rapid Transit District.

SCS 1 silicon-controlled switch *electronics*. **2** Society for Computer Simulation. **3** Soil Conservation Service (of U.S. Department of Agriculture). **4** space communication system.

SCSA standard consolidated statistical area.

SCSI small computer system interface.

SCT surface charge transistor.

Sct the Shield (constellation). [Latin *Scutum*]

SCTR Standing Conference on Telecommunications Research.

sctr. sector.

scty secretary.

SCU 1 also **S.C.U.** Scottish Cycling Union. **2** special care unit.

scuba (skü′bə) self-contained underwater breathing apparatus.

sculp. or **sculpt. 1** also **sculps.** he or she carved or engraved it. [Latin *sculpsit*] **2 a** sculptor. **b** sculpture. **c** sculptural.

SCV State of Vatican City. [Italian *Stato della Città del Vaticano*]

SD 1 also **S.D.** Doctor of Science. [Latin *Scientiae Doctor*] **2** also **S/D a** sea damaged *shipping*. **b** storm damaged *insurance*. **3** Security Service (of the Gestapo in Nazi Germany). [German *Sicherheitsdienst*] **4** also **S.D.** semidiameter (radius). **5** also **S/D** sight draft *commerce*. **6** skin dose (measure of radiation exposure). **7** Social Democrat. **8** solid-drawn (esp. of a process of making metal tubing). **9** South Dakota: **a** (Zip Code). **b** also **S.D.** (in general use). **10** also **S.D.** Special Delivery. **11** Special Duty. **12** stage door. **13** standard deviation *statistics*. **14** also **S.D.** State Department. **15** streptodornase (enzyme to dissolve blood clots, pus, etc.). **16** Supply Department or Depot. **17** without a date (esp. of a publication). [French *sans date*]

sd 1 also **s.d.** same day. **2** also **sd.** sand. **3** also **s.d.** see above. [German *siehe dies*] **4** several dates. **5** also **sd.** sewed (of bookbinding). **6** also **s.d.** sight draft *commerce*. **7** also **sd.** signed (of a document, check, letter, etc.). **8** also **Sd** sound. **9** also **s.d.** standard deviation *statistics*. **10** also **s.d. a** without a date (esp. of a publication). [French *sans date*] **b** indefinitely, without a day being fixed (esp. of an adjournment). [Latin *sine die*]

SDA 1 Scottish Development Agency. **2** also **S.D.A.** Seventh Day Adventists. **3** Source Data Automation *computers*. **4** specific dynamic action (energy expended during digestion and utilization of foods).

S. Dak. South Dakota.

SDAT senile dementia, Alzheimer's type.

SDBL or **S/D B/L** sight draft, bill of lading attached.

SDC 1 signal data converter *electronics*. **2** submersible decompression chamber. **3** System Development Corporation.

SDD 1 also **S-D-D** store to door delivery. **2** *British* subscriber direct dialing (of a telephone system).

SDDC sodium dimethyldithiocarbamate (used esp. as an insecticide).

SDECE Foreign Intelligence and Counterespionage Service (of France). [French *Service de Documentation Extérieure et de Contre-Espionage*]

SDF 1 Self-Defense Forces (of Japan, the armed services). **2** Social Democratic Federation.

sdg. siding (esp. of building materials).

SDI 1 also **S.D.I.** selective dissemination of information (furnishing selected scientists with new technical information). **2** Strategic Defense Initiative, also in combination: *SDIO = Strategic Defense Initiative Organization*.

sdl. saddle.

SDLC synchronous data link control *computers*.

SDLP Socialist and Democratic Labour Party (of Northern Ireland).

SDMJ September, December, March, June (quarterly months, esp. for payments) *commerce*.

SDO Special Development Order (special British Parliamentary bill).

S. Doc. Senate Document (followed by a number).

SDP Social Democratic Party (of various countries).

SDR special drawing rights (privilege of nations to draw from the International Monetary Fund).

SDRM Society for the Protection of Mechanical Rights (recording of music). [French *Société pour l'Administration du Droit de Reproduction Mécanique*]

SDS 1 scientific data system. **2** sodium dodecyl sulphate (used as a detergent). **3** Students for a Democratic Society (any one of several political groups of American students active in the 1960s).

SDU Social Democratic Union.

SDV slowed-down video.

SDWA Safe Drinking Water Act.

SE 1 Sanitary Engineer. **2** self-employment. **3** single entry *accounting*. **4** also **S.E.** or **s.e. a** southeast. **b** southeastern. **5** special equipment. **6** split end *football*. **7** Standard English. **8** standard error *statistics*. **9** *British* Stock Exchange. **10** also **s.e.** straight edge. **11** systems engineer.

Se selenium (chemical element).

SEA 1 Southeast Asia. **2** sudden enhancement of atmospherics (disturbances of the earth's magnetic field).

SEAB Secretary of Energy Advisory Board (of U.S. Department of Energy).

Seabee (sē′bē′) Construction Batallion (of the U.S. Navy). [pronunciation of the initials *C.B.*]

SEAC 1 Southeast Asia Command. **2** Standards Eastern Automatic Computer (Bureau of Standards automatic computer).

SEACOM (sē′kom) South East Asia Commonwealth (telephone cable).

SEALS (sēls) sea, air, and land (teams of members of U.S. Navy trained for unconventional special operations).

SEAQ *British* Stock Exchange Automated Quotations.

SEARCH System for Electronic Analysis and Retrieval of Criminal Histories.

Seasat (sē′sat′) Sea satellite (satellite to gather data about the ocean surface).

SEATO (sē′tō) Southeast Asia Treaty Organization (military pact, disbanded in 1977).

SEbE or **SE by E** southeast by east.

SEbS or **SE by S** southeast by south.

SEC 1 secondary electron conduction *physics*. **2** also **S.E.C.** Securities and Exchange Commission. **3** simple electronic computer. **4** Systems Engineering Coordination.

Sec. 1 Secretary: *Sec. Gen. = Secretary General*. **2** Section. **3** Sector.

sec 1 also **sec.** according to. [Latin *secundum*] **2** secant *mathematics*. **3** also **sec. a** (*also pronounced* sek) second (unit of time). **b** second (unit of angular distance). **4** also **sec.**

secondary. **5** secretary. **6** *also* **sec.** section. **7** *also* **sec.** sector. **8** security.

SECAM (sē'kam) sequential color by memory (French and East European color TV transmission system). [French *Séquentiel Couleur à Mémoire*]

SECAR (sē'kär) secondary surveillance radar (for west European air traffic control).

sec. art. according to art or rule. [Latin *secundum artem*]

sec-ft *or* **sec.-ft.** second-foot.

sech hyperbolic secant *mathematics*.

Sec. Leg. Secretary of the Legation.

sec. leg. according to law. [Latin *secundum legem*]

sec. nat. according to nature. [Latin *secundum naturam*]

SECO 1 a sequential coding *computers*. **b** sequential control *electronics*. **2** sustainer engine cutoff (in a rocket launch).

SECOR sequential collation of range (satellite used in mapping).

sec. reg. according to rule. [Latin *secundum regulam*]

Secs. *or* **secs.** **1** seconds. **2** sections.

Sect. *or* **sect.** **1** section. **2** sector.

Secty *or* **secty.** secretary.

Secy *or* **secy** *or* **sec'y** secretary: *Secy Gen = Secretary General.*

SED 1 Scottish Education Department. **2** skin erythema dose (unit of radiation exposure). **3** Socialist Unity Party (of former East Germany). [German *Sozialistische Einheitspartei Deutschlands*]

sed. 1 sedative. **2** *also* **sed a** sediment. **b** sedimentation.

SEDAR submerged electrode detection and ranging.

sedtn sedimentation.

SEE 1 *also* **see** secondary electron emission. **2** Society of Environmental Engineers.

s.e.e.o. *or* **S.E.e.O.** errors and omissions excepted *commerce, civil engineering*. [Latin *salvis erroribus et omissis*]

SEER Seasonal Energy Efficiency Rating (of air conditioners).

SEG Society of Exploration Geophysicists.

seg. 1 a segment. **b** segmented. **2** segregated. **3** *also* **seg** segue (proceed immediately, following), esp. in music and in broadcasting. [originally Italian *segue*]

segm. segment *botany*.

seis. *or* **seismol.** **1** seismology. **2** seismological.

SEIU Service Employees International Union.

SEL socioeconomic level.

sel. 1 late, deceased. [German *selig*] **2 a** selected. **b** selection. **c** selector.

SELA Latin American Economic System (association of 25 Latin American and Caribbean countries for economic and social cooperation). [Spanish *Sistema Económico Latinoamericano*]

Selk. Selkirk (mountains in Canada).

SELS Severe Local Storm Warning Center.

sels selsyn (self-synchronous unit, as for synchronizing gunfire with a radar scanner).

SEM 1 scanning electron microscope or microscopy. **2** solvent extraction milling process. **3** standard error of the mean *statistics*.

Sem. 1 Seminary. **2** Semitic.

sem. 1 semester. **2** semicolon. **3** seminar.

semi (sem'ē) **1** semicolon. **2** *British* semi-detached house. **3** semitrailer. **4** semifinal.

semih. half an hour. [Latin *semihora*]

semp. the same style throughout *music*. [Italian *sempre*]

sem. ves. seminal vesicle.

Sen. 1 a Senate. **b** Senator. **2** Senior.

sen. 1 senior. **2** without *music*. [Italian *senza*]

SENA French-Belgian Nuclear Group of Ardennes (French and Belgian utilities). [French *Société Nucléaire Franco-Belge des Ardennes*]

Sen. Doc. Senate Document (followed by number).

SENN National Group for Nuclear Electrical Generation. [Italian *Società Elettronucleare Nazionale*]

senr *or* **Senr** senior.

sent. sentence.

s.e.o. *or* **S.E.O.** *or* **s.e.o.o.** *or* **S.e. ou o.** errors and omissions excepted. [French *sauf erreurs ou omissions*]

SEP simplified employee pension.

Sep. 1 September. **2** Septuagint (Greek Translation of the Old Testament done by seventy scholars before time of Christ).

sep. 1 sepal (part of the outer covering of a flower). **2 a** separate. **b** separation.

SEPL *or* **S.E.P.L.** South European Pipeline.

sepn separation.

SEPR French Rocket Society. [French *Société d'Étude de la Propulsion par Réaction*]

Sept. 1 *also* **Sept** September. **2** Septuagint (Greek Translation of the Old Testament done by seventy scholars before time of Christ).

seq. 1 a it follows. [Latin *sequitur*] **b** the following. [Latin *sequens*] **2** sequel. **3** sequence.

seqq. the following. [Latin *sequentia*]

SER 1 smooth-surfaced endoplasmic reticulum *medicine*. **2** Socioeconomic Council (advising body of the Netherlands). [Dutch *Sociaal Economiche Raad*] **3** Spanish Broadcasting Society. [Spanish *Sociedad Española Radiodifusion*]

Ser 1 *also* **Ser.** *or* **SER.** serial: *SER. NO. = serial number.* **2** *also* **Ser.** series. **3** *also* **Ser.** serine (essential amino acid in protein). **4** the Serpent (constellation).

ser. 1 serial. **2** series. **3** serine (essential amino acid in protein). **4** sermon. **5** service.

Serb. 1 Serbia. **2** Serbian.

SERC 1 Science and Engineering Research Council (of Great Britain). **2** Smithsonian Environmental Research Center.

SEREB Society for Development of Rocket Engines. [French *Société pour l'Étude de la Réalisation d'Engins Balistiques*]

Serg. *or* **Sergt.** sergeant.

Serj. *or* **Serjt.** Serjeant *law: Serj. at Arms.*

SERI Solar Energy Research Institute.

SERT Society of Electronic and Radio Technicians (of Great Britain).

serv. 1 preserve. [Latin *serva*] 2 servant. 3 *also* **Serv.** service.

servo (sėr'vō) 1 servomechanism. 2 servomotor.

servt. servant.

SES 1 Senior Executive Service (highest grades of U.S. Civil Service). 2 socioeconomic status (education, income, etc., used to measure rank in sociological studies). 3 Solar Energy Society. 4 Standards Engineers Society. 5 surface effect ship (air-cushion vehicle for use on water).

SESAC Society of European Stage Authors and Composers.

SESL Space Environment Simulation Laboratory.

Sess. *or* **sess.** session.

SETAF Southern European Task Force of Nato.

SETI search for extraterrestrial intelligence.

SEU single event upset (of charged particles in space that affect electronic devices in scientific monitoring satellites).

sev. *or* **sevl.** several.

SEW Safety Equipment Worker.

sew. 1 sewage. 2 sewer (underground drain). 3 sewerage (system of underground drains).

Sex the Sextans (constellation).

sex. 1 *also* **sext.** sextant. 2 sextet. 3 sexual.

Sey *or* **Sey.** Seychelles (republic of islands NE of Madagascar in Indian Ocean): *SeyR = Seychelles Rupee (monetary unit).*

SEZ Special Economic Zone (in China).

SF 1 *also* **S.F.** San Francisco: *the S.F. Bay Area.* 2 *also* **S-F** science fiction: *SF fans.* 3 *also* **S.F.** Senior Fellow. 4 sinking fund *finance.* 5 Sinn Fein. 6 Special Forces: *antiguerrilla training that is SF's major responsibility.*

Sf Svedberg flotation (flotation analysis of sedimentation), esp. in biochemistry.

sf 1 at or with no expense. [French *sans frais*] 2 *also* **s.f.** near the end. [Latin *sub finem*] 3 *also* **s-f** science fiction. 4 signal frequency *electronics.* 5 *also* **s.f.** sinking fund *finance,* also in combination: *s.f.r. = sinking fund rate of return.* 6 **a** square feet. **b** surface feet. 7 with sudden stress *music.* [Italian *sforzando*]

SFA 1 French Astronautical Society. [French *Société Française d'Astronautique*] 2 Scientific Film Association. 3 *also* **S.F.A.** Scottish Football Association.

SFBM Small Farm Business Management Scheme.

SFC 1 *also* **Sfc.** sergeant first class. 2 specific fuel consumption (of aircraft). 3 supercritical fluid chromatography.

sfgd safeguard.

Sfk. Suffolk.

SFL 1 *also* **S.F.L.** Scottish Football League. 2 sequenced flashing lights (of a runway) *aeronautics.*

sfm *or* **s.f.m.** surface feet per minute.

SFOF Space Flight Operations Facility (of NASA).

sfp with sudden stress followed by soft tone *music.* [Italian *sforzando piano*]

sfpm *or* **s.f.p.m.** surface feet per minute.

SFR submarine fleet reactor.

Sfr. Swiss Franc.

S.F.S.A. Steel Founders' Society of America.

SFSS Satellite Field Service Stations (of NASA).

sft. soft (on surveys and navigational charts).

SFTA *or* **S.F.T.A.** Society of Film and Television Arts (of Great Britain).

sftwd. softwood (of lumber).

SFV 1 Saybolt furol viscosity (measure of viscosity). 2 Semliki Forest Virus.

SFX sound effect.

sfz with sudden stress *music.* [Italian *sforzando*]

SG 1 *also* **S-G** Sachs-Georgi (test for syphilis). 2 screen grid *electronics.* 3 *also* **S.G.** *or* **S-G** *or* **S.-G.** Secretary General (of UN). 4 *also* **S.G.** Solicitor General. 5 specific gravity. 6 *also* **S.G.** Surgeon General.

Sg. Surgeon.

sg 1 *also* **s.g.** senior grade. 2 *also* **sg.** singular *grammar,* usually in combination: *1sg. = first person singular.* 3 *also* **s.g.** specific gravity.

S.G.A. Society of Graphic Arts.

SG&A sales and general administration *accounting.*

SGD sliding glass door.

sgd. signed.

S.G.D.G. *or* **s.g.d.g.** without guarantee of the government (of a patent issued by the French government). [French *sans garantie du gouvernement*]

Sge the Arrow (constellation). [Latin *Sagitta*]

SGHW *or* **SGHWR** steam-generating heavy water reactor.

sgl. single.

SGLI Servicemen's Group Life Insurance.

SGML Standard Generalized Markup Language (for coding material to be included in a computer database).

SGN Standing Group of Nato.

SGO Surgeon General's Office.

S.G.O.T. *or* **SGO-T** serum glutamic oxaloacetic transaminase (enzyme in carbohydrate-protein metabolism).

S.G.P.T. *or* **SGP-T** serum glutamic pyruvic transaminase (enzyme in carbohydrate-protein metabolism).

Sgr the Archer, Sagittarius (constellation).

SGT Society of Glass Technology.

Sgt. *or* **sgt.** sergeant.

Sgt. Maj. sergeant major.

SGZ surface ground zero.

SH 1 sacrifice hit *baseball.* 2 *also* **S.H.** schoolhouse, esp. on maps. 3 serum hepatitis. 4 *also* **S.H.** ship's heading *navigation.* 5 social history. 6 somatotrophic hormone (pituitary hormone regulating body growth). 7 *also* **S.H.** Southern Hemisphere. 8 sulfhydryl (univalent radical that inactivates arsenic of lewisite).

S/H shipping and handling *commerce.*

Sh. 1 shells (on navigation charts). **2** *also* **Sh** shilling (monetary unit of Kenya, Somalia, Tanzania, Uganda). **3** show, in horse racing.

sh. 1 *also* **sh** share (of stock). **2** sheep (of bookbinding). **3** *also* **sh** sheet. **4** *also* **sh** shilling (monetary unit of Kenya, Somalia, Tanzania, Uganda). **5** shoal (on navigation charts). **6** short. **7** showers *meterology*.

SHA sidereal hour angle (measured along the celestial equator from the vernal equinox to the hour circle of a star).

SHAB soft and hard acids and bases (identification of the factors that determine the rate of chemical reactions and stability of compounds).

SHAEF Supreme Headquarters, Allied Expeditionary Forces (in WWII).

Shak. *or* **Shaks.** Shakespeare.

SHAPE Supreme Headquarters, Allied Powers in Europe (of Nato).

SHAS Shared Hospital Accounting System.

shd. *or* **shd** should.

Sheff. *or* **Shef.** Sheffield.

Shet. 1 Shetland. **2** Shetland Islands.

SHEX Sundays and Holidays Excepted *commerce*.

SHF *or* **shf** superhigh frequency.

ship. 1 shipping. **2** *also* **shipt.** shipment.

shl. *or* **shl** shoal (esp. on navigation charts).

shld. shoulder.

shlp. shiplap (a rabbeted joint of two running boards).

SHM *or* **s.h.m.** simple harmonic motion *physics*.

sho *or* **Sh.O.** shutout, esp. in baseball.

SHORAN *or* **shoran** (shôr'an) short-range navigation (radio navigational system).

SHOT Society for the History of Technology.

SHP *or* **shp** shaft horsepower.

shpg. shipping.

shpt. shipment.

SHQ station headquarters.

Shr. The Taming of the Shrew (play by Shakespeare).

shr. *or* **Shr** share, shares (of stock).

shrap. shrapnel.

Shrops. Shropshire County, England.

sht. sheet.

shtg. shortage.

sh.tn. short ton (2000 pounds).

s.h.v. under this word. [Latin *sub hoc verbo* or *sub hac voce*]

SI 1 *also* **S.I.** International System of Units (for scientific measurement). [French *Système International d'Unités*] **2** shift in *computers*. **3** Smithsonian Institution. **4** Society of Illustrators. **5** Solomon Islands: *SI$ = Solomon Islands dollar*. **6** *also* **S.I.** South Island (one of the two main islands of New Zealand). **7** special issue *law*. **8** *also* **S.I.** Star of India (decoration). **9** *also* **S.I.** Staten Island.

Si silicon (chemical element).

si *or* **s.i. 1** short interest *commerce*. **2** square inch: *boilers at a pressure of 850 lb./s.i.*

SIA 1 Sanitary Institute of America. **2** Securities Industries Association. **3** standard instrument approach *aeronautics*. **4** Storage Instantaneous Audimeter (tabulating device installed by A.C. Nielsen Co. to monitor television-viewing patterns).

SIAC Securities Industry Automatic Corporation (computer network that processes electronic trading on the New York and American Stock Exchanges).

S.I.A.M. *or* **SIAM** Society for Industrial and Applied Mathematics.

SIAO Smithsonian Institution Astrophysical Observatory.

SIB 1 screen image buffer *computers*. **2** Securities and Investments Board (of Great Britain). **3** Special Investigation Branch (esp. of a British police force).

Sib. 1 Siberia. **2** Siberian.

SIC 1 Scientific Information Center. **2** *also* **sic** semiconductor integrated circuit. **3** specific inductive capacity. **4** Standard Industrial Classification: *SIC codes*.

Sic. 1 Sicily. **2** Sicilian.

SICM scanning ion-conductance microscope.

SID 1 *also* **S.I.D.** his or her spirit rests in God. [Latin *Spiritus in Deo*] **2** seismic intrusion detector (security device). **3** Society for International Development. **4** sports information director. **5** standard instrument departure *aeronautics, navigation*. **6** sudden infant death (syndrome). **7** sudden ionospheric disturbance (as of a solar flare). **8** syntax-improving device (esp. for adjusting a high-level program language to other uses) *computers*.

SIDA (sē'də) Acquired Immune Deficiency Syndrome; AIDS. [French *Syndrome Immune Déficience Acquise*, Spanish *Síndrome de Inmunodeficiencia Adquirida*]

SIDS sudden infant death syndrome.

SIE 1 Science Information Exchange (service of the Smithsonian Institution). **2** *also* **S.I.E.** Society of Industrial Engineers.

SIF 1 selective identification feature *aeronautics*. **2** sound intermediate frequency.

SIFCON slurry-infiltrated fiber-concrete.

si-fi (sī'fī') science fiction.

SIG 1 senior interagency group. **2** special interest group, also in combination: *SIGCUE = Special Interest Group on Computer Science Education*.

Sig. 1 label *pharmaceutics*. [Latin *signa*] **2 a** Mr. [Italian *Signor* or *signore*] **b** Messrs. [Italian *Signori*] **3** signal, also in combination: *Sig.O = Signal Officer*. **4** signature.

sig. 1 let it be labeled *pharmaceutics*. [Latin *signetur*] **2** signal. **3** signature.

sig. fig. significant figures *mathematics*.

sigill. seal (mark or sign). [Latin *sigillum*]

Sigint *or* **SIGINT** (sig'int) signal intelligence (intelligence gathering by monitoring radio and other electronic transmissions).

SIGMA Science in General Management.

sign. signature.

signif. significant.

SIH International Society of Hematology. [French *Société Internationale d'Hématologie*]

SIL 1 speech interference level. **2** surge impedance loading *electronics.*

Sil. Silesia.

sil. silver.

SIM International Society of Musicology. [French *Société Internationale Musicologie*]

sim. 1 similar. **2** simile, esp. in music.

SIMD single instruction multiple data *computers.*

SIMM single in-line memory module (a type of random access memory).

SIMS secondary ion mass spectrometry.

SIMSCRIPT simulation high-level programming language.

simulcast (sī'məl kast') simultaneous broadcast (broadcast on television and AM or FM radio at the same time).

SIN Spanish International Network (Spanish-language television programming service, in New York City).

sin sine *mathematics.*

sin. left hand. [Italian *sinistra*]

Sing. Singapore.

sing. 1 of each *pharmaceutics.* [Latin *singulorum*] **2** singular, esp. in grammar.

Sinh. Sinhalese (principal native people of Sri Lanka or their language).

sinh hyperbolic sine *mathematics.*

SINS Ship's Inertial Navigation System (system of gyroscopes and accelerometers that relates the movement of a ship in all directions to conditions of the sea).

SIO Scripps Institution of Oceanography.

SIOP single integrated operations plan.

SIP 1 Inter-American Society of Psychology. [French *Société Interaméricaine de Psychologie*] **2** single in-line package (arrangement of terminals or lead lines) *electronics.* **3** standard inspection procedure *military.*

SIPC Securities Investor Protection Corporation.

SIPRC Society of Independent Public Relations Consultants.

SIPRE Snow, Ice, and Permafrost Research Establishment (of the U.S. Army Corps of Engineers).

SIPRI Stockholm International Peace Research Institute.

SIR 1 selective information retrieval (used in spectroscopic chemical anaylsis). **2** submarine intermediate reactor.

SIRA Scientific Instrument Research Association (of Great Britain).

Sirs (sèrz) satellite infrared spectrometer.

SIS 1 a Secret Intelligence Service (of Great Britain). **b** Security Intelligence Service (of New Zealand). **2** shaken infant syndrome.

Sis. 1 Sister. **2** *also* **sis** (*pronounced* sis) sister.

SISD single instruction, single data (of a computer processor).

SISI short-increment sensitivity index.

SIT 1 self-induced transparency (transmission of coherent light by a normally opaque medium) *physics.* **2** Society of Industrial Technology. **3** Society of Instrument Technology. **4** spontaneous ignition temperature. **5** static induction transistor *electronics.* **6** *also* **s.i.t. a** stopping in transit. **b** storage in transit.

sit. situation.

SITA 1 *also* **S.I.T.A.** International Society of Aeronautical Telecommunications. [French *Société Internationale de Télécommunications Aéronautiques*] **2** Students International Travel Association.

SITC Standard International Trade Classification.

sitcom (sit'kom) situation comedy.

SITE Satellite Instructional Television Experiment.

SITES Smithsonian Institution Traveling Exhibition Service.

SITPRO *British* Simplification of International Trade Procedures.

SIU Seafarers' International Union.

SIV simian immunodeficiency virus.

SIW self-inflicted wound.

S.J. Society of Jesus (the official name of the Jesuit order).

s.j. under consideration *law.* [Latin *sub judice*]

SJC Standing Joint Committee.

S.J.D. Doctor of Juridical Science. [Latin *Scientiae Juridicae Doctor*]

S.J.Res. Senate Joint Resolution (followed by a number).

SK 1 Saskatchewan (postal code). **2** streptokinase (enzyme used to dissolve clots).

Sk skewness (lack of symmetry in frequency distribution) *statistics.*

sk 1 sack. **2** skein. **3** sketch. **4** skewbald (color of a horse). **5** skip.

SKC *or* **S.K.C.** Scottish Kennel Club.

Skm Stockholm.

s.k.p.o. *or* **skpsso** slip one, knit one, pass slipped stitch over (direction in knitting).

Skr Swedish krona (monetary unit).

Skr. *or* **Skrt.** Sanskrit (ancient sacred and literary language of India).

Skt. 1 Saint. [German *Sankt*] **2** Sanskrit (ancient sacred and literary language of India).

SKU stock-keeping unit (of inventory) *commerce.*

SL 1 salvage loss *insurance.* **2** *also* **S.L.** sea level. **3** searchlight. **4** *also* **S.L.** *British* **a** serjeant-at-law. **b** solicitor-at-law. **5** SL bacterium (cavity-causing streptococcus, after a dental technician named Sandra Lim). **6** sound locator. **7** source language (language from which something is translated or language in which a foreign language is taught). **8** *also* **S.L.** south latitude. **9** *also* **S/L** squadron leader. **10** Standard Location Area; SLA (small official geographical area). **11** statute law. **12** stock length (of lumber).

Sl. 1 Slavic. **2** Slavonic. **3 a** Slovak (person living in Slovakia or their Western Slavic language). **b** Slovakia. **c** Slovakian.

sl. 1 slightly. **2** slip (direction in knitting). **3** slow (condition of the track in horse racing).

s.l. 1 according to law. [Latin *secundum legem*] **2** without place (esp. of a book that does not show where it was printed). [Latin *sine loco*]

SLA 1 Savings and Loan Association. **2** *also* **S.L.A. a** School Library Association. **b** Scottish Library Association. **c** Special Libraries Association. **3** Standard Location Area (small official geographic area, generally a census tract, enumeration district, or political district). **4** State Liquor Authority.

SLAC Stanford Linear Accelerator Center.

SLADE *or* **S.L.A.D.E.** Society of Lithographic Artists, Designers, Engravers and Process Workers (of Great Britain).

S.L.A.E.T. *or* **SLAET** Society of Licensed Aircraft Engineers and Technologists.

s.l.a.n. *or* **SLAN** without place, year, or name (esp. of a book not showing where, when, or by whom it was printed). [Latin *sine loco, anno, vel nomine*]

s.l.&a. without place and year (esp. of a book). [Latin *sine loco et anno*]

SL&C *or* **sl and c** shipper's load and count *commerce*.

SL&T *or* **sl and t** shipper's load and tally *commerce*.

SLANG systems language *computers*.

SLAPP strategic lawsuit against public participation: *SLAPP suit.*

SLAR side-looking airborne radar.

S.Lat. *or* **S.lat.** south latitude.

Slav. 1 Slavic. **2 a** Slavonian. **b** Slavonic.

SLBM submarine-launched ballistic missile.

SLBMDS Sea-Launched Ballistic Missile Detection System.

SLC 1 *British* School Leaving Certificate. **2** Stanford Linear Collider (nuclear accelerator). **3** State Legislative Committee. **4** straight-line capacitance *electronics.*

SLCM submarine-launched cruise missile.

SLD 1 serum lactic dehydrogenase (enzyme). **2 a** Specific Language Disability. **b** Specific Learning Disability.

sld. *or* **sld 1** sailed. **2** sealed. **3** solid.

SLE 1 St. Louis encephalitis. **2** systemic lupus erythematosus (disease characterized by scaly skin lesions).

s.l. et a. without place and year (esp. of a book). [Latin *sine loco et anno*]

SLF 1 Scottish Landowners Federation. **2** straight-line frequency (of a capacitor) *electronics.*

SLFP Sri Lanka Freedom Party.

SLI 1 specific language impairment. **2** starting-lighting-ignition: *SLI battery.*

SLIP Symmetric List Processor (language for computer processing of lists).

SLM ship-launched missile.

SLMA (sal'ē mā') Student Loan Marketing Administration (Sallie Mae).

s.l.n.d. without place or date (esp. of a book). [Latin *sine loco nec data*]

SLO 1 safe laser output (unit of measure). **2** Senior Liaison Officer.

Slorc *or* **SLORC** State Law and Order Restoration Council (ruling junta of Myanmar, formerly Burma).

Slov. 1 a Slovak (person living in Slovakia or their Western Slavic language). **b** Slovakia. **c** Slovakian. **2 a** Slovene (person living in Slovenia or their South Slavic language). **b** Slovenia. **c** Slovenian.

SLP *or* **S.L.P. 1** Scottish Labour Party. **2** Socialist Labor Party. **3** *also* **s.l.p.** without lawful issue. [Latin *sine legitima prole*]

SLR 1 side-looking radar. **2** single-lens reflex (of a camera).

SLS 1 side-looking sonar. **2** strained-layer superlattice (material used in making semiconductors).

SLSA St. Lawrence Seaway Authority.

SLSDC St. Lawrence Seaway Development Corporation (of U.S. Department of Transportation).

SLSI super large-scale integration *computers.*

sl st slip stitch (a stitch in needlework).

SLT 1 searchlight. **2** solid logic technology.

SLV satellite *or* space launching vehicle.

SLW straight-line wavelength (of a capacitor) *electronics.*

sly. 1 sloppy (condition of the track, in horse racing). **2** slowly. **3** *also* **Sly** southerly.

SM 1 *also* **S.M.** Master of Science. [Latin *Scientiae Magister*] **2** *also* **S.M.** of holy memory. [Latin *Sanctae Memoriae*] **3** *also* **S-M** *or* **s-m a** Sadomasochism. **b** Sadomasochist. **4** *also* **S.M.** Saint Mary. **5** Sales Manager. **6** Sergeant Major. **7** service mark. **8** service module (of a spacecraft). **9** servomechanism. **10** *also* **S.M.** short meter (of poetry). **11** signalman. **12** *also* **S.M.** Society of Mary (Marists). **13** Soldier's Medal. **14** stage manager. **15** standard matched (of lumber). **16** *also* **S.M.** State Militia. **17** *also* **sm** statute mile. **18** *British and Canadian* Stipendiary Magistrate (a salaried Justice of the Peace). **19** streptomycin. **20** *also* **S.M.** with the left hand *music.* [Italian *sinistra mano*]

Sm samarium (chemical element).

sm 1 a servomechanism. **b** servomotor. **2** *also* **sm.** small.

SMA Standard Metropolitan Area (former U.S. Census Bureau designation of an area with at least one city of 50,000 or more inhabitants, now *MSA*).

SMATV satellite master antenna television.

S.M.B. Bachelor of Sacred Music.

SMC 1 Scottish Mountaineering Club. **2** sheet molding compound. **3** small magellanic cloud *meteorology.* **4** *also* **S-M-C** sperm or spore mother cell *biology.* **5** *also* **smc** standard mean chord *aeronautical engineering.*

sm.c. *or* **sm.cap.** *or* **sm.caps** small capitals (letters) *printing.*

SMD 1 senile-macular degeneration *medicine.* **2** surface mounting device.

S.M.E. 1 Holy Mother Church. [Latin *Sancta Mater Ecclesia*] **2** *also* **SME** Society of Mining Engineers.

S meter signal-strength meter *electronics.*

SMF System Management Facilities *computers.*

SMG submachine gun.

SMIA Sheet Metal Industries Association.

SMIC Study of Man's Impact on Climate.

SMIS Society for Management Information Systems.

Smith. Inst. Smithsonian Institution.

smk or **smk.** smoke.

SML Symbolic Machine Language.

sml. **1 a** simulate. **b** simulation. **c** simulator. **2** also **sml** small.

S.M.M. Holy Mother Mary. [Latin *Sancta Mater Maria*]

SMO 1 Senior Medical Officer. **2** supplementary meteorological office.

smorz. gradually dying away *music*. [Italian *smorzando*]

SMP 1 also **S.M.P.** Society of Mural Painters. **2** special multiperil (insurance). **3** also **s.m.p.** without male offspring. [Latin *sine mascula prole*]

SMPTE or **S.M.P.T.E.** Society of Motion Picture and Television Engineers.

SMR standard mortality ratio.

SMSA Standard Metropolitan Statistical Area (former U.S. Census Bureau designation, now *MSA*).

SMT 1 ship's mean time. **2** Steiner minimum tree (mathematical model for designing networks, such as computer circuits, manufacturing locations, etc.).

SMV slow-moving vehicle.

SMW standard metal window.

SMWIA Sheet Metal Workers International Association.

SN 1 a also **S/N** serial number. **b** service number. **c** stock number. **2** also **S/N** shipping note. **3** also **S/N** signal-to-noise ratio. **4** supernova.

Sn *I an abbreviation for:* also **Sn. 1 a** sanitary. **b** sanitation. **2** snow.
II a symbol for: tin (chemical element). [Latin *stannum*]

sn 1 also **s.n.** according to nature. [Latin *secundum naturam*] **2** also **sn.** snow. **3** supernova. **4** also **s.n.** without name (esp. a publisher's or printer's name). [Latin *sine nomine*]

SNA Systems Network Architecture *computers*.

snafu (sna fü′) situation normal–all fouled up.

SNAME or **S.N.A.M.E.** Society of Naval Architects and Marine Engineers.

SNAP 1 strong no-trump after passing, in playing bridge. **2** systems for nuclear auxiliary power: *SNAP-8 generates 30,000 watts.*

SNC Supreme National Council (coalition of Cambodian factions forming a transitional government as part of a UN-sponsored peace agreement).

SNCB Belgian National Railway. [French *Société Nationale des Chemins de Fer Belges*]

SNCC (*pronounced* snik) National Coordinating Committee (originally formed as the Student Nonviolent Coordinating Committee).

SNCF French National Railway. [French *Société Nationale des Chemins de Fer*]

SNCV Light Railway Authority. [French *Société Nationale des Chemins de Vicinaux*]

S.N.D. or **SND** Scottish National Dictionary.

snd. sound.

s.n.d. sap no defect (of lumber).

S.N.E. National Organization of Editors. [French *Syndicat National des Éditeurs*]

SNECMA National Society for the Study and Construction of Aircraft Motors. [French *Société Nationale d'Étude et de Construction de Moteurs d'Aviation*]

SNF 1 short-range or strategic nuclear forces. **2** Skilled Nursing Facility. **3** solids, non-fat (esp. of dairy products).

SNFA Standing Naval Force, Atlantic.

SNG 1 Commonwealth of Independent States (of the former Soviet Union). [Russian *Sodruzhestvo Nezavisimykh Gosudarstv*] **2** synthetic or substitute natural gas.

Sng. Singapore.

SNL standard nomenclature list *military*.

S.N.L.R. *British* services no longer required.

SNLV strategic nuclear launch vehicle.

SNM 1 also **S.N.M.** Society of Nuclear Medicine. **2** Somali National Movement (guerrilla group).

SNO 1 Senior Naval Officer. **2** Senior Navigation Officer.

SNOBOL String Oriented Symbolic Language *computers*. [*S*(tri)*n*(g) *O*(riented) (Sym)*bol*(ic) *L*(anguage)]

SNORT Supersonic Naval Ordnance Research Track.

SNP 1 also **S.N.P.** school nurse practitioner. **2** also **S.N.P.** Scottish National Party. **3** soluble nucleoprotein.

SNPO Space Nuclear Propulsion Office.

SNR 1 signal-to-noise ratio. **2** Society for Nautical Research. **3** supernova remnants *astronomy*.

Snr. 1 Mr. [Portuguese *Senhor*, Spanish *Señor*] **2** also **snr.** senior.

Snra. Mrs. [Portuguese *Senhora*, Spanish *Señora*]

snRNA small nuclear ribonucleic acid (particle).

snRNP small nuclear ribonucleoprotein.

Snrta. Miss. [Portuguese *senhorita*, Spanish *Señorita*]

SNS sympathetic nervous system.

SNU solar neutrino unit *astronomy*.

SO *I an abbreviation for:* **1** also **S.O. a** *British* Scientific Officer. **b** Senior Officer. **c** Signal Officer. **d** Staff Officer. **e** Supply Officer. **2** *commerce* **a** seller's option. **b** ship's option. **3** shift out *computers*. **4** also **S.O. a** shipping order. **b** special order. **c** standing order. **5** shut off, also in combination: *SOV = shut-off valve.* **6** Southern Oscillation *meteorology*. **7** strikeout *baseball*.
II a symbol for: classification of galactic nebulae, having a bright nucleus but no distinguishable arms.

So. 1 Sonata. **2** also **so. a** south, esp. in combination: *So.Am. = South America; So.Afr. = South African.* **b** southern.

s.o. 1 see above. [German *siehe oben*] **2** seller's option *commerce*. **3** *commerce* **a** shipping order. **b** special order. **4** strikeout *baseball*.

SOA 1 speed of approach. **2** state-of-the-art.

SOAP Symbolic Optimum Assembly Program *computers*.

SOB 1 Senate Office Building. **2** also **S.O.B.** short of breath *medicine*. **3** also **s.o.b.** son of a bitch (descriptive of a person). **4** also **s.o.b.** souls on board: *the craft has 21 s.o.b.'s.*

SOC Special Operations Command (of U.S. Department of Defense).

Soc. 1 socialist. 2 Society. 3 sociology. 4 Socrates.

soc. 1 social: *soc. sci. = social science; soc. welf. = social welfare.* 2 society. 3 sociology. 4 socket.

Soc. An^e corporation. [French *Société Anonyme*]

Soc. Dem. Social Democrat.

sociol. 1 sociology. 2 sociological. 3 sociologist.

Soc. Is. *or* **Soc. Isl.** Society Islands.

Socred (sok'red) Social Credit Party (of Canada).

Soc.Sec. Social Security.

Socy. Society.

sod. sodium.

SOE 1 *also* **S.O.E.** Special Operations Executive (British intelligence operations in WWII). 2 State Owned Enterprise (of New Zealand).

SOED *Shorter Oxford English Dictionary.*

SOF 1 sound on film. 2 *also* **SOFA** Status of Forces Agreement (governing U.S. Armed Forces personnel).

SOFAA Society of Fine Art Auctioneers.

SOFAR (sō'fär) sound fixing and ranging (system for long-range communications).

SOFCS self-organizing flight control system.

S. of S. Song of Songs (Song of Solomon).

S. of Sol. Song of Solomon (book of the Old Testament).

SOH start of heading *computers, printing.*

SoHo (sō'hō') South of Houston Street (area of New York City noted as a center of avant-garde art, music, film and fashion).

SOHYO General Council of Japanese Trade Unions. [Japanese *(Nihon Rodo Kumiai) Sohy (gikai)*]

SOI 1 silicon-on-insulator *electronics.* 2 space object identification.

SOL 1 *also* **s.o.l.** shipowner's liability *insurance.* 2 solar, esp. in combination: *SOLRAD = solar radiation.*

Sol. 1 Solicitor, also in combination: *Sol. Gen. = Solicitor General.* 2 Solomon: *Song of Sol.*

sol. 1 solar. 2 solenoid. 3 solicitor. 4 soluble. 5 *also* **sol** (*pronounced* sol) solution. 6 solvent.

S.O.L.A.S. Safety of Life at Sea Convention (international treaty mandating high safety standards for new ships).

Sol. Gen. Solicitor General.

solidif. solidification.

SOLINET Southeastern Library Network.

soln. solution.

Solr. *or* **solr.** solicitor.

solut. solution.

solv. 1 dissolve *pharmaceutics.* [Latin *solve*] 2 solvent.

soly. solubility.

SOM 1 serous otitis media (accumulation of fluid and inflammation of the middle ear). 2 *also* **S.O.M.** Society of Occupational Medicine. 3 start of message *communications.*

Som. 1 Somalia, Somali: *Som. Sh. = Somali shilling.* 2 *also* **Soms** Somerset County, England.

SOMPA (som'pə) System of Multicultural Pluralistic Assessment (intelligence testing by comparing scores of those with similar social and cultural backgrounds to eliminate cultural bias).

SON Spear of the Nation (military force of the African National Congress).

Son. 1 sonata. 2 *also* **Sonn.** The Sonnets (by Shakespeare).

sonar *or* **SONAR** (sō'när) sound navigation and ranging (underwater detection device).

Sond. special. [German *Sonder*]

SOP 1 senior officer present *military.* 2 *also* **s.o.p.** standard operating procedure. 3 sum of the products *mathematics, computers.*

Sop. *or* **sop.** soprano.

Soph. 1 Sophocles (Greek tragic poet, 495–406 BC). 2 *also* **soph** Sophomore.

SOR 1 *also* **s.o.r.** sale or return *commerce.* 2 specific operational requirement. 3 *also* **S-O-R** stimulus-organism-response *psychology.*

S.O.R.C. Southern Ocean Racing Conference.

SORD Submerged Object Recovery Device.

sord. a mute *music.* [Italian *sordino*]

SORO Special Operations Research Office (of the U.S. Army).

SOS *I an abbreviation for:* 1 Secular Organizations for Sobriety. 2 Service of Supply (of the U.S. Army). 3 silicon on sapphire *electronics.*
II a symbol for: a call for help (radio signal of distress).

s.o.s. if necessary *pharmaceutics.* [Latin *si opus sit*]

SOSC Smithsonian Oceanographic Sorting Center.

SOSS Shipboard Oceanographic Survey System.

Sost. compiler or editor. [Russian *sostavitel'*]

sost. *or* **sosten.** sustained *music.* [Italian *sostenuto*]

SOSUS *or* **Sosus** Sound Surveillance System (U.S. Navy underwater monitoring system; also used for seismic survey).

S.O.T. *or* **SOT** sound on tape (of sound and picture recorded simultaneously).

SOTA state-of-the-art.

SOTAS stand-off target acquisition system.

SOTUS sequentially operated teletypewriter universal selector *computers.*

SOU Special Operations Unit.

Sou. *or* **sou.** south, southern.

SOV 1 *also* **sov.** *or* **sov** (*pronounced* sov) sovereign (former British gold coin equivalent of £1). 2 shut-off valve.

Sov. Soviet, esp. in relation to the former Soviet Union.

SP 1 self-propelled, esp. in combination: *SPUV = self-propelled underwater vehicle.* 2 selling price. 3 Shore Patrol (police in U.S. Navy). 4 single-phase (of an alternating current). 5 single pole *electricity, electronics.* 6 *also* **S.P.** small paper (ordinary trim size of a book as opposed to the large paper size with extra-wide margins in a deluxe edition). 7 smokeless powder (esp. in an artillery shell). 8 *also* **S.P.** Socialist Party. 9 *also* **S.P.** soil pipe (on a schematic drawing of a plumbing system). 10 solid propellant (esp. of a rocket).

11 Specialist (rank in the U.S. Army): *SP3c = Specialist Third Class.* **12** special purpose, esp. in combination: *SPLA = Special Purpose Local Authority.* **13** standard playback (speed on a videocassette recorder). **14** starting point. **15** starting price (final odds in horse racing or first bidding price in auctioning). **16** State Police. **17** static pressure. **18** stop payment (of a check) *banking.* **19** *also* **S.P.** Supreme Pontiff (the Pope). **20** systolic pressure *medicine.*

Sp 1 *also* **Sp. a** Spain. **b** Spaniard. **c** Spanish. **2** special. **3** Specialist (rank in the U.S. Army): *Sp3c = Specialist Third Class.*

sp 1 *also* **s.p.** short page (of a printed page having fewer than the maximum number of lines). **2** single-phase (of an alternating current). **3** *also* **s.p.** single pole *electricity, electronics: s.p.d.t. = single pole, double throw.* **4** small pica *printing.* **5** *also* **sp.** space. **6** *also* **sp. a** spare. **b** spare part: *sp.no. = spare part number.* **7** special. **8** *also* **sp.** species. **9** *also* **sp.** specific: *sp.gr. = specific gravity.* **10** *also* **sp.** specimen. **11** speech. **12** speed. **13 a** *also* **sp.** spell, spelling. **b** spell out, in reading printer's proofs. **14** spinal. **15** *also* **s.p.** starting price (final odds in horse racing or first bidding price in auctioning). **16** *also* **s.p.** stop payment (of a check) *banking.* **17** supraprotest (payment to the creditor of another who has refused to pay on a note) *banking.* **18** without issue. [Latin *sine prole*]

SPA 1 Society for Personnel Administration. **2** Southwestern Power Administration (agency of U.S. Department of Interior). **3** special purchase allowance (extra discount in retailing). **4** *also* **s.p.a.** subject to particular average *commerce.* **5** sudden phase anomaly (of electrical transmission). **6** Systems and Procedures Association.

S.p.A. corporation. [Italian *Società per Azioni*]

S.P.A.B. Society for the Protection of Ancient Buildings (of Great Britain).

SPADATS Space Detection and Tracking System (used to monitor artificial satellites orbiting earth).

SPAM satellite processor access method *computers.*

Sp. Am. Spanish American.

SPAN Solar Particle Alert Network.

Span. Spanish.

SPANA Society for the Protection of Animals in North Africa.

SPANDAR *or* **spandar** (span'där) space and range radar (monitoring system of NASA).

SPAR 1 superprecision approach radar. **2** U.S. Coast Guard Women's Reserve. [clipped form of its Latin motto *s(emper) par(atus)* "Always Ready"]

SPARC scalable processor architecture *computers.*

SPAS 1 *also* **S.P.A.S.** Fellow of the American Philosophical Society. [Latin *Societatis Philosophicae Americanae Socius*] **2** Shuttle Pallet Satellite (German-built satellite).

SPASUR (spā'sər) space surveillance (radar system to detect communications and surveillance satellites).

SPATC South Pacific Air Transport Council.

SPBs special boiling point, spirits.

SPC 1 South Pacific Commission. **2** stored program control *computers.* **3** Suicide Prevention Center.

SPCA 1 serum prothrombin conversion accelerator (for clotting blood) *medicine.* **2** *also* **S.P.C.A.** Society for the Prevention of Cruelty to Animals.

SPCC *or* **S.P.C.C.** Society for the Prevention of Cruelty to Children.

S.P.C.K. *British* Society for the Promotion of Christian Knowledge.

SPD 1 silicon photodiode. **2** Social Democratic Party (the socialist party of Germany). [German *Sozialdemokratische Partei Deutschlands*] **3** *also* **s.p.d.** south polar distance *astronomy.* **4** *also* **s.p.d.** subject to permission to deal *finance.*

spd. speed.

SPDA single premium, deferred annuity *insurance.*

spdl. spindle.

SPDT *or* **s.p.d.t.** *or* **spdt** single pole, double throw (of an electrical switch).

S.P.E. 1 Society for Pure English. **2** *also* **SPE** Society of Petroleum Engineers. **3** *also* **SPE** Society of Plastics Engineers. **4** *also* **SPE** solar proton event (release of high-energy protons at the peak of a sunspot cycle). **5** *also* **SPE** sucrose polyester.

SPEC 1 (*pronounced* spek *or* speks) specification, specifications. **2** specify (as a command or direction), esp. in computers.

Spec. Specialist (rank in the U.S. Army): *Spec.4 = Specialist Fourth Class.*

spec. 1 a special: *spec. appt. = special appointment.* **b** specially. **2** species. **3 a** specific. **b** specifically. **4** (*pronounced* spek *or* speks) specification, specifications. **5** specimen. **6** *also* **spec** (*pronounced* spek) spectacle, spectacular (a large theatrical or other performance). **7** spectroscopy. **8** spectrum. **9** *also* **spec** (*pronounced* spek) speculation (of a financial venture).

specif. 1 a *also* **specif** (spə sif') specific. **b** specifically. **2** specification.

SPECS switched proton electron channeltron spectrometer (for sorting electrons and protons by spectra).

specs (*pronounced* speks) **1** *also* **SPECS** specifications. **2** spectacles (eyeglasses).

SPECT single photon emission-computed tomography *medicine.*

Sp.Ed. special education (for students with learning disabilities).

SPEDE System for Processing Educational Data Electronically.

S.Petr. Saint Peter.

SPF 1 *also* **S.P.F.** simple process factor (in separation of isotopes) *physics.* **2** Somali Patriotic Front. **3** South Pacific Forum (group of 13 states in the South Pacific Ocean, including Australia and New Zealand, that adopted a nuclear-free zone in 1985). **4** specific pathogen-free (of animal husbandry carried out under disease-free conditions). **5** sun protection factor: *SPF 8 = recommended exposure to the sun of 80 minutes or less.*

SPF/DB superplastic forming, diffusion bonding (of materials).

SPG 1 Special Patrol Group. **2** Spring (in postal address).

Spg. voltage. [German *Spannung*]

spg 1 *also* **sp.g.** specific gravity *physics.* **2** *also* **spg. a** sponge. **b** spring.

SPGA Scottish Professional Golfers Association.

SPGB Socialist Party of Great Britain.

sp. gr. *or* **SPGR** specific gravity *physics*.

SPGS 1 Springs (in postal address). **2** *also* **Spgs.** Springs (in general use).

sph. 1 spherical. **2** spheroid (wedge-shaped).

S.P.H.E. *or* **SPHE** Society of Packaging and Handling Engineers.

SPHER Small Particle Heat Exchange Receiver.

sp. ht. *or* **SPHT** specific heat *physics*.

S.P.I. *or* **SPI** Society of the Plastics Industry.

SPID submerged, portable, inflatable dwelling (underwater base for long dives).

SPIDAC specimen input to digital automatic computer.

spir. spiral.

SPIRE space inertial reference equipment *navigation*.

Spirit. 1 spiritualism. **2** with spirit *music*. [Italian *spiritoso*]

SPIT selective printing of items from tape *computers*.

spiv *or* **Spiv** (*pronounced* spiv) *British* a petty criminal, esp. a thief, blackmailer, etc. [probably from police blotter notation *Suspected Person Itinerant Vagabond*]

SPIW *or* **S.P.I.W.** special purpose individual weapon (gun for firing a dart-shaped projectile or a grenade).

spk. speckled.

Spkr. Speaker (of U.S. House of Representatives).

spkr. 1 speaker. **2** *also* **spkr** sprinkler.

SPL 1 *computers* **a** software programming language. **b** Space Programming Language. **2** sound pressure level (measurement of audible sound). **3** *also* **spl.** special.

s.p.l. without legitimate issue *law*. [Latin *sine prole legitima*]

SPLA 1 Special Purpose Local Authority (for supervision of hospital, electrical, and other local services in New Zealand). **2** Sudan People's Liberation Army.

SPM 1 self-propelled mount. **2** *also* **spm** strokes per minute. **3** *also* **s.p.m.** without male issue *law*. [Latin *sine prole mascula*]

Spn Spanish.

sp. nov. new species. [Latin *species nova*]

SPO 1 *also* **SPÖ** Austrian Socialist Party. [German *Sozialistische Partei Österreichs*] **2** sea post office. **3** System Program Officer.

SPOOL simultaneous peripheral operation on-line *computers*.

sport. 1 sporting. **2** sportscaster. **3** sportsman or sportswoman.

SPOT satellite positioning and tracking.

spot. spotlight, esp. in theater.

SPP 1 severe parental punishment *sociology*. **2** Suicide Prevention Program.

spp. *or* **spp** species (plural).

SPPS stable plasma protein solution.

SPQR 1 *also* **S.P.Q.R.** the Senate and People of Rome (on standards with banners carried by Roman legions). [Latin *Senatus Populusque Romanus*] **2** small profits, quick returns.

SPR 1 simplified practice recommendation. **2** *also* **S.P.R.** Society for Psychical Research. **3** solid propellant rocket. **4** Strategic Petroleum Reserve (oil stockpile of the U.S.).

Spr. 1 sapper (British army engineer trained esp. in defusing munitions). **2** *also* **Spr** Spring.

SPRC Society for the Prevention and Relief of Cancer (of Great Britain).

S.P.R.I. Scott Polar Research Institute.

S.P.R.L. *or* **Sprl.** business firm with limited ownership liability; Inc. or Ltd. [French *Société de Personnes à Responsabilité Limitée*]

Spr.St. extension (of a telephone). [German *Sprechstelle*]

SPS 1 satellite power system. **2 a** secondary propulsion system. **b** service propulsion system (main rocket system in a service module of a spacecraft). **3** Social Democratic Party of Switzerland. [German *Sozialdemokratische Partei der Schweiz*] **4** solar power satellite. **5** Special Services (branch of the U.S. Army). **6** *also* **S.P.S.** standard pipe size. **7** superproton synchrotron (large-particle accelerator at CERN). **8** symbolic programming system *computers*.

s.p.s. without surviving issue *law*. [Latin *sine prole superstite*]

S.P.S.E. *or* **SPSE** Society of Photographic Scientists and Engineers.

SPSL Society for the Protection of Science and Learning.

S.P.S.P. St. Peter and St. Paul (Papal seal).

SPSS Statistical Package for the Social Sciences.

SPST *or* **s.p.s.t.** *or* **spst** single pole, single throw (switch).

SPT 1 *also* **Spt.** *or* **spt.** seaport. **2** shared page table *computers*. **3** *also* **spt.** support.

sptg sporting.

SPU 1 short-procedure unit (of a hospital, for same-day surgery or examination). **2** Social Democratic Party. [German *Sozialdemokratische Partei*]

S.P.U.C. *or* **SPUC** Society for the Protection of the Unborn Child (in Great Britain, etc.).

SPUR space power unit reactor.

SPURV Self-propelled Underwater Research Vehicle.

sp. vol. specific volume.

SPX simplex (one-way electronic communication).

SQ 1 Square (in postal address). **2** *also* **S-Q** stereophonic-quadraphonic (of electronic sound reproduction). **3** survival quotient.

Sq. 1 Squadron. **2** Square: *Union Sq.*

sq. 1 sequence. **2** *also* **sq** square, esp. in combination: *sq.ft.* = *square foot.* **3** the following one (*pl.* sqq.). [Latin singular *sequens* or plural *sequentia*]

SQA software quality assurance *computers*.

SQC statistical quality control.

sq.c. square corners, esp. in construction and bookbinding.

sq.ch. square chain (surveyor's measure).

sq.cm. square centimeter.

sqd. *or* **Sqd.** squad: *Emergency Sqd.*

Sqdn. Squadron: *Sqdn. Ldr. = Squadron Leader.*

sq.ft. *or* **sqft** square foot.

sq.in. square inch.

sq.km. square kilometer.

SQL structural query language *computers.*

sq.m. 1 square meter. 2 *also* **sq.mi.** square mile.

sq.mm. square millimeter.

Sqn. Squadron: *Sqn. Ldr. = Squadron Leader.*

sqq. the following ones. [Latin *sequentia*]

sq.r. *or* **sq.rd.** square rod.

SQUID *or* **squid** (*pronounced* skwid) superconducting quantum interference device (highly sensitive device to detect changes in a magnetic field).

sq.yd. square yard.

SR 1 Saudi Riyal (monetary unit of Saudi Arabia). 2 *also* **S.R.** sedimentation rate. 3 *also* **S/R** send or receive (radio transmission). 4 service record (of military personnel or of machinery or other equipment). 5 shipping receipt. 6 short rate *insurance.* 7 sigma reaction. 8 slow release *electronics.* 9 special regulation. 10 *also* **S-R** *or* **S→R** stimulus-response *psychology.* 11 subject ratio. 12 surveillance radar. 13 Swedish National Radio. [Swedish *Sveriges Radio*] 14 synthetic rubber.

Sr *I an abbreviation for:* 1 *also* **Sr.** Mr. [Italian *Signor*, Portuguese *Senhor*, Spanish *Señor*] 2 *also* **Sr.** senior: *John Baker Franklin Sr.; Sr. Mbr. = Senior Member.* 3 *also* **Sr.** sir: *Sr. John Rogers.* 4 *also* **Sr.** Sister (in a religious order): *Sr. Mary Benedictine.*
II a symbol for: strontium (chemical element): $Sr^{90} = strontium\ 90.$

sr *I an abbreviation for:* 1 *also* **s.r.** shipping receipt. 2 *also* **s.r.** short rate *insurance.*
II a symbol for: steradian (unit of measure of solid angles in geometry).

Sra. Mrs. [Italian *Signora*, Portuguese *Senhora*, Spanish *Señora*]

SRAM 1 short-range attack missile. 2 static random-access memory *computers.*

SR&CC strikes, riots, and civil commotions (clause of exceptions) *insurance.*

S.R.&O. statutory rules and orders.

SRB solid rocket booster (as for the space shuttle).

SRBC sheep red blood cell.

SRBM short-range ballistic missile.

SRC 1 Canadian Broadcasting Corporation service in Quebec. [French *Société Radio-Canada*] 2 sample return container. 3 solvent-refined coal. 4 stored response chain (of computer instructions). 5 *British* Student Representative Council. 6 Swiss Red Cross.

SRCC *or* **s.r.c.c.** strike, riot, and civil commotion (clause of exceptions) *insurance.*

SRCH *or* **Srch** search *computers.*

SRD Statutory Reserve Deposit (of the Australian banking system).

SRDE Signals Research and Development Establishment (of the British Army Signal Corps).

SRDS Standard Rate and Data Service (listing of advertising data).

SRE 1 *also* **S.R.E.** Most Holy Roman Church. [Latin *Sancta Romana Ecclesia* or *Sanctae Romanae Ecclesiae*] 2 surveillance radar element.

S.Rept. Senate Report (followed by a number).

S.Res. Senate Resolution (followed by a number).

Sres. Messrs. [Spanish *Señores*]

SRF 1 Selected Reserve Force (of the Army National Guard). 2 skin-reactive factor. 3 *also* **S.R.F.** Smithsonian Research Foundation.

SRI 1 *also* **S.R.I.** Holy Roman Empire. [Latin *Sacrum Romanum Imperium*] 2 Stanford Research Institute.

SRIF somatotropin-release-inhibiting factor.

Srio. secretary. [Spanish *secretario*]

Srita. Miss. [Spanish *Señorita*]

SRL 1 *also* **S.R.L.** *or* **S.r.l.** corporation. [Italian *Società a Responsabilità Limitata*, Spanish *Sociedad Responsabilidad Limitada*] 2 system reference library *computers.*

SRl Saudi Riyal (monetary unit of Saudi Arabia).

SRM 1 short-range missile. 2 solid rocket motor (as used on the space shuttle). 3 speed of relative movement. 4 Standard Reference Materials.

SRMS structure resonance modulation spectroscopy.

S.R.N. *British* State Registered Nurse (now *RGN*).

sRNA soluble ribonucleic acid (also known as *tRNA*) *biochemistry.*

S.R.O. 1 *British* self-regulatory organisation *commerce.* 2 sex-ratio organism (microorganism causing death of fruit fly male offspring). 3 *also* **SRO** single-room occupancy (welfare lodgings): *SRO hotel, S.R.O. buildings.* 4 *also* **SRO** standing room only (of a theatrical or concert performance). 5 Statutory Rules and Orders.

SRP 1 Savannah River Project (manufacturing facility for nuclear fuel). 2 Socialist Reich Party (neo-Nazi party in Germany). 3 Society for Radiological Protection. 4 suggested retail price. 5 supply refueling point.

SRS 1 *also* **S.R.S.** Fellow of the Royal Society. [Latin *Societatis Regiae Socius*] 2 slow reacting substance *medicine: SRS-A = slow reacting substance-anaphylaxis.* 3 Social and Rehabilitation Service (welfare agency). 4 supplemental restraint system (in an automobile referring to airbags, in addition to seat belts).

SRT *or* **Srt** sort, sorting *computers.*

Srta. Miss. [Italian *Signorita*, Portuguese *Senhorita*, Spanish *Señorita*]

S.R.U. *or* **SRU** Scottish Rugby Union.

S.R.V. surface recombination velocity (of electrons in a semiconductor) *electronics.*

SS 1 *also* **S.S.** His Holiness (the Pope). [French *Sa Sainteté*, Italian *Sua Santita*] 2 *also* **SS.** most holy. [Latin *sanctissimus*] 3 *also* **SS.** namely. [Latin *scilicet*] 4 *also* **SS.** pages. [German *Seiten*] 5 *also* **SS.** Saints: *SS. Peter and Paul.* 6 *also* **S.S.** *or* **S/S** same size (of a photograph or drawing) *printing.* 7 *also* **S/S** Saturday, Sunday *commerce.* 8 *also* **S.S.** Secretary of State. 9 *also* **S.S.** Secret Service. 10 Selective Service (division of government responsible for drafting manpower for the U.S. armed forces). 11 a semi-military force of the Nazi party. [German *Schutzstaffel*] **12** semisteel (scrap steel and pig iron mixture). **13** set screw (esp. in blueprints and other technical drawings). **14** shortstop *baseball*. **15** *also* **S.S.** Silver Star (military decoration). **16 a** single sideband (in radio transmission). **b** single signal *radio, electronics*. **17** social science. **18** Social Security (a federal pension system of the U.S. government). **19** Social Services. **20** solid state *electronics*. **21** stainless steel. **22** standard score, esp. in psychological testing. **23** standard size or sizes. **24** *also* **S.S.** or **S/S** steamship: *SS Lusitania*. **25** sterile solution. **26** *also* **S.S.** Straits Settlements (former British colony in SE Asia). **27** submarine (naval symbol): *SSN = nuclear-powered submarine*. **28** surfaced on side (of lumber): *S2S = surfaced or dressed on two sides*. **29** *also* **S-S** surface-to-surface, esp. in combination: *SSGW = surface-to-surface guided weapon*. **30** suspended sentence *law*. **31** suspended solids (waste products in water) *ecology*. **32** sworn statement *law*. **33 a** *also* **SS.** writers. [Latin *Scriptures*] **b** *also* **S.S.** written above. [Latin *supra scriptum*]

ss 1 half *pharmaceutics*. [Latin *semis*] **2** *also* **ss.** namely. [Latin *scilicet*] **3** *also* **ss.** narrow sense or interpretation, esp. in botany. [Latin *sensu stricto*] **4 a** *also* **ss.** sections. **b** subsection. **5** shortstop *baseball*. **6** *also* **ss.** without mutes *music*. [Italian *senza sordini*]

SSA 1 *also* **S.S.A.** Seismological Society of America. **2** Soaring Society of America. **3** Social Security Administration (of U.S. Department of Health and Human Services). **4** Society of Scottish Artists.

SSADM structural systems analysis and design method (British standard for computer systems).

SSAE or **s.s.a.e.** stamped self-addressed envelope.

S.S.A.F.A. British Soldiers', Sailors', and Airmen's Families Association.

SSAP Statement of Standard Accounting Practices.

SSB 1 *also* **S.S.B.** Bachelor of Sacred Scripture. [Latin *Sacrae Scripturae Baccalaureus*] **2** *also* **ssb** single sideband, in radio transmission. **3** single-strand binding (of a protein). **4** Social Security Board. **5** Space Science Board (of Great Britain).

SSBN nuclear-powered submarine (armed with ballistic missiles). [U.S. naval symbol for *SS* submarine, *B* ballistic, *N* nuclear]

SSC 1 *also* **S.S.C.** Society of the Holy Cross. [Latin *Societas Sanctae Crucis*] **2** *also* **S.S.C.** Solicitor before the Supreme Courts (of Scotland). **3** station selection code (of electronic communication). **4** superconducting supercollider (atomic accelerator).

S.Sc.D. Doctor of Social Science.

SSCI Social Sciences Citation Index.

SSCNS ship's self-contained navigation system.

SSD 1 *also* **S.S.D.** Doctor of Sacred Scripture. [Latin *Sacrae Scripturae Doctor*] **2** *also* **SS.D.** Most Holy Lord (the Pope). [Latin *Sanctissimus Dominus*] **3** Social Services Department. **4** solid-state storage device *electronics*. **5** Space Systems Division (of the U.S. Air Force). **6** State Security Service (formerly East Germany). [German *Staatssicherheitsdienst*] **7** steady-state distribution *physics*.

SS/DD single-sided double-density *computers*.

SS.D.N. Our Most Holy Lord (used of Jesus Christ or the Pope). [Latin *Sanctissimus Dominus Noster*]

ssDNA single-stranded deoxyribonucleic acid *biochemistry*.

SSE or **S.S.E.** or **s.s.e.** south-southeast.

SSEC 1 selective sequence electronic calculator. **2** Social Science Education Consortium.

SSF 1 *also* **S.S.F.** Society of St. Francis. **2** standard Saybolt furol (measure of viscosity).

SSFC Severe Storm Forecast Center (of U.S. Weather Service).

S.S.G.G. Stick, Stone, Grass, Groan (the Vehmgericht, secret tribunals—common in parts of Germany in medieval times—that took over governmental functions in an attempt to establish local order). [German *Stock, Stein, Gras, Grein*]

S/Sgt. or **S.Sgt.** staff sergeant.

SSHRC Social Sciences and Humanities Research Council of Canada.

SSI 1 site of scientific importance. **2** small-scale integration (of computer circuitry containing less than 100 transistors). **3** *also* **S.S.I.** Society of Scribes and Illuminators. **4** Supplemental Security Income (U.S. Federal aid to the needy over 65 or to the disabled).

Ssi. company. [Turkish *Sürekasi*]

SSIE or **S.S.I.E.** Smithsonian Scientific Information Exchange.

S.S.J. Society of Saint Joseph: *Sister Mary Vianney, S.S.J.*

S.S.J.E. Society of St. John the Evangelist.

SSK slip, slip, knit (a direction in knitting).

S.S.L. Licentiate of Sacred Scripture. [Latin *Sacrae Scripturae Licentiatus*]

SS LORAN or **loran** (lôr′an) sky-wave synchronized loran.

SSM 1 single-sideband modulation *electronics*. **2** *also* **S.S.M.** Society of the Sacred Mission. **3** surface-to-surface missile.

SSN 1 nuclear submarine. **2** Social Security number. **3** Standard Serial Number.

S.S.O. British Senior Science Officer.

SSP 1 Society for Scholarly Publishing. **2** *also* **S.S.P.** Society of St. Paul. **3** static spontaneous potential (electrical potential in oil-well drilling to map oil beds).

ssp or **ssp.** subspecies *biology*.

SSPE subacute sclerosing panencephalitis (a chronic brain disease, possibly caused by measles virus).

SSR 1 secondary surveillance radar. **2** solid-state relay. **3** *also* **S.S.R.** Soviet Socialist Republic (of the former Soviet Union).

S.S.R.C. or **SSRC** Social Science Research Council (now ESRC).

S.S.R.I. or **SSRI** Social Science Research Institute.

SSS 1 *also* **S.S.S.** Selective Service System (division of government for drafting manpower for U.S. armed forces).

s.s.s. layer upon layer. [Latin *stratum super stratum*]

SSSA Soil Sciences Society of America.

SSSC or **s.s.s.c.** soft-sized, supercalendered (of paper made very smooth with a soft glaze).

SSSI site of special scientific interest.

SSSR *or* **S.S.S.R.** Union of Soviet Socialist Republics (former Soviet Union). [Russian *Soyuz Sovietskikh Sotsialistickeskikh Respublik*]

SST 1 sea-surface temperature. **2** supersonic transport.

s state condition of no angular momentum *electronics*.

SSTV slow-scan television.

SSU 1 semiconductor storage unit *electronics*. **2** standard or seconds Saybolt universal (measure of viscosity in seconds).

SSV *or* **s.s.v.** under a poison label *pharmaceutics*. [Latin *sub signa veneni*]

SSW *or* **S.S.W.** *or* **s.s.w.** south-southwest.

SSWF sudden short-wave fade-out (of radio).

ST 1 segment table *computers*. **2 a** shipping ton (unit of capacity of about 40 cubic feet). **b** short ton (unit of weight, 2000 pounds). **3** sounding tube (pressure and depth gauge). **4** space telescope *astronomy*. **5** Speech Therapist. **6** standardized test. **7** *also* **S.T. a** Standard Time. **b** Summer Time. **8** *also* **S.T.** static thrust. **9** *also* **S.T.** *computers*: **a** storage capacity. **b** store. **10** Street (in postal address). **11** surface tension.

St 1 *also* **St.** Saint: *St. Thomas.* **2** Stanton number (measure of heat convection). **3** start, esp. in racing. **4** *also* **St.** State. **5** *also* **st.** statute *law*. **6** stokes (metric measure of viscosity). **7** straight, esp. in racing. **8** *also* **St.** Strait. **9** stratus (cloud) *meteorology*. **10** *also* **St.** Street: *Canal St.*

1st *or* **1ˢᵗ** first: *1st/Sgt. = First Sergeant; 21ˢᵗ Ave. = Twenty-first Avenue.*

st 1 *also* **s.t. a** shipping ton (unit of capacity of about 40 cubic feet). **b** short ton (unit of weight, 2000 pounds). **2** stained. **3** stand. **4** *also* **st.** stanza. **5** *also* **st.** statement. **6** *also* **st.** statute, esp. in combination: *st. mi. = statute mile.* **7** steel. **8** stem *botany*. **9** stere (unit of cubic measure, esp. for firewood). **10** stet (direction to a printer to restore original copy). **11** *also* **st.** stitch, in sewing, knitting, and bookbinding. **12** *also* **st.** stock. **13** stone (unit of weight, usually 14 pounds). **14** *also* **st.** strophe. **15** stumped (put out while the batsman is out of the batting area) *cricket*. **16** without time *music*. [Italian *senza tempo*]

STA Station (in postal address).

Sta. 1 *also* **Sta** Saint or Holy. [Spanish or Italian *Santa*] **2** station: *Union Sta.*

sta. 1 stamen *botany*. **2** station. **3 a** stationary. **b** stationery. **4** stator (stationary part, esp. around rotating machinery in a generator or turbine).

STAB *or* **stab. 1** stabilize. **2** stabilizer.

Stabex (stā'beks) stabilized exports (system in the EEC for stabilizing export earnings of developing countries).

stacc. staccato *music*.

STADAN Space Tracking and Data Acquisition Network (of unmanned satellites of all countries by NASA).

Stae. *or* **Ste.** Saints. [Latin feminine *Sanctae*]

Staffs. Staffordshire County, England.

STAG Strategy and Tactics Analysis Group *military*.

STAI State Trait Analysis Inventory.

STALO stabilized local oscillator *electronics*.

sta. mi. statute mile.

stan. *or* **STAN 1** stanchion (an upright support). **2** *also* **stand.** *or* **STAND** standard, also in combination: *STANAG = Standard Agreement.*

staph (*pronounced* staf) *or* **staph.** staphylococcus.

STAR standard terminal arrival route (of aircraft).

STARFIRE System To Accumulate and Retrieve Financial Information with Random Extraction.

STARS Satellite Telemetry Automatic Reduction System.

START 1 Space Technology and Advanced Reentry Tests. **2** Strategic Arms Reduction Talks (for reducing armed forces in Europe).

Stat. 1 Statute *law*. **2** *also* **Stat. L.** Statutes at Large (laws passed and executive orders issued during a session of the U.S. Congress).

stat. 1 *also* **stat** (*pronounced* stat) immediately *medicine, pharmaceutics*. [Latin *statim*] **2** static *electronics, mechanics*. **3** statics (mechanics of bodies at rest and of equal opposing forces). **4** stationary. **5 a** statistics. **b** statistical. **6 a** statuary. **b** statue. **7 a** statute: *stat. mi. = statute mile.* **b** statute miles.

Stat. Off. His or Her Majesty's Stationery Office (British government printing office).

S.T.B Bachelor of Sacred Theology. [Latin *Sacrae Theologiae Baccalaureus*]

stbd. starboard.

STC 1 sensitivity time control. **2** *also* **S.T.C.** Short Title Catalogue (of British books printed 1477–1640). **3** *also* **s.t.c.** single-trip container *shipping*.

Stck. part. [German *Stück*]

STD 1 *also* **S.T.D.** Doctor of Sacred Theology. [Latin *Sacrae Theologiae Doctor*] **2** salinity, temperature, depth (of a measure of ocean water): *STD recorder.* **3** sexually transmitted disease (used in place of *VD*). **4** skin test dose *medicine*. **5** South Tropical Disturbance (of the planet Jupiter). **6** *also* **std.** *or* **Std.** standard: *std.c.f. = standard cubic foot.* **7** Subscriber Trunk Dialing (long-distance telephone system in Great Britain).

Stdy Saturday.

STE Society of Telecommunications Engineers.

Ste. *or* **Ste** Saint. [French feminine *Sainte*]

STED solar turboelectric drive.

STEM 1 a scanning transmission electron microscope (high-resolution instrument giving a three-dimensional image). **b** scanning transmission electron microscopy. **2** storable tubular extendable member (of antennae).

Sten submachine gun: *Sten gun.* [Sheppard, Turpin, England, its inventors]

sten. 1 stencil. **2 a** stenographer. **b** stenography.

steno (sten'ō) *or* **stenog** (stə nog') stenographer.

Steph. Stephen.

STEPS (*pronounced* steps) **1** School-leavers' Training and Employment Preparation Scheme (of the New Zealand Labor Department). **2** solar thermionic electrical power systems.

ster. 1 stereotype (printing plate formerly made from type). **2 a** sterilize. **b** sterilizer. **c** sterilization. **3** *also* **sterl.** sterling.

stereo (ster′ē ō) stereophonic (of sound reproduction).

stev. stevedore.

stew. *or* **Stew.** steward.

St. Ex. stock exchange.

stf. staff.

STG Space Task Group (of NASA).

stg. 1 *also* **STG** stage, staging, esp. in combination: *STGAR = staging area.* **2** sterling. **3** *also* **stge.** storage.

stgr. *or* **STGR** stringer (heavy supporting beam).

STH somatotrophin or somatotrophic hormone (a growth hormone).

Sth. *or* **sth.** south.

Sthn. *or* **sthn.** southern.

STI 1 scientific and technical information. **2** *also* **S.T.I.** Stockholm Institute of Technology.

STID Scientific and Technical Information Division (of NASA).

stim. stimulus.

STINGS stellar inertial guidance system *navigation.*

stip. 1 a stipend. **b** stipendiary. **2** stipulation.

STIS Science and Technology Information System (of National Science Foundation).

stk. 1 sticky (on navigation charts). **2** stock.

Stkm. kilometers per hour. [German *Stundenkilometer*]

STL 1 *also* **S.T.L. a** Licentiate of Sacred Theology. [Latin *Sacrae Theologiae Licentiatus*] **b** Reader of Sacred Theology. [Latin *Sacrae Theologiae Lector*] **2** *also* **stl.** steel. **3** studio transmitter link *electronics.*

stlg. sterling.

STLO Scientific and Technical Liaison Officer.

STLR semitrailer (tractor-trailer combination).

St. Ltg. trunk line (of a telephone). [German *Stammleitung*]

STM 1 *also* **S.T.M.** Master of Sacred Theology. [Latin *Sacrae Theologiae Magister*] **2** scanning tunneling microscope. **3** short-term memory.

Stmt statement *commerce, finance.*

stn. 1 stain. **2** *also* **Stn** station.

stnd. stained.

STO 1 sea transport officer. **2** standing order.

Sto. Saint. [Spanish *Santo*]

STOL short takeoff and landing (of airplanes).

stor. storage.

S-to-S *or* **S to S 1** ship-to-shore (of radio transmission). **2** station-to-station.

STOVL short takeoff, vertical landing (of airplanes).

stow. stowage.

STP 1 dimethoxy-methylamphetamine (hallucinogenic drug). **2** *also* **S.T.P.** Professor of Sacred Theology. [Latin *Sacrae Theologiae Professor*] **3** Scientifically Treated Petroleum (tradename for a gasoline additive). **4** sewage treatment plant. **5** *also* **s.t.p.** standard temperature and pressure *chemistry, physics.*

stp. 1 stamp. **2** stamped.

Stpd. stumped (put out while the batsman is out of the batting area) *cricket.*

St.P. et Miq. St. Pierre et Miquelon (only remaining French holdings in the New World, south of Newfoundland).

STR 1 self-tuning regulator. **2** submarine thermal reactor. **3** synchronous transmitter receiver.

Str. 1 Strait. **2** street. [German *Strasse*] **3** stretch, in horse racing.

str. 1 straight. **2** strainer. **3** strait. **4** strength. **5** streptococcus. **6** string, strings *music.* **7** stroke (of an oar). **8** structural.

STRAC Strategic Army Corps (originally formed as a quick-strike force).

STRAD signal transmitting, receiving, and distributing.

Strad (*pronounced* strad) Stradivarius (family of stringed-instrument makers or an instrument made by them).

STRADAP storm radar data processor (to transmit storm information from all parts of the nation).

STRAF Strategic Army Forces.

STRAT strategic *military:* STRATCOM = *Strategic Communications Command.*

straw. strawberries.

strep *or* **strep.** (*pronounced* strep) streptococcus: *strep sore throat.*

STRESS structural engineering system solver.

STRICOM Strike Command (U.S. forces).

string. accelerating the tempo *music.* [Italian *stringendo*]

STROBE (strōb) satellite tracking of balloons and emergencies.

Str. Set. *or* **Str. Setts.** Straits Settlements (former British colony in Southeast Asia).

struc. *or* **struct.** structure.

STRUDL (strü′dəl) structural design language *computers.*

STS 1 *also* **S.T.S.** Scottish Text Society. **2** serological test for syphilis. **3** ship-to-shore (of radio transmission). **4** significant threshold shift. **5** space transportation system.

sts. 1 stanzas. **2** stems. **3** stitches. **4** streets.

stsm. *or* **Stsm.** statesman.

STU *or* **S.T.U.** skin test unit (as for allergic reaction).

STUC Scottish Trades Union Congress.

stud. student.

Stuka (stü′kə) German dive bomber of WWII. [German *Sturzkampfflugzeug*]

STV 1 Scottish Television. **2** space test vehicle. **3** subscription television.

stwd *or* **Stwd.** steward.

St wgn station wagon.

stwy stairway.

STX start of text *computers.*

SU 1 sensation unit *psychology.* **2** service unit. **3** set up *commerce,* esp. in combination: *SUCL = set up in carloads.* **4** *also* **S.U.** Siemens's unit *electricity.* **5** Special Unitary (symmetry, method of grouping particles) *physics:* SU(3) = *group of three dimensions.* **6** strontium unit.

Su. Sunday.

s.u. see below. [German *siehe unten*]

SUA State Universities Association.

SUB *or* **S.U.B.** supplemental unemployment benefits.

sub. **1** subeditor. **2** subfloor. **3** subject. **4** subjunctive *grammar*. **5** submarine. **6** subordinate. **7** subscription. **8** substitute. **9** *also* **Sub.** **a** suburb. **b** suburban. **10** subway.

subch. subchapter.

subcut. subcutaneous (below the skin).

subd. subdivision.

subgen. subgenus.

subj. **1** subject. **2 a** subjective. **b** subjectively. **3** subjunctive *grammar*.

subpar. subparagraph.

SUBROC submarine rocket.

Subs. subsidiary (of a business).

subs. **1** *also* **subs** subscription. **2** subsidiary (of a business). **3** subsistence: *subs. pay.* **4** substantive. **5** substitute.

subsec. subsection.

subsp. subspecies.

subst. **1 a** substantive. **b** substantively. **2** substitute.

substand. substandard.

subtrop. subtropical.

suc. **1 a** succeeded. **b** successor. **2** suction.

suct. suction.

SUD sudden unexpected death.

Suet. Suetonius (Roman biographer and historian, 75–160 AD).

suf. **1** sufficient. **2** suffix.

Suff. **1** Suffolk. **2** *also* **Suffr.** suffragan (bishop appointed to assist another bishop).

suff. **1** sufficient. **2** suffix.

sug. **1** suggested. **2** suggestion.

Sult. Sultan.

SUM surface-to-underwater missile.

Sum. **1** Sumerian (of Sumer, the ancient region in Euphrates river valley). **2** summer.

sum. *pharmaceutics* **a** take. [Latin *sume* or *sumendus*] **b** let him or her take. [Latin *sumat*]

summ. summary.

SUN *or* **S.U.N.** International Commission on symbols, units, and nomenclature.

Sun. *or* **Sund.** Sunday.

sund. sundries.

SUNFED *or* **Sunfed** (sun'fed) Special United Nations Fund for Economic Development.

SUNS sonic underwater navigation system.

SUNY (sü'nē) State University of New York.

sup. **1** *also* **Sup.** above. [Latin *supra*] **2** super (gauze glued on the spine of a book to reinforce the binding). **3** superfine. **4** superior. **5** superlative, esp. in grammar. **6** *also* **Sup.** **a** supplement. **b** supplementary. **7** supply. **8** support.

Sup.C. *or* **Sup. Ct.** **1** Superior Court. **2 a** Supreme Court. **b** Supreme Court Reporter.

supchg. **1** supercharge. **2** supercharger.

Supdt superintendent.

super (sü'pər) **1** *also* **Super.** superintendent. **2** *British* supermarket.

super. **1** superficial. **2** superfine. **3** superior.

superhet. superheterodyne *electronics*.

superl. superlative, esp. in grammar.

supp. **1** *also* **Supp.** supplement, also in combination: *Supp. Code = Supplement to Code.* **2** supplementary.

suppl. **1** *also* **Suppl.** supplement. **2** supplementary.

suppos. suppository *pharmaceutics*. [Latin *suppositorium*]

Supp. Rev. Stat. Supplement to the Revised Statutes.

supps. *or* **Supps.** supplements.

suppt. **1** *also* **Suppt.** supplement. **2** supplementary.

supr. *or* **Supr.** **1** superintendent. **2** superior, esp. in combination: *Supr. Ct. = Superior Court.* **3** supreme, esp. in combination: *Supr. Ct. = Supreme Court.*

supsd. superseded.

Supt. *or* **supt.** superintendent.

Supvr. *or* **supvr.** supervisor.

Sur. Surrey County, England.

sur. **1** surcharged. **2** *also* **surf.** surface. **3** surplus.

Sur. Ct. Surrogate Court.

surg. **1** *also* **Surg.** surgeon. **2 a** surgery. **b** surgical.

Surg. Gen. Surgeon General.

surj slip, in knitting. [French *surjet*]

Surr. Surrogate (an assistant bishop or a judge in charge of wills and estates).

surr. surrender.

SURV standard underwater research vessel.

surv. **1 a** survey. **b** surveying. **2** *also* **Surv.** surveyor. **3** surviving, esp. in law.

Surv. Gen. *or* **Surv.-Gen.** Surveyor General.

SURWAC surface water automatic computer (automatic processing of records from stream-flow gauging stations).

SUS Saybolt universal seconds (unit of measure of viscosity).

Sus. Susanna (book in the Apocrypha).

sus suspect (as of a crime).

susp. suspended, suspension.

Suss. Sussex (former county in SE England or former early kingdom and later part of Wessex in Anglo-Saxon times).

Suth. Sutherland (former county in Scotland).

SUV **1** Saybolt universal viscosity (measure of viscosity in seconds). **2** Saybolt universal viscosimeter.

SV **1** *also* **S.V.** Holy Virgin. [Latin *Sancta Virgo*] **2** safety valve. **3** *also* **S/V** sailing vessel. **4** simian virus (usually followed by a number): *SV-40 is known to induce cancer in monkeys.* **5** *also* **S.V.** Sons of Veterans. **6** *also* **S.V.** Your Holiness. [Latin *Sanctitas Vestra*]

Sv sievert (unit of absorbed radiation).

s.v. under the word *or* heading. [Latin *sub verbo or sub voce*]

SVC still-video camera (for reproduction on a television screen); SVS.

svc service.

SVD swine vesicular disease (similar to foot-and-mouth disease).

SVGA super video graphics display *computers.*

SVO subject, verb, object (traditional English sentence pattern).

SVP 1 *also* **S.V.P.** if you please. [French *s'il vous plaît*] **2** senior vice-president *commerce.*

S.V.R. *or* **s.v.r.** rectified spirit of wine (alcohol) *pharmaceutics.* [Latin *spiritus vini rectificatus*]

SVS 1 Stamp Ventures (printer of U.S. postage stamps). **2** still-camera video system (for reproduction on a television screen); SVC. **3** *also* **S.V.S.** *British* The Society for Visiting Scientists.

S.V.T. proof spirit (alcohol). [Latin *spiritus vini tenuis*]

SVTP sound velocity, temperature, pressure (measure of sound wave through a specified medium).

svw. equivalent to. [German *soviel wie*]

svy survey.

SW 1 seawater or salt water. **2** shipper's weight *commerce.* **3** shortwave (radio transmission). **4** snow shower *meteorology.* **5** software *computers.* **6** *also* **S.W. a** southwest. **b** southwestern. **7** *also* **S.W.** Southwestern Reporter (publication) *law:* *S.W. (2d)* = *Southwestern Reporter, second series.* **8** specific weight. **9** spot weld. **10** station wagon. **11** *also* **sw.** switch.

Sw. 1 a Sweden. **b** Swedish. **2** *also* **sw.** swell organ. **3** Swiss.

s.w. 1 *also* **s/w** soft water. **2 a** southwest. **b** southwestern. **3** specific weight.

S.W.A. *or* **SWA** South-West Africa (now Namibia).

SWAC Standards Western Automatic Computer (of the National Bureau of Standards).

SWACS Space Warning and Control System.

SWAK 1 sealed with a kiss (esp. on a love letter or the flap of the envelope). **2** *also* **SWALK** sealed with a loving kiss.

SWAMI standing-wave area monitor indicator *electronics.*

SWANU South-West Africa National Union.

SWANUF South-West Africa National United Front.

SWAPO *or* **Swapo** (swä'pō) South-West Africa People's Organization.

SWAT *or* **S.W.A.T.** (*pronounced* swot) Special Weapons and Tactics or Special Weapons Attack Team (civilian police unit trained in the use of military weapons).

SWATH small waterplane area, twin hulled (of a ship).

SWB short wheelbase (of a truck or automobile).

swbd. switchboard.

SWbS *or* **SW by S** southwest by south.

SWbW *or* **SW by W** southwest by west.

SWD sliding watertight door.

swd. *or* **swd** sewed, esp. of a bookbinding.

SWE Society of Women Engineers.

Swe. *or* **Swed. 1** Sweden. **2** Swedish.

SWG 1 *also* **S.W.G.** Screen Writers Guild. **2** *also* **swg a** Standard Wire Gauge. **b** Steel Wire Gauge.

SWGR switchgear (device to operate electrical circuit).

SWIA Southwest Association of Indian Arts.

SWIFT Society of Worldwide Interbank Financial Telecommunication.

Swit. *or* **Switz.** Switzerland.

SWL 1 safe working load (of cables and machinery). **2** short-wave listener.

SWP 1 safe working pressure. **2** Socialist Workers Party.

SWR 1 serum Wassermann reaction. **2** standing wave ratio.

SWS short wave sleep (of the third and fourth stages of sleep).

swtg switching.

SWTL surface wave transmission line.

Swtz. Switzerland.

SX solvent extraction (to recover uranium from uranium ore).

Sx. Sussex (former county in SE England).

sx simplex *mathematics.*

SXAPS soft X-ray appearance potential *spectroscopy.*

SXN *or* **sxn.** Section.

SXR soft X-ray.

SXT *or* **Sxt.** sextant.

Sy. 1 Seychelles (group of small islands in the Indian Ocean off the coast of Africa). **2** Surrey County, England. **3** Syria.

sy. supply.

SYB *Statesman's Year-Book.*

SYd *or* **S.Yd.** Scotland Yard (headquarters of the London Police or, especially, the detective division of the London Police).

Syd. Sydney, Australia.

S.Y.H.A. *or* **SYHA** Scottish Youth Hostels Association.

syll. 1 a *also* **syl.** syllable. **b** syllabication. **2** *also* **syl.** syllabus.

SYLK symbolic link format *computers.*

sym. 1 *also* **Sym a** symbol. **b** symbolic. **2 a** symmetrical *chemistry.* **b** symmetry. **3 a** *also* **Sym.** symphony. **b** symphonic. **4** symptom.

symb. symbol.

Symp. symposium: *Unstable Chemical Species Symp.*

Symph. symphony.

SYN *computers* **1** synchronizing. **2** synchronous.

Syn. 1 Synagogue. **2** Synod (church council or assembly or governing body of a church).

syn. 1 a synchronize. **b** synchronized. **c** synchronizing. **d** synchronous. **2** syndrome. **3** *also* **Syn. a** synonym. **b** synonymous. **c** synonymy. **4** syntax. **5** synthetic.

sync *or* **SYNC** (singk) **1 a** synchronize. **b** synchronizing. **c** synchronization. **2** synchronous.

synch (singk) *or* **synchro. 1 a** synchronize. **b** synchronization. **2** synchronous.

SYNCOM *or* **Syncom** (sin'kom') synchronous communications (series of geostationary space satellites).

synd. 1 a syndicate. b syndicated. 2 *also* **Synd** syndication.

syndet (sin′det′) synthetic detergent.

synfuel (sin′fyü′əl) synthetic fuel.

syngas (sin′gas′) synthetic gas.

synon synonymous.

synop. synopsis.

synth. 1 synthesis. 2 synthesizer *music*. 3 synthetic.

SYNTOL Syntagmatic Organization Language.

syph (*pronounced* sif) syphilis.

Syr. 1 a Syria. b Syrian. 2 Syriac (ancient Semitic language of Syria).

syr. syrup *pharmaceutics*.

sys. 1 *also* **Sys.** system. 2 systematic. 3 systemic.

SYSGEN system generation *computers*.

SYSIN system input *computers*.

SYSOP systems operator *computers*.

SYSOUT system output *computers*.

syst. 1 *also* **Syst.** system. 2 systematic. 3 systemic. 4 systole (contraction of the heart).

sz. size.

T

T *I an abbreviation for:* **1 a** pa'anga (monetary unit of Tonga): *T$.* **b** Taiwan: *T$ = Taiwan dollar.* **c** Tanzania or Tanzanian: *TSh = Tanzania shilling.* **2** *also* **T.** part (of a publication). [German *Teil*] **3** *also* **T.** silence *music.* [Italian *tace*] **4** *also* **T.** tablespoon. **5** tackle *football.* **6** tanker. **7** target. **8** technical foul *basketball.* **9** tee (T-shaped, as a pipe fitting) *engineering.* **10** teeth or tooth (esp. of a gearwheel). **11** telephone, esp. in combination: *NYT = New York Telephone.* **12** temperature: **a** absolute or Kelvin or thermodynamic temperature *physics.* **b** mean temperature *meteorology.* **c** body temperature *medicine.* **13** temporary: *TB = temporary buoy* (in navigation). **14** *also* **T.** tenor (of the voice) *music.* **15** tensile. **16** a tension. **b** surface tension. **17** tera- (one trillion or 10^{12}): *TC = teracycle.* **18** *also* **T.** terminal: *GCT = Grand Central Terminal.* **19** *also* **T.** Territory, in combination: *N.W.T. = Northwest Territories.* **20** thunderstorm. **21** *also* **T.** Thursday. **22 a** thymine (one of the four base compounds of DNA). **b** thymus: *T-Cell* (lymphocyte). **23** tide, in combination: *MST = mean spring tide.* **24** tied (of a game or record of play). **25** time: **a** detonation, starting, or firing time, in combination: *T-40 = firing or takeoff time minus forty minutes.* **b** elapsed time of one cycle, revolution, orbit, vibration, or other periodic phenomena: *Time of passing perihelion, T.* **c** directional time *physics: T stands for time (forward or backward),* see symbols below. **d** setting of a camera shutter, used for long exposures. **26** ton, also in combination: *LT = long ton or 2240 pounds; ST = short ton or 2000 pounds.* **27** torque. **28** total. **29** *also* **T.** township: *sec.4,T. 15N = section 4 of township 15 north.* **30** *also* **T.** trace: **a** of precipitation *meterology.* **b** of an element or substance *chemistry.* **31** transformer. **32** *also* **T.** translation, esp. in library cataloging. **33** transmittance. **34** tranportation, esp. in combination: *MTA = Metropolitan Transportation Authority.* **35** transport number *chemistry.* **36** Treasury (department of the U.S. government), *esp. in T-Bond, T-Note, T-Bill.* **37** tropical. **38** true (of a compass bearing or an answer on a test): *TN = true north; T-F test = true-false test.* **39** truss *engineering.* **40** tube, in combination: *VTVM = vacuum tube voltmeter; PT = pneumatic tube.* **41** *also* **T.** Tuesday. **42** Turkey or Turkish: *T£, LT,* or *TL = Turkish lira.* **43** *also* **T.** volume (part of a set or series of books). [French *Tome,* Latin *Tomus,* Russian *Tom,* Spanish *Tomo*]

II a symbol for: **1** directional time (esp. time reversal, one of the three components of symmetry) *physics.* **2** half-life, of a radioactive substance: $T_{1\ 2}$. **3** kinetic energy. **4** tesla (unit of magnetic induction). **5** thrust *aeronautics.* **6** tritium (isotope of hydrogen). **7** Tropical Load Line (Plimsoll mark to show maximum depth a ship may ride in tropical waters when loaded). **8** twentieth of a series (nineteenth when *J* is omitted).

T₃ T_3 triiodothyronine (amino acid used to treat hypothyroidism).

T₄ T_4 thyroxine (amino acid of thyroid gland, active in metabolism and in growth of children).

2,4,5,-T trichlorophenoxy-acetic acid (a herbicide used esp. in brush control).

t *I an abbreviation for:* **1** *also* **t.** all together (of voices or instruments) *music.* [Italian *tutti*] **2** *also* **t.** in the time of. [Latin *tempore*] **3** *also* **t.** plate *botany.* [Latin *tabula*] **4** *also* **t.** taken. **5** *also* **t.** tare (weight of a container, wrapping, vehicle, etc., other than the goods or substance it contains). **6** target *electronics.* **7** *also* **t.** teaspoon. **8** temperature. **9** *also* **t.** tempo *music.* **10** *also* **t.** temporal *medicine.* **11** tenor (of an instrument) *music.* **12** *also* **t.** tensor esp. in medicine. **13** tentative (as of price, scientific name of a specimen, etc.). **14** terminal: $t^+ = positive\ terminal.$ **15** *also* **t.** tertiary. **16** thickness or depth or, sometimes, height. **17** thunder. **18** time: $r \times t = d =$ *rate times time equals distance.* **19** title, esp. in library cataloging. **20** *also* **t. a** ton, also in combination: *n.t. = net ton.* **b** metric ton (2240.62 pounds). **21** top, esp. in combination: *t quark = top quark* (hypothetical quark with possible mass 13 times that of a proton). **22** transition. **23** *also* **t.** transitive, esp. in combination: *vt = verb transitive.* **24** triode *electronics.* **25** triton *chemistry.* **26** *also* **t.** troy weight. **27** *also* **t.** tun (old unit of liquid measure, esp. for wine and spirits). **28** twist, in knitting: *tb1 = twist back one stitch.* **29** *also* **t.** volume (part of a set or series of books). [French *tome*, Latin *tomus*, Spanish *tomo*]

II *a symbol for:* **1** ratio of a statistic to its standard error *statistics.* **2** twentieth of a series (nineteenth when *j* is omitted).

t- triple bond *chemistry: t-butenyl.*

TA 1 a target *electronics.* **b** target area *military.* **2** Technology Administration (of U.S. Department of Commerce). **3** *also* **T/A a** teaching assistant. **b** temporary assistant. **4** terephthalic acid (used in manufacture of synthetic textile fibers). **5** *British* Territorial Army: *TA units.* **6** therapeutic abortion. **7** *also* **T-A** toxin antitoxin (mixture of toxin with antitoxin, causing only enough reaction to produce immunization). **8** transactional analysis (form of psychoanalysis). **9** Transit Authority (municipal railway system, esp. the one in New York City). **10** travel allowance. **11** *also* **ta** true altitude.

Ta tantalum (chemical element).

t.a. as the acts show *law.* [Latin *testantibus actis*]

TAA 1 Technical Assistance Administration (now *TA*). **2** tumor-associated antigens *medicine.*

TAB 1 *also* **Tab** tabulator (key and mechanism of a typewriter for spacing). **2** Technical Assistance Board (of UN). **3** typhoid, paratyphoid fevers A and B (typhoid = paratyphoid vaccine).

tab. 1 table (arrangement of information in columns or lines). **2** a tablet *pharmaceutics.* **3** tabulate.

TABA The American Book Awards (formerly *NBA* and since 1980 returned to that name).

tabl. tablet, esp. in pharmaceutics.

TABSOL Tabular Systems Oriented Language *computers.*

TAC 1 tactical *military,* esp. in combination: *TACMAR = tactical multifunctional array radar.* **2** Tactical Air Command. **3** Technical Assistance Committee (of UN).

Tac. Tacitus (Roman historian and orator, 55–120 AD).

TACAN *or* **Tacan** (ta'kan') tactical air navigation.

TACS *military* **1** Tactical Air Control System. **2** Theater Area Communications Systems.

TACV tracked air-cushion vehicle (high-speed train riding on a cushion of air over a concrete track).

TAF 1 Tactical Air Force. **2** toxoid-antitoxin floccules *medicine.*

Taf. 1 a table or chart. **b** diagram or index. [German *Tafel*]

TAFE Technical and Further Education (an Australian system of specialized courses to provide instruction that supplements or advances technical skills).

TAG The Adjutant General.

Tag. Tagalog (Austronesian family of languages including those of Malaya, Indonesia, and the Phillippines).

TAI International Atomic Time (measure of time in the ISO system). [French *Temps Atomique International*]

Tai. Taiwan.

TAL Trans-Alpine Pipeline. [Italian *Trans-Alpino Linea*]

Tal. Talmud (Jewish civil and traditional law and commentary on the Old Testament).

TALAR *or* **Talar** (ta'lär') tactical landing approach radio.

tal. qual. average quality (such quality as comes). [Latin *talis qualis*]

TAM 1 Tactical Air Missile. **2** Television Audience Measurement.

Tam. Tamil (a language of southern India and Sri Lanka, having a rich and ancient literature).

TAMS Token and Medal Society.

Tam. Shr. The Taming of the Shrew (play by Shakespeare).

tan tangent.

T&A *or* **T and A 1** taken and accepted *commerce.* **2 a** tonsils and adenoids. **b** tonsillectomy and adenoidectomy (removal) *medicine.*

t&b top and bottom.

t.&d. taps and dies.

T&E 1 test and evaluation. **2** training and education. **3** travel and entertainment (of U.S. Treasury Internal Revenue Service rules and guidelines for figuring taxable business expenditures). **4** *also* **t&e** trial and error.

T&G *or* **t.&g.** tongue and groove (of lumber edges milled to fit together with a tongue and groove joint).

T&M *or* **t&m** time and materials *commerce.*

t.&o. taken and offered, in horse racing.

Tang. 1 Tanganyika. **2** Tangier.

tanh hyperbolic tangent.

TANS terminal area navigation system.

TANU Tanganyika African National Union (after unification of Tanzania, succeeded by *CCM*).

TAN-ZAM Tanzania-Zambia Railway.

TAO Technical Assistance Operation (of UN).

TAOC Tactical Air Operations Center.

TAOR Tactical Area of Responsibility *military.*

TAP 1 Technical Assistance Program. **2** Trans-Alaska Pipeline.

Tapline (tap'lïn') Trans-Arabian Pipeline.

TAPPI Technical Association of the Pulp and Paper Industry.

TAPS (*pronounced* taps) Trans-Alaska Pipeline System.

TAR 1 Tactical Aerial Reconnaissance. **2** terrain-avoidance radar.

tar. tariff.

TARAN test and replace as necessary.

tarp (*pronounced* tärp) tarpaulin.

TAS 1 Target Acquisition Systems (of targets in the former Soviet Union). **2** true air speed.

Tas. 1 Tasmania (state in Australia). **2** Tasmanian.

Taser (tä'zər) tele-active shock electronic repulsion (device temporarily immobilizing a person by electric shock transmitted through dart and wire).

TASI time assignment speech interpolation (telephone switching system regulating speech transmission).

TASM tactical air to surface missile.

Tasm. Tasmania or Tasmanian.

TASNET (taz'net') Tasmanian Network (network of school terminals in a centralized computing facility).

TASS *or* **Tass** (*pronounced* tas) former Soviet News Agency. [Russian *Telegrafnoye Agenstvo Sovetskovo Soyuza*]

TAT 1 tetanus antitoxin. 2 thematic apperception test (storytelling personality test). 3 toxin-antitoxin. 4 transactivation and transcription (of the gene connected with AIDS infection). 5 transatlantic telephone (cables). 6 tyrosine aminotransferase (enzyme active in metabolism and production of thyroid hormones).

TATB triaminotrinitrobenzene (ingredient in explosives).

Tau Taurus, the Bull (constellation).

TAUN Technical Assistance of the UN.

taut. tautology (esp. as an editorial comment).

TAV transatmospheric vehicle (ultrasonic experimental aircraft).

T-a-v. Completely yours (complimentary close in correspondence). [French *Tout-à-vous*]

tav. or **Tav.** tavern.

TAW or **t.a.w.** twice a week (publication schedule of an advertisement; delivery schedules for mail, etc.).

tax. 1 taxation. 2 *also* **taxon. a** taxonomic. **b** taxonomy.

TB 1 tailboard (of a truck). 2 technical bulletin: *TB 6-431.* 3 temporary buoy (on navigation charts). 4 terabyte (unit of one trillion bytes of storage). 5 thymol blue (acid base indicator) *biochemistry.* 6 time base (device controlling wave sweep of a cathode-ray tube). 7 *also* **tb** times at bat *baseball.* 8 Treasury Bill *finance.* 9 trial balance *bookkeeping.* 10 true bearing *navigation.* 11 *also* **T.B. a** tuberculosis. **b** tubercle bacillus.

Tb *I an abbreviation for:* **a** *also* **Tb.** tuberculosis. **b** tubercle bacillus.
II a symbol for: 1 *also* T_b body temperature. 2 terbium (chemical element).

tb 1 *also* **tb. a** tablespoon (measure of about 1/2 ounce). **b** tablespoonful. 2 trial balance *bookkeeping.* 3 **a** *also* **tb.** tuberculosis. **b** tubercle bacillus.

TBA 1 tires, batteries, and accessories, in automotive trade. 2 *also* **T.B.A.** to be announced (esp. on a schedule of events). 3 to be assigned.

TB&S top, bottom, and sides (of lumber).

TBB tenor, baritone, bass (of a musical score).

TBC time base corrector (to filter and stabilize the electronic signal in a television set).

TBD 1 to be determined. 2 to be discontinued.

TBE 1 to be edited. 2 to be expanded.

TBG thyroxine binding globulin (chief thyroid transport protein) *biochemistry.*

TBL or **t B/L** through bill of lading *commerce.*

t.b.l. through back of loops, in knitting.

TBM 1 tactical ballistic missile. 2 *also* **T.B.M.** (advisory) tax board memorandum. 3 *also* **T.B.M.** temporary bench mark (on surveys). 4 tunnel boring machine.

TBO time between overhauls: *to fix every type of engine's TBO.*

TBP 1 tributyl phosphate (esp. used as a solvent). 2 true boiling point.

TBPA thyroxine-binding prealbumin *medicine.*

tbr. or **TBR** timber (esp. a support in building).

TBS 1 talk between ships: *TBS radio.* 2 tetra propylbenzene sulfonate (detergent). 3 tribromosalicylanilide (antiseptic used in soaps). 4 Turner Broadcasting System.

tbs. or **tbsp.** 1 tablespoon (measure of about 1/2 ounce). 2 tablespoonful.

TBT tetrabutyl titanate (adhesive used in paints and for applications of rubber and plastic).

TC 1 *also* **T.C.** (U.S.) Tax Court. 2 *also* **T.C.** Teachers College: *Ball State TC.* 3 *also* **T.C.** technically classified. 4 terra cotta. 5 thermocouple. 6 time check. 7 total cholesterol *medicine.* 8 total cost. 9 town clerk. 10 Transportation Command (of U.S. Department of Defense). 11 true course. 12 Trusteeship Council (of the UN).

Tc 1 technetium (chemical element). 2 *also* **TC** teracycle or teracycles per second.

tc 1 teracycle or teracycles per second. 2 tetracycline (antibiotic). 3 *also* **tc.** tierce: **a** former measure of wines and spirits equal to 42 gallons. **b** fencing stance.

TCA 1 terminal control area (of an airport). 2 tricarboxylic acid (organic acid formed in metabolism). 3 trichloroacetic acid (herbicide). 4 tricyclic antidepressant (one of several compounds used to fight depression).

TCAM telecommunications access method.

TCAS Traffic Collision Avoidance System (for aircraft).

TCB task control block *computers.*

TCC 1 Transport and Communications Commission (of UN). 2 Troop Carrier Command.

TCDC Technical Cooperation Among Developing Countries (of the Colombo Plan, of economic assistance).

TCDD tetrachlorodibenzo-p-dioxin (commonly called dioxin, a persistent herbicide).

TCDF tetrachlorodibenzofuron (chemical related to dioxin).

TCE 1 ton coal equivalent (unit measure for generating energy commercially). 2 trichlorethylene (used in cleaning metals).

TCF 1 tissue coding factor (substance produced by target cells in developing organism). 2 *also* **T.C.F.** Touring Club of France.

tcf trillion cubic feet (of natural gas).

TCGF t-cell growth factor *biology.*

tchg. or **Tchg.** teaching.

tchr. or **Tchr.** teacher.

TCI Touring Club of Italy.

TCIU Transportation Communications International Union.

T.C.N. third-country nationals.

TCNE tetracyanoethylene (a cyanocarbon used in dyes).

TCNQ tetracyanoquinodimethane (used in photographic processes).

TCO 1 Swedish Union of Salaried Employees. [Swedish *Tjänstëmannens Centralorganisation*] 2 Test Control Officer.

TCP 1 Technical Cooperation Program (of the UN). 2 transmission control protocol *computers.* 3 trichlorophenol (fungicide and antiseptic). 4 tricresyl phosphate (gasoline additive).

TCR temperature coefficient of resistance.

TCS 1 target cost system. 2 terminal control system *computers.* 3 traffic control system.

tctl. tactical.

TCTS Trans-Canada Telephone System.

TCXO temperature compensated crystal oscillator *electronics*.

TD 1 *also* **T.D.** Member of Parliament of the Republic of Ireland. [Gaelic *Teachta Dála*] **2** table of distribution. **3** tardive dyskinesia (nervous disorder). **4** Tax Division (of U.S. Department of Justice). **5** *also* **T.D.** technical director. **6** tetanus and diphtheria *medicine*. **7** thoria-dispersed: *TD nickel*. **8** time delay (device to withhold activation of machinery, explosives, etc., for a fixed period of time). **9** *also* **T/D** time deposit *finance*. **10** *also* **T/D** tons per day: *a 200 T/D production plant*. **11** total depth (of an oil field). **12** touchdown *football*. **13** *also* **T.D.** Traffic Director. **14** transmitter distributor *computers*. **15** *also* **T.D. a** Treasury Decision (with a number): *T.D. 8354 1991-30*. **b** Treasury Department. **16** Trinidad and Tobago. **17** tunnel diode *electronics*.

TDA tax deferred annuity.

TDB 1 Barycentric Dynamical Time (system for determining position of celestial bodies based on gravitational center of solar system). [French *Temps Dynamique Barycentrique*] **2** Total Disability Benefit.

t.d.c. *or* **TDC** top dead center (end of stroke farthest from crankshaft).

TDD Telecommunications Device for the Deaf (voice-operated teleprinter that can also be used as a teleprinter operated by a keyboard).

TDDL time division data link *electronics*.

TDE 1 tetrachloro-diphenylethane (insecticide). **2** turned-down edge (fault of an astronomical telescope mirror).

TDF 1 Television of France (government production agency for French television). [French *Télédiffusion de France*] **2** two degrees of freedom (of a gyroscopic mechanism).

TDG Twist Drill Gauge.

TDH total dynamic head *mechanics*.

TDI tolylene diisocyanate (used to make polyurethane foams, rubbers, and surface-coating materials).

TDIS Travel Document and Issuance System (of U.S. State Department Passport Division).

TDM time division multiplexing *computers*.

tdm. tandem.

TDMA time division multiplex access *computers*.

T.D.N. *or* **t.d.n.** total digestible nutrients (as of feed grain nutritional values).

TDO tornado.

TDP 1 *also* **T.D.P.** thermal death point (temperature at which organisms of a culture will die immediately) *biology*. **2** thymidine diphosphate (component of DNA). **3** Trade and Development Program.

TDPOB Thrift Depositor Protection Oversight Board (U.S. government agency for general oversight of the Resolution Trust Corporation).

TDR 1 *also* **t.d.r.** all rights reserved. [French *tous droits réservés*] **2** time domain reflectometer or reflectometry (measure of line and circuit characteristics of electrical equipment). **3** *also* **T.D.R.** torch and drill resisting (of metal): *a T.D.R.*

safe. **4** torque differential receiver *electronics*. **5** transmit data register.

TDRS Tracking and Data Relay Satellite.

TDRSS Tracking and Data Relay Satellite System.

t.d.s. to be taken three times a day *pharmaceutics*. [Latin *ter die sumendum*]

TDT Terrestrial Dynamic Time *astronomy*.

TDTL tunnel diode transistor logic *computers*.

TDWR thermal Doppler weather radar *meteorology, aeronautics*.

TDY temporary duty *military*.

TDZ touchdown zone *aeronautics*.

TE 1 *also* **T/E** table of equipment. **2 a** *also* **T-E** temperature efficiency (classification of climate in particular areas according to favorability of plant growth): *T-E index*. **b** thermal efficiency. **3** tight end (position) *football*. **4** *also* **T.E.** topographical engineer. **5** trailing edge, esp. in aeronautical design. **6** transverse electric (of no electric force along path of transmission): *TE wave*. **7** trial and error *psychology*. **8** turbine engine. **9** *also* **t-e** twin-engine *aeronautics*.

Te *I an abbreviation for:* **1** temperature. **2** tetanus.
II a symbol for: tellurium (chemical element).

TEA 1 *also* **TEAC** tetraethylammonium chloride (nerve block) *medicine*. **2** transferred electron amplifier. **3** transversely excited atmospheric (pressure laser): *TEA laser*.

TEAM Top European Advertising Media (newspapers joined in an organization for single orders in all papers).

teasp. teaspoon or teaspoonful (measure of about 1/6 fluid ounce).

Tec (*pronounced* tek) Technical (of a school): *Georgia Tec*.

tech. *or* **Tech.** (*pronounced* tek) **1 a** *also* **tech** technical: *tech rep = technical representative; Tech. Sgt. = Technical Sergeant*. **b** technically. **2** *also* **tech** technician. **3** technique. **4 a** technology. **b** technological.

techn. *or* **Techn.** **1** technical. **2** technician. **3** technology.

technol. **1** technology. **2** technological.

TEDIS trade electronic data interchange system.

TEE Trans-Europe Express: *TEE trains now link 90 European cities*.

TEFL (tef'əl) Teaching English as a Foreign Language.

Teflon (tef'lon) polytetrafluoroethylene (plastic noted for its slippery composition).

TEFRA Tax Equity and Fiscal Responsibility Act.

TEG 1 *also* **t.e.g.** top edges gilt *bookbinding*. **2** triethylene glycol (solvent and softener in plastic compounds).

TEI Text Encoding Initiative (standard system to code text for electronic storage).

TEL tetraethyl lead (early gasoline additive).

Tel 1 the Telescope (constellation). **2** *also* **Tel.** Telugu (language of eastern India).

tel. **1 a** telegram. **b** telegraph. **c** telegraphic. **d** telegraphy. **2 a** *also* **Tel.** telephone: *Tel. No. = telephone number*. **b** telephony.

tele (tel'ē) *British* television.

Telecom or **telecom.** telecommunications.

teleg. 1 telegram. 2 a telegraph. b telegraphy.

teleph. 1 telephone. 2 telephony.

TELERAN (tel′ə ran′) television radar air navigation (air navigation system).

TELEX or **telex** (tel′eks) teletype exchange (the exchange itself or a message sent by teletype).

telly (tel′ē) *British* television.

TELOPS (tel′ops) Telemetry On-Line Processing System.

Tely (tel′ē) Telegram, esp. in the name of a newspaper.

TEM 1 transmission electron microscope. 2 transverse electromagnetic: *TEM wave.* 3 triethylene melamine (substance used in resin and textile manufacturing and experimental medicine).

TEMA Telecommunication Engineering and Manufacturing Association (of Great Britain).

Temp. 1 temperate zone (one of the divisions of the earth's surface between the Torrid and Frigid Zones). 2 The Tempest (play by Shakespeare).

temp. 1 in the time of. [Latin *tempore*] 2 temperance. 3 (*pronounced* temp) temperature. 4 *also* **TEMP** template. 5 a temporary. b (*pronounced* temp) temporary worker.

ten. 1 held to full time value *music.* [Italian *tenuto*] 2 a tenant. b tenement. 3 *also* **Ten.** tenor *music.*

tency tenancy.

Tenn. 1 Tennessee. 2 Tennyson (Victorian poet).

TENS transcutaneous electrical nerve stimulation or stimulator (used to block pain by stimulating nerves).

tens. 1 tensile: *tens. str. = tensile strength.* 2 tension.

tent. tentative: *tent. std. = tentative standard.*

TEP triethyl phosphate (solvent, softener for plastics, pesticides).

TEPA or **tepa** triethylene phosphoramide (used as chemotherapy in certain forms of cancer).

TEPP tetraethyl pyrophosphate (used as an insecticide, medicine, and nerve gas).

TER Terrace (in postal address).

ter. 1 *also* **Ter.** terrace. 2 terrazzo (flooring usually made of small pieces of broken tile). 3 *also* **Ter.** territory. 4 *also* **Ter.** tertiary *geology.*

terat. teratology (study of abnormal formations in biology).

Tercom terrain contour matching (computerized guidance system in a cruise missile).

TERLS rocket launching station at Thumba (international sounding rocket facility).

term. 1 terminal. 2 termination. 3 terminology.

terr. 1 *also* **Terr.** terrace. 2 a *also* **Terr.** territory. b territorial.

ter. sim. rub together *pharmaceutics.* [Latin *tere simul*]

tert. tertiary.

TESL (tes′əl) Teaching English as a Second Language.

TESOL (tes′ôl, tes′əl) Teaching English to Speakers of Other Languages.

Test. Testament.

test. 1 testament. 2 testamentary. 3 testator. 4 testimonial.

tet. tox. tetanus toxin.

Teut. Teutonic.

TeV teraelectron volts (trillion electronvolts).

TEX Telex (teletype exchange).

Tex. 1 Texan. 2 Texas.

Tex-Mex Texan-Mexican (of the Texas-Mexico border country, combining Texan and Mexican elements).

text. textile.

Text. Rec. the received text of the Greek New Testament (basis of the Authorized Version). [from the publisher's notice declaring the text received by all; Latin *Textus Receptus*]

TF 1 task force. 2 thin film, esp. in combination: *TFT = thin film transistor.* 3 training film. 4 transfer or transcription factor *biochemistry.* 5 Tropical Fresh Water Load Line (Plimsoll mark for loaded ship in tropical waters). 6 *also* **T-F** or **t/f** true, false: *T-F test.*

tf. or **t.f.** till forbidden (indefinite length of time for which an advertisement is placed).

TFA 1 total fatty acids, in blood chemistry. 2 transfer function analyzer *aeronautics.*

TFAP trifluoroacetylprolyl chloride (reagent used in chemical analysis of trace materials).

tfc. or **TFC** traffic.

TFCS Treasury Financial Communication System.

TFE tetrafluoroethylene (resin used to make Teflon).

tfr. transfer.

TFRM Treasury Fiscal Requirements Manual.

TFT *electronics* 1 thin film technology. 2 thin film transistor.

TFX tactical fighter, experimental (originally F-111 fighter aircraft).

TG 1 Theater Guild. 2 *also* **T/G** tongue and groove (of lumber). 3 transformational grammar. 4 triglyceride, in blood chemistry.

tg 1 tangent. 2 *also* **tg.** a telegram. b telegraph. 3 *also* **t.g.** type genus (genus from which family name of classification is taken because type genus is thought to best typify ascribed characteristics).

TGA 1 thermoglobulin antibodies. 2 thermogravimetric analysis.

TGB or **t.g.b.** tongued, grooved, and beaded (of finished lumber).

TGC travel group charter.

TGE 1 total governmental expenditures. 2 transmissible gastroenteritis *medicine.*

TGF transforming growth factors (of cell maturation and reproduction).

TGIF or **tgif** *Informal* thank God it's Friday.

tgl. or **TGL** toggle (esp. of an electrical switch or a mechanical joint).

TG loran traffic guidance loran *aeronautics.*

TGT 1 *also* **tgt.** target. 2 tissue glucose threshold (of blood sugar). 3 turbine gas temperature.

TGTP tuned grid, tuned plate *electronics.*

TGV 1 French high-speed train. [French *Train à Grande Vitesse*] **2** The Two Gentlemen of Verona (play by Shakespeare).

TGWU *or* **T.G.W.U.** *British* Transport and General Workers' Union.

TH 1 *also* **T.H.** (formerly) Territory of Hawaii. **2** *also* **T.H.** Trinity House (organization in England responsible for certain maritime affairs such as lighthouses, ship pilots, etc.).

Th *I an abbreviation for:* **1** *also* **th.** Theater. **2** *also* **Th.** Thomas. **3** *also* **Th.** Thursday.
II a symbol for: thorium (chemical element).

4th *or* **4ᵗʰ** fourth: 4ᵗʰ Ave.; 24ᵗʰ Aug.

th. 1 thermal, also in combination: *th.c. = thermal conductivity.* **2** thoroughbred, in horse racing.

THA tacrine or tetrahydroaminoacridine (drug used to treat Alzheimer's disease).

Thaad theatre high altitude area defense *military.*

Thai. Thailand.

THAM tromethamine (emulsifying agent).

Th.B. Bachelor of Theology. [Latin *Theologiae Baccalaureus*]

THC tetrahydrocannabinol (active marijuana chemical).

THD total harmonic distortion, esp. in recording sound.

TH.D. *or* **ThD** Doctor of Theology. [Latin *Theologiae Doctor*]
thd. thread.

theat. 1 *also* **Thea.** theater. **2** theatrical.

Th-Em thoron or thorium emanation (isotope of thorium).

Theo. 1 Theodore. **2** Theodosia.

theo. 1 theology. **2** theoretical.

theol. 1 theologian. **2 a** theology. **b** theological.

Theoph. 1 Theophilus (early bishop of the Christian church who presided over council that settled custom of finding date of Easter). **2** Theophrastus (ancient Greek philosopher and botanist).

theor. 1 theorem. **2** theoretical. **3** theory.

theoret. theoretical or theoretically.

Theos. *or* **theos. 1** theosophical. **2** theosophist. **3** theosophy.

therap. 1 therapeutic. **2** *also* **Therap.** therapeutics (branch of medicine that deals with the treatment of disease).

therm. 1 *also* **thermom a** thermometric. **b** thermometer. **2** *also* **thermo.** thermostat.

thermochem thermochemistry.

thermodyn thermodynamics.

thes. thesis.

thesp thespian.

Thess. 1 Thessalonians (two books of the New Testament): *I Thess. = One or First Thessalonians; II Thess. = Two or Second Thessalonians.* **2** Thessaly (district of both ancient and modern Greece).

THF 1 tetrahydrofuran, (used esp. as a solvent). **2** *also* **THFA** tetrahydrofurfuryl alcohol (solvent).

THI 1 temperature-humidity index. **2** *also* **t.h.i.** time handed in.

Thia. Theology. [Latin *Theologia*]

thk. *or* **THK** thick (esp. of paper).

Th.L. *or* **ThL** Licentiate in Theology.

THM trihalomethane (any of a group of poisons that form by combining with chlorine in public drinking water).

Th.M. *or* **ThM** Master of Theology. [Latin *Theologiae Magister*]

Tho. *or* **Thom.** *or* **Thos.** Thomas.

thor. 1 thoracic, esp. in combination: *thor. surg. = thoracic surgeon.* **2** thorax.

thoro. thoroughfare.

thou. thousand.

thp *or* **THP** *or* **t.hp.** thrust horsepower.

THPC tetrakishydroxymethyl phosphonium chloride (crystalline compound used in making cotton and rayon fabrics flame-resistant).

thr. 1 their. **2** *also* **Thr** threonine (essential amino acid in protein). **3** through. **4** thrust.

thro B/L through bill of lading *commerce.*

thrombo. thrombosis *medicine.*

throt. throttle.

Thu. Thursday.

Thuc. Thucydides (ancient Greek historian).

THUD thorium, uranium, deuterium.

Thur. *or* **Thurs.** Thursday.

Thwy Thruway.

THz terahertz (trillion hertz).

TI 1 target identification. **2** technical institute. **3** temperature indicator. **4** Trade International (Christian Trade Internationals, associated with the World Confederation of Labor).

Ti titanium (chemical element).

TIA transient ischemic attack (temporary loss of blood flow to part of the body).

TIAA Teachers Insurance and Annuity Association.

Tib. 1 Tibet. **2** Tibetan.

TIBC total iron-binding capacity (measure of iron utilization in the body).

TICCIT Time-shared Interactive Computer-controlled Information Television.

t.i.d. three times a day *pharmaceutics.* [Latin *ter in die*]

T.I.E. totally integrated environment *engineering.*

tier. tierce (old unit of measure for wines and spirits equal to 42 gallons).

TIF 1 International Railway Transports. [French *Transports Internationaux par Chemin de Fer*] **2** telephone influence factor. **3** telephone interference factor.

TIFF tagged image file format *computers.*

TIG tungsten inert-gas (shielded electrode): *TIG welding.*

TIGR Treasury Investment Growth Receipts.

TIL tumor-infiltrating lymphocyte.

TILS Technical Information and Library Service.

Tim. 1 Timon of Athens (play by Shakespeare and some others). **2** Timothy (two books of the New Testament): *I Tim. = One or First Timothy; II Tim. = Two or Second Timothy.*

TIMM thermionic integrated micromodule *electronics*.

timp. timpani *music*.

TIMS 1 The Institute of Management Sciences. 2 thermal infrared multispectral scanner.

TIN taxpayer identification number.

t.i.n. three times a night *pharmaceutics* [Latin *ter in nocte*]

tinct. *or* **tinc.** tincture.

TIO 1 Technical Information Officer. 2 Television Information Office.

TIP 1 tracking and impact prediction. 2 translational inhibitory protein (produced by interferon). 3 **a** tumor inhibitory principle. **b** tumor inducing principle.

Tip. Tipperary County, Ireland.

TIR 1 International Road Transport. [French *Transport International Routiers*] 2 technical information release.

TIRC 1 Tauri Infrared Companion *astronomy*. 2 Tobacco Industry Research Committee.

TIROS (tī′ros) television and infrared observation satellite.

TIS Technical Information Service.

tis. tissue.

Tit. 1 Titus (epistle of the New Testament written by St. Paul to Titus). 2 Titus Andronicus (play by Shakespeare).

tit. 1 patent. [Spanish *título*] 2 title. 3 titular.

Tit.A. Titus Andronicus (play by Shakespeare).

t.j. *or* **T.J.** talk jockey.

TJP turbojet propulsion.

tjrs always. [French *toujours*]

TK *or* **Tk.** taka (monetary unit of Bangladesh).

tk. 1 track. 2 truck.

TKO *or* **t.k.o.** technical knockout, in boxing.

TKPP tetrapotassium pyrophosphate (used esp. in soaps and detergents).

tkr. tanker.

tkt. ticket.

TL 1 target language (language into which something is translated). 2 thermoluminescence or thermoluminescent: *TL dating*. 3 thrust line *engineering*. 4 time limit. 5 *also* **T/L** time loan *finance*. 6 total load. 7 total loss *insurance*. 8 transmission level. 9 transmission line. 10 truckload. 11 Turkish lira (monetary unit of Turkey).

Tl I *an abbreviation for: also* **Tl.** part. [German *Teil*]
II *a symbol for:* thallium (chemical element).

tl. tael (measure common in Asia, of varying weight, but usually approximately an ounce to an ounce-and-a-half).

TLA Theater Library Association.

TLB *or* **tlb** temporary lighted buoy (on navigation charts).

TLC 1 North American Free Trade Agreement. [American Spanish *Tratado de Libre Comercio*] 2 *also* **T.L.C.** tender loving care. 3 thin-layer chromatography. 4 total lung capacity. 5 **a** Trades and Labor Congress (of Canada). **b** Trades and Labour Council (of Australia).

TLD 1 thermoluminescence dosimeter (recording total exposure level to radiation). 2 thermoluminescence dosimetry.

tld tooled.

TLE temporal lobe epilepsy.

TLG Thesaurus of the Greek Language. [French *Thésaurus Linguea Graecae*]

TLI 1 total lymphatic irradiation (used in immunosuppression) *medicine*. 2 translunar injection (orbit around the moon).

TLM *or* **tlm.** telemeter.

TLO 1 Technical Liaison Officer. 2 *also* **t.l.o.** total loss only *insurance*.

TLP 1 time-lapse photography. 2 transient lunar phenomena *astrophysics*.

TLR twin lens reflex (camera).

tlr. 1 teller *banking*. 2 thunderstorm with rain *meteorology*. 3 trailer.

T.L.S. 1 *also* **TLS** Times Literary Supplement (London). 2 *also* **tls** typed letter signed.

tls. 1 taels (measure of weight). 2 thunderstorm with snow *meteorology*.

Tltr. translator.

TLU table look up *computers*.

TLV threshold limit values (of radiation or medicine).

TLZ transfer on less than zero *electronics*.

TM 1 tactical missile. 2 **a** technical manual: *TM 9765 = United States Army Technical Manual 9765*. **b** training manual. 3 technical memorandum. 4 temperature meter. 5 Thayer-Martin culture medium (permitting growth of only certain bacteria): *TM selective medium*. 6 tone modulation. 7 trademark. 8 trainmaster, in railroading. 9 Transcendental Meditation (Hindu system of meditation; trademark for a similar system). 10 transverse magnetic *electronics*: *TM wave*. 11 tropical medicine.

Tm thulium (chemical element).

t.m. 1 time modulation. 2 true mean, esp. in statistics.

TMA 1 total material assets. 2 Toy Manufacturers Association. 3 trimethylamine (used in organic synthesis).

tmbr timber.

T.M.C. target market coverage *advertising*.

TMEDA trimethylethylenediamine (used in manufacture of plastics and textiles).

TMH *or* **t/mh** tons per man-hour.

TMI Three Mile Island (site of industrial nuclear accident in U.S.)

TMJ temporomandibular joint (of the jaw).

tmkpr. timekeeper.

TML 1 tetramethyl lead (former gasoline additive). 2 three-mile limit (distance from shore of a country's jurisdiction over its coastal waters though some countries claim a twelve mile limit). 3 TransManche Link (Eurotunnel or Channel Tunnel between France and England).

T.M.O. *or* **TMO** telegraph money order.

TMP 1 thermomechanical processing. 2 thermomechanical pump. 3 thymidine monophosphate (growth factor in certain bacilli).

Tmp. The Tempest (play by Shakespeare).

tmp. 1 temperature. 2 temporary.

tmr timer.

TMS tetramethylsilane, (used esp. in aviation fuel).

TMT turbomotor train.

TMTD tetramethylthiuram disulfide (substance used in rubber manufacture and as a disinfectant and fungicide).

TMV 1 tobacco mosaic virus (first virus to be chemically identified). 2 true mean value *statistics*.

tMw. or **TMW** or **t.mw.** thermal megawatt.

TMX tandem mirror experiment (of fusion energy).

TN 1 tariff number. 2 technical note. 3 telephone number. 4 Tennessee (Zip Code). 5 *also* **T-N** thermonuclear. 6 trade name. 7 *also* **T.N.** true north. 8 Twelfth Night (play by Shakespeare).

Tn thoron (chemical element).

tn. 1 ton. 2 town. 3 train.

TNA 1 tetranitroaniline (used as an explosive). 2 thermal neutron analysis. 3 total nucleic acid content.

TNF 1 Theater Nuclear Forces (troops and weapons in a potential theater of war). 2 transfer on no overflow *electronics*. 3 tumor necrosis factor (chemical occurring naturally in the body).

TNG The Newspaper Guild.

tng. training.

tnge tonnage.

TNK The Two Noble Kinsmen (a play variously attributed to Shakespeare and Fletcher).

TNM 1 tactical nuclear missile. 2 *also* **T.N.M.** tumors, nodules, metastases (used in a common terminology for the principal forms of cancer).

tno. telephone. [Spanish *teléfono*]

Tnpk. turnpike.

tnr. trainer.

TNT 1 Tactical Narcotics Team. 2 trinitrotoluene (explosive). 3 Turner Network Television.

TNV tobacco necrosis virus.

TNW tactical nulcear weapon.

TNX trinitroxylene (an explosive).

TNZ transfer on non-zero *computers*.

TO 1 *also* **T/O** or **t.o.** table of organization (as of a corporation). 2 takeoff, esp. in combination: *TOGW = takeoff gross weight*. 3 technical order. 4 *also* **T.O.** British Telephone Office. 5 telephone order *commerce*. 6 time opening (as of a safe lock). 7 *also* **t.o.** tincture of opium *pharmaceutics*. 8 *also* **T.O.** Transport Officer. 9 travel orders. 10 **a** *also* **t.o.** or **t/o** turn over, also in combination: *p.t.o. = please turn over*. **b** *also* **T/O** turnover (amount of change or amount of business).

TOA 1 Theater Owners of America. 2 time of arrival. 3 total obligational authority (of government appropriations).

Tob. Tobit (book of the Old Testament: Protestants include it in their Apocrypha, Roman Catholics in their Bible as Tobias).

tob. 1 tobacco. 2 *also* **Tob.** tobacconist.

TOC 1 *also* **t.o.c.** table of contents. 2 total organic carbon (of a sample for analysis).

Toch. Tocharian (group of languages of European peoples living in central Asia during the first thousand years of the Christian era).

TOD 1 time of day. 2 time of delivery. 3 total oxygen demand (consumed oxygen, esp. for combustion).

TOE 1 term of enlistment. 2 *also* **T.O.E.** theory of everything (of the Big Bang theory). 3 ton oil equivalent.

TOEFL (tō'fəl) 1 Teaching of English as a Foreign Language. 2 Test of English as a Foreign Language.

TOF time of flight *aeronautics, physics*, also in combination: *TOFMS = time-of-flight mass spectrometry* (measuring time and distance of motion of nuclear particles in a mass).

TOFC trailer-on-flatcar (piggybacking).

tog. 1 *also* **togr.** together. 2 toggle (of a switch or joint).

TOGW takeoff gross weight *aeronautics*.

Tok Tokyo.

tokamak (tō'kə mak') a device with a magnetic field for producing controlled nuclear power. [Russian *toroidálnaya kámera s magnítnym pólem*]

tol. tolerance *engineering, physics*.

tom. 1 *also* **tom** tomato. 2 *also* **Tom.** volume. [Latin *tomus*, Spanish *tomo*]

TOMS Total Ozone Mapping Spectrometer (for measuring ultraviolet light in the atmosphere).

tonn. tonnage.

t.o.o. or **TOO** time of origin.

TOP 1 *also* **T.O.P.** temporarily out of print. 2 torque oil pressure.

top or **topol.** topology.

topo. 1 topographic or topographical. 2 topography (science of describing surface features).

topog. 1 topographer. 2 topographical. 3 topography.

TOPS Total Operations Processing System (computer monitoring of freight by rail in Britain).

TOPV trivalent oral polio vaccine.

Tor. 1 Toronto. 2 Torrid Zone.

tor torque.

t.o.r. or **TOR** time of receipt or reception.

torn. tornado.

torp. torpedo.

TOS 1 Tape Operating System *computers*. 2 **a** temporarily out of stock. **b** temporarily out of service. 3 term of service.

T.O.S.F. Third Order of St. Francis (Dominican Sisters).

TOSS Tiros Operational Satellite System.

TOT 1 time over target *military*. 2 tip of the tongue (in reference to a temporary inability to recall some word or fact).

tot. total.

Tou. Toulon, France.

tour. 1 tourism. 2 tourist.

Tourn. tournament.

TOW 1 takeoff weight (of an aircraft). 2 tube-launched, optically-tracked, wire-guided missile. 3 *also* **t.o.w.** tug of war.

tox. 1 toxemia. 2 toxic. 3 toxicology.

toxicol. 1 toxicological. 2 toxicologist. 3 toxicology.

TOXLINE Toxicology Line (service of the National Library of Medicine, giving bibliographic references and other information on toxic substances).

TP 1 *also* **T.P.** at Easter. [Latin *tempore Paschale*] 2 target practice. 3 technical paper. 4 **a** telephone. **b** teleprinter. 5 third party, also in combination: *TPI = third party interest.* 6 total points (score of a single game or group of games). 7 total protein. 8 transaction processing *computers.* 9 true position *navigation.* 10 turning point *electronics, surveying.*

Tp. *or* **tp.** 1 township. 2 troop.

t.p. 1 original tempo *music.* [Italian *tempo primo*] 2 *also* **T.P.** title page. 3 *also* **tp** toilet paper.

TPA 1 terephthalic acid (used to produce polyester fibers). 2 *also* **t-PA** tissue plasminogen activator (a clot-dissolving serum).

TPC Time Projection Chamber (of a particle detector) *physics.*

TPCF treponema pallidum complement fixation (test for syphilis).

tpd *or* **TPD** tons per day.

TPER Total Primary Energy Requirements.

T.P.F. Tactical Patrol Force (of a police department).

TPG Tin Plate Gauge.

tph *or* **TPH** tons per hour.

TPHA treponema pallidum hemaglutination assay (test for syphilis).

TPI 1 *also* **t.p.i.** teeth per inch (of a gearwheel). 2 *also* **t.p.i.** threads per inch. 3 tons per inch (immersed). 4 *also* **tpi** tracks per inch *computers.* 5 transpolyisoprene (a synthetic gutta percha). 6 treponema pallidum immobilization test (test for syphilis). 7 triosephosphate isomerase (enzyme). 8 Tropical Products Institute. 9 *also* **t.p.i.** turns per inch (esp. of yarn).

Tpk. *or* **Tpke.** 1 turnpike (in general use). 2 *also* **TPKE** Turnpike (in postal address).

TPLF Tigrean People's Liberation Front.

TPM 1 *also* **t.p.m.** title page mutilated. 2 *also* **tpm** tons per minute. 3 trigger price mechanism *commerce.* 4 turns per minute.

TPN 1 total parenteral nutrition (as by intravenous feeding). 2 *also* **TPNH** triphosphopyridine nucleotide (coenzyme acting as an intermediate agent of metabolism).

TPO Traveling Post Office.

TPP thiamine pyrophosphate (enzyme).

TPR 1 teleprinter. 2 *also* **t.p.r.** temperature, pulse, respiration *medicine.* 3 total pulmonary resistance *medicine.*

Tpr. *or* **tpr.** trooper.

tps. troops.

tpt. 1 *also* **Tpt.** transport. 2 trumpet.

TPTG tuned plated, tuned grid *electronics: TPTG oscillator.*

TPV terminal portal venule (small blood vessel).

TPW *or* **t.p.w.** title page wanting.

T.Q.C. *or* **TQC** total quality control.

TQE technical quality evaluation.

TR 1 tape recorder. 2 technical report. 3 *also* **T.R.** technical representative. 4 **a** test report. **b** test run. 5 *also* **T.R.** Theodore Roosevelt. 6 time of retrofire. 7 *also* **t.r.** tons registered. 8 training regulation. 9 transformer. 10 *radio also* **T/R** or **T-R a** transmit-receive. **b** transmitter-receiver. 11 *also* **T/R** or **T.R.** trust receipt *finance.*

Tr. 1 transactions (proceedings, esp. of a society). 2 **a** translation. **b** translator. 3 Treasurer. 4 Troop. 5 **a** Trust: *Gramatan Tr.Co. = Gramatan Trust Company.* **b** Trustee.

tr 1 tare (weight of container or conveyance). 2 *also* **tr.** tincture (solution in alcohol, esp. of medicine). 3 trace. 4 *also* **tr.** track. 5 *also* **tr.** train. 6 transaction (of money). 7 *also* **tr.** transfer. 8 transistor. 9 *also* **tr.** transitive: *tr.v. = transitive verb.* 10 *also* **tr. a** translated. **b** translation, translation of. **c** translator. 11 transport. 12 *also* **tr.** transpose (esp. of characters in reverse order in printing). 13 travel. 14 *also* **tr.** tray. 15 tread. 16 treble *music.* 17 *also* **tr.** trill *music.* 18 *also* **tr.** trumpet. 19 truss.

TRA Thoroughbred Racing Association.

TrA Southern Triangle (constellation). [Latin *Triangulum Australe*]

trac. tractor.

TRACALS Traffic Control and Landing System *aeronautics.*

TRACE task reporting and current evaluation.

trach. 1 tracheal. 2 tracheotomy.

TRACON terminal radar control *aeronautics.*

trad. 1 **a** tradition. **b** traditional. 2 translated. [French *traduit,* Spanish *traducido*]

traf. traffic.

trag. 1 tragedy. 2 tragic.

TRAIN TeleRail Automated Information Network (computerized system to keep nationwide account of freight cars of members of the Association of American Railroads).

train. *or* **Train.** training.

TRAN transmit *computers.*

Tr.&Cr. Troilus and Cressida (play by Shakespeare).

TRANET Navy Tracking Station Network.

trans. 1 **a** transaction. **b** transactions (proceedings of a society): *Trans. A.I.E.E. = Transactions of the American Institute of Electrical Engineers.* 2 **a** transfer. **b** transferred. 3 transformer. 4 transistor. 5 transit. 6 transitive *grammar.* 7 **a** translated. **b** translation. **c** translator. 8 transparent. 9 **a** transport. **b** transportation. 10 **a** transpose. **b** transposition. 11 transverse: *trans.sect. = transverse section.*

transcr. 1 transcribed by. 2 transcription.

transf. 1 **a** transfer. **b** *also* **transfd** transferred. 2 transformer.

transl. 1 translated. 2 *also* **Transl.** translation. 3 *also* **Transl.** translator.

translit. transliteration.

transp. 1 transparent. 2 transportation.

trav 1 piece of work [French *travail*] 2 *also* **trav. a** travel. **b** traveler.

TRBF total renal blood flow *medicine.*

trbn. trombone.

TRC Tobacco Research Council.

Trd 1 *also* **Trd.** trade or trading: *Western Trd.Co. = Western Trading Company.* **2** Trinidad.

T.R.E. Telecommunications Research Establishment (of Great Britain).

Treas. *or* **treas. 1** treasurer. **2** treasury.

Tree. Trustee.

trem. tremolo *music.*

TREND tropical environment data.

TRF 1 thyrotropin-releasing factor. **2** *also* **trf** *or* **t.r.f.** *or* **t-r-f** tuned radio frequency.

trf. 1 tariff. **2** transfer.

trg. 1 *also* **Trg** training. **2** triangle.

trgt target.

TRH 1 *also* **T.R.H.** Their Royal Highnesses. **2** thyrotropin-releasing hormone (produced by hypothalamus causing release of thyrotropin).

TRI 1 Television Reporters International. **2** Textile Research Institute. **3** total response index. **4** Toxics Release Index (of the Environmental Protection Agency).

Tri the Triangle (constellation).

tri. triode *electronics.*

Trib (*pronounced* trib) Tribune: *Chicago Daily Trib.*

trib. 1 tribal. **2** tribunal. **3** tributary.

TriBeCa (trī′bek′ə) Triangle Below Canal (Street, area in lower New York City).

TRIC trachoma inclusion conjunctivitis (trachoma virus).

tric knit. [French *tricoter*]

Tricap (trī′kap′) Triple-capable (division of U.S. Army composed of tanks, mechanized light infantry, and mobile air support).

trid. three days *pharmaceutics.* [Latin *triduum*]

trig. *also* **trigon. 1** trigonometric or trigonometrical. **2** trigonometry.

TRIGA training, research, isotope production, and general atomic (an older type of uranium atomic reactor).

trik trichloroethylene (solvent).

trim. trimester.

Trin. 1 Trinidad. **2** Trinity.

TRIP transformation induced plasticity (alloys): *TRIP steels.*

trip. 1 triple. **2** *also* **tripl.** triplicate.

TRIS trisaminomethane, triethylamine (used in producton of some polymers, rubber, and as a solvent).

trit. triturate (rub) *music,* (pulverize) *pharmaceutics.*

TRITC tetramethylrhodamine isothiocyanate (textile dye and tissue stain).

trk. 1 track. **2** *also* **TRK a** truck. **b** trucker. **3** trunk.

trlr trailer.

trml. *or* **TRML** terminal.

trmt. treatment.

TRN 1 *also* **trn** technical research note. **2** transfer.

tRNA transfer RNA (codon-recognizing molecule).

TRNC Turkish Republic of North Cyprus.

trng training.

TRO temporary restraining order *law.*

Tro. Troilus and Cressida (play by Shakespeare).

trom. trombone.

tromp. trumpet. [French *trompette*]

trop. 1 *also* **Trop.** tropic, esp. in combination: *Trop. Can. = Tropic of Cancer.* **2 a** tropics. **b** tropical: *trop. med. = tropical medicine.*

TRP *or* **trp. 1** troop *military.* **2** *also* **Trp.** tryptophan (amino acid formed from protein).

TRS tough rubber sheathing (of electric cable insulation).

Trs. Trustees.

trs. 1 traces. **2** transactions. **3** *also* **trs. a** transfer. **b** transferals. **c** transfers. **4** transistors. **5** *also* **Trs. a** translators. **b** translations. **6** transpose, esp. in printing. **7** trumpets.

TRSB time reference scanning beam.

trsd. 1 transferred. **2** transposed.

trsp. transport.

TRSR taxi and runway surveillance radar.

TRT 1 total running time. **2** *also* **trt** treatment *medicine.*

TRTA Traders′ Road Transport Association (of Great Britain).

TRU turbidity reducing unit *medicine.*

TRUMP Target Radiation Measurement Program.

Truron. of Truro (in reference to the Bishop and therefore used as his official signature). [Latin *Truronesis*]

try. 1 truly. **2** *also* **Try.** *or* **tryp.** *or* **Tryp.** tryptophan (amino acid formed from protein).

TS 1 *also* **T-S** temperature, salinity: *T-S diagram.* **2** temperature switch. **3** tensile strength. **4** test solution esp. in chemistry. **5** *also* **T-S** time sharing. **6** tool steel. **7** top secret *military.* **8** *also* **T.S.** transverse section. **9** *also* **T.S.** tub-sized (paper sized with animal gelatin). **10** typescript. **11** *also* **T.S.** without accompanying chords *music.* [Italian *tasto solo*]

ts 1 *also* **t.s.** all by itself *music.* [Italian *tutto solo*] **2** *also* **ts.** teaspoon. **3** tensile strength. **4** *also* **t-s** time sharing. **5** tub-sized (paper sized with animal gelatin).

TSA 1 time series analysis. **2** total survey area *marketing.* **3** tumor specific antigen.

TSB *British* Trustee Savings Bank.

TSC transmitter start code *computers.*

TSE 1 test support equipment. **2** Tokyo Stock Exchange. **3** Toronto Stock Exchange.

T.S.F. French Radio. [French *télégraphie sans fil* wireless telegraphy]

tsfr *or* **Tsfr.** transfer.

T/Sgt *or* **T.Sgt.** Technical Sergeant.

TSH 1 *also* **TSh** Tanzanian shilling (monetary unit). **2** *also* **T.S.H.** Their Serene Highnesses. **3** thyroid stimulating hormone; thyrotropin.

TSI 1 *also* **t.s.i.** tons per square inch. **2** Transportation Safety Institute.

TSO 1 technical standard order. **2** time-sharing option *computers*.

TSP 1 thyroid stimulating hormone of the prepituitary. **2** trisodium phosphate (soap and water softener).

tsp. *or* **tspn** teaspoon or teaspoonful (measure of about 1/6 ounce).

TSPP tetrasodium pyrophosphate (used in well drilling and as a water softener).

TSR 1 telephone sales representative. **2** terminate and stay resident (computer program). **3** Trans-Siberian Railroad. **4** *also* **T.S.R.** Travelling Stock Reserve (land in Australia held by the state to provide access to transportation for livestock drives).

TSS 1 Time Sharing System *computers*. **2** toxic shock syndrome *medicine*. **3** *also* **T.S.S.** **a** turbine steamship. **b** twin screw steamship.

TSTA tumor specific transplantation antigen.

tstr tester.

TSU this side up.

TSVP *or* **t.s.v.p.** please turn over (the page). [French *tournez s'il vous plaît*]

TSWE Test of Standard Written English.

TT 1 technical term. **2** teetotaler. **3** *also* **T.T.** *or* **T/T** *British* telegraphic transfer (dispatch of money or credit by telegraph or cable). **4** teletype. **5** tetanus toxoid. **6** Tourist Trophy (Britain's oldest motor race). **7** transmit time. **8** Trinidad and Tobago: *TT$* = *Trinidad and Tobago dollar*. **9** tuberculin tested (as of milk).

tt. tercentesimal temperature (temperature scale based on a division into 300 parts).

TTAB Trademark Trial and Appeal Board.

TTBT Threshold Test Ban Treaty.

TTC 1 Technical Training Center. **2** Toronto Transit Commission. **3** triphenyl tetrazolium chloride (used for reducing sugars).

TTH thyrotropic hormone (stimulating the thyroid gland).

TTL 1 through-the-lens (of cameras that use the lens as a viewfinder). **2** *also* **t.t.l.** to take leave. **3** transistor transistor logic *computers*.

TTM transit time modulation *electronics*.

Tto Toronto, Canada.

TTP 1 thrombotic thrombocytopenic purpura *medicine*. **2** thymidine triphosphate (constituent of DNA).

T.T.P.I. Trust Territory of the Pacific Islands.

TTR thermal test reactor.

TTS 1 teletypesetter. **2** temporary threshold shift (of sound reception). **3** Tuesday, Thursday, Saturday (frequency of occurrence).

TTU timing terminal unit.

TTY teletypewriter.

TU 1 tape unit *computers*. **2** *also* **T.U.** *or* **t.u.** thermal unit, esp. in combination: *B.t.u.* = *British Thermal Unit.* **3** toxic unit (least amount of toxin that will kill laboratory animal or smallest dose that will cause reaction, as in scarlet fever test). **4** *also* **T.U.** Trade Union, esp. in combination: *WTUC* = *World Trade Union Conference.* **5** traffic unit *communications*.

6 transmission unit (now *decibel*). **7** *also* **T.U.** tuberculin unit *medicine*.

Tu *I* an abbreviation for: **1** Tudor. **2** *also* **Tu.** Tuesday. *II* a symbol for: thulium (chemical element; symbol *Tm*).

TUAC Trade Union Advisory Committee (of Europe).

TUC 1 *also* **T.U.C.** Trades Union Congress (of Great Britain). **2** training for unemployed youth. [French *Traveaux d'Utilité Collective*]

Tuc Toucan (constellation). [Latin *Tucana*]

TUCSA Trade Union Council of South Africa.

Tue. *or* **Tues.** Tuesday.

Tug Tugrik (monetary unit of Mongolia).

TUI Trade Union Internationals (organization within World Federation of Trade Unions).

T.U.L.F. Tamil United Liberation Front (of Sri Lanka).

Tun. 1 Tunisia. **2** Tunnel, also in combination: *Linc. Tun.* = *Lincoln Tunnel.*

tung tungsten.

TUR transurethral resection *medicine*.

TURB turbine.

Turk. 1 Turkey. **2** Turkish.

TURP transurethral resection of the prostate *medicine*.

turp. *or* **turps** (tėrps) turpentine.

tux (*pronounced* tuks) tuxedo.

TV 1 *also* **T.V.** television. **2** terminal velocity. **3** test vehicle. **4** transvestite.

TVA 1 *French also* **T.V.A.** tax on value added; VAT. **2** Tennessee Valley Authority.

TVB *or* **TvB** television bureau (of advertising).

TVC Technical Value Committee.

TVG time-varying gain (system to discriminate between backscatter and cloud echo in radar scanning).

TVHH television households *marketing*.

TVI television interference.

TVL 1 tenth value layer (shielding needed to reduce intensity of radiation to $1/10$). **2** *also* **tvl.** travel.

Tvl. Transvaal (province of Republic of South Africa).

TVM track via missile.

TVNZ Television New Zealand.

TVP textured vegetable protein (trademark for a meat substitute or additive spun from vegetable fiber).

T.V.R. temperature variation of resistance *electricity*.

TVRO television receive only (antenna).

TW 1 *also* **t.w.** tail wind *aeronautics*. **2** *also* **tw** terawatt (trillion watts). **3** *also* **T-W** three-wheeler (three-wheeled motorcycle on balloon tires). **4** traveling wave (particle wave carrying energy from one point to another). **5** Twaddell (hydrometer). **6** *also* **Tw** typewriter *computers*, also in combination: *TWB* = *typewriter buffer.*

TWA time-weighted average.

Twad. Twaddell (hydrometer).

Twel.N. Twelfth Night (play by Shakespeare).

T.W.I. *British* training within industry.

twi. twilight.

TWIMC to whom it may concern.

TWL 1 top water level. **2** total weight loss.

TWO this week only (schedule of advertising in a publication, on television, etc.).

Two Gent. Two Gentlemen of Verona (play by Shakespeare).

TWOV transit without visa (of passengers who travel to a foreign country without documentation, usually seeking political asylum).

twp. or **Twp.** township.

twr. or **Twr.** tower.

TWS 1 timed wire service (of telegraph service). **2** tracking while scanning (of radar).

TWT 1 transonic wind tunnel. **2** also **twt** traveling-wave tube *electronics,* also in combination: *TWTA = traveling-wave tube amplifier.*

TWU Transport Workers' Union.

TWUA 1 Textile Workers' Union of America. **2** Transport Workers' Union of America, or of Australia.

TWX teletypewriter exchange.

twy 1 also **Twy** thruway. **2** twenty.

TX 1 also **tx. a** tax. **b** also **txn.** taxation. **2** telex. **3** Texas (Zip Code). **4 a** also **Tx** transmitter. **b** torque transmitter.

Ty. 1 Territory. **2** also **ty.** truly, as a close in correspondence. **3** also **ty.** type: *rm.ty. = roman type.*

TYMV turnip yellow mosaic virus.

tyo or **t.y.o.** two-year-old, in horse racing.

typ. 1 typewriter. **2** typical. **3** typist. **4** also **Typ. a** typography. **b** typographer. **c** typographical or typographic.

typh. typhoon.

typo. 1 also **typo** (tī′pō) typographical error. **2** also **typog. a** typography. **b** typographer. **c** typographical or typographic.

TYPOE Ten Year Plan for Ocean Exploration.

typw. typewriter.

Tyr. 1 also **Tyrol.** Tyrolean. **2** Tyrone County, Ireland. **3** also **tyr.** tyrosine (amino acid in protein).

TYS tensile yield strength.

TZ 1 tidal zone. **2** also **T.Z.** time zone.

U

U *I an abbreviation for:* **1** also **U.** o'clock. [German *Uhr*] **2** submarine: *U-boat.* [German *Unterseeboot*] **3** Uganda or Ugandan: *USh = Uganda Shilling.* **4** ultra, in combination: *UHF = ultrahigh frequency.* **5** unclassified. **6** also **U.** uncle. **7** under, esp. in combination: *UV = under voltage; Executor U/W = Executor under will.* **8** uniform, esp. in combination: *UCMJ = Uniform Code of Military Justice.* **9** also **U.** Union, in combination: *TWU = Transport Workers' Union.* **10** also **U.** unit, esp. in combination: *AU = angstrom unit; B.T.U. = British Thermal Unit.* **11** also **U.** United, in combination: *USA = United States of America; UAW = United Automobile Workers.* **12** universal, in combination: *UMT = Universal Military Training; UT = universal time.* **13** also **U.** University, in combination: *NYU = New York University.* **14 a** upper, in combination: *UDC = upper dead center.* **b** upper, *esp.* British upper class, and by extension, sophisticated, refined, and cultured, esp. in the compound *non-U.* **c** also **U.** Upper, in combination: *U.C. = Upper Canada.* **15** uracil (base compound of DNA). **16** also **U.** Utah. **17** utility, in combination: *PUC = Public Utilities Commission; the U-2 spy plane.*
II a symbol for: **1** electric potential differential. **2** energy, *esp.* **a** internal energy. **b** potential energy. **c** radiant energy. **d** strain energy. **e** total energy. **3** kilurane (1000 uranium units). **4** overall heat transfer coefficient. **5** twenty-first of a series (twentieth when *J* is omitted). **6 a** unrated (motion picture rating in the U.S. indicating a film that has not been reviewed for rating). **b** unrestricted (motion picture rating

in Great Britain indicating a film suitable for all audiences). **7** uranium (chemical element).
▶The alphabetic distinction between *U* and *V* spread during the Renaissance and was finally established by printers' convention. However, it was not universally applied before the middle of the 19th century, and many older lists intermingled words and abbreviations with *u* and *v*. Even to this day the capital *V* sometimes appears at the beginning of *university* and a few other words to preserve a Latinate effect. The use of *u* for *v* as an abbreviation or symbol is relatively rare: *U* for versor in math and *u* for velocity in engineering.

U (yü) Burmese title of respect, not an abbreviation: *U Nu* or *U Thant.*

u *I an abbreviation for:* **1** also **u.** and. [German *und*] **2** also **u.** unit, in combination: *u./mg. = unit per milligram; Btu = British Thermal Unit.* **3** also **u.** universal, in combination: *u.t. = universal time.* **4** also **u.** upper, in combination: *uc = upper case* (capital letters).
II a symbol for: **1** asymmetrical *chemistry.* **2** energy, *esp.* **a** radiant energy density. **b** specific internal energy. **3** micro- (one millionth or 10^{-6}). ▶Generally in printed and handwritten work the symbol μ for micro- is preserved, as in μv (microvolt). In most typescript *u* is substituted or even *m: uf* and *mf = microfarad.* **4** micron (one millionth of a meter; measure used esp. in microscopy). **5** twenty-first of a series (twentieth when *j* is omitted). **6** ugly or threatening appearance of the sky *me-*

teorology. **7** unified atomic mass unit. **8** velocity *engineering.* **9** wave function.

UA 1 unauthorized absence. **2** *also* **U/A** Underwriting Account *insurance.* **3** unit of account. **4** urinalysis. **5** User Area *computers.*

u.a. *or* **u.A. 1** among others. [German *unter anderem*] **2** and others. [German *und Andere*]

UABS Union of American Biological Societies.

UADW Universal Alliance of Diamond Workers.

UAE United Arab Emirates (area west of Saudi Arabia on the Arabian Peninsula).

U.A.H.C. Union of American Hebrew Congregations.

U.A.I. *or* **UAI 1** International Astronomical Union. [French *Union Astronomique Internationale,* also Spanish, Italian, etc.] **2** Union of International Associations. [French *Union des Associations Internationales*]

UAJAPPFI United Association of Journeymen and Apprentices of the Plumbing and Pipe Fitting Industry of the U.S. and Canada.

UAM underwater-to-air missile.

u.a.m. and so forth; etc. [German *und andere mehr*]

u&lc *or* **u&lc.** upper and lower case (in capital and small letters), in typesetting.

U&O *or* **u. and o.** use and occupancy (esp. of insurance, legal claim, or agreement covering real estate).

UAP 1 unexplained atmospheric phenomenon. **2** United Australian Party.

UAR 1 United Arab Republic (former union of Egypt and Syria, 1958–1961, and name of Egypt until 1971). **2** upper atmospheric research.

UART universal asynchronous receiver transmitter.

UAS *or* **uas** upper airspace.

UAU *British* Universities Athletic Union.

UAUM underwater-to-air-to-underwater missile.

UAW *or* **U.A.W.** United Automobile Workers (United Automobile, Aerospace, and Agricultural Implement Workers of America).

u.A.w.g. an answer is requested. [German *um Antwort wird gebeten*]

UAX unit automatic exchange.

U.B. 1 Union of Burma (now *Union of Myanmar*). **2** United Brethren (either of two Protestant denominations).

Üb. summary. [German *Übersicht*]

UBC Universal Bibliographic Control.

UBCJ *or* **UBC&J** United Brotherhood of Carpenters and Joiners.

übers. translated. [German *übersetzt*]

UBN United States Bank Note (printer of U.S. postage stamps).

U-boat submarine. [German *Unterseeboot*]

UBR University Boat Race (between Cambridge and Oxford).

U.B.S. United Bible Societies (of Great Britain).

UBV ultraviolet-blue-visual *astronomy.*

UC 1 under construction. **2** unemployment compensation, also in combination: *UCB = Unemployment Compensation Board.* **3** *also* **U.C.** United Church. **4** *also* **U.C.** Upper Canada (Ontario, 1791–1841). **5** *also* **U.C.** *British* Urban Council.

u/c 1 undercharge (less than the full charge in fare, gunpowder, etc.). **2** upper-case (in capital letters) in typesetting.

u.c. 1 one string or soft pedal *music.* [Italian *una corda*] **2** *also* **uc** *or* **uc.** upper-case (in capital letters), in typesetting.

UCATT (yü′kət) Union of Construction, Allied Trades and Technicians (of Great Britain).

ucb unless caused by *insurance, commerce.*

UCC 1 Uniform Commercial Code. **2** United Church of Christ. **3** Universal Copyright Convention: *UCC countries.*

UCCA Universities Central Council on Admissions (of Great Britain).

UCG uterine chorionic gonadotropin (hormone measured in pregnancy test).

UCI 1 *also* **U.C.I.** International Cycling Union. [French *Union Cycliste Internationale*] **2** unit construction index.

UCL University College, London.

UCLA University of California, Los Angeles.

UCMJ Uniform Code of Military Justice: *Article 32 U.C.M.J.*

UCP United Country Party (of Australia).

UCR 1 unconditioned response *psychology.* **2** Uniform Crime Report.

UCS 1 unconditioned stimulus *psychology.* **2** *also* **ucs** unconscious. **3** uniform chromaticity scale (of color). **4** Union of Concerned Scientists. **5** universal character set *computers.*

UCSA Uniform Controlled Substances Act (for controlled sale and use of drugs).

UCT ultrasonic computerized tomography (cancer detecting device by sound waves).

UCV uncontrolled variable *psychology.*

U.D. *or* **UD 1** United (Arab Emirates) Dirham (monetary unit). **2** urban district. **3** utility dog (degree of dog performance).

u.d. as directed *pharmaceutics.* [Latin *ut dictum*]

UDA Ulster Defence Association.

UDAG Urban Development Action Grant (funds for revitalizing sections of a city).

UDB (formerly) Yugoslav State Security Directorate. [Serbo-Croatian *Uprava Drzavne Bezbednosti*]

UDC 1 underdeveloped country *or* countries. **2** *also* **U.D.C.** United Daughters of the Confederacy. **3** universal decimal classification *bibliography.* **4** *also* **u.d.c.** upper dead center *engineering.* **5** *also* **U.D.C.** *British* Urban District Council.

UDEAC Central African Economic and Customs Union. [French *Union Douane et Économique l'Afrique Centrale*]

UDEAD Customs Union of West African States. [French *Union Douanière des États de l'Afrique de l'Ouest*]

UDF 1 Ulster Defence Force. **2** unducted fan engine. **3** Union for French Democracy (centrist political party). [French *Union pour la Démocratie Française*] **4** Union of Democratic Forces (political party in Bulgaria). **5** United Democratic Front (political party in South Africa).

u.d.f. and the following. [German *und die folgende*]

udg. edition. [Danish *udgave*]

u. dgl. and the like; etc. [German *und dergleichen*]

UDMH unsymmetrical dimethylhydrazine (rocket fuel).

UDN ulcerative dermal necrosis (of fish).

Udop (yü'dop') ultrahigh frequency Doppler (radar).

UDP 1 United Democratic Party. **2** uridine diphosphate (a glucose carrier).

UDPG uridine diphosphate glucose (UDP compound), also in combination: *UDPGT = uridine diphosphate glucose transferase*.

UDR 1 *also* **U.D.R.** Rural Democratic Union. **2** Ulster Defence Regiment.

UDT 1 *also* **u.d.t.** underdeck tonnage (cubic load capacity of a ship). **2** underwater demolition team. **3** *also* **U.D.T.** utility dog tracking (degree of dog performance).

U.E. *or* **UE** United Electrical, Radio, and Machine Workers of America.

U.E.A. Universal Esperanto Association.

u.e.f. universal extra-fine (screw thread).

UEFA *or* **U.E.F.A.** Union of European Football Association.

U.E.L. United Empire Loyalist (a group of American colonial loyalists who left the colonies around the time of the Revolution to emigrate to Canada or return to England).

UEP European Payments Union. [French *Union Européenne de Paiements*]

UER European Broadcasting Union. [French *Union Européenne de Radiodiffusion*]

UET Universal Engineer Tractor (used as a bulldozer, grader, scraper, armored personnel carrier or general-purpose transport).

UEW *or* **U.E.W.** United Electrical, Radio, and Machine Workers Union.

UF 1 uranium tetrafluoride (used in preparing uranium metal). **2** urea-formaldehyde (resins used in the manufacture of plastics).

UFA 1 unesterified fatty acid. **2** *also* **U.F.A.** Uniformed Firefighter's Association. **3** United Federation of Artists.

UFC 1 uniform freight classification. **2** *also* **U.F.C.** United Free Church of Scotland. **3** Universities Funding Council (of Great Britain). **4** up-front controller (aircraft control panel).

U.F.C.T. United Federation of College Teachers.

UFCW United Food and Commercial Workers (International Union).

UFF Ulster Freedom Fighters.

uff *or* **uff.** official. [Italian *ufficiale*]

UFFI urea-formaldehyde foam insulation (building material).

UFI *or* **U.F.I.** Union of International Fairs. [French *Union des Foires Internationales*]

UFO *or* **U.F.O.** unidentified flying object.

UFSD Unified *or* Union Free School District.

UFT *or* **U.F.T.** United Federation of Teachers.

UFTAA *or* **U.F.T.A.A.** Universal Federation of Travel Agents' Associations.

UFW 1 *also* **UFWA** United Farm Workers of America (formerly *UFWOC* United Farm Workers Organizing Committee). **2** United Furniture Workers.

UG 1 *also* **ug** underground. **2** urogenital *medicine*.

Ug. 1 *also* **Ugan. a** Uganda (country in eastern Africa). **b** Ugandan. **2** Ugric (division of the Finno-Ugric linguistic family).

UGDP University Group Diabetes Program (long-term clinical trial to evaluate glucose-lowering drugs).

UGF unidentified growth factor.

UGGI *or* **U.G.G.I.** International Geodesic and Geophysical Union. [French *Union Géodésique et Géophysique Internationale*]

UGI *or* **U.G.I.** International Geographical Union. [French *Union Géographique Internationale*]

UGS uniform grain storage: *UGS agreements.*

UGT 1 General Workers Union. [Spanish *Union General de Trabajadores*, Portuguese *União Geral de Trabalhadores*] **2** urgent. **3** urogenital tract.

UGTA General Union of Algerian Workers. [French *Union Générale des Travailleurs Algériens*]

UGWA United Garment Workers of America.

UH 1 *also* **uh** ultrahigh, in combination: *UHR = ultrahigh resolution.* **2** upper half, also in combination: *UHM = upper half mean length.* **3** Upper House, also in combination: *UHCC = Upper House of the Convocation of Canterbury.*

UHF *or* **uhf** ultrahigh-frequency (of electromagnetic radio), esp. in broadcasting.

UHT ultrahigh-temperature, also in combination: *UHTM = ultrahigh-temperature milk.*

UHV 1 ultrahigh vacuum. **2** ultrahigh voltage.

UI unemployment insurance.

u.i. as below. [Latin *ut infra*]

UIA 1 International Association of Lawyers. [French *Union Internationale des Avocats*] **2** Union of International Associations.

UIC *Canadian* Unemployment Insurance Commission.

UIE 1 Institute for Education (of UNESCO). **2** International Union of Students. [French *Union Internationale des Étudiants*]

UIEO Union of International Engineering Organizations.

UIHPS *or* **U.I.H.P.S.** International Association of the History and Philosophy of Science. [French *Union Internationale d'Histoire et de Philosophie des Sciences*]

UIL Federation of Italian Labor Unions. [Italian *Unione Italiana del Lavoro*]

UIM Union of International Motorboating.

U.I.O. International Union of Orientalists. [French *Union Internationale des Orientalistes*]

UIP 1 International Skating Union. [French *Union Internationale de Patinage*] **2** International Union of Pure and Applied Physics. [French *Union Internationale de Physique Pure et Appliqué*]

UIPC International Catholic Press Union. [French *Union Internationale de la Press Catholique*]

UIS Unemployment Insurance Service (of U.S. Department of Labor).

UISAE International Union of Anthropological and Ethnological Sciences. [French *Union Internationale des Sciences Anthropologiques et Ethnologiques*]

UISB or **U.I.S.B.** International Union of Biological Sciences. [French *Union Internationale des Sciences Biologiques*]

UISPP International Union of Prehistoric and Protohistoric Sciences. [French *Union Internationale des Sciences Préhistoriques et Protohistoriques*]

UIT 1 International Telecommunications Union. [French *Union Internationale des Télécommunications*] 2 Unit Investment Trust (mutual fund that invests in corporate bonds with a fixed yield over the life of a given trust).

uit. publication. [Dutch *uitgaaf*]

uitg. published. [Dutch *uitgegeven*]

UJ Union Jack (national flag of Great Britain).

UJA or **U.J.A.** United Jewish Appeal.

U.J.D. Doctor of Both Laws (canon and civil). [Latin *Utriusque Juris Doctor*]

UJT unit junction transistor *electronics*.

UK or **U.K.** United Kingdom (of Great Britain and Northern Ireland).

U.K.A. 1 Ulster King at Arms. 2 United Kingdom Alliance.

UKAC United Kingdom Automation Council.

UKADGE United Kingdom Air Defence Ground Environment.

UKAEA United Kingdom Atomic Energy Authority.

UKAPE United Kingdom Association of Professional Engineers.

UKC or **U.K.C.** United Kennel Club.

UKIRT United Kingdom Infrared Telescope.

Ukr. 1 Ukraine. 2 Ukrainian.

UL 1 *also* **U.L.** Underwriters' Laboratories. 2 upper left (a stage direction). 3 *also* **u.l.** upper limit. 4 Urban League.

ULA 1 uncommitted logic array *computers*. 2 Uniform Labor Agreement. 3 *also* **U.L.A.** Uniform Laws Annotated.

ULC upper left center (a stage direction).

ULCA United Lutheran Church in America.

ULCC ultra-large crude carrier (supertanker with a capacity of over 400,000 tons).

ULD unit logic device (transistor).

ULF or **ulf** ultralow frequency (of electromagnetic radiation).

ULM 1 ultrasonic light modulator. 2 universal logic module.

ULMS underwater long-range missile system (submarine-launched ballistic missile).

ULS unsecured loan stock *finance*.

ULSI Ultra-Large-Scale Integration *computers*.

ult. 1 a ultimate. b ultimately. 2 *also* **ulto.** ultimo (in the past month): *your letter of the 25th ult.*

ult. praes. in the last prescription *pharmaceutics*. [Latin *ultimus praescriptus*]

ULV or **ulv** ultra-low volume (as of fluid flow).

UM 1 Ouguiya (monetary unit of Mauritania). 2 utilization management: *UM experience.*

um. unmarried.

UMa Great Bear, the Big Dipper, the Plough (constellation). [Latin *Ursa Major*]

UMB World Billiards Union [French *Union Mondiale de Billard*]

Umb or **Umbr.** Umbrian.

umb. 1 umber. 2 *also* **umbl.** umbilical.

UMC or **U.M.C.** United Methodist Church.

UMF ultramicrofiche.

UMFC or **U.M.F.C.** United Methodist Free Churches.

umgearb. revised. [German *umgearbeitet*]

UMI University Microfilms International (a manuscript and book reproduction service).

UMi Little Bear or the Little Dipper (constellation). [Latin *Ursa Minor*]

U/Min. revolutions per minute. [German *Umdrehungen in der Minute*]

UMNO United Malaysian National Organization (political party).

UMP uridine monophosphate (used in biochemical research).

ump (*pronounced* ump) umpire.

UMS Universal Military Service.

UMT Universal Military Training.

UMTA Urban Mass Transportation Administration (of U.S. Department of Transportation).

UMTS Universal Military Training Service *or* System.

UMW or **UMWA** United Mine Workers of America.

UN or **U.N.** United Nations: a an international organization. b the nations that belong to this organization.

Un. 1 united. 2 university.

un. 1 unified (of bonds). 2 *also* **Un.** union. 3 *also* **Un.** united. 4 unsatisfactory.

UNA or **U.N.A.** United Nations Association.

Unab. or **Unabr.** unabridged.

unacc. unaccompanied.

UNAM (ü'näm) National Autonomous University of Mexico. [Spanish *Universidad Nacional Autónoma de México*]

unan. unanimous.

unasgd. unassigned.

unatt. unattached.

unattrib. unattributed.

unauthd. unauthorized.

UNB universal navigation buoy.

unb. or **unbd.** unbound (of a book).

UNBRO United Nations Border Relief Operation.

UNC United Nations Command.

unc. 1 uncertain. 2 *also* **Unc.** uncirculated (of coins). 3 *also* **Unc.** uncle.

UNCAST United Nations Conference on the Applications of Science and Technology.

UNCC United Nations Cartographic Commission.

UNCCP United Nations Conciliation Commission for Palestine.

UNCDF United Nations Capital Development Fund.

UNCED United Nations Conference on Environment and Development.

uncert. uncertain.

UNCF United Negro College Fund.

UNCHS United Nations Center for Human Settlements.

UNCIO United Nations Conference on International Organization.

UNCIP United Nations Commission for India and Pakistan.

UNCITRAL United Nations Commission on International Trade Law.

unclas. or **unclass.** unclassified.

UNCLOS United Nations Conference on Law of the Sea.

UNCOK United Nations Commission on Korea.

UNCOL Universal Computer Oriented Language.

uncond. 1 unconditional. 2 unconditioned.

UNCOPUOS United Nations Committee on Peaceful Uses of Outer Space.

uncor. or **uncorr.** uncorrected.

UNCSAT United Nations Conference on Science and Technology.

UNCSTD United Nations Conference on Science and Technology for Development.

UNCTAD United Nations Conference on Trade and Development.

UNCURK United Nations Commission for the Unification and Rehabilitation of Korea.

UNDC United Nations Disarmament Commission.

UNDEX or **Undex** United Nations Index (publication).

UNDOF United Nations Disengagement Observer Force.

UNDP United Nations Development Program.

UNDRO United Nations Disaster Relief Organization.

undsgd. undersigned.

UNEC United Nations Education Conference.

UNECA United Nations Economic Commission for Asia.

UNECLA United Nations Economic Commission for Latin America.

UNEDA United Nations Economic Development Administration.

UNEF United Nations Emergency Force.

UNEP United Nations Environment Program.

UNESCO or **Unesco** (yü'nes'kō) United Nations Educational, Scientific, and Cultural Organization.

UNETAS United Nations Emergency Technical Aid Service.

unexpl. 1 unexplained. 2 unexploded. 3 unexplored.

UNFAO United Nations Food and Agricultural Organization.

UNFB United Nations Film Board.

UNFC United Nations Food Conference.

UNFDAC United Nations Fund for Drug Abuse Control.

UNFICYP United Nations Forces in Cyprus.

UNFP National Union of Popular Forces (Moroccan political party). [French *Union Nationale des Forces Populaires*]

UNFPA United Nations Fund for Population Activities.

Ung. Ungava district, Canada (on the Labrador Peninsula).

ung. ointment *pharmaceutics.* [Latin *unguentum*]

UNGA United Nations General Assembly.

Unh unnilhexium (name sometimes associated with chemical element 106).

UNHCR United Nations High Commissioner for Refugees.

UNHQ United Nations Headquarters.

UNIC United Nations Information Center.

UNICE Union of the Industries of the European Community.

UNICEF (yü'nə sef') United Nations Children's Fund (originally called *United Nations International Children's Emergency Fund*).

UNICO Universal Cooperatives, Inc. (in Canada).

UNICOM Universal Communications System.

UNICOR trade name for Federal Prison Industries, Inc. [perhaps originally formed from a clipped blend of *unified corporation*]

UNIDO United Nations Industrial Development Organization.

unif. or **Unif.** uniform.

UNIFEM United Nations Development Fund for Women.

UNIFIL (former) United Nations Interim Force in Lebanon.

Unigov united government (Indianapolis and Marion County).

UNIO United Nations Information Organization.

UNIP United National Independence Party (political party in Zambia).

UNIPEDE International Union of Producers and Distributors of Electric Power. [French *Union Internationale des Producteurs et Distributeurs d'Énergie Électrique*]

UNIPOM United Nations India-Pakistan Observer Mission.

Unis. unison *music.*

UNISIST or **Unisist** (yü'nə sist) United Nations Intergovernmental System of Information in Science and Technology.

Unit. Unitarian.

UNITA or **Unita** (yü nē'tə) National Union for Total Liberation of Angola. [Portuguese *União Nacional para Independência Total de Angola*]

UNITAR United Nations Institute for Training and Research.

Univ. 1 Universalist. 2 University.

univ. 1 a universal. b universally. 2 university.

UNIVAC (yü'nə vak') Universal Automatic Computer (electronic computer designed originally for the U.S. Census Bureau).

unkn. unknown.

UNKRA United Nations Korean Reconstruction Agency.

unl. unlimited.

UNLC United Nations Liaison Committee.

unm. unmarried.

UNMC United Nations Mediterranean Commission.

UNMOGIP United Nations Military Observer Group in India-Pakistan.

UNO *or* **U.N.O.** **1** National Opposition Union (of Nicaragua). [Spanish *Unión Nacional de Oposición*] **2** United Nations Organization.

Unof. unofficial (of law reports).

unop. unopposed.

U.N.P. United National Party (of Sri Lanka).

Unp unnilpentium (name sometimes associated with chemical element 105).

unp. **1** unpaged (of a publication without numbered pages). **2** *also* **unpd.** unpaid.

UNPA **1** National Union of Algerian Workers. [French *Union Nationale des Paysans Algériens*] **2** United Nations Postal Administration.

unperf. unperformed (of a musical composition).

UNPOC United Nations Peace Observation Commission.

UNPROFOR (un'prə fôr') United Nations Protection Force.

unpub. unpublished.

Unq unnilquadium (name sometimes associated with chemical element 104).

UNR Union for the New Republic (French political group of former President de Gaulle). [French *Union pour la Nouvelle République*]

UNREF United Nations Refugee Emergency Fund.

UNREP underway replenishment (an auxiliary warship).

UNRISD United Nations Research Institute for Social Development.

UNRPR United Nations Relief for Palestine Refugees.

UNRRA United Nations Relief and Rehabilitation Administration.

UNRWA United Nations Relief and Works Agency.

Uns unnilseptium (name sometimes associated with chemical element 107).

uns. unsymmetrical.

unsat. **1** unsatisfactory. **2** *also* **unsat** unsaturated.

UNSC United Nations Security Council.

UNSCC United Nations Standards Coordinating Committee.

UNSCCUR United Nations Scientific Conference on the Conservation and Utilization of Resources.

UNSCOB United Nations Special Committee on the Balkans.

UNSCOP United Nations Special Committee on Palestine.

UNSF United Nations Special Fund (for Economic Development).

UNSG United Nations Secretary General.

unsgd. unsigned.

UNSM *or* **UNSvM** United Nations Service Medal.

unsol unsolicited (as of a manuscript).

UNSR United Nations Space Registry.

unsym. unsymmetrical.

UNTAA United Nations Technical Assistance Administration.

UNTAB United Nations Technical Assistance Board.

UNTAM United Nations Technical Assistance Mission.

UNTC United Nations Trusteeship Council.

UNTSO United Nations Truce Supervision Organization.

UNTT *or* **U.N.T.T.** United Nations Trust Territory, also in combination: *UNTTA = United Nations Trust Territory Administration.*

UNU United Nations University.

UNV United Nations Volunteers.

UNWC *or* **U.N.W.C.** United Nations War Crimes Commission.

unwmkd. unwatermarked (of paper).

UOC ultimate operational capability (of a missile).

UOD ultimate oxygen demand.

UP **1** underproof, in distilling. **2** *also* **U.P.** United Presbyterian. **3** United Press (former name of wire service combined with INS to form United Press-International; UPI). **4** university press, esp. in combination: *OUP = Oxford University Press.* **5** Upper Peninsula, Michigan. **6** *also* **U.P.** Uttar Pradesh (state of India, formerly United Provinces in British India).

up. **1** *also* **u.p.** underproof, in distilling. **2** upper.

UPA Uniform Partnership Act.

UPAA Uniform Premarital Agreement Act.

UPC **1** Uganda People's Congress (political party). **2** *also* **U.P.C.** United Presbyterian Church. **3** Universal Product Code (bar code label on a product).

upd unpaid *commerce.*

uphd uphold.

uphol. **1** upholsterer. **2** upholstery.

UPI **1** United Press International. **2** uteroplacental insufficiency *medicine.*

UPIGO International Professional Union of Gynecologists and Obstetricians. [French *Union Professionnelle Internationale des Gynécologues et Obstétriciens*]

UPIN United Paperworkers International Union.

UPONF United Political Organization National Front (in Yemen).

UPOV Union for the Protection of New Varieties of Plants (of the UN to secure rights for the original plant breeder).

uppl. edition. [Swedish *upplaga*]

Upr. Upper (in place names): *Upr. Volta.*

UPRONA Burundi National Party of Unity and Progress. [French *Parti de l'Unité et du Progrès National du Burundi*]

UPS **1** Senegalese Progressive Union (political party). [French *Union Progressiste Sénégalaise*] **2** ultraviolet photoemission spectroscopy. **3** uninterruptible power supply *computers.* **4** United Parcel Service.

UPU *or* **U.P.U.** Universal Postal Union.

UQ upper quartile *statistics.*

UR **1** unconditioned response *psychology.* **2** uniform regulations. **3** unsatisfactory report. **4** up or upper right (a stage direction). **5** utilization review *medicine,* esp. in combination: *UR/DP = utilization review, discharge planning of patient space in hospital.*

Ur. 1 Urdu (official language of Pakistan, form of Hindustani with Arabic and Persian loan words, using Arabic characters). 2 *also* **ur a** urinary. **b** urine. 3 **a** Uruguay. **b** Uruguayan.

URA Urban Renewal Administration.

Uran Uranus *astronomy*.

urb. urban.

URBM ultimate range ballistic missile.

URC upper right center (a stage direction).

URD 1 Republican Democratic Union. [French *Union Républicaine Démocratique*, Spanish *Unión Republicana Democrática*] 2 upper respiratory disease.

Urd. 1 Urdu (official language of Pakistan, form of Hindustani with Arabic and Persian loan words, using Arabic characters). 2 uridine (constituent of nucleic acid).

urg. urgent.

URI upper respiratory infection (esp. in reference to a cold).

URL universal resource locator *computers*.

urol. 1 urological. 2 urologist. 3 urology.

URP unique radiolytic product (chemical compound in food).

URSI (ėr'sē') International Scientific Radio Union (for study of radio transmission). [French *Union Radio Scientifique Internationale*]

URT upper respiratory tract, also in combination: *URTI = upper respiratory tract infection.*

Uru. 1 Uruguay. 2 Uruguayan.

URW *or* **URWA** United Rubber (Cork, Linoleum, and Plastic) Workers of America.

US 1 ultrasound (high-frequency sound waves for internal examination of the body by electronic display). 2 unconditional selection. 3 unconditioned stimulus *psychology*. 4 *also* **U.S.** Under Secretary: *U.S.S. = Under Secretary of State.* 5 uniform system. 6 *also* **U.S. a** United States. **b** United States Highway (used with the number of a highway): *to turn left on US 40.* **c** *United States Supreme Court Reports.* 7 Unit Separator *computers*. 8 *also* **U/S** *or* **u/s** unserviceable.

u.s. 1 as above. [Latin *ut supra*] 2 in the place mentioned above. [Latin *ubi supra*]

USA *or* **U.S.A.** 1 United States Army. 2 United States Attorneys (of Department of Justice). 3 United States of America.

USAAF United States Army Air Force (earlier *USAAC* United States Army Air Corps).

USAC *or* **U.S.A.C.** United States Auto Club.

USACDC United States Army Combat Developments Command.

USACE United States Army Corps of Engineers.

USACIC United States Army Criminal Investigation Command.

USAF United States Air Force.

USAFA United States Air Force Academy.

USAFC United States Army Forces Command.

USAFE United States Air Forces in Europe.

USAFI United States Armed Forces Institute.

USAFR United States Air Force Reserve.

USAHSC United States Army Health Services Command.

USAIC United States Army Intelligence Corps.

USAID United States Agency for International Development.

USAISC United States Army Intelligence and Security Command.

USAMC United States Army Materiel Command.

USAMDW United States Army Military District of Washington.

USAMRIID United States Army Medical Research Institute of Infectious Diseases.

USAN United States Adopted Name (for drug products).

USAR United States Army Reserve.

USAREUR United States Army in Europe.

USARP United States Antarctic Research Program.

USARPAC United States Army in the Pacific.

USART universal synchronous and asynchronous receiver transmitter.

USASCII United States of America Standard Code for Information Interchange.

USASI *or* **U.S.A.S.I.** United States of America Standards Institute.

USAT United States Army Transport.

USATDC United States Army Training and Doctrine Command.

USAWC United States Army Weapons Command.

USB upper sideband *electronics*.

USBC United States Bureau of the Census.

USBE Universal Serials Book Exchange.

USBGN United States Board on Geographic Names (of U.S. Department of Interior).

USBP 1 United States Border Patrol. 2 *also* **U.S.B.P.** United States Bureau of Prisons.

USC 1 *also* **usc** under separate cover. 2 United Somali Conference. 3 *also* **U.S.C.** United States Code (usually with a number): *18 U.S.C. 215.* 4 United States Congress. 5 United States Customs. 6 *also* **U.S.C.** United States of Colombia.

USCA *or* **U.S.C.A.** 1 United States Code Annotated. 2 United States Court of Appeals.

USC&GS United States Coast and Geodetic Survey.

USCC 1 United States Chamber of Commerce. 2 *also* **U.S.C.C. a** United States Circuit Court. **b** United States Claims Court.

USCCA *or* **U.S.C.C.A.** United States Circuit Court of Appeals.

USCCPA *or* **U.S.C.C.P.A.** United States Court of Customs and Patent Appeals.

USCDC United States Civil Defense Council.

USCF United States Chess Federation.

USCG United States Coast Guard.

USCGA United States Coast Guard Academy.

USCGR United States Coast Guard Reserve.

USCGS United States Coast and Geodetic Survey.

USCINCEUR United States Commander in Chief in Europe.

U.S. Const. United States Constitution *law*.

USCS *or* **U.S.C.S.** United States Customs Service.

USCSC *or* **U.S.C.S.C.** United States Civil Service Commission.

U.S.C. Supp. United States Code Supplement.

USD 1 Unified School District. **2** *also* **U.S.D.** United States Dispensatory.

USDA United States Department of Agriculture.

USDAW Union of Shop, Distributive, and Allied Workers (of Great Britain).

USDC United States District Court.

U.S. Dist. Ct. United States District Court.

USE utilized starch equivalent (an index in measuring metabolism).

userid user identification *computers*.

USES United States Employment Service.

U.S.E.T. United States Equestrian Team.

USF United States Forces.

u.s.f. *or* **usf.** and so forth. [German *und so fort*]

USFA 1 United States Fencing Association. **2** United States Fire Administration.

USFHA United States Field Hockey Association.

USFS 1 United States Foreign Service (of U.S. Department of State). **2** United States Forest Service.

USFSA United States Figure Skating Association.

USFWS United States Fish and Wildlife Service.

U.S.G. *or* **USG 1** United States Government. **2** United States Standard Gauge (measure of steel).

USGA *or* **U.S.G.A.** United States Golf Association.

USGCRP United States Global Change Research Program.

USGLI United States Government Life Insurance (for veterans).

USGM United States Government Manual (of organization).

USGPO United States Government Printing Office.

USGS United States Geological Survey.

USh Uganda shilling (monetary unit).

USHA United States Housing Authority.

USI 1 *also* **U.S.I.** United Service Institution. **2** United States of Indonesia.

USIA United States Information Agency.

USINS United States Immigration and Naturalization Service.

USIP United States Import Program.

USIS United States Information Service.

USITC United States International Trade Commission.

USJF United States Judo Federation.

U.S.L. United States Legislation.

USLTA *or* **U.S.L.T.A.** United States Lawn Tennis Association.

USM 1 underwater-to-surface missile. **2** *also* **U.S.M.** United States Marines. **3** United States Marshal. **4** *also* **U.S.M.** United States Mint. **5** *British* Unlisted Securities Market.

USMA 1 United States Maritime Administration. **2** United States Military Academy.

USMC 1 United States Marine Corps. **2** United States Maritime Commission.

USMCR United States Marine Corps Reserve.

USMM United States Merchant Marine.

USMMA United States Merchant Marine Academy.

USMO United States Marshals Office.

USMS 1 United States Maritime Service. **2** United States Marshals Service.

USN *or* **U.S.N.** United States Navy.

USNA 1 United States National Archives. **2** United States Naval Academy.

USNCB United States National Central Bureau (of Interpol).

USNG United States National Guard.

USNHO United States Navy Hydrographic Office.

USNI United States Naval Institute.

USNO United States Naval Observatory.

USNOO United States Naval Oceanographic Office.

USNR United States Naval Reserve.

USNRC United States Nuclear Regulatory Commission.

USNS United States Navy Ship.

USNSA United States National Student Association.

USO United Service Organization.

USOC United States Olympic Committee.

USOE United States Office of Education (now *Department of Education*).

USOM United States Operations Mission.

USP 1 *also* **U.S. Pat.** United States Patent. **2** *also* **U.S.P.** *or* **U.S. Pharm.** *United States Pharmacopoeia.*

USPC United States Parole Commission.

U.S.P.G. United Society for the Propagation of the Gospel.

USPHS *or* **U.S.P.H.S.** United States Public Health Service.

USPO United States Post Office.

USPQ U.S. Patents Quarterly (publication of patent decisions).

USPS 1 United States Postal Service (the independent agency of the U.S. government organized to assume the duties and services of the U.S. Post Office Department). **2** United States Power Squadrons (for boating education and safety).

U.S.R. *United States Supreme Court Reports.*

USRA United States Railway Association.

USRDA United States (Department of Agriculture) Recommended Daily Allowance (of vitamin and food units).

USRS *United States Revised Statutes.*

USRT universal synchronous receiver transmitter.

USS 1 *also* **U.S.S.** Under Secretary of State. **2** *also* **U.S.S.** United States Senate. **3** United States Ship, or United States Steamship. **4** United States standard (a screw thread).

USSA United States Ski Association.

U.S.S.C. *or* **U.S.S.Ct.** United States Supreme Court.

USSCS United States Soil Conservation Service.

USSF United States Soccer Federation.

USSG United States Standard Gauge (for steel).

USSR *or* **U.S.S.R.** (formerly) Union of Soviet Socialist Republics.

USSS 1 *also* **U.S.S.S.** United States Secret Service. **2** United States Steamship.

USSTRICOM United States Strike Command (of the Air Force).

UST undersea technology.

USTA 1 United States Tennis Association. **2** United States Trademark Association. **3** United States Trotting Association.

USTC 1 United States Tariff Commission. **2** *also* **U.S.T.C.** United States Tax Court.

USTFF United States Track and Field Federation.

USTMA United States Trademark Association.

USTR United States Trade Representative.

USTS United States Travel Service.

USTTA United States Travel and Tourism Administration.

usu. 1 usual. **2** usually.

usurp. to be used *pharmaceutics.* [Latin *usurpandus*]

U.S.V. United States Volunteers (Rough Riders of the Spanish American War).

USVA United States Volleyball Association.

USVI *or* **U.S.V.I.** United States Virgin Islands.

USW 1 a ultrashort wave. **b** ultrasonic waves. **2** *also* **U.S.W.** United Steelworkers of America.

usw 1 *also* **u.s.w.** *or* **usw.** and so forth. [German *und so weiter*] **2 a** ultrashort wave. **b** ultrasonic waves.

USWA *or* **U.S.W.A.** United Steelworkers of America.

USWI *or* **U.S.W.I.** United States West Indies.

U.S.W.V. United Spanish War Veterans.

UT 1 *also* **U.T.** universal time *astronomy.* **2** urinary tract. **3** Utah (Zip Code). **4** Union Territory (of India).

Ut. *or* **Ut** Utah.

ut 1 *also* **u.t.** universal time *astronomy.* **2** *also* **ut.** *or* **u/t** untrained. **3** *also* **u.t.** user test. **4** *also* **ut.** utility.

UTC Universal Time Coordinated (an international standard of time). [French *universel temps coordonné*]

UTD undetermined.

Utd *or* **Utd.** United: *Utd Builders.*

ut dict. as directed *pharmaceutics.* [Latin *ut dictum*]

utend. to be used *pharmaceutics.* [Latin *utendium*]

utg. edition. [Norwegian *utgave*]

UTI urinary tract infection.

util. utility.

UTM universal transverse mercator (of a map projection).

UTP uridine triphosphate (coenzyme).

UTS 1 ultimate tensile strength. **2** Universal Time-sharing System.

ut sup. as above [Latin *ut supra*]

UTU United Transportation Union.

UTWA United Textile Workers of America.

U.U. Ulster Unionist, also in combination: *U.U.P. = Ulster Unionist Party.*

UUA Unitarian Universalist Association.

UUM underwater-to-underwater missile.

UUT unit under test.

UUU polyuridylic acid (polymer used in biomedical research).

UUUC United Ulster Unionist Coalition.

UV 1 *also* **U.V.** ultrahigh vacuum. **2** ultraviolet, also in combination: *UV-A = ultraviolet-long wave; UV-B = ultraviolet-short wave.*

u.v. British ultraviolet.

UVAS ultraviolet astronomical satellite.

UVASER ultraviolet laser.

UVF *or* **U.V.F.** Ulster Volunteer Force (Protestant terrorist force in Northern Ireland).

UVL ultraviolet light.

UVR ultraviolet radiation.

UVS ultraviolet spectrometer.

U/W 1 *also* **u/w** *or* **UW** underwater. **2** under will: *Merchants Bank of Mobile, Ala. Executor U/W of Sam Aldridge.* **3** *also* **UW** *or* **u/w** underwriter. **4** *also* **UW** unladen weight.

UWA United Way of America.

UWCE Underwater Weapons and Countermeasures Establishment.

UWF United World Federalists.

UWUA Utility Workers Union of America.

UX unexploded, esp. in combination: *UXM = unexploded missile; UXB = unexploded bomb.*

ux. *or* **Ux.** wife. [Latin *uxor*]

u.X. in the year of the Lord; AD. [Greek μετὰ χριστόν]

Uz. 1 Uzbek. **2** *also* **Uzbek** Uzbekistan (country east of Caspian Sea in former Soviet Union).

u.zw. that is; i.e. [German *und zwar*]

V

V *I an abbreviation for:* **1** *also* **V.** he or she lived. [Latin *vixit*] **2** *also* **V.** valley. **3** valve: *CV = check valve.* **4 a** variable: *VFO = variable frequency oscillator.* **b** variable star. **c** variable stimulus. **5** vector *mathematics, physics.* **6** velocity *physics, chemistry.* **7** verb: *NV = noun verb (description of syntactical order).* **8** *also* **V.** version, in combination: *ASV = American Standard Version; R.S.V. = Revised Standard Version.* **9** verso (back of a sheet of paper, coin, etc., or left-hand page of a two-page spread). **10** vertex. **11** *also* **V.** vertical: *VTOL = Vertical Takeoff and Landing.* **12** very, in combination: *VSW = very short waves.* **13** Veteran: *VFW = Veterans of Foreign Wars.* **14** veterinary: *DVM = Doctor of Veterinary Medicine.* **15** *also* **V.** vibrio (kind of bacteria). **16** *also* **V.** vicar: *VG = vicar general.* **17** *also* **V-** vice, esp. in combination: *VP = vice president; V-C = Vice-Chancellor; V-GIRLS of the night.* **18** *also* **V.** Victoria (referring to Victoria, Queen of England). **19** Victory, esp. of the Allied Nations in WWII: *VE Day = Victory in Europe Day.* **20** video: *VCR = video cassette recorder.* **21** violet: *UV = ultra violet.* **22** *also* **V.** violin. **23 a** visibility. **b** vision or visual, in combination: *VFR = visual flight rules.* **24** volt or voltage. **25** volume: **a** *also* **V.** (space, quantity, or shares offered on a stock exchange). **b** *also* **V.** (book or other publication). **26** *also* **V.** volunteer, in combination: *VFD = Volunteer Fire Department.* **27** vowel: *C-V-C = consonant-vowel-consonant.*
II a symbol for: **1** arrangement of cylinders of an internal combustion engine: *The V-6 with two banks of three cylinders each, slanted to make a V-shape.* **2** blood group antigen. **3** five; 5 (Roman numeral). **4** potential *physics:* **a** electric potential. **b** potential energy. **c** potential difference, esp. in voltage. **5** shearing force *physics.* **6** twenty-second of a series (twenty-first when *J* is omitted). **7** vanadium (chemical element). **8** Verdet constant *physics.*

V̄ five thousand; 5000 (Roman numeral).

Vᵒ verso (back of a sheet of paper, coin, etc., or left-hand page in a book).

V̌ Versicle (verse read by the minister in a responsive reading by the congregation).

v *I an abbreviation for:* **1** *also* **v.** of or from. [German *von*] **2** *also* **v.** see: *v.i. = vide infra, see below.* [Latin *vide*] **3** *also* **v.** turn over. [Latin *verte*] **4** vacuum. **5** *also* **v.** valve, esp. in combination: *ohv = overhead valve.* **6** vapor. **7** variable or variation. **8** *also* **v.** vein. **9** velocity *physics, chemistry, meteorology.* **10** vent. **11** *also* **v.** ventral. **12** *also* **v.** verb or verbal: *vt = verb transitive; v.aux. = verbal auxiliary.* **13** *also* **v.** verse. **14** verso (back of a sheet of paper, coin, etc., or left-hand page of a two-page spread). **15** *also* **v.** versus: *Roe v Wade; conflict of science v. the state.* **16** *also* **v.** vertical. **17** very, in combination: *vhf = very high frequency.* **18** *also* **v.** violin. **19** virus. **20** *also* **v.** vision, esp. visual acuity. **21** voice: *vf = voice frequency.* **22** *also* **v.** volt, voltage. **23** volume: **a** *also* **v.,** esp. specific volume (space, quantity). **b** *also* **v.** (book or other publication).

II a symbol for: **1** coefficient of variation *statistics.* **2** five; 5 (Roman numeral). **3** frequency, as of light waves. **4** twenty-second of a series (twenty-first when *j* is omitted). **5** unusually good visibility *meteorology.* **6** vibrational quantum number *physics.*

V-1 German ramjet flying bomb used in WWII against the British as part of a last effort to inflict damage upon England. [German *Vergeltungswaffe eins* = vengeance weapon one]

V-2 German rocket bomb used in WWII against the British as the final part of a last effort to inflict damage upon England. [German *Vergeltungswaffe zwei* = vengeance weapon two]

V-6 *or* **V-8** an internal combustion engine in an automobile having two rows of three or four cylinders set at angles to each other with the piston rods attached to a single crankshaft.

VA 1 Veterans Administration (now *Department of Veterans Affairs*). **2** *also* **V.A.** Vicar Apostolic (bishop appointed to fill vacant see temporarily or to administer in area not yet created an episcopal see). **3** Vice Admiral. **4** Virginia (Zip Code). **5** visual acuity. **6** *also* **va** volt-ampere (measure of electrical power).

Va. **1** *also* **va.** viola. **2** Virginia (state).

v.a. **1** active verb. **2** he or she lived (so many) years. [Latin *vixit annos*] **3** verbal adjective.

VAB 1 *also* **VAb.** Van Allen Belt *astronomy.* **2** Vehicle Assembly Building (at Kennedy Space Center). **3** Voice Answer Back *computers.*

VABM vertical angle bench mark.

VAC alternating current voltage.

vac 1 vacant. **2** *also* **vac.** vacation. **3** *also* **vac.** vacuum, also in combination: *vac.dist. = vacuum distilled.*

vacc. **1** vaccination. **2** vaccine.

V.Adm. *or military* **VADM** Vice Admiral.

vag. **1** vagina. **2 a** vagrancy. **b** vagrant.

VAH Veterans Adminstration Hospital.

VAL vehicle authorization list (for authorized use).

Val. **1** Valenciennes lace. **2** valine (amino acid in protein). **3** Valley.

val. **1** valence (capacity of an atom or radical to combine with others) *chemistry.* **2** valentine. **3** valine (amino acid in protein). **4** valley. **5 a** value or valued. **b** valuation. **6 a** valve. **b** valvular.

valid. **1** validate. **2** validation.

valn. valuation.

Valpo Valparaiso, Chile.

vamp. vampire.

VAN value-added network (enhanced telecommunications service) *computers.*

van 1 advantage, in tennis. **2** *also* **van.** vanguard. **3** *also* van. vanilla.

Vanc. Vancouver, Canada.

V.&A. *or* **V. and A.** *British* Victoria and Albert (referring esp. to the Victoria and Albert Museum).

V. and T. *or* **v&t** volume and tension (of blood circulation).

v and v verification and validation *computers.*

VAO Veterans Affairs Offices.

vap. 1 vapor, also in combination: *vap.prf.* = *vaporproof.* **2** *also* **vapor.** vaporization.

VAPI visual approach path indicator *aeronautics.*

VAR 1 value-added reseller (distributor of computer systems to which components and applications have been added). **2** *also* **var** volt-ampere reactive unit.

var. 1 *also* **var** variable, also in combination: *var.cond.* = *variable condenser; varactor* = *variable capacitor.* **2 a** variant. **b** *also* **Var.** variation. **c** variety (esp. of species). **3** variometer (any of several instruments to measure magnetic force, electric inductance, or climb and descent in a glider). **4** *also* **var** various.

var. lect. variant reading. [Latin *varia lectio*]

varn. varnish.

vars. varieties (esp. of species).

vas. 1 *also* **vasc.** vascular: *vas.shunt* = *vascular shunt.* **2** vasectomy.

VASI visual approach slope indicator *aeronautics.*

VAT (*pronounced* vat) **1** value-added tax (sales tax). **2** Veterinary Admissions Test.

Vat. Vatican: *Vat.Lib.* = *Vatican Library.*

VATE versatile automatic test equipment.

vaud. *or* **Vaud.** vaudeville.

v. aux. auxiliary verb.

VAV variable air volume.

VAWT vertical axis wind turbine.

VB 1 valence bond *chemistry.* **2** valve box (in blueprints and other technical drawings). **3** *also* **V.B.** vascular bundle (conductive cells in stems and leaves) *botany.*

vb. 1 verb or verbal: *vb.n.* = *verbal noun.* **2** vibration.

VBA Veterans Benefit Adminstration (of U.S. Department of Veterans Affairs).

VBAC vaginal birth after cesarean.

VBC versatile base bus connector *electronics.*

VBE vernacular black English *linguistics.*

VBL vertical block lines (of a magnetic field).

vbl. verbal: *vbl. n.* = *verbal noun.*

VC 1 *also* **v.C.** *or* **V.C.** before Christ; BC. [Dutch *voor Christus*, German *vor Christus*] **2** color vision (in a measure of visual acuity). **3** valuation clause *insurance.* **4** variable capacitor. **5** *also* **V.C. a** Vice-Chairman. **b** Vice-Chamberlain. **c** Vice-Chancellor. **d** Vice-Consul. **6** *usually* **V.C.** Victoria Cross. **7** Vietcong. **8** vinyl chloride (in manufacture of plastics, in organic synthesis, and as refrigerant). **9** vital capacity *medicine.* **10** vitrified clay.

Vc. *or* **vc.** cello or violoncello.

VCA 1 *also* **V.C.A.** Veterans Court of Appeals. **2** voltage control amplifier.

VCCS voltage controlled current source *electronics.*

VCD variable capacitance diode.

VCE variable cycle engine.

Vce Venice, Italy.

VCF 1 vaginal contraceptive film. **2** variable crystal filter *electronics.*

VCG 1 vectorcardiogram. **2** vertical center of gravity.

VCH vinyl cyclohexane (used in formation of polymers and in organic synthesis).

v.Chr. before Christ; BC. [German *vor Christus*]

VCI volatile corrosion inhibitor.

VCL vertical center line.

VCM vinyl chloride monomer.

vcm vacuum.

vcnty vicinity.

VCO voltage controlled oscillator.

vcp vacuum condensing point.

VCR 1 videocassette recorder. **2** visual control room (airport control tower).

Vcr Vancouver, Canada.

VCSEL vertical-cavity surface-emitting laser.

VCT 1 vitrified clay tile (in blueprints and other technical drawings). **2** voltage control transfer.

VD 1 venereal disease; STD. **2** videodisk.

Vd vanadium (chemical element; recognized symbol V).

v.d. 1 vapor density (measure of gas density). **2** various dates.

VDA visual discriminatory acuity *medicine.*

VDC direct current voltage: *VDCW* = *direct current working voltage.*

VDEL Venereal Disease Experimental Laboratory.

VDH *or* **V.D.H.** valvular disease of the heart.

VDI 1 German Institution of Professional Engineers. [German *Verein Deutscher Ingenieure*] **2** vegetation drought index.

VDL Vienna Definition Language (metalanguage for computers).

VDM 1 *also* **V.D.M.** Minister of the Word of God. [Latin *Verbi Dei Minister*] **2** vasodepressor material *medicine.* **3** video display metafile *computers.* **4** Vienna Development Method *computers.*

VDQS wine of superior quality (bottled under supervision of the French Government). [French *vin délimité de qualité supérieure*]

VDR 1 variable diameter rotor. **2** video disk recorder *or* recording. **3** voltage dependent resistor.

VDRL Venereal Disease Research Laboratories (name of a serological test).

VDS variable-depth sonar.

VDT 1 variable density wind tunnel. **2** video display terminal *computers.*

VDU visual display unit (for showing data on an electronic screen).

VE 1 a Value Engineer. **b** Value Engineering. **2** vesicular exanthema (a disease of swine). **3** *also* **V-E** Victory in Europe (victory of the Allied Nations in Europe in WWII): *VE Day.* **4** Vocational Education.

Ve. 1 Venezuela. **2** *also* **v^e** widow. [French *veuve*]

VEA 1 Value Engineers Association. **2** Vocational Education Act.

VEB 1 People's Concern, Factory, *or* Business (formerly in East Germany). [German *Volkseigener Betrieb*] **2** variable elevation beam (of an antenna system).

vec. *or* **vec** vector.

Ved. 1 Vedic (an early form of Sanskrit used in the Veda, a collection of sacred Hindu writing). **2** *also* **ved.** widow. [Italian *vedova*]

VEE Venezuelan equine encephalitis.

veg *or* **veg. 1** (*sometimes pronounced* vej) vegetable or vegetables: *Excellent food, all fresh veg.* **2** *also* **vegan** vegetarian. **3** vegetation.

veggie (vej′ē) **1** vegetable. **2** vegetarian.

veh. 1 vehicle. **2** vehicular.

Vel the Sails (of the ship Argo, an old and very large constellation). [Latin *Vela*]

vel. 1 *also* **Vel.** vellum (fine parchment). **2** velocity. **3** velvet.

Velcro (vel′krō) trade name for a nylon fabric used as a fastener having two strips of tiny hooks and loops that fasten when pressed together. [French *Velours croché* hooked velvet]

VEM vasoexcitor material *medicine*.

Ven. 1 Venerable. **2 a** Venezuela. **b** Venezuelan. **3** Venice. **4 a** Venus. **b** *also* **Ven. & Ad.** Venus and Adonis (poem by Shakespeare).

ven. 1 veneer. **2** venereal. **3 a** venom. **b** venomous. **4** ventral. **5** ventricle.

Venet. Venetian.

Venez. 1 Venezuela. **2** Venezuelan.

vent. 1 a ventilate. **b** ventilation. **c** ventilator. **2** ventral *medicine*. **3 a** ventricle. **b** ventricular.

VEP visual evoked potential.

Ver. 1 Association. [German *Verein*] **2** Vermont. **3** version.

ver. 1 a verification. **b** verify. **2** verse. **3** version. **4** versus. **5** vertex.

VERA versatile experimental reactor assembly.

veränd. revised. [German *verändert*]

verb. improved or corrected. [German and Dutch *verbesserte*]

verb. sap. a word to the wise is sufficient. [Latin *verbum sapienti sat est*]

verdt verdict.

Verf. author. [German *Verfasser*]

Verg. Vergil (Roman poet, author of the *Aeneid*).

verh. married. [German *verheiratet*]

Verl. publisher. [German *Verlag*]

Verm. Vermont.

verm. 1 enlarged. [German *vermehrte*] **2** *also* **verm** vermiculite (mineral used as soil conditioner, insulator, paint, and concrete filler). **3** vermilion.

vern. vernacular.

Vers. 1 experimental. [German *Versuchs-*] **2** version.

vers versed sine *mathematics*.

Ver. St. United States. [German *Vereinigte Staaten*]

verst. died; late. [German *verstorben*]

vert. 1 a vertebra. **b** *also* **Vert.** Vertebrata (the biological name of the group). **c** vertebrate. **2** vertical.

Verz. index, list, or catalog. [German *Verzeichnis*]

ves. 1 a bladder *zoology.* [Latin *vesica*] **b** vesicle (bladder or air sac) *botany.* **2** vessel. **3** *also* **Ves.** vestry.

VESC Vehicle Equipment Safety Commission.

vesp. evening, in the evening. [Latin *vesper*]

vest. vestibule.

vet *or* **Vet** (*pronounced* vet) *or* **vet.** *or* **Vet. 1** veteran. **2 a** veterinarian. **b** *also* **veter.** veterinary: *vet.med.* = *veterinary medicine.*

Vet. Admin. Veterans' Adminstration (now *Department of Veterans Affairs*).

Vet. M.B. Bachelor of Veterinary Medicine.

VETS Veterans' Employment and Training Service (of U.S. Department of Labor).

VF 1 vertical file (of folders in a library collection). **2** very fine (esp. of a pen or pencil point). **3** *also* **V.F.** Vicar Forane (Roman Catholic priest appointed by a bishop to superintend parishes within a see). **4** video frequency. **5** visual field (field of vision). **6** voice frequency *communications*.

v.f. 1 *British* very fair (grade for work done in school). **2** video frequency. **3** voice frequency *communications*.

VFD volunteer fire department.

vfd value for duty.

VFET vertical field effect transistor *electronics*.

VFO *or* **vfo** variable frequency oscillator.

VFP variable factor programming *computers*.

VFR visual flight rules.

VFU Vertical Format Unit *computers*.

V.F.W. *or* **VFW** Veterans of Foreign Wars.

vfy verify.

VG *or* **V.G. 1** very good (grade or condition). **2** vicar general.

v.g. 1 for example. [Latin *verbi gratia*, Spanish *verbigracia*] **2** *also* **vg** vertical grain (of wood). **3** *also* **vg** very good (grade or condition).

VGA 1 variable gain amplifier *electronics*. **2** video graphics array *computers*.

V.G.A.A. Vegetable Growers Association of America.

VGC 1 *also* **v.g.c.** very good condition. **2** viscosity gravity constant.

vgl. compare: *vgl.o.* = *see or compare above.* [Dutch *vergelijk*, German *vergleiche*]

VGLI Veterans Group Life Insurance.

VGO or **VGÖ** Austrian Green Party. [German *Vereinigte Grüne Österreich*]

v.g.u. read, approved, and signed. [German *vorgelesen, genehmigt, unterschrieben*]

VH Vickers hardness number (see *VHN*).

v.H. percent [German *von Hundert*]

VHA Veterans Health Adminstration (of U.S. Department of Veterans Affairs).

VHC very highly commended.

VHD video high density (system for video disks).

VHF or **vhf** very high frequency.

VHN Vickers hardness number (measure of the hardness of metal).

VHO 1 very high operation: *VHO engines.* 2 very high output.

VHP very high performance.

VHS video home system (type of VCR system).

VHSIC very high speed integrated circuit.

VHT very high temperature, also in combination: *VHTR = very high temperature reactor.*

VI 1 *also* **V.I.** Vancouver Island. 2 vertical interval (of contour line in cartography). 3 *also* **V.I.** Virgin Islands: **a** Zip Code. **b** *also* **V.I.** in general use. 4 viscosity index. 5 **a** volume indicator. **b** volume index.

Vi 1 *also* **Vi.** Virginia (state). 2 virginium (name formerly given chemical element *francium*, Fr).

v.i. 1 *also* **vi** intransitive verb. 2 see below. [Latin *vide infra*]

VIA Visually Impaired Association.

viad. viaduct.

VIB vertical integration building *engineering.*

vib. 1 vibrate. 2 vibration.

Vic. 1 **a** Vicar. **b** vicarage. 2 Victoria (esp. Queen of England or state of Australia). 3 victory.

vic. 1 **a** vicinity. **b** vicinal (adjacent or local). 2 *also* **vic** victory.

Vic. Ap. Vicar Apostolic (bishop appointed to fill a vacant see temporarily or to administer in an area not yet created an episcopal see).

Vice Pres. or **Vice-Pres.** Vice-President.

Vic. Gen. Vicar General (assistant of a bishop or archbishop).

VICOM visual communications management.

Vict. 1 Victoria (Queen of England or state of Australia). 2 Victorian.

VID or **Vid.** video.

vid. 1 see. [Latin *vide*] 2 widow. [Latin *vidua*]

VIDAT visual data acquisition.

VIG vaccinia immune globulin (blood fraction used to offset complications from vaccination).

vil. or **Vill.** village.

VIN vehicle identification number.

vin. 1 vinegar. 2 wine. [Latin *vinum*]

vind 1 vindicate. 2 vindication.

vini. viniculture.

VIO *British* Veterinary Investigation Office.

viol. violin. [Italian *violino*]

VIP 1 variable information processing *computers.* 2 vasoactive intestinal polypeptide (found in chemistry of the brain). 3 very important person: *the reception of VIPs.* 4 video integrator and processor (radar device to differentiate by shading its image).

VIPRE visual precision.

VIR vertical interval reference (in television signal transmission).

Vir Virgo, the Virgin (constellation).

vir. green. [Latin *viridis*]

Virg. 1 Virgil (Roman poet, author of the *Aeneid*). 2 *also* **virg.** virgin. 3 Virginia.

v.irr. irregular verb.

Vis. 1 Viscount. 2 Viscountess.

vis. 1 viscosity. 2 **a** visible. **b** visibility. 3 visual.

Visc. 1 Viscount. 2 Viscountess.

visc. 1 viscosity. 2 viscous.

VISTA or **Vista** (vis′tə) Volunteers in Service to America.

VIT value increment taxes.

vit. 1 vital, esp. in combination: *vit. stat. = vital statistics.* 2 vitamin. 3 vitreous.

VITA 1 Volunteer Income Tax Assistance. 2 Volunteers for International Technical Assistance.

vitel. yolk of an egg. [Latin *vitellus*]

viti. viticulture (cultivation of grapes).

vitr. glass. [Latin *vitreum*]

VITS vertical interval test signals *electronics.*

vit. stat. vital statistics.

viv. or **Viv.** quickly, lively *music.* [Italian *vivace*]

viz or **viz.** (*pronounced* viz) namely. [Latin *videlicet*] ▶The *z* is a printing convention rendering a blend of Tironian notation 7 (for Latin *-et*) and a medieval semicolon subsequently rendered in a single stroke ჳ similar to our cursive *ℨ*. In printed form, this character was set as z.

VJ 1 *also* **V-J** victory over Japan (victory of the Allied Nations in the Pacific in WWII): *VJ Day.* 2 *also* **V.J.** or **v.j.** video jockey (announcer for a program of music videos).

v.J. of last year. [German *vorigen Jahres*]

VL or **VLat.** Vulgar Latin (the spoken or popular form of Latin used throughout the later period of the Roman Empire, and the main source of French, Italian, Spanish, Portuguese, and other Romance languages).

vl 1 *also* **v.l.** variant reading. [Latin *varia lectio*] 2 *also* **vl.** violin *music.*

VLA 1 very large array (system of radio telescopes composed of antennas coordinated to function as a unit in the U.S. National Radio Astronomy Observatory). 2 very late activation antigens *biochemistry.* 3 very low altitude.

vla. viola *music.*

Vlad. Vladivostok (Russian port on Sea of Japan).

VLB 1 very long baseline, esp. in combination: *VLBA = very long baseline array* (of a radio telescope); *VLBI = very long baseline interferometry* (measurement of radio source signals in radio astronomy). **2** vertical lift bridge.

VLBC very large bulk carrier (grain or ore ship).

VLCC very large crude carrier (supertanker).

VLCD very low-caloric diet.

VLDL very low-density lipoprotein (large proportion of lipids to protein).

vle. bass viol. [Italian *violone*]

VLF or **vlf** very low frequency: *VLF radio signals.*

Vlg village.

VLIA virus-like infectious agent.

VLLW very low-level waste (of radioactive material).

VLN very low nitrogen: *VLN process for steelmaking.*

vln violin.

VLP virus-like particle.

VLR very long range: *VLR aircraft.*

VLS vapor-liquid-solid: *VLS mechanism for growing crystals.*

VLSI very large-scale integration (technique for fabricating integrated circuits on silicon chips).

VLT 1 very large telescope. **2** video layout terminal.

vltg voltage.

vlv. 1 valve. **2** valvular.

Vly valley.

VM 1 velocity modulation (of beam) *physics.* **2** *computers* **a** virtual machine. **b** virtual memory.

v.M. of last month. [German *vorigen Monats*]

vm. before noon or time from midnight to noon; AM. [German *Vormittag,* Dutch *vormiddag*]

v/m 1 volts per meter (measure of electric field strength). **2** volts per mil (measure of dielectric strength).

VMC visual meteorological conditions.

VMCCA Veteran Motor Car Club of America.

V.M.D. Doctor of Veterinary Medicine. [Latin *Veterinariae Medicinae Doctor*]

VMI Virginia Military Institute.

VMM virtual machine monitor *computers.*

VMOS vertical metal oxide semiconductor *electronics.*

VMS virtual machine system *computers.*

VMT video matrix terminal *computers.*

VN 1 Vietnam, also in combination: *VND = Vietnam dông* (monetary unit). **2** visiting nurse.

vn 1 also **v.n.** neuter verb. **2** also **vn.** violin.

VNA Visiting Nurse Association.

Vna Vienna.

Vno violin. [Italian *violino*]

VNR voltage-controlled differential negative resistance *electronics.*

VNS virtual notebook system *computers.*

VNTSC Volpe National Transportation Systems Center (for research in national transportation and logistics programs).

VO 1 verbal orders. **2** very old (of liquor). **3** virtual office *computers.* **4** voiceover (voice of a narrator or commentator speaking off-camera in motion pictures or television).

Vo. or **vo** or **v°** back of the page or the left-hand page of a two-page spread. [Latin *verso*]

VOA 1 Voice of America. **2** Volunteers of America.

VOC volatile organic compound (toxic emission of automobiles).

voc. 1 vocal. **2** vocational. **3** vocative (grammatical case, esp. in Latin).

vocab. vocabulary.

voc-ed (vok′ed′) or **vo-ed** (vō′ed′) vocational education.

voctl vocational.

VODACOM voice data communications.

VODAT voice-operated device for automatic transmission *electronics.*

VOGAD voice-operated, gain-adjusting device *electronics.*

Vol 1 Flying Fish (constellation). [Latin *Volans*] **2** *also* **vol.** volatile. **3** *also* **vol. a** volcano. **b** volcanic. **4 a** *also* **Vol.** volume, in bibliography: *Vol. 60, pp 313–18.* **b** *also* **vol.** volume (of quantity, space, or intensity): *Vol. control.* **5** *also* **Vol. a** voluntary. **b** volunteer.

VOLAR volunteer army.

volat. volatile.

volc. 1 volcanic. **2** volcano.

vols. or **Vols.** volumes.

volum. volumetric *chemistry, physics.*

Voly Voluntary.

VOM volt-ohm milliammeter (test instrument).

VOP 1 very oldest procurable (of wine). **2** very old pale (brandy and other aged alcohol).

Vopo (vō′pō′) People's Police (of former East Germany). [German *Vo(lks)po(lizei)*]

VOR 1 very high-frequency omnidirectional radio range (standard aid for civil aircraft). **2** voice-operated relay (to control tape recording only when voice activated).

VOR/DME very high-frequency omnirange with distance measuring equipment (for commercial aircraft).

vorm. before noon or time from midnight to noon; AM. [German *vormittags*]

Vorsch. manual. [German *Vorschrift*]

VORTAC (vôr′tak′) very high-frequency omnidirectional range tactical air navigation.

vou. voucher.

VOX 1 voice-operated relay. **2** voice-operated transmission (communications system using a voice-operated relay).

vox pop. voice of the people. [Latin *vox populi*]

VP 1 vapor pressure. **2** *also* **v-p** variable pitch (esp. of propeller aircraft). **3** variable pressure. **4** *also* **V.P.** Vice-President (esp. of the U.S.). **5** vogues proskaner (test to distinguish bacteria).

v.p. **1** passive verb. **2** see below. [Latin *vide post*] **3** vanishing point. **4** vapor pressure. **5** vent pipe. **6** *also* **vp** vice-president: *the v.p. in charge of advertising.*

VPC vapor phase chromatograph.

VPD **1** variation per day. **2** vehicles per day.

VPE vapor phase epitaxy (formation of film on a crystal surface, esp. of a silicon transistor).

VPH **1** variation per hour. **2** vehicles per hour. **3** *also* **v.ph.** vertical photography.

VPI vapor phase inhibitor (to prevent corrosion).

VPM **1** vehicles per mile. **2** vibrations per minute. **3 a** volts per meter (measure of electric field strength). **b** volts per mil (measure of dielectric strength).

vpm volumes per million (measure of substance in a gas).

VPN **1** *also* **vpn** vendor part number. **2** Vickers pyramid number (usually referred to as Vickers hardness number).

VPP viral pneumonia in pigs.

VPRC volume of packed red cells.

V.Pres. *or* **v.pres.** vice-president: *v.pres. for meetings and local sections.*

VPS **1** vibrations per second. **2** volume pressure setting.

VR **1** *also* **V.R.** Queen Victoria. [Latin *Victoria Regina*] **2** variant reading. **3** virtual reality (three-dimensional computer graphics). **4** vocal resonance. **5** voltage regulator. **6** vulcanized rubber.

v.r. **1** reflexive verb. **2** variant reading.

VRA Vocational Rehabilitation Administration (now *Office of Special Education and Rehabilitative Services*).

VRAM video ram (random access memory) *computers.*

vrbl. variable.

VRC **1** vertical redundancy check *computers.* **2** visible records computer.

v.refl. reflexive verb.

V.Rev. Very Reverend.

vrg. veering.

VRI **1** *also* **V.R.I.** Victoria Queen and Empress. [Latin *Victoria Regina et Imperatrix*] **2** visual rules for instrument landing *aeronautics.*

VRL vertical reference line (on blueprints and other mechanical drawings).

VRM variable rate mortgage.

VRR visual radio range.

VS **1** *also* **V.S.** turn over swiftly *music.* [Latin *volti subito*] **2** variable speed. **3** *also* **V.S.** Veterinary Surgeon. **4** volumetric solution *chemistry.*

vs **1** *also* **v.s.** old style (of the calendar). [French *vieux style*] **2** *also* **v.s.** see above. [Latin *vide supra*] **3** *also* **vs.** verse. **4** *also* **vs.** versus: *A baseball game is pitcher vs. batter; Director General of Railroads, Petitioner vs. Mable Green, Administratrix.* **5** *also* **v.s.** vibration seconds (of sound waves).

VSAM Virtual Storage Access Method *computers.*

VSB **1** vestigial sideband *electronics.* **2** *also* **vsb.** visible.

VSBY *or* **vsby.** visibility.

VSCC *or* **V.S.C.C.** Vintage Sports Car Club.

VSCF variable speed constant frequency.

VSD **1** vendor's shipping documents *commerce.* **2** ventricular septal defect *medicine.*

VSI vertical speed indicator.

VSM vibrating sample magnetometer.

VSMF visual search microfilm file (indexed filmed data).

vsn. *or* **VSN** vision.

VSO **1** *also* **V.S.O.** very superior old (of wines and spirits). **2** *British* Voluntary Service Overseas.

VSOP *or* **V.S.O.P.** very superior old pale (of brandy aged about 12 years).

V.S.Q. very special quality.

VSR very short range (radar).

vss. **1** verses. **2** *also* **VSS.** versions.

VSTOL *or* **V/STOL** (vē'stôl) vertical and short takeoff and landing (aircraft).

VSV vesicular stomatitis virus.

VSW very short waves *electronics.*

VSWR voltage standing wave ratio *electronics.*

VT **1** *also* **V.T.** Old Testament. [Latin *Vetus Testamentum*] **2** vacuum technology. **3** vacuum tube: *VTVM = vacuum tube voltmeter.* **4** variable time (esp. of a fuse): *VT shells for airbursts.* **5** Vermont (Zip Code). **6** vertical tabulation *computers.* **7** videotape.

Vt. Vermont.

vt **1** *also* **v.t.** transitive verb. **2** variable transmission. **3** *also* **vt.** voting: *vt.pl. = voting pool.*

V.T.C. voting trust certificate.

VTE **1** vertical tube evaporator (used in distillation of seawater). **2** vicarious trial and error *psychology.*

Vte. Viscomte.

Vtesse. Viscomtesse.

vtg. voting.

VTL variable threshold logic *computers.*

VTO vertical takeoff: *VTO aircraft.*

VTOC Volume Table of Contents *computers.*

VTOL (vē'tôl') vertical takeoff and landing.

VTPR vertical temperature profile radiometer.

VTR videotape recorder or recording.

VTVM vacuum tube voltmeter.

VU *or* **V.U.** volume unit or voice unit (measure of volume for voice or other complex sound wave, esp. on a tape recorder): *V.U. meter.*

Vul the Fox (constellation). [Latin *Vulpecula*]

Vul. *or* **Vulg.** Vulgate (esp. referring to an edition of the Bible).

vulg. **1** vulgar. **2** vulgarly.

v.u.s. see as above. [Latin *vide ut supra*]

VUV vacuum ultraviolet, esp. in combination: *VUVS = vacuum ultraviolet spectroscopy.*

v/v percent volume in volume *chemistry.*

vv 1 also **v.v.** spoken aloud. [Latin *viva voce*] **2** veins *medicine*. **3** also **vv.** verbs. **4** also **vv.** verses. **5** also **v.v.** vice versa. **6** also **vv.** or **VV.** violins (esp. referring to first and second violin sections of an orchestra). **7** also **vv.** or **VV.** volumes (books).

VVA Vietnam Veterans of America.

VVD People's Party for Freedom and Democracy. [Dutch *Volkspartij voor Vrijheid en Democratie*]

v/v/hr. vibration velocity per hour.

vv.ll. variant readings. [Latin *variae lectiones*]

V.V.O. or **VVO** very, very old (of wines and spirits).

V.V.S. or **VVS** very, very superior (of brandy).

V.V.S.O. or **VVSO** very, very superior old (of brandy), esp. in combination: *V.V.S.O.P. = very, very superior old pale.*

VW 1 also **V.W.** *British* Very Worshipful (title of respect for certain judges and ecclesiastics). **2** also **V.W.** vessel wall. **3** Volkswagen (originally a small German two-door automobile).

VWD German News Agency. [German *Vereinigter Wirtschafts Diensf*]

vWF von Willebrand factor (protein found in blood-clotting process).

VX nerve gas (as a military weapon).

vx vertex.

vy 1 also **v.y.** various years, in cataloging. **2** also **vy.** or **Vy.** very: *Vy. Rev. = Very Reverend.*

VZ varicella zoster *medicine*, esp. in combination: *VZIG = varicella zoster immune globulin.*

W *I an abbreviation for:* **1** waist: *34W = 34 inches waist* (in clothing measurements). **2** also **W. a** Wales. **b** Welsh. **3** waste. **4** water, esp. in combination: *MHW = mean high water.* **5** watt: *100W (on a light bulb); KW = kilowatt.* **6** wave: *SW = short wave.* **7** Wednesday: *MWF = Monday, Wednesday, Friday (in scheduling).* **8 a** weight. **b** load, esp. total load. **9** also **W.** West, Western (the compass point, also in combination): *SbW = South by West; Wa£ = West African pound; W.Va. = West Virginia.* **10** also **W.** white. **11 a** wide. **b** width. **12** also **W.** wife. **13** wind. **14** wire, in combination: *AWG = American Wire Gauge.* **15** won: **a** (monetary unit of North and South Korea). **b** (of a game or record of play). **16** wood.
II a symbol for: **1** energy, esp. electric energy. **2** indefinite ceiling *meteorology.* **3** irradiance (radiant flux density). **4** tungsten (chemical element). [German *Wolfram*] **5** twenty-third of a series (twenty-second when *J* is omitted). **6** (originally, weak) an elementary particle thought to be a quantum unit of the weak force or interaction *physics: W particle.* **7** weber (unit of magnetic flux). **8** weber number (of surface tension in a fluid system). **9** wehnelt (measure of X-ray intensity). **10** Winter Load Line (Plimsoll mark to show maximum depth a ship may ride when loaded for winter sea conditions). **11** work *physics.* **12** Wotquenne Catalog (of the music of C.P.E. Bach).

w *I an abbreviation for:* **1** walk *baseball.* **2** wall. **3** also **w.** wanting. **4** warm (of an air mass) *meteorology.* **5** watt: *10-40 w; mw = megawatt.* **6** also **w.** wave, in combination: *w.l. = wave length.* **7** also **w.** week, weekly. **8 a** weight, esp. weight per unit. **b** load, esp. load per unit of area. **9** also **w.** west, western (the compass point, also in combination): *nbw = north by west.* **10** wicket *cricket.* **11 a** wide. **b** width. **12** also **w.** wife. **13** window, in drafting. **14** also **w.** wire, in combination: *3 w. 115/230v service (descriptive of spec-*

ifications for electric service). **15** also **w.** or **w/** with: *liv rm w/fireplace = living room with fireplace.* **16** also **w.** word. **17** wrong, in combination: *wf = wrong font in typesetting.*
II a symbol for: **1** acoustical displacement. **2** angular velocity. **3** dew *meteorology.* **4** mass flow rate *physics.* **5** twenty-third of a series (twenty-second when *j* is omitted). **6** velocity *physics.* **7** water vapor content. **8** work *physics.*

WA 1 also **wa** warm air. **2** Washington (state, Zip Code). **3** also **W.A. a** West Africa. **b** West African: *WA£ = West African pound.* **4** also **W.A.** Western Australia (state in Australia). **5** also **W.A.** with average (of commercial insurance).

WAAC Women's Army Auxiliary Corps (now *Women's Army Corps*, in U.S. and *Women's Royal Army Corps*, in Great Britain).

WAAF *British* Women's Auxiliary Air Force (now the *Women's Royal Air Force*).

WAAS *British* Women's Auxiliary Army Service (now *Women's Royal Army Corps*).

WAB Wage Appeals Board (of U.S. Department of Labor).

WAC 1 also **W.A.C.** Women's Action Coalition. **2** Women's Army Corps. **3** World Aeronautical Chart.

WACK wait before transmitting positive acknowledgment (of a transmission of computer data).

WADEX word and author index.

WADS Wide Area Data Service (system of communication through telephone central dial offices).

WAE or **w.a.e.** when actually employed.

WAF 1 also **w.a.f.** with all faults. **2** Women's Air Force.

W.Afr. 1 West Africa. **2** West African.

WAFS Women's Auxiliary Ferrying Squadron (in WWII).

WAIF Women's Adoption International Fund.

WAIS Wechsler Adult Intelligence Scale *psychology.*

WAK wearable artifical kidney.

Wal. 1 *also* **Walach.** Walachian (esp. referring to a dialect of Romanian spoken in Walachia). **2** Walloon (esp. referring to French dialect of Belgium).

wal. walnut.

Wall. Wallace (U.S. Supreme Court Reports).

WAM wraparound mortgage.

WAN wide-area network (of a computer network).

W&F water and feed (of animals, esp. livestock in transit).

W&I weighing and inspection.

W.&M. William and Mary (King and Queen of England).

W&R water and rail (designated transportation for a shipment).

w&s *or* **W&S** whiskey (whisky) and soda

WAP Women Against Pornography.

WAPA Western Area Power Administration (of U.S. Department of Energy).

WAPDA Water and Power Development Authority (of Pakistan).

WAPOR World Association for Public Opinion Research.

War. 1 Warsaw. **2** *also* **Warks** Warwickshire County, England.

war. warrant.

WARC 1 Western Air Rescue Center (of U.S.). **2** World Administration Radio Conference (to determine use of radio broadcasting frequencies). **3** World Alliance of Reformed Churches.

WARI Waite Agricultural Research Institute (of Australia).

warn. warning.

warr. warranty.

warrtd. warranted.

warrty. warranty.

Wash. Washington (state, American President, and capital of U.S., esp. when used in combination with *D.C.*): *Wash. D.C. = Washington, District of Columbia.*

WASP (*pronounced* wosp) **1** *also* **Wasp** White Anglo-Saxon Protestant. **2** Women's Air Force Service Pilots (to ferry planes in WWII, dissolved 1944).

Wass. Wassermann (test for syphilis).

WAT 1 weight, altitude, temperature *aeronautics.* **2** word association test *psychology.*

Wat. Waterford (type of crystal glassware).

WATA *or* **W.A.T.A.** World Association of Travel Agencies.

WATF Waterloo Fortran (computer program language).

WATS Wide Area Telephone Service (long-distance flat rate telephone service).

W.Aust. Western Australia.

Wave Widows Against Violence Empower (nonsectarian support group for families of victims of political violence in Northern Ireland).

WAVES *or* **Waves** (wāvz) Women Accepted for Volunteer Emergency Service (U.S. Naval Women's Reserve in WWII, no longer an official title).

WAWF World Association of World Federalists.

WAY World Assembly of Youth.

WB 1 *also* **W.B.** warehouse book. **2** water ballast (in a ship). **3** water base (of paint). **4** waveband, esp. in combination: *SWB = short waveband.* **5** *also* **W.B.** *or* **W/B** waybill *commerce.* **6** westbound. **7** wet bulb (esp. of a temperature reading taken with a wet bulb thermometer). **8** wheelbase (esp. as a measurement of relative size of automobiles). **9** Women's Bureau (of U.S. Department of Labor). **10** *also* **W.B.** World Bank (International Bank for Reconstruction and Development).

Wb weber (unit of magnetic flux).

w.b. 1 *also* **w/b** warehouse book. **2** water ballast (in a ship). **3** westbound.

WBA *or* **W.B.A.** World Boxing Association.

WBC 1 *also* **W.B.C.** white blood cells or count. **2** World Boxing Council.

WBF 1 *also* **wb/fp** wood-burning fireplace, in real estate advertising. **2** World Bridge Federation, in cardplaying.

wbi *or* **WBI** will be issued.

WbN west by north.

WBNS water boiler neutron source.

WBO World Boxing Organization.

WBR whole-body radiation (exposure).

WbS west by south.

w.b.s. without benefit of salvage (of commercial insurance).

WBT wet bulb temperature (reading of a thermometer).

W by N west by north.

W by S west by south.

WC 1 *also* **W.C.** War Correspondent (of a publication or broadcast network). **2** *also* **W.C.** water closet (toilet). ▶The abbreviation is common in Europe, esp. in Germany (naturally assimilated as *Wasser Klosett*) and in France (where it is referred to as water closet because no native form corresponds to *W.C.*). **3** wheelchair. **4** will call (in a telephone message). **5** without charge *commerce.* **6** *also* **W.C.** wood casing (of windows). **7** working capital *finance.* **8** workmen's compensation (for injury) *insurance.*

W/C 1 Wing Commander (in the British and Canadian Air Forces). **2** *also* **w/c** with corrections (of printer's proofs).

w.c. 1 water closet (toilet, see *WC*): *small kitchen, and a tiny, clean w.c. and shower.* **2** without charge *commerce.*

WCB Workmen's Compensation Board.

WCC *or* **W.C.C.** World Council of Churches.

WCED World Commission on Environment and Development.

WCEU *or* **W.C.E.U.** World Christian Endeavor Union.

WCL World Confederation of Labor.

WCO Weapons Control Officer.

WCP World Council of Peace.

WCR water-cooled reactor (for nuclear generation of electricity).

WCRA 1 Weather Control Research Association. **2** *also* **W.C.R.A.** Women's Cycle Racing Association.

WCT World Championship Tennis.

W.C.T.U. *or* **WCTU** Women's Christian Temperance Union.

WCWB World Council for the Welfare of the Blind.

WD 1 a water department: *MKWD = Mt Kisco Water Department.* **b** Water District: *CWD = Carmel Water District.* **2** *also* **W.D.** western district (division of Federal Courts). **3** white dwarf (star of low luminosity and great density).

W/D 1 wind direction. **2** withdrawn.

wd. 1 ward. **2** weed. **3** window. **4** wood, also in combination: *wd.sc. = wood screw.* **5** word. **6** would. **7** wound (injury).

4WD four-wheel drive (of a motor vehicle).

WDC World Date Center.

wdg. winding (continuous coil of wire) *electricity.*

WDPS Western Data Processing Center (of U.S.).

wdt. width.

wdwk woodwork.

WDWN well-developed, well-nourished, esp. in combination: *WDWN/NAD = well-developed, well-nourished, and in no acute distress.*

We *or* **We.** Wednesday.

we weekend.

WEA 1 Western European Alliance. **2** *also* **W.E.A.** British Workers' Educational Association.

wea. 1 weapon, weapons. **2** *also* **wea** *or* **WEA** weather, also in combination: *WEARCON = weather reconnaissance* (for weather observation and forecasting).

WEC World Energy Conference.

Wed. *or* **Wednes.** Wednesday.

WEE western equine encephalitis.

w.e.f. with effect from.

WEFAX weather facsimile.

WEFC Western European Fisheries Conference.

WEFT wings, engine, fuselage, tail *aeronautics.*

Wel. Welsh, esp. the Celtic language of Wales.

weld. welding.

Well. Wellington, New Zealand.

WEMA Western Electronic Manufacturers Association.

WEP 1 water-extended polyester. **2** Work Equity Program.

WES 1 Waterway Experiment Station (of U.S. Army Engineers Corps). **2** *British* Women's Engineering Society. **3** World Economic Survey.

Wes. Wesleyan.

wesentl. essential, main, or principal. [German *wesentlich*]

West. *or* **west.** western.

Westm. Westminster.

Westw. westward.

WET *or* **W.E.T.** Western European Time.

WETA Washington Educational Television Association (call letters for Washington, D.C. Public Broadcasting Service station).

WEU Western European Union (organization to promote economic, social, and cultural matters among members and, originally, for collective self-defense).

Wex. Wexford County, Ireland.

WEZ *or* **W.E.Z.** West European Time. [German *westeuropäische Zeit*]

wf *or* **w.f.** wrong font (direction to a printer to change type, esp. a character in the wrong face or style).

W.F.B. World Fellowship of Buddhists.

WFC World Food Council.

WFD World Federation of the Deaf.

w.fd. wool forward (instruction in knitting).

WFEO World Federation of Engineering Organizations.

wff. well-formed formula, in logic.

WFIP Women's Financial Information Program (division of American Association of Retired Persons).

WFL World Football League.

WFMH World Federation for Mental Health.

WFMW *or* **W.F.M.W.** World Federation of Methodist Women.

WFN 1 World Federation of Neurology. **2** World Fund for Nature.

WFNA white fuming nitric acid (component of missile fuel).

WFP World Food Program (of the UN).

WFPA World Federation for the Protection of Animals.

WFS World Future Society.

WFSW World Federation of Scientific Workers.

WFTU *or* **W.F.T.U.** World Federation of Trade Unions.

WFUNA World Federation of United Nations Associations.

WG *or* **W.G. 1** water gauge. **2** *also* **W.Ger.** (formerly) **a** West German. **b** West Germany. **3** wire gauge.

wg 1 *also* **w.g.** water gauge. **2 a** *also* **wg.** weighing. **b** *also* **w.g.** weight guaranteed. **3** *also* **wg.** wing. **4** *also* **w.g.** wire gauge.

W.G.A. Writers Guild of America.

WGI World Geophysical Interval.

WGmc. West Germanic (division of Germanic languages including English, Frisian, Dutch, and German).

WGPMS Warehouse Gross Performance Measurement System (of inventory).

wgt. weight.

WH 1 water heater. **2** *also* **W.h.** watt-hour (unit of electrical energy or unit of work). **3** *also* **W.H.** White House (esp. as office of the President).

wh 1 *also* **w.h.** *or* **wh.** watt-hour (unit of electrical energy or unit of work). **2** which. **3** *also* **Wh.** whistle (esp. of a buoy on navigational charts). **4** white. **5** *also* **w/h** withholding (tax).

WHA World Hockey Association.

WHD *or* **whd** warhead (of a missile).

Wheat. Wheaton (U.S. Supreme Court Reports).

whf. wharf.

whfg. wharfage *commerce.*

WHHA White House Historical Association.

Whis. whistle (esp. of a buoy on navigational charts).

W.H.M.A. Women's Home Missionary Association.

WHO 1 White House Office (chief administrative office of the executive branch of U.S. government). **2** World Health Organization.

WHOI Woods Hole Oceanographic Institution.

Whol. wholesale *commerce.*

whp *or* **WHP** *or* **W.hp.** water horsepower.

whr. **1** *also* **w.hr.** *or* **w-hr** watt-hour (unit of electrical energy or unit of work). **2** whether.

WHRC World Health Research Center.

WHS Washington Headquarters Services.

whs. *or* **whse.** warehouse, also in combination: *whs.rec.* = *warehouse receipt.*

whsle. wholesale.

whsmn. warehouseman.

whsng. warehousing.

wht. *or* **Wht.** white, also in combination: *Wht. Hs.* = *White House.*

whvs. wharves.

WI 1 *also* **W.I. a** West Indies. **b** West Indian. **2** when issued (esp. of stock). **3** *also* **W.I.** Windward Islands. **4** Wisconsin (Zip Code). **5** *British* Women's Institute. **6** wrought iron, esp. in engineering.

w.i. **1** when issued (esp. of stock). **2** wrought iron.

WIA wounded in action.

WIBC Women's International Bowling Congress.

WIC 1 Welfare and Institutions Code. **2** *also* **WICP** Women, Infants, and Children (program of special supplemental support).

Wick. Wicklow County, Ireland.

W.I.D. West India Docks (shipping facilities in the Port of London).

wid. widow, widower.

W.I.F. *or* **WIF** West Indies Federation.

Wilts *or* **Wilts.** Wiltshire County, England.

WIMP 1 weakly interacting massive particle (any of a group of elementary particles thought to be present in the core of the sun and affecting the amount of energy found there). **2** windows, icons, mouse, pull down menus (interfacing to permit easy computer communication with the user).

WIN Work Incentive (federal jobs program for people on welfare).

Winch. Winchester (place name, computer storage disk).

W.Ind. 1 West Indian. **2** West Indies.

Wind.I. Windward Islands.

Winn. Winnipeg, Canada.

Wint. *or* **wint.** winter.

Winton. of Winchester (in reference to the Bishop and therefore used as his official signature). [Latin *Wintoniensis*]

Wint.T. The Winter's Tale (play by Shakespeare).

WIP work in progress.

WIPO World Intellectual Property Organization (intellectual properties include trademark, copyright, and patent rights).

WIPP Waste Isolation Pilot Plant.

WIRA Wool Industries Research Association (of Great Britain).

WIRDS Weather Information Reporting and Display System.

WIS Waste Isolation System.

Wis. *or* **Wisc.** Wisconsin.

WISC Wechsler Intelligence Scale for Children.

Wisd. Wisdom of Solomon (book of the Roman Catholic Old Testament Apocrypha).

WISP wide-range imaging spectrometer.

wit. witness.

WITA Women's International Tennis Association.

withdrl withdrawal.

witht without.

Wiv. The Merry Wives of Windsor (play by Shakespeare).

WIZO Women's International Zionist Organization.

WJC World Jewish Congress.

Wk Walk: *Birdcage Wk (in St. James Park, London).*

wk 1 a weak. **b** *also* **wk.** week. **2** *also* **w.k.** well known (used of species, name, etc.) *biology.* **3** work. **4** *also* **Wk** wreck (on navigational charts).

WKB Wentzel, Kramers, Brillouin (solution for varying potentials in quantum physics): *WKB method.*

wkbk workbook.

wkds weekdays.

wkg working.

wkly weekly.

wkn weaken.

wkr worker.

wks 1 weeks. **2** *also* **Wks** works. **3** *also* **Wks** workshop.

wkt *or* **wkts** wicket, wickets *cricket.*

WL 1 *also* **W.L.** European railway sleeping car. [French *wagon-lit*] **2** waiting list. **3** *also* **w.l.** water line. **4** *also* **wl** wavelength. **5** Women's Liberation (feminist movement).

WLAF World League of American Football.

WLB 1 War Labor Board (of WWII). **2** Wilson Library Bulletin (publication).

wld would.

Wld.Ch. World Champion.

wldr. welder.

W.L.F. Women's Liberal Federation.

WLI workload index.

WLM Women's Liberation Movement.

Wln Wellington, New Zealand.

W.long. west longitude.

W.L.P.S.A. Wild Life Preservation Society of Australia.

W.L.T. *or* **W/L/T** win, lose, tie, in scoring sports.

W.L.U.S. *or* **WLUS** World Land Use Survey (of the International Geographical Union).

Wly or **wly** westerly.

wlz waltz.

WM 1 also **wm** wattmeter. **2** also **W/M** or **w/m** weight and/or measurement commerce. **3** white metal (any of the silver metals having a large amount of tin, esp. some of friction-reducing metals, such as babbitt). **4** wire mesh. **5** word mark computers.

Wm. William.

WMA or **W.M.A.** World Medical Association.

WMAA Whitney Museum of American Art.

WMATA Washington (D.C.) Metropolitan Area Transit Authority.

WMC 1 War Manpower Commission (of WWII). **2** Ways and Means Committee (of U.S. House of Representatives). **3** British Working Men's Club. **4** World Meteorological Center. **5** also **W.M.C.** World Methodist Council.

Wmg. Wilmington, Delaware or North Carolina.

WMI Wildlife Management Institute.

wmk. watermark.

WMO World Meteorological Organization.

WMS 1 also **W.M.S.** Wesleyan Missionary Society. **2** wire mesh screen. **3** World Magnetic Survey.

WNA Winter North Atlantic Load Line (Plimsoll mark to show maximum depth a ship may ride when loaded for passage over North Atlantic sea routes in winter).

WNE Welsh National Eisteddfod (Welsh festival of music and poetry).

wng. warning.

wnl or **WNL** within normal limits.

W.N.P. or **WNP** Welsh Nationalist Party.

WNW or **W.N.W.** or **w.n.w.** west-northwest.

WO 1 also **W.O.** British walkover (easy victory), esp. in sports. **2** also **W.O.** British (formerly) War Office, also in combination: WOCL = War Office Casualty List. **3** Warrant Officer: WO (jg.) = Warrant Officer, junior grade. **4** also **W/O** water in oil (esp. of an emulsion). **5** without, esp. in combination: WOC = without compensation. **6** work order. **7** also **W/O** written off (as a business loss or bad loan). **8** written order.

wo 1 also **w.o.** as above. [German wie oben] **2** also **w/o** without.

WOAR British Women Organized Against Rape.

WOASH Women's Organization Against Sexual Harassment.

WOB or **w.o.b.** washed overboard (of cargo, in an insurance report).

WOC or **W.O.C.** without compensation (esp. of an expert working without pay).

WOCA World Outside Centrally Planned Economic Areas.

WOCE World Ocean Circulation Experiment (international survey of circulation of heat, water, and chemical substances in the oceans).

WOCG weather outline contour generator.

WOE or **w.o.e.** without equipment.

w.o.g. with other goods commerce, insurance.

w.o.l. or **WOL** wharfowners' liability insurance.

WOM 1 Woomera, Australia (NASA tracking station). **2** also **W.O.M.** word of mouth advertising.

WOMAN (wŭm′ən) World Organization for Mothers of All Nations.

w.o.n. wool on needle, in knitting.

WOO World Oceanographic Organization.

woo or **WoO** work without opus (number) music. [German Werke ohne Opuszahl]

WOOOL words out of ordinary language.

WOP 1 with other property. **2** without personnel, also in combination: WOPE = without personnel or equipment.

WORC Washington (D.C.) Operations Research Council.

Worc. or **Worcs** Worcestershire County, England.

WORM Write Once Read Many times (permanent storage computer disk).

WORSE word selection computers.

WOSAC worldwide synchronization of atomic clocks.

WOW 1 waiting on weather. **2** Women Ordnance Workers. **3** also **W.O.W.** Woodmen of the World (fraternal organization).

WP 1 wastepaper, also in combination: WPB = wastepaper basket. **2** also **W.P.** water packed (esp. of canned food). **3** waterproof or weatherproof. **4** weather permitting. **5** wettable powder. **6** white phosphorus (common form of phosphorus). **7** wild pitch baseball. **8** wire payment. **9 a** word processing. **b** word processor. **10** working paper. **11** working point. **12** working pressure.

w.p. 1 waste pipe (on plumbing diagrams). **2** weather permitting. **3** without prejudice insurance, law.

WPA 1 also **w.p.a.** with particular average insurance. **2** Works Projects Administration or earlier, Works Progress Administration (of the administration of Franklin Roosevelt, to provide employment). **3** World Presbyterian Alliance.

WPB 1 War Production Board (of WWII). **2** also **wpb** wastepaper basket.

WPBSA World Professional Billiards and Snooker Association.

WPC 1 also **W/P/C** British Woman Police Constable. **2** wood-plastic composite (wood impregnated with vinyl). **3** World Petroleum Congress.

WPCA Water Pollution Control Act.

WPCF Water Pollution Control Federation (organization of sanitation specialists and municipal officials).

WPE white porcelain enamel.

WPESS Within Pulse Electronic Scanning (for monitoring fish migration).

WPFC Western Pacific Fisheries Commission.

WPGA Women's Professional Golfers' Association.

WPI 1 wholesale price index. **2** also **W.P.I.** World Press Institute.

WPL or **wpl** warning point level.

wpm or **w.p.m.** or **WPM** words per minute.

wpn weapon.

WPP 1 *also* **w.p.p.** waterproof paper packing *commerce*. **2** Witness Protection Program (esp. of U.S. Department of Justice to protect witnesses by providing new identity).

WPPSI Wechsler Preschool and Primary Scale of Intelligence *psychology*.

wpr. waterproof.

WPRL Water Pollution Research Laboratory.

WPS 1 with prior service. **2** *also* **wps** *or* **w.p.s.** words per second.

WPSA World Poultry Science Association.

WQ 1 water quenched *physics*. **2** *also* **Wq.** *or* **wq** Wotquenne catalog (used with a number in cataloging music of C.P.E. Bach).

WR 1 wardroom (officers' quarters on a warship). **2** *also* **W/R** warehouse receipt (receipt for goods in a warehouse, often used as negotiable paper). **3** water repellent. **4** Wassermann reaction (in test for syphilis). **5** *also* **W.R.** West Riding (former administrative division of Yorkshire). **6** wide receiver, in football. **7** with rights *commerce*.

w.r. war risk *insurance*, also in combination: *w.r.i.* = *war risk insurance*.

WRAAC Women's Royal Australian Army Corps.

WRAAF Women's Royal Australian Air Force.

WRAC *British* Women's Royal Army Corps.

WRAF *British* Women's Royal Air Force.

WRANS Women's Royal Australian Navy Service.

WRAP Weapons Readiness Analysis Program.

WRAT Wide-Range Achievement Test.

WRC 1 water retention coefficient. **2** Welding Research Council.

WRE Weapons Research Establishment (in Australia).

w.ref. *or* **w/ref** with reference, esp. in a notation.

WRENS (renz) *British* Women's Royal Navy Service (now *WRNS*).

wrfg. wharfage *commerce*.

W.R.I. Will Rogers Institute.

writ. 1 writer. **2** written.

wrk work, also in combination: *wrk rpt* = *work report*.

WRNR Women's Royal Naval Reserve.

WRNS Women's Royal Naval Service.

wrnt. warrant.

WRO Weed Research Organization.

w.r.o. war risk only *insurance*.

WRP Worker's Revolutionary Party (of Great Britain).

WRSIC Water Resources Scientific Information Center.

wrt wrought: *wrt iron*.

W.R.U. *or* **WRU** Welsh Rugby Union.

WRVS Women's Royal Voluntary Service.

WS 1 *also* **w.s.** water-soluble, esp. in combination: *wsb* = *water-soluble base*. **2** water supply. **3** water surface. **4** weapon system, also in combination: *WSPO* = *Weapon System Project Officer*. **5** weather station. **6** weather stripping.

7 Western Samoa: *WS$* = *Western Samoa tala* (monetary unit). **8** *also* **W.S.** West Saxon. **9** wind speed. **10** working storage *computers*. **11** Writer to the Signet (attorney in Scotland similar in function to English solicitor).

Ws watt-second (unit of energy, one joule).

W.S.A. Weed Society of America.

W.Sam. Western Samoa.

WSB Wage Stabilization Board (of WWII).

WSC 1 Winston Spencer Churchill (British historian and prime minister, 1874–1965). **2** World Series Cricket.

WSEG Weapons System Evaluation Group (of U.S. Department of Defense).

WSI Writers and Scholars International.

WSJ Wall Street Journal (newspaper).

W.S.L.F. *or* **WSLF** Western Somali Liberation Front (political party).

WSP 1 water supply point. **2** working steam pressure.

WSPG White Sands Proving Ground (of U.S. Army).

W.S.P.U. Women's Social and Political Union.

WSTN World Service Television News (British news service).

WSW *or* **W.S.W.** *or* **w.s.w.** west-southwest.

WT 1 The Winter's Tale (play by Shakespeare). **2** *also* **wt** watertight: *WTD* = *watertight door*. **3** *also* **WT.** weight. **4** withholding tax.

wt 1 warrant (right to buy stock at a stipulated price in a given length of time) *finance*. **2** *also* **wt.** weight. **3** without.

WTA 1 Women's Tennis Association. **2** World Trade Association.

WTC World Trade Center (New York City).

Wtf. Waterford (type of glassware).

wth. width.

wthr weather.

WTIS World Trade Information Center.

WTN Worldwide Television News (British news service).

WTO 1 (former) Warsaw Treaty Organization. **2** World Tourism Organization. **3** World Trade Organization.

wtr. 1 waiter. **2** winter. **3** *also* **Wtr.** writer.

WTRC World Textile Research Council.

WTT World Team Tennis.

WU 1 Western Union (telegraph service). **2** *also* **wu** work unit.

W.U.C.T. World Union of Catholic Teachers.

WUJS World Union of Jewish Students.

WUS 1 Western United States. **2** World University Service.

W.U.S.L. Women's United Service League.

WV 1 West Virginia (Zip Code). **2** wind velocity. **3** working voltage, also in combination: *WVDC* = *working voltage direct current*.

w.v. water valve (on plans and diagrams).

w/v weight by volume.

W. Va. West Virginia.

WVD Worldwide Alliance of Diamond Workers. [Dutch *Wereldverband van Diamantbewerkers*]

wvd waived *commerce, law.*

WVE water vapor electrolysis *biology.*

WVF *or* **W.V.F.** World Veterans Federation.

WVS *British* Women's Voluntary Service (now *WRVS*).

WVT water vapor transmission, also in combination: *WVTR = water vapor transmission rate.*

WW 1 walking wounded (war casualties able to get to medical help on their own). **2** *also* **W/W** warehouse warrant (warrant of receipt for goods in a warehouse, often used as a negotiable paper). **3** waterworks. **4** Weight Watchers (trade name for dieters' organization). **5** wire wound *electronics.* **6** *also* **W.W.** World War: *WWI = First World War; WWII = Second World War.* **7** worldwide.

w/w 1 wall-to-wall (of carpet or other floor covering). **2** weight in weight *chemistry, physics.* **3** *also* **ww** with warrants.

WWC World Weather Center.

WWD 1 *also* **wwd** weather working days (accounting for absence). **2** Women's Wear Daily (publication).

WWe widow. [German *Witwe*].

WWF 1 Waterside Workers' Federation (in Australia). **2** World Wildlife Fund (now *Worldwide Fund for Nature*).

WWG Warrington Wire Gauge (for steel and copper).

WWMCCS World Wide Military Command and Control System.

WWSSN Worldwide Standard Seismograph Network.

WWSU World Water Ski Union.

WWV National Bureau of Standards radio station (used as a reference).

WWW 1 *Who Was Who*, in biographical bibliography. **2** World Weather Watch (of the World Meteorological Organization). **3** World Wide Web *computers.*

WX 1 *also* **Wx** weather, also in combination: *WXD =* (symbol for) *weather radar station.* **2** *British* women's extra (extra-large size, of women's clothing).

WY Wyoming (Zip Code).

Wy 1 Way (in postal address). **2** *also* **Wy.** *or* **Wycl.** Wycliffe (English cleric, translated Bible into English, 1320–1384). **3** *also* **Wy.** *or* **Wyo.** Wyoming.

WYSIWYG (wiz'ə wig) what you see is what you get (of a computer screen display in reference to what will appear on a printout).

Wz. trademark [German *Warenzeichen*]

W.Z.O. *or* **WZO** World Zionist Organization.

X *I an abbreviation for: also* **X.** ex, without, in combination: *X.D. = ex dividend* (of stock sold without right to the next dividend).
II a symbol for: **1** abscissa of a coordinate or the longitudinal distance. **2** by (esp. to separate dimensions): *9 × 12 rug = a standard room-sized rug nine feet wide by twelve feet long.* **3** Christ, Christian. [Greek Χριστός *Christós*] **4 a** cross, in combination: *X-ref. = cross reference; XC = cross-country (skiing or running); XQ = cross-question; X out = cross out or delete; X-ing out of names on a list.* **b** crossing (esp. highway, traffic, or railroad crossing). **c** crossed or mated with (esp. in Mendelian notation). **5** crystal. **6 a** error or wrong (used on a test, etc., to mark wrong answers). **b** broken or defective (used as a mark generally and esp. to mark type). **7** experimental or test, in combination: *the X-15 Rocket Plane.* **8 a** explosive. **b** explode, exploded, in combination: *UXB = unexploded bomb.* **9** extra (esp. in marking grade or size): *XL = extra large; XF = extra fine.* **10** gross score *statistics, psychology.* **11 a** halogen or acid radical. **12** kiss (at the end of letters, telegrams, etc.). **13** mark (used as a signature by a person unable to write or as an indication of choice on a ballot, test, etc.). **14** mole or mass fraction (in heavy or unrefined matter) *chemistry.* **15** motion picture rating (indicating a film with material suitable only for adult audiences). **16** reactance *physics:*

a acoustic reactance. **b** electrical reactance: $Xc = capacitive$ *reactance.* **17** sex chromosome (in male and female). **18** ten; 10: **a** Roman numeral (for ten): *XVI = 16.* **b** ten-dollar bill. **19** times: **a** multiply, multiplied by: *7 × 5 = 35.* **b** power of magnification: *35× binoculars.* **20** transistor (esp. in a schematic drawing). **21** transmitter, esp. in combination: *XOff = transmitter off.* **22** twenty-fourth of a series (twenty-third if *J* is omitted). **23 a** unknown: *an incalculable factor, known as X. In 1895 Roentgen discovered penetrating radiation, giving the name X rays because their nature was not known.* **b** unknown quantity (esp. an unknown quantity in algebraic expressions). **24** variable (esp. dependent variable) *physics, statistics, psychology.* **25** volume displacement *physics, chemistry.* **26** X-count in competitive shooting (a bullet landing in the inner circle inside the target 10-ring). **27** xenon (chemical element, alternate for *Xe*).

X̄ predicted gross score *psychology.*

x *I an abbreviation for: also* **x.** ex; without, in combination: *x.d. = ex dividend* (of stock sold without right to the next dividend).
II a symbol for: **1** abscissa of a coordinate or the longitudinal distance. **2** by (esp. to separate dimensions): *2 × 4 = timber originally cut two inches thick by four inches wide.* **3 a** cross:

x-ref. = cross-reference; x out = cross out or delete. **b** crossed or mated with (esp. in Mendelian notation). **4** deviation from the mean *statistics*. **5** haploid generation (see *2×*) *biology*. **6** hoarfrost *meterology*. **7** mole or mass fraction *chemistry*. **8** takes or captures *chess*. **9** ten; 10 (Roman numeral): *xii* = 12. **10** times: **a** multiply, multiplied by: *6 × 8 = 48*. **b** power of magnification: *35 × binoculars*. **11** twenty-fourth of a series (twenty-third if *j* is omitted). **12 a** unknown: *the individual is x number of pounds of chemicals, plus seventy-five percent water*. **b** unknown quantity (esp. an unknown quantity in an algebraic expression).

2x diploid generation: *The number of chromosomes in the cells of any species is the diploid number, expressed 2x. The number of chromosomes in the germ cells is the haploid number, expressed x.*

XA extended architecture (of graphics and text storage on a computer CD-ROM).

xan. 1 xanthene (base of a group of yellow dyes). **2** xanthic (yellow) *botany*. **3** xanthine (nitrogenous substance present in urine, blood, muscle tissue, and plants).

Xbre. or **X^bre** December. [French *décembre*, X from the notation for ten]

XBT expendable bathythermograph.

xbt exhibit.

XC 1 Christ. [Greek Χριστός *Christós*] **2** *also* **X-C** cross-country, in skiing and running. **3** *also* **X.C.** or **x.c.** ex coupon (of stock sold without the most recent dividend coupons).

xch exchange.

xcl excess current liabilities *insurance*.

XCMD external command (of a computer program).

x-cp. ex coupon (of stock sold without the most recent dividend coupons).

xcut. crosscut (of wood, esp. timbers or of a saw blade).

X.D. or **x.d.** or **x-div.** ex dividend (of stock sold without right to the next dividend).

x'd executed (of legal or financial obligation).

Xe xenon (chemical element).

Xen. Xenophon (Greek historian and a leader of the 10,000 Greek soldiers who wandered about the Black Sea area following the battle of Cunaxa, and described in the *Anabasis*).

XES X-ray emission spectroscopy.

XF extra fine.

XFA X-ray fluorescence analysis.

xfer or **XFER** transfer.

xfmr or **Xformer** transformer.

xg crossing.

XH 1 extra-hard. **2** extra-heavy.

XHF or **xhf** extrahigh frequency.

xhst exhaust.

X.I. or **x.i.** or **x-int.** ex interest (of bonds sold without right to the next interest payment due).

XIO execute input and/or output *computers*.

XIST X inactive specific transcriptase (of the female sex chromosome).

XL 1 *also* **xl** crystal. **2 a** extra-large. **b** extra-long.

xlnt excellent.

XLWB extra-long wheelbase (of an automobile or truck).

Xmas (eks′məs or *sometimes* kris′məs) Christmas (the X derives from the Greek Χριστός for Christ to form a hybrid with the English *mas(s)* from *Christmas*).

XMIT or **Xmit** transmit, in radio.

XMP xanthosine monophosphate (nucleotide of purine).

XMs extended memory specification *computers*.

XMSN or **Xmsn** transmission, in radio.

XMTR or **Xmtr** transmitter, in radio.

X.N. or **x.n.** or **x-n.** ex new (of stock sold without right to new shares issued).

Xn. Christian.

XNOR exclusive NOR *computers*: XNOR gate.

Xnty. Christianity.

XO 1 executive officer. **2** xanthine oxidase (enzyme that aids in oxidation). **3** X chromosome missing *genetics*.

XOR exclusive OR *computers*: XOR gate.

XP 1 Christ. [Greek Χριστός *Christós*] **2** express paid. **3** xeroderma pigmentosum (hereditary disease of the skin and eyes).

XPL explosive.

xpn expansion.

XPS X-ray photoelectron spectroscopy.

XQ or **xq** cross-question.

XR 1 *also* **x-r** cross-reference. **2** *also* **X.R.** or **x.r.** ex rights (of stock shares sold without rights incumbent with ownership).

Xr examiner.

XRD X-ray diffraction.

Xrds crossroads.

X-ref. or **Xref** cross-reference (referral to another point in a book or list).

XRF X-ray fluorescence.

XRFS X-ray fluorescence spectrometry.

XRP X-ray polychromator.

X-rts. ex rights (of stock shares sold without rights incumbent with ownership).

XS 1 *also* **xs** extra-small. **2** extra-strength. **3** extra-strong.

Xs or **X's** atmospherics (electrical disturbances in radio communication).

xstr transistor.

Xt. Christ.

xtal or **XTAL** crystal.

Xtian Christian.

xtry extraordinary.

Xty Christianity.

XUV extreme ultraviolet (radiation) *astronomy*.

xw ex warrant (without right to buy stock at a stipulated price) *finance*.

XX 1 double strength, esp. of ale. **2** wrinkled or torn paper.

XXX 1 broken paper. **2** triple strength, esp. of ale.

xyl. or **xylo.** xylophone.

Y

Y *I an abbreviation for:* **1** year. **2** *also* **Y.** yellow. **3** Yemen, in combination: *YRl = Yemen rial (monetary unit).* **4** *also* **¥** yen (monetary unit of Japan). **5 a** Young Men's or Young Women's Christian Association. **b** Young Men's or Young Women's Hebrew Association. **6** *also* **¥** yuan (monetary unit of People's Republic of China).
II a symbol for: **1** admittance *electricity.* **2** gross score *statistics.* **3** one hundred fifty; 150 (medieval Roman numeral). **4** hypercharge (used in designating quantities of strongly interacting particles) *physics.* **5** Planck function *thermodynamics.* **6** prototype (esp. of a missile or aircraft design): *YB-60, the jet version of the B-36 bomber.* **7** sex chromosome (in males). **8** twenty-fifth of a series (twenty-fourth when *J* is omitted). **9** yttrium (chemical element).

y *I an abbreviation for:* **1** yard. **2** year. **3** yellow. **4** youngest.
II a symbol for: **1** depth, height, or altitude *physics.* **2** deviation from the mean *statistics.* **3** dry air *meterology.* **4** one hundred fifty; 150 (medieval Roman numeral). **5** mole or mass fraction (in light or refined matter) *chemistry.* **6** ordinate of a coordinate or the lateral distance. **7** supercompressibility factor *physics.* **8** twenty-fifth of a series (twenty-fourth when *j* is omitted). **9** unknown quantity (esp. an unknown quantity in algebraic expressions). **10** variable *physics, statistics, psychology.*

YA 1 *also* **Y/A** York-Antwerp Rules, in marine insurance. **2** young adult.

YAC yeast artificial chromosome (human DNA grown in cultures of yeast cells).

YAG (*pronounced* yag) yttrium, aluminum, garnet (referring to a synthetic garnet): *YAG laser.*

Y.A.L. Young Australia League.

YAVIS Young, Attractive, Verbal, Intelligent, and Successful (a description similar to yuppie).

YB *or* **Y.B.** yearbook, also in combination: *EBYB = Encyclopedia Britannica Yearbook.*

Yb ytterbium (chemical element, now *Y*).

yb yarn to back (a direction in knitting).

Y.C. Yacht Club: *A.Y.C. = American Yacht Club.*

YCC Youth Conservation Corps.

YCS Young Catholic Students.

yct yacht.

YCW Young Christian Workers.

yd. yard.

y'day *or* **yday** yesterday.

ydg. yardage.

yds. yards.

YE *or* **y.e. 1** *also* **ye** yeast extract, esp. in combination: *yem = yeast extract, malt.* **2** yellow edges (of paper, esp. in a bound book).

yel. yellow.

Yem. Yemen.

Yeo. *or* **yeo. 1** yeoman. **2** yeomanry.

YES 1 *also* **yes** yeast extract sucrose. **2** Youth Employment Service.

yest. *or* **yesty** yesterday.

yf yarn to front (a direction in knitting).

YH youth hostel.

YHA Youth Hostels Association.

YHWH *or* **YHVH** the Tetragrammaton (sacred Hebrew word of four consonants standing for the name of God, transcribed in English as *Yahweh* or *Jehovah*).

Yid 1 *also* **Yid.** Yiddish. **2** yield (esp. of the value of a stock divided in relation to the price paid).

YIG yttrium iron garnet (transmitter and transducer of acoustic energy)

YIP Youth International Party.

Yks. Yorkshire County, England.

yl 1 *also* **yl.** yellow (on navigation charts). **2** yield limit.

yld. yield.

YM Young Men's Christian Association or Young Men's Hebrew Association.

YMC yeast mold count, esp. in dairying.

YMCA *or* **Y.M.C.A.** Young Men's Christian Association.

Y.M.Cath.A. *or* **YMCath.A** Young Men's Catholic Association.

YMCU *or* **Y.M.C.U.** Young Men's Christian Union.

YMFS *or* **Y.M.F.S.** Young Men's Friendly Society.

YMHA *or* **Y.M.H.A.** Young Men's Hebrew Association.

YO 1 *also* **yo** yarn over (a direction in knitting). **2** *also* **y.o.** *or* **y-o** year old (esp. of horses): *race for 2 YO's.* **3** youthful offender *law.*

y.o.b. *or* **YOB** year of birth.

YOC Youth Opportunity Center.

y.o.d. *or* **YOD** year of death.

y.o.m. *or* **YOM** year of marriage.

YOP Youth Opportunity Program.

Yorks *or* **Yorks.** Yorkshire County, England.

YP 1 yellow pine (of lumber). **2** yield point (point of stress, esp. of iron and steel).

YPA 1 Young Pioneers of America. **2** (formerly) Yugoslav People's Army.

YPFB Bolivian State Petroleum Organization (controlling oil production, refining, and distribution). [Spanish *Yacimientos Petrolíferos Fiscales Bolivianos*]

Y.P.S.C.E. Young People's Society of Christian Endeavor.

Y.R. Young Republican (section of the Republican Party).

yr. 1 year: *3-yr. $7 billion school-building program.* **2** younger. **3** your.

Y.R.A. Yacht Racing Association.

yrbk. *or* **Yrbk** yearbook.

yrly yearly.

yrs 1 years. **2** *also* **Yrs.** yours (esp. at the close of correspondence).

YS yield strength (point of stress, esp. of iron or steel).

y.s. yellow spot *medicine.*

YSO young stellar object (faint star highly irregular in its emission spectrum).

YSP Yemeni Socialist Party.

YST *or* **Y.S.T.** Yukon Standard Time.

yst. youngest.

YT *or* **Y.T.** Yukon Territory.

Yt yttrium (chemical element, now Y).

y.t.b. yarn to back (a direction in knitting).

YTD year to date *finance, commerce.*

y.t.f. yarn to front (a direction in knitting).

Yuc. Yucatán (peninsula and state in Mexico).

Yug. *or* **Yugo.** Yugoslavia.

Yuk. Yukon Territory.

yuppie *or* **Yuppie** (yup′ē) Young Urban Professional.

YW Young Women's Christian Association *or* Young Women's Hebrew Association.

YWCA *or* **Y.W.C.A.** Young Women's Christian Association.

Y.W.C.T.U. *or* **YWCTU** Young Women's Christian Temperance Union.

YWES The Year's Work in English Studies (publication).

YWF Young World Federalists.

YWHA *or* **Y.W.H.A.** Young Women's Hebrew Association.

Z

Z *I an abbreviation for:* **1** zaire (monetary unit of Zaire). **2** Zambia: *Z£= Zambia pound.* **3** zenith. **4** zero, esp. in combination: *ZPPR = Zero Power Plutonium Reactor.* **5** Zimbabwe: *Z$ = Zimbabwe dollar.* **6** Zimmermann (used with a number in cataloging music of Henry Purcell). **7** *also* **Z.** zone, esp. in combination: *ZST = Zone Standard Time; NFZ = no-fly zone.*
II a symbol for: **1** atomic number *physics.* **2** gram-equivalent weight *physics.* **3** impedance *physics:* **a** electrical impedance. **b** acoustic impedance. **4** molecular collision frequency *physics.* **5** neutral charge *physics: Z particle.* **6** partition function (distribution in a system of molecules of various states of energy) *physics.* **7** radius of circle of least confusion *physics.* **8** section modulus *physics.* **9** twenty-sixth of a series (twenty-fifth when *J* is omitted). **10** two thousand; 2000 (medieval Roman numeral). **11 a** zenith distance *astronomy.* **b** azimuth angle *surveying.* **12** Zero Mean Time (equivalent of Greenwich Mean Time).

z *I an abbreviation for:* **1** zero. **2** *also* **z.** zone.
II a symbol for: **1** compression factor *chemistry.* **2** cylindrical coordinate *physics.* **3** electrochemical equivalent *physics.* **4** haze *meterology.* **5** standard score *statistics.* **6** twenty-sixth of a series (twenty-fifth when *j* is omitted). **7** two thousand; 2000 (medieval Roman numeral). **8** unknown quantity (esp. unknown quantity in algebraic expressions). **9** valence of an ion *physics.* **10** variable, esp. in physics. **11 a** zenith distance *astronomy.* **b** azimuth angle *surveying.*

Zach. 1 Zachariah. **2** Zacharias.

Zag. Zagreb, Croatia.

Zai. Zaire (country in Africa between Sudan and Angola).

Zam. Zambia (country in Africa between Zaire and Zimbabwe).

ZAMS zero age main sequence.

Zan. Zanzibar (island and port off the east coast of Africa, now part of Tanzania).

ZANU (zä′nü′) Zimbabwe African National Union.

ZANU-PF Zimbabwe African National Union-Patriotic Front.

ZAP zero antiaircraft potential *military.*

Zap. 1 Zapotec (Indian language and people of southern Mexico). **2** Zapotecan (group of related Indian languages of southern Mexico and Guatemala).

ZAPU (zä′pü′) Zimbabwe African People's Union.

ZAS zero access storage (computer storage with immediate access).

ZB 1 a Zen Buddhism. **b** Zen Buddhist. **2** zero beat (of an electrical circuit oscillating in the same frequency as the input signal).

z.B. for example. [German *zum Beispiel*]

ZBB *or* **Z.B.B.** zero-based budgeting (method of preparing a budget by reassessing each year all expenditures of a department, agency, etc.).

ZC Zionist Congress.

ZD 1 Zener diode (semiconductor that acts as a voltage stabilizer). **2** *also* **z.d.** zenith distance (distance of a celestial body from the zenith of a particular place). **3** *also* **Z.D.** Zero Defects, in manufacturing. **4** zone description *navigation.*

ZDA Zinc Development Association.

ZE zero energy, esp. in combination: *ZED = zero energy deuterium oxide reactor; ZETR = zero energy thermal reactor.*

ZEBRA zero energy breeder reactor assembly *physics.*

Zech. Zechariah (book of the Old Testament).

ZEEP zero energy experimental pile.

ZEG zero economic growth (condition of a nation's per capita income showing no appreciable increase).

zen *or* **Zen** zenith.

Zeph. Zephaniah (book of the Old Testament).

zero g. zero gravity (weightlessness, as in a spacecraft).

ZETA zero energy thermonuclear assembly.

ZF 1 *also* **z.f.** zero frequency (of signal) *electricity, telecommunications.* **2** zone of fire *military.*

ZFB signals fading badly, in radio.

ZFS zero field splitting *biology.*

ZG 1 *also* **z.g.** zero gravity (weightlessness), also in combination: *ZGE = zero gravity effect.* **2** *also* **Z.G.** Zoological Garden.

ZGS zero gradient synchrotron.

z.H. in care of. [German *zu Händen*]

ZHR 1 *also* **Z.H.R.** zenithal hourly rate *astronomy.* **2** *also* **ZHr** zero hour (time to begin some action, almost midnight).

ZI 1 *also* **z.i.** zero input. **2** zone of interior, esp. in the military.

ZIP *or* **Zip** (*pronounced* zip) Zone Improvement Plan (of U.S. Postal Service to facilitate delivery of mail by use of a nine-digit number after a two-letter abbreviation of the state).

ZIPRA Zimbabwe Independent People's Republic Army.

ZL 1 freezing drizzle *meterology.* **2** *also* **zl** zero lift *aeronautics.*

Zl *or* **zl** zloty (monetary unit of Poland).

zm zoom: *zm lens.*

Zn *I an abbreviation for:* **1** zenith. **2** *also* **zn** zone. *II a symbol for:* **1** true azimuth. **2** zinc (chemical element).

Z.O.A. Zionist Organization of America.

zod. zodiac.

ZOE zero energy.

zoochem. 1 zoochemical. **2** zoochemistry.

zoogeog. 1 zoogeographical. **2** zoogeography.

zool. 1 zoological. **2** zoologist. **3** zoology.

zoopath. zoopathology (science of animal diseases).

zooph. zoophytology (study of invertebrates usually resembling plants, such as coral and sea anemones).

ZP *or* **zp 1** zero point *physics, chemistry,* also in combination: *ZPE = zero point energy.* **2** zero power, also in combination: *ZPR = zero power reactor.*

ZPG zero population growth (condition in which a population ceases to grow and a balance is reached in the average number of births and deaths).

ZR freezing rain *meterology.*

Zr zirconium (chemical element).

zr zero (of a financial bond giving no periodic interest, a zero-coupon bond).

ZS 1 zero suppress *or* suppression (of digits that are not significant). **2** *also* **Z.S.** Zoological Society (of London), also in combination: *ZSP = Zoological Society of Philadelphia.*

Zs. periodical (publication). [German *Zeitschrift*]

ZST *or* **Z.S.T.** Zone Standard Time (equivalent to Greenwich mean time).

ZT *or* **Z.T.** Zone Time.

Ztr. hundredweight; cwt. [German *Zentner*]

Zur Zurich, Switzerland.

ZZ. number of cylinders. [German *Zylinderzahl*]

z.Z. at present, at this time, acting (in titles). [German *zur Zeit*]

zz zigzag.

A

a good *or* proper deed *law* BF *or* B.F.
a little louder *music* pf *or* p.f.
A Lover's Complaint LC (poem usually attributed to Shakespeare)
A Programming Language APL
abampere abamp.
abandon abnd *or* abnd.
abandoned aband.
abbess Abb. *or* abb. (*OUP:* abb.)
abbey Abb. *or* abb.
Abbot Ab *or* Ab.
abbot Abb. *or* abb.
abbreviate abbr. *or* abbrev.
abbreviated abbr. *or* abbrev.
abbreviation 1 a 2 abbr. *or* abbrev.
abcoulomb aC
abdicated abd.
abdomen 1 abd. 2 abdom.
abdominal abdom.
abeam abm
Aberdeen Aber.
Aberdeen Proving Grounds, Maryland APG
abfarad aF
abhenry aH
ablative abl.
able-bodied seaman 1 AB *or* A.B. 2 ab *or* a.b. 3 ABS *or* A.B.S.
abnormal end ABEND
aboard abd.
aboriginal abo. *or* abor.
aborigines abo. *or* abor.
Aborigines Protection Society A.P.S. (of Australia)
abort ab *or* ab.
abort guidance system AGS
abort sensing-implementation system ASIS
abortion ab *or* ab.
about 1 a 2 ab *or* ab. 3 abt. 4 c *or* c. 5 ca *or* ca. 6 cir. *or* circ. (*OUP:* circ.)
above 1 abv. 2 *Latin* sup. *or* Sup. (*MLA:* supra; *OUP:* sup.)
above ground level *navigation* AGL
above mean sea level AMSL *or* amsl
above proof a.p.
above sea level ASL *or* asl
above water AW
above-named an. *or* an
abrasive abrsv.
abridged Abr. *or* abr.
abridger Abr. *or* abr. (*MLA, CSM, OUP:* abr.)
abridgment Abr.
abscisic acid ABA
abscissa 1 X 2 x
absent 1 a 2 abs.
absent over leave AOL *or* A.O.L.
absent with leave AWL *or* A.W.L. *or* a.w.l. (*GPO:* a.w.l.)
absent without leave 1 AWOL *or* A.W.O.L. *or* a.w.o.l. (*GPO:* a.w.o.l.; *MLA,OUP:*

AWOL) 2 *Australian* AWL *or* A.W.L. *or* a.w.l.
absolute 1 a 2 absol. 3 *chemistry, physics, mathematics* abs. *or* abs
absolute altitude AA
absolute atmosphere atm. a. *or* atma
absolute ceiling A/C
absolute essential equipment AEE
absolute magnitude *astronomy* M
absolute temperature A
absolute value 1 *chemistry, physics, mathematics, computers* ABS 2 *chemistry, physics, mathematics* abs. *or* abs
absolutely 1 abs. *or* abs 2 absol.
absolution Absoluo.
absorption coefficient *a*
absorption rate BET
abstract 1 ab *or* ab. 2 abs. 3 abst. 4 abstr.
abstract expressionism Ab Ex
abstracted abstr.
abundant 1 abund. 2 *biology* a *or* a.
abvolt aV
academic. acad.
Academy of Art and Literature A.A.L.
Academy of Certified Social Workers ACSW
Academy of Dental Prosthetics ADP *or* A.D.P.
Academy of General Dentistry AGD
Academy of Motion Picture Arts and Sciences AMPAS *or* A.M.P.A.S.
Academy of Natural Science Acad. Nat. Sci.
Academy of Physical Medicine A.P.M.
Academy of Science AS *or* A.S.
Academy of Sciences *French* AdS
Academy Acad.
accelerate 1 accel. 2 ACLT
accelerated cost recovery system ACRS
accelerated freeze drying AFD
accelerating the tempo *music* string.
acceleration 1 a 2 a 3 acc.
acceleration of gravity *physics* g
accelerator globulin, factor V AcG
accelerator mass spectroscopy AMS
accept 1 ACPT 2 *commerce* acc.
acceptable daily intake ADI
acceptable quality level AQL
acceptable reliability level ARL
acceptance 1 acce. 2 *commerce* **a** acc. **b** ACPT *or* acpt.
acceptance and transfer A & T
accepted *commerce* 1 a *or* a. 2 acc.
accepted under protest *commerce* 1 ASP *or* asp 2 ASPC *or* aspc
access opening *medicine, architecture* A.O.
access panel *architecture* AP
accession designation number ADN
accessory 1 access. 2 accy.
accessory power supply aps
accident acdnt. *or* acdt.
accident and health *insurance* a & h *or* a. & h.
accident and insurance a & i *or* a. & i.
Accident Compensation Commission ACC *or* A.C.C.
Accident Investigation Branch *British aviation* AIB
accidental death benefit *insurance* ADB *or* adb

accidental injury *insurance* AccI
accommodation 1 accom. 2 *medicine* a
accommodation coefficient *a*
accompanied acc.
accompaniment 1 acc. 2 accomp. *or* accpt.
accompany acmp. *or* acmp
accompanying the solo part *music* cp
accomplishment age AA
accomplishment quotient *education* AQ *or* A.Q.
accomplishment ratio *education* AR *or* A.R.
accordance accdce.
according acc.
according to 1 ap. 2 *Latin* sec *or* sec.
according to art *pharmaceutics* 1 s.a. 2 SA *or* S.A.
according to art *or* rule *Latin* sec. art.
according to custom 1 a.u. 2 *law, commerce* ad us.
according to law *Latin* 1 s.l. 2 sec. leg.
according to rule *Latin* sec. reg.
according to the rules of art s.a.l.
according to the value 1 av *or* a.v. 2 *commerce* **a** ad val. **b** adv. **c** AV *or* A/V *or* a/v
account 1 a 2 *commerce* **a** A/C **b** a/c **c** ac. **d** acc. **e** acct.
account current *commerce* 1 A/C 2 a/c 3 AC
account executive AE
account of 1 A.O. 2 a/o *or* A/o *or* a.o.
account sales AS *or* A.S. *or* A/S
accountant 1 actnt. 2 *commerce* **a** acc. **b** acct.
Accountant General AG *or* A.G. (*OUP:* A.-G.)
Accountant Officer A.O.
Accounting and Finance Office *or* Officer AFO
Accounting Research Bulletin ARB
Accounting Series Release ASR
Accountng Research Bureau ARB
accounts payable 1 A/cs Pay. *or* A/cs pay. 2 A/P 3 AP
accounts receivable 1 A/cs.Rec. *or* A/cs.rec. 2 AR *or* A/R
Accreditation Board for Engineering and Technology ABET
Accreditation Council for Accountancy and Taxation ACAT
accredited accred.
Accredited Record Technician ART
accrued acrd.
accrued interest accrd. int.
accumulate accum.
accumulation 1 Ac 2 accum.
Accuracy in Media AIM
accusative *grammar* 1 acc. 2 accus.
ace A
acetone acet *or* acet.
acetone dicarboxylic acid ADA
acetyl Ac
acetylcholine ACH *or* Ach
acetylcholinesterase AChE *or* ACHE
acetylene acet *or* acet.
acetylsalicylic acid ASA
achievement age AA
achievement quotient *education* AQ *or* A.Q.

achievement ratio *education* AR *or* A.R.
achievement test AT
acid 1 A **2** *medicine* a
acid mucopolysaccharides AMP
acid number AN *or* A.N.
acid radical X
acid value AV
acid, citrate, and dextrose ACD
acid-resistant AR
acidity *medicine* a
acidproof AP
acidproof floor APF
acknowledge 1 ACK **2** ack. *or* ack
acknowledgment 1 ack. *or* ack **2** ackgt *or* ackgt.
acknowledgment of receipt *commerce* **1** a.r. **2** AR *or* A.R.
acoustic ACST *or* acst.
acoustic comfort index ACI
acoustic directed-energy pulse train ADEPT
acoustic impedance *physics* Z
acoustic intensity I
acoustic reactance *physics* X
acoustical displacement w
Acoustical Society of America 1 ACSOC **2** ASA *or* A.S.A.
acoustics acous.
acquire acq *or* acq.
acquired acq *or* acq.
Acquired Immune Deficiency Syndrome 1 AIDS **2** *French, Spanish* SIDA
acquisition of signal *aeronautics, astronautics* AOS
acre 1 A **2** a **3** AC **4** ac.
acre-foot 1 ac.ft. *or* ac.-ft. **2** acre-ft.
across acrs.
acrylonitrile butadiene styrene ABS
acting 1 A *or* A. **2** act. **3** actg.
acting appointment AA
Acting Secretary. Actg. Sec.
actinium 1 Ac **2** Act
actinium emanation Ac Em
actinon An
action 1 actn. **2** *computers* DO **3** *physics* S
action data automation Ada
Action on Smoking and Health ASH
action potential *psychology* AP
action variable *physics* J
activate ACTVT
activated 1 ACT **2** act.
active 1 ACT **2** act. **3** actv. **4** *grammar* a
active duty AD
active duty commitment ADC
active galactic nuclei *astronomy* AGN
active verb v.a.
activities of daily living *medicine* ADL
activity of molar concentration *chemistry* f
actor act.
Actors and Artists of America AAA
Actors Equity Association AEA *or* A.E.A.
Actors' Benevolent Fund A.B.F.
Acts of the Apostolic See AAS *or* A.A.S.
actual 1 ACT **2** act.
actual cash value ACV *or* acv
actual cubic feet per minute a.c.f./min.
actual horsepower AHP *or* A.H.P.
actual time of arrival ATA
actual time of departure ATD *or* atd
actual time of fall ATF

actual weight 1 A/W **2** a/w **3** act. wt.
actuary 1 Act *or* Act. **2** act.
actuate act.
actuating actg.
acute febrile respiratory infection or illness AFRI
acute granulocytic leukemia *medicine* AGL
acute myocardial infarction AMI
acute renal failure *medicine* ARF
acute respiratory disease ARD
acyl carrier protein ACP
adamsite DM
adaptation adapt.
adaptation level *psychology* AL
adapted 1 ad. **2** adap. **3** adapt.
adapted to the principal part *music* col.p.
adapted to the principal voice *music* col.vo.
adapter adpt.
adapter booster AB
adaptor ad.
added value tax AVT *or* A.V.T.
addenda add. *or* Add.
addendum 1 a **2** add. *or* Add.
Addicts Anonymous AA
addition 1 add. **2** addn.
additional 1 add. **2** addl. **3** addnl.
additional living expense *insurance* ALE
additional premium *insurance* a.p.
additional voluntary contribution *British* AVC
additions, alterations, and repairs addns, alts, & reprs
address 1 a **2** add. *or* Add.
addressed addsd.
Adelaide Adel.
adémie Française LAFC
adenine A
adenoid-degenerating AD
adenoidal-pharyngeal-conjunctival APC
adenomatous polyposis coli APC
adenosine deaminase ADA
adenosine diphosphate ADP
adenosine monophosphate AMP
adenosine triphosphate ATP
adenylate energy charge AEC
adenylic acid AA
adhesive adh.
adjacent 1 Adj. **2** adj. **3** adjac.
adjacent channel attenuation *electronics* ACA
adjective 1 a *or* a. **2** adj.
adjoining adj.
adjourned adj. *or* adjd.
adjourned summons adjd. sumns.
adjudged adj.
adjunct 1 adj. **2** Adj.
Adjunct in Arts Adj. A.
adjust adj.
adjustable adj.
adjustable rate mortgage ARM
adjusted adj.
adjusted gross income AGI
adjustment adj.
adjutant 1 Adj. **2** Adjt.
Adjutant General 1 Adj. Gen. *or* Adj.-Gen. **2** AG *or* A.G.
Adjutant General's Corps AGC
Adjutant General's Department AGD
Adjutant General's Office AGO

Adjutant General, The TAG
Adjutant Inspector General AIG
administration 1 adm. *or* Adm. **2** admin.
Administration for Children and Families ACF
Administration for Children, Youth, and Families ACYF
Administration for Native Americans ANA
Administration on Aging AOA *or* AoA (*GPO:* AOA)
Administration on Developmental Disabilities ADD
administrative 1 adm. **2** Adm.
administrative and accounting purposes ad. and ac.
administrative assistant AA
Administrative Conference of the United States ACUS
Administrative Department or Division AD *or* A.D.
administrative district *French* Arron. *or* Arrond.
administrative law judge ALJ
Administrative Officer A.O. *or* AO
Administrative Procedure Act *law* APA *or* A.P.A.
administrative ruling AR
administrator 1 adm. **2** Adm. **3** admin. **4** admr. **5** adms. *or* admstr. **6** admor.
administratrix 1 admix. **2** admrx. **3** admtrx. *or* admx.
Admiral Adml.
admiral 1 Adm. **2** ADM
Admiral Commanding Reserves ACR
Admiral of the Fleet AF
admiralty Adm.
Admiralty Court Adm. Ct.
Admiralty Islands AI *or* A.I.
Admiralty Sailing Directions for the World ASDW
Admiralty Signal and Radar Establishment *British* ASRE
admission adm.
Admissions Test for Graduate Study in Business ATGSB
Admissions Testing Program ATP
admit, admitted adm.
admittance *electricity* Y
admitted to the same degree ad eund.
adoption *law* adop.
adrenal cortical extract ACE
adrenocorticotropic hormone ACTH
adrenocorticotropin ACTH
adrenoglomerulotropin AGTH
adrenoleukodystrophy ALD
adult 1 A **2** a
Adult Children of Alcoholics ACA
adult education AE
Adult Education Association AEA
Adult Education Program AEP
adult respiratory distress syndrome ARDS
adult T-cell leukemia ATL
advance 1 A **2** a
advance corporation tax ACT
advance delivery of correspondence ADC
advance, advanced adv.
advanced 1 A **2** a
advanced aerial fire-support system AAFSS

Advanced Anti-armor Weapon System AAWS
advanced attack helicopter AAH
advanced biomedical capsule ABC
Advanced Biophysical Research Accelerator ABRA
Advanced Cardiology Life Support ACLS
advanced cruise missile ACM
advanced data communications control procedure *computer science* ADCCP
advanced developing country ADC
advanced gas-cooled reactor AGR
advanced graduate certificate AGC
Advanced Individual Training AIT
Advanced Launch System ALS
advanced life support ALS
Advanced Manned Strategic Aircraft AMSA
advanced manufacturing technology AMT
Advanced Orbiting Solar Observatory AOSO
advanced passenger train APT
advanced placement AP
advanced post *military* AP
Advanced Purchase Excursion APEX *or* Apex
Advanced Range Instrumentation Ship ARIS
Advanced Record System ARS
advanced solar turbo-electric conversion ASTEC
Advanced Supplementary *British* AS
Advanced Tactical Fighter ATF
advanced test reactor ATR
advanced video camera system AVCS
advanced waste treatment *ecology* AWT
Advanced X-ray Astronomy Facility AXAF
advantage 1 advtg. 2 *tennis* **a** ad **b** van
Advent Adv.
adverb 1 ad. 2 adv. 3 advb.
adverbial advl.
adverbial, adverbially adv.
adverse possession *law* adv. poss.
advertisement 1 ad. (*OUP:* ad) 2 Adv. 3 adv. 4 advers. 5 advert. *or* Advert. 6 advt.
advertising advtg.
advertising director AD
Advertising Federation of America AFA *or* A.F.A.
Advertising Research Foundation ARF
Advertising Standards Authority *British* ASA
advertising video or videotape advid
advice 1 a 2 adv. 3 *commerce* Adv.
advice of rights *law* AOR
advice, duration, and charge A.D. and C.
advise 1 a 2 adv. 3 *commerce* Adv.
advise status and disposition *commerce* adstadis
advisory adv.
advisory board AB
Advisory Board for Research Councils *British* ABRC
Advisory Center for Education ACE
Advisory Committee on Reactor Safeguards ACRS
Advisory Conciliation and Arbitration Service ACAS
Advisory Council for Applied Research and Development ACARD
Advisory Council on Medical Education ACME

Advisory Council on Scientific Policy ACSP
advocate 1 Adv. 2 adv.
Advocate General 1 Adv. Gen. *or* Adv Gen 2 AG *or* A.G.
Aeneid Aen.
aerial a
aerial combat reconnaisance ACR
Aerial Phenomena Research Organization APRO
aerial port of debarkation APOD
aerial port of embarkation APOE
aerial rocket artillery ARA
aerodrome Aer.
aerodynamic aerodyn.
aerodynamic center AC
aerodynamic decelerator AD
aerodynamics aerodyn.
aerological aerol.
aeromedical aeromed.
aeronautical aero.
aeronautical approach chart AAC
aeronautical center AC
Aeronautical Chart and Information Center ACIC
Aeronautical Engineer 1 AE *or* A.E. 2 Ae. E. *or* Ae E 3 Aer. E. 4 Aero. E.
Aeronautical Engineering Report AER
Aeronautical Fixed Telecommunications Network AFTN
aeronautical material specification AMS
aeronautical national taper pipe threads ANPT
Aeronautical Planning Chart APC *or* A.P.C.
aeronautical recommended practices ARP
Aeronautical Research Laboratory ARL *or* A.R.L.
Aeronautical Society of Great Britain ASGB
Aeronautical Standards Group ASG
aeronautics 1 Aer. *or* aer. 2 aero. 3 aeron.
aerospace control environment ACE
aerospace ground equipment AGE
Aerospace Industries Association AIA *or* A.I.A.
Aerospace Medical Association 1 AMA 2 ASM *or* A.S.M.
Aerospace Medical Division AMD
aerospace plane ASP
Aerospace Research Laboratory *British* ARL
aerothermodynamic structural system environmental tests ASSET
Aeschylus Æsch.
Aesop Aes.
aesthetics aesth.
affidavit afft.
affiliated aff.
affinity *chemistry* **A**
affirmative aff.
affirmative action plan AAP
affirming aff.
affix 1 Af 2 af
Afghani A
afghani Af *or* Af. (*GPO:* Af)
Afghanistan 1 Afg. 2 Afgh.
aforesaid *law* afsd.
Africa 1 Af *or* Af. 2 Afr.
African 1 Af *or* Af. 2 Afr.
African Affairs AA
African and Malagasy Common Organization *French* OCAM

African Development Bank AFDB
African Development Fund AFDF
African Financial Community CFA
African Financial Community franc CFAF
African Methodist Episcopal AME *or* A.M.E.
African Methodist Episcopal Zion A.M.E.Z. *or* AMEZ
African National Congress ANC
African National Congress Party ANCP
African Party for the Independence of Cape Verde PAICV
African Peoples Organization APO
African Postal and Telecommunications Union A.P.T.U.
African swine fever ASF
African Trade Union Confederation ATUC
African, Caribbean, and Pacific Association ACP
African-American Institute AAI
Afrikaans 1 Af *or* Af. 2 Afrik.
after 1 a 2 aft.
after a meal *pharmaceutics* pc *or* p.c.
after Christ AC *or* A.C.
after date *commerce* a.d.
after deducting freight *commerce* ADF
after eating *pharmaceutics* 1 pc *or* p.c. 2 post cib.
after end a.e. (in shipbuilding)
after first shaking the bottle *pharmaceutics* p.p.a.
after meal(s) PP
after noon (time from noon to midnight) 1 p.m. *or* pm 2 PM *or* P.M.
after perpendicular 1 a.p. (in shipbuilding) 2 AP (in shipbuilding)
after receipt of order *commerce* ARO *or* aro
after sight *commerce* AS *or* A/S
after the manner prescribed *pharmaceutics* e.m.p.
afterburner AB
afternoon 1 a 2 aft. 3 aftn. 4 nm *or* n.m. *or* nm.
again agn.
against 1 agst. 2 agt. 3 con 4 cont. 5 *law* adv.
against all risks *insurance* AAR *or* A.A.R. *or* a.a.r.
against medical advice AMA
age a
age-related macular degeneration 1 AMD 2 ARMD
agency agcy.
Agency for Health Care Policy and Research AHCPR
Agency for International Development AID
Agency for Toxic Substances and Disease Registry ATSDR
agent 1 Ag *or* Ag. 2 Agt. 3 agt.
Agent General AG *or* A.G. (*OUP:* A.-G.)
agglutinated agglut.
agglutination agglut.
aggregate agg. *or* aggr.
agreed agd.
agreement 1 Agt. 2 agt.
agricultural 1 Ag *or* Ag. 2 agr. *or* agri. *or* agric.
Agricultural Adjustment Act AAA
Agricultural Adjustment Administration AAA

Agricultural and Mechanical A & M or A. and M.

Agricultural and Technical A & T or A. and T.

Agricultural Conservation and Adustment Administration. ACAA

Agricultural Development and Advisory Service British ADAS

Agricultural Economics Research Institute AERI or A.E.R.I.

Agricultural Engineer 1 AE or A.E. 2 Ag.E.

Agricultural Engineers Association AEA or A.E.A.

Agricultural Marketing Service AMS

Agricultural On Line Access AGRICOLA

Agricultural Research Service ARS

Agricultural Stabilization and Conservation Service ASCS

Agricultural Workers Organizing Committee AWOC

agriculture 1 Ag or Ag. 2 agr. or agri. or agric.

agronomist agron.

agronomy agron.

Aid to Dependent Children ADC

Aid to Families with Dependent Children AFDC

Aid to the Aged, Blind, or Disabled AABD

Aid to the Blind AB

aide-de-camp ADC or A.D.C. or a.d.c.

AIDS Clinical Trials Groups ACTG

AIDS Coalition to Unleash Power ACT UP

AIDS-related complex ARC

AIDS-related virus ARV

aileron AIL or ail.

air 1 A 2 a

Air Base AB

air break switch ABS

Air Carrier Mechanics Association ACMA

Air cavalry Aircav or Air Cav

Air Chief Marshal ACM or A.C.M.

air circuit breaker ACB

air combat information ACI

Air Combat Intelligence Office or Officer ACIO

air command AC

Air Commerce Manual ACM

air commodore AC

air conditioning 1 A/C 2 AC 3 ac

air control center ACC

air control point ACP

Air Corps AC or A.C.

air cushion vehicle ACV

air defense AD

Air Defense Command ADC

Air Defense Control Center ADCC

Air Defense Identification Zone ADIZ

air defense missile ADM

Air Defense of Great Britain A.D.G.B.

Air Depot A Dep

air depot AD

Air Development Center ADC

air division AD

air dried 1 AD 2 ad

Air Efficiency Award AEA or A.E.A.

air encephalogram AEG or aeg

air escape AE

Air Force AF

Air Force Association AFA

Air Force Audit Agency AFAA

Air Force Base AFB or A.F.B. (GPO: AFB)

Air Force Cambridge Research Laboratories AFCRL

Air Force Civilian Appellate Review Agency AFCARA

Air Force Communications Service AFCS

Air Force Cross AFC or A.F.C. (OUP: AFC)

Air Force Depot AFD

Air Force Flight Test Center AFFTC

Air Force Hospital AFH

Air Force Medal AFM or A.F.M. (OUP: AFM)

Air Force Missile AFM

Air Force Office of Scientific Research AFOSR

Air Force Pamphlet AFP

Air Force Personnel and Training Research Center AFPTRC

Air Force Plant Representative AFPR

Air Force Procurement Procedures AFPP

Air Force Program Executive Offices AFPEO

Air Force Records Center AFRC

Air Force Regulation AFR

Air Force Reserve 1 AFR 2 AFRes or AFRES

Air Force Reserve Officers Training Corps AFROTC

Air Force Review Board for Correction of Military Records AFBCMR

Air Force Special Weapons Center AFSWC

Air Force Station AFS

Air Force or Army Post Office APO

Air Force-Navy AN

Air Freight Terminal AFT

Air Headquarters AHQ

air horsepower 1 AHP or ahp 2 air hp.

air intercept missile AIM

Air Land Battle Management ALBM

Air Liaison Officer ALO

Air Line Pilots Association ALPA or A.L.P.A.

Air Marshal AM or A/M

Air Matériel Command AMC

Air Medal AM

air mileage indicator AMI

air mileage unit AMU

Air Ministry AM or A.M.

Air Ministry Order AMO or A.M.O.

air movement data AMD

air movement designator AMD

Air National Guard ANG

Air National Guard of the United States ANGUS

Air Navigation Development Board ANDB

air navigation radio control ANRAC

Air Operations Center AOC

Air Photographic and Charting Service APCS

Air Police AP

air position indicator API

air procurement district APD

air proving ground APG

air quality index AQI

Air Raid Precautions ARP

Air Raid Warden ARW

air raid warning ARW

Air Rescue Service ARS

Air Research and Development Command ARDC

air route traffic control ARTC

air route traffic control center ARTCC

Air Self-Defense Force ASDF

Air Service Command ASC

air speed AS

Air Technical Intelligence ATI

air temperature AT

air traffic control ATC

Air Traffic Control Center ATCC

air traffic controller ATC

Air Training Centre British ATC

air transport AT

Air Transport Association ATA

Air Transport Auxiliary ATA

Air Transport Command ATC

Air Transport Licensing Board ATLB

Air University AU

Air Vice-Marshal of the Canadian Air Force AVM or A/V/M or A.V.M.

Air War College AWC

Air or Air Force attaché AIRA

air-conditioned 1 A/C 2 AC 3 ac

air-cushion landing gear ACLG

air-launched ballistic missile ALBM

air-launched cruise missile ALCM

Air-Sea Rescue ASR or A/SR

air-speed indicator ASI

air-tight AT

air-to-air missile 1 A to A or A-to-A 2 A-A 3 AA 4 AAM

air-to-ground AG or A/G

air-to-ground missile AGM

air-to-ship missile ATS

air-to-surface AS or A-S

air-to-surface ballistic missile ASBM

air-to-surface missile ASM

air-to-underwater missile AU or A-U AUM

air-to-water missile aw

airborne 1 A/B or a/b or a/b. 2 AB 3 abn

Airborne Battle Control and Command Center ABCCC

airborne collision avoidance system ACAS

airborne control ABC

airborne controlled intercept ACI

Airborne Flight Attendants Association AFAA

airborne infantry ABNINF

airborne search equipment ASE

airborne task force ABTF

Airborne Warning and Control System AWACS

airborne or aircraft interception AI

aircraft 1 A 2 AC 3 acft

aircraft and engine A & E or A and E

Aircraft and Engine Mechanic AEM

aircraft commander AC

aircraft control and warning ACW

aircraft direction finder ADF

Aircraft General Standards AGS

Aircraft Industries Association AIA

aircraft on ground ACOG

aircraft out of commission for parts AOCP

Aircraft Owners' and Pilots' Association AOPA

aircraft report AIREP

Aircraft Research Association ARA or A.R.A.

aircraftsman 1 A/C 2 AC

aircraftswoman 1 A/C 2 AC 3 ACW

airdrome adrm. or adrm

airfield AFLD or afld.

airfield surface movement indication ASMI

airframe afr.
airline carriers of passengers ACP
Airline Charter Service ACS
airline transport rating ATR
airlock module AM
Airman AN
airman **1** A **2** A/C **3** Amn. *or* Amn
airman basic **1** A/B **2** AB
airplane **2** a **2** AP
airport APRT
airport surface detection equipment ASDE
airport surveillance radar ASR
airtight **1** a.t. **2** AT
airway, breathing, and circulation *medicine* ABC
Alabama 1 AL (Zip Code) **2** Ala.
alabamine Ab
alanine Ala. *or* ala.
alanine aminotransferase ALT
alanyl Ala. *or* ala.
Alaska 1 AAA **2** AK (Zip Code) **3** Alas. **4** Alsk.
Alaska Defense Command ADC
Alaska-Canada Alcan *or* ALCAN
Alaskan Air Command AAC
Alaskan Communications System ACS
Albania Alb.
Albanian Alb.
Albany Alb.
albedo A
Alberta Union of Provincial Employees AUPE
Alberta, Canada 1 AB **2** Alb. **3** Alba. **4** Alta.
albumin alb.
albumin-globulin AG *or* A/G
alcohol **1** alc. *or* alc **2** alcoh.
Alcohol and Tobacco Tax Division ATTD
alcohol dehydrogenase ADH
Alcohol, Drug Abuse, and Mental Health Administration ADAMHA
alcohol-chloroform-ether ACE
Alcoholic Beverage Control ABC
Alcoholics Anonymous 1 AA *or* A.A. (*GPO:* AA; *NYT:* A.A.) **2** Al-Anon
Alcoholics Anonymous Teens Alateen
alderman Ald. *or* ald. *or* Aldm.
Alexander Alex.
Alfonso Alf.
Alfred Alf.
algebra Alg. *or* alg.
Algeria A
Algerian 1 A **2** Alg.
Algerian Radio and Television (network) RTA
Algiers Alg.
Algorithmic language ALGOL *or* Algol
Alhambra Alh.
alias al
alicyclic ac
alien of declared intention ADI
Alien Property Custodian APC *or* A.P.C.
alkali alk.
alkali-resistant factor ARF
alkaline alk.
alkaline phosphatase *biochemistry* AP
alkyl R
alkyl benzene sulfonate ABS
All but Dissertation ABD
all by itself *music* ts *or* t.s.
all concerned notified ACN

All England *sports* AE
All England Lawn Tennis Club A.E.L.T.C.
All England Women's Hockey Association A.E.W.H.A.
All India Radio AIR
all inertial guidance AIG
all iron a.i.
all points addressable *computers* APA
all points bulletin APB
all risks **1** a.r. **2** a/r
all together *music* t *or* t.
all water *commerce* **1** A/W **2** aw *or* a.w.
all widths aw (of lumber)
All's Well That Ends Well AWW
All-African Trade Union Federation A.A.T.U.F.
All-American Rose Selections A.A.R.S.
All-American Selections AAS
all-purpose vehicle APV
all-terrain bicycle ATB
all-terrain cycle ATC
all-terrain vehicle ATV
all-volunteer force AVF
All-Weather Landing System AWLS
allergic encephalomyelitis AE
Alliance Party AP
Allied Air Headquarters AAHQ
Allied Artists of America AAA
Allied Control Commission ACC
Allied Headquarters AHQ
allowable cabin load ACL
allowable gross weight AGW *or* agw
allowance alw. *or* Alw.
alloy aly.
Allport-Vernon *psychology* AV *or* A-V
Allport-Vernon-Livesey *psychology* AVL *or* A-V-L
alongside AS
Alpes-Maritimes AM *or* A.M. *or* A.-M.
Alpha A
alpha a
alpha-naphthylthiourea ANTU
alphabet ABC
alphafetoprotein AFP
Alphonse Alph.
also known as a.k.a. *or* a/k/a *or* AKA (*GPO:* a.k.a.)
alteration alter.
altered state of consciousness ASC
alternate **1** A **2** alt.
alternate communications facility ACF
alternate day therapy ADT
alternate days *advertising* AD
Alternate Flight Plan AFP
alternate weeks *advertising* A/W
alternating **1** Alt. **2** alt.
alternating continuous waves *electronics* ACW *or* acw
alternating current **1** ac *or* a.c. *or* a-c **2** AC *or* A.C. *or* A-C
alternating current voltage VAC
alternating current, direct current AC/DC *or* ac/dc *or* a-c/d-c
alternating gradient synchrotron AGS *or* A.G.S.
alternation alt.
alternative alt.
Alternative Book Service ASB

alternative delivery system ADS
alternative dispute resolution ADR
alternative minimum tax AMT
alternative operator service AOS
alternative technology AT
alternator alt.
altimeter altm.
altitude **1** alt. **2** d *or* d. **3** H **4** h **5** *physics* y
alto **1** alt. **2** *music, meteorology* a **3** *music* A *or* A.
altocumulus castellatus cloud *meteorology* ACC *or* Acc.
altocumulus cloud *meteorology* **1** AC **2** Ac
altocumulus clouds *meteorology* a-cu
altocumulus clouds standing lenticular *meteorology* ACSL
altostratus cloud *meteorology* As
aluminum **1** Al **2** alum.
aluminum cable, steel reinforced ACSR
aluminum, nickel, cobalt (alloy) alnico
alumna alum.
alumnae alum.
alumni alum.
alumnus alum.
alveolar alv.
always afloat *shipping* **1** a/a **2** aa *or* a.a.
Alzheimer's disease AD
Alzheimer's Disease Education Referral Center ADERC
AM broadcasting BAM
amalgamated amal.
Amalgamated Clothing and Textile Workers Union ACTWU
Amalgamated Engineering Union *British* AEU
Amalgamated Lithographers of America 1 ALA *or* A.L.A. **2** ALOA
Amalgamated Society of Engineers *British* A.S.E.
Amalgamated Transit Union ATU
amateur **1** a **2** A *or* a.
Amateur Athletic Association AAA
Amateur Athletic Association of America AAAA
Amateur Athletic Union AAU *or* A.A.U.
Amateur Bicycle League of America ABLA
Amateur Boxing Association ABA
Amateur Chamber Music Players A.C.M.P.
Amateur Fencers League of America AFLA
Amateur Fencing Association AFA
Amateur Football Association AFA
Amateur Football Club AFC
Amateur Gymnastics Association AGA
Amateur Hockey Association of the United States AHAUS
amateur radio station AR
Amateur Skating Union of the United States ASUUS
Amateur Softball Association of America ASA
Amateur Swimming Association *British* ASA
ambassador Amb.
Ambassador Extraordinary and Plenipotentiary A.E. and P. *or* A.E. & P.
ambient amb
ambulance Amb.
ambulance corps AC
amendment **1** amdt. **2** amend.
America 1 A *or* A. **2** Am *or* Am. **3** Amer.

American 1 A or A. **2** Am or Am. **3** AME
4 Amer.
American Academy for Cerebral Palsy
AACP
American Academy in Rome AAR
American Academy of Advertising AAA
American Academy of Allergy AAA or
A.A.A.
American Academy of Arts and Letters
A.A.A.L.
**American Academy of Arts and Sciences
1** AAAS or A.A.A.S. **2** AAS
American Academy of Asian Studies AAAS
American Academy of Child Psychiatry
AACP or A.A.C.P.
American Academy of Dental Medicine
AADM or A.A.D.M.
American Academy of Dentists AAD or
A.A.D.
American Academy of Dermatology AAD
or A.A.D.
American Academy of Dramatic Arts AADA
or A.A.D.A.
American Academy of Family Physicians
AAFP
American Academy of Forensic Sciences
AAFS
American Academy of General Practice
AAGP
American Academy of Microbiology AAM
American Academy of Neurology AAN
American Academy of Nutrition AAN
American Academy of Ophthalmology
AAO or A.A.O.
**American Academy of Ophthalmology and
Otolaryngology** AAOO or AAO&O
American Academy of Optometry AAO
American Academy of Pediatrics AAP or
A.A.P.
**American Academy of Physical Medicine
and Rehabilitation** A.A.P.M.R.
**American Academy of Political and Social
Science** A.A.P.S.S.
American Accounting Association AAA or
A.A.A.
American Advertising Federation AAF
American Afro-Asian Educational Exchange
AAAEE
American Alpine Club AAC
American Amateur Baseball Congress AABC
American and Foreign Bible Society A.F.B.S.
American and Foreign Christian Union
A.F.C.U.
American Animal Hospital Association
AAHA or A.A.H.A.
American Anthropological Association AAA
American Anti-Vivisection Society AAVS
American Antiquarian Society AAS
American Arbitration Association AAA or
A.A.A.
American Artists Professional League AAPL
**American Association for Artificial
Intelligence** AAAI
American Association for Cancer Research
AACR
American Association for Italian Studies
AAIS
**American Association for Middle East
Studies** AAMES or A.A.M.E.S.

**American Association for Public Opinion
Research** AAPOR
**American Association for State and Local
History** AASLH
**American Association for the Advancement
of Science** AAAS
**American Association for the Advancement
of Slavic Studies**
**American Association for the History of
Medicine** AAHM
**American Association for the Promotion of
Science** AAPS or A.A.P.S.
**American Association for the United
Nations** AAUN
**American Association for Vital Records and
Public Health Statistics** AAVRPHS
**American Association of Advertising
Agencies** AAAA
American Association of Bioanalysts AAB
American Association of Blood Banks
A.A.B.B.
**American Association of Botanical Gardens
and Arboretums** AABGA
**American Association of Classified School
Employees** AACSE
**American Association of Colleges for
Teacher Education** AACTE
**American Association of Community and
Junior Colleges** AACJC
American Association of Dental Examiners
AADE or A.A.D.E.
American Association of Dental Schools
AADS
**American Association of Electrical
Engineers** A.A.E.E. or AAEE
**American Association of Engineering
Societies** AAES
American Association of Engineers A.A.E.
or AAE
American Association of Film Producers
AAFP
American Association of Foot Specialists
AAFS
American Association of Immunologists AAI
**American Association of Industrial
Engineers** A.A.I.E. or AAIE
American Association of Junior Colleges
AAJC or A.A.J.C.
**American Association of Language
Specialists** AALS
American Association of Law Libraries
A.A.L.L. or AALL
**American Association of Marriage
Counselors** AAMC or A.A.M.C.
American Association of Museums AAM
American Association of Nurserymen AAN
or A.A.N.
**American Association of Obstetricians and
Gynecologists** AAOG or A.A.O.G.
**American Association of Oral and
Maxillofacial Surgeons** AAOMS
American Association of Orthodontists
AAO
American Association of Pathologists AAP
or A.A.P.
**American Association of Pathologists and
Bacteriologists** AAPB or A.A.P.B.
**American Association of Petroleum
Geologists** AAPG

American Association of Physics Teachers
AAPT
American Association of Plastic Surgeons
AAPS
**American Association of Poison Control
Centers** AAPCC
American Association of Retired Persons
AARP
**American Association of School
Administrators** AASA
American Association of School Librarians
AASL or A.A.S.L.
**American Association of Schools and
Departments of Journalism** AASDJ
**American Association of State Colleges and
Universities** AASCU
**American Association of State Highway
Officials** AASHO
American Association of State Libraries
AASL or A.A.S.L.
**American Association of Teacher Educators
in Agriculture** AATEA
**American Association of Teachers of
Chinese Language and Culture** AATCLC
American Association of Teachers of French
AATF
**American Association of Teachers of
German** AATG
American Association of Teachers of Italian
AATI
**American Association of Teachers of Slavic
and East European Languages** AATSEEL
**American Association of Teachers of
Spanish and Portuguese** AATSP
**American Association of Textile Chemists
and Colorists** AATCC
**American Association of Theological
Schools** AATS
American Association of University Presses
AAUP
**American Association of University
Professors** AAUP or A.A.U.P.
**American Association of University
Supervisors and Coordinators** AAUSC
American Association of University Women
AAUW or A.A.U.W.
**American Association of Variable Star
Observers** AAVSO or A.A.V.S.O.
**American Association of Zoological Parks
and Aquariums** AAZPA
American Association on Mental Deficiency
AAMD
American Astronautical Federation AAF
American Astronautical Society AAS
American Astronomers Association AAA
American Astronomical Society AAS
American Automobile Association AAA or
A.A.A.
American Automotive Leasing Association
AALA
American Badminton Association ABA
**American Bakery and Confectionery
Workers Union** ABCW
American Ballet Theater ABT
American Bankers Association ABA or
A.B.A.
American Baptist Missionary Union
A.B.M.U.
American Baptist Publishing Society A.B.P.S.

American Bar Association ABA or A.B.A.
(*GPO:* ABA)

American Bar Association Journal A.B.A.J.
or ABAJ

American Battle Monuments Commission
ABMC or A.B.M.C.

American Bible Society ABS or A.B.S.

American Board of Dental Public Health
ABDPH

American Board of Examiners in
Professional Psychology A.B.E.P.P.

American Board of Foreign Missions
A.B.F.M.

American Board of Internal Medicine
A.B.I.M.

American Board of Pediatrics ABP or A.B.P.

American Board of Trial Advocates ABTA

American Book Awards ABA

American Book Collector ABC

American Booksellers Association ABA

American Bowling Congress ABC

American Broadcasting Company ABC

American Bureau of Metal Statistics ABMS

American Bureau of Shipping ABS or A.B.S.

American Business Press ABP

American Campaign Medal ACM

American Camping Association ACA

American Cancer Society ACS

American Canoe Association ACA

American Checkers Federation ACF

American Chemical Society ACS or A.C.S.

American Chiropractic Association ACA

American Choral Directors Association
ACDA

American Choral Foundation ACF or A.C.F.

American Church Union ACU or A.C.U.

American Cinema Editors ACE

American Civil Liberties Union ACLU or
A.C.L.U. (*GPO:* ACLU)

American Clinical and Climatological
Association ACCA

American College of Anesthesiologists ACA

American College of Apothecaries ACA

American College of Cardiology ACC or
A.C.C.

American College of Continuing Medical
Education ACCME

American College of Dentists ACD or A.C.D.

American College of Gastroenterology
A.C.G.

American College of Hospital
Administrators ACHA or A.C.H.A.

American College of Nurse Midwifery
A.C.N.M.

American College of Obstetricians and
Gynecologists ACOG or A.C.O.G.

American College of Pharmacists ACP or
A.C.P.

American College of Physicians ACP or
A.C.P.

American College of Preventive Medicine
ACPM or A.C.P.M.

American College of Radiology ACR or
A.C.R

American College of Surgeons ACS or
A.C.S.

American College of Trial Lawyers ACTL

American College Public Relations
Association ACPRA

American College Testing Program ACT

American Committee for Irish Studies ACIS

American Communications Association ACA

American Comparative Literature
Association ACLA

American Composers Alliance ACA

American Concrete Institute ACI

American Conference of Cantors ACC

American Congregational Association ACA
or A.C.A.

American Congregational Union ACU or
A.C.U.

American Congress on Surveying and
Mapping ACSM

American Conservative Union ACU or
A.C.U.

American Contract Bridge League ACBL

American Corporate Counsel Association
ACCA

American Council for Judaism A.C.J.

American Council of Human Rights ACHR

American Council of Independent
Laboratories A.C.I.L.

American Council of Learned Societies
ACLS or A.C.L.S.

American Council of Teachers of Russian
ACTR

American Council on Education ACE

American Council on NATO. ACN

American Council on Race Relations ACRR

American Council on the Teaching of
Foreign Languages ACTFL

American Craftsmen's Council ACC

American Cycling Union ACU

American Daffodil Society ADS

American Dahlia Society ADS

American Dairy Association ADA

American Dairy Science Association ADSA

American Decisions law Am.Dec.

American Defense Service Medal ADSM

American Dental Association ADA or A.D.A.

American Depositary Receipt *commerce*
ADR

American Diabetes Association ADA

American Dialect Society ADS

American Dietetic Association ADA

American District Telegraph ADT

American Documentation Institute ADI

American Drug Manufacturers Association
ADMA

American Economic Association AEA or
A.E.A.

American Economic Foundation AEF

American Educational Publishers Instiute
AEPI

American Educational Research Association
AERA

American Educational Theatre Association
AETA

American Electrochemical Society AES or
A.E.S.

American Engineering Council AEC

American Engineering Standards
Committee AESC or A.E.S.C.

American English AmE

American Enterprise Institute AEI

American Entomological Society AES

American Epidemiological Society AES

American Ethical Union AEU

American Ethnological Society AES

American Farm Bureau Federation A.F.B.F.

American Farm Economic Association AFEA

American Farm Research Association AFRA

American Federation of Arts AFA or A.F.A.

American Federation of Government
Employees AFGE or A.F.G.E.

American Federation of Information
Processing Societies AFIPS

American Federation of International
Institutes AFII

American Federation of Labor-Congress of
Industrial Organizations AFL-CIO or
A.F.L.C.I.O. (*GPO:* AFL-CIO; *NYT:*
A.F.L.-C.I.O.)

American Federation of Mineralogical
Societies AFMS

American Federation of Musicians AFM or
A.F.M.

American Federation of Musicians of the
United States and Canada AFMUSC

American Federation of Police AFP

American Federation of State, County, and
Municipal Employees AFSCME

American Federation of Teachers AFT or
A.F.T.

American Federation of Television and
Radio Artists AFTRA

American Field Service AFS or A.F.S.

American Film Export Association AFEA

American Film Institute AFI

American Fisheries Society AFS

American Folklore Society AFS or A.F.S.

American Football Conference AFC

American Football League AFL or A.F.L.

American Forces Information Service AFIS

American Forces Press and Publications
Service AFPPS

American Foreign Insurance Association
AFIA

American Foreign Law Association AFLA

American Foreign Service Association AFSA

American Forest Products Industries AFPI

American Foundation for Homeopathy AFH
or A.F.H.

American Foundation for the Blind AFB

American Foundrymen's Association AFA

American Foundrymen's Society AFS

American Friends Service Committee AFSC
or A.F.S.C.

American Gas Association AGA or A.G.A.

American Gear Manufacturers Association
AGMA

American Gem Society AGS

American Geographical and Statistical
Society A.G.S.S.

American Geographical Institute AGI

American Geographical Society AGS or
A.G.S.

American Geological Institute AGI

American Geologists AG

American Geophysical Union AGU

American Graves Registration Service
AGRS

American Group Psychotherapy
Association A.G.P.A. or AGPA

American Guild of Authors and Composers
AGAC

American Guild of Music AGM

American Guild of Musical Artists AGMA or A.G.M.A.
American Guild of Organists AGO or A.G.O.
American Guild of Variety Artists AGVA or A.G.V.A.
American Gynecological Society AGS or A.G.S.
American Hardware Manufacturers Association AHMA
American Heart Association A.H.A. or AHA
American Helicopter Society AHS
American Historical Association A.H.A.
American Historical Review AHR
American Hockey League AHL
American Home Economics Association AHEA
American Home Mission Society A.H.M.S.
American Horse Shows Association A.H.S.A.
American Hospital Association A.H.A. or AHA
American Hotel Association A.H.A.
American Humane Association A.H.A.
American Humane Society AHS or A.H.S.
American Indian 1 Am. Ind. or Am Ind **2** Amerind or AmerInd (*MLA:* AmerInd.)
American Indian Movement AIM
American Industrial Hygiene Association AIHA
American Insitute of Architects AIA or A.I.A.
American Institute of Accountants AIA or A.I.A.
American Institute of Aeronautics and Astronautics AIAA
American Institute of Baking AIB
American Institute of Banking A.I.B.
American Institute of Biological Sciences AIBS or A.I.B.S.
American Institute of Certified Public Accountants AICPA
American Institute of Chemical Engineers 1 A.I.C.E. or AICE **2** A.I.Ch.E. or AIChE
American Institute of Chemists A.I.C. or AIC
American Institute of Consulting Engineers A.I.C.E. or AICE
American Institute of Decorators AID or A.I.D.
American Institute of Electrical Engineers 1 AIEE or A.I.E.E. **2** Am. Inst. E.E.
American Institute of Graphic Arts AIGA
American Institute of Industrial Engineers *French* AIIE or A.I.I.E.
American Institute of Landscape Architects A.I.L.A. or AILA
American Institute of Laundering AIL
American Institute of Management AIM or A.I.M.
American Institute of Marine Underwriters AIMU or A.I.M.U.
American Institute of Mechanical Engineers A.I.M.E.
American Institute of Mining and Metallurgical Engineers 1 A.I.M. & M.E. **2** AIMME or A.I.M.M.E.
American Institute of Mining Engineers A.I.M.E. or AIME

American Institute of Mining, Metallurgical, and Petroleum Engineers A.I.M.M.P.E. or AIMMPE
American Institute of Physics A.I.P. or AIP
American Institute of Real Estate Appraisers AIREA or A.I.R.E.A.
American Institute of Steel Construction AISC or A.I.S.C.
American Institute of Weights and Measures AIWM
American Institutes for Research AIR
American Insurance Association AIA
American Iron and Steel Institute AISI or A.I.S.I.
American Jewish Committee AJC
American Jewish Congress AJC
American Journal of International Law AJIL
American Journal of Science AJS
American Kennel Club AKC
American Labor Party ALP or A.L.P.
American Land Title Association A.L.T.A.
American Law Institute A.L.I.
American Law Reports A.L.R.
American Lawn Bowling Association ALBA
American League *baseball* AL
American Legion AL or A.L.
American Legion of Honor A.L. of H.
American Libraries AL
American Library Association ALA
American Library Institute A.L.I.
American Literary Translators Association A.L.T.A. or ALTA
American Literature Association ALA
American Lutheran Church ALC or A.L.C.
American Management Association AMA or A.M.A.
American Maritime Association AMA or A.M.A.
American Maritime Cases AMC or A.M.C.
American Mathematical Society AMS or A.M.S.
American Meat Institute AMI
American Mechanical Rights Association AMRA
American Medical Association AMA or A.M.A. (*GPO, OUP:* AMA; *NYT:* A.M.A.)
American Medical Political Action Committee AMPAC
American Medical Women's Association AMWA or A.M.W.A.
American Medical Writer's Association AMWA or A.M.W.A.
American Merchant Marine Institute A.M.M.I.
American Meteorological Society AMS or A.M.S.
American Microscopic Society AMS or A.M.S.
American Miscellaneous Society AMSOC
American Montessori Society AMS
American Motorcycle Association AMA
American Museum of Natural History AMNH
American Musicology Society AMS
American Name Society ANS
American National Red Cross ANRC or A.N.R.C.
American National Standards Institute ANSI

American Neurological Association ANA or A.N.A.
American Newspaper Association ANA
American Newspaper Guild ANG
American Newspaper Publishers Association ANPA
American Notes and Queries ANQ
American Nuclear Society ANS or A.N.S.
American Numismatic Association ANA
American Numismatic Society ANS or A.N.S.
American Nurses' Association ANA or A.N.A.
American Occupational Therapy Association A.O.T.A.
American of Japanese Ancestry AJA
American Ophthalmological Society AOS or A.O.S.
American Optometric Association AOA or A.O.A.
American Order of Stationary Engineers A.O.S.E. or AOSE
American Ordnance Association AOA
American Oriental Society AOS or A.O.S.
American Ornithologists Union A.O.U.
American Orthopedic Association AOA
American Osteopathic Association AOA
American Otological Society AOS or A.O.S.
American Peace Society A.P.S.
American Pediatric Society A.P.S.
American Personnel and Guidance Association APGA
American Petroleum Institute API or A.P.I. (*GPO:* API)
American Pharmaceutical Association 1 A.Ph.A. or APhA **2** APA
American Pharmacopeia AP or A.P.
American Philatelic Society A.P.S. or APS
American Philological Association APA or A.P.A.
American Philosophical Association APA
American Philosophical Society A.P.S.
American Physical Society A.P.S. or APS
American Physical Therapy Association APTA or A.P.T.A.
American Physiological Society A.P.S.
American Physiotherapy Association APA
American Plan AP
American Platform Tennis Association APTA
American Political Science Association A.P.S.A.
American Postal Workers Union APWU
American Power Boat Association A.P.B.A. or APBA
American Press Institute API
American Professional Golfers APG or A.P.G.
American Protective Association APA
American Protestant Association APA
American Protestant Society A.P.S.
American Psychiatric Association APA or A.P.A.
American Psychological Association APA or A.P.A.
American Psychological Society A.P.S.
American Public Health Association APHA
American Public Radio APR
American Public Transit Association APTA
American Quarterly AQ

American Radio Relay League ARRL
American Railway Association ARA
American Railway Engineering Association AREA
American Railway Union ARU or A.R.U.
American Red Cross ARC or A.R.C. (GPO: ARC)
American Registry of Radiological Technologists ARRT or A.R.R.T.
American Reports law Am.Repts. or Am.R.
American Revised Version ARV or A.R.V.
American Rocket Society ARS
American Roentgen Ray Society ARRS or A.R.R.S.
American Samoa AS (Zip Code)
American Scholar A Sch
American School Health Association ASHA or A.S.H.A.
American Selling Price ASP or A.S.P.
American Sign Language 1 Ameslan 2 ASL
American Soccer League ASL
American Society for Clinical Investigation ASCI
American Society for Eighteenth-Century Studies ASECS
American Society for Genetics ASG or A.S.G.
American Society for Information Science ASIS
American Society for Metals ASM
American Society for Microbiology ASM
American Society for Quality Control ASQC
American Society for Testing and Materials ASTM or A.S.T.M. (GPO: ASTM)
American Society for the Prevention of Cruelty to Animals ASPCA
American Society for Training and Development ASTD
American Society of Agricultural Engineers ASAE
American Society of Agronomy ASA
American Society of Anesthesiologists ASA or A.S.A.
American Society of Auctioneers ASA
American Society of Bacteriologists ASB
American Society of Biological Chemists ASBC
American Society of Chemical Engineers ASChE or A.S.Ch.E.
American Society of Cinematographers ASC or A.S.C.
American Society of Civil Engineers Am. Soc. C.E. ASCE or A.S.C.E.
American Society of Civil Engineers and Architects ASCEA or A.S.C.E.A.
American Society of Clinical Laboratory Technicians ASCLT
American Society of Clinical Pathologists ASCP
American Society of Composers, Authors and Publishers ASCAP or A.S.C.A.P. or Ascap (MLA: ASCAP)
American Society of Engineers ASE or A.S.E.
American Society of Engineers and Architects ASEA
American Society of Heating, Refrigerating, and Air-Conditioning Engineers ASHRAE
American Society of Hematology ASH

American Society of Ichthyologists and Herpetologists ASIH or A.S.I.H.
American Society of Industrial Designers ASID
American Society of Interior Designers ASID
American Society of Internal Medicine ASIM or A.S.I.M.
American Society of Landscape Architects ASLA or A.S.L.A.
American Society of Limnology and Oceanography ASLO or A.S.L.O.
American Society of Magazine Editors ASME or A.S.M.E.
American Society of Magazine Photographers ASMP or A.S.M.P.
American Society of Mechanical Engineers 1 Am. Soc. M.E. 2 ASME or A.S.M.E. (GPO: ASME)
American Society of Motion Picture and Television Engineers ASMPTE or A.S.M.P.T.E.
American Society of Naval Engineers ASNE
American Society of Newspaper Editors ASNE or A.S.N.E.
American Society of Picture Professionals ASPP
American Society of Radiologic Technologists ASRT or A.S.R.T.
American Society of Refrigerating Engineers ASRE
American Society of Safety Engineers ASSE
American Society of Sanitary Engineering ASSE
American Society of Tool Engineers ASTE
American Society of Travel Agents ASTA
American Society of Tropical Medicine and Hygiene ASTMH or A.S.T.M.H.
American Society of University Composers ASUC
American Sociological Association ASA or A.S.A.
American Speech AS
American Stamp Dealers Association A.S.D.A.
American Standard Code for Information Interchange ASCII
American Standard Version A.S.V.
American Statistical Association. ASA
American Steel and Wire Gauge ASWG
American Stock Exchange 1 Amex or AMEX 2 ASE
American Studies Association ASA
American Sunday School Union A.S.S.U.
American Symphony Orchestra ASO or A.S.O.
American Telephone and Telegraph AT&T
American Temperance Society ATS or A.T.S.
American terms commerce AT or A/T
American Theatre Wing ATW
American Theological Library Association ATLA
American Tract Society ATS or A.T.S.
American Translators Association ATA
American Transport Service ATS
American Trial Lawyers Association ATLA or A.T.L.A.
American Trucking Association ATA
American Type Culture Collection ATCC

American Unitarian Association A.U.A.
American Vecturist Association AVA or A.V.A.
American Veterans AMVETS or Amvets (GPO, NYT: AMVETS)
American Veterans Committee AVC
American Veterinary Medical Association AVMA or A.V.M.A.
American Vocational Association AVA
American Water Ski Association AWSA
American Watercolor Society AWS
American Welding Society AWS
American Wire Gage AWG
American Women in Radio and Television AWRT
American Women's Voluntary Services A.W.V.S.
American World's Boxing Association A.W.B.A.
American Youth Hostels AYH or A.Y.H.
American, British, Canadian ABC
Americans for Democratic Action ADA
Americans with Disabilities Act ADA
americium Am
Ames Research Center ARC
amino adenosine triacid ester biochemistry AATE
2-aminoethylisothiouronium AET
ammeter 1 A 2 Am or Am.
ammonia ammon.
ammonium Am
ammonium nitrate-fuel oil ANFO
ammunition 1 Am or Am. 2 ammo or ammo. 3 amn.
Amnesty International AI
amniolevulinic acid ALA
among amg.
among other things Latin 1 i.a. 2 int. al.
amorphous amorph.
Amos Am or Am.
amount amt.
amperage amp or amp.
ampere 1 A 2 a 3 amp or amp. or Amp
ampere turn 1 a.t. 2 AT
ampere-hour 1 a.h. or a-h. 2 A.H. or AH 3 amp-hr.
amperes per square foot a.s.f. or a./s.f.
amphibian A
amphibian or amphibious AMPH or amph.
amphibious assault vehicle AAV
amphibious corps AC
amplification physics A
amplifier amp or amp.
amplitude 1 am or am. 2 amp or amp. or Amp. 3 physics A
amplitude modulation 1 AM 2 am
amplitude modulation transmitter AMT
amplitude modulation/frequency modulation AM/FM or am/fm
ampule amp or amp.
amputation amp or amp.
Amsterdam Amst.
amyl Am
amyotrophic lateral sclerosis 1 ALS 2 a.l.s.
analog computer AC
analog to digital AD or A/D
analog to digital converter ADC
analogous anal.
analogy anal.

analysis 1 anal. 2 anlys.
analysis of variance ANOVA
analytic anal.
analytical 1 anal. 2 analyt.
analytical chemist AC or A.C.
analytical or analyzed reagent 1 a.r.
 2 *chemistry* AR or A.R.
analyze anal.
analyzed anal.
anatomic anat.
anatomical anat.
anatomist anat.
anatomy anat.
anchor bolt AB
ancient anct.
Ancient Accepted Scottish Rite A.A.S.R.
Ancient and Modern A & M or A. & M.
Ancient Arabic Order of the Nobles of the
 Mystic Shrine AAONMS or A.A.O.N.M.S.
Ancient Free and Accepted Masons
 A.F.A.M. or A.F. & A.M.
Ancient Mystical Order Rosae Crucis
 AMORC or A.M.O.R.C.
Ancient Order of Druids AOD or A.O.D.
Ancient Order of Foresters A.O.F.
Ancient Order of Hibernians A.O.H.
Ancient Order of United Workmen
 A.O.U.W. or AOUW
Ancient York Mason A.Y.M.
ancient or anciently anc.
anciently anct.
and (the) following et seq. (*MLA:* not
 acceptable)
and (those) following et seqq. or et sqq.
 (*MLA:* not acceptable)
and others 1 a/o or A/o or a.o. 2 et al.
and so forth etc. or &c. (*GPO, MLA, OUP:*
 etc.)
and/or a/or
Andorra And.
Andrew And.
androecium A
Andromeda And (constellation)
Angel of the Lord AD
angiotensin-converting enzyme ACE
angle 1 a 2 ang.
angle of incidence *physics* i
angle of reflection *physics* r
angle side angle *geometry* ASA or a.s.a.
angle-measuring equipment AME
Anglican Angl.
Anglican Evangelical Group Movement
 A.E.G.M.
Anglican Theological Review ATR
Anglicized Angl.
Anglo-French 1 AF or A.F. or AF. or A-F
 2 AFr or AFr. (*MLA:* AFr.)
Anglo-Indian A-Ind or A-Ind.
Anglo-Latin AL or AL. or A-L or A.L.
Anglo-Norman AN or AN. or A.N. or A-N
 (*MLA, OUP:* AN)
Anglo-Norman Text Society ANTS
Anglo-Saxon AS or A.S. or AS. or A-S
Anglo-Saxon Protestant ASP
Anglo-Saxon. Ang.-Sax.
Anglo-Welsh Review AWR
Angola Ang.
Angry Young Man or Men A.Y.M.
angstrom unit 1 Å or Å° 2 A 3 a

angular ang.
angular differentiating accelerometer ADA
angular distribution auger microscopy
 ADAM
angular momentum 1 AM 2 *physics* J
angular velocity w
anhydrous anh. or anhyd. or anhydr.
Animal and Plant Health Inspection Service
 APHIS
Animal Breeding Research Organisation
 ABRO
Animal Diseases Research Association ADRA
Animal Liberation Front ALF
animal protein factor APF
ankylosing spondylitis AS
annals ann. or Ann.
Annals of Philosophy AP
Annals of Science AS
Annals of the Association of American
 Geographers A.A.A.G.
annex anx.
anniversary 1 ann. 2 anniv.
annotated 1 An or An. 2 an. 3 annot.
annotation annot.
annotator annot.
annual 1 An or An. 2 an. 3 ann. or Ann.
 4 *botany* A
Annual Delegate Meeting ADM
Annual General Meeting *British* AGM or
 A.G.M.
annual percentage rate APR
annual progress report APR
Annual Register of World Events AR or A.R.
annual return *British* AR or A.R.
Annuale Medievale An M
annually 1 p.a. 2 per an. or per ann.
annuity 1 a 2 ann. 3 *law* anny.
Annunciation Annunc.
annunciator ann.
anodal closing sound *medicine* 1 ACS 2 acs
 or a.c.s.
anodal closure AC
anodal closure contraction *medicine.* ACC
anodal opening contraction AOC or A.O.C.
anode 1 A 2 a 3 AN or AN. 4 an.
anodize anod.
anomalous propagation *meteorology* AP or
 A.P.
anonymous 1 a 2 an. 3 Anon. or anon.
 (*MLA, OUP:* anon.)
anonymously Anon. or anon. (*MLA, OUP:*
 anon.)
another *law* anr.
answer 1 A 2 a 3 ans.
answered ans.
antarctic *meteorology* A
Antarctica 1 Ant. 2 Antarct.
antecedent precipitation index *meteorology*
 API
antenna ant. or ANT
anterior 1 A 2 a 3 ant.
anterior and posterior A & P
anterior pituitary hormone APH
anterior pituitary-like hormone APL or APLH
anthology anth. or anthol.
Anthony Ant.
anthropological anthr. or anthro. or
 anthrop. or anthropol.
Anthropological Institute AI or A.I.

anthropology anthr. or anthro. or anthrop.
 or anthropol.
Anti-Defamation League ADL
anti-detonation injection ADI
anti-icing AI
anti-lock brake system ABS
anti-missile missile AMM
anti-phase domains APD
anti-poaching unit APU
anti-satellite interceptor ASAT
anti-submarine rocket ASROC
Anti-Vivisection Society AVS
anti-vivisectionist AV
antiaircraft 1 AA 2 aa
antiaircraft artillery AAA
antiballistic missile ABM
antibody dependent cellular cytotoxicity
 biochemistry, medicine ADCC
anticipated freight *commerce* ant. frt.
anticyclonic *meteorology* ACYC
antidiuretic hormone ADH
antidote anti or anti.
antifriction bearing AFB
antifriction metal AFM
Antigua Ant.
antihemophilic factor AHF
antihemophilic globulin AHG
antijamming *electronics, communication* AJ
antilog *mathematics* illog.
antilogarithm antilog
antilymphocyte globulin ALG
antilymphocyte serum ALS
antimony Sb
antipersonnel 1 AP 2 apers or APERS
antiphon Ant.
antiproton accumulator *physics* AA
antiquarian 1 ant. 2 antiq. or antiqn.
Antiquarian Booksellers Association of
 America A.B.A.A. or ABAA
antiquary ant.
antique ant.
antiquities 1 ant. 2 antiq.
antiquity antiq.
antiradar missile ARM
antiradiation missile ARM
antisubmarine AS
antisubmarine warfare ASW
antitank AT
antitank missile ATM
antitetanus serum 1 ATS 2 ats
antithymocyte globulin *medicine* ATG
Antitrust Division AD
Antlia Ant (constellation)
Antony and Cleopatra 1 A & C (*MLA:* Ant.)
 2 Ant. 3 Ant. & Cl.
antonym ant.
Antrim, Ireland Ant.
anxiety-tension-state *psychology* ATS
any other business AOB
any quantity 1 AQ 2 aq
any or a good brand a.g.b.
aorist aor.
aortic or arterial pressure *medicine* AP
apartment 1 Apart. 2 apt. or Apt.
aphetic aph.
Apocalypse Apoc.
Apocrypha Apoc. or Apocr.
Apocryphal Apoc.
apogee 1 apo. 2 apog.

apomict *biology* apm.
Apostle 1 Ap. 2 Apost.
Apostles App.
Apostolic Apost.
Apostolic See Ap. Sed.
apostrophe apos.
apothecaries' dram dr.ap.
apothecaries' pound lb. ap.
apothecaries' weight ap. wt.
apothecary Apoth.
Appalachian Mountain Club AMC
Appalachian Regional Commission ARC
apparatus 1 app. 2 appar.
apparent ap.
apparent magnitude *astronomy* m
apparent power S
apparent *or* apparently 1 app. 2 appar.
appeal *law* 1 App. 2 app. 3 appl. *or* Appl.
appeal case AC *or* A.C.
Appeals Court AC *or* A.C.
appellant *law* appl. *or* Appl.
appellate *law* App.
Appellate Court App. Ct.
Appellate Division 1 AD *or* A.D. 2 App. Div.
appellation contrôllée AC *or* A.C.
appended app.
Appendices to the Journals A to J
appendices *or* appendixes apps.
appendix 1 App. 2 app. 3 appx. 4 apx.
appliance leakage current interrupter ALCI
applicable to appl.
applicants-to-acceptance ratio A to A
application 1 appl. 2 appln.
application binary interface ABI
application programming interface API
application specific integrated circuit ASIC
applications portability profile APP
applied app.
Applied Physics Laboratory APL
applied to appl.
applied to the affected part *pharmaceutics* p.a.a.
apply *pharmaceutics* admov.
appoint appt.
appointed 1 app. 2 apptd.
appointment 1 appmt. 2 appt.
appraise app.
appraised appd.
Appraisers Association of America AAA
apprentice 1 app. 2 appr.
apprentice seaman AS
approach control radar ACR
appropriate technology AT
approval 1 app. 2 appro. (*OUP:* appro)
approved 1 a *or* a. 2 app. 3 appd. 5 appr. 5 APR
approximate 1 app. *or* Appr. 2 aprx.
approximate absolute temperature 1 AA 2 aa
approximate *or* approximately 1 appr. 2 approx.
approximately 1 app. 2 c *or* c. 3 ca *or* ca. (*CSM, OUP:* ca.) 4 cir. *or* circ. (*OUP:* circ.)
approximation approx.
appurtenances appurts. *or* appurts
April 1 A 2 Ap. 3 Apl. 4 Apr. *or* Apr (*GPO, OUP:* Apr.)
April and October A & O
April, July, October, January AJOJ

aptitude apt.
aptitude index AI *or* A/I
Aquarius Aqr (constellation)
aqueous aq.
Arab Common Market ACM
Arab Corporation Council ACC
Arab Nationalist Movement ANM
Arab Network of America ANA
Arab Organization of Petroleum Exporting Countries AOPEC
Arab Postal Union A.P.U.
Arab Satellite Arabsat
Arabia Arab.
Arabian 1 Ar *or* Ar. 2 Arab.
Arabian-American Oil Company Aramco *or* ARAMCO (*NYT:* Aramco)
Arabic 1 Ar *or* Ar. 2 Arab.
arabinose Adenine ara-A
arachnology arach.
Aramaic 1 Ar *or* Ar. 2 Aram.
arbitrager arb
arbitrageur arb
arbitrary *or* working origin M'
arbitration arb *or* arb.
arbitrator arb *or* arb.
arboriculture arbor.
archaeological 1 arch. 2 archaeol.
Archaeological Institute of America AIA *or* A.I.A.
archaeology 1 arch. 2 archaeol.
archaic arch.
archaism arch.
Archbishop 1 Abp. 2 Arch. 3 Archbp. (*OUP:* Abp.)
Archdeacon Archd.
archeological archeol.
archeology archeol.
Archer Sgr (constellation)
archery arch.
Archipelago Arch.
archipelago arch.
Architect Arch.
architect 1 arch. 2 Archt.
Architect Member of the Incorporated Association of Architects and Surveyors AIAA *or* A.I.A.A.
architect, engineer, manager AEM
Architectural Arch.
architectural arch.
Architectural Aluminum Manufacturers Association AAMA
Architectural Engineer 1 AE *or* A.E. 2 Arch. E.
Architectural Photographers Association APA
architectural projected window APW
architecture 1 arch. 2 archit.
archives arch.
Archives of American Art AAA *or* A.A.A.
Archivum Linguisticum ALing
Arctic Arc.
arctic *meteorology* A
Arctic Institute of North America AINA
Arctic National Wildlife Refuge ANWR
Arctic Research Laboratory ARL
Arctic *or* Antarctic continental cold air mass cAK
Arctic *or* Antarctic, continental warm air mass cAw

Arctic. Arct.
are 1 a 2 A *or* A.
area 1 A 2 a 3 ar. *or* ar
area code AC
Area Electricity Board AEB *or* A.E.B.
area forecast *meteorology* 1 ARFOR 2 (*in English or traditional units*) ARFORT 3 (*in metric units*) ARMET
Area Forecast Center *meteorology* AFC
area of critical environmental concern ACEC
Area of Outstanding Natural Beauty *British* AONB *or* A.O.N.B.
Area Officer A.O.
area position control APC
Arecibo Ionospheric Observatory AIO
argent 1 a 2 arg. 3 *heraldry* ar.
Argentina Arg.
Argentina, Brazil, Chile ABC
Argentine Arg.
Argentine Republic Arg. Rep.
arginine 1 Arg. 2 arg.
argon 1 A 2 Ar
Argonne National Laboratory ANL
argument *mathematics* arg.
Argyll Arg.
Aries Ari (constellation)
Aristotle Arist.
arithmetic arith.
arithmetic (and) logic unit *computers* ALU
arithmetic age *education* Ar A
arithmetic average AA
arithmetic computation test AC
arithmetic mean 1 AM 2 M
arithmetic progression AP
arithmetic quotient Ar Q
arithmetic ratio Ar R
arithmetical arith.
Arizona 1 Ariz. 2 AZ (Zip Code)
Arkansas 1 Ark. 2 AR (Zip Code)
arm, chest, hip ACH *or* A.C.H.
Armagh Arm.
armament armt.
armature arm.
armature accelerator AA
Armed Forces Institute AFI
Armed Forces Network AFN
Armed Forces Police AFP
Armed Forces Policy Council AFPC
Armed Forces Press Service AFPS
Armed Forces Qualification Test AFQT
Armed Forces Radio and Television Service AFRTS *or* A.F.R.T.S.
Armed Forces Radio Service AFRS *or* A.F.R.S.
Armed Forces Radiology Research Institute AFRRI
Armed Forces Staff College AFSC
Armed Services Procurement Act ASPA
Armed Services Procurement Regulations ASPR
Armed Services Technical Information Agency ASTIA
Armenia *or* Armenian Arm.
Armenian Armen.
armor piercing a.p.
armored *military* armd.
armored combat earthmover ACE

armored personnel carrier APC
Armoric Arm.
arms and armor armor.
Arms Control and Disarmament Agency ACDA
Army Air Force AAF or A.A.F.
Army Air Service AAS
Army and Navy Club A. & N.
Army Chemical Center ACC
Army Clerical Speed Test ACST
Army Contract Adustment Board. ACAB
Army Corps AC or A.C.
Army Corps of Engineers ACE
Army Council AC or A.C.
Army Dental Corps ADC
Army Education Center AEC
Army Electronics Command AEC
Army Emergency Reserve AER or A.E.R.
Army Field Forces AFF
Army General Classification Test AGCT
Army General Staff AGS
Army Ground Forces AGF
Army Headquarters AHQ
Army Hospital Corps AC
Army Map Service AMS
Army Medical Center AMC
Army Medical Department AMD
Army Medical Service AMEDS or AmedS
Army Medical Services AMS
Army Medical Staff AMS
Army Nurse Corps ANC
Army Nursing Service ANS
Army of the United States AUS or A.U.S.
Army Order A.O. or AO
Army Ordnance Army Ord
Army Ordnance Department AOD
Army Package Power Reactor APPR
Army Pay Corps APC
Army Pay Department APD
Army Postal Unit APU
Army Regulation AR
army regulations AR
Army Research Office ARO
Army Routine Order ARO
Army Security Agency ASA
Army Service Forces ASF
Army Service Number ASN or asn or A.S.N. (*GPO:* A.S.N.)
Army Signal Corps ASC
Army Specialized Training Program ASTP
Army Strike Command ARSTRIKE
Army Supply and Maintenance Command ASMC
Army Training Center ATC
Army Transport Service ATS
Army Veteran Department AVD
Army Veterinary Service AVS
Army Volunteer Reserve AVR
Army War College AWC
Army-Navy AN
Army-Navy Munitions Board ANMB
Army-Navy-Air Force ANAF
Arnold Arn.
aromatic ar.
aromatic radical *chemistry* Ar
arpeggio *music* arp
arranged or **arranged by** *music* arr. or Arr.
arrangement arrgt.
arrangement or **arrangements** arr.

arranger *music* arr. or Arr.
arrestor arr.
arrival **1** Ar **2** ar. **3** arr. or ARR
arrival notice *shipping* **1** a.n. **2** AN or A.N.
arrive **1** A **2** a **3** Ar **4** ar. **5** arr. or ARR
arrive at a
arrived arr. or ARR
arrives at A
Arrow Sge (constellation)
arsenic As
Art and Antique Dealers League of America AADLA
art and mechanical A & M
Art Class Teacher's Certificate A.C.T.C.
Art Collectors Club of America ACCA
Art Dealers Association of America A.D.A.A. or ADAA
Art Master's Certificate AMC or A.M.C.
arterial blood pressure ABP
arteriosclerotic heart disease AHD
arteriovenous AV or A-V
arteriovenous malformation AVM
artery *medicine* art.
arthrogryposis multiplex congenita AMC
Arthur **1** Art. **2** Arth.
Arthurian Arth.
article **1** a **2** Art. **3** art.
Article Numbering Association *British* ANA
articles arts.
Articles of War *military* AW
artificial art.
artificial insemination AI
artificial insemination by donor AID
artificial insemination by husband AIH
artificial intelligence AI
artificial rupture of the membrane *medicine* ARM
artillery **1** Art. **2** art. **3** Arty. or arty.
artist art.
artist(s) in residence AIR or A.I.R.
artists and repertory A&R or A. & R. or a. and r.
Artists Equity Fund AEF
Arts Council of Great Britain AC or A.C.
Arts Council of Great Britain. ACGB or A.C.G.B. (*OUP:* ACGB)
Arts Councils of America ACA or A.C.A.
aryl *chemistry* Ar
aryl hydrocarbon hydroxylase AHH
as above **1** *Latin* a u.s. **b** ut sup. **2** *music* co.sa.
as amended by aaby
as before ab or a.b.
as below *Latin* u.i.
as desired **1** *music, pharmaceutics* ad lib. **2** *music* ad libit.
as directed **1** m. dict. **2** *pharmaceutics* **a** la or l.a. **b** mor. dict. **c** mp **d** u.d. **e** ut dict.
as if said *Latin* q.d.
as interest may appear AIMA or a.i.m.a.
as loud as possible *music* fff
as much as necessary *pharmaceutics* **1** q.s. **2** quant. suff.
as much as you please *pharmaceutics* **1** ql or q.l. or q.lib. **2** qp or q.p. or q.pl.
as much as you wish *pharmaceutics* q.v.
as needed *medicine, pharmaceutics* PRN or p.r.n. or P.R.N.
as prescribed *pharmaceutics* **1** mod. praes. **2** mp

as soon as possible **1** ASAP or asap (*OUP:* a.s.a.p.) **2** *British* ASP
as stated *law* AS
as the acts show *law* t.a.
as the book opens a.a.l.
as their respective interests may appear *law* a.t.r.i.m.a.
As You Like It A.Y.L. or A.Y.L.I. (*MLA:* AYL)
asbestos **1** a **2** asb.
ascendance-submission *psychology* AS or A-S
ascending reticular activating system ARAS
Ascheim-Zondek test A-Z test
ascorbic acid factor AAF
Asia As or As. (*OUP:* As.)
Asian As or As. (*OUP:* As.)
Asian and Pacific Council ASPAC or Aspac
Asian Development Bank ADB or A.D.B.
Asian Federation of Library Associations AFLA or A.F.L.A.
Asian-Pacific Economic Cooperation Council Apec
Asiatic As or As. (*OUP:* As.)
asparagine **1** ASN or asn **2** Asp.N or asp.N
aspartate aminotransferase AST
aspartic acid asp. or Asp
aspect ratio **1** *aeronautics* A **2** *electronics, aeronautics* AR
asphalt asph.
aspirin, phenacetin, caffeine *medicine* APC
assault rifle AK
assay ton a.t.
Assembly Ass.
assembly **1** asm. **2** assy. or ass'y
assembly and repair A&R
Assembly Bill AB
Assembly District AD
assented asstd.
assessed assd.
assessment **1** assmt. **2** asst.
assessment paid a.p.
assigned **1** asgd. **2** assd. **3** assnd.
assignment asgmt.
assignment control number ACN
assimilate or **assimilated** assim.
assist *sports* **1** a **2** A or A.
assistant **1** A or A. **2** Ass. or ass. **3** asst. or Asst. or Ass't.
Assistant Adjutant General AAG
Assistant Attorney General AAG or A.A.G.
Assistant Chaplain-General A.C.G.
Assistant Chief of Naval Operations ACNO
Assistant Chief of Staff **1** ACOFS or AC of S **2** ACOS **3** ACS
Assistant Director AD or A.D.
Assistant Director General ADG or A.D.G.
Assistant Director of Medical Services A.D.M.S.
Assistant Director of Nursing ADN
Assistant District Attorney ADA
Assistant District Officer A.D.O. or ADO
assistant instructor AI
Assistant Paymaster A.P.M. APM
Assistant Postmaster General A.P.M.G.
Assistant Provost Marshal A.P.M.
Assistant Scientific Officer ASO
Assistant Secretary AS or A.S.
assisted take-off ATO

assisted *or* assisted by asstd.
associate Assoc. *or* assoc.
Associate Computer Professional ACP
Associate Director AD *or* A.D.
Associate Engraver of the Royal Academy AERA *or* A.E.R.A.
Associate Fellow AF *or* A.F.
Associate Fellow of the Royal Aeronautical Society A.F.R.Ae.S.
Associate in Accounting AA *or* A.A.
Associate in Aeronautical Engineering A.Ae.E.
Associate in Applied Science AAS
Associate in Arts AA *or* A.A.
Associate in Arts in Home Economics A.A.H.E.
Associate in Business Administration ABA *or* A.B.A.
Associate in Education 1 A Ed *or* A. Ed. **2** AE *or* A.E.
Associate in Electrical Technology A.E.T.
Associate in Engineering 1 A. Eng. **2** AE *or* A.E.
Associate in Fine Arts AFA *or* A.F.A.
Associate in General Education AGE *or* A.G.E.
Associate in General Studies AGS *or* A.G.S.
Associate in Home Economics A.H.E.
Associate in Journalism AJ
Associate in Medical Technology AMT *or* A.M.T.
Associate in Nursing AN *or* A.N.
Associate in Public Adminisration APA *or* A.P.A.
Associate in Science 1 A.Sc. **2** AS *or* A.S. **3** Assoc. Sc.
associate instructor AI
Associate Justice AJ *or* A.J.
Associate Member AM *or* A.M.
Associate Member of the Institute of Marine Engineers *British* A.M.I.Mar.E.
Associate Member of the Institution of Automobile Engineers *British* A.M.I.A.E.
Associate Member of the Institution of Chemical Engineers *British* A.M.I.C.E. *or* A.M.I.Chem.E.
Associate Member of the Institution of Civil Engineers *British* A.M.I.C.E.
Associate Member of the Institution of Electrical Engineers A.M.I.E.E.
Associate Member of the Institution of Mechanical Engineers A.M.I.Mech.E.
Associate Member of the Institution of Mining Engineers *British* A.M.I.Min.E.
Associate of Normal School of Science A.N.S.S.
Associate of the American Antiquarian Society AAAS
Associate of the American Guild of Organists A.A.G.O.
Associate of the Association of Certified and Corporate Accountants AACCA *or* A.A.C.C.A.
Associate of the Auctioneers' and Estate Agents' Institute AAI *or* A.A.I.
Associate of the British Archaeological Association ABA *or* A.B.A.

Associate of the British Association of Accountants and Auditors A.B.A.A. *or* ABAA
Associate of the Building Societies Institute ABS *or* A.B.S.
Associate of the Canadian College of Organists A.C.C.O.
Associate of the Chartered Institute of Secretaries ACIS *or* A.C.I.S.
Associate of the City and Guilds of London Institute A.C.G.I.
Associate of the Corporation of Certified Secretaries A.C.C.S.
Associate of the Faculty of Actuaries AFA
Associate of the Faculty of Architects and Surveyors A.F.A.S.
Associate of the Guildhall School of Music A.G.S.M.
Associate of the Incorporated Secretaries Association A.I.S.A. *or* AISA
Associate of the Incorporated Society of Auctioneers and Landed Property Agents A.A.L.P.A.
Associate of the Institute of Actuaries AIA *or* A.I.A.
Associate of the Institute of Arbitrators A.I. Arb.
Associate of the Institute of British Decorators A.I.B.D.
Associate of the Institute of Chartered Accountants ACA
Associate of the Institute of Chartered Shipbrokers A.I.C.S.
Associate of the Institute of Company Accountants A.I.A.C. *or* AIAC
Associate of the Institute of Cost and Management Accountants ACMA
Associate of the Institute of Marine Engineers A.I.Mar.E.
Associate of the Institute of Mechanical Engineers *British* A.I.M.E. *or* A.I.Mech.E.
Associate of the Institute of Municipal Treasurers and Accountants A.I.M.T.A. *or* AIMTA
Associate of the Institute of Physics *British* A.I.P. *or* A.Inst.P.
Associate of the Institution of Automobile Engineers A.I.A.E.
Associate of the Institution of Certified Public Accountants ACPA
Associate of the Institution of Civil Engineers A.I.C.E. *or* AICE
Associate of the Institution of Marine Engineers A.I.M.E.
Associate of the Institution of Mining and Metallurgy *British* A.I.M.E.
Associate of the Institution of Mining Engineers *British* A.I.M.E.
Associate of the Institution of Naval Architects AINA *or* A.I.N.A.
Associate of the Library Association *British* ALA *or* A.L.A.
Associate of the Linnean Society ALS *or* A.L.S.
Associate of the London College of Music ALCM *or* A.L.C.M.
Associate of the National Academy of Design ANA *or* A.N.A.

Associate of the New Zealand Institute of Architects A.N.Z.I.A. *or* ANZIA
Associate of the New Zealand Institute of Chemistry A.N.Z.I.C. *or* ANZIC
Associate of the New Zealand Library Association A.N.Z.L.A. *or* ANZLA
Associate of the Royal Academy ARA *or* A.R.A.
Associate of the Royal Academy of Dancing A.R.A.D. *or* ARAD
Associate of the Royal Academy of Music A.R.A.M. *or* ARAM
Associate of the Royal Aeronautical Society A.R.Ae.S. *or* ARAeS
Associate of the Royal Agricultural College A.R.A.C. *or* ARAC
Associate of the Royal Astronomical Society ARAS *or* A.R.A.S.
Associate of the Royal Australian Chemical Institute A.R.A.C.I. *or* ARACI
Associate of the Royal Australian Institute of Architects A.R.A.I.A. *or* ARAIA
Associate of the Royal Canadian Academy of Arts ARCA *or* A.R.C.A.
Associate of the Royal College of Art ARCA *or* A.R.C.A.
Associate of the Royal College of Music A.R.C.M. *or* ARCM
Associate of the Royal College of Organists A.R.C.O. *or* ARCO
Associate of the Royal College of Science A.R.C.S. *or* ARCS
Associate of the Royal College of Surgeons A.R.C.S. *or* ARCS
Associate of the Royal Hibernian Academy A.R.H.A. *or* ARHA
Associate of the Royal Institute of British Architects A.R.I.B.A. *or* ARIBA
Associate of the Royal Institute of Chartered Surveyors A.R.I.C.S. *or* ARICS
Associate of the Royal Institute of Chemistry A.R.I.C. *or* ARIC
Associate of the Royal Manchester College of Music A.R.M.C.M. *or* ARMCM
Associate of the Royal Photographic Society ARPS *or* A.R.P.S.
Associate of the Royal Red Cross A.R.R.C. *or* ARRC
Associate of the Royal Scottish Academy A.R.S.A. *or* ARSA
Associate of the Royal Scottish Society of Painting in Water Colours A.R.S.W. *or* ARSW
Associate of the Royal Society of Arts A.R.S.A. *or* ARSA
Associate of the Royal Society of British Artists A.R.B.A. *or* ARBA
Associate of the Royal Society of British Sculptors A.R.B.S. *or* ARBS
Associate of the Royal Society of Miniature Painters A.R.M.S. *or* ARMS
Associate of the Royal Society of Painter-Etchers and Engravers A.R.E *or* ARE
Associate of the Royal Society of Painters in Water Colours A.R.W.S. *or* ARWS
Associate of the Society of Art Masters A.S.A.M.

Associate of the Society of Engineers *British* ASE *or* A.S.E.

Associate of the Society of Incorporated Accountants and Auditors A.S.A.A. *or* ASAA

Associate of Theological Study ATS

Associate of Trinity College of Music, London A.T.C.L.

Associate Presbyterian AP

Associate Surveyor Member of the Incorporated Association of Architects and Surveyors A.I.A.S.

associated 1 Assoc. *or* assoc. **2** asstd.

Associated Actors and Artists of America AAAA

Associated Booksellers of Great Britain and Ireland A.B.G.B.I.

Associated British Cinemas ABC

Associated Country Women of the World A.C.W.W. *or* ACWW

Associated Credit Bureaus of America ACB of A

Associated Electrical Industries AEI

Associated Examining Board AEB *or* A.E.B.

Associated Film Distribution AFD

Associated National Press Agency of Italy ANSA

Associated Photographers International API

Associated Press AP *or* AP

Associated Reformed Presbyterian ARP *or* A.R.P.

Associated Society of Locomotive Engineers and Firemen A.S.L.E.F.

Associated Writing Programs AWP

Association Ass.

association 1 Assn. *or* assn. **2** Assoc. *or* assoc.

Association Football Club AFC

Association for Asian Studies AAS

Association for Childhood Education International A.C.E.I.

Association for Children with Learning Disabilities ACLD

Association for Computational Linguistics ACL

Association for Computers and the Humanities ACH

Association for Computing Machinery ACM

Association for Education in Journalism AEJ

Association for Educational Communications and Technology AECT

Association for Educational Data Systems AEDS

Association for Information Management AIM

Association for Library Service to Children ALSC

Association for Literary and Linguistic Computing ALLC

Association for Science Education *British* ASE

Association for Supervision and Curriculum Development ASCD

Association for Systems Management ASM

Association for the Advancement of American Art AAAA *or* A.A.A.A.

Association for the Advancement of Creative Musicians AACM

Association for the Education of Teachers in Science AETS

Association for the Study of Afro-American Life and History ASALH

Association for the Taxonomic Study of African Tropical Flora AETFAT

Association for Women in Computing AWC

Association of Advertising Men and Women AAMW

Association of Air Transport Unions AATU

Association of American Colleges AAC *or* A.A.C.

Association of American Editorial Cartoonists AAEC

Association of American Foreign Service Women AAFSW

Association of American Geographers AAG *or* A.A.G.

Association of American Indian Affairs AAIA

Association of American Law Schools AALS *or* A.A.L.S.

Association of American Library Schools AALS *or* A.A.L.S.

Association of American Medical Colleges AAMC

Association of American Physicians AAP *or* A.A.P.

Association of American Publishers AAP

Association of American Railroads AAR *or* A.A.R.

Association of American Ship Owners AASO

Association of American Steel Manufacturers AASM

Association of American Universities AAU

Association of American Veterinary Medical Colleges AAVMC

Association of Applied Biologists AAB

Association of Average Adjusters of the United States AAAUS

Association of British Archaeologists ABA *or* A.B.A.

Association of British Chambers of Commerce ABCC *or* A.B.C.C.

Association of British Chemical Manufacturers A.B.C.M.

Association of British Science Writers A.B.S.W.

Association of British Travel Agents ABTA *or* Abta

Association of Broadcasting Staff ABS

Association of Canadian Advertisers ACA

Association of Canadian Manufacturers ACM

Association of Canadian Television and Radio Artists ACTRA

Association of Canadian University Teachers of English ACUTE

Association of Casualty Accountants and Statisticians ACAS

Association of Casualty and Surety Companies A.C.S.C.

Association of Catholic Trade Unions ACTU *or* A.C.T.U.

Association of Certified and Corporate Accountants ACCA *or* A.C.C.A.

Association of Chief Officers of Police A.C.O.P.

Association of Choral Conductors ACC

Association of Cinematograph and Television Technicians A.C.T.T.

Association of Classroom Teachers ACT

Association of Clinical Pathologists ACP *or* A.C.P.

Association of Clinical Scientists ACS *or* A.C.S.

Association of College Admission Counselors. ACAC

Association of College and Research Libraries ACRL

Association of College and University Housing Officers A.C.U.H.O.

Association of College Honor Societies ACHS *or* A.C.H.S.

Association of College Unions ACU *or* A.C.U.

Association of Colleges and Universities AC and U

Association of Collegiate Schools of Architecture ACSA

Association of Collegiate Schools of Nursing A.C.S.N. *or* ACSN

Association of Commonwealth Universities ACU *or* A.C.U.

Association of Computer Programmers and Analysts ACPA

Association of Consulting Chemists and Chemical Engineers ACCCE

Association of Consulting Engineers ACE *or* A.C.E.

Association of Consulting Management Engineers ACME

Association of Correctional Psychologists ACP *or* A.C.P.

Association of Correctors of the Press ACP

Association of County Councils ACC

Association of Customers' Brokers ACB

Association of Data Processing Service Organizations ADAPSO

Association of Departments of English ADE

Association of Departments of Foreign Languages ADFL

Association of Education Committees AEC *or* A.E.C.

Association of Food and Drug Officials of the United States AFDOUS

Association of General Contractors AGC

Association of Information Systems Professionals AISP

Association of Intercollegiate Athletics for Women AIAW

Association of International Advertising Agencies AIAA

Association of Iron and Steel Engineers AISE *or* A.I.S.E.

Association of Labor-Management Administrators and Consultants on Alcoholism ALMACA

Association of Lunar and Planetary Observers A.L.P.O. *or* ALPO

Association of Manufacturers and Suppliers for the Graphic Arts AMSGA

Association of Motion Picture and Television Producers AMPTP

Association of National Advertisers ANA

Association of Newspaper Classified Advertising Managers ANCAM

Association of Operating Room Nurses AORN

Association of Polytechnic Teachers APT

Association of Private Hospitals APH

Association of Radio Broadcasters ARB

Association of Research Libraries ARL or A.R.L.

Association of Scientific Workers 1 ASW or A.S.W. 2 *British* AScW or A.Sc.W.

Association of South East Asian Nations ASEAN

Association of State Colleges and Universities ASCU or A.S.C.U.

Association of Supervisory Staffs, Executives, and Technicians ASSET or A.S.S.E.T.

Association of Teachers of Japanese ATJ

Association of Teachers of Mathematics ATM or A.T.M.

Association of Teachers of Russian ATR

Association of the American Antiquarian Society A.A.S.S.

Association of the British Pharmaceutical Industry A.B.P.I.

Association of the Universities of the British Commonwealth A.U.B.C.

Association of Theater Press Agents and Managers ATPAM

Association of Universities for Research in Astronomy AURA

Association of University Teachers AUT or A.U.T.

Association of West European Shipbuilders AWES

association-sensation *psychology* AS or A/S

assorted 1 asst. 2 asstd.

assortment asmt.

assumed position *astronomy, navigation* AP

assumption-based truth maintenance system ATMS

assured assd.

Assyria Assyr.

Assyrian Assyr.

astatine At

astigmatism As

astragal *architecture, medicine* A

astrograph mean time *astronomy* AMT

astrologer astrol.

astrological astrol.

astrology astrol.

astronaut maneuvering unit AMU

astronautics astro.

astronomer 1 astr. 2 astron.

astronomical 1 astr. 2 astron.

Astronomical Association Catalogs *German* AGK

astronomical great circle course ACC

Astronomical Society of the Pacific ASP or A.S.P.

astronomical unit 1 a.u. 2 AU or A.U.

astronomy 1 astr. 2 astron.

astrophysical astrophys.

astrophysics astrophys.

asymmetric 1 as 2 asym. 3 *chemistry* a

asymmetrical 1 asym. 2 *chemistry* u

at 1 @ 2 a

at bat *baseball* 1 ab or a.b. 2 AB or AB. 3 B or B.

at bedtime *pharmaceutics* 1 h.s. 2 hd or h.d.

at or to the end af or a.f.

at own risk AOR

at pleasure 1 *music, pharmaceutics* ad lib. 2 *music* ad libit.

at sight *commerce* 1 as or a.s. 2 AS or A/S

at the age of, aged 1 ae. 2 aet. 3 aetat.

at the direction of the President DP

at the outset *Latin* in lim.

at the place quoted *German* a.a.O. (*MLA:* not acceptable)

at the suit of *law* 1 ads. 2 ATS 3 ats or ats.

at the year ad an.

at this time *Latin* ht or h.t.

at or below AOB

at or on this word a.h.v.

athlete ath.

Athletic Association of Western Universities AAWU

Athletic Club AC

Athletic Director AD

athletics ath.

Atlanta F (in the Federal Reserve system)

Atlantic Atl.

Atlantic Coast Conference (collegiate athletic organization) ACC

Atlantic Daylight Time ADT or A.D.T. or a.d.t.

Atlantic Development Group for Latin America ADELA

Atlantic Merchant Vessel Reporting System AMVER or AMVERS

Atlantic Missile Range AMR

Atlantic Nuclear Force ANF

Atlantic Oceanographic Laboratory or Laboratories AOL

Atlantic Reporter law Atl.

Atlantic Standard Time AST or A.S.T. or a.s.t.

Atlantic Time 1 AT or A.T. 2 At or A.t.

Atlantic to the Urals ATTU

Atlantic Undersea Test and Evaluation Center AUTEC

atmosphere 1 at. 2 atmos. 3 *physics, meteorology* a

atmosphere temperature absolute ata

atmosphere or atmospheres atm. or atm

atmospheric 1 at. 2 atm.

atmospherics Xs or X's

atomic 1 A 2 a 3 at.

atomic absorption spectrometry AAS

Atomic Bomb Casualty Commission ABCC

atomic emission spectroscopy AES

atomic energy AE

Atomic Energy Authority of Great Britain AEA or A.E.A.

Atomic Energy Detection System AEDS

Atomic Energy Establishment AEE or A.E.E.

Atomic Energy of Canada, Limited AECL

Atomic Energy Research Establishment AERE

atomic fission A

atomic force microscopy AFM

atomic mass number A

atomic mass unit AMU or A.M.U. or amu

atomic number 1 at. no. or At. No. 2 *physics* Z

atomic power AP

atomic resolution microscope ARM

Atomic Safety and Licensing Board ASLB

atomic shell of 18 maximum electrons per shell M

atomic shell of 32 maximum electrons per shell N

atomic shell of 50 maximum electrons per shell O

atomic shell of 72 maximum electrons per shell P

atomic shell of 98 electrons per shell Q

atomic shell of eight maximum electrons per shell L

atomic shell of two maximum electrons per shell K

Atomic Time AT

atomic vapor laser isotope separation AVLIS

atomic volume 1 at. vol. 2 av or a.v.

Atomic Weapons Research Establishment AWRE

atomic weight 1 A 2 a 3 at. wt. 4 aw 5 AW or A.W. 6 *physics, chemistry* M

atomic weight unit AWU or awu or A.W.U.

atomic, biological, and chemical ABC

atomic, molecular, and optical *physics* AMO

atrial natriuretic factor ANF

atrial natriuretic peptide ANP

atrioventricular AV or A-V

attach atch.

attach or attached att.

attaché att. or Att.

attachment atch.

Attack Carrier Strike Force ACSF

attack, decay, sustain, release ADSR

attainment age AA

attainment quotient *education* AQ or A.Q.

attainment ratio *education* AR or A.R.

attendance *sports* A

attention 1 att. 2 atten. 3 attn. or Attn. or ATTN (*OUP:* attn.)

attention deficit disorder ADD

attention deficit hyperactive disorder ADHD

attention display AD

attenuation constant *acoustics* A

attitude control system ACS

attitude direction indicator ADI

atto- a

attorney 1 At 2 at. 3 att. or Att. 4 atty. or Atty.

Attorney General AG or A.G. or A-G (*OUP:* A.-G.)

attorney general 1 Att. Gen. (*OUP:* Att.-Gen.) 2 Atty. Gen.

Attorney General's Opinion AGO

attribute attrib. or Attrib. (*MLA:* attrib.)

attributed to attrib. or Attrib. (*MLA:* attrib.)

attributive or attributively *grammar* attrib.

attributively *grammar* attrib.

Auctioneers' and Estate Agents' Institute AI or A.I.

audible aud.

Audio Engineering Society AES

audio frequency 1 AF or A-F (*GPO, OUP:* AF) 2 af or a.f. or a-f

audio frequency modulation AFM

audio media integration standard AMIS

audio response unit *computers* ARU

audiovisual AV or A-V or A/V

audit 1 a 2 aud.

Audit Bureau of Circulation ABC
auditor 1 a **2** aud. or Aud.
Auditor General AG or A.G.
Auger electron spectroscopy AES
augmentative grammar aug. or augm.
augmented aug. or augm.
August 1 A **2** Ag or Ag. **3** Au or Au. **4** Aug. or Aug
August and February A & F
August, November, February, May commerce A.N.F.M.
Augustine Aug. or Aug
Augustinians of the Assumption AA
Augustus Aug. or Aug
aurin tricarboxylic acid ATA
auscultation and percussion A & P
Australasia 1 Austl. **2** Austral.
Australasian 1 Austl. **2** Austral.
Australasian Universities Modern Language Association AUMLA
Australia 1 Aus. **2** Aust. **3** Austl. **4** Austr. **5** Austral.
Australia and New Zealand Army Corps ANZAC
Australia Party AP or A.P.
Australia, New Zealand, and Malaysia ANZAM or Anzam
Australia, New Zealand, and United Kingdom ANZUK
Australia-New Zealand Closer Economic Relations Trade Agreement ANZCERTA
Australian 1 A **2** Aust. **3** Austl. **4** Austr. **5** Austral.
Australian Academy of Science AAS
Australian and New Zealand Association for the Advancement of Science ANZAAS or A.N.Z.A.A.S.
Australian Antarctic Territory A.A.T.
Australian Army Medical Corps AAMC
Australian Associated Press AAP or A.A.P.
Australian Association for the United Nations AAUN
Australian Atomic Energy Commission A.A.E.C.
Australian Automobile Association AAA
Australian Book Publishers Association ABPA
Australian Broadcasting Commission ABC
Australian Broadcasting Corporation ABC
Australian Broadcasting Tribunal ABT
Australian Capital Territory ACT or A.C.T.
Australian College of Dentistry ACD
Australian College of Education ACE
Australian Commonwealth Military Forces A.C.M.F.
Australian Council for Educational Research ACER
Australian Council of Trade Unions ACTU
Australian Country Party ACP
Australian Defence Force Academy ADFA
Australian Democratic Party ADP
Australian Democrats AD
Australian Dental Association ADA or A.D.A.
Australian Department of Agriculture ADA or A.D.A.
Australian Federation of Modern Language Teachers Association A.F.M.L.T.A.

Australian Federation of Travel Agents A.F.T.A. or AFTA
Australian Industry Development Corporation AIDC
Australian Koala Foundation AKF
Australian Labor Party ALP or A.L.P.
Australian Medical Association AMA
Australian Military Forces A.M.F.
Australian National Airways ANA or A.N.A.
Australian National Antarctic Research Expeditions ANARE
Australian National Line ANL
Australian National University A.N.U. or ANU
Australian Natives' Association ANA or A.N.A.
Australian Performing Rights Association APRA or Apra
Australian Radiation Laboratory ARL
Australian Red Cross Society A.R.C.S. or ARCS
Australian Regular Army ARA
Australian Retailers Association ARA
Australian Secret Intelligence Service ASIS
Australian Security Intelligence Organization ASIO
Australian Telecommunications Satellite AUSSAT
Australian Union of Students AUS or A.U.S.
Australian Universities Commission A.U.C. or AUC
Australian Veterinary Association AVA or A.V.A.
Australian Wheat Marketing Board AWB
Australian Wine Research Institute AWRI
Australian Wool Board AWB
Australian Wool Corporation AWC
Australian Workers' Union AWU
Australian-New Zealand Bank Group ANZ
Austria Aust.
Austria, Austrian Aus.
Austrian Aust.
Austrian Cooperative Press Agency APA
Austrian Green Party VGO or VGÖ
Austrian Socialist Party SPO or SPÖ
authentic auth.
author 1 AU **2** Au or Au. or au **3** Aut. **4** aut. **5** auth. or Auth. **6** cataloging, printing a
author's alteration 1 AA or A.A. **2** aa or a.a.
author's correction AC or A.C.
Author's League of America ALA or A.L.A.
author's proof 1 a.p. **2** AP
authority auth. or Auth.
authority for purchase AFP or afp
authority to pay A/P
authority to purchase A/P
authorized auth. or Auth.
authorized pickup shipping APU
authorized selling agent ASR
authorized version AV or A.V.
Authorized Version of the Bible AV or A.V.
auto-oxidation inhibitor AI
autocrine motility factor A.M.F.
autofocus AF
autograph card signed 1 ACS **2** acs or a.c.s.
autograph document 1 a.d. **2** AD
autograph document signed ADS or A.D.S. or a.d.s.
autograph letter al or a.l.

autograph letter signed 1 ALS or A.L.S. **2** a.l.s. (MLA: als)
autograph manuscript signed AMS or A.M.S. or a.m.s.
autograph note 1 a.n. **2** AN or A.N.
autograph note signed 1 a.n.s. **2** ANS
autograph or **autographed 1** aut. **2** autog.
autoimmune hemolytic anemia AIHA
automated camera effects system ACES
automated clearing house ACH
Automated Library Program ALP or A.L.P.
automated or **automatic batch mixing** ABM
automated tracking while scanning ATWS
automated trading system ATS
automatic 1 a **2** aut. **3** auto.
automatic amplitude control AAC
automatic approach control AAC
automatic brightness control ABC
automatic broadcast ABCST
automatic call distribution ACD
automatic calling unit 1 ACU **2** electronics ACU
Automatic Car Identification ACI
automatic carrier landing system ACL
automatic celestial navigation ACN
automatic checkout and readiness equipment ACRE
automatic checkout and recording network ACORN
automatic checkout equipment 1 ACE **2** ACOE
Automatic Chemical Biological Warning System ACBWS
automatic circuit exchange electronics ACE
Automatic Computer-Controlled Electronic Scanning System ACCESS
automatic contrast or **color control** electronics ACC
automatic credit transfer finance ACT
automatic data exchange ADX
automatic data interchange system ADIS
automatic data processing ADP
automatic data processing center ADPC
automatic data processing equipment ADPE
automatic data processing system ADPS
automatic data transmission ADT
automatic debit transfer ADT
automatic dialing recorded message program ADRMP
automatic dialogue replacement ADR
automatic digital computer ADC
automatic direction finder ADF
automatic door seal ADS
automatic fine tuning AFT or aft
automatic flight control AFC
Automatic Flight Control System AFCS
automatic frequency control AFC or A.F.C. or afc
automatic gain control electronics AGC or agc
automatic gain stabilization electronics AGS
automatic ground-controlled approach AGCA
Automatic Ground-to-Air Communications System AGACS
automatic instrument landing approach system AILAS
automatic letter facer British ALF
automatic level control ALC

Automatic Light Aircraft Readiness Monitor ALARM
automatic magnetic guidance AMG
Automatic Meteorological Observation System or **Station** AMOS
automatic mixture control AMC
automatic noise limiter ANL or anl
automatic phase control apc
automatic picture transmission APT
automatic positioning of telemetering antenna APOTA
Automatic Range Tracking Unit ARTU
automatic request for repetition *computers* ARQ
Automatic Retailers of America ARA
automatic rifle AK
automatic sending and receiving ASR
automatic sprinkler AS
automatic terrain recognition and navigation guidance system ATRAN
Automatic Test Equipment ATE
automatic train control ATC
automatic train operation ATO
automatic train stop ATS
automatic train supervision ATS
automatic transition network *communications* ATN
automatic transmission AT or A/T
automatic unattended detection inspection transmitter AUDIT
automatic vehicle monitoring AVM
automatic volume control *electricity* AVC or avc or a.v.c.
automatic volume expansion *electronics* AVE or ave
automatic weapons *military* AW
automatic or **automated teller machine** ATM
automatic-landing system ALS
automatically programmed tool APT

automobile auto.
Automobile Association AA
automobile club AC
Automobile Club de France ACF or A.C.F.
Automobile Club of Great Britain and Ireland A.C.G.B.I. or ACGBI
Automobile Club of Italy ACI or A.C.I.
Automobile Competition Committee for the United States ACCUS
Automobile Legal Association ALA
Automobile Manufacturers Association AMA
Automobile Racing Club of America ARCA
automotive auto.
autonomic nervous system 1 a.n.s. **2** ANS
Autonomous Aut.
auxiliary aux. or auxil. (*MLA:* aux.)
Auxiliary Air Force AAF
Auxiliary Fire Service AFS or A.F.S.
auxiliary power supply aps
auxiliary power unit APU
auxiliary switch closed ASC or asc
auxiliary switch open ASO or aso
auxiliary verb v. aux.
available avail. or aval.
available but not installed abni
available for reassignment *military* AVFR
available supply rate ASR
Avenue 1 Av. **2** AVE or Ave. or ave. (*GPO, NYT, OUP:* Ave.)
avenue av or av.
average 1 A **2** av or av. (*CSM, OUP:* av.) **3** AVE or ave. **4** aver. **5** avg. **6** C
average audience *advertising* AA
average daily attendance ADA
average daily gain ADG
average daily membership ADM
average daily patient load ADPL
average daily traffic ADT

average deviation 1 AD or A.D. **2** *statistics* ad
average freight rate assessment *commerce* AFRA
average length av. l.
average outgoing quality *commerce* AOQ
average quality *Latin* tal. qual.
average quarter hour AQH
average sample number ASN or asn
average value AV
average variability AV
average weekly wage *law* AWW
Avestan Av.
avian leukemia virus ALV
aviation 1 a **2** avn. or Avn.
aviation cadet AC
aviation carrier turbine fuel AVCAT or Avcat
aviation classification test ACT
aviation gasoline *military* AVGAS or avgas
aviation medicine AM or A.M.
Aviation Weather Service AWS
aviator a
Avogadro's number Nor N or N_A
avoid verbal orders AVO
avoirdupois 1 av or av. **2** avdp. **3** avoir.
awaiting action of higher authority *military* AAHA
axial pressure angle apa
axiom ax.
axis ax. or Ax.
Ayrshire, Scotland Ayr.
Azerbaijani Azerb.
azidothymidine AZT
azimuth 1 a **2** AZ **3** az **4** Az. or Az
azimuth angle *surveying* **1** Z **2** z
azimuth error indicator AEI
Azores Az. or Az
azure az or az. (*OUP:* az.)
azure wove AW or A.W.

B'nai B'rith BB or B.B.
baby hamster kidney cells BHK
Babylonian Bab.
Bach, J. S., index of BWV
bachelor Bach. or bach.
Bachelor of Accounting B.Acc.
Bachelor of Aeronautical and Astronautical Engineering BAAE or B.A.A.E.
Bachelor of Aeronautical Engineering 1 B.A.E. or BAE **2** B.Ae.E. or BAeE
Bachelor of Agricultural Engineering B.Eng.A.
Bachelor of Agricultural Science 1 B.A.Sc. **2** B.Agr.Sc. or B.Ag.Sc. or B.Ag.Sci. **3** BAS or B.A.S.

Bachelor of Agriculture 1 B.Ag. or BAg **2** B.Agr.
Bachelor of Applied Arts 1 B.App. Arts **2** BAA or B.A.A.
Bachelor of Applied Mathematics BAM or B.A.M.
Bachelor of Applied Science 1 B.A.Sc. **2** B.App.Sc. **3** B.Sc.App. **4** BAS or B.A.S.
Bachelor of Architectural Engineering B.A.E. or BAE
Bachelor of Architecture 1 B.Ar. **2** B.Arch.
Bachelor of Art and Architecture BAA or B.A.A.
Bachelor of Arts 1 AB or A.B. (*GPO, NYT, CSM:* A.B.; *MLA, OUP:* AB) **2** BA or B.A. (*MLA, OUP:* BA; *CSM:* B.A.)
Bachelor of Arts and Sciences BAS or B.A.S.
Bachelor of Arts in Economics B.A.Econ. or BAEcon
Bachelor of Arts in Education 1 A.B.Ed. **2** B.A.E. or BAE **3** B.A.Ed. or BAEd
Bachelor of Arts in Journalism B.A.J. or B.A.Jour.

Bachelor of Arts in Library Science A.B.L.S.
Bachelor of Arts in Music BAM
Bachelor of Arts in Music Education B.A.Mus.Ed.
Bachelor of Arts in Theology B.A. Theol.
Bachelor of Business Administration BBA or B.B.A.
Bachelor of Business Education B.B.E. or BBE
Bachelor of Business Science BBS or B.B.S.
Bachelor of Business Studies BBS or B.B.S.
Bachelor of Canon Law 1 B.C.L. or BCL **2** J.C.B. or JCB
Bachelor of Chemical Engineering 1 B.C.E. or BCE **2** B.Ch.E. or BChE
Bachelor of Chemical Science BCS or B.C.S.
Bachelor of Chemistry BC or B.C.
Bachelor of Christian Science CSB or C.S.B.
Bachelor of Civil and Canon Law B.U.J. or BUJ
Bachelor of Civil Engineering B.C.E. or BCE
Bachelor of Civil Law 1 B.C.L. or BCL (*CSM:* B.C.L.; *OUP:* BCL) **2** J.C.B. or JCB

Bachelor of Commerce 1 B.Comm. or B.Com. (*CSM, OUP:* B.Com.) **2** BC or B.C.
Bachelor of Commerce and Administration BCA or B.C.A.
Bachelor of Commercial Science 1 B.Com.Sc. **2** BCS or B.C.S.
Bachelor of Dental Service B.D.Sc. or BDSc.
Bachelor of Dental Surgery 1 B.Ch.D. or BChD **2** BDS or B.D.S.
Bachelor of Divinity 1 BD or B.D. (*CSM:* B.D.; *OUP:* BD) **2** DB or D.B.
Bachelor of Domestic Arts ADB or A.D.B.
Bachelor of Dramatic Art BDA or B.D.A.
Bachelor of Economics B.Ec.
Bachelor of Education 1 B. Ed. or BEd (*CSM, OUP:* B. Ed.) **2** B.E. or BE **3** Ed.B.
Bachelor of Electrical Engineering B.E.E. or BEE
Bachelor of Engineering 1 B.A.I. or BAI **2** B.E. or BE (*CSM:* B.E.; *OUP:* BE, B.Eng., or B.A.I.) **3** B.Eng. or BEng
Bachelor of Engineering of Mines BEM or B.E.M.
Bachelor of Engineering Science BES or B.E.S.
Bachelor of Finance BF or B.F.
Bachelor of Fine Arts B.F.A. or BFA (*CSM:* B.F.A.)
Bachelor of Forestry BF or B.F. (*CSM:* B.F.)
Bachelor of Forestry Engineering B.F.E. or BFE (*CSM:* B.F.E.)
Bachelor of Hebrew Letters or Literature B.H.L. or BHL
Bachelor of Home Economics B.H.Ec. or BHEc
Bachelor of Horticultural Science B.Hort.Sc.
Bachelor of Horticulture B.Hort.
Bachelor of Household or **Home Science** B.H.Sc. (*CSM:* B.H.S. or B.H.Sc.)
Bachelor of Humanities BH or B.H.
Bachelor of Hygiene B. Hy.
Bachelor of Industrial Arts BIA or B.I.A.
Bachelor of Industrial Design B.I.D. or BID
Bachelor of Industrial Engineering BIE or B.I.E.
Bachelor of Interior Design B.I.D. or BID
Bachelor of Journalism B.J. or BJ (*CSM:* B.J.)
Bachelor of Jurisprudence B.Jur. or B.Juris.
Bachelor of Landscape Architecture B.L.A. or BLA
Bachelor of Law 1 JB or J.B. **2** *British* B.L. or BL
Bachelor of Laws 1 B.LL. **2** LL.B. (*MLA:* LLB; *OUP:* LL B) **3** *U.S.* B.L. or BL
Bachelor of Letters 1 B.L. or BL **2** B.Litt.
Bachelor of Letters or Literature 1 LB or L.B. **1** Lit.B.
Bachelor of Liberal Arts B.L.A. or BLA
Bachelor of Library Science 1 B.Lib. or B.Lib.Sc. **1** BLS or B.L.S. (*CSM:* B.L.S.)
Bachelor of Literature 1 B.L. or BL **1** B.Lit.
Bachelor of Literature or **Letters** Litt.B.
Bachelor of Marine Science B.M.S. or BMS
Bachelor of Mechancal Engineering B.Mech.E.
Bachelor of Mechanical Engineering BME or B.M.E.
Bachelor of Medical Science 1 B.M.S. or B.M.Sc. **2** B.Med.Sc.

Bachelor of Medical Technology BMT or B.M.T.
Bachelor of Medicine 2 BM or B.M. **1** *British* MB or M.B.
Bachelor of Metallurgy B.Met. or BMet.
Bachelor of Mining Engineering BME or B.M.E.
Bachelor of Music 1 B.Mus. or BMus. **2** Bac. Mus. **3** BM or B.M. **4** MB or M.B. **5** Mus.B. or Mus.Bac.
Bachelor of Music Education 1 B.Mus.Ed. **2** BME or B.M.E. or B.M.Ed.
Bachelor of Natural Science B.N.S. or BNS
Bachelor of Nursing BN or B.N.
Bachelor of Paedagogy *Canadian* B.Paed.
Bachelor of Pedagogy 1 B.Pd. **2** B.Pe. or B.Ped. **3** Pd.B.
Bachelor of Pharmacy 1 B.Pharm. or BPharm **2** BP or B.P. **3** Phm.B.
Bachelor of Philosophy 1 B.Ph. **2** B.Phil. or BPhil **3** BP or B.P. **4** PB or P.B. **5** Ph.B. or PhB
Bachelor of Physical and Health Education B.P.H.E. or BPHE (*CSM:* B.P.H.E.)
Bachelor of Physical Education B.P.E. or BPE
Bachelor of Public Administration BPA or B.P.A. (*CSM:* B.P.A.)
Bachelor of Public Health BPH or B.P.H.
Bachelor of Religious Education BRE or B.R.E.
Bachelor of Sacred Literature BSL or B.S.L.
Bachelor of Sacred Music 1 BSM or B.S.M. **2** S.M.B.
Bachelor of Sacred Scripture SSB or S.S.B.
Bachelor of Sacred Theology 1 BST or B.S.T. **2** S.T.B
Bachelor of Science 1 B.Sc. **2** BS or B.S. (*GPO:* B.S. or B.Sc.; *NYT:* B.S.; *MLA:* BS; *CSM:* B.Sc.; *OUP:* B.Sc. or BS) **3** SB or S.B. **4** Sc.B.
Bachelor of Science in Aeronautical Engineering B.S.A.E. or BSAE
Bachelor of Science in Agricultural Engineering B.S.A.E. or BSAE or B.S.Ag.
Bachelor of Science in Agriculture 1 B.Sc.Ag. or B.Sc.Agr. **2** BSA or B.S.A. (*CSM:* B.Sc. (Agr))
Bachelor of Science in Applied Arts B.S.A.A. or BSAA
Bachelor of Science in Architectural Engineering B.S.A.E. or BSAE
Bachelor of Science in Architecture B.S.Arch.
Bachelor of Science in Business Administration B.S.B.A. or BSBA
Bachelor of Science in Chemical Engineering B.S.Ch.E.
Bachelor of Science in Civil Engineering B.S.C.E. or BSCE
Bachelor of Science in Commerce BSC or B.S.C.
Bachelor of Science in Design B.S.D. or BSD
Bachelor of Science in Economics B.Sc.Econ.
Bachelor of Science in Education BSE or B.S.E. or B.S.Ed.
Bachelor of Science in Electrical Engineering BSEE or B.S.E.E.
Bachelor of Science in Elementary Education BSEE or B.S.E.E.

Bachelor of Science in Engineering 1 B.Sc.Eng. (*CSM:* B.Sc. (Engineering); *OUP:* B.Sc. (Eng.)) **2** BSE or B.S.E. or B.S.Eng.
Bachelor of Science in Foreign Service B.S.F.S.
Bachelor of Science in Forestry 1 B.S.For. **2** B.Sc.F. or B.Sc.For. **3** BSF or B.S.F.
Bachelor of Science in Home Economics B.S.H.E. or B.S.H.Ec.
Bachelor of Science in Industrial Engineering BSIE or B.S.I.E.
Bachelor of Science in Journalism BSJ or B.S.J.
Bachelor of Science in Law BSL or B.S.L.
Bachelor of Science in Library Science BSLS or B.S.L.S.
Bachelor of Science in Linguistics BSL or B.S.L.
Bachelor of Science in Mechanical Engineering BSME or B.S.M.E.
Bachelor of Science in Medical Technology BSMT or B.S.M.T.
Bachelor of Science in Mining Engineering. BSME or B.S.M.E.
Bachelor of Science in Nursing 1 B.Sc.N **2** BSN or B.S.N.
Bachelor of Science in Occupational Therapy BSOT or B.S.O.T.
Bachelor of Science in Pharmacy 1 B.S.Phar. or B.S.Pharm. **2** BSP or B.S.P. (*CSM:* B.S.P.)
Bachelor of Science in Physical Education BSPE or B.S.P.E.
Bachelor of Science in Physical Therapy BSPT or B.S.P.T.
Bachelor of Science in Public Administration BSPA or B.S.P.A.
Bachelor of Science in Public Health BSPH or B.S.P.H.
Bachelor of Science in Secretarial Studies B.S.S.S. or BSSS
Bachelor of Science in Social Science B.S.S.S. or BSSS
Bachelor of Social Science 1 B.S.S. or BSS **2** B.Soc.Sc.
Bachelor of Social Work BSW or B.S.W. (*CSM:* B.S.W)
Bachelor of Surgery 1 B.Ch. or BCh **2** B.Chir. or BChir **3** BC or B.C. **4** BS or B.S. **5** CB or C.B. **6** Ch.B. or ChB **7** Chir. B.
Bachelor of Technical Science B.Sc.Tech.
Bachelor of Technology B.Tech.
Bachelor of Textile Engineering B.T.E. or BTE
Bachelor of Theology 1 B.Th. **2** BT or B.T. **3** Th.B.
Bachelor of Veterinary Medicine 1 B.V.M. **2** Vet. M.B.
Bachelor of Veterinary Science 1 B.Sc.Vet. **2** B.V.S. or BVS or B.V.Sc. (*CSM:* B.V.Sc.)
bachelor officers' quarters *military.* BOQ
bacillary white diarrhea or **Salmonellosis** B.W.D.
bacillus B or B. or B
Bacillus thuringiensis BT or B.t.
back cover BC
back dividend *finance* b.d.
back electromotive force BEMF
back focal length *photography* B.F.L. or BFL
back of a book page b

back of page B
back order 1 b.o. 2 b/o 3 BO
back stage *theater* b.s.
Back-Up Interceptor Control BUIC
background 1 bg. 2 bkgd.
Backus Naur Form BNF
backward bwd.
backward wave amplifier BWA *or* bwa
backward wave oscillator BWO *or* bwo
backwardation 1 *finance* bk. *or* bk 2 *British finance* back. *or* Back.
bacon, lettuce, and tomato BLT
bacteria bact. *or* Bact.
bacterial bact. *or* Bact.
bacteriological bacteriol.
bacteriology 1 bact. *or* Bact. 2 bacteriol.
bad conduct discharge BCD
Badminton Association of England B.A.E.
baffle *architecture, engineering* baf
bag 1 B *or* B. 2 b *or* b. 3 bg.
baggage bag. *or* bag
bags 1 B/S *or* b/s 2 bgs. 3 bs.
Bahama Islands Ba. Is.
Bahamas 1 B 2 Bah.
Bahrain B
baht 2 B 2 b
bail bond b.b.
balance 1 *accounting* BLC *or* blc. 2 *commerce* a Bal. b bal.
balance sheet *commerce* 1 b.s. 2 BS *or* B.S.
balanced unbalanced *electronics* BALUN *or* balun
balanced voltage b.v. *or* bv
balancing bal.
balboa 1 B 2 b
balcony 1 *architecture* bal. 2 *theater* Balc.
bale 1 B *or* B. 2 b *or* b. 3 bl.
Balearic Islands B.I.
bales 1 B/S *or* b/s 2 bls. 3 bs.
balk *baseball* 1 B 2 BK
Balkans Balk.
ball b
ball bearing b.b.
ballast 1 ball. 2 BLST
balled and burlapped *agriculture* B & B *or* b & b
Balling 1 °B. 2 B *or* B.
Balliol College, Oxford Ball.
ballistic electron emission microscopy BEEM
ballistic missile BM
Ballistic Missile Defense BMD *or* B.M.D.
Ballistic Missile Early Warning System BMEWS
Ballistic Missile Interceptor BMI
Ballistic Missile Offensive BMO
Ballistic Research Laboratory BRL
ballistics ball.
ballistocardiogram *medicine* BCG
balloon BLN. *or* bln.
balsam bals *or* bals.
Baltic Balt.
Baltimore Balt.
Baluchistan 1 Bal. 2 Baluch.
band measure b.m.
band pass *electronics* BP
bandwidth *electronics* B
Bangladesh Nationalist Party BNP
Bank Bk *or* Bk.
bank 1 bk. *or* bk 2 bnk.

bank book b.b.
bank clearings bank clgs.
bank debits bank debs.
bank draft 1 B/D 2 BD
Bank for International Settlements 1 BIS *or* B.I.S. (*GPO:* BIS.) 2 *French* BRI *or* B.R.I.
bank note BN *or* B.N.
Bank of England 1 B. of E. 2 B.E.
bank post bills *commerce* B.P.B. *or* b.p.b.
bank rate BR *or* B.R.
banking 1 bank. 2 bkg.
Banking Insurance and Finance Union BIFU
bankrupt bkpt.
bankruptcy 1 bank. 2 Bankr. *or* bankr. 3 bkcy. 4 bkrtcy
Bankruptcy and Insolvency Reports Bank. and Ins. R.
Bankruptcy Cases BC *or* B.C.
Bankruptcy Court BC *or* B.C.
banks bks.
Banque de France BF
Baptist 1 Bap. 2 Bapt.
baptized 1 bap *or* bap. 2 bapt. 3 bp.
bar b *or* b.
Barbados 1 Barb. 2 BDS *or* Bds (*GPO:* Bds)
barbecue BBQ
bare and acid resisting paint b & arp
bare and painted b & p
barge aboard catamaran BACAT
baritone 1 bar *or* bar. 2 Bar. 3 Barit. *or* barit.
barium Ba
bark bk. *or* bk
barn *physics* b
Barnard Barn.
barometer 1 bar *or* bar. 2 BRM
barometric bar *or* bar.
baromil bm.
Baron 1 B *or* B. 2 Bn *or* Bn. 3 *French* Bon.
baroness 1 Bnss. 2 *French* Bonne.
Baronet 1 Bart. 2 Bt *or* Bt.
barracks bks.
barred spiral *astronomy* SB
barrel bar *or* bar. 1 bl. 2 brl.
barrel *or* barrels bbl.
barrels 1 bars. 2 bls.
barrels per charge day b/c.d.
barrels per day 1 b.p.d. 2 b/d
barrister 1 Bar. 2 Barr. *or* barr.
barrister at law B.L.
Bartholomew Bart.
Baruch Bar.
Barycentric Dynamical Time *astronomy* TDB
baryon number B
basal body temperature BBT
basal metabolic rate BMR *or* B.M.R.
basal metabolism BM
base 1 B *or* B. 2 *architecture, baseball, electronics, geometry, mathematics, mechanics* b 3 *baseball* B
base box bb.
base exchange BX
base helix angle *mechanics* bha *or* bh
base hit *baseball* b.h. *or* bh
Base Hospital BH
base line *sports, surveying* 1 B.L. 2 b.l.
base on balls *baseball* BB
base pair *genetics* b.p.
base shield connection BC

base support equipment BSE
Basel Anatomical Nomenclature B.N.A.
baseman *baseball* b
basement Bsmt *or* bsmt
basic BSC *or* bsc
Basic Adult Social Education BASE
basic allowance for subsistence BAS
Basic Armed Forces Communications Plan BAFCOM *or* BAFCom
Basic Essential Skills Training BEST
basic force *aeronautics* b
basic input-output system *computers* BIOS
basic operating system *computers* BDOS
basic oxygen furnace BOF
basic oxygen process BOP
Basic Research in Industrial Technology BRITE
basic sediment and water B.S.&W. *or* b.s.&w.
basic telecommunications access method BTAM
basket 1 bkt. 2 bskt.
baskets bkts.
Basque Country and Liberty (political movement) ETA *or* E.T.A.
bass *music* B *or* B.
bass clarinet 1 b.c. 2 BC
bass viol *music* vle.
Basses-Alpes B.Alp. *or* B.-Alpes
basso 1 B *or* B. 2 Bas. *or* bas
bassoon *music* bn. *or* bn
Basutoland Bas.
bat B *or* B.
bat *or* at bat *baseball* b
bath b
bathroom BTH
bathythermograph BT
battalion 1 bat. 2 batn. 3 batt. 4 Bn 5 bn. 6 btn. *or* Btn.
battens bn.
battery 1 B *or* B. 2 bty. *or* Bty. (artillery) 3 *electronics* a b b bty. 4 *military, electronics* bat. *or* bat 5 *military, music, technology* BTRY *or* btry. 6 *military, music* batt. *or* batt
batting average *baseball* BA
battle dress uniform BDU
Battle Squadron BS
baud 1 Bd. *or* Bd 2 *computers* a B b b c bd. *or* bd
Baumé 1 B *or* B. 2 Bé
Bavaria Bav.
Bavarian Bav.
Bay B *or* B.
Bay Area Rapid Transit BART
bay gelding b.g.
bay horse b.h.
Beach BCH
beacon 1 BCN *or* bcn 2 Bn
beaded one, two, sides B1S, B2S (of lumber)
beam 1 B 2 bm.
beam (of a ship) b *or* b.
beam *or* blind approach beacon system *aeronautics* BABS *or* Babs
beams and stringers *building* b & s
bearer bond *finance* b.b.
bearer depositary receipt *finance* BDR
bearing 1 B 2 *navigation, machinery* br. 3 *navigation* brg. *or* BRG
bearing deviation indicator BDI

bearing (of a compass reading) b or b.
beat bt.
beat frequency *electronics* BF
beat frequency oscillator *electronics* BFO or bfo
Beatrix Bx.
beats per minute *music* bpm
Beaumont and Fletcher Beau. & Fl.
beauty *physics* b
because bec.
becoming slower *music* 1 rall. or rallen. 2 rit. or ritard.
bed bd.
bed and breakfast B & B or b & b (*OUP:* b. & b.)
Bed, Breakfast, and Bath BBB
Bedfordshire, England Bedford. or Beds.
bedroom 1 BDRM or bdrm. 2 BR 3 br.
before 1 *a* 2 *a* 3 bef. 4 *Latin* an.
before Christ 1 a. de J.C. 2 a.Ch. 3 AAC or A.A.C. 4 AC or A.C. 5 BC or B.C. or B.C. or BC (*GPO, NYT, CSM:* B.C.; *OUP:* BC)
before dinner *pharmaceutics* a.p.
before meals *medicine* ac
before noon 1 am or a.m. 2 AM or A.M. (*GPO, MLA, OUP, CSM:* a.m.; *NYT:* A.M.)
before the birth of Christ 1 ACN or A.C.N. 2 ANC or A.N.C.
before the Christian or **common era** B.C.E. or BCE or B.C.E. or BCE
before the day 1 a.d. 2 AD
before the present BP
begin 1 beg. (in needlework) 2 comm.
Beginners All-purpose Symbolic Instruction Code BASIC or Basic
beginning beg. (in needlework)
beginning and ending B & E or b. & e.
beginning of file *computers* BOF
beginning of month *commerce* BOM
beginning of tape *electronics* BOT
behavior *psychology* beh.
behaviorism beh.
bel *acoustics* 1 B 2 b
Belfast Belf.
Belfast Association of Engineers B.A.E.
Belgian 1 Bel. 2 Belg.
Belgian National Railway *French* SNCB
Belgian Radio and Television Company BRT
Belgian Radio and Television in French RTBF
Belgic 1 Bel. 2 Belg.
Belgium 1 Bel. 2 Belg.
Belgium, the Netherlands, and Luxembourg (economic union) Benelux or BENELUX
Belgium-Luxembourg Economic Union BLEU
Belize 1 B 2 Bel.
Bell Telephone Laboratories BTL
Belousov-Zhabotinsky BZ
below 1 bel. 2 *Latin* inf.
below bridges *shipping* b.b.
below proof b.p.
bench mark BM or B.M.
benday BD
benedictine and brandy B & B or B. and B.
benefits bnfts
Benefits Review Board BRB
Benevolent and Protective Order of Elks BPOE or B.P.O.E.
Bengal Beng.

Bengali Beng.
benign prostatic hyperplasia or **hypertrophy** BPH
Benjamin Benj.
bent bt.
benzene Bz
benzene hexachloride BHC
benzoyl Bz
benzylpennicilloyl BPO
Berber Berb.
Berenice's Hair Com (constellation)
Berkeley, California Berk.
berkelium Bk
Berkshire, England Berks.
Berlin Ber.
Bermuda 1 B 2 Ber.
Bermuda Islands 1 B.I. 2 Ber. Is.
Bermuda Plan BP
Berwickshire, Scotland Berw.
beryllium Be
Bessemer Bess.
best opt.
best available technology BAT
best game *billiards* BG
best in show BIS
best of a kind A
best of breed BOB
best offer *commerce* BO or B.O.
best time available *advertising* BTA
Beta B
betalactoglobulin BLG
betanaphthoxyacetic acid NOA
better btr. or BTR
Better Business Bureau BBB or B.B.B.
Better Government Association BGA
between 1 bet. or betw. 2 btwn.
between centers BC
between meals *pharmaceutics* i.c.
between perpendiculars BP or B.P.
beveled bev or Bev.
beverage bev or bev.
6-benzylaminopurine BAP
Bharatiya Janata Party BJP
Bible 1 B or B. 2 Bib.
Bible Churchmen's Missionary Society B.C.M.S.
Bible Version BV or B.V.
Biblical Bibl. (*MLA, OUP:* bib.)
biblical Bib.
bibliographer bibliog.
bibliographic bibliog.
bibliographical 1 bibl. 2 bibliog.
Bibliographical Society BS or B.S.
Bibliographical Society of America BSA or B.S.A.
Bibliographical Society of Canada BSC or B.S.C.
bibliography 1 bibl. (*MLA:* bibliog) 2 bibliog.
Bibliography of American Literature BAL
bicuspid 1 B 2 b
bicycle motocross BMX
bid B
biennial bien.
Big Brothers of America BBA
big man on campus B.M.O.C.
bilingual BIL
bill book *commerce* b.b.
bill for collection *commerce* B/C
bill lodged *banking, commerce* B.L.

bill of entry *commerce* B/E
bill of exchange *commerce* 1 b.e. 2 B.E. or BE 3 B/E
bill of health B/H
bill of lading *commerce* 1 B.L. or B/L 2 b.l. or b/l
bill of material BM or B/M
bill of parcels *commerce* 1 b.p. 2 B/P
bill of sale 1 *commerce* b.s. or b/s (*OUP:* b.s.) 2 B/S
bill of sight *commerce* 1 b.s. 2 B/S 3 B/St or b/st
bill rendered *commerce* b.rend. or b/rend.
billion 1 B 2 b or b. 3 bn.
billion cubic feet bcf
billion electron volts 1 BEV 2 bev or b.e.v. 3 Bev or BeV.
billion years b.y.
bills discounted *commerce* 1 B/D 2 BD or B.D.
bills of lading *commerce* Bs/L
bills payable 1 B.Pay. or b.pay. 2 *French* bap or b. à p. or bàp 3 *commerce* **a** b.p. **b** B/P **c** b/p **d** BP
bills receivable 1 *French* bar or b. à r. or bàr 2 *commerce* **a** b.r. or b/r **b** B.Rec. or b.rec or b/rec. **c** BR or B/R
bimonthly bi-m
binary *electronics* b
binary coded decimal BCD
binary digit *computers* bit
Binary Electronics Sequence Computer BESC
binary rate multiplier *computers* BRM
binary synchronous communication BSC
binder's orders B/Os
binding 1 bdg. 2 bind.
binding margin BM or B/M
biochemical or **biological oxygen demand** BOD or B.O.D.
biochemistry biochem.
Biofeedback Training BFT
biogeography biogeog.
biographer biog.
biographical biog.
biographical summary CV or C.V. (*OUP:* c.v.)
biography 1 bio. or bio (*MLA:* biog.) 2 biog.
biological 1 bio. 2 biol.
Biological Abstract Subjects in Context BASIC
Biological and Toxic Weapons Convention BWC
biological false-positive BFP
Biological Research Institute BRI
Biological Sciences Curriculum Study BSCS
biological or **bacteriological warfare** BW
biologist biol.
biology 1 bio. 2 biol.
Biomedical Communications Network BCN
biopsy Bx.
bipolar complementary metal oxide semiconductor *electronics* BICMOS
Bird of Paradise Aps (constellation)
Birmingham Gage BG
Birmingham Wire Gage BWG
Birmingham, England B'ham
birthplace 1 bp. 2 bpl.
births, deaths, marriages BDM
bisexual *slang* AC/DC or ac/dc or a-c/d-c

Bishop 1 B or B. **2** Bp. **3** *Latin* **a** Ep. or EP. **b** Episc. **c** EPS or Eps. **d** Epus.
bishop *chess* B
Bishopric bhpric.
bismuth Bi
bissextile bis.
bit *computers* b
bitch b or b.
bits or **bytes per inch** bpi
bits or **bytes per second** bps
bituminous 1 b **2** bitum.
bivouac biv.
biweekly bi-w
black 1 B **2** bk. or bk **3** bl. **4** blk.
black and white 1 b & w or B & W or B/W **2** BW or B/W
black English vernacular BEV
black letter *printing* **1** B.L. **2** bklr.
Black Watch BW or B.W.
blank blk.
blend or **blend of** b or b.
Blessed Bl.
Blessed Mary BM
Blessed Mary the Virgin B.M.V.
Blessed Sacrament BS or B.S.
Blessed Virgin BV or B.V.
Blessed Virgin Mary B.V.M.
blessing *Latin* Ben.
blind approach *aviation* BA
blind carbon copy BCC or bcc or b.c.c.
block 1 bk. or bk **2** bl. **3** blk. **4** Blk. (*OUP:* blk.)
block check character BCC
blocks bks.
blood bld.
blood alcohol concentration BAC
blood alcohol level BAL
blood factors ABO
blood group antigen V
blood groups (classification by antigens) MNS
blood pressure BP or B.P.
blood serological test BST
blood sugar *medicine* **1** B/S **2** BS
blood type A A
blood type AB AB
blood type B B
blood type O O
blood volume BV
blood, urea, nitrogen BUN
blood-brain barrier *medicine* BBB
blowing dust BD
blowing snow *meteorology* BS
blue 1 B or B. **2** bl. **3** bu. or bu
Blue Book BB or B.B.
blue sky b
blue star *astronomy* **1** A **2** B
blue stellar objects *astronomy* BSO
blueprint 1 B/P **2** b/p
board 1 Bd. **2** bd. **3** *architecture, bookbinding* brd.
Board Certified 1 B/C **2** BC
Board Examined B.E. or BE
board foot bd.ft.
board measure 1 b.m. **2** BM
Board of Broadcast Governors BBG
Board of Cooperative Educational Services BOCES

Board of Education 1 B. Ed. or BEd **2** B. of E. or B of E or BOE **3** B.E.
Board of Eligibility BE or B/E
Board of Health B of H
Board of Inland Revenue *British* BIR
Board of Ordnance BO
Board of Tax Appeals BTA or B.T.A.
Board of Trade 1 B. of T. **2** BOT
Board of Trade Unit BTU or B.T.U.
boat bt.
Boating Industry Association BIA
boating while intoxicated BWI
boatswain B or B.
bodily injury *law, insurance* B.I. or BI
Bodleian Library 1 B.L. **2** Bod. or Bodl.
body mass index BMI
body odor BO
body of law C.J.
body of the canon law C.J.Can.
body of the civil law C.J.Civ.
body surface area *medicine* BSA
body temperature 1 Tb or T_b **2** *medicine* **a** BT **b** T
body weight *medicine* BW
body-centered cubic BCC or B.c.c.
body-centered cubic BBC
Bohemian Boh. or Bohem.
boil *pharmaceutics* coq.
boiler horsepower b.h. or bh
boiler pressure b.p.
boiling boil.
boiling point 1 b.p. or bp **2** BP
boiling range *chemistry* b.r.
boils or **boils at 1** B or B. **2** b or b.
bold or **boldface** *printing* bld.
boldface *printing* bf or b.f. or bf. (*GPO, CSM:* bf.)
boldface caps *printing* bfc or b.f.c. or bf.c.
bolivar B
Bolivia Bol.
Bolivian Bol.
Bolivian State Petroleum YPFB
boliviano 1 b or b. **2** Ba
bolt circle b.c.
Boltzmann function *physics* H
Boltzmann's constant 1 K **2** k
bomb damage assessment BDA
bomb disposal BD
Bomb Disposal Squad BDS
Bomb Disposal Unit BDU
bombardier Bdr.
bomber B
bona fide occupational qualification BFOQ
bond 1 Bd. **2** bd. **3** *chemistry, finance* B
bonded *chemistry, electricity, finance* B
bonded goods B/G
bonded warehouse BW
bone *medicine* o or o.
bone conduction *medicine* BC
bone marrow transplantation *medicine* BMT
Bonner Durchmusterung BD or B.D.
Bonneville Power Administration BPA
Book 1 Bk or Bk. **2** Lib or Lib.
book 1 B or B. **2** b or b. **3** Bd. **4** bk. or bk (*MLA:* bk.) **5** L or Ll. **6** lib. **7** *Latin, Spanish, French* l or l.
Book Association of Ireland B.A.I.
Book Auction Records BAR or B.A.R.

Book Industry Study Group BISG
Book Manufacturers Institute BMI
Book of Common Prayer B.C.P. or BCP
Book of Reference BR or B.R.
book value *commerce* **1** b.v. **2** BV or B/v
Book-of-the-Month Club BOMC
bookbinder bkbndr.
bookbinding bdg.
bookkeeper BKPR or bkpr.
bookkeeping 1 bkg. **2** bkpg.
booklet bklt.
books 1 bb. or bb **2** bks.
Books in Print BIP
Booksellers Association of Great Britain and Ireland B.G.B.
Booksellers' Association *British* BA or B.A.
booster *aeronautics, aerospace* BSTR
Bordeaux Bdx.
border bdr.
borderline personality disorder BPD
born 1 B or B. **2** b or b. **3** *Latin* n or n.
boron B
boron nitride BN
Borough Bor.
Borough Council BC
Boston Conservatory of Music BCM
Boston Museum of Fine Arts BMFA
Boston Symphony Orchestra BSO
Boston Transportation Authority BTA
Boston University BU
Boston University Studies in English BUSE
botanical bot.
Botanical Society of America BSA or B.S.A.
Botanical Society of London BSL or B.S.L.
Botanical Society of the British Isles B.S.B.I.
botanist bot.
botany bot.
both dates inclusive BDI or b.d.i.
both ears *medicine* AU
both hands *music* BH or B.H.
both sides 1 b.s. **2** *printing* B/S
bottle 1 bot. **2** btl.
bottom 1 bot. **2** *physics* b
bottom dead center b.d.c. or BDC
bottom settlings 1 b.s. **2** BS
bottoms B
bought 1 bgt. **2** bt. **3** *commerce* bot.
Boulevard 1 Bd. **2** BLVD **3** Boul. or boul.
boulevard Blvd. or blvd. (*GPO:* Blvd.)
bound 1 b or b. **2** bd. **3** bnd.
bound in boards bds.
boundary 1 bdry **2** bdy.
boundary layer control *aeronautics* BLC
bovine diarrhea virus BVD
bovine growth hormone bGH or BGH
bovine immunodeficiency virus BIV
bovine somatotrophin BST
bovine spongiform encephalopathy BSE
bowel movement BM
bowels *medicine* B
bowled *sports* b or b.
box bx.
box bark strips BBS or BBS.
box office 1 b/o **2** BO or B.O. (*OUP:* b.o.)
boxed bxd.
boxes bxs.
Boy Scouts of America BSA
Boys' Clubs of America BCA

bracket bkt.
Bradley Fighting Vehicle BFV
Braille Institute of America BIA
brake bk. or bk
brake horsepower bhp or BHP or b.hp.
 (OUP: b.h.p.)
brake mean effective pressure BMEP or
 b.m.e.p.
brake specific fuel consumption BSFC
Branch Br or Br.
branch medicine, aeronautics br.
branch office BO (OUP: b.o.)
brand br.
brass 1 b 2 br.
Brazil or **Brazilian** Braz.
Brazilian Democratic Movement MDB
breadth 1 B 2 b
break bulk commerce b.b.
breakdown voltage physics, electronics BDV
breakfast bkfst.
breaking and entering B & E
breaks in overcast meteorology BINOVC
breath sound or **sounds** medicine BS
Brecknockshire, Wales Brec. or Breck.
breech-loading ordnance 1 B.L. 2 b.l.
breeder reactor BR
Breeding Bird Census BBC
Breeding Bird Survey BBS
Breton 1 Br or Br. 2 Bret.
brevet 1 brev. or Brev. 2 bvt.
brevetted 1 brev. or Brev. 2 bvt.
brevier brev.
brick b
brick piers b.p.
brickwork bwk.
bridge 1 surveying br. 2 brg.
brief law 1 bf or bf. 2 br. 3 brf.
brig br.
Brigade Brig.
brigade Bde.
Brigadier 1 Bdr. 2 Brig.
Brigadier General BG or B.G.
bright 1 a brt.
brightness B
brilliant music brill.
Brinell hardness number 1 BH 2 Bh 3 BHN
 4 Bhn
bring your own booze or **bottle** BYOB
Britain 1 Br or Br. (OUP: Br.) 2 Brit.
Britannia Brit.
Britannica Brit.
Briticism Brit.
British 1 B or B. 2 Br or Br. (OUP: Br.) 3 Brit.
British Academy BA or B.A.
British Academy of Film and Television Arts
 BAFTA
British Actor's Equity Association BAEA or
 B.A.E.A.
British Agricultural Export Council BAEC
British Agricultural History Society B.A.H.S.
British Air Line Pilots Association Balpa or
 BALPA
British Airline Pilots Association B.A.P.A.
British Airports Authority BAA or B.A.A.
British Amateur Athletic Board B.A.A.B.
British America BA
British America or **British American** Br.Am.
British and Foreign Bible Society 1 B. &
 F.B.S. 2 B.F.B.S.

British and Foreign Maritime Agencies
 B.A.F.M.A. or BAFMA
British Antarctic Survey BAS
British Anti-Lewisite BAL or B.A.L.
British Antique Dealers' Association
 B.A.D.A. or BADA
British Approvals Board for
 Telecommunications BABT
British Approved Name chemistry BAN
British Archaeological Association BAA or
 B.A.A.
British Army of the Rhine BAOR or B.A.O.R.
British Association BA or B.A.
British Association for American Studies
 BAAS
British Association for the Advancement of
 Science BAAS or B.A.A.S.
British Association of Accountants and
 Auditors BAA or B.A.A or B.A.A.A.
British Association of Chemists BAC or
 B.A.C.
British Association of Retired Persons BARP
British Association of Social Workers BASW
British Association Thread mechanics B.A.
 Thread
British Astronomical Association BAA or
 B.A.A
British Automobile Racing Club B.A.R.C.
British Bankers Association BBA or B.B.A.
British Board of Film Censors B.B.F.C. or
 BBFC
British Boxing Board of Control BBBC
British Broadcasting Corporation BBC or
 B.B.C. (NYT: BBC)
British Canadian Trade Association BCTA
British Coal Utilization Research Association
 BCURA
British Columbia BC
British Computer Society 1 BBS or BBS. or
 B.B.S. 2 BCS
British Coordinating Committee for
 Biotechnology BCCB
British Council of Churches BCC or B.C.C.
British Cycling Federation BCF
British Dental Association BDA or B.D.A.
British Double Summer Time BDST
British Drama League B.D.L.
British Drug Houses BDH
British Electrical Approvals Board BEAB
British Electrotechnical Committee BEL
British Empire Medal BEM or B.E.M.
British Empire Service League B.E.S.L.
British Engineering Standards Association
 B.E.S.A. or BESA
British Engineers Association BEA or B.E.A.
British English BrE
British Expeditionary Forces B.E.F.
British Federation of Master Printers
 B.F.M.P.
British Federation of University Women
 B.F.U.W.
British Film Institute B.F.I.
British Forces Post Office BFPO
British Frontier Service BFS
British Gaming Association BGA
British Geriatrics Society BGS or B.G.S.
British Gliding Association BGA or B.G.A.
British High Commissioner BHC or B.H.C.
British Hotels Association BHA

British Indian Ocean Territory BIOT
British Information Service BIS or B.I.S.
British Institute of Electrical Engineers BIEE
British Institute of Engineering Technology
 BIET
British Institute of Management B.I.M.
British Institute of Radiology BIR or B.I.R.
British Institute of Recorded Sound BIRS
British Institution of Radio Engineers
 B.I.R.E.
British Insurance Association BIA
British Interplanetary Society BIS
British Iron and Steel Federation BISF
British Iron and Steel Research Association
 BISRA
British Israel World Federation BIWF
British Joint Communications Electronics
 Board BJCEB
British Lawn Tennis Association B.L.T.A.
British Library B.L. or BL
British Library Association B.L.A.
British Library Automated Information
 Service BLAISE
British Industrial Biological Research
 Association BIBRA or Bibra
British Medical Association B.M.A. or BMA
British Medical Journal BMJ
British Museum 1 BM or B.M. (MLA, OUP:
 BM) 2 Brit. Mus.
British Museum Library BML or B.M.L.
British Museum Quarterly BMQ
British National Bibliography B.N.B.
British National Export Council B.N.E.C.
British National Formulary pharmaceutics
 BNF or B.N.F.
British National Oil Corporation BNOC
British National Opera Company BNOC or
 B.N.O.C.
British Naturalists' Association B.N.A.
British Nuclear Fuels Limited BNF or BNFL
British Numismatic Society B.N.S.
British Olympic Association B.O.A. or BOA
British Optical Association B.O.A.
British Ornithologists' Union B.O.U. or BOU
British Orthopaedic Association B.O.A. or
 BOA
British patent Brit. Pat.
British Pediatric Association BPA or B.P.A.
British Pharmaceutical Codex B.P.C.
British Pharmacopoeia 1 B.Ph. 2 BP or B.P.
 3 PB or P.B.
British Philatelic Association BPA or B.P.A.
British Racing Drivers' Club B.R.D.C.
British Racing Motors BRM or B.R.M.
British Rail BR
British Rail Board BRB or B.R.B.
British railway guide ABC
British Record Society B.R.S.
British Records Association B.R.A.
British Red Cross Society B.R.C.S.
British Revision medicine BR
British Road Services B.R.S. or BRS
British Safety Council BSC
British Sailors' Society B.S.S.
British Satellite Beam BSB
British School of Archaeology at Athens
 B.S.A.A.
British Ship Research Association B.S.R.A.
British Show Jumping Association BSJA

British Society for Research on Ageing
  B.S.R.A.
British Society for the History of Science
  B.S.H.S.
British Society for the Study of
  Orthodontics B.S.S.O. *or* BSSO
British Sound Recording Association B.S.R.A.
British Standard BS *or* B.S.
British Standard Beam BSB
British Standard Channel BSC
British Standard Code of Practice BSCP
British Standard Fine BSF
British Standard Gage BG
British Standard Gauge BSG *or* B.S.G.
British Standard Pipe thread BSP
British Standard Sizes B.S.S. *or* BSS
British Standard Specification B.S.S. *or* BSS
British Standard Time BST *or* B.S.T.
British Standard Whitworth screw thread
  BSW
British Standards Institution BSI *or* B.S.I.
British Sub-Aqua Club BSAC
British Summer Time BST *or* B.S.T.
British Tax Review B.T.R.
British Technology Group BTG
British Technology Index BTI
British Telecom BT
British thermal unit 1 B 2 B.Th.U. *or* B.th.u.
  3 BTU *or* B.T.U *or* Btu *or* B.t.u. *or* btu *or*
  b.t.u. (*NYT:* B.T.U)
British Tourist Authority BTA
British Trust for Ornithology BTO *or* B.T.O.
British Union Catalogue of Periodicals
  BUCOP *or* B.U.C.O.P.
British United Press BUP *or* B.U.P.
British Universities North America Club
  BUNAC
British Veterinary Association B.V.A. *or* BVA
British Virgin Islands B.V.I.
British Watercolour Society B.W.S. *or* BWS
British Waterways Board BWB
British West Indies BWI *or* B.W.I.
British Women's Temperance Association
  B.W.T.A.
Britons (of the) Britt. *or* BRITT (*OUP:* Britt.)
broadcast 1 B 2 b.c. *or* bc 3 BC 4 BCST
broadcast band BC
Broadcast Education Association BEA
broadcast interference BCI
Broadcast Music Incorporated BMI
Broadcasting Confederation of Germany
  ARD
Broadcasting Corporation of New Zealand
  BCNZ
broadcasting station BS
Broadcasting, Entertainment, and
  Cinematograph Technicians Union BECTU
Broadway B'way
broken X
broken paper XXX
broker's order *commerce* 1 b.o. 2 BO
  (*OUP:* b.o.)
bromine Br
bromoform-allyl-phosphate BAP
bronchial asthma BA
Bronx Bx. *or* Bx
bronze 1 br. 2 brz.
bronze medal *or* medalist BM
Brookhaven National Laboratory BNL

Brooklyn Bklyn.
Brooklyn Academy of Music BAM
Brother 1 B *or* B. 2 Br *or* Br. (*OUP:* Br.)
brother 1 b 2 br. 3 Bro. *or* bro.
Brother (a religious) Fr
Brotherhood B *or* B.
brotherhood Bro. *or* bro.
Brotherhood of Locomotive Engineers B.L.E.
  or BLE
Brotherhood of Locomotive Firemen and
  Enginemen B.L.F.E.
Brotherhood of Painters, Decorators, and
  Paperhangers of America B.P.D.P.A.
Brotherhood of Railroad Trainmen BRT *or*
  B.R.T.
Brotherhood of Railway Carmen of
  America B.R.C.A.
Brotherhood of the Holy Name of Jesus
  B.H.N.
Brothers FF *or* FF.
brothers Bros. *or* bros.
Brothers of St. Francis Xavier C.F.X.
Brothers of the Christian Schools FSC *or*
  F.S.C.
brought brt.
brought down *accounting* 1 b.d. 2 B/D
  3 b/d 4 BD
brought forward *accounting* 1 bf *or* b.f. *or*
  b/f 2 BF *or* B/F (*CSM:* B.F.; *OUP:* b.f.)
brought over *accounting* 1 b.o. 2 b/o 3 BO
  or B/O (*OUP:* b.o.)
brown 1 br. *or* br 2 brn
brown adipose tissue BAT
Brown and Sharpe *or* Brown and Sharpe
  Gauge B & S *or* B & SG
Browning Automatic Rifle BAR *or* B.A.R.
Brunei B
Brussels Brux.
Brussels Tariff Nomenclature BTN *or* B.T.N.
Brussels Tariff Nomenclature for the Latin
  American Free Trade Association NABLOC
bryology bryol.
Buckinghamshire, England Bucks.
buckram 1 bkm 2 buck.
Budapest Budpst
Buddhist Era B.E. *or* B.E. *or* BE *or* B.E.
Buenos Aires BA
buffer index *biochemistry* B.I.
builder bldr.
builder's risk *insurance* 1 b.r. 2 BR
building 1 bldg. *or* Bldg. (*GPO:* Bldg.;
  CSM: bldg.) 2 blg.
building and loan association B & L *or* B
  and L
Building Research Establishment BRE
Building Societies Association BSA *or* B.S.A.
Building Societies' Institute BSI *or* B.S.I.
buildings bldgs.
built blt.
Bulgaria Bulg.
Bulgarian Bulg.
Bulgarian Socialist Party BSP
bulk blk.
bulk modulus *physics* K
bulkhead 1 bhd. 2 blkd.
bulletin 1 bul. (*MLA, CSM, OUP:* bull.)
  2 bull.
bulletin board system *computers* BBS
Bulletin of Bibliography BB

Bulletin of the Bureau of Standards BBS *or*
  B.B.S.
*Bulletin of the Geological Society of
  America* BGSA
Bulletin of the Geological Survey BGS
Bulletin of the National Research Council
  BNRC
Bulletin of the New York Public Library
  BNYPL
*Bulletin of the Philosophical Society of
  Washington* BPSW
*Bulletin of the School of Oriental and
  African Studies* BSOAS
bulwark bwk.
bunch bch.
bundle 1 bd. 2 bdl. *or* bdle.
bundled bdl.
bundles bds.
bunt *baseball* b
buoyancy B
Bureau 1 Bu *or* Bu. 2 Bur.
bureau bu.
Bureau of Agricultural Economics BAE
Bureau of Alcohol, Tobacco, and Firearms
  ATF
Bureau of American Ethnology BAE
Bureau of Child Welfare BCW
Bureau of Criminal Investigation BCI
Bureau of Economic Analysis BEA
Bureau of Employment Security BES
Bureau of Engraving and Printing BEP
Bureau of Foreign Commerce BFC
Bureau of Indian Affairs BIA
Bureau of Insular Affairs BIA
Bureau of International Broadcasting BIB
Bureau of International Expositions BIE
Bureau of International Labor Affairs BILA
Bureau of International Whaling Statistics
  BIWS
Bureau of Justice Assistance BJA
Bureau of Justice Statistics BJS
Bureau of Labor Statistics BLS
Bureau of Labor-Management Relations
  and Cooperative Programs BLMRCP
Bureau of Labor-Management Reports
  B.L.M.R.
Bureau of Land Management BLM
Bureau of Mines BOM *or* BoM
Bureau of Mines Information Circular BMIC
Bureau of Mines Technical Paper BMTP
Bureau of Narcotics BN
Bureau of Narcotics and Dangerous Drugs
  BNDD
Bureau of Personnel Management BPM
Bureau of Plant Industry BPI
Bureau of Prisons BOP
Bureau of Product Safety BPS
Bureau of Public Roads BPR
Bureau of Radiological Health BRH
Bureau of Reclamation BOR
Bureau of Sport Fisheries and Wildlife BSFW
Bureau of the Budget 1 BB 2 BOB
Bureau of the Census BOC
Bureau of Veterans Affairs B.V.A.
burgess Burg.
burgomaster Burg.
buried bur.
Burkitt's lymphoma B.L.
burlap brlp.

burlesque burl.
Burma Bur. (now *Myanmar*)
Burma Socialist Programme Party BSPP
Burmese Bur.
burning rate BR
bursar Burs.
Burundi National Party of Unity and Progress *French* UPRONA
bushel 1 bsh. 2 bu. 3 bus. 4 bush.
bushing *mechanics, electricity* bush.
Business Busn
business 1 Bus. 2 *informal* biz or biz.
Business Administration Bus. Admin.
Business Equipment Manufacturers Association BEMA
Business Experience Training BET
Business Information System *computers* BIS
Business Manager Bus. Mgr.

business office must BOM or bom
business owner's policy *insurance* BOP
business reply envelope BRE
Business Service Center BSC
Business Services and Defense Administration BSDA
Buteshire Bute.
butter but.
button 1 btn. 2 but.
butyl Bu
butylated hydroxyanisole 1 BHA 2 BTA
butylated hydroxytoluene BHT
buyer has 7, 10, 15 days to take up stock b7d, b10d, b15d
buyer's option *commerce* 1 b.o. 2 BO (*GPO, OUP:* b.o.)
buyer's risk c.e.
by 1 b or b. 2 X 3 x

by agent per pro. or per proc.
by agent or **proxy** *commerce, law* pp or p.p.
by aid and counsel *law* OC or O.C.
by authority of the office ex off.
by or on the information of *law* ex rel or ex rel.
by procuration per pro. or per proc.
by proxy per pro. or per proc.
by the day, per diem 1 PD or P.D. 2 pd or p.d. or p/d
by the way BTW
by weight 1 P 2 p 3 pond.
bye *sports* b
bypass *computers* byp. or BYP
byte b
Byzantine Byz.
Byzantium Byz.

C-reactive protein *biochemistry* CRP
cabin cab.
cabinet 1 cab. 2 cabt. or cabnt.
Cabinet Council on Economic Affairs CCEA
cable 1 cab. 2 CBL or cbl. 3 *electronics* ca
Cable News Network CNN
Cable Satellite Public Affairs Network C-Span
cable television 1 CATV 2 CTV
cable transfer CT or C/T
cadenza *music* cad.
Cadet 1 Cad. 2 CDT or Cdt.
cadet cad.
cadmium 1 Cad. 2 Cd
Caernarvonshire, Wales Caern.
Caesar Caes.
cafeteria caf
Caithness County, Scotland Caith.
calcium Ca
calcium in the solar spectrum *astronomy* K
calcium line in solar spectrum H
calculate calc.
calculated 1 C 2 calcd.
calculation 1 C 2 caln.
Calcutta, India Cal.
calendar cal.
calendar year CY
calendered paper Cal.
calends 1 K 2 kal.
calf cf. (book binding)
Calgary, Canada Calg.
caliber cal.
calibrate calibr.
calibrated air speed CAS
calibration calibr.
California 1 CA 2 Ca or Ca. 3 Cal. (*NYT, OUP:* Calif.) 4 Calif.
California Achievement Test CAT or C.A.T.

California Association of Student Councils CASC
California Institute of Technology 1 Caltech or Cal. Tech. 2 CIT or C.I.T.
California Redwood Association CRA
California Rural Legal Assistance C.R.L.A.
californium Cf
call c
Call Directing Code CDC
call of more *finance* C/m
call signal C/S
call waiting CW
called *commerce* cld.
calm *meteorology* c or c.
Calmette-Guérin bacillus BCG
calorie c
calorific value CV
calyx *botany* K
Cambridge 1 Cam or Cam. 2 Camb.
Cambridge Bibliography of English Literature C.B.E.L. or CBEL
Cambridge History of English Literature C.H.E.L. or CHEL
Cambridge Language Research Unit CLRU
Cambridge University CU or C.U.
Cambridge University Press CUP or C.U.P.
Cambridgeshire, England Cambs
Camden Society Camd. Soc.
camera control unit CCU
camera-ready copy *printing* CRC
camouflage cam.
Camp CP
Campaign for Nuclear Disarmament CND
Campeche Camp.
can C or C.
Canada 1 Ca or Ca. 2 Can. or CAN 3 CDN 4 CN
Canada Assistance Plan CAP
Canada East CE or C.E.
Canada Emergency Measures Organization CEMO
Canada Medal CM or C.M.
Canada Pension Plan CPP
Canada Standard Size CSS
Canada, United Kingdom, and United States CANUKUS

Canada-U.S. Regional Planning Group CUSRPG
Canadian 1 Ca or Ca. 2 Can. or CAN 3 Canad. 4 CDN or Cdn.
Canadian Aeronautical Institute CAI or C.A.I.
Canadian Air Line Pilots Association CALPA
Canadian Amateur Hockey Association CAHA
Canadian Armament Research and Development Establishment CARDE
Canadian Armed Forces CAF or C.A.F.
Canadian Army Medical Corps CAMC
Canadian Army Operational Research Group CAORG
Canadian Army Post Office CAPO
Canadian Association for Adult Education CAAE
Canadian Association of Advertising Agencies CAAA
Canadian Association of Broadcasters CAB or C.A.B.
Canadian Association of College and University Libraries CACUL
Canadian Association of Radiologists CAR
Canadian Authors' Association CAA
Canadian Automoile Sports Club CASC
Canadian Bankers Association CBA or C.B.A.
Canadian Bar Association CBA or C.B.A.
Canadian Biochemical Society CBS or C.B.S.
Canadian Book Publishers Council CBPC or C.B.P.C.
Canadian Booksellers Association CBA or C.B.A.
Canadian Broadcasting Corporation CBC
Canadian Broadcasting Corporation service in Quebec *French* SRC
Canadian Brotherhood of Railway, Transport, and General Workers Union CBRT
Canadian Cancer Society CCS
Canadian Chamber of Commerce. CCC
Canadian Council of Professional Engineers C.C.P.E. or CCPE

Canadian Dental Association CDA or C.D.A.

Canadian deuterium uranium CANDU

Canadian Development Corporation CDC or C.D.C.

Canadian Electrical Code CEC

Canadian Engineering Standards Association CESA

Canadian Federation of Agriculture CFA

Canadian Figure Skating Association CFSA

Canadian Football League CFL

Canadian Forces CF

Canadian Forces Communication Command CFCC

Canadian Forces Decoration CD or C.D.

Canadian Forces Europe CFE

Canadian French Can.F. or Can.Fr.

Canadian Geographical Society CGS

Canadian Government Office of Tourism CGOT

Canadian Hydrographic Service CHS or C.H.S.

Canadian Information Processing Society CIPS

Canadian Institute of Forestry CIF or C.I.F.

Canadian Institute of Mining CIM or C.I.M.

Canadian Institute on Public Affairs CIPA or C.I.P.A.

Canadian Labor Congress CLC or C.L.C.

Canadian Labor Relations Board CLRB

Canadian Law Times CLT

Canadian Library Association 1 CLA or C.L.A. 2 French ACB

Canadian Manufacturers' Association CMA

Canadian Maritime Union CMU

Canadian Medical Association CMA or C.M.A.

Canadian Mental Health Association C.M.H.A. or CMHA

Canadian Meteorological Center CMC

Canadian Music Council CMC

Canadian Musical Reproduction Rights Agency CMRRA

Canadian National Committee for Mental Hygiene CNCMH

Canadian National Library CNL

Canadian National Railways 1 CN 2 CNR

Canadian Nurses Association CNA or C.N.A.

Canadian Officers' Training Corps COTC

Canadian Ophthalmological Society COS or C.O.S.

Canadian Pacific Railroad CPR

Canadian patent Can. pat.

Canadian Pharmaceutical Association 1 CPA or C.P.A. 2 CPhA or C.Ph.A.

Canadian Press CP

Canadian Psychological Association CPA or C.P.A.

Canadian Public Health Association CPHA or C.P.H.A.

Canadian Radio-television and Telecommunications Commission CRTC

Canadian scientific ship CSS

Canadian Society for the Prevention of Cruelty to Animals CSPCA or C.S.P.C.A.

Canadian Society of Laboratory Technologists CSLT or C.S.L.T.

Canadian Society of Landscape Architects and Town Planners CSLATP or C.S.L.A.T.P.

Canadian Standard Freeness CSF or C.S.F.

Canadian Standards Association CSA

Canadian Steel Industries Construction Council CSICC

Canadian Teachers' Federation CTF

Canadian Television CTV

Canadian Transport Commission CTC

Canadian Tuberculosis Association CTA

Canadian Underwriter Association CUA or C.U.A.

Canadian Union of Public Employees CUPE

Canadian Union of Students CUS

Canadian University Students Overseas CUSO

Canadian Veterinary Medical Association C.V.M.A.

Canadian Wildlife Service CWS

canal 1 Can. 2 can.

Canal Zone CZ or C.Z.

Canary Islands Can.I.

Canberra, Australia Can.

cancel computers CNCL or Cncl

cancel or canceled can. or CAN

canceled canc.

canceled to order CTO or c.t.o.

cancellation 1 can. or CAN 2 canc.

cancelled commerce, computers, meteorology cld. or CLD

cancer Ca

candela physics cd

candle physics 1 C 2 c or c.

candle hour 1 c.h. or c-h. 2 chr. or c-hr.

candlepower 1 CP 2 cp or cp. or c.p. 3 I

candlepower second cp.s.

canine K-9

canine parvo virus CPV

canine tooth c or c.

Canis Major CMa (constellation)

Canis Minor CMi (constellation)

cannon can.

cannot find c/f

canoe C or C-

Canon 1 Can. (a religious) 2 Cn or Cn.

canon music can.

Canterbury Cant.

Canticles Cant.

Canto 1 Can. 2 Cant. or cant.

canto can.

Canton 1 Cant. 2 Ct or Ct.

Cantonese Cant.

canvas canv or canv.

Canyon CYN

capacitance 1 C or C. 2 cap

capacitor 1 C 2 cap

capacity 1 C 2 cap or cap. 3 cy or cy. 4 electricity k or k.

Cape 1 C or C. 2 CPE

Cape Breton Island, Nova Scotia 1 CB or C.B. 2 CBI

Cape of Good Hope C.G.H.

Cape Verde Islands CVI or C.V.I.

capital 1 Cap or Cap. 2 caps or Caps

capital account C/A

Capital Cost Recovery System CCRS

capital gains tax finance CGT

Capital Issues Committee CIC

capital letter 1 Cap 2 cap or cap. (MLA: cap.)

capital stock finance 1 c.s. or cs 2 CS or C.S.

capital transfer tax British CTT

capitalize 1 Cap 2 cap or cap. (MLA: cap.) 3 caps or Caps

capitals and lower case 1 c & lc (CSM: c. & lc.; OUP: c. and l.c.) 2 caps and lc

capitals and small capitals 1 c & sc (GPO: c. and sc.; CSM: c. & s.c.) 2 caps and sc

Capricorn 1 Cap (constellation) 2 Caprice (constellation)

capsule 1 caps. 2 pharmaceutics cap or cap.

capsule communicator CAPCOM

Captain 1 Cap or Cap. (NYT: Capt.) 2 Capt. or Captn. 3 Cpt.

Captain General CG or C.G.

Captain of the Guard CG

Captain of the Horse CH or C.H.

caption cap

captured air bubble CAB

captures chess x

carat 1 c or c. 2 car. 3 ct. or ct 4 K 5 k or k. 6 kt or kt.

carats cts.

carbine CBN or cbn

carbohydrate 1 CHO 2 COH

carbohydrate-nitrogen ratio C/N or C:N

carbohydrates carbo.

carbon 1 C 2 carb.

carbon dioxide CO_2

carbon monoxide CO

carbon star astronomy N

carbon stars astronomy R

carbon steel CS

carbon tetrachloride CTC

carbon^{12} ^{12}C

carbon^{14} ^{14}C or C$_{14}$

carbon, nitrogen, oxygen CNO

carbon-nitrogen CN

carbon-nitrogen ratio chemistry C/N

carbonate or calcite compensation depth CCD

carboxymethylcellulose CMC

carburetor carb.

carcinoembryonic antigen CEA

Card Random Access Memory computers CRAM

cardiac index CI

cardiac output CO

Cardiac or Coronary Care Unit CCU

Cardiganshire, Wales Card.

Cardinal Card.

cardinal point CP

Cardinals PP. AA. (of Roman Catholic Church)

cardiokymograph CKG

cardiopulmonary resuscitation CPR

cardiovascular CV

cardiovascular system CVS

Career Minister CM

career trainee c.t. or C.T.

Careers Research and Advisory Centre CRAC

caressing or coaxing music Lusing.

cargo 1 C 2 car. 3 cgo.

cargo aircraft C or C-

cargo's proportion of general average *commerce* c.g.a. *or* cga
Caribbean Carib.
Caribbean Basis Initiative CBI
Caribbean Common Market *or* **Caribbean Community** CARICOM *or* Caricom
Caribbean Community CC
Caribbean Marine Biological Institute CMBI
Caribbean Research Institute CRI *or* C.R.I.
Caribbean Tourist Association CTA *or* C.T.A.
carload *commerce* cl *or* cl.
carload lots *commerce* c.l.
Carlow Car *or* Car.
Carmarthenshire, Wales Carm.
Carmelite Friars *Latin* OCC *or* O.C.C.
Carnegie Institute of Technology CIT *or* C.I.T.
Carnegie Institute of Washington CIW *or* C.I.W.
Carnegie United Kingdom Trust CUKT *or* C.U.K.T.
carpal tunnel syndrome CTS
Carpathian Mountains Carp.
carpel cpl.
carpenter 1 carp. 2 cptr.
carpentry carp.
carpeting carp.
carriage 1 carr. 2 *commerce* cge.
carriage and packing *commerce* c & p
Carriage of Goods by Sea Act COGSA *or* C.O.G.S.A.
carriage paid *commerce* 1 CP 2 cp *or* c.p.
carriage return *computers* CR
carried down *finance* 1 C/D 2 c/d 3 cd *or* c.d.
carried forward *accounting* 1 c.f. 2 c/f 3 CF *or* C/F
carried over *accounting* C/O *or* c/o *or* c.o.
carrier 1 *commerce* carr. 2 *computers* CARR
carrier frequency *electronics* CF
carrier sense multiple access *computers* CSM *or* CSMA
carrier wave *electronics* CW
carrier's risk *commerce* CR *or* C.R. *or* C/R
carrier-operated device, anti-noise codan
cartage 1 ctg. *or* ctge. 2 *commerce* cart.
carte blanche CBL *or* c.bl.
Carthusian Order O.Cart.
cartilage derived inhibitor CDI
carting to shipside *commerce* c. to s.
cartographer Cartog.
cartography Cartog.
carton 1 c *or* c. 2 ct. 3 ctn *or* ctn.
cartons cts.
cartridge ctg. *or* ctge.
case 1 c *or* c. 2 *commerce, law* ca (*OUP*: ca.) 3 *commerce* cs. 4 *law* Cs *or* Cs.
casehardened CH
cases *commerce* C/S
cash against documents *commerce* CAD
cash before delivery CBD *or* C.B.D. *or* cbd (*GPO*: c.b.d.)
cash credit CC *or* C.C.
cash discount *commerce* cd *or* c.d.
cash letter *commerce* CL *or* C/L
cash on hand *accounting* COH *or* c.o.h.
cash on shipment *commerce* 1 COS *or* C.O.S. 2 cos *or* c.o.s.

cash *or* **collect on delivery** COD *or* C.O.D. *or* c.o.d. (*GPO, NYT*: c.o.d.; *CSM*: c.o.d. *or* COD; *OUP*: COD)
cash order 1 C/O 2 CO *or* C.O.
cash versus documents *commerce* CVD *or* c.v.d.
cash with order *commerce* CWO *or* c.w.o. *or* C.W.O.
cashbook *accounting* 1 C/B 2 CB
cashier cash.
cashier's check CC
casing 1 cas. 2 csg.
cask 1 ck. 2 *commerce* csk. *or* csk
casks cks.
cassette cass *or* Cass
cassette camera recorder CCR
Cassiopeia 1 Cas (constellation) 2 Cp. (constellation)
cast copper CC
cast in brass *foundry* CB
cast iron CI
cast steel CS
Castile Cast.
casting cstg.
castle Cas *or* Cas.
casualty cas.
Casualty Clearing Station CCS
catabolite activator protein *genetics* CAP
Catalan 1 Cat. 2 Catal.
catalog cat.
cataloging in publication CIP
cataloging in source CIS *or* cis.
catalysis cat. *or* cat
cataplasm cat.
catapult cat.
cataract *medicine* cat.
catch basin CB
catcher *baseball* c *or* c.
catechism cat.
category cat.
category development index *marketing, advertising* CDI
cathartic cath.
Cathedral Cath.
Catherine Cath.
catheter cath.
catheterize cath.
cathodal opening contracture *medicine* CaOC.
cathode 1 C 2 ca *or* ca. 3 cath. 4 K 5 k 6 Ka 7 ka.
cathode ray CR
cathode-ray oscilloscope CRO
cathode-ray tube CRT
Catholic Cath.
Catholic Action CA *or* C.A.
Catholic Information Society CIS *or* C.I.S.
Catholic Library Association CLA *or* C.L.A.
Catholic Women's League C.W.L. *or* CWL
Catholic Young Men's Society CYMS *or* C.Y.M.S.
Catholic Youth Organization CYO *or* C.Y.O.
Caucasian Cauc.
caught *cricket* 1 c *or* c. 2 ct.
caught and bowled *cricket* c & b
cauliflower mosaic virus CaMV
caulking clkg.
causative *grammar* caus.
cause of death COD

cause to be done *Latin* fi.fa.
Causeway CSWY
Cavalier Cav.
Cavalry Cav. *or* Cav
Cavalry Brigade CB
caveat cav.
cavity cav.
Cayman Islands CI
cedi ¢
ceiling 1 ceil. 2 clg.
ceiling and visibility unlimited *aviation* CAVU
celebrated cel.
celesta *music* cel.
cell activity G
cell therapy CT
cell-mediated immunity CMI
cello Vc. *or* vc.
cellular-automata *or* **-automation machine** CAM
celluloid cel.
cellulose cel.
cellulose acetate butyrate CAB
Celsius 1 Cel. 2 Cels.
Celsius scale; centigrade C *or* C. *or* °C
Celsius *or* **centigrade thermal unit** CTU *or* C.T.U.
Celtic Celt.
celtium Ct
cement cem. *or* cem
cement base CB
cemetery cem.
Cenozoic *geology, biology* 1 CZ 2 Cz
censor cens.
censorship cens.
census cs.
Census Bureau CB
Census Metropolitan Area CMA
cent 1 c *or* c. 2 ct.
cental ctl.
Centaur Cen (constellation)
centavo 1 c *or* c. 2 Ctvo.
Center 1 Cr *or* Cr. 2 CTR
center 1 C *or* C. 2 c *or* c. 3 cen. 4 cent. 5 cntr *or* Cntr. 6 cr *or* cr. 7 ctr. *or* Ctr.
center back *sports* 1 CB 2 cb
center field *or* **center fielder** *baseball* CF
Center for Applied Linguistics CAL
Center for Bibliographical Services CBS
Center for Brain Research CBR
Center for Computer Sciences and Technology CCST
Center for Democratic Renewal CDR
Center for Educational Research and Innovation CERI
Center for Intercultural Documentation CIDOC
Center for International Studies CIS
Center for Measurement Science CMS *or* C.M.S.
Center for Science in the Public Interest CSPI
Center for Short Lived Phenomena CSLP
Center for UFO Studies CUFOS
Center for Utilization of Federal Technology CUFT
center forward *sports* CF
center halfback *sports* CH
center line *sports, printing, theater, mechanical drawing* CL

center matched cm or c.m.
center of buoyancy 1 CB 2 cb
Center of Experimentation in the Pacific Ocean CEP
center of flotation CF
center of gravity 1 CG or c.g. 2 cog or c.o.g. or COG
center of mass physics 1 CM 2 cm or c.m.
center of pressure 1 CP 2 cp or c.p.
center of resistance engineering 1 CR 2 cr or c.r.
center tap electronics CT
center to center c. to c. or c-to-c
center tracon automation system CTAS
Center Union Party of Greece EK
Center(s) For Disease Control CDC
centered cent.
centesimo Ctmo.
centi- c
centiare 1 ca or ca. 2 cent. or cent
centibar meteorology cb
centigrade cent.
centigrade heat unit CHU
centigram cg. or cg
centigram or centigrams cgm. or cgm
centiliter cl
centime 1 c or c. 2 cent. or cent 3 ct.
centimes cts.
centimeter 1 C 2 c 3 cent. 4 cm or cm.
centimeter-gram-second CGS or cgs or c.g.s.
centimeters ccm
centimeters per second 1 cm/s or cm./s 2 cm/sec or cm./sec. 3 cmps or cm.p.s.
centimo Ctmo.
centimorgan cM
centipoise 1 cp or cp. 2 cpe. 3 cps. 4 cpse.
centistoke 1 ck. or ck 2 cs. 3 cst.
Central 1 C 2 Cent. 3 CTL or Ctl.
central 1 cen. 2 cent. 3 Centr.
Central African Democratic Assembly RDC
Central African Economic and Customs Union French UDEAC
Central African Republic CAR or C.A.R.
central air data computer CADC
Central America CA or C.A.
Central American Bank for Economic Integration 1 BCIE 2 CABEI or Cabei
Central American Common Market CACM
Central American Standard Tariff Terminology Spanish NAUCA
Central Arbitration Committee CAC
Central Bureau for Astronomical Telegrams CBAT
Central Bureau of Identification CBI
central business district CBD or C.B.D.
Central Computer Complex CCC
Central Computing and Telecommunications Agency CCTA
Central Criminal Court CCC or C.C.C
Central Daylight Time CDT or C.D.T. or c.d.t.
Central Electricity Authority CEA or C.E.A.
Central Electricity Board British CEB
Central Electricity Generating Board CEGB
Central Electricity Research Laboratory CERL
Central European Line CEL
Central European Time CET
Central Flying School CFS or C.F.S.

central heating c.h. or ch
central information file computers CIF
Central Intelligence Agency CIA
Central Intelligence Board CIB
Central London Railway CLR
Central Medical Board CMB or C.M.B.
Central Mortgage and Housing Corporation CMHC
central nervous system CNS or C.N.S. or c.n.s.
central office CO
Central Office of Information COI or C.O.I.
central processing unit CPU
central processor computers CP
Central Radio Propagation Laboratory CRPL
Central Security Service CSS
Central Standard Time CST or C.S.T. or c.s.t.
Central Statistical Board CSB
Central Statistical Office CSO
Central Time 1 c.t. 2 CT or C.T.
Central Tumor Registry medicine CTR
Central Unit for Scientific Photography CUSP
central venous pressure medicine CVP
centralized engine room control CERC
Centralized Traffic Control CTC
centrifugal cent.
centrifugal force CF
centripetal force CF
cents 1 ¢ 2 cts.
centuries cc or cc.
century 1 C or C. 2 cen. 3 cent. 4 centy. or Centy. 5 French s or s.
cephalic index anthropology, medicine CI or C.I.
Cepheus Cep (constellation)
Ceramic Cer.
Ceramics Cer.
ceramics ceram.
cerebral blood flow CBF
cerebral infarction CI
cerebral palsy CP
cerebrospinal fluid medicine CSF or c.s.f.
cerebrospinal meningitis CSM
cerebrovascular accident CVA
cerificate of deposit C/D
cerium Ce
certainty factor mathematics CF
Certificate Ct or Ct.
certificate 1 cert. or Cert. 2 certif. 3 ctf.
Certificate in Computer Programming CCP
Certificate in Data Processing CDP or C.D.P.
Certificate in Library Science CLS or C.L.S.
Certificate in Public Health C.P.H.
Certificate in Social Work CSW or C.S.W.
Certificate of Advanced Graduate Study C.A.G.S. or CAGS
Certificate of Advanced Study CAS or C.A.S.
certificate of airworthiness C. of A.
Certificate of Clinical Competence CCC or C.C.C.
certificate of deposit CD or C.D.
certificate of disability for discharge military CDD
Certificate of Extended Education CEE or C.E.E.
certificate of insurance CI or C/I
certificate of maintenance aeronautics C of M

certificate of management accounting CMA
Certificate of Merit CM or C.M.
Certificate of Origin C/O or C.O.
Certificate of Physical Education CPE
Certificate of Qualification in Social Work CQSW or C.Q.S.W.
certificated certif.
certificates cts.
certification cert. or Cert.
certified 1 cert. or Cert. 2 ctf.
Certified General Accountant CGA or C.G.A.
Certified Internal Auditor CIA
Certified Kitchen Designer CKD or C.K.D.
Certified Management Consultant CMC or C.M.C.
Certified Medical Assistant CMA or C.M.A.
Certified Nurse Midwife CNM
Certified Occupational Therapist OTR or O.T., Reg.
Certified Occupational Therapy Assistant COTA
certified official government business British COGB
Certified Pediatric Worker CPW
Certified Professional Secretary CPS or C.P.S.
Certified Public Accountant CPA or C.P.A. (GPO, NYT: C.P.A.)
Certified Record Librarian C.R.L. or CRL
Certified Reference Librarian C.R.L. or CRL
Certified Registered Nurse Anesthetist C.R.N.A.
Certified Rehabilitation Counselor CRC
Certified Respiratory Therapy Technician CRTT
Certified Shorthand Reporter C.S.R. or CSR
Certified System Professional computers CSP
certified teacher CT or C.T.
certified technician CT or C.T.
Certified Tumor Registrar medicine CTR
certify 1 cert. or Cert. 2 certif. 3 ctf.
certiorari cert.
cervical cerv.
cervical spinal nerve C or C.
Cesarean section medicine CS
cesium Cs
chain 1 ch. or ch (surveyor's measure and needlework) 2 chn. (surveyor's measure)
chair C or C.
Chairman 1 Ch. 2 Chm. 3 Chn. 4 Chn. or Chmn. 5 Chrm. or Chrmn.
chairman C or C.
Chairperson 1 Chn. 2 Chrp.
chairperson 1 C or C. 2 Chpn
Chaldean Chal. or Chald.
Challenge Certificate CC
chamber 1 Ch. 2 chm.
Chamber of Commerce 1 C of C 2 CC or C.C. 3 COC
Chamberlain Chamb.
Chameleon Cha (constellation)
champion 1 Ch. or Ch 2 champ. or champ or Champ.
championship CHP or chp.
Championship Auto Racing Team CART
Chancellor 1 Canc. 2 Ch. 3 Chanc. or Chanc
Chancery 1 Ch. 2 Chanc.

Chancery Reports *law* CR *or* C.R.
change chg.
change of course C/C
change over C/O *or* c.o. *or* c/o
change point *surveying* CP *or* C.P.
changed chgd.
Channel Cha *or* Cha.
channel 1 chan. *or* Chan. **2** *television,*
   navigation Ch. *or* Ch **3** *television* ch. *or* ch
channel for orders *commerce* CFO *or* C.F.O.
Channel Islands CI *or* C.I.
channel status table *computers* CST
channel status word *computers* CSW
Channel Tunnel CHUNNEL *or* Chunnel
Chapel Chap.
chapel *Latin* capel.
Chaplain 1 Ch. **2** Chap.
Chaplain to the Forces *British* CF *or* C.F.
chapter 1 C **2** c *or* c. **3** cap *or* cap. **4** ch.
   5 Ch. *or* Ch (*MLA:* ch., chap.; *CSM:* chap.;
   OUP: ch.) **1** Chap. *or* chap. **2** *Latin,*
   Spanish Cap *or* Cap. (*OUP:* cap.)
chapters 1 cc *or* cc. **2** chs.
character *printing, computers* char. *or* CHAR
characteristic char.
characters per inch *printing* CPI *or* cpi
characters per line *computers, printing* CPL
   or cpl
characters per minute 1 CPM **2** cpm *or*
   c.p.m.
characters per pica *printing* CPP *or* c.p.p.
characters per second 1 CPS **2** cps *or* c.p.s.
charge 1 chg. **2** *physics* C
charge conjugation *physics* C
charge conjugation, parity CP
charge conjugation, parity, time *physics* CPT
Charge of Quarters CQ *or* C.Q.
charge-coupled device CCD
charge-injection device *electronics* CID
charged chgd.
Charged Particle Beam CPB
charges prepaid ch.ppd.
Charioteer Aur (constellation)
charity char.
Charity Organization Society COS *or*
   C.O.S.
Charles 1 Ch. **2** Chas. **3** *Latin* Car *or* Car.
charter char. *or* Char.
charter party CP
Chartered Accountant CA *or* C.A. (*CSM:*
   C.A.; *OUP:* CA)
chartered engineer CEng
Chartered Financial Analyst CFA *or* C.F.A.
Chartered Institute of Building CIOB
Chartered Institute of Patent Agents CIPA
   or C.I.P.A.
Chartered Insurance Institute C.I.I. *or* CII
Chartered Life Underwriter C.L.U. *or* CLU
Chartered Patent Agent CPA *or* C.P.A.
Chartered Property and Casualty
   Underwriter C.P.C.U *or* CPCU
Chartered Public Accountant CPA *or* C.P.A.
Chartered Society of Massage and Medical
   Gymnastics C.S.M.M.G.
Chartered Stenographic Reporter C.S.R. *or*
   CSR
charterers pay dues *commerce* CPD *or*
   C.P.D.
Chaucer Chauc.

chauffeur chauf.
Chautauqua Literary and Scientific Circle
   C.L.S.C.
Chawa Cha Mapinduzi CCM
check 1 CHK *or* chk. **2** ck. **3** *chess* **a** Ch. *or*
   Ch **b** ch. *or* ch
check valve CV
checker CHKR *or* chkr
checkmate *chess* chm.
checks *commerce* cks.
chemical 1 chem. **2** cml. *or* Cml
Chemical Abstract Service CAS
Chemical Abstracts CA
Chemical Addiction Certification CAC *or*
   C.A.C.
chemical and biological CB
chemical and biological warfare CBW
Chemical Engineer 1 CE *or* C.E. **2** ChE *or*
   Ch.E. *or* Che.E. **3** Chem.E. *or* ChemE
chemical engineering optimization system
   CHEOPS
chemical field effect transistor chemfet
Chemical Industry Institute of Toxicology
   CIIT
Chemical Institute of Canada CIC
Chemical Notation Association CNA *or*
   C.N.A.
chemical oxygen demand COD
chemical stimulation of the brain *medicine*
   CSB
chemical vapor deposition CVD
chemical warfare CW
Chemical Workers Union CWU
chemical, biological, radiological CBR
chemical-atomic-biological CAB
Chemical-Biological Coordination Center
   CBCC
chemically pure 1 CP *or* C.P. **2** cp *or* c.p.
   (*GPO:* c.p.)
chemist chem.
chemistry 1 Ch. **2** chem.
chemotherapeutic index *pharmaceutics,*
   medicine CI
cheque chq.
Cheshire, England Ches. *or* Chesh.
chest 1 cht. **2** *dressmaking, tailoring,*
   medicine ch.
chestnut ch.
Chevalier Chev.
chevron chev.
Chicago 1 Chi. *or* Chic. **2** G(in the Federal
   Reserve banking system) **3** *finance* Chgo
Chicago Board of Trade 1 CBOT **2** CBT
Chicago Board Options Exchange CBOE
Chicago Daily News CDN
Chicago Mercantile Exchange CME
Chicago Review Chi. R.
Chicago Symphony Orchestra CSO *or*
   C.S.O.
Chicago Transit Authority CTA
Chicago Tribune Chi. Trib.
Chichester Cicestr.
chicken cell agglutination CCA
Chief 1 C *or* C. **2** Ch. *or* Ch
chief Chf.
chief accountant CA *or* C.A.
Chief Accounting Officer CAO
Chief Administrative Officer CAO *or* C.A.O.
Chief Baron CB

Chief Clerk 1 CC *or* C.C. **2** Ch. Clk.
Chief Clerk of the Admiralty CCA *or* C.C.A.
Chief Commissioner CC *or* C.C.
Chief Counsel CC
Chief Education Officer CEO
Chief Engineer 1 CE *or* C.E. **2** ChE
Chief Executive Officer CEO
Chief Financial Officer CFO
Chief Inspector CI
Chief Instructor CI
Chief Judge C.J.
Chief Justice 1 C.J. **2** Ch.J.
Chief Medical Officer CMO
Chief of Finance C of F
Chief of Naval Operations CNO *or* C.N.O.
Chief of Section 1 COFS *or* C of S **2** COS *or*
   C.O.S.
Chief of Staff 1 COFS *or* C of S **2** COS *or*
   C.O.S. **3** CS
Chief of the Air Staff CAS
Chief of the Defense Staff *British* CDS *or*
   C.D.S.
Chief of the General Staff CGS *or* C.G.S.
Chief or Company Quartermaster CQM
Chief Patriarch CP *or* C.P.
Chief Petty Officer CPO
Chief Scientific Officer CSO *or* C.S.O.
Chief Signal Officer CSO *or* C.S.O.
Chief Staff Officer CSO *or* C.S.O.
Chief Technical Officer CTO
chief value c.v.
Chief Warrant Officer CWO
Chihuahua Chih.
child 1 Ch. **2** ch.
child development research CDR
Child Study Association CSA *or* C.S.A.
Child Welfare CW
Child Welfare League C.W.L. *or* CWL
Child Welfare Service CWS
Child or Children In Need of Supervision
   CINS
children 1 Ch. **2** ch.
Children's Aid Society CAS
Children's Apperception Test CAT
Children's Book Council CBC *or* C.B.C.
Children's Hospital Medical Center CHMC
Children's Services Division CSD
Children's Television Workshop CTW
chimney 1 ch. **2** chy. *or* chy
China 1 Ch. **2** Chin.
Chinese 1 Ch. **2** Chin.
Chinese Bridge Association CBA
Chinese Communist Party CCP
Chinese People's Political Consultative
   Conference CPPCC
Chino-Japanese Chino-Jap.
Chisel Cae (constellation)
chloride 1 chl *or* chlo. **2** Cl
chlorine Cl
chloroacetophenone CN
chlorofluorocarbon CFC
chlorofluoromethane CFM
chloroform chl *or* chlo. *or* chloro.
chlorophenyldimethylurea CMU
chloroprene CR
chlortetracycline CTC
chocolate choc.
choir Ch.
choirmaster Chm. *or* CHM

choke coil *electronics* CHC
choke *or* choke coil *electronics* CH
cholecystokinin CCK
cholesterol chol.
cholesterol, saturated-fat index CSI
cholinesterase ChE *or* chE
Choral Chor.
chord *mathematics* chd.
chorioallantoic membrane CAM
chorionic villus sampling CVS
chorus Chor.
chrestomathy chr.
Christ 1 Chr. 2 X 3 XC 4 XP 5 Xt.
Christian 1 Chr. 2 Christ. 3 X 4 Xn.
Christian Broadcasting Association CBA
Christian Broadcasting Network CBN
Christian Brothers FSC *or* F.S.C.
Christian Democratic Party CDP *or* C.D.P.
Christian Democratic People's Party of
  Switzerland CUP
Christian Democratic Union CDU *or* C.D.U.
Christian Education CE *or* C.E.
Christian Endeavor CE *or* C.E.
Christian Endeavour Union C.E.U.
Christian Era CE *or* C.E. *or* CE *or* C.E. *(OUP:*
  CE)
Christian Methodist Episcopal CME *or*
  C.M.E.
Christian People's Party (of Flemish
  Belgium) CVP
Christian Science CS *or* C.S.
Christian Science Monitor CSM
Christian Social Union CSU
Christian Trade Union Federation of
  Germany CGD
Christian. Xtian
Christianity 1 Xnty. 2 Xty
Christmas 1 Chr. 2 Christ. 3 Xmas
Christopher Chr.
chromium Cr
chronic 1 ch. 2 chr.
chronic active hepatitis CAH
chronic brain syndrome *medicine* CBS
chronic coronary insufficiency *medicine* CCI
chronic fatigue syndrome *medicine* CFS
chronic granulomatosis disease CGD
chronic lymphocytic leukemia CLL
chronic migrating red rash ECM
chronic myelocytic leukemia CML
chronic obstructive pulmonary disease
  COPD
chronic pulmonary disease CPD
chronic pulmonary emphysema CPE
chronic renal failure *medicine* CRF
chronic respiratory disease CRD
chronic ulcerative colitis CUC
Chronicle Chron.
Chronicles Chron.
chronological age *psychology* CA
chronological *or* chronologically chron. *or*
  chronol. *(OUP:* chron.)
chronology chron. *or* chronol. *(OUP:* chron.)
chronometry Chron. *(OUP:* chron.)
Church C
church 1 Ch. 2 ch.
Church Missionary Society CMS *or* C.M.S.
Church of England 1 C. of E. 2 CE *or* C.E.
  or C. of E.
Church of England Men's Society C.E.M.S.

Church of England Temperance Society
  CETS *or* C.E.T.S.
Church of England Working Men's Society
  C.E.W.M.S. *or* CEWMS
Church of Ireland C. of I.
Church of Scotland C. of S.
churchwarden Chwdn.
Cicero Cic.
Cincinnati 1 Cin. 2 Cinn.
Cincinnati Symphony Orchestra CSO *or*
  C.S.O.
Circle CIR
circle cir. *or* circ. *or* Cir.
circle of equal probability CEP
circuit 1 cir. *or* circ. *or* Circ. 2 ckt. 3 ct.
circuit breaker 1 C/B 2 cb *or* c.b. *or* c/b
Circuit Judge C.J.
Circuit *or* County Court Judge CCJ *or* C.C.J.
circular cir. *or* circ.
circular mil 1 cir mil *or* cir. mil 2 cm *or* cm.
circular note C/N
circular pitch cp *or* c.p.
circular probable error 1 *mathematics* CEP
  2 *navigation* CPE *or* c.p.e.
circular wave number *physics* k
circulating hot water HWC
circulation cir. *or* circ.
circulation manager CM
circumference 1 C 2 cir. *or* circ. 3 circum.
circumstance circe.
circumstances *British* circs
cirrocumulus Cc
cirrostratus Cs
cirrus *meteorology* 1 c 2 Ci
citation cit.
cited cit.
citizen cit.
Citizen Military Force CMF
Citizens Band CB
Citizens for Decent Literature CDL
Citizens Military Training Camp C.M.T.C.
Citizens' Advice Bureau CAB *or* C.A.B.
Citizens' Civic Action Association CCAA
Citizens' Training Corps CTC
citrate cit.
City 1 C 2 Cty.
City and Guilds of London Institute CGIL *or*
  C.G.I.L. *or* C.G.I.
City College of New York CCNY *or*
  C.C.N.Y. *(NYT: not acceptable)*
City Council CC *or* C.C.
City Councilor CC *or* C.C.
City of Birmingham Symphony Orchestra
  CBSO
City Planning Commission CPC
City University of New York CUNY
civil civ. *or* Civ.
Civil Aeronautics Administration CAA
Civil Aeronautics Board CAB
Civil Air Patrol CAP *or* C.A.P. *(GPO:* CAP;
  OUP: cap.)
Civil Air Regulations CAR
Civil Air Transport CAT
Civil and Public Services Association CPSA
  or C.P.S.A.
Civil Aviation Authority CAA
civil cases *law* CC *or* C.C.
civil code *law* CC *or* C.C.
civil commotion CC

Civil Cooperation Bureau C.C.B.
Civil Court CC *or* C.C.
Civil Defense CD
Civil Defense Act CDA
Civil Defense Services *British* CDS
Civil Division CD
Civil Engineer CE *or* C.E.
Civil Engineering Research Association CERA
Civil Law CL *or* C.L.
Civil Pilot Training Program CPTP
Civil Procedure CP *or* C.P.
Civil Reserve Air Fleet CRAF
Civil Rights Commission CRC *or* C.R.C.
Civil Rights Division CRD
Civil Servant CS *or* C.S.
Civil Service CS *or* C.S.
Civil Service Commission CSC *or* C.S.C.
Civil Service Commission of Canada CSCC
  or C.S.C.C.
Civil Service Employees Association
  C.S.E.A. *or* CSEA
Civil Technical Corps CTC *or* C.T.C.
Civil Works Administration CWA
civilian civ.
Civilian Conservation Corps CCC
Civilian Health and Medical Program of the
  Veterans Administration CHAMPVA
Civilian Review Board CRB
civilian war dead CWD
civilization civ.
claim 1 Cl *or* Cl. 2 cl *or* cl.
claim agent CA *or* C.A.
claims Cl *or* Cl.
clarendon Clar. *or* clar.
Clarendon Press CP *or* C.P.
clarinet 1 Clar. *or* clar. 2 *music* cl
clarinetist Clst. *or* clst.
class 1 C 2 Cl *(OUP:* cl) 3 cl *or* cl.
class interval *statistics, psychology* CI *or* c.i.
class interval or width *statistics* i
classic class.
Classical Cl *or* Cl.
classical class.
classical gyromagnetic ratio *physics* g
Classical Latin Cl Lat.
Classical Philology CP
classification 1 cl *or* cl. 2 class.
classified class.
classroom Clrm.
clause 1 cl *or* cl. 2 Cl *or* Cl. *(OUP:* cl.)
clavichord *music* clvd
clay Cl
clean pur.
clean and jerk C & J
Clean Water Act CWA *or* C.W.A.
clear 1 clr. 2 *computers* CLR
clear air turbulence CAT
clear to send *computers* CTS
clearance 1 cl 2 clr.
cleared 1 *commerce* cld. 2 *computers* cld. *or*
  CLD 3 *meteorology* cld.
clearing *finance* clg.
clearing house CH *or* C.H.
clergyman 1 Cl 2 Clerg.
cleric Cl
clerical, administrative, and fiscal
  accounting CAF
clerk 1 Cl *or* Cl. 2 clk.
Clerk of Petty Sessions CPS *or* C.P.S.

Clerk of Session *or* **Sessions** CS *or* C.S.
Clerk of the Peace *British* CP *or* C.P.
Clerk of the Privy Council CPC *or* C.P.C.
Cleveland 1 Clev. *or* Cleve. **2** CLV *or* Clv. **3** D(in the Federal Reserve system)
Cleveland Open Cup *chemistry* COC
climate clim.
climatological climat
climatology climat
Clinic Clin.
clinical Clin. *or* clin.
Clinical Fellow Year C.F.Y.
Clinical Orthopedic Society COS *or* C.O.S.
Clinical Pathological Conference *medicine* CPC
Clock Hor (constellation)
clock clk. *or* CLK
clockwise 1 ckw. **2** CW **3** cw
close *computers* CLS
close-in weapons system CIWS
close-up *photography* CU
close-up shot *photography* CS
closed caption CC
closed user group CUG
closed-circuit television CCTV
Closer Economic Relations CER (Australian-New Zealand trade agreement)
closet 1 cl **2** clo.
cloth cl *or* cl. (*OUP:* cl.)
cloth sides *bookbinding* CS *or* C.S.
clothing clo.
cloudy *meteorology* c
club Cl *or* Cl.
cluster bomb unit CBU
cluster of differentiation *or* **cluster designation** *immunology* CD
clutter-operated anti-clutter COAC
co-edition Co-edn.
Coadjutor Coad.
Coal Mining Institute of America C.M.I.A.
coal water slurry CWS
coal-oil-gas Cogas
coast Cst.
Coast and Geodetic Survey 1 C & GS **2** CGS
Coast Artillery CA
Coast Guard CG *or* C.G.
Coast Guard Academy CGA *or* C.G.A.
Coast Guard Auxiliary CGA *or* C.G.A.
Coast Guard Cutter C.G.C. *or* CGC
coastal defense CD
Coastal Motor Boat CMB
coated both sides *printing* C2S
coated one side *printing* C1S
coated tablet *pharmaceutics* CT
coaxial 1 co. **2** coax
coaxial cable coax
cobalt Co
code cod. *or* Cod.
code division multiple access CDMA
code division multiplex CDM
Code Napoleon CN *or* C.N.
Code of Civil Procedure CCP *or* C.C.P.
Code of Criminal Procedure CCP *or* C.C.P.
Code of Federal Regulations CFR
Code of Military Justice CJM *or* C.J.M.
Code of Procedure *law* CP *or* C.P.
code wave CW
Coder and Decoder Codec

codices codd.
codicil cod. *or* Cod.
coeducational coed
coefficient 1 C **2** c **3** coef. *or* coeff.
coefficient of alienation *statistics* k
coefficient of correlation *statistics* CC
coefficient of friction *physics* CF
coefficient of impact e
coefficient of performance *physics* COP
coefficient of thermal expansion *engineering, physics* CTE *or* cte
coefficient of variation 1 *psychology, statistics* CV **2** *statistics* v
coenzyme Co
cognate *linguistics* cog *or* cog. (*MLA:* cog.)
cognate with *linguistics* c *or* c.
cognitive behavioral modification *psychology* CBM
cognizant cog *or* cog.
cohabit co-hab
cohabitation co-hab
coherent oscillator *electronics* COHO
coin-operated coin-op
colatitude 1 co. **2** *astronomy, navigation* col. *or* col
cold 1 C **2** c
cold air mass *meteorology* k
cold maritime Polar air mass *meteorology* mPk
Cold Region Research and Engineering Laboratory CRREL
cold rolled CR
cold weld *mechanics, engineering* CW
cold-punched cp
cold-rolled steel CRS
Coldstream Guards CG
collaborate collab.
collaboration collab.
collaborator collab.
collated 1 col. **2** coll.
collated and perfect *bookbinding* c & p
collateral 1 coll. **2** collat.
Collateralized Mortgage Obligation CMO
colleague coll.
collect 1 col. **2** coll.
collected 1 col. **2** coll.
collection coll.
collection and delivery *commerce* C & D *or* c & d
collective 1 coll. **2** collect.
collective call sign CCS
Collective Measures Committee CMC
collective reserve unit CRU *or* cru
collective volume *chemistry* coll.vol.
collector 1 col. **2** coll.
College 1 Col *or* Col. **2** Coll.
college coll.
College Ability Test CAT
College Achievement Test CAT
College English CE
College English Association CEA
College Entrance Examination Board CEEB
College Football Association CFA
College Language Association CLA
College Level Examination Program CLEP
College of Advanced Technology *British* CAT
College of American Pathologists CAP *or* C.A.P.
Collegiate 1 Col *or* Col. **2** Coll.

Collider Detector at Fermilab CDF
Collision Waiver CDW
collision-avoidance system CAS
colloidal coll.
colloquial 1 col. **2** coll. **3** colloq.
colloquialism colloq.
colloquially colloq.
cologarithm colog
Colombia Col *or* Col.
colon Col
colón ¢ *or* ₡
Colonel Col *or* Col.
Colonial Col *or* Col.
Colonial Dames of America CDA *or* C.D.A.
colonies cols.
Colony Col *or* Col.
colony col.
colony stimulating factor CSF
colony-forming cells *biology* CFC
colony-forming unit *biology* CFU
colophon col.
color 1 C **2** clr. **3** col.
color code CC
color correction CC
color graphics *computers* CG
color graphics adaptor *computers* CGA
Color Index CI
color phase alternation CPA
color response *psychology* CR
color reversal intermediate *photography, printing* CRI
color separation *printing* CS
color vision VC
Color-Sergeant Col.-Sgt.
Colorado 1 CO (Zip Code) **2** Co *or* Co. **3** Col *or* Col. **4** Colo.
Colorado River Authority CRA *or* C.R.A.
colored 1 cld. **2** col.
Colossians 1 Col *or* Col. **2** Coloss.
Columbia Col *or* Col.
Columbia Broadcasting System CBS
Columbia Journalism Review CJR
Columbia University CU
Columbia University Press CUP
Columbia Valley Authority CVA
column 1 clm. **2** col *or* col (*MLA:* col.) **3** colm. **4** *bibliography* c *or* c.
columns cols.
Combat Air Patrol CAP
Combat Information Center CIC
Combat Operations Center COC
combat zone *military* CZ
combination 1 comb. **2** combo **3** *British* combi
combination export manager CEM
combinations combs.
combine comb.
combined comb.
Combined Chiefs of Staff CCS
combined diesel and gas CODAG
Combined Forces Command CFC
combined heat and power CHP
combined immunodeficiency *medicine* CID
Combined Programming Language *computers* CPL
Combined State Unions CSU (of New Zealand)
combined steam and gas COSAG *or* Cosag
combining comb.

combustible comb.
combustion comb.
Comédie Française CF
comedy com.
Comedy of Errors, The 1 Com.Err. 2 Err.
comma com.
Command 1 Cmd. 2 Comd.
command *computers* COM
command and data acquisition CDA
command and data-handling console
  computers CDC
Command and General Staff C & GS
Command Center *military* CC
command language interpreter *computers*
  CLI
command module CM
Command Paper 1 Cmd. 2 Cmnd.
Command Post CP
command service module CSM
Commandant 1 CDT *or* Cdt. 2 Cmdt.
  3 Comdt.
Commandant of the Marine Corps CMC *or*
  C.M.C.
Commander 1 C 2 CDr. *or* CDR (*OUP:* Cdr.)
  3 Cmdr. 4 Comd. 5 Comdr. 6 Comm.
  7 *military* **a** COM **b** Com.
Commander in Chief CIC *or* C-I-C
Commander of the Order of the British
  Empire CBE *or* C.B.E.
Commander of the Royal Victorian Order
  C.V.O. *or* CVO
Commander-in-Chief 1 C-in-C *or* CinC
  2 Com.-in-Chf. 3 *military* CINC
Commanding 1 Cmdg. 2 Comdg. 3 *military*
  COMD
Commanding District Officer DOC *or* D.O.C.
Commanding General CG *or* C.G.
Commanding Officer CO *or* C.O. (*GPO,*
  OUP: CO)
commemorative commem.
commence comm.
comment com.
commentary 1 com. 2 comm.
commentator comm.
Commerce Comm.
commerce com.
Commerce Clearing House CCH
Commercial 1 Com. 2 Comm.
commercial 1 cml. 2 cmml. 3 com. 4 coml.
  5 comm.
commercial agent CA *or* C.A.
commercial air movement CAM *or* C.A.M.
commercial bill of lading CBL *or* CB/L *or*
  cb/l
commercial demonstration fast reactor
  CDFR
commercial quality CQ
commercial standard CS
commercial weight CW
commercial zone 1 cmmz 2 CZ
Commissary 1 Com. 2 Comm.
Commissary General CG
Commission 1 Com. 2 Comm. 3 Commn.
commission CMN *or* Cmn.
Commission for Industry and Manpower
  CIM *or* C.I.M.
Commission for Local Administration CLA
Commission for Synoptic Meteorology CSM
Commission of Fine Arts CFA

Commission of the Churches on
  International Affairs CCIA
Commission on Civil Rights CCR
Commission on Intergroup Relations COIR
commissioned Cd *or* Cd.
commissioned officer Com.Off.
Commissioner 1 Com. 2 Comm. 3 Commr.
  4 Comr.
Commissioner of Metropolitan Police CMP
Commissioners of the District of Columbia
  CDC *or* C.D.C
Committee 1 Cmte 2 Com. (*CSM:* comm.)
  3 Comm. 4 Cttee.
Committee for Economic Development CED
  or C.E.D.
Committee for Economic Development of
  Australia CEDA *or* C.E.D.A.
Committee for Environmental Conservation
  COENCO
Committee for Exploitation of the Oceans
  COMEXO
Committee for the Defense of the
  Revolution CDR *or* C.D.R.
Committee of Agricultural Organizations
  C.O.P.A. *or* COPA
Committee of European Shipowners CES
Committee of National Institutes of Patent
  Agents CNIPA
Committee of the International Socialist
  Conference COMISCO
Committee on Academic Science and
  Engineering CASE
Committee on Extraterrestrial Exploration
  CETEX
Committee on Fisheries COFI
Committee on National Library and
  Information Systems CONLIS
Committee on Political Education COPE *or*
  C.O.P.E.
Committee on Scholarly Communication
  with the People's Republic of China
  CSCPRC
Committee on Science and Public Policy
  COSPUP
Committee on Scientific and Technical
  Information COSATI
Committee on Space Research COSPAR *or*
  Cospar
Committee on the Peaceful Uses of Outer
  Space CPUOS
Committee on Uniform Securities
  Identification Procedures CUSIP
Committee on Water Research COWAR
Commodities Trading Advisor CTA
Commodity Credit Corporation CCC
Commodity Exchange COMEX *or* Comex
Commodity Exchange Authority CEA
Commodity Futures Trading Commission
  CFTC
Commodity Stabilization Service CSS
Commodore 1 Cmdre. 2 Com.
Common Com.
common 1 com. 2 cs. 3 *music* C
Common Agricultural Policy CAP
Common Algorithmic Language COMAL
common applications environment CAE
Common Bench *British law* CB *or* C.B.
common bile duct *medicine* CBD
common brick *construction* cb *or* c.b.

Common Business Oriented Language
  COBOL
common carrier CC
common channel signaling *communications*
  CCS
Common Council CC *or* C.C.
Common Councilman CC *or* C.C.
Common Entrance CE *or* C.E.
Common Entrance Examination CEE
Common Era CE *or* C.E. *or* CE *or* C.E. (*OUP:*
  CE)
common external tariff CXT
Common Fisheries Policy CFP
Common Law CL *or* C.L.
Common Law Procedure Acts C.L.P.A. *or*
  CLPA
Common Market CM
common meter *music* CM *or* C.M.
Common Meter Double *music* CMD
common mode *electronics* CM
common mode rejection CMR
common particular meter *music* CPM *or*
  C.P.M.
Common Plea CP *or* C.P.
Common Prayer CP *or* C.P.
common stock *finance* 1 c.s. *or* cs 2 CS *or*
  C.S.
common variable immunodeficiency CVI
Common Version 1 Com. Ver. (of the Bible)
  2 CV *or* C.V.
commonly com.
Commons, Open Spaces and Footpaths
  Preservation Society COSFPS
Commonweal Comm.
Commonwealth 1 Com. 2 Comm.
  3 Commw. 4 Cwlth. *or* C'wealth
Commonwealth Arbitration Reports CAR *or*
  C.A.R.
Commonwealth Bureau of Census and
  Statistics C.B.C.S. *or* CBCS
Commonwealth Economic Committee CEC
  or C.E.C.
Commonwealth National Library CNL
Commonwealth of Australia Bureau of
  Meteorology C.A.B.M. *or* CABM
Commonwealth of Independent States
  1 CIS 2 SNG
Commonwealth Parliamentary Association
  CPA *or* C.P.A.
Commonwealth Press Union CPU *or* C.P.U.
Commonwealth Science Council CSC
Commonwealth Scientific and Industrial
  Research Organization CSIRO
Commonwealth Serum Laboratories CSL
Commonwealth-Pacific COMPAC
communicate com.
communicated com.
communication 1 com. 2 comm. 3 commun.
communication line adapter for teletype
  computers CLAT
communication line terminal *computers* CLT
communication with extraterrestrial
  intelligence CETI
communications COM
communications electronics instructions CEI
communications for on-line systems
  computers COLS
communications input and output control
  system *computers* CIOCS

communications intelligence COMINT
Communications of the Association for Computing Machinery CACM
communications satellite COMSAT or Comsat (GPO, NYT: Comsat)
Communications Workers of America CWA
communications zone indicator COZI
Communist 1 Com. 2 Comm.
Communist International Comintern
Communist Party CP
Communist Party of Cuba Spanish PCC
Communist Party of Greece KKE or K.K.E.
Communist Workers Party CWP
Community 1 Com. 2 Comm.
Community Action Agency CAA
community antenna television 1 CAT 2 CATV
Community College CC or C.C.
Community Development Block Grant CDBG
community mental health center CMHC
Community of European Writers Comes
Community Relations Service CRS
community service volunteer CSV or C.S.V.
Community Services Administration CSA
compact disc-interactive CDI or CD-I
compact disk CD
compact disk television CDTV
compact disk video CDV
compact disk–read only memory CD-Rom
Compact Ignition Tokamak CIT or C.I.T.
compact molecular cloud chemistry CMC
compact source iodide CSI
companies Cos. or cos.
companion comp.
companion dog CD or C.D.
Companion of Honour CH or C.H.
Companion of Literature C.Lit. or C.Litt.
Companion of the Order of Australia AC or A.C.
Companion of the Order of Canada CC or C.C.
Companion of the Order of St. Michael and St. George C.M.G. or CMG
Companion of the Order of the Bath CB or C.B.
Company 1 Co or Co. (GPO, NYT, OUP: Co.) 2 commerce Com.
company Coy.
Company Commander military CC
company's risk commerce CR or C.R. or C/R
comparative 1 comp. 2 compar.
Comparative Literature Studies CLS
compare 1 cf. 2 comp. 3 conf. 4 cp or cp. 5 computers CMP or cmp
comparison 1 comp. 2 compar.
compartment compt.
Compass Pyx (constellation)
compass comp.
compass bearing CB
compass course cc
compass error c.e.
compass heading CH
compass north CN
compatible single side-band transmission electronics CSSB
compensating comp.
compensation comp.
competency-based education CBE
competitive protein binding biology CPB
compilation comp.

compiled Comp.
compiled by 1 Comp. 2 comp.
compiler 1 Comp. 2 comp.
compilers comps.
complainant complt.
complement 1 compl. 2 computers CMPL or Cmpl
complement fixation CF
complement fixation test medicine CFT
complement fixing antigen CFA
complementary metal oxide semiconductor electronics CMOS
complete 1 compl. 2 cpl.
complete background investigation CBI or c.b.i.
complete blood count CBC
complete marked inversion CMI
completed compl.
completed games pitched baseball CG
completely knocked down commerce CKD
complex instruction set computer CISC
Compliance and Investigations Group CIG
component comp.
compose comp.
composed by comp.
composer comp.
Composers and Authors Guild CAG
Composers, Authors, and Publishers Association of Canada CAPAC or C.A.P.A.C.
composite comp.
composite cost-effectiveness index CCEI or ccei
composition 1 comp. 2 compn. or compo.
compositor comp.
compound 1 cmpd or CMPD 2 comp. 3 cpd. 4 chemistry, pharmaceutics compd.
compounded 1 cmpd or CMPD 2 chemistry, pharmaceutics compd. 3 pharmaceutics comp.
comprehensive comp.
Comprehensive Assessment of Treatment Outcome Research CATOR
Comprehensive Certificate of Origin C.C.O. or CCO
Comprehensive Drug Abuse Prevention and Control Act CDAPC
Comprehensive Employment and Training Act CETA
Comprehensive Environmental Response, Compensation and Liability Act, the Superfund CERCLA
Comprehensive Test Ban Treaty CTB or CTBT
comprehensives comps. or comps
compress comp.
compressed comp.
compressed air energy storage CAES
compressed natural gas CNG
compressibility factor physics k
compression factor chemistry z
compression ignition CI or C.I. or c.i.
compression in transit cit. or c.i.t.
compression ratio engineering CR
compression scanning array radar COSAR
compression yield strength engineering CYS
comprising comp.
compromise cmp.
comptometer compt.
Comptroller Comp.

comptroller Compt.
Comptroller General Comp.Gen.
Comptroller's Decisions Comp.Dec
compute computers CMPT or Cmpt
computer COM
computer entry device CED
computer graphics CG
computer graphics metafile CGM
Computer Information Delivery Service CIDS
computer input microfilm CIM
computer interface unit CIU
computer language Ada
computer language recorder CLR
computer language translator CLT
computer numerical control CNC
computer or computerized tomography CT
computer output microfilm COM or com
computer performance evaluation CPE
Computer Science Association CSA
Computer Services and Bureaus Association COSBA
computer simulation language CSL
computer systems simulator CSS
computer terminal having a cathode-ray tube CRT
computer-aided design and computer-aided manufacturing CAD-CAM
computer-aided design and drafting CADD
computer-aided design and manufacturing CADAM
computer-aided engineering CAE
computer-aided manual operation CAMO
computer-aided manufacture CAM
computer-aided production CAP
computer-aided software engineering CASE
computer-aided or -assisted design CAD
computer-assisted acquisition and logistic support CALS
computer-assisted instruction CAI
computer-assisted learning CAL
computer-assisted menu planning CAMP
computer-assisted retrieval CAR
computer-assisted teaching CAT
computer-assisted testing engineering CAT
computer-assisted training CAT
computer-assisted typesetting CAT
computer-assisted writing CAW
computer-based instruction CBI
computer-based learning CBL
computer-based training CBT
computer-directed communications CODIC
computer-integrated factory CIF
computer-integrated manufacturing CIM
computer-integrated production CIP
computer-integrated telephony CIT or C.I.T.
computer-managed instruction CMI
computer-oriented language COL
computerized axial tomography CAT
Computerized Vocational Information System CVIS
Computing Services Association CSA
Computing System M.I.T. COMIT
concentrate conc.
concentrated 1 conc. 2 concd. or concentr.
concentration 1 C or $\underline{C}$ 2 conc. 3 concn. 4 chemistry ^{c}
concentric conc.

conceptual or creativity quotient CQ or C.Q.
concerning 1 con. 2 conc.
Concert Artists Guild CAG
concerto 1 con. 2 conc. 3 cto.
conchology conch.
Concise Oxford Dictionary COD
conclusion 1 con. 2 concl.
concrete 1 conc. 2 construction con.
concurrent cncr. or Cncr.
concurrent DOS CDOS
concurrent peripheral operation computers CPO
concurrent processing operation computers CPO
concurrent program operation computers CPO
condensation physics s
condensation or vapor trail meteorology contrail
condense cond.
condensed cond.
condenser cond.
condition cond.
conditional cond.
conditionally qualified CQ
conditioned avoidance response psychology CAR
conditioned emotional response CER
conditioned response or reflex psychology CR
conditioned stimulus psychology CS
conditioner cond.
conduct cond.
conductance physics Gor G
conductance of heat or electricity C
conducted by music cond.
conductivity cond.
conductor 1 condr. 2 music cond. or Cond. 3 physics c
Confederacy Confed.
Confederate Confed.
Confederate States Army CSA
Confederate States of America CSA
Confederation 1 Conf. 2 Confed.
Confederation of British Industry CBI
Confederation of Health Service Employees COHSE or C.O.H.S.E.
Confederation of Latin American Travel Organizations COTAL
Confederation of National Trade Unions (of Canada) CNTU
Confederation of North, Central American, and Caribbean Association Football CONCACAF
Conference Conf.
conference conf.
Conference Board of Mathematical Sciences CBMS
Conference of Jewish Organizations COJO
Conference on College Composition and Communication CCCC
Conference on Data Systems Languages CODASYL
Conference on Security and Cooperation in Europe CSCE
Confessor Conf.
confidence con

confidence and security-building measures CSBM
confidential conf.
Confidential Book CB
confidential document CD or C.D.
configuration config.
confined to barracks military CB
confined to camp military CC
confirm CFM or cfm.
confirmation of balance banking C. of B. or C of B
confirmation of broadcast order advertising CBO
Confraternity of the Blessed Sacrament CBS or C.B.S.
Confucius Conf.
congenital adrenal hyperplasia CAH
congenital heart disease CHD
congenital rubella syndrome CRS
Congressional Cong.
congestive cardiac failure CCF or ccf
congestive heart disease CHD
congestive heart failure CHF
Congregation Cong.
Congregation of St. Paul CSP or C.S.P.
Congregation of the Holy Cross CSC
Congregational Cong.
Congregational Publishing Society CPS
Congregational Union of England and Wales C.U.E.W.
Congregationalist Cong.
Congress 1 C 2 Cong.
Congress of Industrial Organizations Political Action Committee CIO-PAC
Congress of Racial Equality CORE
Congress Of South African Trade Unions COSATU
Congress Party CP
Congressional Budget Office CBO
Congressional District CD
Congressional Medal of Honor C.M.H. or CMH
Congressional Record Cong. Rec.
Congressional Research Service CRS
conic con.
conic section con.sec. or con.sect.
conics con.
conjectural cj.
conjugate mathematics, grammar conj.
conjugation grammar conj.
conjunction conj.
conjunctive conj.
connected conn.
Connecticut 1 Conn. 2 CT 3 Ct or Ct.
connection 1 con. 2 conn.
connection-oriented network service CONS
connectionless network service CLNS
connector conn.
connotation conn.
conscientious objector CO
conscious medicine, psychology Cs
consciousness raising CR
consecrated 1 Cons. 2 cons.
consecration Cons.
consecutive 1 cons. 2 consec.
consequence cons.
Conservation Conserv. or conserv.
conservation cons.

Conservation Reserve Program CRP
Conservative 1 C 2 Cons. 3 politics Con.
Conservatory 1 Cons. 2 Conserv.
conserve medicine cons.
consider all factors CAF
consigned cons.
consignment commerce 1 cons. 2 consgt.
consignment note 1 c.n. 2 C/N 3 CN
console 1 con. 2 computers a CNSL or Cnsl b CON
Consolidated Con. or Con
consolidated 1 con. 2 cons. 3 consol.
Consolidated Annuities Consols or consols
Consolidated Freight Classification CFC
Consolidated Metropolitan Area CMA
Consolidated Metropolitan Statistical Area CMSA
consols British 1 con. 2 cons.
consonant cons.
consonant, vowel, consonant education c-v-c or cvc or CVC
consort law con.
Consortium for the Education of Non-Traditional Students CENTS
Conspicuous Gallantry Medal British CGM or C.G.M.
Constable 1 Cons. 2 Const.
constant 1 C 2 cons. 3 const. 4 computers con.
constant angular velocity CAV
constant boiling mixture CBM or cbm
constant error psychology CE
constant frequency CF
constant hot water chw or c.h.w.
constant linear velocity computers CLV
constant or continuous variable transmission CVT (of automobiles)
constant phase angle CPA
constant pressure 1 CP 2 cp or c.p.
constant rate of solution CRS or crs
constant speed drive engineering CSD
constant speed unit engineering CSU or c.s.u.
constant or continuous astronomy K
Constantinople Const.
constituency const.
Constituency Labour Party CLP
constituent constit.
Constitution 1 Cons. 2 Const.
constitution 1 cons. 2 const.
Constitutional 1 Cons. 2 Const.
constitutional 1 cons. 2 const.
construction 1 cons. 2 const. 3 constr.
Construction Battalion Seabee
Construction Battalion military CB
construction permit CP
Construction Specifications Institute CSI
constructive total loss insurance CTL or c.t.l.
construed constr.
Consul 1 Con. 2 Cons. 3 Cos.
Consul General 1 CG 2 Cons.Gen.
Consular Affairs CA or C.A.
Consular Agent CA or C.A.
Consular Clerk CC or C.C.
consular invoice CI
Consuls Coss.
Consultation Committee for the Definition of the Metre CCDM
Consultation on Church Union COCU

Consultative Commitee for Photometry and Radiometry CCPR
Consultative Committee for Electricity CCE
Consultative Committee for the Definition of the Second CCDS
Consultative Committee for the Standards of Measurement of Ionizing Radiations CCEMRI
Consultative Committee for Thermometry CCT
Consultative Committee for Units CCU
Consultative Group on International Agricultural Research CGIAR
consulting cons.
Consumer Advisory Council CAC
Consumer and Marketing Service CMS
Consumer Federation of America CFA
Consumer Information Center CIC
Consumer News and Business Channel CNBC
Consumer Price Index CPI or C.P.I. (*GPO:* CPI)
Consumer Product Safety Commission CPSC
Consumer Protection Agency CPA
Consumer Reports CR
Consumers Association of Canada CAC
Consumers Cooperative Association CCA
Consumers' Union CU
Consumers' Research CR
contact QSO (in amateur radio)
contact potential difference *electronics* CPD
contact-inhibiting factor CIF
contagious or communicable disease *medicine* CD or C.D.
contain cntn
container cntr or Cntr.
container unit *commerce* CU
containing 1 cont. 2 contg.
contaminate contam.
Contamination by Extraterrestrial Exploration CETEX
contango *finance* cgo.
contemporary 1 Cont. 2 contemp.
Contemporary Art Society of Australia CASA or C.A.S.A.
content-addressable memory *computers* CAM
contents cont.
Contextual Indexing and Faceted Taxonomic Access System CIFT
Continent Cont.
continent cont.
Continental Cont.
continental 1 CON 2 cont. 3 contl. or Contl.
Continental Air Command 1 CAC 2 CONAC
Continental Air Defense Command CONAD
continental air mass *meteorology* c
continental air mass having antarctic air within it. cA
Continental Army Command CONARC
continental polar air cP
continental polar cold air mass cPk
continental polar warm air mass cPw
Continental United States CONUS (*GPO:* Conus)
contingent negative variation *biology* CNV
Contingent Value Rights CVR
continuation 1 cont. 2 contn.
continuation clause CC

continue 1 Cont. 2 cont.
continued 1 con. (*MLA:* cont., contd.; *CSM, OUP:* cont.) 2 Cont. 3 cont. 4 contd. or Contd.
continuing contg.
Continuing Education CE
continuing medical education CME
continuous 1 Cont. 2 cont.
continuous aircraft reliability evaluation CARE
continuous ambulatory peritoneal dialysis *medicine* CAPD
continuous casting concast
continuous cycling peritoneal dialysis *medicine* CCPD
Continuous Electron Beam Accelerator Facility CEBAF
continuous positive airway pressure *medicine* CPAP
continuous seismic wave *geology* CSW
continuous wave *electronics* 1 CW 2 cw or c.w.
continuous welded rail CWR or c.w.r.
contraband contbd.
contrabass *music* CB or C.B.
contract 1 cont. 2 contr.
Contract Appeals Board CAB or C.A.B.
contract change notice or notification CCN
contracted contr.
Contracting Officers Technical Representation COTR
contraction contr.
contractor contr. or Contr.
contractor performance evaluation CPE
Contractor Weighted Average Share CWAS
contractor-furnished equipment CFE
contraindication *medicine* contra.
Contralto *music* Con.
contralto 1 C 2 c 3 contr. or Contr.
contrary 1 cont. 2 contr.
contrary to good manners contr. bon. mor.
contraterrene CT
contributing 1 Contbg. 2 contrib. or Contrib.
contribution 1 cntr or cntr. 2 contr. 3 contrib.
contributor 1 contr. or Contr. 2 contrib. or Contrib.
control 1 con. 2 cont. 3 contr. 4 *computers* CTR or CTRL
Control and Reporting Center CRC
control leader *computers* CL
control panel CP
Control Program for Microcomputers CP/M
Control Read Only Memory *computers* CROM
control routine *computers* CR
control unit *computers* CU
control unit end *computers* CUE
controlled con.
controlled circulation audit CCA
Controlled Materials Plan CMP
controlled thermonuclear reaction CTR
controlled thermonuclear reactor CTR
Controlled Underwater Recovery Vehicle CURV
controlled variable *psychology* CV
controller 1 Cont. 2 cont. or Cont. 3 contr. or Contr.
controller of accounts CA or C.A.

convalescent conv.
conveniences *British* 1 con. 2 cons.
convenient conv.
convent Conv.
convention conv.
Convention on International Trade in Endangered Species CITES
conventional conv.
Conventional Arms Transfer CAT
Conventional Forces in Europe CFE
conventional takeoff and landing *aeronautics* CTOL
conversation 1 con. 2 conv.
Conversational Monitor System *computers* CMS
conversion factor CF
convert to *chemistry, commerce, computers, mathematics, physics* Cnvt or cnvt.
converted conv.
converter conv.
convertible 1 conv. 2 cv 3 *commerce* CVT or cvt. or cv't.
convex cx.
Conveyor Equipment Manufacturers Association CEMA
convict con
convocation Conv.
convulsive disorder *medicine* CD or C.D.
cook ck.
cooled cld.
Cooper Union CU
cooperation coop. or co-op.
cooperative coop. or co-op.
cooperative average fuel economy CAFE
Cooperative for American Relief Everywhere, Inc. CARE
Cooperative Fuel Research CFR or C.F.R.
Cooperative Holocene Mapping Project COHMAP
Cooperative Merchandising Agreement CMA or C.M.A.
Cooperative State Research Service CSRS
coordinate coord.
coordinate geometry COGO
Coordinating Board of Jewish Organizations CBJO
Coordinating Council of Community Organizations CCCO
Coordinating Research Council CRC or C.R.C.
coordination coord.
coordination of benefits C.O.B.
Copenhagen Cpn
copies cc or cc.
copilot CoP
copper 1 cop. 2 cpr. 3 Cu
Coptic 1 Cop. 2 Copt.
copulative *grammar.* cop.
copy 1 c or c. 2 cop.
Copyright ©
copyright 1 c 2 cop. 3 copr. or copy.
copyrighted cop.
coral Co or Co.
cord cd or cd.
cord foot cd.ft.
cordillera Cord.
cordoba ¢ or ₡
Corinthians Cor.
Coriolanus 1 Cor. 2 Coriol.

corn, soya, milk CSM
Cornell Aeronautical Laboratory CAL
Cornell University CU
corner 1 cnr. or cnr **2** cor.
cornet *music* cor.
Cornish *linguistics* Corn.
Cornwall Corn. or Cornw.
corolla C
corollary corol. or coroll.
coronal mass ejection CME
coronary artery disease CAD
coronary heart disease CHD
Coroner Cor.
coroner cor.
Corporal 1 Corp. **2** Corpl. **3** Cpl.
Corporation 1 Corp. **2** *Italian* EA
corporation 1 *French* Soc. Anᵉ **2** *Italian,* *Spanish* SRL or S.R.L. or S.r.l. **3** *Italian* S.p.A.
Corporation for Economic and Industrial **Research** CEIR or C.E.I.R.
Corporation for Public Broadcasting CPB
Corps Headquarters CHQ
Corps of Engineers 1 CE or C.E. **2** COE
Corps of Military Police CMP
Corpus Corp.
corpus cor.
Corpus Christi College CCC
corpus luteum c.l.
corpus luteum stimulating hormone CLSH
correct 1 C **2** cor. **3** corr. **4** cx. or CX
corrected 1 cor. **2** corr.
correction 1 C **2** cor. **3** corr.
corrections corrs.
corrective cor.
Corrective Action Commission or **Committee** CAC
correlation coefficient *statistics* **1** R **2** r
correlation, detection, and ranging CODAR
correlative 1 cor. **2** corr. **3** correl.
correspond corr.
correspondence 1 cor. **2** corr. **3** corresp.
correspondent 1 cor. **2** corr.
corresponding 1 cor. **2** corr. **3** corresp.
Corresponding Fellow 1 CF or C.F. **2** Corr. Fell.
Corresponding Member 1 CM or C.M. **2** Corr. Mem.
corresponding member Cor. Mem.
Corresponding Secretary 1 Cor. Sec. **2** Corr. Sec.
corresponds corresp.
corrigenda corr.
corrosion corr.
corrosion resistant CRE
corrugated 1 cor. **2** corr.
corrugated galvanized iron c.g.i.
corrugated iron CI or c.i.
corrupt *linguistics* corr.
corrupted *linguistics* **1** cor. **2** corr.
corruption *linguistics* **1** cor. **2** corr.
Corsica 1 Cor. **2** Cors.
cortex cort.
corticosteroid *medicine* CS
corticotropin releasing factor *medicine* CRF
corticotropin releasing hormone CRH
cosecant *mathematics* **1** cosec **2** csc
cosine cos
Cosmic Background Explorer COBE

cosmography cosmog.
cosmopolitan Cosmop.
cost and freight 1 CAF or c.a.f. **2** *commerce* **a** C & F or c & F **b** c.f.
cost and insurance *commerce* **1** C & I or c & i **2** CI or c.i.
cost benefit *finance* C/B
cost effectiveness index CEI
cost of living 1 C of L or COFL **2** COL or col or c.o.l.
cost per thousand CPM
cost plus fixed fee CPFF or c.p.f.f.
cost plus incentive fee CPIF or cpif
cost reimbursable CR or C.R.
cost, assurance, and freight CAF or c.a.f.
cost, freight, and insurance *commerce* CFI or c.f.i.
cost, insurance, and freight *commerce* CIF or c.i.f.
cost, planning, and appraisal CPA or c.p.a.
cost-benefit ratio CBR
cost-of-living allowance or **adjustment** COLA
cost-of-living index CLI
Costa Rica CR or C.R.
Costa Rican CR or C.R.
cotangent *mathematics* **1** cot **2** ctn
cottage ctg. or ctge.
cotter pin cot or cot.
cotton cot or cot.
couchant *heraldry* couch.
could cld.
coulomb 1 C **2** Q
Council 1 Cncl. **2** Conc. **3** Coun.
Council for Basic Education CBE
Council for Cultural Cooperation CCC
Council for Economic and Environmental **Development** CEED or C.E.E.D.
Council for European Economic Cooperation CEEC or C.E.E.C.
Council for Exceptional Children CEC
Council for International Exchange of **Scholars** CIES
Council for International Organizations of **Medical Sciences** CIOMS
Council for International Progress in **Management** CIPM
Council for Scientific and Industrial **Research** CSIR
Council for Scientific Policy CSP
Council for Small Industries in Rural Areas CoSIRA
Council for Social Service Data Archives CSSDA
Council for Technical Education and Training **for Overseas Countries** CTETOC
Council for the Advancement of Science **Writing** CASW
Council for the Advancement of Small **Colleges** CASC
Council for the Encouragement of Music and **the Arts** CEMA or C.E.M.A.
Council for the Preservation of Rural **America** CPRA
Council for the Preservation of Rural **England** CPRE or C.P.R.E.
Council for the Promotion of Field Studies CPFS
Council of Economic Advisers CEA

Council of Energy Resources Tribes CERT
Council of Engineering Institutions CEI or C.E.I.
Council of Europe CE or C.E.
Council of European Industrial Federations CEIF or C.E.I.F.
Council of European Municipalities CCE or C.C.E.
Council of Federated Organizations COFO
Council of Foreign Ministers CFM
Council of Industrial Design CID
Council of Technical Examining Bodies CTEB
Council of the National Library Association CNLA
Council on Chiropractic Education CCE
Council on Environmental Quality CEQ
Council on Foreign Affairs CFA
Council on Foreign Relations CFR
Council on Hemispheric Affairs COHA
Council on Industrial Relations CIR
Council on Library Resources CLR or C.L.R.
Councillor *British* Cllr.
Councilor 1 Cnclr. **2** Coun.
Counsel Coun.
Counselor Coun.
Count Ct or Ct.
count 1 ct. **2** *commerce, computers* CNT or Cnt
counter ctr.
counter electromotive force counter emf
counter-electromotive force cemf or CEMF
counterclockwise 1 CC **2** cckw. **3** CCW or ccw.
countercurrent distribution *chemistry* CCD
counterespionage CE
counterimmunoelectrophoresis *medicine* CIE
counterinsurgency 1 CI or C.I. **2** COIN
counterintelligence CI or C.I.
Counterintelligence Corps CIC
counterintelligence program Cointelpro
countermeasure CM
counterpoint *music* **1** cpt. **2** ctp or ctpt
countersink csk. or csk
countertenor *music* Ct
Countess Ctss.
counties Cos. or cos.
Country and Western *music* CW
country and western *music* C&W
Country Music Association CMA
Country Party CP or C.P.
counts per million cpm or c.p.m.
counts per minute cpm or c.p.m.
counts per minute per gram c./m./g. or c/m/g
County 1 Co or Co. **2** Ct or Ct. **3** Cty. **4** Cy or Cy.
County Agricultural Committee CAC
County Agricultural Officer *British* CAO
County Alderman CA or C.A.
county borough CB or C.B.
County Clerk CC or C.C.
County Commissioner CC
County Council CC or C.C.
County Councilor CC or C.C.
County Court CC or C.C.
County Court of Appeals CCA or C.C.A.
County Recorders Office CRO
County Registrars Office CRO

coupling *electronics* coup.
coupon cp *or* cp.
coupons cps.
course CSE *or* cse
course line computer *navigation* CLC
course of action C/A
Court 1 C *or* C. 2 Crt *or* Crt. 3 CT 4 Ct *or* Ct. (*GPO*: Ct.)
court 1 cur. *or* Cur. 2 *sports* ct.
court desires to consider *law* CAV *or* C.A.V.
Court of Appeals CA *or* C.A.
Court of Claims 1 C.Cls. 2 Ct. Cls.
Court of Common Pleas CCP *or* C.C.P.
Court of Customs and Patent Appeals C.C.P.A.
Court of First Instance CFI *or* C.F.I.
Court of Military Appeals CMA
Court of Probate CP *or* C.P.
Court of Session *or* **Sessions** CS *or* C.S.
Courthouse 1 CH *or* C.H. 2 Ct.Ho. *or* Cths.
courtmartial CM *or* C.M.
Courts CTS
Courts of London Sessions CLS *or* C.L.S.
Cove CV
Covenant Cov.
cover note CN
coversed sine *mathematics* covers
coxswain Cox. *or* cox.
Crab Cnc (constellation)
craft cft.
craft loss *insurance* CL *or* c/l
Cranch's Reports Cr *or* Cr.
Crane Gru (constellation)
craniology craniol.
crassulacean acid metabolism CAM
crate 1 cr *or* cr. 2 crt 3 ct.
crater *astronomy, geology* 1 Crt 2 crt
crates cts.
cream cr
created cr
creatine kinase CK
creatine phosphokinase CPK
creatinine Cr
credit 1 Cr *or* Cr. 2 cr *or* cr. (*GPO*: cr.; *OUP*: Cr.)
credit account C/A
credit card purchase *or* **purchases** CCP *or* ccp
credit card *or* **cards** CC
credit note C/N
credit rating CR *or* C.R.
Credit Union National Association CUNA
creditor 1 Cr *or* Cr. 2 cr *or* cr. (*GPO*: cr.; *OUP*: Cr.)
creditors CRS *or* crs.
credits CRS *or* crs.
Creek 1 Cr (watercourse, American Indian tribe) 2 CRK
crescendo *music* cres. *or* cresc.
Cretaceous-Tertiary KT *or* K-T *or* K/T
Creutzfeldt-Jakob Disease CJD *or* C-J disease
crew cr
Crimean Astrophysical Observatory CAO *or* C.A.O.
Criminal Cr *or* Cr.
criminal *law* crim. *or* Crim.
criminal cases CC *or* C.C.
Criminal Division CD

Criminal Investigation Branch CIB *or* C.I.B.
Criminal Investigation Department CID *or* C.I.D. (*OUP*: CID)
Criminal Justice Institute CJI
criminal offense CO *or* C.O.
Criminal Records Office CRO *or* C.R.O.
criminologist criminol.
criminology criminol.
crimson cr
critic crit.
critical crit.
critical flicker frequency *psychology* CFF
critical list CL
critical micelle concentration *chemistry* CMC
critical path analysis CPA
critical path method CPM
critical path planning *computers* CPP
critical ratio CR
critical success factor CSF
critical trauma care *medicine* CTC
criticism crit.
criticized crit.
Croatia Croat.
Croatian Croat.
crochet cr
Croix de Guerre 1 C.de G. 2 CG
Crop Research Division CRD
cropping index *agriculture* CI
cross x
cross section S
Cross, Iddings, Pirsson, and Washington C.I.P.W. *or* CIPW (classification of rocks)
cross-country XC *or* X-C
cross-over value *genetics* c.o.v.
cross-question XQ *or* xq
cross-reacting material CRM
cross-reference 1 X-ref. *or* Xref 2 XR *or* x-r
crosscut xcut. (of wood or a saw blade)
crossed (in Mendelian notation) 1 X 2 x
crossing 1 cross. 2 X 3 xg
crossroads 1 CR 2 Xrds
crosstalk unit *electronics* CU
croup associated viruses CA
Crow Crv (constellation)
Crown Cr
crown cr *or* cr. (paper size)
Crown Agent CA *or* C.A.
Crown Clerk CC *or* C.C.
Crown Office CO *or* C.O.
crude CRD *or* crd (grade of oil)
cruise missile CRM
crushed stone cr.st.
cruzeiro 1 Cr 2 Cruz. 3 Cz
cryptographic crypto. *or* CRYPTO
cryptography crypto. *or* CRYPTO *or* Crypto.
crystal 1 cryst. 2 X 3 XL *or* xl 4 xtal *or* XTAL
crystal oscillator *electronics* CO
crystal unit *electronics* CU
crystalline cryst.
crystallization crystn.
crystallized cryst.
crystallography cryst. *or* crystall.
cubic cu.
cubic capacity of holds CCH
cubic centimeter cu.cm.
cubic centimeter *or* **centimeters** 1 CC 2 cc *or* cc. *or* c.c.
cubic centimeters ccm *or* c.cm.

cubic close packed *or* **packing** *chemistry* CCP
cubic contents cc *or* c.c.
cubic feet per day cfd *or* c.f.d.
cubic feet per hour cfh *or* c.f.h.
cubic feet per minute cfm *or* c.f.m.
cubic feet per second cfs *or* c.f.s.
cubic foot 1 c.ft. 2 cu.ft.
cubic inch cu.in.
cubic meter 1 CBM *or* cbm 2 cu.m.
cubic millimeter 1 c.mm. 2 cu.mm.
cubic second cusec
cubic yard cu.yd.
cuisine cuis.
culinary cul.
Culinary Institute of America CIA
cultivar cv *or* cv. (*OUP*: cv.)
cultivated cult.
cultivation cult.
cultural cult.
cultural resource management CRM
culture *anthropology, law* cult.
cum dividend *commerce* cd (*OUP*: c.d.)
Cumberland, England Cumb. *or* Cumbld.
cumulative 1 cu. 2 cum *or* cum.
Cumulative Bulletin CB *or* C.B.
Cumulative Book Index CBI
cumulative preference *commerce* cum. pref.
cumulative preferred stock *finance* cm.pf.
cumulonimbus 1 Cb 2 Cn
cumulus Cu
cuneiform cun.
Cup Crt (constellation)
cup c *or* c.
curative dose *medicine* CD
Curia Regis Roll C.R.R.
curie c *or* c.
curium Cm
currency 1 cur. 2 curr. 3 *commerce* cy *or* cy.
currency bond CB
Currency Transaction Report CTR
current 1 ct. 2 cur. (this month or instant) 3 curr. *or* curt. (this month or instant) 4 *physics* I
current account C/A
current cost accounting CCA
current density S
current density of electricity CD
Current List of Medical Literature CLML
current mode logic *computers* CML
current purchasing power CPP *or* cpp
current rate *commerce* CR *or* C.R.
current resistance IR
current strength *or* **intensity** *electronics* CS
current transformer CT
current value c.v.
current year CY
Curriculum Development Centre CDC *or* C.D.C.
curvature *physics* K
cuspid c *or* c.
custodian cust. *or* Cust. *or* Custod.
custody cust.
custom of the port C/P
customer cust.
Customer Engineer *computers* CE
customer information control system CICS
customer owned and maintained COAM

customer's own merchandise COM
customer-owned property *commerce* COP
customs 1 cust. *or* Cust. **2** *French* d *or* d.
Customs Cooperation Council CCC
Customs Declaration CD
Customs House CH *or* C.H.
Customs Union of West African States *French* UDEAD
cut out CO
cut-off frequency *electronics* f
Cutaneous T-Cell Lymphoma CTCL
cutoff CO
cyan, magenta, yellow, key CMYK
cyanide 1 Cy **2** cy
cyanogen 1 Cy **2** cy
cybernetic organism cyborg
cybernetics cyber. *or* Cyber.
cycle 1 c **2** *physics, chemistry, electronics, medicine* cy **3** *physics, chemistry* cyc
cycles per hour c.p.h.
cycles per minute 1 CPM **2** cpm *or* c.p.m.

cycles per second 1 c/s **2** cps *or* c.p.s. **3** *physics, electronics* CPS
cyclic adenosine monophosphate cAMP
cyclic GMP cGMP
cyclic redundancy check *computers* CRC
Cyclists' Touring Club CTC *or* C.T.C.
cyclonite RDX
cyclopedia 1 cyc *or* cyc. *or* Cyc. (*OUP:* cyc.) **2** cycl. *or* cyclo. *or* Cycl. *or* Cyclo.
cyclopedic cyc *or* cyc. *or* Cyc. (*OUP:* cyc.)
cyclorama cyc
cyclosporin CS
cyclotron cycl. *or* cyclo.
cycocel CCC
Cygnus, the Swan Cyg (constellation)
cylinder cyl.
cylinder head temperature CHT
cylindrical cyl.
cylindrical coordinate *physics* z
Cymbeline Cym. *or* Cymb. (*MLA:* Cym.)
Cymric Cym.

Cyprian Cyp.
Cypriot Cyp.
Cyprus 1 C **2** Cyp.
cysteine cys. *or* Cys.
cystic fibrosis CF
cystine cys. *or* Cys.
cystology cysto
cytidine diphosphate CDP
cytidine monophosphate CMP
cytidine triphosphate *biochemistry* CTP
cytochrome cyt
cytological cyt *or* cytol.
cytology *biology* cyt *or* cytol.
cytomegalic inclusion disease CID
cytomegalovirus CMV
cytopathic effect *medicine* CPE
cytosine C
cytosine arabinoside ara-C
cytotoxic T-lymphocyte CTL
Czech Cz *or* Cz.
Czechoslovakia 1 Cz *or* Cz. **2** Czech.
Czechoslovakian 1 Cz *or* Cz. **2** Czech.

D day D
Dahomey Dah.
daily 1 dly. *or* Dly. **2** *pharmaceutics* **a** in d. **b** quotid.
daily proceedings *law* AD *or* A.D.
daily subsistance allowance DSA
daily subsistance allowance rates DSAR
Daily Weather Report DWR
dairy herd improvement DHI
Dairy Society International DSI
Dakota Dak.
dalasi D
Dallas 1 D **2** K (in Federal Reserve banking system)
Dallas Symphony Orchestra DSO
Dallas's United States Supreme Court Reports Dall.
dalton unit *biochemistry* **1** d **2** Da. *or* Da
dam 1 D *or* D. **2** d *or* d.
damage 1 dmg. **2** *commerce, insurance* dam.
damage free *commerce* d.f.
damaged *commerce, insurance* dam.
Dame D *or* D.
Dame Commander of the Order of the British Empire D.B.E. *or* DBE
Dame Commander of the Royal Victorian Order D.C.V.O.
Dame of the Order of Australia AD
damp proof dp
damp proof course *British* d.p.c.
damper dmpr.
Dance Masters of America DMA *or* D.M.A.

Daniel 1 Dan. **2** Danl.
Danish 1 D **2** Da. **3** Dan.
Danish krone Dkr (*GPO:* DKr)
Danube Commission DANCOM
dark dk *or* dk.
dark matter *astronomy* DM *or* dM
Dartmouth Drt.
data acquisition *computers* DA
data acquisition and control *computers* DAC
Data Acquisition System *computers* DAS
data circuit terminal equipment *computers* DCE
data collection form DCF
data communication *computers* DC
data communication interrogate *computers* DCI
data communications equipment DCE
data conversion *computers* DC
Data Description Language *computers* DDL
data encryption standard DES
data entry unit *computers* DEU
data exchange format DXF
data interchange format *computers* DIF
data link *computers* DL *or* D/L
data link escape *computers* DLE
data loop transceiver *computers* DLT
data management system *computers* DMS
data manipulation language *computers* DML
data processing *computers* DP
Data Processing Management Association DPMA
Data Processing Supplies Association DPSA
data set *computers* DS
data set control block *computers* DSCB
data terminal equipment *computers* DTE
data transmission DT
data transmission control unit *computers* DTCU
data transmission terminal unit *computers* DTTU

data transmission *or* **transfer unit** *computers* DTU
data-processing control *computers* DPC
data-processing system DPS
data-to-synchro converter *computers* DSC *or* D/Sc
data-undervoice DUV
database *computers* **1** DB **2** db
Database Administrator *computers* DBA
database management system *computers* DBMS
date 1 D *or* D. **2** d *or* d.
date and place of birth dpob
date book 1 d.b. **2** DB *or* D.B.
date of birth DOB *or* d.o.b.
date of death DOD *or* d.o.d.
dated 1 dd *or* d.d. **2** dtd *or* dtd.
dative *grammar* dat.
daughter 1 D *or* D. **2** d *or* d. **3** da *or* da. **4** dau.
Daughters of the American Revolution DAR *or* D.A.R. (*NYT:* D.A.R.; *OUP:* DAR)
David Dav.
day 1 d **2** D *or* D. **3** da *or* da.
day book 1 d.b. **2** DB *or* D.B.
day of sale *commerce* DOS *or* d.o.s.
day's date dd *or* d.d.
daylight exposure DX
Daylight Saving Time DST *or* D.S.T. *or* d.s.t.
Daylight Time DT *or* D.T.
days after acceptance *commerce* D/A *or* d/a
days after date *commerce* **1** dd **2** DD *or* D/D
days after delivery *commerce* **1** dd *or* d.d. *or* d/d **2** DD *or* D/D
days after sight *commerce* **1** DS **2** ds *or* d.s.
days' sight *commerce* **1** ds *or* d.s. **2** DS *or* D/S
daytime running lights DRL
Deacon 1 D *or* D. **2** Dea.

deactivated war trophy DEWAT
dead d *or* d.
dead center *engineering* d.c. *or* dc
dead freight *commerce* d.f.
dead heat *sports* DH
dead letter box DLB
Dead Letter Office DLO
dead of injuries *medicine* DOI *or* d.o.i.
dead on arrival *medicine* DOA *or* d.o.a.
   (*OUP:* DOA)
dead reckoning *navigation* DR *or* D/R
dead reckoning tracer DRT
dead weight 1 d.w. *or* dw **2** DW *or* D/W
deadhead *transportation* dh
deadline data dld
deadweight capacity DWC *or* d.w.c.
deadweight ton *commerce* DWT *or* d.w.t.
   (*OUP:* d.w.t.)
dealer dlr.
deals and battens DB
deals, battens, and boards DBB
Dean Dec.
Dean and Chapter D & C *or* D. and C.
Dean of the Faculty DF *or* D.F.
death and dying D and D *or* D&D
death by accidental injury DAI *or* d.a.i.
death certificate DC *or* D.C.
Death on High Seas Act DOHSA
debenture deb. *or* deben. (*OUP:* deb.)
debit 1 D **2** dbt. **3** deb. **4** Dr *or* Dr. **5** dr *or*
   dr. (*GPO:* dr.)
debit note *commerce* D/N
debt liquidation schedule *law, commerce*
   DLS *or* D.L.S.
debtor 1 Dr *or* Dr. **2** dr *or* dr. (*GPO:* dr.)
debutante Deb
deca dk
deca- da
decaffeinated decaf
decagram 1 dag. **2** dcg. **3** dkg *or* dkg.
decaliter 1 dal. **2** dcl. **3** dkl *or* dkl.
decaliters dal.
decameter 1 dam. **2** dcm. **3** dkm *or* dkm.
decastere dks *or* dks.
decayed, missing, and filled teeth 1 DMF
   2 *dentistry* DFM
deceased 1 D *or* D. **2** d *or* d. **3** dec. **4** decd.
   5 def.
December 1 D **2** Dec. *or* Dec (*NYT:* Dec.)
December and June *accounting* D. & J.
December, March, June, September
   accounting DMJS
deci- d
decibel 1 dB **2** db *or* db.
decibels 1 db *or* db. **2** dBk *or* dbk **3** dBm *or*
   dbm (by milliwatt) **4** dBv *or* dbv (by volt)
   5 dBw *or* dbw (by watt)
decibels above reference noise dBrn *or*
   DBRN
decibels adjusted dba
decibels at A-level dBA
deciduous 1 decid. **2** *botany, dentistry* d *or* d.
decigram dg *or* dg.
decile *statistics* Dec.
deciliter dl *or* dl.
decimal dec.
decimal classification DC *or* D.C. (of library
   cataloging)

decimeter 1 dec. **2** decim. **3** dm *or* dm.
decimillimeter dmm *or* dmm.
decision *law* decn. *or* Decn.
decision support system *computers* DSS
Decision-Making Ability Test *psychology*
   DMAT
decision-making device DMD
decision-making unit DMU
decistere ds *or* ds.
deck dk *or* dk.
deckle edge DE *or* D.E.
declaration 1 dec. **2** decl. **3** *commerce,*
   insurance, law dcl. *or* Dcl.
declared 1 dec. **2** decd.
declension *grammar* **1** dec. **2** decl.
declination 1 dec. **2** decl.
decompose 1 decomp. **2** *chemistry, physics*
   dec.
decomposition decomp. *or* decompn.
decontamination decn. *or* decon
decontamination and deconstruction D and
   D *or* D&D
decontamination factor DF
decorated dec.
decoration dec.
decorative dec.
decrease dec.
decreased decd.
decree 1 D *or* D. **2** d *or* d.
decrescendo *music* **1** dec. **2** decres.
dedicated 1 DD *or* D.D. **2** dd *or* dd.
dedicated to ded.
dedication ded.
deduct 1 ded. **2** *commerce* ddt.
deduction ded. *or* deduct.
Deep Diving System DDS
deep ocean survey vessel DOSV
deep scattering layer DSL
Deep Sea Drilling Project DSDP
Deep Space Information Facility DSIF
Deep Space Network *astronautics* DSN
deep tendon reflex *medicine* DTR *or* D.T.R.
Deep Underground Support Center *military*
   DUSC
deep X-ray DXR *or* D.X.R. *or* DX-R
Deep-Submergence Rescue Vehicle DSRV
Deep-Submergence Search Vehicle DSSV
Deep-Submergence Systems Project DSSP
deepwater motion-picture system DMPS
defamation of dignity *law* scan. mag.
defeated *sports* d *or* d.
defecation *medicine* def.
defective 1 def. **2** defect. **3** X
defective interfering particle DI particle
defective material report DMR
Defence Research and Development
   Organization DRDO
defendant 1 def. **2** deft. **3** dft.
defendant being absent abs. re.
defendant being absent, the abse. re.
Defender of the Faith 1 DF *or* D.F. **2** FD *or*
   F.D.
Defense D
defense 1 def. **2** *sports* D
Defense Activity for Non-Traditional
   Education Support DANTES
Defense Advanced Research Projects
   Agency Darpa

Defense Air Transportation Administration
   DATA
Defense Communications Agency DCA
Defense Communications System DCS
defense condition DEFCON *or* Defcon
Defense Contract Administration Services
   Region DCASR
Defense Contract Audit Agency DCAA
Defense Electric Power Administration DEPA
Defense Finance and Accounting Service
   DFAS
Defense Industrial Plant Equipment Center
   DIPEC
Defense Information School DINFOS
Defense Information Services Activity DISA
Defense Information Systems Agency DISA
Defense Institute of Security Assistance
   Management DISAM
Defense Intelligence Agency DIA
Defense Intelligence School DIS
Defense Investigative Service DIS
Defense Language Institute DLI
Defense Legal Services Agency DLSA
Defense Logistics Agency DLA
Defense Mapping Agency DMA
Defense Mapping System DMS
Defense Materials Procurement Agency
   DMPA
Defense Materials System DMS
Defense Medical Facilities Office DMFO
Defense Medical Support Activity DMSA
Defense Medical Systems Support Center
   DMSSC
Defense Notice *British* D Notice *or* D notice
Defense Nuclear Agency DNA
Defense Order DO
Defense Research Board DRB
Defense Research Establishment DRE
Defense Research Institute DRI
Defense Research Telecommunications
   Establishment DRTE
Defense Security Assistance Agency DSAA
Defense Supply Agency DSA
Defense Systems Acquisition Review Council
   DSARC
Defense Technology Security Administration
   DTSA
Defense Waste Processing Facility DWPF
defensive end DE
defensive tackle DT
deferred def.
deferred payment account DPA *or* d.p.a.
deficiency report DR
deficit def.
defined def.
definite def.
definition def.
degauss DG
degeneracy *physics* g
degeneration *medicine* deg.
degeneration reaction *physiology* DR *or*
   D.R.
degenerative joint disease DJD
degree 1 d *or* d. **2** deg.
degree of freedom *physics, chemistry,*
   statistics DOF *or* dof
degree of polymerization *chemistry* **1** DP
   2 dp

degree of substitution *chemistry* DS *or* D.S.
degrees before top dead center
  engineering °BTDC
degrees Fahrenheit °F
degrees of freedom *statistics* df
dehydroepiandrosterone DHA
Delaware 1 DE (Zip Code) 2 Del *or* Del.
  (*NYT, OUP:* Del.)
delayed action DA
delayed allergic response DAR
delayed broadcast DB
delayed delivery *commerce* dd *or* d.d.
delayed matching to sample *psychology*
  DMTS
delayed sleep phase syndrome DSPS
delayed type hypersensitivity *medicine* DTH
Delegate 1 Del *or* Del. 2 Deleg.
delegate del.
Delegation Del *or* Del.
delete 1 d *or* d. 2 del. 3 *computers* DEL
delicatessen deli
delinquent *commerce, law* delin. *or* delinq.
deliquescent *chemistry* deliq. *or* deliquesc.
delirium tremens 1 d.t.'s 2 DT 3 dt *or* d.t.
deliver 1 del. 2 dlvr.
delivered 1 dd *or* dd. 2 del. *or* DEL 3 deld.
  4 dld *or* dld. 5 dlvd.
delivered alongside ship *commerce* DAS *or*
  das
delivered at dock *commerce* dd *or* d.d. *or*
  d/d
delivered sound dd/s
delivery 1 del. 2 delvy. *or* dely. 3 dlvr. *or*
  dlvy. 4 dly. 5 dy.
delivery order *commerce* DO *or* D/O
delivery point *commerce* DP
deluxe edition e.d.l.
demand *commerce, law* dem *or* dem.
demand and supply *economics*
  d. and s.
Demand Deposit Account DDA
demand draft *commerce* 1 dd *or* d.d. 2 DD
  or D.D. *or* D/D
demand loan *commerce* DL *or* D/L
demethylchlortetracycline DMCT
demilitarized zone DMZ
demise *law* dem *or* dem.
demobilization demob.
democracy dem *or* dem.
Democrat 1 D *or* D. 2 Dem. 3 Demo
Democrat Liberal D.-Lib.
Democratic 2 D *or* D. 2 Dem.
Democratic Leadership Council DLC *or*
  D.L.C.
Democratic National Committee DNC
Democratic Party DP
Democratic Party of Angola PDA *or* P.D.A.
Democratic Party of Guinea PDG
Democratic People's Republic of Korea
  DPRK
Democratic Socialist Party DSP
Democratic Unionist Party DUP (of Northern
  Ireland)
demodulator *electronics* dem
demolition DML *or* dml
demonstration 1 demo 2 dmst. *or* dmstn.
demonstrative 1 demon. 2 *grammar* dem
demonstrator dmstr.

demurrage dem *or* dem.
demy *printing* dem *or* dem.
dendrology dend. *or* Dend.
denier den. *or* den
Denmark 1 D 2 Den.
denomination denom.
denotation den.
density 1 D 2 d 3 dens. *or* dens
dental dent.
Dental Assistant DA *or* D.A.
Dental Corps DC
Dental Surgeon 1 D.Surg. 2 DS *or* D.S.
Dental Technician DT *or* D.T.
dentist 1 Dent. 2 dent.
dentistry dent.
Denver D(on coins)
Denver Developmental Screening Test
  DDST
deoxycorticosterone DOC
deoxycorticosterone acetate 1 DCA
  2 DOCA
deoxyribonuclease DNase *or* DNAase
deoxyribonucleic acid DNA
depart dep.
Department 1 D *or* D. 2 Dep. 3 dept. *or*
  Dept.
department 1 dep. 2 dpt.
Department of Agriculture 1 DA 2 DOA
Department of Civil Aviation DCA
Department of Commerce DOC *or* DoC
Department of Defense DOD *or* DoD (*GPO:*
  DOD)
Department of Defense Dependents Schools
  DODDS
Department of Defense Support DDS
Department of Education DOE *or* DoE
Department of Education and Science DES
  or D.E.S.
Department of Employment DE
Department of Energy 1 DE 2 DOE *or* DoE
Department of Energy, Mines and
  Resources EMR
Department of Environmental Protection
  DEP
Department of Environmental Resources
  DER
Department of Health DOH *or* DoH
Department of Health and Human Services
  DHHS
Department of Housing and Urban
  Development HUD (*GPO:* HUD; *NYT:*
  H.U.D.)
Department of Industry DOI *or* DoI
Department of Justice 1 DJ 2 DOJ *or* DoJ
Department of Labor 1 DL 2 DOL *or* DoL
Department of Labor Academy DLA
Department of Motor Vehicles DMV
Department of National Defense DND
Department of Overseas Trade DOT *or*
  D.O.T.
Department of Public Health DPH *or* D.P.H.
  (*GPO, CSM:* D.P.H.; *OUP:* DPH)
Department of Public Services DPS
Department of Public Welfare DPW
Department of Public Works DPW *or*
  D.P.W.
Department of Regional Economic
  Expansion DREE

Department of Regional Industrial
  Expansion DRIE
Department of Social Welfare DSW
Department of State 1 DOS *or* DoS 2 DS
Department of the Army 1 DA 2 DOA *or*
  DoA
Department of the Environment DOE *or*
  DoE (*OUP:* D.o.E.)
Department of the Interior 1 DI *or* D.I.
  2 DOI *or* DoI
Department of the Navy D.N. *or* DN
Department of Trade and Industry DTI
Department of Transport DOT *or* D.O.T.
Department of Transportation 1 DOT *or*
  DoT (*GPO:* DOT) 2 DT
departs 1 d 2 dep.
departure 1 dep. 2 dept.
departure point *commerce* DP
dependent dep.
dependent variable *statistics* DV
Depo-Provera DMPA
deponent *grammar, law* 1 dep. 2 dept.
  3 dpt.
deposed dep.
deposit 1 dep. 2 *banking* Dep.
deposit account *commerce* 1 D/A 2 DA *or*
  D.A.
deposit passbook *commerce* DPB
deposit receipt *commerce* DR *or* D/R
deposition dpt. *or* Dpt.
depositor dep.
Depot Dep.
depreciation *commerce* depr.
depression *geology, medicine* depr.
depth 1 d *or* d. 2 dpt. 3 H 4 h 5 t 6 *physics* y
depth charge DC
depth over all OAD *or* o.a.d.
Deputy 1 D *or* D. 2 Dep. 3 dept. *or* Dept.
deputy dpty. *or* Dpty.
Deputy Adjutant General DAG
Deputy Assistant Adjutant General DAAG
  or D.A.A.G.
Deputy Assistant Advocate General DAAG
  or D.A.A.G.
Deputy Assistant Director DAD
Deputy Chief of Staff 1 DCofS 2 DCS
Deputy Clerk of Sessions DCS *or* D.C.S.
Deputy Consul DC (diplomatic corps)
Deputy Director DD
Deputy Master DM *or* D.M.
Derbyshire County, England Derby. *or*
  Derbys.
derivation 1 der. 2 deriv.
derivative 1 der. (*MLA, OUP:* der.) 2 deriv.
  3 *mathematics* D *or* D
derivative differential thermal analysis
  DDTA
derived der.
dermatitis derm.
dermatologist derm.
dermatology derm. *or* dermatol.
descendant desc.
describe desc.
described as follows daf *or* d.a.f.
Descriptive Video Service DVS
Desert Des.
Desert Locust Information Service DLIS *or*
  D.L.I.S.

desertion des.
desferrioxamine DFO
design 1 des. **2** dsgn or dsgn.
Design and Industries Association DIA or D.I.A.
design change *engineering* DC
design waterline DWL
designated hitter *baseball* **1** DH **2** dh
designated market area *advertising* DMA
designated order turnaround *finance* DOT
designation 1 des. **2** *computers* dsgn or dsgn.
Designer Des.
designer dsgn or dsgn.
Designers Lighting Forum DLF
desired mean point of impact *military* DMPI
desired or **designated ground zero** DGZ
desk accessory *computers* DA
desktop publishing *computers* DTP
desmethylimipramine DMI
despatch desp.
dessert des.
destination 1 destn. **2** dstn.
destructive read-out *computers* DRO
desynchronized D
detach det.
detached det.
detached service DS or D.S.
detachment *military* det.
detail det.
detective Det.
Detective Inspector DI or D.I.
detector det.
deterioration quotient DQ
determination detn.
determiner *grammar* det.
Detroit Symphony Orchestra DSO
deuterated potassium dihydrogen phosphate *electronics* DKDP
deuterium 1 D **2** H^2
deuteron d
Deuteronomy Deut.
Deutsch 1 D or D. or D **2** D or D. or D
Deutsche D
Deutsche mark 1 dem **2** DM or DM.
develop 1 dev. **2** devp.
develop and print *photography* D. and P. or D&P
Developer Dev.
developer dev.
developer inhibitor release DIR
Development 1 Dev. **2** Devt.
development 1 dev. or devel. (MLA: dev.) **2** devpt.
Development Assistance Committee DAC
Development Assistance Group DAG or D.A.G.
Development Finance Corporation DFC
Development Loan Fund DLF or D.L.F.
Developmental Age *medicine, psychology* DA
developmental flight instrumentation DFI
developmental quotient *psychology* DQ or D.Q.
deviation 1 dev. **2** *statistics* D
deviation clause *insurance* **1** d.c. **2** DC or D/C
deviation from the mean *statistics* **1** x **2** y

device status word *computers* DSW
device to enhance electromagnetic signals compander
Devonian *geology* Dev.
Devonshire County, England 1 Dev. **2** Devon.
dew *meteorology* w
dew point DP
Dewey Decimal Classification DDC
Dexedrine dex
dextro *chemistry* **1** d or d **2** D or D
dextro- *chemistry* d- or d-
dextro- and **levorotatory molecules** dl
dextrorotatory *chemistry* **1** d or d **2** D or D
dextrose and water *medicine* d.w. or d/w or DIW
dextrose to nitrogen ratio *medicine* D/N or D:N
diabetes insipidus *medicine* DI
diabetes mellitus *medicine* DM
diabetic ketoacidosis *medicine* DKA
diagnosis 1 diag. **2** *medicine* DX or Dx
Diagnosis Related Group DRG
diagnosis undetermined *electronics, medicine* DU
diagnostic diag.
Diagnostic and Statistical Manual DSM or D.S.M.
Diagnostic Function Test DFT
diagnostic rhyme test *psychology* DRT
diagonal diag.
diagram 1 dia. **2** diag. or diagr.
dialect dial.
dialectal dial.
dialectic dial.
dialectical dial.
diallyl phthalate DAP
dialogue dial.
diameter 1 D **2** d **3** di or di. **4** dia. **5** diam.
diameter breast high *forestry* d.b.h.
diametral pitch DP
diaminodiphenyl sulfone DDS
diamond pyramid hardness DPH or D.P.H.
diapason *music* diap.
diarrheic shellfish poison *medicine* DSP
diastolic blood pressure *medicine* DBP
diastolic murmur *medicine* DM
diastolic pressure *medicine* DP
diathermy *medicine* dia.
dichlorobenzidine DCB
dichlorodiphenyl-trichloroethane DDT
dichlorophenoxyacetic acid 2,4-D or 2:4-D
dichloropropane-dichloroprene DD
dictated dict.
dictation dict.
diction dict.
dictionary dict. or Dict.
Dictionary of American Biography DAB or D.A.B. (MLA, OUP: DAB)
Dictionary of American English DAE or D.A.E.
Dictionary of American History DAH or D.A.H
Dictionary of American Regional English DARE
Dictionary of Americanisms DA or D.A.
Dictionary of National Biography DNB or D.N.B. (MLA, OUP: DNB)

Dictionary of Occupational Titles DOT
Dictionary of the Scottish Tongue D.O.S.T.
Dictionary Society of North America DSNA
did not finish *sports* DNF
dideoxyinosine DDI
didymium 1 D **2** Di
died 1 D or D. **2** d or d.
died in his or **her father's life** DVP or d.v.p.
died of disease DOD or d.o.d.
died of wounds *military* DOW or d.o.w.
died without issue 1 DSP or d.s.p. **2** DWI or D.W.I.
died without issue, he or **she** OSP or O.S.P. or o.s.p. (OUP: ob. s.p.)
dielectric constant K
dielectric flux density D or D
diesel engine DE
dietary diet.
diethanolomine DEA
diethyl phthalate DEP
diethyl sulfate *chemistry* DS
diethylenetriaminepentaacetic acid *chemistry* DTPA
diethylstilbestrol DES
diethyltoluamide 1 Deet **2** DET
diethyltryptamine DET
diethylzinc DEZ
dietician diet. or Diet.
difference 1 dif. or diff. **2** *statistics* D or D
difference limen *psychology* DL
difference of or **in latitude** DLAT or D.Lat.
difference of or **in longitude** DLONG or D.Long.
different dif. or diff.
differential 1 dif. or diff. **2** DX or dx **3** *mathematics* d or d
differential absorption lidar DIAL
Differential Aptitude Test *psychology* DAT
differential generator *electricity* DG
differential phase shift keying DPSK
differential scatter DISC
differential thermal analysis DTA
diffused metal oxide semiconductor *electronics* DMOS
diffusing capacity *medicine* DCO
diffusion coefficient *physics* D or D
difluorodiphenyl-trichloroethane DFDT
digest dig. or Dig.
digit 1 dig. **2** *mathematics, computers* dgt
digital dig.
digital audiotape DAT
digital compact cassette DCC
digital computer DC
digital data service *computers* DDS
digital differential analyzer *computers* DDA
Digital Information Display System *computers* DIDS
Digital Integrated Attack Navigation Equipment DIANE
digital microcircuit *electronics* DMC
digital mobilized radio DMR
digital modulation DM
digital multimeter DMM
digital signal processor *computers* DSP
Digital Sound Processing DSP
digital subtraction angiography *medicine* DSA
digital termination system *computers* DTS

digital unit DU
digital video interactive *computers* DVI
Digital Voice Privacy network DVP
digital voltmeter DVM
digital-to-analog converter *computers* DAC
or D/AC or D-AC
digital-to-analog *computers* D/A or D-A
diglyceride *medicine* dg
dihydroxyacetone DHA
dihydroxyphenylalanine DOPA *or* dopa
diisodecyl adipate DIDA
diisodecyl phthalate DIDP
diisopropanolamine DIPA
diisopropyl fluorophosphate DFP
dilatation dilat.
dilation and curettage D & C
dilation and evacuation D and E or
D & E
dilute dil.
dilute strength *medicine, chemistry* DS
dilute volume DV
diluted dild.
dilution 1 dil. 2 *chemistry* diln.
dilution units du or du.
dilution units per milligram du./mg.
dime d or d.
dimension 1 dim. 2 dmn
dimensional D
dimethoxy-diphenyl-trichloro-ethane
DMDT
dimethoxy-methylamphetamine STP
dimethoxybenzene DMB
dimethoxyphenylethylamine DMPE
dimethyl dichlorovinyl phosphate DDVP
dimethyl sulfoxide DMSO
dimethylacetamide DMAC
dimethylamine DMA
dimethylaminoethyl chloride hydrochloride
DMC
dimethylbenzanthracene DMBA
dimethylformamide *chemistry* DMF
dimethylhydantoin formaldehyde DMHF
dimethylnitrosamine DMN *or* DMNA
dimethylol ethylene urea DMEU
dimethylolpropionic acid DMPA
dimethylolurea DMU
dimethylphenylpiperazinium iodide DMPP
dimethylphthalate DMP
dimethylsulfide DMS
dimethylterephthalate DMT *or* D.M.T.
dimethyltryptamine DMT
diminish in tone and tempo *music* cal.
diminished *music* dim. *or* dimin.
diminuendo *music* dim. *or* dimin.
diminutive dim.
dinar 1 D 2 DA 3 Din
dining din. *or* din
dining room DR
dinitro-ortho-cresol DNOC
dinitrobenzene DNB
dinitrochlorobenzene DNCB
dinitrocresol DNC
dinitrophenol DNP
dinitrophenyl DNP
dinitrotoluene DNT
dinner din.
dinner jacket DJ
Diocesan Dioc.
Diocese Dioc.

dioctyl sodium sulfosuccinate d.s.s.
diode d
diode transistor logic *electronics* DTL
diopter d
diphenylamine DPA
diphenylaminochloroarsine DM
diphenylpicrylhydrazyl DPPH
diphosphoglyceric acid DPG *or* DPGA
diphosphothiamine DPT
diphtheria diph.
diphtheria, tetanus, pertussis DTP
diploid generation 1 2 *n* 2 2x
diploid number of chromosomes 2 *n*
Diploma 1 Dipl. 2 Dpl.
diploma Dip. (*OUP:* Dip.)
Diploma in Business Management DBM *or*
D.B.M.
Diploma in Child Health DCH *or* D.C.H.
Diploma in Clinical Pathology DCP *or* D.C.P.
Diploma in Clinical Psychology DCP *or*
D.C.P.
Diploma in Dental Health DDH *or* D.D.H.
Diploma in Dermatological Medicine DDM
or D.D.M.
Diploma in Gynaecology and Obstetrics
British D.G.O.
Diploma in Industrial Health DIH
Diploma in Industrial Management DIM
Diploma in Medical Jurisprudence DMJ *or*
D.M.J.
Diploma in Medical Laboratory Technology
DMLT *or* D.M.L.T.
Diploma in Medical Radiology DMR *or*
D.M.R.
Diploma in Medical Radiology and
Electrology DMRE *or* D.M.R.E.
Diploma in Nursing D.N. *or* DN
Diploma in Nutrition D.N. *or* DN
Diploma in Occupational Therapy DOT *or*
D.O.T.
Diploma in Ophthalmic Medicine and
Surgery DOMS *or* D.O.M.S.
Diploma in Ophthalmology DO *or* D.O.
Diploma in Physical Education DPE
Diploma in Plant Pathology DPP *or* D.P.P.
Diploma in Psychological Medicine DPM *or*
D.P.M.
Diploma in Public Health DPH *or* D.P.H.
Diploma in Therapeutic Radiology DTR *or*
D.T.R.
Diploma in Tropical Hygiene DTH *or* D.T.H.
Diploma in Tropical Medicine DTM *or* D.T.M.
Diploma in Tropical Medicine and Hygiene
D.T.M.H.
Diploma in Tropical Veterinary Medicine
D.T.V.M. *or* DTVM
Diploma in Tuberculosis and Chest Disease
D.T.C.D.
Diploma in Venereology and Dermatology
D.V. & D.
Diploma in Veterinary Hygiene D.V.H.
Diploma of Art DA *or* D.A.
Diploma of Child and Educational
Psychology DCEP *or* D.C.E.P
Diploma of the Imperial
College DIC *or* D.I.C.
Diploma of the Royal Scottish Academy of
Music and Dance DRSAMD *or*
D.R.S.A.M.D.

Diploma of the Sydney Conservatory of
Music DSCM *or* D.S.C.M.
diplomacy dipl.
Diplomat 1 Dip. 2 Dipl.
diplomat 1 dipl. 2 Dpl. *or* DPL
Diplomatic Dipl.
diplomatic 1 dipl. 2 Dpl. *or* DPL
Diplomatic Corps CD
diplomatic immunity DI
Diplomatic Security DS
Diplomatic Service Administration Office
D.S.A.O.
dipotassium phosphate DKP
diptheria, pertussis, tetanus DPT
Dirac's constant ℏ
direct dir. *or* dir (*MLA:* dir.)
direct access *computers* DA
direct access storage *computers* DAS
direct access storage device DASD
direct action da
direct broadcast satellite DBS
direct broadcasting by satellite DBS
direct coupled *computers* DC
Direct Coupled System DCS
direct current 1 DC *or* D.C. *or* d-c
2 *electricity* d.c. *or* dc (*OUP:* d.c.)
direct current voltage VDC
direct current working voltage DCWV *or*
dcwv
direct digital control *computers* DDC
Direct Distance Dialing DDD
Direct Information Access Network for
Europe DIANE
direct inward dialing DID
direct manufacturing cost *commerce* DMC
direct marketing DM
Direct Marketing Association DMA
direct memory access *computers* DMA
direct operating cost *commerce* DOC
direct order *commerce, military* DO *or* D.O.
direct outward dialing DOD
direct port *commerce* DP
direct question DQ
direct reduction DR
direct reduction process DRP
Direct Selling Association DSA
direct to consumer DTC
direct view storage tube *computers*
DVST
direct *or* distributed numerical control
computers DNC
direct-coupled transistor logic *computers*
DCTL
directed by 1 Dir. 2 Dr *or* Dr.
direction dir.
direction finder DF *or* D/F
direction of relative movement *navigation*
DRM
directional gyro *navigation* DG
directional time *physics* T
directly reduced iron DRI
Director 1 D *or* D. 2 Dir. 3 Dr *or* Dr.
Director General DG *or* D.G. *or* D-G
Director of Central Intelligence DCI
Director of Education DOE
Director of Information DOI
Director of Medical Services DMS *or* D.M.S.
Director of Military Intelligence DMI
Director of Military Operations DMO

Director of Military Training DMT
Director of Naval Intelligence *British* DNI
Director of Naval Recruiting D.N.R. *or* DNR
Director of Operations D.Ops.
Director of Public Instruction *British* D.P.I.
Director of Public Prosecutions *British* DPP *or* D.P.P.
Director of Public Relations DPR
Director of Scientific Research DSR *or* D.S.R.
Directorate of Atomic Research DAR (of Canada)
Directorate of Intelligence DDI *or* D.D.I.
Directorate of Military Survey DMS
Directorate of Operations DDO
Directorate of Security and Intelligence S&I
Directorate of Technical Development DTD
Directors Guild of America DGA
directory and officers D&O
dirham DH
disability disab.
disability insurance DI
disabled 1 dis. **2** disab.
Disabled American Veterans D.A.V. *or* DAV
Disabled Income Group *British* D.I.G.
disabled person DP
Disabled Veterans Administration DVA
disbursements *accounting* disbs.
discharge 1 dis. **2** disch. *or military* DISCH
discharged 1 d *or* d. **2** dis. **3** disch. *or military* DISCH
Discharged Prisoners' Aid Society D.P.A.S.
Disciples of Christ DC *or* D.C.
discipline dis.
discography disc. *or* Disc.
discoid lupus erythematosus DLE
discomfort index DI *or* D.I.
discomfort-relief quotient *psychology* DRQ
disconnect 1 dis. **2** disc. **3** discon
disconnected dis.
discontinue disc.
discontinued dis.
discontinuity *geology, mathematics, physics* dis. *or* dis
discotheque 1 disc. *or* disc **2** disco
discount 1 dis. **2** disc. **3** disct.
discounted cash flow *British* DCF *or* d.c.f.
Discover America Travel Organizations DATO
discovered disc.
discoverer disc.
discrete address beacon system *aeronautics* DABS
discrete Fourier transform DFT
dishonorable dishon.
dishonorable discharge *military* DD
dishwasher DW
disintegrations per minute *physics* dpm *or* d.p.m.
disjunctive *grammar* disj.
disk file *computers* DF
disk file check *computers* DFC
disk filing system *computers* DFS
disk jockey DJ *or* dj
disk operating system DOS
dismissed 1 dismd. **2** Dsmd. *or* dsmd.
disodium methylarsonate DSMA
disordered action of the heart *medicine* DAH

disorderly conduct discon
dispatch loading only *commerce* DLO *or* d.l.o.
dispensary disp. *or* Disp.
Dispensatory of the United States of America DUSA
dispense quickly *pharmaceutics* cito disp.
dispenser disp.
disperse disp.
dispersion disp.
displaced person DP
displacement 1 displ. **2** *physics* **a** D **b** s
displacement ton 1 DT **2** dt *or* d.t.
display and keyboard DSKY
display unit *computers, aeronautics* DU
disposable tape reel *computers* DTR
disposal dspl.
disqualified *sports, law* DQ
disqualify *sports, law* DQ
disseminated intravascular coagulation *medicine* **1** DIC **2** DIS
dissertation diss. *or* Diss. (*MLA:* diss.)
Dissertation Abstracts International **1** DA **2** DAI (*MLA:* DA)
dissipation factor *electronics* DF
dissolve 1 dil. **2** diss. **3** *pharmaceutics* solv.
dissolved dild.
dissolved oxygen DO
distal *anatomy* d
distal tingling on percussion *medicine* DTP
distance 1 D **2** d **3** dis. **4** dist. **5** DX *or* D.X. **6** *physics* s
distance-measuring equipment DME
distant 1 dis. **2** dist. **3** DX *or* D.X.
distill dstl.
distillation distn.
distilled dist.
distilled water DW
Distillery, Wine and Allied Workers Union DWU
distinguish dist.
distinguished dist.
Distinguished Conduct Medal *British* D.C.M. *or* DCM
Distinguished Flying Cross DFC *or* D.F.C.
Distinguished Flying Medal DFM *or* D.F.M.
Distinguished Service Award DSA *or* D.S.A.
Distinguished Service Cross DSC *or* D.S.C.
Distinguished Service Medal DSM *or* D.S.M.
Distinguished Service Order DSO *or* D.S.O.
distinguished visitor DV
distortion D
distribute 1 dis. **2** distr. *or* distrib. *or military* DISTR (*MLA:* distr.; *OUP:* dis.)
distributed 1 dis. **2** dist.
distributed data processing *computers* DDP
Distributing Post Office DPO *or* D.P.O.
distribution 1 dis. **2** distr. *or* distrib. *or military* DISTR **3** dstrib
distribution function *physics* F
distribution tape reel *computers* DTR
distributive *mathematics* distr. *or* distrib.
Distributor Dist.
distributor 1 dist. **2** distr. *or* distrib. *or military* DISTR (*MLA:* distr.; *OUP:* dis.)
District Dist.
district 1 D *or* D. **2** dist. *or* Dist.

District Attorney 1 DA *or* D.A. (*NYT:* D.A.; *OUP:* DA) **2** Dist. Atty.
District Commissioner DC *or* D.C.
District Court 1 DC *or* D.C. **2** Dist. Ct.
District Court Judge DCJ
District Director DD
District Inspector DI
District Judge DJ *or* D.J.
District Medical Officer DMO
District of Columbia 1 DC (Zip Code) **2** DC *or* D.C. (*OUP:* DC)
District of Columbia Appeal Cases *law* App. D.C.
District Office DO *or* D.O.
District Officer DO *or* D.O.
District Registry DR
ditto do. *or* dº (*GPO, CSM, OUP:* do.)
divergence *mathematics, meteorology* div.
diverse div.
diversion div.
divide div.
divided div.
dividend 1 d *or* d. **2** *commerce, law, mathematics* div. *or* divd. **3** *commerce, law* Div. *or* Div
dividend reinvestment program *finance* DRIP
dividends divs
Divine Div.
Divinity Div.
Division 1 D **2** Div.
division 1 div. **2** divn *or* Divn.
Division Headquarters *military* DHQ
Division of Law Enforcement Sciences DLES
Division of Substance Abuse Services DSAS
division service area *military* DSA
Divisional Divnl.
divorce div.
divorced div.
dizygotic DZ
do not resuscitate D.N.R. *or* DNR
do-it-yourself DIY *or* d.i.y. (*OUP:* DIY)
dock dk *or* dk.
dock receipt *commerce* DR *or* D/R
dock warrant *commerce* DW *or* D/W
docket dkt. *or* Dkt.
Dockyard Dkyd.
dockyard dy. *or* dyd.
Doctor 1 D *or* D. **2** Doc. **3** Dr *or* Dr. (*GPO, NYT, CSM:* Dr.; *OUP:* Dr)
Doctor of Agriculture D. Agr.
Doctor of Architecture D.Arch.
Doctor Of Arts DA *or* D.A. (*MLA:* DA)
Doctor of Both Canon and Civil Laws J.U.D. *or* JUD
Doctor of Both Laws *Latin* U.J.D.
Doctor of Business Administration DBA *or* D.B.A.
Doctor of Canon Law 1 D.C.L. *or* DCL **2** D.Cn.L. **3** J.C.D. *or* JCD
Doctor of Chemical Engineering D.Ch.E. *or* DChE
Doctor of Chemistry 1 Ch.D. *or* ChD **2** Dr.Chem.
Doctor of Chiropractic DC *or* D.C.
Doctor of Christian Science 1 CSD *or* C.S.D. **2** DCS *or* D.C.S.
Doctor of Christian Theology DCT *or* D.C.T.

Doctor of Civil Engineering DCE or D.C.E.
Doctor of Civil Law 1 C.L.D. or CLD
2 D.C.L. or DCL 3 J.C.D. or JCD
Doctor of Commercial Law D.Com.L.
Doctor of Commercial Science DCS or
D.C.S.
Doctor of Comparative Law D.Comp.L.
Doctor of Comparative Medicine D.C.M. or
DCM
Doctor of Dental Medicine 1 DDM or
D.D.M. 2 DMD or D.M.D. (NYT: D.M.D.)
Doctor of Dental Science DDS or D.D.S. or
D.D.Sc.
Doctor of Dental Surgery DDS or
D.D.S.(GPO, NYT, CSM: D.D.S.; OUP:
DDS)
Doctor of Divinity DD or D.D. (GPO, NYT,
CSM: D.D.; OUP: DD)
Doctor of Economics D.Ec. or D. Econ.
Doctor of Education 1 D.Ed. 2 Ed.D. (MLA:
EdD)
Doctor of Engineering 1 D.Eng. 2 D.Ing.
3 DE or D.E. 4 Dr.Eng. 5 Dr.Ing. 6 ED or
E.D. 7 Eng.D.
Doctor of Engineering Science Eng.Sc.D.
Doctor of Fine Arts 1 AED or A.E.D. 2 AFD
or A.F.D. 3 DFA or D.F.A.
Doctor of Forestry DF or D.F.
Doctor of Hebrew Literature or Letters
D.H.L. or DHL
Doctor of Holy Scripture DSS or D.S.S.
Doctor of Humane Letters 1 D.H.L. or DHL
2 Latin L.H.D.
Doctor of Hygiene 1 D.Hy. 2 Dr.Hy.
Doctor of Juridical Science 1 DJS or D.J.S.
2 S.J.D.
Doctor of Jurisprudence 1 DJ or D.J. 2 DJur
or D.Jur. 3 Dr.Jur. 4 JD or J.D.
Doctor of Juristic Science J.S.D. or JSD
(NYT: J.S.D.)
Doctor of Law 1 DJ or D.J. 2 DL or D.L.
3 Dr.Jur. 4 Jur. D.
Doctor of Laws 1 JD or J.D. (GPO, NYT: J.D.;
OUP: JD) 2 LL.D. (MLA: LLD; OUP: LL D)
Doctor of Letters LD or L.D.
Doctor of Letters in Economic Studies DLES
or D.L.E.S.
Doctor of Letters or Literature 1 D.Lit. or
DLit. or D.Litt. or DLitt. (GPO, CSM, OUP:
D.Lit. or D.Litt.) 2 Lit.D.
Doctor of Library Science DLS or D.L.S or
DLSc. or D.L.Sc.
Doctor of Literature or Letters Litt.D.
Doctor of Mathematics 1 DM or D.M.
2 DMath. or D.Math.
Doctor of Mathematics and Didactics DMD
or D.M.D.
Doctor of Medical Science 1 DMS or D.M.S.
or D.M.Sc. 2 M.Sc.D. 3 Med.Sc.D. 4 MSD
or M.S.D.
Doctor of Medicine 1 DM or D.M.
2 Dr.Med. 3 MD or M.D. (GPO, NYT:
M.D.; MLA, OUP: MD)
Doctor of Metallurgy DMet. or D.Met.
Doctor of Meteorology DMet. or D.Met.
Doctor of Modern Languages DML or
D.M.L.
Doctor of Music 1 D.Mus or DMus 2 DM or
D.M. 3 Mus.D. or Mus.Doc.

Doctor of Natural Science Dr.Nat.Sci.
Doctor of Nursing Science D.N.Sc.
Doctor of Optical Science DOS
Doctor of Optometry 1 DO or D.O. 2 OD
or O.D. (GPO: O.D.) 3 Opt.D.
Doctor of Oratory DO
Doctor of Oriental Learning DOL or D.O.L.
Doctor of Osteopathy and Surgery DO or
D.O.
Doctor of Pedagogy 1 Pd.D. 2 Ped.D.
Doctor of Pediatric Medicine DPM or D.P.M.
Doctor of Pharmacy 1 D.Pharm. 2 DP or
D.P. 3 PD or P.D.
Doctor of Philosophy 1 D.Ph. or D.Phil.
2 Dr.Phil. 3 PD or P.D. 4 Ph.D. or PhD
(GPO, NYT, OUP: Ph.D.; MLA: PhD)
Doctor of Podiatric Medicine DPM or D.P.M.
Doctor of Podiatry Pod.D.
Doctor of Political Science 1 D.Pol.Sc. 2 DPS
or D.P.S. 3 Dr.Pol.Sc. 4 R.P.D. or RPD
Doctor of Public Administration DPA or
D.P.A.
Doctor of Public Health 1 DPH or D.P.H.
2 Dr.P.H. 3 P.H.D. or PHD
Doctor of Public Hygiene Dr.P.H.
Doctor of Religious Education DRE or
D.R.E.
Doctor of Sacred Music DSM or D.S.M.
Doctor of Sacred Scripture SSD or S.S.D.
Doctor of Sacred Theology 1 DST or D.S.T.
2 STD or S.T.D.
Doctor of Science 1 D.Sc. 2 Dr.Sc. or
Dr.Sci. 3 DS or D.S. (OUP: D.Sc.) 4 Sc.D.
5 SD or S.D.
Doctor of Science in Economics DSE or
D.S.E.
Doctor of Science in Engineering D.Sc.Eng.
Doctor of Social Science 1 D.Soc.Sci. 2 DSS
or D.S.S. or D.S.Sc. 3 S.Sc.D.
Doctor of Social Welfare DSW or
D.S.W.
Doctor of Social Work DSW or D.S.W.
Doctor of Surgery D.Ch.
Doctor of Surgical Chiropody DSC or
D.S.C.
Doctor of Technology D.Tech. or DTech.
Doctor of the Humanities 1 D.Hum. 2 DH or
D.H. 3 HH.D. 4 Latin L.H.D.
Doctor of the Science of Law J.S.D. or JSD
(NYT: J.S.D.)
Doctor of the University D.Univ.
Doctor of the University of Paris DUP or
D.U.P.
Doctor of Theology 1 D.Th. or D.Theol.
2 Dr.Theol. 3 DT or D.T. 4 TH.D. or ThD
Doctor of Tropical Medicine DTM or D.T.M.
Doctor of University of Paris Dr.Univ.Par.
Doctor of Veterinary Medicine 1 DMV or
D.M.V. 2 DVM or D.V.M. (GPO, CSM:
D.V.M) 3 M.D.V. or MDV 4 MVD or
M.V.D. 5 V.M.D.
Doctor of Veterinary Medicine and Surgery
D.V.M.S.
Doctor of Veterinary Science DVS or D.V.S
or D.V.Sc. (CSM: D.V.Sc.; OUP: DVS)
Doctor of Veterinary Surgery DVS or
D.V.S.
Doctor of Zoology DZ or D.Z. or D. Zool.
Doctors Without Frontiers French MSF

document 1 DCT or dct 2 Doc. or doc.
3 docu or docu. or docum.
document content architecture computers
DCA
Document Interchange Architecture DIA
document signed 1 DS or D.S. 2 ds or d.s.
documentary docu or docu.
Documentation of Molecular Spectroscopy
DMS
documents against payment commerce
1 DAP or d.a.p. 2 DP or D/P
documents attached or **for acceptance**
commerce 1 D/A 2 DA
doing business as dba or d.b.a. or d/b/a
(GPO: d.b.a)
Dolby noise reduction electronics DBX or
dbx
dollar 1 $ 2 d or d. 3 dlr. or dlr 4 dol.
dollars dls.
Dolphin Del (constellation)
Domesday Book DB
Domestic Dom.
domestic dom.
Domestic and Foreign Missionary Society
D.F.M.S.
domestic credit expansion DCE
Domestic International Sales Corporation
DISC or D.I.S.C. (NYT: DISC)
domestic satellite domsat or Domsat
domicile dom.
dominant 1 A 2 A 3 d 4 dom.
dominant wavelength DWL
Dominican Republic 1 Dom. Rep. 2 RD
Dominican Revolutionary Party PRD
Dominion Dom.
don't answer DA
don't know commerce dk or DK
Donegal, Northern Ireland Don.
dong D
door 1 D or D. 2 d or d. 3 dr or dr.
Doppler Microwave Landing System
aviation DMLS
Doppler ranging DORAN
Doppler sonar DS
Doppler velocity and position DOVAP
Dorado Dor (constellation)
Doric Dor or Dor. (OUP: Dor.)
dormitory dorm or dorm.
dorsal d or d.
dorsal column stimulator DCS
Dorset, England Dors.
dorsiventral botany DV
dosage dos.
dose 1 dos. 2 medicine **a** D or D.
b d or d.
dose-reduction factor DRF
dots per inch dpi
Douay Bible D.Bib.
Douay Version DV or D.V.
double 1 D or D. 2 dbl. or dble.
(OUP: dbl.)
double bass 1 music, German KB or KB.
2 music d.b.
double bassoon music dbn
Double British Summer Time DBST or
D.B.S.T.
double column d.c. or d/c
double column inch advertising DCI or dci
double crochet 1 d.c. 2 DC

double declining balance *commerce* DDB
double entry *accounting* DE
double foolscap D.Cap. *or* d cap.
double gummed d.g.
double hung *building* dh
double play DP
double point *needlework* dp *or* d.p.
double pole 1 *electricity, electronics* DP **2** *electricity* dp
double pole, double throw *electricity* DPDT *or* dpdt
double pole, single throw *electricity* DPST *or* dpst
double reduced DR
double sideband *radio* DSB
double silk covered DSC *or* dsc
double spacing DSP *or* d/sp.
double strength 1 XX **2** *building* ds *or* d.s.
Double Summer Time *British* DST
double throw 1 DT (of an electrical switch) **2** dt (of an electrical switch)
double time dt
double vibration DV *or* d.v.
double-break DB
double-breasted 1 DB **2** db (*OUP:* d.b.)
double-stranded *biology* ds
Dounias D
Dove Col (constellation)
Dow Jones *commerce* DJ *or* D.-J.
Dow Jones Index DJI
Dowager 1 D *or* D. **2** DOW.
dowel dwl
doweling dwl
Down dwn *or* Dwn *or* Dwn.
down 1 d- *or* d- **2** dn. **3** dwn *or* Dwn
Down's Syndrome DS *or* D.S.
Downs Dns *or* Dns. *or* dns
downward d- *or* d-
dozen 1 doz. **2** dz.
drachma 1 D **2** dr *or* dr. **3** Dr *or* Dr. (*GPO:* Dr; *OUP:* dr.) **4** drch.
Draco, the Dragon Dra (constellation)
draft 1 df **2** dft. *or* Dft.
drag *aeronautics.* D
drain, waste, and vent *plumbing* DWV
dram dr *or* dr.
dramatic dram.
dramatis personae dram. pers.
dramatist dram.

draperies *astronomy* D
Draughtsmen's and Allied Technicians' Association DATA
Dravidian Drav.
Draw a Person test *psychology* DAP *or* DAPT
drawback *commerce* dbk.
Drawer dwr (esp. in postal address)
drawer 1 Dr *or* Dr. **2** dr *or* dr. **3** dwr
drawing 1 dr *or* dr. **2** drg. **3** dwg.
drawn 1 dr *or* dr. **2** drn.
drawn by dr *or* dr.
dressed and headed D & H (of lumber)
dressed and matched D&M (of lumber)
dressed sides DS (of lumber)
drill dr *or* dr.
drill instructor *military* DI *or* D.I.
drilling mud emulsifier DME
drilling mud surfactant DMS
drink *pharmaceutics* bib.
Drive (in address) **1** DR **2** Dr *or* Dr. (*GPO, CSM:* Dr.)
drive 1 dr *or* dr. **2** *computers* DR **3** *psychology* D
driver Dvr.
driving d *or* d.
driving under the influence DUI *or* D.U.I.
driving while intoxicated DWI *or* D.W.I.
drizzle *meteorology* **1** d *or* d. **2** L
drop *pharmaceutics* gt *or* gt.
drop forge DF
drop zone *military* DZ
dropping mercury electrode *electronics* DME
drops *pharmaceutics* **1** gtt. **2** gutt.
Drug Abuse Resistance Education DARE
Drug Amendments Act DAA
Drug Enforcement Administration DEA
Drug Supervisory Board DSB
drum *mechanics, music* dr *or* dr.
drunk and disorderly D and D
dry air *meterology* y
dry bulb DB
dry bulb temperature DBT
drydock dd
dual employed with kids DEWK
dual in-line package *electronics* DIP
dubious dub.
Dublin, Ireland Dub. *or* Dubl.

Duchennes Muscular Dystrophy *medicine* DMD
Duchess D *or* D.
Duck Embryo Virus DEV
due date *commerce, obstetrics* DD
Duke 1 D *or* D. **2** Du.
Duluth, Minnesota Dul.
Dumfries, Scotland Dumf.
dummy section *computers* DSECT *or* DSect.
dun dn.
Dundee, Scotland Dun.
dunnage dun.
duodecimo 1 D *or* D. **2** *printing* duo.
duodenal ulcer *medicine* DU
duplex 1 dpl. *or* dplx **2** *commerce, biology* dup *or* dup. *or* dupl. **3** *electronics* DX
duplicate 1 DUP **2** dup *or* dup. *or* dupl.
durable press DP
duration *medicine* d *or* d.
Durban, South Africa Dur.
Durham Dunelm.
Durham, England Dur.
during the night *pharmaceutics* noct.
Düsseldorf, Germany Dsf
dust 1 *meteorology* D **2** *pharmaceutics* consperg.
dust jacket DJ *or* dj *or* d.-j.
dust storm *meteorology* KZ *or* kz
dust wrapper 1 d.w. *or* d-w **2** DW
Dutch 1 D *or* D. **2** Du. **3** Dut.
Dutch florin D.fl.
Dutch Reformed Church D.R.C.
duty dy.
Duty Officer DO
duty paid *commerce* DP
dwelling dwg. *or* dwel.
dying away *music* perd.
dynamic address translator *computers* DAT
dynamic pressure q
dynamic programming *computers* DP
dynamic random-access memory *computers* DRAM
dynamic spatial reconstructor *medicine* DSR
dynamics dyn. *or* dynam.
dynamite dyn.
dynamo dyn.
dyne 1 d *or* d. **2** dyn. *or* dyn
dysprosium Dy

each ea.
each eye *medicine* OU *or* o.u.
Eagle Aql (constellation)
ear *medicine* aur.
ear, nose, and throat *medicine* ENT
Earl Marshal EM *or* E.M. (*OUP:* EM)
earliest arrival time EAT

earliest practicable date *commerce* EPD
earliest start time EST
Early Childhood Education ECE
Early English E.E. *or* EE (*OUP:* EE)
Early English Text Society E.E.T.S.
early lunar flare ELF *or* elf *or* e.l.f.
Early Modern English 1 E.MnE. **2** E.Mod.E.
early pregnancy test EPT
early receptor potential ERP
early warning radar EWR
earned income credit EIC
earned points EP
earned runs *baseball* ER
earned-run average *baseball* ERA
earnings after taxes *finance* EAT

earnings before interest and taxes *finance* EBIT
earnings per share *commerce* EPS *or* eps
earth continuity conductor *electricity* ECC
Earth Observing System EOS *or* EoS *or* Eos
Earth Orbiting Satellite EOS
earth parking orbit EPO
Earth Resources Observation Satellite EROS
earth satellite vehicle ESV
earth's mean orbital speed EMOS *or* emos
Easel Pic (constellation)
East E *or* E.
east e *or* e.
East African Freshwater Fisheries Organization EAFFRO

East African Marine Fisheries Research Organization EAMFRO
East African Veterinary Research Organization EAVRO
East Asian and Pacific Affairs EAPA
east by north 1 E by N 2 EbN
east by south 1 E by S 2 EbS
East Caribbean EC
East Indian EI or E.I.
East Indies EI or E.I.
east longitude E.long.
East Riding, Yorkshire ER or E.R.
East River ER
east-northeast ENE or E.N.E. or e.n.e.
east-southeast ESE or E.S.E. or e.s.e.
eastbound EB
Easter Term *British* ET or E.T.
easterly Ely
Eastern E or E.
eastern 1 e or e. 2 East. or east.
Eastern College Athletic Conference ECAC or E.C.A.C.
Eastern Daylight Saving Time EDST or E.D.S.T. or e.d.s.t.
Eastern Daylight Time EDT or E.D.T. or e.d.t.
eastern equine encephalomyelitis EEE
Eastern European Time EET or E.E.T.
Eastern Fishermen's Association EFE
Eastern Hockey League EHL
Eastern Orthodox EO or E.O.
Eastern Standard Time EST or E.S.T. or e.s.t.
Eastern Test Range ETR
Eastern Time ET or E.T. or e.t.
eastward Eastw.
easy EZ or E-Z
eat-in kitchen EIK
eccentric geophysical observatory EGO
eccentricity *mathematics, physics* e
eccentricity of the orbit *astronomy* e
Ecclesiastes Eccl. (*MLA, OUP:* Eccles.) Eccles.
Ecclesiastic *or* Ecclesiastical Eccl.
Ecclesiasticus Ecclus.
ecclesiology eccles.
echelon *military* Ech.
echo ranging ER
echo sounding device ESD
eclectic eclec.
eclecticism eclec.
eclipse ecli.
ecological 1 eco. or eco 2 ecol.
Ecological Society of America 1 Ecol. Soc. Am. 2 ESA
ecology ecol.
economic econ. or Econ.
economic advisor EA or E.A.
Economic and Monetary Union EMU
Economic and Planning Council EPC
Economic and Social Commission for Asia and the Pacific ESCAP
Economic and Social Commission for Western Asia ESCWA
Economic and Social Council 1 ECOSOC 2 ESC
Economic and Social Research Council ESRC
Economic Commission for Africa ECA
Economic Commission for Europe ECE

Economic Commission for Latin America and the Caribbean ECLAC
Economic Commission for Western Africa ECWA
Economic Commission of West African States ECOWAS
Economic Cooperation Administration ECA
Economic Development Administration EDA or E.D.A.
Economic Development Committee *British* EDC
Economic Information Service EIS
Economic Policy Committee EPC
Economic Research Council ERC
Economic Research Service ERS
Economic Society of Australia and New Zealand ESANZ or E.S.A.N.Z.
economical econ.
economical order quantity *commerce* EOQ
economics 1 eco. 2 econ. or Econ.
economist econ. or Econ.
Economist Intelligence Unit EIU or E.I.U.
economy econ.
Ecuador 1 Ec. 2 Ecua.
eddy diffusivity *chemistry, physics* E
edetic acid EDTA
edge E
edge and center E&C (of lumber)
edges gilt e.g.
edible structural material ESM
Edinburgh Review ER
Edinburgh, Scotland Edin.
Edison Electric Institute EEI
edited 1 ed. or Ed. (*MLA, OUP:* ed.) 2 edit. or Edit.
edition 1 ed. or Ed. (*MLA:* ed.; *OUP:* Edn.) 2 edit. or Edit. 3 Edn.
edition cited ed.cit. (*MLA:* not acceptable)
editions eds.
editor 1 ed. or Ed. (*MLA, OUP:* ed.) 2 edit. or Edit.
Editor and Publisher E&P
Editor-in-Chief E-in-C
editorial 1 ed. or Ed. 2 edit. or Edit.
editors eds.
educable mentally retarded EMR
educated 1 ed. 2 educ.
education 1 ed. or Ed. (*MLA:* educ.) 2 educ.
Education Department ED
Education Officer EO or E.O.
Education Writers Association EWA or E.W.A.
educational 1 ed. or Ed. (*MLA:* educ.) 2 educ.
educational age EA or E.A.
educational and vocational training EVT
Educational Council for Foreign Medical Graduates ECFMG
Educational Film Library Association EFLA
Educational Foundation for Nuclear Science EFNS
Educational Foundation for Visual Aids EFVA
Educational Media Research Information Center EMRIC
Educational Opportunity Fund EOF
Educational Opportunity Grant EOG or E.O.G.

educational priority area EPA or E.P.A.
Educational Products Information Exchange EPIE
Educational Publishers Council EPC
educational quotient EQ or E.Q.
educational ratio ER or E.R.
Educational Research Information Center ERIC
Educational Specialist ES or E.S.
Educational Television ETV
Educational Testing Service ETS
educational therapy ET
Educational, Scientific, and Cultural Organization ESCO
educationally subnormal *British* ESN
Edward Edw.
Edward Grey Institute of Field Ornithology EGIFO
Edwards Flight Research Center EFRC
Eelam People's Revolutionary Liberation Front EPRLF
effect eff. or Eff.
effective eff.
effective address *computers* EA
effective date of change EDOC
effective dose ED
effective half-life *nuclear physics* EHL or ehl
effective horsepower ehp or EHP
effective perceived noise decibel EPNdB
effective radiated power *communications* ERP
effective renal plasma flow *medicine* ERPF
effectiveness report ER
Effects of Atomic Weapons EAW
Effects of Nuclear Weapons ENW
efferens *biology* eff.
efferent *biology* eff.
efficiency 1 E 2 eff. 3 *physics* n
Efficiency Decoration ED or E.D.
efficient deck hand EDH
effluent flow per hour e.f.p.h.
effluent gas analysis *chemistry* EGA
effluent gas detection EGD
effort E
egg transfer *medicine* ET
Egypt Eg.
Egyptian 1 E 2 Eg. 3 Egypt.
Egyptian General Petroleum Corporation EGPC
Egyptian Intelligence Service EIS
Egyptian pound £E
Egyptologist Egyptol.
Egyptology Egyptol.
einsteinium Es
either or both a/or
El Niño-Southern Oscillation *meteorology* ENSO
El Salvador 1 El Salv. 2 Salv.
elapsed time ET or e.t.
elapsed time indicator ETI or eti
elapsed time of one cycle T
elastance S
elasticity elas.
elder eld.
eldest 1 e or e. 2 eld.
elected 1 el. 2 elect.
election elect.
election district ED

electric 1 el. 2 elec. or Elec. 3 elect. or Elect.
Electric and Musical Industries EMI
electric charge e or e
electric current density J
electric dipole moment 1 p 2 physics EDM
electric displacement chemistry D or D
electric field strength E
electric horsepower ehp or EHP
electric potential V
electric potential differential U
Electric Power Research Institute EPRI
electric primer ep
electric vehicle EV
electrical 1 el. 2 elec. or Elec. 3 elect. or Elect.
electrical engineer E.E. or EE
electrical engineering E.E.
electrical impedance physics Z
electrical impedance tomography medicine EIT
electrical kilowatt ekw
Electrical Manufacturers Standards Council EMSC
electrical metallic tubing EMT
electrical reactance physics X
Electrical Research Association ERA
electrical resistance gauge ERG
electrical stimulation of the brain ESB
Electrical Trades Union ETU or E.T.U.
electrical or electronic discharge machining EDM
Electrical or Electronic Technicians Certificate ETC or E.T.C.
electrically alterable read-only memory computers EAROM
electrically erasable programmable read-only memory computers EEPROM
electrically erasable read-only memory computers EEROM
electrically polarized 1 EP 2 ep
electrically suspended gyroscope ESG
electrician 1 elec. or Elec. 2 elect. or Elect.
electricity 1 el. 2 elec. 3 elect.
electrocardiogram 1 ECG 2 EK 3 EKG
electrocardiograph 1 ECG 2 EKG
electrochemical electrochem.
electrochemical diffused collector transistor ECDC
electrochemical equivalent physics z
electrochemical machining ECM
electrochemistry electrochem.
electroconvulsive shock ECS
electroconvulsive therapy ECT
electrodermal response EDR
electroencephalogram EEG
electroencephalograph EEG
electroencephalography EEG
electrofluid-dynamic EFD
electrogasdynamic EGD
electrogastrogram EGG
electrogastrograph EGG
electrohydrodynamic physics EHD
electrokymogram medicine EKY
electroluminescent display ELD
electromagnetic 1 EM 2 em or e.m.
electromagnetic field EMF
electromagnetic intelligence ELMINT
electromagnetic interference EMI

electromagnetic pulse EMP
electromagnetic radiance astronomy, physics L
electromagnetic resonance EMR
electromagnetic unit EMU or emu
electromagnetic vector potential physics EVP
electromechanical aid ELMA
Electromechanical Experimental Module MOSE
electromolecular propulsion EMP
electromotive 1 EM 2 em or e.m.
electromotive difference of potential EMDP or e.m.d.p.
electromotive force 1 E or E 2 EMF or e.m.f.
electromyogram EMG
electromyography EMG
electron 1 E 2 e 3 e or e
electron beam EB
electron beam ion source electronics, physics EBIS
electron beam machining EBM
electron beam recording EBR
electron beam welding EBW
electron bombardment induced conductivity EBICON
electron capture physics, chemistry EC
electron cyclotron resonance physics ECR
electron dipole moment nuclear physics EDM
electron energy loss spectroscopy chemistry, physics EELS
electron microprobe analysis EMA
electron microscope EM
Electron Microscope Society of America EMSA
electron microscopy EM
electron nuclear double resonance ENDOR
electron paramagnetic resonance EPR
electron probe microanalysis EPM
electron ring accelerator physics ERA
electron spectroscopy for chemical analysis ESCA
electron spin polarization physics ESP
electron spin resonance ESR or e.s.r.
electron stimulated desorption ion angular distribution ESDIAD
electron transport particles physics ETP
electron volt EV or eV or e.v.
electron-beam addressed memory computers EBAM
electron-coupled oscillator ECO
electronic 1 E 2 e
electronic accounting machine EAM
electronic altitude direction indicator aeronautics EADI
electronic article surveillance EAS
electronic automatic exchange computers, communications EAX
electronic cash register ECR
Electronic Circuit Analysis Program computers ECAP
electronic coding machine ECM
electronic components board ECB
Electronic Components Quality Assurance Committee ECQAC
electronic counter-countermeasures ECCM
electronic countermeasures ECM

electronic data interchange EDI
electronic data processing EDP
electronic data processing equipment EDPE
electronic data processing system EDPS
electronic fetal monitor medicine EFM
electronic field production EFP
electronic flash approach system EFAS
electronic fuel injection EFI
electronic funds transfer EFT
electronic funds transfer at point of sale EFTPOS or Eftpos or Eft/pos
electronic funds transfer system EFTS
electronic ground automatic destruct sequencer EGADS
electronic ignition system EIS
Electronic Industries Association EIA
electronic intelligence ELINT
electronic interference communications QRM
electronic mail e-mail
electronic news gathering ENG
electronic parts of assessed quality EPAQ
electronic point of sale computers EPOS
electronic position indicator surveying, navigation EPI
electronic program guide EPG
Electronic Random Number Indicating Equipment ERNIE
electronic recorder ER
electronic reporting ER
electronic setup ESU
electronic sports gathering ESG
electronic still store ESS
Electronic Switching System communications ESS
electronic video recording EVR
electronic view finder EVF
electronic warfare EW
electronics 1 elct. 2 electron.
Electronics Research Center ERC
electronystagmograph ENG
electrooculogram EOG
electrooculograph EOG
electrophoretic light scattering physics ELS
electrophysical electrophys.
electrophysical study EPS
electroplate EP
electroplated nickel silver EPNS
electroreflectance physics ER
electroretinogram ERG
electrorheological physics ER
electrorheological fluid physics ERF
electrosensitive pattern ESP
electroshock therapy EST
electrostatic ES
electrostatic unit physics ESU or esu
electrothermal chemical ETC
electuary 1 elec. 2 elect.
element 1 el. 2 elem.
elementary elem.
Elementary and Secondary Education Act ESEA
elementary body EB or E.B.
elementary charge chemistry e
elementary-high school El-hi
elevated railway el. or el or El
elevation 1 EL 2 el. or El. 3 elev.
elevation finder EF

elevation position indicator EPI
elevator elev.
Elijah Eli. or Elij.
eliminated elim.
elixir pharmaceutics elix.
Elizabeth Eliz.
Elizabethan Eliz.
elliptical ellipt.
elliptical nebula E
elocution elo. or eloc.
elongation elong.
eloquence elo. or eloq.
elsewhere ali.
Elzevir Elz.
emalangeni E
emanation 1 Em 2 em
Emanuel Em or Em.
embargo emb.
embark emb.
embarkation emb.
embassy Emb.
embassy officer emboff
embossed emb.
embroider embr.
embroidered emb.
embroidery embr.
embryo 1 emb. 2 embr.
embryological embr. or embryol.
embryology 1 emb. 2 embr. or embryol.
emendation or emendations emend. or Emend.
emergency Emer. or emer. or emerg.
emergency action file EAF
Emergency Action Notification EAN
Emergency Broadcast System EBS
emergency core cooling system ECCS
emergency field ration K-ration
Emergency Health Service EHS
emergency locator transmitter ELT
emergency maintenance EM
emergency maternity and infant care EMIC
Emergency Measures Organization EMO
emergency medical care EMC
Emergency Medical Service EMS
emergency medical technician EMT
emergency medicine EM
emergency operating center EOC
Emergency Operating Facility EOF
emergency operations plan EOP
Emergency Petroleum Allocation Act EPAA
Emergency Powers Act EPA
Emergency Powers Defense Act EPDA
Emergency Public Information EPI
emergency room ER
Emergency Technician ET
emergency ward EW
emergency water supply EWS
emerging technology ET
Emeritus Emer.
Eminence Em or Em.
emissivity physics e
emitter electronics e
emitter coupled logic electronics ECL
emitter-coupled logic operator electronics ECLO
emitter-follower logic computers EFL
emmetropia E or E.
Emperor 1 Emp. 2 I or I. 3 Imp or Imp.

Empire Emp.
Employee Assistance Program EAP
employee ownership plan EOP
Employee Retirement Income Security Act ERISA
Employee Stock Ownership Plan ESOP
Employees' Compensation Appeals Board ECAB
Employees' Compensation Commission ECC
Employers Identification Number EIN
employment emp.
Employment and Standards Administration ESA
Employment and Training Administration ETA
Empress 1 Emp. 2 I 3 Imp or Imp.
empty MT (of a container or railroad car)
emulsion emul.
en route ER or E/R
enamel covered e.c.
enameled enam.
encapsulated PostScript computers EPS
encapsulated PostScript format computers EPSF
encephalization quotient EQ or E.Q.
encephalomyocarditis EMC
enclosed enc. or encl. (OUP: enc.)
enclosure enc. or encl. (OUP: enc.)
Encyclopaedia Britannica EB
encyclopedia 1 enc. or Enc. 2 ency. or Ency. 3 encyc. or Encyc. or encycl. or Encycl.
end football E
end center matched ECM (of lumber)
end diastolic volume medicine EDV
end of address computers EOA
end of block computers EOB
end of cycle EOC
end of file computers EOF
end of job computers EOJ
end of line computers EOL
end of medium computers EM
end of message computers EOM
end of record computers EOR
end of tape computers EOT
end of text computers ETX
end of the month accounting EOM or e.o.m. (GPO: e.o.m.)
end of transmission computers EOT
end of transmission block computers ETB
end paper 1 end p. or endp. 2 ep
end point EP or E.P.
end, the fin.
end to end E to E (in blueprints)
endocardial fibroelastosis EFE
endoplasmic reticulum biology ER
endorsed end or end.
endorsement end or end.
endorsement irregular banking EI or E.I. or E/I
endosperm end
endothelium-derived relaxing factor EDRF
ends matched EM (of lumber)
ends standard matched ESM (of lumber)
enema en.
enemy en.
enemy aircraft EA
enemy prisoner of war EPW
energy 1 E 2 U 3 u 4 W

energy conservation vehicle ECV
energy efficiency ratio EER
Energy Information Administration EIA
Energy Policy and Conservation Act EPCA
Energy Rate Input Controller ERIC
Energy Regulatory Administration ERA
Energy Research and Development Administration ERDA
Energy Research Center ERC
Energy Resources Advisory Board ERAB
Energy Supply and Environmental Coordination Act ESECA
Energy Technology Support Unit ETSU
energy utilization index EUI
engine eng. or eng
engine room ER
engine test vehicle ETV or etv
engine-pressure ratio EPR
Engineer 1 E 2 En. or En
engineer 1 eng. 2 engr.
Engineer and Architects Association EAA or E.A.A.
Engineer Buyers and Representatives Association EBRA
Engineer of Metallurgy E.Met.
Engineer of Mines EM or E.M.
Engineer Officer EO
Engineer-in-Chief E-in-C
Engineered Performance Standard EPS
Engineering 1 E 2 Eng.
engineering 1 eng. 2 engg. or Engg. 3 engin.
engineering change order ECO
engineering change proposal ECP
Engineering Committee on Ocean Resources ECOR
Engineering Data Information System EDIS
Engineering Institute of Canada EIC
Engineering Research and Development Laboratory ERDL
engineering setup ESU
engineering test ET
Engineering Test Reactor ETR
engineering time ET
Engineers Council for Professional Development ECPD
Engineers Joint Council EJC or E.J.C.
England 1 Eng. (MLA: E or Eng.) 2 Engl.
English 1 E or E. 2 En. or En 3 Eng. (MLA: E or Eng.) 4 Engl.
English as a foreign language EFL
English as a Second Language ESL
English Bookplate Society EBS or E.B.S.
English Bowling Association EBA
English Chamber Orchestra ECO
English Church Union ECU or E.C.U.
English Dialect Dictionary EDD or E.D.D.
English Dialect Society EDS or E.D.S.
English finish EF
English Folk Dance and Song Society EFDSS or E.F.D.S.S.
English for Speakers of Other Languages ESOL
English for Special Purposes ESP
English Golf Union EGU or E.G.U.
English Historical Review EHR
English horn 1 eng hn or Eng hn 2 music EH

English Journal EJ
English Language Book Society ELBS or E.L.B.S.
English Language Notes ELN
English Language Teaching ELT
English language teaching ELT
English Literature Eng. Lit.
English National Opera ENO
English Newspaper Association ENA
English Philological Studies EPS
English Place-Name Society EPNS or E.P.N.S.
English Revised Version ERV or E.R.V.
English Rugby Union ERU or E.R.U.
English Speaking Union ESU or E.S.U.
English Standard Gauge ESG
English Studies ES
English translation ET or E.T. (OUP: ET)
English Universities Press EUP or E.U.P.
English Version EV or E.V. (of the Bible)
engraved 1 Eng. 2 eng. 3 Engr. 4 engr.
engraver 1 Eng. 2 eng. 3 Engr. 4 engr.
engraving 1 eng. 2 engr.
enhanced *electronics, medicine* E
enhanced expanded memory specification *computers* EEMS
enhanced graphics adaptor *computers* EGA
enhanced oil recovery EOR
enhanced radiation ER
enhanced radiation weapon ERW
enhanced small device interface ESDI
enhancement *electronics, medicine* E
enlarged enl.
enlisted enl.
enlisted man or men EM
enquiry ENQ or enq
ensemble *music* ens
enter left *theater* EL
entered ent. or entd.
enteric cytopathogenic human orphan ECHO or Echo
enterotoxigenic E. coli ETEC
entertainment ent. or Ent.
Entertainment and Sports Network ESPN
enthalpy H
entomological entom. or entomol.
Entomological Society of America ESA
Entomological Society of Canada ESC
entomology 1 ent. 2 entom. or entomol.
entrance 1 ent. or Ent. 2 *theater* e or e.
entropy *physics* 1 S 2 s
entropy unit EU or E.U. or e.u.
envelope env.
Environment and Natural Resources Division ENR
environmental 1 Env. 2 env. or envtl.
environmental analysis EA
environmental assessment EA
environmental control EC
environmental control system ECS
environmental control unit ECU
Environmental Data Service EDS
Environmental Defense Fund EDF
Environmental Equipment Institute EEI
environmental impact assessment EIA
environmental impact report EIR
Environmental Impact Statement EIS
Environmental Investigation Agency EIA

Environmental Protection Agency EPA (*NYT*: E.P.A.)
Environmental Protection Board EPB
environmental quality index EQI
Environmental Research Institute of Michigan ERIM
Environmental Research Laboratory ERL
Environmental Science Services Administration ESSA
Environmental Survey Satellite ESSA
environmental tobacco smoke ETS
Envoy Env.
Envoy Extraordinary E.E.
Envoy Extraordinary and Minister Plenipotentiary E.E.&M.P.
Enzyme Commission (Number) EC(No.)
enzyme substrate *biochemistry* ES
enzyme-linked immunosorbent assay ELISA or Elisa
Eocene Eoc.
eosin methylene blue EMB
eosinophil eos.
eosinophilia-myalgia syndrome EMS
eosinophilic chemotactic factor *medicine* ECF
ephemeris time ET
Ephesians Eph. or Ephes. (*MLA, OUP*: Eph.)
Ephraim Eph.
epidemic epid.
Epidemic Intelligence Service EIS
epidermal growth factor EGF
epigram epig.
epigraphy epig.
epilogue epil.
Epiphany Epiph.
Episcopal 1 Epis. 2 Episc.
Episcopal Church EC or E.C.
Episcopalian 1 Epis. 2 Episc.
Epistle 1 Ep. or ep. 2 Epis.
epitaph epit. or Epit.
epitome epit.
epoch *astronomy, geology* e
epsilon amino caproic acid EACA
Epstein-Barr EB
Epstein-Barr virus EBV
equal 1 aeq. or æq. 2 eq.
equal employment opportunity EEO
Equal Opportunities Commission EOC
Equal Opportunity and Civil Rights EOCR
equal opportunity employer EOE
equal parts 1 p. ae. 2 *pharmaceutics* part. aeq. or p.e.
Equal Rights Amendment ERA or E.R.A.
equal section ES or es (of blueprints)
equalization *electronics, engineering* EQ
equalizer *electronics, engineering* EQ
equals aeq. or æq.
equation 1 eq. 2 eqn.
Equator Eq.
Equatorial 1 Eq. 2 Equat.
equatorial *meteorology* E
Equerry Eq.
equilibrium constant *chemistry* K
equilibrium peritoneal dialysis *medicine* EPD
equipment 1 eq. 2 equip.
equitable eq.
equity eq. or eq

Equity Principle Auditions *theater* EPA
equivalence 1 EQ 2 equiv.
equivalent 1 eq. 2 equiv.
equivalent air speed *aeronautics* EAS
equivalent direct radiation edr
equivalent focal length EFL or E.F.L.
equivalent full-power day EFPD
equivalent full-power hour EFPH
equivalent isotropic radiated power *communications* EIRT
equivalent megatons EMT
equivalent residual dose ERD
equivalent shaft horsepower ESHP or eshp
erasable programmable read-only memory *computers* EPROM
Erasmus Eras.
erbium Er
erg *physics* e
ergonomics ergon.
ermine erm.
erroneous erron.
erroneously erron.
error 1 Err. or err. 2 X 3 *statistics, sports* E
error correction or corrected EC
error detection and correction EDC or edc
error detection or detecting ED
error frequency limit *computers* EFL
error function ERF or erf
error recovery *computers* ER
errors and omissions excepted 1 *commerce, civil engineering* a E.&O.E. or E.&o.e. (*OUP*: E.&O.E.) b s.e.e.o. or S.E.e.O. 2 *commerce* EOE or E.O.E. or e.o.e.
errors excepted E.E. or EE or e.e.
errors or omissions excepted e.o.o.e. or EOOE
erythema dose *medicine* ED
erythema nodosum leprosum ENL
erythroblastosis fetalis EF
erythrocyte maturing factor *medicine* EMF
erythrocyte sedimentation rate *medicine* ESR
erythrocyte with antigen EA
erythrocyte with antigen and complement EAC
erythropoietic stimulating factor *biochemistry* ESF
erythropoietin EPO
erythrose phosphate *biochemistry* EP
escape 1 esc. or esc 2 *computers* ESC
escaped esc. or esc
escaping esc. or esc
eschatology eschat.
Escherichia coli E. coli
escudo ESC or esc.
Esdras Esd.
Eskimo Esk.
especially esp. or espec. (*NYT, OUP*: esp.)
Esquire Esq. or Esqr. or Esqre.
essence ess.
essential ESN or esn
essential elements of information EEI
essential fatty acid or acids *biochemistry* EFA
Essex County, England Ess.
established 1 Est. 2 est. 3 Estab. or estab. 4 estd. or Estd.
Established Church EC

Establishment Estab. *or* estab.
estate est.
Estates EST (in postal address)
Esther 1 Es *or* Es. **2** Esth.
estimate est.
estimated 1 E **2** est. **3** estd.
estimated completion date ECD
estimated position *navigation* EP
estimated time at *or* **over next position** ENP
estimated time en route *navigation* ETE
estimated time of arrival ETA *or* e.t.a.
    (*OUP:* ETA)
estimated time of completion ETC
estimated time of departure ETD *or* e.t.d.
estimated time of return ETR
estimated time of separation *military* ETS
estimated turnaround point ETP
estimated value of agricultural operations
    EVAO
estimating estg.
estimation est.
Estonia Est.
Estonian Est.
estradiol cyclopentylpropionate ECP
estrogen-replacement therapy *medicine*
    ERT
Estuary Est.
estuary est.
ethambutol EMB
ether eth.
ethical eth.
ethics eth.
Ethiopia Eth.
Ethiopian Eth.
Ethiopian birr EB
Ethiopic Eth.
ethnographic ethnog.
ethnography ethnog.
ethnological 1 ethn. **2** ethnol.
ethnology 1 ethn. **2** ethnol.
ethyl Et
ethyl alcohol EtOH
ethyl hydroxyethyl cellulose EHEC
ethyl mercury phosphate EMP
ethyl tertiary butyl ether ETBE
ethylene bisdithiocarbamate EBDC
ethylene dibromide EDB
ethylene glycol EG
ethylene propylene diene monomer EPDM
ethylene propylene terpolymer EPT
ethylene thiourea ETU
ethylene vinyl acetate EVA
ethylene-propylene rubber EPR
ethylparanitrophenyl EPN
etiology etiol.
Etruscan Etr.
etymological ety. *or* etym. *or* etymol.
etymology ety. *or* etym. *or* etymol.
euphemism euphem.
Europe 1 Eu *or* Eu. **2** Eur.
European 1 E **2** Eu *or* Eu. **3** Eur.
European Academic Network EAN
European Academic Research Network
    EARN
European Agricultural Guidance and
    Guarantee Fund 1 EAGGF **2** *French*
    FEOGA
European and Canadian Affairs ECA

European and Mediterranean Plant
    Protection Organization EPPO
European Association for Animal
    Production EAAP
European Association for Research on Plant
    Breeding EUCARPIA
European Association of Exploration
    Geophysicists EAEG
European Association of Music Festivals
    EAMF
European Atomic Energy Community
    1 EAEC **2** Euratom
European Atomic Energy Society EAES
European Bank for Reconstruction and
    Development EBRD
European Boxing Union EBU *or* E.B.U.
European Brewery Convention EBC
European Broadcasting Union 1 EBU
    2 *French* UER
European Bureau of Consumers Unions
    French BEUC
European Center for Population Studies
    1 CEEP *or* C.E.E.P. **2** ECPS
European Central Inland Transport
    Organization ECITO
European Civil Aviation Conference ECAC
European Coal and Steel Community ECSC
European Committee for Future
    Accelerators ECFA
European Committee for Standardization
    CEN
European Communications Satellite ECS
European Community 1 CE *or* C.E. **2** EC
European Computer Manufacturers
    Association ECMA
European Confederation of Agriculture
    1 CEA **2** ECA
European Conference of Ministers of
    Transport ECMT
European Conference on Satellite
    Communications CETS
European Court of Justice ECJ
European Cultural Center ECC
European Cultural Foundation *French* FEC
European Currency Unit ECU *or* ecu
European Democratic Union EDU
European Depositary Receipts EDR *or* E.D.R.
European Development Fund 1 EDF **2** FED
European Documentation and Information
    System in Education EUDISED
European Economic Area EEA
European Economic Community EEC *or*
    E.E.C. (*NYT:* E.E.C.; *OUP:* EEC)
European Environmental Bureau EEB
European Federalist Movement EFM
European Federation for the Protection of
    Waters EFPW
European Federation of Corrosion EFC
European Federation of Sea Anglers EFSA
European Fighter Aircraft EFA
European Football Union EFU
European Forestry Commission EFC
European Free Trade Association EFTA
European Golf Association EGA *or* E.G.A.
European Hockey Federation EHF
European Industrial Research Management
    Association EIRMA
European Investment Bank EIB

European Large Orbiting Instrumentation
    for Solar Experiment ELOISE
European Launching Development
    Organization CECLES
European Long Lines Agency ELLA
European Meteorological Satellite
    EUMETSAT
European Molecular Biology Organization
    EMBO
European Monetary Agreement EMA
European Monetary System EMS
European Monetary Unit EMU
European Network Euronet
European Nuclear Energy Agency ENEA
European Nuclear Force ENF *or* E.N.F.
European Organization for Nuclear
    Research CERN
European Organization for Quality Control
    EOQC
European Organization for Research on
    Treatment of Cancer EORTC
European Parliament EP
European patent Eur. pat.
European Patent Office EPO
European Payments Union 1 EPU **2** *French*
    UEP
European People's Party EPP
European Petro-Chemical Association EPCA
European Plan EP
European Productivity Agency EPA
European Radio Frequency Agency ERFA
European Railway Pass EURAILPASS
European Recovery Program ERP *or* E.R.P.
    (*GPO:* ERP)
European Regional Organization (of Free
    Trade Unions) E.R.O.
European Satellite Tracking and Telemetry
    Network ESTRACK
European Science Foundation ESF *or* E.S.F.
European Society of Haematology E.S.H.
European Southern Observatory ESO
European Space Agency ESA
European Space Data Center ESDAC
European Space Operation Center ESOC
European Space Research Institute ESRIN
European Space Research Laboratory
    ESLAB
European Space Research Organization
    ESRO
European Space Technology Center ESTEC
European Strategic Research Program in
    Information Technology ESPRIT
European Teachers Association 1 ETA
    2 *French* A.E.D.E. *or* AEDE
European Telecommunications Satellite
    EUTELSAT
European Theater of Operations ETO
European Trade Union Confederation ETUC
European Translation Center ETC *or* E.T.C.
European Union EU *or* E.U.
European Union of Film and Television
    Technicians EUFTT
European Union of Women EUW
European Unit of Account EUA
European Weed Research Council EWRC
European Youth Center EYC
europium Eu
Eusebius Eus.

Euthanasia Society of America ESA
evacuated evac.
evacuation evac.
evaluate eval.
evaluated eval.
evaluation eval.
evangelical Evang. *or* evang.
Evangelical (Protestant) Church of Germany EKD
Evangelical and Reformed Church E and R
Evangelical Christians and Baptists ECB *or* E.C.B.
Evangelical Lutheran Church in America ELCH
Evangelical Union EU *or* E.U.
Evangelical United Brethren E.U.B.
evangelist Evang. *or* evang.
evaporate evap.
evaporated evap.
evaporation 1 E 2 evap. *or* evapn.
evaporation water loss EWL
evening 1 Eve *or* eve 2 evg.
evening, in the evening *Latin* vesp.
evenings Eves.
event-related potential ERP
every 1 evy 2 *pharmaceutics* q
every day *pharmaceutics* q.d.
every four hours *pharmaceutics* q.q.h.
every hour *pharmaceutics* 1 o.h. 2 omn. hor. 3 q.h. 4 qq.hor.
every morning *pharmaceutics* 1 o.m. 2 omn. man. 3 q.m.
every night *pharmaceutics* 1 o.n. 2 omn. n oct. 3 qn *or* q.n.
every other day 1 EOD *or* e.o.d. (*OUP:* e.o.d.) 2 *pharmaceutics* alt. dieb.
every other hour *pharmaceutics* alt. hor.
every other month *advertising* EOM *or* e.o.m.
every other night *pharmaceutics* alt. noc.
every other week *advertising* EOW *or* e.o.w.
every two hours *pharmaceutics* omn. bih.
everyday ED (of an advertisement in a publication)
evidence *law* Ev. *or* Evid.
evolution evol.
evolutionary operation *engineering* EVOP
ex 1 X *or* X. 2 x *or* x.
ex coupon 1 ex cp. 2 x-cp. 3 *finance* XC *or* X.C. *or* x.c.
ex dividend 1 ex d. *or* ex div. 2 *finance* a e.d. b X.D. *or* x.d. *or* x-div. (*OUP:* x.d. *or* x-div.)
ex interest 2 ex int. 1 X.I. *or* x.i. *or* x-int. (*OUP:* x.i. *or* ex int.)
ex new *finance* X.N. *or* x.n. *or* x-n. (of stock) (*OUP:* x.n. *or* ex n.)
ex rights *finance* 1 X-rts. (of stock) 2 XR *or* X.R. *or* x.r. (of stock)
ex warrant *finance* xw
exa- E
examination 1 ex. 2 exam.
examination under anesthesia *medicine* EUA
examined 1 ex. 2 exam. 3 exd.
examiner 1 Exam. 2 Exmr. 3 Xr
examining Examg.

example 1 Ex *or* Ex. 2 ex.
examples exx.
excellence E
Excellency Exc.
excellent 1 A-1 2 E 3 Ex 4 exc. 5 excl. *or* Excl 6 xlnt
except 1 ex. 2 exc.
except as otherwise herein provided *commerce, law* e.o.h.p. *or* EOHP
except as otherwise noted EAON *or* e.a.o.n.
excepted exc.
exception 1 ex. 2 exc.
exceptions noted EN
excerpt Ex
excess current liabilities *insurance* xcl
excess profits duty *commerce* EPD
excess-profits tax EPT
Exchange 1 EX 2 Ex *or* Ex. 3 Exch.
exchange 1 ex. 2 xch
exchange rate mechanism ERM (of the European Community)
exchangeable disk store *computers* EDS
Exchequer Exch. *or* Exchq. (*OUP:* Exch.)
excitatory postsynaptic potentials EPSP
exciter *electronics* 1 EXC 2 exc.
exclamation excl. *or* exclam.
exclamatory excl. *or* exclam.
exclude excl.
excluding 1 ex. 2 excl.
exclusive excl.
Exclusive Economic Zone EEZ
exclusive NOR *computers* XNOR
exclusive OR *computers* XOR
exclusively excl.
excommunicated Exc.
excommunication Exc.
excursion ex.
execute *computers* EXEC
execute input and/or output *computers* XIO
executed 1 ex. 2 exec. 3 *law, finance* x'd
execution exec.
Executive 1 Ex *or* Ex. 2 Exec.
executive *computers* EXEC
Executive Committee 1 EC *or* E.C. 2 Ex.Com.
executive document Ex.Doc.
Executive Office Building EOB
Executive Office for Immigration Review EOIR
Executive Office for United States Attorneys EOUSA
Executive Office for United States Trustees EOUST
Executive Office of the President EOP
Executive Officer EO
executive officer XO
Executive Order EO *or* E.O.
Executive Schedule ES (of U.S. Civil Service)
executive support system *computers* ESS
executor 1 ex. 2 exor. 3 exr. 4 *law* exec.
executrix 1 exx. 2 *law* exrx.
exempt ex.
exercise 1 ex. 2 exer.
Exeter, England Exon.
exhaust 1 exh. 2 xhst
exhaust gas recirculation EGR
exhaust gas temperature EGT

exhaust valve EV
exhibit 1 exh. 2 exhib. 3 xbt
Exhibition Exhib. *or* Exhbn.
exhibition exh. *or* Exh.
existence doubtful ED
Exoatmospheric Reentry Vehicle Interceptor System ERIS *or* Eris
Exodus 1 Ex 2 Exod.
exophthalmos-producing substance *medicine* EPS
Expanded In-home Services for the Elderly Program EISEP
expanded memory specification *computers* EMS
expanded metal EM
Expanded Program of Technical Assistance EPTA
Expanded Technical Assistance Program ETAP
expansion 1 exp. *or* EXP 2 xpn
expatriate expat
expected date of confinement *medicine* EDC
expected date of delivery *obstetrics, commerce* EDD
expected value *mathematics* EV
expedition Expdn.
Expeditionary Force EF
expendable bathythermograph XBT
Expendable Launch Vehicle ELV
expense exp.
expenses *accounting* exs
experience 1 exp. *or* Exp 2 exper.
experienced 1 exp. *or* Exp *or* expd. *or* Expd 2 expd *or* edp'd 3 exper. *or* experd.
experiment 1 exp. 2 expt.
experimental 1 EX 2 exp. *or* EXP 3 exper. 4 exptl. 5 X
Experimental Aircraft Program EAP
experimental allergic neuritis EAN
Experimental Assembly of Structures in Extravehicular Activity EASE
experimental boiling-water reactor EBWR
experimental data handling equipment EDHE
experimental gas-cooled reactor EGCR
experimental manned space station EMSS
Experimental Prototype Community of Tomorrow EPCOT
Experimental Research Society ERS
Experimental Satellite Communication Earth Station ESCES
Experimental Use Permit EUP
expiratory reserve volume ERV
expired exp.
expires expr.
explanation expl.
Explanation of Medical Benefits EOMB
explanatory expl.
explode X
exploded X
explosion expl.
explosive 1 expl. 2 X 3 XPL
Explosive Ordnance Disposal EOD
Explosives Research and Development Establishment ERDE
exponent *mathematics* exp.
exponential *mathematics* exp.

export 1 E **2** ex. **3** exp. **4** expt.
Export Credits Guarantee Department E.C.G.D.
export licensing regulations ELR
Export-Import Bank 1 EIB **2** Ex-Im *or* Eximbank
exportation exp.
exported exp.
exporter Exptr.
exposition Expn. *or* Expo
exposure *photography, physics, medicine* exp.
exposure index *photography* EI *or* E.I.
exposure-value system *photography* EV *or* E-V
Express Ex
express 1 ex. **2** exp. **3** expr. *or* Expr.
express paid XP
Expressway 1 Expwy **2** EXPY (in postal address)
expurgated exp.
exsecant *mathematics* exsec
extant ext.
extend ext.
extended extd. *or* Extd. *or* EXTD
extended architecture *computers* XA
extended area service EAS
extended binary coded decimal interchange code *computers* EBCDIC
extended care facility *medicine* ECF
extended coverage *broadcasting* EC
extended coverage endorsement ECE
extended industry standard architecture EISA
extended memory specification *computers* XMs

Extended Range Intercept Technology Erint
extended X-ray absorption fine structure *physics* EXAFS
extended *or* **enhanced definition television** EDTV
Extension EXT (in postal address)
extension 1 ext. *or* Ext. **2** extn.
extension course *education* EC
exterior 1 EXT **2** ext. **3** exte
external ext.
external archival storage *computers* EAS
external command *computers* XCMD
External Financing Limits *commerce* EFL
external resistance *medicine* ER
external symbols dictionary *computers* ESD
externally 1 ext. **2** *medicine* extern.
externally specified index *computers* ESI
extinct ext.
extinguisher EXT
extra 1 E **2** Ex *or* Ex. **3** ex. **4** ext. **5** X
extra duty ED
extra fine 1 EF **2** XF
extra–large XL
extra–long XL
extra–small XS *or* xs
extra–strength XS
extra–strong XS
extra-hard XH
extra-heavy XH
extra-high tension EHT *or* eht
extra-high voltage *electronics* EHV *or* ehv
extra-long wheelbase XLWB
extra-low frequency *astronomy, physics, electronics* ELF *or* elf
extra-low voltage ELV *or* elv
extracellular fluid *medicine* ECF

extracorporeal membrane oxygenation ECMO
extracorporeal shock wave lithotripsy *medicine* ESWL
extracranial-intracranial *medicine* EC/IC
extract 1 ex. **2** *pharmaceutics* ext.
extracted *medicine, dentistry* extd.
extraction *dentistry* ext.
extradition extrad.
extrahigh frequency XHF *or* xhf
extraordinary 1 extr. **2** xtry
Extraordinary and Plenipotentiary E&P *or* E. and P.
extraordinary general meeting EGM
extrasensory perception ESP
extraterrestrial ET
extraterrestrial intelligence ETI
extravehicular activity EVA
extreme ext.
extreme closeup ECU (of a photograph)
extreme low water ELW
extreme pressure EP
extreme ultraviolet 1 *astronomy* XUV **2** *physics* EUV
Extreme Ultraviolet Explorer EUVE
extremely high frequency *electronics* EHF *or* ehf (*GPO:* EHF)
extremely-low frequency *astronomy, physics, electronics* ELF *or* elf
extruded extr.
eye 1 E *or* E. **2** *medicine* O *or* O.
eye lotion *pharmaceutics* collyr.
Ezekiel Ezek.
Ezra Ez. *or* Ezr.

F

Fabian Society 1 Fab.Soc. **2** FS *or* F.S.
fabric fab.
fabricate fab. *or* fabr.
fabricated fab. *or* fabr.
face F
face-centered cubic *chemistry* FCC
facetiae facet.
facetious facet.
facility facil. *or* Facil.
facing fcg *or* fcg.
facing matter fm
facsimile 1 fac. (*MLA:* facsim, facs; *OUP:* fac.) **2** fax **3** fs *or* fs.
facsimile copy *or* **machine 1** FACS *or* facs **2** facsim. *or* facsm. (*MLA:* facsim. *or* facs.) **3** fax
factor fac.
factor analysis system FAST
factor of safety 1 FS *or* f/s **2** *physics* N

Factories and Workshops Act (of Great Britain) FWA
factory 1 fac. **2** fact. **3** fcty.
faculty fac. *or* Fac. (*MLA:* fac.)
fade in FI
fade out 1 f/o **2** FO
Faerie Queene FQ
Faeroe Islands Faer.
Faeroese Fa.
Fahrenheit 1 F *or* F. **2** Fah. *or* Fahr.
faint ft.
fair F *or* F.
fair average quality FAQ *or* f.a.q.
fair copy f.co.
fair employment practices FEP
Fair Labor Standards Act FLSA
fair market value *commerce* FMV
Falkland Islands 1 Falk.Is. **2** FI *or* F.I.
falls Fls
false F
false reading fl *or* f.l.
familial adenomatous polyposis FAP
familial hypercholesterolemia FH
Familial Mediterranean Fever *medicine* FMF
familiar fam.
family 1 f *or* f. **2** fam. *or* Fam.
family allowance FA
Family Assistance Program FAP

family history FH *or* F.H.
Family Income Supplement *British* FIS
Family Planning Association FPA
family practitioner *medicine* FP *or* F.P.
family room FR
Family Service Unit *British* FSU
Family Welfare Association (of Great Britain) FWA *or* F.W.A.
fancy fcy *or* fcy.
far infrared space telescope FIRST
far point PR (focus of eyes)
farad 1 F **2** f *or* f. **3** Far. *or* far.
Faraday constant *or* **faraday** F
faradic Far. *or* far.
farewell *Latin* BV *or* B.V.
farm 1 fm **2** Fm *or* Fm.
Farm Credit Administration FCA
Farm Credit System FCS
Farm Security Administration FSA
Farmers Home Administration 1 FHA **2** FmHA
farthing f *or* f.
fascicle fasc.
Fashion Institute of Technology FIT *or* F.I.T.
fast 1 F **2** fst.
fast atom bombardment FAB *or* F.A.B.
fast breeder reactor FBR
fast forward FF

Fast Fourier Transform FFT
fast interactive retrieval system technology FIRST
fast reaction integrated submarine control FRISCO
fast scan television FSTV
fast time constant FTC or ftc
Father 1 F or F. **2** Fr or Fr. **3** P or P.
father f or f.
Fathers (priests) PP or PP.
fathom 1 f or f. **2** fath. **3** fm or fm. (OUP: fm.) **4** fth. or fthm.
fatigue crack propagation FCP (in refining)
fatty acid FA
fatty acid fraction biochemistry FAF
fatty acid methyl ester biochemistry FAME
favorable fav.
favorite fav.
fear, tension, pain psychology FTP or F.T.P.
feasibility study FS
Feather River Project Association FRPA
featherweight fwt. (in boxing)
February 1 F or F. **2** Feb. (NYT, OUP: Feb.)
Federal 1 F or F. **2** Fed. or fed.
Federal Acquisition Regulations FAR
Federal Agricultural Mortgage Corporation Farmer Mac
Federal Aviation Administration FAA (NYT: F.A.A.)
Federal Aviation Regulation FAR
Federal Bar Association FBA or F.B.A.
Federal Bureau of Investigation FBI or F.B.I. (GPO, OUP: FBI; NYT: F.B.I.)
Federal Bureau of Prisons FBP or F.B.P.
Federal Capital Territory FCT or F.C.T.
Federal Civil Defense Administration FCDA
Federal Communications Commission FCC or F.C.C. (GPO: FCC; NYT: F.C.C.)
Federal Council for Science and Technology FCST or F.C.S.T.
Federal Council of Churches FCC or F.C.C.
Federal Credit Union FCU
Federal Crop Insurance Corporation FCIC or F.C.I.C. (GPO: FCIC)
Federal Deposit Insurance Corporation FDIC or F.D.I.C. (GPO: FDIC; NYT: F.D.I.C.)
Federal Detention Center FDC
Federal Disaster Assistance Administration FDAA or F.D.A.A.
Federal District 1 DF (in Mexico) **2** Fed. or fed.
Federal Election Commission FEC
Federal Emergency Management Agency FEMA
Federal Emergency Relief Administration FERA
Federal Employees' Compensation Act FECA or F.E.C.A.
Federal Employer Identification Number FEIN
Federal Employer's Liability Act FELA or F.E.L.A.
Federal Energy Office FEO or F.E.O.
Federal Energy Regulatory Commission FERC
Federal Estate Tax FET
Federal Excise Tax FET

Federal Executive Association FEA
Federal Executive Board FEB
Federal Executive Institute FEI
Federal Express Fedex or FEDEX or FedEx
Federal Financing Bank FFB or F.F.B.
Federal Food, Drug, and Cosmetic Act FFDCA
Federal Gift Tax FGT
Federal Government FG or F.G.
Federal Grain Inspection Service FGIS
Federal Highway Administration 1 FHA **2** FHWA
Federal Home Loan Bank FHLB
Federal Home Loan Bank Board FHLBB
Federal Home Loan Mortgage Corporation 1 FHLMC **2** Freddie Mac
Federal House of Representatives FHR
Federal Housing Administration FHA (NYT: F.H.A.)
Federal Housing Finance Board FHFB
Federal Income Tax FIT
Federal Income Tax Withheld FITW or fitw
Federal Information Center FIC
Federal Information Processing Standards FIPS
Federal Information Relay Service FIRS
Federal Insecticide, Fungicide, and Rodenticide Act FIFRA
Federal Insurance Administration FIA
Federal Insurance Contributions Act FICA
Federal Investigative Strike Team FIST
Federal Labor Relations Authority FLRA
Federal Land Bank FLB
Federal Law Enforcement Training Center FLETC
Federal Library and Information Network FEDLINK
Federal Loan Agency FLA
Federal Maritime Board FMB
Federal Maritime Commission FMC
Federal Mediation and Conciliation Service FMCS
Federal Motor Vehicle Safety Standards FMVSS
Federal National Mortgage Association 1 Fannie Mae **2** FNMA
Federal Open Market Committee FOMC
Federal Power Commission FPC (NYT: F.P.C.)
Federal Prison Industries FPI
Federal Prison Industries, Inc. UNICOR
Federal Property Management Regulation FPMR
Federal Property Resources Service FPRS
Federal Public Housing Authority FPHA
Federal Quarantine Service FQS
Federal Radiation Council FRC
Federal Railroad Administration FRA
Federal Register 1 Fed. Reg. **2** FR or F.R. (GPO: FR)
Federal Reporter Fed. or fed.
Federal Republic of Germany 1 B.R.D. or BRD **2** BD **3** FRG
Federal Research in Progress FEDRIP
Federal Reserve Bank 1 Fed **2** FRB or F.R.B.
Federal Reserve Board 1 Fed **2** FRB or F.R.B.
Federal Reserve Branch FRB or F.R.B.
Federal Reserve District Fed

Federal Reserve System FRS
Federal Rules Decisions F.R.D.
Federal Rules of Appellate Procedure FRAP or F.R.A.P.
Federal Rules of Civil Procedure F.R.C.P. or FRCP
Federal Safety Council FSC
Federal Savings and Loan Insurance Corporation FSLIC
Federal Secure Telephone Service FSTS
Federal Security Agency FSA
Federal Specification FS or F.S.
Federal Stock Number FSN
Federal Stock or **Supply Code** FSC
Federal Supplement law F.Supp.
Federal Supply Catalog FSC
Federal Supply Service FSS
Federal Supreme Court FSC
Federal Tax Deposit FTD
federal tax included FTI
Federal Telecommunications System FTS
Federal Trade Commission FTC or F.T.C. (GPO: FTC; NYT: F.T.C.)
Federal Transfer Surcharge FTS
Federal Unemployment Tax Act FUTA
Federal Water Pollution Control Administration FWPCA
Federal Wildlife Service FWS
Federal Works Agency FWA
Federal Writers Project FWP
Federalist Fed. or fed.
Federated Fed. or fed.
Federated States of Micronesia 1 FM (in postal address) **2** FSM
Federation Fed. or fed.
Federation of American Scientists FAS or F.A.S.
Federation of Asian Women's Associations FAWA or F.A.W.A.
Federation of Astronomical and Geophysical Services FAGS
Federation of Australian Commercial Broadcasters FACB
Federation of Australian Commercial Television Stations FACTS
Federation of British Film Makers FBFM or F.B.F.M.
Federation of Canadian Artists FCA or F.C.A.
Federation of Engineering Design Consultants FEDC
Federation of European Biochemical Societies FEBS
Federation of International Amateur Cycling FIAC or F.I.A.C.
Federation of Labour FOL (of New Zealand)
Federation of Societies for Paint Technology FSPT
Federation of Union Representatives FOUR
Federation of West Indies F.W.I. or FWI
feedback electronics f.b. or f/b
feet 1 f or f. **2** ft. or ft (CSM, OUP: ft.)
feet per minute fpm or f.p.m.
feet per second 1 fps or f.p.s. **2** fs or f.s. or f-s or f/s **3** ft/s or ft/sec
feet per second per second fpsps or f.p.s.p.s.

Feline Acquired Immune Deficiency Syndrome FAIDS

feline infectious enteritis FIE

feline leukemia virus FeLV

feline T-lymphotropic lentivirus FTLV

Fellow F or F.

Fellow of American Public Health Association F.A.P.H.A. or FAPHA (*CSM:* F.A.P.H.A.)

Fellow of Australian Academy FAA or F.A.A.

Fellow of the American Academy AAS

Fellow of the American Academy of Allergy FAAA or F.A.A.A.

Fellow of the American Academy of Arts and Sciences 1 AAS 2 FAAAS or F.A.A.A.S.

Fellow of the American Academy of Optometry FAAO or F.A.A.O.

Fellow of the American Academy of Orthopedic Surgeons FAAOS or F.A.A.O.S.

Fellow of the American Academy of Pediatrics FAAP or F.A.A.P.

Fellow of the American Association FAA or F.A.A.

Fellow of the American Association for the Advancement of Science FAAAS or F.A.A.A.S.

Fellow of the American College of Anesthesiologists FACA or F.A.C.A.

Fellow of the American College of Cardiology FACC or F.A.C.C.

Fellow of the American College of Dentists FACD or F.A.C.D.

Fellow of the American College of Gastroenterology FACG or F.A.C.G.

Fellow of the American College of Hospital Administration FACHA or F.A.C.H.A.

Fellow of the American College of Obstetricians and Gynecologists FACOG or F.A.C.O.G.

Fellow of the American College of Otolaryngology FACO or F.A.C.O.

Fellow of the American College of Pathologists FACP or F.A.C.P.

Fellow of the American College of Physicians FACP or F.A.C.P.

Fellow of the American College of Radiology FACR or F.A.C.R.

Fellow of the American College of Sports Medicine FACSM or F.A.C.S.M.

Fellow of the American College of Surgeons FACS or F.A.C.S. (*CSM:* F.A.C.S.)

Fellow of the American Geographical Society FAGS or F.A.G.S.

Fellow of the American Guild of Organists F.A.G.O. or FAGO

Fellow of the American Institute of Architects F.A.I.A. or FAIA

Fellow of the American Institute of Chemists FAIC or F.A.I.C.

Fellow of the American Medical Association FAMA or F.A.M.A.

Fellow of the American Oriental Society A.O.S.S.

Fellow of the American Philosophical Society *Latin* SPAS or S.P.A.S.

Fellow of the American Physical Society F.A.P.S. or FAPS

Fellow of the American Societies for Experimental Biology FASEB or F.A.S.E.B.

Fellow of the American Society of Civil Engineers FASCE or F.A.S.C.E.

Fellow of the Anthropological Society FAS or F.A.S.

Fellow of the Antiquarian Society FAS or F.A.S.

Fellow of the Association of Certified and Corporate Accountants FACCA or F.A.C.C.A.

Fellow of the Association of Mining, Electrical, and Mechanical Engineers FAMEME or F.A.M.E.M.E.

Fellow of the Australian College of Education FACE or F.A.C.E.

Fellow of the Botanical Society FBS or F.B.S.

Fellow of the British Academy FBA or F.B.A.

Fellow of the British Association of Accountants and Auditors FBAA or F.B.A.A.

Fellow of the British Computer Society FBCS

Fellow of the British Horological Institute FBHI or F.B.H.I.

Fellow of the British Institute of Management FBIM or F.B.I.M.

Fellow of the British Ornithologists' Union F.B.O.U. or FBOU

Fellow of the Canadian Aeronautics and Space Institute FCASI or F.C.A.S.I.

Fellow of the Canadian College of Organists F.C.C.O. or FCCO

Fellow of the Canadian Institute of Actuaries FCIA or F.C.I.A.

Fellow of the Canadian Psychological Association FCPA or F.C.P.A.

Fellow of the Chartered Association of Certified Accountants FCCA or F.C.C.A.

Fellow of the Chartered Institute of Secretaries F.C.I.S. or FCIS

Fellow of the Chartered Insurance Institute FCII or F.C.I.I.

Fellow of the Chemical Institute of Canada FCIC or F.C.I.C. (*CSM:* F.C.I.C.)

Fellow of the City and Guilds of London Institute F.C.G.I.

Fellow of the College of American Pathologists FCAP or F.C.A.P.

Fellow of the College of General Practitioners FCGP or F.C.G.P.

Fellow of the College of Physicians and Surgeons FCPS or F.C.P.S.

Fellow of the Connecticut Academy of Arts and Sciences CAS

Fellow of the Corporation of Certified Secretaries FCCS or F.C.C.S.

Fellow of the Corporation of Insurance Agents FCIA or F.C.I.A.

Fellow of the Entomological Society FES or F.E.S.

Fellow of the Ethnological Society FES or F.E.S.

Fellow of the Faculty of Actuaries FFA or F.F.A.

Fellow of the Faculty of Architects and Surveyors F.F.A.S. or FFAS

Fellow of the Faculty of Physicians and Surgeons FFPS or F.F.P.S.

Fellow of the Faculty of Radiologists FFR or F.F.R.

Fellow of the Geographical Society FGS or F.G.S.

Fellow of the Geological Society FGS or F.G.S.

Fellow of the Geological Society of America FGSA or F.G.S.A.

Fellow of the Guild of Organists F.G.O.

Fellow of the Historical Society H.S.S. or HSS

Fellow of the Incorporated Association of Architects FIAA or F.I.A.A.

Fellow of the Incorporated Guild of Church Musicians FIGCM

Fellow of the Incorporated Secretaries Association FISA or F.I.S.A.

Fellow of the Institute of Actuaries FIA or F.I.A.

Fellow of the Institute of Chartered Accountants FCA or F.C.A.

Fellow of the Institute of Chartered Shipbrokers FICS or F.I.C.S.

Fellow of the Institute of Chemistry FIC or F.I.C.

Fellow of the Institute of Company Accountants FIAC or F.I.A.C.

Fellow of the Institute of Electronic and Radio Engineers FIERE or F.I.E.R.E.

Fellow of the Institute of Industrial Administration FIIA or F.I.I.A.

Fellow of the Institute of Information Scientists FIInfSc or F.I.Inf.Sc.

Fellow of the Institute of Journalists F.J.I. or FJI

Fellow of the Institute of Linguistics FIL

Fellow of the Institute of Physics F.Inst.P.

Fellow of the Institute of Radio Engineers F.I.R.E. or FIRE

Fellow of the International College of Dentists FICD or F.I.C.D.

Fellow of the International College of Surgeons FICS or F.I.C.S.

Fellow of the Library Association FLA or F.L.A.

Fellow of the Library Association of Australia F.L.A.A. or FLAA

Fellow of the Linnean Society F.L.S. or FLS

Fellow of the London College of Music FLCM or F.L.C.M.

Fellow of the National Association of Auctioneers FNAA or F.N.A.A.

Fellow of the National Institute of Sciences of India F.N.I.

Fellow of the New Zealand Institute of Architects FNZIA or F.N.Z.I.A.

Fellow of the New Zealand Institute of Chemistry FNZIC or F.N.Z.I.C.

Fellow of the New Zealand Institution of Engineers FNZIE or F.N.Z.I.E.

Fellow of the New Zealand Library Association FNZLA or F.N.Z.L.A.

Fellow of the New Zealand Society of Accountants FNZSA or F.N.Z.S.A.

Fellow of the Philological Society FPS or F.P.S.

Fellow of the Philosophical Society (of America) FPS *or* F.P.S.

Fellow of the Philosophical Society (of Great Britain) F.Ph.S.

Fellow of the Physical Society F.Phys.S.

Fellow of the Royal Academy of Music F.R.A.M. *or* FRAM

Fellow of the Royal Academy of Physicians FRAP *or* F.R.A.P.

Fellow of the Royal Aeronautical Society FRAeS *or* F.R.Ae.S.

Fellow of the Royal Agricultural Societies FRAgS *or* F.R.Ag.S.

Fellow of the Royal Anthropological Institute F.R.A.I.

Fellow of the Royal Architectural Institute of Canada FRAIC *or* F.R.A.I.C.

Fellow of the Royal Asiatic Society F.R.A.S. *or* FRAS

Fellow of the Royal Astronomical Society F.R.A.S. *or* FRAS

Fellow of the Royal Australian Chemical Institute FRACI *or* F.R.A.C.I.

Fellow of the Royal Australian College of General Practitioners FRACGP *or* F.R.A.C.G.P.

Fellow of the Royal Australian College of Physicians FRACP *or* F.R.A.C.P. (*CSM:* F.R.A.C.P.; *OUP:* FRACP)

Fellow of the Royal Australian College of Surgeons FRACS *or* F.R.A.C.S.

Fellow of the Royal Australian Historical Society F.R.A.H.S.

Fellow of the Royal Australian Institute of Architects FRAIA *or* F.R.A.I.A.

Fellow of the Royal Botanic Society F.R.B.S. *or* FRBS

Fellow of the Royal College of Art FRCA *or* F.R.C.A.

Fellow of the Royal College of Music F.R.C.M. *or* FRCM

Fellow of the Royal College of Obstetricians and Gynaecologists FRCOG *or* F.R.C.O.G.

Fellow of the Royal College of Organists F.R.C.O. *or* FRCO

Fellow of the Royal College of Physicians F.R.C.P. *or* FRCP

Fellow of the Royal College of Science FRCSc *or* F.R.C.Sc.

Fellow of the Royal College of Surgeons F.R.C.S. *or* FRCS (*CSM:* F.R.C.S.; *OUP:* FRCS)

Fellow of the Royal College of Veterinary Surgeons F.R.C.V.S. *or* FRCVS

Fellow of the Royal Economic Society F.R.Econ.S

Fellow of the Royal Entomological Society FRES *or* F.R.E.S.

Fellow of the Royal Faculty of Physicians and Surgeons FRFPS *or* F.R.F.P.S.

Fellow of the Royal Geographical Society FRGS *or* F.R.G.S.

Fellow of the Royal Historical Society 1 F.R.H.S. 2 F.R.Hist.S.

Fellow of the Royal Horticultural Society 1 F.R.H.S. *or* FRHS 2 F.R.Hort.S.

Fellow of the Royal Institute of British Architects FRIBA *or* F.R.I.B.A.

Fellow of the Royal Institute of Chemistry FRIC *or* F.R.I.C.

Fellow of the Royal Institution of Chartered Surveyors FRICS *or* F.R.I.C.S.

Fellow of the Royal Irish Academy FRIA *or* F.R.I.A.

Fellow of the Royal Manchester College of Music FRMCM *or* F.R.M.C.M.

Fellow of the Royal Meteorological Society F.R.Met.S.

Fellow of the Royal Microscopical Society F.R.M.S. *or* FRMS

Fellow of the Royal Numismatic Society F.R.N.S. *or* FRNS

Fellow of the Royal Philatelic Society F.R.P.S.L. *or* FRPSL

Fellow of the Royal Photographic Society F.R.P.S. *or* FRPS

Fellow of the Royal Scottish Geographical Society F.R.S.G.S. *or* FRSGS

Fellow of the Royal Scottish Society of Arts F.R.S.S.A. *or* FRSSA

Fellow of the Royal Society 1 FRS *or* F.R.S. (*CSM:* F.R.S; *OUP:* FRS) 2 *Latin* **a** RSS *or* R.S.S. **b** SRS *or* S.R.S.

Fellow of the Royal Society of Antiquaries A.R.S.S.

Fellow of the Royal Society of Antiquaries of Ireland F.R.S.A.I. *or* FRSAI

Fellow of the Royal Society of Arts F.R.S.A. *or* FRSA

Fellow of the Royal Society of British Sculptors F.R.B.S.

Fellow of the Royal Society of Canada F.R.S.C. *or* FRSC

Fellow of the Royal Society of Chemistry F.R.S.C. *or* FRSC

Fellow of the Royal Society of Edinburgh F.R.S.E. *or* FRSE

Fellow of the Royal Society of Literature F.R.S.L. *or* FRSL

Fellow of the Royal Society of London F.R.S.L. *or* FRSL (the *L* is generally omitted)

Fellow of the Royal Society of Medicine F.R.S.M. *or* FRSM

Fellow of the Royal Society of New Zealand F.R.S.N.Z. *or* FRSNZ

Fellow of the Royal Statistical Society F.R.S.S. *or* FRSS

Fellow of the Royal Zoological Society F.R.Z.S. *or* FRZS

Fellow of the Society of Antiquaries FSA *or* F.S.A.

Fellow of the Society of Arts 1 FAS *or* F.A.S. 2 FSA *or* F.S.A.

Fellow of the Society of Company and Commercial Accountants FSCA

Fellow of the Society of Engineers FSE *or* F.S.E.

Fellow of the Society of Incorporated Accountants and Auditors FSAA *or* F.S.A.A.

Fellow of the Society of Industrial Artists FSIA *or* F.S.I.A.

Fellow of the Statistical Society FSS *or* F.S.S.

Fellow of the Zoological Society F.Z.S.

Fellowship of Christian Athletes FCA

female 1 F *or* F. 2 f *or* f. 3 fem.

feminine 1 F *or* F. 2 fem. *or* Fem (*MLA, OUP:* fem.) 3 *grammar* f *or* f.

femto- f

femtometer *physics* fm

femtovolt fV *or* fv

fencing fenc.

Fenian Brotherhood FB *or* F.B.

Ferdinand Ferd.

Fermanagh County, Ireland 1 Fer. 2 Ferm.

fermi *physics* f

Fermi National Accelerator Laboratory Fermilab

fermium Fm

ferredoxin fd

ferrohydrodynamic FHD

ferry 1 fry *or* Fry. 2 Fy. *or* fy.

fertility F

festival Fest.

fetal alcohol syndrome *medicine* FAS

fetal heart heard *medicine* FHH

fetal heart rate *medicine* FHR

feudal feud.

feudalism feud.

fever FEV *or* fev.

fever of unknown origin *medicine* 1 FUO *or* F.U.O. 2 PUO

fever, in absence of *medicine* abs. feb.

Fianna Fáil FF

fiber fbr.

fiber distributed data interface *computers* FDDI

fiber reinforced plastic FRP

fiber saturation point FSP *or* F.S.P.

fibrillation *medicine* fib.

fibrin degradation products *medicine* FDP

fiction 1 F 2 fic. 3 fict.

fictitious 1 fic. 2 fict.

fidelity fid.

fiduciary fid.

field 1 fd *or* fd. 2 fld. *or* FLD 3 *medicine, mathematics, military* F

field ambulance FA

field artillery FA

Field Artillery Computer Equipment FACE *or* Face

field artillery guided missile FAGMS

Field Developed Program *computers* FDP

field effect transistor *electronics* FET

field engineer FE

field focusing nuclear magnetic resonator FONAR

field goal FG

Field Hockey Association of America FHAA

field hospital *military* FH

Field Information Agency, Technical (report) FIAT

Field Intelligence Department FID

field ion mass spectroscopy FIMS

field ion microscope FIM

field magnet FM *or* F.M.

field manual (U.S. Army) FM (with number)

Field Marshall FM *or* F.M.

field of view FOV

field of vision *medicine* F

field office FO *or* F.O.

Field Officer FO

Field Operations Bureau FOB

field order FO
Field Post Office FPO
field programmable logic array *computers* FPLA
Field Project Office FPO
Field Security Officer FSO
Field Service FS
Field Service Regulations FSR
Field Service Representative FSR
field support equipment FSE
Field Survey Association FSA
field test FT *or* F.T.
field trial FT *or* F.T.
fielder's choice *baseball* FC
fielding average *baseball* FA
Fifeshire County, Scotland Fife.
fifth *Latin* quint.
fifty A
fighter F-
fighter bomber FB
figurative fig *or* fig.
figuratively fig *or* fig.
figure fig *or* Fig. *or* fig. (*MLA, CSM, OUP:* fig.)
figure of merit *statistics* FOM
figure reading electronic device FRED
figured bass BC *or* BC
figures figs.
figures shift *computers* FIGS
Fiji *or* **Fijian** F
filament 1 F 2 f (esp. as a subscript) 3 fil.
filament center tap *electronics* FCT *or* fct
file allocation table *computers* FAT
file control block *computers* FCB
file transfer protocol *computers* FTP
file transfer, access, and management *computers* FTAM
filial generation F
fillet fil.
filly f *or* f.
film F
Film and Television Production Association of Australia FTPAA *or* F.T.P.A.A.
film emulsion speed H & D
Film Entertainments National Service Association FENSA
film input to digital automatic computer FIDAC
film strip fs
filter 1 fil. 2 filt. 3 flt.
filtration fil.
final 1 fin. 2 fnl.
final approach fix *aeronautics* FAF
final boiling point FBP *or* fbp
final common pathway *anatomy* FCP
final form text FFT
finally fnl.
finance fin.
Finance and Accounts Office FAO
Finance and Management Policy FMP
Finance Office of the U.S. Army FOUSA
Finance *or* **Financial Officer** FO *or* F.O.
financial 1 fin. 2 Fincl *or* fincl
Financial Accounting Standards Board FASB
Financial Adviser FA *or* F.A.
Financial Community of the Pacific CFP
Financial Crimes Enforcement Network FINCEN

Financial Futures Exchange *French* MATIF
financial interest and syndication fin-syn *or* fin/syn
Financial Management Service FMS
Financial News Network FNN
Financial Secretary Fin.Sec.
financial statement FS
Financial Times Institute of Actuaries FTIA (stock index)
Financial Times, The FT
Financing Corporation FICO
fine F (of pencils or pens)
fine arts FA
fine copy bel ex.
fine error sensor FES
Fine Gael FG
fine grain 1 f.g. 2 FG
fine measurement fm
fine paper FP *or* F.P.
finish 1 Fin. 2 fin.
finish all over FAO *or* f.a.o.
finished fin.
finished floor level F.F.L.
finite intersect property *mathematics* FIP *or* f.i.p.
Finland 1 Fi. (*OUP:* Fin.) 2 Fin.
Finnish 1 Fi. (*MLA:* Finn.; *OUP:* Fin.) 2 Fin. 3 Finn.
finsen unit FU
Fiord Fd.
fire F
fire and theft *insurance* F&T
fire brigade FB
fire control FC
fire department FD *or* F.D.
Fire Direction Center FDC
fire hydrant FH
fire insurance FI
Fire Prevention Officer FPO
fire resistant FR
fire risk on freight *insurance* f.r.o.f.
fire vent f.v.
fire wall FW *or* f.w.
fireplace 1 FP 2 fpl *or* fplc
fireproof 1 FPRF 2 FRPF
firkin fir.
firm F (of pencil lead)
firm fixed price *commerce, law* FFP
firm offer *commerce* FO *or* f.o.
first 1st *or* 1st
first aid FA
First Aid Nursing Yeomanry F.A.N.Y.
First Aid Post FAP
first class 1 A-1 *or* A1 2 FC *or* F/C
first class certificate FCC
first edition fe *or* f.e.
First Families of Virginia F.F.V. *or* FFV
first in a series a
first in, first out *commerce* FIFO *or* fifo (*NYT:* FIFO)
first in, last out *commerce, computers* FILO *or* filo
first level interrupt handler *computers* FLIH
first of a series A
first open water *shipping* f.o.w.
first section A
first signature of a book *printing* A
first-class 1 A No.1 2 A one

first-day cover *philately* FDC
firsts and seconds FAS *or* f.a.s. (of lumber)
fiscal fisc.
fiscal quarter *accounting* FQ *or* f.q.
fiscal year FY
Fish and Wildlife Service FWS
fish protein concentrate FPC
Fisheries Research Board FRB *or* F.R.B.
fishery fish.
Fishery Board FB
fishing fish.
fitting ftg.
fittings and fixtures *insurance* f&f *or* f. and f.
five 1 V (Roman numeral) 2 v (Roman numeral)
five hundred 1 A 2 D
fixed 1 F 2 FX *or* Fx 3 fxd.
fixed action pattern *psychology* FAP
fixed base operator FBO
fixed focus ff. *or* f.f. *or* f/f
fixed price FP *or* F.P.
fixed price contract *commerce* FPC *or* F.P.C.
fixed price incentive *commerce* FPI *or* F.P.I.
fixed price tenders *commerce* FPT
fixture fix.
Fjord Fj. *or* Fjd.
Flag Officer fp *or* f.p.
flameproof fp *or* f.p.
Flanders Fl *or* Fl. (*OUP:* Fl.)
flange flg.
flash point 1 fl.pt. 2 FP
flashing 1 FL 2 Fl
flat 1 ft. 2 *construction* F
flat back f.bk. (of lumber)
flat bar f.b.
flat grain FG
flat head FH (of screws)
flat plate collector *engineering* FPC
flavin adenine dinucleotide FAD
flavin mononucleotide FMN
flavoprotein FP
fleet 1 FLT 2 Flt.
Fleet Air Arm *British* FAA *or* F.A.A.
fleet ballistic missile FBM
Fleet Marine Forces FMF
Fleet Post Office FPO
Flemish 1 Fl *or* Fl. (*OUP:* Fl.) 2 Flem.
flexible 1 flex. *or* FLEXBL 2 flx. *or* flx
flexible armored electrical cable BX
Flexible Loan Insurance Program FLIP
flexible manufacturing system FMS
flexible working hours fwh *or* FWH
flicker fusion threshold FFT *or* F.F.T.
flight 1 Flt. 2 flt.
Flight Advisory Weather Service FAWS
flight control center *aeronautics* FCC
flight data acquisition unit FDAU
flight data recorder *aeronautics* FDR
flight director computer FDC
Flight Dynamics Officer FIDO *or* Fido
Flight Engineers' International Association FEIA
flight forecast *meteorology* FIFOR
Flight Information Center FIC
flight information region FIR
Flight Information Service FIS
Flight Lieutenant FL *or* F/L
Flight Model Discharge System FMDS

Flight Research Center FRC
Flight Safety Foundation FSF
Flight Test Center FTC
flight test vehicle FTV
flip-flop *electronics* FF or F-F
float flt.
floating fltg.
Floating Instrument Platform FLIP
floating point operation FLOP
floating point operations per second FLOPS
floating point processor *computers* FPP
floating policy *insurance* FP or F.P.
floor 1 fl or fl. 2 flr. or Flr
flooring flg.
floppy disk *computers* FD
floppy disk, high density *computers* FDHD
Florence Nightingale International Foundation FNIF or F.N.I.F.
floret fl or fl.
Florida 1 Fa. (*OUP:* Fla.) 2 FL (Zip Code) 3 Fla.
florin 1 F 2 fl 3 fl or fl. 4 flr.
Florists' Transworld Delivery FTD
flotation 1 flot. 2 flt.
flour fl
flourished 1 fl or fl. (*MLA, OUP:* fl.) 2 flor.
flower 1 fl or fl. 2 flr.
flowered fld. (of plants)
flowers fls.
fluctuate fluc.
fluctuation fluc.
flue gas desulfurization *engineering* FGD
fluid 1 f or fl. 2 fld.
fluid catalytic cracking FCC
fluid dram fl.dr.
fluid ounce 1 F or F. 2 f or fl. 3 fl.oz.
Fluid Power Society FPS or F.P.S.
fluid. fl or fl.
fluidized bed combustion *engineering* FBC
fluorescein isothiocyanate *biochemistry* FITC
fluorescence activated cell sorter *biochemistry* FACS
fluorescence digital imaging microscopy FDIM
fluorescent fluor.
fluorescent antibody *medicine* FA
fluorescent antibody test *biochemistry* FAT
fluorescent indicator analysis FIA
fluorescent treponemal antibody FTA
fluorinated ethylene propylene FEP
fluorine 1 F 2 Fl
fluorine and liquid oxygen FLOX
fluorine, uranium, and nitrogen *archaeology* FUN
fluoro-immuno-assay *biochemistry* FIA
fluorodinitrobenzene FDNB
fluorouracil 1 5-FU 2 FU
flush 1 FL (even) 2 fl or fl. (even)
flush valve f.v.
flute *music* fl
flux unit FU or fu
Fly Mus (constellation)
Flying Fish Vol (constellation)
Flying Officer FO or F/O
flying spot microscope FSM
focal distance FD or f/d

focal length 1 FL or F/L 2 *optics, photography* f or f. 3 *photography* f:
fog f or f.
fog bell f.b.
fog horn 1 f.h. 2 FH
Fog Investigation Dispersal Operations FIDO
fog over low ground fg.
folded and gathered f&g or f&gs or F&G or F&Gs (of pages for bookbinding)
folded flat FF
folded, trimmed, and packed FTP (in bookbinding)
folding fldg.
folic acid FA
folio 1 f or f. 2 fo. or fᵒ (*GPO:* fᵒ; *OUP:* fo. or fol.; *MLA:* not acceptable) 3 fol.
folios 1 ff. 2 foll. 3 fols.
follicle-stimulating hormone FSH
follow copy 1 fc or f.c. 2 *printing* FC
follow on forces attack *military* FOFA
followed fol.
following 1 f or f. 2 ff. (*MLA:* not acceptable) 3 fol. 4 foll.
following items not available *commerce* FINA or f.i.n.a.
following one sq.
following, the *Latin* 1 seq. 2 seqq.
Food and Agriculture Organization 1 FAO (*NYT:* F.A.O.; *OUP:* FAO) 2 *French, Spanish* OAA
Food and Agriculture Technical Information Service FATIS
food and beverage F&B
Food and Drug Administration FDA or F.D.A. (*GPO:* FDA)
Food and Drug Directorate FDD
Food and Nutrition Service FNS
Food Marketing Institute FMI
Food Safety and Inspection Service FSIS
food stamp program FSP
Food, Drug, and Cosmetic Act FD&C
foolscap 1 fcp. (*OUP:* fcp.) 2 *printing* **a** cap (*OUP:* cap.) **b** fcap. or f/cap
foot 1 f or f. 2 ft. or ft (*CSM, OUP:* ft.)
foot and mouth disease F&M
foot board measure 1 fbm 2 f.b.m.
foot candle 1 FC 2 fc
foot surface measure Ft.s.m. (of lumber)
foot-and-mouth disease FMD or f.m.d.
foot-candle ft-c or ftc
foot-lambert 1 FL 2 fl or f-l or fL 3 ftL or ft-l
foot-pound 1 FP 2 ft-lb or ft lb
foot-pound-second fps or f.p.s. or FPS
foot-second fs or f.s. or f-s
Football Association *British, Australian, Irish* FA or F.A.
Football Club FC or F.C.
footings *building* foot.
footnote fn or f.n.(*OUP:* f.n. or fn.; *MLA:* not acceptable)
for @
for example 1 e.g. 2 ex.gr. 3 *Latin, Spanish* v.g.
for further assignment FFA
for information only FIO or f.i.o.
for instance f.i.
for orders *commerce* f/o

for private circulation f.p.c.
for sale by owner *real estate* fsbo or FSBO
for the meantime a.i.
for the occasion *medicine, pharmaceutics* PRN or p.r.n. or P.R.N.
for the sake of honor h.c.
for your eyes FYE
for your information FYI
force F
force and rhythm *medicine* F. and R.
force constant *physics* k
force, length, time FLT
force, mass, length, time FMLT
forced expiratory volume *medicine* FEV
forced vital capacity *medicine* FVC
Forces Mobile Command FMC
fore and aft f&a or f. and a.
foreground-initiated background FIB
foreign 1 fgn. or Fgn. 2 for. or For. 3 Forgn.
Foreign Agricultural Service FAS
Foreign and Commonwealth Office FCO
foreign body *medicine* f.b.
Foreign Broadcast Information Service FBIS
Foreign Claims Settlement Commission FCSC or F.C.S.C. (*GPO:* FCSC)
foreign consul FC
Foreign Credit Insurance Association FCIA or F.C.I.A.
foreign duty pay FDP
foreign exchange FX or F/X
foreign freight agent *commerce* FFA or F.F.A.
Foreign Funds Control FFC
foreign general average *insurance* FGA or f.g.a.
Foreign Investment Review Agency FIRA
Foreign Language FL
Foreign Language Annuals FLA
Foreign Language in the Elementary Schools FLES
Foreign Language Program FLP
Foreign Licensing Examination *medicine* FLEX
foreign medical graduate FMG
Foreign Member of the Royal Society FMRS or F.M.R.S.
Foreign Minister FM or F.M.
Foreign Missions FM or F.M.
foreign object damage *aeronautics* FOD
Foreign Office FO
Foreign Personal Holding Company FPHC
Foreign Policy Association FPA or F.P.A.
Foreign Press Association FPA or F.P.A.
Foreign Relations Council FRC
foreign rights For. Rts
Foreign Secretary FS
Foreign Service FS
Foreign Service Institute FSI
Foreign Service Officer FSO
foreign service pay FSP
Foreign Trade Zone FTZ
forensic for.
forest for. or For.
Forest Service FS
forestry for.
foreword Frwd.
forint Ft.
Fork Fk. (in place names)

form fm or fm.
form feed or **form feeding** computers FF
formal dining room FDR
formal offer FO
formation 1 fmn. **2** form
former 1 fmr. **2** form **3** frm.
formerly 1 fmr. **2** form
formerly known as FKA or fka
formula 1 F or F. **2** f or f.
Formula Translation computers FORTRAN or
  Fortran (OUP: FORTRAN)
formula weight chemistry FW or f.w.
Fornax, the Furnace For (constellation)
Fort 1 FT (in postal address) **2** Ft.
fortification 1 fort. **2** ft.
fortified 1 fort. **2** ft.
forward 1 for'd. **2** fwd.
Forward Air Controller FAC
forward observation post military FOP
forward observer military FO
forward pass football FP
forward perpendicular FP
forward propagation ionospheric scatter
  electronics, physics FPIS
forward-based system military FBS
forward-looking infrared FLIR
forwarding fwdg.
Foster Grandparent Program FGP
foul sports F
found fnd.
Foundation Found.
foundation 1 fdn. **2** fnd. or Fnd.
founded 1 Fd. **2** fnd. or fdd.
founder 1 Fdr. **2** fndr. or Fndr
foundry 1 fdry. **2** fndry. or Fndry
four quat.
four hundred CCCC
four times a day pharmaceutics **1** q.d. or
  Q.D. **2** q.i.d.
four-wheel brakes FWB or f.w.b.
four-wheel drive 1 4×4 **2** 4WD **3** FWD
Fourier transform mathematics FT
Fourier transform infrared FTIR or FT-IR
fourth 4th or 4th
fourth-generation language 4-GL
Fox Vul (constellation)
foxed 1 FX or fx. **2** fxd.
fractional frl.
fractional horsepower fhp or FHP
Fractional Orbital Bombardment System
  FOBS
fractional test meal FTM
fragile frag.
fragment 1 fr. **2** frag. or frag **3** biochemistry
  F **4** law Fr
fragmentation frag. or frag
frame computers, construction, photography
  fr.
frame check sequence computers FCS
framed construction frd. (of a building)
frames per foot photography FPF or fpf
frames per second photography fps or f.p.s.
framework frwk
framing construction frm.
franc 1 F **2** f or f. **3** fc or fc. **4** fr. or fr
France 1 F or F. **2** Fr
Franciscan Franc.
francium Fr

francs 1 fcs or fcs. **2** frs. or frs
Frank Fk.
Frankish Frank.
Franklin Delano Roosevelt FDR
Fraternal Order of Eagles FOE or F.O.E.
fraternity Frat.
fraudulent fraud.
Frederic or **Frederick** Fred.
Frederick Fredk.
free 1 f **2** Latin grat.
free air delivered commerce FAD or f.a.d.
free alongside quay FAQ or f.a.q.
free alongside ship 1 FAS or F.A.S. or f.a.s.
  (GPO: f.a.s.) **2** commerce f.a.
Free and Accepted Masons 1 F. and A.M.
  2 F.A.M. or F.& A.M. (OUP: FAM)
free and independent travelers FIT
free association psychology FA
Free Baptist FB or F.B.
free cholesterol biochemistry FC
Free Church FC (of Scotland)
free delivery FD or f.d.
free dispatch FD or f.d.
free electron laser FEL
free energy physics F
free fatty acids FFA
free foreign agency commerce FFA
free from alongside ship commerce FFA or
  f.f.a.
free from chlorine chemistry FFC
free from infection medicine F.F.I.
free in commerce FI
free in and out commerce FIO or f.i.o.
free in and out stowage commerce FIOS or
  f.i.o.s.
free in and trim shipping FIT or f.i.t.
free in bunker commerce FIB or f.i.b.
free in truck commerce FIT or f.i.t.
free into barge commerce FIB or f.i.b.
free of all average commerce FAA or f.a.a.
free of capture and seizure commerce
  1 f.c.& s. **2** f.c.s.
free of charge commerce FOC or f.o.c.
free of damage commerce FOD or f.o.d.
free of general average insurance FGA or
  f.g.a.
free of income tax FIT
free of knots f.o.k. or FOK (of lumber)
free of particular average insurance FPA or
  f.p.a.
free of riot and civil commotion insurance
  f.r.&c.c.
free of tax commerce FOT or f.o.t.
free on board commerce FOB or F.O.B. or
  f.o.b. (GPO, NYT: f.o.b.)
free on quay shipping FOQ
free on rails commerce FOR or f.o.r.
free on station or **ship** commerce FOS or
  f.o.s.
free on truck commerce FOT or f.o.t.
free on wagon commerce f.o.w.
free overside shipping FO or f.o.
free piston vessel FPV or F.P.V.
Free Sons of Israel FSI or F.S.I.
free standing insert FSI
Free Trade Zone FTZ
Free Will Baptists FWB or F.W.B.
Freedom of Choice Act FOCA

freedom of information FOI
Freedom of Information Act 1 FIA **2** FOIA
freehold Fhld
freeholder FH or F/H
Freestanding Emergency Clinic FEC
freeway 1 frwy. **2** fry or Fry.
freeze fz. or FZ
freezing fz. or FZ
freezing drizzle meterology ZL
freezing point 1 fp (OUP: f.p.) **2** FP (OUP:
  f.p.)
freezing rain meterology ZR
freight 1 FGT or fgt. **2** frgt. **3** frt.
freight agent FA
freight and demurrage commerce f&d or f.
  and d.
freight bill f.b.
freight release commerce FR
freight ton 1 f.t. **2** FT
French 1 F or F. **2** Fr or Fr. (MLA, OUP: Fr.)
French Academy 1 AF or A.F. **2** LAF
French Army AF or A.F.
French Association for Standardization
  AFNOR
**French Association for the Advancement of
  the Sciences** A.F.A.S.
French Astronautical Society SFA
French Carbon Research Center CERCHAR
French Communist Party PCF or P.C.F.
French corporation of limited liability
  S.A.R.L.
French Democratic Confederation of Labor
  CFDT
French fried FF
French Geographers' Association AGF or
  A.G.F.
French Government Printing Office Impr.
  Nat.
French Information Agency ADI
French National Radio and Television RTF
French National Railway French SNCF
**French Office for the Export of
  Aeronautical Material** OFEMA
French Press Agency AFP or A.F.P.
French Radio T.S.F.
French Red Cross CRF or C.R.F.
French Republic RF or R.F.
French Security or **Riot Police** CRS
French Standard Book Number Agency
  AFNIL
French Television Company CFT
French-Canadian Academy ACF or A.C.F.
**French-Canadian Association for the
  Advancement of Science** A.C.F.A.S. or
  ACFAS
frequency 1 F **2** f **3** fqcy **4** freq. **5** v
frequency control and analysis aeronautics
  FCA
frequency division multiplex FDM
frequency interface control communications
  FIC
frequency modulation electronics **1** FM **2** fm
frequency modulation-continuous wave
  FM-CW
frequency-shift keying computers FSK
frequent 1 fr. **2** freq. **3** frq. or FRQ
  4 biology f

Frequent Flier Bonus FFB
Frequent Flier Program FFP
frequentative freq.
frequently 1 freq. **2** frq. *or* FRQ
frequently asked questions FAQ
fresh *pharmaceutics* Rec.
fresh air intake *construction, refining* FAI
fresh frozen plasma *medicine* FFP
fresh water FW *or* f.w.
fresh water damage FWD *or* fwd
Fresh Water Load Line F
Friar Fr
fricative *phonetics* fric.
friction fric.
friction glazed 1 f.g. **2** FG *or* F.G.
friction horsepower fhp *or* FHP *or* F.H.P.
friction *or* **friction factor** f
Friday 1 F *or* F. **2** Fr **3** Fri.
Friend Leukemia Virus FLV
friend of the court *law* am. cur.
friendly aircraft *military* FA *or* F/A
Friends of the Earth FOE *or* FoE
Friesland 1 Fries. **2** Fris.
Frisia Fris.
Frisian 1 Fris. **2** Frs.
from 1 f *or* f. **2** fm *or* fm. **3** fr. **4** frm.
from day to day 1 d.d. in d. **2** de d. in d.
from the beginning ab init.
from the library *or* **books of** ex lib.
from the sign *music* **1** Dal S. **2** DS *or* D.S. **3** ds *or* d.s.
from without ab ex.
front fr.
front matter fm
front-end processor *computers* FEP
front-wheel drive FWD *or* f.w.d.
frontal bovine serum *medicine* FBS
frontispiece 1 Fp. *or* fp. **2** front.

Froude number *physics* Fr
fructose fru.
fructose diphosphate FDP
fructose-monophosphate *biochemistry* FMP
fruit 1 frt. **2** *botany* fr.
fruits *botany* frs. *or* frs
fuel injection FI
fuel oil FO *or* f.o.
fuel oil equivalent FOE
fuel reprocessing plant FRP
fuel research station FRS
fuel-air explosive FAE
fugacity *botany, thermodynamics* f
full charge FC *or* F/C
full duplex 1 *computers* FD **2** *electronics* FDX
full interest admitted *commerce* FIA *or* f.i.a.
full motion video FMV
full name unknown FNU
full orchestra *music* rip
full organ *music* FO *or* F.O.
full out *commerce* f/o
full scale *or* **size** fs *or* f.s.
full terms *commerce* f.t.
full time value *music* ten.
full width at half maximum fwhm *or* FWHM (in spectroscopy)
full-fashioned FF
full-power hours fph
full-scale deflection *electronics, physics, engineering* FSD
full-screen video *electronics* FSV
full-time FT *or* F/T
full-time employee FTE
full-time equated FTE (of student funding)
full-time equivalent FTE (measure of working time)
full-time or part-time FT/PT
fullback *sports* **1** f.b. **2** FB **3** LB

fully automatic compiler translator FACT
fully good *commerce* f.g.
fully good, fair *commerce* f.g.f.
fully paid *commerce* **1** FP *or* F.P. **2** fp *or* f.p.
fume tight FT
function 1 F **2** func. *or* funct.
function (of) f
functional electronic block *computers* FEB
functional residual capacity *medicine* FRC (of resting lung)
fund fd *or* fd.
fundamental fund.
Fundamentally Analyzable Simplified English FASE
funding Fdg. *or* fdg.
funds fd *or* fd.
furlong 1 f *or* f. **2** fur.
furlough furl.
furnace furn.
furnished 1 f *or* f. **2** fur. **3** furn.
furniture furn.
furniture and fixtures 1 FF **2** *insurance* f&f *or* f. and f.
Furniture Industry Research Association FIRA
furring *construction* fr.
further fur.
fuse F
fuselage fus.
fusion 1 f (as a subscript) **2** fn *or* fn.
Fusion Engineering Device FED
fusion point 1 FNP *or* fn.p. **2** fu.p.
future fut.
Future Farmers of America FFA
Future Homemakers of America FHA
Future Teachers of America FTA
futures commission merchant FCM

g-factor g
Gabon Gab
gadolinium Gd
gaelic Gael.
Gaelic Society A.C.G. *or* ACG
gain *electronics, statistics* G
galactic latitude *astronomy* b
galactose *biochemistry* Gal
Galatians Gal *or* Gal. (*MLA, OUP:* Gal.)
gallbladder *medicine* GB
gallery gall. *or* Gall.
Gallic Ga *or* Ga.
gallium Ga
gallium arsenide GaAs
gallium phosphide *electronics* GaP
gallon 1 gal. **2** gall. **3** *pharmaceutics* **a** C **b** c *or* c. **c** cong.
gallons gals.

gallons per day GPD *or* g.p.d.
gallons per hour GPH *or* g.p.h.
gallons per minute 1 gal/min. **2** GPM *or* g.p.m.
gallons per second 1 g/s **2** GPS *or* g.p.s.
Gallup Poll GP *or* G.P.
galvanic galv.
galvanic skin response GSR
galvanism galv.
galvanized 1 gal. *or* gal **2** galv.
galvanized iron GI *or* g.i.
Galvanized Sheet Steel Gauge GSG
galvanometer galv.
Gambia Gam.
Gamblers Anonymous GA *or* G.A.
games G
gamete intra-fallopian transfer GIFT
gamma globulin GG *or* G.G.
gamma ray GR
Gamma Ray Observatory GRO
gamma rays GR
gamma-aminobutyric acid GABA
gamma-ray burst *astronomy* GRB
garage gar.
garbage garb.
garbage in, garbage out GIGO

garden 1 gard. **2** gdn.
Gardens 1 Gard. **2** GDNS (in postal address) **3** Gdns.
gargle garg.
Garrison *military* G
garter stitch *knitting* gst
gas G (as a subscript)
gas amplification GA
gas chromatography GC
gas chromatography mass spectrometry *or* **spectrometer** GCMS *or* GC/MS
gas constant *physics, chemistry* R
gas controlled fast reactor GCFR
gas dynamic laser GDL
gas evolution analysis *chemistry* GEA
gas generator GG
gas horsepower GHP *or* ghp
gas operated GO
gas tight gt *or* g.t.
gas tungsten arc GTA
gas turbine ship GTS
gas turbine vessel GTV
gas-liquid chromatograph *or* **chromatography** GLC
gas-solid chromatography GSC
gaseous oxygen 1 GAX **2** GOX *or* gox

gastric ulcer GU
gastroenterology 1 Gastroent. 2 GE
gastrointestinal GI or G.I.
gate G
gate turnoff GTO
gate valve gv
gauge 1 G or G. 2 g or g.
gauge atmosphere g.a.
Gaulish Gaul.
gauss 1 G 2 Gs
Gay Academic Union GAU
Gay Activists' Alliance GAA
Gay Liberation Front GLF
Gay Men's Health Crisis GMHC
gazette gaz. or Gaz.
gazetted gaz.
gazetteer gaz. or Gaz.
Gdansk, Poland Gdk
gelatin gel.
gelatinous gel.
gelding g or g.
geminate gem.
Gemini, the Twins Gem. (constellation)
Gemological Institute of America GIA or
 G.I.A.
gender 1 g or g. 2 gen.
gene protein biochemistry g.p. or gp
genealogical 1 gen. 2 geneal.
genealogy 1 gen. 2 geneal.
genera gen.
General 1 Gen. 2 Genl.
general 1 G or G. 2 g or g. 3 gen. 4 genl.
 5 gn. or Gn. 6 Gnl. or gnl.
General Accounting Office GAO
general adaptation syndrome GAS or
 G.A.S.
general address reading device GARD
General Advisory Committee GAC
General Agent GA or G.A.
General Agreement on Tariffs and Trade
 GATT or Gatt
General Agreement or Arrangements to
 Borrow GAB
General Agricultural Union CGA or
 C.G.A.
General American GA (speech area)
General and Complete Disarmament GCD
General Aptitude Test Battery psychology
 GATB
General Assembly GA or G.A.
General Assembly Program computers
 GAP
general assistance GA
general average insurance 1 g.a. 2 GA or
 G/A
general aviation GA
general call preceding a message QST (in
 amateur radio)
general call to receive CQ
General Catalog of Variable Stars GCVS
General Certificate of Education GCE or
 G.C.E.
General Certificate of Secondary Education
 1 GCSE or G.C.S.E. 2 GSCE
general circulation model meteorology
 GCM
General College Entrance (examination)
 GCE
general compiler computers GECOM

General Conference on Weights and
 Measures CGPM
General Council of British Shipping GCBS
 or G.C.B.S.
General Council of Japanese Trade Unions
 SOHYO
general counsel law GC or G.C.
general court-martial GCM
general data group computers GDG
General Delegation for Scientific and
 Technical Research DGRST
general delivery GD
general duties GD
General Duty GD
General Educational Development Test GED
 or GED test or GEDT
general election GE
General Electric GE
General Equivalency Certificate G.E.C.
General Equivalency Diploma GED
General Extrasensory Perception GESP
general factor G (in intelligence testing)
General Federation of Trade Unions GFTU
General Federation of Women's Clubs
 GFWC
General Freight Agent GFA
General Headquarters military GHQ
general headquarters GH
general hospital GH
general intelligence psychology g
general issue law GI
general ledger accounting GL or G/L
general maintenance system computers
 GMS
general manager GM or G.M.
General Mathematical Aptitude Test
 GMAT
General Medical Council G.M.C.
general merchandise GM
general mortgage GM
General Motors GM
general notice GENOT
General of the Army GA
General Office GO or G.O.
General Officer military GO
general officer commanding British GOC or
 G.O.C.
general operational requirement GOR
general order or orders military GO
General Ordination Examination G.O.E.
general paralysis medicine GP
general paralysis of the insane medicine
 GPI
general passenger agent GPA or G.P.A.
general pause music GP
General Post Office GPO or G.P.O.
general practitioner (of medicine) GP or
 G.P.
General Practitioners' Association British
 GPA or G.P.A.
general public GP or G.P.
general purpose GP
general purpose computer GPC
general purpose digital computer GPDC
general purpose oscillograph GPO
General Purpose Simulation System
 engineering GPSS
general quarters GQ or G.Q. (alarm on
 shipboard)

general reconnaissance military GR
General Register Office British GRO or
 G.R.O.
General Reserve GR
general rule (of the court) reg. gen.
general rule or order of court law RG or
 R.G.
General Sales Manager GSM
General Schedule (of the civil service)
 GS
General Secretary GS
General Service or Services GS
General Services Administration
 GSA
General Sessions law GS or G.S.
General Staff 1 G 2 military GS
General Staff Corps GSC
General Studies education GS
General Theological Seminary GTS
General Traffic Manager GTM
general with parents' consent GP
 (motion-picture rating)
General, Municipal, Boilermakers (trade
 union) German GMB
generalized coordinate physics q
Generalized Information System computers
 GIS
Generalized System of Preferences GSP
generally gen.
generally accepted accounting principles
 GAAP
generally accepted auditing standards
 GAAS
generally recognized as effective medicine
 GRAE
generally regarded as safe GRAS (USFDA
 list of substances)
generate genr.
generation 1 gen. 2 genr.
generator 1 gen. 2 genr.
generator control unit GCU
generic gen.
Genesis Gen.
Genetic Manipulation Advisory Group
 GMAG
genetics gen.
Geneva Gen.
Genevan Gen.
genitive 1 g or g. 2 grammar a gen. b genit.
genitourinary GU or G.U.
gentleman or gentlemen Gent. or gent.
Gentlemen Messrs.
genuine gen.
genus gen.
geodesy geod.
geodetic geod.
Geoffrey Geoff.
geographer geog. or geogr. (OUP: geogr.)
geographic position GP
geographic or geographical geog. or
 geogr. (OUP: geogr.)
Geographical Information System
 computers GIS
Geographical Section of the British General
 Staff GSGS or G.S.G.S.
Geography G
geography geog. or geogr. (OUP: geogr.)
geologic or geological geol.
Geological Society GS

Geological Society of America GSA or G.S.A.
Geological Society of London GSL or G.S.L.
Geological Survey GS
Geological Survey of Great Britain GSGB or G.S.G.B.
Geological Survey of India GSI or G.S.I.
geologist geol.
geology geol.
geomagnetic electrokinetograph GEK
geometer geom.
geometric mean GM
geometric progression GP
geometric or **geometrical** geom.
geometrical dilution of precision navigation GDOP
geometry geom.
geophysical geophys.
geophysics geophys.
geopolitics geopol.
geopotential meter GPM
George Geo.
George Bernard Shaw GBS or G.B.S.
George Cross British GC or G.C.
George Medal British GM or G.M.
George Washington GW
George William Russell Æ or A.E.
Georgia 1 GA (Zip Code) **2** Ga or Ga. (NYT, OUP: Ga.) **3** Geo.
Georgia Review Ga R
Georgian Georg.
geostationary meteorological satellite GMS
geostationary operational environmental satellite GOES
geostationary satellite GSS
geosynchronous orbit GEO
geosynchronous or **geostationary transfer orbit** GTO
German 1 G or G. **2** Ger. **3** Germ. **4** French All
German Academic Exchange Service DAAD
German Aerospace Research Center DFVLR
German Committee on Standards DNA
German Communist Party KPD
German Federal or **Central Bank** DB
German Federal Patent DBP
German Federal Railways DB
German Industrial Standards DIN
German patent DRP or D.R.P.
German Pharmacopoeia Ph.G. or DAB
German Red Cross DRK
German registered design DRGM or D.R.G.M.
German Research Institute for Soaring DFS or D.F.S.
German Trade Unions Federation DGB
German-American Securities Corporation GASC
Germanic 1 Ger. **2** Gmc.
germanium Ge
Germany 1 G or G. **2** Ger. **3** Germ.
germination grm.
gerund ger.
gerundive ger.
Ghana Gh or Gh.
giant slalom GS
gibberellin GA
Gibbs function physics G or G

Gibraltar Gib.
giga- G
giga-electron-volt GEV or GeV or Gev or g.e.v. (NYT: Gev; OUP: GeV)
gigabyte computers GB
gigacycle kMc or kmc or kmc.
gigahertz 1 GHz **2** Gz
gigawatt GW or gw
gilbert 1 g **2** Gb or gb
Gilbert and Sullivan G & S
gill (unit of measure) **1** gi. **2** gl.
gilt 1 g or g. **2** glt.
gilt beveled edge GBE or g.b.e.
gilt edged g.e.
gilt top gt or g.t.
gilt top edges GTE or g.t.e.
Giorgi system mksa or MKSA
Giraffe Cam (constellation)
girder gir.
Girl Guides GG or G.G.
Girl Guides Association G.G.A.
Girl Scouts GS or G.S.
Girl Scouts of America GSA or G.S.A.
Girls Clubs of America GCA
Girls Training Corps GTC
Girls' Friendly Society GFS or G.F.S.
give pharmaceutics d or d.
glabrous botany glab.
Glamorganshire, Wales Glam.
Glasgow Glas. or Glasg.
glass 1 gl. **2** Latin vitr.
glass fiber reinforced plastic GFRP
glass plasma display electronics GPD
glass reinforced plastic or **polyester** GRP or grp
glass tube gt
glassful pharmaceutics cyath.
glaucous botany glau.
glazed imitation parchment British GIP
glissando music gliss.
global Glo. or Glo
Global Atmospheric Research Program GARP
Global Environmental Monitoring System GEMS
global horizontal sounding technique GHOST
Global Oscillation Network Group GONG
Global Positioning System GPS
global surveillance system GSS
global telecommunications system GTS (of World Meteorological Organization)
Global-Range Ballistic Missile GRBM
globin insulin medicine GI or G.I.
glomerular filtration rate GFR
gloom meteorology g or g.
gloss gl. (of a surface or a text giving equivalent words)
glossary 1 gl. **2** Glo. or glo. **3** Gloss. or gloss.
glossy gl.
Gloucester 1 Glos. **2** Gloss.
Gloucestershire 1 Glos. **2** Gloss. **3** Gloucester.
glucose glu.
glucose nitrogen ratio G:N
glucose phosphate dehydrogenase 1 GPD **2** GPDH

glucose tolerance test GTT
glucosyltransferase genetics GTF
glutamate dehydrogenase biochemistry GDH
glutamate synthase GOGAT
glutamic acid 1 GA **2** glu. or Glu.
glutamic acid decarboxylase GAD
glutamic-oxaloacetic transaminase GOT
glutamine 1 gln. or Gln. **2** GluN
glutamine synthetase biochemistry GS
glutathione GSH
glyceric acid GA
glycine gly. or Gly.
glycosaminoglycan GAG
go ahead communications GA
goal for sports GF
goalkeeper sports **1** G **2** GK
goals sports G
God D or D.
God the Lord of all D.O.M.
God willing DV
Goddard Space Flight Center GSFC
gold 1 Au **2** g or g.
gold medal GM or G.M.
Golfers' Association GA
gonadotropic hormone GTH
gonadotropin-releasing hormone GnRH
gonococcus medicine GC
good 1 G **2** g **3** gd or gd.
good at sight commerce b. à v.
Good Conduct Medal GCM
good fair average commerce GFA or g.f.a.
good manufacturing practices GMP
good merchandisable brand commerce GMB or g.m.b.
good merchandisable quality GMQ or g.m.q.
good ordinary brand GOB or g.o.b.
good service pension military GSP or G.S.P.
good this month commerce GTM or g.t.m.
good this week commerce GTW or g.t.w.
good till canceled or **countermanded** finance GTC or g.t.c.
goods gds.
goods and services tax GST (of Canada and New Zealand)
goods in bad order commerce GBO or g.b.o.
Gothic Got. or Goth. (MLA, OUP: Goth.)
Gothic letter or **letters** printing GL
gourde 1 G **2** gde. (monetary unit of Haiti)
Government 1 Gov. or gov. (MLA: govt.; OUP: gov. or Govt.) **2** Govt. or govt.
government GVT or Gvt. or gvt
Government and Relief in Occupied Areas GARIOA
government bill of lading GB/L or GBL
Government Communications Headquarters GCHQ
government form GF
government furnished GF
Government Information Service GIS
Government issue GI or G.I. (GPO, NYT, OUP: GI)
Government Laboratory GL
Government National Mortgage Association 1 Ginnie Mae **2** GNMA
Government of American Samoa GAS

Government of the Ryukyu Islands GRI
Government Printing Office GPO or G.P.O. (GPO, MLA: GPO)
Government Service GS
Government Training Center GTC
government-furnished equipment GFE
government-furnished materials GFM
government-furnished part or parts GFP
government-owned GO
government-owned contractor-operated GOCO
government-owned materials GOM
Governor Gov. or gov. (GPO, NYT: Gov.; OUP: gov.)
Governor General 1 GG or G.G. 2 Gov. Gen.
grade 1 Gr. 2 gr.
grade-point average education GPA
gradient grad.
gradual grad.
gradual increase in tempo music accel.
gradually decreasing music manc.
gradually diminishing music mor.
gradually dying away music smorz.
graduate grad. or grad
graduate assistant GA
Graduate Business Admissions Test GBAT
Graduate in Pharmacy 1 G.Ph. 2 GP or G.P. 3 Ph.G.
Graduate Management Admission Test GMAT
Graduate Nurse G.N.
Graduate of the Guildhall School of Music GGSM or G.G.S.M.
Graduate of the Institute of Automobile Engineers Grad.I.A.E.
Graduate of the Institute of Metallurgists Grad.I.M.
Graduate of the Institute of Physics Grad.Inst.P.
Graduate of the Institution of British Engineers Grad.Inst.B.E.
Graduate of the London College of Music GLCM or G.L.C.M.
Graduate of the Royal College of Music G.R.C.M. or GRCM
Graduate of the Royal Schools of Music GRSM or G.R.S.M.
Graduate of the Society of Engineers Grad.S.E.
graduate practical nurse GPN
Graduate Record Examination GRE
Graduate School Foreign Language Test GSFLT
graduate teaching assistant GTA or G.T.A.
graduated grad.
graduated interest rate finance GIR
graduated length method GLM
graduated payment mortgage GPM
Graduated Pension Scheme British GPS or G.P.S.
graft-versus-host medicine GVH
grain 1 G or G. 2 g or g. (unit of measure) 3 gr. or gr (unit of measure)
Grain and Feed Trade Association GAFTA
grain-consuming animal unit GCAU
grains grs.

gram 1 G or G. 2 g or g. 3 gm or gm. 4 gr. or gr 5 grm. (CSM: g. or gm.; OUP: g)
gram calorie g.cal. or g-cal
gram molecule g mol or g.-mol.
gram-equivalent weight J physics Z
gram-force physics gf
gram-mass gm
gram-molecular volume GMV or g.m.v.
gram-molecular weight GMW or g.m.w.
gram-negative grn. or gr.n. or GRN
gram-positive GRP or grp or gr.p.
grammar 1 gr. 2 gram.
grammatical gram.
grams 1 gms or gms. 2 gr. or gr
grams per gallon g.p.g. or GPG
grams per liter g./l. or g/l
grams per square meter GSM or gsm
Gran Turismo GT (automobile model)
Grand 1 G or G. 2 Gd or Gd. 3 Gr.
Grand Army of the Republic G.A.R.
Grand Chancellor GC or G.C.
Grand Chaplain GC or G.C.
Grand Chapter GC or G.C.
Grand Commander GC or G.C.
Grand Commander of the Star of India G.C.S.I. or GCSI
Grand Conductor GC or G.C.
Grand Council GC or G.C.
Grand Cross British GC or G.C.
Grand Cross of the Legion of Honor G.C.L.H. or GCLH
Grand Cross of the Order of St. Michael and St. George G.C.M.G.
Grand Cross of the Order of the Bath G.C.B. or GCB
Grand Cross of the Order of the British Empire GBE or G.B.E.
Grand Cross of the Victorian Order G.C.V.O. or GCVO
Grand Duchess GD or G.D.
Grand Duchy GD or G.D.
Grand Duke GD or G.D.
Grand Lodge GL or G.L.
Grand Marshal GM
Grand Master GM or G.M.
Grand Master of the Order of St. Michael and St. George G.M.M.G. or GMMG
Grand Master of the Order of the Bath GMB or G.M.B.
Grand Master of the Order of the Indian Empire G.M.I.E. or GMIE
Grand Master of the Order of the Star of India G.M.S.I. or GMSI
Grand Old Man GOM or G.O.M. (Gladstone)
grand old man GOM or G.O.M.
Grand Old Party GOP or G.O.P. (NYT: G.O.P.; OUP: GOP)
Grand Old Party Political Action Committee GOPAC
Grand Past Master GPM or G.P.M.
Grand Prix GP
Grand Recorder GR or G.R.
grand speed GS
grand total GT
Grand Touring GT (automobile model)
grand unification theories GUTS
Grand Unified Theory physics GUT

granddaughter gd or g.d.
grandson g.s.
granular activated carbon GAC
granulocyte colony stimulating factor G-CSF
granulocyte macrophage colony stimulating factor GM-CSF
granulosis virus GV
graphic arts composing equipment printing GRACE
Graphic Arts Technical Foundation GATF
Graphic Arts Trade Association GATA or G.A.T.A.
Graphical Evaluation and Review Technique computers GERT
graphical user interface computers GUI
Graphics Communication International Union GCIU
Graphics Interchange Format computers GIF
graphics or graphical kernel system GKS
Grashof number Gr.
grass grs. or Grs.
gravel 1 G or G. 2 gvl.
Graves Registration Service GRS or G.R.S.
gravimetric density gd or g.d.
gravimetric volume gv or g.v.
gravitational constant Gor G
gravitational force G
gravitational lens effect GLE
gravity 1 G 2 g 3 gr. or gr
gravity-vacuum transportation GVT
Gray botany Gr.
gray 1 gr. 2 GY or gy.
Great 1 Gr. 2 Gt.
great 1 gr. 2 advertising Grt or grt
Great Atlantic and Pacific Tea Company A & P
Great Bear, the Big Dipper, the Plough UMa (constellation)
Great Britain 1 GB or G.B. 2 Gr. Br. or Gr. Brit. 3 Gt. Br. or Gt. Brit.
Great Britain and Ireland G.B. & I. or GB & I
great circle navigation, geography GC
great granddaughter g.gd.
great grandson g.gs.
great gross (144 dozen) 1 g.gr. 2 GG 3 gr. gro.
great organ music GO or G.O.
great primer 1 g.p. 2 GP or G.P.
great red spot GRS
Great Universal Stores GUS or G.U.S.
Greater Gtr.
greater than mathematics, computers GT
greatest common divisor mathematics GCD or g.c.d.
greatest common factor mathematics GCF or g.c.f.
greatest common measure mathematics GCM or g.c.m.
greatest common multiple mathematics GCM or g.c.m.
Grecian Gr.
Greece Gr.
Greek 1 G or G. 2 Gk or Gk. (MLA, OUP: Gk.) 3 Gr.
Greek New Testament (received text) Text. Rec.

Greek Orthodox Church GOC *or* G.O.C.
green 1 G *or* G. **2** g *or* g. **3** gn. *or* gn
  4 grn.
Greenland Green. *or* Greenl.
greens in regulation GIR
Greenwich Apparent Time GAT *or* G.A.T.
Greenwich civil time *astronomy, navigation*
  GCT *or* G.C.T. *or* G.c.t.
Greenwich hour angle *navigation,*
  astronomy GHA
Greenwich mean astronomical time GMAT
  or G.M.A.T. *or* G.m.a.t.
Greenwich mean time GMT *or* G.M.T. *or*
  G.m.t.
Greenwich Royal Observatory GRO *or*
  G.R.O.
Greenwich sidereal time *astronomy,*
  navigation GST *or* G.S.T. *or* G.s.t.
Greenwich time signal GTS
Gregorian Greg.
Gregory Greg.
Grenadier Guards GG
grid 1 G **2** *physics* g
grid bias *electronics* GB
grid heading *navigation* GH
grievous bodily harm G.B.H. *or* GBH
grind grd.
Grocery Manufacturers of America GMA
Grocery Manufacturers of Australia GMA
gross 1 g (144) **2** Gr. (144) **3** gr. (144)
  4 gr. (whole, entire) **5** gro. (144)
gross agricultural product *economics*
  GAP
gross annual value GAV
gross domestic product *economics* GDP
gross earnings deflator *economics* GED
gross energy GE
gross global product GGP
gross leasable area GLA
gross national income GNI *or* G.N.I.
gross national product *economics* GNP *or*
  G.N.P. (*GPO, OUP:* GNP; *NYT:* G.N.P.)
gross rating point *commerce* GRP
gross redemption yield gry *or* g.r.y.
gross registered tons *or* **tonnage** GRT *or*
  g.r.t.
gross score 1 *statistics, psychology* X
  2 *statistics* Y
gross social product *economics* GSP
gross ton 1 GT **2** gt *or* g.t.
gross tons GRT *or* grt
gross vehicle weight GVW
gross weight 1 gr.wt. **2** GW
gross world product *economics* GWP
ground 1 G **2** gnd. *or* GND **3** grd. *or* GRD
  4 *electronics* gd *or* gd.
ground control approach *aviation* GCA
ground control interception GCI
ground control landing *aviation* GCL
ground detector GD
ground effect machine GEM
ground effect vehicle GEV

ground effects takeoff and landing
  aeronautics GETOL
ground elapsed time *navigation* GET
ground electro-optical deep space
  surveillance GEODSS
Ground Electronics Engineering Installation
  Agency GEEIA
ground fault circuit interrupter *electricity*
  GFCI
ground fog *meteorology* GF
ground level GL
ground mapping radar GMR
ground or sea-launched GSL *or* G/SL
ground position indicator *aeronautics* GPI
ground power unit GPU
Ground Self-Defense Force GSDF (army of
  Japan)
ground speed g.s.
ground speed indicator GSI
ground station GS
ground support equipment GSE
Ground Wave Emergency Network
  GWEN
ground zero GZ
ground-controlled radar GCR
ground-launched cruise missile GLCM
ground-to-air GA *or* G/A *or* G-A
ground-to-air pilotless aircraft GAPA *or*
  Gapa
ground-to-ground GG *or* G/G *or* G-G
group 1 G *or* G. **2** Gp. *or* gp. **3** gr. **4** Grp.
Group Against Smokers Pollution GASP
Group Captain GC *or* G/C
Group for the Advancement of Psychiatry
  GAP
Group Health Insurance GHI
Group Inclusive Tour GIT
group mark *computers* GM
Group of Seven G-7
Group of Three G-3
group projective test *psychology* GPT
group repetition frequency *electronics* GRF
  or grf.
group separator *computers* GS
Grove GRV (in postal address)
growing equity mortgage GEM
growth and development hormone
  biochemistry GDH
growth and income *finance* G & I
growth hormone GH
growth-hormone releasing factor GHRF *or*
  GRF
Guam GU (Zip Code)
guanine G
guanine and cytosine GC
guanine, adenine, thymine, cytosine
  genetics GATC *or* gatc
guanosine diphosphate *biochemistry* GDP
guanosine monophosphate GMP
guanosine triphosphate GTP
guarani Gs *or* Gs. (monetary unit of
  Paraguay)

guarantee *or* **guaranteed** guar.
guaranteed gtd.
guaranteed annual income GAI
guaranteed annual wage GAW *or* G.A.W.
  or Gaw
Guaranteed Income Supplement GIS
guaranteed investment contract GIC
guaranteed minimum value GMV *or* gmv
guaranteed retirement income GRI
guaranteed student loan GSL
Guaranteed Student Loan Program GSLP
Guard Gd *or* Gd.
guard 1 grd. **2** *sports* G
guard ring GR (of an electric field)
guardian gdn. *or* Gdn.
Guardsman Gdsm.
Guatemala Guat.
guessed mean *psychology* GM
Guggenheim Aeronautical Laboratory of
  the California Institute of Technology
  GALCIT
Guggenheim Foundation GF
Guiana Gui.
guidance guid.
guidance and navigation G & N
Guidance Officer *astronautics* GUIDO *or*
  Guido
guide g *or* g.
guide book GB *or* G.B.
Guide Dogs for the Blind Association GDBA
guide RNA gRNA
guided aircraft missile GAM
guided aircraft rocket GAR
guided missile GM
guided space vehicle GSV
guided weapon GW
Guild of Air Pilots and Air Navigators
  GAPAN
Guild of Air Traffic Control Officers GATCO
Guild of Radio Service Engineers GRSE *or*
  G.R.S.E.
guilder Gld. *or* gld. *or* gldr.
Guildhall School of Music and Dance GSMD
  or G.S.M.D.
Guinea Guin.
guitar gui.
Gulf G *or* G.
Gulf Cooperation Council GCC
gummed all over flap *British* g.a.o.f. (of
  envelopes)
gummed only g.o. (of envelopes)
gunner 1 Gnr. **2** *British* Gr.
gunner's mate GM
gunnery gun.
gunshot wound GSW
Guyana G
gymnasium gym
gymnastics gym
gynecological GYN *or* gyn. *or* gynecol.
gynecology GYN *or* gyn. *or* gynecol.
gynoecium G
gypsum Gyp

Habakkuk Hab.
habeas corpus hab. corp.
habitat 1 hab. **2** habit.
habitation hab.
habitual criminal HC or H.C.
had been drinking HBD or H.B.D.
hafnium Hf
Hageman factor HF
Haggai Hag.
hagiology hagiol.
hahnium Ha
Haifa, Israel Hfa
hail 1 h or h. **2** *meteorology* A
hail and rain *meteorology* HR
Hail, Mary! AM
hairspace hr.
Haiti Ha or Ha.
half 1 h **2** hf or hf. **3** *Latin* s or s.
  4 *pharmaceutics* **a** dim. **b** ss
half calf hf.cf. (bookbinding)
half duplex *computers* **1** HD **2** HDX
half hard *metallurgy* hh or h.h.
half morocco hf.mor. (bookbinding)
half pay hp or h.p.
half title *printing* HT
half-bound hf.bd.
half-hardy annual hha. or HHA
half-hardy biennial hhb. or HHB
half-hardy perennial hhp. or HHP
half-life *physics, chemistry* T
half-power beamwidth *electronics* HPBW
half-time HT
halfback *sports* **1** h.b. **2** HB
halftone *photography, printing* **1** HT **2** ht
Halifax, Nova Scotia 1 Hal. **2** Hfx
hallmark HM
halogen 1 hal or hal. **2** R **3** X
Hamburg, Germany Hamb.
Hamiltonian function *physics* H
hamlet hmlt.
Hamlet, Prince of Denmark Ham. or Haml.
  (*MLA:* Ham.)
Hampshire County, England Hants or Hants.
hand 1 hd or hd. **2** hnd **3** *music* h or h.
hand control HC
hand-held maneuvering unit HHMU
handbook 1 HB **2** HBK or h.bk. or hbk
  3 hdbk. **4** hndbk.
handful *Latin* m or m.
handicap 1 hcap **2** hcp
handily h or h. (in horse racing)
handkerchief 1 hdkf. **2** hkf.
handle hdl.
handling hdlg.
handmade HM or H.M.
handmade paper HMP or hmp
hands or **hands high** hh
hangar hgr or Hgr
hanger hgr
Hansen's disease HD

haploid generation 1 n **2** *biology* x
haploid number of chromosomes n
Happy, Healthy, Holy Organization 3HO
harassment and interdiction *military* H.& I.
Harbor HBR
harbor 1 H or H. **2** Har. or har. **3** hbr. or
  Hbr.
Harbor Master HM or H.M.
hard 1 H **2** hrd. **3** *geology* h
hard and black HB (of pencil lead)
hard copy HC
hard disk HD
hard drive HD
hard firm HF (of lead pencil)
hard tissue replacement HTR
hard—coal equivalents h.c.e.
hard-drawn *metallurgy* HD
hardback 1 h.b. **2** HBK or hbk
hardcover HC
harden hdn.
hardness 1 H **2** *geology* h
hardware 1 hard. **2** hdw. or hdwe.
hardwood hdwd.
hardwood floor HWF
hardy annual 1 HA or H.A. **2** ha or ha.
hardy biennial *botany* **1** HB **2** hb.
hardy perennial 1 HP or hp. **2** hp or hp.
Hardy-Rand-Ritter H-R-R (color blindness
  test)
harmonic distortion HD
harmonic mean *mathematics* HM
harmonics *music* Harm.
Harold Har.
harpsichord 1 harp. **2** hpcd or hpch
Harry S Truman HST or H.S.T. or
  H.S T.
Hartford Hart.
Harvard Harv.
Harvard College Observatory HCO
Harvard Educational Review HER
Harvard Library Bulletin HLB
Harvard Theological Review HTR
Harvard University Press HUP
Hashemite Kingdom of Jordan HKJ
hatchback 1 HB or H/B **2** Htbk or htbk
Haute Loire HL or H-L
Haute-Garonne HG or H-G
Haute-Marne HM or H-M
Hautes Pyrénées HP or H-P
Hautes-Alpes HA or H.A.
have the record before the court Re.fa.lo.
haversine *mathematics* hav
having concealed nectar AB
Hawaii 1 Ha or Ha. **2** Haw. **3** HI (Zip Code)
Hawaii Time HT or H.T.
Hawaiian Islands HI or H.I.
Hawaiian Standard Time HST or H.S.T. or
  h.s.t.
hazard haz.
hazard analysis critical control point
  HACCP
hazardous haz.
hazardous materials HM
hazardous waste HW or H.W.
haze 1 hz. **2** *meteorology* **a** H **b** z
hazy 1 hzy. **2** *spectroscopy* h
he or **she died without issue** ob.s.p.
he or **she lived so many years** av or a.v.

Head Hd. (in place names)
head 1 hd or hd. **2** *physics, chemistry* h
head nurse HN or H.N.
Head Office H.O. or HO
head-down display HDD
head-up display HUD
heading Hdg. or hdg
headline *printing* hed
headmaster or **headmistress** HM
Headmasters' Association H.M.A.
headquarters 1 Hdqrs. **2** HQ or hq.
headwaiter HW
Health Advisory Service HAS
Health and Human Services HHS or H.H.S.
  (*GPO:* HHS)
Health Care Financing Administration HCFA
Health Insurance Plan HIP
Health Insurance Purchasing Cooperative
  HIPC
Health Maintenance Organization HMO
Health Officer H.O. or HO
Health Opportunity for People Everywhere
  HOPE
Health Resources Administration HRA
Health Resources and Services
  Administration HRSA
Health Sciences Advancement Award
  HSAA
hearing distance HD or H.D.
heart hrt.
heart rate *medicine* HR
heartwood hrtwd.
heat 1 h **2** ht or ht.
heat engine HE
heat resistant HR
heat resistant plastic HRP
heat stress index HSI
heat transfer coefficient HTC
heat transfer medium *engineering* HTM
heat transfer unit HTU
heat treatment HT
heat-generating waste HGW
heated Htd or htd.
heater 1 htr. **2** *electronics* **a** H **b** h (as a
  subscript)
heating htg.
heating and ventilating HV or H&V
Heating and Ventilating Contractors
  Association HVCA
Heating and Ventilating Research
  Association HVRA
heating, ventilation, and air conditioning
  HVAC
heavier than air HTA
heavy 1 H **2** hvy. or hvy **3** hy.
heavy artillery HA
heavy duty HD
heavy equipment transporter HET
heavy free gas HFG
heavy fuel oil HFO
heavy goods vehicle *British* HGV
heavy hydrogen HH
heavy ion plasma accelerator *physics*
  HIPAC
heavy sea H or H.
heavy water HW
heavy water reactor HWR
heavy-duty vehicle HDV

heavy-ion linear accelerator HILAC or Hilac
heavy-lift launch vehicle *aeronautics* HLLV
Hebraic Heb. or Hebr.
Hebrew Heb. or Hebr. (*MLA, OUP*: Heb.)
Hebrew Immigration Aid Society HIAS
Hebrew Young Men's Association HYMA
Hebrews Heb. or Hebr. (*MLA, OUP*: Heb.)
Hebrides Heb. or Hebr.
hectare 1 ha **2** hect.
hecto- 1 H **2** h
hectogram 1 hectog. **2** Hg **3** hg or hg.
hectoliter 1 hectol. **2** hl or hl.
hectometer 1 hectom. **2** hm or hm.
hed or **headline to come** HTK
heel H (on organ music)
Heifer Project International HPI
height 1 d or d. **2** H **3** h **4** hgt. **5** ht or ht.
  6 *physics* y
height above airport HAA
height above touchdown *aeronautics* HAT
height equivalent of theoretical plate
  chemical engineering HETP
height of an arc h
height of instrument *surveying* HI
height of transfer unit *engineering* HTU
height over all OAH or o.a.h.
height-range indicator HRI
Heights 1 Hgts **2** HTS (in postal address)
  3 Hts.
heir 1 h or h. **2** *Latin* her.
held covered *insurance* HC or H/C
held on charge HOC or h.o.c.
helicopter 1 H **2** H- **3** hcptr **4** hel or heli
helicopter electronic landing path HELP
heliocentric Julian date *astronomy* HJD
heliport helo.
helium He
helium underwater speech translating
  equipment HUSTLE
helium-neon He-Ne (laser)
Hellenic Hellen.
Hellenism Hellen.
Hellenistic Hellen.
Helm H or H. or н
Helmholtz function A
helper Hlpr.
Helsinki, Finland Hel.
hemagglutination inhibition or **inhibiting**
  medicine HI
hemaglutinin HA
hematocrit HCT or Hct.
hemoglobin 1 Hb or hb. **2** hem. or hemo.
  3 Hg **4** hg **5** Hgb
hemolytic disease of newborns HDN
Hemophilus or **Haemophilus influenza type**
  B HIB
hemorrhage hem. or hemo.
hence 1 H or H. **2** h or h.
Henry Hen. (*King Henry* in listing
  Shakespeare's plays)
henry *electricity* **1** H **2** h **3** hy. or Hy.
Henry Draper 1 H.D. (astronomical catalog)
  2 HD
heparan sulfate protoglycan HSPG
heparin-binding growth factor HBGF
hepatitis A virus HAV
hepatitis B HB
hepatitis B virus HBV

hepatitis infectious mononucleosis *medicine*
  HIM
hepatitis-associated antigen HAA
Her Grace HG or H.G.
Her Highness HH or H.H.
Her Magesty HM or H.M.
Her or **His Britannic Majesty** HBM or H.B.M.
Her Royal Highness HRH or H.R.H.
Her Serene Highness HSH or H.S.H.
Her Serene Majesty HSM or H.S.M.
Her or **His Majesty's New Zealand Ship**
  HMNZ
Her or **His Majesty's Australian Ship** HMAS
  or H.M.A.S.
Her or **His Majesty's Canadian Ship** HMCS
  or H.M.C.S.
Her or **His Majesty's Civil Service**
  Commissioners HMCSS or H.M.C.S.S.
Her or **His Majesty's Customs** H.M.C. or
  HMC
Her or **His Majesty's Forces** HMF or H.M.F.
Her or **His Majesty's Government** HMG or
  H.M.G.
Her or **His Majesty's Inspector** HMI or
  H.M.I.
Her or **His Majesty's Land Registry** HMLR or
  H.M.L.R.
Her or **His Majesty's Office of Works**
  HMOW or H.M.O.W.
Her or **His Majesty's Prison** HMP or H.M.P.
Her or **His Majesty's Service** HMS or H.M.S.
Her or **His Majesty's Ship** HMS or H.M.S.
Her or **His Majesty's Stationery Office**
  HMSO or H.M.S.O. (*MLA, OUP*: HMSO)
heraldic her.
heraldry her.
Heralds' College HC or H.C.
herbarium Herb.
Herbig-Haro *astronomy* HH
Hercules Her (constellation)
Herdsman Boo (constellation)
here and there (in a book, article, or other
  work) pass. (*MLA*: not acceptable)
here is buried *Latin* **1** H.S.E. or HSE **2** HS or
  H.S.
here lies 1 HI or H.I. **2** *Latin* **a** HJ or H.J.
  b HS or H.S. **c** i.h.
here lies buried *Latin* **1** H.I.S. **2** HJS or
  H.J.S.
here rests in peace H.R.I.P. or HRIP
heredity hered.
Herefordshire County, England Heref or
  Heref. or Hereford.
hereinafter described had.
herewith hw
hermetic-integrating gyroscope *navigation*
  HIG
Herodotus Herod.
heroin H
herpes simplex virus HSV
herpetology herp. or herpet.
Hertfordshire County, England Herts or
  Herts.
hertz Hz or Hz. (*OUP*: Hz)
Hertzsprung-Russell diagram H-R diagram
heterogeneous nuclear RNA HnRNA
hexachlorobenzene HCB
hexachlorocyclohexane HCH

hexachlorophene G_{11} or G-11
hexachord hex.
hexadecimal *computers* HEX or hex
hexaethyl tetraphosphate HETP
hexagon hex.
hexagonal hex.
hexagonal close-packed hcp or HCP
Hezekiah Hzk.
hibernation trigger HT
Hibernian Hib.
hierarchical database management system
  computers HDBMS
hierarchy plus input-process-output
  computers HIPO
hieroglyphics or **hieroglyphic** hier.
high H
high accuracy HIAC or hi. ac.
high altitude HA
high altitude, high opening HAHO (of
  parachuting)
high altitude, low opening HALO (of
  parachuting)
high band HB
high blood pressure HBP or hbp
high breaking capacity *engineering* HBC
high capacity HC
high carbohydrate and fiber HCF
High Church HC
High Command Hi. Com.
High Commissioner 1 HC or H.C. **2** Hi.
  Com. or Hi-Com
high compression HC
high cost of living HCL or h.c.l.
High Court of Justice H.C.J.
high current density HCD or hcd
high definition HD
high density HD
high duty alloy HDA
high energy HE
high energy phosphate HEP
High Energy Physics Laboratory HEPL
high explosive HE
high fidelity 1 HF **2** hf **3** hi-fi or Hi-Fi
High Flux Beam Reactor HFBR
High Flux Isotope Reactor HFIR
high frequency 1 hf or h-f **2** HF or H-F (*GPO*,
  OUP: HF)
high frequency recombination HFR
  or Hfr
High German HG
high grade HG
high intensity HI or H.I.
high latitude HILAT or Hilat (satellite)
high molecular weight *chemistry* HMW
high oxygen pressure HOP
high performance HP
high potency HP
high potential hipot.
high power HP or H.P.
high pressure 1 HP or H.P. **2** hp or h.p.
high quality HQ
high resolution 1 hi-res **2** HR
high run HR (in billiards)
High School HS or H.S.
high speed HS
high technology hi-tech
high temperature HT
high tension 1 ht or h.t. **2** *electricity* HT

high tide HT
high vacuum HV
high velocity HV
high voltage HV or h.v.
high water HW or H.W.
high-abrasion furnace HAF
high-altitude bombing HAB
high-altitude clear air turbulence HICAT
high-altitude fluorescence HAF
high-alumina cement *construction* HAC
high-carbon steel HCS or hcs
high-definition television HDTV
high-definition TV hi-def
high-definition video HDV
high-density air traffic zone HDATZ
high-density data system *computers* HDDS
high-density lipoprotein HDL
high-density polyethylene HDP or HDPE
high-duty metal HDM
high-efficiency particulate air HEPA (filter)
high-electron mobility transistor HEMT
High-Energy Astronomy Observatory
  HEAO
high-energy electron diffraction HEED
high-energy fuel HEF
high-energy laser HEL
high-energy rate forming HERF
high-explosive incendiary HEI
high-explosive plastic HEP
high-frequency current HFC or hfc
high-frequency direction finder or finding
  HF-DF or HF/DF
high-frequency oscillation *electronics* HFO
high-fructose corn syrup HFCS
high-grade tax-exempt *finance* HGT (of
  bonds)
high-impact plastic HIP
high-impact polystyrene HIPS
high-intensity discharge HID
high-level data link control *computers* HDLC
high-level forecast HIFOR
high-level language HLL
high-level nuclear waste HLNW
high-level waste HLW
high-maneuverable aircraft technology
  HIMAT
High-Mobility, Multiple-purpose Wheeled
  Vehicle HMMWV
high-occupancy vehicle HOV
high-pass *electronics* hp
high-performance liquid chromatography
  chemistry HPLC
high-performance navigation system
  HIPERNAS
high-power acquisition radar HIPAR
high-power amplifier HPA
high-precision short-range navigation
  HIRAN
high-pressure area *meteorology* H
high-pressure mercury vapor HPMV
high-pressure nervous syndrome HPNS
high-pressure oceanographic equipment
  HIPOE
high-pressure steam HPS
high-pressure test HPT
high-protein supplement HPS
High-Resolution Electron Microscope HREM
high-resolution gas chromatography HRGC

High-Resolution Infrared Radiometer HRIR
high-resolution mass spectrometry HRMS
High-Resolution Scanning Electron
  Microscope HRSEM
high-speed anti-radiation missile HARM
High-Speed Civil Transport HSCT
high-speed data acquisition *computers*
  HSDA
high-speed diesel (oil) HSD
high-speed ground transport HSGT
high-speed memory *computers* HSM
High-Speed Multichannel Data Recorder
  HSMCDR
high-speed printer *computers* HSP
high-speed rail HSR
high-speed reader *computers* HSR
high-speed train HST
high-strength low-alloy HSLA
high-temperature gas-cooled reactor HTGC
  or HTGCR or HTGR
high-temperature reactor HTR
high-temperature short-time
  (pasteurization) HTST
high-tensile steel HTS
high-tension battery HTB
high-test hypochlorite HTH
high-voltage electron microscope HVEM
high-voltage power supply HVPS
high-water interval HWI
high-water line HWL or hwl
high-water mark HWM or hwm
high-yield tax-exempt *finance* HYT
Higher Education Act HEA
Higher National Certificate *education*
  H.N.C.
Higher National Diploma *education* H.N.D.
highest common factor *mathematics* HCF or
  h.c.f.
highest grade AA
highest occupied molecular orbital
  chemistry HOMO
highest possible frequency HPF
highest price quoted of a stock *finance* H
highest priority DX
highest rating *finance* 1 AAA 2 Aaa
highest spring tide HST or hst
highest useful compression ratio
  engineering HUCR
Highly Eccentric Orbital Satellite HEOS
highly leveraged transactions *finance* HLT
Highway HWY (in postal address)
highway 1 Hgwy. 2 Hwy. or hwy. 3 hy. or
  Hy
Highway Contract Route HCR
Highway Safety Research Institute HSRI
Hilary Hil. (term)
Hilda Doolittle H.D.
Hindi Hi.
Hindu Hind.
Hindustan Hind.
Hindustani Hind. or Hindu.
Hippocrates Hipp.
hire purchase *British* 1 HP 2 hp
His Eminence HE or H.E.
His Grace HG or H.G.
His Highness HH or H.H.
His Holiness HH or H.H.
His Majesty HM or H.M.

His Master's Voice HMV (recording label)
His Royal Highness HRH or H.R.H.
His Serene Highness HSH or H.S.H.
His Serene Majesty HSM or H.S.M.
His or Her Excellency HE or H.E.
His or Her Majesty's Stationery Office Stat.
  Off.
Hispanic Institute of the United States
  H.I.U.S.
histamine *biochemistry* H
histamine receptor H
histidine his. or His.
histocompatibility locus antigen HLA
histocompatibility Y-chromosome H-Y
histology 1 hist. 2 histol.
historian hist. or histn (*MLA, OUP:* hist.)
historic hist. or Hist.
Historic American Buildings Survey HABS
historical hist. or Hist.
Historical Manuscripts Commission H.M.C.
history hist.
history of present complaint *medicine*
  HPC
history of present illness *medicine* HPI
hit *baseball* H
hit by ball *baseball* HB
hit by pitched ball HBP
hit by pitcher *baseball* HP
hit wicket *cricket* 1 ht. wkt. 2 hw or h.w.
Hittite Hitt.
hoarfrost *meterology* x
Hoboken 1 H or H. or H 2 Hob.
Hodgkin's disease HD
Hoffer-Osmond Diagnosis H.O.D.
hogshead 1 hd or hd. 2 hhd.
hold for money *commerce* HFM
hold for release HFR
hold or held over *theater, commerce* h.o.
holder in due course *commerce, law* HDC
  or hdc
holiday hol or hol.
holidays hols or hols.
Holland 1 Hol. 2 Holl.
hollow hol or hol.
hollow back HBK (of lumber)
hollow metal door *construction* HMD
holmium Ho
Holtzman Inkblot Technique H.I.T.
Holy H or H.
Holy Communion HC
Holy Mother Church S.M.E.
Holy Mother Mary S.M.M.
Home Box Office HBO
Home Civil Service *British* HCS or H.C.S.
Home Energy Assistance Program HEAP
Home fleet *British* HF
Home forces *British* HF
Home Grown Cereals Authority HGCA
Home Guard *British* HG or H.G.
Home Loan Bank Board HLBB or H.L.B.B.
Home Mission HM
Home Office *British* H.O. or HO
Home Owners' Association HOA
Home Owners' Loan Corporation HOLC
Home Relief HR
Home Rule HR
home run *baseball* HR
Home Secretary *British* HS or H.S.

Home Service Force *British* HSF
home video HV
homeopathic 1 homeo. **2** homo.
homeopathy 1 homeo. **2** homo.
Homer Hom. (Greek poet)
homes using radio *advertising* Hur
homes using television *advertising* HUT
homestead Hmstd
homing beacon HB
Homing Overlay Experiment HOE
homo sapiens hom. sap.
homogeneous staining region *biochemistry* HSR
homonym hom
homosexual homo.
homosexuality homo.
homovanillic acid HVA
Honduras Hond.
Hong Kong HK
honor hon.
Honorable 1 Hon. *or* Hon **2** Honble.
honorable hon.
Honorable Artillery Company HAC *or* H.A.C.
honorable discharge *military* HD
honorably hon.
Honorary Hon. *or* Hon
honorary hon.
Honorary Doctor Dr.h.c.
Honorary Fellow of the Royal Academy H.F.R.A. *or* HFARA
Honorary Foreign Associate of the Royal Academy H.F.A.R.A. *or* HFARA
Honorary Member of Royal Hibernian Academy HRHA *or* H.R.H.A.
Honorary Member of the Royal Academy HRA *or* H.R.A.
Honorary Member of the Royal Scottish Academy HRSA *or* H.R.S.A.
Honorary Member Royal Cambrian Academy HRCA *or* H.R.C.A.
honors Hnrs
Honours *British* Hons.
Honours List HL
Horace Hor. (Roman poet)
horizon hor.
horizontal 1 H *or* H. **2** h *or* h. **3** hor.
horizontal axis wind turbine HAWT
horizontal band HB
horizontal center line HCL *or* h.c.l.
horizontal equivalent HE
horizontal force (of the magnetic field of the earth) *physics, electronics, astronomy* H
horizontal parallax *astronomy* hp *or* h.p.
horizontal radiation pattern *communications* HRP
horizontal takeoff and landing HOTOL
hormone replacement therapy HRT
horn *music* **1** H **2** h **3** hn *or* Hn
horological hor.
Horological Institute of America H.I.A.
horology 1 hor. **2** horol.
horse h *or* h.
Horse Artillery HA *or* H.A.
Horse Guards *British* HG *or* H.G.
horsepower 1 Ch. *or* Ch **2** cv **3** HP *or* H.P. **4** hp *or* h.p. (*CSM:* hp.; *OUP:* hp)

horsepower nominal *mechanics* HPN *or* hp.n.
horsepower-hour HPH *or* hph *or* hp-hr
horticultural hort.
Horticultural Marketing Council H.M.C.
horticulture hort.
Hosea Hos.
hospital 1 H **2** Hosp.
Hospital Corps HC *or* H.C.
hospital information system HIS
hospital *or* **hospitalization insurance** HI
hospital-acquired infection HAI
Hostage Rescue Team HRT
hostilities only H.O. *or* HO
hot 1 H **2** h
hot and cold h.and c. (*OUP:* h.& c.)
hot and cold water 1 h.c. *or* h/c **2** HC *or* H/C
hot dry rock HDR
hot water 1 HW **2** hw *or* h.w.
hot water soluble HWS
hot-pressed HP *or* H.P. (of paper)
hot-rolled paper HR *or* H.R.
hot-rolled steel HR
Hotel and Catering Trades Benevolent Association HCTBA
Hotel Employees and Restaurant Employees International Union HEREIU
Hounds CVn (constellation)
hour 1 H *or* H. **2** h *or* h. **3** hr.
hour angle *astronomy* HA
hourly difference *navigation, astronomy* HD
hours hrs.
hours, minutes, seconds HMS *or* h/m/s *or* hms
House Hse.
house 1 h **2** Ho *or* Ho. *or* ho. (*OUP:* ho.) **3** HS
House Bill HB
House Committee HC *or* H.C.
House Concurrent Resolution H.Con.Res. (with a number)
House Conference Report H.Conf.Rept. (with a number)
House Document H.Doc. (with a number)
House Joint Resolution H.J.Res. *or* HJR (with number; *GPO:* H.J.Res.)
House of Commons 1 H of C *or* HoC **2** HC *or* H.C. (*GPO:* H.C.; *OUP:* HC)
House of Commons Bill HCB (with number)
House of Commons Paper hcp *or* HCP
House of Keys HK *or* H.K.
House of Lords 1 *Latin* DP *or* D.P. **2** *law* Dom. Proc. **3** H of L *or* HoL **4** HL *or* H.L. (*GPO:* H.L.; *OUP:* HL)
House of Representatives 1 H of R **2** H *or* H. **3** HR
House of Representatives Bill HR (with number; *GPO:* H.R.; *OUP:* HR)
House of Representatives Ways and Means Committee HRWMC
house *or* **home equity loan** HEL
house physician HP
House Report H.Rept. (with number)
House Resolution H.Res. (with number)
household furniture *insurance* HHF
household goods *insurance* HHG
housekeeper hskpr
Houses of Parliament HP *or* H.P.

housing hsg.
Housing and Home Finance Agency HHFA
Housing Implementation Fund HIF
Houston Automatic Spooling Program HASP
Howard How. (U.S. Supreme Court Reports)
howitzer how.
hub end HE
Hubble constant H_o
Hubble Space Telescope HST
human 1 hum. **2** Hum. *or* HUM
human albumin microspheres *medicine* HAM
human being h.b.
human chorionic gonadotrophin HCG
human chorionic somatomammotrophin HCS
Human Genome Organization HUGO
Human granulocytic ehrlichiosis HGE
human growth hormone HGH
human herpes virus HHV
human immunodeficiency virus 1 HIV *or* HIV-1 **2** HIV-2
human intelligence humint *or* HUMINT
human interest HI *or* H.I.
human leucocyte antigen HLA
human menopausal gonadotrophin *biochemistry* HMG
Human Nutrition and Information Service HNIS
human papillomavirus HPV
Human Relations Areas Files HRAF
Human Resources Administration HRA
Human Rights and Humanitarian Affairs HRHA (bureau of U.S. Department of State)
Human Rights Commission HRC
Human Sciences and Advanced Technology HUSAT (Institute)
human serum albumin *medicine* HSA
human T-cell lymphotropic virus HTLV
human-caused error h.c.e.
human-powered vehicle HPV
human-ras H-ras
humane Hum.
Humane Society of the United States HSUS
Humanities 1 Hum. **2** *Latin* Lit. Hum.
humanities H (library cataloging)
Humboldt and Bonpland *botany* H.& B.
Humboldt, Bonpland, and Kunth *botany* H.B. & K.
humidity H
humidity index HI
humorous hum.
hundred 1 C **2** cent. **3** H *or* H. **4** h *or* h. **5** hd **6** hnd *or* HND **7** hun. *or* hund.
hundred cubic feet HCF
hundred thousand hunth.
(in) hundreds hd *or* hds (of a stock transaction)
hundredweight 1 cent. **2** cwt. *or* cwt **3** hwt.
Hungarian 1 Hg *or* Hg. **2** Hun. *or* Hung. (*MLA, OUP:* Hung.)
Hungarian Democratic Forum HDF
Hungarian News Agency MTI
Hungary Hun. *or* Hung. (*MLA, OUP:* Hung.)
Hunter and Driffield HD *or* H-D (film speed)
hunter-killer HUK (search group for enemy submarines)
Hunting Dogs CVn (constellation)

Huntingdonshire County, England Hunts or Hunts.
Huntington's disease HD
hurricane Hur or hur. or HURCN
Hurricane Warning System HWS
husband 1 H or H. **2** h or h.
husband and wife h/w
husbandry Husb. or husb.
Hute-Saône HS or H-S
hyaline membrane disease HMD
hyaluronic acid HA
hybrid hyb.
hybrid computer translator HYCOTRAN
hybrid electromagnetic HEM
hybrid integrated circuit electronics HIC
Hydra, the Water Snake Hya (constellation)
hydrant hydt.
hydraulic hyd.
hydraulic cement concrete HCC or hcc
hydraulic cycling unit HCU
hydraulic mean depth HMD
hydraulics 1 hyd. **2** hydr. or hydraul.
hydrocarbon HC
hydrochloric acid HCl
hydrochlorofluorocarbon HCFC
hydrodynamic hydro.
hydroelectric hydro.
Hydroelectric Power Commission HEPC
hydroelectric unit HEU
hydrofluorocarbon HFC
hydrogen H
hydrogen bomb H-bomb
hydrogen cyanide HCN

hydrogen embrittlement HE
hydrogen fluoride HF
hydrogen ion H^+ or H^-
hydrogen ion concentration $H°$
hydrogen ion concentration in solution pH or pH
hydrogen line in the solar spectrum F
hydrogen nicotinamide adenine dinucleotide NADH
hydrogen nicotinamide adenine dinucleotide phosphate NADPH
hydrographer Hydr.
hydrographic 1 hyd. **2** hydro. or hydrog.
Hydrographic Office 1 H.O. or HO **2** hydro. or HYDRO
hydrography hyd.
hydrography, Atlantic Ocean HYDROLANT
hydrography, Pacific Ocean HYDROPAC
hydrolysis physics h
hydrophilic-lipophilic balance chemistry HLB
hydrostatic hyd.
hydrostatics 1 hyd. **2** hydros.
hydroxybutyric dehydrogenase HBD
hydroxycorticosteroid OHCS
hydroxyindole-O-methyltransferase HIOMT
hydroxyl OH
hydroxymethanesulfonate HMSA
hydroxymethyl phenylalanine HP
hydroxyproline Hyp
hydroxytryptophan HTP
Hydrus Hyi (constellation)
hygiene Hyg. or hyg.

hymns ancient and modern 1 H.A.& M. **2** HAM or H.A.M.
hyperbolic amplitude mathematics amh
hyperbolic cosecant mathematics csch
hyperbolic cosine mathematics cosh
hyperbolic cotangent mathematics **1** coth **2** ctgh **3** ctnh
hyperbolic secant mathematics sech
hyperbolic sine mathematics sinh
hyperbolic tangent tanh
hypercharge physics Y
hyperfine biology HF
hyperfine structure hfs or HFS (spectral lines in chemical analysis)
hyperfine structure quantum number physics F
hyperglycemic factor HGF
hypermetropic astigmatism ah.
Hypersonic Test Vehicle HTV
hypersonic transport HST
hyphenation and justification H & J (OUP: H.& J.)
hypodermic 1 hyp. **2** hypo.
hypotenuse hyp.
hypothalamic-pituitary-adrenal HPA
hypothesis 1 hyp. **2** hypoth.
hypothetical 1 hyp. **2** hypoth.
hypoxanthine, aminopterin, thymidine HAT (medium for tissue culture)
hypoxanthine-guanine phosphoribosyltransferase PRTase
hypoxanthine-guanine phosphoribosyl transferase HGPRT or HGPTase
hysteria hys. or hyst.

I

I owe you IOU or I.O.U. (GPO, OUP: IOU; NYT: i.o.u.)
Iceland 1 I **2** Ice.
Icelandic 1 I **2** Ice. **3** Icel. (MLA: Icel.; OUP: Ice.)
ichthyology ich. or ichth. or ichthyol.
icing ICG
iconography icon.
Idaho 1 I or I. **2** ID (Zip Code) **3** Id. **4** Ida.
identification 1 ID or I.D. **2** iden. or ident.
identification point IP
identification, friend or foe IFF (of aircraft)
identified flying object IFO
identifier sequence biochemistry ID
identity iden. or ident.
identity card IC
idiopathic hypertrophic subaortic stenosis IHSS
if and only if mathematics IFF or iff
if necessary pharmaceutics s.o.s.
ignition 1 ig. **2** ign.
Iliad Il or Il.
illegitimate illegit.

illicit diamond buyer or **buying** I.D.B. or IDB
illicit gold dealer IGD or i.g.d.
Illinois 1 IL (Zip Code) **2** Ill.
Illinois Institute of Technology IIT
illiterate illit.
illuminated 1 ill. **2** illum.
Illuminating Engineering Society IES
illumination physics E
illustrated 1 il or il. **2** ill. **3** illus. or illust. (MLA, OUP: illus.)
Illustrated London News ILN
illustration 1 il or il. **2** ill. **3** illus. or illust. (MLA, OUP: illus.)
illustrator ill. or Ill.
illustrious men CC.VV.
image intelligence IMINT
image maximum Imax
image motion compensation photography IMC
image orthicon IO
imaginary imag.
imaginary number mathematics i
imaginary number $\sqrt{-1}$ j
iminodiacetic acid IDA
imitation imit.
imitative imit.
immature im.
immediate immed.
immediate access storage computers IAS
immediate constituent IC (of a sentence)

immediately 1 imdt. **2** medicine, pharmaceutics stat. or stat
immediately available commerce IA
Immigration and Nationality Department Electronic Computer System INDECS
Immigration and Naturalization Service INS
immune complex IC
immune renal disease medicine IRD
immune response Ir
immunity test medicine IT
immunizing unit IU or I.U.
immunoglobulin Ig
immunoglobulin-binding factor biochemistry IBF
immunology immun. or immunol.
IMP(act) Avalanche Transit Time computers IMPATT
impact point IP
impedance physics Z
impedance angle IA
imperative 1 imp. **2** imper.
imperfect 1 imp. **2** imperf. **3** grammar impf. (MLA: imperf.; OUP: imp. or imperf.)
imperforate imperf.
imperial 1 Imp (paper size) **2** imp. (esp. in measure)
imperial bushel imp. bu.
Imperial Cancer Research Fund I.C.R.F. or ICRF

Imperial Chemical Industries *British* ICI *or* I.C.I.
Imperial College of Science and Technoloy I.C.S.T. *or* ICST
imperial gallon imp. gal.
Imperial Order of the Daughters of the Empire *Canadian* I.O.D.E.
imperial standard gallon ISG *or* isg
Imperial Standard Wire Gauge ISWG *or* i.s.w.g.
impersonal imp.
implement impl.
implementation, planning, and control techniques *computers* IMPACT
import imp.
import certification, delivery verification *commerce* IC/DV
import license IL *or* I/L
import quota IQ
important 1 imp. **2** impt.
imported imp.
importer 1 imp. **2** imptr.
impression imp.
imprint imp.
improper *or* **improperly** improp.
improved 1 imp. **2** impr.
Improved Order of Red Men I.O.R.M.
improvement 1 imp. **2** impr.
improvised explosive device IED *or* I.E.D.
impulse 1 im. **2** *aeronautics* I
in a marked or emphatic way *music* marc.
in accordance with IAW *or* i.a.w.
in arguing *law* arg.
in bond *commerce* IB *or* I.B.
in care of C/O *or* c/o *or* c.o.
in charge i/c
in collaboration with collab.
in connection with ICW *or* icw
in divided doses or parts *pharmaceutics* part. vic.
in English Ang. *or* angl.
in equal parts 1 AA **2** A **3** $\overline{aa}$ **4** $\overline{a}$ **5** a
in expectation of death cm *or* c.m.
in good faith *Latin* BF *or* B.F.
in its place *Latin* in loc.
in lieu of ILO *or* ilo
in memory of in mem.
in my humble opinion INMHO
in octaves *music* Coll'ott.
in one's own person *law* PP *or* P.P.
in passing 1 *Latin* **a** in trans. **b** ob *or* ob. **2** *chess* ep *or* e.p. (*OUP*: e.p.)
in peace *Latin* INP
in proportion in pro
in status quo ISQ *or* isq
in the Hebrew year A.H.
in the last prescription *pharmaceutics* ult. praes.
in the name of Christ INC *or* I.N.C.
in the name of God *Latin* I.D.N.
in the place cited 1 lc *or* l.c. **2** *Latin* **a** in loc. cit. **b** l.l. **c** loc. cit. (*GPO, CSM*: loc. cit.; *OUP*: l.c. *or* loc. cit.; *MLA*: not acceptable)
in the place first cited *Latin* loc. primo cit.
in the place mentioned above *Latin* u.s.
in the presence of the Lords of Session *law* IPD *or* I.P.D.

in the same place 1 ibid. *or* ibid **2** *Latin* ib. (*GPO*: ibid.; *CSM, OUP*: ib. *or* ibid.; *MLA*: not acceptable)
in the time of 1 t *or* t. **2** *Latin* temp.
in the usual manner *pharmaceutics* mor. sol.
in the work cited *Latin* o.c.
in the work cited *or* **article** *or* **book referred to** op. cit. (*MLA*: not acceptable)
in the year *Latin* **1** an. **2** ann. *or* Ann
in the year after the birth of Christ A.P.C.N.
in the year after the founding of Rome A.P.R.C.
in the year of human salvation AHS *or* A.H.S.
in the year of Our Lord *French* AJC *or* A.J.C.
in the year of our redemption ARS
in the year of salvation AS *or* A.S.
in the year of the Creation AOC
in the year of the discovery AI *or* A.I.
in the year of the Hegira A.H.
in the year of the King's *or* **Queen's reign** A.R.R.
in the year of the Lord 1 apr. J.-C. **2** u.X.
in the year of the reign AR *or* A.R.
in the year of the world 1 am **2** AM (*GPO*: A.M.; *OUP*: AM)
in the year since the founding of the city A.U.C.
in this year *Latin* h.a.
in time, resume tempo *music* a temp.
in transit i.t.
in vitro fertilization IVF
in *or* **of this month** *Latin* hm *or* h.m.
in *or* **of this place** hl *or* h.l.
in *or* **at the beginning** *Latin* in pr.
inactivated poliovirus vaccine IPV
inaugurated inaug.
inboard inbd.
inboard-outboard I/O *or* I-O (of a motorboat)
inbound inbd. *or* IB
incentive pay IP
inch in. *or* in (*CSM, OUP*: in.)
inch-pound in.-lb. *or* in-lb
inches ins.
inches per hour IPH *or* iph
inches per minute IPM *or* ipm
inches per revolution IPR *or* ipr
inches per second IPS *or* ips (*MLA*: ips; *OUP*: i.p.s.)
inches per year ipy
inchoate *law, grammar* inch. *or* incho.
inchoative *law, grammar* inch. *or* incho.
incision and drainage *medicine* I and D *or* I & D
incisor i *or* i.
inclination i
incline incl.
inclined incl.
inclosure 1 inc. *or* inc **2** incl.
included 1 inc. **2** incl.
including 1 inc. **2** incl. (*MLA*: inc.; *OUP*: incl.)
including particular average *insurance* i.p.a.
inclusion body IB

inclusive 1 inc. **2** incl.
inclusive tour IT *or* I.T.
incognito incog.
income inc.
Income Eligibility Verification Systems IEVS
income tax IT
incompatibility incompat.
incomplete 1 i **2** inc. **3** incompl.
Incorporated 1 Inc. **2** Incorp.
incorporated inc. (*NYT, OUP*: Inc.; *MLA*: inc.)
incorporated accountant IA
Incorporated Association of Architects and Surveyors I.A.A.S.
Incorporated Practitioners in Radio and Electronics IPRE
Incorporated Society of Authors, Playwrights, and Composers I.S.A.P.C. *or* ISAPC
Incorporated Society of British Advertisers ISBA
Incorporated Society of Musicians ISM
incorrect incorr.
increase 1 inc. *or* inc **2** incr.
increased incr.
increased value i.v.
increasing incr.
increasing tempo and tone *music* incalz. *or* Incalz
increment incr.
incremental incr.
incremental velocity indicator IVI
incumbent inc. *or* inc
incunabula incun. *or* Incun.
indefinite indef.
indefinite ceiling *meteorology* W
indefinite number *mathematics* n
indefinitely, without a day being fixed *Latin* sd *or* s.d.
indemnity indem.
Independence Ind.
independence ind.
Independent 1 IND (division of the New York City subway system) **2** Ind.
independent 1 I **2** ind.
Independent Bankers Association IBA
Independent Broadcasting Authority IBA
independent distributor ID (of magazines and newspapers)
Independent Grocers Alliance IGA
Independent Labour Party I.L.P.
Independent Literary Agents Association ILAA
independent local radio *British* ILR
Independent News Network INN
Independent Order of Foresters IOF *or* I.O.F.
Independent Order of Good Templars I.O.G.T.
Independent Order of Odd Fellows I.O.O.F.
Independent Order of the Sons of Malta I.O.S.M.
Independent Petroleum Association of America IPAA
independent power producer IPP
Independent Radio News IRN

independent rear suspension IRS or i.r.s. (of a car)
independent sales organization ISO
independent school IS
Independent Schools Association ISA
Independent Schools Information Service ISIS
independent sideband electronics i.s.b. or ISB
independent software vendor computers ISV
Independent Television ITV or I.T.V. (OUP: ITV)
Independent Television News ITN
independent variable statistics IV
indeterminate mass particle 1 IMP 2 Imp
index 1 I 2 ind.
Index Catalogue astronomy IC
index correction IC
index error IE
index number I
index of precision statistics h
index of refraction n
index word IW
indexed ind.
indexed and paged 1 I & P or i. and p. 2 IP or I&P
indexed sequential access method computers ISAM
indexed, paged, and titled IPT or i.p.t.
India 1 In 2 Ind.
India paper IP or I.P.
India Tourist Office ITO
Indian 1 In 2 Ind. 3 Ind. or Ind (constellation)
Indian Administrative Service IAS or I.A.S.
Indian Agricultural Research Institute IARI
Indian Air Force IAF
Indian Army IA or I.A.
Indian Council of Agricultural Research ICAR
Indian Educational Service IES
Indian Forest Service IFS
Indian Health Service IHS (for Native Americans)
Indian Housing Authority IHA (for Native Americans)
Indian Institute of Technology IIT
Indian Medical Service IMS
Indian National Army INA
Indian National Committee for Space Research INCOSPAR
Indian National Congress INC or I.N.C.
Indian National Democratic Congress INDC
Indian National Trades Union Congress INTUC
Indian Navy IN
Indian Ocean and Southern Hemisphere Analysis Center INOSHAC
Indian Ocean Biological Center IOBC
Indian Order of Merit IOM or I.O.M.
Indian Police Service IPS
Indian Space Research Organization ISRO
Indian Standard Time IST
Indian Standards Institute ISI
Indiana 1 IN (Zip Code) 2 Ind.
indicated 1 I 2 ind. 3 indic.

indicated air speed IAS
indicated altitude aeronautics, surveying, geography IA
indicated horsepower IHP or ihp or i.hp.
indicated mean effective pressure IMEP or i.m.e.p.
indicating indic.
indication ind.
indicative grammar 1 ind. 2 indic. (MLA: indic.)
Indicative World Plan IWP
indicator indic.
Indies Ind.
indigenous botany Indig.
indigo ind.
indirect ind.
indirect target damage assessment ITDA
indirect waste IW
indium In
individual 1 ind. 2 indiv. or individ. or indiv'l
individual education plan IEP
Individual Housing Account IHA or I.H.A.
individual package delivery IPD
Individual Practice Association medicine IPA
individual protection equipment I.P.E. or IPE
Individual Retirement Account IRA
individual retirement mortgage account IRMA
Individualized Guided Education IGE
Indo-European 1 IE or I.E. 2 Indo-Eur. (MLA: IE; OUP: IE or Indo-Eur.)
Indo-Germanic 1 IG or I-G 2 Indo-Ger. (OUP: IG)
Indo-Hittite IH or I-H
Indo-Pacific Fisheries Council IPFC
indole, methyl red, Voges-Proskauer, and citrate tests bacteriology IMVIC
indoleacetic acid IAA
indolebutyric acid IBA
Indonesia 1 Ind. 2 Indon.
Indonesia Nationalist party PNI
Indonesian Indon.
indorsement irregular II
induced-draft ID or I.D.
inductance electricity L
inductance capacitance ratio electricity LC
inductance, resistance, capacitance electronics IRC
induction 1 b 2 induc.
inductively coupled plasma physics ICP
Industrial Ind.
industrial 1 I 2 ind. 3 indust.
Industrial Advisory Board IAB
Industrial and Commercial Finance Corporation I.C.F.C. or ICFC
industrial and organizational I/O
Industrial College of the Armed Forces ICAF
Industrial Council for Educational and Training Technology ICETT
industrial design ID
industrial design technology IDT
Industrial Development Certificate IDC
Industrial Engineer 1 IE or I.E. 2 Ind.E.
Industrial Engineering Institute IEI
Industrial Hygiene Foundation IHF
Industrial Injuries Advisory Council IIAC
industrial methylated spirits IMS

industrial operations unit IOU
industrial process control IPC
Industrial Production Index finance IPI
industrial relations IR
Industrial Relations Advisory Committee IRAC
Industrial Relations Counselors IRC or I.R.C.
Industrial Reorganization Corporation IRC
Industrial Research and Development Authority IRDA
Industrial Research Information Service IRIS
Industrial Research Institute IRI or I.R.I.
industrial space facility ISF
Industrial Television ITV
Industrial Training Council ITC or I.T.C.
Industrial Union Department IUD
Industrial Workers of the World IWW or I.W.W.
industrialized building IB
Industry Ind.
industry 1 ind. 2 indust.
Industry Advisory Committee IAC
Industry Council for Tangible Assets ICTA
inert nitrogen protection INP or I.N.P.
inertia physics, chemistry I
inertia survey system ISS
inertial confinement fusion ICF
inertial guidance IG
inertial guidance system aeronautics IGS
inertial measurement unit IMU
inertial navigation IN or I.N.
Inertial Navigation System INS
infant mortality rate IMR
Infantry Inf.
infected area IA
infectious inf.
infectious bovine rhinotracheitis IBR
infectious disease ID
infectious hepatitis IH
infectious laryngotracheitis ILT
infectious mononucleosis IM
infectious pancreatic necrosis IPN
infective dose ID
inferior inf.
infinite inf.
infinitive 1 inf. 2 infin. (MLA: infin.; OUP: inf. or infin.)
infinity inf.
Infirmary Infirm.
inflammable infl.
inflorescence botany infl.
influence infl.
influenced infl.
Information Infm.
information 1 inf. 2 info
information and retrieval I and R or I & R
information bit infobit
information center IC
Information Council of America INCA
information feedback IF
Information Industry Association IIA
Information Management System computers IMS
information officer IO

Information Processing Society of Japan IPSJ

information request IR

information requested in. req.

Information Resource Manager *computers* IRM

Information Resources Management Service IRMS

information retrieval IR

information retrieval language IRL

information retrieval system *computers* IRS

information science IS

Information Sciences Technology IST

information service IS

information storage and retrieval *computers* ISR

information system IS

Information Systems Office ISO (of Library of Congress)

information technology IT

information theory IT

information-processing language *computers* IPL

infralow frequency ILF

infrared 1 IR **2** *British* i.r.

Infrared Astronomical Satellite IRAS

infrared laser IRASER

infrared radiation IR

infrared rays IRR

infrared star IRS (with number)

infrequent infreq.

infuse *medicine, pharmaceutics* inf.

infusion *medicine, pharmaceutics* inf.

inground IG

inhabitants inhab.

inhabited inhab.

inhibitor *medicine* Inh

inhibitory postsynaptic potential *medicine* IPSP

initial boiling point IBP *or* i.b.p. *or* ibp

initial graphics exchange specification *computers* IGES

Initial Operational Capability IOC

initial orbit time IOT

initial phase *or* **point** IP

initial program load *or* **loading** *computers* IPL

initial public offering IPO (of stock)

initial velocity 1 i.v. **2** IV

initial (beginning) init.

initiative and referendum I and R *or* I & R

inject inj.

injection inj. *or* inject.

Inland Revenue *British* IR *or* I.R.

Inland Revenue Office *or* **Officer** *British* IRO *or* I.R.O.

Inland Waterways Association IWA

innate releasing mechanism *psychology* IRM

Inner In *or* In.

inner bottom IB (in shipbuilding)

innings *cricket* inns.

innings pitched *baseball* IP

inorganic inorg.

inorganic phosphate Pi

inorganic pyrophosphate *biochemistry* PP

inosine I

inosine diphosphate IDP

inosine monophosphate IMP

inpatient IP (in a hospital)

input *electronics* IN *or* in

input and output *computers* I & O

input preparation unit *computers* IPU

input, process, output *computers* IPO

input/output 1 *computers* IO **2** *electronics,* *computers* I/O *or* i/o

input/output buffer *computers* IOB *or* i/ob

input/output control system *computers* IOCS

input/output controller *computers* IOC

input/output processor *computers* IOP

inquiry inq.

inscribed 1 ins. **2** Inscr. *or* inscr.

inscription Inscr. *or* inscr.

inseparable insep.

insertion phase delay *electronics* IPD

insertion sequence *genetics* IS

inside I

inside air temperature IAT

inside back cover *advertising* IBC

inside edge IE *or* I.E.

inside height i.h. *or* ih

inside left *sports* IL

inside length 1 IL **2** il *or* i.l.

inside radius 1 i.r. **2** IR

inside right *sports* IR

inside width *or* **diameter** IW *or* i.w.

inside *or* **inner diameter 1** ID **2** id *or* i.d. (*OUP:* i.d.)

insoluble insol.

insolvent insolv.

inspected and condemned IC *or* I & C

Inspection Service IS (of U.S. Internal Revenue Service)

Inspector 1 Ins. **2** Insp. **3** I

Inspector General IG *or* I.G.

Inspector General's Department IGD

Inspectorate of Electrical and Mechanical Engineering IEME

inspiratory capacity IC

inspiratory reserve volume IRV (of the lungs)

installation instl.

installation and checkout *electronics* I & C *or* I and C

installation and service I & S *or* I and S

installment inst.

installment credit selling ICS

installment plan IP

instant inst.

instantaneous inst.

instantaneous current i

instantaneous replay IR

Institute Inst.

institute inst.

Institute for Advanced Study IAS

Institute for American Indian Arts IAIA

Institute for Defense Analyses IDA

Institute for Education UIE (of UNESCO)

Institute for Educational Innovation IEI

Institute for Environmental Research IER

Institute for Industrial Reconstruction *Italian* IRI

Institute for Latin American Studies ILAS

Institute for Local Self-Reliance ILSR

Institute for Motivational Research IMR

Institute for New Generation Computer Technology ICOT

Institute for Research on Animal Diseases IRAD

Institute for Social Research ISR

Institute for the Study of Animal Behavior ISAB

Institute of Actuaries IA

Institute of Aviation Medicine IAM *or* I.A.M.

Institute of Boiler and Radiator Manufacturers IBR

Institute of British Architects IBA *or* I.B.A.

Institute of British Engineers IBE *or* I.B.E.

Institute of British Geographers IBG *or* I.B.G.

Institute of British Photographers I.B.P.

Institute of Business Designers IBD

Institute of Cancer Research ICR

Institute of Chartered Accountants ICA *or* I.C.A.

Institute of Child Welfare ICW

Institute of Comparative Biology ICB

Institute of Contemporary Arts ICA *or* I.C.A.

Institute of Economic Affairs IEA *or* I.E.A.

Institute of Educational Research IER

Institute of Electrical and Electronics Engineers IEEE

Institute of Electrical Engineers IEE

Institute of Electronics IE

Institute of Environmental Engineers IEE

Institute of Food Service and Technology IFST

Institute of Geophysics and Planetary Physics IGPP

Institute of Highway Engineers IHE

Institute of Historical Research IHR

Institute of Industrial Engineers IIE

Institute of Information Scientists 1 I.Inf.Sc. **2** IIS

Institute of International Education IIE *or* I.I.E.

Institute of Journalists IOJ *or* IoJ

Institute of Laboratory Animal Resources ILAR

Institute of Landscape Architects ILA

Institute of Local Government Administration ILGA

Institute of Management Consultants IMC

Institute of Management Sciences, The TIMS

Institute of Marine Biology IMB

Institute of Marine Engineers 1 I.Mar.E. **2** IME **3** Inst.M.E. **4** IOME

Institute of Masters of Wine IMW

Institute of Medical and Veterinary Science IMVS

Institute of Medical Research IMR

Institute of Metals IOM

Institute of Museum Services IMS

Institute of Nuclear Engineering I.Nuc.E.

Institute of Nuclear Power Operations INPO

Institute of Nutrition of Central America and Panama INCAP

Institute of Office Management IOM

Institute of Painters in Oil Colors IOP or I.O.P.
Institute of Personal Management IPM
Institute of Petroleum IP or I.P.
Institute of Physics 1 Inst.P. 2 IOP
Institute of Plant Engineers I.P.E.
Institute of Population Studies IPS
Institute of Practitioners in Advertising IPA or I.P.A.
Institute of Production Engineers I.P.E.
Institute of Public Relations IPR
Institute of Quality Assurance IQA
Institute of Quantity Surveyors IQS
Institute of Race Relations IRR
Institute of Radio Engineers IRE
Institute of Space and Aeronautical Science ISAS
Institute of Space Sciences ISS
Institute of Sports Medicine ISM
Institute of Technical Authors and Illustrators ITAI
Institute of Telecommunications Engineers ITE
Institute of Terrestrial Ecology ITE
Institute of the Aerospace Sciences IAS or I.A.S.
Institute of Trade Mark Agents ITMA
Institute of Traffic Engineers ITE
Institute of Transport IOT or IoT
Institute of Welding IOW
Institute of World Affairs IWA
Institute of World Economics and International Affairs IMEMO
Institution 1 Inst. 2 Instn
institution inst.
Institution of Automobile Engineers IAE
Institution of Automotive and Aeronautical Engineers IAAE
Institution of Chemical Engineers 1 I.Chem.E. 2 ICE
Institution of Civil Engineers 1 ICE 2 Inst.C.E.
Institution of Electrical and Electronics Incorporated Engineers IEEIE
Institution of Electrical and Electronics Technician Engineers IEETE
Institution of Electrical Engineers 1 IEE 2 Inst.E.E.
Institution of Electronic and Radio Engineers IERE
Institution of Engineering Designers IED
Institution of Mechanical Engineers 1 IME or I.Mech.E. 2 Inst.M.E. or Inst. Mech.E.
Institution of Mining and Metallurgy 1 IMM 2 Inst.M.M.
Institution of Mining Engineers I.Min.E.
Institution of Naval Architects 1 INA or I.N.A. 2 Inst.N.A.
Institution of Professional Civil Servants IPCS
Institution of Structural Engineers ISE
Institutional instl. or Instl.
Institutional Review Board medicine IRB
Institutional Revolutionary Party Spanish PRI or P.R.I. (of Mexico)
instruction inst.
instruction address register computers IAR
instruction book IB

instructional television ITV
Instructional Television Fixed Service ITFS
instructions 1 instns. 2 instr. 3 instrns
Instructor 1 In 2 Inst. 3 Instr.
instructor inst.
instrument 1 inst. 2 instr.
instrument approach system aeronautics IAS
instrument flight rules IFR
instrument landing aviation IL
instrument landing approach aviation ILA
instrument landing system aviation ILS
instrument meteorological conditions aviation IMC
Instrument Society of America ISA
instrument unit IU or I.U.
instrumental 1 inst. 2 instr.
instrumental neutron activation analysis INAA
instrumentation and communications officer INCO
instrumentation digital on-line transcriber computers IDIOT
instrumented test vehicle ITV
instruments for the evaluation of photographs IEP
insular ins.
insulated ins.
insulated gate field effect transistor IGFET
insulation ins.
insulator ins.
insulin coma therapy ICT
insulin shock therapy medicine IST
insulin tolerance test ITT
insulin-dependent diabetes mellitus IDD or IDDM
insulin-like growth factor IGF
insurance 1 Ins. 2 ins.
Insurance Rating Board IRB
insured deposits transferred IDT
integral int.
integral boiling reactor IBR
integral fast reactor physics IFR
integrated circuit electronics IC
Integrated Civil Engineering System ICES
integrated data processing IDP
Integrated Data Store computers IDS
integrated drive generator electronics IDG
integrated information system computers IIS
Integrated Information-Processing System INTIPS
integrated injection logic electronics IIL or I^{2}L
Integrated Mission Control Center IMCC (of NASA)
integrated optical circuit electronics IOC
integrated pest management IPM
integrated program support environment computers IPSE
integrated-services digital network ISDN
integrated trajectory system ITS
intellectually gifted child or children IGC or I.G.C.
intelligence 1 Int. 2 int.
Intelligence and Research IR (bureau of U.S. Department of State)
Intelligence Department ID or I.D.

intelligence officer IO
intelligence quotient IQ or I.Q. (GPO, OUP: IQ; NYT, CSM: I.Q.)
intelligence ratio IR or I.R.
intelligent character recognition computers ICR
Intense Neutron Generator ING
intensity 1 I 2 astronomy, physics J
intensity of magnetic field strength H
intensive intens.
Intensive Care Unit ICU
Intensively Supervised Probation law ISP
Inter-American Affairs IAA
Inter-American Commission on Human Rights IACHR
Inter-American Council of Commerce and Production IACCP
Inter-American Defense Board IADB
Inter-American Development Bank 1 I.D.B. or IDB 2 IADB
Inter-American Economic and Social Council IA-ECSOC
Inter-American Foundation IAF
Inter-American Geodetic Survey IAGS or I.A.G.S.
Inter-American Labor Organization Spanish ORIT
Inter-American Nuclear Energy Commission IANEC or I.A.N.E.C.
Inter-American Press Association IAPA
Inter-American Society of Cardiology ISC
Inter-American Society of Psychology 1 ISP 2 French SIP
Inter-American Statistical Institute IASI
Inter-Parliamentary Union IPU or I.P.U.
Inter-Union Commission on Solar Terrestrial Physics IUCSTP
interactive computer graphics ICG
Interagency Committee on Oceanography ICO
Interagency Communications System ICS
Interagency Group for International Aviation IGIA
Interagency Noise Abatement Program IANAP
interband magneto-optic IMO
interblock gap computers IBG
Interborough Rapid Transit IRT (division of New York City subway system)
intercept ground optical recorder astronautics IGOR
Intercollegiate Association of Amateur Athletes of America 1 IAAAA 2 ICAAAA or IC4A
intercom 1 i/c 2 ICOM
intercommunication intercom or intercom.
intercommunication system intercom
intercontinental ballistic missile 1 IBM 2 ICBM
intercostal space medicine IS or I.S.
Interdepartmental Committee for Atmospheric Sciences ICAS
Interdepartmental Radio Advisory Committee IRAC
interest 1 i or i. 2 in. or in 3 int.
interest equalization tax I.E.T.
Interface Message Processors computers IMP

interference frequency rejection unit
  electronics IFRU
interferon *biochemistry* IF
**Intergovernmental Committee for
  Migration** ICM
**Intergovernmental Committee on Science
  and Technology** IGST
Intergovernmental Conference IGC *or*
  I.G.C.
**Intergovernmental Conference on Oceanic
  Research** ICOR
Intergovernmental Copyright Committee
  1 CIDA *or* C.I.D.A. **2** IGCC
**Intergovernmental Oceanographic
  Commission** IOC
Intergovernmental Organization IGO *or*
  I.G.O.
**Intergovernmental Panel on Climate
  Change** IPCC
interim int.
interim report IR
interior int.
interior communications IC
Interior Design Educators Council IDEC
Interior Design Society IDS *or* I.D.S.
interjection 1 interj. **2** *grammar* int.
interleave inter.
interleukin IL
Intermarket Trading System *finance* ITS
Intermediate Inter.
intermediate 1 int. **2** inter.
intermediate distribution frame IDF (for
  circuits)
intermediate frequency 1 i.f. **2** IF *or* I-F *or* i-f
  (*GPO, OUP:* IF)
intermediate level waste ILW
intermediate peritoneal dialysis *medicine*
  IPD
intermediate power amplifier IPA
intermediate pressure IP *or* i.p.
Intermediate Range Ballistic Missile IRBM
intermediate range missile IRM
intermediate school IS *or* I.S. (*NYT:* I.S.)
intermediate-density lipoprotein
  biochemistry IDL
Intermediate-Range Nuclear Forces INF
intermedin MSH
intermittent intmt.
**intermittent commercial and amateur
  service** ICAS
intermittent mandatory ventilation IMV
intermittent positive pressure breathing
  medicine IPPB
Internal Int. *or* INT
internal 1 int. **2** intern.
internal browning IB (of fruits and
  vegetables)
internal combustion IC
internal combustion engine ICE
internal energy U
internal function register *computers* IFR
internal pipe thread IPT *or* ipt
internal rate of return *finance* IRR
internal resistance *medicine* Ir
Internal Revenue Int. Rev.
Internal Revenue Bulletin IRB *or* I.R.B.
Internal Revenue Code IRC
Internal Revenue Office *or* **Officer** IRO

Internal Revenue Service IRS (*GPO:* IRS;
  NYT: I.R.S.)
internal shield *electronics* IS
internal thread IT (in machining)
International 1 I **2** Int. **3** Inter.
international 1 int. **2** intern. *or* Intern.
  3 internat. *or* Internat. **4** intl. *or* Intl.
International Academy of Astronautics IAA
International Academy of Pathology IAP
International Advertising Association IAA
**International Advisory Committee on
  Bibliography** IACB
**International Advisory Committee on
  Marine Sciences** IACOMS
International Aeronautical Federation
  French FAI
International African Institute IAI
International African Law Association
  IALA
**International Agency for Research on
  Cancer** IARC
International Air Carriers Association IACA
International Air Safety Association IASA
International Air Transport Association
  IATA
International Airline Navigators Council
  I.A.N.C.
International Algebraic Language IAL
**International Alliance of Theatrical Stage
  Employees and Moving Picture Machine
  Operators** IATSE
**International Allied Printing Trades
  Association** I.A.P.T.A.
International Amateur Athletic Federation
  IAAF
**International Amateur Basketball
  Federation** *French* F.I.B.A.
International Amateur Boxing Association
  French A.I.B.A. *or* AIBA
International Amateur Radio Union IARU
International Amateur Rugby Federation
  French FIRA
**International Amateur Swimming
  Federation** *French* FINA *or* F.I.N.A.
international analysis code *meteorology*
  IAC
international angstrom IA *or* I.A.
International Antarctic Analysis Center
  IAAC
**International Association for Bridge and
  Structural Engineering** IABSE
**International Association for Child
  Psychiatry and Allied Professions** IACP *or*
  IACP & AP
**International Association for Classical
  Archaeology** *French* A.I.A.C.
**International Association for Dental
  Research** IADR
**International Association for Hydraulic
  Research** IAHR
**International Association for Medical
  Assistance to Travelers** IAMAT
**International Association for Physical
  Sciences of the Oceans** IAPSO
**International Association for Plant
  Taxonomy** IAPT
**International Association for Prevention of
  Blindness** I.A.P.B.

**International Association for Religious
  Freedom** IARF
**International Association for Vocational
  Guidance** *French* A.I.O.P.
**International Association of Aerospace
  Equipment Manufacturers** *French*
  A.I.C.M.A.
**International Association of Aircraft
  Brokers and Agents** IABA
**International Association of Aircraft
  Owners and Pilots Association** IAAOPA
**International Association of Allergology
  1** IAA **2** *French* AIA
**International Association of Analog
  Computation** *French* AICA
**International Association of Applied
  Psychology** *French* A.I.P.A.
**International Association of Bridge,
  Structural, and Ornamental Iron Workers**
  IABSIW
**International Association of Cancer
  Registries** IACR
International Association of Chiefs of Police
  I.A.C.P.
**International Association of Culinary
  Professionals** IACP
**International Association of Department
  Stores** *French* A.I.G.M. *or* AIGM
**International Association of Earthquake
  Engineers** IAEE
**International Association of Financial
  Consultants** IAFC
International Association of Fire Fighters
  IAFF
**International Association of Genito-Urinary
  Surgeons** I.A.G.U.S.
**International Association of Geodesy
  1** IAG **2** *French* AIG *or* A.I.G.
**International Association of Geomagnetism
  and Aeronomy 1** IAGA **2** *French* AIGA *or*
  A.I.G.A.
International Association of Gerontology
  IAG
**International Association of Horticultural
  Producers** IAHP
International Association of Hydrology
  IAH
International Association of Lawyers
  French UIA
International Association of Legal Science
  IALS
**International Association of Machinists and
  Aerospace Workers** IAM *or* I.A.M.
International Association of Meteorologists
  IAM *or* I.A.M.
**International Association of Meteorology
  and Atmospheric Physics 1** IAMAP
  2 *French* A.I.M.P.A. *or* AIMPA
**International Association of Microbiological
  Societies** IAMS
International Association of Microbiologists
  IAM *or* I.A.M.
**International Association of Philatelic
  Journalists** *French* AIJP
**International Association of Physical
  Geography** IAPG
**International Association of Physical
  Oceanography** IAPO

International Association of Poets, Playwrights, Editors, Essayists, and Novelists PEN or P.E.N.
International Association of Professional Numismatists I.A.P.H.
International Association of Scientific Hydrology 1 IASH 2 French A.I.H.S.
International Association of Seismology and Physics of the Earth's Interior IASPEI
International Association of Sheet Metal Workers IASMW
International Association of Soil Science IASS
International Association of Teachers of English as a Foreign Language IATEFL
International Association of Technical University Libraries IATUL
International Association of the History and Philosophy of Science French UIHPS or U.I.H.P.S.
International Association of Theoretical and Applied Limnology French AIL or A.I.L.
International Association of Universities IAU
International Association of University Professors and Lecturers IAUPL
International Association of Volcanology 1 IAV 2 French A.I.V.
International Association of Water Pollution Research IAWPR
International Association of Workers French AIT
International Association on Quaternary Research INQUA
International Astronautical Federation IAF
International Astronomical Union 1 IAU 2 French U.A.I. or UAI
International Atomic Energy Agency 1 IAEA 2 French AIEA or A.I.E.A.
International Atomic Time 1 IAT 2 French TAI
International Automobile Federation French FIA
International Badminton Federation IBF
International Bank for Economic Cooperation IBEC
International Bank for Reconstruction and Development 1 BANK or Bank 2 BIRD 3 IBRD
international banking facilities IBF
International Bar Association IBA
International Bauxite Association IBA
International Bibliographical Description IBID
International Biological Program 1 I.B.P. 2 IBP
International Board for Plant Genetic Resources IBPGR
International Bobsleighing and Tobogganing Federation French FIBT or F.I.B.T.
International Bowling Federation French FIQ
International Boxing Federation IBF
International Brotherhood of Boilermakers (Iron Shipbuilders, Blacksmiths, Forgers and Helpers) IBB

International Brotherhood of Bookbinders IBB
International Brotherhood of Electrical Workers IBEW
International Brotherhood of Painters and Allied Trades IBPAT
International Brotherhood of Teamsters (Chauffeurs, Warehousemen, and Helpers of America) IBT
International Bureau for Registration of Mechanical Rights French BIEM
International Bureau of Education 1 French BIE 2 IBE
International Bureau of Exhibition IBE
International Bureau of Time French BIH
International Bureau of Weights and Measures 1 French BIPM 2 IBWM
International Business Machines IBM or I.B.M.
International Cargo Handling Association ICHA
International Cartographic Association ICA or I.C.A.
International Cartographic Bibliography French BCI or B.C.I.
International Catholic Press Union French UIPC
International Center for Criminological Studies ICCS
International Center for Theoretical Physics ICTP
International Center for Tropical Agriculture French CIAT
International Central Bureau of Seismology French BCIS
International Chamber of Commerce 1 French CCI or C.C.I. 2 ICC or I.C.C.
International Chemical Workers Union ICWU
International Chess Federation French FIDE
International Children's Emergency Fund ICEF
International Circulation Managers Association ICMA
International Civil Aviation Organization 1 French, Spanish OACI 2 ICAO
International Classification of Diseases ICD (with a number)
International Code of Botanical Nomenclature ICBN
International Code Use ICU
International Coffee Organization ICO
International College of Surgeons ICS or I.C.S.
International Commercial Arbitration ICA or I.C.A.
International Commission for Agricultural Industries ICAI
International Commission for Air Navigation ICAN
International Commission for Northwest Atlantic Fisheries ICNAF
International Commission for Optics ICO
International Commission for the Prevention of Alcoholism ICPA
International Commission for Weights and Measures ICWM

International Commission of Jurists ICJ or I.C.J.
International Commission on Agricultural Engineering ICAE
International Commission on Glass ICG
International Commission on Illumination 1 French CIE or C.I.E. 2 ICI or I.C.I.
International Commission on Irrigation and Drainage ICID
International Commission on Radiological Protection ICRP
International Commission on Radiological Units and Measurements ICRU
International Commission on Rules for the Approval of Electrical Equipment CEE
International Commission on symbols, units, and nomenclature SUN
International Commission or Code on Zoological Nomenclature ICZN
International Committee of Onomastic Sciences I.C.O.S.
International Committee of Scientific Management French C.I.O.S.
International Committee of the Red Cross ICRC or I.C.R.C.
International Committee of Weights and Measures French CIPM
International Committee on Geophysics French CIG
International Committee on Laboratory Animals ICLA
International Communication Agency ICA or I.C.A.
International Communication Association ICA or I.C.A.
International Communications and Information Policy ICIP
International Community of Booksellers Associations ICBA
International Comparative Literature Association ICLA
International Confederation of Free Trade Unions 1 French CISL 2 ICFTU or I.C.F.T.U.
International Confederation of Labor ICL
International Confederation of Midwives ICM
International Confederation of Professional and Intellectual Workers French CITI
International Confederation of Societies of Authors and Composers French CISAC or C.I.S.A.C.
International Conference of Agricultural Economists ICAE
International Conference on Information Processing ICIP
International Conference on Large Electric Systems French CIGRE
International Conference on Scientific Information ICSI
International Congregational Council ICC
International Congress of Building Officials ICBO
International Congress of Modern Architecture French C.I.A.M.
International Congresses on Tropical Medicine and Malaria ICTMM
International Consultative Council for Radio Communications ICCR

International Consumer Credit Association
ICCA
International Container Bureau 1 ICB
2 *French* BIC
**International Convention for Safety of Life
at Sea** ICSLS
International Cooperation Administration
ICA *or* I.C.A.
International Cooperative Alliance ICA *or*
I.C.A.
**International Cooperative Investigations of
the Tropical Atlantic** ICITA
International Copyright Convention ICC *or*
I.C.C.
International Correspondence Schools ICS
International Council for Bird Preservation
ICBP
**International Council for Building Research,
Studies, and Documentation** *French* CIB
**International Council for Educational
Development** ICED
**International Council for Philosophy and
Humanistic Studies** ICPHS
**International Council for Philosophy and
the Humanities** *French* CIPSH *or* C.I.P.S.H.
**International Council for the Exploration of
the Sea** ICES
**International Council of Aeronautical
Sciences** ICAS
International Council of Aerospace Science
ICAS
International Council of Ballroom Dancing
ICBD
International Council of Film and Television
French CICT
International Council of Industrial Editors
ICIE
International Council of Jewish Women
ICJW
**International Council of Monuments and
Sites** ICOMOS
International Council of Museums ICOM
International Council of Nurses ICN
International Council of Psychologists ICP
International Council of Scientific Unions
1 *French* CIUS **2** ICSU *or* I.C.S.U.
International Council of Social Welfare
ICSW
**International Council of Societies of
Industrial Design** ICSID
**International Council of Sport and Physical
Recreation** ICSPE
International Council of Travel Agents ICTA
International Council of Voluntary Agencies
ICVA
International Council of Women ICW
International Council on Archives 1 *French*
CIA **2** ICA *or* I.C.A.
International Court of Justice ICJ *or* I.C.J.
International Cricket Conference ICC
International Criminal Police Organization
1 ICPO **2** Interpol
International Critical Tables ICT
International Cultural Exchange ICE
International Cycling Union *French* UCI *or*
U.C.I.
International Dairy Federation IDF
International Dancing Masters Association
IDMA

International Date Line IDL
International Dendrology Union IDU
International Dental Federation *French* FDI
International Development Association IDA
**International Development Cooperation
Agency** IDCA
International Development Research Center
IDRC
International Diabetes Federation IDF
**International Diamond Security
Organization** IDSO *or* I.D.S.O.
international direct dialing IDD
International Disarmament Organization
IDO
International Distillers and Vintners IDV *or*
I.D.V.
international drawing rights *commerce*
IDR
International Driving Permit IDP
International Economic Association IEA *or*
I.E.A.
International Economic Science Association
French AISE *or* A.I.S.E.
International Electronic Post INTELPOST
International Electrotechnical Commission
1 *French* CEI **2** IEC
International Energy Agency IEA
International Equestrian Federation
1 *French* FEI *or* F.E.I. **2** I.E.F.
International Farm Youth Exchange IFYE
International Federation for Documentation
French FID
**International Federation for Housing and
Planning** IFHP
International Federation of Actors IFA
**International Federation of Agricultural
Producers** IFAP
**International Federation of Air Traffic
Controllers' Association** IFATCA
**International Federation of Airline Pilots'
Association** IFALPA
International Federation of Archery *French*
FITA
**International Federation of Association
Football** *French* FIFA
**International Federation of Automatic
Control** IFAC
**International Federation of Automotive
Sports** *French* FISA
International Federation of Bodybuilders
IFBB
**International Federation of Business and
Professional Women 1** IFBPW **2** *French*
FIFCLC
**International Federation of Camping and
Caravanning 1** IFCC **2** *French* FICC *or*
F.I.C.C.
**International Federation of Christian Trade
Unions** CISC
**International Federation of Commercial,
Clerical, and Technical Employees** IFCCTE
**International Federation of Computer
Sciences** IFCS
**International Federation of Consulting
Engineers** *French* F.I.D.I.C. *or* FIDIC
**International Federation of Cotton and
Allied Textile Industries** IFCATI
**International Federation of Electron
Microscope Societies** IFEMS

**International Federation of Film Archives
1** IFFA **2** *French* FIAF
International Federation of Gymnastics
French FIG
**International Federation of Gynecology
and Obstetrics 1** IFGO **2** *French* FIGO *or*
F.I.G.O.
International Federation of Hospitals
French FIH *or* F.I.H.
**International Federation of Information
Processing** IFIP
**International Federation of Journalists
1** *French* FIJ **2** I.F.J. *or* IFJ
**International Federation of Landscape
Architects** IFLA
**International Federation of Library
Association** IFLA *or* I.F.L.A.
International Federation of Musicians
French FIM *or* F.I.M.
**International Federation of Newspaper
Publishers and Editors** *French* F.I.E.J. *or*
FIEJ
**International Federation of Operational
Research Societies** IFOR
**International Federation of Petroleum
Workers** IFPW
**International Federation of Physical
Medicine** IFPM
International Federation of Social Workers
IFSW
International Federation of Surveyors
IFS
International Federation of Teachers Union
French FISE *or* F.I.S.E.
International Federation of Translators
1 IFT **2** *French* FIT *or* F.I.T.
International Federation of Travel Agencies
French FIAV *or* F.I.A.V.
**International Federation of University
Sports** *French* FISU *or* F.I.S.U.
**International Federation of University
Women 1** IFUW *or* I.F.U.W. **2** *French*
FIFDU
International Federation of Youth Hostels
French FIAJ *or* F.I.A.C.
International Fencing Federation *French*
FIE
International Fertility Association IFA
International Film and Television Council
IFTC
International Finance Corporation IFC *or*
I.F.C. (*GPO, OUP:* IFC)
International Fiscal Association IFA
International Fisheries Commission IFC
**International Fisheries Cooperative
Organization** IFCO
International Flame Research Foundation
IFRF
International Freighting Corporation IFC
International Frequency Registration Board
IFRB
**International Fund for Agricultural
Development 1** IFAD **2** IFDA
International Fund for Animal Welfare
IFAW
International Game Fish Association IGFA
International Gas Union IGU
**International Geodesic and Geophysical
Union** *French* UGGI *or* U.G.G.I.

International Geographical Association
IGA
International Geographical Bibliography
French B.G.I.
International Geographical Union 1 IGU
2 *French* UGI *or* U.G.I.
International Geophysical Cooperation IGC
International Geophysical Year IGY
International Graphic Arts Society IGAS
International Grassland Congress IGC
International Hockey Federation 1 IHF
2 *French* FIH
International Horticultural Advisory Bureau
IHAB
International Hospital Federation IHF
International Hotel Association *French* AIH
International Hydrographic Bureau
1 *French* B.H.I. *or* BHI 2 IHB
International Hydrological Decade IHD
International Ice Hockey Federation IIHF
International Ice Patrol IIP
International Indian Ocean Expedition
IIOE
International Information Administration
IIA
International Institute for Conservation of
Historic and Artistic Works IIC
International Institute for Educational
Planning IIEP
International Institute for Environmental
Affairs IIEA
International Institute of African Languages
and Culture IIALC
International Institute of Arts and Letters
IIAL
International Institute of Embryology IIE
International Institute of Interpreters III
International Institute of Philosophy IIP
International Institute of Welding IIW
International Joint Commission IJC
International Judo Federation *French* FIJ
International Labor Office 1 *French* BIT
2 ILO *or* I.L.O.
International Labor Organization 1 ILO *or*
I.L.O. (*NYT:* I.L.O.; *OUP:* ILO) 2 *French*
OIT
International Ladies' Garment Workers'
Union ILGWU *or* I.L.G.W.U. (*NYT:*
I.L.G.W.U.)
International Landworkers Federation ILF
International Language for Aviation ILA
International Latitude Service ILS
International Law Association ILA *or* I.L.A.
International Law Commission ILC
International Lawn Tennis Federation ILTF
or I.L.T.F.
International League of Antiquarian
Booksellers ILAB
International Legal Aid Association ILAA
International Longshoremen's and
Warehousemen's Union ILWU *or* I.L.W.U.
International Longshoremen's Association
ILA *or* I.L.A. (*NYT:* I.L.A.)
International Lunar Society ILS
International Magnetospheric Study IMS
International Map of the World IMW
International Marine and Shipping
(Conference) IMAS
International Maritime Committee IMC

International Maritime Organization IMO
International Maritime Satellite
Organization INMARSAT
International Match Point IMP *or* I.M.P. (in
scoring contract bridge)
International Material Management Society
IMMS
International Mathematical Union IMU
International Meteorological Organization
IMO
International Metered Communication
Service IMCO
International Molders' and Allied Workers'
Union IMAWU
International Monetary Fund IMF *or* I.M.F.
(*GPO, OUP:* IMF; *NYT:* I.M.F.)
International Monetary Market IMM
International Motorcycle Federation *French*
FIM
International Music Council 1 *French* CIM
2 IMC
International Musicological Society IMS
International Narcotics Control Board
INCB
International Naturalist Federation INF
International network Internet
International Neurological Association INA
or I.N.A.
International News Photo INP
International Non-Governmental
Organization INGO
International Nonproprietary Name
INN
international normal atmosphere 1 INA
2 *French* a.n.i.
International Nuclear Information System
INIS
International Nuclear Law Association
INLA
International Oceanographic Foundation
IOF
International Olympic Committee IOC *or*
I.O.C.
International Oranization of Consumers
Unions IOCU
International Organization Affairs IOA
International Organization for Migration
IOM
International Organization for Pure and
Applied Biophysics IOPAB
International Organization for
Standardization IOS
International Organization for Vacuum
Science and Technology IOVST
International Organization of Citrus
Virologists IOCV
International Organization of Employers
IOE
International Organization of Journalists
1 IOJ 2 *French* O.I.J.
International Organization of Masters,
Mates and Pilots MMP *or* M.M.P.
International Patent Institute *French* IIB
International Permanent Bureau of Motor
Manufacturers IPBMM
International Pharmacopoeia *French* PI *or*
P.I.
International Philatelic Federation *French*
FIP *or* F.I.P.

International Phonetic Alphabet IPA
International Phonetic Association IPA *or*
I.P.A.
International Planned Parenthood
Federation IPPF
International Polar Commission IPC
International Police Association IPA
International Political Science Association
IPSA
International Practical Temperature Scale
IPTS
International Press Association IPA *or*
I.P.A.
International Press Institute IPI *or* I.P.I.
International Printing Pressmen and
Assistants' Union I.P.P.A.U.
International Prisoners Aid Association
IPAA
International Professional Tennis Players
Association IPTPA
International Professional Union of
Gynecologists and Obstetricians *French*
UPIGO
International Project for the Evaluation of
Educational Achievement IEA
International Psychoanalytical Association
IPA
International Public Relations Association
IPRA
International Publishers' Association IPA *or*
I.P.A.
International Quiet Sun Year IQSY
International Radiation Protection
Association IRPA
International Radio and Television
Organization *French* OIRT
International Radio and Television Society
IRTS
International Radio Communication
Consultative Committee *French* CCIR
International Radio Medical Center *French*
CIRM
international radium unit IRU
International Railway Transports *French*
TIF
International Reading Association IRA *or*
I.R.A.
International Red Cross IRC *or* I.R.C.
international registration IR
International Relief Organization IRO
International Rescue Committee IRC
International Research and Exchange
Board IREX
International Research and Training
Institute for the Advancement of Women
INSTRAW
International Research Council IRC
International Review of Applied Linguistics
IRAL
International Rice Research Institute IRRI
International Road Federation IRF
International Road Transport *French* TIR
International Road Transport Union IRU
International Rorschach Society IRS *or*
I.R.S.
International Rowing Federation 1 IRF
2 *French* FISA
International Satellites for Ionospheric
Studies ISIS

International Schools Association *French*
AEI *or* A.E.I.
International Science and Engineering Fair
ISEF
International Science Foundation ISF
International Science Organization ISO
International Scientific Film Association
ISFA
International Scientific Radio Union *French*
URSI
International Scientific Vocabulary ISV
International Seamen's Union ISU
International Secretariat of Entertainment
Trade Unions ISETU
International Seed Testing Association ISTA
International Seismological Summary ISS
International Seismology Center ISC
International Shipping Federation ISF
International Shipping Information
Services ISIS
International Shoe and Leather Workers
Federation ISLWF
International Skating Union 1 ISU *or* I.S.U
2 *French* UIP
International Ski Federation *French* FIS
International Social Science Council ISSC
International Social Security Association
ISSA
International Society for Bioclimatology
and Biometeorology ISBB
International Society for Cell Biology ISCB
International Society for Christian
Endeavor ISCE *or* I.S.C.E.
International Society for Clinical and
Experimental Hypnosis ISCEH
International Society for Contemporary
Music I.S.C.M. *or* ISCM
International Society for Education through
Art INSEA
International Society for Horticultural
Science ISHS
International Society for Human and
Animal Mycology ISHAM
International Society for Music Education
ISME
International Society for Musicology ISM
International Society for Prosthetics and
Orthotics ISPO
International Society for Rehabilitation of
the Disabled I.S.R.D.
International Society for Testing Materials
ISTM *or* I.S.T.M.
International Society for the Protection of
Animals ISPA
International Society of Aeronautical
Telecommunications *French* SITA *or*
S.I.T.A.
International Society of Appraisers ISA
International Society of Cardiology ISC
International Society of Chemotherapy ISC
International Society of Clinical Pathology
ISCP
International Society of Gastroenterology
ISGE
International Society of Hematology 1 ISH
2 *French* SIH
International Society of Interior Designers
I.S.I.D.

International Society of Internal Medicine
ISIM
International Society of Musicology *French*
SIM
International Society of Phonetic Science
ISPHS
International Society of Radiology ISR
International Society of Soil Science ISSS
International Society of Tropical
Dermatology ISTD
International Society of Urology ISU
International Sociological Association ISA
international solar terrestrial physics ISTP
International Space Station ISS
International Special Committee on Radio
Interference *French* CISPR
International Sports Commission *French*
CSI
International Standard Atmosphere ISA
international standard bibliographic
description ISBD
International Standard Book Number ISBN
International Standard Classification of
Occupations ISCO
international standard depth ISD
International Standard Serial Number ISSN
International Standards Association ISA
International Standards Organization ISO
International Statistical Institute ISI
International Statistical Programs Office
ISPO
International Stock Exchange ISE
International Student Identity Card ISIC
International Student Service ISS
international subscriber dialing ISD
International System of Units *French* SI *or*
S.I. (*GPO, OUP:* SI)
International Table calorie ITcal
International Table Tennis Federation
I.T.T.F. *or* ITTF
International Technical Institute ITI
International Telecommunications Satellite
INTELSAT (*NYT, OUP:* Intelsat)
International Telecommunications Union
1 ITU 2 *French* UIT
International Telegraph and Telephone
Consultative Committee *French* CCITT
International Telephone and Telegraph
Corporation 1 I.T. & T. 2 ITT
International Telephone Consultative
Committee *French* CCIF
International Tennis Federation I.T.F.
International Theater Institute ITI *or* I.T.I.
International Thermonuclear Experimental
Reactor ITER
International Time Bureau ITB
International Tin Council ITC *or* I.T.C.
international tolerance *engineering* IT
International Tourism Alliance *French* AIT
International Trade Administration ITA (of
U.S. Department of Commerce)
International Trade Commission ITC
International Trade Federations I.T.F.
International Trade Organization 1 ITO *or*
I.T.O. (*GPO, OUP:* ITO) 2 *French* OIC
International Trade Secretariats ITS
International Traffic in Arms Regulations
ITAR

International Transport Workers'
Federation *German* I.T.F.
International Tropical Timber Organization
ITTO
International Typographical Union ITU *or*
I.T.U. (*GPO:* ITU)
International Ultraviolet Explorer IUE
International Union for Conservation of
Nature and Natural Resources IUCN
International Union for the Study of Social
Insects IUSSI
International Union of Air Pollution
Prevention Associations IUAPPA
International Union of Anthropological and
Ethnological Sciences 1 IUAES 2 *French*
UISAE
International Union of Architects I.U.A. *or*
IUA
International Union of Bakery,
Confectionery, and Tobacco Workers
IUBCTW
International Union of Biochemistry IUB
International Union of Biological Sciences
1 IUBS 2 *French* UISB *or* U.I.S.B.
International Union of Chemistry IUC
International Union of Crystallography
IUCr
International Union of Electrical Workers
IUE *or* I.U.E.
International Union of Food and Allied
Workers Associations IUF
International Union of Forest Research
Organizations IUFRO
International Union of Geodesy and
Geophysics IUGG
International Union of Geological Sciences
IUGS
International Union of Local Authorities
I.U.L.A.
International Union of Mine, Mill, and
Smelter Workers IUMMSW
International Union of Nutritional Sciences
IUNS
International Union of Official Travel
Organizations IUOTO
International Union of Operating Engineers
IUOE
International Union of Orientalists *French*
U.I.O.
International Union of Physiological
Sciences IUPS
International Union of Police Associations
IUPA
International Union of Prehistoric and
Protohistoric Sciences *French* UISPP
International Union of Producers and
Distributors of Electric Power *French*
UNIPEDE
International Union of Pure and Applied
Biophysics IUOPAB
International Union of Pure and Applied
Chemistry IUPAC
International Union of Pure and Applied
Physics 1 IUPAP 2 *French* UIP
International Union of Scientific Psychology
IUSP
International Union of Students 1 I.U.S.
2 *French* UIE

International Union of the History and Philosophy of Science IUHPS

International Union of Theoretical and Applied Mechanics IUTAM

international unit *medicine* IU or I.U.

International University Bureau *French* BIU

international vehicle registration IVR

International Voluntary Service I.V.S. or IVS

International Water Supply Association IWSA

International Whaling Commission IWC or I.W.C.

International Wheat Agreement IWA

International Wheat Council IWC

International Women's Year IWY

International Woodworkers of America IWA

International Wool Secretariat IWS

International Yacht Racing Union I.Y.R.U.

International Youth Hostels Federation IYHF

internetwork Internet

interpersonal orientation IO

interplanetary monitoring platform IMP

interplanetary monitoring probe IMP

Interpol OIPC

interposed abdominal compressions IAC

interpreter 1 int. 2 intpr.

interpretive programming system *computers* IPS

interpupillary distance PD

interrecord gap *computers* IRG

interrogate intgr.

interrogation 1 inter. 2 interrog.

interrogation prisoner of war IPW

interrogation recording location system *navigation* IRLS

interrogative 1 inter. 2 interrog.

interrogator intgr.

interrupted continuous wave *electronics* ICW or i.c.w.

interruptions per minute IPM

intersecting storage rings *physics* ISR

Interstate Commerce Commission ICC or I.C.C. (*GPO:* ICC; *NYT:* I.C.C.)

interstate highway I (with a number)

interstellar matter ISM

interstitial cell-stimulating hormone ICSH

interstitial nuclei of the anterior hypothalamus INAH

Intertropical Convergence Zone ITC or ITCZ

intertropical front *meteorology* I.T.F.

interval int.

interval of uncertainty *psychology* IU or I.U.

intracellular fluid ICF

intracranial self-stimulation ICSS

intradermal *medicine* ID

intramuscular *or* intramuscularly *medicine* IM or i.m.

intransitive 1 i or i. 2 intr. 3 intrans.

intransitive verb v.i. or vi (*MLA, OUP:* v.i.)

intrauterine device IUD

intravehicular transfer IVT

intravenous oxygenator IVOX

intravenous pyelogram IVP

intravenous urography *medicine* IVU

intravenous *or* intravenously 1 i.v. 2 IV or I.V.

intraventricular conduction delay IVCD

introduce 1 intr. 2 intro. or introd. (*MLA, OUP:* introd.)

introduced 1 intr. 2 intro. or introd. (*MLA, OUP:* introd.)

introducing 1 intr. 2 intro. or introd. (*MLA, OUP:* introd.)

introduction 1 intr. 2 intro. or introd. or Intro. or Introd. (*MLA, OUP:* introd.)

introductory 1 intr. 2 intro. or introd. or Intro. or Introd.

invented inv.

invented by inv.

invention inv.

inventor inv.

inventory 1 inv. 2 invt. or invty.

inventory and inspection II

inventory of land use ILU

Inverness Inv.

inversion inv.

invertebrate invert.

investigating *or* investigation officer 1 I/O 2 IO

investigation invest.

Investigation Service IS (of Canadian Post Office)

investigational new drug IND

Investigative Dermatological Society IDS or I.D.S.

Investigative Reporters and Editors IRE

investment 1 inv. 2 invest.

Investment Bankers Association IBA

Investment Counsel Association of America ICAA

investment tax credit ITC

investor-owned utilities IOU

invitation for bid *commerce* IFB

invitation to send *computers* ITS

invoice 1 Inv. 2 inv.

invoice book IB

invoice book inwards *accounting* IBI or i.b.i.

invoice book outwards *accounting* IBO or i.b.o.

invoice value i.v.

involuntary invol.

inward wide-area telephone service INWATS

iodinated human serum albumin IHSA

iodine I

iododeoxyuridine IDU or IdU

ion cyclotron resonance *physics* ICR or icr

ion exchange 1 IE 2 *chemistry* IX

ion neutralization spectroscopy INS

ion-scattering spectroscopy ISS

Ionic Ion.

ionic strength I

ionium Io

ionosphere sounding satellite ISS

Iowa 1 IA (Zip Code) 2 Ia. 3 Io or Io.

Iran Ir or Ir.

Iranian Iran.

Iraq 1 I 2 Iq.

Iraq Petroleum Company IPC

Iraqi I

Iraqi dinar ID

Ireland 1 I or I. 2 IR 3 Ir or Ir. 4 Ire. (*MLA, OUP:* Ir.)

iridescent *biology* irid.

iridium Ir

Irish 1 I or I. 2 IR 3 Ir or Ir. (*MLA, OUP:* Ir.)

Irish Academy of Letters IAL or I.A.L.

Irish Agricultural Organization Society I.A.O.S.

Irish Amateur Athletic Association IAAA

Irish Congress of Trade Unions ICTU

Irish Free State IFS or I.F.S.

Irish National Liberation Army INLA

Irish Republican Army IRA

Irish Society IS or I.S.

Irish Tourist Board ITB

iron 1 Fe 2 I

Iron and Steel Institute ISI

iron line in solar spectrum *astronomy* G

iron pipe size IPS or ips

iron, in solar spectrum *astronomy* E

irradiance 1 W 2 *physics* **a** E **b** H

irredeemable *finance* irr.

irregular 1 I 2 irr. or irreg. (*MLA, OUP:* irreg.)

irregular verb v.irr.

irregularly irr. or irreg. (*MLA, OUP:* irreg.)

irrigation irrig.

Isaiah Is. or Isa. (*MLA, OUP:* Isa.)

ischemic heart disease IHD

Islam Is.

Islamic Is.

Islamic Conference Organization ICO

Islamic Democratic Alliance IDA (of Pakistan)

Islamic Foundation for Science, Technology and Development IFSTAD

Islamic Jihad for Liberation of Palestine IJLP

Islamic Republican Party IRP

Islamic Salvation Front *French* FIS or F.I.S.

Island 1 I or I. 2 Id. 3 IS (in postal address)

island 1 Is. or is. 2 Isl. or isl.

Islands ISS (in postal address)

islands Isls. or isls.

Isle I or I.

isle 1 Is. or is. 2 Isl. or isl.

Isle of Man 1 IM or I.M. 2 IOM or I.O.M.

Isle of Wight 1 IOW or I.O.W. 2 IW or I.W.

isles Isls. or isls.

isobutyl isobutyrate IBIB

isobutylene-isoprene rubber IIR

isobutylphenylpropionic acid ibuprofen

isolated iso or iso.

isolation isoln

isoleucine Ile or ileu.

isoniazid INH

isonicotinic acid hydrazide 1 INAH 2 INH

isopropyl alcohol IPA

isopropylphenylcarbamate IPC

isosceles isos.

isothermal remanent magnetization *physics* IRM or irm

isotope iso or iso.

isotopic weight IW or i.w.

Israel 1 I 2 Is. 3 Isr.

Israel Defense Forces IDF

Israel Society of Special Libraries and Information Centers ISLIC

Israeli 1 I **2** Is. **3** Isr.
issue iss. (of a publication)
issuing office IO
isthmus Isth. *or* isth.
it follows *Latin* seq.
Italian 1 It. **2** Ital. **3** Itl. (*MLA, OUP:* It.)
Italian Alpine Club CAI
Italian Central Statistical Institute ISTAT
Italian Communist Party PCI

Italian Confederation of Trades Union Workers CISL
Italian corporation *Italian* SAI *or* S.A.I.
Italian Free Trades Union Confederation CISL
Italian General Confederation of Labor *Italian* CGIL
Italian limited liability partnership *or* **corporation** *Italian* SAS

Italian Red Cross CRI *or* C.R.I.
Italian Republican Party *Italian* PRI
Italian Social Movement *Italian* MSI
Italian Socialist Party *Italian* PSI
italic *or* **italics** ital *or* ital.
Italy 1 It. **2** Ital. (*MLA, OUP:* It.)
item it.
itinerary itin.

J

J particle *physics* J
jack J (plug or playing card)
jacket jkt.
Jacobean J
Jacobean *or* **Jacobus** Jac.
Jacobian *mathematics* J
Jamaica 1 J **2** Jam.
Jamaica Agricultural Society JAS
Jamaica Broadcasting Corporation JBC
Jamaica Labour Party JLP
Jamaican J
James 1 J *or* J. **2** Jam. **3** Jas. (*MLA:* Jas.)
janitor jan.
January 1 J **2** Ja **3** Jan. *or* Jan (*NYT, OUP:* Jan.)
Japan 1 J *or* J. **2** Jap.
Japan Aeronautic Association J.A.A.
Japan Association JA
Japan Atomic Energy Commission JAEC
Japan Atomic Energy Research Institute JAERI
Japan Atomic Fuel Corporation JAFC
Japan Atomic Power Company JAPC *or* JAPAC
Japan Communist Party JCP
Japan Defense Agency JDA
Japan Development Bank JDB
Japan Engineering Standards Association JESA
Japan External Trade Organization JETRO
Japan Fishery Society JFS
Japan Industrial Robot Association JIRA *or* J.I.R.A.
Japan Industrial Standard JIS
Japan Information Center of Science and Technology JICST
Japan Institute of Metals JIM
Japan Maritime Self-Defense Force JMSDF
Japan Medical Association JMA
Japan Meteorological Agency JMA
Japan National Tourist Organization JNTO
Japan Nuclear Fuel JNF
Japan Oceanographic Data Center JODC
Japan Science Council JSC
Japan Socialist Party JSP *or* J.S.P.
Japan Society JS

Japan Society for the Promotion of Science JSPS
Japan Times JT
Japan Union of Scientists and Engineers J.U.S.E.
Japanese 1 Jap. *or* Japan. **2** Jpn. (*MLA, NYT, OUP:* Jap.)
Japanese Fisheries Resources Conservation Association JFRCA
Japanese National Broadcasting Station NHK
Japanese National Railways JNR
Japanese Red Army JRA
Japanese Standard Time JST
japanned jap.
jargon jar.
jaundice jaund.
Javanese Jav.
javelin Jav.
Jehovah's Witnesses J.W. *or* JW
jen min piao *or* **yuan** J.M.P. (People's Money of China)
jeopardy Jep
Jeremiah Jer.
Jersey Jer.
Jerusalem 1 Jer. **2** *Latin* Hier.
Jesus 1 IHS *or* I.H.S.; see usage note in abbreviations list. **2** Jes.
Jesus Christ 1 JC *or* J.C. **2** JX **3** *Greek* IX *or* I.X. **4** *Latin* IC *or* I.C.
Jesus of Nazareth, King of the Jews *Latin* INRI *or* I.N.R.I.
Jesus, Mary, and Joseph J.M.J.
Jesus, Savior of Men JHS
Jesus, Savior of the World *Latin* ISM *or* I.S.M.
jet 1 J **2** *engineering* j
jet engine J- (with number)
jet propellant JP (with number)
jet propulsion JP
Jet Propulsion Laboratories JPL
jettison and washing overboard *commerce, insurance* j. & w.o.
jeweler jwlr.
jewelry jew.
jewels *horology* j
Jewish Jew.
Jewish American Princess JAP *or* J.A.P.
Jewish Community Center JCC
Jewish Community Relations Council JCRC
Jewish Defense League JDL *or* J.D.L.
Jewish Librarians Association JLA
Jewish National Fund JNF
Jewish Publication Society JPS
Jewish War Veterans J.W.V. *or* JWV

Jewish Welfare Board J.W.B. *or* JWB
Job Control Language *computers* JCL
job data sheet JDS
job descriptor language JDL *or* J.D.L.
job entry subsystem JES
job hazard analysis JHA
job instruction training JIT
job knowledge test JKT
job methods training JMT
job order JO
job safety analysis JSA
Job Training Partnership Act JTPA
job training standards JTS
jocose joc.
jocular joc.
Joel Jo.
Johannesburg, South Africa Johan.
John 1 J *or* J. **2** Jn. **3** Jno. **4** Jo.
John (book of the New Testament) Jn.
John Fitzgerald Kennedy JFK
John the Baptist Jo. Bapt.
Johnson Space Center JSC
join jn
joined jd
joinery join.
joint 1 jnt. *or* jnt **2** Jt. *or* jt.
Joint Academic Network *computers* JANET
joint account *commerce* JA *or* J.A. *or* J/A
joint agent JA
Joint Air Defense Board *military* JADB
Joint Air Traffic Control Radar Unit JATCRU
Joint and Combined Staff Officer School JCSOS
joint Army-Navy JAN
Joint Atomic Information Exchange Group JAIEG
Joint Chiefs of Staff JCS
Joint Command, Control, and Electronic Warfare School JCEWS
Joint Commission on Accreditation of Healthcare Organizations JCAHO
Joint Commission on Accreditation of Hospitals JCAH
Joint Commission on Rural Reconstruction JCRR
Joint Committee on Atomic Energy JCAE
Joint Communications Center JCC
Joint Council for the Welfare of Immigrants *British* JCWI
Joint Council on Economic Education JCEE
Joint Distribution Committee JDC
Joint Economic Committee JEC
Joint Electron Device Engineering Council JEDEC

Joint Electron Tube Engineering Council JETEC

Joint Electronic Research Committee JERC

Joint Engineering Management Conference JEMC

Joint European Torus JET

joint export agent JEA

Joint Industrial Council J.I.C.

Joint Information Bureau J.I.B. or JIB (news pool of reporters)

Joint Intelligence Bureau British J.I.B.

Joint Intelligence Center J.I.C. or JIC

Joint Intelligence Committee J.I.C. or JIC

joint occupancy date JOD

Joint Oceanographic Institutions Deep Earth Sampling JOIDES

joint operating agreement JOA

joint operations center JOC

Joint Planning Council J.P.C.

Joint Planning Group J.P.G.

Joint Production Council J.P.C.

Joint Research Council JRC

Joint Resolution 1 J.R. **2** J.Res. (GPO: J.Res.)

joint services standard JSS

joint stock company JSC

Joint Tactical Command, Control, and Communications Agency JTCCCA or JTC³A

Joint Tactical Information Distribution System JTIDS

Joint Task Force JTF

joint technical committee JTC

joint use JU or j.u.

Joint Users Group JUG

joint venture commerce J.V. or JV

jointly jtly.

Jonah Jon.

Jonathan Jon. or Jona.

Jordan J

Jordan dinar JD

Jordanian J

Joseph Jos.

Joshua Jos. or Josh. (MLA: Josh.)

Josiah Jos.

joule physics **1** J **2** j

Journal 1 J or J. **2** Jl or Jl. **3** Jour. **4** Jr.

journal Jnl. (NYT, OUP: jour.)

Journal of General Education JGE

Journal of English Literary History ELH

Journal of the American Chemical Society JACS

Journal of the American Medical Association JAMA

Journal of the History of Ideas JHI

journalism jour.

journalist jour.

journey jour.

journeyman jour.

Judge J or J.

judge jud.

Judge Advocate JA or J.A.

Judge Advocate General JAG or J.A.G. (GPO: JAG or Judge Adv. Gen.; OUP: JAG)

Judges 1 JJ. **2** Jud. (book of the Old Testament) **3** Judg.

judgment **1** jud. **2** judgt.

judgment notwithstanding verdict law J.N.O.V.

judgment summons law JS

judicial jud.

judiciary jud.

Judith 1 Jth. **2** Jud. (esp. in the Bible)

Julian Jul.

Julian Day astronomy JD or J.D.

Julius Caesar JC

Julius Caesar (Shakespeare) **1** JC or J.C. **2** Jul. Caes. or Jul. C.

July 1 J **2** Jl **3** Ju **4** Jul.

Junction 1 Jc. **2** JCT (in postal address) **3** Jn. (in place names) **4** Jnc. (in place names) **5** Junc. or junc.

junction **1** jct. or jctn. **2** jn **3** electronics, communication J

junction box JB

junction field-effect transistor JFET

June 1 J **2** Je **3** Ju **4** Jun.

Junior 1 Jr. or Jr or jr. **2** Jun. (GPO, NYT, MLA, CSM: Jr.; OUP: jun.)

junior Jnr. or jnr.

Junior Achievement JA

Junior Association of Commerce JAC

Junior Chamber (of Commerce) International JCI

Junior Chamber of Commerce 1 JC of C **2** JCC

Junior Deacon JD

Junior Girls' Training Corps J.G.T.C.

junior grade jg. or j.g. (NYT: j.g.)

Junior Grand Warden J.G.W.

Junior High School JHS (NYT: J.H.S.)

junior officer JO or J.O.

Junior Red Cross JRC

junior varsity sports J.V. or JV or j.v.

Jupiter Jup (planet)

juridical jur.

jurisdiction Juris. or jurisd.

jurisprudence Juris. or jurisp.

Juror Jr.

jury duty JD

just in time JIT (computer inventory system)

just noticeable difference psychology JND or j.n.d.

Justice 1 J or J. **2** Jus. **3** Just.

Justice Clerk British JC or J.C.

Justice Department JD

Justice Management Division JMD

Justice of Appeal JA or J.A.

Justice of the Peace JP or J.P.

Justices JJ.

Justinian Just.

Juvenal Juv.

juvenile **1** J **2** Juv. or juv.

juvenile court JC

juvenile delinquency JD or j.d.

juvenile delinquent JD or J.D.

juvenile hormone biochemistry JH

Juvenile In Need of Supervision law, social work JINS

juxtaglomerular apparatus JGA

juxtaposition jux or jux.

Kampuchean National United Front for National Salvation KNUFNS

Kansas 1 Kan. or Kans. **2** Kas. **3** KS (Zip Code) (NYT, OUP: Kan.)

Kansas Bureau of Investigation K.B.I. or KBI

Kansas City 1 J (in Federal Reserve banking system) **2** KC or K.C.

Kaohsiung Export Processing Zone KEPZ

kaolin kao.

Kaposi's sarcoma medicine KS

Karachi, Pakistan Kar.

karat **1** K **2** k or k. **3** kt or kt.

Kasatuan Aksi Mahasiswa Indonesia KAMI (political party)

Kasatuan Aksi Peladjar Indonesia KAPI (political party)

Kashmir Kash.

Katharine Kath.

kayak K- (with number)

Keel Car (constellation)

keel K

keep standing KS or K.S. (of printing forms)

keeper Kpr.

Keeper of the Privy Seal CPS or C.P.S.

Keeper of the Rolls CR or C.R.

Keeper of the Seal CS or C.S.

keg **1** k or k. **2** kg

Kelvin calorie Kcal. or kcal

Kelvin scale K or K.

kelvins k

Kennedy Space Center KSC

Kennel Club KC

Kensington Ken. or Kens

Kentucky 1 Ken. **2** KY (Zip Code) **3** Ky. (NYT, OUP: Ky.)

Kenya K

Kenya African National Union KANU (political party)

Kenya African Union KAU

Kenya shilling KSh.

Kenyon Review KR

Kerr constant K

Kerry County, Ireland Ker.

ketogenic steroid medicine KGS

ketosteroid medicine KS

key k

Key Word in Context KWIC

keyboard **1** KB **2** kybd

keyboard send and receive KSR

keyed sequential access method computers KSAM

keyhole limpet hemocyanin biology KLH or klh

Keyword and Context KWAC

Keyword in Title KWIT
Keyword out of Context KWOC
Khmer Rouge KR
kicker *football* K
kickoff *football* KO
kidney kid.
kidney, ureter, bladder *medicine* KUB
Kildare County, Ireland Kild.
kilderkin 1 kil. **2** kild.
Kilkenny County, Ireland Kilk.
killed kd
killed in action KIA
kiln-dried KD
kilo- 1 K **2** k
kiloampere kA
kilobar *meteorology* kb *or* kbar
kilobase *genetics* kb
kilobit *computers* **1** Kb **2** kb **3** Kbit
kilobits per second kbps *or* kb/s
kilobyte *computers* **1** K **2** k **3** K byte **4** KB
(*MLA:* KB)
kilocalorie kcal.
kilocurie 1 kc. **2** kCi
kilocycle KC
kiloelectron volt KEV *or* keV *or* kev
kilogauss kg *or* kg. *or* kG
kilograin kgr.
kilogram 1 K *or* k **2** kg *or* kg. **3** kgm *or* kgm.
4 kil. **5** kilo. *or* kilo **6** kilog.
kilogram-calorie kg. cal. *or* kg-cal
kilogram-force kgf
kilogram-meter 1 kgm *or* kgm. **2** kg. m. *or*
kg-m
kilograms per second kgps
kilohertz kHz *or* kHz.
kilojoule kj. *or* kJ
kiloliter 1 kilol. **2** kl. *or* kl
kilomega kM
kilomegacycle kMc *or* kmc *or* kmc.
kilomegawatt kmw *or* kMw
kilometer 1 kil. **2** kilo. **3** kilom. **4** km *or* km.
kilometers per hour 1 km/h **2** KPH *or* kph
kilometers per second km/s
kiloparsec kpc
kilopascal kPa
kilopound kip
kilorad kr
kiloton kt *or* kT.
kilovar kVAr *or* kvar
kilovolt 1 KV *or* K.V. **2** kV *or* kv.
kilovolt peak KVP *or* kVp *or* kvp
kilovolt-ampere KVA *or* kVA *or* kva
kilovolt-ampere reactive kilovar
kilovolt-ampere-hour kVAH *or* kvah
kilowatt kW *or* kw.
kilowatt electrical kWe *or* KWE *or* kwe
kilowatt thermal kWt *or* kwt
kilowatt-hour 1 kWh *or* KWH *or* kwh
2 kWhr *or* kw-hr *or* kwhr.
kilurane U
kina K
Kindergarten K

kindergarten kind.
Kindergarten Teachers Association KTA
kinetic K
kinetic energy 1 KE **2** T
King K *or* K.
King George GR
King Henry H (in plays by Shakespeare)
King James J.R.
King James Version K.J.V.
King John Jn. (Shakespeare)
King Lear Lr *or* Lr. (Shakespeare; *MLA:* Lr.)
King of Arms K.A.
King Richard R (in plays by Shakespeare)
King's Bench KB *or* K.B.
King's Bishop *chess* KB
King's Bishop's Pawn *chess* KBP
King's Counsel KC *or* K.C.
King's Knight *chess* **1** K.Kt. *or* KKt **2** KN
King's Knight's Pawn *chess* **1** K.Kt.P. *or*
KKtP **2** KNP
King's or Queen's Bench Banc. Sup.
King's Pawn *chess* KP
King's Rook *chess* KR
King's Rook's Pawn *chess* KRP
Kingdom 1 King. *or* Kingd. **2** Km. *or* Km
kingdom Kdm
Kingdom of Denmark KD
Kingdom of Sweden KS
Kingdom of the Netherlands *Dutch* KdN
Kings (books of the Old Testament) **1** K **2** Ki.
kip K *or* K.
Kirkpatrick K *or* K. *or* K *or* κ (with number
in cataloging music of Domenico Scarlatti)
kitchen 1 K **2** ki. **3** kit. *or* kitch
kitchen police KP *or* K.P.
knee jerk *medicine* KJ
Knight 1 K *or* K. **2** Knt. **3** *chess* **a** Kt. *or* Kt
b N
Knight Bachelor 1 KB **2** Knt. **3** Kt. **4** Kt.
Bach.
Knight Commander KC *or* K.C.
**Knight Commander of the Order of Saint
Michael and Saint George** K.C.M.G.
**Knight Commander of the Order of the
Bath** K.C.B. *or* KCB
**Knight Commander of the Order of the
British Empire** K.B.E *or* KBE
**Knight Commander of the Order of the
Indian Empire** K.C.I.E.
**Knight Commander of the Royal Victorian
Order** K.C.V.O.
Knight Commander of the Star of India
K.C.S.I.
Knight Grand Commander K.G.C. *or* KGC
Knight of Gustavus Vasa K.G.V.
Knight of Malta K.M.
Knight of the Golden Circle K.G.C. *or* KGC
Knight of the Grand Cross K.G.C. *or* KGC
Knight of the Legion of Honor KLH *or* K.L.H.
Knight of the Order of Australia AK
**Knight of the Order of St. John of
Jerusalem** K.St.J.

Knight of the Order of the Bath KB
Knight of the Order of the Garter KG *or*
K.G.
Knight of the Order of the Thistle *Scottish*
KT *or* K.T.
Knight of the Red Cross. K.R.C.
Knight Templar KT *or* K.T.
Knights of Columbus 1 K. of C. **2** KC *or* K.C.
Knights of Pythias 1 K. of P. **2** KP
knit 1 K **2** k **3** *French* tric
knit into back of stitch Kb
knock down *boxing* KD
knocked down *commerce* KD *or* kd.
knocked down flat *commerce* KDF
knocked down, in carloads *commerce* KDCL
knocked down, in less than carloads
commerce KDLCL
knockout *boxing* KO *or* K.O. *or* k.o.
Knoop hardness number KHN
knot (unit of nautical and wind speed) **1** k *or*
k. **2** kn **3** kt
knots equivalent airspeed KEAS *or* keas.
knots indicated airspeed KIAS *or* kias.
knots true airspeed KTAS *or* ktas.
knotty pine KP
knowledge 1 knwldg. **2** Kwl *or* kwl
knowledge representation language
computers KRL
Kobe Marine Observatory KMO
Köchel K *or* K. (with number in cataloging
music of Mozart)
Köchel catalog KV *or* K.V. (of Mozart's
music)
kopeck K
Koran Kor. *or* Kor
Korea Kor.
Korean Kor.
Korean Central Intelligence Agency KCIA
Korean Service Medal KSM
koruna Kč *or* Kc
kosher K
króna 1 kn *or* kn. **2** kr *or* kr. (monetary unit
of Iceland; *GPO:* IKr; *OUP:* kr.)
krona 1 kn *or* kn. **2** Kr (monetary unit of
Sweden; *GPO:* SKr; *OUP:* kr.)
krone 1 kn *or* kn. **2** Kr (monetary unit of
Norway; *GPO:* NKr; *OUP:* kr.) **3** kr *or* kr.
(monetary unit of Denmark; *GPO:* DKr;
OUP: kr.)
krypton Kr
Ku Klux Klan KKK *or* K.K.K.
kurchatovium Ku (Russian name of element
104)
Kurtosis *statistics* Ku
kurus Krs
Kuwait 1 K **2** Kuw.
Kuwait Theater of Operations KTO
Kuwaiti dinar KD
kwacha K
kwanza Kz
kyat K
Kyoto, Japan Kyo

L

label 1 lab. 2 pharmaceutics a S or S. b Sig.
labor 1 lab. 2 lbr.
Labor Management Reporting and Disclosure Act LMRDA
Labor Party or Labour Party LP or Lab.
Laboratory Lab.
laboratory lab.
laboratory computer on-line inquiry LACONIQ
laboratory instrument computer LINC
laborer lab.
Laborers International Union of North America LIUNA
Laborite Lab.
Labour Exchange British LE
Labourite Lab.
Labrador 1 Lab. 2 LB
lacquer lac.
lacrosse lax
lactation lac.
lactic dehydrogenase LDH
lactobacillus L
lactobacillus lactis Dorner factor LLD factor
ladder lad.
Ladies Professional Bowlers Tour LPBT
Ladies Professional Golfers' Association L.P.G.A.
Ladies' Golf Union LGU
Lady L or L.
Lady Day LD or L.D.
Lady Margaret Hall LMH
Lady of the Order of the Garter LG or L.G.
Ladyship 1 Ladp. 2 Ldp. 3 Lp.
lager lgr. (beer)
Lagoon 1 Lag. 2 Lg.
Lagrangian function physics L
Lahore, Pakistan Lah.
laid in this place Latin H.L.S. or HLS
laid to rest D or D.
Lake 1 L or L. 2 Lk 3 LK (in postal address)
lake l or l.
Lake Superior L. Sup.
Lakes LKS (in postal address)
Lamarck biology Lam. (name of species)
lambert physics l
Lamentations Lam.
laminar flow control LFC
laminar navigation, anticollision LANAC
laminated lam.
laminated-veneer lumber LVL
lamination lam.
Lamont Geological Observatory LGO
Lancashire or Lancaster County, England Lancs or Lancs.
Lance Corporal L Cpl
land 1 L or L. 2 ld.
Land satellite Landsat
Land Trust Commission LTC
Land Use Commission LUC
Land Utilization Survey L.U.S. or LUS
land value LV

land-based test site LBTS
Landé factor g
landed terms commerce 1 LT 2 lt or l.t.
Landing Lndg. (in place names)
landing ldg.
landing craft LC
landing craft air cushion LCAC
landing craft infantry LCI
landing craft tank LCT
landing guidance system LGS
landing helicopter assault LHA
landing ship dock LSD
landing ship tank LST
landing signal officer LSO
landing vehicle tracked military LVT
landing zone military LZ
landmark Ldmk
landscape lndsc
Lane LN (in postal address)
lane La or La.
langley astronomy, physics ly
Language 1 L 2 lg.
language 1 L 2 lang. 3 lg. or lg
lanthanide or lanthanide series chemistry Ln
lanthanum La
laparotomy lap.
Lapland Lap.
laptop LT (small computer)
large 1 L 2 lg. or lg 3 lge. 4 lrg. 5 Latin a Mag. b Magn. or magn.
large aperture seismic array LASA
large astronomical satellite LAS
large automatic navigational buoy LANBY
large calorie physics, medicine Cal.
large closeup photography LCU
large electron-positron LEP
large grain LG or L.G. or l.g.
Large Magellanic Cloud astronomy LMC
large orbiting telescope LOT
large paper (edition) LP or L.P.
large post printing LP or L.P.
large print LP or L.P.
large space telescope LST
large-object salvage system LOSS
large-scale integration electronics LSI or L.S.I.
large-screen display LSD
larger lgr.
laryngology laryngol.
laser detection and ranging ladar or LADAR
Laser Inertial Navigation System LINS
laser mass spectrometry chemistry LMS
laser printer computers LP
laser-energized explosive device LEED
laser-induced fluorescence LIF
last 1 la or la. (weight of wool) 2 finance L
last complete program computers LCP
last in, first out 1 commerce LIFO or Lifo (method of inventory) (NYT: LIFO) 2 computers LIFO or Lifo (of a data file)
last in, last out 1 commerce LILO (method of inventory) 2 computers LILO (of a data file)
last menstrual period medicine LMP
late L or L.
Late Greek or Low Greek LGk or LGk.
Late Latin 1 LL or L.L. 2 LLat.
late-bottled vintage LBV
latent lat.
latent heat physics L

latent hyperopia medicine Hl
lateral lat.
lateral distance of a coordinate y
lateral eye movement LEM
Latin 1 L or L. 2 Lat.
Latin America LA or L.A.
Latin American LA or L.A.
Latin American Association of Development Financing Institutions Spanish ALIDE
Latin American Banking Federation Spanish FELABAN
Latin American Common Market LATCOM
Latin American Economic System Spanish SELA
Latin American Integration Association 1 LAIA 2 Spanish ALADI
Latin American Regional Office LARO
Latin American Solidarity Organization LASO
Latin American Studies Association LASA or L.A.S.A.
Latin-American Forestry Commission LAFC
latitude 1 l 2 L 3 lat. (GPO, OUP: lat.)
latitude and longitude indicator LLI
Latter-day Saints L.D.S.
Latvia 1 Lat. 2 Latv. 3 Lv
Latvian 1 Lat. 2 Latv. 3 Lv
launch acoustic measuring system LAMS
Launch Control Officer LCO
launch escape system LES
Launch Operation Center LOC
launch platform LP
launch telemetry station LTS
launch tracking system LTS
launch umbilical tower LUT
launch vehicle LV
launched laun.
laundry ldry.
lavatory lav.
law 1 J or J. 2 L or L. 3 l or l.
Law Courts LC
law enforcement LE or L.E.
Law Enforcement Assistance Act LEAA
Law Enforcement Assistance Administration LEAA
Law Journal LJ or L.J.
Law Latin LL or L.L.
Law of the Sea LOS
Law Reports LR or L.R.
Law School Admission Test LSAT
Law Student Division LSD
law-abiding citizen LAC or L.A.C.
Lawn Tennis Association LTA
Lawn Tennis Association of Australia LTAA
lawrencium Lr
laws 1 J or J. 2 ll.
Lawyer's Edition L.Ed.
laxative lax.
layer of the atmosphere D
leach-precipitate float LPF
lead 1 ld. 2 Pb
lead covered LC (of cable)
lead lanthanum zirconate titanate PLZT
lead zirconate titanate 1 PZT 2 metallurgy LZT
leader ldr.
leading ldg.
leading aircraftsman LAC

leading aircraftswoman LACW
leading cases *law* LC or L.C.
leading economic indicators LEI
leading edge *aeronautics, computers, meteorology* LE
Leading Seaman *British* LS or L.S.
leaf 1 L or L. (of a book) **2** l or l. **3** *botany* lf or lf.
leaf area index LAI
leaf mold LMD or lmd
leaf protein concentrate LPC
leaflet *botany* lft or lft.
league 1 lea. **2** lge or Lge.
League of Advertising Agencies LAA
League of American Writers LAW
League of Arab States LAS
League of British Dramatists LBD or L.B.D.
League of Conservative Voters LCV
League of Red Cross Societies L.R.C.S. or LRCS
League of United Latin-American Citizens LULAC
League of Women Voters LWV
leakage lkg or lkge
learner L
learning disability LD
learning disabled LD
leased lsd.
least fatal dose *medicine* LFD
least recently used *computers* LRU
least significant bit *computers* LSB
least significant character *computers* LSC
least significant digit *mathematics, computers* LSD
least upper bound *mathematics* l.u.b.
least voltage coincidence detection LVCD
leather 1 lea. **2** lthr
leave l or l. (on a timetable)
leave of absence LOA
leave without pay lwop or l.w.o.p.
leave or **leave at 1** L **2** Lv or lv or lv.
leaved *botany* lvd.
leaves 1 ll. **2** *botany* lvs.
Lebanese 1 L **2** Le or Le. **3** Leb.
Lebanese pound LL or £L
Lebanon 1 Le or Le. **2** Leb.
lecithin cholesterol acyltransferase LCAT
lecture lect.
lecturer lect. or Lect.
ledger 1 ldr. **2** led.
ledger folio *accounting* LF or l.f.
Leeward Islands 1 Le. Is. **2** LI or L.I.
left 1 L or L. **2** *Latin* s or s. **3** *chemistry* l- or L- **4** *music* l or l.
left atrium LA
left back *sports* LB
left bundle branch block LBBB
left center LC or L.C.
left ear *medicine* as or a.s.
left end *football* LE
left eye *medicine* **1** LE or L.E. **2** o.s. **3** OL or O.L. **4** OS or O.S.
left field *baseball* LF
left foot (in dance notation) **1** LF **2** L or L.
left forward *sports* LF
left fullback *sports* **1** LF **2** LFB or l.f.b.
left guard *sports* LG or l.g.
left halfback *sports* **1** LH **2** LHB or l.h.b.

left hand 1 lh or l.h. **2** *French* MG or M.G. or m.g. **3** *music* **a** L or L. **b** LH or L.H. **c** MS or M.S. **d** S or S.
left on base *baseball* LOB
left side l.s.
left side of a stage *theater* L or L.
left tackle *football* LT
left upper entrance L.U.E. (stage direction)
left ventricle or **ventricular** LV
left ventricular hypertrophy *medicine* LVH
left-hand side lhs or LHS
left-to-right l. to r. or l-to-r
Leftist Revolutionary Movement MIR or M.I.R.
leg before wicket *cricket* LBW or l.b.w.
leg bye *cricket* lb or l.b.
legal leg.
Legal Advisor LA or L.A.
Legal Aid Society LAS or L.A.S.
legal currency LC
Legal Defense Fund LDF
legally Legit.
Legate Leg.
Legation Leg.
legend leg.
Legion of Honor 1 L.d'H. **2** LH or L.H.
Legion of Merit LM
legislation 1 leg. **2** legis. (*MLA*: legis.)
Legislative Leg.
legislative legis.
Legislative Assembly LA or L.A.
Legislative Reference Service LRS
Legislature Leg.
legislature legis. or Legis.
legitimate 1 Legit. **2** legit.
Leicestershire County, England Leic. or Leics.
Leipzig, Germany Lpz
leisurely *music* adgo.
lek L
lempira L
lender LNDR
length 1 L **2** l **3** lgth. **4** lng. **5** *physics* s
length at water line LWL or l.w.l.
length between perpendiculars LBP (in shipbuilding)
length over all 1 LOA or l.o.a. **2** OAL or o.a.l.
length, breadth, height LBH or lbh
length, mass, time *physics* LMT or l.m.t.
length-to-diameter ratio *engineering* L/D
lens-modulated oscillator LMO
leone Le
Lepus, the Hare Lep (constellation)
less than carload lot *commerce* LCL or l.c.l.
less than container load *commerce* LCL or l.c.l.
less than truckload *shipping* LTL or l.t.l.
less-developed country LDC
lesson lect. (from the Bible)
let a mixture be made *pharmaceutics* m.ft.
let him have *pharmaceutics* habt.
let it be labeled *pharmaceutics* sig.
let it be made *pharmaceutics* f or f.
let it be printed *Latin* imp.
let it be repeated *pharmaceutics* repet.
let the buyer beware c.e.
let the remedy be continued *pharmaceutics* cont. rem.

lethal concentration LC
lethal dose LD
letter 1 let. **2** ltr. or Ltr.
letter of advice *commerce* LA or L/A or l/a
letter of agreement LOA
letter of authority *commerce, law* LA or L/A
letter of credit 1 l/cr. **2** LOC **3** *commerce* LC or L/C
letter of deposit *finance* L/D
Letter Service LS or L.S.
letter shift *computers* LTRS
letter signed 1 l.s. **2** LS or L.S.
lettered lett'd (of the spine of a book)
letters lett.
Lettish Lett.
leu L
leucine leu. or Leu.
Leukemia Society of America LSA
leukocytosis-promoting factor *medicine* LPF
lev 1 L **2** Lv
Levant. Lev.
Level Nor. or Nor (constellation)
level crossing LC
leveraged buyout *finance* LBO
Leviticus Lev. or Levit. (*MLA, OUP*: Lev.)
levo- *chemistry* **1** l **2** L or L- **3** l- or l-
levodopa or **L-dihydroxyphenylalaline** L-DOPA
levorotatory l- or L-
lexical lex.
lexicographer lexicog.
lexicographical lexicog.
lexicography lexicog.
Lexicography Information Service Lexis
Lexicon Lex.
Leyden, Netherlands Ley or Leyd.
liaison ln or ln.
Liaison Officer LO or L.O.
Liberal 1 L (political party) **2** Lib or Lib.
Liberal Country League LCL
Liberal National Country Party LNCP
Liberal Party 1 Lib or Lib. **2** LP
Liberal-Country Party LCP or L.C.P.
Liberal-Democratic Party LDP
liberation 1 Lib **2** lib. or lib
Liberation Front of Quebec *French* FLQ
Liberation Tigers of Tamil Eelam LTTE
Liberia Lib or Lib.
Liberia Produce Marketing Corporation LPMC
Liberian Bank of Development and Investment LBDI
Liberian, American, Swedish Mineral Corporation LAMCO
Libra 1 Lib (constellation) **2** *astrology* L
Librarian Lib or Lib.
librarian 1 lib. **2** Libn. or Libr.
Library Lib or Lib.
library lib.
Library Association of Australia LAA or L.A.A.
Library Association of Ireland LAI or L.A.I.
Library Association of the United Kingdom L.A.U.K. or LAUK
library catalog lib. cat.
Library Information Service LIS
Library Journal LJ
Library of Congress 1 L of C **2** LC or L.C. **3** Lib. Cong. **4** LOC (*GPO, MLA, OUP*: LC)

Library of Congress Catalog Card LCCC or L.C.C.C.
library on-line acquisition LOLA
Library Science LS or L.S.
libretto lib. or lib
Libyan L
Libyan Broadcasting Service LBS
Libyan dinar LD
License Lic.
Licensed Lic.
Licensed Counseling Social Worker L.C.S.W.
Licensed Driver's Waiver LDW
Licensed Motor Vehicle Dealer L.M.V.D.
Licensed Practical Nurse LPN or L.P.N.
Licensed Surveyor LS or L.S.
Licensed Vocational Nurse LVN or L.V.N.
Licentiate Lic.
Licentiate in Canon Law JCL or J.C.L.
Licentiate in Medicine 1 LM or L.M. 2 ML or M.L.
Licentiate in Midwifery LM or L.M.
Licentiate in Surgery Latin L.Ch.
Licentiate in Theology 1 L.Th. 2 LT or L.T. 3 Th.L. or ThL
Licentiate of Instruction LI or L.I.
Licentiate of Laws LLL or LL.L.
Licentiate of Sacred Scripture S.S.L.
Licentiate of Sacred Theology STL or S.T.L.
Licentiate of the Apothecaries' Company LAC or L.A.C.
Licentiate of the Guildhall School of Music L.G.S.M. or LGSM
Licentiate of the Incorporated Society of Musicians L.I.S.M.
Licentiate of the Institute of Building L.I.O.B.
Licentiate of the London College of Music L.L.C.M.
Licentiate of the Royal Academy of Music L.R.A.M. or LRAM
Licentiate of the Royal College of Music L.R.C.M. or LRCM
Licentiate of the Royal College of Physicians L.R.C.P. or LRCP
Licentiate of the Royal College of Surgeons L.R.C.S. or LRCS
Licentiate of the Royal College of Veterinary Surgeons L.R.C.V.S. or LRCVS
Lieutenant 1 Lieut. 2 Lt. 3 military LT
Lieutenant Colonel Lt.Col.
Lieutenant Commander 1 LCDR 2 Lt.Com. or Lt.Comdr.
Lieutenant General Lt.Gen.
Lieutenant Governor Lt.Gov.
Life Assurance Advertisers LAA
life cycle cost accounting LCC
life cycle management computers LCM
Life Guards LG (British cavalry regiment)
life insurance policy LIP or l.i.p.
life jacket LJ or l.j.
Life Underwriters Association LUA
life-support system LSS
lift aeronautics L
lift-drag or lift-drag ratio aeronautics L/D
lifting condensation level meteorologyendl LCL
ligament 1 lig. 2 biology L or L.
Light Lt.

light 1 L (illumination, shade, consistency, weight) 2 lgt. or Lgt. 3 lt or lt. 4 lx
light airborne multipurpose system LAMPS
light alcohol LA
light amplification by stimulated emission of radiation laser
light and accommodation medicine L & A
light and rapid or light and lively music legg.
light and variable meteorology LV
Light Antitank Weapon LAW
light armored vehicle LAV
light detection and ranging lidar
light difference medicine LD
light distillate spirit L.D.S. or LDS
light fuel oil LFO
Light Infantry Lt.Inf.
light machine oil LMO or lmo
light metal LM
light microscope LM
light observation helicopter LOH
light rapid transit LRT
light transmission index LTI
light value system LVS
light vessel LV or L/V (ship)
light-activated silicon-controlled rectifier LASCR
light-activated silicon-controlled switch LASCS
light-dependent resistor electronics LDR
light-emitting diode LED
light-rail vehicle LRV
light-water reactor LWR
light-year astronomy 1 lt-yr 2 ly or l.y.
lighter ltr. (barge)
lighter aboard ship LASH
lighter-than-air LTA
lightface printing lf or lf. or l.f. (GPO, CSM: lf.)
lighthouse 1 LH 2 lh
lighting ltg
lightning 1 ltng. 2 meteorology l or l.
lightning arrester LA
lightweight LW
lilangeni L
liminal sensitivity physiology LS
limit 1 lim. 2 LMT or lmt
limit address register computers LAR
limit of flocculation medicine LF
limit of impurities chemistry LOI or l.o.i.
Limited 1 Ld. 2 commerce Ltd.
limited 1 LMTD or lmtd 2 commerce Ltd. or ltd. (GPO, OUP: Ltd.; MLA: ltd.)
limited duty officer LDO
limited liability commerce, insurance LL
limited liability company German 1 e.G.m.b.H. 2 G.m.b.H. or GmbH
Limited Liability Partnership L.L.P. or LLP
limited partnership commerce, law LP
limited signed edition L.S.E. or LSE or l.s.e.
limited space charge accumulation electronics LSA
Limited Test Ban Treaty LTBT
limited voting LV (stock rights)
limousine limo or limo.
Lincoln Linc.
Lincolnshire County, England Lincs or Lincs.
line l or l.

line buffer computers LB
line by line LL or L/L
line feed computers LF
line of balance LOB
line of communications L of C
line of duty 1 LD 2 LOD
line of least resistance LLR
line of position navigation LOP
line of scrimmage football LOS
line of sight LOS
line replacement unit LRU
line squall meteorology Kq
line termination unit computers LTU
line voltage regulator LVR
lineal lin.
linear lin.
linear acceleration a
linear accelerator LINAC or linac
Linear Accelerator Laboratory LAL
linear accelerator regenerator reactor LARR
linear accelerator–driven reactor LADR
linear aeronautical chart LAC
linear alkylate sulfonate LAS
linear combination of atomic orbitals physics, chemistry LCAO
linear elastic fracture mechanics LEFM
linear energy-transfer LET
linear foot or feet 1 lin. ft. 2 lft or l.ft.
linear induction motor LIM or L.I.M.
Linear Information Programming Language LIPL
linear integrated circuit LIC
linear predictive coding computers LPC
linear programming computers LP
linear strain E
linear synchronous motor LSM
linear variable-differential transformer LVDT
lineman lmn.
lines ll.
lines of communication LOC
lines per inch lpi
lines per minute LPM
Linguistic Atlas of France ALF
Linguistic Society of America LSA
linguistics ling.
liniment lin.
lining lng.
link li. (in surveyor's measure)
Linnaeus Linn.
Linnean 1 L 2 Linn.
Linnean Society LS or L.S.
linotype lino. or Lino.
Linz-Donawitz LD
lipopolysaccharide LPS or lps
lipotropic hormone LPH
liquefied natural gas LNG
liquefied petroleum LP
liquefied petroleum gas 1 LGP 2 LPG
liquid liq.
liquid air cycle engine LACE
liquid chromatography LC
liquid crystal LC or L.C.
liquid crystal diode LCD
liquid crystal display LCD
liquid crystal polymer LCP
liquid extract pharmaceutics ext.liq.
liquid hourly space velocity engineering LHSV

Liquid Metal Engineering Center LMEC
liquid metal fast breeder reactor LMFBR
liquid metal fuel reactor LMFR
liquid metal reactor LMR
liquid nitrogen LN or LN$_2$
liquid oxygen 1 LO or LO$_2$ 2 LOX or lox
  (GPO: lox)
liquid ozone LOZ
liquid phase epitaxy LPE
liquid propellant LP
liquid propellant rocket LPR
liquid protein diet LPD
liquid scintillation counter LSC
liquid scintillation detector LSD
liquid or liquefied propane LP
liquor liq.
Liquor Control Board LCB
lira 1 L 2 l or l. 3 li. 4 lr.
lira Italy or lira italiana Lit
Lisbon, Portugal Lis.
list price LP
list processing computers Lisp or LISP
List Processing Language computers LPL
liter 1 l or l. 2 lit. or lit
Literacy Volunteers of America LVA
literal lit.
literally lit.
literary 1 lit. or Lit. 2 lt or lt.
literary criticism lit.crit.
Literary Market Place LMP
literature 1 lit. or Lit. 2 lt or lt.
lithium 1 L 2 Li
lithograph lith. or litho.
Lithographers and Printers National
  Association LPNA
lithography lith. or lithog.
lithology geology, medicine lithol.
Lithuania Lith.
Lithuanian Lith.
little music p or p.
Little Bear UMi (constellation)
Little Dipper UMi (constellation)
little green man or men LGM
Little Horse Equ (constellation)
Little League LL
Little Lion LMi (constellation)
liturgical liturg.
liturgics liturg.
Liturgies Liturg.
Liturgy Liturg.
live load LL
lively music 1 allo. 2 anim. 3 Scherz. 4 viv.
  or Viv.
Liverpool 1 Liv. 2 Lpool or L'pool
Liverpool Marine Biological Committee
  LMBC
living room 1 liv. rm. 2 LR or L.R.
Lizard Lac (constellation)
Lloyd's machinery certificate LMC or L.M.C.
Lloyd's Register LR or L.R.
load 1 ld. 2 W or w
load accumulator electronics LAC
load classification number LCN
load factor aeronautics n
load on call computers LOCAL
load water line LWL or l.w.l.
load-limiting resistor electronics LLR
loading ldg.
loan ln

loans and discounts L & D
local 1 L 2 l 3 lcl. 4 loc.
Local Access and Transport Area LATA
local and remote printing computers LARP
local apparent noon navigation LAN or
  l.a.n.
local apparent time LAT or l.a.t.
local area network computers LAN
local area networks computers LANS
Local Authorities Management Services and
  Computer Committee LAMSAC
Local Authority LA
local board LB or L.B.
local civil noon LCN
local civil time LCT or l.c.t.
Local Defence Volunteers or Volunteer LDV
  or L.D.V.
Local Education Authority British L.E.A.
local excitatory state physics LES or les
local government board L.G.B.
local hour angle astronomy, navigation LHA
local mean time LMT or l.m.t. or lmt
local origination LO
local sidereal time astronomy LST or l.s.t.
local standard time LST or l.s.t.
local sunset LS
local time 1 LT 2 lt or l.t.
locality lcty.
localizer directional aid aeronautics LDA
location 1 loc. 2 locn
locked lkd
locker Lkr.
locking lkg
locomotion loco.
locomotive loco.
Lodge LDG (in postal address)
lodging 1 ldg. 2 lodg
lodgings lodg
log run LR (of timber)
logarithm log. or log (GPO, OUP: log)
logarithmic decrement physics log-dec
logarithmic mean temperature difference
  LMTD
logic log.
logic design translator LDT
logic unit computers lu or LU
logic or logical commands computers
  LOGANDS
logical inferences per second computers
  LIPS or lips
logical input-output control system
  computers LIOCS
logical program computers LOGRAM
logistic log.
logistical log.
logistics log. or Log.
Lombardy, Italy Lomb.
London 1 L 2 Ln. 3 Lon. 4 Lond.
London Academy of Music L.A.M.
London Academy of Music and Dramatic
  Art L.A.M.D.A.
London Bankers Clearing House LBCH
London College of Music LCM or L.C.M.
London International Financial Futures
  Exchange LIFFE
London Mathematical Society LMS or L.M.S.
London Metal Exchange L.M.E.
London Missionary Society LMS or L.M.S.
London Passenger Transport Board LPTB

London Pharmacopoeia PL or P.L.
London Philharmonic Orchestra LPO or
  L.P.O.
London School of Economics L.S.E. or LSE
London Stock Exchange L.S.E. or LSE
London Symphony Orchestra LSO or L.S.O.
London Transport LT
London Underwriters Association LUA
London Weekend Television LWT
Londonderry, Northern Ireland Lond.
long 1 l 2 lg. or lg 3 physics L
Long Duration Exposure Facility LDEF
long instruction format engine computers
  LIFE
Long Island LI (NYT: L.I.; OUP: LI)
Long Island Expressway LIE
long jump sports LJ
long meter music LM or L.M.
long meter double music LMD or L.M.D.
long particular meter music LPM or L.P.M.
long primer LP or L.P.
long range LR
long run LR
long shot photography LS
long terminal repeat biology LTR
long ton 1 lg. tn. 2 LT 3 lt
long ton unit LTU
long wave LW
long wheelbase LWB or lwb
long-acting thyroid stimulator LATS
long-baseline radar LOBAR
long-chain fatty acid chemistry LCFA
long-distance call LDC
Long-Distance Xerography LDX
long-range accuracy LORAC
long-range active detection LORAD
long-range air antisubmarine capability
  aircraft LRAACA
long-range ballistic missile LRBM
long-range data computers LRD
Long-Range Intermediate Nuclear Forces
  LRINF
long-range navigation LORAN or loran
  (GPO: loran)
long-range planning LRP
Long-Range Theater Nuclear Forces LRTNF
Long-Term and Expanded Program of
  Oceanic Research and Exploration LEPORE
long-term memory LTM
long-tube vertical LTV (distillation process)
longer lgr.
longer combination vehicles LCV (tandem
  trailer trucks)
longitude 1 L 2 l 3 lon. 4 long. (GPO, CSM,
  OUP: long.)
longitudinal longl.
longitudinal center of buoyancy LCB or
  l.c.b.
longitudinal center of flotation LCF or l.c.f.
longitudinal center of gravity LCG or l.c.g.
longitudinal distance of a coordinate X or x
longitudinal interval LI or l.i.
longitudinal redundancy check computers
  LRC
longitudinal section biology LS
longitudinal video recording LVR
Longo L (in cataloging keyboard
  compositions of Domenico Scarlatti)
loop test electricity lt or l.t.

loose leaf l.l. or l/l.
Lord 1 DNUS or Dnus 2 Dom. 3 D or D.
   4 Ld. (part of title)
Lord Advocate of Scotland LAS or L.A.S.
Lord Chamberlain British LC or L.C.
Lord Chancellor British LC or L.C.
Lord Chief Justice L.C.J.
Lord Justice LJ or L. J.
Lord Justices L.JJ.
Lord Mayor LM or L.M.
Lord Privy Seal LPS or L.P.S.
Lordship 1 Ldp. 2 Lp.
Los Alamos National Laboratory
   LANL
Los Angeles LA
loss and damage insurance L & D
loss of coolant accident LOCA
loss of fluid mechanics, medicine LOF
loss of fluid test LOFT
loss of signal LOS
loss on ignition LOI or loi
lost sports L
lot tolerance percent defective engineering
   LTPD
Lothian Loth.
loti L
lotion pharmaceutics lot.
Lou Gherig's disease ALS or a.l.s.
loud music F or f
loud and then soft music fp
loudspeaker LS
Louisiana 1 LA (Zip Code) 2 La or La. 3 Lou.
   (NYT, OUP: La.)
Love's Labor's Lost LLL or L.L.L. (MLA: LLL)
Low linguistics L or L.
low finance, meteorology L
low alcohol LA
low altitude LA
low birth weight medicine LBW
low blood pressure LBP
low calorie LC
low carbon LC
low data rate input computers LDRI
low density LD
Low Dutch LD
low earth orbit LEO
low frequency 1 lf or l-f 2 LF or L-F (GPO: LF;
   OUP: LF or l.f.)
Low German 1 L.Ger. 2 LG or LG.
Low Greek or Late Greek LGr.
low level LL
low middling clause LMC or l.m.c.
low pass electronics LP
low power LP
low pressure LP or L.P. or l.p.
low speed LS
low temperature meteorology, physics LT
low tension engineering, physics 1 LT 2 lt or
   l.t.
low viscosity index LVI
low voltage LV or l.v.
low water LW

low-altitude bombing system LABS
low-altitude coverage radar LACR
low-altitude navigation and targeting
   infrared system LANTIRN
low-altitude space platform LASP
low-cost automation LCA
low-cost production LCP
low-density data system LDDS
low-density lipoprotein LDL
low-density polyethylene LDP or LDPE
Low-Energy Anti-Proton Ring LEAR
low-energy electron diffraction LEED
low-energy positron diffraction LEPD
low-fat diet LFD or L.F.D.
low-frequency current LFC or lfc
low-frequency oscillator LFO
low-frequency radio telescope LOFT
low-level exposure LLE
low-level logic computers LLL
low-level waste LLW
low-light television LLTV
low-power acquisition radar LOPAR
low-power television LPTV
low-pressure chamber LPC
low-pressure coolant LPC
low-speed logic computers LSL
low-water line LWL
low-water mark LWM
Lower Lr or Lr.
lower back disorder LBD
lower back pain LBP
lower case lc or lc. or l/c (GPO, CSM: lc.;
   OUP: l.c.)
lower control limit LCL
lower court decision LCD or L.C.D.
lower dead center engineering LDC or l.d.c.
lower esophageal sphincter LES
lower half 1 LH 2 lh
lower hour angle astronomy LHA
lower left LL
lower left center LLC or llc
lower limit electronics LL
lower right LR
lower-body negative pressure LBNP
lowest finance L
lowest effective power LEP
lowest quartile statistics LQ
lowest required radiating power LRRP
lowest useful or usable high frequency LUF
   or LUHF or luhf
lowest or least common denominator
   mathematics LCD or l.c.d.
lowest or least common factor mathematics
   LCF or l.c.f.
lowest or least common multiple
   mathematics LCM or l.c.m.
Loyal Order of Moose 1 L.O.M. or LOM
   2 L.O.O.M.
loyalty loy.
Lübeck, Germany Lbc
lubricant lub.
lubricate lub.

lubricating lub.
lubricating oil LO
luggage lug.
Luke Lk or Lk.
lumbar puncture LP
lumber 1 lbr. 2 lum. or lumb.
lumen 1 l 2 lm 3 lu
lumen per watt lm/w
lumen-hour 1 lhr or l-hr. 2 lmhr or lm-hr.
lumens per watt 1 l/w 2 LPW or l.p.w.
luminance B
luminosity lum.
luminous lum.
luminous efficiency K
luminous emittance M
luminous flux F
luminous intensity I
Lunar Analysis and Mapping Program
   LAMP
Lunar Excursion Module LEM
Lunar Excursion Vehicle LEV
lunar logistic system LLS
lunar mapping system LUMAS
Lunar Module LM
lunar orbit insertion LOI
Lunar Polar Orbiter LPO
Lunar Receiving Laboratory LRL
lunar surface inspection LUSI
Lunar-Roving Vehicle LRV
luncheon voucher LV or L.V.
lupus erythematosus LE
luteinizing hormone LH
luteinizing hormone releasing factor LHRF
luteinizing hormone releasing hormone
   LHRH or LH-RH
luteinizing releasing factor LRF
luteotrophic hormone LTH or LtH
lutetium Lu
Lutheran Luth.
Lutheran Church in America LCA
Lutheran Council in the United States of
   America LCUSA
Lutheran Free Church LFC
Lutheran World Federation LWF
lux lx (unit of illumination)
Luxembourg Lux.
lying down medicine decub.
Lyme Disease LD
lymph node medicine LN
lymphadenopathy-associated virus LAV
lymphocytic choriomeningitis medicine LCM
lymphogranuloma venereum LGV
lymphokine activated killer LAK
Lyndon Baines Johnson LBJ
Lynx Lyn (constellation)
Lyra, the Lyre Lyr (constellation)
lyric lyr.
lyrical lyr.
lyricist lyr.
lysergic acid diethylamide LSD
lysine lys. or Lys.

Mac 1 M' 2 Mc-
macadam mac.
Macbeth Mac. or Macb. (*MLA:* Mac.)
Maccabees Mac. or Macc.
Macedonia Maced.
Macedonian Maced.
macerate mac.
Mach M
Mach number Ma
machine mach.
machine direction MD
machine finish MF
machine glazed MG or m.g.
machine gun MG
machine language ML
machine made MM or M.M. (of paper)
Machine Readable Catalog or Cataloging MARC
machine screw *mechanics* MS
machine stress-graded lumber *building* MSR
Machine Tool Industry Research Association MTIRA
machine translation MT
machine-aided cognition *computers* MAC
machine-aided translation MAT
Machine-Oriented Language *computers* MOL
machinery 1 mach. 2 mchy
Machinery and Allied Products Institute MAPI
machinery certificate MC or M.C.
machinery survey MS or M.S.
machinist mach.
Machinist's Mate MM
Mackenzie Mackenz.
macro assembly program *computers* MAP
macrodefect-free cement MDF
macroeconomics macroeco.
macrophage activating factor *biology, medicine* MAF
macrophage migration inhibition *biology, medicine* MMI
Madagascar Mad. or Madag.
Madam 1 Mad. 2 Madm.
madam Mdm.
Madame 1 Me. 2 Mme. 3 *British* Mdme.
made of copper or bronze aen.
Mademoiselle 1 Mdlle. 2 Mlle.
Madrid Mad.
Maelzel's metronome *music* MM or M.M.
magazine mag.
Magazine Publishers Association MPA
Magistrate M or M.
magnesium 1 MAG 2 mag. or mag 3 Mg
magnet mag.
magnetic 1 m 2 mag. or mag
magnetic amplifier MAGAMP
Magnetic Anomaly Detection MAD
Magnetic Anomaly Detector MAD
magnetic bearing *navigation, surveying* MB or m.b.

magnetic circular dichromism *physics* MCD
magnetic course *navigation* MC
magnetic direction indicator MDI
magnetic drum receiving equipment MADRE
magnetic flux density or induction b or B
magnetic heading MH
magnetic ink character recognition MICR
magnetic levitation maglev
magnetic levitation vehicle MLV
magnetic moment m
magnetic north MN
magnetic oxide conversion MOC
magnetic polarization *physics, electronics* J
magnetic pole strength m
magnetic quantum number of *spin* m_s or *orbit* m_l
magnetic resonance *physics* MR
magnetic resonance imaging MRI
magnetic resonance spectroscopy MRS
magnetic resonance tomography MRT
magnetic surface wave MSW
magnetic susceptibility *physics* k
magnetic tape MT
magnetic tape unit *computers* MTU
magnetic vector potential A
magnetic-particle inspection MPI
magnetism mag.
magnetization *physics* M
magneto mag.
magneto-encephalograph meg
magneto-motive force F
magnetocardiograph *medicine* MCG
magnetohydrodynamic 1 MHD 2 *physics* MDH
magnetohydrodynamics MHD
magnetomotive force MMF or m.m.f.
magneton mag. or mag
magnetoplasmadynamic MPD
magnetron mag.
magnification m
magnifying power (times) X or x
magnitude mag.
magnum mag.
Magyar Mag.
mahogany mah. or mahog.
maiden over *cricket* m or m.
mail *British* 1 Ml. 2 ml.
mail order 1 MO or M.O. 2 mo or m.o.
mail order department MOD
mail preference service MPS
mail transfer MT or M/T
main battle tank MBT
main distribution frame MDF
main engine cutoff MECO
main floor of a theater parq or Parq.
main hatch MH
main line of resistance *military* MLR
main meteorological office MMO
main storage unit *computers* MSU
main switch MS
main urban area MUA
Maine 1 ME (Zip Code) 2 Me.
Maine-et-Loire M-et-L
maintenance 1 maint. 2 mntn.
maintenance and repairs M&R
maintenance and supply M&S
maintenance manual MM
Maintenance Unit MU

maintenance, assembly, and disassembly MAD
maintenance, repair, and operating MRO
majestically *music* Maesto.
Majesties MM
Majesty M or M.
Major Maj.
major 1 *music, military* Ma 2 *music* magg.
major basic protein MBP
Major General Maj.Gen.
major histocompatibility complex MHC
Major Soccer League MSL
majority Maj.
make *pharmaceutics* ft.
make a mixture *pharmaceutics* fm or f.m.
make a pill *pharmaceutics* 1 f.pil. 2 fp or f.p.
make good all works distributed *law* mgawd or MGAWD
Malachi Mal.
malacology malac.
Malay Mal.
Malaya Mal.
Malayan Mal.
Malaysia 1 M 2 Mal.
Malaysian 1 M 2 Mal.
male 1 M or M. 2 m or m.
male chauvinist pig MCP (epithet)
male, female m/f
male, female, handicapped, veteran m/f/h/v (in advertisements for employment)
maleic hydrazide MH
Mali M
malignant tertian MT
malignant tumor MT
malleable mall
malleable cast iron MCI
malleable iron MI
maloti M
Malta Mal.
Maltese lira Lm
mammary tumor virus MTV
man on the street *advertising* MOS
management 1 Mang. 2 Mgmt. 3 Mgt
Management and Personnel Office MPO
management by objective MBO
Management Consultants Association MCA or M.C.A.
Management Information System MIS
management job description MJD
Manager 1 Mgr. or mgr. 2 Mngr.
Managing Mng.
managing Man. or Man
Managing Director MD or M.D.
Managing Editor ME or M.E.
Manchester Mch
Manchester Guardian Weekly MGW
Manchester Ship Canal MSC or M.S.C.
Maneuverable Reentry Vehicle MARV
manganese Mn
Manhattan School of Music MSM
manifest hypermetropia *medicine* Hm
Manila Man. (of paper)
Manila, Philippines Mnl.
Manitoba MB
Manitoba, Canada 1 Man. or Man 2 Manit.
manned maneuvering unit MMU
Manned Orbital Laboratory MOL

Manned Orbital Research Laboratory MORL
Manned Spacecraft Center MSC
Manned Underwater Station MUST
Manor Mnr.
Manpower Development and Training Act MDTA
Manpower Services Commission MSC
manual 1 m or m. **2** man. **3** Man. or MAN. **4** music M or M.
manual direction finder MDF
manually man.
manually operated MO
manufacture 1 manuf. **2** mf. **3** mfr.
manufactured 1 Man. **2** manuf. **3** mfd.
manufacturer 1 Man. **2** manf. **3** manuf. **4** mfr.
manufacturing 1 manuf. **2** mfg.
manufacturing automated protocol MAP
Manufacturing Chemists Association MCA or M.C.A.
manuscript 1 cod. or Cod. **2** Ms **3** ms **4** MS **5** Script. or script. (GPO: ms; NYT, OUP: MS; MLA: ms.; CSM: MS.)
manuscripts MSS or Mss or mss (GPO, NYT, OUP: MSS; MLA: mss.; CSM: MSS.)
many-body theory physics MBT
map distance MD
map reference MR
mapping unit mu (of genes)
marbled edges ME
marbled paper sides MPS
March 1 M (the month) **2** Mar. **3** Mch **4** Mr (month)
March, June, Setember, December accounting MJSD
Marchioness March.
mare m or m. (in horse racing)
margarine marg
margin 1 marg **2** mg.
margin of safety 1 M/S **2** MS
marginal 1 marg or marg. **2** mg.
marginal credit finance, commerce M/C
marine mar.
Marine Automatic Meteorological Observing Station MAMOS
Marine Biological Laboratory M.B.L. or MBL
Marine Corps MC
Marine Corps League MCL
Marine Ecosystems Analysis MESA
Marine Engineer ME or M.E.
Marine Engineers Beneficial Association MEBA
Marine Insurance Policy MIP
Marine Resources Monitoring Assessment and Prediction MARMAP
Maritime Marit.
maritime 1 mar. **2** mrtm.
Maritime Administration 1 MA **2** MARAD (GPO: MarAd)
Maritime Air Group MAG
maritime air mass meteorology m
maritime antarctic air mass meteorology ma.
maritime Arctic cold air meteorology mAk
maritime Arctic warm air mass meteorology mAw
Maritime Command MARCOM
Maritime Defense Zone M.D.Z.

Maritime Mobile Phone MMP
maritime polar air meteorology mP
maritime satellite Marisat
Maritime Self-Defense Force MSDF (Japanese Navy)
Maritime tropical air mass meteorology mT
Mark 1 Mk or MK (car model) **2** Mk or Mk. (book of New Testament)
mark 1 a M or M. **b** Mk or mk. (monetary unit of Germany) **2** pharmaceutics S or S.
marked mkd.
marker 1 mkr. **2** mrkr.
Market Mrkt.
market mkt.
Market and Opinion Research Institute MORI
market quotation Cs
market value 1 MV **2** mv or m.v.
marketing mktg or mktg.
Marketing Board MB
markka 1 Fmk **2** Mk or mk. or mk
marksman mkm. or Mkm.
Marquess Marq.
Marquis 1 M or M. **2** Marq.
marriage matr.
marriage encounter ME
married 1 M or M. **2** m or m. **3** mar.
marshal Mshl
Marshall Islands MH (in postal address)
Marshall Space Flight Center MSFC
Martinique 1 Mart. **2** Mqe
martyr Mart.
martyrology Mart.
martyrs MM or MM. or Mm.
Maryknoll Missioner MM or M.M.
Maryland 1 MD (Zip Code) **2** Md or Md.
Marylebone Cricket Club MCC or M.C.C.
masculine 1 m or m. **2** masc. (MLA: masc.; OUP: m. or masc.)
Masoretic Text MT or M.T.
mass physics **1** m **2** (electron mass) m_e **3** (neutron mass) m_n **4** (proton mass) m_p
mass concentration maskon
mass flow rate physics w
mass fraction chemistry X or x
mass fraction (in light or refined matter) chemistry y
mass observation (survey) British MO
mass spectrometry astronomy, chemistry MS
mass storage system computers MSS
mass transportation MT
mass velocity aeronautics G
mass, length, time MLT
Massachusetts 1 MA (Zip Code) **2** Mass.
Massachusetts General Hospital M.G.H.
Massachusetts Institute of Technology MIT or M.I.T. (NYT: M.I.T.; OUP: MIT)
massively parallel processor MPP
Master 1 Dom. **2** M or M.
master Mstr. or Mstr
master bedroom MBR
Master Chief Petty Officer M/CPO
master control MC
master control program MCP
master control routine computers MCR
Master in Hospital Administration MHA
Master in Landscape Architecture MLA or M.L.A.

Master in Regional Planning MRP or M.R.P.
Master in Surgery CM or C.M.
master instruction tape computers MIT
Master Mason MM or M.M.
master mechanic MM or M.M.
Master of Aeronautical Engineering M.A.E. or MAE
Master of Agriculture 1 M.Ag. **2** M.Agr.
Master of Applied Science 1 M.A.S. or M.A.Sc. **2** M.App.Sc. (CSM: M.A.Sc.)
Master of Architecture 1 Ar.M. **2** M.Arch.
Master of Art Education M.A.E. or MAE
Master of Arts 1 AM or A.M. (GPO: A.M. or M.A.; CSM: A.M.; MLA, OUP: AM) **2** MA or M.A. (NYT, CSM: M.A.; MLA, OUP: MA)
Master of Arts in Economics M.A.Econ.
Master of Arts in Education M.A.E. or MAE or M.A.Ed
Master of Arts in Law and Diplomacy M.A.L.D. or MALD
Master of Arts in Liberal Studies MALS or M.A.L.S.
Master of Arts in Library Science 1 AMLS or A.M.L.S. **2** MALS or M.A.L.S.
Master of Arts in Obstetrics British MAO or M.A.O.
Master of Arts in Social Work AMSW or A.M.S.W.
Master of Arts in Teaching MAT or M.A.T.
Master of Arts Teaching Certificate A.M.T.C.
Master of Business Administration MBA
Master of Business Management MBM
Master of Business Science M.B.Sc. or MBSc
master of ceremonies 1 m.c. **2** MC or M.C. (GPO, OUP: MC)
Master of Chemical Engineering M.Ch.E.
Master of City Planning MCP
Master of Civil Engineering MCE or M.C.E.
Master of Civil Law MCL or M.C.L.
Master of Commerce M.Com.
Master of Commercial Science MCS or M.C.S.
Master of Comparative Law MCL or M.C.L.
Master of Computer Science MCS or M.C.S.
Master of Dental Science M.D.Sc.
Master of Dental Surgery 1 MDS or M.D.S. **2** British M.Ch.D.
Master of Design M.Des.
Master of Divinity M.Div.
Master of Economics 1 M.Ec. **2** M.Econ.
Master of Education 1 Ed.M. **2** M.Ed.
Master of Electrical Engineering M.E.E.
Master of Engineering 1 M.Eng. **2** Ma.E. or MaE **3** MAI or M.A.I.
Master of Engineering Physics MEP or M.E.P.
Master of Fine Arts MFA or M.F.A.
Master of Food Science MFS or M.F.S.
Master of Foreign Study MFS or M.F.S.
Master of Forestry MF or M.F. (CSM: M.F.)
Master of Hebrew Literature M.H.L.
Master of Horticulture M.Hort.
Master of Hygiene M.Hy.
Master of Laws LL.M.
Master of Letters or Literature M.Lit. or M.Litt.
Master of Liberal Arts Latin L.A.M. or LAM

Master of Library Science 1 M.Lib.Sc. **2** MLS or M.L.S. (*CSM:* M.L.S.)
Master of Literature or **Letters** Litt.M.
Master of Mathematics M.Math.
Master of Mechanical Arts AMM or A.M.M.
Master of Mechanical Engineering M.M.E. or MME or M.Mech.Eng.
Master of Medical Science M.M.Sc.
Master of Music 1 M.Mus. **2** MM or M.M. **3** Mus.M.
Master of Music Education M.M.E. or MME or M.M.Ed.
Master of Nursing 1 M.Nurs. **2** MN or M.N.
Master of Nursing Administration MNA or M.N.A.
Master of Oriental Languages MOL or M.O.L.
Master of Patent Law MPL or M.P.L.
Master of Pedagogy 1 M.Pd. **2** Pd.M.
Master of Pharmacy M.Pharm.
Master of Philosophy 1 M.Ph. **2** M.Phil. **3** Ph.M.
Master of Physical Education MPE or M.P.E.
Master of Psychology M.Ps. or M.Psych.
Master of Public Administration MPA or M.P.A.
Master of Public Health M.P.H. or MPH (*CSM:* M.P.H.)
Master of Public Services MPS or M.P.S.
Master of Radiology M.Rad.
Master of Religious Education MRE or M.R.E.
Master of Sacred Music MSM or M.S.M.
Master of Sacred Theology 1 MST or M.S.T. **2** STM or S.T.M.
Master of Science 1 M.Sc. or MSc (*CSM, OUP:* M.Sc.) **2** MS or M.S. (*GPO, NYT, CSM:* M.S.; *MLA:* MS) **3** Sc.M. **4** SM or S.M.
Master of Science and Arts MSA or M.S.A.
Master of Science in Agriculture MSA or M.S.A. or M.S.Agr. (*CSM:* M.S.A.)
Master of Science in Business Administration MSBA or M.S.B.A. or MSBus or M.S.Bus.
Master of Science in Chemical Engineering MS.Ch.E.
Master of Science in Civil Engineering MSCE or M.S.C.E.
Master of Science in Dentistry MSD or M.S.D.
Master of Science in Economics M.Sc.Econ.
Master of Science in Education 1 M.S.Ed. or MSEd. **2** MSE or M.S.E.
Master of Science in Electrical Engineering MSEE or M.S.E.E.
Master of Science in Engineering 1 M.Sc.Eng. **2** MSE or M.S.E.
Master of Science in Engineering Mechanics MSEM or M.S.E.M.
Master of Science in Forestry MSF or M.S.F.
Master of Science in Home Economics MSHE or M.S.H.E.
Master of Science in Hospital Administration MSHA or M.S.H.A.
Master of Science in Hygiene M.S.Hyg.
Master of Science in Journalism M.S.J. or MSJ

Master of Science in Library Science MSLS or M.S.L.S.
Master of Science in Linguistics MSL or M.S.L.
Master of Science in Mechanical Engineering M.S.M.E. or MSME
Master of Science in Music M.S.Mus.
Master of Science in Nursing M.S.N. or MSN
Master of Science in Pharmacy MSP or M.S.P. or M.S.Pharm.
Master of Science in Public Health MSPH or M.S.P.H.
Master of Science in Public Health Engineering MSPHE or M.S.P.H.E.
Master of Science in Sanitary Engineering M.S.S.E. or MSSE
Master of Science in Social Work MSSW or M.S.S.W.
Master of Science in Taxation MST
Master of Science in Teaching MST or M.S.T.
Master of Social Science 1 M.Soc.Sc. **2** MSS or M.S.S.
Master of Social Work MSW or M.S.W. (*CSM:* M.S.W.)
Master of Statistics M.Stat.
Master of Surgery 1 Ch.M. **2** *British* **a** M.Ch. **b** MC or M.C.
Master of Surveying M.Surv.
Master of Technology M.Tech.
Master of the Liberal Arts A.L.M. or ALM
Master of the Rolls MR or M.R.
Master of Theology 1 M.Th. **2** Th.M. or ThM
Master of Town Planning M.T.P.
Master of Veterinary Science M.V.Sc.
master oscillator *electronics* MO
master oscillator power amplifier *electronics* MOPA
Master Sergeant M.Sgt. or M/Sgt.
Master or **Mistress of English Literature** MEL
Master's Degree in Teaching AMT or A.M.T.
master-at-arms MAA
masters MM or MM.
mated with X or x
material 1 matl. **2** MTL or mtl. **3** *military* MAT
material recovery facility MRF
material requirements planning MRP
Materials Command *military* MATCOM
Materials Testing Reactor MTR
Materials Transportation Bureau MTB
Maternal and Child Health MCH
maternal resistance factor MRF
maternity Mat
mathematical math.
Mathematical Association of America MAA
mathematician math.
mathematics math. or *British* maths
matinee 1 Mat or Mat. **2** mat.
matins mat.
matriculated Matric.
matriculation Matric.
matrimony matr.
Matthew 1 Mat **2** Matt.
Matthias Matt.
mature M
maturity 1 mat. **2** *finance* Mat
Maudsley Personality Inventory *psychology* MPI
Mauna Kea Observatory MKO

Mauritian Militant Movement MMM
Mauritius Mau or Mau.
Max Planck Institute MPI
maxim max.
Maximilian Max.
maximum 1 max. or MAX **2** mxm (*CSM, OUP:* max.)
maximum acceptable daily intake MADI
maximum allowable concentration MAC
maximum available gain *electronics* MAG
maximum average price MAP
maximum breathing capacity *medicine* MBC
maximum contaminant level MCL
maximum continuous thrust MCT
maximum efficient rate MER
maximum effort ME
maximum gross weight MGW or mgw
maximum legal rent MLR or M.L.R.
maximum likelihood estimate *statistics* MLE
maximum loss expectancy MLE
maximum permissible amount MPA
maximum permissible concentration MPC or mpc
maximum permissible dose MPD
maximum permissible exposure MPE
maximum permissible level MPL
maximum stress MS (of materials)
maximum sustainable yield MSY (in resource planning)
maximum tolerated dose MTD
maximum undistorted power output *electronics* MUPO
maximum usable frequency MUF or muf
maximum working pressure MWP
maximum working voltage MWV
Maxwell or **maxwell 1** M **2** Mx or mx (unit of magnetic flux)
May 1 M **2** My (the month)
may he or **she rest in peace 1** RIP or R.I.P. **2** Q.I.P.
may he or **she rest well** B.Q.
may he rest with all good souls C.O.B.Q.
May, August, November, February *finance* MANF
meals, ready to eat MRE (army field rations)
mean M or m (average)
mean aerodynamic chord MAC
mean annual increment MAI or mai
mean arterial pressure MAP
mean blood pressure MBP
mean body temperature MBT
mean corpuscular diameter MCD
mean corpuscular hemoglobin MCH
mean corpuscular volume MCV
mean deviation *navigation, statistics* MD
mean downtime MDT
mean effective pressure MEP or mep
mean free path 1 *physics, chemistry* l **2** *physics* MFP
mean high tide MHT
mean high water MHW
mean horizontal candlepower MHCP or mhcp
mean indicated pressure MIP or M.I.P. or m.i.p.
mean length per turn *electronics* MLT
mean level ML or m.l.
mean low tide MLT

mean low water MLW
mean point of impact MPI
mean sea level MSL or m.s.l. (GPO, OUP: m.s.l.)
mean solar time MST or mst
mean spherical candlepower m.s.c.p. or MSCP
mean square *mathematics* MS
mean square error *mathematics* MSE
mean survival time MST or mst
mean temperature T
mean temperature difference MTD
mean tidal level MTL
mean tide MT
mean time MT (average time)
mean time between failures MTBF
mean time to failure MTTF
mean time to repair MTTR
mean time to restore MTR
mean variation 1 MV 2 mv or m.v.
meanwhile ad int.
measles, mumps, and rubella MMR (inoculation)
measurable meas.
measure 1 m or m. (size, quantity, bar of music) 2 meas.
measure of effectiveness *computers* MOE
measured ceiling *meteorology* M
Measure for Measure 1 Meas. for M. 2 MM
measurement mst.
measurement information data analysis system MIDAS
mechanic mech. or MECH
mechanical mech. or MECH
Mechanical Aptitude Test MAT
mechanical computer-aided engineering MCAE
Mechanical Engineer 1 M.Eng. 2 ME or M.E. 3 Mech.E.
Mechanical Power Transmission Association MPTA
mechanical time fuse MTF
mechanical transport MT
mechanical wood pulp MWP
mechanically operated MO
mechanically recovered meat MRM
mechanics mech. or MECH
mechanism mech. or MECH
mechanized mech. or MECH
Medal for Merit MM or M.M.
Medal of Freedom MF
Medal of Honor MH or M.H.
medalist med.
median 1 Md 2 mdn. or Mdn 3 med.
median deviation *statistics* Md D
median lethal dose MLD or m.l.d.
median lethal time MLT
Medical Med.
medical 1 M or M. 2 *military* med. or MED
Medical Advisory Board MAB
medical aid post MAP
Medical Assistance Program MAP
Medical Bank Medibank
Medical Board MB or M.B.
Medical Center MC
medical certificate MC
Medical College Admission Test MCAT
Medical Committee for Human Rights M.C.H.R.

Medical Corps MC
Medical Department MD or M.D.
medical evacuation MEDEVAC or medevac
Medical Examiner ME or M.E.
medical internal radiation dose MIRD
Medical International Cooperation Organization MEDICO
Medical Library Association MLA
Medical Literature Analysis and Retrieval System MEDLARS or Medlars
Medical Officer MO
Medical Officers Reserve Corps MORC
medical record MR
medical records indexing MRI
Medical Records Librarian MRL or M.R.L.
Medical Research Council *British* MRC or M.R.C.
Medical Research Council of Canada MRCC or M.R.C.C.
Medical Research Council standard of units of measurement *British* MRC or M.R.C.
Medical Reserve Corps MRC
Medical Review Board MRB
Medical Services MS
Medical Social Worker MSW
Medical Subject Headings MeSH
medical technologist MT or M.T.
Medical Television Network MTN
Medical Women's Federation MWF
Medical Women's International Association MWIA
medical-dental service MDS
Medicare, Medicaid Assistance Program MMAP
medicine 1 M or M. 2 *military* med. or MED
Medieval Med.
Medieval Academy of America MAA or M.A.A.
Medieval Latin ML or ML.
Medieval or Middle Greek 1 MGk. 2 MGr.
Mediterranean 1 Med. 2 Medit.
Mediterranean Association of Marine Biology and Oceanography MAMBO
medium 1 M (size) 2 med.
medium assault weapon MAW
medium close shot *photography* MCS
medium close-up *photography* MCU
medium frequency *electronics* MF or mf (GPO, OUP: MF)
medium large ML
medium machine oil MMO
medium pressure MP
medium range MR
medium shot *photography, television* MS
medium standard frequency MSF
medium steel MS
medium voltage 1 MV 2 mv
medium wave *electronics* MW
Medium or Minimum Intensity Approach Lights System MALS
medium-power loop range *electronics* MRL
Medium-Range Ballistic Missile MRBM
medium-resolution infrared radiometer MRIR
medium-scale integration *electronics* MSI
medium-scan television MSTV
MEDLARS on-line MEDLINE
medullary ray MR or M.R.
meeting mtg. or mtg

mega meg or MEG
mega roentgen equivalent physical megarep.
mega- M
megabit 1 MB or Mb 2 mbit
megabits per second Mbps
megabyte 1 MB 2 a Mbyte b meg
megabytes meg
megacurie MCi
megacycle mc. or Mc. or mc
megagauss-oersted MGOe
megagram Mg or Mg.
megahertz MHz
megahertz per second MHz/s
megajoule mj. or MJ
megaparsec Mpc or mpc
megapascal MPa or mpa
megarad mr.
megasecond 1 Ms or Ms. 2 ms or ms.
megaton 1 MT 2 mt or mt.
megavar MVAR or mvar
megavolt 1 MV 2 mv or Mv
megavolt-ampere MVA or mv.a.
megawatt 1 MW 2 mw or Mw
megawatt day MWD or Mwd or mwd
megawatt year of electricity MWYE or Mwye or mwye
megawatt, thermal MWT or Mwt or mwt
megawatt-hour MWH or Mwh or mwh
megawatts of electrical power MWE or MWe or Mw(e)
megawatts of electricity eMW
megohm meg
melamine-formaldehyde MF
Melanesia Mel or Melan.
Melanesian Mel or Melan.
melanocyte-stimulating hormone MSH
Melbourne Mel or Melb
melting at m or m.
melting point 1 MP 2 mp
member 1 M or M. 2 Mbr. or mbr. 3 mem.
member of a local Junior Chamber of Commerce JC
Member of Congress MC or M.C.
Member of Council *British* MC or M.C.
Member of Parliament 1 MOP or MoP 2 MP or M.P. (GPO, NYT, CSM: M.P.; OUP: MP)
Member of Parliament of the Republic of Ireland TD or T.D.
Member of Parliament, Canada MPC or M.P.C.
Member of the American Academy of Arts and Sciences MAAS or M.A.A.S.
Member of the European Parliament MEP
Member of the Executive Council M.E.C.
Member of the General Assembly MGA or M.G.A.
Member of the German Parliament M.d.B.
Member of the House of Assembly MHA or M.H.A.
Member of the House of Keys M.H.K. or MHK
Member of the House of Representatives M.H.R. or MHR
Member of the Japan Society M.J.S.
Member of the Legislative Assembly MLA or M.L.A.
Member of the Legislative Council MLC or M.L.C.

Member of the National Academy of Sciences M.N.A.S. *or* MNAS
Member of the National Assembly (of Quebec) MNA *or* M.N.A.
Member of the Numismatic Society MNS *or* M.N.S.
Member of the Order of Australia AM
Member of the Order of Canada CM *or* C.M.
Member of the Order of Military Merit MMM
Member of the Order of the British Empire MBE *or* M.B.E.
Member of the Provincial Parliament MPP *or* M.P.P. (in Canada)
Member of the Real Estate Institute of New Zealand M.R.E.I.N.Z.
Member of the State Parliament M.d.L.
membranoproliferative glomerulonephritis MPGN
membranous glomerulonephritis MGN
memento mem.
memoir mem.
memorandum 1 M 2 mem. 3 memo
memorandum (of) receipt *commerce* MR *or* M/R
memorandum of a conversation memcon
memorandum of agreement *commerce* MOA
memorandum of deposit *commerce* 1 M/D 2 MD *or* M.D.
memorandum of partnership *commerce, law* MP *or* M/P
memorandum of understanding *commerce, law* MOU *or* m.o.u.
memorial mem. *or* Mem.
memory address register *computers* MAR
memory buffer *computers* MB
memory buffer register *computers* MBR
memory data register *computers* MDR
memory information register *computers* MIR
memory management unit *computers* MMU
mendelevium Md *or* Mv
mensuration mensur.
mental age *psychology* MA
Mental Health MH
mental retardation MR
mentally deficient MD
Mentally Ill Chemical *or* **Chronic Abuser** MICA
mentally retarded and developmentally disabled MR/DD
mentioned mentd
mercantile merc.
mercaptobenzothiazole MBT
Mercator's Projection MP
mercenary merc. *or* merc
merchandise mdse
merchandising mdsg. *or* Mdsg
merchant mcht
Merchant Marine MM
Merchant Navy MN *or* M.N.
Merchant Navy Establishment M.N.E.
Merchant of Venice, The 1 Merch.V. 2 MV
mercury 1 Hg 2 mer. 3 merc.
merged transistor logic *computers* MTL
mergers and acquisitions *finance* M&A
meridian 1 M *or* M. 2 m *or* m. 3 mer.

Merit Systems Protection Board MSPB
Meritorious Service Medal MSM
Merry Wives of Windsor, The 1 Merry W. 2 MWW 3 Wiv.
Mesdames Mmes.
Mesdemoiselles Mlles.
mesh M *or* m
mesothorium Ms-Th *or* MsTh
message 1 mge 2 msg.
message authentication code *computers* MAC
messenger 1 msgr. 2 msngr.
messenger ribonucleic acid mRNA *or* m-RNA
Messerschmitt Me.
Messier (catalog) *astronomy* M
Messieurs 1 Messrs. 2 MM *or* MM.
meta- *chemistry* m-
metabolic clearance rate *medicine* MCR
metabolic index MI
metabolic rate MR
metabolism met. *or* metab.
metabolizable energy ME
metachromatic leukodystrophy MLD
metal base transistor MBT
metal insulator semiconductor MIS
metal insulator semiconductor field effect transistor MISFET
metal *or* **metallic oxide semiconductor** MOS
metal oxide semiconductor field effect transistor MOSFET
metal oxide semiconductor transistor MOST
metal oxide sensor MOS
metal oxide silicon MOS
metal semiconductor field-effect transistor *electronics* MESFET
metal-inert gas MIG
metal-matrix composite MMC
metal-nitride-oxide semiconductor *electronics* MNOS
metal-organic chemical vapor deposition MOCVD
metallic met.
metallurgical 1 met. 2 metal. *or* metall.
Metallurgical Engineer Met.E.
metallurgy 1 met. 2 metal. *or* metall.
metaphor 1 met. 2 metaph.
metaphorical 1 met. 2 metaph.
metaphysical 1 met. 2 metaph.
metaphysics 1 met. 2 metaph.
meteorological 1 met. *or* met 2 meteor. *or* meteorol.
Meteorological Automatic Reporting Station MARS
Meteorological Office MO *or* M.O.
Meteorological Operational Telecommunications Network Europe MOTNE
meteorological satellite 1 Meteosat 2 metsat
meteorology 1 met. *or* met 2 meteor. *or* meteorol.
meter m *or* m. (unit of measure)
meter-gram-second mgs *or* m.g.s. *or* MGS
meter-kilogram 1 mk *or* MK 2 mkg *or* m-kg.
meter-kilogram-second mks *or* MKS
meter-kilogram-second-ampere system mksa *or* MKSA
meters per minute MPM *or* mpm
meters per second MPS *or* mps
methamphetamine meth

methane meth *or* meth.
methanol extraction residue MER
methionine 1 Met *or* Met. 2 met.
method of operation 1 MO *or* M.O. 2 mo *or* m.o.
Methodist Meth.
Methodist Episcopal Church M.E.C. *or* M.E.Ch.
Methodist Episcopal Church, South MES *or* M.E.S.
methods time measurement MTM
methoxyethylmercury chloride MEMC
methoxypsoralen MOP
methyl Me
methyl ethyl ketone MEK
methyl methanesulphonate *biochemistry* MMS
methyl tert-butyl ether MTBE
methylated 1 meth *or* Meth. 2 *British* meths.
methylchlorophenoxyacetic acid MCPA
methylcyanoacrylate MCA
methylcyclopentadienyl manganese tricarbonyl MMT
methylenedioxy-amphetamine MDA
methylenedioxy-methamphetamine MDMA
metol quinal *photography* MQ
metonymy meton.
metric m *or* m.
metric carat 1 m.c. 2 cm *or* c.m.
metric system MS
metric ton 1 MT 2 mt *or* m.t. 3 t *or* t.
Metro-Goldwyn-Mayer MGM (*NYT:* M-G-M; *OUP:* MGM)
metrology metrol.
metronome met.
metropolis metrop.
Metropolitan 1 M 2 Met *or* Met.
metropolitan metrop. *or* metropol
Metropolitan Applied Research Center MARC
metropolitan area 1 MA 2 metro *or* Metro
Metropolitan Boston Transit Authority MBTA
Metropolitan Fire Brigade *British* M.F.B. *or* MFB
Metropolitan Museum of Art MMA
Metropolitan Opera House *or* **Company, New York** Met
Metropolitan Police MP (of London)
Metropolitan Police Office MPO *or* M.P.O.
Metropolitan Statistical Area MSA
Metropolitan Transportation Authority M.T.A. *or* MTA (*NYT:* M.T.A.)
Meurthe-et-Moselle M-et-M
Mexican Mex.
Mexican Communist Party PCM *or* P.C.M.
Mexican Federation of Labor CTM
Mexico Mex.
mezzanine Mezz. (in a theater)
mezzo *music* mez
Micah Mic.
Michael Mich.
Michaelmas Mich.
Michigan 1 MI (Zip Code) 2 Mich.
micro- 1 m 2 u 3 μ
microalloy diffused-base transistor MADT
microalloy transistor MAT
microanalytical reagent *chemistry* MAR

Microbiological Research Establishment MRE
microcalorie mcal.
microchannel architecture *computers* MCA
microchannel plate *biology* MCP
microcom networking protocol MNP
microcrystalline microcryst.
microfarad 1 mf. *or* mf *or* mF **2** mfd. *or* mfd
microfiche MF
microgram 1 mcg **2** mg. *or* mg
microinch min
micrometer mm
micron 1 mu **2** u **3** μ
Micronesia Micro.
Micronesian Micro.
microprocessor system MPS
microprocessor unit MPU
microprogrammed control unit MCU
microroentgen mr. *or* mr *or* m/R
Microscope Mic (constellation)
microscopic micr.
microscopy micros.
Microsoft Disk Operating System *trademark* MS/DOS *or* MS-DOS
microtubule-organizing center MTOC
microvolt muv
microwatt muw
Microwave Aircraft Digital Guidance Equipment MADGE
microwave amplification by stimulated emission of radiation maser
microwave integrated circuit MIC
Microwave Landing System MLS
midcourse correction *navigation* MCC
Middle M *or* M.
middle 1 mdl. *or* Mdl. **2** mid.
Middle Ages MA *or* M/A.
Middle District MD *or* M.D.
Middle Dutch 1 MD **2** MDu *or* MDu.
Middle East ME
Middle East Defense Organization MEDO
Middle English ME *or* ME. *or* M.E.
Middle English Dictionary MED *or* M.E.D.
Middle European Time MEZ *or* M.E.Z.
Middle Flemish MFlem
Middle French 1 M.Fr. **2** MF *or* MF.
Middle High German MHG *or* M.H.G.
Middle Irish M.Ir. *or* MIr
Middle Low German MLG *or* MLG.
middle of the month *accounting, finance* MOM *or* m.o.m.
middle-of-the-road MOR
Middlesex County, England 1 Mddx. **2** Middx. **3** Mx
Midlands Mid. (Midland counties of England)
midnight 1 mdnt. **2** mid. **3** Mn *or* Mn.
Midshipman Mid. *or* Mid
Midsummer Night's Dream, A **1** Mids.N.D. **2** MND
Midwest Modern Language Association MMLA
Midwest Universities Research Association MURA
migration inhibitory factor *medicine* MIF
mild upper-respiratory infection MURI
mile 1 m *or* M **2** mi. *or* mi **3** ml.
mileage 1 mi. **2** mil.
miles per gallon mpg *or* m.p.g.

miles per hour mph *or* m.p.h. (*NYT, OUP:* m.p.h.; *CSM:* mph)
miles per hour per second mphps *or* mphp/s
military 1 mil. *or* Mil. **2** MIL **3** Milit.
Military Advisory Group MAG
Military Affiliated Radio System MARS
Military Agency for Standardization MAS
military aid to the civilian community MACC
Military Air Transport Service MATS
Military Airlift Command MAC
Military Assistance Advisory Group MAAG
Military Assistance Program MAP
Military Attaché MA
military compact reactor MCR
Military Cross *British* MC *or* M.C.
Military Government MG
Military Health Services System MHSS
Military Hospital MH
Military Intelligence MI
military intelligence division MID
Military Interdepartmental Purchase Request MIPR
Military Liaison Officer MLO
Military Observer MO *or* M.O.
military occupational specialty MOS
Military Operations and Intelligence MOI
Military Order of the Purple Heart MOPH
military payment certificate MPC
Military Police *or* **Policeman** MP
Military Police Corps MPC
Military Representatives Committee MRC
military science MS
Military Sea Transportation Service MSTS
Military Sealift Command MSC (*GPO:* MSC; *NYT:* M.S.C.)
Military Specification MS
Military Standard MS (with number)
military-industrial complex MIC
Militia mil. *or* Mil.
milk of magnesia MOM *or* m.o.m.
mill 1 mi. **2** m *or* m. (U.S. monetary unit)
mill cull outs MCO (of lumber)
mill finish MF (of lumber)
mill run MR (of lumber)
milled in transit MIT *or* m.i.t.
Miller Analogy Test MAT
milli- m
milli-International Unit mIU
milliampere 1 mA. **2** ma.
milliampere second MAS *or* mAs
milliangstrom mA. *or* mÅ
millibar *meteorology* **1** mb *or* mb. **2** mbar
millibarn *nuclear physics* mb *or* mb.
millicurie 1 mc. *or* mc **2** mCi
millidarcy md *or* mD
millielectron volt meV
millieme mil. (one thousandth of a country's monetary unit)
milliequivalent 1 me. **2** meq *or* m.eq. *or* mEq.
millifarad 1 mf. *or* mf *or* mF **2** mfd. *or* mfd
millifoot lamberts *physics* mftL
milligal mgal.
milligauss mg. *or* mG
milligram 1 M **2** mg. *or* mg **3** mgm. *or* mgm
milligram hour mgh
milligrams per square decimeter per day mdd

millihenry mh. *or* mh *or* mH
millihertz mHz
millijoule mj. *or* mj *or* mJ
millikelvin mk *or* mK
millilambert mL
milliliter 1 mL **2** ml. *or* ml
millimass unit mmu
millimeter mm *or* mm. (*NYT, OUP:* mm.)
millimeter of mercury mmHg
millimicron 1 mm **2** mu
millimole mM
million 1 M **2** m **3** mil. **4** mill. **5** mn
million acre-feet MAF
million barrels per day mbd
million electron volts MEV *or* MeV *or* Mev *or* mev (*NYT:* Mev; *OUP:* MeV)
million floating-point operations per second *computers* mflops
million gallons Mgal
million gallons per day m.g.d. *or* MGD
million instructions per second *computers* MIPS
million kilowatt hours Mkw.h. *or* MkWh
million years *astronomy, anthropology, geology* my *or* m.y.
million years ago *geology* mya
milliosmol mOsm
millipoise mp *or* mp.
millirad mrad
millirem 1 MR **2** mrem
milliroentgen 1 MR **2** mr. *or* mr *or* m/R
millisecond 1 millisec **2** ms *or* ms. **3** msc *or* MSc **4** msec. *or* msec
millisiemens mS
millivolt mv *or* mV
milliwatt mw *or* mW
Milton Milt. (English poet)
Milwaukee Milw.
Mine Safety and Health Administration MSHA
mineral min *or* min.
mineral lease ML *or* M.L.
mineralogical 1 min *or* min. **2** Min. **3** mineral.
Mineralogical Society of America MSA
mineralogy 1 min *or* min. **2** Min. **3** mineral.
Minerals Management Service MMS
mini disk MD
minim 1 min **2** mor m.
minimal brain dysfunction MBD
minimal identifiable odor MIO
minimum 1 min *or* min. **2** mnm *or* mnm. (*CSM, OUP:* min.)
minimum admissible flow MAF
minimum adult daily requirement *nutrition* MADR
minimum audible field MAF
minimum audible pressure MAP
minimum daily requirement MDR *or* mdr
minimum data set *medicine* MDS
minimum detectable activity MDA
minimum discernible signal *electronics* MDS
minimum effective dose *medicine* MED
minimum erythema dose *medicine* MED
minimum fatal dose *medicine* M.F.D. *or* MFD
minimum hemolytic dose MHD
minimum infective dose *medicine* MID *or* M.I.D.

minimum lending rate MLR
minimum lethal dose MLD or m.l.d.
minimum reacting dose *medicine* MRD
minimum reception altitude *aeronautics* MRA
minimum spanning tree MST
mining min or min.
Mining Engineer 1 M.Eng. **2** ME or M.E.
Minister 1 M **2** Min.
Minister Plenipotentiary 1 Min.Plen. **2** MP or M.P.
Minister Resident MR or M.R.
Ministry 1 M **2** Min.
Ministry of Agriculture, Fisheries, and Food M.A.F.F.
Ministry of Aircraft Production MAP or M.A.P.
Ministry of Defence MOD or MoD
Ministry of Housing and Local Government M.H.L.G. or MHLG
Ministry of International Trade and Industry M.I.T.I. or MITI
Ministry of Overseas Development MOD
Ministry of Transport MOT or MoT
Ministry of Transport and Civil Aviation MTCA
Minneapolis I (in Federal Reserve banking system)
Minneapolis Grain Exchange *commerce* MGE
Minnesota 1 MN (Zip Code) **2** Minn.
Minnesota Multiphasic Personality Inventory MMPI
Minnesota Scholastic Aptitude Test MSAT
minor 1 m **2** min or min. **3** Min. **4** *astronomy, music, military* Mi.
Minor In Need of Supervision *law, social work* MINS
Minority Business Development Administration MBDA
Minority Business Enterprise MBE
Minority Rights Group MRG
Minority Small Business MSB
minority-enterprise small-business investment company MESBIC
mint state MS (of coins)
minute 1 mi. **2** min or min. **3** m or m. (*CSM, OUP:* min.)
miscellaneous 1 misc or misc. or miscl. **2** msc (*MLA, CSM, OUP:* misc.)
Miscellaneous Document Misc.Doc. (with number)
miscellany 1 misc or misc. **2** miscl.
miscible misc or misc.
misnumbered misn.
Miss Ms or Ms. (*GPO, NYT:* Ms.; *OUP:* Ms)
missile M
Missile Technology Control Regime MTCR
missile, experimental MX
missile-site radar MSR
missing in action MIA
Missing Persons Bureau MPB
missing, believed killed MBK
Mission Miss. or Msn.
Mission Control MC
Mission Control Center MCC
mission-planning program MPP
Missionary Miss. or miss.
Mississippi 1 Miss. **2** MS (Zip Code)

Mississippi Test Facility MTF
Mississippi Valley Authority MVA
Missouri 1 MO (Zip Code) **2** Mo or Mo. (*NYT, OUP:* Mo.)
Missouri Pacific Railroad Mopac
Missouri Valley Authority MVA
mist *meteorology* mor m.
mister Mr or Mr. (*GPO, NYT:* Mr.; *OUP:* Mr)
mistranslation mistrans.
mistress Mrs. or Mrs (*GPO, NYT:* Mrs.; *OUP:* Mrs)
mistress, miss, Mrs Ms or Ms. (used before the name of a woman either married or unmarried; *GPO, NYT:* Ms.; *OUP:* Ms)
mitochondrial DNA 1 MLDNA **2** mtDNA
mitotic index *biology* MI
mitral stenosis MS
mix *pharmaceutics* **1** M or M. **2** m or m.
mix and write a label *pharmaceutics* m. et sig.
mix well *pharmaceutics* mb or m.b.
mixed mxd. or mxd
mixed lengths ML or m.l. or M/L (of lumber)
mixed lymphocyte culture MLC
mixed lymphocyte reaction MLR
mixed widths MW (of lumber)
mixed or **multi-language system** MLS
mixture 1 mixt. **2** *Latin* mist.
mobile 1 mbl. **2** mob. or Mob.
Mobile Army Surgical Hospital MASH
Mobile Atlantic Range Stations MARS
mobile control room *military* MCR
mobile digital computer *military* Mobidic
mobile field hospital *military* MFH
Mobile Homes Manufacturers Association MHMA
Mobile Intensive Care Unit MICU
mobile medium-range ballistic missile MMRBM
mobile repair unit MRU
Mobile Strike Force MSF
mobile unit MU
mobilization mob.
mobilization day *military* M-day
mobilized mob.
mode *statistics* Mo
model 1 M (with number) **2** mdl. or Mdl. **3** mod.
Model Secondary School for the Deaf MSSD
modem sharing device MSD
moderate 1 M **2** mdt. **3** mod.
moderately loud *music* m.f.
moderately quick *music* mod.
moderately slow *music* and.
moderately soft *music* mp or m.p.
moderator mod. or Mod.
modern mod. or mod or Mod.
Modern English MnE or MnE.
Modern Language Association MLA
Modern Language Journal MLJ
Modern Language Notes MLN
Modern Language Quarterly MLQ
Modern Language Review MLR
modern large ballistic missile MLBM
Modern Woodmen of America M.W.A.
modification mod. or mod
modified mod. or mod
Modified American Plan MAP

modified atmospheric packaging MAP
modified frequency modulation MFM
modulated continuous wave *electronics* MCW
modulation 1 m **2** M
modulation factor *electronics* m
modulation transfer function *photography* MTF
modulation-doped field effect transistor MODFET
modulator *electronics* MOD
Modulator-Demodular modem or MODEM
module M
modulus 1 *mathematics, physics* m or m. **2** *physics, mathematics* mod.
modulus of elasticity E
modulus of rigidity 1 *mechanics* G or G **2** *physics* n
Mohorovicic discontinuity Moho
moisture and ash free MAF or m.a.f.
molality m
molar 2 *physics, chemistry, dentistry* M **1** *physics, chemistry* m
molar extinction coefficient *chemistry* e
molar mass *physics* M
mold line ML
molded mld.
molder mldr.
molding 1 mld. or mldg. **2** mold.
mole mol (amount of substance)
mole fraction *chemistry* x or X
mole fraction (in light or refined matter) *chemistry* y
molecular mol or mol.
molecular beam epitaxy *physics* MBE
molecular cloud *astronomy* MC
molecular collision frequency *physics* Z
molecular emission cavity analysis *biology* MECA
molecular heat C
molecular orbital MO
molecular weight 1 mol wt **2** MW or M.W. **3** mw or m.w. or m.wt. **4** *physics, chemistry* M
molecule mol or mol.
molybdenum Mo
moment *physics* M
moment of area Q
moment of inertia *physics* **1** J **2** MI
momentum *physics* p
Monaco Mon or Mon.
Monastery Mon
monaural mono
Monday 1 M **2** Mo **3** Mon or Mon.
Monday through Friday M-F
Monday, Wednesday, Friday MWF
monetary mon.
monetary allowance for quarters MAQ
monetary compensatory amounts MCA
money *economics* M
money (in circulation) MO
money market deposit account MMDA
money order 1 MO or M.O. **2** mo or m.o.
Mongol People's Revolutionary Party MPRP
Mongolia Mong.
Mongolian Mong.
Mongolian People's Republic MPR
monitor mon.

monitored retrievable storage *computers* MRS

monoamine oxidase MAO

monoamine oxidase inhibitor MAOI

monobasic sodium phosphate MSP

monochrome display adaptor *computers* MDA

monocotyledon *biology* monocot.

monocyte colony stimulating factor *medicine, biology* M-CSF

monoethanolamine MEA

monograph monog. *or* monogr.

monoiodotyrosine MIT

monolithic microwave integrated circuit *electronics* MMIC

monomethyl aniline MMA

monomethyl hydrazine MMH

mononucleosis mono

monophonic 1 M 2 mono

Monopolies and Mergers Commission MMC

monosodium acid methanearsenate MSMA

monosodium glutamate MSG

monotype mono.

monozygotic MZ

Monseigneur 1 Mgr. *or* Mngr. (French title of honor) 2 Msgr.

Monsieur 1 M *or* M. 2 Mons.

Monsignor 1 Mgr. *or* Mngr. (title in Roman Catholic Chucrh) 2 Mon 3 Mons. 4 Monsig. 5 Msg. 6 Msgr. (*GPO, NYT:* Msgr.; *OUP:* Mgr.)

monsoon mon. *or* mon

monsoon air *meteorology* M *or* M.

Montana 1 Mon *or* Mon. 2 Mont. 3 MT (Zip Code)

Monte Carlo method *mathematics, physics* MCM

month 1 M 2 mo *or* mo. 3 mth. *or* mth (*GPO:* mo.; *OUP:* m.)

month's date *commerce* 1 M/D 2 m/d *or* m.d.

month's sight *or* months after sight *commerce* 1 M/S 2 m/s *or* m.s.

monthly 1 M 2 mo *or* mo.

Monthly Investment Plan MIP

months mos.

months after date *commerce* 1 M/D 2 m/d *or* m.d.

Montreal Stock Exchange MSE

Monument Mon

moon m *or* m.

Moral Re-Armament MRA

morale, welfare, and recreation MWR (program of U.S. Army)

More Developed Country MDC

morning 1 M *or* M. 2 morn. 3 mrng

Morning Report *military* MR

Moroccan Mor.

Morocco 1 Mco. (leather) 2 Mor.

morocco mor. (leather)

morphine morph.

morphological morph. *or* morphol.

morphology morph.

Morse Automatic Decoder MAUDE

Morse Code MC

mortar 1 mor. 2 mort.

mortgage 1 mort. 2 mtg. *or* mtg 3 mtge. *or* mtge

mortgage interest relief at source MIRAS

mortgage-backed security MBS

mortgaged mtgd. *or* mtgd

mortgagee mtgee. *or* mtgee

mortgagor mtgor. *or* mtgor

mortuary mort.

Moscow Mos.

mosque Mq *or* mq.

Mössbauer Emission Spectroscopy *chemistry* MES

Mössbauer Effect *nuclear physics.* ME

most favored nation MFN

Most Fortunate Brothers FF *or* F.F.

Most Holy Father BP *or* B.P.

Most Holy Lord SSD *or* SS.D.

Most Holy Roman Church SRE *or* S.R.E.

most probable number *mathematics* MPN

most probable position *navigation* MPP

Most Reverend Mt. Rev.

most significant bit *computers* MSB

most significant digit *computers* MSD

most valuable player *sports* MVP

Most Worshipful MW *or* M.W.

Most Worshipful Grand Master MWGM

Most Worthy MW *or* M.W.

Most Worthy Patriarch MWP *or* M.W.P.

Mother M *or* M. (in a religious order)

mother of pearl m.o.p.

mother/daughter M/D

Mothers Against Drunk Driving MADD

motion analysis camera *biophysics* MAC

Motion Picture Association of America MPA *or* MPAA

Motion Picture Experts Group MPEG

Motion Picture Producers and Distributors of America MPPDA

motivational research MR

motocross MX

motor 1 M 2 mot. 3 MTR *or* mtr

Motor Agents' Association *British* MAA *or* M.A.A.

motor freight tariff *commerce* MFT

motor generator MG

Motor Industry Research Association MIRA

motor launch ML

motor neurone disease *or* diseases MND

motor octane number MON

motor torpedo boat MTB

motor transport *British military* MT

motor turbine ship MTS

Motor Vehicles Department MVD

motor vessel MV *or* M/V

motor yacht MY

motorbicycle moped

motorcycle MC

Motorcycle Operator Skills Test MOST

motorized mot.

motorship M/S *or* MS

motorway *British* 1 M (with number) 2 M-way

Mount 1 MT (in postal address) 2 Mt.

Mount Wilson Observatory MWO

Mountain MTN (in postal address)

mountain 1 M *or* M. 2 Mt. 3 mtn.

mountain daylight saving time MDST *or* M.D.S.T. *or* m.d.s.t.

mountain daylight time MDT *or* M.D.T. *or* m.d.t.

mountain standard time MST *or* M.S.T. *or* m.s.t.

mountain time 1 MT 2 mt

mountains Mts. *or* mts.

mounted Mtd. *or* Mtd

mounting mtg. *or* mtg

mouse unit *biology* MU *or* M.U. *or* m.u.

Mouth *geography* Mth. *or* Mth

mouthwash *pharmaceutics* collut.

moved, seconded, and carried 1 MSC 2 msc *or* m.s.c.

movement 1 mvt. 2 *music* mov *or* movt

moving coil m.c. *or* mc

moving-target indicator MTI

Mozambique 1 Moz. *or* Mozamb. 2 *Portuguese* Moçam.

Mozambique escudo M. Esc

Mozambique National Resistance Renamo *or* RENAMO

Mozart Moz.

Mr. and Mrs. MM *or* M/M

Mr. and Ms. MM *or* M/M

Much Ado About Nothing Ado

mucilage muc.

mucocutaneous lymph node syndrome *medicine* MLNS

mucopolysaccharidoses MPS

mucous membrane MM *or* M.M.

mud M *or* M.

muddy track my (in horse racing)

Multi-Launch Rocket System MLRS

multichannel analyzer *electronics* MCA

multichannel data recorder *computers* MDR

multicolor graphics array *computers* MCGA

multidimensional access *computers* MDA

Multifiber Arrangement MFA

multifrequency MF

Multifunction Array Radar MAR

multilateral trade negotiations MTN

multilevel marketing MLM

multimedia personal computer MPC

multimission modular spacecraft MMS *or* M.M.S.

multinational corporation MNC

Multinational Peacekeeping Force MFO

multinetwork area *advertising* MNA

multiple mult.

multiple (linear) regression *statistics* MLR

multiple airborne target trajectory system Matts

multiple chemical sensitivities *medicine* MCS *or* M.C.S.

multiple contact *electronics* MC

multiple endocrine neoplasia *medicine* MEN

Multiple Independently-targeted Reentry Vehicle MIRV

Multiple Instruction, Multiple Data *computers* MIMD

Multiple Instruction, Single Data MISD

Multiple Listing Board *or* Bureau MLB

Multiple Listing Service MLS

Multiple Mirror Telescope MMT

multiple module access *computers* MMA

multiple on-line programming MOP

Multiple Orbit Bombardment System MOBS

multiple personality disorder *psychiatry* MPD

multiple reentry vehicle MRV

multiple sclerosis MS

multiple systems operator *communications* MSO

multiple unit MU
multiple-access computer MAC
multiple-frequency-shift keying *computers* MFSK
multiple-track radar MTR
multiple-unit steerable antenna MUSA
multiplex 1 MPX **2** MX **3** Mx *or* mx
multiplex interferometric Fourier spectroscopy MIFS
multiplexed analog components MAC
multiplexer 1 MPX **2** *computers* MUX
multiplication *or* **reproduction factor** *physics* k
multiplicity of infection *biology, medicine* MOI
multiplied by X *or* x
multiplier quotient *computers* MQ
multiply 1 mult. **2** X *or* x
multipoint distribution service MDS
multipolar MP
multiprocessor MP
Multiprogramming for Variable Tasks *computers* MVT
multiprogramming system *computers* MPS
multiprogramming with fixed task *computers* MFT
multipurpose food M.P.F. *or* MPF
multirole combat aircraft MRCA
multispectral scanner *medicine, photography* MSS
Multistate Bar Examination MBE
multivibrator *electronics* MVBR
municipal 1 mun. *or* Mun. **2** munic. *or* Munic.
Municipal Assistance Corporation MAC *or* M.A.C. (*NYT:* M.A.C.)

Municipal Borough MB *or* M.B.
municipality munic. *or* Munic.
munitions *military* MUN
murine leukemia virus MLV
murine sarcoma virus MSV
Murrumbidgee Irrigation Area MIA *or* M.I.A.
muscle m *or* m.
muscular dysgenesis MDG
muscular dystrophy MD
Muscular Dystrophy Association MDA
museum mus. *or* Mus.
Museum of Modern Art MOMA (in New York City)
music mus. *or* Mus.
music and effects M&E
music director MD *or* M.D.
Music Educators National Conference MENC
Music Information Retrieval MIR
Music Library Association MLA
Music Operators of America MOA
Music Publishers Association MPA
Music Television MTV
Music Wire Gauge MWG *or* m.w.g.
musical mus. *or* Mus.
musical instrument digital interface MIDI
musician mus. *or* Mus.
Muslim mus. *or* Mus.
mustered out MO *or* M.O.
mustering-out pay MOP *or* M.o.P.
mutation mut.
mutatis mutandis m.m.
mute *music* sord.
mutilated mut.

mutual mut. *or* Mut.
mutual and balanced force reduction MBFR
Mutual Assistance Program MAP
Mutual Assured Destruction MAD
Mutual Broadcasting System MBS
mutual conductance *or* **transconductance** gm *or* Gm
Mutual Improvement Association MIA *or* M.I.A.
mutual inductance *physics* M
Mutual Insurance Rating Bureau MIRB
Mutual Reduction in Forces MRF
Mutual UFO Network MUFON
muzzle velocity 1 MV **2** mv
muzzle-loading ML *or* M.L.
muzzle-loading rifle MLR
myasthenia gravis MG
Mycenaean Myc.
mycobacterium aviumintracellulare complex MAC
mycological myc. *or* mycol.
mycology myc. *or* mycol.
myeloperoxidase *biochemistry* MPO
myocardial infarction MI *or* M.I.
myofascial pain dysfunction MPD
myopia my *or* my.
myriagram myg *or* myg.
myrialiter myl *or* myl.
myriameter mym *or* mym.
myriare mya *or* mya.
mystery myst.
Mystery Writers of America M.W.A.
mythological myth. *or* mythol.
mythology myth.

N

N(negative)-channel metal oxide semiconductor *electronics* NMOS
N-acetylglucosamine NAG
N-acetylmuramic acid NAM
N-acetylneuraminic acid NANA
N-acrylonitrile-butadiene rubber NBR
N-methyl-D-aspartate NMDA
nadir N
Nahum Nah.
nail n *or* n. (cloth measure)
naira N
name 1 N *or* N. **2** n *or* n.
name alone *taxonomy* nom. nud.
name unknown n.u.
namely 1 scil. **2** viz *or* viz. (*CSM, OUP:* viz.; *MLA:* not acceptable) **3** *Latin* sc *or* sc. (*GPO, OUP:* sc. or ss)
names nn. *or* NN.
nano- n
nanoampere nA
nanocurie nCi

nanofarad *electronics* nf *or* nF
nanogram ng *or* ng. *or* nG
nanohenry nh. *or* nH
nanometer nm
nanosecond 1 nanosec. **2** ns **3** nsec.
nanowatt nW
Naperian base e
naphtha nap. *or* naph.
naphthoxyacetic acid BNOA
naphthylacetic acid NAA
Naples Nap
Napoleon Nap *or* Nap.
narcotic narc *or* narc.
Narcotic Drugs Supervisory Body NDSB
narcotics narc *or* narc.
narcotics agent narc
Narcotics Anonymous NA *or* N.A.
narrated by narr.
narrator narr.
narrow 1 N (shoe size) **2** nar *or* nar.
narrow band *electronics* NB
narrow band frequency modulation 1 NBFM **2** NFM *or* nFM
narrow sense *or* **interpretation** ss *or* ss.
narrow-beam transducer NBT
nasal *medicine* n *or* n.
Nashville Nash.
Nassau Nass.
Natal Nat.

Nathaniel Nath.
National 1 N *or* N. **2** Nat. **3** Nl
national Natl. *or* natl.
National Abortion Rights Action League NARAL
National Academician NA *or* N.A.
National Academy of Design NAD *or* N.A.D.
National Academy of Engineering NAE
National Academy of Recording Arts and Sciences NARAS
National Academy of Science Committee on Oceanography NASCO
National Academy of Science–National Research Council NAS-NRC
National Academy of Sciences NAS
National Academy of Television Arts and Sciences NATAS
National Accelerator Laboratory NAL
National Achievement Scholarship Program NASP
National Acid Precipitation Assessment Program NAPAP
National Action Party PAN (of Mexico)
National Ad Hoc Committee Against Censorship NAHCAC
National Advisory Committee for Aeronautics NACA

National Advisory Committee on Radiation NACOR

National Advisory Council NAC

National Aero-Space Plane NASP

National Aeronautics and Space Administration NASA

National Aeronautics and Space Center NASC

National Aeronautics and Space Council NASC

National Aeronautics Association NAA

National Aerospace Education Council NAEC

National Aerospace Laboratory NAL

National Aerospace or Aircraft Standards NAS

National Agricultural Advisory Service NAAS

National Agricultural Research Center NARC

National Agricultural Statistics Service NASS

National Air Carrier Association NACA

National Air Pollution Control Administration NAPCA

National Air Traffic Controllers Association NATCA

National Aircraft Noise Abatement Council NANAC

National Airport System Plan NASP

National Airspace System NAS

National Alliance of Businessmen NAB

National Amalgamated Stevedores and Dockers NASD or N.A.S.D.

National Ambient Air Quality Standards NAAQS

National and Local Government Officers' Association NALGO

National Archery Association NAA

National Archives and Records Administration NARA

National Archives and Records Service NARS

national arrangements for incidents involving radioactivity NAIR

National Assembly NS (of Bulgaria)

National Assessment of Educational Progress NAEP

National Association for Children of Alcoholics NACA

National Association for Gifted Children N.A.G.C.

National Association for Mental Health NAMH

National Association for Practical Nurse Education and Service NAPNES

National Association for the Advancement of Colored People NAACP (NYT: N.A.A.C.P.)

National Association for the Prevention of Addiction to Narcotics NAPAN

National Association of Attorneys General NAAG

National Association of Biology Teachers NABT

National Association of British Manufacturers N.A.B.M.

National Association of Broadcast Employees and Technicians NABET

National Association of Broadcasters NAB

National Association of Business Economists NABE

National Association of Childbearing Centers NACC

National Association of Civil Service Employees NACSE or N.A.C.S.E.

National Association of College Admissions Counselors NACAC

National Association of Corn and Agricultural Merchants NACAM

National Association of Cost Accountants NACA or N.A.C.A.

National Association of Counties NAC

National Association of County Administrators NACA

National Association of Dealers in Antiques NADA

National Association of Dental Laboratories NADL

National Association of Educational Broadcasters NAEB

National Association of Emergency Medical Technicians NAEMT

National Association of Engine and Boat Manufacturers N.A.E.B.M.

National Association of Food Chains NAFC

National Association of Funeral Directors N.A.F.D.

National Association of Government Employees NAGE

National Association of Greeting Card Publishers NAGCP

National Association of Home Builders NAHB

National Association of Independent Schools N.A.I.S.

National Association of Insurance Agents NAIA or N.A.I.A.

National Association of Insurance Brokers N.A.I.B.

National Association of Intercollegiate Athletics NAIA

National Association of Letter Carriers NALC

National Association of Life Underwriters N.A.L.U.

National Association of Magazine Publishers NAMP

National Association of Manufacturers NAM or N.A.M.

National Association of Marine Engineers NAME

National Association of Marine Surveyors NAMS

National Association of Medical Examiners NAME or N.A.M.E.

National Association of Paper Merchants NAPM

National Association of Pediatric Nurse Associates and Practitioners NAPNAP

National Association of Pension Funds NAPF

National Association of Performing Artists NAPA or N.A.P.A.

National Association of Photo Lithographers N.A.P.L.

National Association of Photographic Manufacturers NAPM or N.A.P.M.

National Association of Physical Therapists NAPT

National Association of Police Organizations NAPO

National Association of Printers and Lithographers N.A.P.L. or NAPL

National Association of Probation Officers NAPO

National Association of Property Owners NAPO

National Association of Purchasing Agents NAPA

National Association of Purchasing Management NAPM

National Association of Radio and Television Broadcasters NARTB

National Association of Real Estate Boards N.A.R.E.B. or NAREB

National Association of Realtors NAR

National Association of Record Merchandisers NARM

National Association of Retail Druggists N.A.R.D.

National Association of Rocketry NAR

National Association of School Psychologists NASP

National Association of Schools of Music NASM

National Association of Schools of Public Affairs and Administration NASPAA

National Association of Science Writers NASW

National Association of Securities Dealers NASD (NYT: N.A.S.D)

National Association of Securities Dealers Automated Quotations NASDAQ

National Association of Social Workers NASW

National Association of State Purchasing Officials NASPO

National Association of Stationary Engineers NASE

National Association of Stock Car Auto Racing NASCAR

National Association of Student Councils NASC

National Association of Tax Accountants NATA

National Association of Testing Authorities NATA

National Association of Theater Owners NATO

National Association of Trade and Technical Schools NATTS

National Association of Transportation Advertisers NATA

National Association of Travel Organizations NATO

National Association of University Women NAUW

National Associations of Workshops for the Blind NAWB

National Audio-Visual Association NAVA

National Audubon Society NAS or N.A.S.

National Automobile Dealers Association NADA

National Automobile Theft Bureau N.A.T.B.

National Autonomous University of Mexico UNAM

National Aviation Facilities Experimental Center NAFEC
National Bankers Association NBA *or* N.B.A.
National Bar Association NBA *or* N.B.A.
National Basketball Association NBA
National Battlefield NB
National Battlefield Park NBP
National Battlefield Site NBS
National Better Business Bureau NBBB
National Biscuit Company NABISCO
National Blood Transfusion Service NBTS
National Board for Prices and Incomes N.B.P.I.
National Board for Respiratory Therapy NBRT
National Board of Fire Underwriters NBFU
National Book Awards NBA *or* N.B.A.
National Book League NBL *or* N.B.L.
National Book Week NBW
National Bowling League NBL
National Boxing Association NBA
National Broadcasting Company NBC *or* N.B.C. (*NYT*: NBC)
National Broadcasting Service NBS
National Bureau of Economic Research NBER
National Bureau of Standards radio station WWV
National Cable Television Association NCTA
National Cancer Institute NCI
National Capital Planning Commission NCPC
National Cartographic Information Center NCIC
National Catholic Education Association NCEA *or* N.C.E.A.
National Catholic Office for Motion Pictures N.C.O.M.P.
National Catholic Welfare Conference N.C.W.C. *or* NCWC
National Cattle Breeders Association NCBA
National Cattlemen's Association NCA
National Cemetery System NCS
National Center for Atmospheric Research NCAR
National Center for Biotechnology Information NCBI
National Center for Disease Control NCDC
National Center for Earthquake Research NCER
National Center for Educational Statistics NCES
National Center for Health Statistics NCHS
National Center for Human Genome Research NCHGR
National Center for Nursing Research NCNR
National Center for Research Resources NCRR
National Center for Scientific Research *French* CNRS
National Center for Space Research *French* CNES
National Center for the Study of Telecommunications *French* CNET
National Center for Foreign Commerce *French* CNCE *or* C.N.C.E.
National Chemical Laboratory NCL

National Chiropractic Association NCA
National Cholesterol Education Program NCEP
National Climatic Data Center NCDC
National Climbing Classification System NCCS (for rating rock climbing routes)
National Coal Association NCA
national coarse fine NC (of screw thread)
National Coffee Association NCA
National Collection of Type Cultures *medicine* NCTC
National Collegiate Athletic Association NCAA
National Commission on Accrediting NCA *or* N.C.A.
National Commission on Teacher Education and Professional Standards NCTEPS
National Committee for a Sane Nuclear Policy SANE
National Committee for Commonwealth Immigrants NCCI
National Committee on Radiation Protection NCRP
National Communicable Disease Center NCDC
National Communications System NCS
National Communications Union NCU
National Companies and Securities Commission NCSC
National Computing Centre NCC
National Conference of Bar Examiners NCBE
National Conference of Christians and Jews N.C.C.J.
National Conference of Editorial Writers NCEW
National Conference of English Teachers NCET
National Congress of American Indians NCAI
National Congress of Mothers NCM
National Congress of Parents and Teachers NCPT
National Conservative Political Action Committee NCPAC
National Consumer Testing Institute NCTI
National Coordinating Committee NCC
National Copyright Advisory Committee NCAC
National Council for Educational Research and Training NCERT
National Council for Educational Technology NCET
National Council for Geographic Education NCGE
National Council for the Accreditation of Teacher Education NCATE *or* N.C.A.T.E
National Council for the Arts NCA
National Council for the Social Studies NCSS
National Council Licensing Examination NCLEX (for nursing)
National Council of Churches NCC *or* N.C.C.
National Council of Nigerian Citizens N.C.N.C.
National Council of Senior Citizens NCSC
National Council of Teachers of English NCTE

National Council of Teachers of Mathematics NCTM
National Council of Technical Schools NCTS
National Council of Women N.C.W.
National Council on Adult Education NCAE
National Council on Aging NCA
National Council on Crime and Delinquency NCCD
National Credit Association NCA
National Credit Union Administration NCUA
National Cricket Association NCA
National Crime Information Center NCIC
National Crime Survey NCR
National Criminal Justice Reference Service NCJRS
national currency MN (of Argentina)
national cycling proficiency NCP
National Cyclists' Union NCU *or* N.C.U.
National Dairy Association NDA
National Dairy Council NDC
National Data Processing Service NDPS
National Debt ND
National Defence Headquarters NDHQ
National Defense Advisory Commission NDAC
National Defense Education Act NDEA
National Defense Mediation Board NDMB
National Defense Research Committee NDRC
National Defense Transportation Agency NDTA
National Defense University NDU
National Democratic Committee NDC
National Democratic Party 1 NDP (of Germany) **2** NPD *or* N.P.D. (of Germany)
National Dental Association NDA *or* N.D.A.
National Earthquake Information Center NEIC
National Economic Development Council NEDC (of Great Britain)
National Economic Development Office NEDO (of Great Britain)
National Editorial Association NEA
National Education Association NEA *or* N.E.A.
National Educational Television NET
National Electric Light Association NELA
National Electrical Code NEC
National Electrical Code Standards NECS
National Electrical Manufacturers Association NEMA
National Electrical Safety Code NESC
National Electricity Board NEB
National Electronics Conference NEC
National Electronics Laboratory NEL
National Electronics Research Council NERC (of Great Britain)
National Emergency NE
National Emergency Airborne Command Post NEACP
National Emergency Coordination Center NECC
National Emergency Management Training Center NEMTC
National Employment Service NES (of Canada)
National Endowment for the Arts NEA *or* N.E.A.

National Endowment for the Humanities NEH

National Energy Board NEB

National Engineering Laboratory NEL

National Environmental Policy Act NEPA

National Environmental Satellite Center NESC

National Environmental Satellite, Data, and Information Service NESDIS

National Environmental Study Area NESA

National Executive Committee NEC

National Eye Institute NEI

National Farm Workers Association NFWA

National Farmers Organization N.F.O. or NFO

National Farmers' Union NFU or N.F.U.

National Federation of Business and Professional Women's Clubs N.F.B.P.W.C or NFBPWC

National Federation of Federal Employees N.F.F.E. or NFFE

National Federation of Independent Business N.F.I.B.

National Federation of Music Clubs NFMC

National Federation of Professional Workers N.F.P.W. or NFPW

National Federation of Science Abstracting and Indexing Services NFSAIS

National Federation of the Blind NFB

National Film Board NFB (of Canada)

National Film Library NFL

National Film Unit NFU

national fine NF (screw thread)

National Fire Protection Association NFPA

National Fire Service NFS or N.F.S. (of Great Britain)

National Flood Insurance NFI

National Flood Insurance Program NFIP

National Fluid Power Association NFPA

National Football Conference NFC

National Football League NFL or N.F.L.

National Football League Players Association NFLPA

National Foreign Intelligence Program NFIP

National Foreign Trade Council N.F.T.C.

National Forest Products Association NFPA

National Forest System NFS

National Formulary NF or N.F. (GPO: N.F.)

National Foundation for Educational Research N.F.E.R. (of Great Britain)

National Foundation for the Arts and Humanities NFAH

National Futures Association NFA

National Gallery *British* NG

National Gallery of Art NGA or N.G.A.

National Gas Turbine Establishment NGTE

National Geodetic Survey Information Center NGSIC

National Geographic Society NGS

National Geophysical and Solar Terrestrial Data Center NGSDS

National Geophysical Data Center NGDC

National Governors Association NGA

National Guard NG

National Guard of the United States NGUS

National Harbours Board *British* NHB

National Hazardous Chemicals Information Center NHCIC

National Health and Medical Research Council of Australia NHMRCA

National Health and Nutrition Examination Survey NHANES

National Health Association NHA

National Health Council NHC

National Health Insurance NHI or N.H.I.

National Health Service NHS or N.H.S.

National Health Service Corps NHSC

National Heart, Lung, and Blood Institute NHLBI

National Higher Education Association NHEA

National Highway Traffic Safety Administration NHTSA

National Historic Park NHP

National Historic Site NHS

National Historical Publication and Records Commission NHPRC

National Hockey Association NHA

National Hockey League NHL or N.H.L.

National Honor Society NHS or N.H.S.

National Hospice Organization NHO

National House Builders' Registration Council NHBRC

National Housing Agency *or* Act NHA

National Hurricane Center NHC

National Hurricane Research Project NHRP

National Incomes Commission NIC

National Industrial Conference Board NICB

National Industrial Recreation Association NIRA

National Industrial Relations Court NIRC

National Institute for Biological Standards Control NIBSC

National Institute for French Language INaLF

National Institute for Human Genome Research NIHGR

National Institute for Medical Research *British* NIMR

National Institute for Occupational Safety and Health NIOSH

National Institute for Research in Nuclear Science NIRNS

National Institute of Agricultural Botany NIAB

National Institute of Allergy and Infectious Diseases NIAID

National Institute of Arthritis and Musculoskeletal Diseases NIAMSD

National Institute of Child Health and Human Development NICHHD or NICH

National Institute of Corrections NIC

National Institute of Dental Research NIDR

National Institute of Diabetes NID

National Institute of Diabetes and Digestive and Kidney Diseases NIDDKD

National Institute of Dramatic Art NIDA

National Institute of Economic and Social Research N.I.E.S.R.

National Institute of Education NIE

National Institute of Environmental Health Sciences NIEHS

National Institute of General Medical Sciences NIGMS

National Institute of Justice NIJ

National Institute of Mental Health NIMH

National Institute of Names of Origin (of wine) *French* INAO

National Institute of Neurological Disorders and Stroke NINDS

National Institute of Oceanography NIO

National Institute of Public Health NIPH

National Institute of Radiological Science NIRS

National Institute of Research in Dairying NIRD

National Institute of Standards and Technology NIST

National Institute on Aging NIA

National Institute on Deafness NID

National Institute on Deafness and Other Communication Disorders NIDCD

National Institute on Drug Abuse NIDA or Nida

National Institutes of Health NIH

National Insurance NI or N.I.

National Insurance Crime Bureau NICB

National Intelligence Authority NIA

National Intelligence Test NIT

National Investor Relations Institute NIRI

National Invitational Tournament NIT

National Joint Advisory Council *British* N.J.A.C. or NJAC

National Junior College Athletic Association NJCAA

National Kitchen and Bath Association N.K.B.A. or NKBA

National Labor Board NLB

National Labor Relations Board NLRB or N.L.R.B. (GPO: NLRB; NYT: N.L.R.B.)

National Lakeshore NL or N.L.

National League *baseball* NL or N.L.

National League for Democracy NLD (of Burma or Myanmar)

National League for Nursing NLN

National Lending Library for Science and Technology N.L.L. or NLL or NLLST

National Liberation Front *French, Spanish* F.L.N.

National Library for the Blind NLB

National Library of Australia NLA

National Library of Canada N.L.C.

National Library of Ireland N.L.I.

National Library of Medicine NLM

National Library of Music, in Paris B.N.C.M

National Library of Scotland N.L.S.

National Library (of France, Italy, or Spain) BN

National Lubricating Grease Institute NLGI

National Lumbermen's Association NLA

National Machine Tool Builders' Association NMTBA

National Management Association NMA or N.M.A.

National Marine Fisheries Service NMFS

National Maritime Board NMB

National Maritime Union NMU

National Market System NMS

National Market Traders' Federation NMTF

National Marketing Council NMC

National Measurement Laboratory NML

National Mediation Board NMB

National Medical Association NMA or N.M.A.

National Merit Scholarship NMS

National Meteorological Center NMC
National Military Command Center NMCC
National Military Command System NMCS
National Military Establishment NME
National Mortgage Association NMA or N.M.A.
National Museum of Anthropology of Mexico MNAM
National Museum of Natural History NMNH
National Music Publishers Association NMPA
National Newspaper Association NNA
National Newspaper Publishers Association NNPA
National Ocean Service NOS
National Ocean Survey NOS
National Oceanic and Atmospheric Administration NOAA
National Oceanographic Data Center NODC
National Office for Decent Literature NODL
National Office Management Association NOMA
National Office of Vital Statistics NOVS
National Office Products Association NOPA
National Oil Fuel Institute NOFI
National Olympic Committee NOC
National Opera Association NOA or N.O.A.
National Operational Meteorological Satellite System NOMSS
National Ophthalmic Treatment Board NOTB
National Opinion Polls British NOP
National Opinion Research Center NORC or Norc
National Opposition Union UNO or U.N.O. (of Nicaragua)
National Optical Astronomy Observatories NOAO
National Organization for Public Health Nursing NOPHN
National Organization for Women NOW
National Organization of Cypriot Struggle EOKA or Eoka
National Paper Trade Association NPTA
National Park 1 Nat. Pk. 2 NP
National Park Service NPS
National Parks and Wildlife Service N.P.W.S.
National Patriotic Front of Liberia NPFL
National People's Congress NPC (of China)
National Personnel Authority NPA
National Pest Control Association NPCA
National Petroleum Association NPA
National Petroleum Council NPC
National Pharmaceutical Union NPU
National Physical Laboratory British NPL or N.P.L.
National Planned Parenthood Federation NPPF
National Planning Association NPA
National Portrait Gallery NPG or N.P.G.
National Portrait Society NPS or N.P.S.
National Postal Union NPU
National Press Club NPC
National Press Photographers Association NPPA

National Production Authority NPA
National Program for Acquisition and Cataloging NPAC
National Public Radio NPR
National Radiation Laboratory NRL
National Radio Astronomy Observatory NRAO
National Radio Institute NRI or N.R.I.
National Radio of Angola RNA
National Railroad Passenger Corporation NRPC
National Railway Historical Society N.R.H.S.
National Reactor Testing Station NRTS
National Reclamation Association NRA
National Records Management Council NRMC
National Recovery Act or Administration NRA or N.R.A.
National Recreation Association NRA
National Recreational Area NRA
National Reference Library NRL or N.R.L.
National Relief Fund N.R.F.
National Religious Party NRP or N.R.P. (of Israel)
National Repertory Theater NRT or N.R.T.
National Republican Campaign Committee NRCC
National Republican Convention NRC (of Nigeria)
National Research Council NRC
National Research Council of Canada NRCC
National Research Development Corporation NRDC or N.R.D.C.
National Resistance Movement NRM (of Uganda)
National Resources Evaluation Center NREC
National Resources Planning Board NRPB
National Restaurant Association NRA
National Retail Credit Association NRCA
National Retail Merchants Association N.R.M.A.
National Retired Teacher Association N.R.T.A.
National Rifle Association NRA or N.R.A.
National Rural Electric Cooperative Association NRECA
National Safety Council NSC
National Sample Survey NSS
National Sanitary Foundation NSF
National Scholastic Press Association NSPA
National Science Board NSB
National Science Foundation NSF or N.S.F. (GPO: NSF)
National Science Library NSL or N.S.L.
National Science Teachers Association NSTA
National Sculpture Society NSS
National Seashore NS
National Security Agency NSA
National Security Council NSC
National Security Decision Directive NSDD
National Security Industrial Association NSIA
National Security Resources Board NSRB
National Security Traders Association NSTA
National Service NS
National Service Armed Forces Act British NSAFA
National Service Center NSC

National Service Life Insurance NSLI
National Severe Storm Forecast Center NSSFC
National Severe Storms Laboratory NSSL
National Shipping Authority NSA
National Skating Association NSA
National Ski Association NSA
National Ski Federation NSF
National Socialist German Workers Party Nazi
National Society for Autistic Children NSAC
National Society for Crippled Children N.S.C.C. or NSCC
National Society for Medical Research NSMR
National Society for the Prevention of Blindness N.S.P.B. or NSPB
National Society for the Prevention of Cruelty to Animals NSPCA or N.S.P.C.A.
National Society for the Prevention of Cruelty to Children NSPCC or N.S.P.C.C.
National Society of Art Education NSAE
National Society of Interior Designers N.S.I.D.
National Society of Professional Engineers NSPE or N.S.P.E.
National Solid Waste Management Association NSWMA
National Space Development Agency NASDA or Nasda (of Japan)
National Space Technology Laboratories NSTL
National Sportscasters and Sportswriters Association NSSA
National Standard Reference Data System NSRDS
National Standards Association NSA
National Standards Laboratory NSL or N.S.L.
National Student Association NSA
National Student Nurses Association N.S.N.A. or NSNA
National Synchrotron Light Source NSLS
National Taxpayers Union NTU
National Technical Association NTA
National Technical Information Service NTIA
National Technical Institute for the Deaf NTID
National Telecommunications and Information Administration NTIA
National Telephone Company of Spain CTNE
National Television System Committee NTSC
National Traffic System NTS
National Transportation Safety Board NTSB
National Trust British NT
National Trust for Historic Preservation NTHP or N.T.H.P.
National Tuberculosis Association NTA or N.T.A.
National Union NU or N.U.
National Union for Total Liberation of Angola Portuguese UNITA or Unita
National Union of Agricultural and Allied Workers NUAAW
National Union of Algerian Workers French UNPA

National Union of Bank Employees N.U.B.E. or NUBE (of Great Britain)
National Union of General and Municipal Workers NUGMW (of Great Britain)
National Union of Journalists N.U.J. or NUJ (of Great Britain)
National Union of Mineworkers NUM (of Great Britain)
National Union of Public Employees NUPE (of Great Britain)
National Union of South African Students NUSAS
National Union of Students NUS (of Great Britain)
National Union of Teachers NUT (of Great Britain)
National Union of Trained Nurses NUTN (of Great Britain)
National Union of Women Workers NUWW (of Great Britain)
National University Continuing Education Association NUCEA
National University of Ireland NUI or N.U.Irel.
National Urban League NUL or N.U.L.
National Vegetable Research Station NVRS
National Veterinary Medical Association NVMA or N.V.M.A.
National Vocational Guidance Association NVGA or N.V.G.A.
National War College NWC
National Warning System NAWAS
National Water and Soil Conservation Agency NWSCA
National Water Quality Surveillance System NWQSS
National Weather Satellite Center NWSC
National Weather Service NWS
National Wildlife Federation NWF
National Wildlife Refuge NWR
National Wildlife Reserve NWR
national wire gauge NWG
National Women's Political Caucus NWPC
National Women's Studies Association NWSA
National Youth Administration NYA
National Youth Orchestra NYO
Nationalist Party of Mexico Spanish PNM
native nat.
native language NL or N.L.
Nativity Nativ.
Nativity of the Virgin Mary NVM or N.V.M.
NATO Defense College NDC
Natural Nat.
natural nat. or nat.
Natural Environment Research Council NERC (of Great Britain)
natural family planning NFP
natural gas NG
natural gas liquids NGL
natural gas vehicle NGV
natural history Nat. Hist.
natural killer NK (of a cell)
natural language processing computers NLP
natural log or logarithm 1 n.l. 2 $\log_e$ 3 mathematics ln
natural order 1 Nat. Ord. 2 botany NO or N.O.
natural philosophy Nat. Phil.

natural remanent magnetization NRM
Natural Resources Defense Council NRDC
natural rubber NR
Natural Science 1 NS 2 Nat. Sci. or Nat. Sc.
Natural Science and Engineering Research Council NSERC
naturalist 1 nat. or nat. 2 natur.
naturalized 1 nat. 2 Natzd.
Nature Conservancy 1 Nat. Con. 2 NC
Nature Conservancy Council NCC
nautical naut.
nautical air miles NAM or nam
Nautical Almanac NA or N.A.
nautical mile 1 n.mi. or n.mi 2 NM or nm
Navaho Nav.
naval military nav. or NAV
Naval Academy NA or N.A.
Naval Air NAVAIR
Naval Air Base NAB
Naval Air Station NAS
Naval Air Transport Service NATS
Naval Architect NA or N.A.
Naval Attaché NA
Naval Base NB
Naval Electronics Laboratory NEL
Naval Engineer NE or N.E.
Naval Hospital NH
naval intelligence NI
Naval Intelligence Department NID
Naval Investigation Service NIS
Naval Medical Center NMC
Naval Observatory NAVOBSY
Naval Oceanographic Office NOO
naval officer NO
Naval Ordnance Laboratory NOL
Naval Ordnance Research Computer NORC
Naval Personnel Training Research Laboratory NPTRL
Naval Proving Grounds NPG
Naval Radiological Defense Laboratory NRDL
Naval Research Laboratory NRL
Naval Reserve Officer Training Corps NROTC or N.R.O.T.C.
naval staff officer NSO
Naval Standard NS (with number)
Naval Transport Service NTS
Naval Underwater Systems Center NUSC
navigable nav.
navigation 1 nav. 2 navig.
navigation and radar NAVAR
Navigation Computer Unit NCU
navigation data assimilation computer NAVDAC
Navigation Officer NO
navigation satellite NAVSAT
navigation system based on time and ranging NAVSTAR
navigational aid navaid
navigator 1 nav. 2 navig.
Navy N
Navy Cross NC
Navy Department ND
Navy Hydrographic Office NHO
Navy League British NL or N.L.
Navy Navigation Satellite System NNSS
Navy Oceanographic Meteorological Automatic Device NOMAD

Navy Post Office NPO
Navy Regulations NR (with number)
Navy Tracking Station Network TRANET
Navy, Army, and Air Force Institutes British NAAFI
near 1 nr. 2 medicine p or p.
Near Eastern and South Asian Affairs NESAA (bureau of U.S. Department of State)
near face engineering NF
near letter quality computers NLQ
near point (focus of the eyes) PP
near side NS (left-hand side)
near-death experience NDE
Nebraska 1 NE (Zip Code) 2 Neb. or Nebr. (NYT: Neb.; OUP: Nebr.)
necessary 1 nec or nec. 2 necy
neck nk. (in horse racing)
necrology necrol.
necrotizing ulcerative gingivitis medicine NUG
needle valve nv
needle French aig. (in knitting)
negation neg.
negative 1 N 2 neg.
negative acknowledgment communications NAK
negative binomial distribution statistics NBD
negative electron affinity NEA
negative feedback or no feedback electronics 1 B 2 NFB
negative income tax NIT
negative input, positive output electronics NIPO
negative temperature coefficient electronics NTC or n.t.c.
negative-positive-negative electronics NPN or npn
negative-positive-negative-positive electronics NPNP or npnp
negatively neg.
negligence neg.
negligent neg.
negotiable neg.
negotiated order of withdrawal NOW
Nehemiah Neh.
Neighborhood Improvement Association NIA
neighborhood loan program NLP
Neighborhood Watch Group NWG
neodium Nd
neologism neol.
neon Ne
neonatal intensive care unit NICU
Nepal 1 N 2 Nep.
Nepalese rupee NR
neper 1 n 2 Np
nephelometric turbidity unit NTU
nephew n or n.
Neptune Nep.
neptunium Np
nerve medicine n or n.
nerve cell adhesion molecule NCAM
nerve gas 1 VX 2 BZ 3 (sarin) GB
nerve growth factor biochemistry NGF
nerves medicine nn.
Net Ret (constellation)
net 1 n 2 nt or nt.
net annual gain commerce NAG or n.a.g.

net asset value *finance* n.a.v. *or* NAV
net assimilation rate *biology* nar *or* n.a.r.
Net Book Agreement NBA
net book value *commerce* NBV *or* n.b.v.
Net Domestic Product *economics* NDP
net economic welfare NEW
net financial assets *commerce* NFA *or* nfa
net material product NMP
Net National Product *commerce* NNP
net positive suction head NPSH (of a pump)
net present value *finance* NPV *or* n.p.v.
net proceeds n.p. *or* n/p
net quick assets *finance* n.q.a.
net rating point *or* **points** NRP
net realizable value *commerce* NRV
net register *shipping* NR
net registered tonnage *shipping* NRT *or* nrt
net reproductive rate NRR
net sales value NSV
net tangible assets *finance* NTA
net ton NT *or* n.t.
net ton mile NTM *or* n.t.m.
net weight 1 n.wt. *or* nwt 2 nt wt *or* nt.wt.
3 nw *or* n.w. *or* n/w (*GPO, CSM:* net wt.)
net worth nw *or* n/w
Netherlands 1 Neth. 2 Nth 3 *Dutch* Ndl.
Netherlands West Indies N.W.I. *or* NWI
network 1 NET *or* net *or* Net 2 ntwrk
network interface card *computers* NIC
network user identifier *computers* NUI
networking netwrkg
neuraminidase NA
neurocirculatory asthenia NCA
neurodevelopmental treatment NDT
neurofibromatosis NF
neuroleptic malignant syndrome NMS
neurological neur. *or* neurol.
Neurological Society of America NSA *or*
N.S.A.
neurology neur.
neuron-specific enolase NSE
Neuropathic Doctor ND
neuropsychiatric NP
neuropsychiatry NP
neuter 1 n *or* n. 2 neut.
neuter verb vn *or* v.n.
neutral 1 N 2 neut.
neutral charge *physics* Z
neutral density ND
neutral protein Hagedorn NPH
neutralization number *chemistry* NN *or*
N.N.
neutralize neut.
neutron 1 N 2 *physics* n
neutron activation analysis NAA
neutron flux nv
neutron flux time integral nvt
neutron number N
Nevada 1 Nev. 2 NV (Zip Code)
Nevada Proving Ground NPG
Nevada Test Site NTS
New N *or* N.
new *pharmaceutics* Rec.
New American Bible NAB
New and Nonofficial Drugs N.N.D.
New and Nonofficial Remedies N.N.R.
New British Standard NBS *or* N.B.S.
New Brunswick NB (postal code)
New China News Agency NCNA

new college graduate NCG
New Community Instrument NCI
new cruzado NCz
New Democratic Party NDP (of Canada)
new drug application NDA
new edition NE *or* N.E.
new edition pending NEP *or* n.e.p.
New England 1 N. Eng. 2 NE *or* N.E.
3 New Eng. (*OUP:* N. Eng.)
New England Conservatory of Music NEC
or NECM
New English NE *or* NE.
New English Bible NEB
New English Dictionary NED
New General Catalogue NGC
new genus *biology* 1 n.gen. 2 ng *or* n.g.
New Greek NGk. *or* NGk *or* NGr.
New Guinea NG *or* N.G.
New Hampshire NH (Zip Code) *or* N.H. (in
general use) (*NYT:* N.H.; *OUP:* NH)
New Hebrew N.Heb.
New Hebrides N.Heb.
New High German NHG. *or* NHG
new impression ni *or* n/i
New Jersey NJ (Zip Code) *or* N.J. (in
general use) (*NYT:* N.J.; *OUP:* NJ)
New Latin NL *or* N.L. *or* NL.
new line 1 *computers* NL *or* N.L. 2 *printing*
n.l.
New Linguistic Atlas of France NALF
New Mexico 1 N. Mex. 2 New M. 3 NM
(Zip Code) *or* N.M. (in general use) (*NYT:*
N.M.; *OUP:* N. Mex.)
new moon nm *or* n.m.
new name *taxonomy* 1 n. nov. 2 nom. nov.
new obligation authority NOA
New Orleans 1 NO *or* N.O. 2 O (mint
mark)
new paragraph n.p. *or* np
new pence *British* p
New Programming Language *computers*
NPL
New Progressive Party *Spanish* PNP *or*
P.N.P. (of Puerto Rico)
New Providence, Bahamas NP *or* N.P.
New Scotland Yard N.S.Y. *or* NSY
New Series NS *or* N.S. (*OUP:* NS)
new series ns *or* n.s. (*MLA:* ns)
new shekel £
New South Wales N.S.W. *or* NSW
New South Wales Government N.S.W.G.
or NSWG
new species 1 sp. nov. 2 *biology* n.sp.
New Style (Gregorian calendar) NS *or* N.S.
(*MLA, OUP:* NS)
New Technology Telescope NTT
new terms *commerce* N/t
New Testament 1 New Test. 2 NT *or* N.T. *or*
NT. (*MLA, OUP:* NT)
New Testament Greek NTGk *or* N.T.Gk
new translation NT *or* N.T.
New Version NV *or* N.V.
New World Order N.W.O. (of the post
Cold War)
New Year NY
New York NY (Zip Code) *or* N.Y. (in
general use) (*NYT:* N.Y.; *OUP:* NY)
New York Board of Fire Underwriters
N.Y.B.F.U.

New York Bureau of State Building Codes
N.Y.B.S.C.
New York Cash Exchange NYCE
New York City NYC *or* N.Y.C.
New York City Ballet NYCB
New York Cocoa Exchange NYCE
New York Commodity Exchange NYCE
New York Cotton Exchange CTN
New York Futures Exchange NYFE
New York Historical Society N.Y.H.S.
New York Mercantile Exchange NYME
New York Public Library NYPL
New York Racing Association N.Y.R.A.
New York State NYS *or* N.Y.S.
New York State Athletic Commission
NYSAC
New York Stock Exchange NYSE *or*
N.Y.S.E.
New York Telephone Company NYNEX
New York Times NYT
New York Zoological Society NYZS
New York (City) Police Department NYPD
New York (City) Transit Authority NYTA
New York (in Federal banking system) B
New Zealand 1 NZ *or* N.Z. *or* N.Zeal.
2 NZL
New Zealand Associated Press NZAP
New Zealand Atomic Energy Committee
NZAEC
New Zealand Broadcasting Corporation
NZBC *or* N.Z.B.C.
New Zealand Council of Trade Unions
NZCTU
New Zealand Educational Institute NZEI *or*
N.Z.E.I.
New Zealand Forest Service NZFS
New Zealand Labour Party NZLP
New Zealand Medical Association
N.Z.M.A.
New Zealand Post Office NZPO *or*
N.Z.P.O.
New Zealand Press Association N.Z.P.A. *or*
NZPA
New Zealand Railways NZR *or* N.Z.R.
New Zealand Registered Nurse NZRN
New Zealand Rugby Football Union NZRFU
New Zealand University Students
Association NZUSA *or* N.Z.U.S.A.
New Zealand Wool Board NZWB
New Zealand, Australia Free Trade
Agreement NAFTA
newborn NB
Newfoundland 1 Newf. 2 NF (postal code)
or N.F. *or* NF. (in general use) 3 Nfd.
4 Nfld. 5 Nwfld (*OUP:* NF *or* Nfld.)
Newfoundland Standard Time NST *or*
N.S.T.
newly industrialized country NIC
News Press Agency of Russia APN
Newspaper Advertising Bureau NAB
Newspaper Association of America NAA
Newspaper Enterprise Association NEA *or*
N.E.A.
Newspaper Guild, The TNG
Newspaper Publishers Association NPA *or*
N.P.A.
newton 1 nt 2 *physics* N
newton meter *physics* Nm
next nx *or* nxt

next day *commerce* ND *or* N/D
next in, first out *commerce* NIFO
next month *prox.*
next of kin nok *or* NOK
next to reading matter *advertising* NRM
Ngultrum Nu *or* N
Nicaragua Nic. *or* Nicar.
Nicaraguan Nic. *or* Nicar.
nickel Ni
nickel-cadmium nicad *or* NiCad
nicotinamide adenine dinucleotide NAD
nicotinamide adenine dinucleotide
    phosphate NADP
nicotinamide mononucleotide *biochemistry*
    NMN
Nielsen Television Index NTI
Niger Progressive Party *French* PPN
Nigeria Nig.
Nigerian 1 N 2 Nig.
night 1 n *or* n. 2 ni *or* ni. 3 nt
night and morning 1 *French* n. et m.
    2 *pharmaceutics* nm *or* n.m.
night observation device NOD
night vision NV
nimbostratus *meteorology* Ns
nimbus *meteorology* Nb
nimbus cloud N
nineteen-hundred indexing and cataloging
    computers NIC
ninety N
niobium Nb
Nippon Nip.
Nippon Telegraph and Telephone
    Corporation NTT
Nippon Television NTV
Nipponese Nip.
nit nt (unit of luminance)
nitrilotriacetic acid NTA
nitrocellulose NC *or* N.C. *or* n.c.
nitrogen N
nitrogen oxide NO_x
nitrogen-fixing *biology* nif
nitrogen-phosphorous-potassium NPK *or*
    N-P-K (of fertilizer)
nitroglycerine NG
nitrophenyl pentadienal NPPD
no 1 N 2 n *or* n.
no account *banking* n/a
no advice *banking* NA *or* N/A
no angular momentum *electronics* s state
no answer NA
no appreciable disease NAD *or* n.a.d.
no ball *cricket* n.b.
no bias *electronics* NB
no bid NB
no bone injury *medicine* NBI *or* n.b.i.
no carbon required NCR
no change NC
no charge NC *or* n/c
no comment NC
no commercial value n.c.v. *or* NCV
no commission until paid *commerce* n.c.u.p.
    or NCUP
no common interest NCI *or* n.c.i.
no connection *electronics* NC
no copies available NCA *or* n.c.a.
no credit *commerce* NC *or* N/C
no date 1 n.d. 2 ND *or* N.D.
no decision ND *or* N.D. *or* N/D

no deed ND *or* N.D.
no discount *commerce* ND *or* N.D. *or* N/D
    or n/d
no effects *banking* N/E
no evidence of disease *medicine* NED
no fixed date n.f.d.
no funds *banking* 1 nf *or* n.f. *or* n/f 2 NF *or*
    N/F *or* N.F.
no further action NFA *or* n.f.a.
no further requirements NFR *or* n.f.r.
no good 1 NG *or* N.G. *or* N/G 2 ng *or*
    n.g. *or* n/g
no load *commerce* NL *or* N.L. *or* N.L.
no mark *commerce* N/m *or* n/m
no middle initial NMI *or* nmi
no more credit *commerce* n.m.c.
no name n.n.
no one dissenting *law* N.C.D.
no operation *computers* 1 no op *or* No op
    2 NOP
no orders *commerce* NO *or* N/O
no paging *printing* n.p. *or* np (*MLA:* n.pag.)
no par value *finance* NPV *or* n.p.v.
no paragraph no par.
no passed proof *printing* n.p.p.
no pathologic diagnosis *medicine* NPD
no personal liability *insurance* NPL
no place of publication n.p.
no place or date 1 n.p. *or* d. 2 np/d
no prior service NPS
no protest NP *or* N/P
no protest nonacceptance *banking* n.p.n.a.
    or NPNA
no publisher n.p.
no response or return NR *or* N.R.
no risk *insurance* NR *or* N/R
no risk after discharge *insurance* NRAD *or*
    n.r.a.d.
no service ns *or* n/s
no significant difference n.s.d.
no time lost n.t.l.
no title page NTP *or* n.t.p.
no voltage release NVR
no-claim bonus *insurance* NCB
no-fly zone *military* NFZ
no-trump NT *or* N.T.
NOAA Weather Radio NWR
Nobel Prize NP *or* N.P.
nobelium No
noble Nob.
nobody dissenting nem. dis.
nobody opposing nem. con.
nocturne *music* Noct.
Noise Abatement Society NAS
noise and number index NNI *or* n.n.i.
noise equivalent power NEP *or* nep
noise exposure forecast NEF
noise factor 1 NF 2 *electronics* F
noise figure *electronics* NF
noise load ratio NLR
noise pollution level NPL
noise ratio NR
noise reduction NR
noise transmission impairment NTI
noise-power ratio *electronics* NPR
nomenclature 1 nom. 2 nomen.
nominal nom.
nominal capital *commerce* nom. cap.
nominal horsepower NHP *or* nhp *or* n.hp.

nominated nom.
nominative 1 n *or* n. 2 *grammar* a nom.
    b nomin.
Non-Aligned Movement NAM *or* nam
non-OPEC NOPEC
non-REM NREM
Non-Self-Governing territory NSGT
Nonaccelerating Inflation Rate of
    Unemployment NAIRU
nonacceptance 1 *commerce* n/a 2 NA *or*
    N/A
nonbank financial institutions NBFI
noncomissioned officer 1 noncom *or* *military*
    NONCOM 2 NCO *or* n.c.o.
nondelivery 1 n.d. 2 ND *or* N/D
nondestructive analysis *chemistry,*
    engineering NDA *or* n.d.a.
nondestructive evaluation NDE
nondestructive inspection NDI
nondestructive readout *computers* NDRO
nondestructive testing NDT
nondeterministic polynomial NP
nondirectional ND
nondirectional beacon *aeronautics* NDB
nonequivalence *computers* NEQ
nones N
nonesterified fatty acid NEFA
nonfat dry milk NFDM
nonferrous NF
nonfundable NF
nongonococcal urethritis *medicine* NGU
nongovernmental organization NGO
noninsulin-dependent diabetes NIDD
noninsulin-dependent diabetes mellitus
    NIDDM
noninterference basis NIB
nonoperation NOP
nonoperational 1 no op *or* No op 2 NOP
nonparticipating n.p. *or* np (of stock rights)
nonpolice NP
Nonprofessional Staff NPS
nonprofit NP
nonproliferation treaty NPT *or* N.P.T.
nonprotein nitrogen NPN
nonreactive *electronics* NR
nonresident NR *or* N.R. *or* N-R
nonreturn to zero *computers* NRZ
nonreturn valve NRV *or* nrv
nonspecific urethritis *medicine* NSU
nonstandard 1 nonstand *or* nonstd 2 ns
    (*MLA:* nonstand.)
nonsteroidal anti-inflammatory drug
    NSAID
nonstop ns
Nontariff Barrier NTB
nonutility generator NUG
nonvintage NV *or* N.V. *or* N/V
nonvolatile matter NVM
nonvoting NV (of stock rights)
nonwatertight door NWTD *or* nwtd
noon 1 N *or* N. 2 n *or* n. 3 *Latin* m *or* M
nordihydroguaiaretic acid NDGA
Norfolk County, England Norf.
normal 1 N 2 n- (in a straight-chain structure)
    3 nor. 4 norm. 5 nrml 6 *chemistry* n *or* n
normal allowed time nat. *or* n.a.t.
normal boiling point NBP *or* nbp
normal circular pitch *engineering* NCP *or*
    n.c.p.

normal lymphocyte transfer NLT
normal pressure 1 n.p. **2** NP
normal pressure and temperature NPT or n.p.t.
normal saline solution *medicine* NSS or n.s.s.
normal temperature and pressure NTP or ntp
normal water surface NWS or nws
normal-mode rejection ratio *electronics* NMRR
normalize norm.
normalized norm.
normally closed NC
normally open NO or n.o.
Norman (French) **1** Nor. **2** Norm.
Norman-French NF or N.F. or N-F
North 1 Nor. **2** Nth **3** N or N.
north 1 No or No. **2** no or no. **3** nor.
North Africa N. Afr.
North African N. Afr.
North America 1 N. Am. **2** NA or N.A. (OUP: N. Amer.)
North American 1 N. Am. **2** NA or N.A.
North American Air Defense Command NORAD
North American Data Airborne Recorder Nadar
North American Free Trade Agreement 1 NAFTA **2** *Spanish* TLC
North American Newspaper Alliance NANA or N.A.N.A.
North American Presentation Level Protocol Syntax *computers* NAPLPS
North American Soccer League NASL
North American Water and Power Alliance NAWAPA
North Atlantic Council NAC
North Atlantic Free Trade Area NAFTA
North Atlantic Treaty Organization NATO or Nato (GPO, NYT: NATO; OUP: NATO or Nato)
north by east NbE or N by E
north by west NbW or N by W
North Carolina 1 N. Car. **2** NC (Zip Code) or N.C. (in general use) (NYT: N.C.; OUP: NC)
North Dakota 1 N. Dak. **2** ND (Zip Code) or N.D. (in general use) (NYT: N.D.; OUP: N. Dak.)
North East Atlantic Fisheries Commission NEAFC
North Island (New Zealand) NI or N.I.
north latitude 1 N.Lat. or N.lat. **2** NL or N.L.
North Pacific *military* NORPAC
north polar distance NPD or n.p.d.
North Wales NW or N.W.
north-northeast NNE or N.N.E. or n.n.e.
north-northwest NNW or N.N.W. or n.n.w.
North-West Frontier Province N.W.F.P. (of Pakistan)
North-West Provinces N.W.P. (of India)
Northamptonshire County, England Northants
northbound 1 n.b. or n/b **2** NB
northeast 1 NE or N.E. **2** n.e. (GPO: NE.; OUP: NE)
northeast by east NEbE or NE by E

northeast by north NEbN or NE by N
Northeast Modern Language Association NEMLA
Northeast Radio Observatory Corporation NEROC
northeastern 1 NE or N.E. **2** n.e.
Northern 1 Nor. **2** N or N.
northern 1 No or No. **2** no or no. **3** nor. **4** North. or north. **5** Nthn or nthn.
Northern Crown CrB (constellation)
Northern District ND or N.D.
Northern Hemisphere NH or N.H.
Northern Ireland 1 N.Ir. or N.Ire. **2** NI
Northern Mariana Islands MP (in postal address)
Northern Region Headquarters NRHQ
Northern Rocky Mountains NRM
Northern Territory NT or N.T. (of Australia)
Northumberland County, England Northum. or Northumb.
northward Northw. or northw.
northwest 1 NW or N.W. **2** n.w. (GPO: NW.; OUP: NW)
Northwest Atlantic Fisheries Organization NAFO
northwest by north NWbN or NW by N
northwest by west NWbW or NW by W
Northwest Territories 1 N.W.T. or NWT (of Canada) **2** NT (Canada, postal code)
northwestern 1 NW or N.W. **2** n.w.
Norway 1 Nor. **2** Norw. **3** *Norwegian* KN
Norwegian 1 N **2** Ng. **3** Nor. **4** Norw. **5** Nrw.
Norwegian krone Nkr
Norwegian Lutheran Church of America N.L.C.A.
nose no (in horse racing)
nose cone NC
not 1 N **2** n or n.
not allowed NA
not always afloat *shipping* naa
Not AND *computers* NAND
not applicable 1 n/a or n.a. **2** NA or N/A (GPO: NA.; OUP: n/a)
not assigned NA
not available 1 n/a or n.a. **2** NA or N.A. (GPO: NA.; OUP: n/a)
not cataloged NC
not dated 1 n.d. **2** ND or N.D.
not earlier than NET or n.e.t.
not elsewhere classified nec or n.e.c. (GPO: n.e.c.)
not elsewhere indicated n.e.i.
not elsewhere mentioned NEM or n.e.m.
not elsewhere specified NES or n.e.s. (GPO: n.e.s.)
not essential NE
not exceeding n.e. or n/e
not favorably considered NFC or nfc
not for sale NFS
not guilty *law* non cul.
not guilty, insanity NGI
not in contact *electronics* NIC or nic
not in my back yard NIMBY or Nimby
not in stock *commerce* NIS or n.i.s.
not known NK or N.K. or nk
not later than NLT or n.l.t.
not less than NLT or n.l.t.
not marked *commerce* N/m or n/m

not more than NMT or nmt
not on active duty NAD
not operating NO or N/O
not operationally ready NOR
not otherwise authorized NOA or n.o.a.
not otherwise classified NOC or n.o.c.
not otherwise enumerated NOE or n.o.e.
not otherwise herein provided NOHP or n.o.h.p.
not otherwise indexed by name *commerce* NOIBN or n.o.i.b.n. (GPO: n.o.i.b.n.)
not otherwise provided for NOP or n.o.p. (GPO, OUP: n.o.p.)
not otherwise specified n.o.s.
not our publication NOP
not out *cricket* no or n.o.
not out yet N.O.Y. or n.o.y. (of a publication)
not passed urine *medicine* NPU or npu
not provided for n.p.f.
not published and no date 1 n.p. or d. **2** n.p./n.d.
not reported NR or N.R. or n/r
not scheduled ns
not significant NS or N.S.
not specifically provided for n.s.p.f. or nspf (GPO: n.s.p.f.)
not specified ns
not sufficient *banking* **1** NS or N/S **2** ns or n/s
not sufficient funds *banking* NSF or nsf
not taken out n.t.o. or NTO
not to be noted *commerce* N/N or n/n
not to be omitted *music* obb. or obbl.
not to be repeated *pharmaceutics* NR or n.r.
not to scale NTS or ntc
not traded *commerce* **1** nt **2** r
not under control NUC
not yet diagnosed *medicine* NYD
not yet published NYP or n.y.p.
not yet returned NYR or n.y.r.
NOT-OR *mathematics, computers* NOR
Notary Not.
Notary Public NP or N.P.
note n or n.
note well 1 n.b. **2** *Latin* NB (MLA, OUP: NB; CSM: N.B.)
notes nn.
Notes and Queries 1 N.&Q. **2** NQ
nothing abnormal discovered NAD or n.a.d.
nothing by mouth *medicine* NPO or n.p.o.
nothing to report NTR
notice Not. or not.
notice to airmen NOTAM
notify ntfy
Nottinghamshire County, England Notts.
notwithstanding 1 notwg **2** *Latin* non obs. or non obst.
notwithstanding the verdict *law* n.o.v. or N.O.V.
noun n or n.
noun feminine *grammar* nf or n.f.
noun phrase *grammar* n.p. or np
noun plural n.pl.
noun-verb NV
Nova Scotia NS (in postal code) or N.S. (in general use)
novel Nov. or nov.

novelist Nov. or nov.
November 1 N **2** Nov. or Nov (*NYT, OUP:* Nov.)
novice Nov. or nov.
nozzle **1** n **2** noz
nuclear **1** N **2** nuc
nuclear, biological, chemical NBC (of weapons)
Nuclear Defense Affairs Committee NDAC
nuclear detonation or **detection system** NUDETS
Nuclear Emergency Search Team NEST
Nuclear Energy Agency NEA
Nuclear Engine for Rocket Vehicle Applications NERVA
nuclear galaxy NG
nuclear generating station NGS
nuclear gyromagnetic ratio g
Nuclear Industry Radioactive Waste Executive NIREX
nuclear magnetic resonance (scanner) *medicine* NMR
Nuclear Materials Equipment Corporation NUMEC
nuclear paramagnetic resonance *physics* NPR
Nuclear Planning Group NPG
nuclear polyhedrosis virus NPV

nuclear power plant NPP
nuclear quadrupole resonance *physics* NQR
nuclear reaction spectrometry NRS
Nuclear Regulatory Commission NRC
Nuclear Rocket Development Station NRDS
nuclear science NS
nuclear ship NS
nuclear submarine SSN (naval symbol)
nuclear warfare NW
nuclear waste material NWM
Nuclear Weapons Storage Facility NWSF
nuclear or **isotopic spin** I
nuclear-powered submarine SSBN (naval symbol)
nucleoprotein NP
nucleoside diphosphate NDP
nucleus 1 N **2** *astronomy* b or c
nucleus (of nebula) *astronomy* a
nudism nud.
nudist nud.
null character *computers* NUL
number 1 N **2** n or n. **3** num. **4** *Latin* **a** no or no. **b** No (*GPO, NYT, CSM:* No.; *MLA:* no.; *OUP:* No. or no.)
number of components n
number of conductors *electronics* N
number of factors or **variables** N
number of grating lines of an atom N

number of observation N
number of variables n
number of windings of a coil N
number or name changed NCH
number unobtainable 1 n.u. **2** NU
numbered numb.
Numbers Num. (book of the Old Testament)
numbers Nos. or nos. (*GPO:* Nos.; *OUP:* Nos. or nos.)
numeral num.
numeric *computers* NUM
numerical num.
numerical aperture NA (of a microscope)
numerical control NC or n/c
numerical weather prediction NWP
numismatics or **numismatic** numis. or numism.
nun N or N.
Nurse Corps NC or N.C.
Nurse Practitioner NP
nurse's aide NA
Nursery School Association *British* NSA
Nursing Auxiliary Service NAS
nursing procedure NP
nutrients nut.
nutrition nutr.
nylon nyl

oak leaf cluster *military* OLC
Oak Ridge Institute for Nuclear Studies ORINS
Oak Ridge National Laboratory ORNL
Obadiah 1 Ob **2** Obad.
obedient 1 obdt. **2** obt.
obituary obit or obit.
object obj.
object-oriented programming *computers* OOP
objection obj.
objective obj. or object. (*MLA, OUP:* obj.)
Oblates of Mary Immaculate O.M.I.
obligation obl.
oblique obl.
oblique photograph *surveying* ob. ph.
oblong 1 Ob **2** obl.
oboe ob or ob.
obscure obs.
obscured *navigation* obsc. or Obsc.
observation 1 O **2** ob **3** obs.
Observation Officer OO
observation post *military* OP
observatory obs. or Obs.
observe obs.
observed 1 obs. **2** Obs. or OBS
observer O
obsessive compulsive disorder *medicine* OCD

obsolescent obsol. or obsoles.
obsolete obs. or Obs. (*MLA, CSM, OUP:* obs.)
obstacle obs.
obstetrical 1 OB or OB. **2** obstet.
obstetrician 1 OB or OB. **2** Obs. or OBS
obstetrician and gynecologist OB/GYN
obstetrics 1 OB or OB. **2** Obs. or OBS **3** obstet.
obstetrics and gynecology OB/GYN
obtained obtd.
obverse obv.
occasion occn.
occasional or **occasionally 1** o or o. **2** occ. or occas.
occupation 1 occ. **2** occup.
occupational occup.
occupational health nurse OHN
Occupational Safety and Health Administration OSHA
Occupational Safety and Health Review Commission OSHRC
occupational therapy OT or O.T.
occupied territories OT (by Israel)
Ocean 1 O or O. **2** Oc. or oc.
Ocean Data Station ODS
Ocean Drilling Program ODP
Ocean Research Institute ORI
Ocean Resources Conservation Association ORCA
ocean station OS
ocean station vessel OSV
ocean thermal energy conversion OTEC
Ocean Weather Service OWS
Oceanic Air Traffic Control OATC
oceanographic research buoy ORB
oceanography oceanog.

Oceans and International Environmental and Scientific Affairs OIESA
ochre och.
octagon oct.
octane number ON
octant Oct
octave 1 oct. **2** *music* ott.
octaves *music* ova.
octavo 1 O or O. **2** o or o. **3** oct. **4** ovo.
October 1 O or O. **2** Oct or Oct. (*NYT, OUP:* Oct.)
October and April *accounting* O&A
October, January, April, July *accounting* OJAJ
octomethyl pyrophosphoramide OMPA
ocular hypertension indicator OHI
Odd Fellows OF or O.F.
oersted Oe or Oe.
of Cambridge Cantab.
of Canterbury Cantaur.
of Carlisle Carliol.
of Chester Cestr.
of each *pharmaceutics* sing.
of Exeter Exon.
of Oxford Oxon. or oxon.
of Rochester Roffen
of Salisbury Sarum
of the current month cour. or Cour.
of the goods not yet administered *law* D.B.N. or d.b.n.
of this year *Latin* h.a.
of which *pharmaceutics* cuj.
of Winchester Winton.
off o or o.
off and on OAO or o.a.o.
off-Broadway OB or oB
off-off-Broadway OOB or ooB

off-road vehicle ORV
off-the-film OTF
off-track betting OTB
offered off.
office 1 ofc. or Ofc. 2 off. or Off.
Office and Professional Employees International Union OPEIU
Office Appliance and Business Equipment Trade Association OABETA
office automation OA
office copy OC
office document architecture *computers* ODA
Office Employees International Union OEIU
Office for Equal Opportunity OEO
Office For the Aging OFA
Office for Victims of Crime OVC
office hours OH
Office of Administration OA
Office of Administrative Appeals OAA
Office of Administrative Law OAL
Office of Advanced Research and Technology OART
Office of Aeronautics and Space Technology OAST
Office of Aerospace Research OAR
Office of Airline Statistics OAS
Office of Alcoholism and Substance Abuse Services OASAS
Office of Alien Property OAP
Office of Automated Tariffs OAT
Office of Business Economics OBE
Office of Challenge Grants OCG
Office of Child Support Enforcement OCSE
Office of Civil Rights OCR
Office of Civilian Health and Medical Program of the Uniformed Services OCHAMPUS
Office of Civilian Radioactive Waste Management OCRWM
Office of Commercial Space Transportation OCST
Office of Community Services OCS
Office of Computer Services OCS
Office of Congressional and Legislative Affairs OCLA
Office of Consumer Affairs OCA
Office of Contract Settlement OCS
Office of Coordinator of Inter-American Affairs OCIAA
Office of Defense Resources ODR
Office of Defense Transportation ODT
Office of Dependency Benefits ODB
Office of Economic Adjustment OEA
Office of Economic Opportunity OEO
Office of Education OE
Office of Employment Stability OES
Office of Energy Conservation OEC
Office of Energy Research OER
Office of Environmental Affairs OEA
Office of Environmental Restoration and Waste Management OERWM
Office of Exploration OE (of NASA)
Office of Fair Trading OFT
Office of Family Assistance OFA
Office of Federal Contract Compliance OFCC
Office of Federal Procurement Policy OFPP
Office of Federal Records Centers OFRC

Office of Financial Management OFM
Office of Foreign Missions OFM
Office of Government Ethics OGE
Office of Grants and Program Systems OGPS
Office of Health Economics OHE or O.H.E.
Office of Hearings and Appeals OHA
Office of Highway Safety OHS
Office of Human Development Services HDS
Office of Impact Analysis OIA
Office of Independent Counsel OIC
Office of Intelligence Policy and Review OIPR
Office of International Affairs OIA
Office of International Cooperation and Development OICD
Office of International Scientific Affairs OISA
Office of International Trade OIT
Office of International Trade Fairs OITF
Office of Job Training Programs OJTP
Office of Justice Programs OJP
Office of Juvenile Justice and Delinquency Prevention OJJDP
Office of Labor-Management Standards OLMS
Office of Legal Counsel OLC
Office of Legislative Affairs OLA
Office of Liaison Service OLS
Office of Management and Administration OMA
Office of Management and Budget OMB or O.M.B. (*GPO:* OMB; *NYT:* O.M.B.)
Office of Management and Information Systems OMIS
Office of Mental Health OMH
Office of Minority Business Enterprise OMBE
Office of Minority Economic Impact OMEI
Office of Minority Institutions Program OMIP
Office of Naval Intelligence ONI
Office of Naval Research ONR
Office of New Production Reactors ONPR
Office of Nuclear Safety ONS
Office of Operations OO
Office of Ordnance Research OOR
Office of Personnel Management OPM
Office of Planning and Budget OPB
Office of Planning and Research OPR
Office of Policy Coordination OPC
Office of Policy Development OPD
Office of Policy Planning and Analysis OPPA
Office of Policy, Planning, Research, and Budget OPPRB
Office of Presidential Libraries OPL
Office of Primary Responsibility OPR
Office of Program and Fiscal Integrity OPFI
Office of Program Organization OPO
Office of Public Affairs OPA
Office of Public Information OPI
Office of Public Programs OPP
Office of Publications and Public Affairs OPPA
Office of Quartermaster General O.Q.M.G.
Office of Records Administration ORA
Office of Refugee Resettlement ORR

Office of Regional Management ORM
Office of Saline Water OSW or O.S.W.
Office of Science and Technology Policy OSTP
Office of Scientific and Technical Information or **Infrastructure** OSTI
Office of Scientific Integrity OSI
Office of Small and Disadvantaged Business Utilization OSDBU
Office of Space Communications OSC
Office of Space Flight OSF
Office of Space Science and Applications OSSA
Office of Space Systems Development OSSD
Office of Special Counsel OSC
Office of Special Investigations OSI
Office of Substance Abuse Prevention OSAP
Office of Surface Mining Reclamation and Enforcement OSM or OSMRE
Office of Surface Transportation Safety OSTS
Office of Technical Services OTS
Office of Technology Assessment OTA
Office of Telecommunications Oftel or OFTEL
Office of the Assistant Secretary for Technology Policy OASTP
Office of the Attorney General OAG
Office of the Chief of Engineers of the U.S. Army OEC
Office of the Controller of the Currency OCC
Office of the Federal Register OFR
Office of the Inspector General OIG
Office of the National Archives ONA
Office of the Pardon Attorney OPA or O.P.A.
Office of the Secretary of Defense OSD
Office of the Secretary of Labor OSL
Office of the Secretary of the Air Force OSAF
Office of the Secretary of the Army OSA
Office of the Secretary of the Navy OSN
Office of the Status of Women OSW or O.S.W.
Office of the Vice President of the United States OVP or OVPUS
Office of Thrift Supervision OTS
Office of Trade Adjustment Assistance OTAA
Office of Transportation OT
Office of Treatment Improvement OTI
Office of U.S. Trade Representative OTR
Office of Visas and Registration OVIR (in Russia)
Office of Volunteerism Initiatives OVI
Office of Women's Business Ownership OWBO
Office of Work-Based Learning OWBL
Office of Worker Retraining and Adjustment Programs OWRAP
Office of Workers' Compensation Programs OWCP
officer 1 off. or Off. 2 offr. or Offr.
Officer Candidate OC
Officer Candidate School OCS
Officer Commanding *British* OC or O.C.
officer efficiency report OER
officer in tactical command OTC

Officer of the Day 1 OD **2** OOD or O.O.D.
Officer of the Deck OOD or O.O.D.
Officer of the Guard 1 OG **2** OOG or O.O.G.
Officer of the Order of Australia A.O. or AO
Officer of the Watch OOW or O.O.W.
Officer Training Corps British OTC or O.T.C.
Officer Training School OTS
Officer-in-Charge OIC
Officers Reserve Corps ORC or O.R.C.
Officers' Emergency Reserve OER
Offices of Medical Services MED
official 1 ofcl. or Ofcl. **2** off. or Off. **3** offic. or Offic.
Official Airline Guide OAG
official classification OC
Official Development Assistance ODA
Official Gazette Off. Gaz.
Official Hostess OH
Official Secrets Act British OSA or O.S.A.
official test insecticide OTI
officially ex off.
officiating offg.
officinal off.
offshore procurement OSP
offside British OS (right-hand side)
ogee architecture OG or O.G.
O-Gravity OG or O-G (weightlessness)
Ohio 1 O or O. **2** OH (Zip Code)
Ohio College Library Center OCLC
Ohio Improved Chester White OIC
ohm 1 O **2** o
oil 1 O/O **2** Latin ol.
oil circuit breaker engineering OCB
Oil Heat Institute of America OHIA
oil immersed OI
oil in water O/W
oil switch OS
Oil, Chemical and Atomic Workers International Union OCAW or OCAWIU
oiltight OT
ointment 1 oint. **2** pharmaceutics ung.
Oklahoma 1 OK (Zip Code) **2** Okla.
Old O or O.
old account OA
Old Age Assistance OAA
Old Age Pension or **Pensioner** OAP
Old Age Security OAS (of Canada)
Old Age, Survivors, Disability, and Health Insurance OASDHI
Old Bulgarian OBulg.
Old Catholic OC
Old Church Slavic OSl. or OSlav.
Old Danish ODan.
Old Dutch OD or OD.
Old English OE or O.E.
old face OF or O.F. (printing type)
Old Flemish OFlem.
Old French 1 OF or O.F. **2** OFr or O.Fr.
Old Frisian OFris.
Old High German OHG or O.H.G.
Old Icelandic 1 OI **2** OIcel.
Old Irish OIr.
Old Italian OIt.
Old Latin OL or O.L.
Old Low German OLG or O.L.G.
old measurement o.m.
Old Norman French ONF or O.N-F.

Old Norse ON or O.N.
Old Persian OPer. or OPers.
Old Provençal OProv.
Old Prussian OPr. or OPruss.
Old Russian ORuss.
Old Saxon OS or OS.
Old Series law **1** o.s. **2** OS or O.S. (MLA: os; OUP: OS)
Old Slavic OSl. or OSlav.
Old Spanish OSp.
old style 1 (printing type) OS or O.S. **2** (calendar) vs or v.s.
old term or **terminology** medicine OT or O.T.
old terms commerce OT or O/t or O/T
Old Testament 1 Old Test. **2** OT or O.T. or OT. (MLA, OUP: OT) **3** Latin VT or V.T.
old tuberculin OT
Old Welsh OW
Older Americans Act OAA
Older Women's League OWL
Olduvai Hominid anthropology OH
oleoresin capsicum OC
olive drab OD
Olympiad 1 Ol. **2** Olym.
Olympic Games 1 OG or O.G. **2** Olym.
Olympics Olym.
ombudsman Swedish JO or J.O.
omissions excepted 1 o.e. **2** OE or O.E.
omnibearing direction navigation OBD
omnibearing indicator navigation OBI
omnidirectional radio beacon ORB
omnidirectional ranging navigation ODR
on account commerce O/A or o/a or o.a.
on active service military OAS
on behalf Latin ex p.
on board ob or o.b.
on camera OC or O/C (in television)
on center o.c.
on course OC
on demand finance **1** OD or O/D **2** od or o/d
on duty OD
on hand 1 o.h. **2** OH
On His or **Her Britannic Majesty's Service** O.H.B.M.S. or OHBMS
On His or **Her Majesty's Service** O.H.M.S. or OHMS
on or about O/A or o/a or o.a.
on or **at this passage 1** ad h.l. **2** ad loc.
on order O/O or o/o
on request OR or O/R or o/r
on sale OS or O/S
on schedule OS or O/S
on station OS
on the back of the page f.v. or FV (OUP: f.v.)
on time o.t. or ot
on or **at this passage** a.h.l.
on-line computers OL
on-line communications driver computers OCD
on-line computer OLC
On-line Cryptanalytic Aid Language computers OCAL
on-line real time operation computers OLRT
On-Site Inspection Agency OSIA
on-the-job training OJT
oncological Onco or Oncol.

oncology Onco or Oncol.
one hundred call seconds CCC
one side OS
one string or **soft pedal** music u.c.
one thousand circular mils MCM
one thousand pounds per square inch K.s.i. or ksi
one time only advertising OTO
one way (of a fare) **1** O/W **2** OW or O.W.
one-stop-inclusive tour charter OTC or O.T.C.
Online Computer Library Center OCLC
only child o.c.
only son o.s.
onomatopoeia onomat.
Ontario 1 O or O. **2** ON (postal code) **3** Ont.
Ontario Provincial Police OPP
Ontario Society of Artists OSA or O.S.A.
open charter commerce OC or O/C
open circuit OC
open circuit voltage OCV
open end o.e.
open hearth OH
open hearth steel OHS
open joint building OJ
open policy insurance OP
open systems interconnection OSI
open to buy commerce OTB
open-circuit television OCTV
open-close-open electronics OCO
opening opg.
opening of books OB or O/B
opening price O
opening snap medicine OS or O.S.
opera (works) Opp.
operate opr.
operating characteristic OC
Operating Forces military OF
operating instructions OI or O.I.
operating nursing procedure medicine ONP
operating procedure OP
operating room medicine OR
operating system computers OS
operating under the influence law OUI
operation 1 OP **2** op or op. **3** opn. or OPN **4** opt.
operation and maintenance OM or O.M. or o/m
Operation or **Operations** Op or Op.
operation or **operations control** OPCON or op con or ops-con
operational 1 OP **2** opl.
operational amplifier op-amp
operational conversion unit OCU
Operational Executive and Administrative Personnel OPEX
operational requirement OR
Operational Research OR or O.R.
Operational Research Society ORS
operational support equipment OSE
operational taxonomic unit OTU
Operational Training Unit OTU
Operations Ops. or Ops
operations analysis OA
Operations and Maintenance O&M
Operations Control Center OCC
operations order O/O
operations per minute computers OPM

operations research OR
Operations Research Society of America O.R.S.A.
operations room *military* OR
operator 1 Op *or* Op. **2** opr. *or* Opr.
ophthalmic oph.
ophthalmologist 1 oph. *or* Oph. **2** ophth. *or* ophthal. *or* Ophth. *or* Ophthal.
ophthalmology 1 oph. *or* Oph. **2** ophth. *or* ophthal. *or* Ophth. *or* Ophthal.
ophthalmoscope oph.
opinion opn.
Opinions of the U.S. Attorney General Op. Atty. Gen.
Opportunities Industrialization Center OIC *or* O.I.C.
opportunity 1 opp. **2** oppy.
opposed opp.
Opposing Forces OPFOR
opposite 1 op *or* op. **2** opp.
Opposite Editorial Op-Ed (page)
opposite prompter *theater* OP *or* O.P.
opposition opp.
optative opt.
opthalmoscope ophth. *or* ophthal.
opthalmoscopy ophth. *or* ophthal.
optical 1 Op **2** op **3** opt.
optical character reader *computers* OCR
optical character recognition *computers* OCR
optical character scanner *computers* OCS
optical density *biology, chemistry, medicine* OD
Optical Direction and Ranging OPDAR
optical emission spectroscopy OES
Optical Mark Reading *or* **Recognition** OMR
optical pulse transmitter using laser *electronics* OPTUL
optical rotary dispersion ORD
Optical Society of America OSA
optical-to-tactile converter Optacon
optician opt.
optics opt.
optimal opt.
optimum opt.
optimum working frequency *electronics* **1** FOT **2** OWF
option opt.
optional opt.
options income Opinc
opto-electronic pulse amplifier OPA
Optometry College Admissions Test OCAT
opus 1 Op **2** op *or* op. (*MLA, OUP:* op.)
opuses Opp.
or best offer *advertising* OBO
or the nearest offer *advertising* ONO *or* o.n.o.
oral contraceptive OC
oral glucose tolerance test *medicine* OGTT
oral polio vaccine OPV
oral rehydration therapy ORT
orally *medicine* po *or* p.o.
orange 1 O **2** or *or* or. **3** Or.
orange juice OJ *or* o.j.
oration orat.
orator orat.
oratorio orat. *or* Orat.
oratory orat.

orbital angular momentum quantum number *physics* L
Orbital Attitude Maneuvering System OAMS
orbital escape system OES (of a spacecraft)
Orbital Satellite Carrying Amateur Radio OSCAR
Orbital-Maneuvering System OMS
Orbiting and Landing Approach Flight Simulator OLAFS
Orbiting Astronomical Observatory OAO
Orbiting Geophysical Observatory OGO
orbiting observatory OO
Orbiting Radio Beacon Ionospheric Satellite ORBIS
Orbiting Solar Observatory OSO
Orchard ORCH (in postal address)
orchard orch.
orchestra orch. *or* Orch. (*MLA:* orch.)
orchestral orch.
orchestrated by orch. *or* Orch. (*MLA:* orch.)
Ordained Ord.
order 1 O *or* O. **2** Ord. **3** ord. *or* ORD
order canceled OC *or* O/C
order number ON
order of O/O *or* O/o
Order of Australia OAM
Order of Canada OC *or* O.C.
Order of Friars Minor OFM *or* O.F.M.
Order of Jacques-Cartier OJC
Order of Leopold OL *or* O.L.
Order of Merit OM *or* O.M.
Order of Preachers OP *or* O.P.
Order of Saint Benedict O.S.B.
Order of Saint Dominic OSD *or* O.S.D.
Order of Saint Francis OSF *or* O.S.F.
Order of St. Augustine OSA
Order of St. Ursula O.S.U.
Order of the British Empire OBE *or* O.B.E.
Order of the Eastern Star OES *or* O.E.S.
Order of the Servants of Mary OSM *or* O.S.M.
Order of United American Mechanics O.U.A.M.
ordered back OB
orderly marketing agreement OMA
ordinal ord.
Ordinance Ord.
Ordinary Ord.
ordinary 1 O **2** ord.
ordinary general meeting OGM
ordinary least squares *statistics* OLS
Ordinary National Certificate O.N.C.
Ordinary National Diploma O.N.D.
ordinary portland cement OPC *or* opc
Ordinary Seaman OS *or* O.S.
ordinary spring tides OST *or* o.s.t.
ordinary, reasonable, and prudent *law* ORP
ordinate y
Ordination Ord.
ordnance 1 Ord., *military* ORD **2** Ordn. *or* ordn.
ordnance data OD
Ordnance Department OD
ordnance map OM *or* O.M.
Ordnance Officer OO
Ordnance Survey OS *or* O.S. (with number)
Ordnance Survey Department *British* OSD *or* O.S.D.

ore O/O
ore-bulk-oil (carrier) O/B/O
Oregon 1 O *or* O. **2** OR (Zip Code) **3** Or. **4** Ore. *or* Oreg. (*NYT:* Ore.; *OUP:* Oreg.)
organ org. *or* org
Organ Procurement Organization OPO
organ tolerance dose *medicine* OTD
organic org.
organic acid-soluble phosphorus OASP
organic heart disease OHD
organic liquid-moderated reactor OLMR
organic matter *biology* OM
organism org.
Organist Org.
organist org.
Organization 1 O **2** Org. *or* Orgn.
organization org. *or* org *or* orgn.
Organization and Method O&M *or* O. & M.
Organization for Economic Cooperation and Development 1 OECD (*NYT:* O.E.C.D.; *OUP:* OECD) **2** *French* O.C.D.E.
Organization for Rehabilitation through Training ORT
Organization for Trade Cooperation OTC
Organization for Tropical Studies OTS
Organization of African Unity OAU
Organization of Afro-American Unity OAAU
Organization of American States 1 OAS *or* O.A.S. (*GPO, OUP:* OAS; *NYT:* O.A.S.) **2** *Spanish* OEA *or* O.E.A.
Organization of Arab Petroleum Exporting Countries OAPEC (*NYT:* OAPEC)
Organization of Central American States 1 OCAS **2** *Spanish* ODECA *or* O.D.E.C.A.
Organization of Cooperatives of America OCA
Organization of Eastern Caribbean States OECS
Organization of European States OES
Organization of Petroleum Exporting Countries OPEC *or* Opec (*GPO, NYT, OUP:* OPEC)
Organization of the Islamic Conference OIC
organizational org.
organizational development OD
organized org.
Organized Crime Bureau OCB
Organized Reserve Corps ORC *or* O.R.C.
organophosphorus OP
Oriental Or.
oriental Orient. *or* orient.
oriented polypropene OPP
origin orig.
origin and destination OD
original 1 Or. **2** orig. *or* Orig.
original cover *philately* OC *or* O.C.
original equipment 1 o.e. **2** OE
original equipment manufacturer OEM
original error 1 o.e. **2** OE
original gravity OG (in brewing)
original gum OG *or* o.g. (of a postage stamp)
original tempo *music* t.p.
original-issue discount *commerce* OID
originally orig.
originated orig.
originator orig. *or* Orig.

Orion Ori (constellation)
Orkney Islands Ork.
ornament orn.
ornithine transcarbanylase *biochemistry* OTC
ornithological orn. or ornithol.
ornithology orn. or ornith.
Orphan Drug Act ODA
orphanage Orph.
ortho o-
Orthodox Orth.
orthography orth. or ortho.
Orthopedic Orth.
orthopedic nurse ON or O.N.
Orthopedics Orth.
orthophosphate Pi
oscillate OSC or osc.
oscillation 1 O **2** OSC or osc.
oscillator OSC or osc.
osmium Os
osmotic pressure *chemistry* OP
osteoarthritis OA
osteogenesis imperfecta OI or O.I.
osteopath Osteo.
osteopathy Osteo. or osteo. or osteop.
Othello, the Moor of Venice Oth.
other or or or.
other ranks *military* OR
other things being equal cet. par.
other valuable considerations *commerce* ovc or o.v.c.
others ors.
otherwise known as o.k.a. or o/k/a
otolaryngologist OTO
otolaryngology OTO
otology otol.
Ottawa, Canada Ott.
Ouguiya UM
ounce oz. or oz (*CSM, OUP:* oz.)
ounce apothecaries' weight oz. ap. or oz. apoth.
ounce avoirdupois oz. av.
ounce troy oz. t.
ounces ozs.
Our Lady *French* ND or N.D.
Our Lord D.N.
Our Lord Jesus Christ D.N.J.C.
Our Lord the Pope D.N.P.P.
Our Most Holy Lord SS.D.N.
Our Saviour Jesus Christ *Latin* NSIC or N.S.I.C.
out of Ex
out of bed *medicine* OOB
out of bounds ob or o/b
out of print 1 OOP or o.o.p. **2** OP or o.p. (*CSM, OUP:* o.p.)
out of print at present OPP or O.P.P. or o.p.p.
out of range or
out of stock 1 o.s. or o/s **2** OOS or o.o.s. **3** OS or O/S

out of stock indefinitely OSI or o.s.i.
out of town OOT
out-of-body experience OBE
out-of-pocket (expenses) OOP
outboard 1 ob or o/b or o.b. **2** otbd. **3** outbd.
Outboard Boating Club OBC
Outdoor Advertising Association OAA
Outdoor Advertising Association of America OAAA
Outer Continental Shelf OCS
outer or **outside back cover** *advertising* OBC
outfield *baseball* OF
outgassing OG
outlet out.
outpatient OP
Outpatient Clinic OPC
Outpatient Department OPD
output out.
output control pulses *electronics* OCP
output per man shift OMS
output secondary *electronics* OS
outs *baseball* o or o.
outside 1 exte **2** OS
outside air temperature OAT
outside broadcast OB
outside diameter 1 OD or O.D. **2** od or o/d or o.d.
outside dimensions 1 OD or O.D. **2** od or o/d or o.d.
outside guard OG
outside left *sports* OL
outside radius 1 OR **2** or or o.r.
outside right *sports* OR
outsides OS or O.S. (endsheets of a ream)
outsize OS (of clothing)
outstanding *banking* OS or o/s
outward bound OB
ovary ov or ov.
over 1 O **2** ov **3** *cricket* o or o.
over, short, and damaged *commerce* **1** o. s. & d. **2** OSD or OS/D
over all OA or o.a.
over voltage OV or o.v.
over-horizon detection system OHDETS
over-the-counter 1 OC or O-C **2** OTC
over-the-horizon OTH
overall heat transfer coefficient U
overboard ovbd
overcast *meteorology* **1** o or o. **2** OCST **3** ovc or ovc. or ovcst
overcharge OC or O/C or o/c
overdose 1 OD (*GPO:* OD) **2** od or o.d.
overdraft *banking* OD or O/D
overdrawn *banking* OD or O/D
Overeaters Anonymous OA or O.A.
overflow ovfl.
overflow level OL
overhaul and repair or or o/r or o&r

overhead 1 ovhd. **2** *accounting* OH or O/H
overhead camshaft OHC or o.h.c.
overhead line OL
overhead projector OHP
overhead valve OHV or o.h.v.
overhead vent OHV
overload 1 ovld. **2** *electricity* OL
overpaid *commerce* ovpd.
overprint OP or o.p. or O.P.
overproof OP or O.P. (*CSM, OUP:* o.p.)
override ovrd.
Overseas Education Association OEA
Overseas Press Club OPC or O.P.C.
Overseas Private Investment Corporation OPIC
Overseas Telecommunications Commission of Australia OTC
Overture *music* Ov or Ov. or ov
Ovid Ov or Ov. (Roman poet)
ovonic memory switch *electronics* OMS
owned and operated O&O
owner O
owners, landlords, and tenants OL and T or OL&T
owner's risk *insurance* **1** OR or O.R. **2** or or o.r.
owner's risk of breakage *insurance* ORB or O.R.B. or o.r.b.
owner's risk of damage *insurance* ORD or o.r.d.
owner's risk of fire *insurance* ORF
owner's risk of leakage *insurance* ORL or o.r.l.
owner's risk of shifting *insurance* ORS or o.r.s.
owner's risk of wetting *insurance* ORW or o.r.w.
owner's risk rates *insurance* ORR or o.r.r.
Oxford 1 Ox. **2** Oxf. **3** *Latin* Oxon. or oxon.
Oxford and Cambridge Universities Oxbridge
Oxford Committee for Famine Relief Oxfam or OXFAM
Oxford English Dictionary OED
Oxford University Press OUP or O.U.P.
Oxfordshire, England 1 Oxf. **2** *Latin* Oxon. or oxon.
oxidation reduction OR or O-R
oxidation-reduction potential E
oxide dispersion strengthened ODS (of steel)
oxidizer ox
oxidizing flame OF
oxygen 1 O **2** O_2 **3** ox or Ox
oxygen-free high-conductivity OFHC
oxygeny oxy
oxytetracycline OTC
oysters oys.
ozone 1 O_3 **2** Oz

P(positive) channel metal oxide
  semiconductor *electronics* PMOS
pa'anga T (monetary unit of Tonga)
Pacific **1** Pac. *or* PAC **2** Pacif.
Pacific Area Communications System PACS
Pacific Area Travel Association PATA
Pacific Coast Conference PCC
Pacific Command *military* PC
Pacific Daylight Saving Time PDST *or*
  P.D.S.T. *or* p.d.s.t.
Pacific Daylight Time PDT *or* P.D.T. *or* p.d.t.
Pacific Missile Range PMR
Pacific newly industrializing countries
  PACNIC
Pacific Ocean Pac. O. *or* Pac. Oc.
Pacific Oceanograph Laboratory POL
Pacific Reporter law Pac.
Pacific Standard Time PST *or* p.s.t. *or* P.S.T.
Pacific Stock Exchange PSE
Pacific time PT *or* P.T.
pack pk. *or* pk
package pkg.
packaged assembly circuit *electronics* PAC
packaged disaster hospital PDH
packed cell volume PCV
packed weight PW *or* p.w.
packer pkr. *or* Pkr.
packet pkt.
packet assembler and disassembler
  computers PAD
padding pad.
padlock pad.
page **1** p *or* p. **2** pg *or* p.g. (*MLA, CSM,*
  OUP: p.)
page description language *computers* PDL
page down *computers* PgDn
page footing *computers* PF
page format *printing* PF
page heading *computers* PH
page up *computers* PgUp
page view terminal *computers* PVT
paged memory management unit
  computers PMMU
pages pp *or* pp.
pages per hour pph
paid pd *or* pd.
pain, unit of *medicine* dol
painted pntd
painted by pntd
Painter Pic (constellation)
painter **1** paint. **2** pntr. **3** ptr.
painting paint.
pair pr *or* pr.
Pair of Compasses Cir (constellation)
pairs prs.
pajamas pjs *or* p.j.'s
Pakistan Pak.
Pakistan Council of Scientific and Industrial
  Research PCSIR
Pakistan People's Party PPP
Pakistani Pak.

Palau PW (in postal address)
paleobotany paleob.
paleography **1** pal. **2** paleog.
paleontology **1** pal. **2** paleon. *or* paleont.
  or paleontol.
Palestine Pal.
Palestine Liberation Army PLA
Palestine Liberation Organization PLO *or*
  P.L.O. (*NYT:* P.L.O.; *OUP:* PLO)
Palestine National Council PNC *or* P.N.C.
palladium Pd
pamphlet **1** p **2** pam. *or* pamph. **3** pph *or*
  pph.
Pan Africanist Congress PAC *or* P.A.C.
Pan American Technical Standards
  Commission COPANT
Pan American Union P.A.U. *or* PAU
Pan-African Telecommunications
  PANAFTEL
Pan-American Congress PAC *or* P.A.C.
Pan-American Health Organization PAHO
Pan-American Medical Association
  P.A.M.A. *or* PAMA
Pan-American Pharmaceutical and
  Biochemical Federation PPBF
Pan-American satellite system PANAMSAT
Pan-Indian Ocean Science Association
  PIOSA
Panama Pan.
Panama Canal **1** Pan. Can. *or* PanCan **2** PC
  or P.C.
Panama Canal Commission PCC
Panama Canal Zone PCZ
Panamanian Pan.
panchromatic pan.
panel pnl.
paneled PNLD *or* pnld.
Panhellenic Socialist Movement PASOK (of
  Greece)
panoramic pan.
pantomime pan.
Pantone matching system *printing* PMS
pantry pan.
Papanicolaou Pap
paper **1** pa. **2** pap. **3** ppr. *or* Ppr. **4** pr
  5 *pharmaceutics* chart.
paper equilibrium tester PET
Paper Industries Research Association PIRA
paper radioimmunosorbent test PRIST
paper, printing, and binding PPB
paperback **1** PB **2** PBK *or* pbk
Papers in English Language and Literature
  PELL
papers under consideration PUC *or* p.u.c.
Papers of the Biographical Society of
  America PBSA
papillary, marginal, attached *medicine*
  PMA *or* P.M.A.
Papua New Guinea **1** PNG *or* P.N.G. **2** Pap
  or Pap.
Papuan Pap *or* Pap.
para *chemistry* p-
para aminohippuric acid PAH
para-aminobenzoic acid PAB *or* PABA *or*
  paba
para-aminosalicylic acid PAS *or* PASA
para-aminosalicylic acid and isonicotinic
  acid hydrazide PAS-INAH
para-chlorophenoxyacetic acid PCPA

para-chlorophenylalanine PCPA
parabola para. *or* parab.
parabolic **1** par. **2** para. *or* parab.
parachloromercuribenzoate PCMB
paradichlorobenzene PDB
paraffins, olefins, naphthenes, aromatics
  PONA (constituents in octane rating)
paragraph **1** par. **2** para.
paragraphs pars.
Paraguay **1** Par. **2** Para. *or* Parag.
Paraguay Confederation of Workers
  Spanish CPT
Paraguayan Para. *or* Parag.
parallax **1** p **2** par.
parallax second parsec
parallel par.
parallel distributed processing *computers*
  PDP
parameter param
parameters param
parametric amplifier paramp
paraphrase para.
parathyroid hormone PTH
parcel pcl.
parcel airlift mail PAL
Parcel Post PP *or* P.P.
parchment parch.
Parent, Adult, Child PAC *or* P-A-C (in
  transactional analysis)
Parent Effectiveness Training PET *or* P.E.T.
Parent-Teacher Association PTA (*GPO,*
  OUP: PTA; *NYT:* P.T.A.)
Parent-Teacher-Student Association PTSA
parental P
parental guidance PG
Parental Kidnapping Prevention Act PKPA
parenthesis, *pl.* parentheses **1** par. **2** paren,
  pl. parens
Parents' National Educational Union
  P.N.E.U.
Paris Anatomical Nomenclature *Latin* N.A.P.
Parish Par.
parity *physics* P
park pk. *or* Pk.
parking P
Parkinson's disease PD
Parkway **1** P **2** Pkwy *or* Pkwy. **3** PKY (in
  postal address)
Parliament Parl. *or* parl.
Parliamentary Parl. *or* parl.
Parliamentary Cases *law* PC *or* P.C.
Parliamentary Commissioner for
  Administration PCA *or* P.C.A.
Parliamentary Conservative Party *British*
  PCP *or* P.C.P.
Parliamentary Labour Party PLP *or* P.L.P. (of
  Great Britain)
Parliamentary Private Secretary *British* PPS
  or P.P.S.
Parliamentary Question PQ *or* P.Q.
Parliamentary Report PR *or* P.R.
Parliamentary Secretary *British* PS *or* P.S.
Parliamentary Undersecretary *British* PUS
  or P.U.S.
parochial par.
parole officer PO *or* P.O.
paroxysmal atrial tachycardia *medicine* PAT
parquet parq
parsec pc *or* pc.

part 1 p or p. 2 pt 3 Pt or Pt.
  4 *pharmaceutics* par. (*MLA, OUP:* pt.)
part control number PCN
part number PN or P/N
part time 1 pt or p.t. or p/t 2 PT or P/T
  3 pt/tm or pt tm
partial loss *insurance* 1 p.l. 2 PL
partial thermoremanent magnetization
  geophysics PTRM
partial thrombin time *medicine* PTT
partial water vapor pressure *meteorology*
  e or e.
partial zonal drilling *medicine* PZD
partially oriented yarn POY
partially stabilized zirconia PSZ
participating part.
participation certificate PC (in Government
  loans)
Participative Management Program PMP
participial part.
participial adjective *grammar* p.a.
participle 1 part. 2 ppl.
particle 1 p or p. 2 part.
particle beam fusion accelerator PBFA
particle board PBD or PBd or pbd
particular part.
particular average *insurance* 1 p.a. 2 PA
Partisan Review PR
partition 1 pn. 2 Ptn. or ptn.
partition function 1 *chemistry* f 2 *physics* Z
partly paid *commerce* pp or p.p.
partly soluble p sol
partner 1 part. 2 Ptnr.
partnership part. or Part.
parts pts
parts data-processing system PDPS
parts per billion PPB or ppb or p.p.b.
parts per hundred pph
parts per million PPM or ppm or p.p.m.
parts per thousand ppt or p.p.t.
parts per trillion ppt or p.p.t.
party Pty. or pty.
party election broadcast *British* PEB
Party for Peace and Democracy PPD (of
  South Korea)
pascal Pa or Pa.
pass P
pass slipped stitch over p.s.s.o. or PSSO (in
  knitting)
Passage Pass.
passage 1 pas. 2 pass.
passbook *banking* PB
passed pd or pd.
passed ball or balls *baseball* PB or pb
passenger 1 pass. 2 psgr.
passenger liability *insurance* PL
passenger-car unit pcu
passing showers *meteorology* p or p.
Passionate Pilgrim, The 1 Pilgr. 2 PP (poems,
  some attributable to Shakespeare)
passive *grammar* 1 pas. 2 pass.
passive optical surveillance system POSS
passive verb v.p.
Passover Pass.
Passport Office PO
past pt
Past Chief Patriarch PCP or P.C.P.
Past Grand Master PGM or P.G.M.
past history *medicine* PH

past participle *grammar* pp or pp. or p.p.
  (*MLA, OUP:* p.p.)
Past President PP or P.P.
past tense *grammar* 1 pa.t. 2 pt or p.t.
paste grain PG or P.G.
Pastor P or P.
Patagonia Pata.
patch test for tuberculosis OT
patent pat. or Pat.
Patent and Trademark Office PTO
Patent Cases *law* PC or P.C.
Patent Cooperation Treaty PCT
Patent Depository Library PDL
Patent Licensing Bulletin Board PLBB
Patent Office 1 Pat.Off. 2 PO or P.O.
patent pending pat. pend.
patented 1 pat. or Pat. 2 patd.
pathological path. or pathol.
pathologist path. or pathol.
pathology path. or pathol.
patient 1 pat. 2 pt
patient-controlled analgesia *medicine* PCA
patient-operated selector mechanism
  POSM
Patrol Hydrofoil Missileship PHM
patrol torpedo (boat) PT
patrolman Ptl.
Patrolmen's Benevolent Association PBA or
  P.B.A.
pattern 1 pat. 2 patt.
pattern recognition system *computers* PRS
pawn *chess* P or p
pay as you enter PAYE
pay on delivery POD or p.o.d.
pay on return POR or p.o.r.
pay-as-you-earn *British* PAYE or P.A.Y.E.
pay-per-view PPV
payable after death *insurance* PAD
payable on death *commerce, insurance*
  POD
payable on receipt POR or p.o.r.
paying guest PG or p.g. or P.G.
payload Pld or pld
payload assist module PAM
Paymaster 1 Paymr. or Payr. 2 PM or P.M.
Paymaster General PMG or P.M.G.
payment 1 payt. 2 pmt 3 pt or pt. 4 pymt.
payment by results *commerce* PBR
payment in kind PIK
payment in lieu PIL
payments pts or pts.
payroll 1 PR or P/R 2 pr or p/r
Peace Corps PC
Peace Corps Volunteer PCV
Peaceful Nuclear Explosions Treaty PNET
Peacock Pav (constellation)
peak pk. or Pk.
peak envelope power *communications* PEP
peak flow rate PFR
peak inverse voltage PIV or piv
peak reverse voltage PRV
peak to peak PP or p-p
peck pk. or pk (unit of measure; *CSM:* pk.)
pecky pky. (of lumber)
pedal ped. or PED. or Ped.
pedestal ped.
pedestrian ped.
Pediatric Nurse Practitioner PNP or P.N.P.
pediatrician ped. or Ped.

pediatrics ped. or Ped.
peer review organization PRO
Pegasus Peg (constellation)
pelvic inflammatory disease PID
Penal Code PC
penal code C.Pen.
pending pndg
penicillin Pen. or pen.
peninsula Pen. or pen.
penitentiary Pen. or pen.
Pennsylvania 1 PA (Zip Code) 2 Pa or Pa.
  3 Penn. or Penna. (*NYT, OUP:* Pa.)
Pennsylvania Avenue Development
  Corporation PADC
Pennsylvania, New Jersey, Maryland
  Interconnection P.J.M.
penny 1 d or d. 2 p or p. (nail size)
pennyweight 1 DWT or dwt. 2 pwt. (*CSM,
  OUP:* dwt.)
penology penol.
pension and welfare P&W
Pension and Welfare Benefits
  Administration PWBA
Pension Benefit Guaranty Corporation
  PBGC
pentachloronitrobenzene PCNB
pentachlorophenol PCP
pentaerythritol PE
pentaerythritol tetranitrate PETN
Pentagon Pnt (U.S. Department of Defense
  or building housing it)
pentagon pent.
Pentateuch Pent.
Pentecost Pent.
pentose nucleic acid PNA
People United to Serve Humanity PUSH
People's Consultative Assembly MPR (in
  Indonesia)
People's Currency RMB (of People's
  Republic of China)
People's Democratic Party of Afghanistan
  PDPA
People's Liberation Army PLA (China's
  single-service armed forces)
People's National Congress PNC or P.N.C.
People's National Movement PNM (of
  Trinidad and Tobago)
People's National Party PNP or P.N.P. (of
  Jamaica)
People's Progressive Party PPP (of Gambia
  and Guyana)
People's Republic of China PRC
pepper pep.
peppermint pep.
per P or p
per capita per cap.
per gross ton PGT or pgt
per gyrocompass PGC or pgc
per power of attorney p.p.a.
per standard compass PSC or psc
per thousand per M
per thousand words ptw
per unit of time, area, etc. k
perceived noise decibel PNdb or PNdB
percent 1 pc or p.c. 2 pct. or Pct. (*NYT:*
  pct.; *OUP:* p.c.)
percent volume in volume *chemistry* v/v
percentage 1 p 2 pct. or Pct. 3 *sports* pc or
  p.c. or Pc

percentile P
percentile rank *statistics* PR
perception pcpt.
perception of light PL
perceptual quotient PQ
perch p *or* p. (unit of measure)
percussion *medicine, music* perc.
perennial per.
perfect 1 perf. 2 pf *or* pf.
perforated 1 p 2 perf.
performance 1 perf. 2 pfce. *or* Pfce (*NYT:* Pfc.)
performance and cost evaluation *commerce* PACE
performance report PR
performed by perf.
Performing Right Society PRS *or* P.R.S.
perhaps perh.
perianth P
periaqueductal gray matter *medicine* PAG
Pericles, Prince of Tyre Per *or* Per. (*MLA:* Per.)
perigee peri. *or* perig.
perihelion peri. *or* perih.
perihelion distance *astronomy* q
perimeter 1 P 2 peri. *or* perim.
perimeter acquisition radar PAR
Perimeter Acquisition Radar Attack Character System PARCS
perimeter acquisition radar sites PARS
period 1 P (of time, motion, etc.) 2 per.
periodic acid Schiff PAS
periodic reverse PR (of electric current)
periodic review instrument PRI (in health care)
periodical (of a publication) 1 per. 2 period.
Periodical Publishers Association PPA *or* P.P.A.
peripheral address field *computers* PAF
peripheral arterial disease PAD
peripheral artherosclerotic disease PAD
peripheral availability list *computers* PAL
Peripheral Interchange Program *computers* PIP
peripheral interface adapter *computers* PIA
peripheral nervous system PNS
peripheral vascular disease PVD
perishable 1 p *or* p. 2 persh.
Perlsucht tuberculin original *medicine* PTO *or* P.T.O.
permanent perm *or* perm.
permanent bench mark *surveying* PBM
permanent change of station PCS
Permanent Committee of International Zoological Congresses *French* CPCIZ
Permanent Committee on Geographical Names PCGN
Permanent Court of Arbitration PCA
Permanent Court of International Justice *French* C.P.J.I.
permanent echo PE
Permanent International Association of Navigation Congresses PIANC
Permanent International Association of Road Congresses PIARC
Permanent International Committee for Genetic Congresses PICGC
Permanent International Committee of Linguists *French* C.I.P.L.

permanent magnet PM
permanent personal registration P.P.R.
Permanent Secretary *British* PS *or* P.S.
Permanent Service for Mean Sea Level PSMSL
Permanent Undersecretary *British* PUS *or* P.U.S.
permanent wave perm
permeability quotient PQ
permeable base transistor *electronics* PBT
permeance *physics* P
permissible accumulated dose PAD
permissive action link PAL
permissive action link system *computers* PALS
permittivity *physics* e
permutate *British* perm
pernicious anemia *medicine* PA *or* P.A.
peroxyacetyl nitrate PAN
perpendicular perp.
perpetrator perp. *or* perp
perpetual perp.
perquisite perq *or* perk
Perseus Per (constellation)
Persia 1 Per *or* Per. 2 Pers.
Persian 1 Per *or* Per. 2 Pers. (*MLA:* Per.)
persistent internal polarization PIP
persistent vegetative state *medicine* PVS *or* P.V.S.
person 1 per. 2 pers.
person of the opposite sex sharing living quarters posslq *or* POSSLQ
person with AIDS PWA
Person *or* **Persons In Need of Supervision** *law* PINS
persona non grata PNG *or* p.n.g.
personal pers.
personal assistant *British* PA
personal communication service PCS
personal communications network *computers* PCN
personal computer 1 PC 2 pc *or* p.c.
personal corporation PC *or* P.C.
personal digital assistant *computers* PDA
personal effects PE
personal effects floater *insurance* PEF
personal flotation device PFD
personal foul 1 *basketball* P 2 *sports* PF *or* pf
personal identification code PIC
personal identification device PID
personal identification number PIN
personal income PI
personal injury *law, insurance* PI
personal property *insurance* PP
personal property floater *insurance* PPF
personal rapid transit PRT
personal word processor PWP
personality quotient PQ *or* P.Q.
personalized system of instruction PSI
personnel pers.
Personnel and Administrative P&A
personnel carrier *military* PC
Personnel Officer PO
perspective persp.
pertaining pert.
Peruvian Peruv.
Peruvian Confederation of Labor CTP
peseta 1 P 2 pes. 3 Ps. *or* ps. 4 Pta. *or* pta. (*GPO:* Pta; *OUP:* pta.)

peso $ *or* P
peta- P
Peter Pet. (books of the New Testament)
Peters law Pet.
petite P (size)
petition petn.
petitioner *Latin* orat.
petrified petr.
petrochemical petro
petrography petrog.
petroleum 1 pet. 2 petr.
Petroleum Engineer PE *or* P.E.
petroleum, oil, and lubricant POL
petrologist pet.
petrology 1 pet. 2 petrol.
petty cash pc *or* p/c
petty cash book PCB *or* p/cb.
Petty Officer PO
pfennig 1 pf *or* Pf. 2 pfg.
pharmaceutical 1 Phar. *or* phar. 2 Pharm. *or* pharm.
Pharmaceutical Chemist Ph.C.
Pharmaceutical Manufacturers' Association PMA
Pharmaceutical Manufacturers' Association of Canada PMAC
pharmacist 1 Phar. *or* phar. 2 Pharm. *or* pharm.
pharmacology 1 Pharm. *or* pharm. 2 pharmacol.
pharmacopoeia 1 Ph 2 Phar. *or* phar. 3 Pharm. *or* pharm.
Pharmacopoeia of the United States PUS *or* P.U.S.
pharmacy 1 Phar. *or* phar. 2 Pharm. *or* pharm.
phase 1 PH 2 ph
phase modulation *electronics* PM
Phase Shift Keying *electronics* PSK
phase time modulation PTM
phase-alternating line *communications* PAL
phase-change material PCM
phase-locked loop *electronics* PLL
phenacetin, aspirin, caffeine PAC
phenolsulfonphthalein PSP
phenomenon phenom
phenyl *chemistry* Ph
phenylalanine Phe *or* Phe. *or* phe.
phenylcycloexylpiperidine PCP
phenylketonuria PKU
phenylmercuric acetate PMA
phenylpropanolamine PPA
phenylthiocarbamide PTC
phenyltoloxamine PRN
Phi Beta Kappa PBK
Philadelphia 1 C (in Federal Reserve system) 2 P (mint mark) 3 Phil. 4 Phila.
Philemon 1 Phil. 2 Philem. (*MLA, OUP:* Philem.)
Philharmonic Phil.
Philharmonic Society Phil. Soc.
Philip Phil.
Philippians Phil.
Philippine Phil.
Philippine Islands 1 Phil.I. *or* Is. 2 PI *or* P.I.
Philippines 1 Phil. 2 Philipp.
philological 1 Phil. *or* phil. 2 philol. *or* Philol (*MLA:* philol.)
Philological Society Phil. Soc.

philologist philol. *or* Philol
philology 1 Phil. *or* phil. **2** philol. *or* Philol
philosopher philos. *or* Philos
philosophical 1 Phil. *or* phil. **2** philos. *or* Philos (*MLA:* philos.)
Philosophical Society Phil. Soc.
Philosophical Transactions Phil. Trans.
philosophy 1 Phil. *or* phil. **2** philos. *or* Philos
philosophy, politics, and economics PPE
Phoenix Phe (constellation)
Phoenix and the Turtle, The PhT (poem by Shakespeare)
phone ph *or* ph.
phone line PL
phonetics phon. *or* phonet.
phonocardiogram *medicine* PCG
phonograph phono.
phonology phon. *or* phonol.
phosphate phos.
phosphate to oxygen PO *or* P/O (ratio of atoms)
phosphate-buffered saline PBS
phosphocreatine PC
phosphoenolpyruvic acid PEP
phosphofractokinase PFK
phosphoglycerate kinase PGK
phosphoglyceric acid PGA
phosphomolybdic acid PMA
phosphor ph *or* ph.
phosphor bronze ph.bz.
phosphorescence phos.
phosphoribosylamine PRA
phosphorus P
phosphotungstic acid PTA
phot ph
photo interpretation PI
photo interpreter PI
photo-reactive keratectomy PRK
photo-type composition PTC
photoacoustic spectroscopy PAS
photochromic microimage PCMI
photoelectric cell PEC *or* pec
photoelectric scanner PES
photoelectrochemical cell PEC
photoelectromagnetic PEM
photograph 1 phot. **2** photo *or* photo.
photographer 1 phot. **2** photog.
photographic 1 phot. **2** photog.
photographic intelligence PHOTINT
Photographic Society of America PSA *or* P.S.A.
photography 1 phot. **2** photog.
photomagnetoelectric effect PME
photomechanical transfer PMT
photometrical photom.
photometry photom.
photomultiplier tube PMT
phrase phr.
phrase structure *grammar* PS
phraseology phr.
physical phys.
physical education 1 PE **2** phys. ed.
physical examination 1 PE **2** PX
physical fitness index PFI
physical input/output control system *computers* PIOCS
physical quality of life index PQLI
physical therapy *or* **therapist** PT *or* P.T.
Physical Training Instructor PTI

physician phys.
physician's assistant PA
Physician's Desk Reference PDR
physics phys.
physiological 1 phys. **2** physiol.
physiologist physiol.
physiology 1 phys. **2** physiol.
physiotherapist PT *or* P.T.
physiotherapy PT *or* P.T.
phytogeography phytogeog.
phytohemagglutinin PHA
pianoforte 1 pf **2** Pft. *or* Pfte
piaster 1 P **2** pi *or* Pi.
pica 1 pc **2** pi
piccolo pic.
pick up and delivery *or* **deliveries** P&D
pick your own PYO
pickup *electronics* PU *or* P/U
pickup and delivery PUD
pico- p
picoampere pA
picofarad 1 pF **2** pf
picogram pg
picosecond 1 ps **2** psec. *or* psec
picowatt pw *or* pw.
pictorial pict.
picture 1 pic. **2** pict. **3** pix
picture description instruction *computers* PDI
picture element 1 pixel **2** *computers* pel *or* PEL
picture in picture *electronics* PIP
picture postcard p.p.c.
piece pc *or* pc.
pieces 1 pcs **2** ps *or* ps.
pigment pig. *or* pigm.
pigmentation pig. *or* pigm.
Pilgrim's Progress, The Pilgr.
pill *pharmaceutics* **1** bol. **2** pil.
pilot plt.
pilot officer PO *or* P/O
pilot report PIREP
Pilot's Electronic Eye-level Presentation PEEP
pi-meson pion
pin grid array *computers* PGA
pinch hitter *baseball* PH
Pincherle P (with number, catalog of Vivaldi's music)
Pindar Pind. (Greek poet)
pint 1 p *or* p. **2** pt *or* pt. (*CSM, OUP:* pt.) **3** *pharmaceutics* **a** O *or* O. **b** o *or* o.
pints pts *or* pts.
pipe p *or* p.
pipe size PS
Pisces *or* **Fishes** Pisc (constellation)
pistil pist.
pistillate pist.
pitch p (inclination)
pitch circle PC
pitch ratio PR
pitcher *baseball* p *or* p.
Pittsburgh Pitts.
pituitary adrenotrophic hormone *biochemistry* PATH
pizzicato *music* pizz.
Place PL (in postal address)
place 1 pl. *or* Pl. **2** *Latin* **a** l **b** L *or* L. (*GPO, NYT:* Pl.; *OUP:* pl.)

place of the seal *Latin* **1** l.s. **2** LS *or* L.S.
plain 1 pl. **2** pln.
plain chant *music* c.f.
plain face pf (as of a hammer, molding, etc.)
plain paper copier *commerce* PPC
plaintiff 1 plf. *or* plff. **2** pltf.
plan position indicator PPI
Planck constant *physics* h
Planck function *thermodynamics* Y
planed P (of lumber)
planet plan.
planetarium plan.
planetary plan. *or* planet.
planetary radio astronomy PRA
Planned Parenthood PP
Planned Parenthood Federation of America PPFA
Planned Parenthood World Population PPWP
planned unit development PUD
planning plng
planning and operations P&O
Plant Engineer PE
plant unit *botany* p.u.
plaque-forming cells PFC
plaque-forming unit *virology* pfu
plasma pl. *or* Pl.
plasma desorption mass spectrometry PDMS
plasma thromboplastin antecedent PTA
plasma thromboplastin component PTC
plasma thromboplastin factor PTF
plasma-wave sensor PWS
plasmacrit test PCT
plaster 1 plas. **2** *Latin* emp.
plaster of paris POP
plastic plas.
plastic surgery p.surg
Plastics Institute of America PIA
plate 1 p *or* p. (electrode) **2** pl. *or* Pl. **3** plt. **4** *botany* t *or* t. (*MLA, CSM:* pl.; *OUP:* Pl.)
plate glazed PG *or* P.G.
plateau plat. *or* Plat.
platelet-activating factor *medicine* PAF
platelet-derived growth factor PDGF
platelet-rich plasma *medicine* PRP
platform plat. *or* platf.
platinum Pt
platinum group metals PGM
platoon 1 pl. *or* Pl. **2** plat.
Plautus Plaut. (Roman writer of comedies)
playroom PLYRM
Plaza 1 Pla. **2** PLZ (in postal address)
Pleas of the Crown *law* PC *or* P.C.
please pls. *or* Pls.
please exchange PX *or* P.X.
please note PN *or* p.n. *or* P/N
please turn over PTO *or* p.t.o.
plenipotentiary Plen. *or* plen.
plenum chamber burning PCB
pleuropneumonia-like organism PPLO
Plimsoll Line PL *or* P.L.
plow steel rope PSR
plug-compatible manufacturer PCM
Plumbers and Pipefitters Union PPF
plumbing plmb.
pluperfect *grammar* plup. *or* plupf.
plural 1 pl. **2** plu. **3** plur.
plurality plur.

plutonium Pu
Plymouth Ply.
Plymouth Brethren PB or P.B.
plywood 1 plwd **2** pwd. or pwd
pneumatic pneu. or pneum.
pneumocystis carinii pneumonia PCP
pneumoencephalogram PEG
pneumothorax *medicine* PX or Px
pocket pkt.
poetic poet.
poetry poet.
Point Pt or Pt.
point pt (period)
point after touchdown *football* PAT
point of maximal impulse *medicine* PMI
point of purchase POP or P.O.P.
point of sale POS
point of subjective equality *psychology* PSE
point of view POV
point to point *electronics* PTP or p-t-p
points 1 P **2** pts
points against *sports* PA
points for *sports* PF
poise P (unit of viscosity)
Poison Control Center PCC
poison ivy pi
poisonous pois.
Poland Pol.
polar 1 pol. **2** *meteorology, astronomy* P
polar cap absorption *communications* PCA
Polar Orbiting Geophysical Observatory POGO
polar stratospheric cloud PSC
polarity *physics* po
polarization 1 pol. **2** polar. **3** *physics* P
pole 1 po or po. (unit of measure) **2** *physics* p or P
Police Athletic League PAL or P.A.L.
Police Commissioner PC
Police Constable *British* PC
Police Department PD or P.D.
Police Justice P.J.
Police Magistrate PM or P.M.
Police Sergeant PS
policy Plcy
Policy Planning Council PPC
policy proof of interest *insurance* PPI or p.p.i.
Polish Pol.
polished pol.
political 1 pol. **2** polit.
Political Action Committee PAC
political advisor pol. ad. or Pol. Ad.
Political and Economic Planning *British* PEP
political party broadcast *British* PPB
politically correct 1 pc **2** PC or P.C.
politician pol. or pol
Politico-Military Affairs PMA
politics 1 pol. **2** polit.
pollen index pol ind
pollutants poll.
pollution poll.
Pollution Standard Index PSI
pollution-added tax PAT
polonium Po
poly p-phenylene vinylene PPV
polyacrylamide PAM
polyacrylonitrile PAN
polychlorinated biphenyl PCB or pcb

polychlorinated dibenzo- PCD
polychlorinated fluorocarbon PFC
polychloroethylene PCE
polychlorotrifluoroethylene PCTFE
polycyclic aromatic compound *chemistry* PAC
polycyclic aromatic hydrocarbon PAH
polyester fiber poly.
polyethylene 1 PE **2** poly.
polyethylene glycol PEG
polyethylene oxide PEO
polyethylene terephthalate PET
polygalacturonase PG
polyhalogenated aromatic hydrocarbon PAH
polyinosinic:polycytidylic acid poly I:C
polyisobutylene PIB
polymer poly.
polymerase pol.
polymerase chain reaction PCR
polymethylmethacrylate PMMA
polymorphonuclear leukocyte PMN
Polynesia Poly.
Polynesian Poly.
polynuclear aromatic hydrocarbon PAH
polyoxymethylene POM
polyphenylene or **polyphene oxide** PPO
polystyrene PS
polytechnic poly.
polytechnical 1 poly. **2** polytech
polytechnical school or **institute 1** Poly. **2** *British* poly.
polytetrafluoroethylene 1 PTFE **2** Teflon
polytrifluorochloroethene PTFCE
polyunsaturated fatty acids PUFA
polyurethane PU
polyuridylic acid UUU
polyvinyl acetate PVA
polyvinyl alcohol PVA
polyvinyl chloride PVC
polyvinyl dichloride PVDC
polyvinyl ethyl ether PVE
polyvinyl fluoride PVF
polyvinyl isobutyl ether PVI
polyvinyl methyl ether PVM
polyvinyl pyrrolidone PVP
polyvinyl toluene PVT
polyvinylidene difluoride PVDF
pomological pom.
pomology pom.
pond pd
Pontiff Pont.
Pontificate Pont.
pontoon pon or pont.
pool test reactor PTR
Poop Pup (constellation)
poor p
Pope 1 P or P. **2** PP or PP.
popular pop. or pop
Popular Alliance *French, Spanish* AP
Popular Democratic Front for the Liberation of Palestine PDFLP
Popular Democratic Party *Spanish* PPD (of Puerto Rico)
Popular Front for the Liberation of Palestine PFLP
Popular Movement of the Revolution *French* MPR (in Zaire)
Popular Republican Movement *French* MRP

Popular Revolutionary Party of Benin *French* PRPB
Popular Socialist Party *Spanish* PPS (of Mexico)
popularly pop.
population 1 p or p. **2** pop.
population growth rate PGR
porcelain porc.
pornographic porn or porn. or porno
pornography porn or porn.
porosity por.
porous por.
Port 1 PRT **2** Pt or Pt.
port 1 P **2** pt
port and starboard P&S or p&s
Port Authority PA or P.A.
Port Authority Trans-Hudson Corporation PATH
port dues *shipping* PD
port of call POC or P.O.C.
port of debarkation 1 PD **2** POD or P.O.D.
port of embarkation 1 P/E **2** PE **3** POE or P.O.E.
port of entry POE or P.O.E.
Port of London Authority PLA or P.L.A.
portable 1 port. **2** ptbl.
portable common tools environment *computers* PCTE
portable electronic traffic analyzer *British* Peta
Portable Life-Support System PLSS
Portable Operating System Interface POSIX (standard of the Institute of Electrical and Electronic Engineers)
portage por.
portfolio port.
portion por.
portland cement PC
portrait 1 por. **2** port. or portr.
Portugal 1 Pg. **2** Port. **3** Ptg.
Portuguese 1 Pg. **2** Port. **3** Ptg.
Portuguese National Radio RDP
Portuguese National Radio and Television RTP
position 1 P or P. **2** pos **3** posn. **4** PSN or psn
position doubtful PD (of a vessel or aircraft)
position indicator PI
Position Operational Meteorological Aircraft Report POMAR
position or **radius vector** *physics* r
position-fixing device PFD
positive 1 p **2** P (electric pole) **3** pos
positive crankcase ventilation PCV
positive infinity variable PIV or P.I.V.
positive input, negative output *electronics* PINO
positive temperature coefficient PTC
positive-intrinsic-negative *electronics* PIN
positive-negative *electronics* PN or P-N or p-n
positive-negative-intrinsic-negative *electronics* PNIN or p-n-i-n
positive-negative-intrinsic-positive *electronics* PNIP or p-n-i-p
positive-negative-positive *electronics* PNP or p-n-p
positive-negative-positive-negative *electronics* PNPN or p-n-p-n

positively vet *British* PV *or* P.V.
positron emission transverse tomography PETT
positron-emission tomograph *or* tomography PET
possession 1 pos 2 poss.
possessions poss.
possessive 1 pos 2 *grammar* poss.
possibility 1 pos 2 poss.
possible 1 pos 2 poss.
possibly 1 pos 2 poss.
Post Adjutant *military* PA
Post Commander PC
Post Exchange PX
Post Office PO *or* P.O. (*GPO:* P.O.; *OUP:* PO)
Post Office Box POB *or* P.O.B.
post position PP (in horse racing)
Post-Anesthesia Care Unit PACU
post-menopausal estrogen and progestin intervention PEPI
post-polio sequelae PPS
post-traumatic amnesia PTA
post-traumatic stress disorder PTSD
post-tuning drift PTD (of radio reception)
Post-Vietnam Syndrome PVS *or* P.V.S.
postage and handling *commerce* P&H
postage due PD
postal 1 post. 2 Pstl.
Postal Inspection Service PIS
postal order *British* 1 PO 2 po *or* p.o.
Postal Rate Commission PRC
postcard pc *or* p.c.
postdated 1 PD *or* P.D. *or* P/D 2 pd *or* p/d
postdeflection acceleration *physics* PDA
posterior 1 P 2 p 3 post.
postgraduate PG
Postgraduate Certificate of Education PGCE
posthumous posth.
postmark pmk
postmarked pmkd
Postmaster PM *or* P.M.
Postmaster General PMG *or* P.M.G.
postmortem 1 p.m. 2 PM *or* P.M.
postmortem dump *computers* PMD
postpaid 1 PP 2 ppd.
postprandial 1 PP 2 pp *or* p.p.
postscript 1 PS *or* P.S. 2 ps *or* p.s. (*GPO, CSM:* P.S.; *MLA, OUP:* PS)
postscripts PSS *or* P.SS. *or* p.ss.
poststreptococal glomerulonephritis PSGN
postsynaptic potential p.s.p.
potash pot.
potassium 1 K 2 potass.
potassium, rare-earth elements, and phosphorus KREEP
potential 1 pot. 2 *physics* V
potential difference 1 PD 2 pd *or* p.d. 3 V
potential energy 1 U 2 V
potential transformer PT
potentially responsible parties *insurance, law* PRP
potentiometer pot. *or* pot
pottery pot.
(made of) pottery, earthenware fict.
pound 1 £(monetary unit) 2 a lb *or* lb. (*CSM, OUP:* lb.) b pd *or* pd. (weight) 3 *Latin* L
pound avoirdupois lb. av.
pound troy weight lb. t.

pound-foot lb-ft
pound-force lbf
pound-inch lb-in
pound-mass lbm *or* lb-m
poundal *physics* pdl
pounds lbs.
pounds per cubic foot PCF *or* pcf
pounds per horsepower PHP *or* p/hp
pounds per linear foot plf *or* p.l.f.
pounds per linear inch pli *or* p.l.i.
pounds per minute PPM *or* p.p.m. *or* p/m
pounds per second 1 p.p.s. *or* p/s 2 PPS
pounds per square foot psf *or* p.s.f.
pounds per square inch psi *or* p.s.i.
pounds per square inch gauge psig *or* p.s.i.g.
pounds per square inch, absolute psia *or* p.s.i.a.
pounds per square inch, differential psid *or* p.s.i.d.
pounds static thrust PST *or* p.s.t. *or* pst.
poverty datum line *British* PDL
powder 1 pdr. *or* pdr 2 pwd. 3 *pharmaceutics* pulv.
power 1 pr 2 PWR *or* pwr. *or* pwr 3 *physics* P
power amplifier PA
power brakes PB
power control unit pcu *or* PCU
power cord pc
power distribution unit PDU
power factor pf
power line carrier PLC
power locks PL (on automobiles)
power of attorney PA *or* P.A. *or* P/A
power oscillator PO
power plant PP
power steering PS *or* P/S
power supply PS
power supply unit PSU
power take-off PTO
power windows PW (on automobiles)
powered pwd. *or* pwd
powered underwater research vehicle PURV
Poynting vector S
Practical Nurse PN *or* P.N.
practice prac.
practitioner prac. *or* Prac.
pragmatic prag.
pragmatism prag.
Prairie Farm Rehabilitation Act *Canadian* PFRA
Prandtl number Pr
praseodymium Pr
Prausnitz-Küstner reaction PK *or* P-K
Prayer Book PB *or* P.B.
pre-eradication program *medicine* PEP
pre-impregnation prepreg
Pre-Raphaelite Brotherhood P.R.B.
preamplifier preamp
prebend Preb. *or* preb.
prebendary Preb. *or* preb.
preceded prec.
preceding prec.
Precentor Prec.
precinct pct. *or* Pct.
precipitate 1 precip. 2 *chemistry* ppt *or* ppt.
precipitated *chemistry* pptd *or* pptd.

precipitating *chemistry* pptg *or* pptg.
precipitation 1 *chemistry* pptn *or* pptn. 2 *meteorology* precip.
precipitation, evaporation P/E *or* P-E
precision prec.
precision altitude and landing monitor PALM
precision analog computing equipment PACE
precision approach radar PAR
precision depth recorder PDR
precision plan-position indicator PPPI
precision-guided munition PGM
preconscious *psychology* pcs *or* Pcs.
predelivery inspection *commerce* PDI
predicate pred.
predicative pred.
predicted drift angle *navigation* PDA
predicted gross score *psychology* X̄
prefabricated prefab
Preface Pref. (*MLA, OUP:* pref.)
Prefect Pref.
preference pref.
preferred 1 pfd. *or* pfd 2 Pr (of stock) 3 pr *or* pr. (of stock) 4 pref. *or* prefd 5 *commerce* pf (of stock)
Preferred Policyholders' Discount *British* PPD
preferred provider organization PPO (for health care)
preferred stock *commerce* Pref.
prefix 1 pfx. 2 pre. 3 pref.
prefixed pref.
preflight PF
pregnancy urine PU *or* P.U.
pregnant preg.
pregnant mare's serum *veterinary medicine* PMS
pregnant mare's urine *veterinary medicine* PMU
prehistoric prehist. *or* prehis.
prejudice prej.
preliminary prel. *or* prelim.
preliminary flight rating test PFRT
preliminary proofs *or* pages of a book prel. *or* prelim. *or* prelims
preliminary report PR
Preliminary Scholastic Aptitude Test PSAT
premature prem. *or* prem
premature infant 1 prem. *or* prem 2 preemie *or* preemy
premature rupture of the membranes *medicine* PROM
premature ventricular contraction *medicine* PVC
premedical premed *or* premed.
premedical student premed
premenstrual syndrome PMS
premenstrual tension PMT
Premier Prem.
premium 1 pm. 2 prem. 3 prm.
Premium Advertising Association of America PAAA
premolar 1 P 2 pm.
preoperation preop *or* preop.
preoperative preop *or* preop.
prepaid 1 PP 2 ppd.
preparation 1 prep. *or* prep 2 prepn.
preparatory prep. *or* prep

prepare prep. *or* prep
prepared prep. *or* prep *or* prepd
preposition *grammar* prep. *or* prep (*MLA, OUP*: prep.)
prepublication prepub
prerequisite prereq.
presbyopia Pr *or* Pr.
Presbyterian Pres. *or* Presb. *or* Presbyt.
prescription Rx
present 1 pr *or* pr. **2** pres.
present illness *medicine* PI
present participle 1 ppr. *or* p.pr. **2** pr.p.
Presentation Pres.
preservation presv.
preserved context index system PRECIS
presidency pres.
President Pres.
president pres.
President of the Royal Academy PRA *or* P.R.A.
President of the Royal Society PRS *or* P.R.S.
President of the Royal Society of Edinburgh P.R.S.E.
President of the United States POTUS
President's Intelligence Oversight Board PIOB
President's Science Advisory Committee PSAC
Presidential Special Representative PSR *or* P.S.R.
Presiding Bishop PB *or* P.B.
Presiding Elder PE *or* P.E.
Presiding Judge P.J.
Press Pr *or* Pr.
Press Agent PA *or* P.A.
Press Association PA *or* P.A.
press release PR *or* P.R.
Press Secretary PS *or* P.S.
Press Trust of India PTI
pressed prsd
pressure 1 pres. **2** press. *or* press **3** *physics, chemistry, geology* P **4** *physics* p
pressure line of position PLOP
pressure sensitive ps
pressure silver ion pAg
pressure, volume, temperature *chemical engineering* PVT
pressure-reducing valve PRV
pressure-zone microphone PZM
pressurization control unit pcu *or* PCU
pressurized fluidized bed combustion PFBC
pressurized water reactor PWR
prestressed concrete PC
presumptive pres.
preterit *grammar* **1** pret. **2** pt *or* pt.
pretrial intervention PTI
preventive detention PD *or* P.D.
preventive maintenance PM
previous prev.
previous medical history PMH
previous question PQ *or* P.Q. *or* p.q.
previously prev.
previously taxed income PTI
price 1 pc *or* pc. **2** pr
price current pc *or* pc. *or* p/c
price–level adjusted mortgage PLAM
price-to-earnings ratio P/E *or* P-E
Priest 1 P *or* P. **2** Pr
primary 1 pri. **2** prim.

primary atypical pneumonia PAP
primary control program *computers* PCP
primary health care PHC
primary health center PHC
primary human amnion PHA
primary mental abilities *psychology* PMA
primate prim.
Prime Minister 1 PM *or* P.M. **2** Pr.Min.
Prime Minister's Question *British* PMQ
prime time PT
primer pri.
primipara primip.
primitive prim.
Prince 1 P *or* P. **2** Pr
Prince Edward Island 1 P.E.I. **2** PE (postal code)
principal prin. *or* Prin.
Principal Clerk of Session PCS *or* P.C.S.
principal component analysis *mathematics* PCA
principal investigator PI (in a scientific experiment or study)
Principal Medical Officer PMO
principal neutralizing determinant PND
principal quantum number n
principal, interest, taxes, insurance *commerce* PITI *or* p.i.t.i.
Principality prin. *or* Prin.
principally prin. *or* Prin.
principle prin.
print prt
print contrast signal PCS
print numerically PRN *or* prn
print-out *or* **printing-out paper** POP
printed 1 pr *or* pr. **2** print. **3** Ptd.
printed by 1 pr *or* pr. **2** print.
printed circuit *electronics* PC
printed circuit board *electronics* PCB *or* pcb
printer 1 a Pr *or* Pr. **b** pr *or* pr. **2** print. **3** prntr **4** ptr. *or* Ptr.
printer control language *computers* PCL
printer's error 1 p.e. *or* pe **2** PE
Printers Prs.
printing 1 pr **2** print. **3** Ptg. *or* ptg.
Printing Industries of America PIA *or* P.I.A.
Printing Industry Research Association PIRA
prion protein PRP *or* Prp
prior pr *or* pr.
prior notice required *commerce* p.n.r.
prior to admission *medicine* PTA
prism diopter pd
prismatic prism.
prisoner pris.
prisoner of war 1 POW *or* P.O.W. *or* PoW (*GPO, OUP*: POW) **2** PW *or* P.W.
Private 1 Pr *or* Pr. **2** Pvt. **3** *British* Pte. (in the Army) (*NYT*: Pvt.; *OUP*: Pte.)
private 1 pri. **2** priv. **3** pvt. *or* pvt
private account *banking, commerce* PA *or* P.A. *or* P/A
private automatic branch exchange PABX
private automatic exchange *communications* PAX
private branch exchange *communications* PBX
private first class *military* Pfc *or* pfc
private investigator PI *or* P.I.
private line PL

private manual exchange *communications* PMX
private pilot license PPL
private property PP
private resolution Private Res. (with number)
Private Retirement Account PRA
private secretary PS *or* P.S.
private telephone exchange PX
private wire *communications* PW
privately priv.
privately owned vehicle POV *or* pov
privately printed pp *or* p.p.
privative *grammar* priv.
privilege priv.
Privy Council *British* PC
Privy Councilor *British* PC
Privy Seal PS *or* P.S.
pro forma pf
pro rata pr *or* p.r. *or* p/r
pro tem pt *or* p.t.
probabilistic risk assessment PRA
probability 1 P **2** prob.
probability density function *engineering* PDF
probability distribution analyzer PDA
probability state variable PSV
probable prob.
probable error 1 ep **2** *statistics* **a** p.e. **b** PE *or* P.E.
probable maximum flood PMF
probable maximum loss *insurance* PML
probably prob.
probate prob. *or* Prob.
Probate Judge P.J.
probation prob. *or* Prob.
probation officer PO *or* P.O.
problem prob.
Problem Resolution Officer PRO
problem-oriented language *computers* POL
problem-oriented medical record POMR
procaine penicillin in oil and aluminum monostearate PAM
procedure 1 pro *or* pro. **2** proc.
procedure library *computers* PROCLIB
Procedures for Air Navigation Services PANS
proceedings Proc. (*MLA, CSM*: proc.; *OUP*: Proc.)
Proceedings of the British Academy PBA
Proceedings of the Royal Society of Edinburgh P.R.S.E.
Proceedings of the Royal Society PRS *or* P.R.S.
process proc.
process automatic monitor *computers* PAM
Process Inherent Ultimate Safety PIUS (nuclear reactor)
process operator's console *computers* POC
processing proc'g
processing elements *computers* PE
processor controller *computers* PC
processor unit *computers* PU
processor-memory-switch *computers* PMS
Proclamation Proc.
Proctor Proc.
Procurator-Fiscal PF *or* P.F.
procure Proc. *or* PROC
procurement Proc. *or* PROC
procurement lead time *military* PROLT

Procurement Services Office PSO
produce prod.
produced prod.
producer prod.
Producer Price Index PPI
product prod.
product liability PL
product manager PM
product of sums *mathematics* POS
product sales manager PSM
production prod.
Production and Marketing Administration PMA
production assistant PA
Production Code Administration PCA
Production Engineering Research Association PERA
production environmental test PET
production man-hour PMH *or* pmh
profession prof.
professional 1 pro *or* pro. **2** Prof. **3** prof.
Professional and Administrative P&A
professional association PA *or* P.A.
Professional Association of Teachers PAT
Professional Bowlers Association PBA *or* P.B.A.
Professional Coin Grading Service PCGS
professional corporation PC *or* P.C.
Professional Engineer 1 P.Eng. **2** PE *or* P.E.
Professional Engineers in Private Practice PEPP
Professional Golfers' Association PGA *or* P.G.A. (*NYT:* P.G.A.; *OUP:* PGA)
Professional Photographers of America PPA
Professional Services Section PSS
professional standards review organization PSRO *or* P.S.R.O.
Professional, Administrative, Clerical, Technical, and Other PACTO (Civil Service categories)
professor Prof. *or* Prof (*GPO, NYT, OUP:* Prof.)
Professor of Sacred Theology STP *or* S.T.P.
profit and loss *commerce* **1** P&L *or* p&l **2** PL *or* P/L *or* P-L
profits before taxes *finance* PBT
prognosis *medicine* prog.
program 1 pgm. **2** prog.
program appraising and review PAR
program control register *computers* PCR
program controller *computers* PC
program counter *computers* PC
Program Development Plan PDP
program director PD *or* P.D.
Program Evaluation Procedure *computers* PEP
Program Evaluation Review Technique *computers* PERT
program for integrated shipboard electronics PRISE
program for numerical tool operation PRONTO
Program for the Advancement of Industrial Technology PAIT
program indicator *computers* PI
program interrupt control *computers* PIC
program manager PM
program reference table *computers* PRT

program reliability information system for management PRISM
program reporting and evaluation system for total operation PRESTO
program status word *computers* PSW
program-controlled computer PCC
Programmable Logic Array *computers* PLA
programmable logic controller *computers* PLC
programmable read-only memory *computers* PROM
programmed prog.
programmed control interrupt *computers* PCI
Programmed Inquiry, Learning or Teaching *computers* PILOT
programmed instruction PI
Programmed Logic for Automatic Teaching Operations PLATO *or* Plato
programming assembly language PAL
programming documentation standards *computers* PDS
Programming in Logic PROLOG
programming language PL
programming language for automatic checkout equipment PLACE
programming language for microprocessors PLM *or* PL/M
programming, planning, and budgeting PPB
progress prog.
progress report PR
Progressive Prog.
progressive 1 pro *or* Pro. **2** prog.
Progressive Australia Party PAP
Progressive Conservative PC
Progressive Federal Party PFP (of South Africa)
Progressive Labor Movement PLM
progressive multifocal leukoencephalopathy PML
progressive patient care *medicine* PPC
progressive rubella panencephalitis PRP
project proj. *or* proj *or* Proj.
Project Management System *commerce* PMS
project manager PM
Project Operations Director POD *or* P.O.D.
Project Operations Manager POM
projection proj. *or* proj
projector proj. *or* proj
prolactin inhibitory factor PIF
prolactin releasing factor PRF
prolapsed intervertebral disk *medicine* PID
proline PRO *or* Pro.
prologue prol.
promenade 1 prom. *or* prom **2** *British* prom. *or* prom *or* Prom (concert)
promethium Pm
promissory note *commerce* PN *or* P/N *or* p.n.
promontory prom. *or* Prom.
promoted prom.
promotion prom. *or* promo
prompt side *theater* PS *or* P.S.
prompter *theater* P *or* P.
pronominal pron.
pronoun pron.
pronounced pron.

pronunciation 1 pr *or* pr. **2** pron. (*MLA:* pronunc.; *OUP:* pron.)
proof 1 pf **2** Pf. (of coins) **3** prf.
Proof and Experimental Establishment *British* PEE
proof spirit S.V.T.
propellant utilization PU
propeller prop
proper prop *or* prop.
proper forms being observed PP
proper motion *astronomy* PM *or* P.M.
properly prop *or* prop.
properties *theater* props. *or* props
property 1 ppty *or* Ppty **2** prop *or* PROP *or* prop.
property damage *insurance* PD
proportion 1 p **2** propn.
proportional propl.
proportional representation PR *or* P.R.
proportionality limit PL
proposed prop *or* prop.
proposition prop *or* prop.
proprietary 1 prop **2** Pty. *or* Pty *or* pty.
proprietor 1 prop *or* Prop. **2** Propr.
propyl 1 pro *or* pro. **2** *chemistry* Pr
propylthiouracil PTU
Prosecuting Attorney Pros. Atty
prosody pros.
prostacycline PGI_2
prostaglandin PG
prostaglandin group PGE *or* PGF
prostate prost.
prostate-specific antigen PSA
prostatic acid phosphatase PAP
prosthetic valve endocarditis PVE
prostitution prost.
protactinium Pa
protamine insulin PI
protamine zinc insulin PZI
protected prot.
protection prot.
protection and indemnity *insurance* P&I
Protectorate Prot.
protein pro
protein efficiency ratio *agriculture* PER
protein-bound iodine PBI
protein-calorie malnutrition PCM
protein-nitrogen unit PNU
proteinaceous infectious particle prion
pro tem *or* **Pro tem.** (*GPO:* pro tem; *CSM:* pro tem.; *OUP:* p.t. *or* pro tem)
Protestant Prot. *or* Protest.
Prothonotary Apostolic PA *or* P.A.
prothrombin time *medicine* PT
protium H^1
Proto-Indo-European PIE
proton 1 p **2** H^{1+}
proton exchange membrane PEM
proton magnetic resonance PMR
proton synchrotron *physics* PS
proton-induced X-ray emission PIXE
protopam chloride PAM
prototype Y
prototype fast reactor PFR
proved pr
proven as safe PAS
Provençal 1 Pr **2** Prov.
provenance Prov.
Provence Prov.

proverb prov.
proverbial prov.
Proverbs Prov.
Province Prov.
Province of Ontario PO or P.O.
Province of Quebec PQ or P.Q.
Provincial Prov.
provincialism prov.
proving ground PG
provision prov.
Provisional Provo
provisional prov.
provocateur Provo or provo
Provost 1 Pro or Pro. 2 Prov.
Provost Marshal PM
Provost Marshal General PMG or P.M.G.
pruritic urticarial papules and plaques
    PUPP
Prussia Prus. or Pruss.
Prussian Prus. or Pruss. (*MLA:* Pruss.)
Psalm 1 Ps. 2 Psa.
Psalms 1 Ps. (book of the Old Testament)
    2 Psa. (book of the Old Testament) 3 Pss.
pseudo-random pulse *electronics* PRP
pseudonym 1 ps or ps. 2 pseud.
pseudorandom binary sequence *computers*
    PRBS
pseudorandom noise *computers* PN
pseudostatic spontaneous potential
    engineering PSP
Psoralen Ultraviolet A PUVA
psychiatric psych.
psychiatric social worker PSW
psychiatry 1 psy. 2 psych.
psychic psych.
psychoanalysis psy.
psychogalvanic response PGR
psychokinesis PK
psychological psych. or psychol.
psychological saline solution PSS
psychological warfare 1 psywar 2 PW
psychological warfare operations psyop
psychologist psych. or psychol.
psychology 1 psy. 2 psych. or psychol.
psychoneurotic PN
psychotherapist PT or P.T.
psychotherapy PT or P.T.
pteroylglutamic acid PGA
Public Pub.
public pub. or publ.
public address 1 p.a. 2 PA
Public Affairs PA
Public Affairs Information Service PAIS
Public Affairs Officer PAO
public assistance PA
Public Assistance Committee *British* PAC
Public Broadcasting Service PBS
Public Broadcasting System PBS
Public Buildings Administration PBA
Public Buildings Service PBS
public data network PDN
public defender PD or P.D.
public document Pub. Doc.
public domain PD (of intellectual material)
Public Education Association P.E.A.
public good, the b.p.
Public Health PH or P.H.

Public Health Engineer PHE
public health nurse PHN or P.H.N.
Public Health Service PHS
Public Housing Administration PHA or
    P.H.A.
Public Information PI
public information office *or* **officer** PIO
Public Interest Research Group PIRG
Public Law PL or P.L. (with number)
public liability *insurance* PL
Public Library PL or P.L.
Public Limited Company PLC
Public Message Service *computers* PMS
Public Record Office PRO or P.R.O.
public relations PR or P.R. or p.r.
public relations officer PRO
Public Relations Society of America PRSA or
    P.R.S.A.
Public Resolution Public Res. (with number)
public school PS (with number) (*NYT:* P.S.)
public sector borrowing requirement
    PSBR
public service announcement PSA
Public Service Commission PSC or P.S.C.
Public Service Vehicle PSV
Public Services International PSI (trade
    union alliance)
Public Statutes PS or P.S.
Public Switched Network *computers* PSN
public television PTV
Public Trustee Office PTO or P.T.O.
Public Utilities Commission PUC or P.U.C.
public utility district PUD
public works PW or P.W.
Public Works Loans Board P.W.L.B.
public, educational, and governmental PEG
    (of cable TV)
public-address system 1 p.a. 2 PA
publication 1 Pub. (often with number)
    2 pub. or publ. (*MLA:* pub or publ.; *OUP:*
    pub.) 3 Pubn or pubn.
Publication Board PB (of U.S. Department of
    Commerce)
Publications of the Modern Language
    Association PMLA
publicity 1 Pub. 2 pub. or publ.
published 1 pp or p.p. 2 pub. or publ. or
    pubd.(*MLA:* pub or publ.; *OUP:* pub.)
publisher pub. or publ. (*MLA:* pub or publ.;
    OUP: pub.)
Publishers Information Bureau PIB
Publishers Weekly PW
publishing pub. or publ.
pudding pud.
Puerto Rico PR (Zip Code) or P.R. (in
    general use) (*NYT:* P.R.; *OUP:* PR)
pugilist pug.
pula P
pull next stitch over pnso or PNSO (in
    knitting)
pull switch PS
pulmonary pul. or pulm.
pulmonary infiltrates with eosinophilia
    medicine PIE or P.I.E.
pulsar PSR (with number)
pulse P
pulse acquisition radar PAR

pulse amplitude modulation *electronics*
    PAM or pam
Pulse Code Modulation *communications*
    PCM or pcm
pulse duration modulation *electronics* PDM
pulse frequency *electronics* PF
pulse frequency modulation *electronics* PFM
    or pfm
pulse generator *electronics* PG
pulse height analyzer *electronics* PHA
pulse interval modulation *electronics* PIM
pulse length modulation *electronics* PLM
pulse modulation *electronics* PM
pulse position modulation *communications*
    PPM
pulse recurrence *or* **repetition frequency**
    PRF
pulse repetition period *electronics* PRP
pulse repetition rate *electronics* PRR
pulse repetition time *electronics* PRT
pulse time modulation PTM
pulse width *electronics* PW
pulse width modulation *electronics*
    PWM
pulses per second p.p.s. or pps
pulverized pulv.
pulverized fuel ash PFA
pump horsepower PHP or php
punch off *computers* PF
punctuation punc.
punish pun.
punishment pun.
pupil *medicine* P or P.
pupil-teacher PT
purchase pur.
Purchase and Resale Agreement *finance*
    PRA
purchase order PO
purchase tax *British* 1 PT 2 pt or p.t.
purchaser pur.
purchasing pur. or purch
Purchasing Agent PA or P.A.
purchasing power parity PPP
pure pur.
pure parental type *biology* F_o
purification pur.
purified protein derivative PPD
purl 1 P 2 p
purl into back of stitch Pb
purple purp
Purple Heart *military* PH or P.H.
pursuit pur.
push-pull pp or p-p (of a circuit)
pushbutton PB or p/b
put p (option to sell stock)
put and call 1 P&C 2 PAC (option to sell or
    buy stock)
putout *baseball* 1 PO 2 po or p.o.
pyrazinamide PZA
pyribenzamine PBZ
pyridine Py
pyrogallol pyro. or pyro
pyromaniac pyro. or pyro
pyromellitic dianhydride PMDA
pyrometric cone equivalent PCE or pce
pyrotechnic pyro. or pyrotech.
pyroxylin pyro. or pyrox.

Qatar Q
quad in-line *electronics* QUIL
quadrangle quad. *or* quad *or* Quad
quadrant quad.
quadraphonic quad.
quadratic sieve *computers* QS
quadrature amplitude modulation *communications* QAM
quadrilateral quad.
quadruple quad.
quadruplicate quad.
quadrupole moment *physics* Q
qualification qual.
qualification approval QA
qualified qual.
qualified (to work with) mentally retarded people QMRP
qualified nurse QN *or* Q.N.
qualified products list QPL
qualified scientist and engineer *British* QSE
Qualified Voluntary Employee Contribution Plan QVEC
qualify qual.
qualitative qual.
qualitative material requirement QMR
qualitative operational requirement QOR
qualitative personnel information QPI
qualitative personnel requirements information QPRI
quality 1 Q **2** qlty. **3** qual.
quality assurance QA
quality control QC
quality control engineering QCE
quality control technology QCT
quality factor 1 Q **2** QF
quality improvement QI
quality of life QOL
quality of working life QWL
quality reliability assurance QRA
quality test QT
quality-adjusted life years QALY
quality-protein maize QPM
quantitative quant.
quantitative computed tomography *medicine* QCT
quantitative fluorescence image analysis QFIA
quantity 1 A *or* a **2** C **3** Q *or* q **4** qnty **5** qt *or* qt. **6** qty. **7** quant. **8** *mathematics* B *or* b
quantity discount agreement *commerce* q.d.a. *or* QDA
quantity not sufficient QNS *or* q.n.s.
quantity of electricity *or* **electric charge** q *or* Q
quantity of heat Q
quantity of light Q
quantity of reactive power Q
quantity *or* **rate of flow** q

quantum chromodynamics QCD
quantum electrodynamics QED
quantum electronics QE
quantum field theory *physics* QFT
quantum mechanics QM
quantum number of total angular momentum *British, physics* F
quark *physics* q
quart 1 q *or* q. **2** qt *or* qt. (*CSM, OUP*: qt.) **3** qu.
quarter 1 q *or* q. **2** qtr. **3** qtr. **4** qu. **5** quar. *or* quart.
Quarter Journal of Speech QJS
quarter section (of land) **1** q.s. **2** QS
quarter session QS *or* Q.S. (of a court of law)
quarter ton qr.
quarterback *sports* QB *or* q.b.
quartered qtd.
quarterly 1 Q (in stock report) **2** q *or* q. **3** qr. **4** qtly. *or* Qtly **5** qtr. *or* Qtr. **6** qu. **7** quar. *or* quart.
Quarterly Review QR
Quartermaster 1 QM **2** QMR *or* Qmr.
Quartermaster Corps 1 QC **2** QMC
Quartermaster General 1 QG **2** QMG *or* QMGen.
quarternary phase-shift keying *computers* QPSK
quarters 1 qrs. *or* Qrs **2** qtrs. *or* Qtrs
quarters allowance *British* QA
quartet *music* qt
quartile Q
quartile deviation *statistics* Q
quarto 1 Q *or* Q. **2** q *or* q. **3** qto. *or* Qto.
quartos Qq *or* Qq.
quarts qts.
quartz 1 qtz. **2** qz.
quasi-autonomous national government organization *British* quango
quasi-autonomous nongovernmental organization *British* quango
quasi-biennial oscillation *meteorology* QBO
quasi-stellar galaxy *astronomy* QSG
quasi-stellar object *astronomy* **1** quasar **2** QSO
quasi-stellar radio source (quasar) *astronomy* QSR *or* QSS
quasiperiodic object *astronomy* QPO
quaternary quat. *or* Quat.
Quay Qy.
Quebec 1 Q *or* Q. **2** Qbc **3** Que.
Quebec Party PQ
Quechua Que.
Queen 1 Q *or* Q. **2** Qn. **3** Qu.
Queen Alexandra's Royal Air Force Nursing Service *British* QA *or* QARAFNS
Queen Alexandra's Royal Army Nursing Corps *British* QA *or* QARANC
Queen Alexandra's Royal Navy Nursing Service *British* QA *or* QARNNS
Queen Anne's Bounty *British* Q.A.B.
Queen Elizabeth ER *or* E.R.
Queen Elizabeth the Second QE 2 (British ocean liner)
Queen's Bench *British law* QB *or* Q.B.
Queen's Bench Division *British law* Q.B.D.

Queen's Bishop *chess* QB
Queen's Bishop's Pawn *chess* QBP
Queen's Counsel *British law* QC *or* Q.C.
Queen's evidence *British law* QE
Queen's Honorary Chaplain Q.H.C.
Queen's Honorary Physician Q.H.P.
Queen's Honorary Surgeon Q.H.S.
Queen's Knight *chess* **1** QKt *or* Qkt **2** QN
Queen's Knight's Pawn *chess* **1** QKtP *or* Qktp **2** QNP *or* QNp
Queen's Messenger QM *or* Q.M.
Queen's Pawn *chess* QP
Queen's Regulations QR *or* Q.R.
Queen's Rook *chess* QR
Queen's Rook's Pawn *chess* QRP *or* QRp
Queensland 1 Q *or* Q. **2** Qld. **3** Qnsld. **4** Queens. *or* Queensl.
Quell basic oxygen process Q-BOP
quench frequency *electronics* QF
Querwellen Q
query 1 q **2** Qu. *or* Qu **3** qu. *or* qu **4** Qy. *or* qy.
query by example *computers* QBE
query language *computers* QL
question 1 Q **2** q **3** qn *or* qn. *or* q^n **4** Qu. *or* Qu **5** qu. *or* qu (*CSM*: ques.; *OUP*: qu.) **6** ques.
question and answer QA *or* Q/A *or* Q&A *or* Q. and A. (*NYT*: Q. and A.)
questioned trade *commerce* QT *or* Q.T.
questionnaire questn
questions qq *or* qq.
quetzal Q
queue control block *computers* QCB
queued access method *computers* QAM
queued indexed sequential access method *computers* QISAM
queued sequential access method *computers* QSAM
queued telecommunications access method *computers* QTAM
queueing theory *computers* QT
quick Qk
quick connect QC
quick freeze QF
quick make-and-break *electronics* QMB
quick response *commerce* QR
quick-firing QF
quickchange QC
quickly *music* viv. *or* Viv.
quiet room QR
quiet short takeoff and landing (aircraft) QSTOL
quiet takeoff and landing (aircraft) QTOL
quinone Q
quintal 1 q *or* q. **2** ql
quintet *music* qnt
quintuple quint.
quintuplicate quint.
quire 1 Q *or* Q. **2** q *or* q. **3** qr. *or* qr
quires qrs. *or* qrs
quitclaim *law* QC
quorum quor. *or* Quor
quotation 1 qn *or* qn. **2** quot.
quoted quot.
quotient Q

Rabbi Rab.
rabbi R or R.
Rabbinate Rabb.
Rabbinic Rabb.
Rabbinical Rabb.
Rabbinical Alliance of America R.A.A.
Rabbinical Council of America RCA or R.C.A.
Racketeer Influenced and Corrupt Organizations RICO
rad rd
radar 1 R 2 rdr 3 military RAD
Radar Altimeter and Doppler Velocity Sensor RADVS
Radar Approach Control RAPCON
radar beacon racon or RACON (GPO: racon)
radar control or controlled RC or R/C
radar countermeasures RCM
radar coverage indicator RCI
radar cross section RCS
radar data RADAT
radar dome radome
radar marker RAMARK
radar navigation RADAN
radar operator RO
radar report meteorology RAREP
radar signature analysis RSA
radar warning circuits RAWARC (of National Weather Service)
radar wind measurements RAWIN
radar-absorbing material RAM
radar-equipped inertial navigation system REINS
radial rad or rad.
radial keratotomy medicine RK or rk
radian rad
radiance physics R
radiancy physics R
radiant energy U
radiant energy density u
radiation radn
radiation danger zone RDZ
Radiation Protection Guides RPG
Radiation Safety Officer RSO
Radical Rad.
radical 1 chemistry R 2 mathematics rad or rad.
radio 1 rad or rad. 2 military RAD
Radio Advertising Bureau RAB
Radio Amateur Civil Emergency Service RACES
Radio and Electronic Component Manufacturers Federation RECMF
Radio and Electronics Measurements Committee REMC
Radio and Television Agency of Italy RAI
Radio and Television of Ireland RTE
Radio and Television Retailers Association RTRA
radio astronomy explorer RAE

radio astronomy observatory RAO
radio beacon R.Bn.
radio bearing or beacon RB
Radio Chemical Center RCC
radio code RC
radio coding RC
radio common carrier RCC
radio controlled RC or R/C
Radio Corporation of America RCA
radio countermeasures RCM
radio direction finder or finding RDF
radio distress signal CQD or C.Q.D.
Radio Free Europe RFE
radio frequency 1 RF or R-F (GPO: RF) 2 rf or r.f. or r-f
radio frequency choke electronics RFC or rfc
radio frequency interference RFI
radio inertial (guidance) RI
Radio Intelligence Division RID
Radio Liberty RL
radio location RL
radio magnetic indicator RMI
Radio New Zealand RNZ or R.N.Z.
radio observation RAOB
radio operator RO
radio range RR
Radio Society of Great Britain RSGB
radio station RS
Radio Technical Committee for Aeronautics RTCA
Radio Technician RT
radio teletype 1 RATT 2 RTTY
radio, television aid to navigation RATAN
radio-frequency radiation RFR
Radio-Television News Directors Association RTNDA
radioacoustic ranging RAR
radioactive RA
radioactive iodine I^{131}
radioactive iodine serum albumen RISA
radioactivity RA
radioactivity concentration guide RCG
radioactivity detection, identification, and computation radiac
radioallergosorbent test medicine RAST
radioimmunoassay RIA
radioisotope thermoelectric generator RTG
radiological military RAD
radiological emergency medical team REMT
Radiological Emergency Response Plan RERP
Radiological Society of North America RSNA or R.S.N.A.
radiological warfare RW
radionavigation RN
radiosonde balloon RABAL
radiotelephone RT or R/T
radiotelephone operator RTO
radiotelephony RT or R/T
radiothorium RdTh
radium Ra
radium emanation RE
radius 1 R or r 2 rad or rad.
radius gyration physics k
radius of circle of least confusion physics Z
radix (root) mathematics rad or rad.
radon Rn
ragged right rr (margin in printing)
rail and water commerce R&W or r. and w.
rail rapid transit RRT

rail-diesel-car RDC
railroad 1 R or R. 2 RR
Railroad Retirement Board RRB
railroad retirement tax RRTA
railway 1 R or R. 2 Rly. or rly. 3 RW 4 Rwy. 5 Ry or Ry. (GPO: Ry.; OUP: R. or rly.)
Railway Association of Canada RAC
rain r or r.
rain shower meteorology RW
raised ranch architecture RR or R/R
Rajasthani Raj.
Raleigh wave R
ram-air turbine RAT
rand R (monetary unit of South Africa)
random rdm.
random access and correlation for extended performance computers RACEP
random access and discrete address RADA
random access discrete address system computers RADAS
random access memory computers RAM
random access memory accounting RAMAC
random access plan position indicator RAPPI
random access programming computers RAP
random communication satellite system RCSS
random digit dialing RDD
random length RL (of lumber)
random widths RW (of lumber)
Range 1 Ra or Ra. 2 Rge 3 Rng.
range R or r
range and elevation guidance for approach and landing aeronautics REGAL
range finder RF
range of jamming communications ROJ
range safety beacon RSB
Range Safety Officer RSO
range-height indicator RHI
Rankine °R or R
Rape of Lucrece, The Luc. or Lucr. (MLA: Luc.)
rapid rap.
rapid automatic checkout equipment electronics RACE
Rapid Deployment Force RDF or R.D.F.
rapid eye movement REM
rapid eye movement sleep REMS
rapid plasma reagin RPR
rapid plasma reagin test RPRT
rapid speech transmission index RASTI
rapid-fire 1 RF 2 rf or r.f.
rare biology r or r.
rare bird alert RBA
rare earth RE (chemical element)
rare earth element REE
rare earth permanent magnet REPM
raster image file format computers RIFF
raster image processor computers RIP
rat unit biology, biochemistry RU or R.U.
rate R or r
rate of energy loss REL
rate of exchange 1 r.e. or r/e 2 RE or R/E
rated horsepower rhp or r.h.p.
rating rat.
ratio R
ratio of a statistic to its standard error statistics t

ration rat.
reactance 1 *electricity* react. 2 *physics* X
reaction R
reaction control jet RCJ
reaction control system RCS
reaction injection molding RIM
reaction of degeneration 1 DER 2 *medicine* RD
reaction time RT
reactive volt ampere rva *or* RVA
reactor react. *or* reac.
Reactor Centrum Netherlands RCN *or* R.C.N.
reactor containment building RCB
reactor cooling system RCS
Reactor Safety Advisory Committee RSAC
read in *computers* RI
read, write *computers* RW *or* R/W
read-only memory ROM
read-only storage *computers* ROS
Reader of Sacred Theology STL *or* S.T.L.
Reader's Guide to Periodical Literature RG
readiness potential RP
reading rdg.
Reading Is Fundamental RIF
ready rdy
ready money down r.m.d.
ready-to-wear r-t-w *or* rtw
reaffirmed R
real 1 Re 2 *mathematics* R
real estate RE
real estate investment trust REIT
Real Estate Settlement Procedures Act RESPA
real time RT
real time data system *computers* RTDS
real time disk operating system *computers* RDOS
realised ultimate reality piton rurp
Realtor Rltr.
realty rty *or* Rty
ream rm. (of paper)
reams rms *or* rms. (of paper)
Rear Admiral 1 RA *or* R.A. 2 Rear Adm. 3 *military* R.Adm. *or* RADM
rear projection RP (in motion-picture making)
rear-wheel brakes r.w.b. *or* RWB
rear-wheel drive r.w.d. *or* RWD
reason rsn
Réaumur 1 R *or* R. 2 Réaum. *or* Réau.
Rebuttable Presumption Against Registration RPAR
recapitulate recap
recapitulation recap
receipt 1 rcpt. 2 rct. 3 rec. 4 rect. 5 rept.
receipt of goods *commerce* r.o.g. *or* ROG
receipt, inspection, and maintenance RIM
receive 1 rec. *or* REC 2 RX
received 1 R (of radio message) 2 rcd. *or* Rcd 3 recd. *or* rec'd. 4 *commerce* r *or* r.
received on account *commerce* ROA
Received Pronunciation RP
receiver 1 RCVR *or* rcvr 2 rec. *or* REC 3 recr. 4 RX
receiver operator characteristic *communications* ROC
Receiving Office RO *or* R.O.
Receiving Officer RO *or* R.O.
receiving station RS

recent rec.
reception 1 rec. 2 recep. 3 recp.
receptor-destroying enzyme RDE
recessive *genetics* a *or* a
recidivism recid.
recidivous recid.
recipe rec.
reciprocal 1 recip. 2 recp.
reciprocal recurrent selection RRS (in stock breeding)
Reciprocal Trade Agreement RTA *or* R.T.A.
reciprocating 1 recip. 2 recp.
reciprocity recip.
recirculating recirc.
recirculating single pass RSP
recirculation recirc.
recitation recit.
recitative *music* recit. *or* Recit.
reclamation reclam.
recognition recog.
recognize recog.
recognized professional body RPB
Recollect Augustinian Fathers AR *or* A.R.
recombinant organism RO (of a virus)
recombinant tissue plasminogen activator r-tPA
recombination activation gene RAG
recommend recm. *or* recom.
recommended daily allowance *nutrition* RDA
recommended dietary allowance *nutrition* RDA
recommended retail price RRP
recommended *or* requirement standard RS
reconcentration recon.
reconciliation recon.
recondition recon.
reconnaissance recon. *or* RECON
reconsignment recon.
reconstruction recon. *or* reconst.
reconveyance recon.
record rec.
Record Office RO
recorded rec.
recorded demand RD
Recorder Rec.
recorder rec.
Recording Rec.
recording rec.
Recording for the Blind RFB
Recording Industry Association of America RIAA
Recording Optical Tracking Instrument ROTI
Recording Secretary 1 Rec. Sec. 2 RS *or* R.S.
recovery room 1 Rec. Rm. 2 RR *or* R.R.
recreation rec.
recreational therapy RT
recreational vehicle 1 rec.v. *or* recvee 2 RV *or* R/V
recruit RCT *or* Rct.
Recruiting Officer RO
recrystallization recrystn
recrystallize recryst.
rectangle rect.
rectangular rect.
rectified rect.

rectified spirit of wine *pharmaceutics* S.V.R. *or* s.v.r.
rectifier rect.
rectifying-demodulating phonopneumograph RDP
recto 1 R 2 r 3 ro. *or* r°
recto leaf *botany* a
Rector Rect.
Rectory Rect.
recurrent recur.
recurrent abdominal pain RAP
recurring recur.
red 1 r 2 R *or* R. 3 rd 4 rub.
red blood cell RBC
red blood corpuscle RBC
red blood count RBC
Red Cross RC *or* R.C.
red star of maximum intensity of metal *astronomy* K
red star of prominent titanium oxide intensity *astronomy* M
red, green, and ultraviolet *astronomy* RGU (of star magnitude)
red-green RG
red-green-blue RGB (of color separation)
redactor 1 R *or* R. 2 red. *or* Red.
redeemable red.
rediscount redisc.
reduced red.
reduced instruction set computer RISC
reduced layer formation RLF
reduced takeoff and landing RTOL
reducer red.
reducing flame *chemistry* rf
reduction 1 rd 2 red.
reduction in force RIF *or* R.I.F. (*GPO:* RIF)
reduction in forces RIF
reduction of area RA
reduction oxidation redox.
redundancy adjustment of probability RAP
reduplication redup. *or* redupl.
reentry control system RCS
reentry flight demonstration RFD
reentry vehicle RV *or* R/V
refashioned refash.
refer ref. *or* Ref.
refer to ref. *or* Ref.
refer to acceptor *commerce* RA *or* R/A
refer to drawer *British* RD *or* R/D (in banking)
referee ref. *or* Ref. *or* ref
reference 1 R 2 ref. *or* Ref. *or* ref
Reference and Adult Services Division (of the ALA) RASD *or* R.A.S.D.
reference library RL
referred 1 ref. *or* ref *or* Ref. 2 refd. 3 rfrd
referred by ref. *or* ref *or* Ref.
refined ref.
refining ref.
reflection refl.
reflection high-energy electron diffraction RHEED
reflective refl.
reflex refl.
reflexive *grammar* refl.
reflexive verb 1 v.r. 2 v.refl.
Reform Party RP
Reformation (movement in 16th century Europe) ref.

reformation ref.
Reformatory Reform.
reformed ref.
Reformed Church Ref. Ch.
Reformed Presbyterian 1 Ref. Pres. **2** RP or R.P.
Reformed Protestant Episcopal RPE or R.P.E.
Reformed Spelling RS
reformed spelling Ref.Sp.
reformulated gas (of gasoline) RFG
refraction 1 R **2** ref. **3** refr.
refractive index 1 r.i. **2** RI
refrigerate refr. or refrig.
refrigerated 1 ref. **2** refg.
refrigeration 1 ref. **2** refg. **3** refr. or refrig.
refuel rfl.
refund 1 ref. **2** refd.
refunded refd.
regenerate regen.
regeneration regen.
Regent 1 Reg. **2** Regt.
Regiment 1 Reg. **2** Regt. **3** Rgt.
Regimental Regtl.
regimental combat team RCT
Regimental Headquarters RHQ
Regimental Order RO or R.O. (with number)
Regimental Sergeant Major RSM
Region Reg.
region 1 reg. **2** Rgn or rgn
Regional Commissioner (of U.S. Customs Service) RC
Regional Customs Representative RCR
Regional Economic Planning Council REPC
regional holding company (satellite telephone company) RHC
Regional Planning Association RPA
regional seat of government RSG
Regional Transportation Authority RTA
Register Reg.
register reg.
register and arithmetic logic unit computers RALU
register book Reg. Lib.
register of judicial writs law Reg. Jud.
Registered Reg.
registered 1 R or R. **2** reg. **3** regd. **4** Rgd. **5** German Ges. or ges.
registered at the United States Patent Office Reg. US Pat. Off.
Registered Clinical Nurse Teacher RCNT
registered company German e.G.
Registered Dietitian RD
Registered Fever Nurse RFN or R.F.N.
Registered General Nurse RGN or R.G.N.
Registered Laboratory Technician RLT
Registered Maternity Nurse RMN or R.M.N.
Registered Medical Technician RMT
Registered Midwife RM
Registered Nurse RN or R.N. (GPO: R.N.)
Registered Occupational Therapist OTR
Registered Pharmacist R.Ph.
Registered Physical Therapist RPT
Registered Psychiatric Nurse RPN
Registered Record Librarian RRL
Registered Respiratory Therapist RRT
Registered Retirement Savings Plan Canadian RRSP
Registered Technician RT or R.T.
registered trademark 1 Reg.TM **2** RTM

Registrar 1 Reg. **2** Regr.
registrar reg.
registration reg.
Registry Reg.
registry reg.
Registry of Toxic Effects of Chemical Substances RTECS
Regius Professor 1 Reg. Prof. **2** RP or R.P.
regression coefficient statistics b
Regular Reg.
regular reg.
Regular Army RA
Regular Officer Training Plan Canadian ROTP
regular oil (grade of motor oil) ML
regular variable star astronomy RV
regularly reg.
Regulation Reg.
regulation reg.
Regulations 1 Reg. **2** Regs
regulator reg.
rehabilitation rehab. or Rehab
Rehabilitation Services Administration RSA
reichsmark RM or r.m.
Reid vapor pressure aeronautics RVP
reinforced reinf.
reinforced concrete RC
reinforced concrete pipe RCP
reinforcing 1 reinf. **2** music **a** rf **b** rfz **c** rinf.
reinforcing stimulus psychology RS
reinsurance RI
Reiter Protein Complement Fixation RPCF
reject rej.
rejection rej.
rejection slip RS or R/S
related rel.
related subjects RS
relating rel.
relation rel.
relational database management system computers RDBMS
relative rel.
relative atomic mass RAM or r.a.m.
relative bearing RB
relative biological effectiveness RBE
relative centrifugal force RCF
relative heat physics L
relative humidity 1 f **2** RH **3** rh or r.h. **4** meteorology r
relative molecular mass r.m.m. or rmm
relatively rel.
relativistic electron beam physics REB
relay rel.
release rel.
release clause r.c.
released rel.
released on own recognizance law ROR or R.O.R.
releasing factor (of a hormone) RF
reliability performance measure RPM
relic or **relics** rel.
relief rel.
relief pitcher baseball RP
relief valve RV
relieve or **relieved** rel.
religion 1 rel. or Rel. **2** Relig.
religious 1 rel. or Rel. **2** Relig. or relig.
religious education RE
religious instruction RI or R.I.

reluctance 1 rel. **2** physics R
remainder rem.
remaining rem.
remaining on board shipping rob
remarks rem.
remedial occupational therapy ROT
remittance rem.
remote augmented lift system RALS
remote automatic telemetry equipment RATE
remote call forwarding RCF
remote computing service RCS
remote control oscillator RCO
remote control system RCS
remote control unit RCU
remote control or **controlled** RC or R/C
remote instrument package RIP
Remote Interactive Communications computers RIC
remote job entry computers RJE
remote manipulator system (of a spacecraft) RMS
remote pickup unit communications RPU
remote position control RPC
remote sensing RS or rs
remote terminal unit computers RTU
Remote Underwater Manipulator RUM
remote-association test RAT
remotely operated vehicle ROV
remotely piloted vehicle RPV
removed rem.
Renaissance Ren.
renal plasma flow medicine RPF
renal pressor substance RPS
renal tubular acidosis RTA
renal vein renin activity medicine RVRA
rendezvous 1 rdv or rdvu. **2** RV or Rv
renegotiable rate mortgage RRM
renovate renv.
renovation renv.
reorganization reorg.
repair rep.
repeat 1 R **2** rep. **3** rpt.
repeat from the beginning music d.c. or DC
repeating unit (of identical integers) repunit
repertory Rep or rep
Repertory Company or **Theater** Rep or rep
repetitive stress or **strain injury** RSI
replace repl.
replacement repl.
replicating form genetics RF
reply postcard RPC
report 1 rep. **2** rept. or Rept. **3** RPRT or rprt. **4** rpt. or Rpt. (MLA: rept.; OUP: rep. or rept.)
Report Program Generator RPG
reported rep. (MLA: rept.)
reporter rep. (OUP: rep. or rept.)
repossess repo
repossessed property repo
repossession repo
Representative Rep or Rep.
representative rep
representative fraction cartography RF
represented repr.
representing repr.
reprint 1 R **2** repr. **3** RP or R.P. **4** rpt.
reprinted 1 repr. **2** RP or R.P.
reproduction repro or repro.

reprogrammable programmable ROM
computers RPROM
reptile rept.
Republic 1 Rep *or* Rep. **2** Repub.
Republic of Argentina RA *or* R.A.
Republic of Bolivia RB
Republic of China (Taiwan) ROC *or* R.O.C.
Republic of Korea ROK
Republic of Panama RP *or* R.P.
Republic of Portugal RP *or* R.P.
Republic of Romania RR
Republic of South Africa RSA
Republic of the Ivory Coast *French* RCI
Republican 1 R **2** Rep *or* Rep. **3** Repub.
Republican Democratic Union *French,*
Spanish URD
Republican National Committee RNC
Republican Party *French* PR *or* P.R.
Republican Party of Quebec *French* PRQ
republication repub
reputation rep.
request req.
request for authority to negotiate RAN
request for information RFI
request for price quotation *commerce* RPQ
request for proposals RFP
request for quotation *commerce* **1** RFQ
2 RQ *or* R/Q
require req.
require better information RBI
required req. *or* req'd
requirement rqmt *or* Rqmt
requisition req. *or* reqn
rerun R (in TV schedule)
resale price maintenance *British* RPM *or*
R.P.M.
resawed res. (of lumber)
rescue res. *or* resc.
rescue and recovery R&R *or* R and R
Rescue Coordination Center RCC
Research Res.
research 1 res. **2** Rsch *or* rsch
Research Analysis Corporation RAC
research and development 1 R&D *or* R and
D (*GPO, MLA:* R & D) **2** Rand *or* RAND
3 RD
Research and Development Board RDB
Research and Development Establishment
British RDE
Research and Development in Advanced
Communications Technology in Europe
RACE
Research and Special Programs
Administration RSPA
Research Applied to National Needs RANN
research, development, and demonstration
RD&D
research, development, and engineering
RD&E
research, development, testing, and
evaluation RDT&E
Research Institute of America RIA *or* R.I.A.
research laboratory RL
Research Libraries Information Network
RLIN
Research Open Systems in Europe
computers ROSE
research paper RP
Research Report RR

research safety vehicle RSV
Research Society of America RESA
research vessel RV *or* R/V
Reservation Res.
Reserve 1 R **2** Res.
reserve res.
Reserve Corps RC
Reserve Force RF *or* R.F.
Reserve Officers' Training Corps R.O.T.C.
or ROTC (*GPO:* ROTC; *NYT:* R.O.T.C.)
reserved res.
Reservoir Res.
reservoir 1 res. **2** Rsvr. *or* rsvr
residence 1 r *or* r. **2** res.
Resident Res.
resident res.
Resident Advisor RA
resident alien RA *or* R.A.
Resident Medical Officer R.M.O.
resident utilization group RUG
resides *or* **resides at 1** res. **2** r *or* r.
residual res. *or* res *or* resid
residual gas analyzer RGA
residual volume (of the lungs) *medicine* RV
residue res. *or* res
resignation res. *or* resign.
resigned res. *or* resgn'd
resin coated RC
resistance 1 *physics, biology, construction* R
2 *physics, electronics* res. *or* resist.
3 *physics* r
resistance temperature detector *physics*
RTD
resistance-capacitance *electronics* RC *or* R-C
resistance-capacitance coupling *electronics*
RCC
Resistance-Inducing Factor RIF
resistance-transfer factor *genetics* RTF
resistor 1 R **2** *physics, electronics* res. *or*
resist.
resistor transistor logic *computers* RTL
resistor-capacitor-transistor logic
electronics RCTL
Resolution Res.
resolution *optics* res.
Resolution Funding Corporation REFCORP
Resolution Trust Corporation RTC
resonant gate transistor RGT
resonator *electronics* res.
resorcinol diglycidyl ether RDGE
resorcylic acid lactone RAL
resource allocation in multiprocess
scheduling RAMPS
Resource Conservation and Recovery Act
RCRA
respective resp.
respectively resp.
respiration 1 R *or* R. **2** resp. *or* respir.
respiration rate RR
respiratory resp. *or* respir.
respiratory distress syndrome RDS
respiratory enteric orphan (virus) reo
respiratory infection *or* **illness** RI
respiratory quotient RQ *or* r.q.
respiratory syncytial RS
respiratory syncytial virus RSV
Respiratory Therapist RT
respond R *or* R.
respondent resp.

response R *or* R.
responsible resp.
rest and recreation *or* **rehabilitation** R&R *or*
R and R
rest in proportion RIP
restartable solid variable pulse RSVP
restaurant rest. *or* restr.
resting heart rate RHR
resting metabolic rate *medicine* RMR
restoration rest.
restore *computers* RES
restored rest.
restrict rest.
restricted 1 R **2** RSTR *or* Rstr
restricted use, publication, etc. ltd. *or* Ltd.
restriction 1 R **2** rest. *or* restr.
restriction fragment-length polymorphism
1 RFLP **2** riflip *or* RIFLIP
resubmit resub.
résumé CV *or* C.V. (*OUP:* c.v.)
Resurrection Resurr.
retail display agreement RDA
retail price index RPI
retain ret.
retained retd.
retainer (fee for services) **1** ret. **2** retnr.
retard 1 R **2** ret.
retarder R
reticular activating system RAS
reticuloendothelial r.e.
reticuloendothelial system RES
retinal pigmented epithelium RPE
retinitis pigmentosa RP
retired 1 r *or* r. **2** ret. **3** retd.
Retired Senior Volunteer Program RSVP
Retired Teachers Association RTA
retroactive retro *or* retro.
retroactive inhibition *psychology* RI
retrofire retro *or* retro.
retrofire officer RETRO *or* Retro
retrofit retro *or* retro.
retrograde rocket system RRS
retrogressive retrog.
retrolental fibroplasia RLF
retrorocket retro *or* retro.
return 1 R **2** ret. **3** rtn
return on assets *commerce* ROA
return on capital *commerce* ROC
return on equity *commerce* ROE
return on investment *commerce* ROI
return premium *insurance* RP
return to base *military* RTB
return to bias *computers* RB
return to zero RZ *or* rz
return trip RT *or* R/T
returned 1 ret. **2** retd. *or* ret'd. **3** rtd.
Returned by Post Office RPO
Returned Letter Office R.L.O.
Returned Services Association RSA
Returned Services League of Australia RSL
or RSLA
returned to author RA *or* R/A
returned to unit *military* RTU
reusing junk as something else rejasing
Revelation Rev.
Revenue Rev. (of the U.S. Internal Revenue
Service)
revenue rev.
revenue agent's report RAR (of the IRS)

reverberation time *acoustics* rt or r.t.
reverberation-controlled gain *electronics* RCG or rcg
Reverend 1 Rev. **2** Revd. (*GPO, NYT:* Rev.; *OUP:* Revd.)
Reverend Father RP or R.P.
reverse 1 R **2** rev.
reverse annuity mortgage RAM
reverse course RC
reverse field pinch *physics* RFP
reverse osmosis RO
reverse Polish notation RPN
reversed rev.
reversing Rev'g.
Review Rev.
review rev.
review of symptom *medicine, psychology* ROS
reviewed rev.
revise rev.
revised rev. or Rev.
revised edition RE or R.E.
Revised Laws RL or R.L.
Revised Standard Version RSV or R.S.V.
Revised Statutes 1 Rev. Stat. **2** RS or R.S.
Revised Version (of the Bible) **1** Rev. Ver. **2** RV or R.V.
revision rev.
Revolution 1 Rev. **2** Revol.
revolution 1 rev. or rev **2** revol.
Revolutionary Revol. or revol.
Revolutionary Command Council RCC
Revolutionary Democratic Party PRD (of Mexico)
revolutions 1 n **2** revs
revolutions per hour rph or r.p.h.
revolutions per minute 1 r/m **2** r/min **3** RPM or rpm or r.p.m. (*MLA:* rpm; *OUP:* r.p.m.)
revolutions per minute indicator RPMI
revolutions per second 1 r/s **2** r/sec. **3** RPS or rps or r.p.s.
revolver rev.
revolving rev. or rev
reward Rew.
rewind Rew. or REW
rewind and unload *computers* RUN
rewritable optical disk *computers* ROD
Reynolds number 1 NRe **2** Re **3** RN **4** *aerodynamics* R
rhapsody rhap.
rhenium Re
rheostat rheo.
Rhesus factor Rh
rhetoric rhet.
rhetorical rhet.
rheumatic rh or rh.
rheumatic fever RF
rheumatoid arthritis RA
rheumatoid factor RF
Rhode Island RI (Zip Code) or R.I. (in general use) (*NYT:* R.I.; *OUP:* RI)
rhodium Rh
rhombic rhom
rhomboid rhom
rhombus rhom
rhythm and blues 1 R&B or R and B or r&b **2** *music* r'n'b
rial R
ribbon rib.

ribonuclease RNAase or RNase
ribonucleic acid RNA or rna
ribonucleic acid phosphorus RNAP
ribonucleoprotein RNP
ribose rib.
ribose phosphate RP
ribosomal DNA *biology* rDNA
ribosomal ribonucleic acid rRNA
ribulose biphosphase RUBP or RuBP
ribulose biphosphate carboxylase oxygenase RUBISCO or RuBisCO
Richard Rich. (in plays by Shakespeare)
Richmond E (in Federal Reserve banking system)
ridge rdg. or Rdg.
riel CR
Rifle Brigade RB
right 1 r or r. **2** R (correct) **3** rt or rt. **4** *music* R or R.
right ascension *astronomy* **1** AR or A.R. **2** RA or R.A.
right ascension of the mean sun *navigation* R.A.M.S.
right atrium *medicine* RA
right back *sports* RB
right center *theater* RC or R.C.
right center entrance RCE (stage direction)
right ear *medicine* a.d.
right end *football* RE
right eye *medicine* **1** OD or O.D. **2** RE or R.E.
right field *baseball* RF
right fielder *baseball* RF
right foot 1 RF **2** *dancing* R or R.
right forward *sports* RF
right fullback *sports* **1** RF **2** RFB or r.f.b. **3** RB
right guard *sports* RG or r.g.
right halfback *sports* **1** RH **2** RHB or r.h.b.
right hand 1 RH or R.H. **2** rh or r.h. **3** *music* c/d or MD
Right Honourable Rt. Hon.
right of admission reserved ROAR
right of way 1 R.O.W. **2** RW or R/W
Right Reverend 1 RR or R.R. **2** Rt. Rev.
right side RS or r.s.
right side of a stage *theater* R or R.
right side up with care *shipping* RSWC or R.S.W.C.
right tackle *football* RT
right upper entrance R.U.E. (stage direction)
right ventricle or **ventricular** *medicine* RV
right ventricular hypertrophy *medicine* RVH
right when tested R.W.T.
Right Worshipful RW or R.W.
Right Worthy RW or R.W.
right-hand side rhs
right-hand side of a two-page spread f.r.
Right-to-Life RTL
rights Rts.
rim-fire RF
ring *chemistry* R
ring micrometer r.m.
ringgit $
ripped rip or rip. (of lumber)
rises r or r.
river 1 riv. or Riv. **2** R or R.
River Eridanus Eri (constellation)
Rivest-Shamir-Adleman RSA (system of algorithmic notation)

riyal R
road 1 Rd or Rd. **2** R or R. **3** RD (in postal address)
Road Racing Drivers Championship RRDC
roan ro.
Robert Robt. or Rob.
Robert Louis Stevenson RLS
robotic excavator REX
rock Rk or rk
rock'n'roll 1 r.'n'r. **2** R&R or R and R or r&r
rocket 1 R **2** rkt.
rocket engine analyzer and decision instrumentation READI
rocket launcher RL
rocket powered RP
rocket projectile RP
rocket propellant RP
Rocket Propulsion Department R.P.D.
rocket-assisted homing torpedo RAT
rocket-assisted takeoff *aeronautics* RATO or rato (*GPO:* rato)
rocket-on-rotor ROR
Rockwell hardness RH
rocky rky or Rky.
Rocky Mountains RM
rod (measure of length) **1** r or r. **2** rd or rd.
roentgen 1 R **2** r
Roentgen Satellite Rosat or ROSAT
roentgens per hour r/hr
roentgens per hour at one meter distance RHM
roll-on roll-off ro-ro or RO/RO (type of sea ferry)
rolled steel beam RSB
rolled steel joint RSJ
Rolls Series RS or R.S.
Roman Rom.
roman rom. (type)
Roman Catholic 1 RC or R.C. **2** Rom. Cath.
Roman Catholic Church RCC or R.C.C. or R.C.Ch.
Romance Rom.
Romania Rom.
Romanian Rom.
Romanic Rom.
Romans Rom. (book of the New Testament)
Romeo and Juliet Rom. or Rom. & Jul.
rood (unit of measure) **1** r or r. **2** ro.
roof rf
roofing rfg.
Rook *chess* **1** R **2** r or r.
room rm.
room temperature RT
root mean square *mathematics* **1** RMS **2** rms or r.m.s.
root mean square error *mathematics* RMSE or rmse or r.m.s.e.
root-sum-squares *mathematics* RSS or rss
roots R
rotary rot.
rotary combustion RC
rotary engine RE
Rotary International RI or R.I.
rotating rot. or Rot.
rotating platinum electrode RPE
rotation 1 rot. **2** rotn.
rotational quantum number *physics* K
rotations n
rotor rot.

Rotterdam Rhine Pipeline RRP or R.R.P.
Rotterdam, Netherlands Rot.
rough R
rough cut RC (of lumber)
rough finish RF
rough-surfaced endoplasmic reticulum
   medicine RER
roulette roul. (of postage stamps)
Roumania Roum.
Roumanian Roum.
round **1** rd or rd. **2** rnd. or rnd
round trip RT or R/T
roundhead (of a screw or bolt) **1** rd hd **2** RH
roundheaded screw rhs
Rous sarcoma virus RSV
Rous-associated virus RAV
Route Rte.
route forecast *meteorology* ROFOR
row rg
Royal Roy.
royal **1** r or r. (paper size) **2** R or R.
Royal Academician *British* RA or R.A.
Royal Academy *British* RA or R.A.
Royal Academy of Arts R.A.A.
Royal Academy of Dramatic Art RADA or
   R.A.D.A.
Royal Academy of Music RAM or R.A.M.
Royal Aero Club R.Ae.C.
Royal Aeronautical Society **1** R.Ae.S. **2** RAS
   or R.A.S.
Royal Agricultural College RAC or R.A.C.
Royal Agricultural Society RAS or R.A.S.
Royal Air Force RAF (*NYT:* R.A.F.; *OUP:*
   RAF)
Royal Air Force Volunteer Reserve RAFVR
Royal Albert Hall RAH
Royal and Ancient Golf Club R&A
Royal Arch Mason *British* RAM
Royal Architectural Institute of Canada
   RAIC
Royal Armoured Corps RAC
Royal Army Educational Corps RAEC
Royal Army Medical Corps RAMC
Royal Army Ordnance Corps RAOC
Royal Army Veterinary Corps RAVO
Royal Artillery *British* RA
Royal Astronomical Society RAS or R.A.S.
Royal Australian Air Force RAAF
Royal Australian Historical Society R.A.H.S.
Royal Australian Institute of Architects
   RAIA
Royal Australian Naval College RANC
Royal Australian Naval Reserve RANR or
   R.A.N.R.
Royal Australian Navy RAN
Royal Automobile Club RAC or R.A.C.
Royal Automobile Club of Australia RACA
   or R.A.C.A.
Royal Belgian Air Force RBAF
Royal Canadian Academy of Arts RCA or
   R.C.A.
Royal Canadian Institute RCI
Royal Canadian Mounted Police RCMP or
   R.C.M.P.
Royal College of Art RCA or R.C.A.
Royal College of Defence Studies RCDS or
   R.C.D.S.
Royal College of Music RCM or R.C.M.
Royal College of Nursing RCN

Royal College of Obstetricians and
   Gynecologists RCOG or R.C.O.G.
Royal College of Organists RCO or R.C.O.
Royal College of Physicians RCP or R.C.P.
Royal College of Science RCS or R.C.S.
Royal College of Surgeons RCS or R.C.S.
Royal College of Veterinary Surgeons RCVS
   or R.C.V.S.
Royal Corps of Naval Constructors RCNC
Royal Danish Navy *Danish* KDM
Royal Drawing Society RDS or R.D.S.
Royal Electrical and Mechanical Engineers
   R.E.M.E. or REME
Royal Engineers **1** R.Eng. **2** *British* RE
Royal Festival Hall RFH
Royal Field Artillery RFA
Royal Fine Art Commission R.F.A.C.
Royal Geographical Society R.G.S. or RGS
Royal Greenwich Observatory RGO or
   R.G.O.
Royal Grenadier Guards RGG
Royal Highland Regiment RHR
Royal Highness RH or R.H.
Royal Historical Society **1** R.H.S. or RHS
   2 R.Hist.S.
Royal Horticultural Society R.H.S. or RHS
Royal Humane Society R.H.S. or RHS
Royal Incorporation of Architects of
   Scotland RIAS or R.I.A.S.
Royal Institute of Architects of Ireland RIAI
   or R.I.A.I.
Royal Institute of British Architects RIBA or
   R.I.B.A.
Royal Institute of International Affairs
   R.I.I.A. or RIIA
Royal Institute of Oil Painters **1** RIOP or
   R.I.O.P. **2** ROI or R.O.I.
Royal Institute (of Painters in Water Colours)
   RI or R.I.
Royal Institution (for scientific knowledge) RI
Royal Irish Academy RIA
Royal Irish Academy of Music RIAM or
   R.I.A.M.
Royal Irish Constabulary RIC or R.I.C.
Royal Mail RM or R.M.
Royal Mail Service RMS
Royal Mail Steamship RMS or R.M.S.
Royal Manchester College of Music
   R.M.C.M.
Royal Marine Reserve RMR
Royal Marines RM or R.M.
Royal Melbourne Institute of Technology
   R.M.I.T.
Royal Meteorological Society **1** R.Met.S.
   2 RMS
Royal Microscopical Society RMS or R.M.S.
Royal Military Academy R.M.A.
Royal Military Police RMP
Royal National Lifeboat Institution R.N.L.I.
Royal Naval Auxiliary Service RNXS
Royal Naval College RNC or R.N.C.
Royal Naval Reserve RNR or R.N.R.
Royal Naval Scientific Service RNSS or
   R.N.S.S.
Royal Naval Staff College R.N.S.C. or
   RNSC
Royal Naval Training Establishment
   RNTE
Royal Navy RN or R.N.

Royal New Zealand Air Force RNZAF or
   R.N.Z.A.F.
Royal New Zealand Armoured Corps
   RNZAC
Royal New Zealand Astronomical Society
   RNZAS
Royal New Zealand Infantry Regiment
   RNZIR
Royal New Zealand Navy RNZN or
   R.N.Z.N.
Royal Northern College of Music RNCM
Royal Norwegian Navy KNM
Royal Philharmonic Orchestra RPO or
   R.P.O.
Royal Philharmonic Society RPS or R.P.S.
Royal Photographic Society RPS
Royal Red Cross R.R.C.
Royal Research Ship RRS
Royal Sanitary Institute RSI or R.S.I.
Royal Scottish Academician RSA or R.S.A.
Royal Scottish Academy RSA or R.S.A.
Royal Scottish Geographical Society
   R.S.G.C. or RSGS
Royal Shakespeare Company RSC
Royal Signals and Radar Establishment RSRE
Royal Society RS or R.S.
Royal Society for the Prevention of
   Accidents Rospa
Royal Society for the Prevention of Cruelty
   to Animals RSPCA or R.S.P.C.A.
Royal Society of Antiquarians RSA
Royal Society of Arts RSA
Royal Society of Australia RSA or R.S.A.
Royal Society of British Artists RBA or
   R.B.A.
Royal Society of British Sculptors RBS or
   R.B.S.
Royal Society of Canada RSC or R.S.C.
Royal Society of Chemistry RSC
Royal Society of Dublin RSD or R.S.D.
Royal Society of Edinburgh RSE or R.S.E.
Royal Society of Literature RSL or R.S.L.
Royal Society of Medicine RSM or R.S.M.
Royal Society of New Zealand R.S.N.Z. or
   RSNZ
Royal Society of Painter-Etchers and
   Engravers RSPE or R.S.P.E.
Royal Society of Painters in Water Colours
   R.W.S.
Royal Society of Portrait Painters **1** RP
   2 RSPP or R.S.P.P.
Royal Statistical Society RSS or R.S.S.
Royal Swedish Navy *Swedish* KSM
Royal Ulster Constabulary RUC or R.U.C.
Royal United Kingdom Beneficent
   Association RUKBA
Royal Veterinary College R.V.C.
Royal Victorian Order R.V.O.
Royal Welsh Fusiliers R.W.F.
rub together *pharmaceutics* conter.
rubber **1** r or r. **2** rub.
rubber band rb
rubber insulated r.i.
rubber insulation r.i.
rubidium Rb
ruble **1** R **2** rbl.
rudder rud.
Rugby Football Club RFC or R.F.C.
Rugby Football Union RFU

Rugby Union RU
rule R or R.
rule of pleading *law* Reg. Pl.
rule then example *computers* RULEG
Rules of Procedure RP
ruling case law RCL
Rumania Rum.
Rumania, Rumanian Ru or Ru.
Rumanian Rum.
run *baseball, cricket* **1** R **2** r or r.
run of kiln RK (of pottery)
run of paper *advertising* ROP
run of press ROP
run-length limited *computers* RLL
run-of-schedule *advertising* ROS
run-of-station *advertising* ROS
run-on *printing* RO
running back *sports* RB

running days rd or r.d.
running head RH
running time RT
running-down clause *insurance* RDC
runover *printing* RO
runs batted in *baseball* RBI or rbi
runway 1 rnwy **2** RW
runway visual range *aviation* RVR
rupee 1 R **2** Re
rupees Rs
rupiah Rp or Rp.
rupture rupt.
rural R or R.
Rural Delivery RD or R.D.
Rural Democratic Union UDR or U.D.R.
Rural Development Administration RDA
Rural District Council *British* RDC or R.D.C.

Rural Electrification Administration REA (*GPO:* REA; *NYT:* R.E.A.)
Rural Electrification and Telephone Revolving Fund RETRF
Rural Free Delivery RFD (*GPO, NYT:* R.F.D.)
rural route RR (*NYT:* R.R.)
Rural Telephone Bank RTB
Russia or **Russian 1** Rus. or Russ. **2** Ru or Ru.
ruthenium Ru
rutherford rd
rutherford backscattering spectrometry *physics* RBS
Rutherford High Energy Laboratory RHEL
Rydberg *physics* Ry or ry
Rydberg constant *astronomy* R
Ryom R
Ryom-Vivaldi *music* RV

S

Sabbath 1 S or S. **2** Sab.
sabin S
sable Sa (in heraldry)
Sachs-Georgi SG or S-G
sack sk
Sacred Congregation of Bishops and Regulars *Latin* S.C.EE.RR.
sacred to the memory of MS or M.S.
sacrifice hit *baseball* SH
saddle sdl.
sadism and masochism S and M or S&M
sadist and masochist S and M or S&M
Sadomasochism or **Sadomasochist** SM or S-M or s-m
Safe Drinking Water Act SDWA
safe laser output SLO (unit of measure)
safe working load SWL
safe working pressure SWP
safeguard sfgd
safety 1 saf. **2** *football* S
safety analysis report SAR
Safety Equipment Worker SEW
Safety of Life at Sea Convention S.O.L.A.S.
safety valve SV
Sagittarius Sgr (constellation)
sailed sld. or sld
sailing vessel SV or S/V
Saint St or St. (*GPO, MLA, NYT, CSM:* St.; *OUP:* S. or St.)
saint S or S.
Saint Mary SM or S.M.
Saint Peter S.Petr.
Saints SS or SS. (*GPO, NYT:* SS.; *MLA, OUP:* SS)
salary sal.
sale or return *commerce* SOR or s.o.r.
sales and general administration *accounting* SG&A
sales book *commerce* SB or S.B.

Sales Manager SM
salinity S
salinity, temperature, depth STD (measure of ocean water)
salt water SW
salvage salv.
salvage loss *insurance* SL
Salvation Army SA
samarium 1 Sa **2** Sm
same *pharmaceutics* ead.
same as given before eidem
same case *law* SC or S.C.
same day sd or s.d.
same size *printing* SS
same style throughout *music* semp.
same, the *Latin* id or id. (*GPO, CSM, OUP:* id.)
Samoa Sam. or Sam
Samoan Sam. or Sam
sample return container SRC
sampling and automatic measurement SAM
Samuel 1 Sam. **2** Saml. (books of the Old Testament)
San Francisco 1 L (in Federal Reserve banking system) **2** S (mint mark) **3** San Fran. **4** SF or S.F.
sand 1 S or S. **2** sd or sd.
Sandinista National Liberation Front *Spanish* FSLN
sandstorm *meteorology* KZ or kz
sanitarium san.
sanitary 1 san. **2** sanit. **3** Sn or Sn.
Sanitary Corps SC or S.C.
Sanitary Engineer SE
Sanitary Institute of America SIA
sanitation 1 sanit. **2** Sn or Sn.
sans serif Sans. or sans
Sanskrit 1 Sans. or Sansk. **2** Skr. or Skrt. **3** Skt. (*MLA, OUP:* Skt.)
sap no defect s.n.d. (of lumber)
saponification sap. or sapon.
sapper Spr.
sapwood sap.
Sarawak Sar.
Sardinia Sar.
Sardinian Sar.
Saskatchewan 1 Sask. **2** SK (postal code)

satellite 1 SAT **2** Sat.
satellite and missile observation system SAMOS
satellite communications SATCOM
Satellite Field Service Stations SFSS (of NASA)
satellite infrared spectrometer Sirs
Satellite Instructional Television Experiment SITE
satellite master antenna television SMATV
satellite positioning and tracking SPOT
satellite power system SPS
satellite processor access method *computers* SPAM
Satellite Telemetry Automatic Reduction System STARS
satellite tracking of balloons and emergencies STROBE
satellite or **space launching vehicle** SLV
satisfactory 1 S **2** Sat.
saturated sat. or satd.
saturated adiabatic lapse rate *meteorology* SALR
saturated solution sat. sol.
saturation sat. or satn.
Saturday 1 S or S. **2** Sa or Sa. **3** Sat. **4** Stdy
Saturday, Sunday *commerce* SS or S/S
Saturn Sat.
Saudi Arabia SA or S.A.
Saudi Arabian SA or S.A.
Saudi Arabian Monetary Agency SAMA
Saudi Riyal 1 SR **2** SRI
Savannah River Project SRP
save as you earn *British* SAYE
Save the Children Fund SCF
savings sav.
Savings and Loan Association 1 S&L **2** SLA
Savings Association Insurance Fund SAIF
Savings Bank SB
Savings Bank Life Insurance SBLI
Saxon Sax. (*MLA:* S.; *OUP:* Sax.)
Saxony Sax.
saxophone sax
Saybolt furol viscosity SFV
Saybolt universal seconds SUS
Saybolt universal viscosimeter SUV
Saybolt universal viscosity SUV

scalable processor architecture *computers* SPARC

scalar *mathematics, physics* S

scale **1** sc **2** scl.

Scales Lib (constellation; Libra)

Scandinavia **1** Sc. **2** Scan. *or* Scand. (*MLA, OUP:* Scand.)

Scandinavian Scan. *or* Scand. (*MLA, OUP:* Scand.)

Scandinavian Council for Applied Research SCAR

scandium Sc

scanning acoustic microscope SAM

scanning electron microscope *or* microscopy SEM

scanning ion-conductance microscope SICM

scanning transmission electron microscope STEM

scanning transmission electron microscopy STEM

scanning tunneling microscope STM

scene (of a play) **1** sc *or* sc. **2** Sc.

schedule **1** Sch. *or* SCH **2** sched.

schedule compliance evaluation SCE

scheduled Scd. *or* scd

schematic schem.

schilling (monetary unit of Austria) **1** S *or* S. **2** Sch.

Schmieder S *or* S. (catalog of J. S. Bach's music)

Scholar Sch.

scholarship schol.

scholastic schol.

Scholastic Aptitude Test SAT

School Sch.

school **1** S *or* S. **2** sch.

School and College Ability Test SCAT

School Bus Manufacturers Institute SBMI

school certificate SC

School Leaving Certificate *British* SLC

School Library Association SLA *or* S.L.A.

school nurse practitioner SNP *or* S.N.P.

School of American Ballet S.A.B. *or* SAB

School-leavers' Training and Employment Preparation Scheme STEPS

schoolhouse SH *or* S.H.

schools, colleges, and departments of education SCDE

schooner **1** Sch. **2** Schr. *or* schr.

science **1** Sc. **2** Sci. *or* sci.

Science Advisory Board S.A.B.

Science Advisory Committee SAC

Science and Engineering Research Council SERC

science and technology S&T

Science and Technology Information System STIS

Science Citation Index SCI

Science Clubs of America SCA

Science Council of Canada SCC

science fiction **1** sci-fi **2** SF *or* S-F **3** sf *or* s-f **4** si-fi

Science in General Management SIGMA

Science Information Exchange SIE

scientific Sci. *or* sci.

scientific and technical S&T

scientific and technical information STI

Scientific and Technical Information Division STID

Scientific and Technical Information Facility SATIF

Scientific and Technical Liaison Officer STLO

Scientific Apparatus Makers Association SAMA

Scientific Committee on Oceanic Research SCOR

Scientific Committee on the Effects of Atomic Radiation SCEAR

scientific data system SDS

Scientific Film Association SFA

Scientific Information Center SIC

Scientific Instrument Research Association SIRA

Scientific Officer *British* SO *or* S.O.

scoring scg

Scorpius *or* Scorpio Sco (constellation)

Scotch **1** Sc. **2** Scot. (*MLA:* Scot.)

Scotch Gaelic Sc. Gael.

Scotland **1** Sc. **2** Scot. **3** Scotl.

Scotland Yard SYd *or* S.Yd.

Scots Sc.

Scott Polar Research Institute S.P.R.I.

Scottish **1** Sc. **2** Scot. (*MLA:* Scot.)

Scottish Central Library S.C.L.

Scottish Certificate of Education SCE *or* S.C.E.

Scottish Cycling Union SCU *or* S.C.U.

Scottish Development Agency SDA

Scottish Education Department SED

Scottish Football Association SFA *or* S.F.A.

Scottish Football League SFL *or* S.F.L.

Scottish Kennel Club SKC *or* S.K.C.

Scottish Labour Party SLP *or* S.L.P.

Scottish Landowners Federation SLF

Scottish Library Association SLA *or* S.L.A.

Scottish Mountaineering Club SMC

Scottish National Dictionary S.N.D. *or* SND

Scottish National Party SNP *or* S.N.P.

Scottish Professional Golfers Association SPGA

Scottish Rugby Union S.R.U. *or* SRU

Scottish Television STV

Scottish Text Society STS *or* S.T.S.

Scottish Trades Union Congress STUC

Scottish Youth Hostels Association S.Y.H.A. *or* SYHA

screen scrn

Screen Actors' Guild SAG

screen grid *electronics* SG

screen image buffer *computers* SIB

Screen Writers Guild SWG *or* S.W.G.

screw **1** sc **2** scr. *or* scr

screwed SCD *or* scd. (of construction)

scrip *commerce* scr.

Scripps Institution of Oceanography SIO

Scriptural Script.

Scripture Script. *or* Scrip.

Scriptures Script. *or* Scrip.

scruple (weight) **1** sc *or* sc. **2** scr.

Sculptor Scl (constellation)

sculptor sculp. *or* sculpt.

sculptural sculp. *or* sculpt.

sculpture sculp. *or* sculpt.

Sea S *or* S.

sea damaged *shipping* SD *or* S/D

sea level SL *or* S.L.

sea post office SPO

Sea satellite Seasat

sea transport officer STO

Sea-Launched Ballistic Missile Detection System SLBMDS

sea-surface temperature SST

Seafarers' International Union SIU

seal *Latin* sigill. (mark or sign)

sealed sld. *or* sld

seaman S *or* S.

seaman apprentice SA

seaport SPT *or* Spt. *or* spt.

search *computers* SRCH *or* Srch

search and rescue SAR

Search and Rescue Automatic Homing SARAH

Search and Rescue Beacon Equipment SARBE

search and rescue satellite-aided tracking SARSAT

search and rescue using satellites SARUS

search for extraterrestrial intelligence SETI

searchlight **1** SL **2** SLT

seasonal affective disorder SAD

Seasonal Energy Efficiency Rating SEER (of air conditioners)

seawater SW

secant *mathematics* sec

second **1** s **2** S (in a series) **3** sec *or* sec. (unit of time or angular distance) (*CSM:* sec.; *OUP:* s. or sec.)

second class E (in Lloyd's Register)

second drive on a multidisk system *computers* B

second postscript **1** p.p.s. **2** PPS *or* P.P.S.

second-foot sec-ft *or* sec.-ft.

secondary **1** S **2** sec *or* sec.

secondary audio program SAP

Secondary Audio Program Services SAPS

secondary electron conduction *physics* SEC

secondary electron emission SEE *or* see

secondary input *electronics* IS

secondary ion mass spectrometry SIMS

secondary propulsion system SPS

secondary surveillance radar SSR

seconds Secs. *or* secs.

secret S

Secret Intelligence Service SIS

Secret Service SS *or* S.S.

Secretary Sec.

secretary **1** scty **2** sec **3** Secty *or* secty. **4** Secy *or* secy *or* sec'y

Secretary General SG *or* S.G. *or* S-G *or* S.-G.

Secretary of Energy Advisory Board SEAB

Secretary of State SS *or* S.S.

Secretary of the Legation Sec. Leg.

Section **1** Sec. **2** SXN *or* sxn.

section **1** s *or* s. **2** S *or* S. (with number) **3** sec *or* sec. (*CSM:* sec.; *OUP:* s. or sect.) **4** Sect. *or* sect.

section modulus *physics* Z

sections **1** Secs. *or* secs. **2** ss *or* ss.

Sector Sec.

sector **1** sctr. **2** sec *or* sec. **3** Sect. *or* sect.

Secular Organizations for Sobriety SOS

Securities and Exchange Commission SEC *or* S.E.C. (*GPO:* SEC; *NYT:* S.E.C.)

Securities and Investments Board SIB

Securities Industries Association SIA (*NYT:* S.I.A.)

Securities Industry Automatic Corporation SIAC (for electronic trading on New York and American Stock Exchanges)
Securities Investor Protection Corporation SIPC
security sec
security control of air traffic SCAT
Security Council SC or S.C.
Security Intelligence Service SIS
sedative sed.
sediment sed. or sed
sedimentation 1 sed. or sed 2 sedtn
sedimentation rate SR or S.R.
see Latin vid.
see above Latin vs or v.s.
see below Latin v.i.
segment 1 2 botany segm.
segment table computers ST
segmented seg.
segregated seg.
segue seg. or seg
seismic intrusion detector SID
seismocardiography SCG or S.C.G.
seismological seis. or seismol.
Seismological Society of America SSA or S.S.A.
seismology seis. or seismol.
selected sel.
Selected Reserve Force SRF
selection sel.
selective catalytic reduction SCR
selective conscientious objector SCO
selective dissemination of information SDI or S.D.I.
selective identification feature aeronautics SIF
selective information retrieval chemistry SIR
selective printing of items from tape computers SPIT
selective sequence electronic calculator SSEC
Selective Service SS
Selective Service System SSS or S.S.S. (GPO: SSS)
selector sel.
selenium Se
self-addressed stamped envelope SASE or s.a.s.e.
Self-Defense Forces SDF (of Japan)
self-employment SE
self-induced transparency physics SIT
self-inflicted wound SIW
self-organizing flight control system SOFCS
self-propelled SP
self-propelled mount SPM
Self-propelled Underwater Research Vehicle SPURV
self-regulatory organisation British commerce S.R.O.
self-tuning regulator STR
Selkirk Selk.
seller's option commerce 1 s.o. 2 SO
selling price SP
semester sem.
semi-detached house British semi
semiannual 1 s.a. 2 SA
semiautomatic SA (of a weapon)
semiautomatic rifle SAR
semicolon 1 sem. 2 semi

semiconductor integrated circuit SIC or sic
semiconductor storage unit electronics SSU
semidiameter SD or S.D.
semifinal semi
semimajor axis astronomy 1 a 2 a
seminal vesicle sem. ves.
seminar sem.
Seminary Sem.
semisteel SS
Semitic Sem.
semitrailer 1 semi 2 STLR
Semliki Forest Virus SFV
sen S or S.
Senate 1 S or S. 2 Sen.
Senate Armed Services Committee SASC
Senate bill 1 S or S. (with number) 2 SB (with number)
Senate concurrent resolution S.Con.Res. (with number)
Senate Document 1 S. Doc. (with number) 2 Sen. Doc. (with number)
Senate Joint Resolution S.J.Res. (with number)
Senate Office Building SOB
Senate Report S.Rept. (with number)
Senate Resolution S.Res. (with number)
Senator Sen.
send or receive SR or S/R (radio transmission)
Senegalese Progressive Union French UPS
senile dementia, Alzheimer's type SDAT
senile-macular degeneration medicine SMD
Senior Sen.
senior 1 sen. 2 senr or Senr 3 Snr. or snr. 4 Sr or Sr. (GPO, NYT, MLA, CSM: Sr.; OUP: sen.)
senior appointments selection committee SASC
Senior Chief Petty Officer S/CPO
Senior Executive Service SES (of U.S. Civil Service)
Senior Fellow SF or S.F.
senior grade sg or s.g.
senior interagency group SIG
Senior Liaison Officer SLO
Senior Medical Officer SMO
Senior Naval Officer SNO
Senior Navigation Officer SNO
Senior Officer SO or S.O.
senior officer present military SOP
Senior Science Officer British S.S.O.
senior vice-president commerce SVP
sensation psychology S
sensation unit psychology SU
sensitivity physics S
sensitivity time control STC
sentence 1 sent. 2 linguistics S
sepal sep.
separate sep.
separation 1 sep. 2 sepn
September 1 S 2 Sep. 3 Sept. or Sept
September, December, March, June commerce SDMJ
Septuagint 1 LXX or LXX. 2 Sep. 3 Sept.
sequel seq.
sequence 1 seq. 2 sq.
sequenced flashing lights aeronautics SFL
sequential coding computers SECO
sequential control electronics SECO

sequential controlled automatic transmitter start computers SCATS
sequentially operated teletypewriter universal selector computers SOTUS
Serbia Serb.
Serbian Serb.
sergeant 1 Serg. or Sergt. 2 Sgt. or sgt.
sergeant first class SFC or Sfc.
sergeant major 1 Sgt. Maj. 2 SM
serial 1 Ser or Ser. or SER. 2 ser.
Serial Copy Management System electronics SCMS
serial number SN or S/N
series 1 s or s. 2 Ser or Ser. 3 ser.
serine 1 Ser or Ser. 2 ser.
Serjeant law Serj. or Serjt.
serjeant-at-law British SL or S.L.
sermon ser.
serological test for syphilis STS
serotonin HT
serous otitis media medicine SOM
Serpent Ser (constellation)
Serpent Holder Oph (constellation)
serum glutamic oxaloacetic transaminase S.G.O.T. or SGO-T
serum glutamic pyruvic transaminase S.G.P.T. or SGP-T
serum hepatitis SH
serum insulin-like activity ILA
serum lactic dehydrogenase SLD
serum prothrombin conversion accelerator medicine SPCA
serum Wassermann reaction SWR
servant 1 serv. 2 servt.
service 1 ser. 2 serv. or Serv. 3 svc
service charge commerce SC
Service Corps of Retired Executives SCORE
Service Employees International Union SEIU
service mark SM
service module SM
service number SN
Service of Supply SOS
service propulsion system SPS
service record SR
service unit SU
Servicemen's Group Life Insurance SGLI
services no longer required British S.N.L.R.
servomechanism 1 servo 2 SM 3 sm
servomotor 1 servo 2 sm
session Sess. or sess.
set sports, mathematics s or s.
set screw SS
set up commerce SU
sets sports, mathematics S
Seventh Day Adventists SDA or S.D.A.
several sev. or sevl.
several dates sd
severe combined immunodeficiency disease SCID
Severe Local Storm Warning Center SELS
severe parental punishment sociology SPP
Severe Storm Forecast Center SSFC
sewage sew.
sewage treatment plant STP
sewed (of bookbinding) 1 sd or sd. 2 swd. or swd
sewer sew. (underground drain)
sewerage sew.

sex chromosome 1 X **2** Y (in males)
sex chromosome abnormalities SCA
sex-ratio organism *biology* S.R.O.
Sextans Sex (constellation)
sextant 1 sex. *or* sext. **2** SXT *or* Sxt.
sextet sex.
sexual sex.
sexually transmitted disease STD
Seychelles 1 Sey *or* Sey. **2** Sy.
shaft horsepower SHP *or* shp
shake or stir *pharmaceutics* agit.
shaken baby syndrome SBS
shaken infant syndrome SIS
Shakespeare Shak. *or* Shaks.
share *or* **shares** (of stock) **1** sh. *or* sh
    2 shr. *or* Shr
shared appreciation mortgage SAM
Shared Hospital Accounting System SHAS
shared page table *computers* SPT
shear modulus *mechanics* G*or* G
shearing force *physics* V
sheep (of bookbinding) sh.
sheep cell agglutination test SCAT
sheep red blood cell SRBC
sheet 1 sh. *or* sh **2** sht.
Sheet Metal Industries Association SMIA
Sheet Metal Workers International
    Association SMWIA
sheet molding compound SMC
Sheffield Sheff. *or* Shef.
shells Sh. (on navigation charts)
Shetland Shet.
Shetland Islands Shet.
Shield Sct (constellation)
shield *electronics* s
shift in *computers* SI
shift out *computers* SO
shilling (former coin of Great Britain) **1** s
    2 Sh. *or* Sh **3** sh. *or* sh (GPO, OUP: sh)
ship's heading *navigation* SH *or* S.H.
Ship's Inertial Navigation System SINS
ship's mean time SMT
ship's option *commerce* SO
ship's self-contained navigation system
    SSCNS
ship-launched missile SLM
ship-to-shore 1 S-to-S *or* S to S **2** STS
Shipboard Oceanographic Survey System
    SOSS
shiplap shlp.
shipment 1 ship. *or* shipt. **2** shpt.
shipowner's liability *insurance* SOL *or* s.o.l.
shipper and carrier S&C *or* S.&C.
shipper's load and count *commerce* SL&C
    or sl and c
shipper's load and tally *commerce* SL&T *or*
    sl and t
shipper's weight *commerce* SW
shipping 1 ship. **2** shpg.
shipping and forwarding agents S.&F.A.
shipping and handling *commerce* **1** S/H
    2 S&H
shipping note SN *or* S/N
shipping order *commerce* **1** SO *or* S.O.
    2 s.o.
shipping receipt 1 SR **2** sr *or* s.r.
shipping ton 1 ST **2** st *or* s.t.
ships apparent time *navigation* SAT *or*
    S.A.T.

shoal 1 sh. **2** shl. *or* shl
Shore Patrol SP
short 1 S (clothing size) **2** sh.
Short Airfield for Tactical Support SATS
short bill *commerce* SB
short circuit SC *or* S/C
short interest *commerce* si *or* s.i.
short meter SM *or* S.M. (of poetry)
short of breath *medicine* SOB *or* S.O.B.
short page *printing* sp *or* s.p.
short rate *insurance* **1** SR **2** sr *or* s.r.
short takeoff and landing STOL
short takeoff, vertical landing STOVL
Short Title Catalogue STC *or* S.T.C.
short ton 1 sh.tn. **2** ST **3** st *or* s.t.
short wave sleep SWS
short wheelbase SWB
short-increment sensitivity index SISI
short-procedure unit SPU
short-range attack missile SRAM
short-range ballistic missile SRBM
short-range missile SRM
short-range navigation SHORAN *or* shoran
    (GPO: shoran)
short-range nuclear forces SNF
short-term memory STM
shortage shtg.
Shorter Oxford English Dictionary SOED
shortstop *baseball* **1** SS **2** ss
shortwave *radio* SW
shortwave listener SWL
should shd. *or* shd
should be sb *or* s/b
shoulder shld.
show Sh. (in horse racing)
showers *meterology* sh.
shrapnel shrap.
Shropshire County, England Shrops.
shut off SO
shut-off valve SOV
shutout sho *or* Sh.O.
Shuttle Pallet Satellite SPAS
Siberia Sib.
Siberian Sib.
Sicilian Sic.
Sicily Sic.
sickle S (of a gene)
sickle cell anemia SCA
side S
side, angle, side *geometry* SAS *or* s.a.s.
side-looking airborne radar SLAR
side-looking radar SLR
side-looking sonar SLS
sidereal hour angle SHA
sidereal period of revolution *astronomy* [P] sid
siding sdg. (of building materials)
siemens S
Siemens's unit *electricity* SU *or* S.U.
Sierra Sa
sievert Sv
sight draft *commerce* **1** sd *or* s.d. **2** SD *or*
    S/D
sight draft, bill of lading attached SDBL *or*
    S/D B/L
sigma reaction SR
signal 1 Sig. **2** sig.
signal automatic air traffic control SATCO
Signal Corps SC *or* S.C.
Signal Corps Engineering Laboratories SCEL

signal data converter *electronics* SDC
signal frequency *electronics* sf
signal intelligence Sigint *or* SIGINT
Signal Officer SO *or* S.O.
signal transmitting, receiving, and
    distributing STRAD
signal-strength meter *electronics* S meter
signal-to-noise ratio 1 SN *or* S/N **2** SNR
signalman SM
signals fading badly ZFB
Signals Research and Development
    Establishment SRDE
signature 1 S (in bookbinding) **2** Sig. **3** sig.
    4 sign.
signed 1 S **2** s *or* /s/ **3** sd *or* sd. **4** sgd.
significant signif.
significant figures *mathematics* sig. fig.
significant threshold shift STS
silence *music* T *or* T.
silent, compact auxiliary power SCAP
Silesia Sil.
silicon Si
silicon controlled avalanche transistor
    electronics SCAT
silicon on sapphire *electronics* SOS
silicon photodiode SPD
silicon-controlled rectifier SCR
silicon-controlled switch *electronics* SCS
silicon-on-insulator *electronics* SOI
silver 1 a **2** a **3** Ag **4** arg. **5** s **6** sil.
    7 *heraldry* Ar
Silver Star SS *or* S.S.
simian AIDS SAIDS
simian immunodeficiency virus SIV
simian virus SV (usually with number)
similar sim.
simile *music* sim.
simple electronic computer SEC
simple harmonic motion *physics* SHM *or*
    s.h.m.
simple process factor *physics* SPF *or* S.P.F.
simplex 1 *electronics* SPX **2** *mathematics* sx
Simplification of International Trade
    Procedures *British* SITPRO
simplified employee pension SEP
simplified practice recommendation SPR
simulate sml.
simulation sml.
simulation high-level programming
    language SIMSCRIPT
simulator sml.
simultaneous broadcast 1 SB **2** simulcast
simultaneous peripheral operation on-line
    computers SPOOL
sine *mathematics* sin
Singapore 1 S **2** Sing. **3** Sng.
single 1 S **2** sgl.
single channel per carrier *electronics*
    SCPC
single column sc *or* s.c. *or* s/c
single column inch SCI *or* sci
single crochet sc *or* s.c.
single entry *accounting* SE
single event upset *electronics* SEU
single in-line memory module *computers*
    SIMM
single in-line package *electronics* SIP
single instruction multiple data *computers*
    SIMD

single instruction, single data *computers* SISD

single integrated operations plan SIOP

single photon emission-computed tomography *medicine* SPECT

single pole *electricity, electronics* **1** SP **2** sp or s.p.

single pole, double throw *electricity* SPDT or s.p.d.t. or spdt

single pole, single throw *electricity* SPST or s.p.s.t. or spst

single premium, deferred annuity *insurance* SPDA

single sideband *radio* **1** SS **2** SSB or ssb

single signal *radio, electronics* SS

single-breasted *British* SB

single-cell protein SCP or S.C.P.

single-lens reflex SLR

single-phase *electricity* **1** SP **2** sp

single-room occupancy S.R.O. or SRO

single-sideband modulation *electronics* SSM

single-sided double-density *computers* SS/DD

single-strand binding SSB (of a protein)

single-stranded deoxyribonucleic acid *biochemistry* ssDNA

single-trip container *shipping* STC or s.t.c.

singular **1** s or s. **2** *grammar* **a** sg or sg. **b** sing.

Sinhalese Sinh.

sinking fund *finance* **1** SF **2** sf or s.f.

Sinn Fein SF

sinoatrial SA or S.A.

sir Sr or Sr.

sire (in pedigrees) **1** S or S. **2** s or s.

Sister **1** S or S. (in a religious order) **2** Sis. **3** Sr or Sr. (in a religious order)

sister **1** s or s. **2** Sis. or sis

Site Activation Task Force SATF

site of scientific importance SSI

site of special scientific interest SSSI

situation sit.

situation comedy sitcom

situation normal—all fouled up snafu

size sz.

sized and calendered **1** S&C or s.andc. **2** sc or s.c.

sized and supercalendered S&SC or s.ands.c.

skein sk

sketch sk

skewbald sk

skewness *statistics* Sk

Ski Club of Great Britain SCGB or S.C.G.B.

Skilled Nursing Facility SNF

skin dose SD (radiation exposure)

skin erythema dose SED (radiation exposure)

skin test dose *medicine* STD

skin test unit STU or S.T.U.

skin-reactive factor SRF

skip sk

sky-wave synchronized loran SS LORAN or ss loran

SL bacterium SL

Slavic **1** Sl. **2** Slav. (*MLA, OUP:* Slav.)

Slavonian Slav.

Slavonic Sl. or Slav.

sleet *meteorology* rs.

sleet shower *meteorology* EW

sliding glass door SGD

sliding watertight door SWD

slightly sl.

slip **1** sl. **2** surj (in knitting) **3** *physics* s

slip one, knit one, pass slipped stitch over s.k.p.o. or skpsso

slip stitch sl st (in needlework)

slip, slip, knit SSK

sloppy sly. (in horse racing)

Slovak **1** Sl. **2** Slov.

Slovakia **1** Sl. **2** Slov.

Slovakian **1** Sl. **2** Slov.

Slovene Slov.

Slovenia Slov.

Slovenian Slov.

slow **1** S **2** sl. (in horse racing)

slow reacting substance *medicine* SRS

slow release *electronics* SR

slow-moving vehicle SMV

slow-scan television SSTV

slowed-down video SDV

slower *music* riten.

slowly **1** sly. **2** *music* adag.

slurry-infiltrated fiber-concrete SIFCON

small **1** S **2** sm or sm. **3** sml. or sml

small acid-soluble spore protein SASP

small arms SA

small arms ammunition SAA

small astronomical satellite SAS

small bore SB

Small Business Administration SBA

small business computer SBC

Small Business Investment Company SBIC

small calorie *physics, medicine* cal. (*OUP:* cal)

small capitals **1** s.caps. **2** sc or s.c. **3** sm.c. or sm.cap. or sm.caps (*GPO, CSM, OUP:* s.c.)

small computer system interface SCSI

small cytoplasmic RNA scRNA

Small Farm Business Management Scheme SFBM

small magellanic cloud *meteorology* SMC

small nuclear ribonucleic acid snRNA

small nuclear ribonucleoprotein snRNP

small paper *printing* SP or S.P.

Small Particle Heat Exchange Receiver SPHER

small pica *printing* sp

small profits, quick returns SPQR

small waterplane area, twin hulled SWATH

small-angle scattering *physics, electronics* SAS

small-scale integration *computers* SSI

Smithsonian Astrophysical Observatory SAO

Smithsonian Environmental Research Center SERC

Smithsonian Institution **1** SI **2** Smith. Inst.

Smithsonian Institution Astrophysical Observatory SIAO

Smithsonian Institution Traveling Exhibition Service SITES

Smithsonian Oceanographic Sorting Center SOSC

Smithsonian Research Foundation SRF or S.R.F.

Smithsonian Scientific Information Exchange SSIE or S.S.I.E.

smoke **1** smk or smk. **2** *meteorology* K

smokeless powder SP (in munitions)

smooth **1** S **2** *music* leg.

smooth bore SB

smooth or flowing manner *music* cantab.

smooth-surfaced endoplasmic reticulum *medicine* SER

snow **1** s **2** Sn or Sn. **3** sn or sn.

snow shower *meteorology* SW

Snow, Ice, and Permafrost Research Establishment SIPRE

Soaring Society of America SSA

social soc.

Social and Rehabilitation Service SRS

Social Christian Party PSC (of French Belgium)

Social Credit Party **1** SCP (of Canada) **2** Socred

Social Democrat **1** SD **2** Soc. Dem.

Social Democratic Federation SDF

Social Democratic Party **1** P.S.D. (of France, Italy, etc.) **2** SPU (of Germany) **3** *German* SPD

Social Democratic Party of Switzerland SPS

Social Democratic Union SDU

social history SH

social science SS

Social Science Education Consortium SSEC

Social Science Research Institute S.S.R.I. or SSRI

Social Sciences and Humanities Research Council of Canada SSHRC

Social Sciences Citation Index SSCI

Social Security **1** Soc.Sec. **2** SS

Social Security Administration SSA

Social Security Board SSB

Social Security number SSN

Social Services SS

Social Services Department SSD

social-accounting matrix SAM

Socialist S

socialist Soc.

Socialist and Democratic Labour Party SDLP (of Northern Ireland)

Socialist Labor Party SLP or S.L.P.

Socialist Party **1** SP or S.P. **2** *French* PS

Socialist Party of Great Britain SPGB

Socialist Reich Party SRP (German neo-Nazi party)

Socialist Workers Party SWP

society **1** S or S. **2** soc. or Soc. **3** Socy.

Society for American Baseball Research SABR

Society for Army Historical Research SAHR

Society for Biological Rhythm SBR

Society for Checking the Abuses of Public Advertising SCAPA or S.C.A.P.A.

Society for Computer Simulation SCS

Society for Industrial and Applied Mathematics S.I.A.M. or SIAM

Society for International Development SID

Society for Management Information Systems SMIS

Society for Nautical Research SNR

Society for Personnel Administration SPA

Society for Psychical Research SPR or S.P.R.

Society for Pure English S.P.E.

Society for Radiological Protection SRP
Society for Scholarly Publishing SSP
Society for the History of Technology SHOT
Society for the Prevention and Relief of Cancer SPRC
Society for the Prevention of Cruelty to Animals SPCA or S.P.C.A.
Society for the Prevention of Cruelty to Children SPCC or S.P.C.C.
Society for the Promotion of Christian Knowledge British S.P.C.K.
Society for the Protection of Ancient Buildings S.P.A.B.
Society for the Protection of Animals in North Africa SPANA
Society for the Protection of Mechanical Rights French SDRM
Society for the Protection of Science and Learning SPSL
Society for the Protection of the Unborn Child S.P.U.C. or SPUC
Society for the Study of Multi-Ethnic Literature of the United States MELUS
Society for Visiting Scientists British SVS or S.V.S.
Society Islands Soc. Is. or Soc. Isl.
Society of American Bacteriologists S.A.B.
Society of American Etchers SAE or S.A.E.
Society of American Foresters SAF
Society of American Graphic Artists SAGA
Society of American Historians SAH or S.A.H.
Society of American Military Engineers S.A.M.E. or SAME
Society of American Travel Writers SATW
Society of Authors SA or S.A.
Society of Authors' Representatives SAR or S.A.R.
Society of Authors, Composers, and Editors of Music French SACEM
Society of Automotive Engineers SAE
Society of British Aeronautics Companies SBAC
Society of Civil and Public Servants SCPS
Society of Electronic and Radio Technicans SERT
Society of Environmental Engineers SEE
Society of European Stage Authors and Composers SESAC
Society of Exploration Geophysicists SEG
Society of Film and Television Arts SFTA or S.F.T.A.
Society of Fine Art Auctioneers SOFAA
Society of Glass Technology SGT
Society of Graphic Arts S.G.A.
Society of Illustrators SI
Society of Independent Public Relations Consultants SIPRC
Society of Industrial Engineers SIE or S.I.E.
Society of Industrial Technology SIT
Society of Instrument Technology SIT
Society of Jesus S.J.
Society of Licensed Aircraft Engineers and Technologists S.L.A.E.T. or SLAET
Society of Lithographic Artists, Designers, Engravers and Process Workers SLADE or S.L.A.D.E.
Society of Mary SM or S.M.
Society of Mining Engineers S.M.E. or SME

Society of Motion Picture and Television Engineers SMPTE or S.M.P.T.E.
Society of Mural Painters SMP or S.M.P.
Society of Naval Architects and Marine Engineers SNAME or S.N.A.M.E.
Society of Nuclear Medicine SNM or S.N.M.
Society of Occupational Medicine SOM or S.O.M.
Society of Packaging and Handling Engineers S.P.H.E. or SPHE
Society of Petroleum Engineers S.P.E. or SPE
Society of Photographic Scientists and Engineers S.P.S.E. or SPSE
Society of Plastics Engineers. S.P.E. or SPE
Society of Priests of the Sacred Heart of Jesus S.C.J.
Society of Saint Joseph S.S.J.
Society of Scottish Artists SSA
Society of Scribes and Illuminators SSI or S.S.I.
Society of St. Francis SSF or S.S.F.
Society of St. John the Evangelist S.S.J.E.
Society of St. Paul SSP or S.S.P.
Society of Telecommunications Engineers STE
Society of the Chemical Industry SCI or S.C.I.
Society of the Holy Cross SSC or S.S.C.
Society of the Plastics Industry S.P.I. or SPI
Society of the Sacred Mission SSM or S.S.M.
Society of Women Engineers SWE
Society of Worldwide Interbank Financial Telecommunication SWIFT
socioeconomic level SEL
socioeconomic status SES
sociological sociol.
sociologist sociol.
sociology 1 Soc. 2 soc. 3 sociol.
socket soc.
Socrates Soc.
sodium 1 Na 2 sod. 3 (line in solar spectrum) D
sodium alkane sulfonate SAS
sodium aluminum sulfate SAS
sodium bicarbonate bicarb or bicarb.
sodium carboxymethylcellulose CMC-CT
sodium dimethyldithiocarbamate SDDC
sodium dodecyl sulphate SDS
sodium thiosulphate hypo. or hypo
soft 1 S 2 s 3 sft. (on charts and surveys) 4 music p
soft and hard acids and bases SHAB
soft water s.w. or s/w
soft X-ray SXR
soft X-ray appearance potential spectroscopy SXAPS
soft-sized, supercalendered SSSC or s.s.s.c.
softly music dol.
software computers SW
software programming language computers SPL
software quality assurance computers SQA
softwood sftwd.
Soil Conservation Service SCS
soil horizons ABC
soil pipe SP or S.P.

Soil Sciences Society of America SSSA
sol S (monetary unit)
solar 1 SOL 2 sol.
solar absorption index K
Solar Energy Research Institute SERI
Solar Energy Society SES
solar neutrino unit astronomy SNU
Solar Particle Alert Network SPAN
solar power satellite SPS
solar proton event astronomy S.P.E. or SPE
solar thermionic electrical power systems STEPS
solar turboelectric drive STED
Soldier's Medal SM
Soldiers', Sailors', and Airmen's Families Association British S.S.A.F.A.
solenoid sol.
solicitor 1 sol. or Sol. 2 Solr. or solr.
Solicitor before the Supreme Courts (of Scotland) SSC or S.S.C.
Solicitor General 1 SG or S.G. 2 Sol. Gen.
solicitor-at-law British SL or S.L.
solid 1 s 2 sld. or sld
solid logic technology SLT
solid propellant SP
solid propellant rocket SPR
solid rocket booster SRB
solid rocket motor SRM
solid state electronics SS
solid-drawn SD
solid-state relay SSR
solid-state storage device electronics SSD
solidification solidif.
solids, non-fat SNF
solo S or S.
Solomon Sol.
Solomon Islands SI
solubility 1 s 2 soly.
soluble 1 s 2 sol.
soluble nucleoprotein SNP
soluble ribonucleic acid biochemistry sRNA
solution 1 sol. or sol 2 soln. 3 solut.
solvent 1 sol. 2 solv.
solvent extraction SX
solvent extraction milling process SEM
solvent-refined coal SRC
Somali Som.
Somali National Movement SNM
Somali Patriotic Front SPF
Somalia Som.
soman GD
somatotrophic hormone SH
somatotrophin or somatotrophic hormone STH
somatotropin-release-inhibiting factor SRIF
Somerset County, England Som. or Soms
somewhat softly music mv or m.v.
son 1 F or F. 2 S or S. 3 s or s.
Sonar British Asdic or asdic or A.S.D.I.C.
sonata So. or Son.
song and dance S&D
Song of Solomon S. of Sol.
Song of Songs S. of S.
sonic underwater navigation system SUNS
Sonnets, The (by Shakespeare) Son. or Sonn. (MLA: Son.)
Sons of the American Revolution SAR or S.A.R. (GPO: SAR)
Sons of Veterans SV or S.V.

soon as possible SAP *or* s.a.p.
Sophocles Soph. (Greek poet)
Sophomore Soph. *or* soph
soprano 1 S *or* S. **2** s *or* s. **3** Sop. *or* sop.
soprano, alto, bass *music* S.A.B.
soprano, alto, tenor, bass *music* S.A.T.B.
sort *computers* SRT *or* Srt
sorting *computers* SRT *or* Srt
souls on board SOB *or* s.o.b.
sound 1 snd. **2** *geography* sd *or* Sd
sound effect SFX
sound fixing and ranging SOFAR
sound intermediate frequency SIF
sound locator SL
sound on film SOF
sound on tape SOT *or* S.O.T.
sound pressure level SPL
Sound Surveillance System SOSUS *or* Sosus
sound velocity, temperature, pressure SVTP
sounding tube ST
Source Data Automation *computers* SDA
source language SL
South S *or* S.
south 1 s *or* s. **2** So. *or* so. **3** Sou. *or* sou. **4** Sth. *or* sth.
South Africa *or* **South African 1** S.Af. *or* SAfr *or* S.Afr. **2** SA *or* S.A.
South African Air Force SAAF
South African Atomic Energy Board SAAEB
South African Black Alliance SABA
South African Broadcasting Corporation SABC
South African Bureau of Racial Affairs SABRA
South African Bureau of Standards SABS
South African Communist Party SACP
South African Confederation of Labour SACOL
South African Congress of Trade Unions SACTU
South African Council for Scientific and Industrial Research SACSIR
South African Defense Force SADF
South African Development Co-ordination Council SADCC
South African Industrial Federation SAIF *or* S.A.I.F.
South African Institute of Medical Research S.A.I.M.R.
South African Labour Party SALP
South African Police SAP
South African Press Association SAPA *or* S.A.P.A.
South African Publishers' Association SAPA *or* S.A.P.A.
South African Republic SAR *or* S.A.R.
South America *or* **South American 1** S.Am. *or* S.Amer. **2** SA *or* S.A.
South Asian Association for Regional Cooperation SAARC
South Atlantic SAt *or* S.At.
South Atlantic Anomaly SAA *or* S.A.A.
South Australia *or* **South Australian 1** S.Aus. **2** SA *or* S.A.
South Britain SB *or* S.B.
south by east S by E *or* SbE
south by west S by W *or* SbW
South Carolina SC (Zip Code) *or* S.C. (in general use)(*NYT:* S.C.; *OUP:* SC)

South Dakota 1 S. Dak. **2** SD (Zip Code) *or* S.D. (in general use)(*NYT:* S.D.; *OUP:* S. Dak.)
South East Asia Commonwealth SEACOM
South European Pipeline SEPL *or* S.E.P.L.
South Island (New Zealand) SI *or* S.I.
south latitude 1 S.Lat. *or* S.lat. **2** SL *or* S.L.
South of Houston Street SoHo
South Pacific Air Transport Council SPATC
South Pacific Commission SPC
South Pacific Forum SPF
south polar distance *astronomy* SPD *or* s.p.d.
South Tropical Disturbance *astronomy* STD
south-southeast SSE *or* S.S.E. *or* s.s.e.
south-southwest SSW *or* S.S.W. *or* s.s.w.
southbound SB
southeast SE *or* S.E. *or* s.e. (*GPO:* SE.; *OUP:* SE)
Southeast Asia SEA
Southeast Asia Command SEAC
southeast by east SE by E *or* SEbE
southeast by south SE by S *or* SEbS
southeastern SE *or* S.E. *or* s.e.
Southeastern Library Network SOLINET
southerly sly. *or* Sly
Southern S *or* S.
southern 1 s *or* s. **2** So. *or* so. **3** Sou. *or* sou. **4** Sthn. *or* sthn.
Southern Association of Colleges and Schools SACS
Southern Baptist Convention SBC *or* S.B.C.
Southern California Rapid Transit District SCRTD
Southern Christian Leadership Conference SCLC
Southern Command SC (of U.S. Department of Defense)
Southern Cross Cru (constellation)
Southern Crown CrA (constellation)
Southern European Task Force of Nato SETAF
Southern Fish PsA (constellation)
Southern Hemisphere SH *or* S.H.
Southern Ocean Racing Conference S.O.R.C.
Southern Oscillation *meteorology* SO
Southern Triangle TrA (constellation)
southwest SW *or* S.W. *or* s.w. (*GPO, OUP:* SW)
Southwest Association of Indian Arts SWIA
southwest by south SW by S *or* SWbS
southwest by west SW by W *or* SWbW
southwestern 1 s.w. **2** SW *or* S.W.
Southwestern Reporter *law* SW *or* S.W.
Southwestern Power Administration SPA
space sp *or* sp.
Space and Missile Test Center SAMTEC
space and range radar SPANDAR *or* spandar
space at will *advertising* SAW
space available mail SAM
Space Command SC (of U.S. Department of Defense)
space communication system SCS
Space Detection and Tracking System SPADATS
Space Environment Simulation Laboratory SESL

Space Flight Operations Facility SFOF (of NASA)
space inertial reference equipment *navigation* SPIRE
Space Nuclear Propulsion Office SNPO
space object identification SOI
space power unit reactor SPUR
Space Programming Language *computers* SPL
Space Science Board SSB
space surveillance SPASUR
Space Systems Division SSD
Space Task Group STG
Space Technology and Advanced Reentry Tests START
space telescope *astronomy* ST
space test vehicle STV
Space Tracking and Data Acquisition Network STADAN
space transportation system STS
Space Warning and Control System SWACS
Spain 1 S *or* S. **2** Sp *or* Sp. (*MLA, OUP:* Sp.)
span 1 B **2** b
Spaniard Sp *or* Sp.
Spanish 1 S *or* S. **2** Sp *or* Sp. **3** Span. **4** Spn (*MLA, OUP:* Sp.)
Spanish American Sp.Am.
Spanish Broadcasting Society SER
Spanish Communist Party PCE *or* P.C.E.
Spanish International Network (in New York City) SIN
Spanish National Radio and Television RTVE
Spanish Socialist Workers Party PSOE
spar S *or* S.
spare sp *or* sp.
spare part sp *or* sp.
Speaker Spkr. (of U.S. House of Representatives)
speaker spkr.
Spear of the Nation SON (military force of the ANC)
special 1 Sp **2** sp **3** spec. **4** SPL *or* spl.
special agent SA
Special Air Service SAS
special boiling point, spirits SPBs
Special Branch *British* SB (of police)
Special Broadcasting Service SBS
special care baby unit SCBU
special care unit SCU
Special Committee on Antarctic Research SCAR
Special Delivery SD *or* S.D.
Special Development Order SDO
special drawing rights SDR (*NYT:* S.D.R.; *OUP:* SDR)
Special Duty SD
Special Economic Zone SEZ (in China)
special education Sp.Ed.
special effects FX *or* F/X
special equipment SE
Special Forces SF
special interest group SIG
Special Investigation Branch SIB
special issue *law* SI
Special Libraries Association SLA *or* S.L.A.
special multi-peril (insurance) SMP
Special Operations Command SOC
Special Operations Research Office SORO
Special Operations Unit SOU

special order 1 SO *or* S.O. **2** *commerce* s.o.
Special Patrol Group SPG
special purchase allowance *commerce* SPA
special purpose SP
special purpose individual weapon SPIW *or* S.P.I.W.
Special Purpose Local Authority SPLA
special regulation SR
Special Services SPS
Special Unitary *physics* SU
Special United Nations Fund for Economic Development SUNFED *or* Sunfed
Special Weapons and Tactics SWAT *or* S.W.A.T. (*GPO:* SWAT)
Special Weapons Attack Team SWAT *or* S.W.A.T. (*GPO:* SWAT)
Specialist 1 SP **2** Sp **3** Spec.
Specialist in Education Ed.S.
specially spec.
species 1 sp *or* sp. **2** spec. **3** spp. *or* spp
specific 1 sp *or* sp. **2** spec. **3** specif. *or* specif
specific dynamic action SDA
specific energy *physics* e
specific enthalpy h
specific fuel consumption SFC
specific gravity 1 SG **2** sg *or* s.g. **3** spg *or* sp.g. **4** *physics* sp.gr. *or* SPGR (*GPO:* sp. gr.)
specific heat *physics* sp.ht. *or* SPHT
specific heat capacity *physics* c
specific heat capacity of water *physics* J
specific inductive capacity SIC
specific internal energy u
Specific Language Disability SLD
Specific Language Impairment SLI
Specific Learning Disability SLD
specific operational requirement SOR
specific pathogen-free SPF
specific refraction r
specific volume sp. vol.
specific weight 1 s.w. **2** SW
specifically 1 spec. **2** specif.
specification 1 SPEC **2** spec. **3** specif.
specifications 1 SPEC **2** spec. **3** specs *or* SPECS
specify *computers* SPEC
specimen 1 sp *or* sp. **2** spec.
specimen input to digital automatic computer SPIDAC
speckled spk.
spectacle spec. *or* spec
spectacles specs (eyeglasses)
spectacular spec. *or* spec
spectroscopy spec.
spectrum spec.
speculation spec. *or* spec (of a financial venture)
speech sp
Speech Association of America SAA
speech interference level SIL
Speech Therapist ST
speed 1 sp **2** spd.
speed of approach SOA
speed of light c *or* c
speed of relative movement SRM
spell sp *or* sp.
spell out sp
spelling sp *or* sp.

sperm or spore mother cell *biology* SMC *or* S-M-C
spherical 1 S *or* S. **2** sph.
spherical candlepower SCP *or* scp *or* s.cp. *or* s.c.p.
spheroid sph.
spin quantum number *physics* S
spinal sp
spindle spdl.
spiral 1 spir. **2** *astronomy* S
spiritualism Spirit.
split *finance* s
split end *football* SE
spoken aloud *Latin* vv *or* v.v.
sponge spg *or* spg.
spontaneous ignition temperature SIT
spoonful *pharmaceutics* coch. *or* cochl.
sporting 1 sport. **2** sptg
sportive *music* Scherz.
Sports Car Club of America S.C.C.A. *or* SCCA
sports information director SID
sportscaster sport.
sportsman sport.
sportswoman sport.
spot weld SW
spotlight spot.
Spring 1 SPG (in postal address) **2** Spr. *or* Spr
spring spg *or* spg.
Springs 1 SPGS (in postal address) **2** Spgs. (in general use)
sprinkle *pharmaceutics* consperg.
sprinkler spkr. *or* spkr
squad sqd. *or* Sqd.
Squadron 1 Sq. **2** Sqdn. **3** Sqn.
squadron leader SL *or* S/L
squalls *meteorology* q
Square 1 SQ (in postal address) **2** Sq. (*GPO, NYT:* Sq.; *CSM, OUP:* sq.)
square sq. *or* sq
square centimeter sq.cm.
square chain sq.ch.
square corners sq.c.
square foot 1 sq.ft. *or* sqft **2** sf
square inch 1 si *or* s.i. **2** sq.in.
square kilometer sq.km.
square meter sq.m.
square mile sq.m. *or* sq.mi.
square millimeter sq.mm.
square rod sq.r. *or* sq.rd.
square yard sq.yd.
Sri Lanka Freedom Party SLFP
St. Bartholomew's Hospital Bart's *or* Barts
St. Basilius. Bas.
St. Catherine's College Cath.
St. Lawrence Seaway Authority SLSA
St. Lawrence Seaway Development Corporation SLSDC
St. Louis H (in Federal Reserve banking system)
St. Louis encephalitis SLE
St. Pierre et Miquelon St.P. et Miq.
stability augmentation system SAS
stabilize STAB *or* stab.
stabilized exports (of the EEC) Stabex
stabilized local oscillator *electronics* STALO
stabilizer STAB *or* stab.

stable plasma protein solution SPPS
staccato *music* stacc.
Staff 1 *military* S **2** stf.
Staff College SC
Staff Corps SC *or* S.C.
Staff Officer SO *or* S.O.
Staff Sergeant S/Sgt. *or* S.Sgt.
Staffordshire County, England Staffs.
stage 1 S (of a rocket) **2** *theater* stg. *or* STG
stage door SD
stage manager SM
staging stg. *or* STG
stain stn.
stained 1 st **2** stnd. *or* Stn
stainless steel SS
stairway stwy
stamen *botany* sta.
stamp stp.
stamped stp.
stamped addressed envelope SAE *or* s.a.e.
stamped self-addressed envelope SSAE *or* s.s.a.e.
stanchion stan. *or* STAN
stand st
stand-off target acquisition system SOTAS
standard 1 S *or* S. **2** s *or* s. **3** stan. *or* STAN *or* stand. *or* STAND **4** STD *or* std. *or* Std.
Standard & Poor S&P
standard address number *computers* SAN
standard advertising unit SAU
Standard Beam Approach SBA
standard calomel electrode *physics* SCE
Standard Consolidated Area SCA
Standard Consolidated Statistical Area SCSA
standard cubic foot scf *or* s.c.f.
standard deviation *statistics* **1** SD **2** sd *or* s.d.
Standard English SE
standard error *statistics* SE
standard error of the mean *statistics* SEM
Standard Generalized Markup Language *computers* SGML
Standard Industrial Classification SIC
standard inspection procedure *military* SIP
standard instrument approach *aeronautics* SIA
standard instrument departure *aeronautics, navigation* SID
Standard International Trade Classification SITC
Standard Location Area 1 SL **2** SLA
standard matched SM (of lumber)
standard mean chord *aeronautical engineering* SMC *or* smc
standard metal window SMW
standard mortality ratio SMR
standard nomenclature list *military* SNL
standard operating procedure SOP *or* s.o.p. (*GPO:* SOP)
standard pipe size SPS *or* S.P.S.
standard playback *electronics* SP
Standard Rate and Data Service SRDS
Standard Reference Materials SRM
standard Saybolt furol SSF
standard score 1 SS **2** *statistics* z
Standard Serial Number SSN
standard size *or* sizes SS

standard temperature and pressure *chemistry, physics* STP *or* s.t.p. (*GPO, OUP:* STP)
standard terminal arrival route STAR
Standard Time ST *or* S.T.
standard underwater research vessel SURV
Standard Wire Guage SWG *or* swg
standard *or* **seconds Saybolt universal** SSU
standardized test ST
standards and recommended practices SARPS
Standards Association of Australia SAA
Standards Association of New Zealand SANZ
Standards Eastern Automatic Computer SEAC
Standards Engineers Society SES
Standards Western Automatic Computer SWAC
Standing Conference on Telecommunications Research SCTR
Standing Group of Nato SGN
Standing Joint Committee SJC
Standing Naval Force, Atlantic SNFA
standing order 1 SO *or* S.O. **2** STO
standing room only S.R.O. *or* SRO
standing wave ratio SWR
standing-wave area monitor indicator *electronics* SWAMI
Stanford Linear Accelerator Center SLAC
Stanford Linear Collider SLC
Stanford Research Institute SRI
Stanford-Binet SB *or* S-B
Stanton number St
stanza st *or* st. (*MLA, OUP:* st.)
stanzas sts.
staphylococcus staph *or* staph.
star classification in order of luminosity Mk *or* MK
starboard stbd.
start St
start of heading *computers, printing* SOH
start of message *communications* SOM
start of text *computers* STX
starting point SP
starting price 1 SP **2** sp *or* s.p.
starting-lighting-ignition SLI
State St *or* St.
State and Regional Disaster Airlift SARDA
State Department SD *or* S.D.
State Law and Order Restoration Council Slorc (ruling junta of Myanmar)
State Legislative Committee SLC
State Liquor Authority SLA
State Militia SM *or* S.M.
state-of-the-art 1 SOA **2** SOTA
State Owned Enterprise SOE
State Police SP
State Trait Analysis Inventory STAI
State Universities Association SUA
State University of New York SUNY
statement 1 st *or* st. **2** *commerce, finance* Stmt
Statement of Additional Information *finance* SAI
statement of billing SB *or* S/B
Statement of Standard Accounting Practices SSAP
Statesman's Year-Book SYB

Staten Island SI *or* S.I. (*NYT:* S.I.; *OUP:* SI)
statesman stsm. *or* Stsm.
static *electronics, mechanics* stat.
static induction transistor *electronics* SIT
static pressure SP
static random-access memory *computers* SRAM
static spontaneous potential SSP (of oil-well exploration)
static thrust ST *or* S.T.
statics stat.
Station STA (in postal address)
station 1 Sta. **2** sta. **3** stn. *or* Stn
station headquarters SHQ
station selection code SSC
station wagon 1 St wgn **2** SW
station-to-station S-to-S *or* S to S
stationary 1 sta. **2** stat.
stationery sta.
statistical stat.
Statistical Package for the Social Sciences SPSS
statistical quality control SQC
statistical weight *physics* g
statistics stat.
stator sta.
statuary stat.
statue stat.
Status of Forces Agreement SOF *or* SOFA
statute 1 st *or* st. **2** stat. **3** *law* **a** St *or* st. **b** Stat.
statute law SL
statute mile 1 SM *or* sm **2** sta. mi. **3** stat.
Statutes at Large Stat. *or* Stat. L. (*GPO:* Stat.; *OUP:* stat)
Statutory Reserve Deposit SRD
Statutory Rules and Orders S.R.O.
statutory rules and orders S.R.&O.
steady-state distribution *physics* SSD
steam-generating heavy water reactor SGHW *or* SGHWR
steamship SS *or* S.S. *or* S/S (*GPO, OUP:* SS; *NYT:* S.S.)
steel 1 s **2** S *or* S. **3** st **4** STL *or* stl.
steel alloy protective plating ASPP
Steel Boiler Institute SBI
steel casting SC *or* S.C.
Steel Founders' Society of America S.F.S.A.
Steel Wire Gauge SWG *or* swg
Steiner minimum tree SMT
stellar inertial guidance system *navigation* STINGS
stem *botany* **1** s *or* s. **2** st
stems sts.
stencil sten.
stenographer 1 sten. **2** steno *or* stenog
stenography sten.
Stephen Steph.
steradian 1 S **2** sr
stere 1 s **2** st
stereo S
stereophonic stereo
stereophonic-quadraphonic SQ
stereotype ster.
sterile solution SS
sterilization ster.
sterilize ster.
sterilizer ster.
sterling 1 ster. *or* sterl. **2** stg. **3** stlg.

stet st
stevedore stev.
steward 1 stew. *or* Stew. **2** stwd *or* Stwd.
sticky stk. (on navigation charts)
stilb sb
still-camera video system SVS
still-video camera SVC
stimulus 1 S **2** stim.
stimulus-organism-response *psychology* SOR *or* S-O-R
stimulus-response *psychology* SR *or* S-R *or* S → R
stipend stip.
stipendiary stip.
Stipendiary Magistrate *British and Canadian* SM
stipulation stip.
stitch 1 m(in knitting) **2** st *or* st.
stitches sts.
stock 1 st *or* st. **2** stk.
stock and fixtures *insurance* S&F *or* s.andf.
stock at value *British* SAV
Stock Exchange 1 SE **2** St. Ex.
Stock Exchange Automated Quotations *British* SEAQ
stock length SL (of lumber)
stock number SN
stock-keeping unit *commerce* SKU
Stockholm Skm
Stockholm Institute of Technology STI *or* S.T.I.
Stockholm International Peace Research Institute SIPRI
stoke S (unit of viscosity)
stokes St
stolen base *or* **bases** *baseball* **1** SB **2** sb *or* s.b.
stone st (unit of weight)
stop payment *banking* **1** SP **2** sp *or* s.p.
stopping in transit SIT *or* s.i.t.
storable tubular extendable member STEM (of antennae)
storage 1 stg. *or* stge. **2** stor.
storage capacity *computers* ST *or* S.T.
storage in transit SIT *or* s.i.t.
Storage Instantaneous Audimeter SIA (for Nielsen ratings)
store *computers* ST *or* S.T.
store to door delivery SDD *or* S-D-D
stored program control *computers* SPC
stored response chain SRC
storm damaged *insurance* SD *or* S/D
storm of drifting snow *meteorology* KS *or* KS.
storm radar data processor STRADAP
stowage stow.
Stradivarius Strad
straight 1 St **2** str.
straight edge SE *or* s.e.
straight-line capacitance *electronics* SLC
straight-line frequency *electronics* SLF
straight-line wavelength *electronics* SLW
strain *pharmaceutics* col. *or* col
strain energy U
strain of a virus A
strained-layer superlattice SLS
strainer str.
Strait 1 St *or* St. **2** Str.
strait str.

strange *physics* s
strapped, corded, and sealed *shipping* SC&S *or* s.c. and s.
strategic *military* STRAT
Strategic Air Command SAC
Strategic Air Force SAF
Strategic Arms Limitation Talks SALT
Strategic Arms Reduction Talks START
Strategic Army Corps STRAC
Strategic Army Forces STRAF
strategic business unit SBU
Strategic Defense Initiative SDI
strategic lawsuit against public participation SLAPP
strategic nuclear forces SNF
strategic nuclear launch vehicle SNLV
Strategic Petroleum Reserve SPR
Strategy and Tactics Analysis Group *military* STAG
stratocumulus *meteorology* Sc
stratus 1 s 2 *meteorology* St
strawberries straw.
Street 1 ST (in postal address) 2 St *or* St. (GPO, NYT, CSM, OUP: St.)
streets sts.
strength str.
strength of association *psychology* Asn
streptococcus 1 str. 2 strep *or* strep.
streptodornase SD
streptokinase SK
streptomycin SM
stress corrosion cracking *engineering* SCC
stretch Str. (in horse racing)
Strike Command STRICOM
strike price *finance* s
strike, riot, and civil commotion *insurance* SRCC *or* s.r.c.c.
strikeout 1 *baseball* K 2 s.o. 3 SO
strikes, riots, and civil commotions *insurance* SR&CC
string *music* str.
String Oriented Symbolic Language *computers* SNOBOL
stringer stgr. *or* STGR
strings *music* str.
stroke str.
strokes per minute SPM *or* spm
strong no-trump after passing SNAP (in bridge)
strontium Sr
strontium unit SU
strophe st *or* st.
structural str.
structural design language *computers* STRUDL
structural engineering system solver STRESS
structural query language *computers* SQL
structural systems analysis and design method *British* SSADM
structure struc. *or* struct.
structure resonance modulation spectroscopy SRMS
student stud.
Student Christian Movement SCM *or* S.C.M.
Student Loan Marketing Administration 1 Sallie Mae 2 SLMA
Student of Civil Law S.C.L.

Student Representative Council *British* SRC
Students Against Drunk Driving SADD
Students International Travel Association SITA
studio transmitter link *electronics* STL
Study of Man's Impact on Climate SMIC
stumped *cricket* 1 st 2 Stpd.
styrene acrylonitrile SAN
styrene-butadiene rubber SBR
subacute bacterial endocarditis *medicine* SBE
subacute sclerosing panencephalitis SSPE
subarachnoid hemorrhage *medicine* SAH
subchapter subch.
subcutaneous 1 subcut. 2 *medicine* sc *or* s.c.
subdivision subd.
subeditor sub.
subfloor sub.
subgenus subgen.
subject 1 S 2 sub. 3 subj. (MLA, OUP: subj.)
subject ratio SR
subject to approval s.a.
subject to approval, no risk SANR *or* s.a.n.r.
subject to particular average *commerce* SPA *or* s.p.a.
subject to permission to deal *finance* SPD *or* s.p.d.
subject to the rule of the institution *Latin* in stat. pup.
subject, verb, object SVO (sentence pattern)
subjective subj.
subjectively subj.
subjunctive *grammar* 1 sub. 2 subj. (MLA, OUP: subj.)
submachine gun SMG
submarine 1 SS (naval symbol) 2 sub.
Submarine Celestial Altitude Recorder SCAR
submarine fleet reactor SFR
submarine intermediate reactor SIR
submarine rocket SUBROC
submarine thermal reactor STR
submarine-launched ballistic missile SLBM
submarine-launched cruise missile SLCM
submerged electrode detection and ranging SEDAR
Submerged Object Recovery Device SORD
submerged, portable, inflatable dwelling SPID
submersible decompression chamber SDC
subordinate sub.
subparagraph subpar.
Subscriber Direct Dialing *British* SDD
Subscriber Trunk Dialing STD
subscription 1 sub. 2 subs. *or* subs
subscription television STV
subsection 1 ss 2 subsec.
subsidiary 1 Subs. 2 subs.
subsiding *music* perd.
subsistence subs.
subsistence allowance SA
subspecies 1 subsp. 2 *biology* ssp *or* ssp.
substandard. substand.
substantive 1 s *or* s. 2 subs. 3 subst. 4 *grammar* sb *or* sb.
substantively subst.
substitute 1 sub. 2 subs. 3 subst.
substitute natural gas SNG

subtropical subtrop.
suburb sub. *or* Sub.
suburban sub. *or* Sub.
subway sub.
succeeded 1 s *or* s. 2 suc.
successor suc.
sucre S
sucrose polyester S.P.E. *or* SPE
suction 1 suc. 2 suct.
Sudan S
Sudan People's Liberation Army SPLA
Sudanese S
Sudanese pound LS *or* £S
sudden cardiac death *medicine* SCD
sudden commencement type *astronomy* SC *or* S-C
sudden cosmic noise absorption SCNA
sudden enhancement of atmospherics SEA
sudden infant death (syndrome) SID
sudden infant death syndrome SIDS
sudden ionospheric disturbance SID
sudden phase anomaly *electricity* SPA
sudden short-wave fade-out SSWF
sudden unexpected death SUD
Suetonius Suet. (Roman historian)
sufficient 1 suf. 2 suff.
sufficient quantity *pharmaceutics* 1 q.s. 2 quant. suff.
suffix 1 suf. 2 suff.
Suffolk 1 Sfk. 2 Suff.
suffragan Suff. *or* Suffr.
Suffragan Bishop 1 Bp. Suff. 2 BS
suggested sug.
suggested retail price SRP
suggestion sug.
Suicide Prevention Center SPC
Suicide Prevention Program SPP
sulfhydryl SH
sulfur S
sulphonamide, type of *British* M&B
Sultan Sult.
sum of the products *mathematics, computers* SOP
summary summ.
Summary Court-Martial SCM
summer Sum.
Summer Load Line S
Summer Time ST *or* S.T.
sun 1 S *or* S. 2 s *or* s.
sun protection factor SPF
Sunday 1 S *or* S. 2 Su. 3 Sun. *or* Sund.
Sundays and holidays S&H
Sundays and Holidays Excepted *commerce* SHEX
sundries sund.
super sup. (in bookbinding)
super large-scale integration *computers* SLSI
super video graphics display *computers* SVGA
super-proton synchrotron SPS
supercalendered 1 SC 2 sc *or* s.c.
supercharge supchg.
supercharger supchg.
supercompressibility factor *physics* y
superconducting quantum interference device SQUID *or* squid
superconducting supercollider SSC
superconductivity, theory of BCS

supercritical fluid chromatography SFC
superficial super.
superfine 1 sup. **2** super.
superheterodyne *electronics* superhet.
superhigh frequency SHF *or* shf (*GPO:* SHF)
superintendent 1 Supdt **2** super *or* Super. **3** supr. *or* Supr. **4** Supt. *or* supt. (*GPO:* Supt.; *OUP:* supt.)
superior 1 S **2** sup. **3** super. **4** supr. *or* Supr.
Superior Court Sup.C. *or* Sup. Ct.
superlative 1 sup. **2** superl. (*MLA, OUP:* superl.)
supermarket *British* super
supernova 1 SN **2** sn
supernova remnants *astronomy* SNR
superplastic forming, diffusion bonding SPF/DB
superprecision approach radar SPAR
superseded supsd.
supersonic commercial air transport SCAT
Supersonic Naval Ordnance Research Track SNORT
supersonic transport SST
Supervising Customs Agent SCA
supervisor Supvr. *or* supvr.
supplement 1 sup. *or* Sup. **2** supp. *or* Supp. **3** suppl. *or* Suppl. **4** suppt. *or* Suppt. (*MLA, CSM:* supp.; *OUP:* suppl.)
Supplement to the Revised Statutes Supp. Rev. Stat.
supplemental restraint system SRS
Supplemental Security Income SSI
Supplemental Unemployment Benefits SUB *or* S.U.B.
supplementary 1 sup. *or* Sup. **2** supp. **3** suppl. **4** suppt.
supplementary airways weather-reporting station SAWRS
supplementary meteorological office SMO
supplements supps. *or* Supps.
supply 1 sup. **2** sy.
Supply Department *or* **Depot** SD
Supply Officer SO *or* S.O.
supply refueling point SRP
support 1 SPT *or* spt. **2** sup.
suppository *pharmaceutics* suppos.
suprachiasmatic nucleus *biology* SCN
supraprotest *banking* sp
supreme supr. *or* Supr.
Supreme Allied Command *or* **Commander, Atlantic** SACLANT
Supreme Allied Command *or* **Commander, Europe** SACEUR
Supreme Allied Headquarters SAH
Supreme Commander Allied Forces SCAF
Supreme Court 1 SC *or* S.C. **2** Sup.C. *or* Sup. Ct.
Supreme Court of the U.S. SCOTUS
Supreme Court Reporter Sup.C. *or* Sup. Ct. (*GPO:* Sup.Ct.)
Supreme Headquarters, Allied Powers in Europe SHAPE
Supreme Pontiff SP *or* S.P.
surcharged sur.
surface 1 S **2** s **3** sur. *or* surf.
surface acoustic wave *electronics* SAW
surface area 1 S **2** SA
surface barrier diffused transistor *electronics* SBDT

surface barrier transistor *electronics* SBT
surface charge transistor SCT
surface effect ship SES
surface feet sf
surface feet per minute 1 sfm *or* s.f.m. **2** sfpm *or* s.f.p.m.
surface ground zero SGZ
surface mounting device SMD
surface recombination velocity *electronics* S.R.V.
surface tension 1 ST **2** T
surface water automatic computer SURWAC
surface wave transmission line SWTL
surface-to-air SA
surface-to-air missile SAM *or* S-A-M (*NYT, OUP:* SAM)
surface-to-surface SS *or* S-S
surface-to-surface missile SSM
surface-to-underwater missile SUM
surfaced on side SS (of lumber)
surge impedance loading *electronics* SIL
surgeon 1 Sg. **2** surg. *or* Surg. (*GPO:* Surg.; *OUP:* surg.)
Surgeon General 1 SG *or* S.G. **2** Surg. Gen.
Surgeon General's Office SGO
surgery surg.
surgical surg.
surplus 1 S *or* S. **2** sur.
surrender surr.
Surrey County, England 1 Sur. **2** Sy.
Surrogate Surr.
Surrogate Court Sur. Ct.
surveillance radar SR
surveillance radar element SRE
survey 1 surv. **2** svy
survey analysis language SAL
surveying surv.
surveyor surv. *or* Surv.
Surveyor General Surv. Gen. *or* Surv.-Gen.
survival quotient SQ
surviving surv.
Susanna Sus. (book of Apocrypha)
susceptance *electricity* B *or* b
suspect sus
suspended susp.
suspended sentence *law* SS
suspended solids *ecology* SS
suspension susp.
Sussex 1 Suss. **2** Sx.
sustained *music* sost. *or* sosten.
sustainer engine cutoff SECO
Svedberg flotation Sf
Svedberg unit S
swath-sounding sonar SASS
Sweden 1 S **2** Sw. **3** Swe. *or* Swed.
Swedish 1 S **2** Sw. **3** Swe. *or* Swed. (*MLA:* Swed.; *OUP:* Sw.)
Swedish krona Skr
Swedish National Radio SR
sweetly *music* dol.
swell organ Sw. *or* sw.
swine vesicular disease SVD
Swiss Sw.
Swiss Franc Sfr.
Swiss National Railroad CFF *or* C.F.F.
Swiss Red Cross SRC
switch SW *or* sw.
switchboard swbd.

switched proton electron channeltron spectrometer SPECS
switchgear *electricity* SWGR
switching swtg
switching, conference, and monitoring arrangements SCAMA (of telephones)
Switzerland 1 Hel. **2** Helv. **3** Swit. *or* Switz. **4** Swtz.
sworn statement *law* SS
Sydney, Australia Syd.
syllabication syll.
syllable syll. *or* syl.
syllabus syll. *or* syl.
symbol 1 S *or* S. **2** s *or* s. **3** sym. *or* Sym **4** symb.
symbolic sym. *or* Sym
symbolic link format *computers* SYLK
Symbolic Machine Language SML
Symbolic Optimum Assembly Program *computers* SOAP
symbolic programming system *computers* SPS
Symmetric List Processor *computers* SLIP
symmetrical 1 *botany, chemistry, mathematics* s **2** *chemistry* sym.
symmetry sym.
sympathetic nervous system SNS
symphonic sym.
symphony 1 sym. *or* Sym. **2** Symph.
symposium Symp.
symptom sym.
Synagogue Syn.
synchronization 1 sync *or* SYNC **2** synch *or* synchro.
synchronize 1 syn. **2** sync *or* SYNC **3** synch *or* synchro.
synchronized 1 S **2** syn.
synchronizing 1 syn. **2** sync *or* SYNC **3** *computers* SYN
synchronous 1 syn. **2** sync *or* SYNC **3** synch *or* synchro. **4** *computers* SYN
synchronous alternating current ACS
synchronous amplitude modulation SAM
synchronous communications SYNCOM *or* Syncom
synchronous data link control *computers* SDLC
synchronous transmitter receiver STR
syndicate synd.
syndicated synd.
syndication synd. *or* Synd
syndrome syn.
Synod Syn.
synodic time of revolution *astronomy* ^{P}syn
synonym syn. *or* Syn. (*MLA, OUP:* syn.)
synonymous 1 syn. *or* Syn. **2** synon
synonymy syn. *or* Syn.
synopsis synop.
Syntagmatic Organization Language SYNTOL
syntax syn.
syntax-improving device *computers* SID
synthesis synth.
synthesizer *music* synth.
synthetic 1 syn. **2** synth.
synthetic detergent syndet
synthetic fuel synfuel
synthetic gas syngas
synthetic natural gas SNG

synthetic rubber SR
synthetic-aperture radar SAR
syphilis syph
Syria 1 S 2 Sy. 3 Syr.
Syriac or Syrian Syr.
Syrian pound LS or £S
syrup *pharmaceutics* syr.
system 1 sys. or Sys. 2 syst. or Syst.
System Assurance Program *computers* SAP
System Development Corporation SDC
System for Electronic Analysis and Retrieval of Criminal Histories SEARCH
System for Processing Educational Data Electronically SPEDE
system generation *computers* SYSGEN
system input *computers* SYSIN

System Management Facilities *computers* SMF
System of Multicultural Pluralistic Assessment *education* SOMPA
system output *computers* SYSOUT
System Program Officer SPO
system reference library *computers* SRL
System to Accumulate and Retrieve Financial Information with Random Extraction STARFIRE
systematic 1 sys. 2 syst.
Systematic Alien Verification for Entitlement SAVE
systematic assertiveness training SAT or S.A.T.
Systematic Assessment of Licensee Performance SALP

systemic 1 sys. 2 syst.
systemic lupus erythematosus SLE
Systems and Procedures Association SPA
systems application architecture *computers* SAA or S.A.A.
Systems Computer Evaluation and Review Technique SCERT
systems engineer SE
Systems Engineering Coordination SEC
systems for nuclear auxiliary power SNAP
systems language *computers* SLANG
Systems Network Architecture *computers* SNA
systems operator *computers* SYSOP
systole syst.
systolic blood pressure SBP
systolic pressure *medicine* SP

T

table tab.
table look up *computers* TLU
Table Mountain Men (constellation)
table of contents TOC or t.o.c.
table of distribution TD
table of equipment TE or T/E
table of organization TO or T/O or t.o.
tablespoon 1 T or T. 2 tb or tb. 3 tbs. or tbsp. (*CSM, OUP:* tbsp.)
tablespoonful 1 tb or tb. 2 tbs. or tbsp.
tablet *pharmaceutics* 1 tab. 2 tabl.
Tabular Systems Oriented Language *computers* TABSOL
tabulate tab.
tabulator TAB or Tab
Tacitus Tac. (Roman historian)
tackle *football* T
tacrine or tetrahydroaminoacridine THA
tactical 1 tctl. 2 *military* TAC
Tactical Aerial Reconnaissance TAR
Tactical Air Command TAC
Tactical Air Control System *military* TACS
Tactical Air Force TAF
Tactical Air Missile TAM
tactical air navigation TACAN or Tacan
Tactical Air Operations Center TAOC
tactical air to surface missle TASM
Tactical Area of Responsibility *military* TAOR
tactical ballistic missile TBM
tactical fighter, experimental TFX
tactical landing approach radio TALAR or Talar
tactical missile TM
Tactical Narcotics Team TNT
tactical nuclear missile TNM
tactical nulcear weapon TNW
Tactical Patrol Force T.P.F.
tael tl. (unit of weight)
Tagalog Tag.
tagged image file format *computers* TIFF

tail wind *aeronautics* TW or t.w.
tailboard TB
Taiwan 1 T 2 Tai.
taka TK or Tk. (*GPO:* Tk)
take *pharmaceutics* 1 R_x or Rx 2 cap or cap. 3 sum.
taken t or t.
taken and accepted *commerce* T&A or T and A
taken and offered t.&o. (in horse racing)
taken elsewhere *construction* E.W.T. or EWT
takeoff TO
takeoff gross weight *aeronautics* TOGW
takeoff weight TOW
talk between ships TBS
Talmud Tal.
Tamil Tam.
Tamil United Liberation Front T.U.L.F.
Taming of the Shrew, The 1 Shr. 2 Tam. Shr.
tandem tdm.
tandem mirror experiment TMX (of fusion energy)
tangent 1 tan 2 tg
Tangier Tang.
tanker 1 T 2 tkr.
tantalum Ta
Tanzania or Tanzanian T
Tanzania-Zambia Railway TAN-ZAM
Tanzanian shilling TSH or TSh
Tape Operating System *computers* TOS
tape recorder TR
tape unit *computers* TU
taps and dies t.&d.
tardive dyskinesia TD
tare 1 t or t. 2 tr (weight of container or conveyance)
target 1 T 2 TGT or tgt. 3 trgt 4 *electronics* a t b TA
Target Acquisition Systems TAS
target area *military* TA
target cost system TCS
target identification TI
target language TL
target market coverage *advertising* T.M.C.
target practice TP
Target Radiation Measurement Program TRUMP

tariff 1 tar. 2 trf.
tariff number TN
tarpaulin tarp
task control block *computers* TCB
task force TF
task reporting and current evaluation TRACE
Tasmania 1 Tas. 2 Tasm.
Tasmanian 1 Tas. 2 Tasm.
Tasmanian Network TASNET
Tauri Infrared Companion *astronomy* TIRC
Taurus, the Bull Tau (constellation)
tautology taut.
tavern tav. or Tav.
tax TX or tx.
tax board memorandum TBM or T.B.M.
tax deferred annuity TDA
Tax Division TD (of U.S. Department of Justice)
Tax Equity and Fiscal Responsibility Act TEFRA
taxation 1 tax. 2 TX or tx. or txn.
taxi and runway surveillance radar TRSR
taxonomic tax. or taxon.
taxonomy tax. or taxon.
taxpayer identification number TIN
t-cell growth factor *biology* TCGF
teacher tchr. or Tchr.
Teachers College TC or T.C.
Teachers Insurance and Annuity Association TIAA
teaching tchg. or Tchg.
teaching assistant TA or T/A
Teaching English as a Foreign Language TEFL
Teaching English as a Second Language TESL
Teaching English to Speakers of Other Languages TESOL
Teaching of English as a Foreign Language TOEFL
teaspoon 1 t or t. 2 teasp. 3 ts or ts. 4 tsp. or tspn (*CSM, OUP:* tsp.)
teaspoonful 1 teasp. 2 tsp. or tspn (*CSM, OUP:* tsp.)
technetium Tc
Technical Tec
technical 1 tech. or tech or Tech. 2 techn. or Techn.
Technical and Further Education TAFE

Technical Assistance Board TAB
Technical Assistance Bureau *French* BAT *or* B.A.T.
Technical Assistance Committee TAC
Technical Assistance Committee of the United Nations *French* CAT *or* C.A.T.
Technical Assistance of the UN TAUN
Technical Assistance Operation TAO
Technical Assistance Program TAP
Technical Association of the Pulp and Paper Industry TAPPI
technical bulletin TB
Technical Cooperation Among Developing Countries TCDC
Technical Cooperation Program TCP (of the UN)
technical director TD *or* T.D.
technical foul *basketball* T
Technical Information and Library Service TILS
Technical Information Officer TIO
technical information release TIR
Technical Information Service TIS
technical institute TI
technical knockout TKO *or* t.k.o. (*OUP:* TKO)
Technical Liaison Officer TLO
technical manual TM
technical memorandum TM
technical note TN
technical order TO
technical paper TP
technical quality evaluation TQE
technical report TR
technical representative TR *or* T.R.
technical research note TRN *or* trn
Technical Sergeant T/Sgt *or* T.Sgt.
technical standard order TSO
technical term TT
Technical Training Center TTC
Technical Value Committee TVC
technically tech. *or* Tech.
technically classified TC *or* T.C.
technician 1 Tech. *or* tech. *or* tech 2 Techn. *or* techn.
technique tech. *or* Tech.
technological 1 tech. *or* Tech. 2 technol.
technology 1 tech. *or* Tech. 2 techn. *or* Techn. 3 technol.
Technology Administration TA
tee *engineering* T
teeth T
teeth per inch TPI *or* t.p.i. (of a gearwheel)
teetotaler TT
Telecommunication Engineering and Manufacturing Association TEMA
telecommunications Telecom *or* telecom.
telecommunications access method TCAM
Telecommunications Device for the Deaf TDD
Telecommunications Research Establishment T.R.E.
Telegram Tely
telegram 1 tel. 2 teleg. 3 tg *or* tg.
telegraph 1 tel. 2 teleg. 3 tg *or* tg.
telegraph money order T.M.O. *or* TMO
telegraphic tel.
telegraphic transfer *British* TT *or* T.T. *or* T/T
telegraphy 1 tel. 2 teleg.

telemeter TLM *or* tlm.
Telemetry On-Line Processing System TELOPS
telephone 1 T 2 tel. *or* Tel. 3 teleph. 4 TP
telephone influence factor TIF
telephone interference factor TIF
telephone number TN
Telephone Office *British* TO *or* T.O.
telephone order *commerce* TO
telephone sales representative TSR
telephony 1 tel. 2 teleph.
teleprinter 1 TP 2 TPR
TeleRail Automated Information Network TRAIN
Telescope Tel (constellation)
teletype TT
teletype exchange TELEX *or* telex
teletypesetter TTS
teletypewriter TTY
teletypewriter exchange TWX
television 1 TV *or* T.V. (*GPO, NYT, OUP:* TV) 2 *British* **a** tele **b** telly
television and infrared observation satellite TIROS
Television Audience Measurement TAM
television bureau TVB *or* TvB
television households *marketing* TVHH
Television Information Office TIO
television interference TVI
Television New Zealand TVNZ
Television of France TDF
television radar air navigation TELERAN
television receive only TVRO
Television Reporters International TRI
Telex TEX
telex TX
teller *banking* tlr.
tellurium Te
Telugu Tel *or* Tel.
temperance temp.
temperate zone Temp.
temperature 1 t 2 Te 3 temp. 4 tmp. 5 *physics* T
temperature coefficient of resistance TCR
temperature compensated crystal oscillator *electronics* TCXO
temperature efficiency TE *or* T-E
temperature indicator TI
temperature meter TM
temperature switch TS
temperature variation of resistance *electricity* T.V.R.
temperature, pulse, respiration *medicine* TPR *or* t.p.r.
temperature, salinity TS *or* T-S
temperature-humidity index THI
Tempest, The 1 Temp. (*MLA:* Tmp.) 2 Tmp.
template temp. *or* TEMP
tempo *music* t *or* t.
temporal *medicine* t *or* t.
temporal lobe epilepsy TLE
temporarily out of print TOP *or* T.O.P.
temporarily out of service TOS
temporarily out of stock TOS
temporary 1 T 2 temp. 3 tmp.
temporary assistant TA *or* T/A
temporary bench mark TBM *or* T.B.M. (on surveys)
temporary buoy TB

temporary duty *military* TDY
temporary lighted buoy TLB *or* tlb
temporary restraining order *law* TRO
temporary threshold shift TTS (of sound reception)
temporary worker temp.
temporomandibular joint TMJ
ten X *or* x
Ten Year Plan for Ocean Exploration TYPOE
tenancy tency
tenant ten.
tenderly *music* affret. *or* affrett.
tenement ten.
Tennessee 1 Tenn. 2 TN (Zip Code)
Tennessee Valley Authority TVA *or* T.V.A. (*GPO, OUP:* TVA; *NYT:* T.V.A.)
Tennyson Tenn.
tenor *music* 1 t 2 T *or* T. 3 ten. *or* Ten.
tenor, baritone, bass TBB (of a musical score)
tens of rupees Rx *or* rx
tensile 1 T 2 tens.
tensile strength 1 TS 2 ts
tensile yield strength TYS
tension 1 T 2 tens.
tensor t *or* t.
tentative 1 t 2 tent.
tenth value layer TVL (of radiation shielding)
tera- T
terabyte *computers* TB
teracycle *or* **teracycles per second** 1 Tc *or* TC 2 tc
teraelectron volts TeV
terahertz THz
teratology terat.
terawatt TW *or* tw
terbium Tb
tercentesimal temperature tt.
terephthalic acid 1 TA 2 TPA
term of enlistment TOE
term of service TOS
terminal 1 T *or* T. 2 term. 3 trml. *or* TRML 4 *electricity* t
terminal area navigation system TANS
terminal control area TCA
terminal control system *computers* TCS
terminal portal venule TPV
terminal radar control *aeronautics* TRACON
terminal velocity TV
terminate and stay resident *computers* TSR
termination term.
terminology term.
terra cotta TC
Terrace TER (in postal address)
terrace 1 ter. *or* Ter. (*GPO, OUP:* Ter.) 2 terr. *or* Terr.
terrain contour matching Tercom
terrain-avoidance radar TAR
terrazzo ter.
Terrestrial Dynamic Time *astronomy* TDT
territorial terr.
Territorial Army *British* TA
territory 1 T *or* T. 2 Ty. 3 ter. *or* Ter. 4 terr. *or* Terr.
tertiary 1 t *or* t. 2 tert. 3 *geology* ter. *or* Ter.
tesla T
test X
test and evaluation T&E

test and replace as necessary TARAN
Test Control Officer TCO
Test of English as a Foreign Language TOEFL
Test of Standard Written English TSWE
test report TR
test run TR
test solution *chemistry* TS
test support equipment TSE
test vehicle TV
Testament Test.
testament test.
testamentary test.
testator test.
tester tstr
testimonial test.
tetanus Te
tetanus and diphtheria *medicine* TD
tetanus antitoxin TAT
tetanus toxin tet.tox.
tetanus toxoid TT
tetra propylbenzene sulfonate TBS
tetrabutyl titanate TBT
tetrachloro-diphenylethane TDE
tetrachlorodibenzo-p-dioxin TCDD
tetrachlorodibenzofuron TCDF
tetracyanoethylene TCNE
tetracyanoquinodimethane TCNQ
tetracycline tc
tetraethyl lead TEL
tetraethyl pyrophosphate TEPP
tetraethylammonium chloride *medicine* TEA or TEAC
tetrafluoroethylene TFE
Tetragrammaton 1 JHVH or JHWH 2 YHWH or YHVH
tetrahydrocannabinol THC
tetrahydrofuran THF
tetrahydrofurfuryl alcohol THF or THFA
tetrakishydroxymethyl phosphonium chloride THPC
tetramethylrhodamine isothiocyanate TRITC
tetramethylsilane TMS
tetramethylthiuram disulfide TMTD
tetranitroaniline TNA
tetrapotassium pyrophosphate TKPP
tetrasodium pyrophosphate TSPP
Teutonic Teut.
Texan Tex.
Texas 1 Tex. 2 TX (Zip Code)
Text Encoding Initiative TEI
textile text.
Textile Research Institute TRI
Textile Workers' Union of America TWUA
textured vegetable protein TVP
Thailand Thai.
thallium Tl
that is *Latin* 1 h.e. 2 i.e.
that which is to be proved *Latin* i.q.e.d.
Thayer-Martin culture medium *bacteriology* TM
The Book Collector BC
theater 1 Th or th. 2 theat. or Thea. 3 T
Theater Area Communications Systems *military* TACS
Theater Guild TG
Theater Library Association TLA
Theater Nuclear Forces TNF
Theater Owners of America TOA

theatre high altitude area defense *military* Thaad
theatrical theat.
their thr.
Their Royal Highnesses TRH or T.R.H.
Their Serene Highnesses TSH or T.S.H.
thematic apperception test *psychology* TAT
Theodore Theo.
Theodore Roosevelt TR or T.R.
Theodosia Theo.
theologian theol.
theological theol.
Theology *Latin* Thia.
theology 1 theo. 2 theol.
Theophilus Theoph.
Theophrastus Theoph. (Greek philosopher)
theorem theor.
theoretical 1 theo. 2 theor. 3 theoret.
theoretically theoret.
theory theor.
theory of everything TOE or T.O.E. (of the Big Bang theory)
theosophical Theos. or theos.
theosophist Theos. or theos.
theosophy Theos. or theos.
therapeutic therap.
therapeutic abortion TA
therapeutics therap. or Therap.
therefore *Latin* Igr.
thermal th.
thermal conductivity k
thermal death point *biology* TDP or T.D.P.
thermal Doppler weather radar *meteorology, aeronautics* TDWR
thermal efficiency TE
thermal infrared multispectral scanner TIMS
thermal megawatt tMw. or TMW or t.mw.
thermal neutron analysis TNA
thermal test reactor TTR
thermal unit TU or T.U. or t.u.
thermionic integrated micromodule *electronics* TIMM
thermochemistry thermochem
thermocouple TC
thermodynamics thermodyn
thermoelectric power *physics* Q
thermoglobulin antibodies TGA
thermogravimetric analysis TGA
thermoluminescence TL
thermoluminescence dosimeter TLD
thermoluminescence dosimetry TLD
thermoluminescent TL
thermomechanical processing TMP
thermomechanical pump TMP
thermometer therm. or thermom
thermometric therm. or thermom
thermonuclear TN or T-N
thermostat therm. or thermo.
thesis thes.
thespian thesp
Thessalonians Thess.
Thessaly Thess.
thiamine pyrophosphate TPP
thick thk. or THK (esp. of paper)
thick fog *nautical, meteorology* FF
thickness 1 H or h 2 t
thin film TF
thin film technology *electronics* TFT

thin film transistor *electronics* TFT
thin-layer chromatography TLC
third 3rd or 3rd
Third Order of St. Francis T.O.S.F.
third party TP
third-class ship in Lloyd's Register Æ
third-country nationals T.C.N.
this is *Latin* h.e.
this side up TSU
this week only *advertising* TWO
Thomas 1 Th or Th. 2 Tho. or Thom. or Thos.
thoracic thor.
thorax thor.
thoria-dispersed TD
thorium th.
thorium emanation Th-Em
thorium, uranium, deuterium THUD
thoron 1 Th-Em 2 Tn
thoroughbred th.
Thoroughbred Racing Association TRA
thoroughfare thoro.
thousand 1 M 2 thou.
thousand board feet MBF or mbf
thousand cubic feet Mcf or M c.f. or MCF
thousand feet surface measure MSM or M s.m.
thousand feet or foot board measure 1 MBM or m.b.m. 2 MFBM or m.f.b.m.
thousands mm
thread thd.
threads per inch TPI or t.p.i.
three days *pharmaceutics* trid.
three hundred 1 B 2 CCC
Three Mile Island TMI
three times a day *pharmaceutics* 1 t.d.s. 2 t.i.d.
three times a night *pharmaceutics* t.i.n.
three-dimensional television 3-DTV
three-mile limit TML
three-wheeler TW or T-W
threonine thr. or Thr
threshold limit values *medicine* TLV
Threshold Test Ban Treaty TTBT
Thrift Depositor Protection Oversight Board TDPOB
thrombosis *medicine* thrombo.
thrombotic thrombocytopenic purpura *medicine* TTP
throttle throt.
through thr.
through back of loops t.b.l. (in knitting)
through bill of lading *commerce* 1 TBL or t B/L 2 thro B/L
through-the-lens TTL (of a camera)
thrust 1 F 2 thr. 3 *aeronautics* T
thrust horsepower thp or THP or t.hp.
thrust line *engineering* TL
thruway 1 Thwy 2 twy or Twy
Thucydides Thuc. (Greek historian)
thulium Tm
thunder t
thunderstorm T
thunderstorm with rain *meteorology* tlr.
thunderstorm with snow *meteorology* tls.
Thursday 1 T or T. 2 Th or Th. 3 Thu. 4 Thur. or Thurs.
thymidine diphosphate TDP
thymidine monophosphate TMP
thymidine triphosphate TTP

thymine T
thymol blue *biochemistry* TB
thymus T
thyroid stimulating hormone TSH
thyroid stimulating hormone of the prepituitary TSP
thyrotropic hormone TTH
thyrotropin TSH
thyrotropin-releasing factor TRF
thyrotropin-releasing hormone TRH
thyroxine T_4
thyroxine binding globulin *biochemistry* TBG
thyroxine-binding prealbumin *medicine* TBPA
Tibet Tib.
Tibetan Tib.
ticket tkt.
tidal zone TZ
tide T
tied T
tierce tc *or* tc.
tight end *football* TE
Tigrean People's Liberation Front TPLF
till forbidden *advertising* tf. *or* t.f.
timber 1 tbr. *or* TBR 2 tmbr
time T *or* t
time and materials *commerce* T&M *or* t&m
time assignment speech interpolation TASI (regulating telephone speech transmission)
time base TB (of a cathode-ray tube)
time base corrector *electronics* TBC
time between overhauls TBO
time check TC
time delay TD
time deposit *finance* TD *or* T/D
time division data link *electronics* TDDL
time division multiplex access *computers* TDMA
time division multiplexing *computers* TDM
time domain reflectometer *or* **reflectometry** TDR
time handed in THI *or* t.h.i.
time limit TL
time loan *finance* TL *or* T/L
time modulation t.m.
time of arrival TOA
time of day TOD
time of delivery TOD
time of flight *aeronautics, physics* TOF
time of origin t.o.o. *or* TOO
time of receipt *or* **reception** t.o.r. *or* TOR
time of retrofire TR
time opening TO
time over target *military* TOT
Time Projection Chamber *physics* TPC
time reference scanning beam TRSB
time series analysis TSA
time sharing 1 TS *or* T-S 2 ts *or* t-s
Time Sharing System *computers* TSS
time zone TZ *or* T.Z.
time-lapse photography TLP
Time-shared Interactive Computer-controlled Information Television TICCIT
time-sharing option *computers* TSO
time-varying gain TVG
time-weighted average TWA
timed wire service TWS

timekeeper tmkpr.
timer tmr
times X *or* x
times at bat *baseball* TB *or* tb
Times Literary Supplement TLS *or* T.L.S.
timing terminal unit TTU
Timon of Athens Tim.
Timothy Tim. (books of the New Testament)
timpani *music* timp.
tin Sn
Tin Plate Gauge TPG
tincture 1 tinct. *or* tinc. 2 tr *or* tr.
tincture of opium *pharmaceutics* TO *or* t.o.
tip of the tongue *psychology* TOT (of recall)
Tipperary County, Ireland Tip.
tires, batteries, and accessories TBA (in automobile trade)
Tiros Operational Satellite System TOSS
tissue tis.
tissue coding factor *biology* TCF
tissue glucose threshold TGT
tissue plasminogen activator TPA *or* t-PA
titanium Ti
title 1 t 2 tit.
title page t.p. *or* T.P.
title page mutilated TPM *or* t.p.m.
title page wanting TPW *or* t.p.w.
titular tit.
Titus Tit. (in New Testament)
Titus Andronicus 1 Tit. 2 Tit.A.
to be added 1 addend 2 *medicine* **a** ad. **b** add.
to be announced TBA *or* T.B.A.
to be assigned TBA
to be determined TBD
to be discontinued TBD
to be edited TBE
to be expanded TBE
to be used 1 *medicine* adhib. 2 *pharmaceutics* **a** usurp. **b** utend.
to infinity ad inf. *or* ad infin.
to *or* **at the beginning** ad init.
to *or* **at the place** ad loc.
to take leave TTL *or* t.t.l.
to the end 1 ad fin. 2 fin.
to the greater glory of God A.M.D.G.
to the man ad hom.
to whom it may concern TWIMC
tobacco tob.
Tobacco Industry Research Committee TIRC
tobacco mosaic virus TMV
tobacco necrosis virus TNV
Tobacco Research Council TRC
tobacconist tob. *or* Tob.
Tobit Tob.
Tocharian Toch.
together tog. *or* togr.
toggle 1 tgl. *or* TGL 2 tog.
toilet paper t.p. *or* tp
Token and Medal Society TAMS
Tokyo Tok
Tokyo Stock Exchange TSE
tolerance *engineering, physics* tol.
tolylene diisocyanate TDI
tomato tom. *or* tom
tomorrow morning *pharmaceutics* cm *or* c.m.
tomorrow morning, to be taken *pharmaceutics* c.m.s.

tomorrow night *pharmaceutics* c.n.
ton 1 T 2 t *or* t. 3 tn.
ton coal equivalent TCE
ton oil equivalent TOE
tone modulation TM
tongue and groove 1 T&G *or* t.&g. 2 TG *or* T/G
tongued, grooved, and beaded TGB *or* t.g.b.
tonnage 1 tnge 2 tonn.
tons per day 1 TD *or* T/D 2 tpd *or* TPD
tons per hour tph *or* TPH
tons per inch TPI
tons per man-hour TMH *or* t/mh
tons per minute TPM *or* tpm
tons per square inch TSI *or* t.s.i.
tons registered TR *or* t.r.
tonsillectomy and adenoidectomy *medicine* T&A *or* T and A
tonsils and adenoids T&A *or* T and A
tool steel TS
tooled tld
tooth T
top t
top and bottom t&b
top dead center *mechanics* t.d.c. *or* TDC
top edges gilt *bookbinding* TEG *or* t.e.g.
Top European Advertising Media TEAM
top secret *military* TS
top water level TWL
top, bottom, and sides TB&S (of lumber)
topographer topog.
topographic *or* **topographical** topo.
topographical topog.
topographical engineer TE *or* T.E.
topography 1 topo. 2 topog.
topology top *or* topol.
torch and drill resisting TDR *or* T.D.R.
tornado 1 TDO 2 torn.
Toronto 1 Tor. 2 Tto
Toronto Stock Exchange TSE
Toronto Transit Commission TTC
torpedo torp.
torque 1 T 2 tor
torque differential receiver *electronics* TDR
torque oil pressure TOP
torque transmitter TX
Torrid Zone Tor.
torsion constant *physics* k
total 1 T 2 tot.
total cholesterol *medicine* TC
total cost TC
total depth TD (of an oil field)
total digestible nutrients T.D.N. *or* t.d.n.
Total Disability Benefit TDB
total dynamic head *mechanics* TDH
total energy U
total fatty acids TFA
total governmental expenditures TGE
total harmonic distortion THD
total iron-binding capacity TIBC
total load TL
total loss *insurance* TL
total loss only *insurance* TLO *or* t.l.o.
total lung capacity TLC
total lymphatic irradiation *medicine* TLI
total material assets TMA
total nucleic acid content TNA
total obligational authority TOA

Total Operations Processing System *British railroading* TOPS
total organic carbon TOC
total oxygen demand TOD
Total Ozone Mapping Spectrometer TOMS
total parenteral nutrition TPN
total points TP
Total Primary Energy Requirements TPER
total protein TP
total pulmonary resistance *medicine* TPR
total quality control T.Q.C. *or* TQC
total renal blood flow *medicine* TRBF
total response index TRI
total running time TRT
total survey area *marketing* TSA
total weight loss TWL
totally integrated environment *engineering* T.I.E.
Toucan Tuc (constellation)
touchdown *football* TD
touchdown zone *aeronautics* TDZ
tough rubber sheathing TRS (of electric cable insulation)
Toulon, France Tou.
Touring Club of France TCF *or* T.C.F.
Touring Club of Italy TCI
tourism tour.
tourist tour.
Tourist Trophy TT
tournament Tourn.
tower twr. *or* Twr.
town tn.
town clerk TC
township 1 T *or* T. 2 Tp. *or* tp. 3 twp. *or* Twp. (*GPO:* T. *or* Tps.; *CSM:* tp.; *OUP:* t.)
toxemia tox.
toxic tox.
toxic shock syndrome *medicine* TSS
toxic unit TU
toxicological toxicol.
toxicologist toxicol.
toxicology 1 tox. 2 toxicol.
Toxicology Line TOXLINE (service of National Library of Medicine)
toxin antitoxin 1 TA *or* T-A 2 TAT
toxoid-antitoxin floccules *medicine* TAF
Toy Manufacturers Association TMA
trace 1 tr 2 *chemistry* T *or* T. 3 *meteorology* T *or* T.
traces trs.
tracheal trach.
tracheotomy trach.
trachoma inclusion conjunctivitis TRIC
track 1 tk. 2 tr *or* tr. 3 trk.
track via missile TVM
tracked air-cushion vehicle TACV
Tracking and Data Relay Satellite TDRS
Tracking and Data Relay Satellite System TDRSS
tracking and impact prediction TIP
tracking while scanning TWS
tracks per inch *computers* TPI *or* tpi
tractor trac.
trade *or* **trading** Trd *or* Trd.
Trade and Development Program TDP
trade electronic data interchange system TEDIS
Trade International TI
trade name TN

Trade Union TU *or* T.U.
Trade Union Advisory Committee TUAC
Trade Union Council of South Africa TUCSA
Trade Union Internationals TUI
trademark 1 TM 2 Wz.
Trademark Trial and Appeal Board TTAB
Traders' Road Transport Association TRTA
Trades and Labor Congress TLC
Trades and Labour Council TLC
Trades Union Congress *British* TUC *or* T.U.C.
tradition trad.
traditional trad.
traffic 1 tfc. *or* TFC 2 traf.
Traffic Collision Avoidance System TCAS (for aircraft)
Traffic Control and Landing System *aeronautics* TRACALS
traffic control system TCS
Traffic Director TD *or* T.D.
traffic guidance loran *aeronautics* TG loran
traffic unit *communications* TU
tragedy trag.
tragic trag.
trailer 1 tlr. 2 trlr
trailer-on-flatcar TOFC
trailing edge TE
train 1 tn. 2 tr *or* tr.
trainer tnr.
training 1 tng. 2 train. *or* Train. 3 trg. *or* Trg 4 trng
training and education T&E
training film TF
training manual TM
training regulation TR
training within industry *British* T.W.I.
trainmaster TM
Trans-Alaska Pipeline TAP
Trans-Alaska Pipeline System TAPS
Trans-Alpine Pipeline *Italian* TAL
Trans-Arabian Pipeline Tapline
Trans-Canada Telephone System TCTS
Trans-Europe Express TEE
Trans-Siberian Railroad TSR
transaction 1 tr (of money) 2 trans.
transaction processing *computers* TP
transactional analysis TA
transactions 1 Tr. (proceedings, as of a society) 2 trans. (proceedings, as of a society) 3 trs.
transactivation and transcription *genetics* TAT
transatlantic cable to Britain from Canada CANTAT
transatlantic telephone TAT
transatmospheric vehicle TAV
Transcendental Meditation TM
transcribed by transcr.
transcription transcr.
transcription factor *biochemistry* TF
transcutaneous electrical nerve stimulation *or* **stimulator** TENS
transfer 1 tfr. 2 tr *or* tr. 3 trans. 4 transf. 5 trf. 6 TRN 7 trs. *or* trs. 8 tsfr *or* Tsfr. 9 xfer *or* XFER
transfer factor *biochemistry* TF
transfer function analyzer *aeronautics* TFA
transfer on less than zero *electronics* TLZ
transfer on no overflow *electronics* TNF

transfer on non-zero *computers* TNZ
transfer RNA tRNA
transferals trs. *or* trs.
transferred 1 trans. 2 transf. *or* transfd 3 trsd.
transferred electron amplifier TEA
transfers trs. *or* trs.
transformation induced plasticity TRIP
transformational grammar TG
transformer 1 T 2 TR 3 trans. 4 transf. 5 xfmr *or* Xformer
transforming growth factors TGF
transient ischemic attack TIA
transient lunar phenomena *astrophysics* TLP
transistor 1 tr 2 trans. 3 X 4 xstr
transistor transistor logic *computers* TTL
transistors trs.
transit trans.
Transit Authority TA
transit time modulation *electronics* TTM
transit without visa TWOV
transition t
transitional antarctic coastal air mass *meteorology* nA
transitive *grammar* 1 t *or* t. 2 tr *or* tr. 3 trans. (*MLA:* trans. *or* tr.; *OUP:* trans. *or* transit.)
transitive verb vt *or* v.t. (*MLA, OUP:* v.t.)
translated 1 tr *or* tr. 2 trans. 3 transl. (*MLA:* trans. *or* tr.; *OUP:* tr.)
translation 1 T *or* T. 2 tr *or* tr. 3 Tr. 4 trans. 5 transl. *or* Transl. (*MLA:* trans. *or* tr.; *OUP:* tr.)
translational inhibitory protein TIP
translator 1 Tltr. 2 tr *or* tr. 3 Tr. 4 trans. 5 transl. *or* Transl. (*MLA:* trans. *or* tr.; *OUP:* tr.)
transliteration translit.
translunar injection TLI
TransManche Link TML
transmissible gastroenteritis *medicine* TGE
transmission XMSN *or* Xmsn
transmission control protocol *computers* TCP
transmission electron microscope TEM
transmission level TL
transmission line TL
transmit 1 XMIT *or* Xmit 2 *computers* TRAN
transmit data register TDR
transmit time TT
transmit-receive *radio* 1 TR 2 T/R *or* T-R
transmittance T
transmitter 1 X 2 XMTR *or* Xmtr 3 TX *or* Tx
transmitter distributor *computers* TD
transmitter start code *computers* TSC
transmitter-receiver *radio* 1 TR 2 T/R *or* T-R
transonic wind tunnel TWT
transparent 1 trans. 2 transp.
transpolyisoprene TPI
transport 1 tpt. *or* Tpt. 2 tr 3 trans. 4 trsp.
Transport and Communications Commission TCC (of the UN)
Transport and General Workers' Union *British* TGWU *or* T.G.W.U.
transport number *chemistry* T
transport number of an ion n
Transport Officer TO *or* T.O.
Transport Organization of Ireland CIE
Transport Workers' Union TWU

Transport Workers' Union of America *or* of Australia TWUA
transportation 1 trans. 2 transp. 3 T
Transportation Command TC (of U.S. Department of Defense)
Transportation Communications International Union TCIU
Transportation Safety Institute TSI
transpose 1 trans. 2 trs. 3 *printing* tr *or* tr. (*CSM:* trs.; *OUP:* trs)
transposed trsd.
transposition trans.
transurethral resection *medicine* TUR
transurethral resection of the prostate *medicine* TURP
Transvaal Tvl.
transverse trans.
transverse electric TE
transverse electromagnetic TEM
transverse magnetic *electronics* TM
transverse section TS *or* T.S.
transversely excited atmospheric TEA
transvestite TV
travel 1 tr 2 trav *or* trav. 3 TVL *or* tvl.
travel allowance TA
travel and entertainment T&E (in figuring taxable business expenditures)
Travel Document and Issuance System TDIS (of U.S. Department of State)
travel group charter TGC
travel orders TO
traveler trav *or* trav.
Traveling Post Office TPO
Traveling Stock Reserve TSR *or* T.S.R.
traveling wave *electronics* TW
traveling-wave tube *electronics* TWT *or* twt
tray tr *or* tr.
tread tr
Treasurer 1 Tr. 2 Treas. *or* treas.
Treasury 1 T 2 Treas. *or* treas.
Treasury Bill *finance* TB
Treasury Decision TD *or* T.D. (with number) (*GPO:* T.D.)
Treasury Department TD *or* T.D.
Treasury Financial Communication System TFCS
Treasury Fiscal Requirements Manual TFRM
Treasury Investment Growth Receipts TIGR
treatment 1 trmt. 2 *medicine* TRT *or* trt
treble *music* tr
tremolo *music* trem.
treponema pallidum complement fixation TPCF
treponema pallidum hemaglutination assay TPHA
treponema pallidum immobilization test TPI
trial and error 1 T&E *or* t&e 2 *psychology* TE
trial balance *bookkeeping* 1 TB 2 tb
triaminotrinitrobenzene TATB
triangle trg.
Triangle Below Canal TriBeCa
Triangle, the Tri
tribal trib.
tribromosalicylanilide TBS
tribunal trib.
Tribune Trib
tributary trib.
tributyl phosphate TBP

tricarboxylic acid TCA
trichlorethylene TCE
trichloroacetic acid TCA
trichloroethylene trik
trichlorophenol TCP
trichlorophenoxy-acetic acid 2,4,5,-T
tricresyl phosphate TCP
tricyclic antidepressant TCA
triethyl phosphate TEP
triethylamine TRIS
triethylene glycol TEG
triethylene melamine TEM
triethylene phosphoramide TEPA *or* tepa
trifluoroacetylprolyl chloride TFAP
trigger price mechanism *commerce* TPM
triglyceride TG
trigonometric *or* trigonometrical *trig. or trigon.*
trigonometry trig. *or* trigon.
trihalomethane THM
triiodothyronine T$_3$
trill *music* tr *or* tr.
trillion cubic feet tcf
trimester trim.
trimethylamine TMA
trimethylethylenediamine TMEDA
Trinidad 1 Trd 2 Trin.
Trinidad and Tobago 1 TD 2 TT
trinitrotoluene TNT
trinitroxylene TNX
Trinity Trin.
Trinity House TH *or* T.H.
triode *electronics* 1 t 2 tri.
triosephosphate isomerase TPI
triphenyl tetrazolium chloride TTC
triphosphopyridine nucleotide TPN *or* TPNH
triple trip.
triple bond *chemistry* t-
triple strength XXX
Triple-capable Tricap (mechanized division of the U.S. Army)
triplicate trip. *or* tripl.
trisaminomethane TRIS
trisodium phosphate TSP
tritium 1 H^3 2 T
triton *chemistry* t
triturate *music, pharmaceutics* trit.
trivalent oral polio vaccine TOPV
Troilus and Cressida 1 Tr.&Cr. 2 Tro.
trombone 1 trbn. 2 trom.
Troop 1 Tr. 2 trp. *or military* TRP 3 Tp. *or* tp.
Troop Carrier Command TCC
trooper Tpr. *or* tpr.
tropic trop. *or* Trop.
tropical 1 T 2 trop.
tropical continental air mass cT
tropical continental cold air mass cTk
tropical continental warm air mass cTw
tropical environment data TREND
Tropical Fresh Water Load Line TF
Tropical Load Line T
Tropical maritime cold air mass *meteorology* mTk
Tropical maritime warm air mass *meteorology* mTw
tropical medicine TM
Tropical Products Institute TPI
tropics trop.

troy weight t *or* t.
truck 1 tk. 2 trk. *or* TRK
trucker trk. *or* TRK
truckload TL
true T
true air speed TAS
true altitude TA *or* ta
true azimuth Zn
true bearing *navigation* TB
true boiling point TBP
true course TC
true mean t.m.
true mean value *statistics* TMV
true north TN *or* T.N.
true position *navigation* TP
true, false TF *or* T-F *or* t/f
truly 1 try. 2 Ty. *or* ty. (as a close in correspondence)
trumpet 1 tpt. 2 tr *or* tr. 3 *French* tromp.
trunk trk.
truss 1 tr 2 *engineering* T
Trust Tr.
trust receipt *finance* TR *or* T/R *or* T.R.
Trust Territory of the Pacific Islands T.T.P.I.
Trustee 1 Tr. 2 Tree.
Trustee Savings Bank *British* TSB
Trusteeship Council TC (of the UN)
tryptophan 1 TRP *or* Trp. 2 try. *or* Try. *or* tryp. *or* Tryp.
tub-sized 1 ts 2 TS *or* T.S. (of paper)
tube T
tube-launched, optically-tracked, wire-guided missile TOW
tubercle bacillus 1 Tb 2 tb 3 TB *or* T.B.
tuberculin tested TT
tuberculin unit *medicine* TU *or* T.U.
tuberculosis 1 TB *or* T.B. 2 Tb *or* Tb. 3 tb *or* tb. (*GPO, OUP:* TB)
Tudor Tu
Tuesday 1 T *or* T. 2 Tu *or* Tu. 3 Tue. *or* Tues.
Tuesday, Thursday, Saturday TTS
tug of war TOW *or* t.o.w.
Tugrik Tug
tumor inducing principle TIP
tumor inhibitory principle TIP
tumor necrosis factor TNF
tumor specific antigen TSA
tumor specific transplantation antigen TSTA
tumor-associated antigens *medicine* TAA
tumor-infiltrating lymphocyte TIL
tumors, nodules, metastases TNM *or* T.N.M.
tuned grid, tuned plate *electronics* TGTP
tuned plated, tuned grid *electronics* TPTG
tuned radio frequency TRF *or* trf *or* t.r.f. *or* t-r-f
tungsten 1 tung 2 W
tungsten inert-gas TIG
Tunisia Tun.
Tunnel Tun.
tunnel boring machine TBM
tunnel diode *electronics* TD
tunnel diode transistor logic *computers* TDTL
turbidity reducing unit *medicine* TRU
turbine TURB
turbine engine TE
turbine gas temperature TGT
turbine steamship TSS *or* T.S.S.
turbojet propulsion TJP

turbomotor train TMT
Turkey 1 T 2 Turk.
Turkish 1 T 2 Turk.
Turkish lira TL
Turkish Republic of North Cyprus TRNC
turn over TO *or* t.o. *or* t/o
turn over swiftly *music* VS *or* V.S.
turn page PTO
turned-down edge TDE (of a telescope)
Turner Broadcasting System TBS
Turner Network Television TNT
turning point *electronics, surveying* TP
turnip yellow mosaic virus TYMV
turnover TO *or* T/O (amount of change or business)
turnpike *or* Turnpike 1 Tnpk. 2 Tpk. *or* Tpke. (in general use) *or* TPKE (in postal address)
turns per inch TPI *or* t.p.i. (esp. of yarn)
turns per minute TPM
turpentine turp. *or* turps
tuxedo tux

Twaddell (hydrometer) 1 TW 2 Twad.
Twelfth Night 1 TN 2 Twel.N.
twenty twy
twice a day 1 *medicine* b.d. *or* b.d.s. 2 *pharmaceutics* b.i.d.
twice a night *pharmaceutics* b.i.n.
twice a week TAW *or* t.a.w.
twilight twi.
twin engine *aeronautics* TE *or* t-e
twin lens reflex TLR
twin screw steamship TSS *or* T.S.S.
twist t (in knitting)
Twist Drill Gauge TDG
two degrees of freedom TDF (of a gyroscope)
Two Gentlemen of Verona, The 1 TGV 2 Two Gent.
two hundred CC
Two Noble Kinsmen, The TNK
two thousand MM
two-year-old tyo *or* t.y.o. (in horse racing)

type Ty. *or* ty.
type genus tg *or* t.g.
typed letter signed T.L.S. *or* tls (*MLA:* tls)
typescript TS (*MLA:* ts.; *OUP:* TS)
typewriter 1 typ. 2 typw. 3 *computers* TW *or* Tw
typhoid (fevers A and B) TAB
typhoon typh.
typical typ.
typist typ.
typographer 1 typ. *or* Typ. 2 typo. *or* typog.
typographical error typo. *or* typo
typographical *or* typographic 1 typ. *or* Typ. 2 typo. *or* typog.
typography 1 typ. *or* Typ. 2 typo. *or* typog.
Tyrolean Tyr. *or* Tyrol.
Tyrone County, Ireland Tyr.
tyrosine Tyr. *or* tyr.
tyrosine aminotransferase TAT

Uganda *or* Ugandan 1 U 2 Ug. *or* Ugan.
Uganda People's Congress UPC (political party)
Uganda shilling USh
ugly *or* threatening appearance of the sky u
Ugric Ug.
Ukraine Ukr.
Ukrainian Ukr.
ulcerative dermal necrosis UDN
Ulster Defence Association UDA
Ulster Defence Force UDF
Ulster Defence Regiment UDR
Ulster Freedom Fighters UFF
Ulster King at Arms U.K.A.
Ulster Unionist U.U.
Ulster Volunteer Force UVF
ultimate ult.
ultimate operational capability UOC
ultimate *or* perfect state n.p.u.
ultimate oxygen demand UOD
ultimate range ballistic missile URBM
ultimate tensile strength UTS
ultimately ult.
ultimo (in the past month) ult. *or* ulto.
ultra U
ultra-large crude carrier ULCC
Ultra-Large-Scale Integration *computers* ULSI
ultra-low volume ULV *or* ulv
ultrahigh UH *or* uh
ultrahigh frequency UHF *or* uhf (*GPO, NYT, OUP:* UHF)
ultrahigh frequency Doppler Udop
ultrahigh temperature UHT
ultrahigh vacuum 1 UHV 2 UV *or* U.V.
ultrahigh voltage UHV

ultralow frequency ULF *or* ulf
ultramicrofiche UMF
ultrashort wave 1 USW 2 usw
ultrasonic computerized tomography UCT
ultrasonic light modulator ULM
ultrasonic waves 1 USW 2 usw
ultrasound US
ultraviolet 1 UV 2 *British* u.v. (*OUP:* UV)
ultraviolet astronomical satellite UVAS
ultraviolet blue visual *astronomy* UBV
ultraviolet laser UVASER
ultraviolet light UVL
ultraviolet photoemission spectroscopy UPS
ultraviolet radiation UVR
ultraviolet spectrometer UVS
umber umb.
umbilical umb. *or* umbl.
Umbrian Umb *or* Umbr.
umpire ump
unabridged Unab. *or* Unabr.
unaccompanied unacc.
unanimous unan.
unassigned unasgd.
unattached unatt.
unattributed unattrib.
unauthorized unauthd.
unauthorized absence UA
unbound unb. *or* unbd. (of a book)
uncertain 1 unc. 2 uncert.
uncirculated unc. *or* Unc. (of coins)
unclassified 1 U 2 unclas. *or* unclass.
uncle 1 U *or* U. 2 unc. *or* Unc.
uncommitted logic array *computers* ULA
unconditional uncond.
unconditional selection US
unconditioned uncond.
unconditioned response *psychology* 1 UCR 2 UR
unconditioned stimulus *psychology* 1 UCS 2 US
unconscious UCS *or* ucs
uncontrolled variable *psychology* UCV
uncorrected uncor. *or* uncorr.

undated *Latin* s.a.
under U
under a poison label *pharmaceutics* SSV *or* s.s.v.
under consideration *law* s.j.
under construction UC
Under Secretary US *or* U.S.
Under Secretary of State USS *or* U.S.S.
under separate cover USC *or* usc
under the word *or* heading s.v.
under the year *Latin* s.a.
under will U/W
undercharge u/c
underdeck tonnage UDT *or* u.d.t.
underdeveloped country *or* countries UDC
underground UG *or* ug
underproof 1 UP (in distilling) 2 up. *or* u.p. (in distilling)
undersea technology UST
undersigned undsgd.
underwater U/W *or* u/w *or* UW
underwater demolition team UDT
underwater long-range missile system ULMS
Underwater Weapons and Countermeasures Establishment UWCE
underwater-to-air missile UAM
underwater-to-air-to-underwater missile UAUM
underwater-to-surface missile USM
underwater-to-underwater missile UUM
underway replenishment UNREP
underwriter U/W *or* UW *or* u/w
Underwriters' Laboratories UL *or* U.L.
Underwriting Account *insurance* UA *or* U/A
undetermined UTD
undignified infra dig *or* infra. dig.
unducted fan engine UDF
unemployment compensation UC
unemployment insurance UI
Unemployment Insurance Commission *Canadian* UIC
Unemployment Insurance Service UIS
unesterified fatty acid UFA

unexplained unexpl.
unexplained atmospheric phenomenon UAP
unexploded 1 unexpl. **2** UX
unexplored unexpl.
Ungava district, Canada Ung.
Unicorn Mon (constellation)
unidentified flying object UFO *or* U.F.O. (*NYT:* U.F.O.; *OUP:* UFO)
unidentified growth factor UGF
unified un. (of bonds)
unified atomic mass unit u
Unified School District USD
Unified *or* **Union Free School District** UFSD
uniform 1 U **2** unif. *or* Unif.
uniform chromaticity scale UCS
Uniform Code of Military Justice UCMJ
Uniform Commercial Code UCC
Uniform Controlled Substances Act UCSA
Uniform Crime Report UCR
uniform freight classification UFC
uniform grain storage UGS
Uniform Labor Agreement ULA
Uniform Laws Annotated ULA *or* U.L.A.
Uniform Partnership Act UPA
Uniform Premarital Agreement Act UPAA
uniform regulations UR
uniform system US
Uniformed Firefighter's Association UFA *or* U.F.A.
uninterruptible power supply *computers* UPS
Union U *or* U.
union un. *or* Un.
Union for French Democracy UDF
Union for the New Republic (of France) UNR
Union for the Protection of New Varieties of Plants UPOV
Union Jack UJ
Union of American Biological Societies UABS
Union of American Hebrew Congregations U.A.H.C.
Union of Burma U.B.
Union of Concerned Scientists UCS
Union of Construction, Allied Trades and Technicians *British* UCATT
Union of Democratic Forces UDF (of Bulgaria)
Union of European Football Association UEFA *or* U.E.F.A.
Union of International Associations 1 UIA **2** *French* U.A.I.
Union of International Engineering Organizations UIEO
Union of International Fairs *French* UFI *or* U.F.I.
Union of International Motorboating UIM
Union of Shop, Distributive, and Allied Workers USDAW
Union of Soviet Socialist Republics CCCP
Union of the Industries of the European Community UNICE
Union Territory UT
unique radiolytic product URP
unison *music* Unis.
unit 1 U *or* U. **2** u *or* u.
unit automatic exchange UAX
unit construction index UCI
Unit Investment Trust UIT

unit junction transistor *electronics* UJT
unit logic device ULD
unit of acceleration (of gravity) **1** Gal **2** gal. (*OUP:* Gal)
unit of account UA
unit of radiation 1 RAD **2** rad
Unit Separator *computers* US
unit under test UUT
Unitarian Unit.
Unitarian Universalist Association UUA
United 1 U *or* U. **2** Utd *or* Utd.
united un. *or* Un.
United (Arab Emirates) Dirham U.D. *or* UD
United Arab Emirates UAE
United Association of Journeymen and Apprentices of the Plumbing and Pipe Fitting Industry of the U.S. and Canada UAJAPPFI
United Australian Party UAP
United Automobile Workers UAW *or* U.A.W. (*NYT:* U.A.W.)
United Bible Societies U.B.S.
United Brethren U.B.
United Brotherhood of Carpenters and Joiners UBCJ *or* UBC&J
United Church UC *or* U.C.
United Church of Christ UCC
United Confederation of Workers C.U.T.
United Country Party UCP
United Daughters of the Confederacy UDC *or* U.D.C.
United Democratic Front UDF (of South Africa)
United Democratic Party UDP
United Electrical, Radio, and Machine Workers of America U.E. *or* UE
United Electrical, Radio, and Machine Workers Union UEW *or* U.E.W.
United Empire Loyalist U.E.L.
United Farm Workers of America UFW *or* UFWA
United Federation of Artists UFA
United Federation of College Teachers U.F.C.T.
United Federation of Teachers UFT *or* U.F.T.
United Food and Commercial Workers UFCW
United Free Church of Scotland UFC *or* U.F.C.
United Furniture Workers UFW
United Garment Workers of America UGWA
united government Unigov (of Indianapolis and Marion County)
United Jewish Appeal UJA *or* U.J.A.
United Kennel Club UKC *or* U.K.C.
United Kingdom UK *or* U.K.
United Kingdom Air Defence Ground Environment UKADGE
United Kingdom Alliance U.K.A.
United Kingdom Association of Professional Engineers UKAPE
United Kingdom Atomic Energy Authority UKAEA
United Kingdom Automation Council UKAC
United Kingdom Infrared Telescope UKIRT
United Lutheran Church in America ULCA
United Malaysian National Organization UMNO

United Methodist Church UMC *or* U.M.C.
United Methodist Free Churches UMFC *or* U.M.F.C.
United Mine Workers of America UMW *or* UMWA
United National Independence Party UNIP (of Zambia)
United National Party U.N.P. (of Sri Lanka)
United Nations 1 UN *or* U.N. **2** *French* NU **3** *French, Spanish* ONU *or* O.N.U. (*GPO, NYT:* U.N.; *OUP:* UN)
United Nations Association UNA *or* U.N.A.
United Nations Border Relief Operation UNBRO
United Nations Capital Development Fund UNCDF
United Nations Cartographic Commission UNCC
United Nations Center for Human Settlements UNCHS
United Nations Children's Fund UNICEF
United Nations Command UNC
United Nations Commission on International Trade Law UNCITRAL
United Nations Committee on Peaceful Uses of Outer Space UNCOPUOS
United Nations Conference on Environment and Development UNCED
United Nations Conference on International Organization UNCIO
United Nations Conference on Law of the Sea UNCLOS
United Nations Conference on Science and Technology UNCSAT
United Nations Conference on Science and Technology for Development UNCSTD
United Nations Conference on the Applications of Science and Technology UNCAST
United Nations Conference on Trade and Development UNCTAD
United Nations Development Fund for Women UNIFEM
United Nations Development Program UNDP
United Nations Disarmament Commission UNDC
United Nations Disaster Relief Organization UNDRO
United Nations Disengagement Observer Force UNDOF
United Nations Economic Commission for Asia UNECA
United Nations Economic Commission for Latin America UNECLA
United Nations Economic Development Administration UNEDA
United Nations Education Conference UNEC
United Nations Educational, Scientific, and Cultural Organization UNESCO *or* Unesco (*GPO, OUP:* Unesco; *NYT:* UNESCO)
United Nations Emergency Force UNEF
United Nations Emergency Technical Aid Service UNETAS
United Nations Environment Program UNEP
United Nations Film Board UNFB
United Nations Food and Agricultural Organization UNFAO
United Nations Food Conference UNFC

United Nations Forces *French* FNU

United Nations Fund for Drug Abuse Control UNFDAC

United Nations Fund for Population Activities UNFPA

United Nations General Assembly UNGA

United Nations Headquarters UNHQ

United Nations High Commissioner for Refugees UNHCR

United Nations Index UNDEX *or* Undex

United Nations Industrial Development Organization UNIDO

United Nations Information Center UNIC

United Nations Information Organization UNIO

United Nations Institute for Training and Research UNITAR

United Nations Intergovernmental System of Information in Science and Technology UNISIST *or* Unisist

United Nations Liaison Committee UNLC

United Nations Mediterranean Commission UNMC

United Nations Narcotics Commission NARCO

United Nations Organization 1 UNO *or* U.N.O. 2 *French, Spanish* ONU

United Nations Peace Observation Commission UNPOC

United Nations Postal Administration UNPA

United Nations Protection Force UNPROFOR

United Nations Refugee Emergency Fund UNREF

United Nations Relief and Rehabilitation Administration UNRRA

United Nations Relief and Works Agency UNRWA

United Nations Research Institute for Social Development UNRISD

United Nations Scientific Conference on the Conservation and Utilization of Resources UNSCCUR

United Nations Secretary General UNSG

United Nations Security Council UNSC

United Nations Service Medal UNSM *or* UNSvM

United Nations Space Registry UNSR

United Nations Special Committee on the Balkans UNSCOB

United Nations Special Fund UNSF

United Nations Standards Coordinating Committee UNSCC

United Nations Technical Assistance Administration 1 UNTAA 2 *French* AATNU

United Nations Technical Assistance Board UNTAB

United Nations Technical Assistance Mission UNTAM

United Nations Truce Supervision Organization UNTSO

United Nations Trust Territory UNTT *or* U.N.T.T.

United Nations Trusteeship Council UNTC

United Nations University UNU

United Nations Volunteers UNV

United Nations War Crimes Commission UNWC *or* U.N.W.C.

United Negro College Fund UNCF

United Paperworkers International Union UPIN

United Parcel Service UPS

United Political Organization National Front UPONF (in Yemen)

United Presbyterian Church UPC *or* U.P.C.

United Press International UPI

United Rubber Workers of America URW *or* URWA

United Service Institution USI *or* U.S.I.

United Service Organization USO (*NYT:* U.S.O.)

United Society for the Propagation of the Gospel U.S.P.G.

United Somali Conference USC

United Spanish War Veterans U.S.W.V.

United States 1 US *or* U.S. 2 USA *or* U.S.A. (*NYT:* U.S.; *OUP:* US)

United States Adopted Name USAN (for drug products)

United States Agency for Industrial Science and Technology AIST

United States Agency for International Development USAID

United States Air Force USAF

United States Air Force Academy USAFA

United States Air Force Reserve USAFR

United States Air Forces in Europe USAFE

United States Antarctic Research Program USARP

United States Armed Forces Institute USAFI

United States Army USA *or* U.S.A.

United States Army Combat Developments Command USACDC

United States Army Corps of Engineers USACE

United States Army Criminal Investigation Command USACIC

United States Army Forces Command USAFC

United States Army Health Services Command USAHSC

United States Army in Europe USAREUR

United States Army in the Pacific USARPAC

United States Army Information Radio Service AIRS

United States Army Intelligence and Security Command USAISC

United States Army Intelligence Corps USAIC

United States Army Materiel Command USAMC

United States Army Medical Research Institute of Infectious Diseases USAMRIID

United States Army Military District of Washington USAMDW

United States Army Reserve USAR

United States Army Training and Doctrine Command USATDC

United States Army Transport USAT

United States Army Weapons Command USAWC

United States Attorneys USA *or* U.S.A.

United States Auto Club USAC *or* U.S.A.C.

United States Board on Geographic Names USBGN *or* BGN

United States Border Patrol USBP

United States Bureau of Alcohol, Tobacco, and Firearms BATF *or* ATF

United States Bureau of Commercial Fisheries BCF

United States Bureau of Criminal Statistics BCS

United States Bureau of Employees' Compensation BEC

United States Bureau of International Commerce BIC

United States Bureau of Prisons USBP *or* U.S.B.P.

United States Bureau of the Census USBC

United States Business and Defense Services Administration BDSA

United States Chamber of Commerce USCC

United States Chess Federation USCF

United States Circuit Court 1 USCC *or* U.S.C.C. 2 CC *or* C.C.

United States Circuit Court of Appeals 1 USCCA *or* U.S.C.C.A. 2 CCA *or* C.C.A. (*GPO:* C.C.A.)

United States Civil Defense Council USCDC

United States Civil Service Commission USCSC *or* U.S.C.S.C.

United States Claims Court USCC *or* U.S.C.C.

United States Coast and Geodetic Survey 1 USC&GS 2 USCGS

United States Coast Guard USCG

United States Coast Guard Academy USCGA

United States Coast Guard Reserve USCGR

United States Coast Guard Women's Reserve SPAR

United States Code USC *or* U.S.C. (*GPO:* U.S.C.)

United States Code Annotated USCA *or* U.S.C.A. (*GPO:* U.S.C.A.)

United States Code Supplement U.S.C.Supp.

United States Combat and Development Command CDC

United States Commander in Chief in Europe USCINCEUR

United States Congress USC

United States Constitution *law* U.S. Const.

United States Court of Appeals USCA *or* U.S.C.A.

United States Court of Customs and Patent Appeals USCCPA *or* U.S.C.C.P.A.

United States Customs USC

United States Customs Service USCS *or* U.S.C.S.

United States Department of Agriculture USDA

United States Dispensatory USD *or* U.S.D.

United States District Court 1 U.S. Dist. Ct. 2 USDC

United States Employment Service USES

United States Equestrian Team U.S.E.T.

United States European Command EUCOM

United States Fencing Association USFA

United States Field Hockey Association USFHA

United States Figure Skating Association USFSA

United States Fire Administration USFA

United States Fish and Wildlife Service USFWS

United States Forces USF

United States Foreign Service USFS
United States Forest Service USFS
United States Geological Survey USGS
United States Global Change Research Program USGCRP
United States Golf Association USGA or U.S.G.A.
United States Government U.S.G. or USG
United States Government Life Insurance USGLI
United States Government Manual USGM
United States Government Printing Office USGPO or GPO
United States Highway US or U.S. (with number)
United States Housing Authority USHA
United States Immigration and Naturalization Service USINS or INS
United States Import Program USIP
United States Information Agency USIA (GPO: USIA; NYT: U.S.I.A.)
United States Information Service USIS (NYT: U.S.I.S.; OUP: USIS)
United States International Trade Commission USITC
United States Judo Federation USJF
United States Lawn Tennis Association USLTA or U.S.L.T.A.
United States Legislation U.S.L.
United States Marine Corps USMC
United States Marine Corps Reserve USMCR
United States Marines USM or U.S.M.
United States Maritime Administration USMA
United States Maritime Commission USMC
United States Maritime Service USMS
United States Marshal USM
United States Marshals Office USMO
United States Marshals Service USMS
United States Merchant Marine USMM
United States Merchant Marine Academy USMMA
United States Military Academy USMA
United States Mint USM or U.S.M.
United States National Archives USNA
United States National Central Bureau USNCB (of Interpol)
United States National Guard USNG
United States National Student Association USNSA
United States Naval Academy USNA
United States Naval Institute USNI
United States Naval Observatory USNO
United States Naval Oceanographic Office USNOO
United States Naval Reserve USNR
United States Navy USN or U.S.N. (GPO, OUP: USN)
United States Navy Hydrographic Office USNHO
United States Navy Papers NAVPERS
United States Navy Ship USNS
United States Nuclear Regulatory Commission USNRC
United States of America USA or U.S.A.
United States of America Standard Code for Information Interchange USASCII

United States of America Standards Institute USASI or U.S.A.S.I.
United States of Colombia USC or U.S.C.
United States of Indonesia USI
United States of Mexico Spanish EUM
United States Olympic Committee USOC
United States Operations Mission USOM
United States Parole Commission USPC
United States Patent USP or U.S. Pat.
United States Pharmacopoeia USP or U.S.P. or U.S. Pharm. (GPO: U.S.P.)
United States Post Office USPO
United States Postal Service USPS
United States Power Squadrons USPS
United States Public Health Service USPHS or U.S.P.H.S.
United States Railway Association USRA
United States Recommended Daily Allowance USRDA
United States Revised Statutes USRS
United States Secret Service USSS or U.S.S.S.
United States Senate USS or U.S.S. (GPO: U.S.S.)
United States Ship USS (GPO, NYT: U.S.S.)
United States Ski Association USSA
United States Soccer Federation USSF
United States Soil Conservation Service USSCS
United States standard USS (screw thread)
United States Standard Gauge 1 U.S.G. or USG 2 USSG (measure of steel)
United States Steamship 1 USS 2 USSS (GPO, NYT: U.S.S.)
United States Strike Command USSTRICOM
United States Supreme Court U.S.S.C. or U.S.S.Ct.
United States Supreme Court Reports 1 U.S.R. 2 US or U.S. (GPO: U.S.)
United States Tariff Commission USTC
United States Tax Court 1 USTC or U.S.T.C. 2 TC or T.C.
United States Tennis Association USTA
United States Track and Field Federation USTFF
United States Trade Representative USTR
United States Trademark Association 1 USTA 2 USTMA
United States Travel and Tourism Administration USTTA
United States Travel Service USTS
United States Trotting Association USTA
United States Virgin Islands USVI or U.S.V.I.
United States Volleyball Association USVA
United States West Indies USWI or U.S.W.I.
United Steelworkers of America 1 USW or U.S.W. 2 USWA or U.S.W.A.
United Textile Workers of America UTWA
United Transportation Union UTU
United Ulster Unionist Coalition UUUC
United Way of America UWA
United World Federalists UWF
universal 1 U 2 u or v. 3 univ.
Universal Alliance of Diamond Workers UADW
universal asynchronous receiver transmitter UART

Universal Bibliographic Control UBC
universal character set computers UCS
Universal Communications System UNICOM
Universal Computer Oriented Language UNCOL
Universal Cooperatives, Inc. UNICO
Universal Copyright Convention UCC
universal decimal classification bibliography UDC
Universal Engineer Tractor UET
Universal Esperanto Association U.E.A.
Universal Exhibition of Rome Italian E.U.R.
universal extra-fine u.e.f. (screw thread)
Universal Federation of Travel Agents' Associations. UFTAA or U.F.T.A.A.
universal logic module ULM
Universal Military Service UMS
Universal Military Training UMT
Universal Military Training Service or System UMTS
universal navigation buoy UNB
Universal Postal Union UPU or U.P.U.
Universal Product Code UPC
universal resource locator computers URL
Universal Serials Book Exchange USBE
universal synchronous and asynchronous receiver transmitter USART
universal synchronous receiver transmitter USRT
universal time astronomy 1 UT or U.T. 2 ut or u.t.
Universal Time Coordinated French UTC
Universal Time-sharing System UTS
universal transverse mercator UTM (map projection)
Universalist Univ.
universally univ.
Universities Athletic Union British UAU
Universities Central Council on Admissions UCCA
Universities Funding Council UFC
University 1 U or U. 2 Univ.
university 1 Un. 2 univ.
University Boat Race UBR
University College, London UCL
University Group Diabetes Program UGDP
university master British mag.
University Microfilms International UMI
University of California, Los Angeles UCLA
university press UP
unknown 1 unkn. 2 X or x 3 Latin ign. or Ign.
unknown quantity 1 X or x 2 y 3 z
unladen weight U/W or UW
unlawful entry law QCF
unless before 1 ni. pri. 2 law NP or N.P.
unless caused by insurance, commerce ucb
unless otherwise noted Latin n.a.n.
unlimited unl.
Unlisted Securities Market British USM
unmarked commerce a.u.n. or AUN
unmarried 1 um. 2 unm.
unnilhexium Unh (chemical element, 106)
unnilpentium Unp (chemical element 105)
unnilquadium Unq (chemical element 104)
unnilseptium Uns (chemical element 107)
unofficial Unof.
unopposed unop.

unpaged unp.
unpaid 1 unp. *or* unpd. **2** *commerce* upd
unperformed unperf. (of a musical composition)
unpublished unpub.
unrated U (of a motion picture)
unrestricted *British* U (of a motion picture)
unsatisfactory 1 un. **2** unsat.
unsatisfactory report UR
unsaturated unsat. *or* unsat
unsecured loan stock *finance* ULS
unserviceable US *or* U/S *or* u/s
unsigned unsgd.
unsolicited unsol (as of a manuscript)
unsymmetrical 1 uns. **2** unsym.
unsymmetrical dimethylhydrazine UDMH
until effective *medicine* ad effect.
untrained ut *or* ut. *or* u/t
unwatermarked unwmkd.
up *or* **upper right** UR (stage direction)
up-front controller UFC
uphold uphd
upholsterer uphol.
upholstery uphol.
Upper 1 U *or* U. **2** Upr. (in place names)
upper 1 u *or* u. **2** up.
upper airspace UAS *or* uas
upper and lower case u&lc *or* u&lc. (*CSM:* u&l)
upper atmospheric research UAR
upper dead center *engineering* UDC *or* u.d.c.
upper half UH
Upper House UH
upper ionized layer of the ionosphere F

upper left UL (stage direction)
upper left center ULC (stage direction)
upper limit UL *or* u.l.
Upper Peninsula, Michigan UP
upper quartile *statistics* UQ
upper respiratory disease URD
upper respiratory infection URI
upper respiratory tract URT
upper right center URC (stage direction)
upper sideband *electronics* USB
upper-case 1 u.c. *or* uc *or* uc. (*GPO:* uc.; *OUP:* u.c.) **2** u/c
uracil U
uranium U
uranium tetrafluoride UF
Uranus *astronomy* Uran
urban urb.
Urban Council *British* UC *or* U.C.
Urban Development Action Grant UDAG
urban district U.D. *or* UD
Urban District Council *British* UDC *or* U.D.C.
Urban League UL
Urban Mass Transportation Administration UMTA
Urban Renewal Administration URA
Urdu 1 Ur. **2** Urd.
urea-formaldehyde UF
urea-formaldehyde foam insulation UFFI
urgent 1 UGT **2** urg.
uridine Urd.
uridine diphosphate UDP
uridine diphosphate glucose UDPG
uridine monophosphate UMP
uridine triphosphate UTP

urinalysis UA
urinary Ur. *or* ur
urinary tract UT
urinary tract infection UTI
urine Ur. *or* ur
urogenital *medicine* UG
urogenital tract UGT
urological urol.
urologist urol.
urology urol.
Uruguay 1 Ur. **2** Uru.
Uruguayan 1 Ur. **2** Uru.
use and occupancy U&O *or* u. and o.
User Area *computers* UA
user identification *computers* userid
user test ut *or* u.t.
U.S. Patents Quarterly USPQ
usual usu.
usually usu.
Utah 1 U *or* U. **2** UT (Zip Code) **3** Ut. *or* Ut
uterine chorionic gonadotropin UCG
uteroplacental insufficiency *medicine* UPI
utility 1 U **2** ut *or* ut. **3** util.
utility dog U.D. *or* UD (degree of dog performance)
utility dog tracking UDT *or* U.D.T. (degree of dog performance)
Utility Workers Union of America UWUA
utilization management UM
utilization review *medicine* UR
utilized starch equivalent USE
Uttar Pradesh UP *or* U.P.
Uzbek Uz.
Uzbekistan Uz. *or* Uzbek

vacant vac
vacation vac *or* vac.
vaccination vacc.
vaccine vacc.
vaccinia immune globulin VIG
vacuum 1 v **2** vac *or* vac. **3** vcm
vacuum condensing point vcp
vacuum technology VT
vacuum tube VT
vacuum tube voltmeter VTVM
vacuum ultraviolet VUV
vagina vag.
vaginal contraceptive film VCF
vagrancy vag.
vagrant vag.
valence *chemistry* val.
valence bond *chemistry* VB
valence of an ion *physics* z
Valenciennes lace Val.
valentine val.
validate valid.
validation valid.

valine 1 Val. **2** val.
valley 1 V *or* V. **2** val. *or* Val. **3** Vly
Valparaiso, Chile Valpo
valuation 1 val. **2** valn.
valuation clause *insurance* VC
value val.
Value Engineer VE
Value Engineering VE
Value Engineers Association VEA
value for duty vfd
value increment taxes VIT
value-added network *computers* VAN
value-added reseller VAR
value-added tax 1 VAT **2** *Spanish* IVA **3** *French* TVA *or* T.V.A.
valued val.
valve 1 V **2** v *or* v. **3** val. **4** vlv.
valve box VB
valvular 1 val. **2** vlv.
valvular heart disease VDH *or* V.D.H.
vampire vamp.
Van Allen Belt *astronomy* VAB *or* VAb.
van der Waals constant *a*
Van't Hoff factor i
vanadium V
Vancouver Island VI *or* V.I.
Vancouver, Canada 1 Vanc. **2** Vcr
vanguard van *or* van.
vanilla van *or* van.
vanishing point v.p.

vapor 1 v **2** vap.
vapor density v.d.
vapor phase chromatograph VPC
vapor phase epitaxy VPE
vapor phase inhibitor VPI
vapor pressure 1 v.p. **2** VP
vapor pressure constant *physics* i
vapor-liquid-solid *crystallogenesis* VLS
vaporization vap. *or* vapor.
variable 1 V *or* v **2** var. *or* var **3** vrbl. **4** z **5** *physics, statistics, psychology* X *or* y
variable air volume VAV
variable capacitance diode VCD
variable capacitor VC
variable crystal filter *electronics* VCF
variable cycle engine VCE
variable density wind tunnel VDT
variable diameter rotor VDR
variable elevation beam VEB
variable factor programming *computers* VFP
variable frequency oscillator VFO *or* vfo
variable gain amplifier *electronics* VGA
variable information processing *computers* VIP
variable pitch VP *or* v-p
variable pressure VP
variable rate mortgage VRM
variable speed VS
variable speed constant frequency VSCF

variable star V
variable stimulus V
variable threshold logic *computers* VTL
variable time VT
variable transmission vt
variable-depth sonar VDS
variant var.
variant reading 1 v.r. **2** var. lect. **3** vl *or* v.l. **4** VR
variant readings *Latin* vv.ll.
variation 1 v **2** var. *or* Var.
variation per day VPD
variation per hour VPH
varicella zoster *medicine* VZ
varieties vars. (esp. of species)
variety var. (esp. of species)
variometer var.
various var. *or* var
various dates v.d. (*MLA:* not acceptable; *OUP:* v.d)
various years vy *or* v.y.
varnish varn.
vascular vas. *or* vasc.
vascular bundle VB *or* V.B.
vasectomy vas.
vasoactive intestinal polypeptide VIP
vasodepressor material *medicine* VDM
vasoexcitor material *medicine* VEM
Vatican Vat.
vaudeville vaud. *or* Vaud.
vector 1 vec. *or* vec **2** *mathematics, physics* V
vectorcardiogram VCG
Vedic Ved.
veering vrg.
vegetable 1 veggie **2** veg *or* veg.
Vegetable Growers Association of America V.G.A.A.
vegetarian 1 veg *or* veg. **2** vegan **3** veggie
vegetation veg *or* veg.
vegetation drought index VDI
vehicle veh.
Vehicle Assembly Building VAB (at Kennedy Space Center)
vehicle authorization list VAL
Vehicle Equipment Safety Commission VESC
vehicle identification number VIN
vehicles per day VPD
vehicles per hour VPH
vehicles per mile VPM
vehicular veh.
vein v *or* v.
veins *medicine* vv
vellum vel. *or* Vel.
velocity 1 k **2** vel. **3** *engineering* u **4** *physics, chemistry* V *or* v **5** *meteorology* v **6** *physics* w
velocity modulation *physics* VM
velvet vel.
vendor part number VPN *or* vpn
vendor's shipping documents *commerce* VSD
veneer ven.
Venerable Ven.
venereal ven.
venereal disease VD (*NYT:* V.D.; *OUP:* VD)
Venereal Disease Experimental Laboratory VDEL

Venereal Disease Research Laboratories VDRL (serological test)
Venetian Venet.
Venezuela 1 Ve. **2** Ven. **3** Venez.
Venezuelan 1 Ven. **2** Venez.
Venezuelan Communist Party *Spanish* PCV *or* P.C.V.
Venezuelan Confederation of Workers *Spanish* CTV
Venezuelan equine encephalitis VEE
Venice 1 Ven. **2** Vce
venom ven.
venomous ven.
vent v
vent pipe v.p.
ventilate vent.
ventilation vent.
ventilator vent.
ventral 1 v *or* v. **2** ven. **3** *medicine* vent.
ventricle 1 ven. **2** vent.
ventricular vent.
ventricular septal defect *medicine* VSD
Venus Ven.
Venus and Adonis Ven. *or* Ven. & Ad. (*MLA:* Ven.)
verb 1 V *or* v *or* v. **2** vb. (*MLA, OUP:* vb.)
verbal 1 v *or* v. **2** vb. (*MLA, OUP:* vb.) **3** vbl.
verbal adjective v.a.
verbal orders VO
verbs vv *or* vv.
Verdet constant *physics* V
verdict verdt
Vergil Verg. (Roman poet)
verification ver.
verification and validation *computers* v and v
verify 1 ver. **2** vfy
vermiculite verm. *or* verm
vermilion verm.
Vermont 1 Ver. **2** Verm. **3** VT (Zip Code) **4** Vt.
vernacular vern.
vernacular black English *linguistics* VBE
versatile automatic test equipment VATE
versatile base bus connector *electronics* VBC
versatile experimental reactor assembly VERA
verse 1 v *or* v. **2** ver. **3** vs *or* vs.
versed sine *mathematics* vers
verses 1 vss. **2** vv *or* vv. (*MLA:* vv. *or* vss.; *OUP:* vv.)
Versicle V̸
version 1 V *or* V. **2** Ver. **3** ver. **4** Vers.
versions vss. *or* VSS.
verso 1 V *or* v **2** V°
versus 1 v *or* v. **2** ver. **3** vs *or* vs. (*NYT, OUP:* v. *or* vs.; *MLA:* vs. *or* v.; *CSM:* vs.)
vertebra vert.
Vertebrata vert. *or* Vert.
vertebrate vert.
vertex 1 V **2** ver. **3** vx
vertical 1 V *or* V. **2** v *or* v. **3** vert.
vertical and short takeoff and landing VSTOL *or* V/STOL
vertical angle bench mark VABM
vertical axis wind turbine VAWT
vertical block lines VBL
vertical center line VCL

vertical center of gravity VCG
vertical field effect transistor *electronics* VFET
vertical file VF
Vertical Format Unit *computers* VFU
vertical grain v.g. *or* vg (of wood)
vertical integration building *engineering* VIB
vertical interval *cartography* VI
vertical interval reference *electronics* VIR
vertical interval test signals *electronics* VITS
vertical lift bridge VLB
vertical metal oxide semiconductor *electronics* VMOS
vertical photography VPH *or* v.ph.
vertical redundancy check *computers* VRC
vertical reference line VRL (on blueprints and other mechanical drawings)
vertical speed indicator VSI
vertical tabulation *computers* VT
vertical takeoff VTO
vertical takeoff and landing VTOL
vertical temperature profile radiometer VTPR
vertical tube evaporator VTE
vertical-cavity surface-emitting laser VCSEL
very 1 V *or* v **2** vy *or* vy. *or* Vy.
very fine VF
very good 1 v.g. *or* vg **2** VG *or* V.G.
very good condition VGC *or* v.g.c.
very hard (of lead pencil) **1** HH **2** HHH
very high frequency VHF *or* vhf (*GPO, OUP:* VHF)
very high operation VHO
very high output VHO
very high performance VHP
very high speed integrated circuit VHSIC
very high temperature VHT
very high-frequency omnidirectional radio range VOR
very high-frequency omnidirectional range tactical air navigation VORTAC
very high-frequency omnirange with distance measuring equipment *aeronautics* VOR/DME
very highly commended VHC
very important person VIP
very large array VLA
very large bulk carrier VLBC
very large crude carrier VLCC
very large telescope VLT
very large-scale integration *electronics* VLSI
very late activation antigens *biochemistry* VLA
very long baseline VLB
very long range VLR
very loud *music* ff. *or* ff
very low altitude VLA
very low frequency VLF *or* vlf
very low nitrogen VLN
very low-caloric diet VLCD
very low-density lipoprotein VLDL
very low-level waste VLLW
very old VO (of liquor)
very old pale VOP (of liquor)
very oldest procurable VOP (of liquor)
very rare rr *or* rr.
Very Reverend 1 Adm. Rev. **2** V.Rev.
very short range VSR

very short waves *electronics* VSW
very softly *music* 1 dolciss. 2 pp
very special quality V.S.Q. (of liquor)
very superior old VSO *or* V.S.O. (of liquor)
very superior old pale VSOP *or* V.S.O.P. (of liquor)
very sweetly *music* dolciss.
Very Worshipful *British* VW *or* V.W.
very, very old V.V.O. *or* VVO (of liquor)
very, very softly *music* ppp.
very, very superior V.V.S. *or* VVS (of liquor)
very, very superior old V.V.S.O. *or* VVSO (of liquor)
vesicle *botany* ves.
vesicular exanthema VE
vesicular stomatitis virus VSV
vessel ves.
vessel wall VW *or* V.W.
vestibule vest.
vestigial sideband *electronics* VSB
vestry ves. *or* Ves.
veteran 1 V 2 vet *or* Vet *or* vet. *or* Vet.
Veteran Motor Car Club of America VMCCA
Veterans Administration VA (*NYT:* V.A.)
Veterans Adminstration Hospital VAH
Veterans Affairs Offices VAO
Veterans Benefit Adminstration VBA
Veterans Court of Appeals VCA *or* V.C.A.
Veterans Group Life Insurance VGLI
Veterans Health Adminstration VHA
Veterans of Foreign Wars V.F.W. *or* VFW
Veterans' Adminstration Vet. Admin.
Veterans' Employment and Training Service VETS
veterinarian vet *or* Vet *or* vet. *or* Vet.
veterinary 1 V 2 vet *or* Vet *or* vet. *or* Vet. 3 veter.
Veterinary Admissions Test VAT
Veterinary Investigation Office *British* VIO
Veterinary Physician MV *or* M.V.
Veterinary Surgeon VS *or* V.S.
viaduct viad.
vibrate vib.
vibrating sample magnetometer VSM
vibration 1 vb. 2 vib.
vibration seconds vs *or* v.s.
vibration velocity per hour v/v/hr.
vibrational quantum number *physics* v
vibrations per minute VPM
vibrations per second VPS
vibrio V *or* V.
Vicar 1 Vic. 2 V *or* V.
Vicar Apostolic 1 VA *or* V.A. 2 Vic. Ap.
Vicar Forane VF *or* V.F.
Vicar General 1 Vic. Gen. 2 VG *or* V.G.
vicarage Vic.
vicarious trial and error *psychology* VTE
vice V *or* V-
Vice Admiral 1 V.Adm. *or military* VADM 2 VA
vice versa vv *or* v.v.
Vice-Chairman VC *or* V.C.
Vice-Chamberlain VC *or* V.C.
Vice-Chancellor VC *or* V.C.
Vice-Consul VC *or* V.C.
vice president 1 v.p. *or* vp 2 V.Pres. *or* v.pres.

Vice-President 1 Vice Pres. *or* Vice-Pres. 2 VP *or* V.P.
vicinal vic.
vicinity 1 vcnty 2 vic.
Vickers hardness number 1 VH 2 VHN
Vickers pyramid number VPN
Victoria 1 V *or* V. (Queen of England) 2 a Vic. b Vict. (Queen of England or state of Australia)
Victoria and Albert *British* V.&A. *or* V. and A. (museum)
Victoria Cross V.C. *or* VC
Victorian Vict.
victory 1 Vic. 2 vic. *or* vic 3 V
video 1 V 2 VID *or* Vid.
video disk recorder *or* recording VDR
video display metafile *computers* VDM
video display terminal *computers* VDT
video frequency 1 v.f. 2 VF
video graphics array *computers* VGA
video high density VHD
video home system VHS
video integrator and processor VIP
video jockey VJ *or* V.J. *or* v.j.
video layout terminal VLT
video matrix terminal *computers* VMT
video RAM *computers* VRAM
videocassette recorder VCR
videodisk VD
videotape VT
videotape recorder *or* recording VTR
Vienna Vna
Vienna Definition Language *computers* VDL
Vienna Development Method *computers* VDM
Vietnam VN
Vietnam Veterans of America VVA
village 1 vil. *or* Vill. 2 Vlg
vindicate vind
vindication vind
vinegar vin.
viniculture vini.
Vintage Sports Car Club VSCC *or* V.S.C.C.
vinyl chloride VC
vinyl chloride monomer VCM
vinyl cyclohexane VCH
viola 1 Va. *or* va. 2 *music* vla.
violet V
violin 1 V *or* V. 2 v *or* v. 3 viol. 4 vln 5 vn *or* vn. 6 *music* a vl *or* vl. b Vno
violins vv *or* vv. *or* VV.
violoncello Vc. *or* vc.
viral pneumonia in pigs VPP
Virgil Virg. (Roman poet)
virgin Virg. *or* virg
Virgin Islands VI (Zip Code) *or* V.I. (in general use)(*NYT:* V.I.)
Virginia 1 VA (Zip Code) 2 Va. 3 Vi *or* Vi. (state) 4 Virg.
Virginia Military Institute VMI
Virgo, the Virgin Vir (constellation)
virtual machine *computers* VM
virtual machine monitor *computers* VMM
virtual machine system *computers* VMS
virtual memory *computers* VM
virtual notebook system *computers* VNS
virtual reality *computers* VR
Virtual Storage Access Method *computers* VSAM

virus v
virus-like infectious agent VLIA
virus-like particle VLP
viruses that produce cancers in animals C
Viscomte Vte.
Viscomtesse Vtesse.
viscosity 1 vis. 2 visc.
viscosity gravity constant VGC
viscosity index VI
Viscount 1 Vis. 2 Visc.
Viscountess 1 Vis. 2 Visc.
viscous visc.
visibility 1 V 2 vis. 3 VSBY *or* vsby.
visibility (unusually good) *meteorology* v
visible 1 vis. 2 VSB *or* vsb.
visible records computer VRC
vision 1 V 2 v *or* v. 3 vsn. *or* VSN
visiting card c.d.v.
visiting nurse VN
Visiting Nurse Association VNA
visual 1 V 2 vis.
visual acuity VA
visual approach path indicator *aeronautics* VAPI
visual approach slope indicator *aeronautics* VASI
visual communications management VICOM
visual control room VCR
visual data acquisition VIDAT
visual discriminatory acuity *medicine* VDA
visual display unit VDU
visual evoked potential VEP
visual field VF
visual flight rules VFR
visual meteorological conditions VMC
visual precision VIPRE
visual radio range VRR
visual rules for instrument landing *aeronautics* VRI
visual search microfilm file VSMF
Visually Impaired Association VIA
vital vit.
vital capacity *medicine* VC
vital statistics vit. stat.
vitamin vit.
vitamin B_2 G
vitamin D D
viticulture viti.
vitreous vit.
vitrified clay VC
vitrified clay tile VCT
Vladivostok Vlad.
vocabulary vocab.
vocal voc.
vocal resonance VR
vocational 1 voc. 2 voctl
Vocational Education VE
vocational education voc-ed *or* vo-ed
Vocational Education Act VEA
vocative *grammar* voc.
vogues proskaner VP
voice v
Voice Answer Back *computers* VAB
voice data communications VODACOM
voice frequency *communications* 1 v.f. 2 VF
Voice of America VOA
voice of the people *Latin* vox pop.
voice unit VU *or* V.U.

voice-operated device for automatic transmission *electronics* VODAT
voice-operated relay 1 VOR **2** VOX
voice-operated transmission VOX
voice-operated, gain-adjusting device *electronics* VOGAD
voiceover VO
volatile 1 Vol *or* vol. **2** volat.
volatile corrosion inhibitor VCI
volatile organic compound VOC
volcanic 1 Vol *or* vol. **2** volc.
volcano 1 Vol *or* vol. **2** volc.
Volkswagen VW
Volpe National Transportation Systems Center VNTSC
volt 1 V **2** v *or* v.
volt-ampere VA *or* va (*GPO:* VA)
volt-ampere reactive unit VAR *or* var (*GPO:* var)
volt-ohm milliammeter VOM
voltage 1 e **2 a** V **b** v *or* v. **3** vltg
voltage control amplifier VCA
voltage control transfer VCT
voltage controlled current source *electronics* VCCS

voltage controlled oscillator VCO
voltage dependent resistor VDR
voltage regulator VR
voltage standing wave ratio *electronics* VSWR
voltage-controlled differential negative resistance *electronics* VNR
volts per meter 1 v/m **2** VPM
volts per mil 1 v/m **2** VPM
volume 1 a V *or* V. **b** v *or* v. **c** Vol *or* Vol. (in bibliography) **2** Vol *or* vol. (of quantity, space, or intensity) (*MLA, CSM, OUP:* vol.)
volume and tension V. and T. *or* v&t
volume displacement *physics, chemistry* X
volume index VI
volume indicator VI
volume of packed red cells VPRC
volume pressure setting VPS
Volume Table of Contents *computers.* VTOC
volume unit VU *or* V.U.
volume (tome) 1 T *or* T. **2** t *or* t. **3** tom. *or* Tom.
volumes per million vpm
volumes (books) 1 vv *or* vv. *or* VV. **2** vols. *or* Vols.

volumetric *chemistry, physics* volum.
volumetric solution *chemistry* VS
voluntary 1 Voly **2** Vol *or* Vol.
Voluntary Service Overseas *British* VSO
volunteer 1 V *or* V. **2** Vol *or* Vol.
volunteer army VOLAR
volunteer fire department VFD
Volunteer Income Tax Assistance VITA
Volunteers for International Technical Assistance VITA
Volunteers in Service to America VISTA *or* Vista
Volunteers of America VOA
von Willebrand factor vWF
voting 1 vt *or* vt. **2** vtg.
voting trust certificate V.T.C.
voucher vou.
vowel V
vulcanized rubber VR
vulgar vulg.
Vulgar Latin VL *or* VLat. (*MLA:* VL)
vulgarly vulg.
Vulgate Vul. *or* Vulg.

Wage Appeals Board WAB
waist W
Waite Agricultural Research Institute WARI
waiter wtr.
waiting list WL
waiting on weather WOW
waived *commerce, law* wvd
Walachian Wal. *or* Walach.
Wales W *or* W.
Walk Wk (in place names)
walk *baseball* w
walking wounded WW
walkover *British sports* WO *or* W.O.
wall w
Wall Street Journal WSJ
wall-to-wall w/w (of floor covering)
Wallace Wall.
Walloon Wal.
walnut wal.
waltz wlz
wanting w *or* w.
War Correspondent WC *or* W.C.
war risk *insurance* w.r.
war risk only *insurance* w.r.o.
ward wd.
wardroom WR
warehouse whs. *or* whse.
warehouse book w.b. *or* w/b WB *or* W.B.
Warehouse Gross Performance Measurement System WGPMS (of inventory)
warehouse receipt WR *or* W/R

warehouse warrant *commerce, finance* WW *or* W/W
warehouseman whsmn.
warehousing whsng.
warhead WHD *or* whd
warm *meteorology* w
warm air WA *or* wa
warm maritime Polar air mass *meteorology* mPw
warmed *pharmaceutics* calef.
warning 1 warn. **2** wng.
warning point level WPL *or* wpl
warrant 1 war. **2** wrnt. **3** *finance* wt
Warrant Officer WO
warranted warrtd.
warranty 1 warr. **2** warrty.
Warrington Wire Gauge WWG
Warsaw War.
Warwickshire County, England War. *or* Warks
washed overboard *insurance* WOB *or* w.o.b.
Washington 1 WA (state, Zip Code) **2** Wash.
Washington (D.C.) Operations Research Council WORC
Washington (D.C.) Educational Television Association WETA
Washington Headquarters Services WHS
Washington (D.C.) Metropolitan Area Transit Authority WMATA
Wassermann Wass.
Wassermann reaction *medicine* WR
waste W
Waste Isolation Pilot Plant WIPP
Waste Isolation System WIS
waste pipe w.p.
wastepaper WP
wastepaper basket WPB *or* wpb
water 1 a 2 a 3 aq. **4** W
water and feed W&F (of livestock in transit)

Water and Power Development Authority WAPDA
water and rail *commerce* W&R
water ballast 1 w.b. (in a ship) **2** WB
water base WB (of paint)
water boiler neutron source WBNS
water closet 1 w.c. **2** WC *or* W.C.
Water Department WD
Water District WD
water gauge 1 WG *or* W.G. **2** wg *or* w.g.
water heater WH
water horsepower whp *or* WHP *or* W.hp.
water in oil WO *or* W/O
water line WL *or* w.l.
water packed WP *or* W.P.
Water Pollution Control Act WPCA
Water Pollution Control Federation WPCF
Water Pollution Research Laboratory WPRL
water quenched *physics* WQ
water repellent WR
Water Resources Scientific Information Center WRSIC
water retention coefficient WRC
water supply WS
water supply point WSP
water surface WS
water valve w.v.
water vapor content w
water vapor electrolysis *biology* WVE
water vapor transmission WVT
water-cooled reactor WCR
water-extended polyester WEP
water-soluble WS *or* w.s.
Waterford 1 Wat. (glassware) **2** Wtf. (glassware)
Waterloo Fortran WATF
watermark wmk.
waterproof 1 WP **2** wpr.
waterproof paper packing *commerce* WPP *or* w.p.p.

Waterside Workers' Federation WWF
watertight WT or wt
Waterway Experiment Station WES
waterworks WW
watt 1 W 2 w
watt-hour 1 WH or W.h. 2 wh or w.h. or wh. 3 whr. or w.hr. or w-hr (GPO: Wh)
watt-second Ws
wattmeter WM or wm
wave 1 W 2 w or w.
wave function u
waveband WB
wavelength WL or wl
Way Wy (in postal address)
waybill commerce WB or W.B. or W/B
Ways and Means Committee WMC (of U.S. House of Representatives)
weak wk
weak force or interaction physics W
weaken wkn
weakly interacting massive particle astrophysics WIMP
weapon 1 wea. 2 wpn
weapon system WS
Weapons Control Officer WCO
Weapons Readiness Analysis Program WRAP
Weapons Research Establishment WRE
Weapons System Evaluation Group WSEG
wearable artifical kidney WAK
weather 1 wea. or wea or WEA 2 wthr 3 WX or Wx
Weather Control Research Association WCRA
weather facsimile WEFAX
Weather Information Reporting and Display System WIRDS
weather outline contour generator WOCG
weather permitting 1 w.p. 2 WP
weather station WS
weather stripping WS
weather working days WWD or wwd
weatherproof WP
weber 1 W 2 Wb
weber number W
Wechsler Adult Intelligence Scale psychology WAIS
Wechsler Intelligence Scale for Children WISC
Wechsler Preschool and Primary Scale of Intelligence psychology WPPSI
Wednesday 1 W 2 We or We. 3 Wed. or Wednes.
weed wd.
Weed Research Organization WRO
Weed Society of America W.S.A.
week 1 wk or wk. 2 w or w.
weekdays wkds
weekend we
weekly 1 wkly 2 w or w.
weeks wks
wehnelt W
weighing wg or wg.
weighing and inspection W&I
weight 1 W or w 2 wgt. 3 WT or WT. 4 wt or wt. 5 Latin P or p 6 physics F (CSM, OUP: wt.)
weight and/or measurement commerce WM or W/M or w/m

weight by volume w/v
weight guaranteed wg or w.g.
weight in weight chemistry, physics w/w
Weight Watchers WW
weight, altitude, temperature aeronautics WAT
welder wldr.
welding weld.
Welding Research Council WRC
Welfare and Institutions Code WIC
well known biology wk or w.k.
well-developed, well-nourished WDWN
well-formed formula wff. (in logic)
Wellington, New Zealand 1 Well. 2 Wln
Welsh 1 W or W. 2 Wel.
Welsh National Eisteddfod WNE
Welsh Nationalist Party W.N.P. or WNP
Welsh Rugby Union W.R.U. or WRU
Wentzel, Kramers, Brillouin physics WKB
Wesleyan Wes.
Wesleyan Missionary Society WMS or W.M.S.
west 1 W or W. 2 w or w.
West Africa or West African 1 W.Afr. 2 WA or W.A.
West African Economic Community CEAO
west by north 1 W by N 2 WbN
west by south 1 W by S 2 WbS
West Germanic WGmc.
West India Docks W.I.D. (in port of London)
West Indian 1 W.Ind. 2 WI or W.I.
West Indies 1 W.Ind. 2 WI or W.I.
West Indies Federation W.I.F. or WIF
west longitude W.long.
West Saxon WS or W.S.
West Virginia 1 W. Va. 2 WV (Zip Code)
west-northwest WNW or W.N.W. or w.n.w.
west-southwest WSW or W.S.W. or w.s.w.
westbound 1 w.b. 2 WB
westerly Wly or wly
western 1 West. or west. 2 a W or W. b w or w.
Western Air Rescue Center WARC
Western Area Power Administration WAPA
Western Australia 1 W.Aust. 2 WA or W.A. (state)
Western Data Processing Center WDPS
western district WD or W.D. (division of Federal Courts)
Western Electronic Manufacturers Association WEMA
western equine encephalitis WEE
Western European Alliance WEA
Western European Fisheries Conference WEFC
Western European Time WET or W.E.T.
Western European Union WEU
Western Pacific Fisheries Commission WPFC
Western Samoa 1 W.Sam. 2 WS
Western Somali Liberation Front W.S.L.F. or WSLF
Western Union WU (telegraph service)
Western United States WUS
Westminster Westm.
westward Westw.
wet air without rain meteorology e or e.
wet bulb WB
wet bulb temperature WBT

wet fog meteorology fe or fe.
wettable powder WP
Wexford County, Ireland Wex.
Whale CET or Cet (constellation)
wharf whf.
wharfage commerce 1 whfg. 2 wrfg.
wharfowners' liability insurance w.o.l. or WOL
wharves whvs.
what you see is what you get WYSIWYG
Wheaton Wheat.
wheelbase WB
wheelchair WC
when actually employed WAE or w.a.e.
when issued 1 w.i. 2 WI
wherefore execution should not be issued law Q.E.N.
whether whr.
which wh
which is Latin q.e.
which see Latin 1 q.v. 2 qq.v.
which was to be done Latin Q.E.F. or q.e.f.
which was to be found out Latin Q.E.I. or q.e.i.
which was to be proved Latin QED or Q.E.D. or q.e.d.
whiskey (whisky) and soda w&s or W&S
whistle 1 wh or Wh. 2 Whis.
white 1 Alb. or Alb 2 W or W. 3 wh 4 wht. or Wht.
White Anglo-Saxon Protestant WASP or Wasp (NYT, OUP: WASP)
white blood cells or count WBC or W.B.C.
white dwarf astronomy WD
white fuming nitric acid WFNA
White House WH or W.H.
White House Historical Association WHHA
White House Office WHO
white metal WM
white phosphorus WP
white porcelain enamel WPE
White Sands Proving Ground WSPG
Whitney Museum of American Art 1 WMAA 2 MMA
who is calling QRZ (in amateur radio)
who sues law QT or Q.T.
Who Was Who WWW
whole-body radiation WBR
wholesale 1 whsle. 2 commerce Whol.
wholesale price index WPI
wicket cricket w or wkt
Wicklow County, Ireland Wick.
wide 1 W 2 w
Wide Area Data Service WADS
Wide Area Telephone Service WATS
wide receiver football WR
wide-area network WAN (of computers)
Wide-Range Achievement Test WRAT
wide-range imaging spectrometer WISP
widow wid.
widower wid.
Widows Against Violence Empower Wave
width 1 B or b 2 W or w 3 wdt. 4 wth.
wife 1 W or W. 2 w or w. 3 Latin ux. or Ux. 4 law con.
Wild Life Preservation Society of Australia W.L.P.S.A.
wild pitch baseball WP
Wildlife Management Institute WMI

will be issued wbi or WBI
will call WC
Will Rogers Institute W.R.I.
William Wm.
William and Mary W.&M.
Wilmington, Delaware or **North Carolina** Wmg.
Wilson Library Bulletin WLB
Wiltshire County, England Wilts or Wilts.
win, lose, tie sports W.L.T. or W/L/T
Winchester Winch.
wind W
wind direction W/D
wind speed WS
wind velocity WV
winding electricity wdg.
window 1 w **2** wd.
windows, icons, mouse, pull down menus computers WIMP
Windward Islands 1 WI or W.I. **2** Wind.I.
wing wg or wg.
Wing Commander W/C
wings, engine, fuselage, tail aeronautics WEFT
Winnipeg, Canada Winn.
Winston Spencer Churchill WSC
winter 1 Wint. or wint. **2** wtr.
Winter Load Line W
Winter North Atlantic Load Line WNA
Winter's Tale, The **1** Wint.T. **2** WT
wire 1 W **2** w or w.
wire gauge 1 WG **2** wg or w.g.
wire mesh WM
wire mesh screen WMS
wire payment WP
wire wound electronics WW
Wisconsin 1 WI (Zip Code) **2** Wis. (*NYT, OUP:* Wis.)
Wisdom of Solomon Wisd. (*MLA:* Wisd. Sol. or Wisd.; *OUP:* Wisd.)
with 1 w or w. or w/ **2 a** pharmaceutics c **b** music, law c. **3** C or C.
with all faults WAF or w.a.f.
with average insurance WA or W.A.
with corrections W/C or w/c
with coupon commerce cum cp.
with dividend commerce cum d. or cum div.
with double flowers botany fl.pl.
with effect from w.e.f.
with expression music **1** con esp. **2** esp. or esp
with force music fz.
with force or **emphasis** music forz.
with interest commerce cum int.
with other goods commerce, insurance w.o.g.
with other property WOP
with particular average insurance WPA or w.p.a.
with prior service WPS
with reference w.ref. or w/ref
with rights commerce WR
with spirit music Spirit.
with sudden stress music **1** sf **2** sfz
with sudden stress followed by soft tone music sfp
with the bass music CB or C.B.
with the bow music ca or c.a.
with the left hand music **1** c.s. **2** SM or S.M.

with the necessary changes m.m.
with the right hand music DM or D.M.
with the voice music **1** c.v. **2** C.Voc. or c.voc.
with the will annexed law CTA or C.T.A. or c.t.a.
with warrants w/w or ww
withdrawal withdrl
withdrawn W/D
withholding wh or w/h
withholding tax WT
within normal limits wnl or WNL
Within Pulse Electronic Scanning WPESS (monitoring fish migration)
without 1 witht **2** WO **3** wo or w/o **4** wt **5** X or X. **6** x or x. **7** music sen. **8** pharmaceutics s or s.
without accompanying chords music TS or T.S.
without annotation bibliography a.u.n. or AUN
without benefit of salvage insurance w.b.s.
without charge commerce **1** w.c. **2** WC
without compensation WOC or W.O.C.
without equipment WOE or w.o.e.
without issue Latin sp
without lawful issue Latin SLP or S.L.P. or s.l.p.
without legitimate issue law s.p.l.
without male issue or **offspring** Latin SMP or s.m.p.
without mutes music ss or ss.
without name Latin sn or s.n.
without personnel WOP
without place Latin s.l.
without place and year Latin **1** s.l. et a. **2** s.l.&a.
without place or date Latin s.l.n.d.
without place, year, or name Latin s.l.a.n. or SLAN
without prejudice insurance, law w.p.
without surviving issue law s.p.s.
without time music st
without year Latin s.a.
witness wit.
Witness Protection Program WPP
Wolf Lup (constellation)
Woman Police Constable British WPC or W/P/C
Women Against Pornography WAP
Women Ordnance Workers WOW
Women Organized Against Rape British WOAR
Women's Action Coalition WAC or W.A.C.
Women's Adoption International Fund WAIF
Women's Air Force WAF
Women's Army Corps WAC
Women's Bureau WB
Women's Christian Temperance Union W.C.T.U. or WCTU (*NYT:* W.C.T.U.)
Women's Cycle Racing Association WCRA or W.C.R.A.
Women's Engineering Society British WES
women's extra British WX (of clothing size)
Women's Financial Information Program WFIP
Women's Home Missionary Association W.H.M.A.

Women's Institute British WI
Women's International Bowling Congress WIBC
Women's International Tennis Association WITA
Women's International Zionist Organization WIZO
Women's Liberal Federation W.L.F.
Women's Liberation WL
Women's Liberation Movement WLM
Women's Organization Against Sexual Harassment WOASH
Women's Professional Golfers' Association WPGA
Women's Royal Air Force British WRAF
Women's Royal Army Corps British WRAC
Women's Royal Australian Air Force WRAAF
Women's Royal Australian Army Corps WRAAC
Women's Royal Australian Navy Service WRANS
Women's Royal Naval Reserve WRNR
Women's Royal Naval Service WRNS
Women's Royal Voluntary Service WRVS
Women's Social and Political Union W.S.P.U.
Women's Tennis Association WTA
Women's United Service League W.U.S.L.
Women's Wear Daily WWD
Women, Infants, and Children WIC or WICP
won W (monetary unit of N. and S. Korea; record of a game)
wood 1 W **2** wd.
wood casing WC or W.C.
wood-burning fireplace WBF or wb/fp
wood-plastic composite WPC
Woodmen of the World WOW or W.O.W.
Woods Hole Oceanographic Institution WHOI
woodwork wdwk
wool forward w.fd. (in knitting)
Wool Industries Research Association WIRA
wool on needle w.o.n.
Woomera, Australia WOM
Worcestershire County, England Worc. or Worcs
word 1 w or w. **2** wd.
word and author index WADEX
word association test psychology WAT
word mark computers WM
word of mouth advertising WOM or W.O.M.
word processing WP
word processor WP
word selection computers WORSE
words out of ordinary language WOOOL
words per minute wpm or w.p.m. or WPM (*OUP:* w.p.m.)
words per second wps or w.p.s. or WPS
work 1 wk **2** wrk **3** physics **a** A **b** W or w
Work Equity Program WEP
work in progress WIP
work order WO
work unit WU or wu
work without opus (number) music woo or WoO

workbook wkbk
worker wkr
Worker's Revolutionary Party WRP
Workers' Educational Association *British* WEA *or* W.E.A.
Workers' Party of the Congo *French* PCT
working wkg
working capital *finance* WC
Working Men's Club *British* WMC
working paper WP
working point WP
working pressure WP
working steam pressure WSP
working storage *computers* WS
working voltage WV
workload index WLI
workmen's compensation *insurance* WC
Workmen's Compensation Board WCB
works wks *or* Wks
workshop wks *or* Wks
World Administration Radio Conference WARC
World Aeronautical Chart WAC
World Alliance of Reformed Churches WARC
World Assembly of Youth 1 WAY **2** *French* A.M.J.
World Association for Public Opinion Research WAPOR
World Association of Travel Agencies WATA *or* W.A.T.A.
World Association of World Federalists WAWF
World Bank WB *or* W.B.
World Billiards Union *French* UMB
World Boxing Association WBA *or* W.B.A.
World Boxing Council WBC
World Boxing Organization WBO
World Bridge Federation WBF (in cardplaying)
World Champion Wld.Ch.
World Championship Tennis WCT
World Christian Endeavor Union WCEU *or* W.C.E.U.
World Commission on Environment and Development WCED
World Confederation of Labor WCL
World Council for the Welfare of the Blind WCWB
World Council of Churches WCC *or* W.C.C.
World Council of Peace WCP
World Date Center WDC
World Economic Survey WES
World Energy Conference WEC
World Federation for Mental Health WFMH

World Federation for the Protection of Animals WFPA
World Federation of Engineering Organizations WFEO
World Federation of Methodist Women WFMW *or* W.F.M.W.
World Federation of Neurology WFN
World Federation of Scientific Workers WFSW
World Federation of the Deaf WFD
World Federation of Trade Unions 1 WFTU *or* W.F.T.U. **2** *French* FSM
World Federation of United Nations Associations WFUNA
World Fellowship of Buddhists W.F.B.
World Food Council WFC
World Food Program WFP
World Football League WFL
World Fund for Nature WFN
World Future Society WFS
World Geographic Reference System GEOREF
World Geophysical Interval WGI
World Health Organization WHO (*NYT:* W.H.O.; *OUP:* WHO)
World Health Research Center WHRC
World Hockey Association WHA
World Intellectual Property Organization WIPO
World Jewish Congress WJC
World Land Use Survey W.L.U.S. *or* WLUS
World League of American Football WLAF
World Magnetic Survey WMS
World Medical Association 1 WMA *or* W.M.A. **2** *French* AMM *or* A.M.M.
World Meteorological Center WMC
World Meteorological Organization WMO
World Methodist Council WMC *or* W.M.C.
World Ocean Circulation Experiment WOCE
World Oceanographic Organization WOO
World Organization for Mothers of All Nations WOMAN
World Outside Centrally Planned Economic Areas WOCA
World Petroleum Congress WPC
World Poultry Science Association WPSA
World Presbyterian Alliance WPA
World Press Institute WPI *or* W.P.I.
World Professional Billiards and Snooker Association WPBSA
World Series Cricket WSC
World Service Television News *British* WSTN
World Team Tennis WTT

World Textile Research Council WTRC
World Tourism Organization WTO
World Trade Association WTA
World Trade Center WTC (New York City)
World Trade Information Center WTIS
World Trade Organization WTO
World Union of Catholic Teachers W.U.C.T.
World Union of Jewish Students WUJS
World University Service WUS
World Veterans Federation WVF *or* W.V.F.
World War WW *or* W.W.
World Water Ski Union WWSU
World Weather Center WWC
World Weather Watch WWW
World Wide Military Command and Control System WWMCCS
World Wide Web *computers* WWW
World Zionist Organization W.Z.O. *or* WZO
worldwide WW
Worldwide Alliance of Diamond Workers *Dutch* WVD
Worldwide Standard Seismograph Network WWSSN
worldwide synchronization of atomic clocks WOSAC
Worldwide Television News *British* WTN
Wotquenne Catalog 1 W **2** WQ *or* Wq. *or* wq (cataloging music of C.P.E. Bach)
would 1 wd. **2** wld
wound (injury) wd.
wounded in action WIA
wraparound mortgage WAM
wreck wk *or* Wk
wrinkled *or* **torn paper** XX
writ of execution Ca. Sa. *or* ca. sa.
write *pharmaceutics* S
Write Once Read Many times *computers* WORM
writer 1 writ. **2** wtr. *or* Wtr.
Writer to the Signet WS
Writers and Scholars International WSI
Writers Guild of America W.G.A.
written writ.
written off WO *or* W/O
written order WO
wrong 1 w **2** X
wrong font wf *or* w.f. (*CSM:* wf; *OUP:* w.f.)
wrought wrt
wrought iron 1 w.i. **2** WI
Wycliffe Wy *or* Wy. *or* Wycl. (medieval English cleric)
Wyoming 1 WY (Zip Code) **2** Wy *or* Wy. *or* Wyo. (*NYT, OUP:* Wyo.)

X chromosome missing *genetics* XO
X inactive specific transcriptase XIST
X-count in competitive shooting X

X-ray diffraction XRD
X-ray emission spectroscopy XES
X-ray fluorescence XRF
X-ray fluorescence analysis XFA
X-ray fluorescence spectrometry XRFS
X-ray photoelectron spectroscopy XPS
X-ray polychromator XRP
xanthene xan.

xanthic *botany* xan.
xanthine xan.
xanthine oxidase XO
xanthosine monophosphate XMP
xenon 1 X **2** Xe (*GPO, OUP:* Xe)
Xenophon Xen.
xeroderma pigmentosum XP
xylophone xyl. *or* xylo.

Y

yacht yct
Yacht Club Y.C.
Yacht Racing Association Y.R.A.
yard **1** y **2** yd.
yardage ydg.
yards yds.
yarn over YO or yo (in knitting)
yarn to back (in knitting) **1** y.t.b. **2** yb
yarn to front (in knitting) **1** y.t.f. **2** yf
year **1** Y **2** y **3** yr.
year of birth y.o.b. or YOB
year of death y.o.d. or YOD
year of marriage y.o.m. or YOM
year of the Lord **1** a.D. **2** AD or A.D. or A.D. or AD (GPO, CSM: A.D.; MLA, OUP: AD)
year old YO or y.o. or y-o (of horses)
year to date finance, commerce YTD
yearbook **1** YB or Y.B. **2** yrbk. or Yrbk **3** Y
yearly yrly
years **1** ann. or Ann **2** yrs
Year's Work in English Studies, The YWES
yeast artificial chromosome YAC
yeast extract YE or y.e. or ye
yeast extract sucrose YES or yes
yeast mold count YMC
yellow **1** y **2** Y or Y. **3** yel. **4** yl or yl. **5** pharmaceutics flav.

yellow edges YE or y.e.
yellow pine YP
yellow spot medicine y.s.
Yemen **1** Y **2** Yem.
Yemeni Socialist Party YSP
yen Y or ¥
yeoman Yeo. or yeo.
yeomanry Yeo. or yeo.
yesterday **1** y'day or yday **2** yest. or yesty
Yiddish Yid or Yid.
yield **1** yld. **2** finance Yid
yield limit yl
yield point YP
yield strength YS
yolk of an egg Latin vitel.
York Ebor.
York-Antwerp Rules insurance YA or Y/A
Yorkshire County, England **1** Yks. **2** Yorks or Yorks.
young adult YA
Young Australia League Y.A.L.
Young Catholic Students YCS
Young Men's Catholic Association Y.M.Cath.A. or YMCath.A
Young Men's Christian Association **1** YM **2** YMCA or Y.M.C.A. **3** Y
Young Men's Christian Union YMCU or Y.M.C.U.
Young Men's Friendly Society YMFS or Y.M.F.S.
Young Men's Hebrew Association **1** YM **2** YMHA or Y.M.H.A. **3** Y
Young People's Society of Christian Endeavor Y.P.S.C.E.

Young Pioneers of America YPA
Young Republican Y.R.
young stellar object YSO
Young Urban Professional yuppie or Yuppie
Young Women's Christian Association **1** YW **2** YWCA or Y.W.C.A. **3** Y
Young Women's Christian Temperance Union Y.W.C.T.U. or YWCTU
Young Women's Hebrew Association **1** YW **2** YWHA or Y.W.H.A. **3** Y
Young World Federalists **1** YWF **2** French JFM
younger yr.
youngest **1** y **2** yst.
your yr.
Your Holiness **1** BV or B.V. **2** SV or S.V.
yours yrs or Yrs.
Youth Employment Service YES
youth hostel YH
Youth Hostels Association YHA
Youth International Party YIP
Youth Opportunity Center YOC
Youth Opportunity Program YOP
youthful offender law YO
yttrium Y
yttrium iron garnet electronics YIG
yttrium, aluminum, garnet YAG (of a synthetic garnet)
yuan Y or ¥
Yucatán Yuc.
Yugoslavia Yug. or Yugo.
Yukon Standard Time YST or Y.S.T.
Yukon Territory **1** YT or Y.T. **2** Yuk.

Z

Zachariah Zach.
Zacharias Zach.
Zagreb, Croatia Zag.
Zaire Zai.
zaire Z (monetary unit of Zaire)
Zambia **1** Z **2** Zam.
Zanzibar Zan.
Zapotec Zap.
Zapotecan Zap.
Zechariah Zech. (book of the Old Testament)
Zen Buddhism ZB
Zen Buddhist ZB
Zener diode ZD
zenith **1** Z **2** zen or Zen **3** Zn
zenith distance astronomy **1** Z or z **2** ZD or z.d.
zenithal hourly rate astronomy ZHR or Z.H.R.
Zephaniah Zeph.
zero **1** Z or z **2** zr
zero access storage computers ZAS
zero age main sequence ZAMS
zero antiaircraft potential military ZAP

zero beat ZB (of an electrical circuit)
Zero Defects ZD or Z.D.
zero economic growth ZEG
zero energy **1** ZE **2** ZOE
zero energy breeder reactor assembly physics ZEBRA
zero energy experimental pile ZEEP
zero energy thermonuclear assembly ZETA
zero field splitting biology ZFS
zero frequency electricity, telecommunications ZF or z.f.
zero gradient synchrotron ZGS
zero gravity **1** zero g. **2** ZG or z.g.
zero hour ZHR or ZHr
zero input ZI or z.i.
zero lift aeronautics ZL or zl
Zero Mean Time Z
zero point physics, chemistry ZP or zp
zero population growth ZPG
zero power ZP or zp
zero suppress or suppression ZS
zero-based budgeting ZBB or Z.B.B.
zigzag zz
Zimbabwe Z
Zimbabwe African National Union ZANU
Zimbabwe African National Union-Patriotic Front ZANU-PF
Zimbabwe African People's Union ZAPU
Zimbabwe Independent People's Republic Army ZIPRA

Zimmermann Z (in cataloging Purcell's music)
zinc Zn
Zinc Development Association ZDA
Zionist Congress ZC
Zionist Organization of America Z.O.A.
zirconium Zr
zloty Zl or zl
zodiac zod.
zone **1** Z or Z. **2** z or z. **3** Zn or zn
zone description navigation ZD
Zone Improvement Plan ZIP or Zip
zone of fire military ZF
zone of interior ZI
Zone Standard Time ZST or Z.S.T.
Zone Time ZT or Z.T.
zoochemical zoochem.
zoochemistry zoochem.
zoogeographical zoogeog.
zoogeography zoogeog.
zoological zool.
Zoological Garden ZG or Z.G.
Zoological Society ZS or Z.S.
zoologist zool.
zoology zool.
zoom zm
zoopathology zoopath.
zoophytology zooph.
Zurich, Switzerland Zur
zytron DMPA